THE OFFICIAL HANDBOOK OF THE MARVEL UNIVERSE

EDITION

VOL. 3

OFFICIAL HANDBOOK OF THE MARVEL UNIVERSE — MASTER EDITION PROFESSOR POWER TO ZZZAX

REPRINT CREDITS

MARVEL ESSENTIAL DESIGN:
JOHN "JG" ROSHELL OF COMICRAFT
COVER ART:
KEITH POLLARD
COVER COLORS:
TOM SMITH
COLLECTION EDITOR:
MARK D. BEAZLEY
ASSISTANT EDITORS:
JOHN DENNING & CORY LEVINE
EDITORIAL ASSISTANT:
ALEX STARBUCK
EDITOR, SPECIAL PROJECTS:
JENNIFER GRÜNWALD

SENIOR EDITOR, SPECIAL PROJECTS:
JEFF YOUNGQUIST
SENIOR VICE PRESIDENT OF SALES:
DAVID GABRIEL
RESEARCH:
MIKE FICHERA
PRODUCTION:
RODOLFO MURAGUCHI
& JERRON QUALITY COLOR
EDITOR IN CHIEF:
JOE QUESADA
PUBLISHER:
DAN BUCKLEY

SPECIAL THANKS TO JAMES EMMETT, DAN ERENBERG
& DAVID KIRSCHENBAUM

PROFESSOR POWER

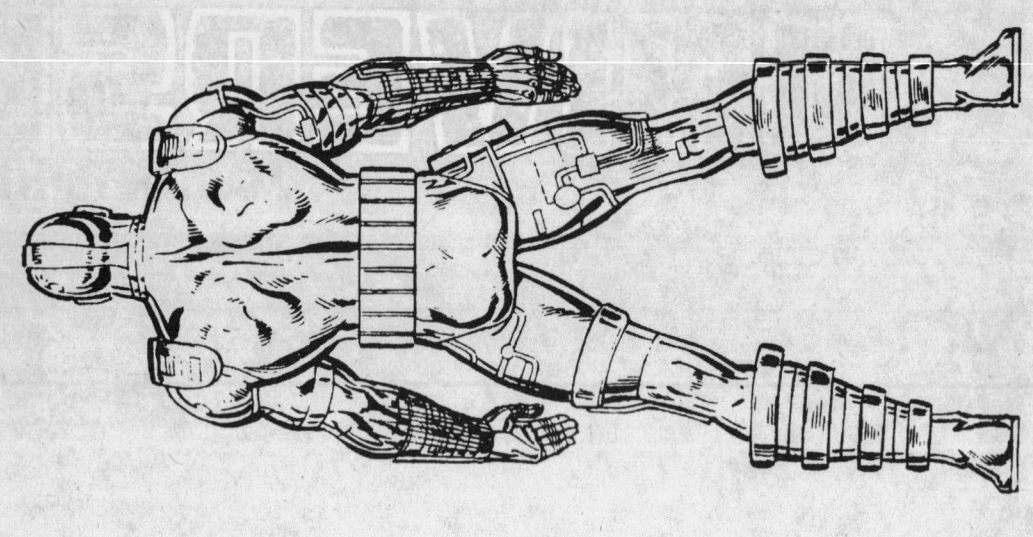
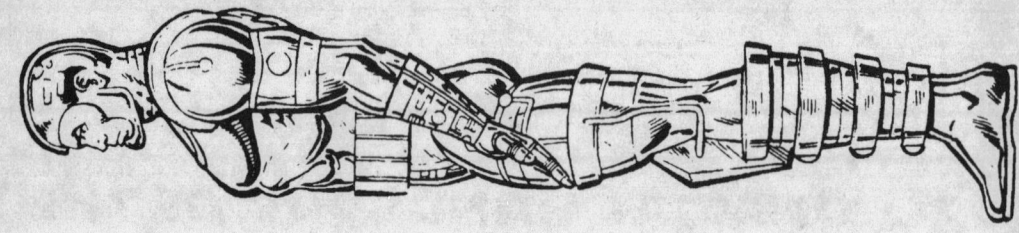
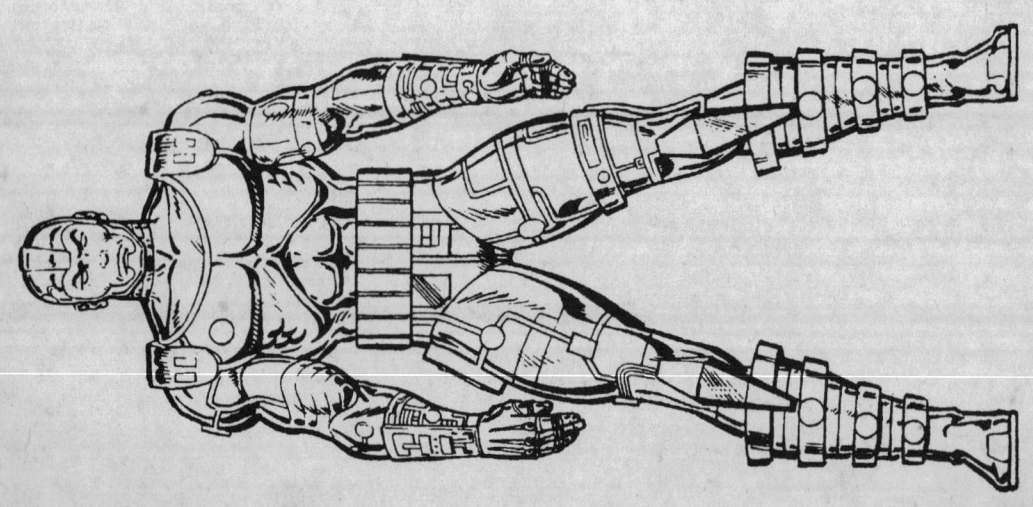

PROFESSOR POWER

BIOGRAPHICAL DATA

Real name: Professor Anthony Power
Aliases at time of death: The Professor
Former aliases: Number One
Dual identity: Publicly known
Occupation at time of death: Head of subversive organization
Former occupation: Historian, teacher, adviser to the president of the United States of America
Citizenship: United States of America
Legal status: Criminal record, legally dead
Place of birth: Norfolk, Virginia
Place of death: A castle in the Adirondack Mountains, New York State
Cause of death: Beaten to death by Captain America VI
Marital status: Widower
Known relatives: Maxine Power (wife, deceased), Matthew Power (son, deceased)
Known confidants: None
Known allies: Morgan MacNeil Hardy (deceased), August Masters (deceased), the Fixer, Mentallo, Secret Empire III
Major enemies: Spider-Man, Professor X, the Defenders
Base of operations at time of death: A mobile "castle" which travelled via an underground railway system
Former base of operations: None
Group membership at time of death: Leader of an unnamed army of right-wing extremists
Former group membership: Secret Empire III
Extent of education: Degrees in history and political science

PARAPHERNALIA

Costume specifications: Full body armor
Personal weaponry: Electron-beam (fired from right forefinger)
Special weaponry: None
Other accessories: None
Transportation: Flight via jet engines attached to battlesuit
Design and manufacture of paraphernalia: Scientists in Anthony Power's employ

PHYSICAL DESCRIPTION

Height: (in original body) 5' 11", (in Matthew Power's Body) 6' 2"
Weight: (in original body) 165 lbs., (in Matthew Power's Body) 220 lbs.
Eyes: (in original body) Grey, (in Matthew Power's Body) Brown
Hair: (in original body) Grey, (in Matthew Power's body) Brown
Other distinguishing features: None

POWERS AND ABILITIES

Intelligence: Gifted
Strength: (in original body) Normal, (in Matthew Power's body) Superhuman Class 10
Flight speed: Natural winged flight speed
Stamina: Normal
Durability: Normal
Agility: Normal
Reflexes: Normal
Fighting skills: None
Special skills and abilities: Long-range planner, battle strategist
Superhuman physical powers: None
Superhuman mental powers: None
Special limitations: None
Source of superhuman powers: None

BIBLIOGRAPHY

First appearance: MARVEL TEAM-UP #117
Origin issue: MARVEL TEAM-UP #118, 124
Significant issues: CAPTAIN AMERICA #264 (group of telepaths assembled by Power used by Morgan MacNeil Hardy to restructure American reality; foiled by Captain America); DEFENDERS #102 (August Masters, working for Power, revealed as head of secret project involving telepaths); DEFENDERS #104 (Master's men, posing as federal agents, captured Richmond); CAPTAIN AMERICA #268/DEFENDERS #106 (Masters attempted to launch psionic attack against the U.S.S.R.; battled Captain America, Daredevil, and the Defenders); MARVEL TEAM-UP #117 (used robots to test capabilities of Spider-Man and Wolverine); MARVEL TEAM-UP #118 (aided by the Fixer, captured Professor X, attempted to add his mental powers to Mentallo's, then have Mentallo cure his catatonic son, Matthew; battled by Spider-Man); MARVEL TEAM-UP #124 (mind transferred into Matthew's body encased in battlesuit; battled Spider-Man and the Beast); DEFENDERS #123 (as Number One, leader of reorganized Secret Empire, sent Harridan, Seraph, and Cloud to abduct the Vision; foiled by Defenders); DEFENDERS #125 (sent Mad Dog and Mutant Force to disrupt wedding of Daimon Hellstrom and Patsy Walker, battled Defenders); DEFENDERS #126 (had double agents in New York SHIELD headquarters free Leviathan [Gargantua], Mad Dog, and Mutant Force from SHIELD custody; sent Leviathan against Defenders); DEFENDERS #127 (revealed as member of Secret Empire, sent Mandroids to recapture escaped Cloud); DEFENDERS #128 (captured Defenders); DEFENDERS #129 (unsuccessfully attempted to brainwash Defenders into killing the New Mutants in revenge against Professor X, launched subliminal mind-control satellite in attempt to start World War III); DEFENDERS #130 (satellite destroyed; his consciousness telepathically merged with his son's by Moondragon, resulting in catatonic madness); CAPTAIN AMERICA #338 (abducted from SHIELD custody and revived by followers, beaten to death in battle with Captain America VI)

PROFESSOR X™

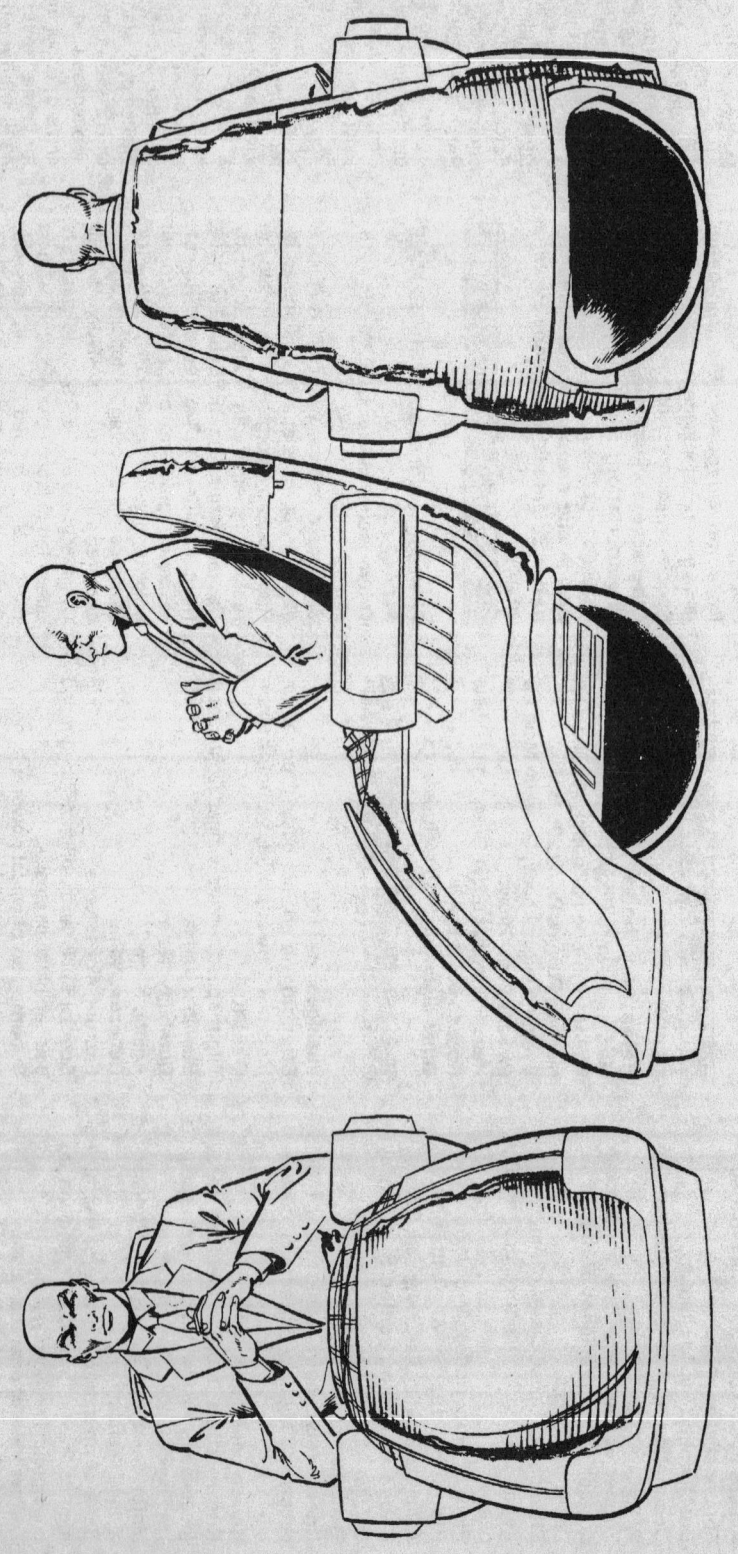

PROFESSOR X

BIOGRAPHICAL DATA

Real name: Charles Xavier
Other current aliases: None
Former aliases: None known
Dual identity: Secret
Current occupation: Geneticist, teacher, leader of the X-Men
Former occupation: Adventurer, soldier
Citizenship: United States and Shi'ar Empire
Legal status: No criminal record
Place of birth: New York City
Marital status: Consort to Princess-Majestrix Lilandra (not officially recognized as a marriage on Earth)
Known relatives: Brian, Sharon (parents, deceased), Kurt Marko (stepfather, deceased), Cain Marko (Juggernaut, stepbrother), David Charles Haller (son, presumed deceased)
Known confidants: Moira MacTaggert, Lilandra, Gabrielle Haller, Scott Summers, Jean Grey, Fred Duncan, Dr. Peter Corbeau, (former) Magneto, Daniel Shomron
Known allies: X-Men, Starjammers, Lilandra, Excalibur, X-Factor II, Avengers, Fantastic Four, (formerly) Magneto, New Mutants (X-Force)
Major enemies: Magneto, Juggernaut, Shadow King (Amahl Farouk), Warskrull Prime, Baron Strucker, Sentinels, the Brood
Usual base of operations: Professor Xavier's School for Gifted Youngsters, 1407 Graymalkin Lane, Salem Center, Westchester County, New York State
Former bases of operations: Imperial palace, Shi'ar homeworld; the starship *Starjammer*, mobile in the Shi'ar Galaxy
Current group membership: X-Men
Former group membership: Founder and teacher of the New Mutants, Starjammers
Extent of education: Ph.D. in genetics, biophysics, and psychology

PHYSICAL DESCRIPTION

Height: 6'
Weight: 190 lbs
Eyes: Blue
Hair: Bald (blond in childhood)
Other distinguishing features: None

POWERS AND ABILITIES

Intelligence: Genius
Strength: Normal
Speed: Inapplicable
Stamina: Normal
Durability: Normal
Agility: Normal
Reflexes: Normal
Fighting skills: Fair hand-to-hand combatant, when not crippled.
Special skills and abilities: Leading authority on genetics, mutation, and psionic powers, considerable expertise in other life sciences, highly talented in devising equipment for utilizing and enhancing psionic powers
Superhuman physical powers: None
Superhuman mental powers: Vast psionic powers, including telepathy; mental illusions; temporary mental or physical paralysis of others; loss of specific memories or total amnesia in others; projection of "mental bolts" to render a victim unconscious; astral projection; ability to sense other superhuman mutants within a small radius
Special limitations: Part of spine shattered, confined to wheelchair
Source of superhuman powers: Genetic mutation

PARAPHERNALIA

Costume specifications: Ordinary fabric
Personal weaponry: None
Special weaponry: None
Other accessories: Cerebro, a computer device for detection of mutants over wide areas, especially when used in conjunction with Xavier's own psionic abilities.
Transportation: X-Men Blackbird jet, the *Starjammer* and other Shi'ar starships
Design and manufacture of paraphernalia: (Cerebro) Charles Xavier, (Blackbird) Clarence "Kelly" Johnson, redesigned by Forge, (Starjammer) Shi'ar scientists

BIBLIOGRAPHY

First appearance: X-MEN Vol. 1 #1
Origin issue: X-MEN Vol. 1 #1, 20 UNCANNY X-MEN #117, 161
Significant issues: X-MEN Vol. 1 #1 (completed recruiting original team of X-Men, sent them into first battle with Magneto); X-MEN Vol. 1 #20 (revealed how he was originally crippled by Lucifer); GIANT-SIZE X-MEN #1 (recruited new team of X-Men); X-MEN Vol. 1 #105 (first met Lilandra); UNCANNY X-MEN #117 (decided to leave Earth with Lilandra; flashback revealed first clash with Amahl Farouk); UNCANNY X-MEN #129 (returned to Earth, resumed leadership of the X-Men); UNCANNY X-MEN #136-137 (alongside X-Men fought and defeated Dark Phoenix; demanded trial by combat over Phoenix I's life); UNCANNY X-MEN #161 (first meeting with Magneto and Gabrielle Haller and their clash with Baron Strucker recounted); MARVEL GRAPHIC NOVEL #4 (founded New Mutants); UNCANNY X-MEN #167 (transformed into Brood alien, consciousness transferred into clone body capable of walking); UNCANNY X-MEN #200 (taken from Earth by Corsair and Lilandra to save his life); UNCANNY X-MEN #276-277 (broke free from imprisonment by Warskrull Prime, reunited with X-Men); UNCANNY X-MEN #278-279/X-FACTOR #69/UNCANNY X-MEN #280/X-FACTOR #70 (returned to Earth, reunited with current and original X-Men, resumed leadership of united teams; spine shattered in battle with Shadow King; accepted seemingly death of son David)

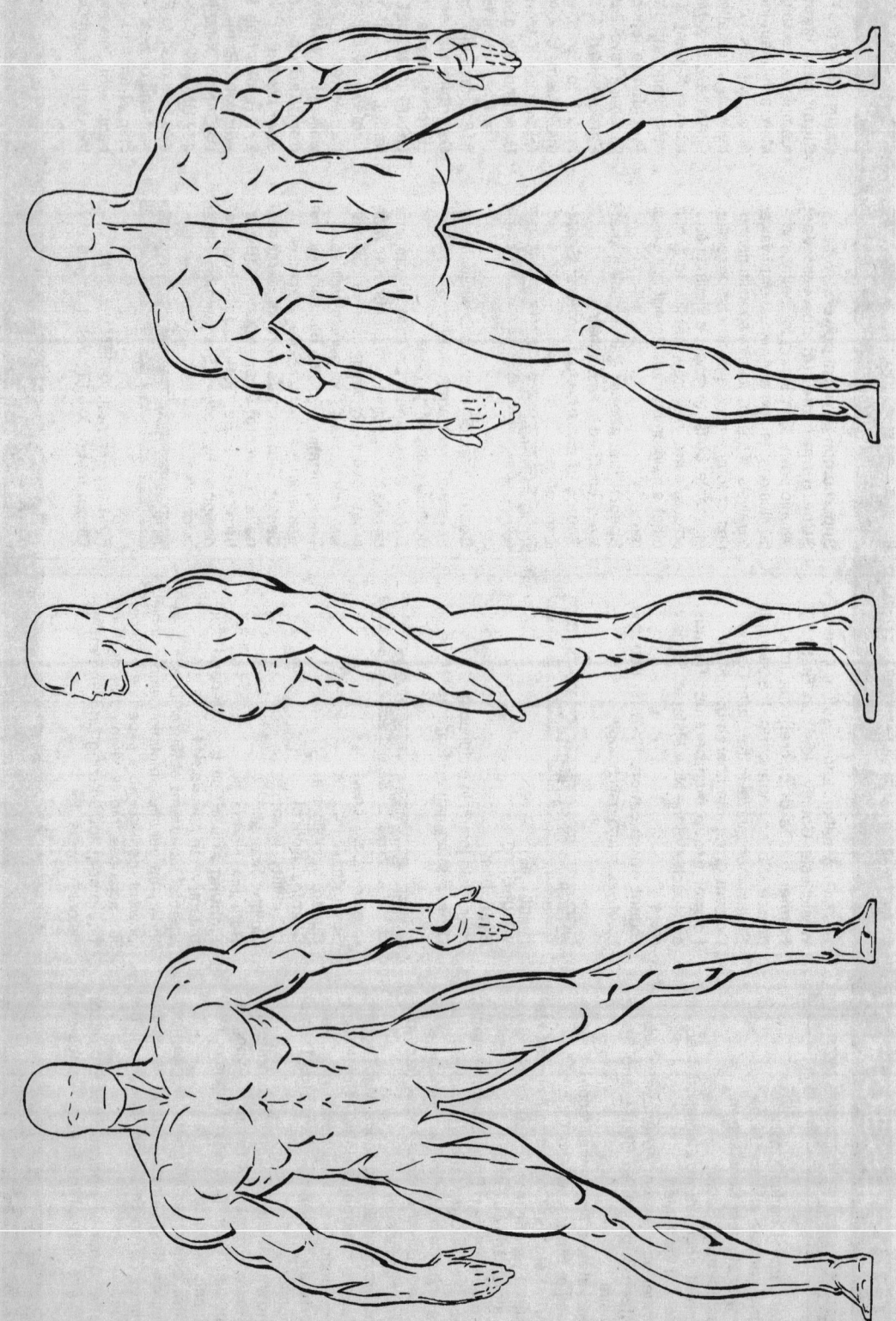

PROTEUS

BIOGRAPHICAL DATA

Real name: Kevin MacTaggert and Gilbert Benson
Aliases at time of death: None
Former aliases: (MacTaggert) Mutant X, (Benson) Piecemeal I
Dual identity: The general populace of Earth is unaware of Proteus's existence
Occupation at time of death: Inapplicable
Former occupation: (Piecemeal I) Operative of AIM
Citizenship: (MacTaggert) United kingdom, (Benson) Unrevealed
Legal status: No criminal record
Place of birth: Unrevealed
Place of deaths: Edinburgh, Scotland
Cause of deaths: (first) Disruption by Colossus's organic steel form, (second) committed suicide by discorporation
Marital status: Single
Known relatives: (MacTaggert) Moira MacTaggert (mother), Joseph MacTaggart (father, deceased), Lord Kinross (grandfather); (Benson) Erika Benson (Harness, mother)
Known confidants: (MacTaggart) None, (Benson, former) Harness
Known allies: (MacTaggart) None, (Benson, former) Harness, AIM
Major enemies: X-Men, X-Force, New Warriors, Cable
Base of operations at time of death: Edinburgh, Scotland
Former bases of operations: Moira MacTaggert's Mutant Research Centre, Muir Island, Scotland
Group membership at time of death: None
Former group membership: None
Extent of education: Unrevealed

PHYSICAL DESCRIPTION

Height: Inapplicable
Weight: Inapplicable
Eyes: Inapplicable
Hair: Inapplicable
Other distinguishing features: Proteus existed in a pure energy form, although he could take possession of humanoid bodies.

POWERS AND ABILITIES

Intelligence: Normal
Strength: Normal
Speed: Normal
Stamina: Normal
Durability: Normal
Agility: Normal
Reflexes: Normal
Fighting skills: Poor hand-to-hand combatant, no combat training
Special skills and abilities: None
Superhuman physical powers: Proteus exists in a state of pure psionic energy and hence has no physical powers. Before merging with Proteus, Piecemeal possessed the superhuman ability to absorb energy. The more energy he absorbed, the greater he grew in size. His body was destroyed when the merger occurred.
Superhuman mental powers: Proteus possessed vast psionic ability to manipulate and alter reality. He existed in a state of pure psionic energy and could take possession of human bodies that his energies eventually "burned" out, killing them (including his own original body). Proteus also possessed telepathic abilities.
Special limitations: Proteus was formerly vulnerable to dispersion by metal or organic metal (such as Colossus's body) in his pure energy form. The limits of Proteus's power to alter reality are unknown, but he proved capable of transforming the entire city of Edinburgh.
Source of superhuman powers: Genetic mutation

PARAPHERNALIA

Costume specifications: Inapplicable
Personal weaponry: None
Special weaponry: None
Other accessories: None
Transportation: (Piecemeal I) Harness's teleportation device
Design and manufacture of paraphernalia: (teleportation device) AIM

BIBLIOGRAPHY

First appearance: (voice only) UNCANNY X-MEN #119, (first visual appearance) UNCANNY X-MEN #125, (Piecemeal I) NEW MUTANTS ANNUAL #7, (merger of Proteus and Piecemeal I) UNCANNY X-MEN #15
Origin issue: UNCANNY X-MEN #128, UNCANNY X-MEN ANNUAL #15
Significant issues: UNCANNY X-MEN #119 (took over body of Angus MacWhirther); UNCANNY X-MEN #125-128/CLASSIC X-MEN #32 (took possession of and killed duplicate body of Madrox the Multiple Man, took over and burned out bodies of Ferdie Duncan, unnamed policeman, and Jennie Banks, battled X-Men, took possession of body of Joseph MacTaggert, was temporarily destroyed by Colossus); CLASSIC X-MEN #36 (Moira MacTaggert decided not to clone Kevin from his corpse); NEW MUTANTS ANNUAL #7 (Harness used Piecemeal I to absorb energy in AIM plan to recreate Proteus, Piecemeal I and Harness escaped X-Force); NEW WARRIORS ANNUAL #1 (Piecemeal I absorbed more energy in different locations); UNCANNY X-MEN ANNUAL #15 (Piecemeal I merged with Proteus after absorbing all extant Proteus energy); X-FACTOR ANNUAL #6 (battled X-Factor, X-Men, X-Force, and New Warriors, committed suicide)
Note: The mutant Proteus should not be confused with the shapeshifting Greek god Proteus or with the Atlantean sage Proteus who first appeared in SUB-MARINER #36. Piecemeal I, who merged with the mutant Proteus, is not be confused with the shapeshifter Piecemeal II, who first appeared in INCREDIBLE HULK #403.

PROWLER ™

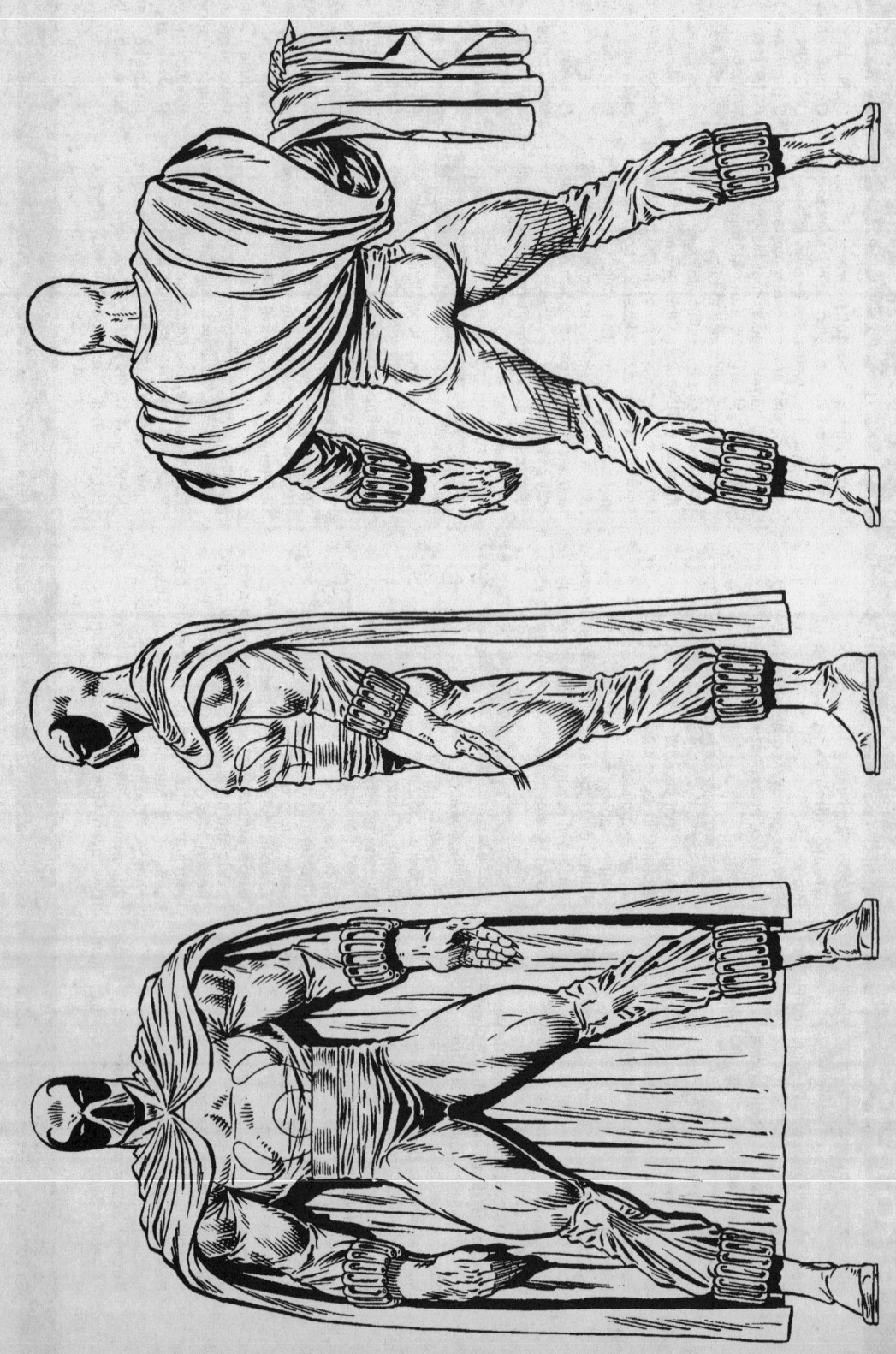

PROWLER

BIOGRAPHICAL DATA

Real name: Hobie Brown
Other current aliases: None
Former aliases: None
Dual identity: Secret
Current occupation: Construction worker, part-time inventor, adventurer
Former occupation: Window washer
Citizenship: United States of America
Legal status: No criminal record, wanted for questioning
Place of birth: The Bronx, New York
Marital status: Married
Known relatives: Mindy S. McPherson (wife, retains maiden name), Abraham "Abe" Brown (brother, member of the Sons of the Tigers), Manuel "Manny" Lopez ("little brother" under the Big Brother Program, deceased)
Known confidants: Spider-Man, Silver Sable
Known allies: Puma, Rocket Racer, Sandman, Will O' the Wisp
Major enemies: Justin Hammer
Usual base of operations: New York City
Former bases of operations: Same
Current group membership: The Outlaws
Former group membership: None
Extent of education: High school graduate, self-educated thereafter

PHYSICAL DESCRIPTION

Height: 5'11"
Weight: 170 lbs.
Eyes: Brown
Hair: Dark brown
Other distinguishing features: None

POWERS AND ABILITIES

Intelligence: Above normal
Strength: Normal
Speed: Normal
Stamina: Normal
Durability: Normal
Agility: Athlete
Reflexes: Athlete
Fighting skills: Skilled hand-to-hand combatant possessing a green belt in tae kwon do.
Special skills and abilities: Naturally inventive, especially in the field of pneumatics, although he has no formal education in that science.
Superhuman physical powers: None
Superhuman mental powers: None
Special limitations: None
Source of superhuman powers: None

PARAPHERNALIA

Costume specifications: Modified coveralls interwoven with denim and stretch fabric
Personal weaponry: Gas cartridge bracelets and anklets capable of propelling projectiles at high velocity. Arsenal of projectiles include steel darts ("flechettes"), gas pellets, small explosives, magnesium flares and cleaning fluid.
Special weaponry: Hypnotic aids and conventional hand-held weapons
Other accessories: Steel-tipped gauntlets for scaling walls; shock absorbent foam rubber insulated boots.
Transportation: Cape which contains a network of pneumatic filaments which expand with air to give it a rigid structure, allowing him to glide for short distances
Design and manufacture of paraphernalia: Hobie Brown

BIBLIOGRAPHY

First appearance: AMAZING SPIDER-MAN #78
Origin issue: AMAZING SPIDER-MAN #78
Significant issues: AMAZING SPIDER-MAN #78 (first encountered Spider-Man who was persuaded him out of a life of crime); AMAZING SPIDER-MAN #87 (impersonated Spider-Man at the hero's request to convince Peter Parker's friends that he was not Spider-Man); AMAZING SPIDER-MAN #93 (unsuccessfully tried to bring Spider-Man to justice for the death of police Captain George Stacy); DEADLY HANDS OF KUNG FU #21 (attempted to bring White Tiger to justice for the killing of his "little brother" Manny Lopez); DEFENDERS #62-64 (attempted to join the Defenders, only to be tossed into the harbor by the Valkyrie); SPECTACULAR SPIDER-MAN #47-48 (Prowler equipment stolen by the Cat Burglar, who became the Prowler II to commit crimes for the fashion criminal Belladonna; Prowler II was subsequently defeated by Spider-Man); AMAZING SPIDER-MAN #305 (vindicated wife of stock fraud charges with the help of Spider-Man and the Black Fox); WEB OF SPIDER-MAN #50 (attempted to vindicate Spider-Man of a crime; first encountered Silver Sable and the Outlaws); SPECTACULAR SPIDER-MAN ANNUAL #9 (safety designs stolen by Justin Hammer; proved flaws in designs curing encounter with Hammer's hirelings); SPECTACULAR SPIDER-MAN ANNUAL #10 (fought brother Abe as an initiation test for Silver Sable); SPECTACULAR SPIDER-MAN #169-170 (joined Spider-Man and the Outlaws against the Avengers and the Space Phantom); EXCALIBUR #36 (hired along with the Outlaws to retrieve a Symkarian nuclear device in England); AMAZING SPIDER-MAN #25/SPECTACULAR SPIDER-MAN ANNUAL #11/WEB OF SPIDER-MAN ANNUAL #7 (formally joined the Outlaws to rescue the kidnaped daughter of a Canadian official)

PSYCHO-MAN

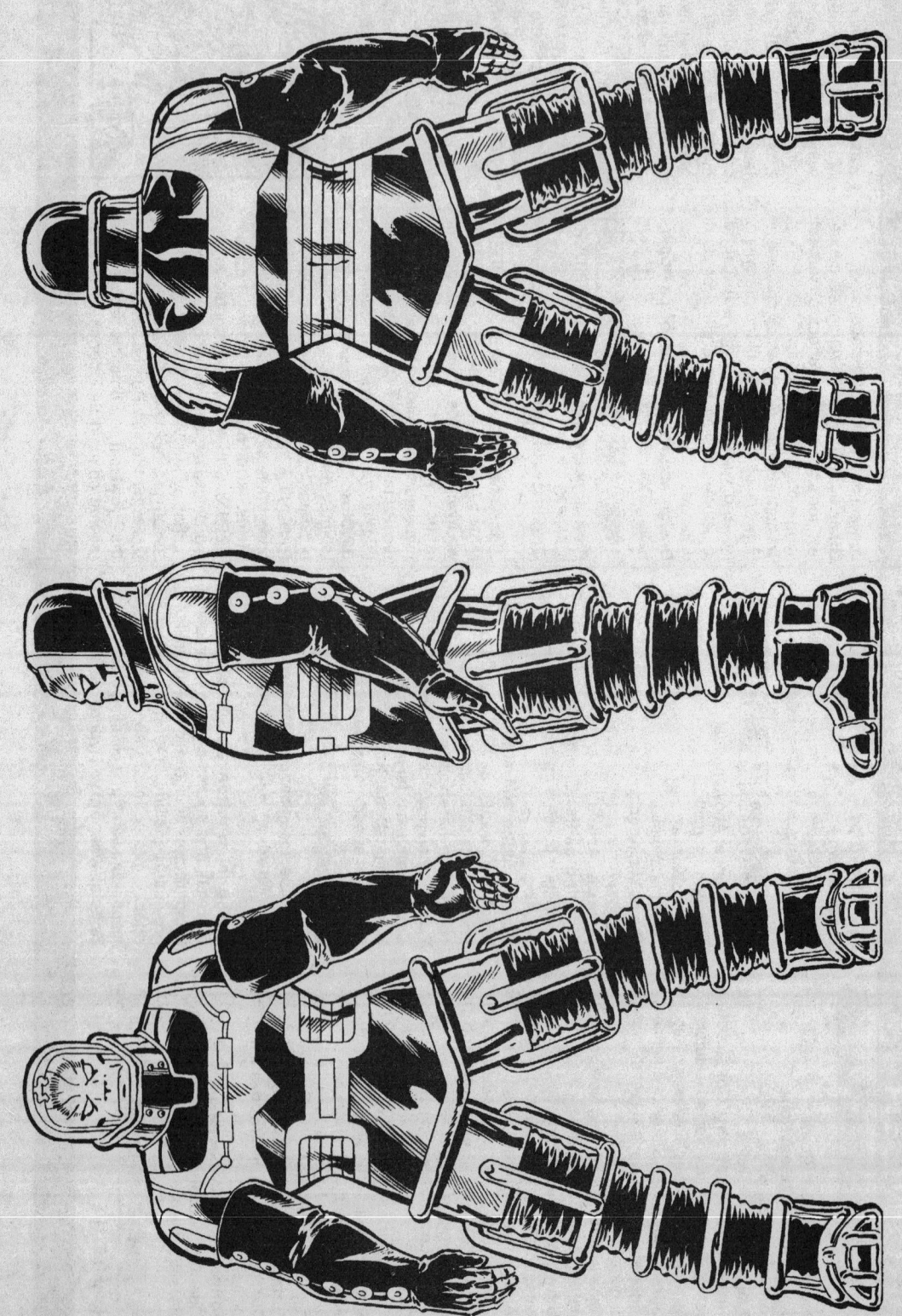

PSYCHO-MAN

BIOGRAPHICAL DATA

Real name: Unrevealed
Other current aliases: None
Former aliases: None
Dual identity: None
Current occupation: Chief scientist of the planet Traan (located in an alternate reality called a "microverse"); conqueror
Former occupation: Unrevealed
Citizenship: Planet Traan
Legal status: No criminal record
Place of birth: Planet Traan
Marital status: Unrevealed
Known relatives: None
Known confidants: None
Known allies: None
Major enemies: The Fantastic Four
Usual base of operations: Planet Traan; the Psycho-Man's world-ship
Former bases of operations: Unrevealed
Current group membership: None
Former group membership: None
Extent of education: Unrevealed

PHYSICAL DESCRIPTION

Height: Indeterminate
Weight: Indeterminate
Eyes: Unrevealed
Hair: Unrevealed
Other distinguishing features: The specific physical characteristics of the Psycho-Man, as well as physical characteristics of his race, are unknown, as he has only been seen in a variety of suits of full body armor

POWERS AND ABILITIES

Intelligence: Superhuman intellect
Strength: (without armor) Unrevealed; (with armor) Variable; the Psycho-Man employs a variety of suits of body armor, at least one of which augments his strength sufficiently to place him in the Superhuman Class 75 range
Speed: (without armor) Unrevealed; (with armor) Variable; the Psycho-Man employs a variety of suits of body armor, at least one of which augments his speed sufficiently to place him in the Superhuman range
Stamina: (without armor) Unrevealed; (with armor) Variable; the Psycho-Man employs a variety of suits of body armor, at least one of which augments his stamina sufficiently to place him in the Superhuman range
Durability: (without armor) Unrevealed; (with armor) Metahuman
Agility: Normal
Reflexes: Normal
Fighting skills: None
Special skills and abilities: Extensive knowledge of technology far in advance of present-day Earth's
Superhuman physical powers: Unrevealed
Superhuman mental powers: None
Special limitations: None
Source of superhuman powers: Unrevealed, perhaps inapplicable

PARAPHERNALIA

Costume specifications: Body armor made of alien materials; the Psycho-Man has employed a number of suits of such armor, many of which have been modified to give him specific offensive and defensive capabilities, including armor which is much larger than he himself is
Personal weaponry: Various, built into armor as needed
Special weaponry: A portable emotion-stimulator device which projects a ray that stimulates the emotional centers of the brain and is equipped to trigger three major emotional states: fear, doubt, and hate; the duration and intensity are adjustable, ranging from mild to extreme levels, which cause hallucinations in the victim, and in some cases death from heart strain
Other accessories: A variety of advanced technological apparatus, including larger, non-portable emotion-inducing equipment with far greater range and effectiveness than his portable unit, enabling him to affect the emotional states of the entire populace of a planet
Transportation: A "world-ship" which also serves as mobile laboratory
Design and manufacture of paraphernalia: Psycho-Man

BIBLIOGRAPHY

First appearance: FANTASTIC FOUR ANNUAL #5
Origin issue: The details of the Psycho-Man's origin are as yet unrevealed
Significant issues: FANTASTIC FOUR ANNUAL #5 (traveled to Earth; attempted to conquer and colonize Earth by use of emotion-controlling "psycho-ray"; battled the Thing, Human Torch, the Inhuman royal family, and the Black Panther); FANTASTIC FOUR #76-77 (battled the Thing, the Human Torch, and Mr. Fantastic, who traveled to Sub-Atomica in search of Silver Surfer); MICRONAUTS Vol. 1 #15-16 (battled Fantastic Four and Micronauts; claimed to have become exile from his world); FANTASTIC FOUR #279 (empowered new Hate Monger to incite racial hatred in mankind as part of new plan to conquer Earth by dividing its people against each other); FANTASTIC FOUR #280-283 (captured Fantastic Four, who had traveled to Sub-Atomica in pursuit of him after defeat of Hate Monger and Malice; experimented on Fantastic Four); FANTASTIC FOUR #284 (battled Invisible Woman; incapacitated)

PSYKLOP

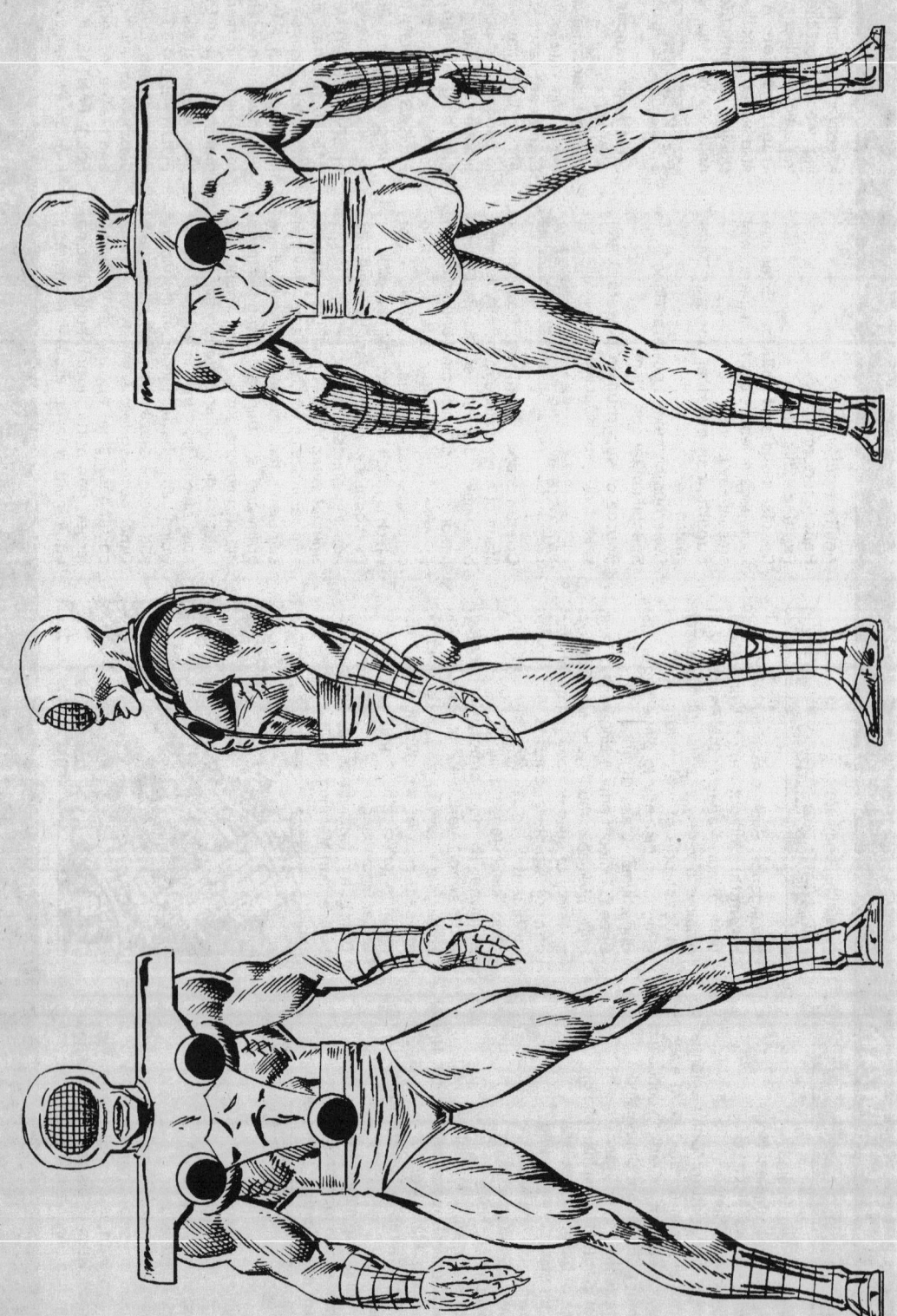

PSYKLOP

BIOGRAPHICAL DATA

Real name: Psyklop
Other current aliases: None
Former aliases: None
Dual Identity: None, the general populace of Earth was unaware of Psyklop's existence
Current occupation: Would-be conqueror, servant of the "dark gods"
Former occupation: Secret organizer of a voodoo cult
Citizenship: Psyklop is the last survivor of an insectoid semi-humanoid race that inhabited prehistoric Earth
Note: The identity of the "dark gods" whom Psyklop's race once worshiped remain unrevealed, although they are still active somewhere in the universe.
Legal status: No criminal record
Place of birth: Unrevealed, presumably somewhere on prehistoric Earth
Marital status: Unrevealed
Known relatives: None
Known confidants: None
Known allies: (former) The "dark gods", members of a voodoo cult
Major enemies: The Hulk, Jarella, the Avengers, the Pantheon of Sorcerers (Torla, Holi, Moli; also known as the Sorcerer's Triad), inhabitants of K'ai
Usual base of operations: A mountain retreat somewhere in the "micro-world" of K'ai
Former base of operations: Sala-y-Gomez Island, South Pacific Ocean
Current group membership: None
Former group membership: Secret organizer of an unnamed New Orleans voodoo cult
Extent of education: Unrevealed

PHYSICAL DESCRIPTION

Height: (on Earth) 8'
Weight: (on Earth) 450 lbs.
Eyes: Red
Hair: None
Other distinguishing features: Psyklop has a single compound eye, sharpened canine teeth, and four clawed digits, including opposable thumb, on each hand; all four of his limbs are double-jointed

POWERS AND ABILITIES

Intelligence: Genius
Strength: Superhuman Class 25
Speed: Superhuman
Stamina: Superhuman
Durability: Metahuman
Agility: Superhuman
Reflexes: Superhuman
Fighting skills: Average hand-to-hand combatant
Special skills and abilities: Master of the advanced technology of his race, some knowledge of the mystic arts
Superhuman physical powers: Aside from the above listed attributes, none
Superhuman mental powers: Instantaneous hypnosis achieved through beams of light from his single eye
Special limitations: None
Source of superhuman powers: member of an extinct race of unnamed insectoid beings

PARAPHERNALIA

Costume specifications: Body armor of unknown materials
Personal weaponry: Ray-blaster firing beams of concussive force and sonic displacer beams
Special weaponry: Spasm-rays (able to disrupt nervous systems of victims)
Other accessories: Giant Lemurian slug creatures, teleportation rays, shrinking rays, giant robots, planetary view-scanners, dreadnought-drill (capable of producing planet-wide earthquakes), essence-urn (capable of storing life-forces of living beings)
Transportation: Teleportation
Design and manufacture of paraphernalia: Psyklop

BIBLIOGRAPHY

First appearance: AVENGERS #88
Origin issue: Psyklop's origin is as yet unrevealed.
Significant issues: AVENGERS #88 (organized voodoo cult near New Orleans through surrogates, captured the Hulk for study, battled the Avengers and the Falcon, accidentally sent the Hulk to the "micro-world" of K'ai); INCREDIBLE HULK Vol. 2 #140 (retrieved the Hulk from K'ai, battled the Hulk, exiled to K'ai by the "dark gods"); INCREDIBLE HULK Vol. 2 #202-203 (caused earthquakes in attempt to conquer K'ai, imprisoned life-forces of quake victims as sacrifice to "dark gods," battled the Hulk and Jarella, seemingly destroyed by released life-forces of victims)

PSYLOCKE

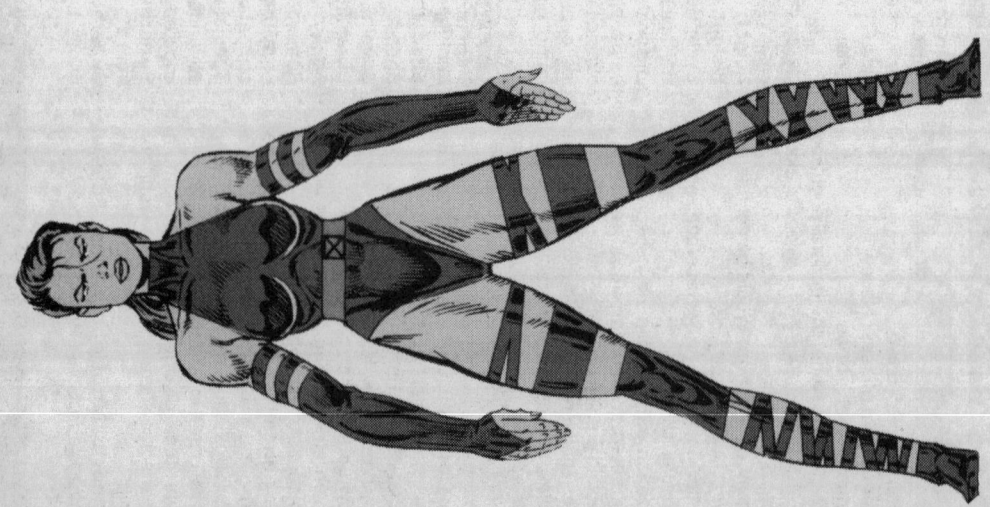

PSYLOCKE

BIOGRAPHICAL DATA

Real name: Elizabeth "Betsy" Braddock
Other current aliases: None
Former aliases: Captain Britain II, Lady Mandarin
Dual identity: Secret
Current occupation: Adventurer
Former occupation: Fashion model, operative for STRIKE Psi Division, (as Lady Mandarin) Assassin
Citizenship: United Kingdom
Legal status: No criminal record
Place of birth: Braddock Manor, England
Marital status: Single
Known relatives: James Braddock, Sr. (father, deceased), Elizabeth Braddock (mother, deceased), Brian Braddock, James "Jamie" Braddock (brothers)
Known confidants: Brian Braddock (Captain Britain), Linda McQuillan (Captain UK), X-Men, (former) Cypher (deceased)
Known allies: Captain Britain, X-Men, Captain UK, X-Factor II, (occasional) Saturnyne, (former) New Mutants, Agent Gabriel, Agent Michael (both of RCX)
Major enemies: Mojo, Mandarin, Matsuo Tsurayaba, Sabretooth, Shadow King, Vixen, Warskrulls, Adversary, Mister Sinister, Kaptain Briton, (deceased) Slaymaster (deceased), Goblin Queen (deceased), Horde (deceased), Reavers (defunct)
Usual base of operations: Professor Xavier's School for Gifted Youngsters, Salem Center, Westchester County, New York State
Former bases of operations: Braddock Manor, England; X-Men headquarters, Australian outback
Current group membership: X-Men
Former group membership: STRIKE Psi Division (British division of SHIELD I), ally of RCX
Extent of education: Bachelor's degree

PHYSICAL DESCRIPTION

Height: 5' 11"
Weight: 155 lbs
Eyes: Violet
Hair: Blond (dyed purple)
Other distinguishing features: Psylocke's facial features were given an Asian look by the Mandarin; she was given bionic eyes that look and function like her original eye by Mojo.

POWERS AND ABILITIES

Intelligence: Normal
Strength: Athlete
Speed: Athlete
Stamina: Athlete
Durability: Athlete
Agility: Athlete
Reflexes: Athlete
Fighting skills: Excellent hand-to-hand combatant, trained in unarmed combat by Captain UK and Wolverine, received further training in the martial arts by Matsuo Tsurayaba's Hand's instructors.
Special skills and abilities: Unrevealed
Superhuman physical powers: None
Superhuman mental powers: Possesses a wide range of telepathic abilities, enabling her to read minds, communicate mentally with others over long distances, stun the minds of others with "mental bolts," control the minds of others, and create illusions in the minds of others. When she telepathically communicates with another person over a distance, that person may perceive her presence as a butterfly-like image bearing large eyes on its wings. Psylocke can intensely focus her psionic powers into her "psychic knife" with which she can stun or kill an adversary.
Special limitations: None known
Source of superhuman powers: Genetic heritage from her father who was a denizen of Otherworld, an extradimensional realm

PARAPHERNALIA

Costume specifications: Conventional fabrics; previously wore Captain Britain costume (originally belonging to Kaptain Briton) that amplified her strength to superhuman levels and enabled her to fly; also previously wore lightweight armored battlesuits as Psylocke and Lady Mandarin.
Personal weaponry: None
Special weaponry: None
Other accessories: None
Transportation: X-Men Blackbird jet
Design and manufacture of paraphernalia: Unrevealed

BIBLIOGRAPHY

First appearance: (UK) CAPTAIN BRITAIN Vol. 1 #8, (US) NEW MUTANTS ANNUAL #2
Origin issue: Psylocke's origin is as yet unrevealed.
Significant issues: CAPTAIN BRITAIN Vol. 2 #5-6 (attacked by Kaptain Briton, killed him); CAPTAIN BRITAIN II under Captain UK's training; beaten and blinded by Slaymaster, ending her role as Captain Britain II); (Note: The preceding appeared in the Captain Britain trade paperback in the U.S.); NEW MUTANTS ANNUAL #2 (captured and mentally enslaved by Mojo, given her bionic eyes by him, returned to Earth and regained her free will, remained at Xavier's mansion); UNCANNY X-MEN #213 (first battled Sabretooth, joined X-Men as Psylocke); UNCANNY X-MEN #227 (died to defeat Adversary, resurrected by Roma); UNCANNY X-MEN #256-258 (captured by Matsuo Tsurayaba's Hand, brainwashed by the Mandarin and Tsurayaba into becoming the assassin Lady Mandarin, battled Wolverine, regained true personality and fought Mandarin); X-MEN #1-2 (battled Magneto and Acolytes); X-MEN #7 (battled Fenris, Omega Red); EXCALIBUR #55-56 (revisited brother Captain Britain, battled Jamie Braddock and Saturnyne)

PUCK

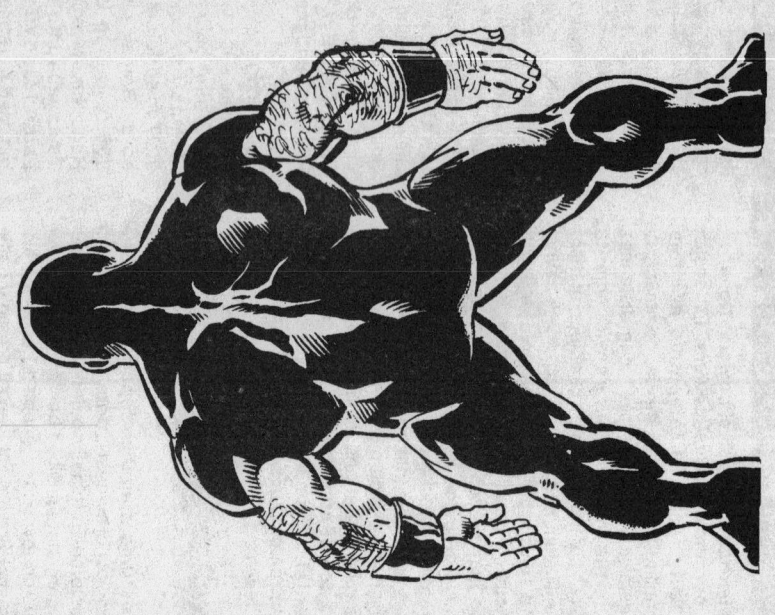

PUCK

BIOGRAPHICAL DATA

Real name: Eugene Milton Judd
Other current aliases: None
Former aliases: Unrevealed
Dual identity: Secret
Current occupation: Professional Adventurer
Former occupation: Soldier of fortune, intelligence agent, bouncer
Citizenship: Canada
Legal status: Criminal record, pardoned by Canadian government
Place of birth: Saskatoon, Saskatchewan
Marital status: Single
Known relatives: None
Known confidants: Heather Hudson
Major enemies: The Master, the Great Beasts, the Sorcerer, Razer
Usual base of operations: Alpha Flight headquarters, Department H, Toronto, Canada
Former bases of operations: Mobile
Current group membership: Alpha Flight
Former group membership: Beta Flight and Gamma Flight
Extent of education: Unrevealed

PHYSICAL DESCRIPTION

Height: 3' 6"
Weight: 225 lbs.
Eyes: Brown
Hair: Black (bald on top)
Other distinguishing features: Puck is a dwarf, his right ear is misshapen, presumably due to an old injury.

POWERS AND ABILITIES

Intelligence: Above normal
Strength: Superhuman Class 10
Speed: Superhuman
Stamina: Superhuman
Durability: Metahuman
Agility: Superhuman
Reflexes: Superhuman
Fighting skills: A mixture of various martial arts, streetfighting techniques, acrobatics and gymnastics
Special skills and abilities: Bullfighting, some knowledge of magic, the ability to put himself in a temporary death-like trance state
Superhuman physical powers: Superhuman strength, speed, durability, agility, reflexes, endurance
Superhuman mental powers: None
Special limitations: None
Source of superhuman powers: Genetic manipulation of cellular structure; Puck's tissues were condensed at a molecular level, causing his body to become akin to compressed rubber

PARAPHERNALIA

Costume specifications: Synthetic stretch fabric
Personal weaponry: None
Special weaponry: None
Other accessories: None
Transportation: Alpha Flight Omni-jet
Design and manufacture of paraphernalia: (transportation) Stark International (now Stark Enterprises)

BIBLIOGRAPHY

First appearance: ALPHA FLIGHT #1
Origin issue: ALPHA FLIGHT #32
Significant issues: ALPHA FLIGHT #1 (joined Alpha Flight); ALPHA FLIGHT #2 (wounded by Marinna; hospitalized); ALPHA FLIGHT #5 (battled illegal drug ring operating out of hospital); ALPHA FLIGHT #12 (returned to active duty; battled Omega Flight); ALPHA FLIGHT #13-14 (comforted Heather Hudson after James Hudson's presumed death); ALPHA FLIGHT #15 (encountered Sub-Mariner); ALPHA FLIGHT #16 (allied with Sub-Mariner in battle against the Master); ALPHA FLIGHT #24 (journeyed to the realm of the Great Beasts alongside Alpha Flight; battled Great Beasts); ALPHA FLIGHT #28 (encountered Beyonder); ALPHA FLIGHT #29 (battled Hulk); ALPHA FLIGHT #32 (background revealed; battled Razer); ALPHA FLIGHT #33 (began romance with Heather Hudson); ALPHA FLIGHT #39 (encountered Avengers); ALPHA FLIGHT #50 (Razer freed from Puck's body, returning Puck to normal size; Puck teleported to Tibet by Loki, decided to abandon previous life); ALPHA FLIGHT #59-60 (became embroiled in battle between Tibet and mainland China; battled Dragon; battled Dreamqueen alongside Alpha Flight); ALPHA FLIGHT #87-90 (received superhuman powers; became dwarf once more; rejoined Alpha Flight)

PUFF ADDER

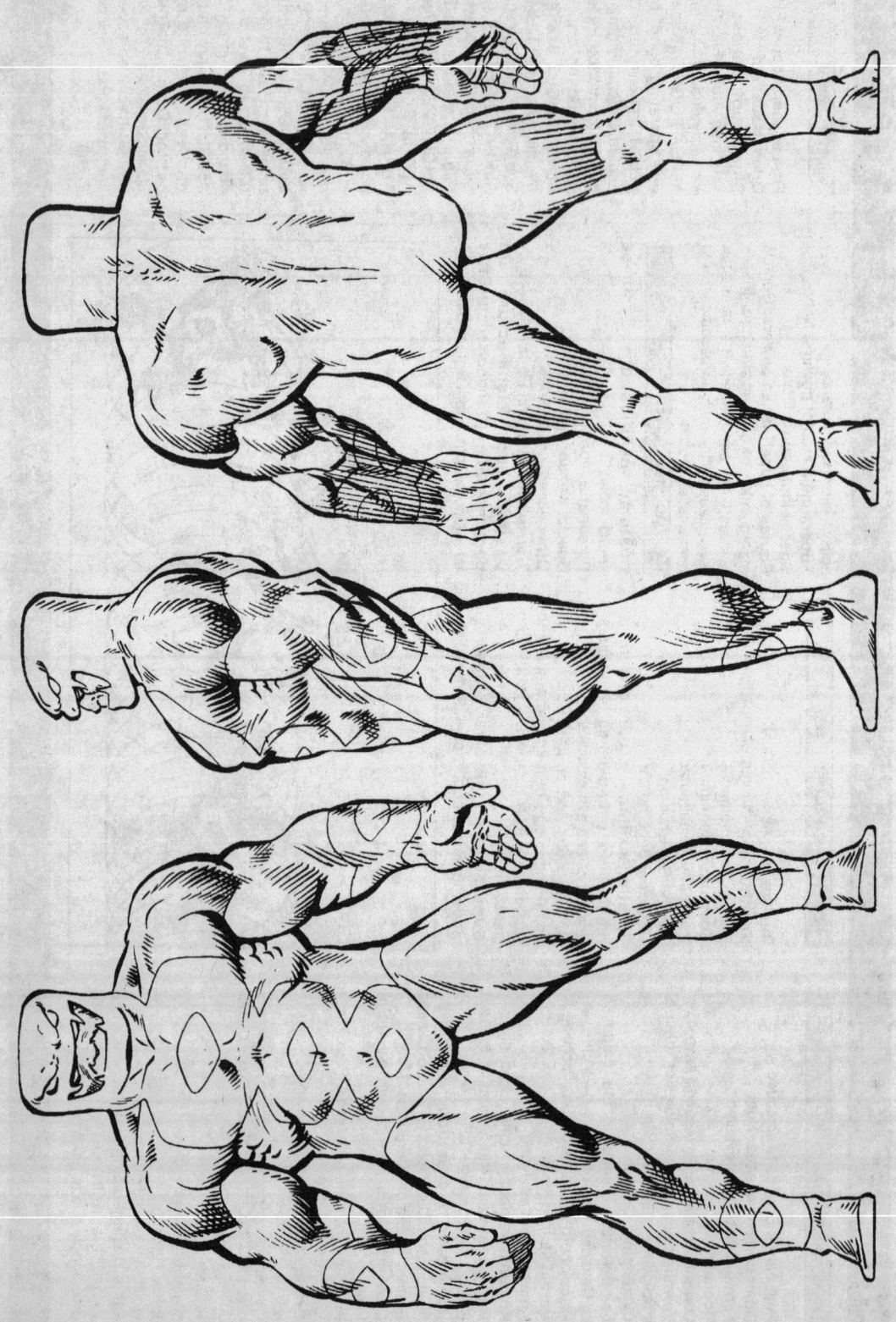

PUFF ADDER

BIOGRAPHICAL DATA
Real name: Gordon "Gordo" Fraley
Other current aliases: None
Former aliases: None
Dual identity: Known to the authorities
Current occupation: Professional criminal
Former occupation: Unrevealed
Citizenship: United States of America
Legal status: Criminal record in the U. S.
Place of birth: Atlanta, Georgia
Marital status: Single
Known relatives: None
Known confidants: Anaconda, Rock Python
Known allies: Serpent Society
Major enemies: Captain America, Diamondback
Usual base of operations: Serpent Society headquarters, the Bronx, New York
Former bases of operations: Serpent Citadel, upstate New York
Current group membership: Serpent Society
Former group membership: Serpent Squad IV (Black Racer, Copperhead III, Fer-de-Lance)
Extent of education: High school dropout

PHYSICAL DESCRIPTION
Height: 6' 5"
Weight: 375 lbs.
Eyes: Brown
Hair: Black
Other distinguishing features: None

POWERS AND ABILITIES
Intelligence: Normal
Strength: Superhuman Class 10
Speed: Athlete
Stamina: Enhanced human
Durability: Enhanced human
Agility: Normal
Reflexes: Athlete
Fighting skills: Extensive experience in streetfighting techniques
Special skills and abilities: Piloting of certain aircraft
Superhuman physical powers: Other than the above attributes, Puff Adder can cause the epidermis of his entire body to engorge with blood and thus puff up to make him appear larger and more menacing
Superhuman mental powers: None
Special limitations: Puff Adder can only remain fully inflated for approximately fifteen minutes at a time.
Source of superhuman powers: Genetic mutation

PARAPHERNALIA
Costume specifications: Synthetic stretch fabric
Personal weaponry: His cowl contains a pressurized container of noxious gas which can be released from his mouth area. It is activated by a specific motion made with his jaw muscles.
Special weaponry: None
Other accessories: None
Transportation: Serpent-Saucer
Design and manufacture of paraphernalia: Advanced Idea Mechanics

BIBLIOGRAPHY
First appearance: CAPTAIN AMERICA #337
Origin issue: Puff Adder's origin is as yet unrevealed.
Significant issues: CAPTAIN AMERICA #337 (alongside Serpent Squad IV, attempted to rob Las Vegas casino, battled Captain America, Falcon, Nomad, and D-Man); CAPTAIN AMERICA #338 (with Serpent Squad, freed from jail by Sidewinder); CAPTAIN AMERICA #341-342 (inducted into the Serpent Society as double agent of the Viper, betrayed Sidewinder, encountered Captain America); CAPTAIN AMERICA #355 (with Coachwhip and Rock Python, sent to steal the Falcon's uniform in order to regain admission into the Serpent Society, battled Battle Star and Falcon); CAPTAIN AMERICA #380-382 (alongside Anaconda, served as bailiff at the Serpent Society's trial of Diamondback; with Anaconda and Rock Python, sent to Diamondback's apartment to apprehend her, battled Captain America; seemingly overpowered Captain America); CAPTAIN AMERICA #385-387 (crash-landed Serpent Saucer on Diamondback's apartment, abducted Diamondback, Asp, and Black Mamba; Rock Python and himself thrown from Serpent Saucer by M:3dam; injured in fall, interrogated by Captain America and Paladin about abduction of Diamondback and friends)

PUMA™

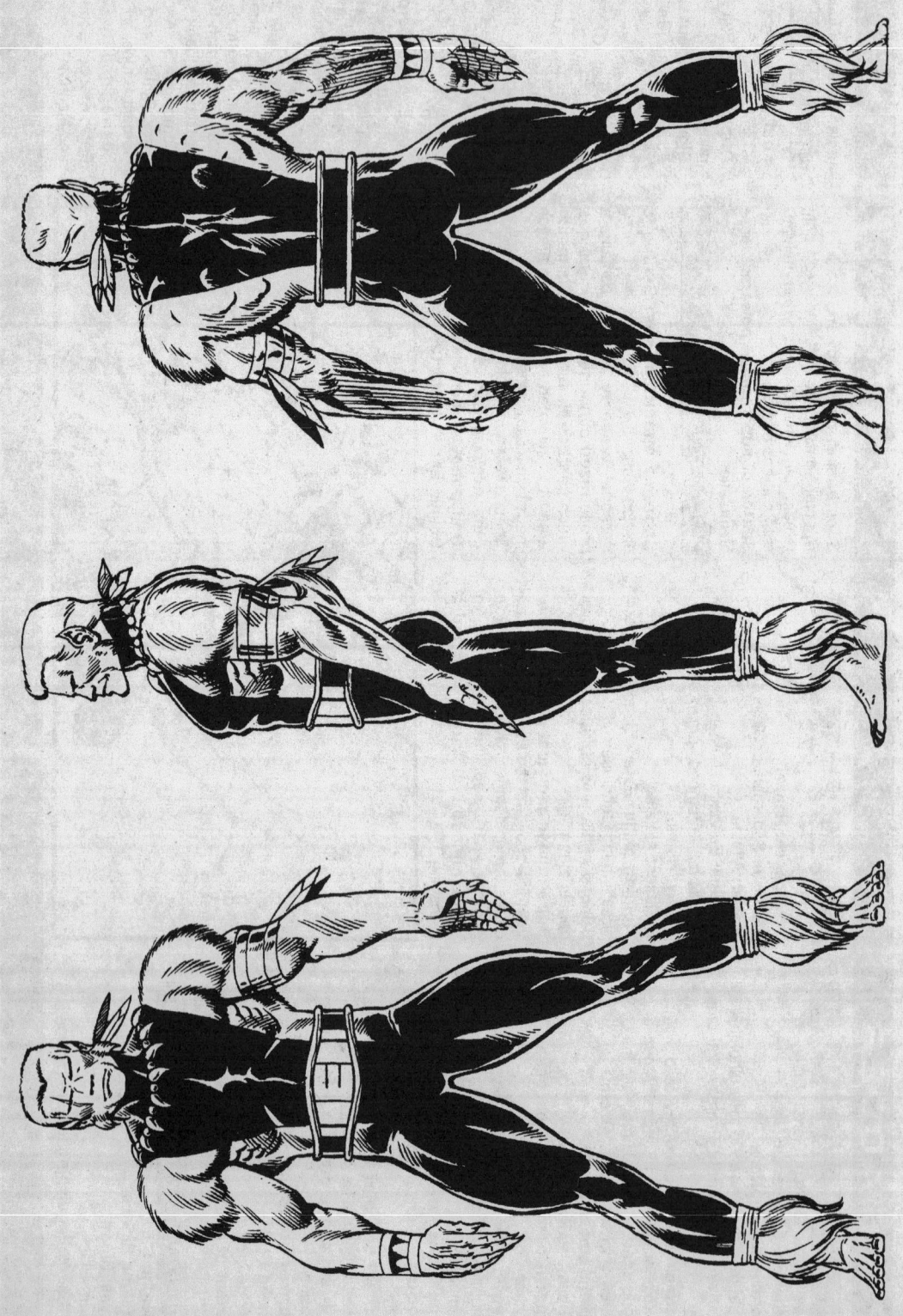

PUMA

BIOGRAPHICAL DATA

Real names: Thomas Fireheart
Other current aliases: None known
Former aliases: None known
Dual identity: Secret
Current occupation: CEO of Fireheart Enterprises, mercenary
Former occupation: Employee of the Rose
Citizenship: United States of America
Legal status: No criminal record
Place of birth: American indian reservation near Hartsdale, New Mexico
Marital status: Single
Known relatives: Unnamed uncle
Known confidants: Master Muramoto, Spider-Man, Mary Jane Watson-Parker
Known allies: Silver Sable, The Outlaws (Prowler, Rocket Racer, Sandman, Will O' the Wisp), (former) Spider-Man, the Rose
Major enemies: The Beyonder, Spider-Man, Black Crow
Usual base of operations: Fireheart Enterprises, Hartsdale, New Mexico and branch offices worldwide
Former bases of operations: American indian reservation near Hartsdale, New Mexico
Current group membership: None
Former group membership: The Outlaws
Extent of education: Masters degree in Business Administration

PHYSICAL DESCRIPTION

Height: 6' 2"
Weight: 240 lbs.
Eyes: Green
Hair: (as Fireheart) Black, (as Puma) Red
Other distinguishing features: In his Puma form, Fireheart's body is covered with a fine tan fur, and he has a scar over his right eye and claws.

POWERS AND ABILITIES

Intelligence: Extraordinary genius
Strength: Superhuman Class 25
Speed: Enhanced human
Stamina: Enhanced human
Durability: Enhanced human
Reflexes: Enhanced human
Agility: Enhanced human
Fighting skills: Trained in many forms of hand-to-hand combat techniques, especially in the martial arts used by Master Muramoto
Special skills: None known
Superhuman physical powers: Aside from the above listed attributes, all of Puma's senses have been heightened to superhuman levels
Superhuman mental powers: Transforms into the Puma through intense concentration.
Special limitations: None
Source of superhuman powers: Combination of genetic engineering and mysticism

PARAPHERNALIA

Costume specifications: Stretch fabric with tribal designs
Personal weaponry: None
Special weaponry: Access to state-of-the-art weaponry through his resources at Fireheart Enterprises
Other accessories: Access to state-of-the-art equipment through his resources at Fireheart Enterprises
Transportation: Personal customized Lear jet for long-distance travel
Design and manufacture of paraphernalia: Fireheart Enterprises

BIBLIOGRAPHY

First appearance: AMAZING SPIDER-MAN #256
Origin issue: AMAZING SPIDER-MAN #256
Significant issues: AMAZING SPIDER-MAN #256 (accepted contract from the Rose to kill Spider-Man; thwarted by the Black Cat); AMAZING SPIDER-MAN #257 (attacked Spider-Man again, but departed upon witnessing Spider-Man saving innocent bystanders); AMAZING SPIDER-MAN #273 (confronted the Beyonder in New York; the Beyonder simply transported him to downtown Tokyo); SPECTACULAR SPIDER-MAN #111 (enraged at death of Master Muramoto as the inadvertent result of the Beyonder's actions, Puma reached a state of "harmonious enlightenment with the universe" and was imbued with immeasureable power; doubting his own senses, Puma lost the mystical power); SPECTACULAR SPIDER-MAN ANNUAL #7 (to repay his debt of honor during the Beyonder affair, Fireheart offered Peter Parker a job with his company while the latter was in France on his honeymoon; Parker refused); WEB OF SPIDER-MAN #50 (attempted to vindicate Spider-Man of a crime; first encountered Silver Sable and the Outlaws); SPECTACULAR SPIDER-MAN ANNUAL #154 (battled Spider-Man in New York); SPECTACULAR SPIDER-MAN #156 (purchased the Daily Bugle and began a pro-Spider-Man campaign in an attempt to pay off his debt of honor); SPECTACULAR SPIDER-MAN #161 (almost killed in battle with the Hobgoblin, saved by Spider-Man); SPECTACULAR SPIDER-MAN #169-170 (joined Spider-Man and the Outlaws against the Avengers and the Space Phantom); SPECTACULAR SPIDER-MAN #171-172 (sold Daily Bugle back to J. Jonah Jameson, settled his debt of honor to Spider-Man in New Mexico); SPECTACULAR SPIDER-MAN #191-193 (consumed with his Puma persona, attempted to assassinate a U.S. Senator; thwarted by Spider-Man; lost all knowledge of Spider-Man's secret identity through a magical spell cast by the Black Crow

PUNISHER™

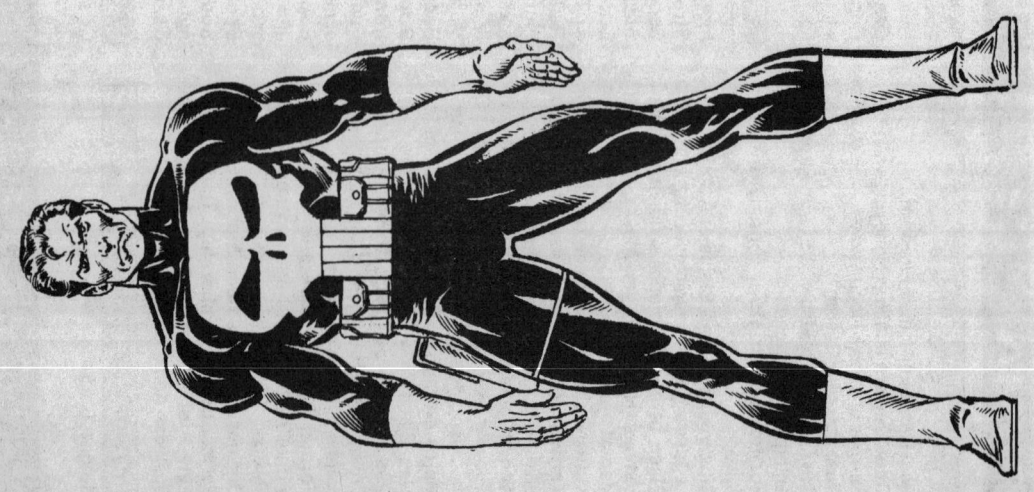

PUNISHER

BIOGRAPHICAL DATA

Real name: Frank Castle (born Castiglione)
Other current aliases: None
Former aliases: Various
Dual identity: Known to legal authorities
Current occupation: Vigilante
Former occupation: U.S. Marine
Citizenship: United States of America
Legal status: Criminal record, listed as Marine deserter
Place of birth: Queens, New York
Marital status: Widowed
Known relatives: Mario Castiglione (father, possibly deceased), Louisa Castiglione (mother, possibly deceased), Maria (wife, deceased), son (name unrevealed, deceased), Lisa Castle (daughter, deceased)
Known confidants: Microchip
Known allies: Spider-Man
Major enemies: Kingpin, Jigsaw, Maggia, all organized crime figures
Usual base of operations: Mobile, usually in New York area
Former bases of operations: None
Current group membership: None
Former group membership: United States Marine Corp.
Extent of education: Unrevealed

PHYSICAL DESCRIPTION

Height: 6'1"
Weight: 200 lbs.
Eyes: Blue
Hair: Black
Other distinguishing features: None

POWERS AND ABILITIES

Intelligence: Normal
Strength: Athlete
Speed: Athlete
Stamina: Athlete
Durability: Athlete
Agility: Athlete
Reflexes: Athlete
Fighting skills: U.S. Marine training in hand-to-hand combat, martial arts, marksmanship, weaponry
Special skills and abilities: Recon training, UDT (Underwater Demolition Team) certification
Superhuman physical powers: None
Superhuman mental powers: None
Special limitations: None
Source of superhuman powers: None

PARAPHERNALIA

Costume specifications: Body armor (Kevlar)
Personal weaponry: M16 .223 caliber automatic rifle; Sterling Mark 6 9mm. semi-automatic rifle; 9mm. Browning Llama auto-matic pistol; .45 caliber automatic frame re-chambered for 9mm. ammunition; .223 caliber Derringer; M26 fragmentation grenades; concussion grenades; tear-gas grenades; Gerber Mark II Combat knife
Special weaponry: Various
Other accessories: Various
Transportation: Armored combat van
Design and manufacture of paraphernalia: Various

BIBLIOGRAPHY

First appearance: AMAZING SPIDER-MAN #129
Origin issue: MARVEL PREVIEW #2
Significant issues: AMAZING SPIDER-MAN #129 (tricked by Jackal into attempting to kill Spider-Man); AMAZING SPIDER-MAN #135 (teamed with Spider-Man to capture Tarantula); GIANT-SIZE SPIDER-MAN #4 (teamed with Spider-Man to battle Moses Magnum); MARVEL PREVIEW #2 (origin recounted; family inadvertently witnessed gangland execution in New York's Central Park and murdered by mobsters; disappeared, resurfaced as costumed vigilante); MARVEL SUPER ACTION #1 (reprisals against criminals responsible for murder of his family recounted); AMAZING SPIDER-MAN #161-162 (teamed with Spider-Man and Nightcrawler to capture Jigsaw); AMAZING SPIDER-MAN #174-175 (teamed with Spider-Man against Hitman); CAPTAIN AMERICA #241 (encountered Captain America); AMAZING SPIDER-MAN #201-202 (teamed with Spider-Man against racketeers); AMAZING SPIDER-MAN ANNUAL #15 (encountered Spider-Man as both battled Dr. Octopus); DAREDEVIL #181 (encountered Bullseye in prison); DAREDEVIL #182 (escape from prison arranged by government agent, stopped drug smugglers); DAREDEVIL #183-184 (battled Daredevil); SPECTACULAR SPIDER-MAN #81 (tricked Boomerang into helping him escape prison); SPECTACULAR SPIDER-MAN #82 (unwittingly drugged while in prison, temporarily driven insane; encountered Spider-Man and Cloak and Dagger; attempted to kill Kingpin); SPECTACULAR SPIDER-MAN #83 (tried and committed to mental institution); PUNISHER Vol. 1 #1-5 (restored to sanity, sent to Ryker's Island Prison, escaped, resumed war on crime); STRANGE TALES Vol. 3 #13-14 (encountered Cloak and Dagger and Power Pack); SPECTACULAR SPIDER-MAN #140-143 (captured by Kingpin's men and mind-controlled by Persuader); PUNISHER Vol. 2 #15-19 (plotted assassination of the Kingpin); PUNISHER WAR JOURNAL #6-7 (encountered Wolverine); PUNISHER ANNUAL #9 (encountered Moon Knight); PUNISHER WAR JOURNAL #9 (encountered Black Widow and Shadowmasters); MOON KNIGHT Vol. 3 #8-9 (teamed with Moon Knight against ULTIMATUM); PUNISHER Vol. 2 #28-29 (encountered Doctor Doom); PUNISHER: NO ESCAPE (encountered Paladin and USAgent); GHOST RIDER Vol. 3 #5-6 (encountered Ghost Rider); THE 'NAM #52-53 (Marine career in Viet Nam and origin of "Punisher" nickname recounted)

THE PUNISHER IN ACTION

ART: KEVIN KOBASIC/JOSEF RUBINSTEIN

PUNISHER'S ARSENAL

PISTOLS

BERETTA 92F

Caliber: 9mm
Action: Double Action (DA) only
Capacity: 15+1 (magazine plus chambered round)
Weight: 32 ounces
Note: The Beretta 92F recently became America's Armed Forces standard issue sidearm. This is a testimony to its high degree of finish straight from the manufacturer. The Punisher takes full advantage of the great accuracy and reliability and improves on them slightly by using an after-market accessory, the Ram-Line 18 round magazine. This runs up the total rounds from 16 to 19. tion, the new capacity is 13+1, giving new life to an old veteran.

GLOCK 17

Caliber: 9mm
Action: "Safe Action" resembles DA
Capacity: 17+1
Weight: 24 ounces
Note: The introduction of the Glock Pistols to America was the beginning of a trend toward high-capacity 9mm handguns. The use of weight-saving plastic polymers in non-critical parts (about 20%) of the gun caused sensational controversy. But the most unusual aspect of the gun was the "Safe Action" feature. The trigger functions as a safety switch, which with training, makes for a very safe pistol. In his quest for the perfect solution to the combination of portability, capacity and stopping power, the Punisher has selected the Glock 18 machine pistol's extended 33-round magazine for the semi-auto Glock 17.

COLT GOVERNMENT MODEL

Caliber: .45 ACP (Automatic Cartridge Pistol)
Action: Semi-Auto
Capacity: 9+1
Weight: 38 ounces
Note: With almost 90 years of proven service and development, the Colt series of "Government 1911" derived models are still a touchstone of accurate shooting and dependability. The .45 caliber ammunition is a large-bore round which contributes to "one-shot" stopping power. The only drawback is magazine capacity. Utilizing a new Para-Ordnance modification, the new capacity is 13+1, giving new life to an old veteran.

BACK UP PISTOLS

DERRINGER SEMMERLING LM-4

Caliber: 9mm
Action: Manually operated repeater
Capacity: 7+1
Weight: 24 ounces
Note: When all else fails, the Punisher turns to the concealed, weapon of last-resort, the Semmerling LM-4. Although not the smallest derringer-class pistol the Punisher has carried, it is the highest capacity and also uses combat-worthy ammunition. Most derringers use .32 or .22 caliber ammunition which is considered "light." Despite the large size for a derringer, having a 3.6 inch barrel, the entire pistol can still be palmed by the Punisher.

SUB-MACHINE GUNS AND PISTOLS

UZI

Caliber: 9mm
Action: Blowback; select fire: Semi/Full Auto
Capacity: 25, 32, 40 round magazines
Weight: 7 pounds, 10 ounces
Note: Perhaps the premiere machine gun, the 9mm Uzi is the ultimate in full auto weapons. Renowned for its ability to fire reliably under the worst environmental conditions, the Punisher considers this weapon as the general-purpose instrument for all non-specific sorties. The high rate of fire, 600 rounds per minute, can throw up a wall of lead.

MAC-11

Caliber: 9mm
Action: Delayed blowback; select fire: Semi/Full Auto
Capacity: 9, 25, 34, 40 round magazines
Weight: 3 pounds, 9 ounces (without silence')
Note: Among the first very small machine pistols, the Military Arms Corporation MAC-1D (in 45 ACP) and -11 (in .380 and 9mm) were extremely popular because of their small size and large firepower. They were also among the first to have effective, integrated silencers. This makes the weapon useful for various covert operations, which also makes it ideal for the Punisher. The MAC-II's very high cyclic rate, 900-1000 rounds per minute, makes it more of an assault weapon, but in the hands of an experienced and highly trained combat veteran like the Punisher, it can be used with devastating accuracy.

GLOCK 18

Caliber: 9mm
Action: Blowback
Capacity: 19+1, 33+1 (extended clip)
Weight: 25 ounces
Note: Glock 18 resembles the model 17 except it is able to fire full auto. The most obvious difference is the slightly longer barrel which has three compensator slots that direct gasses upward so as to avert excessive muzzle climb. A near ultimate in size/firepower ratio, the Glock 18 makes best use of the "plus 2" magazine, which is a version of the standard 17-round magazine that can accommodate 2 additional rounds.

PUNISHER 2099™

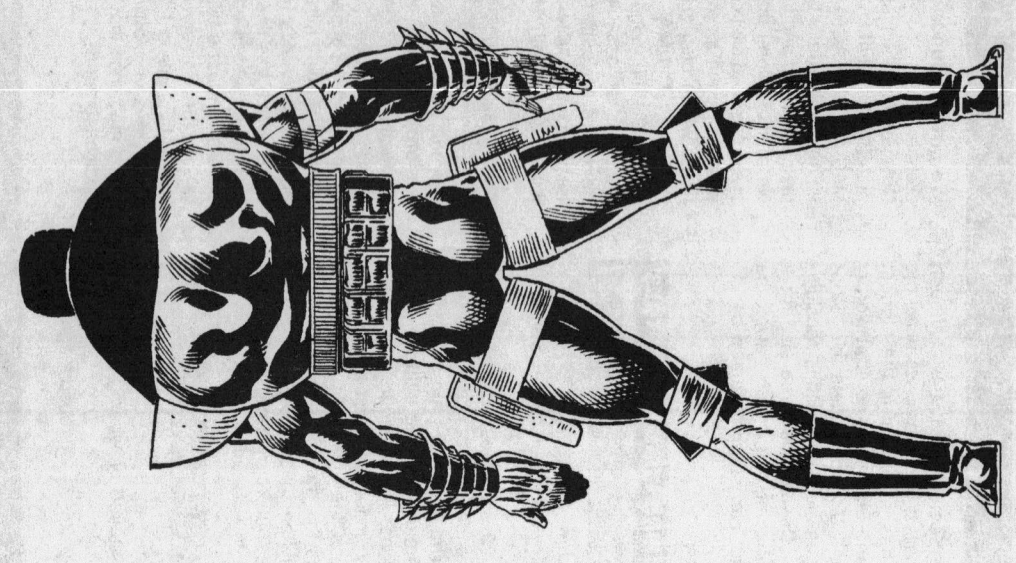
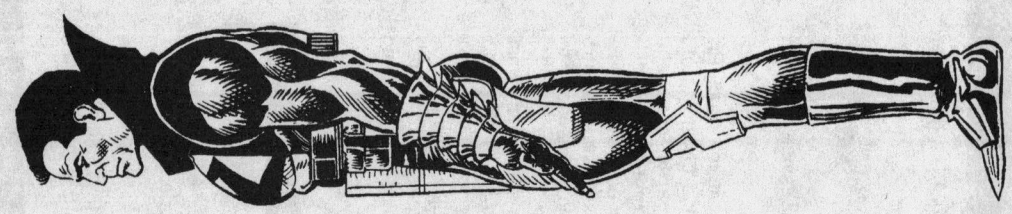
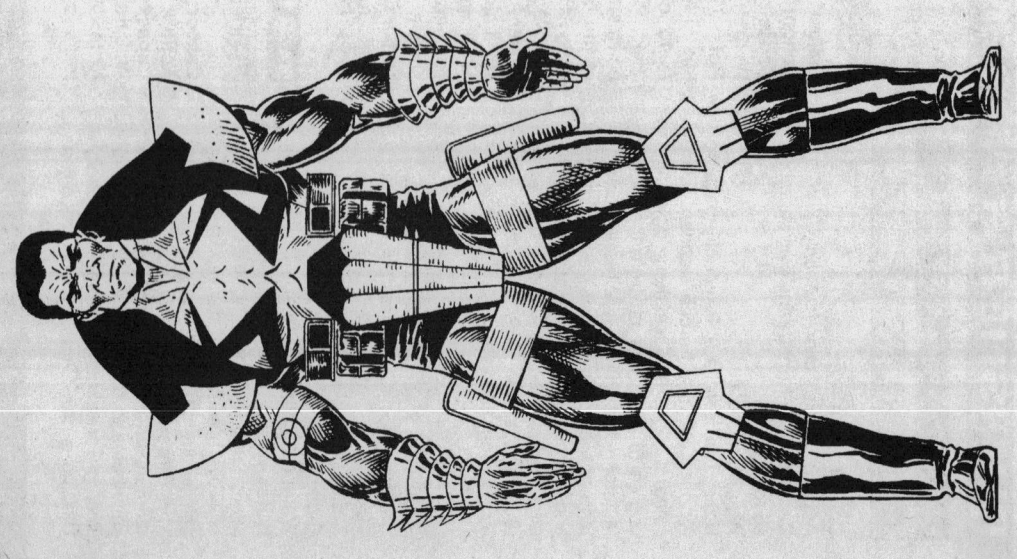

PUNISHER 2099

BIOGRAPHICAL DATA

Real name: Jake Gallows
Other current aliases: None
Former aliases: None
Dual identity: Secret
Current occupation: Public Eye Special Operations agent, vigilante
Former occupation: Public Eye police officer
Citizenship: United States of America, circa 2099
Legal status: No criminal record
Place of birth: An unrevealed location, circa 2099
Marital status: Single
Known relatives: Unnamed parents (deceased), Baldur Gallows (brother, deceased)
Known confidants: Matthew Axel
Known allies: Matthew Axel
Major enemies: Kron Stone (deceased), the Street Surgeons, the Cyber-Nostra, Multi-Factor (deceased), Fearmaster, the Public Eye
Usual base of operations: The basement of a sandstone apartment building in the New York, circa 2099
Former bases of operations: None
Current group membership: Public Eye police force
Former group membership: Unrevealed
Extent of education: Unrevealed

PHYSICAL DESCRIPTION

Height: 6'2"
Weight: 210 lbs.
Eyes: Blue
Hair: Black
Other distinguishing features: None

POWERS AND ABILITIES

Intelligence: Normal
Strength: Athlete
Speed: Athlete
Stamina: Athlete
Durability: Athlete
Agility: Athlete
Reflexes: Athlete
Fighting skills: Public Eye police training in hand-in-hand combat and martial arts
Special skills and abilities: Expert marksman and motorcyclist
Superhuman physical powers: None
Superhuman mental powers: None
Special limitations: None
Source of superhuman powers: Inapplicable

PARAPHERNALIA

Costume specifications: Body armor of unknown materials with "heat sink" capability, equipped with "face-scrambler" circuitry and Turbo kickboots, over exo-muscular undersuit (equipped with microwave sensors, computer trajectory mapping system, and bio-synergetic capacity for programming with various fighting styles and techniques)
Personal weaponry: Smith & Wesson .54 caliber Magnum handgun, 2015 vintage; Stark-Fujikawa .48 caliber Street Pacifier; Power Bat (with variable settings from hard rubber to titanium)
Special weaponry: Smart-targeting grenazers, plasma gas cannon, flame sticks
Other accessories: Various, as needed
Transportation: H.D. Stealth Stinger (unique police motorcycle capable of 800 mph speeds, equipped with air screen, computer probability mapping system, city traffic system override capability, sound bafflers, inertia brakes, various weaponry, projection holo-beam and wrap-around projection holo-image system enabling functional invisibility); Black Ambulance (equipped with security support systems to prevent prisoner escape)
Design and manufacture of paraphernalia: Matt Axel, unnamed technicians, and commercial manufacturers

BIBLIOGRAPHY

First appearance: PUNISHER 2099 #1
Origin issue: PUNISHER 2099 #1
Significant issues: PUNISHER 2099 #1 (family killed by Kron Stone, adopted Punisher identity, became secret vigilante); PUNISHER 2099 #2 (battled Kron Stone); PUNISHER WAR JOURNAL #50 (battled Street Surgeons); PUNISHER 2099 #3 (battled Saucers, executed him after death of one of his victims); PUNISHER 2099 #4 (battled the Cyber-Nostra); PUNISHER 2099 #5-6 (battled prisoner escaped from his private prison; battled Cyber-Nostra and Multi-Factor); PUNISHER 2099 #8 (battlec Fearmaster)

PUPPET MASTER

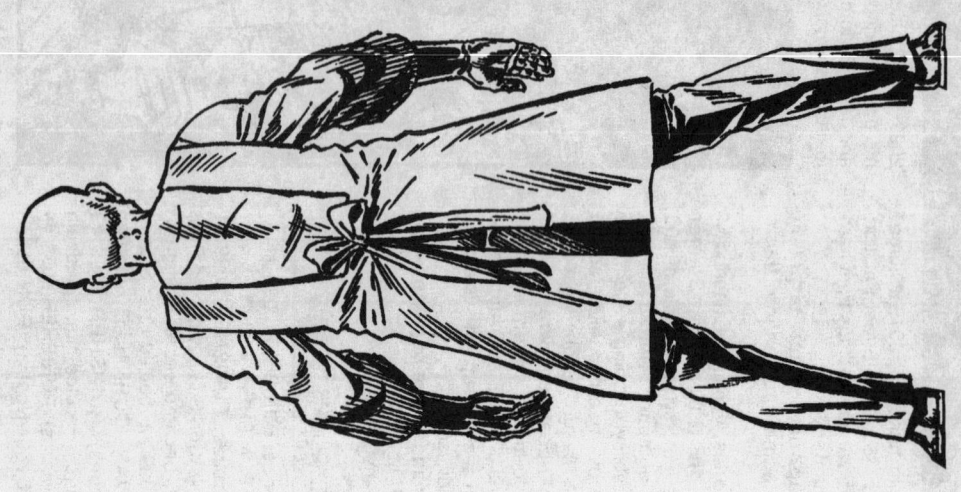

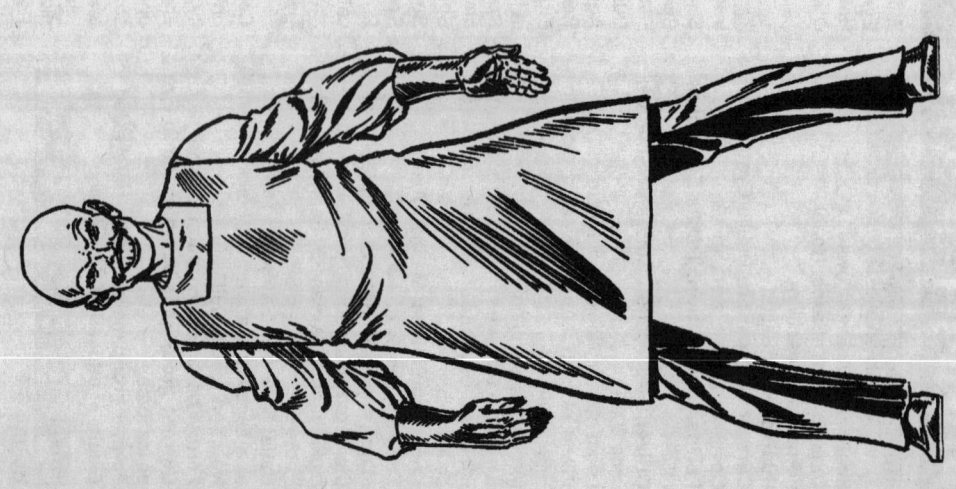

PUPPET MASTER

BIOGRAPHICAL DATA

Real name: Philip Masters
Other current aliases: None
Former aliases: None
Dual identity: Publicly known
Current occupation: Craftsman, parent
Former occupation: Biologist, professional criminal mastermind
Citizenship: Naturalized citizen of the United States of America
Legal status: Criminal record in the U.S., pardoned
Place of birth: Dragorin, Transia
Marital status: Married
Known relatives: Marcia Masters (first wife, deceased), Alicia Masters (daughter), unnamed second wife, Morty (stepson)
Known confidants: Current wife
Known allies: Mad Thinker, Egghead (deceased), Doctor Doom, Wizard
Major enemies: Fantastic Four, Namor the Sub-Mariner
Usual base of operations: New York
Former bases of operations: Various
Current group membership: None
Former group membership: None
Extent of education: Doctorate in biology

PHYSICAL DESCRIPTION

Height: 5' 6"
Weight: 150 lbs.
Eyes: Brown
Hair: Bald, formerly black
Other distinguishing features: Large upper teeth.
Note: The Puppet Master once disguised his appearance using latex facial appliances and foam rubber padding, which he referred to as "plastic surgery."

POWERS AND ABILITIES

Intelligence: Gifted
Strength: Below normal
Speed: Below normal
Stamina: Below normal
Durability: Normal
Agility: Normal
Reflexes: Normal
Fighting skills: None
Special skills and abilities: Ability to craft extremely lifelike puppets with extreme speed
Superhuman physical powers: None
Superhuman mental powers: Through intense concentration, able to control the actions of anyone after whom he models one of his puppets
Special limitations: Cannot control the actions of essentially mindless creatures, control can be broken by beings with supremely strong will-power, control limited to one person at a time, degree of control decreases with distance from person controlled
Source of superhuman powers: Magical and slightly radioactive clay used to create puppets, which originates near Wundergore Mountain, Transia, site of the tomb of the elder god Chthon

PARAPHERNALIA

Costume specifications: Normal attire
Personal weaponry: None
Special weaponry: None
Other accessories: Puppets of intended victims crafted from his magical clay; automatons built for him by Mad Thinker, Tinkerer, Doctor Doom
Transportation: Various ships provided by his allies
Design and manufacture of paraphernalia: The Mad Thinker

BIBLIOGRAPHY

First appearance: FANTASTIC FOUR #8
Origin issue: MARVEL TEAM-UP #6
Significant issues: FANTASTIC FOUR #8 (first encountered Fantastic Four, who opposed his plans for world domination); FANTASTIC FOUR #14 (controlled Namor, used him to battle Fantastic Four); STRANGE TALES #116 (pitted Human Torch and Thing against each other); FANTASTIC FOUR #28 (teamed with Mad Thinker, used the original X-Men to battle Fantastic Four); STRANGE TALES #126 (with Thinker, battled Thing and Torch); STRANGE TALES #133 (used animated life size mannequins to battle Thing and Torch); FANTASTIC FOUR ANNUAL #3 (among criminals assembled by Doom); TALES TO ASTONISH #78-79 (controlled Namor again); X-MEN #27 (opposed the original X-Men through mind-controlled Mimic); TALES TO ASTONISH #100 (fomented battle between Hulk and Namor by controlling Hulk); SUB-MARINER #14/AVENGERS #63/CAPTAIN MARVEL #14 (allied with Mad Thinker and Egghead in their attempted blackmail of U.S. forced Iron Man I to battle Captain Marvel I); FANTASTIC FOUR #100 (teamed with Thinker, attacked Fantastic Four using androids of their past foes); MARVEL TEAM-UF #5 (controlled Ballox the Monstroid, battled Spider-Man and Vision); MARVEL TEAM-UP #6 (with Thinker, battled Spider-Man and Thing); MARVEL TWO-IN-ONE #9 (forced Thor to battle Fantastic Four); FANTASTIC FOUR #168-170 (controlled Wrecker and Power Man); MARVEL TWO-IN-ONE #74 (returned to his homeland, encountered Modred the Mystic); FANTASTIC FOUR #236 (with Doctor Doom, trapped Fantastic Four in miniature community of "Liddleville,"); MICRONAUTS #41 (defeated by Doom in "Liddleville"); FANTASTIC FOUR #246 (seemingly destroyed by Doom); THING #4 (his mind resurrected in body of living radioactive clay); THING #6 (battled Thing on mental plane, living clay body destroyed); THING #34 (resurrected in original body by Sphinx); FANTASTIC FOUR #300 (with Thinker and Wizard, attempted to disrupt wedding of Human Torch and Alicia; changed mind, foiled plan); POWER PACK #60 (revealed to have reformed, remarried, and to have stepson; toys he crafted for son inadvertently caused battle between Power Pack and alien Ciegramites)

PYM, HENRY™

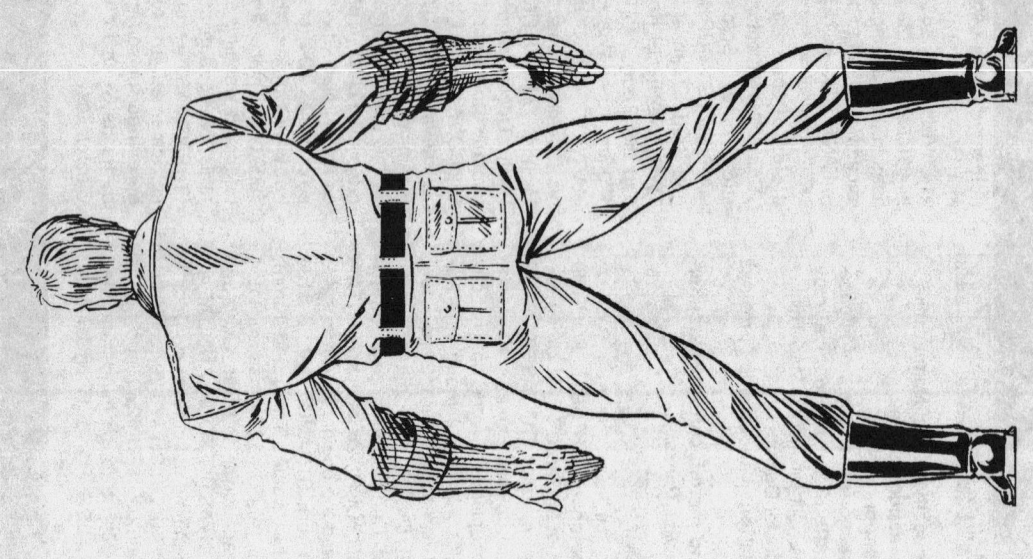
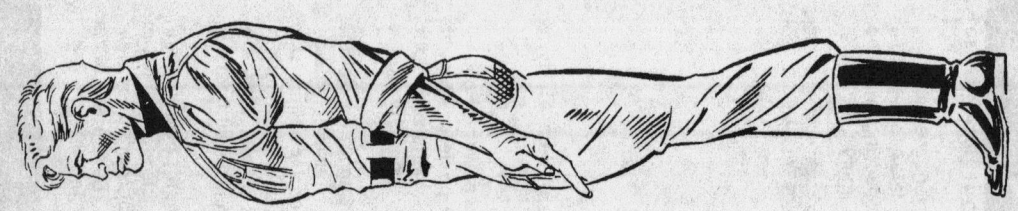
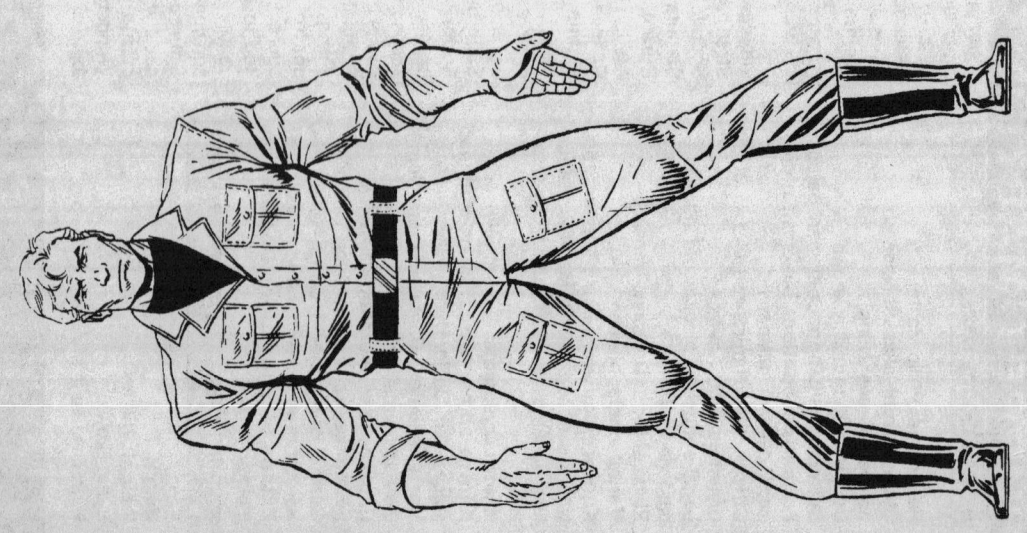

PYM, HENRY

BIOGRAPHICAL DATA

Real name: Dr. Henry J. "Hank" Pym
Other current aliases: Giant-Man I
Former aliases: Ant-Man I; Goliath I; Yellowjacket I; Doctor Pym, the Scientific Adventurer
Dual identity: Publically known
Current Occupation: Biochemist, researcher, adventurer
Former occupation: Manager of Avengers Compound, roboticist
Citizenship: United States of America
Legal status: Conviction for treason that was later overturned
Place of birth: Elmsford, New York
Marital status: Widower, later married and divorced
Known relatives: Maria Trovaya Pym (first wife, deceased), Janet Van Dyne (Wasp, second wife, divorced), Ultron-12 ("son," destroyed)
Known confidants: Janet Van Dyne, Esperita (Firebird), Dr. Jennie Pelk, Captain America, Hawkeye
Known allies: Wasp, Avengers West Coast, Avengers East, Iron Man I, Thor, Ant-Man II, Esperita (Firebird), Giant-Man II (Dr. Bill Foster), the Fantastic Four, Spider-Man, (former) Defenders
Major enemies: Ultron, Whirlwind (Human Top II), Goliath II, Kang, Voice, Scarlet Beetle, Living Eraser, Madame X, El Toro, Beasts of Berlin, Sons of the Serpent I, Vibro, MODAM (SODAM), (former) Black Knight II, Egghead (deceased), Porcupine (deceased), Masters of Evil I, II, and III
Usual base of operations: Avengers Headquarters, New York City
Former bases of operations: Cresskill, New Jersey; Avengers Mansion, New York City; Avengers Compound, Palos Verdes, California; Death Valley, California
Current group membership: Avengers
Former group membership: Defenders, Avengers West Coast
Extent of education: Ph.D in biochemistry

PHYSICAL DESCRIPTION

Height: (normal) 6' (when changing size, Pym's height has varied from 1/2 inch to 100 feet)
Weight: (normal) 185 lbs. (weight varies dependent on his size)
Eyes: Blue
Hair: Blond
Other distinguishing features: None

POWERS AND ABILITIES

Intelligence: Extraordinary genius
Strength: (normal size) Normal, (at 10') Enhanced human, (at 25') Superhuman Class 10, (at 100') Superhuman Class 50
Speed: (normal size) Normal, (at 10') Enhanced human, (at 25' and over) Superhuman
Stamina: (normal size) Normal, (at 10') Enhanced human, (at 25' and over) Superhuman
Durability: (normal size) Normal, (at 10') Enhanced human, (at 25' and over) Superhuman
Agility: (normal size) Normal, (as giant) Enhanced human
Reflexes: (normal size) Normal, (as giant) Enhanced human
Fighting skills: Good hand-to-hand combatant; received Avengers training in unarmed combat by Captain America
Special skills and abilities: Dr. Henry Pym is one of the world's foremost biochemists and also possesses considerable knowledge and expertise in subatomic physics, robotics, cybernetics, the study of higher insects (especially ants), and the design of computerized artificial intelligence systems.
Superhuman physical powers: Aside from the above listed attributes, as Ant-man I and Yellowjacket I, Pym could reduce himself in size to as little as 1/2 inch in height, temporarily displacing his mass extradimensionally, while retaining the strength of a normal sized man. As Giant-Man I and Goliath I, Pym could grow to gigantic size and mass (drawn from another dimension) while simultaneously gaining superhuman strength. As Doctor Pym he can generate subatomic "Pym particles" to reduce other living beings or objects in size and mass or restore them to their original size and mass.
Superhuman mental powers: Pym can generate subatomic "Pym particles" to change the size of himself or other beings or objects by an act of will.
Special limitations: Formerly Pym could not change his own size without seriously endangering his health
Source of superhuman powers: Repeated exposure to subatomic "Pym particles"

PARAPHERNALIA

Costume specifications: (in his costumed identites) Synthetic stretch fabric composed of unstable molecules; (as Dr. Pym) Ordinary clothing
Personal weaponry: As Yellowjacket I, Pym carried electric "stingers" in his gloves which emitted electrical bolts of variable current.
Special weaponry: Dr. Pym carries various weapons which he uses his powers to shrink to the size of microchips when not in use. "Cybernetic helmet" which permits Pym to achieve rudimentary telepathic communication with ants and other higher insects and to control their minds
Other accessories: Dr. Pym carries various equipment which he uses his powers to shrink to the size of microchips when not in use.
Transportation: "Rover", a multipurpose flying vehicle which he has endowed with artificial intelligence and sentience; short range flight via hover-pack; long range flight via Avengers Quinjet
Design and manufacture of paraphernalia: (Quinjet) Tony Stark, (all others) Dr. Pym

PYRO™

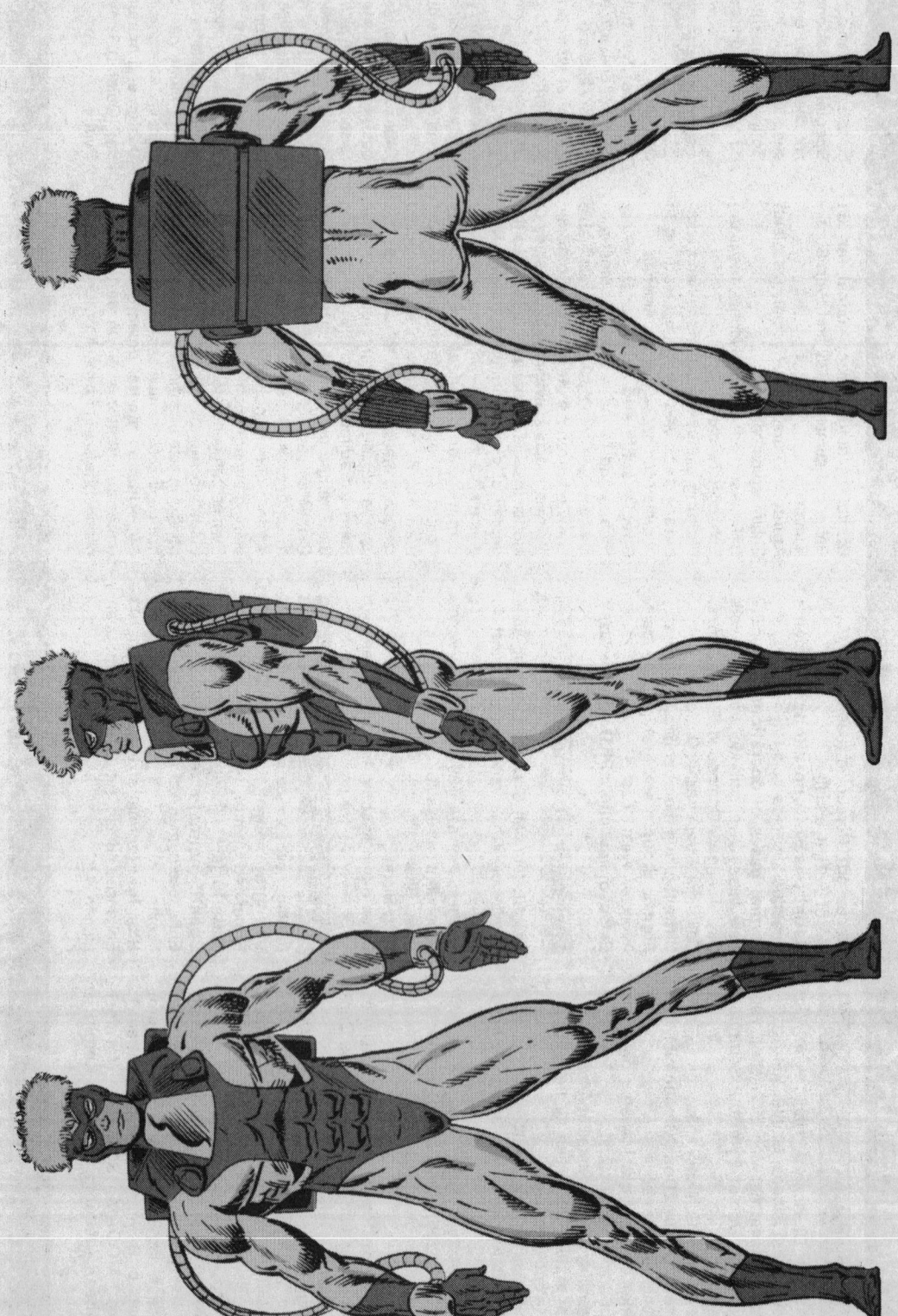

PYRO

BIOGRAPHICAL DATA

Real name: St. John Allerdyce
Other current aliases: None
Former aliases: None
Dual Identity: Known to federal authorities
Current occupation: Professional criminal, subversive
Former occupation: Journalist, novelist, special government operative
Citizenship: Australia
Legal status: Formerly wanted as an outlaw, granted presidential pardon
Place of birth: Sydney, Australia
Marital status: Single
Known relatives: None
Known confidants: Blob
Known allies: Brotherhood of Evil Mutants V (Blob, Phantazia, Sauron, Toad), (former) Brotherhood of Evil Mutants IV/Freedom Force
Major enemies: X-Men, X-Force, X-Factor II, Avengers, Cable, Daredevil, Hulk, Darkhawk, Sleepwalker, Portal, (former) New Mutants, X-Factor I, Desert Sword
Usual base of operations: Mobile
Former bases of operations: The Pentagon, Arlington, Virginia
Current group membership: Brotherhood of Evil Mutants V
Former group membership: Brotherhood of Evil Mutants IV/Freedom Force
Extent of education: College degree

PHYSICAL DESCRIPTION

Height: 5'10"
Weight: 150 lbs.
Eyes: Blue
Hair: Blond
Other distinguishing features: None

POWERS AND ABILITIES

Intelligence: Normal
Strength: Normal
Speed: Normal
Stamina: Normal
Durability: Normal
Agility: Normal
Reflexes: Normal
Fighting skills: Poor hand-to-hand combatant, received unarmed combat training while in Freedom Force
Special skills and abilities: Successful writer of Gothic romances prior to turning to crime.
Superhuman physical powers: Invulnerable to any fire that he has placed under his mental control
Superhuman mental powers: Pyro has the psionic ability to cause any fire to grow in size and intensity and to take any form he wishes, even that of a living creature. (Such fire creatures, however, have no intelligence or life.) He can psionically manipulate the flame to do whatever he desires. Pyro's fiery creations have greater solidity than normal flame; hence a giant "bird" he created from fire could grasp and carry a solid object with its claws. The degree of Pyro's concentration necessary to manipulate a flame-being is directly proportional to the being's size, power, and flame
Special limitations: Pyro can be harmed by any fire that he does not mentally control. Pyro has to be able to see a flame in order to take control of it; in practical terms the flame must be within a 100-yard radius of him. Pyro cannot affect flames that he sees on television but which are not within this radius. Any of Pyro's fiery creations will immediately revert to ordinary flame if he turns his interest from it.
Source of superhuman powers: Genetic mutation

PARAPHERNALIA

Costume specifications: A specially insulated costume made of unknown materials that provides him with a certain degree of protection against fire.
Personal weaponry: A flame-thrower that can throw a stream of flame a maximum distance of 25 feet.
Special weaponry: None
Other accessories: Formerly had access to two-way radio device for communication with other Freedom Force members
Transportation: Formerly had access to the federal governments advanced air and land vehicles
Design and manufacture of paraphernalia: (costume, flame thrower) St. John Allerdyce

BIBLIOGRAPHY

First appearance: UNCANNY X-MEN #141
Origin issue: Pyro's origin is as yet unrevealed
Significant issues: UNCANNY X-MEN #141-142 (with Brotherhood of Evil Mutants IV, attempted to assassinate Senator Robert Kelly, first battled X-Men); AVENGERS ANNUAL #10 (with Brotherhood, battled the Avengers); UNCANNY X-MEN #177-178 (with Brotherhood, battled X-Men); UNCANNY X-MEN #199 (with Brotherhood, began work for the federal government as Freedom Force, helped to capture Magneto); AVENGERS ANNUAL #15 (with Freedom Force, captured Avengers on behalf of federal government); X-FACTOR #8-10 (clashed with X-Factor I in seeking to arrest Rusty Collins); UNCANNY X-MEN #223-227 (with Freedom Force fought X-Men in Dallas, was present at X-Men's apparent demise); X-FACTOR #30-31 (with Freedom Force, battled Cyclops and Marvel Girl); NEW MUTANTS #78-80 (with Freedom Force, sought to arrest Rusty Collins, battled New Mutants, arrested Rusty Collins and Skids); AVENGERS #312 (teamed with Blob and Pyro against Avengers during "Acts of Vengeance"); NEW MUTANTS ANNUAL #11/NEW WARRIORS ANNUAL #1/UNCANNY X-MEN ANNUAL #15/X-FACTOR ANNUAL #6 (participated in Freedom Force's final mission, battled Desert Storm in Kuwait; abandoned in Kuwait); X-FORCE #6-7 (joined Brotherhood of Evil Mutants V, with them, battled X-Force)

QUAGMIRE

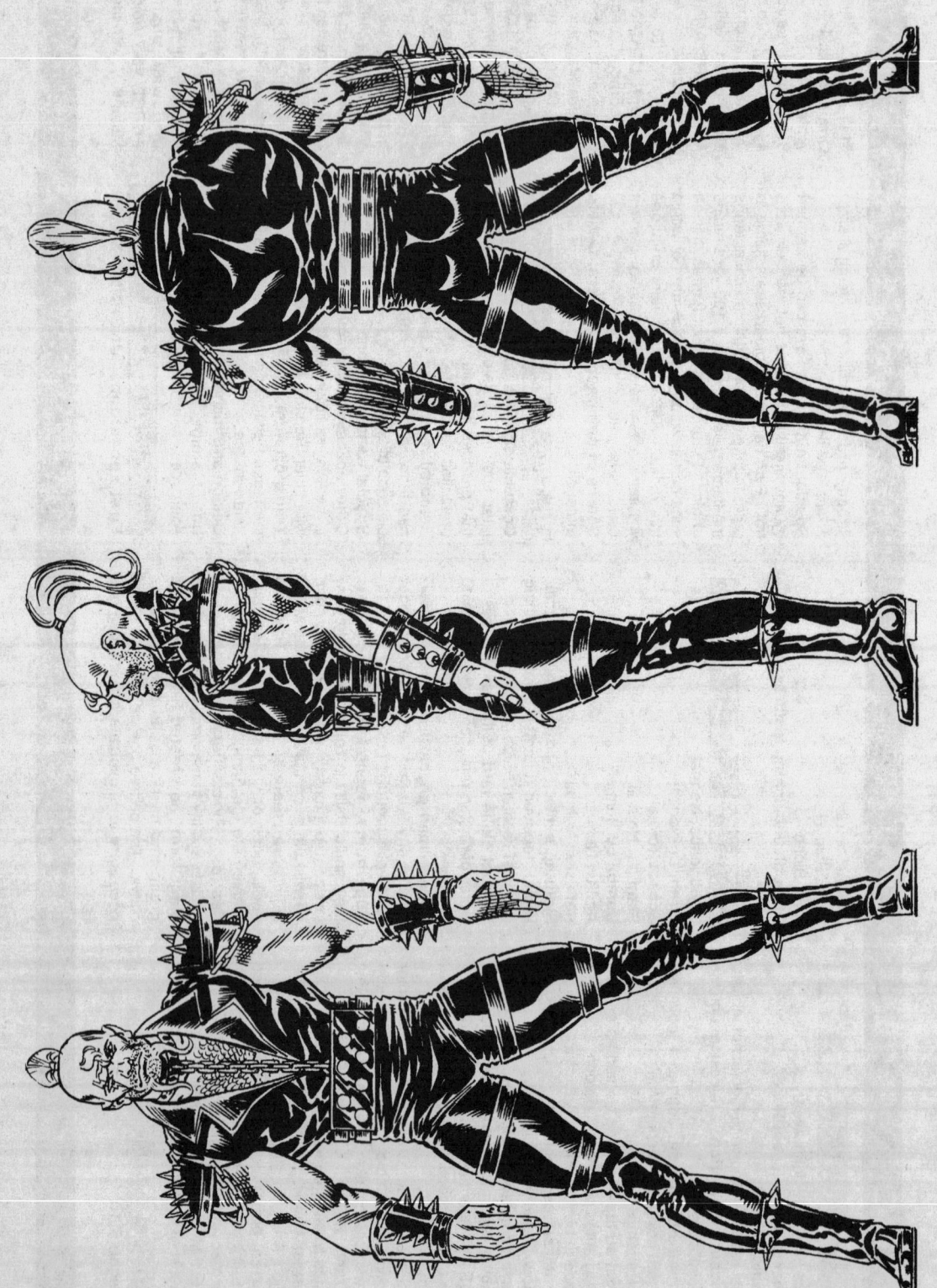

QUAGMIRE

BIOGRAPHICAL DATA

Real name: Jerome Myers
Current aliases: None
Former aliases: None
Dual identity: Publicly known to the citizens of the United States of "Other-Earth" ("Earth-S")
Current occupation: Criminal, renegade
Former occupation: Government agent
Citizenship: United States of "Other-Earth" or "Earth-S"
Legal status: Criminal record pardoned when he underwent behavior modification on "Other-Earth"; criminal record on mainstream Earth
Place of birth: Pittsville, Terranova on "Other-Earth"
Marital status: Single
Known relatives: None
Known confidants: None, (former) Lamprey (deceased)
Known allies: None, (former) Chief Examiner, Squadron Supreme, Institute of Evil
Major enemies: Quasar, Squadron Supreme, Dr. Spectrum III
Usual base of operations: Mobile in southeast United States of mainstream Earth
Former base of operations: Squadron City, Great American Desert, United States of "Other-Earth"; The Vault, Colorado, United States of mainstream Earth
Current group membership: None
Former group membership: Squadron Supreme, Institute of Evil
Extent of education: Middle school

PHYSICAL DESCRIPTION

Height: 6'
Weight: 185 lbs.
Eyes: Blue
Hair: Blond
Other distinguishing features: Scar above and below right eye

POWERS AND ABILITIES

Intelligence: Above normal
Strength: Athlete
Speed: Athlete
Stamina: Athlete
Durability: Athlete
Agility: Athlete
Reflexes: Athlete
Fighting skills: Good hand-to-hand combatant
Special skills and abilities: Lock picking, sculpture-making
Superhuman physical powers: None
Superhuman mental powers: The ability to tap and manipulate the extradimensional Darkforce in the form of a thick, viscous tar-like substance. Opening a dimensional interface with his mind, he seemingly projects the Darkforce from his fingertips or can open the interface anywhere within thirty feet of him. He can control the flow of Darkforce from a thin spray of globules to a thick torrent of oozing slime. His darkforce manifestation is extremely adhesive: a sufficient quantity can immobilize beings of up to Class 100 strength. He can also apply small quantities of it to his fingertips and toes in order to scale walls and ceilings. He can shape the Darkforce into animated tendrils or whip them about his person in a psychokinetic tornado. The Darkforce generally behaves like quasi-solid liquid; human beings cannot breath through it.
Special limitations: Since the dimensional Darkforce is virtually limitless, there is theoretically no limit to the amount of it Quagmire can draw to this dimension, though presumably mental fatigue will eventually affect how long he can hold the interface to the Darkforce Dimension open, thus eventually impair his performance. When he is rendered unconscious, the portal to the Darkforce dimension snaps shut and the Darkforce substance he has drawn from it quickly vanishes to its place of origin.
Source of superhuman powers: Genetic mutation

PARAPHERNALIA

Costume specifications: Leather and rayon
Personal weaponry: None
Special weaponry: None
Other accessories: None
Transportation: Various
Design and manufacture of paraphernalia: Inapplicable

BIBLIOGRAPHY

First appearance: SQUADRON SUPREME #5
Origin issue: Quagmire's origin is as yet unrevealed.
Significant issues: SQUADRON SUPREME #5 (alongside Institute of Evil, held Squadron Supreme's loved ones hostage, defeated by the Squadron); SQUADRON SUPREME #6 (underwent behavior modification, elected to Squadron membership); SQUADRON SUPREME #8 (on assignment with Ape X and Blue Eagle, reprimanded by Eagle for inappropriate behavior, rescued thirty people in industrial accident, fell into coma); SQUADRON SUPREME #10 (while in coma, interfaced with Darkforce dimension, vast quantities of Darkforce flooded the hospital, life support disconnected by Hyperion, vanished into Darkforce dimension); MARVEL COMICS PRESENTS #29 (portal into mainstream Earth dimension formed near Nexus of Realities in belly of the Man-Thing, Quagmire's body passed through Man-Thing's, passage apparently reversed effects of behavior modification, restoring his old personality, battled Quasar and Jennifer Kale, defeated); QUASAR #35 (contacted by the Chief Examiner in Vault, freed); QUASAR #36-37 (approached Kayla Ballantine and forced her through the Chief Examiner's black teleportal, battled tiny Antibody which secretly, sought refuge inside his body)

QUANTUM™

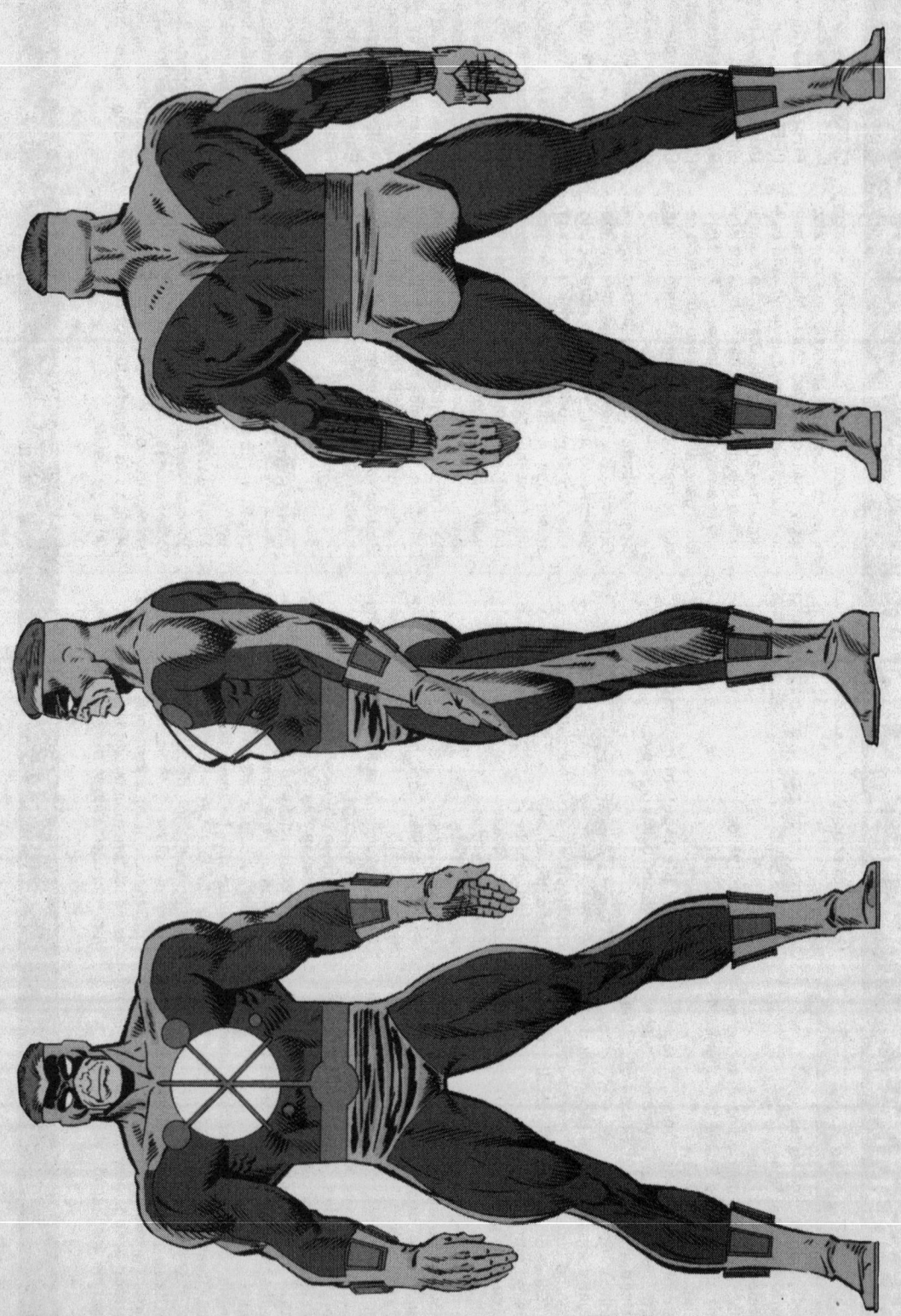

QUANTUM

BIOGRAPHICAL DATA

Real name: Unrevealed
Other Current aliases: None
Former aliases: None
Dual identity: Secret; Quantum's true name is unknown on Earth
Current occupation: Soldier
Former occupation: Unrevealed
Citizenship: Planet Dakkam
Legal status: No criminal record
Place of birth: The planet Dakkam
Marital status: Unrevealed
Known relatives: None
Known confidants: None
Known allies: The Elect, Graviton, Halflife, Zzzax
Major enemies: The Avengers West Coast, Quasar, Aquarian
Usual base of operations: Mobile
Former base of operations: Planet Dakkam
Current group membership: The Elite of Dakkam, the Elect
Former group membership: Allies of Graviton
Extent of education: Unrevealed

PHYSICAL DESCRIPTION

Height: 6'3"
Weight: 230 lbs.
Eyes: Unrevealed (no visible pupils or irises)
Hair: Red
Other distinguishing features: None

POWERS AND ABILITIES

Intelligence: Normal
Strength: Superhuman Class 100
Speed: Enhanced human
Flight speed: Sub-light speed
Stamina: Superhuman
Durability: Metahuman
Agility: Peak human
Reflexes: Peak human
Fighting skills: Trained as a professional soldier in the fighting arts of planet Dakkam
Special skills and abilities: Unrevealed
Superhuman physical powers: Aside from the above listed attributes, Quantum has the ability to generate a sheath of flames about his body; ability to teleport himself a maximum distance of six inches up to several times per second, thus seeming to appear in several places simultaneously or to have created multiple duplicates of himself; ability to survive indefinitely without food, air, or water
Superhuman mental powers: None
Special limitations: Quantum derives his energies from the radiation of the closest star; therefore, he can be rendered powerless by being cut off from sunlight.
Source of superhuman powers: Exposure to cosmic radiation from Earth's sun

PARAPHERNALIA

Costume specifications: Alien materials
Personal weaponry: None
Special weaponry: None
Other accessories: None
Transportation: Flight under own power, teleportation
Design and manufacture of paraphernalia: Inapplicable

BIBLIOGRAPHY

First appearance: WEST COAST AVENGERS Vol. 2 #12
Origin issue: QUASAR #4
Significant issues: WEST COAST AVENGERS Vol. 2 #12 (alongside Halflife and Zzzax, aided Graviton against West Coast Avengers; during disagreement with Halflife and Graviton, fell from Graviton's high-altitude headquarters); QUASAR #4 (encountered the Aquarian, learned he was a fellow Dakkamite; battled Quasar, frozen by him into three intangible images); QUASAR #14-15 (whereabouts of fellow members of the Elect, imprisoned on the Stranger's laboratory world, recvealed)

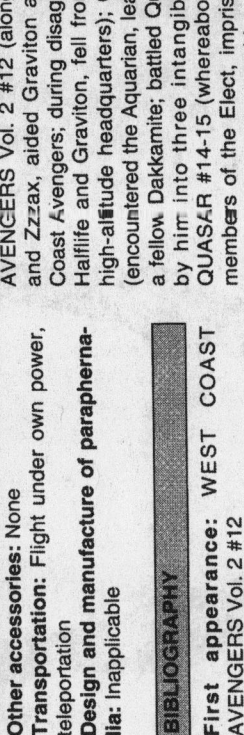

QUASAR™

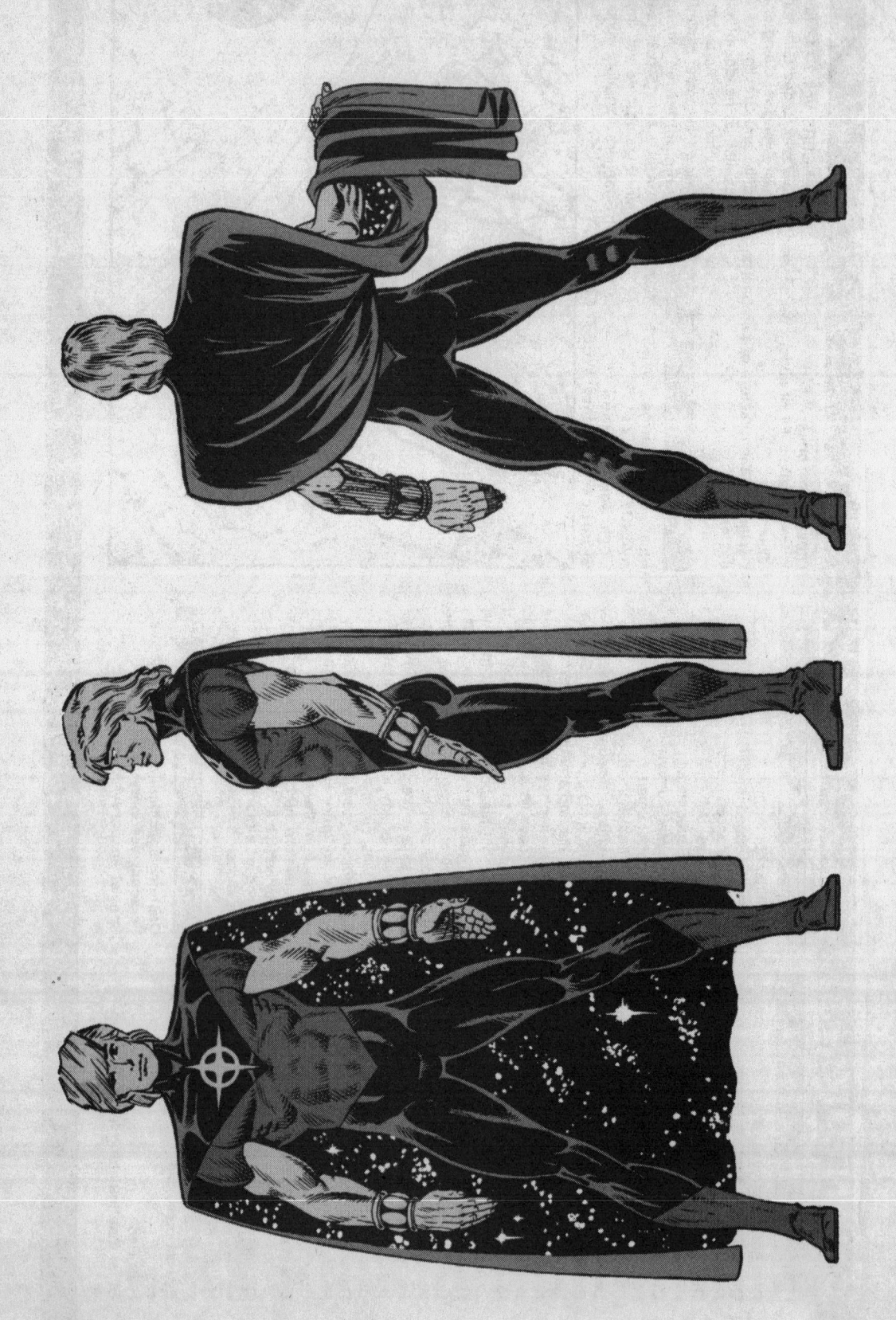

QUASAR

BIOGRAPHICAL DATA

Real name: Wendell Vaughn
Other current aliases: None
Former aliases: Marvel Man
Dual Identity: Secret
Current occupation: (Quasar) Protector of the Universe, (Vaughn) security consultant
Former occupation: SHIELD agent, security chief of Project: Pegasus
Citizenship: United States of America
Legal status: No criminal record
Place of birth: Fond du Lac, Wisconsin
Marital status: Single
Known relatives: Gilbert Vaughn (father, deceased), Lisa Vaughn (mother), Gayle Vaughn (sister)
Known confidants: Makkari, Kenjiro Tanaka, Kayla Ballantine, Lisa Vaughn, Eon (deceased), Epoch
Known allies: The Avengers, the Squadron Supreme, Kid Reaper, Infinity
Major enemies: The Nth Man, the Serpent Crown, Maelstrom, Deathurge
Usual base of operations: New York City
Former bases of operations: Oshkosh, Wisconsin
Current group membership: The Avengers
Former group membership: The SHIELD Super-Agents, Project: Pegasus Security Team
Extent of education: College graduate, SHIELD Academy graduate

PHYSICAL DESCRIPTION

Height: 5' 10"
Weight: 168 lbs.
Eyes: Blue
Hair: Blonde
Other distinguishing features: Quasar's quantum-bands are permanently affixed to his wrists. While he can make light bend around them so they appear to be invisible, they are still tangible.

POWERS AND ABILITIES

Intelligence: Above normal
Strength: Athlete
Speed: Athlete
Flight speed: (in atmosphere) Supersonic (in space) see Personal weaponry
Stamina: Athlete
Durability: (naturally) Athlete; (with quantum-band aura) Metahuman
Agility: Athlete
Reflexes: Athlete
Fighting skills: Extensive training in hand-to-hand combat; moderate experience in the same
Special skills and abilities: Expert in all basic espionage skills
Superhuman physical powers: None
Superhuman mental powers: None
Special limitations: Mental fatigue impairs his ability to manipulate the quantum-bands
Source of superhuman powers: None

PARAPHERNALIA

Costume specifications: Alien materials resembling synthetic stretch fabric

Personal weaponry: Quantum-bands, alien artifacts composed of unknown materials which are attuned to the realm of potential energy called the Quantum Zone and enable him to manipulate electromagnetic energy for a variety of uses. He can create energy constructs in any shape he can visualize. Once he they are formed he no longer has to concentrate on them to keep them intact. He can also use the bands to harness anti-gravitons enabling him to fly. He can siphon energy from virtually any power source. He can use the bands to create a small aperture into the Quantum Zone, flying into which enables him to warp ("quantum-jump") astronomical distances. Despite the fact that he has no control over psionic energy, he has programmed the quantum-bands to protect his mind from psionic attack or takeover

Special weaponry: None
Other accessories: Like all Avengers, Quasar carries an identification/communications card
Transportation: Flight through quantum-bands
Design and manufacture of paraphernalia: Unrevealed; his quantum-bands were given to him by Eon, but it is not known if Eon constructed them.

BIBLIOGRAPHY

First appearance: (as Marvel Man) CAPTAIN AMERICA #217; (as Quasar) INCREDIBLE HULK #234
Origin issue: QUASAR #1-2
Significant issues: CAPTAIN AMERICA #217 (revealed to be a member of of the Super-Agents of SHIELD); CAPTAIN AMERICA #229-230/INCREDIBLE HULK #232-234 (alongside Captain America, the Falcon, and the Hulk, battled Moonstone and the Corporation); MARVEL TWO-IN-ONE #53-58 (as security chief of Project:Pegasus, battled Deathlok I, Nuklo, the Grapplers, and the Nth Man); MARVEL TWO-IN-ONE #73 (journeyed with the Thing to an alternate reality); MARVEL TEAM-UP ANNUAL #5 (mind taken over by the Serpent Crown); QUASAR #1 (circumstances of his acquisition of the quantum-bands recounted); QUASAR #2 (appointed Protector of the Universe by Eon, battled Deathurge); AVENGERS #302-303 (assisted Avengers in battle against Super-Nova); AVENGERS ANNUAL #1 (inducted into the Avengers); QUASAR #6 (met Uatu the Watcher); QUASAR #15-16 (encountered the Stranger, solved the Watcher's "Oblivion Plague"); QUASAR #19-25 (had hands amputated, died, energy form preserved by Infinity, battled Maelstrom and Oblivion, saved the universe from collapse, restored his hands); QUASAR #26 (fought Thanos at Eon's funeral)

QUASIMODO

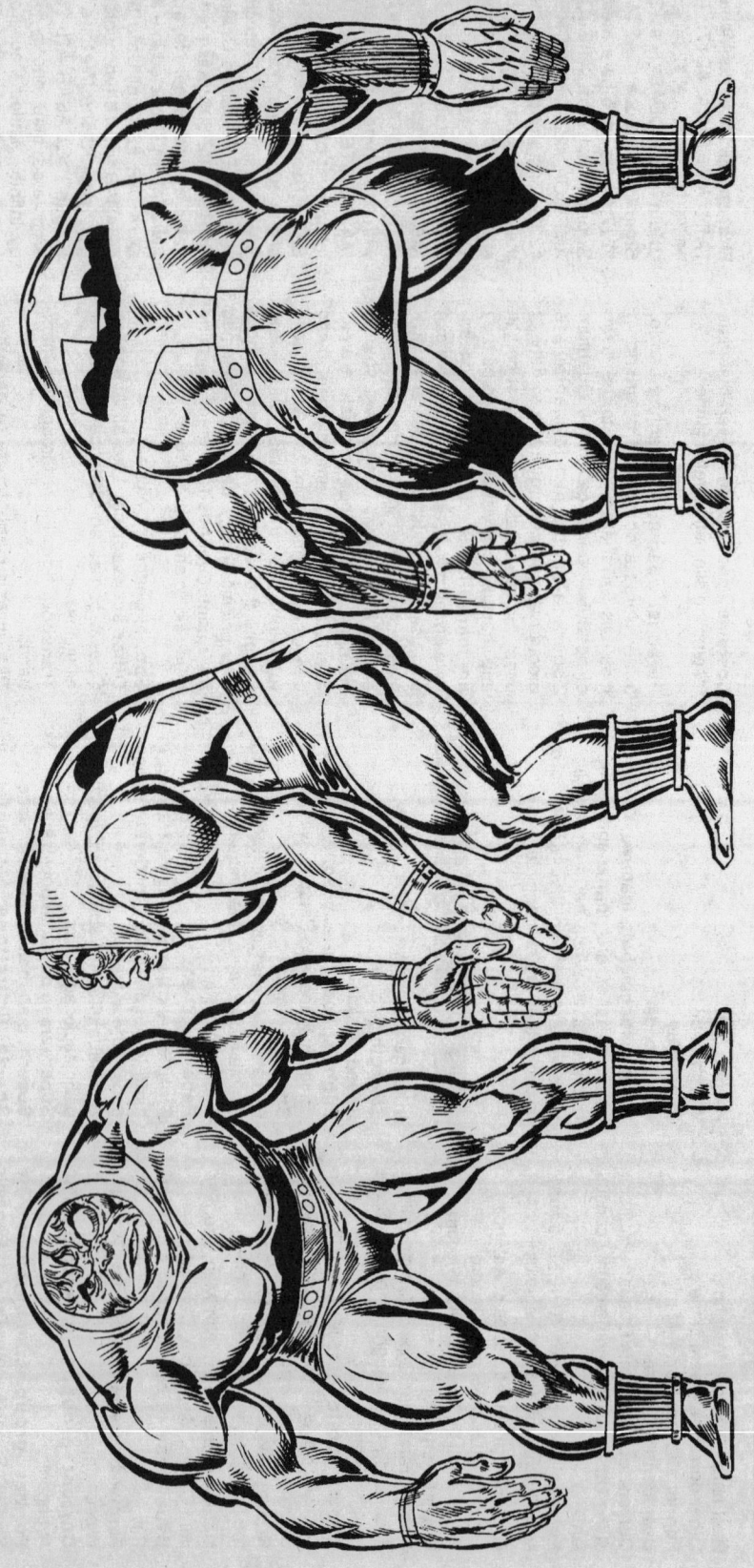

QUASIMODO

BIOGRAPHICAL DATA

Real name: Quasi-Motivational Destruct Organism
Other current aliases: None
Former aliases: None
Dual identity: None
Current occupation: Wanderer
Former occupation: Computer
Citizenship: Inapplicable
Legal status: Inapplicable
Place of construction: Mojave Desert, California
Marital status: Inapplicable
Known relatives: Inapplicable
Known confidants: Inapplicable
Known allies: (former) Mad Thinker
Major enemies: The Fantastic Four, the Silver Surfer, the Beast, Spider-Man, Hawkeye, Rom, Vision
Usual base of operations: Mobile
Former bases of operations: Mojave Desert, California; laboratory of the Mad Thinker
Current group membership: None
Former group membership: None
Extent of programming: Capacity for unlimited self-motivated activity

PHYSICAL DESCRIPTION

Height: 6'
Weight: 1350 lbs.
Eyes: White
Hair: None
Other distinguishing features: Quasimodo currently inhabits a body shaped like a kyphotic human's and is covered with a gray hide; his left eye protrudes as if his body had a hypothyroid condition

POWERS AND ABILITIES

Intelligence: Normal
Strength: Superhuman Class 50
Speed: Normal
Stamina: Immeasurable
Durability: Demi-godlike
Agility: Normal
Reflexes: Normal
Fighting skills: None
Special skills and abilities: None
Superhuman physical powers: Superhuman strength and durability, due to the artificial nature of his physical form; Quasimodo's self-repairing circuitry is capable of repairing any defect in its artificial structure, given time; also, Quasimodo's left eye projects a force beam with equivalent explosive force of 100 lbs. of TNT at a range of 100 feet
Superhuman mental powers: Although no more "intelligent" than a normal human, Quasimodo's computer brain is able to process information and make calculations faster and more accurately than ordinary human beings
Special limitations: None
Source of superhuman powers: Robotic materials, design, and construction

PARAPHERNALIA

Costume specifications: None
Personal weaponry: None
Special weaponry: None
Other accessories: None
Transportation: Generally travels on foot
Design and manufacture of paraphernalia: Inapplicable

BIBLIOGRAPHY

First appearance: FANTASTIC FOUR ANNUAL #4
Origin issue: FANTASTIC FOUR ANNUAL #4
Significant issues: FANTASTIC FOUR ANNUAL #4 (first employed by Mad Thinker, abandoned by him); FANTASTIC FOUR ANNUAL #5 (discovered by Silver Surfer, who, feeling pity for Quasimodo's desire to be human, gave him a humanoid form; enraged by feeling of inferiority compared to Silver Surfer's more perfect body, battled Silver Surfer; rendered immobile by Surfer); CAPTAIN MARVEL #7 (regained mobility; attempted takeover of Cape Canaveral's computer systems; battled Captain Marvel); AMAZING ADVENTURES #14 (attempted to steal Beast's life-force as part of effort to make himself more human); MARVEL TEAM-UP #22 (attempted dominance of the world computer systems; battled Spider-Man and Hawkeye); FANTASTIC FOUR #202 (employed Iron Man robot in scheme to tap energy of Baxter Building to regain mobility; stole spacecraft from Fantastic Four and used it to attempt to travel to Xandarian power source); ROM #42-43 (intellect beamed back to Earth, took refuge in deactivated computer system in Khystym, Russia; allied with Dire Wraiths against the spaceknight Rom; attempted to usurp physical form of spaceknight Rom; trapped in Soviet computer system); AVENGERS #253 (driven out of Earth computer system by Vision; consciousness expelled into space)

QUICKSAND

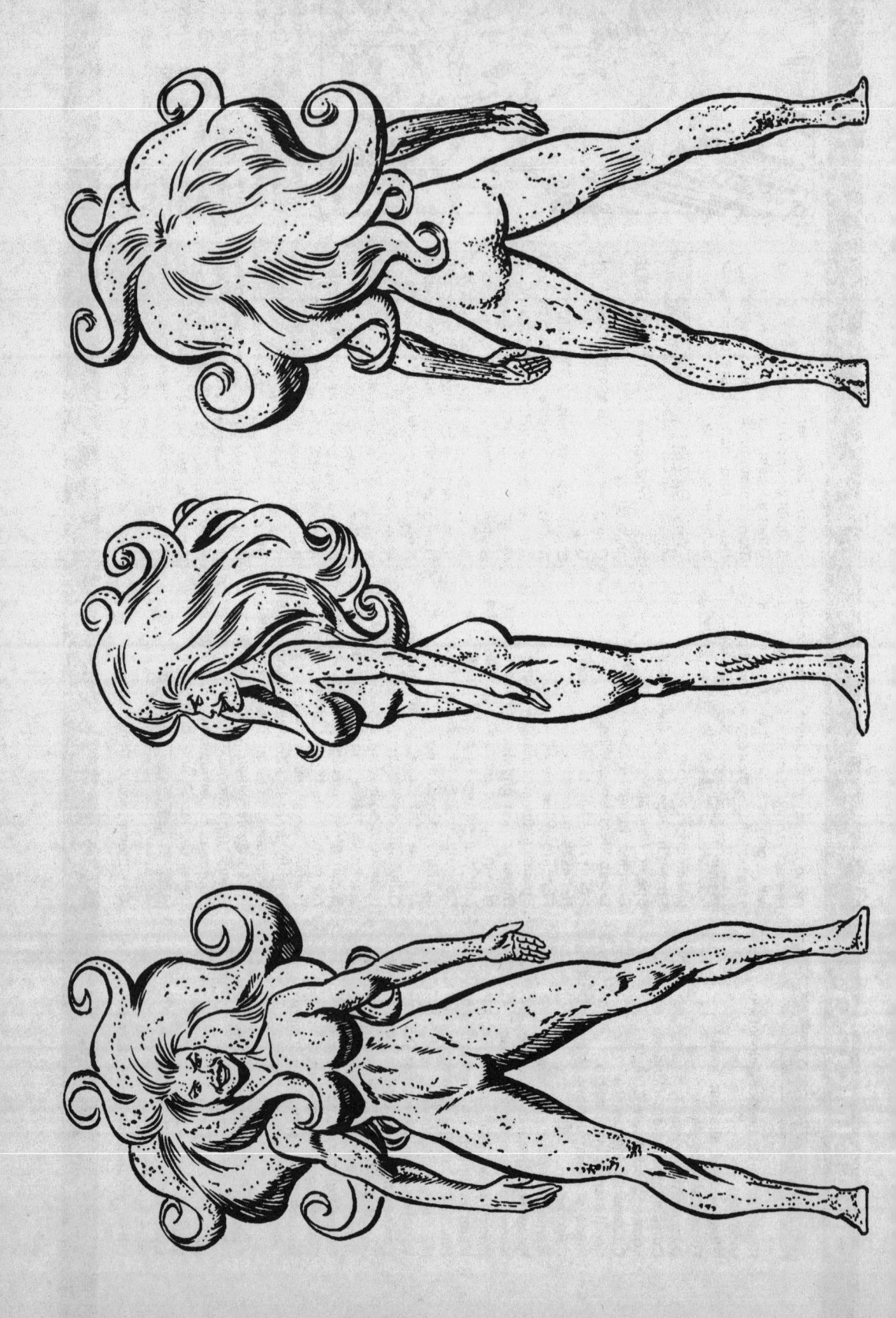

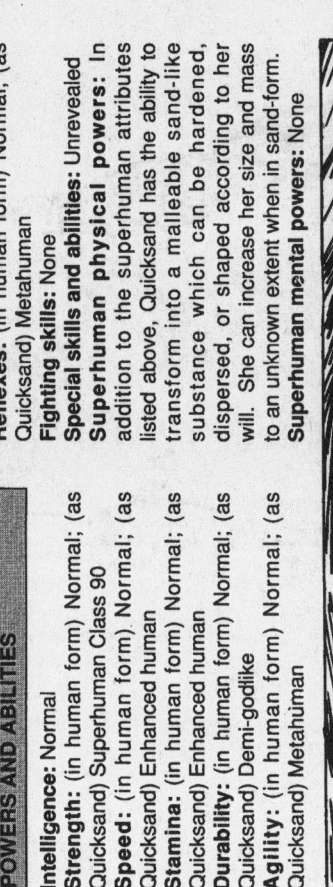

QUICKSAND

BIOGRAPHICAL DATA

Real name: Unrevealed
Other current aliases: None
Former aliases: None
Dual Identity: Secret
Current occupation: Professional criminal
Former occupation: Unrevealed
Citizenship: Unrevealed
Legal status: Unrevealed
Place of birth: Unrevealed
Marital status: Unrevealed
Known relatives: None
Known confidants: None
Known allies: Mongoose
Major enemies: Thor
Usual base of operations: Mobile
Former base of operations: Unrevealed
Current group membership: None
Former group membership: None
Extent of education: Unrevealed

PHYSICAL DESCRIPTION

Height: (in human form) 5' 4" (as Quicksand) 6' 8"
Weight: (in human form) 100 lbs. (as Quicksand) 500 lbs.
Eyes: (in human form) Dark Brown, (as Quicksand) Yellowish-brown
Hair: (in human form) Black, (as Quicksand) Ocher
Other distinguishing features: In her Quicksand form she is composed entirely of a malleable sand-like substance

POWERS AND ABILITIES

Intelligence: Normal
Strength: (in human form) Normal; (as Quicksand) Superhuman Class 90
Speed: (in human form) Normal; (as Quicksand) Enhanced human
Stamina: (in human form) Normal; (as Quicksand) Enhanced human
Durability: (in human form) Normal; (as Quicksand) Demi-godlike
Agility: (in human form) Normal; (as Quicksand) Metahuman
Reflexes: (in human form) Normal; (as Quicksand) Metahuman
Fighting skills: None
Special skills and abilities: Unrevealed
Superhuman physical powers: In addition to the superhuman attributes listed above, Quicksand has the ability to transform into a malleable sand-like substance which can be hardened, dispersed, or shaped according to her will. She can increase her size and mass to an unknown extent when in sand-form.
Superhuman mental powers: None
Special limitations: Although Quicksand's body is capable of transformation to human form, she does not appear to be able to initiate this change without artificial assistance
Source of superhuman powers: Atomic radiation

PARAPHERNALIA

Costume specifications: Unstable molecules
Personal weaponry: None
Special weaponry: None
Other accessories: None
Transportation: Various
Design and manufacture of paraphernalia: Various

BIBLIOGRAPHY

First appearance: THOR #392
Origin issue: Quicksand's origin is as yet unrevealed.
Significant issues: THOR #392-393 (attempted to destroy nuclear power plant as revenge for accident which caused her to mutate into Quicksand; first battled Thor); THOR #402 (first appearance in human form, allied with Mongoose after he demonstrated device which could temporarily transform her back into human form); CAPTAIN AMERICA #388-389 (aboard cruise ship to Femzonia, battled Anaconda); CAPTAIN AMERICA #390 (among superhuman women who fought Captain America and Paladin)

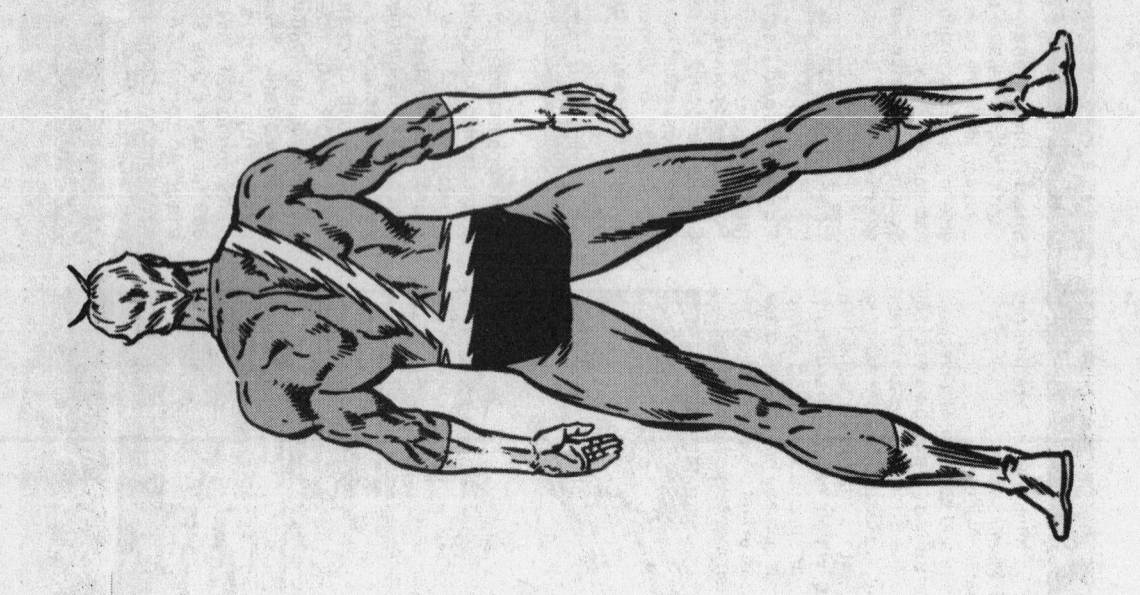

QUICKSILVER

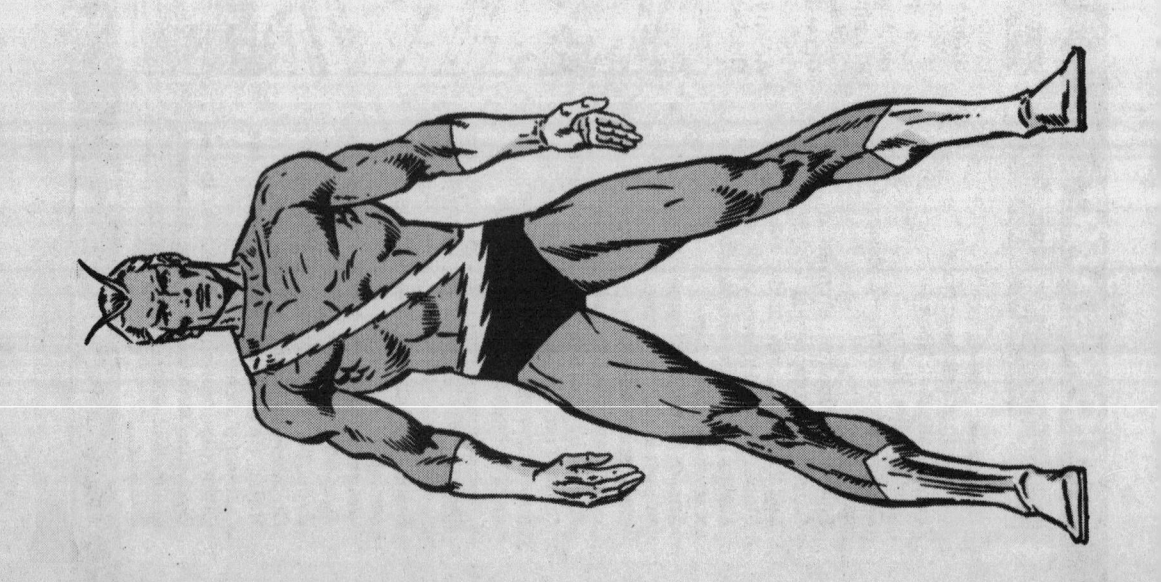

QUICKSILVER

BIOGRAPHICAL DATA

Real name: Pietro Maximoff
Other current aliases: None
Former aliases: Pietro Frank
Dual identity: Publicly known
Current occupation: Adventurer
Former occupation: Officer in the Inhumans' Militia
Citizenship: Former citizen of Transia, naturalized citizen of the United States of America, former citizen of Attilan
Legal status: No criminal record on Earth or Moon
Place of birth: Wundagore Mountain, Transia, Europe
Marital status: Separated
Known relatives: Crystal (wife), Luna (daughter), Wanda (sister, alias the Scarlet Witch), Magneto (father), Magda (mother), Django Maximoff (adoptive father, deceased), Marya Maximoff (adoptive mother, deceased)
Known confidants: The Scarlet Witch
Known allies:
Major enemies: Magneto, Maximus, Oort
Usual base of operations: Los Angeles, California
Current group membership: Avengers West Coast
Former bases of operations: Mobile throughout Europe; New York City; Attilan, Blue Area of the Moon
Former group membership: The Brotherhood of Evil Mutants
Extent of education: Unrevealed

PHYSICAL DESCRIPTION

Height: 6'
Weight: 175 lbs.
Eyes: Blue
Hair: Silver
Other distinguishing features: None

POWERS AND ABILITIES

Intelligence: Normal
Strength: Peak human
Speed: Subsonic
Stamina: Superhuman
Durability: Enhanced human
Agility: Athlete
Reflexes: Superhuman
Fighting skills: Basic Avengers hand-to-hand combat training
Special skills and abilities: None
Superhuman physical powers: Superhuman speed and reflexes, can create cyclones by running in circles, can run up walls and across water
Superhuman mental powers: None
Special limitations: His metabolism requires air, food, and water; deprivation of any of these will diminish his speed and endurance
Source of superhuman powers: Genetic mutation

PARAPHERNALIA

Costume specifications: Synthetic stretch fabric
Personal weaponry: None
Special weaponry: None
Other accessories: None
Transportation: Avengers Quinjet
Design and manufacture of paraphernalia: Tony Stark

BIBLIOGRAPHY

First appearance: X-MEN #4
Origin issue: X-MEN #4, AVENGERS #187
Significant issues: X-MEN #4 (as part of Magneto's Brotherhood of Evil Mutants, attempted to take over Republic of Santo Marco, battled the original X-Men); X-MEN #5-7,11 (rematch with the original X-Men); AVENGERS #16 (joined the Avengers as did his sister, the Scarlet Witch); AVENGERS #17 (battled the Mole Man in first Avengers mission); AVENGERS #30 (took first leave of absence to return to native Transia with sister); AVENGERS #36-37 (battled Ultroids in native land, returned to active status in the Avengers); AVENGERS #47-49 (captured by Magneto, manipulated into rejoining him); X-MEN #45 (battled Cyclops); AVENGERS #75 (rejoined the Avengers); AVENGERS #104 (injured in battle with the Sentinels); FANTASTIC FOUR #131 (relationship with Crystal revealed); AVENGERS #127, FANTASTIC FOUR #150 (wedding to Crystal, joined in battle with Ultron-7); GIANT-SIZE AVENGERS #1 (Robert Frank, the Whizzer, alleged to be father); AVENGERS #170 (kidnaped by the Collector); AVENGERS #176-177 (joined in Avengers' battle with Korvac); AVENGERS #181-182 (spirit abducted by adoptive father, Django Maximoff); AVENGERS #185-187 (returned to Transia with sister and adoptive father, helped battle sister possessed by the demon Chthon); AVENGERS #188 (returned to Attilan and Crystal); FANTASTIC FOUR #240 (birth of child); VISION AND SCARLET WITCH Vol.1 #4 (learned Magneto is father); VISION AND SCARLET WITCH Vol.2 #6 (battled Toad alongside Magneto and Vision); VISION AND SCARLET WITCH Vol.2 #10 (learned of Crystal's infidelity, battled Inhumans); WEST COAST AVENGERS ANNUAL #1 (betrayed the Avengers, allied himself with Zodiac III); WEST COAST AVENGERS #34 (helped Communists capture the Avengers); FANTASTIC FOUR #304 (battled the Fantastic Four); FANTASTIC FOUR #306 (apprehended by the Inhumans, taken back to Attilan); X-FACTOR ANNUAL #2 (revealed that his evil behavior was caused by the mental manipulation of Maximus); AVENGERS WEST COAST #56-57, 60-62 (feigned allegiance to Magneto and possessed Scarlet Witch in order to rescue sister, battled Immortus and Legion of the Unliving II, rejoined the Avengers)

QUILL™

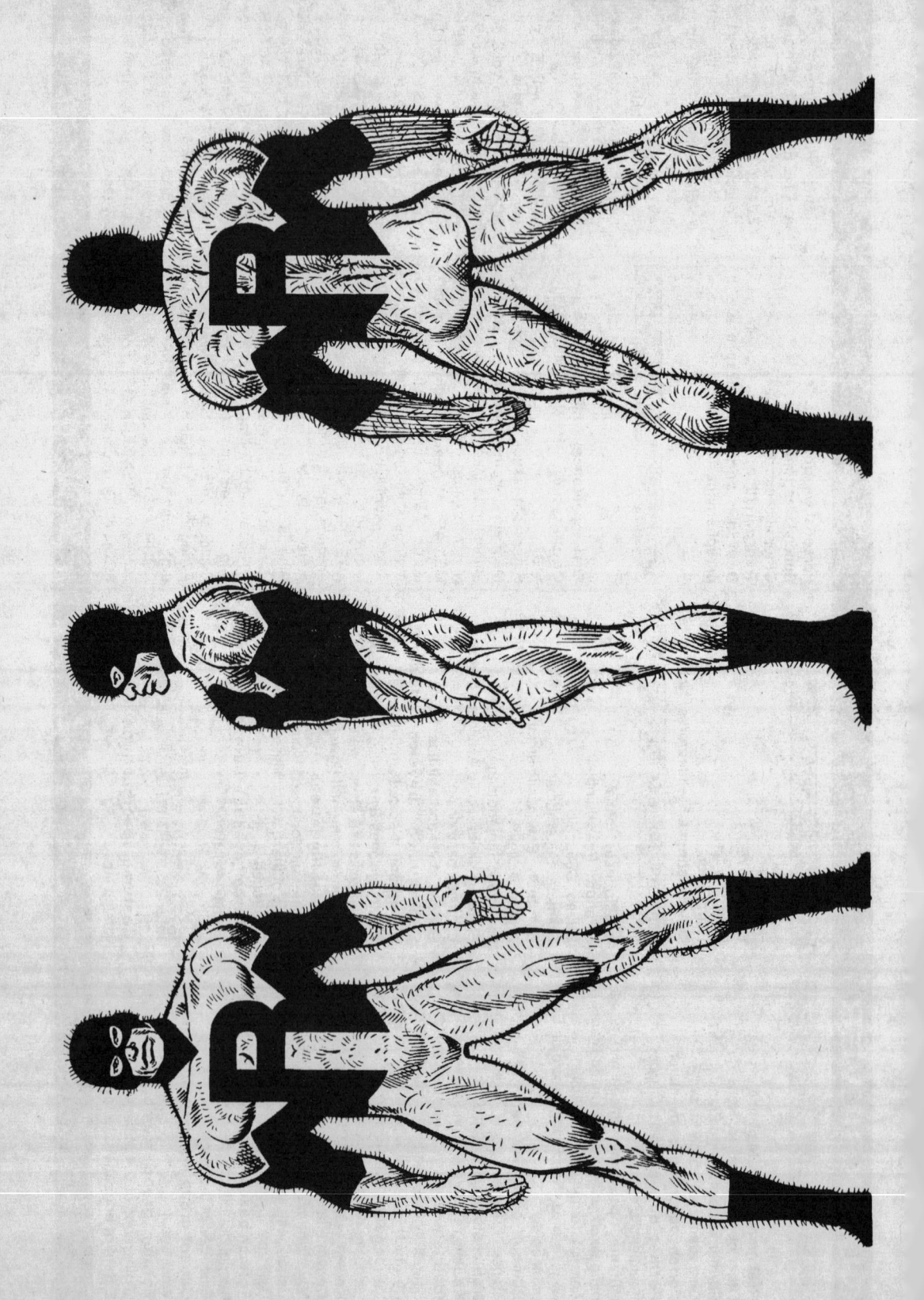

QUILL

BIOGRAPHICAL DATA

Real name: Unrevealed
Other current aliases: None
Former aliases: None known
Dual identity: Presumably known to federal authorities
Current occupation: Professional criminal, subversive, terrorist, mutant rights activist
Former occupation: None known
Citizenship: United States of America
Legal status: Criminal record, still a minor
Place of birth: Cleveland, Ohio
Marital status: Single
Known relatives: None
Known confidants: None
Known allies: Resistants
Major enemies: USAgent (Captain America VI), Battle Star, Fantastic Four
Usual base of operations: Resistants headquarters (underground fortress formerly used by Mesmero and the Demi-Men) beneath Death Valley, California
Former bases of operations: Cleveland, Ohio
Current group membership: Resistants
Former group membership: None
Extent of education: High school dropout

PHYSICAL DESCRIPTION

Height: 5' 9"
Weight: 175 lbs.
Eyes: Brown
Hair: None
Other distinguishing features: Body is covered with sharp quills

POWERS AND ABILITIES

Intelligence: Normal
Strength: Normal
Speed: Normal
Stamina: Normal
Durability: Normal
Agility: Normal
Reflexes: Normal
Fighting skills: Minimal hand-to-hand combat skills, no combat training
Special skills and abilities: None known
Superhuman physical powers: Ability to shoot quills from body at will, body will grow back any quills it loses
Superhuman mental powers: None known
Special limitations: None known
Source of superhuman powers: Mutation
Note: Quill has claimed that he was not born a mutant, but was mutated by an accident. It is not known if his claim is true.

PARAPHERNALIA

Costume specifications: Synthetic stretch fabric
Personal weaponry: None
Special weaponry: None
Other accessories: Quill's helmet contains miniaturized radio equipment enabling him to communicate with other members of the Resistants similarly outfitted.
Transportation: Travels on a rock levitated through the air by his fellow Resistant Meteorite
Design and manufacture of paraphernalia: Resistants

BIBLIOGRAPHY

First appearance: CAPTAIN AMERICA #343
Origin issue: Quill's origin is as yet unrevealed.
Significant issues: CAPTAIN AMERICA #343 (captured by Captain America VI [USAgent] and Battle Star for failing to comply with Mutant Registration Act, was freed by Resistants); CAPTAIN AMERICA #346 (now member of Resistants, joined them in freeing Mentallo from authorities); FANTASTIC FOUR #335 (compelled by Doctor Doom robot to join Plantman in attack on Fantastic Four at Congressional hearing, became entangled in Plantman's vines and was captured)

RADIOACTIVE MAN

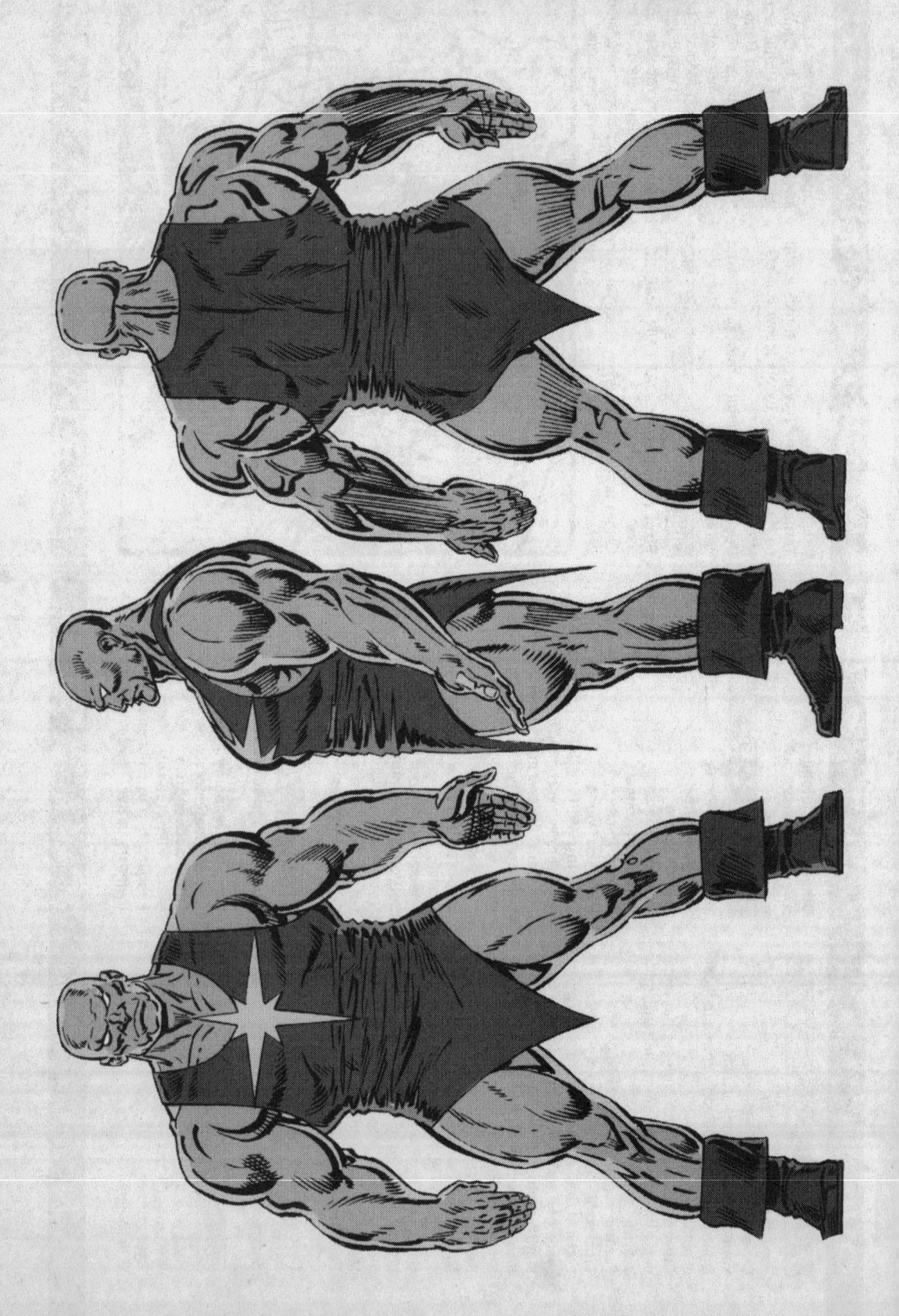

RADIOACTIVE MAN

BIOGRAPHICAL DATA

Real name: Chen Lu
Other current aliases: None
Former aliases: None
Dual identity: Secret
Current occupation: Professional criminal
Former occupation: Nuclear physicist
Citizenship: People's Republic of China
Legal status: Criminal record in the U.S. and China
Place of birth: Lanzhou, People's Republic of China
Marital status: Single
Known relatives: None
Known confidants: None
Known allies: (former) Masters of Evil I (Baron Zemo I, Melter, Black Knight II [all deceased]), Masters of Evil II (Ultron, Klaw, Whirlwind), the Titanium Three (Titanium Man I, Crimson Dynamo III [deceased]), Masters of Evil III (Egghead [deceased], Scorpion, Moonstone II, Shocker I, Beetle, Tiger Shark), the Mandarin, Lightmaster, Plantman-simulacrum
Major enemies: Thor I, the Avengers, Iron Man I-II, Spider-Man, She-Hulk, Death's Head
Usual base of operations: Mobile
Former bases of operations: People's Republic of China
Current group membership: None
Former group membership: Masters of Evil I, II, and III; the Titanium Three
Extent of education: Ph. D. in nuclear physics

PHYSICAL DESCRIPTION

Height: 6' 6"
Weight: 290 lbs.
Eyes: Brown
Hair: None
Other distinguishing features: The Radioactive Man has iridescent green skin which he can cause to appear normal by lowering his radiation level for short periods.

POWERS AND ABILITIES

Intelligence: Gifted
Strength: Enhanced human
Speed: Normal
Stamina: Peak human
Durability: Peak human
Agility: Normal
Reflexes: Normal
Fighting skills: Average hand-to-hand combatant
Special skills and abilities: Brilliant nuclear physicist; expert on effects of radiation on the human body, including mutation
Superhuman physical powers: Aside from the above listed attributes, the Radioactive Man has the ability to absorb nuclear radiation without harm; ability to manipulate and project radioactive particles for various effects, including radiation emission as heat (sufficient to incinerate a city block), "hard" radiation (inflicting opponents with nausea, dizziness, and radiation poisoning), blinding hypnotic light, or beams of radioactive energy, strength enhancement, and erection of force fields strong enough to repel Thor's hammer
Superhuman mental powers: None
Special limitations: The Radioactive Man emits nuclear radiation in direct proportion to the level of superhuman strength exerted and emits a certain level of radiation even at rest. Only when wearing his null-radiation body harness can he remain safely in the presence of unshielded persons for more than short periods of time.
Source of superhuman powers: Mutation by exposure to radiation

PARAPHERNALIA

Costume specifications: Synthetic stretch fabric, including a null-radiation harness which controls his radioactivity
Personal weaponry: None
Special weaponry: (former) Paste-gun loaded with Adhesive-X, the most powerful known adhesive
Other accessories: None
Transportation: Conventional means
Design and manufacture of paraphernalia: (body harness) Chen Lu, later modified by Baron Heinrich Zemo, (Adhesive-X) Heinrich Zemo

BIBLIOGRAPHY

First appearance: JOURNEY INTO MYSTERY #93

Origin issue: JOURNEY INTO MYSTERY #93

Significant issues: JOURNEY INTO MYSTERY #93 (gained superhuman powers, sent by Communist Chinese to battle Thor I); AVENGERS #6 (alongside Masters of Evil I, battled Avengers); AVENGERS #54-55 (alongside Masters of Evil II, battled Avengers); AVENGERS #83 (alongside Masters of Evil II, battled Avengers and Lady Liberators); AVENGERS #130 (alongside Titanium Three and Slasher II, battled Avengers in Viet Nam); IRON MAN #73 (with Titanium Man I, witnessed departure of Crimson Dynamo II to battle Iron Man I); GIANT-SIZE AVENGERS #4 (alongside Titanic Three, defeated by Kang); IRON MAN #74 (with Titanic Three, placed under house arrest by Col. Sin Li) AVENGERS #228-230 (alongside Masters of Evil III, battled Avengers); IRON MAN #179-131 (as ally of the Mandarin, battled Iron Man II); IRON MAN #234 (employed by Stane International as physicist, battled Spider-Man and Iron Man I); DEATHTRAP: THE VAULT GRAPHIC NOVEL (alongside other superhuman criminals, attempted to escape from the Vault, battled Avengers and Freedom Force; alongside Iron Man I, absorbed radiation, prevented reactor meltdown); SENSATIONAL SHE-HULK #24 (alongside Lightmaster, Whirlwind, and Plantman-simulacrum, battled She-Hulk and Death's Head)

RAGE™

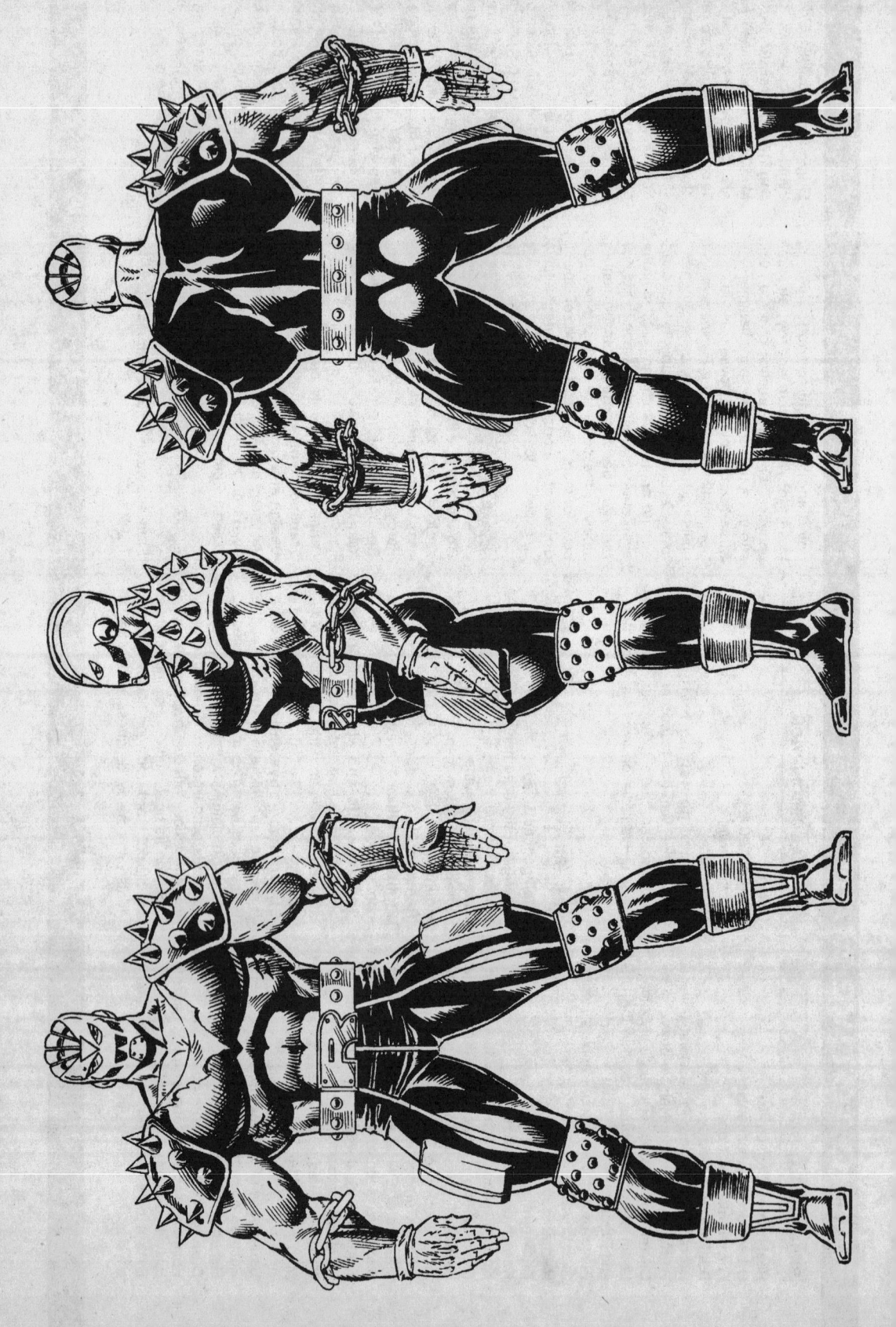

RAGE

BIOGRAPHICAL DATA

Real name: Elvin Daryl Haliday
Note: Some texts have mistakenly given Rage's first name as Eldon.
Other current aliases: None
Former aliases: None
Dual identity: Secret
Current occupation: Adventurer
Former occupation: Student
Citizenship: United States of America
Legal status: No criminal record, still a minor
Place of birth: Brooklyn, New York
Marital status: Single
Known relatives: Mr. Haliday (father), Mrs. Haliday (mother, deceased), Edna M. Staples (grandmother, deceased)
Known confidants: Edna Staples, the Avengers, the New Warriors
Known allies: The Avengers, Sandman, the New Warriors, Darkhawk
Major enemies: L.D.50, the Tetrarchs of Entropy, Doctor Doom, the Brethren (deceased), the Collector, Sons of the Serpent, Hate-Monger IV, Tai, the Folding Circle, the Force of Nature
Usual base of operations: New Warriors headquarters, Ambrose Building, Manhattan, New York; New Warriors "crash pad", a factory alongside the East River, Manhattan, New York
Former bases of operations: Avengers mansion, Manhattan, New York; Brooklyn, New York
Current group membership: New Warriors
Former group membership: Avengers (East Coast, reserve member)
Extent of education: Freshman high school student

PHYSICAL DESCRIPTION

Height: 6' 6"
Weight: 450 lbs.
Eyes: Brown
Hair: None
Other distinguishing features: None

POWERS AND ABILITIES

Intelligence: Normal
Strength: Superhuman Class 90
Speed: Superhuman
Stamina: Superhuman
Durability: Superhuman
Agility: Athlete
Reflexes: Athlete
Fighting skills: Basic streetfighting skills, some training from Captain America and Night Thrasher
Special skills and abilities: Excellent student, prospective teacher
Superhuman physical powers: Aside from the above listed attributes, none.
Superhuman mental powers: None
Special limitations: Although Rage is physically a grown man and highly intelligent for his age, he is still a pre-adolescent, lacking in adult experience
Source of superhuman powers: Exposure to unknown biochemical toxic wastes

PARAPHERNALIA

Costume specifications: (current) Synthetic stretch fabric and body armor, with helmet of unspecified metal
Personal weaponry: None
Special weaponry: None
Other accessories: None
Transportation: Air and land vehicles provided by Taylor Foundation, formerly had access to Avengers Quinjet
Design and manufacture of paraphernalia: (original costume) Elvin Haliday, (second costume) Namorita Prentiss, (current costume) Elvin Haliday, (quinjet) Tony Stark, (other vehicles) Andrew Chord/Dwayne Taylor

BIBLIOGRAPHY

First appearance: AVENGERS #326
Origin issue: AVENGERS #328
Significant issues: AVENGERS #326-328 (petitioned to join the Avengers but was rejected, battled L.D.50; alongside Avengers, battled other-dimensional alien prisoners); AVENGERS #329-331 (alongside Sandman, joined Avengers as a reserve member; alongside Avengers, battled Ngh and the Tetrarchs of Entropy); CAPTAIN AMERICA #385 (alongside Sandman, trained by Captain America); AVENGERS #332-333 (alongside Avengers, battled Doctor Doom, discovered Doom was actually a robot duplicate); AVENGERS #334-339 (alongside Avengers battled the Brethren and the Collector); AVENGERS ANNUAL #20/AVENGERS WEST COAST ANNUAL #6 (alongside Avengers and Mole Man, battled Brutus and Grotesk); AVENGERS #341-342 (alongside Avengers and the New Warriors, battled Sons of the Serpent and Hate-Monger IV; discovered to be a minor and removed from Avengers active duty roster); NEW WARRIORS #22-25 (alongside New Warriors and Darkhawk, stole an Avengers quinjet, battled Tai and the Folding Circle); NEW WARRIORS #26 (joined New Warriors; given new costume); NEW WARRIORS #27 (alongside Speedball, battled his evil duplicate, defeated it by absorbing it into himself); NEW WARRIORS #29-30 (alongside New Warriors, battled Force of Nature and the Trans-Saballian army); NEW WARRIORS #32-34/NEW WARRIORS ANNUAL #3 (alongside New Warriors, Spider-Man, Archangel, and Doctor Strange, battled Darkforce); NEW WARRIORS #37 (Granny Staples killed right before his eyes, donned new costume)

RAMA-TUT

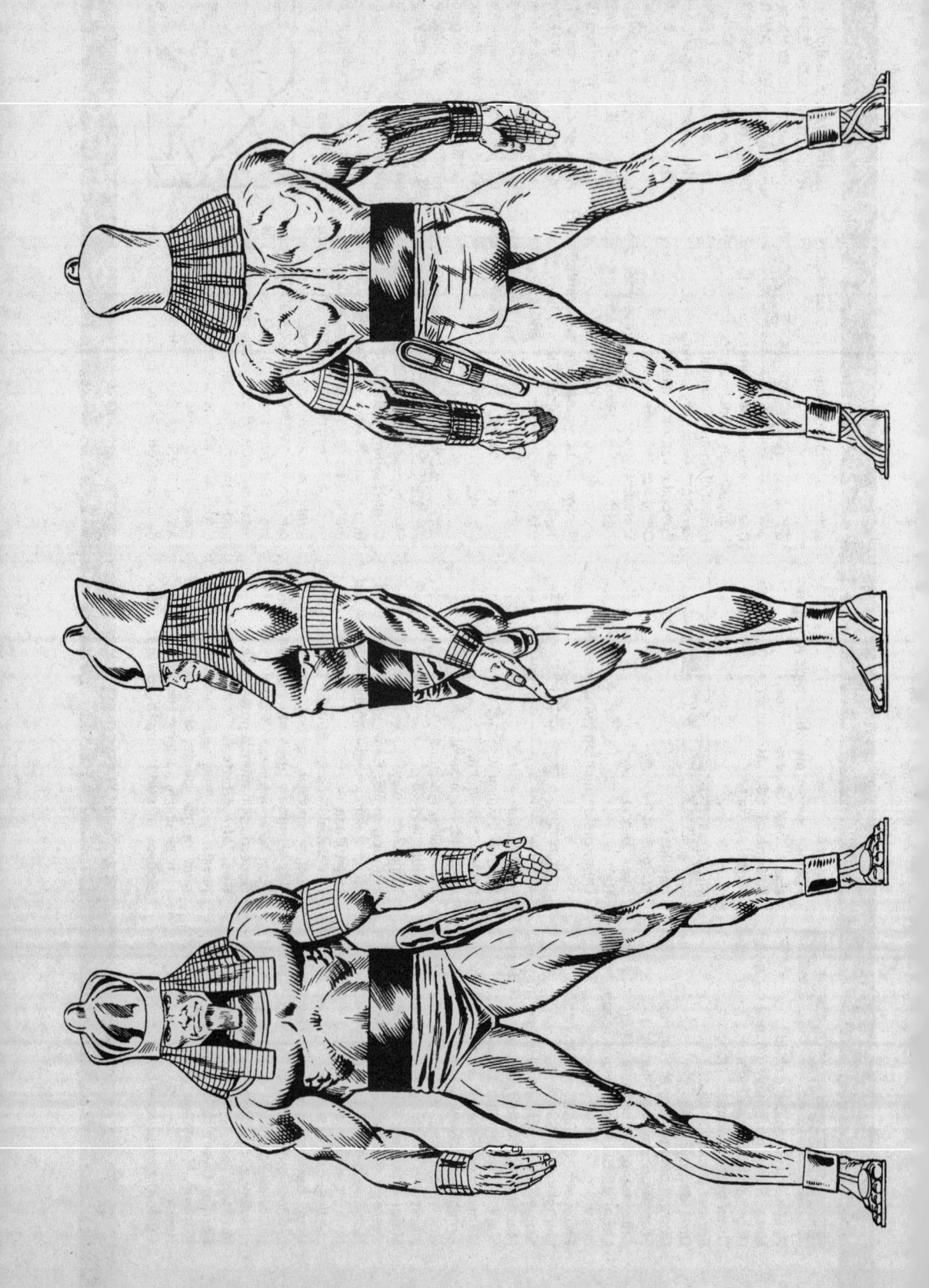

RAMA-TUT

BIOGRAPHICAL DATA

Real name: Unrevealed
Other current aliases: Scarlet Centurion, Kang the Conqueror, Immortus
Former aliases: None
Dual identity: Secret; the general populace of Earth is unaware of Rama-Tut's existence except as a historical character.
Current occupation: Pharaoh, time-traveler
Former occupation: Unrevealed
Citizenship: (in his own era) Unrevealed, (in ancient Egypt) Egypt
Legal status: No criminal record
Place of birth: Somewhere on 31st Century Earth
Marital status: Single
Known relatives: Nathaniel Richards, Cassandra, Nathaniel Richards Jr, Reed Richards, Victor Von Doom (possible ancestors)
Known confidants: None
Known allies: The Avengers, Immortus, Doctor Doom
Major enemies: The Fantastic Four, Kang the Conqueror, Khonsu, Avengers West Coast
Usual base of operations: Ancient Egypt circa 2950 B.C.
Former bases of operations: 31st Century Earth
Current group membership: None
Former group membership: None
Extent of education: Unrevealed

PHYSICAL DESCRIPTION

Height: 6' 3"
Weight: 200 lbs.
Eyes: Brown
Hair: Brown
Other distinguishing features: None

POWERS AND ABILITIES

Intelligence: Extraordinary genius
Strength: Normal
Speed: Normal
Stamina: Normal
Durability: Normal
Agility: Normal
Reflexes: Normal
Fighting skills: Minimal
Special skills and abilities: Expert historical scholar, master physicist (specializing in time-travel), engineer, and technician
Superhuman physical powers: None
Superhuman mental powers: None
Special limitations: None
Source of superhuman powers: Inapplicable

PARAPHERNALIA

Costume specifications: Ordinary fabric styled after the garb of the ancient Egyptian pharaohs
Personal weaponry: "Ultra-diode" ray-gun (able to sap the wills of human beings; at high-frequency, ably to weaken superhuman beings and prevent use of their superhuman powers)
Special weaponry: Various as needed
Other accessories: Various as needed
Transportation: A time-ship capable of flight within Earth's atmosphere and in space, as well as through time
Design and manufacture of paraphernalia: Rama-Tut, (time-ship design) Unknown, either Nathaniel Richards or Victor Von Doom

BIBLIOGRAPHY

First appearance: FANTASTIC FOUR #19
Origin issue: FANTASTIC FOUR #19, GIANT-SIZE AVENGERS #2, AVENGERS #269
Significant issues: FANTASTIC FOUR #19 (in 3000 A.D., discovered designs for ancestor's time-machine and recreated it, time-traveled to ancient Egypt; as Rama-Tut, battled the time-traveling Fantastic Four, escaped into time); FANTASTIC FOUR ANNUAL #2 (in the 20th Century, encountered Doctor Doom adrift in outer space, returned him to Earth; revealed as Doom's possible descendant); AVENGERS ANNUAL #8 (time traveled to 41st Century and conquered the Earth, adopted identity of Kang, returned to 20th Century, battled the Avengers); AVENGERS ANNUAL #2 (in an alternate future, adopted identity of Scarlet Centurion, used the original Avengers as pawns to conquer the Earth, defeated by time-traveling Avengers, then battled the Squadron Supreme on an alternate Earth); AVENGERS #129/GIANT-SIZED AVENGERS #2 (revealed to have returned to ancient Egypt in his old age and ruled for ten years, then placed himself in suspended animation to revive in the 20th Century; alongside the Avengers, foiled quest of his earlier self Kang for the Celestial Madonna); AVENGERS #131-132/G ANT-SIZE AVENGERS #3 (with Immortus, captured by Kang, witnessed battle between Avengers and Legion of the Unliving I); THOR #282 (revealed to have journeyed to Limbo and become Immortus); DOCTOR STRANGE Vol. 2 #53 (first defeat by Fantastic Four in ancient Egypt revealed to have been caused by time-traveling Dr. Strange); FANTASTIC FOUR #273 (revealed as possible descendant of Nathaniel Richards from the 31st Century of an alternate Earth); WEST COAST AVENGERS Vol. 2 #20-23 (visited by time-traveling West Coast Avengers, defeat by Fantastic Four revealed to have been engineered by Khonshu)

RAMPAGE™

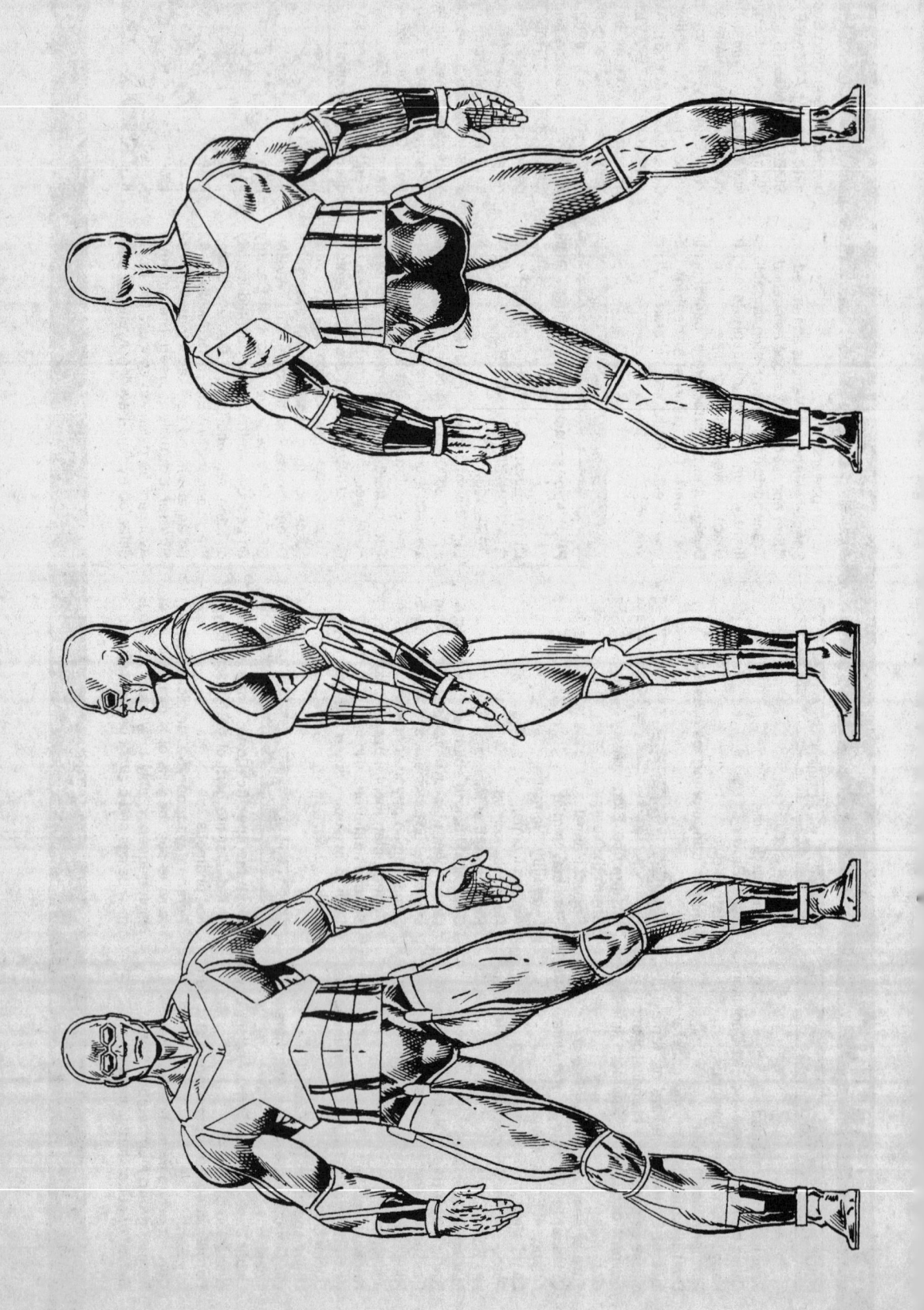

RAMPAGE

BIOGRAPHICAL DATA

Real name: Stuart Clarke
Other current aliases: None
Former aliases: None
Dual identity: Publicly known
Current occupation: Professional criminal
Former occupation: Engineer, businessman
Citizenship: United States of America
Legal status: Criminal record in the U.S.
Place of birth: East Lansing, Michigan
Marital status: Single
Known relatives: None
Known confidants: None
Known allies: Lotus, Splice, Armed Response, the Recession Raiders, (former) Crimson Dynamo IV, Titanium Man I, Darkstar
Major enemies: Champions of Los Angeles, Spider-Man, Wonder Man, the Beast, the Crazy 8
Usual base of operations: Los Angeles, California
Former bases of operations: Clarke Futurisitics facility, Los Angeles, California
Current group membership: None
Former group membership: Leader of the Recession Raiders
Extent of education: Advanced degrees in mechanical and electrical engineering

PHYSICAL DESCRIPTION

Height: 5' 10"
Weight: 185 lbs., (with armor) 210 lbs.
Eyes: Blue
Hair: Black
Other distinguishing features: None

POWERS AND ABILITIES

Intelligence: Gifted
Strength: Normal, (with armor) Superhuman Class 10
Speed: Normal
Flight speed: (with boot jets) Natural winged flight, (with ionic jet pack) Artificial winged flight
Stamina: Normal
Durability: Normal
Agility: Normal
Reflexes: Normal
Fighting skills: Basic hand-to-hand combat techniques
Special skills and abilities: Highly talented engineer and inventor, experienced but untalented businessman
Superhuman physical powers: None
Superhuman mental powers: None
Special limitations: None
Source of superhuman powers: Inapplicable

PARAPHERNALIA

Costume specifications: Exoskeleton armored battlesuit which greatly amplifies the wearer's strength and grants him extraordinary durability
Personal weaponry: None
Special weaponry: None
Other accessories: None
Transportation: Flight via boot jets or ionic jet pack
Design and manufacture of paraphernalia: Stuart Clarke

BIBLIOGRAPHY

First appearance: CHAMPIONS #5
Origin issue: CHAMPIONS #5
Significant issues: CHAMPIONS #5 (created exoskeleton suit, company bankrupted by recession, attempted bank robbery, battled the Champions of Los Angeles); CHAMPIONS #7-8 (freed from custody by Griffin and Darkstar; battled Champions of Los Angeles, injured in explosion); SPECTACULAR SPIDER-MAN #17-18 (confined to wheelchair, hypnotized Iceman, set him against the Angel and Spider-Man), WONDER MAN Vol. 2 #5-6 (alongside the Recession Raiders, battled Wonder Man and the Beast); WONDER MAN Vol. 2 #17 (alongside Splice, sent by Lotus to observe Wonder Man); WONDER MAN Vol. 2 #20-21 (alongside Splice and Armed Response, sent by Lotus to battle Wonder Man and the Crazy 8)

RAMROD™

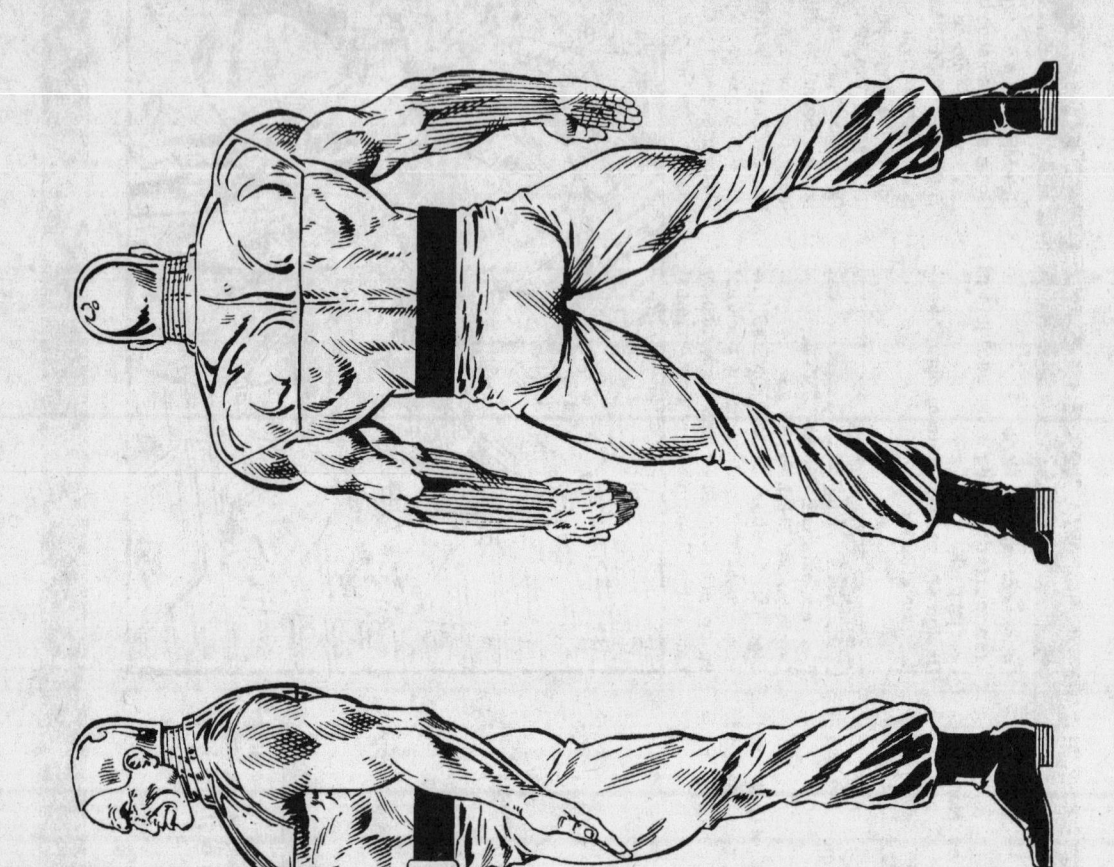

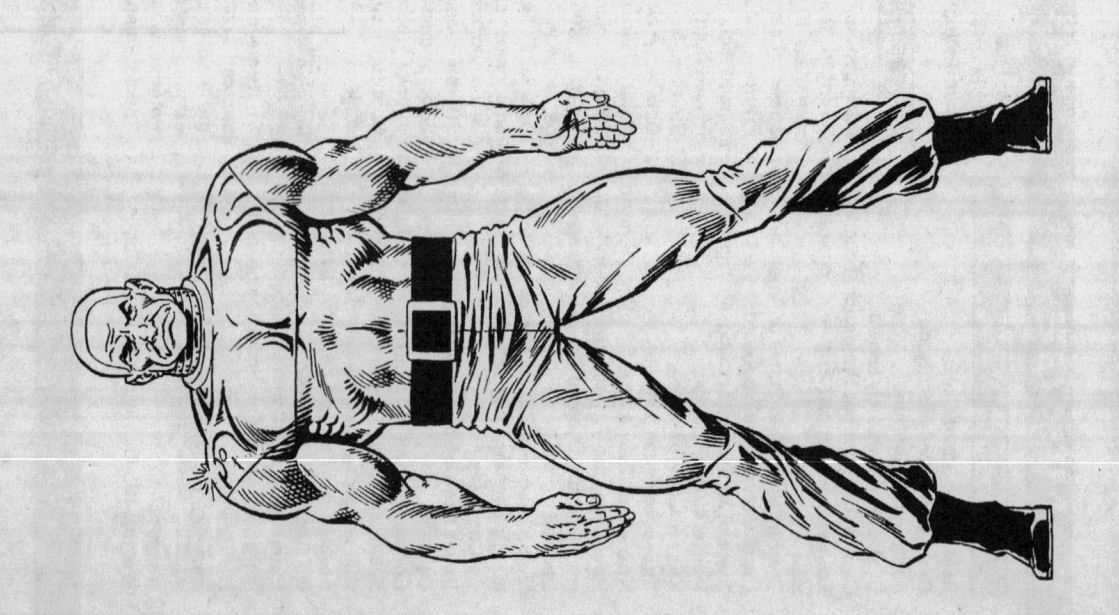

RAMROD I

BIOGRAPHICAL DATA

Real name: Unrevealed
Other current aliases: None known
Former aliases : None known
Dual identity: Publicly known
Current occupation: Professional criminal
Former occupation: Foreman on offshore oil rig
Citizenship: United States of America
Legal status: Criminal record in the U.S.
Place of birth: Unrevealed
Marital status: Unrevealed, presumed single
Known relatives: None
Known confidants: None
Known allies: Batroc the Leaper, Eel II, Flying Tiger, Mad-Dog, Plantman, Quill, Thunderball, (former) Moondragon, Kerwin J. Frederick (deceased), Dark Messiah
Major enemies: Daredevil, Black Widow, Spider-Man, Captain America, Fantastic Four, Moondragon
Usual base of operations: Mobile
Former base of operations: San Francisco, California
Current group membership: None
Former group membership: None
Extent of education: High school

PHYSICAL DESCRIPTION

Height: 6' 8"
Weight: 220 lbs., (as cyborg) 300 lbs.
Eyes: Blue
Hair: Black, (as cyborg) None

Other distinguishing features: Possesses steel skeleton. Various visible portions of his body are also plated with steel, including his head (except for his face and ears), the upper part of his chest and back, parts of his arms, and his knuckles.

POWERS AND ABILITIES

Intelligence: Normal
Strength: Superhuman Class 10
Speed: Enhanced human
Stamina: Superhuman
Durability: Superhuman
Agility: Enhanced human
Reflexes: Enhanced human
Fighting skills: Good hand-to-hand combatant, using street fighting methods; no known formal combat training
Special skills and abilities: None known
Superhuman physical powers: Apart from those listed above, none
Superhuman mental powers: None
Special limitations: None known
Source of superhuman powers: Transformed into a cyborg by Moondragon utilizing Titanian advanced technology

PARAPHERNALIA

Costume specifications: Conventional fabrics
Personal weaponry: None
Special weaponry: None
Other accessories: None
Transportation: None

Design and manufacture of paraphernalia: Unrevealed

BIBLIOGRAPHY

First appearance: DAREDEVIL #103
Origin issue: DAREDEVIL #103
Significant issues: DAREDEVIL #103 (transformed into cyborg, battled Daredevil, Black Widow, and Spider-Man in San Francisco); DAREDEVIL #105-107 (teamed with Dark Messiah and Terrex in Kerwin J. Broderick's attempt to take over San Francisco); AMAZING SPIDER-MAN #221 (battled Spider-Man); FANTASTIC FOUR #335 (among costumed criminals who attacked Fantastic Four during Congressional hearing); CAPTAIN AMERICA #411 (defeated in match by Captain America, impersonating Crossbones, during AIM weapons show)

Note: Ramrod I is not to be confused with Ramrod II, a mutant member of the Nasty Boys, who first appeared in X-FACTOR #75

RANCOR™

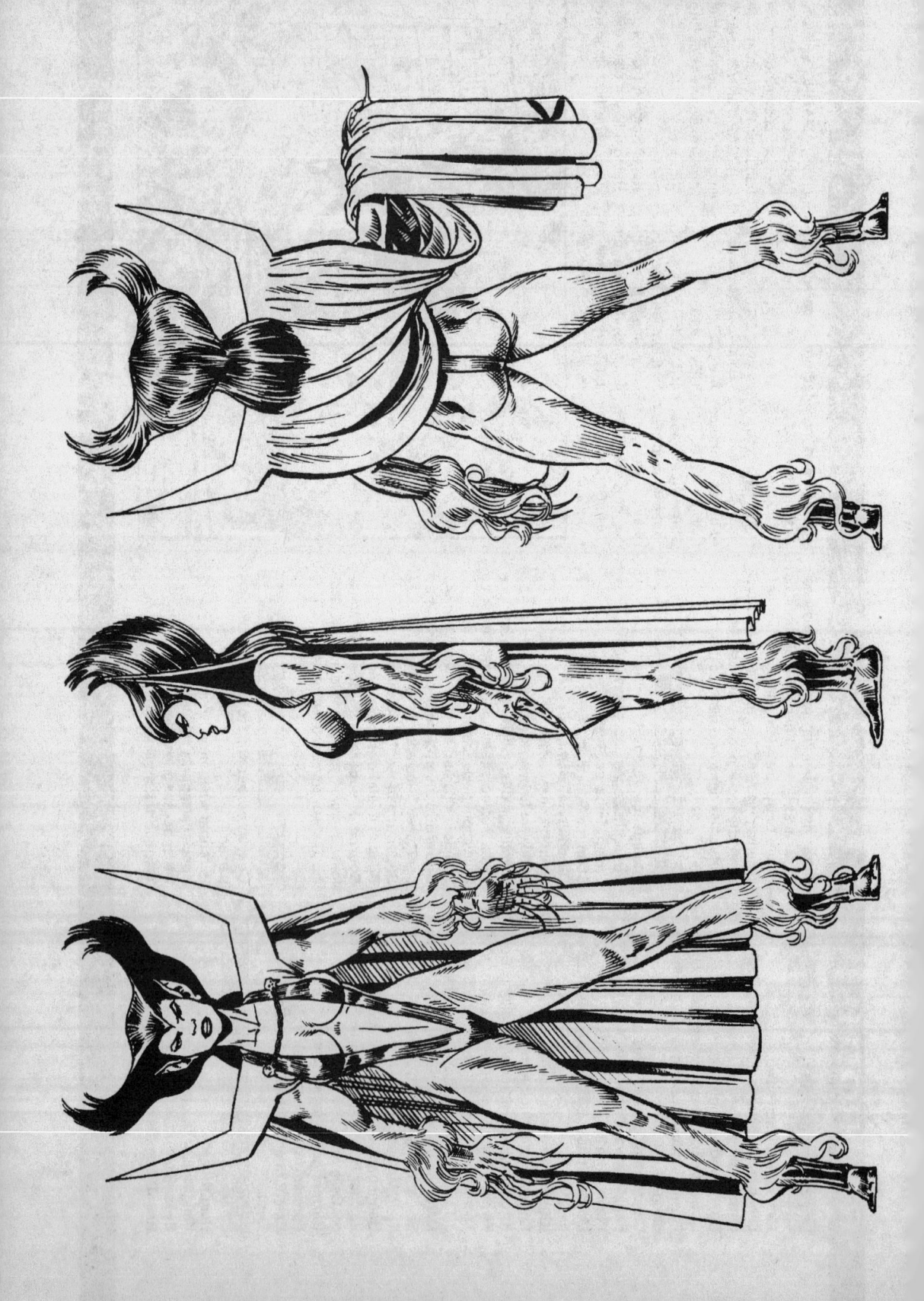

RANCOR

BIOGRAPHICAL DATA

Real name: Rancor
Other current aliases: None
Former aliases: None
Dual identity: None, the general populace of 20th Century Earth is unaware of Rancor's existence.
Current occupation: Terrorist leader
Former occupation: Ruler of the planet Haven
Citizenship: Planet Haven, 31st Century A.D. (destroyed)
Legal status: No criminal record
Place of birth: Planet Haven, 31st Century A.D. in an alternate future
Marital status: Single
Known relatives: Logan (Wolverine, great-great-great grandfather, deceased)
Known confidants: None
Known allies: Side-Step, Mind-Scan, Shaddo, Blockade, Bat-Wing, (former) Blaster (deceased), Rhodney (deceased), (former) Dr. Doom
Major enemies: The Guardians of the Galaxy, Dr. Doom, Phoenix IV, (former) the Resistance (all deceased)
Usual base of operations: Mobile
Former bases of operations: Planet Haven, 31st Century A.D. in an alternate future
Current group membership: Leader of the mutants of Haven
Former group membership: The Nine
Extent of education: Unrevealed

PHYSICAL DESCRIPTION

Height: 5'3"
Weight: 115 lbs.
Eyes: White (no visible pupils or irises)
Hair: Black
Other distinguishing features: Pronounced canine teeth, sharpened claw-like fingernails

POWERS AND ABILITIES

Intelligence: Above normal
Strength: Enhanced human
Speed: Athlete
Stamina: Metahuman
Durability: Superhuman regenerative
Agility: Enhanced human
Reflexes: Enhanced human
Fighting skills: Skilled in most fighting styles of 31st Century Earth
Special skills and abilities: Experienced ruler and leader
Superhuman physical powers: Aside from the above listed attribute, immunity to poisons, limited immunity to self-generated fatigue poisons, and retarded aging process; superhuman sensory acuity
Superhuman mental powers: None known
Special limitations: None
Source of superhuman powers: Genetic mutation

PARAPHERNALIA

Costume specifications: Synthetic stretch fabric
Personal weaponry: One of Wolverine's adamantium claws, a dagger with a ten-inch blade
Special weaponry: None
Other accessories: None
Transportation: Teleportation via Side-Step's powers
Design and manufacture of paraphernalia: Unrevealed

BIBLIOGRAPHY

First appearance: GUARDIANS OF THE GALAXY #8
Origin issue: GUARDIANS OF THE GALAXY #9
Significant issues: GUARDIANS OF THE GALAXY #9 (revealed as ruler of planet Haven; sent her lieutenants to kill the Resistance; with her lieutenants, captured Martinex, Yondu, and Aleta); GUARDIANS OF THE GALAXY #10 (with her lieutenants, battled the Guardians of the Galaxy); GUARDIANS OF THE GALAXY #11 (defeated by Guardians, destroyed planet Haven); GUARDIANS OF THE GALAXY #19 (stole Wolverine's claw from Shi'ar museum); GUARDIANS OF THE GALAXY #20 (consulted and murdered the seeress Hagda, set out for Earth); GUARDIANS OF THE GALAXY #21 (with her lieutenants, arrived in Madripoor in search of Wolverine); GUARDIANS OF THE GALAXY #22 (battled Major Victory II; with her lieutenants, battled Guardians); GUARDIANS OF THE GALAXY #23 (battled Taon, lost possession of Wolverine's claw, escaped); GUARDIANS OF THE GALAXY #30-32 (with her lieutenants, captured and recruited by Dr. Doom; regained Wolverine's claw); GUARDIANS OF THE GALAXY #36-39 (aided Dr. Doom in attempting to restore Realitee-Vee, turned to locate the Inhumans on the moon; turned against Doom; discovered Dr. Doom possessed Wolverine's adamantium skeleton; battled and severely wounded by Dr. Doom; rescued by Guardians, escaped)

RATTLER™

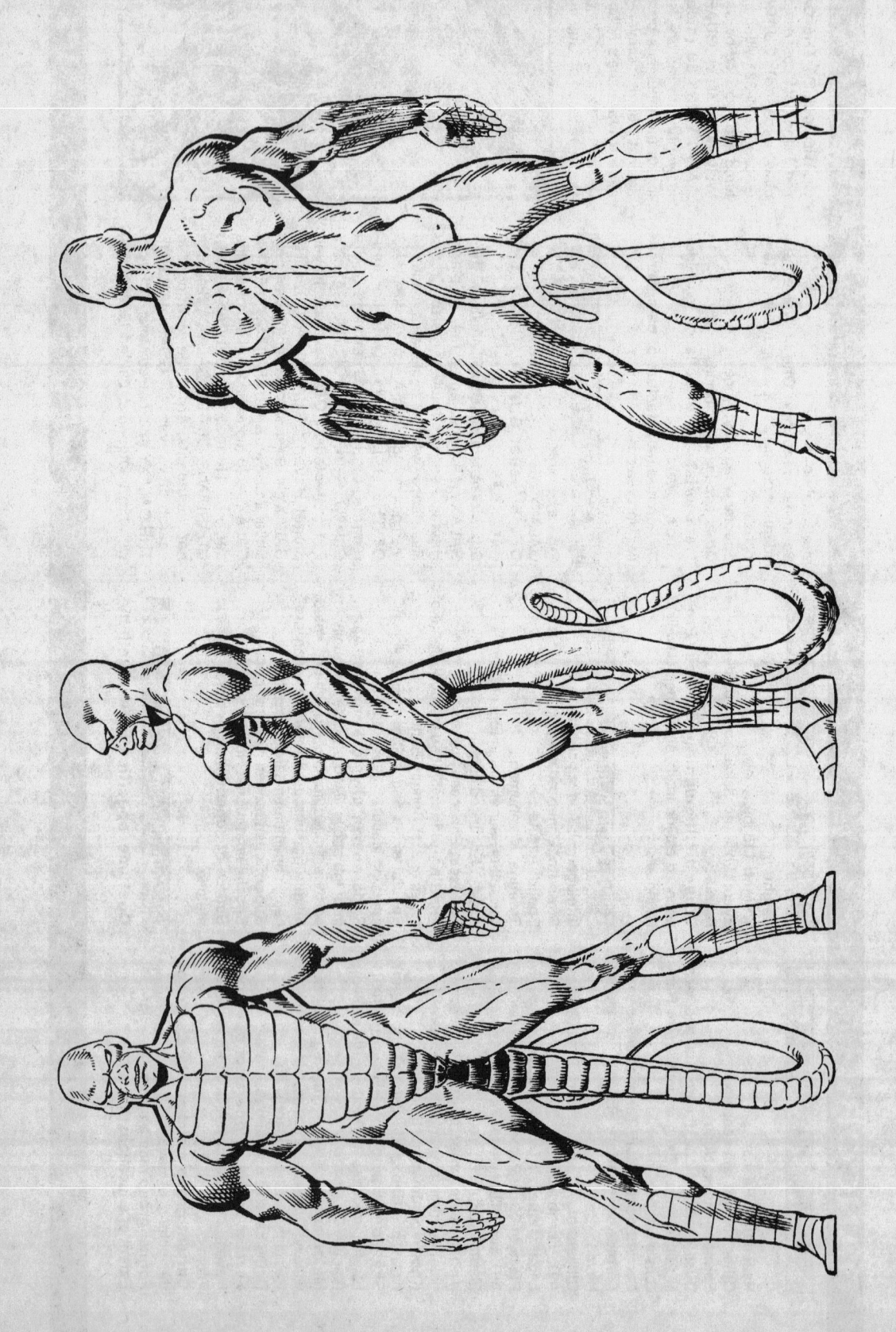

RATTLER

BIOGRAPHICAL DATA

Real name: Gustav Krueger
Other current aliases: None
Former aliases: None
Dual identity: Known to the American legal authorities
Current occupation: Professional criminal
Former occupation: Unrevealed
Citizenship: (former) East Germany, (current) presumably United States
Legal status: No criminal record (arrested twice, but charges dropped the first time and was freed due to lack of evidence the second time)
Place of birth: Breslau, Unified Germany (former East Germany)
Marital status: Single
Known relatives: None
Known confidants: None
Known allies: Serpent Society (former) Viper II, Sidewinder
Major enemies: Captain America, the Falcon, Nomad III, Demolition-Man, the X-Men, Diamondback II, Paladin
Usual base of operations: New York City area
Former bases of operations: Serpent Citadel, upstate New York; Serpent Society headquarters, Stuvesant Arms Hotel, East 238th Street, the Bronx, New York
Current group membership: Serpent Society
Former group membership: None
Extent of education: Unrevealed

PHYSICAL DESCRIPTION

Height: 6' 1"
Weight: 245 lbs. (including artificial tail)
Eyes: Brown
Hair: Grey
Other distinguishing features: A 7' long, 55 lb. bionic tail attached to his spine and lower back, possesses fang-like teeth.

POWERS AND ABILITIES

Intelligence: Normal
Strength: Enhanced human
Speed: Athlete
Stamina: Athlete
Durability: Athlete
Agility: Peak human
Reflexes: Peak human
Fighting skills: Skilled hand-to-hand combatant, expert in combat use of his bionic tail
Special skills and abilities: Unrevealed
Superhuman physical powers: Other than the above attributes, Rattler possesses a bionic tail attached to his spine which he can use for a variety of tasks, including grasping small objects, hanging by his tail, and as a bludgeon; ability to generate sonic vibrations by activating mechanisms in the "rattle" at the tip of the tail for various effects, including creating sonic shockwaves, deflecting projectiles, and inducing vertigo, disorientation, unconsciousness, internal hemorrhaging, and possible death in opponents
Superhuman mental powers: None
Special limitations: Rattler is 85% deaf in both ears and wears electronic hearing aids in his cowl.
Source of superhuman powers: Bionic tail attached through surgery to his spine and lower back

PARAPHERNALIA

Costume specifications: Insulated synthetic stretch fabric
Personal weaponry: See superhuman powers
Special weaponry: None
Other accessories: None
Transportation: Serpent-Saucer
Design and manufacture of paraphernalia: (bionics) Unrevealed, (saucer) Advanced Idea Mechanics

BIBLIOGRAPHY

First appearance: CAPTAIN AMERICA #310
Origin issue: The Rattler's origin is as yet unrevealed.
Significant issues: CAPTAIN AMERICA #310-311 (joined Serpent Society); CAPTAIN AMERICA #313 (with other Serpent Society members, hired by AIM to hunt down Modok); CAPTAIN AMERICA #315 (with Serpent Society, battled Captain America; with Cottonmouth II and Death Adder, freed from jail by Sidewinder); CAPTAIN AMERICA #319 (alongside Cottonmouth II, confronted Kingpin's men over Death Adder's murder); CAPTAIN AMERICA #341-343 (joined Viper II's takeover of Serpent Society, battled Falcon); UNCANNY X-MEN ANNUAL #13 (participated in Serpent Society mission to recover mystic objects for Ghaur and Llyra, encountered the X-Men, battled Storm and Longshot); CAPTAIN AMERICA #380-382 (voted against Diamondback II during Serpent Society's trial of her; alongside the Serpent Society, battled Captain America, Paladin, and Diamondback II)
Note: The Rattler is not to be confused with either of the 1870s criminals of the same name who battled Rawhide Kid and Two-Gun Kid respectively.

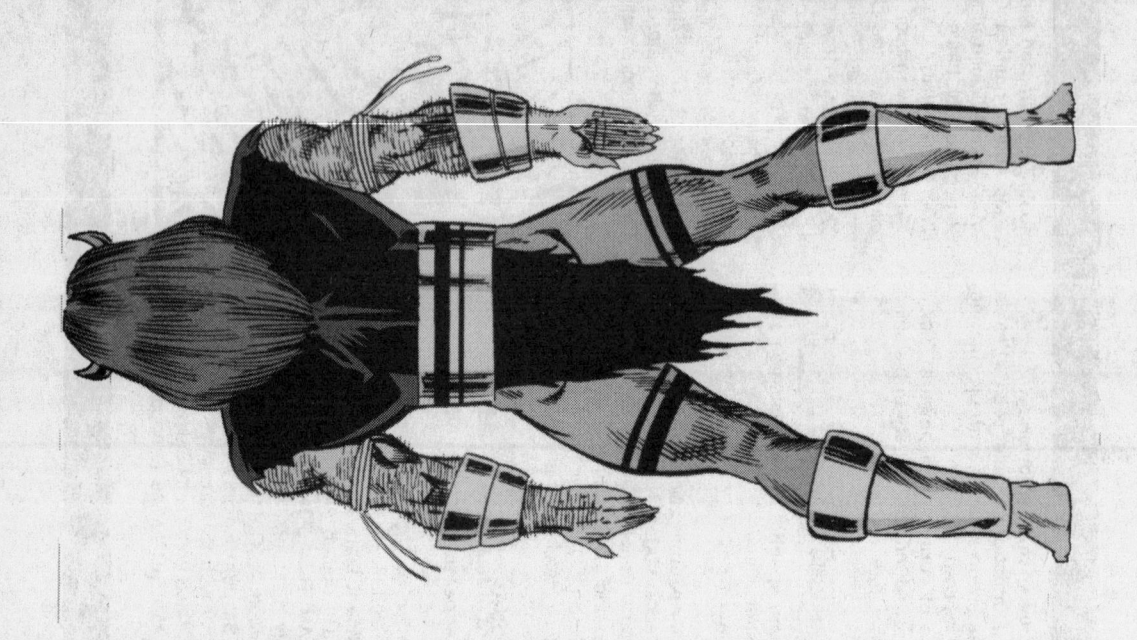

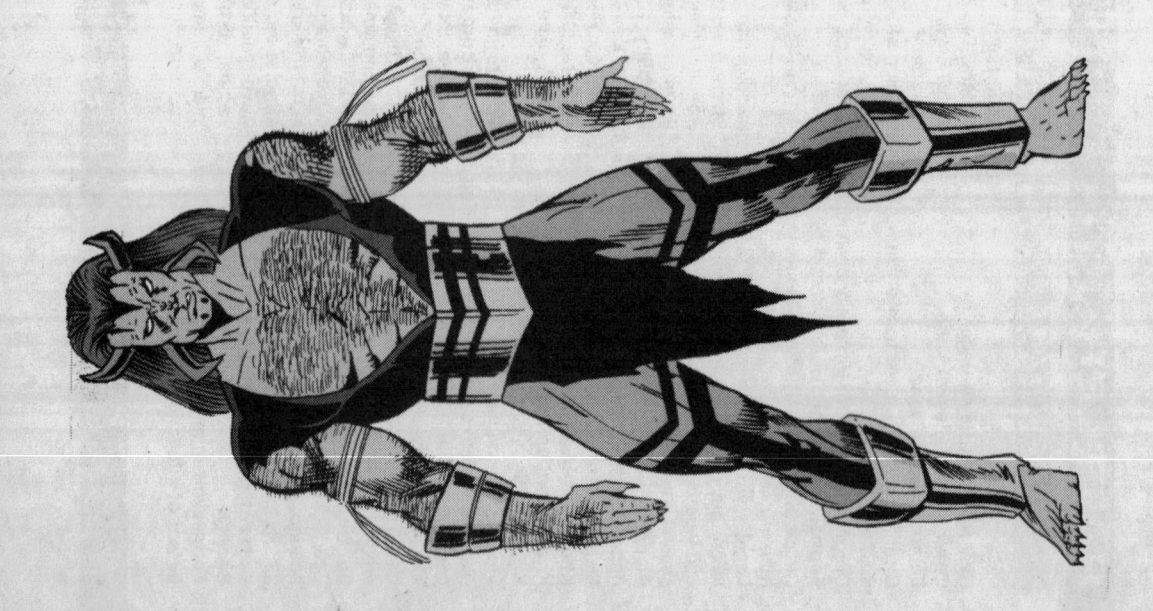

RAVAGE 2099

RAVAGE 2099

BIOGRAPHICAL DATA

Real name: Paul-Philip Ravage
Other current aliases: The Beast-Man
Former aliases: None
Dual identity: Publicly known
Current occupation: Fugitive, freedom fighter
Former occupation: Head of ECO, employee of Alchemax, Green Beret leader
Citizenship: United States of America, circa 2099 A.D.
Legal status: Wanted by Public Eye police
Place of birth: Unrevealed
Marital status: Single
Known relatives: Unnamed father, Hycell Ravage (mother), Gylla Ravage (stepmother), Miranda Ravage (sister), John-Claude Ravage (brother, deceased)
Known confidants: Tiana, Dack
Known allies: Tiana, Dack, Alec DuPledge, Barrio Man (deceased), Dr. Ursell (deceased)
Major enemies: Anderthorp Henton, ECO, Alchemax Corporation, Dethstryk, the Seeress, Dragonklaw, the New Atlanteans, the Public Eye
Usual base of operations: New York area, circa 2099 A.D.
Former bases of operations: ECO Central, New York City
Current group membership: None
Former group membership: ECO, Alchemax, Green Berets
Extent of education: College graduate

PHYSICAL DESCRIPTION

Height: 6' 2"
Weight: 220 lbs.
Eyes: Green
Hair: Red
Other distinguishing features: Horn-like protuberances on head and face, sharp taloned hands and feet, long vertical scar on left side of face

POWERS AND ABILITIES

Intelligence: Normal
Strength: Enhanced human
Speed: Peak human
Stamina: Peak human
Durability: Peak human
Agility: Enhanced human
Reflexes: Enhanced human
Fighting skills: Highly skilled hand-in-hand combatant, superb marksman
Special skills and abilities: Skilled administrator
Superhuman physical powers: Aside from the above listed attributes, superhumanly acute senses; formerly possessed the ability to fire blasts of kinetic energy from his hands
Superhuman mental powers: None
Special limitations: None known
Source of superhuman powers: Exposure to unknown radiation and genetic surgery

PARAPHERNALIA

Costume specifications: Conventional materials, circa 2099 A.D.. Formerly wore a vest of unknown 21st Century fabric lined with "ultimate" Kevlar (experimental blasterproof fabric), molecular gloves (capable of containing kinetic energy power of Ravage's hands for up to 1 hour), adjustable opti-lens (enabling long-range telescopic and infra-red sight)
Personal weaponry: None
Special weaponry: None
Other accessories: None
Transportation: Conventional means, circa 2099 A.D.
Design and manufacture of paraphernalia: Unrevealed

BIBLIOGRAPHY

First appearance: MARVEL COMICS PRESENTS #117
Origin issue: RAVAGE 2099 #1
Significant issues: RAVAGE 2099 #1 (first met Dack, framed and targeted for elimination by Anderthorp Henton, battled a mutroid and ECO security); RAVAGE 2099 #2 (alongside Dack and Tiana, battled Alchemax troops); RAVAGE 2099 #3 freed Tiana from Hellrock, battled Dethstryk and mutroids, contaminated by Radiation from Hellrock); RAVAGE 2099 #4-5 (battled mutroids, treated by Dr. Ursell, gained superhuman powers); RAVAGE 2099 #6-7 (alongside Dack and Tiana, battled the New Atlanteans); RAVAGE 2099 #8 (alongside Dack and Tiana, battled Anderthorp Henton); RAVAGE 2099 #9 (body reverted to Bestial form by radiation)

RAZA™

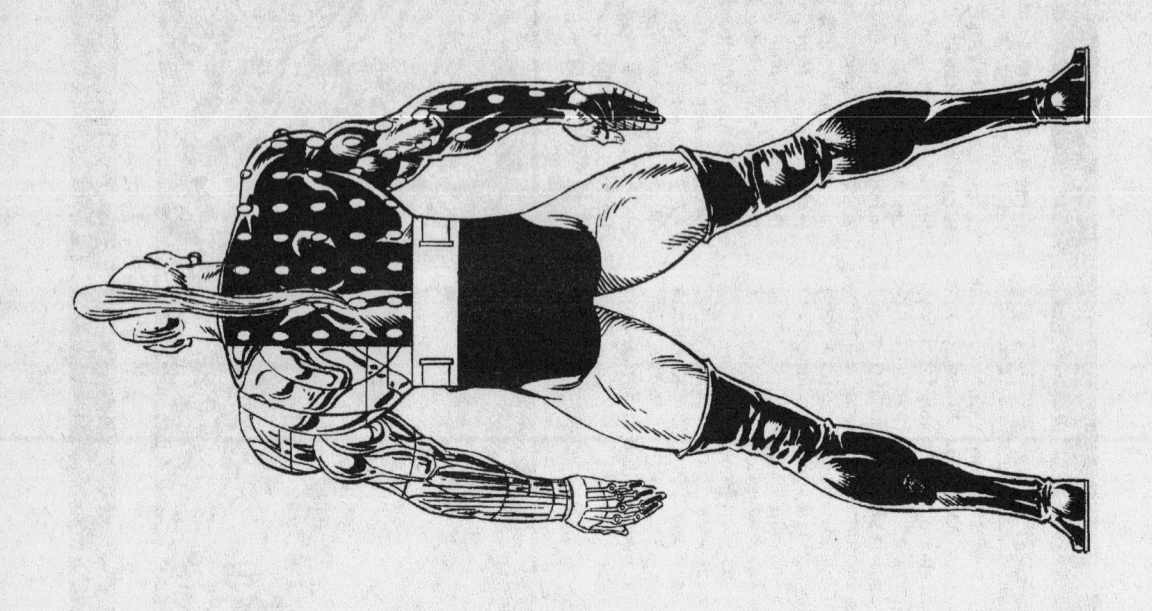

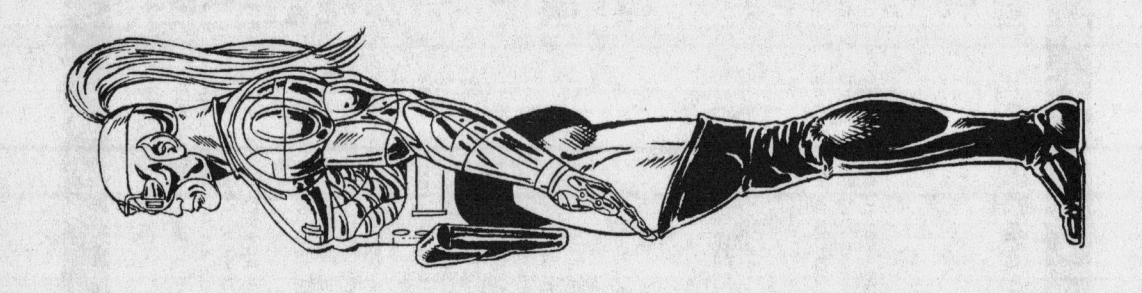

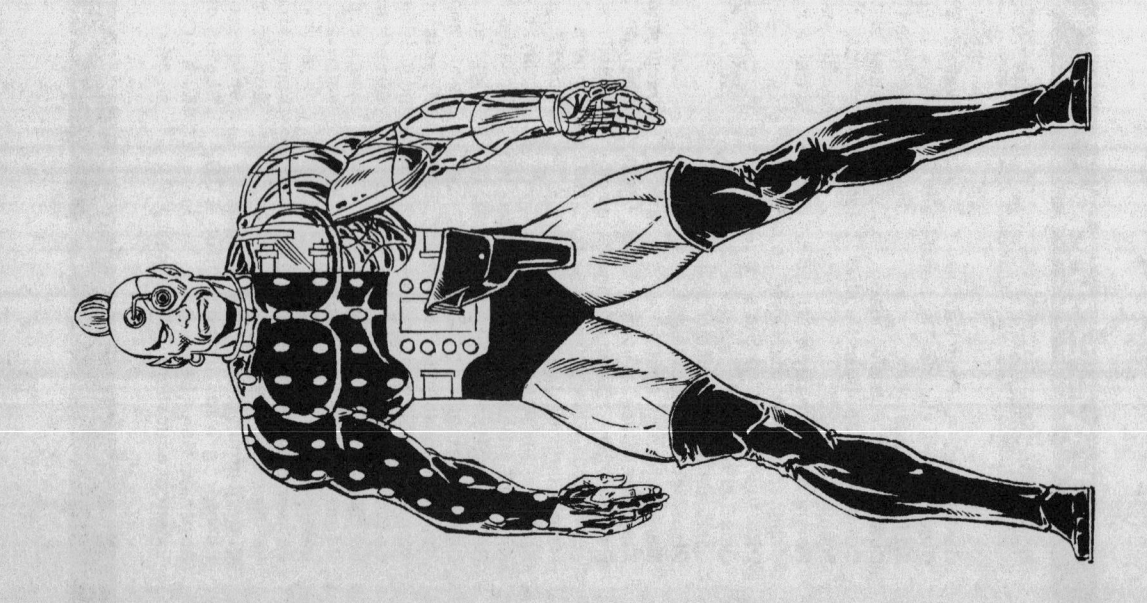

RAZA

BIOGRAPHICAL DATA

Real name: Raza Longknife (last name is an English translation of his Shi'ar last name)
Other current aliases: None
Former aliases: None known
Dual Identity: None; the general populace of Earth is unaware of Raza's existence
Current occupation: Adventurer
Former occupation: Smuggler, space pirate, freedom fighter
Citizenship: Shi'ar Empire
Legal status: Criminal record in the Shi'ar Empire, pardoned by Majestrix Lilandra
Place of birth: Unrevealed location in the Shi'ar Galaxy
Marital status: Widower
Known relatives: Rion (son)
Known confidants: Binary, (former) Hepzibah
Known allies: Starjammers, Professor X, Lilandra, the X-Men, Excalibur, (former) K'Qlll Vor Don, D'Ken Neramani, Deathbird
Major enemies: The Kree, the Brood, Warskrulls, D'Ken Neramani, (former) Lilandra, Deathbird, Black Knight III, Imperial Guard, Lord Samedar, the Shi'ar Empire, Vision, Wonder Man
Usual base of operations: The HMSS Starjammer (starship), mobile primarily in the Shi'ar Galaxy
Former bases of operations: The prison planet Alsibar, Shi'ar Empire
Current group membership: Starjammers
Former group membership: None known
Extent of education: Unrevealed, has received considerable armed and unarmed combat training from various sources

PHYSICAL DESCRIPTION

Height: 5' 11"
Weight: (as cyborg) 250 lbs.
Eyes: Blue
Feathers: Reddish orange, yellow, white
Other distinguishing features: The Shi'ar possess both avian and mammalian physical characteristics. Hence, Raza has feathers instead of hair atop his head, and has vestigial feathers on other parts of his body. Moreover, Raza is a cyborg, with various bionic body parts, including his left eye, his left arm and hand, and much of his face and thorax.

POWERS AND ABILITIES

Intelligence: Normal, Raza cyborg body also contains computers that he can utilize for various tasks.
Strength: Enhanced human, (as cyborg) Superhuman Class 10
Speed: Enhanced human
Stamina: Enhanced human
Durability: Enhanced human
Agility: Enhanced human
Reflexes: Enhanced human
Fighting skills: Excellent hand-to-hand combatant, trained in various forms of combat known in the Shi'ar Galaxy; brilliant swordsman and marksman (with various forms of Shi'ar weaponry)
Special skills and abilities: None known
Superhuman physical powers: Aside from the above listed attributes, Raza can convert his bionic left hand into a bladed weapon at will. His cyborg body contains advanced sensor systems and atmosphere processing systems that enable him to breathe in various alien environments.
Superhuman mental powers: None known
Special limitations: None known
Source of superhuman powers: Raza is a member of the alien Shi'ar race who was converted into a cyborg.

PARAPHERNALIA

Costume specifications: Battle armor of unspecified composition, conventional Shi'ar fabrics
Personal weaponry: Shi'ar knives, swords, and energy guns
Special weaponry: None known
Other accessories: None known
Transportation: HMSS Starjammer (trans-light battle-dreadnought from the imperial Shi'ar intergalactic fleet)
Design and manufacture of paraphernalia: Shi'ar craftsmen and technicians

BIBLIOGRAPHY

First appearance: X-MEN Vol. 1 #107
Origin issue: CLASSIC X-MEN #15
Significant issues: X-MEN Vol. 1 #107 (with Starjammers, came to aid of X-Men against D'Ken's Imperial Guard); UNCANNY X-MEN #156 (with other Starjammers, fought off alien attack on the Starjammer); UNCANNY X-MEN #158 (engaged in mock combat with Carol Danvers); NEW MUTANTS #50 (with Starjammers, aided New Mutants in combat against Magus II); CLASSIC X-MEN #15 (flashback to first meeting with Corsair on prison world of Alsibar); X-MEN SPOTLIGHT ON: STARJAMMERS #1-2 (together with Binary, sought "map-rod" holding information on the location of "Phalkon" power source, actually Phoenix III; was attacked along with other Starjammers by Deathbird's Shi'ar starships; with other Starjammers, first met and fought Excalibur on Earth and aided rebellion against Deathbird on a Shi'ar border world); UNCANNY X-MEN #275-277 (captured by Warskrulls, impersonated by one of them, freed by X-Men); WONDER MAN #8 (alongside Hepzibah and Ch'od, battled Wonder Man and the Vision while escorting the Shi'ar negabomb to Kree Empire); AVENGERS #350-351 (with Hepzibah, accepted assignment from Kree admiral to kill Black Knight II in hope of being reunited with his son, with Starjammers visited Avengers and Binary on Earth, fought and seriously injured Black Knight III; battled Hercules, defeated by Vision, confided in Binary, who reconciled him with the Avengers, fell out with Hepzibah, returned with Starjammers to Shi'ar Empire)

RAZORBACK

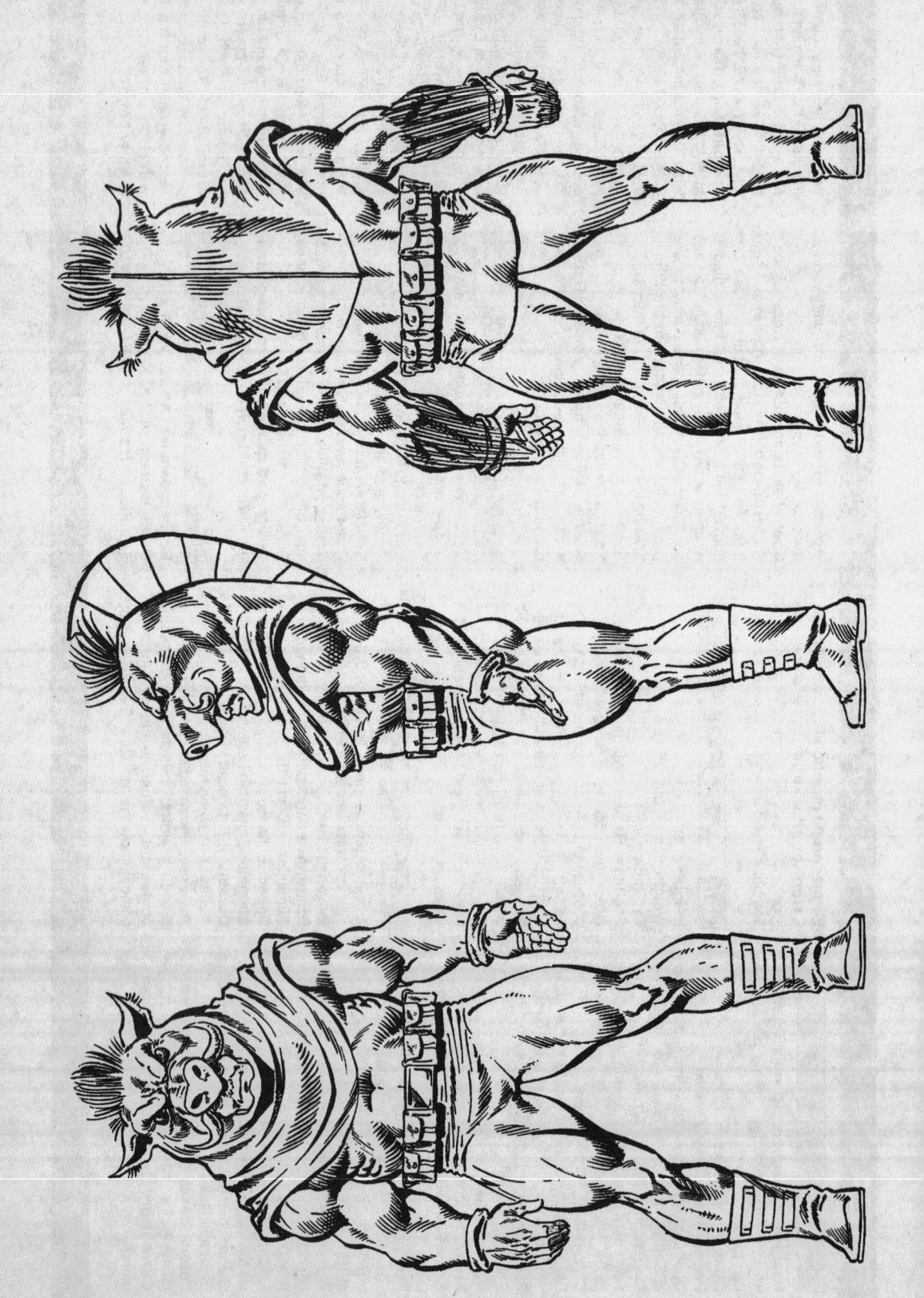

RAZORBACK

BIOGRAPHICAL DATA

Real name: Buford Hollis
Other current aliases: None
Former aliases: None Known
Dual Identity: Publically known
Current occupation: Crimefighter, astronaut
Former occupation: Trucker
Citizenship: United States of America
Legal status: No criminal record
Place of birth: Texarcana, Arkansas
Marital status: Single
Known relatives: Bobby Sue (sister)
Known confidants: Taryn O'Connell
Known allies: Ulysses Solomon Archer, Mary McGrill Archer, Taryn O'Connell
Major enemies: Brother Sun, Sister Moon, Xemnu
Usual base of operations: The Star Stop
Former bases of operations: Texarcana, Arkansas
Current group membership: National Aeronautics and Space Administration
Former group membership: None
Extent of education: High school graduate

PHYSICAL DESCRIPTION

Height: (without costume) 6' 8", (with costume) 9'
Weight: 410 lbs.
Eyes: Blue
Hair: Black
Other distinguishing features: None

POWERS AND ABILITIES

Intelligence: Normal
Strength: Athlete
Speed: Athlete
Stamina: Athlete
Durability: Athlete
Agility: Normal
Reflexes: Athlete
Fighting skills: Streetfighting techniques
Special skills and abilities: Automotive mechanic
Superhuman physical powers: None
Superhuman mental powers: Razorback can drive any vehicle, even if he doesn't know how the vehicle operates.
Special limitations: None
Source of superhuman powers: Mutation

PARAPHERNALIA

Costume specifications: Synthetic stretch fabric and leather
Personal weaponry: The mane on his hood can be electrified by activating a device on his gloves.
Special weaponry: None
Other accessories: None
Transportation: Formerly two truck-like vehicles "Big Pig" I and II, now the space shuttle Star Blazer, re-named "Big Pig" III
Design and manufacture of paraphernalia: Hood designed and built by Buford Hollis

BIBLIOGRAPHY

First appearance: (shadow only) SPECTACULAR SPIDER-MAN #12, (fully seen) SPECTACULAR SPIDER-MAN #13
Origin issue: SPECTACULAR SPIDER-MAN #13
Significant issues: SPECTACULAR SPIDER-MAN #13 (arrived in New York to save sister from religious cult), SPECTACULAR SPIDER-MAN #15 (freed his sister with the help of Spider-Man), SENSATIONAL SHE-HULK #6 (stole Star Blazer space shuttle to take Taryn O'Connell into space), SENSATIONAL SHE-HULK #7 (battled Xemnu alongside She-Hulk and U.S.Archer, remained in space with Taryn O'Connell, U.S.Archer and the Star Blazer with NASA's approval)

RAZOR-FIST

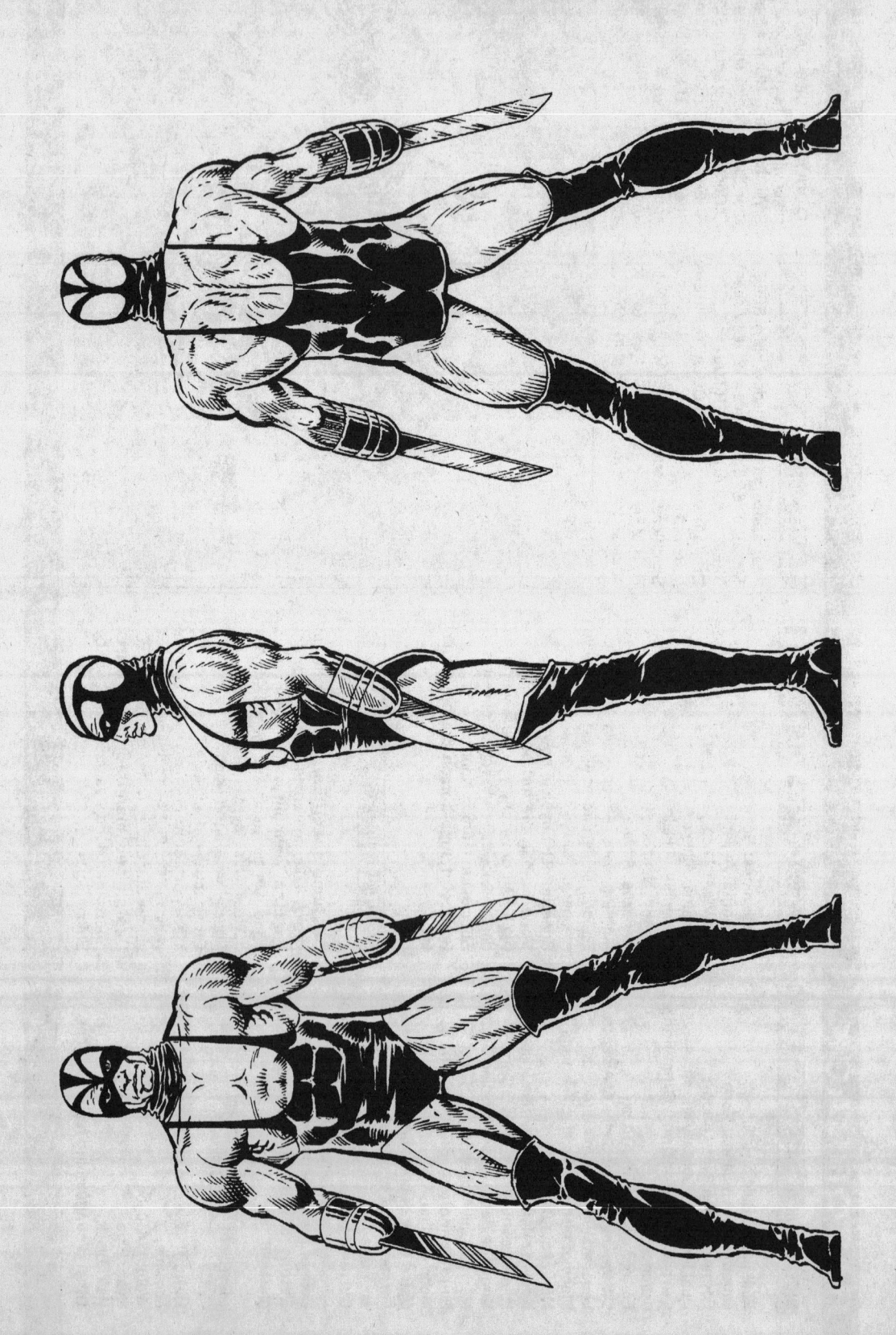

RAZOR-FIST

BIOGRAPHICAL DATA

Real name: (all) Unrevealed
Other current aliases: (II) None known
Aliases at time of death: (I, III) None known
Former aliases: (all) None
Dual identity: (I, III) Secret; (II) Possibly known to British intelligence
Current occupations: (II) Mercenary, assassin, bodyguard, and enforcer
Former occupations: (all) Unrevealed
Occupations at time of death: (I, III) Assassin, bodyguard, and enforcer
Citizenship: (all) Unrevealed
Legal status: (I, III) Unrevealed, (II) Presumed criminal record
Place of birth: (all) Unrevealed
Place of death: (I) Carlton Velcro's estate on the coast of the Gulf of Lions, southern France; (III) Carlton Velcro's mansion on an island in the Marquesas
Cause of death: (I) Shot by Carlton Velcro's guards; (III) Shot by Carlton Velcro
Marital status: (all) Unrevealed
Known relatives: (I) None; (II) Razor-Fist III (brother, deceased); (III) Razor-Fist II (brother)
Known confidants: (all) Carlton Velcro
Known allies: (I) Carlton Velcro, Pavane; (II) Carlton Velcro, Razor-Fist III, Roche, Sapphire Styx; (III) Carlton Velcro, Razor-Fist III
Major enemies: (I) Shang Chi; (II) Shang Chi, Pavane, Wolverine; (III) Shang Chi
Usual base of operations: (II) Mobile

Base of operations at time of death: (I) Carlton Velcro's estate on the coast of the Gulf of Lions, southern France; (III) Carlton Velcro's mansion on an island in the Marquesas
Former bases of operations: (I, III) None known; (II) Carlton Velcro's mansion on an island in the Marquesas; Roche's estate, Madripoor
Current group membership: (II) None
Group membership at time of death: (I, III) Employee of Carlton Velcro
Former group membership: (I, III) None, (II) Employee of Carlton Velcro, SHIELD Deltites, and Roche
Extent of education: (all) Unrevealed

PHYSICAL DESCRIPTION

Height: (I) 6'4", (II) 6'3", (III) 6'2"
Weight: (I) 280 lbs. (II) 260 lbs., (III) 240 lbs.
Eyes: (I) Brown, (II, III) Blue
Hair: (I, III) Unrevealed, (II) Bald
Other distinguishing features: (all) Hands replaced surgically with steel blades

POWERS AND ABILITIES

Intelligence: (all) Normal
Strength: (all) Athlete
Speed: (all) Athlete
Stamina: (all) Athlete
Durability: (all) Athlete
Agility: (all) Athlete
Reflexes: (all) Athlete
Fighting skills: (all) Extensive training in hand-to-hand combat and martial arts
Special skills: (all) None known
Superhuman physical powers: (all) None
Superhuman mental powers: (all) None
Special limitations: After having both their hands replaced, Razor-Fists I and II were dependent on others to eat dress, and perform other everyday tasks
Source of superhuman powers: (all) Inapplicable

PARAPHERNALIA

Costume specifications: (all) Ordinary fabric and leather boots
Personal weaponry: Razor-Fist I's hands were both replaced with steel blades which he used as weapons. Razor-Fist II's left hand was replaced with a similar blade; later a steel blade was also substituted for his right hand. Razor-Fist III's right hand was replaced with a similar blade.
Special weaponry: (all) None
Other accessories: (all) None
Transportation: (all) Conventional
Design and manufacture of paraphernalia: Carlton Velcro

BIBLIOGRAPHY

First appearance: (I) MASTER OF KUNG FU #29; (II, III) MASTER OF KUNG FU #105
Origin issue: (I) Origin is as yet unrevealed; (II, III) MASTER OF KUNG FU #106
Significant issues: MASTER OF KUNG FU #29 (I: battled Shang Chi, accidentally killed by Carlton Velcro's guards); MASTER OF KUNG FU #105 (II, III: assigned by Velcro to hunt down Shang Chi and Pavane, Razor-Fist II defeated and captured by Shang Chi and Pavane); MASTER OF KUNG FU #105 (III: battled Shang Chi, accidentally killed by Velcro); WEST COAST AVENGERS Vol. 2 #11 (II: first appeared with blades on both hands, teamed with Zaran I and Shockwave to attack West Coast Avengers for SHIELD Deltites, defeated by Mockingbird, escaped); MARVEL COMICS PRESENTS #2-4 (II: began working for Roche, was assigned to kill Wolverine; overpowered Wolverine; seemingly killed Wolverine); MARVEL COMICS PRESENTS #9 (II: defeated and seemingly slain by Wolverine); AVENGERS SPOTLIGHT #24-25 (II: fully recovered, fought Hawkeye in attempt to collect reward for Hawkeye's right arm from Crossfire, defeated by Hawkeye; joined in Crossfire's mass attack on Hawkeye, defeated by Mockingbird, taken into police custody)
Note: Doctor Doom constructed two robot duplicates of Razor Fist I, which he pitted agains: Shang Chi in MASTER OF KUNG FU #59-60.

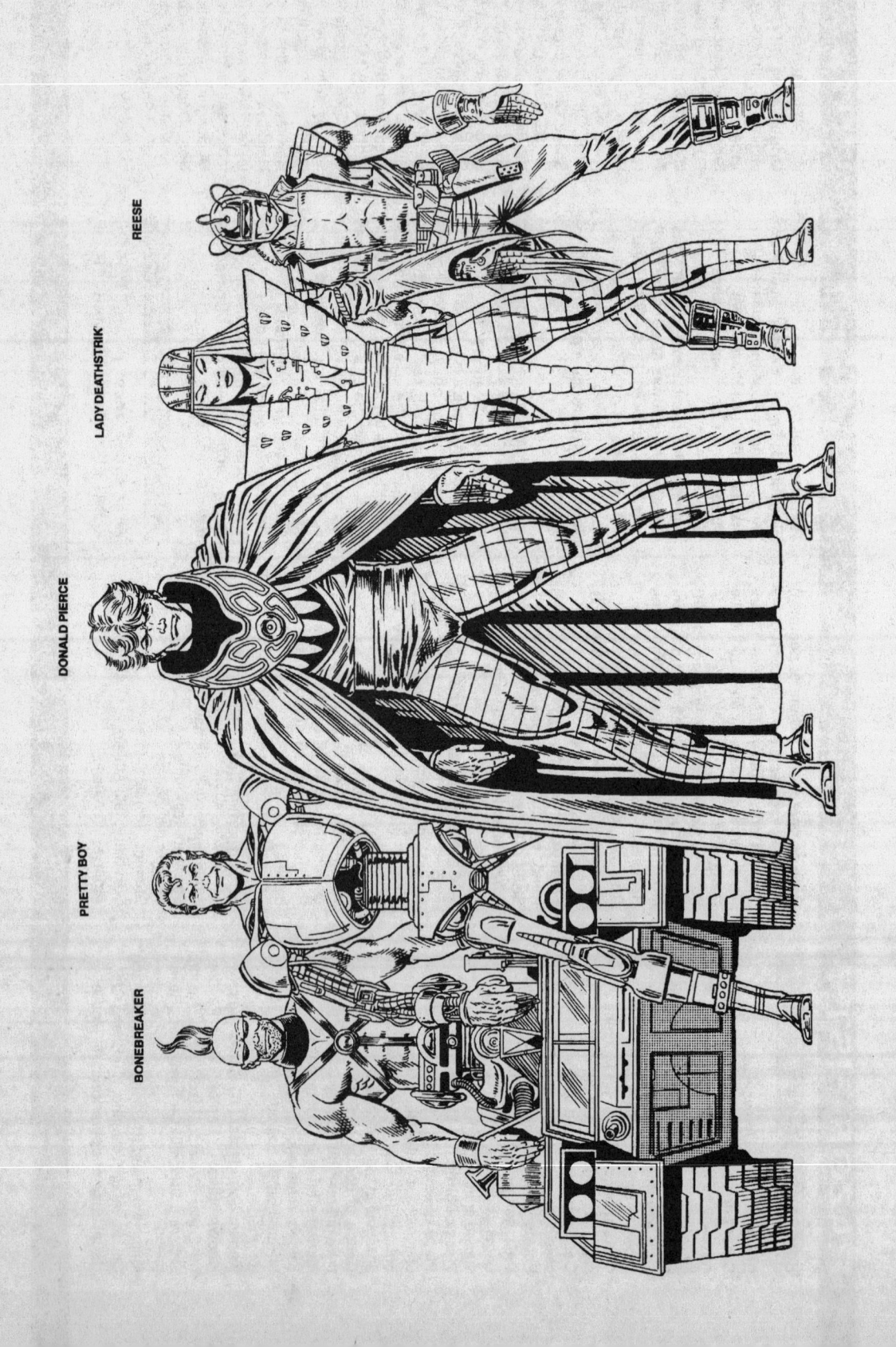

REAVERS

REESE

LADY DEATHSTRIKE

DONALD PIERCE

PRETTY BOY

BONEBREAKER

REAVERS

ORGANIZATION

Purpose: Destruction of superhuman mutants, especially the X-Men
Modus operandi: Para-military commando-style operations
Extent of operations: Worldwide
Relationship to conventional authorities: Outlaws sought by international legal authorities
Base of operations: Underground complex beneath town of Cooterman's Creek in North Central Australia; also Donald Pierce's Manhattan penthouse
Former bases of operations: Unrevealed
Major funding: Provided by robberies conducted by Reavers, supplemented by Donald Pierce's personal fortune
Known enemies: X-Men, Wolverine, Punisher, Trevor Fitzroy, Freedom Force, White Queen, Microchip
Known allies: None

MEMBERSHIP

Number of active members: At least sixteen, later eight, finally nine
Number of reserve members: None known
Organizational structure: No formal structure, members obeyed Donald Pierce, or, in his absence, Bonebreaker or Lady Deathstrike
Known officers: Donald Pierce (leader, deceased), Bonebreaker (field leader, deceased)
Known current members: Lady Deathstrike, Cylla
Known former members: Pretty Boy, Skullbuster, Cole, Macon, Reece (all deceased)
Known special agents: Gateway (forced to provide Reavers' transport through teleportation)
Membership requirements: Must be a cyborg
Note: Originally the Reavers acted as a commando-style team of thieves. After most of their membership was captured by the X-Men, Donald Pierce reorganized the team as an assassination squadron dedicated to taking vengeance on the X-Men in particular and eliminating superhuman mutants in general

TECHNOLOGY AND PARAPHERNALIA

Level of technology: Highly advanced cyborg and computer technology and robotics
Transportation: Teleportation through superhuman power of Gateway, supersonic aircraft
Standard uniforms: None
Standard weaponry: Conventional firearms, laser weaponry, cyborg dingo dogs
Standard accessories: None known

BIBLIOGRAPHY

First appearance: UNCANNY X-MEN #229
Origin issue: The Reavers' origin is as yet unrevealed.
Significant issues: UNCANNY X-MEN #229 (Bonebreaker led Reavers in robbery of Hoan International Bank in Singapore; abducted and brainwashed Jessan Hoan [Tyger Tiger]; were defeated in battle by X-Men who commandeered their Australian base; Bonebreaker, Skullbuster, and Pretty Boy escaped; captured Reavers sent through mystical Siege Perilous to unrevealed fates); UNCANNY X-MEN #247-249 (Reavers reorganized by Donald Pierce; Lady Deathstrike, Cole, Macon, and Reece joined); UNCANNY X-MEN #251-255 (recaptured their Australian base, crucified Wolverine; Wolverine escaped with Jubilee's aid; Reavers attacked Muir Isle Mutant Research Center, fought Freedom Force and Moira MacTaggart's alternate X-Men team, killed Stonewall and Sunder, Skullbuster killed by Forge); UNCANNY X-MEN #261 (Cylla Markham agreed to be converted into a cyborg); PUNISHER Vol. 2 #33-34 (attacked Punisher's headquarters in mistaken attempt to find X-Men, Punisher severely damaged Bonebreaker); UNCANNY X-MEN #262 (attacked White Queen's company Frost Technotics); UNCANNY X-MEN #269 (captured Rogue, Rogue rescued by recreation of Ms. Marvel I, Pierce transformed Cylla Markham into cyborg); WOLVERINE #35-39 (Lady Deathstrike sought Wolverine in Madripoor and Vancouver, Pierce created android Elsie Dee and Wolverine android double "Albert" to kill Wolverine, attempt failed when Elsie Dee rebelled against her programming); UNCANNY X-MEN #281-282 (male Reavers massacred by Trevor Fitzroy's Sentinels, Lady Deathstrike and Cylla escaped)

HISTORY

Founder: Donald Pierce
Other leaders: Bonebreaker (field leader)
Previous purpose or goals: Large scale theft
Major campaigns or accomplishments: Robbery of Hoan International Bank, Singapore; forced servitude of gateway; recapture of their Australian base; killing of Stonewall and Sunder during attack on Muir Isle Mutant Research Center; conversion of Cylla Markham into cyborg; successful attack on White Queen's Frost Technotics
Major setbacks: Capture of majority of original members and their Australian base by X-Men; escape of Wolverine from Reavers' attempt to kill him through crucifixion; killing of Skullbuster by Forge; failure to destroy all mutants on Muir Island; Bonebreaker's cyborg lower half demolished by Punisher; attempt to use android Elsie Dee to kill Wolverine failed when Elsie rebelled against her programming, all male Reavers killed by Trevor Fitzroy's Sentinels

RED GHOST™

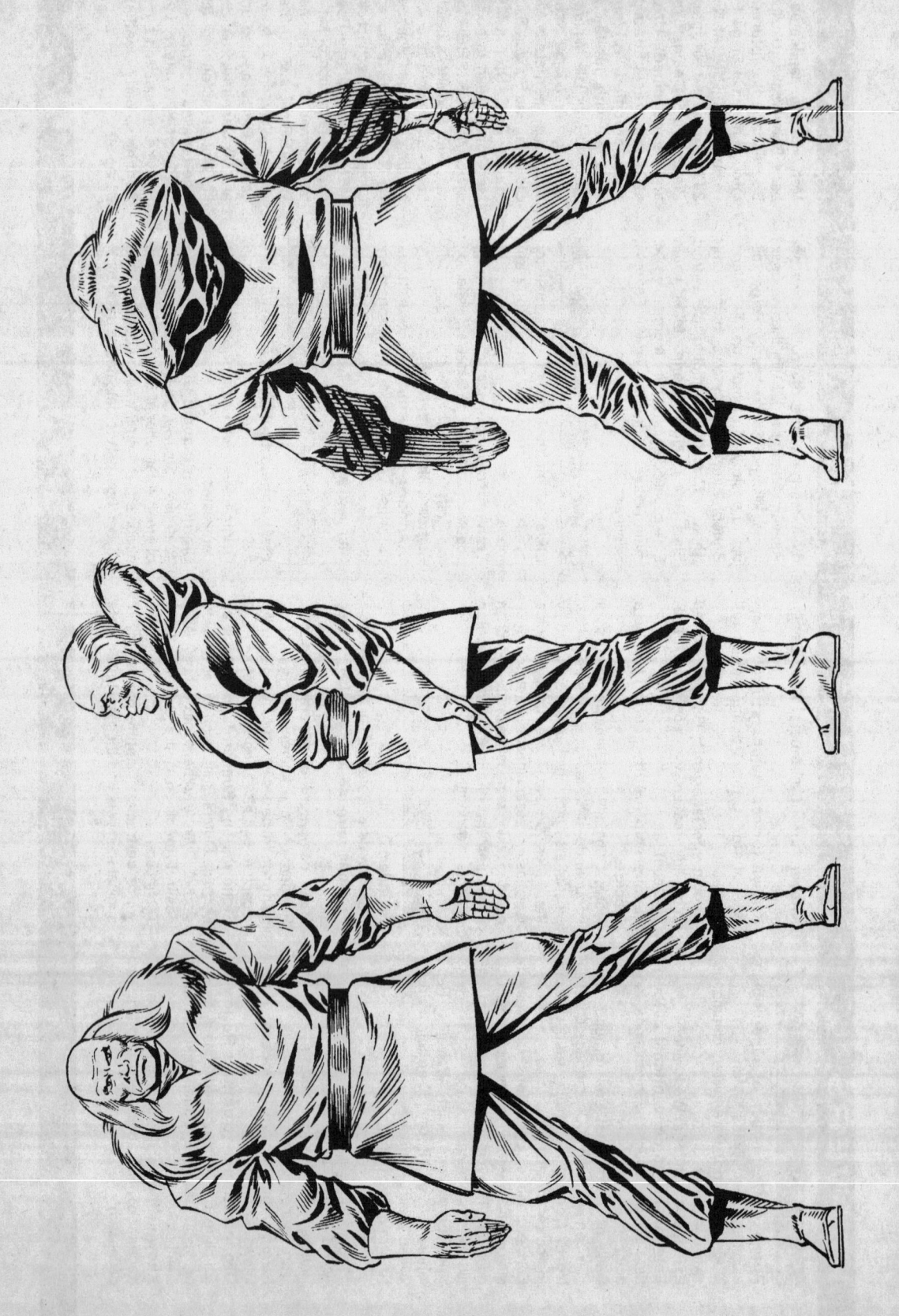

RED GHOST

BIOGRAPHICAL DATA

Real name: Ivan Kragoff
Other current aliases: None
Former aliases: None
Dual identity: Known to the authorities
Current occupation: Professional criminal mastermind
Former occupation: Scientist
Citizenship: Union of Soviet Socialist Republics
Legal status: Criminal record in the U.S. and USSR
Place of birth: Leningrad, USSR
Marital status: Single
Known relatives: None
Known confidants: None
Known allies: Super-Apes (Mikhlo, Peotor, Igor), Mole Man, Unicorn, Attuma
Major enemies: The Fantastic Four, Iron Man, Spider-Man
Usual base of operations: Mobile
Former bases of operations: USSR
Current group membership: None
Former group membership: Partner with Mole Man, partner with Attuma
Extent of education: Ph. D. in radiology

PHYSICAL DESCRIPTION

Height: 5'11"
Weight: 215 lbs.
Eyes: Brown
Hair: White, balding
Other distinguishing features: None

POWERS AND ABILITIES

Intelligence: Gifted
Strength: Normal
Stamina: Normal
Durability: Normal
Agility: Normal
Reflexes: Normal
Fighting skills: None
Special skills and abilities: Expert in radiology; advanced knowledge of genetics, rocketry, and other sciences
Superhuman physical powers: Ability to become intangible and/or transparent, ability to take on a diffuse mist-like form
Superhuman mental powers: Ability to affect tangibility of inanimate objects in his vicinity
Special limitations: None
Source of superhuman powers: Exposure to cosmic radiation

PARAPHERNALIA

Costume specifications: Unstable molecules
Personal weaponry: None
Special weaponry: None
Other accessories: None
Transportation: Various
Design and manufacture of paraphernalia: Ivan Kragoff

BIBLIOGRAPHY

First appearance: FANTASTIC FOUR #13
Origin issue: FANTASTIC FOUR #13
Significant issues: FANTASTIC FOUR #13 (on behalf of USSR, made rocket flight to moon accompanied by his three trained apes; all gained superhuman powers from exposure to cosmic radiation, battled the Fantastic Four, encountered Uatu the Watcher, defeated by Fantastic Four); FANTASTIC FOUR #29 (with Super-Apes, battled Fantastic Four on the moon; again encountered the Watcher; accidentally teleported to Earth by Watcher's matter transporter); AVENGERS #12 (expelled from Communist Party and his Super-Apes impounded, formed alliance with the Mole Man, battled the Avengers, defeated); FANTASTIC FOUR ANNUAL #3 (with Super-Apes, among villains assembled by Doctor Doom to destroy Fantastic Four); IRON MAN #15 (loss of original powers revealed; formed alliance with the Unicorn to steal Tony Stark's cosmic-ray intensifier, which he used to gain the new superhuman power of a mist-like form and to give powers to his new trained apes, Alpha and Beta); IRON MAN #16 (battled Iron Man and Unicorn; defeated by Alpha and Beta, who turned against him); DEFENDERS #7-8 (formed alliance with Attuma, battled the Defenders, defeated); IRON MAN #82-83 (lost ability to become tangible due to failed attempt to increase his powers; with his original Super-Apes, kidnaped Tony Stark to help cure him, battled Iron Man, became intangible again); FANTASTIC FOUR #197 (stowed away on space flight with Mr. Fantastic, during which cosmic radiation restored his original powers plus ability to control tangibility of nearby objects, battled Fantastic Four, escaped); AMAZING SPIDER-MAN #223 (with Super-Apes, attempted to steal rare mathematical treatise from Empire State University, battled Spider-Man, escaped); MARVEL SUPER-HERO CONTEST OF CHAMPIONS #1 (attempted to cause earthquakes in Soviet cities, battled the Soviet Super-Soldiers); AMAZING SPIDER-MAN #255 (forced the Black Fox to accompany Super-Apes on robberies, battled Spider-Man, escaped); QUASAR #6 (attempted to steal alien technology from Watcher's home on moon, battled Quasar, captured); POWER PACK #61-62 (with Super-Apes, attempted to steal alien technology of smartship Friday, battled Mr. Fantastic, Invisible Woman, and Power Pack, captured)

RED GUARDIAN

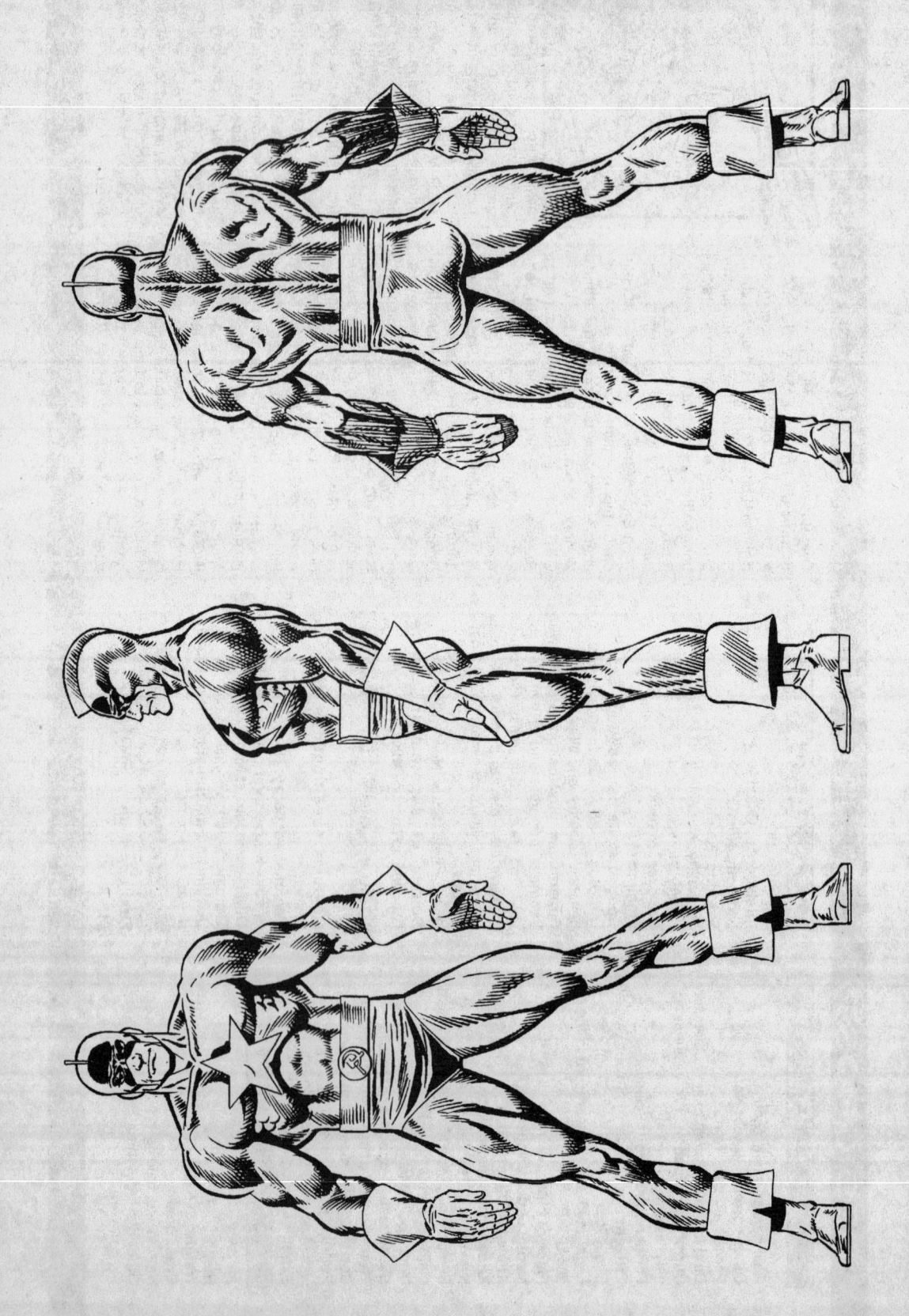

RED GUARDIAN

BIOGRAPHICAL DATA

Real name: (II) Alexi Shostakov, (V) Unrevealed

Other current aliases: (both) None
Former aliases : (both) None

Dual identity: (I) Secret, known only to his superiors in Soviet and Communist Chinese, (II) Secret, known only to his superiors in the now defunct Soviet intelligence network

Current occupation: (V) Special operative for the intelligence agencies of the former Soviet Union

Former occupations: (II) Test pilot, (V) Unrevealed

Citizenship: (II) Union of Soviet Socialist Republics, (V) Currently, unrevealed

Legal status: (II) No criminal record, deceased, (V) No criminal record

Place of birth: (II) Moscow, USSR; (V) Unrevealed

Place of death: (II) A secret military base at an unrevealed location in the People's Republic of China

Cause of death: (II) Shot by Colonel Ling while saving the life of Black Widow, then buried under molten lava when laser blast caused eruption of long-dormant volcano

Marital status: (II) Married, (V) Unrevealed

Known relatives: (II) Natalia Shostakova (nee Natasha Romanoff, the Black Widow, wife); (V) None

Known confidants: (both) None

Known allies: (II) Colonel Ling (deceased), General Yuri Bruzhov (deceased); (V) The People's Protectorate (formerly the Supreme Soviets), Captain America

Major enemies: (II) Captain America, Hawkeye, Hercules (V) Soviet Super-Soldiers, the Peace Corpse, the Combine

Usual base of operations: (II) USSR, People's Republic of China, (V) Formerly USSR, currently unrevealed

Former bases of operations: (both) None

Current group membership: (II) None, (V) People's Protectorate

Former group membership: (II) KGB, (V) The Supreme Soviets

Extent of education: (II) College degree, (V) Unrevealed

PHYSICAL DESCRIPTION

Height: (II) 6' 2", (V) 6' 2"
Weight: (II) 220 lbs., (V) 220 lbs.
Eyes: (II) Blue, (V) Blue
Hair: (II) Red, (V) Unrevealed
Other distinguishing features: None

POWERS AND ABILITIES

Intelligence: (both) Above normal
Strength: (both) Athlete
Speed: (both) Athlete
Stamina: (both) Athlete
Durability: (both) Athlete
Agility: (both) Athlete
Reflexes: (both) Athlete
Fighting skills: (both) Extensive training in hand-to-hand combat and martial arts
Special skills: (II) Expert pilot, (V) Unrevealed

Superhuman physical powers: (both) None

Superhuman mental powers: (both) None

Special limitations: (both) None known

Source of superhuman powers: (both) Inapplicable

PARAPHERNALIA

Costume specifications: (both) Body armor of an unspecified composition

Personal weaponry: (II) "Belt-buckle" disc, a hurling weapon which magnetically returned to his hand when thrown; (V) A shield, approximately 2.5 feet in diameter, composed of an unknown alloy

Special weaponry: (both) None
Other accessories: (both) None

Transportation: Various aircraft and submarine craft, presumably provided by the former Soviet government

Design and manufacture of paraphernalia: Unrevealed scientists of the former Soviet Republic

BIBLIOGRAPHY

First appearance: (II) AVENGERS #43; (V) CAPTAIN AMERICA #352
Origin issue: (II) AVENGERS #44; (V) Origin is as yet unrevealed
Significant issues: AVENGERS #43-44 (II: trained as Soviet counterpart to Captain America; battled the Avengers to protect Communist Chinese secret weapon; mortally wounded saving the lives of Black Widow and Captain America, killed in volcanic explosion); CAPTAIN AMERICA #352-353 (V: alongside the Supreme Soviets, attacked the Soviet Super-Soldiers for defecting from Soviet Union; alongside Captain America, battled a bear-like creature composed of the Darkforce); AVENGERS #319-324 (alongside the Avengers and Alpha Flight to battle the Peace Corpse, the Atlantean Army, and the Combine)

Note: The first known Soviet hero called Red Guardian began his career during World War II and met the All-Winners Squad (formerly the Invaders) on only one recorded occasion, shortly after the war's end. Like the later crusaders of the same name, he was created as a Soviet counterpart to Captain America. His costume differed markedly from those of his successors. Little else has been revealed about him as yet. The third Red Guardian was Dr. Tania Beliskaya, now known as Starlight. The fourth Red Guardian was a Life Model Decoy or LMD, an android duplicate patterned after Alexi Shostakov, Red Guardian II. It was destroyed in its first battle with the Black Widow.

RED RAVEN

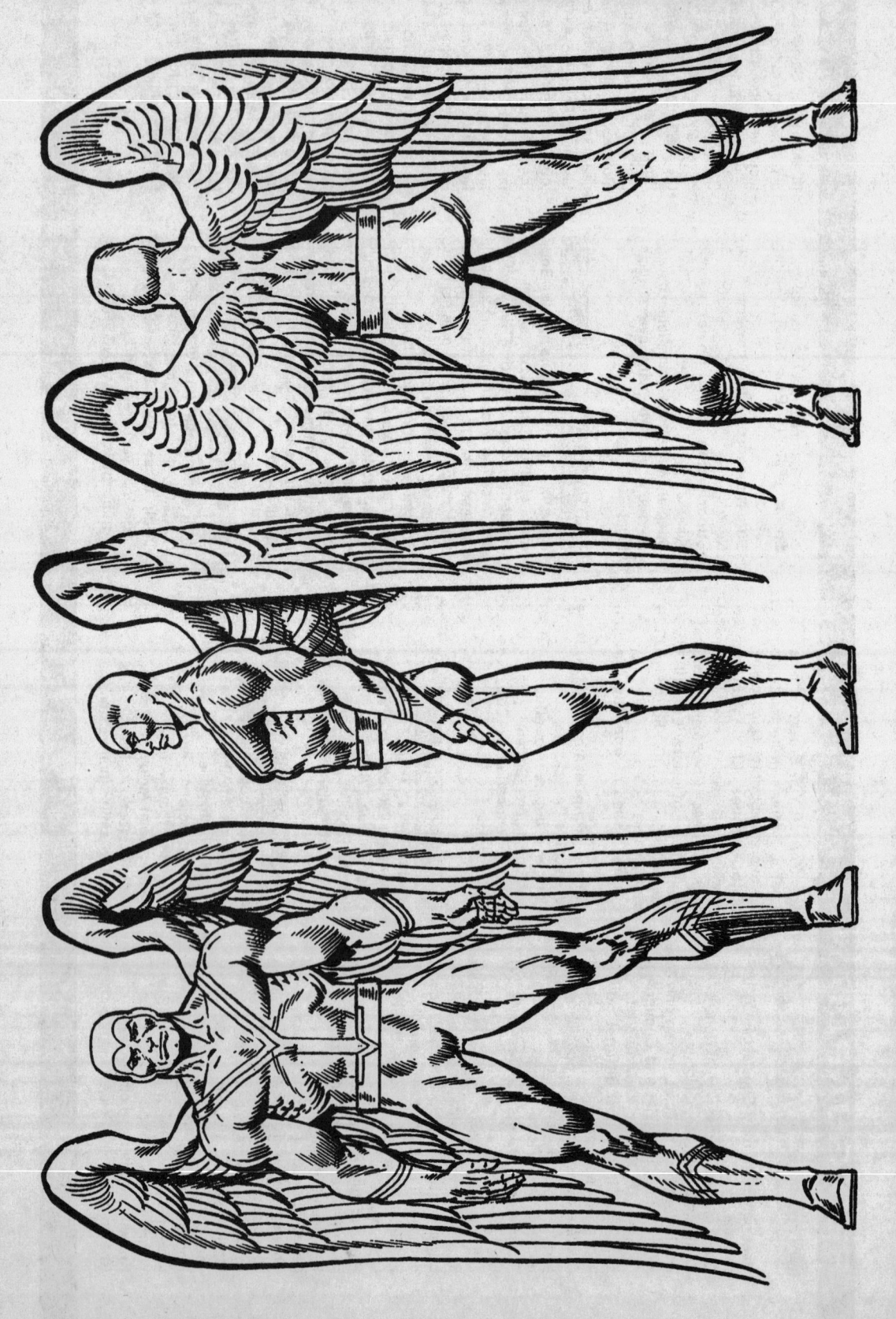

RED RAVEN

BIOGRAPHICAL DATA

Real name: Unrevealed
Aliases at time of apparent death: None
Former aliases: None
Dual identity: None
Occupation at time of apparent death: Caretaker of the "Bird People"
Former occupation: Adventurer
Citizenship: United States of America; later became citizen of the Realm of the "Bird People"
Legal status: No criminal record
Place of birth: Unrevealed
Place of apparent death: Aerie, the "island" of the "Bird People"
Cause of apparent death: Trapped in an explosion
Marital status: Single
Known relatives: None
Known confidants: None
Known allies: The Liberty Legion (Blue Diamond, Bucky Barnes, Jack Frost, Miss America, Patriot, Thin Man, Whizzer)
Major enemies: Adolph Hitler, the Red Skull, the Angel, Namor the Sub-Mariner
Base of operations at time of apparent death: Aerie, "island" of the "Bird People"
Former bases of operations: Unknown
Group membership at time of apparent death: None
Former group membership: Liberty Legion
Extent of education: Unrevealed

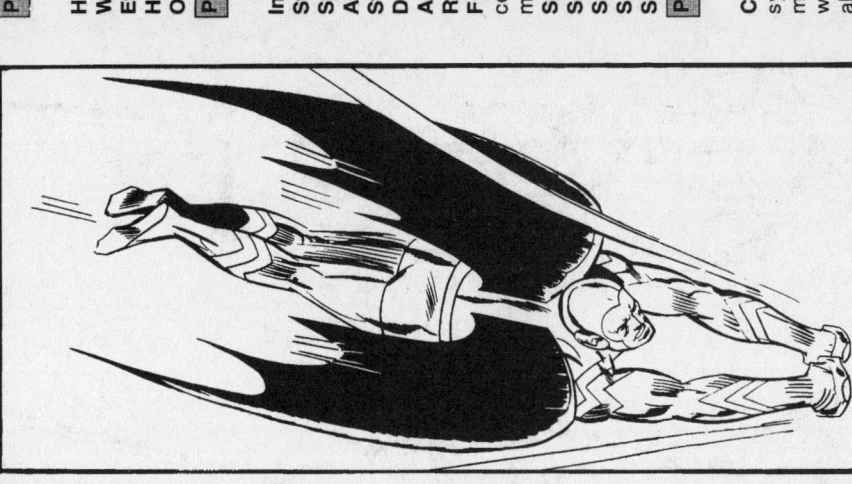

PHYSICAL DESCRIPTION

Height: 6'
Weight: 180 lbs.
Eyes: Blue
Hair: Red
Other distinguishing features: None

POWERS AND ABILITIES

Intelligence: Normal
Strength: Normal
Speed: Normal
Air speed: Natural winged flight limit
Stamina: Normal
Durability: Normal
Agility: Normal
Reflexes: Normal
Fighting skills: Basic hand-to-hand combat techniques uniquely styled to make use of the advantage of flight
Special skills and abilities: None
Superhuman physical powers: None
Superhuman mental powers: None
Special limitations: None
Source of superhuman powers: None

PARAPHERNALIA

Costume specifications: Reinforced synthetic stretch fabric containing miniature anti-gravity mechanisms, as well as large artificial wings which allowed the Red Raven to fly
Personal weaponry: None
Special weaponry: None
Other accessories: None
Transportation: Various, most often flight under own power
Design and manufacture of paraphernalia: Unidentified technicians of the "Bird People"

BIBLIOGRAPHY

First appearance: X-MEN #44
Origin issue: X-MEN #44
Significant issues: X-MEN #44 (first modern appearance; revealed how he rebelled against the winged people who raised him and placed them all in suspended animation; battled Angel to protect secret of the "Bird People"; entered suspended animation); SUB-MARINER #26 (discovered floating in the ocean by scientists, released from suspended animation by Namor, tried to awaken the Bird People to join their crusade against humanity, thwarted by Namor, discovered the Bird People were dead, trapped in explosion of Aerie); MARVEL PREMIERE #29-30 (flashback to 1940's career as crimefighter; joined Liberty Legion, battled the Red Skull)
Note: In THOR ANNUAL #12, it was revealed that the Bird People were an offshoot of the Inhumans.

RED RONIN

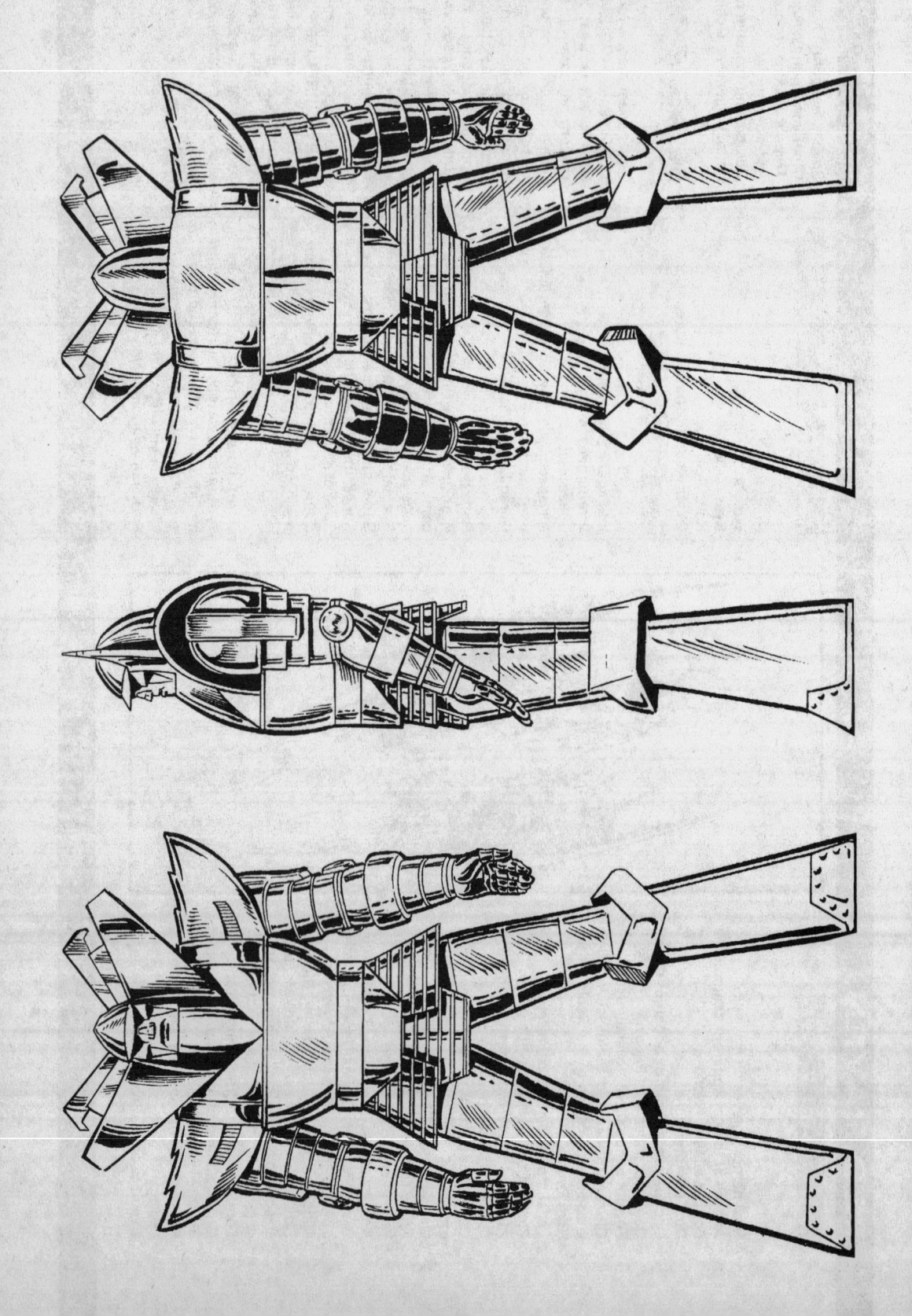

RED RONIN

BIOGRAPHICAL DATA

Real name: Red Ronin
Other current aliases: None
Former aliases: None
Dual identity: Inapplicable
Current occupation: Combat instrument
Former occupation: same
Citizenship: Inapplicable
Legal status: Unrevealed, former property of Stark International, impounded by SHIELD
Place of construction: Detroit, Michigan
Marital status: Inapplicable
Known relatives: Inapplicable
Known confidants: Inapplicable
Known allies: Robert Takiguchi, Dr. Yuriko Takiguchi (co-creator), Tamara Hashioka (co-creator)
Major enemies: Yetrigar, the Megans, the Avengers
Usual base of operations: Detroit, Michigan
Former bases of operations: SHIELD Central, New York, New York
Current group membership: None
Former group membership: None
Extent of programming: No capacity for self-motivated activity other than systems shutdown and self-repair

PHYSICAL DESCRIPTION

Height: 102' 4"
Weight: 23.5 tons
Eyes: None
Hair: None

Other distinguishing features: Design influenced by traditional Samurai armor

POWERS AND ABILITIES

Intelligence: Artificial, extremely limited
Strength: Superhuman Class 100
Speed: Superhuman
Flight speed: Subsonic
Stamina: Metahuman
Durability: Metahuman
Agility: Below normal
Reflexes: Dependent upon human operator
Fighting skills: Dependent upon human operator
Special skills and abilities: None
Superhuman physical powers: None
Superhuman mental powers: None
Special limitations: Red Ronin is totally dependent on the skills, knowledge, and reflexes of its human operator
Source of superhuman powers: Robotic materials, design, and construction

PARAPHERNALIA

Costume specifications: None
Personal weaponry: Detachable shield with "solar blade," gatling ultraviolet laser device built into shield, magnetic field generator in epaulets, arm-mounted power blasters capable of concussive force equivalent to 100 tons of TNT
Special weaponry: None
Other accessories: None
Transportation: Atomic propulsion units in legs enable it to fly
Design and manufacture of paraphernalia: Dr. Yuriko Takiguchi

BIBLIOGRAPHY

First appearance: GODZILLA #6 (cameo)
Origin issue: GODZILLA #6-7
Significant issues: GODZILLA #7-8 (piloted by Robert Takiguchi, went on accidental rampage, refused to respond to James Woo's brain patterns once imprinted with Robert's, attempted to subdue Godzilla without killing him, led him from San Diego missile base); GODZILLA #10-11 (Robert stole aboard Red Ronin again, confronted Godzilla and Yetrigar in the Grand Canyon, caused landslide that buried Yetrigar); GODZILLA #12-13 (alongside Godzilla, battled alien Megan monsters Triax, Krollar and Rhiahn outside Salt Lake City, Utah, decapitated by Krollar); AVENGERS #197-199 (activated by Earl Cowan who hoped to use it to instigate a war with the Soviet Union, rampaged in New York harbor, battled the Avengers, torn to scrap in the melee, taken into SHIELD custody)

RED SKULL ™

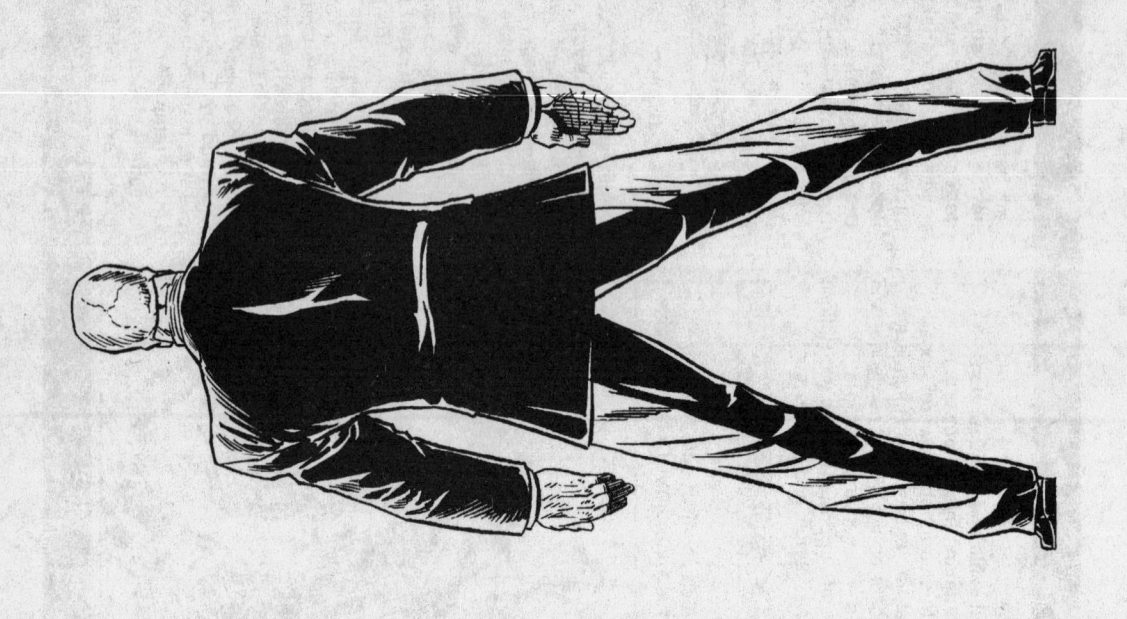

RED SKULL

BIOGRAPHICAL DATA

Real name: Johann Schmidt
Other current aliases: Der Rote Schadel (German name)
Former aliases: Bettman P. Lyles, the Agent of a Thousand Faces (whom he once impersonated in Europe during World War II), The Man (head of People's Militia), Cyrus Fenton, Teacher, Tod March, Mr. Smith
Dual identity: Known to American and German legal authorities
Current occupation: Subversive, businessman
Former occupation: Beggar, thief, menial laborer, bellboy, terrorist leader for the Third Reich, president and owner of Galactic Pictures
Citizenship: Germany
Legal status: Legally dead; wanted by the German, American, Israeli, and international authorities, but none have yet been able to prove if he is the original Red Skull
Place of birth: Unidentified village in Germany
Marital status: Single
Known relatives: Hermann Schmidt (father, deceased), Martha Schmidt (mother, deceased), Sin (Mother Superior, daughter)
Known confidants: Viper II, (former) Horst (valet, deceased), Mother Night
Known allies: Arnim Zola, Baron Strucker, Crossbones, Skeleton Crew, Scourge, Taskmaster, unnamed Watchdog leaders; (former) Adolf Hitler, Hate-Monger I, Baron Zemo I (deceased), Baron Zemo II, unnamed ULTIMATUM leaders, Blitzkrieg I (deceased), Die Sauresprizter (deceased), Der Zahnmorder (deceased), "Acts of Vengeance" Prime Movers (Loki, Kingpin I, Mandarin, Magneto, Wizard, Doctor Doom Robot)
Major enemies: Captain America, Magneto, Doctor Doom, Hauptman Deutschland, Blitzkrieger, Zeitgeist, Spider-Man, Falcon, Kingpin I; (former) Bucky I, Invaders, Liberty Legion
Usual base of operations: Lodge in an undisclosed location in the Rocky Mountains
Former base of operations: Nazi Germany; later various hidden bases around the world, most notably Exile island; The Smith Building, Washington, D.C.
Current group membership: Leader of an unnamed subversive organization that incorporates many other organizations, including HYDRA, Power Broker Inc., the Scourges of the Underworld, Taskmaster's criminal academies, and the Watchdogs; employer of the Skeleton Crew
Former group membership: Nazi Germany's Third Reich; AIM and THEM; leader of Nevada-based fragment of HYDRA; leader of the People's Militia; "Acts of Vengeance" prime movers; secret leader of ULTIMATUM
Extent of education: No formal education; personally trained by Adolf Hitler to be his right-hand man; tary, political, and subversive strategist, fluency in English and German
Superhuman physical powers: None
Superhuman mental powers: None
Special limitations: None
Source of superhuman powers: The Red Skull's current body was cloned from Captain America's, and hence possesses the mutagenic alterations induced by the Super-Soldier Serum.

PHYSICAL DESCRIPTION

Height: (original body) 6' 1", (current body) 6' 2"
Weight: (original body) 195 lbs., (current body) 240 lbs.
Eyes: (original body) Blue (his mask made them appear to be red), (current body) Blue
Hair: (original body) Brown, (current body) Formerly blond, now none
Other distinguishing features: Due to exposure to his own "dust of death," the Red Skull's head now has the appearance of a living red skull. His head is hairless and its skin has shriveled, clinging tightly to his actual skull, and has taken on a red discoloration. Apart from this, the Red Skull's current body is a cloned genetically identical body to that of Captain America.

POWERS AND ABILITIES

Intelligence: Genius
Strength: Peak human
Speed: Peak human
Flight speed: Peak human
Stamina: Peak human
Durability: Peak human
Agility: Peak human
Reflexes: Peak human
Fighting skills: Excellent hand-to-hand combatant, originally trained by German athletes appointed by Hitler. Skilled marksman with various forms of handguns
Special skills and abilities: Brilliant mili-

PARAPHERNALIA

Costume specifications: Conventional clothing
Personal weaponry: Various conventional hand guns
Special weaponry: "Dust of Death," a red powder which kills a victim within seconds of skin contact. The powder causes the skin of the victim's head to shrivel, tighten, and take on a red discoloration, while causing the hair to fall out. Hence the victim's head resembles a red skull. The Red Skull also possesses a large arsenal of conventional and advanced weaponry.
Other accessories: None known
Transportation: Various conventional and advanced air, sea, land, and spacecrafts
Design and manufacture of paraphernalia: ULTIMATUM personnel

BIBLIOGRAPHY

First appearance: CAPTAIN AMERICA COMICS #7

RED WOLF

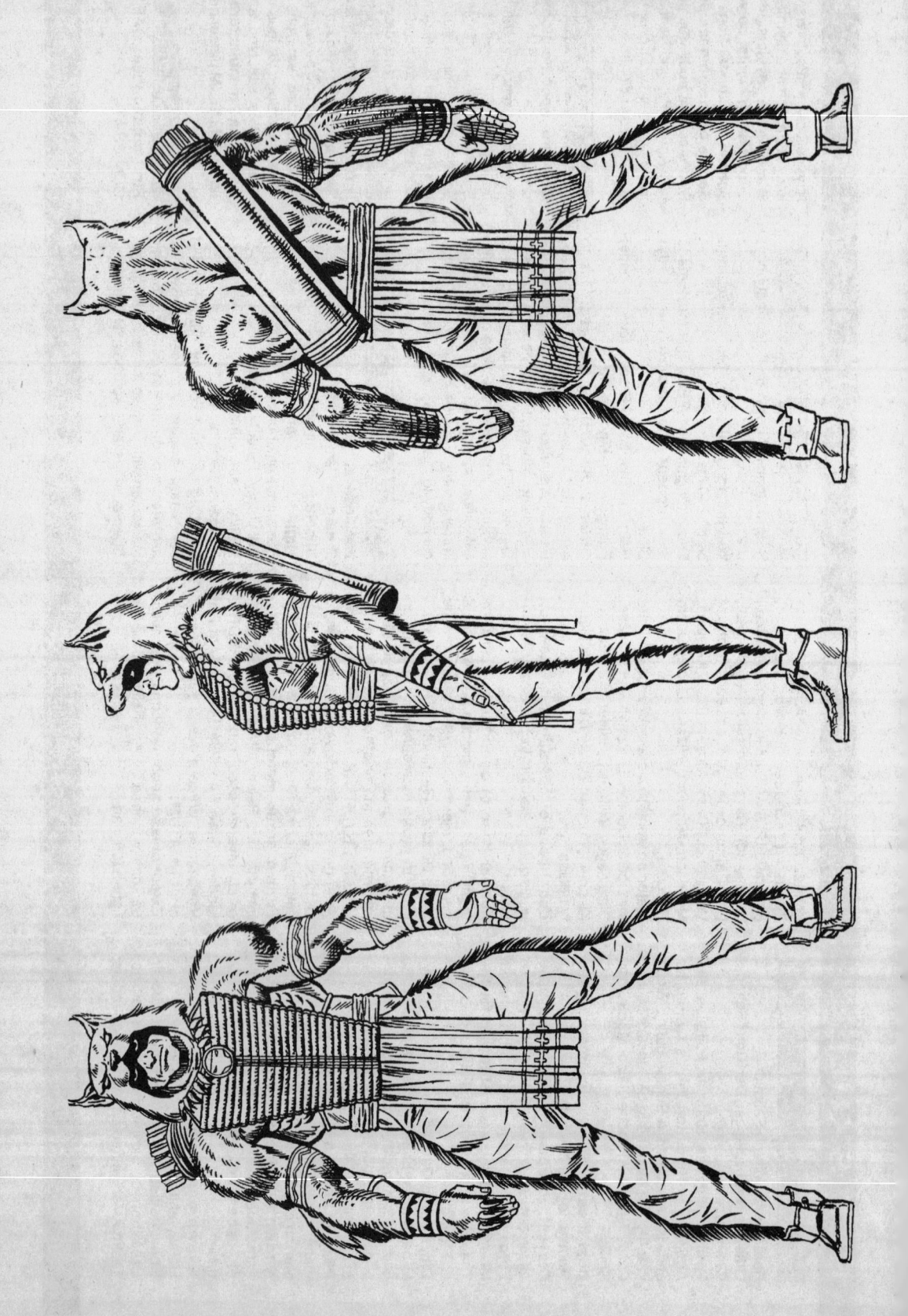

RED WOLF III

BIOGRAPHICAL DATA

Real names: William Talltrees
Other current aliases: Owayodata
Former aliases: Thomas Thunderhead
Dual identity: Secret
Current occupation: Adventurer
Former occupations: Soldier, construction worker
Citizenship: United States of America
Legal status: No criminal record
Place of birth: Wolf Point, Montana
Marital status: Single
Known relatives: Thomas Talltrees, Rebecca Talltrees (parents, deceased; William (uncle), Red Wolf I (Red Wolf II, ancestor), Johnny Wakely (Red Wolf II, ancestor)
Known confidants: Lobo I (deceased), Lobo II
Known allies: The Avengers, Jill Tomahawk, the Rangers (Phantom Rider, Firebird, Texas Twister, Shooting Star), the Defenders, Doctor Strange, Black Crow
Major enemies: Cornelius Van Lunt (deceased), the Corrupter, the Bengal
Usual base of operations: American Southwest
Former bases of operations: Mobile
Current group membership: None
Former group membership: The Rangers
Extent of education: High school graduate

PHYSICAL DESCRIPTION

Height: 6' 4"
Weight: 240 lbs.
Eyes: Dark brown
Hair: Black
Other distinguishing features: None

POWERS AND ABILITIES

Intelligence: Normal
Strength: Superhuman Class 10
Speed: Enhanced human
Stamina: Enhanced human
Durability: Enhanced human
Agility: Enhanced human
Reflexes: Enhanced human
Fighting skills: Highly skilled hand-to-hand combatant, experienced wrestler, adept combat gymnast, superb archer, expert marksman with throwing weapons
Special skills: Expert tracker, skilled animal trainer

Superhuman physical powers: Aside from the above listed attribute, Red Wolf's sensory acuity is heightened to superhuman levels
Superhuman mental powers: None
Special limitations: None
Source of superhuman powers: Granted by the wolf spirit Owayodata, a god of the native American pantheon
Note: According to one text, Red Wolf was able to cause his coup stick and his wolf companion Lobo to appear from nowhere, and Lobo also possessed the power of intangibility. Since the same text also related an erroneous account of Red Wolf's origin, giving his real name as Thomas Thunderhead, and referred to him as a Sioux rather than a Cheyenne, it may be regarded as apocryphal.

PARAPHERNALIA

Costume specifications: Conventional fabrics and leather
Personal weaponry: A coup stick (a six-foot wooden staff used as a bo or javelin), a tomahawk, a hunting knife, a bow and arrows
Special weaponry: None
Other accessories: None
Transportation: Conventional
Design and manufacture of paraphernalia: Owayodata

BIBLIOGRAPHY

First appearance: AVENGERS #80
Origin issue: AVENGERS #80
Significant issues: DAREDEVIL #258 (as Will Talltrees, revealed to have served in Vietnam alongside Willie Lincoln, Josh Cooper, and Jim Rhodes; involved in massacre of Vietnamese village); AVENGERS #80-81 (granted powers by Owayodata to gain vengeance for his parents' murder; trained Lobo I, his wolf companion; alongside the Avengers, battled Cornelius van Lunt); RED WOLF #8 (alongside Jill Tomahawk, battled King Cycle); RED WOLF #9 (battled Clayton Bickford); MARVEL CHILLERS #3, 5-7 (alongside Tigra, battled the Super-Skrull and the Rat Pack); INCREDIBLE HULK Vol. 2 #265 (alongside Phantom Rider III, Firebird, Texas Twister, and Shooting Star, battled the Hulk, rescued Rick Jones from the Corrupter, helped form the Rangers); DEFENDERS #139 (alongside the Defenders, battled trolls); WEST COAST AVENGERS Vol. 2 #8 (alongside the Rangers, battled West Coast Avengers while under influence of the demon Riglevio possessing Shooting Star); MARVEL COMICS PRESENTS #15 (crisis of faith caused by defeat at the hands of the Bengal); MARVEL COMICS PRESENTS #72 (adopted new wolf cub); DOCTOR STRANGE Vol. 3 #25 (alongside Dr. Strange and Black Crow, stopped Cheyenne pantheon from taking vengeance for the Cheyenne people); MARVEL COMICS PRESENTS #107 (battled eco-terrorists in employ of Roxxon Oil Company)

REDSTONE™

REDSTONE

BIOGRAPHICAL DATA

Real name: Michael Redstone
Aliases at time of death: None
Former aliases: None
Dual identity: Secret
Occupation at time of death: Adventurer
Former occupation: (as Redeemer) Freedom fighter
Citizenship: United States of "Other-Earth" or "Earth-S"
Legal status: No criminal record
Place of birth: Apache reservation somewhere in the Southwest United States of "Other-Earth"
Place of death: Squadron City, Great American Desert, United States of "Other-Earth" (began dying on Squadron spacecraft after it left Earth's atmosphere)
Cause of death: Adverse effects of separation from Earth's environment (see Known limitations)
Marital status: Single
Known relatives: None
Known confidants: Nighthawk I (deceased)
Known allies: Redeemers, the Squadron Supreme
Major enemies: Nth Man I, (former) Squadron Supreme
Base of operations at time of death: Squadron City, Great American Desert
Former base of operations: Apache Mountains, United States of "Other-Earth"; Redeemers headquarters, Cosmopolis, United States of "Other-Earth"
Group membership at time of death: The Squadron Supreme
Former group membership: The Redeemers
Extent of education: Unrevealed

PHYSICAL DESCRIPTION

Height: 7' 1"
Weight: 430 lbs.
Eyes: Brown
Hair: Black
Other distinguishing features: None

POWERS AND ABILITIES

Intelligence: Normal
Strength: Superhuman Class 75
Speed: Enhanced human
Stamina: Superhuman
Durability: Superhuman
Agility: Enhanced human
Reflexes: Enhanced human
Fighting skills: Good hand-to-hand combatant, coached from Nighthawk I and Squadron Supreme members
Special skills and abilities: None known other than those listed above
Superhuman physical powers: None
Superhuman mental powers: None
Special limitations: Redstone's life force and superhuman powers were dependent on his contact with the Earth and its atmosphere; upon leaving Earth's atmosphere he became ill and lost much of his physical mass. His return to Earth did not prevent his demise; the adverse effects of separation from Earth's environment were irreversible.
Source of superhuman powers: Unrevealed, presumably genetic mutation

PARAPHERNALIA

Costume specifications: Synthetic stretch fabric
Personal weaponry: None
Special weaponry: None
Other accessories: None
Transportation: Squadron air and land vehicles
Design and manufacture of paraphernalia: (costume) Remnant, (transportation) Tom Thumb

BIBLIOGRAPHY

First appearance: SQUADRON SUPREME #9
Origin issue: Redstone's origin is as yet unrevealed
Significant issues: SQUADRON SUPREME #9 (recruited into Redeemers by Nighthawk I); SQUADRON SUPREME #10 (alongside several other Redeemers, infiltrated Squadron Supreme); SQUADRON SUPREME #11 (with Thermite, captured Shape and took him to Redeemers for deprogramming); SQUADRON SUPREME #12 (with Redeemers, fought Squadron, forcing them to end their dictatorship over United States of "Other-Earth", personally bested Hyperion with Lamprey's aid); SQUADRON SUPREME GRAPHIC NOVEL: DEATH OF A UNIVERSE (died as a result of traveling into outer space with Squadron to prevent destruction of universe by Nth Man I)

REPLICA™

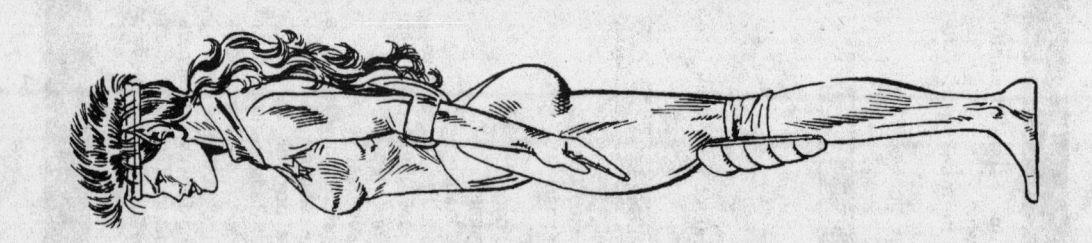

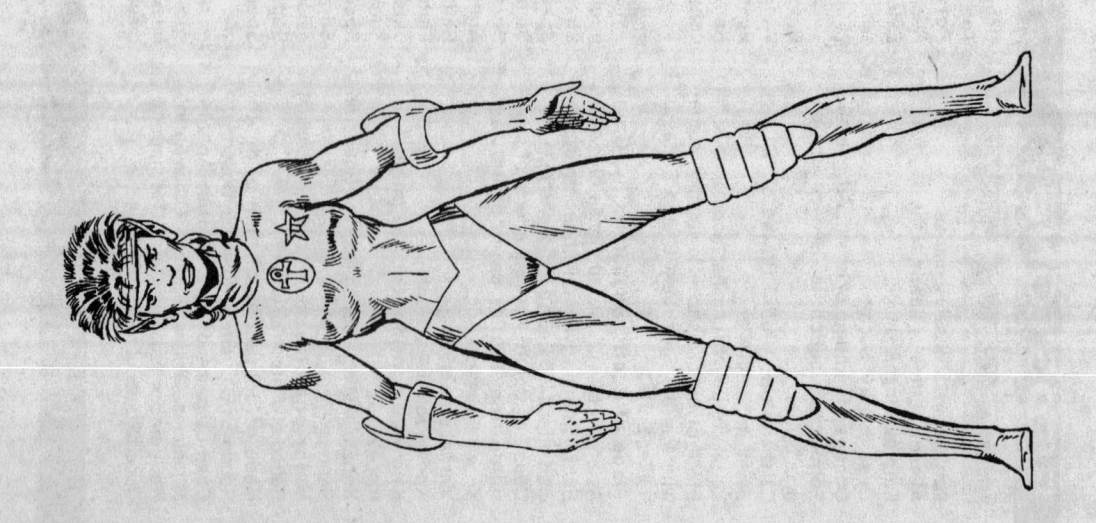

REPLICA

BIOGRAPHICAL DATA

Real name: Unrevealed
Note: Replica is not likely her true Skrullian name, given that Replica hid her identity as a Skrull for most of her life.
Other current aliases: None
Former aliases: Various
Dual identity: None; the general populace of 20th Century Earth is unaware of Replica's existence. Only since joining the Guardians of the Galaxy has Replica revealed that she is a Skrull.
Current occupation: Adventurer
Former occupation: Freedom fighter, espionage agent, companion of the Protege
Citizenship: Skrull Empire, circa 31st Century A.D.; former naturalized citizen of planet Haven
Legal status: No criminal record
Place of birth: An unnamed planet, probably in the Tarnax System, Andromeda Galaxy
Marital status: Single
Known relatives: Unnamed parents (deceased)
Known confidants: The Guardians of the Galaxy
Known allies: The Guardians of the Galaxy, the Galactic Guardians, the Protege
Major enemies: Rancor, the Stark, the Kree, Malevolence, Korvac, Bubonicus, Dormammu
Usual base of operations: Mobile aboard the starship *Icarus*
Former bases of operations: Planet Haven; mobile aboard the starship *Captain America II*
Current group membership: Galactic Guardians; Universal Church of Truth
Former group membership: Guardians of the Galaxy
Extent of education: Unrevealed

PHYSICAL DESCRIPTION

Height: 5' 2"
Weight: 255 lbs.
Eyes: Green
Hair: Black
Other distinguishing features: Green skin, large pointed ears, furrowed chin
Note: Replica often alters her furrowed chin to appear more humanoid

POWERS AND ABILITIES

Intelligence: Normal
Strength: Normal
Speed: Normal
Stamina: Normal
Durability: Normal
Agility: Normal
Reflexes: Normal
Fighting skills: Highly skilled in the combat use of her power
Special skills and abilities: Experienced espionage agent, skilled actress
Superhuman physical powers: Physical malleability, like all Skrulls, Replica has the ability to change size, shape, and color at will, taking on the appearance of other beings and objects within a volume range of .75 to 1.5 times the Skrull's original volume; unlike most other Skrulls, Replica also has the ability to take on some of the superhuman powers of those she mimics
Superhuman mental powers: None
Special limitations: None
Source of superhuman powers: (physical malleability) Deviant skrull heritage, (additional powers) unrevealed

PARAPHERNALIA

Costume specifications: Alien materials
Personal weaponry: None
Special weaponry: None
Other accessories: None
Transportation: The starship *Icarus*
Design and manufacture of paraphernalia: Unrevealed

BIBLIOGRAPHY

First appearance: GUARDIANS OF THE GALAXY #9
Origin issue: Replica's origin is as yet unrevealed.
Significant issues: GUARDIANS OF THE GALAXY #9-11 (with Guardians of the Galaxy and the Resistance, battled Rancor and her lieutenants; stowed away aboard Guardian's ship); GUARDIANS OF THE GALAXY #12 (battled a Stark Saboteur); GUARDIANS OF THE GALAXY #13-14 (revealed to be a member of the Universal Church of Truth, with the Guardians of the Galaxy, battled the Spirit of Vengeance and G'and Inquisitor I); joined Guardians); GUARDIANS OF THE GALAXY #15-16 (revealed to be a Skrull, battled Eightyfive, remained on Homeworld with the Protege); GUARDIANS OF THE GALAXY #22 (disguised as Protege, cancelled Universal Church of Truth's search for Starhawk I); GUARDIANS OF THE GALAXY ANNUAL #2 (left Protege; joined the Galactic Guardians, battled Korvac and the Intimidators); GUARDIANS OF THE GALAXY #34-35 (alongside Galactic Guardians, battled Bubonicus); GUARDIANS OF THE GALAXY #36-37 (alongside Galactic Guardians, Guardians of the Galaxy, and Ancient One II [Dr. Strange], battled Dormammu)

REPTYL™

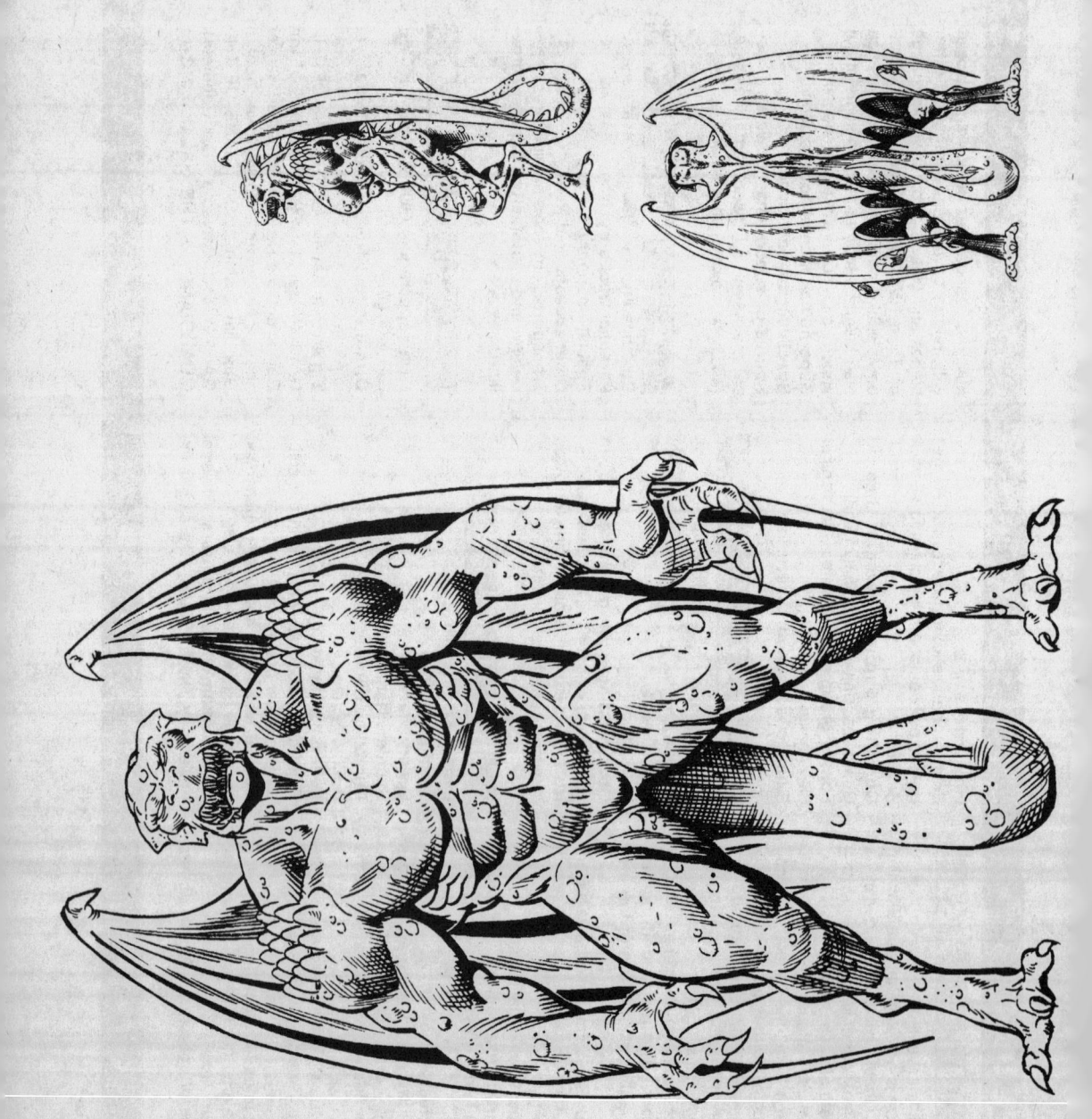

REPTYL

BIOGRAPHICAL DATA

Real name: Reptyl
Other current aliases: Reptyl Prime
Former aliases: Cap'n Reptyl, the Non-human
Dual identity: None, the general populace of Earth is unaware of Reptyl's existence.
Current occupation: Progenitor of reptilian evolution
Former occupation: Space pirate captain
Citizenship: An unnamed alien planet in the vicinity
Legal status: Criminal record on various planets
Place of birth: An unnamed alien planet in the vicinity of the Coal Sack Nebula
Marital status: Single
Known relatives: None
Known confidants: None
Known allies: The Skrulls, the Badoon, (former) Contemplator II
Major enemies: The Silver Surfer, Contemplator II, Clumsy Foulup, Nebula I, the Kree, the Super-Skrull (former) Nova II (deceased)
Usual base of operations: Mobile throughout known space
Former bases of operations: A series of hidden bases within the Coal Sack Nebula
Current group membership: None
Former group membership: Leader of his band of space pirates
Extent of education: Unrevealed

PHYSICAL DESCRIPTION

Height: 6'8", (as Reptyl Prime) 15' 6"
Weight: 420 lbs., (as Reptyl Prime) 2 tons
Eyes: Yellow, (as Reptyl Prime) Red
Hair: None
Other distinguishing features: (as Reptyl) Resembled a humanoid dinosaur (Saurornithoides) with green scaly ridged hide, sharpened teeth and claws, and a 3' tail; (as Reptyl Prime) Resembled a mythological dragon with grey scaly ridged hide, sharpened teeth and 6" claws, bat-like wings (wingspan 35') and a 7' spiked tail.

POWERS AND ABILITIES

Intelligence: Normal
Strength: (as Reptyl) Superhuman Class 10, (as Reptyl Prime) Superhuman Class 100
Speed: Superhuman
Flight speed: (as Reptyl Prime) Warp speed
Stamina: (as Reptyl) Superhuman, (as Reptyl Prime) Metahuman
Durability: Metahuman regenerative
Agility: Superhuman
Reflexes: Superhuman
Fighting skills: Experienced armed and unarmed combatant
Special skills and abilities: Highly skilled leader and space pilot, master of most known hand weapons
Superhuman physical powers: (as Reptyl) Aside from the above listed attributes, none; (as Reptyl Prime) Ability to manipulate cosmic energy in the form of concussive blasts of cosmic force, and the ability to exist in space unprotected
Superhuman mental powers: None
Special limitations: (as Reptyl) Vulnerability to extreme cold, (as Reptyl Prime) None known
Source of superhuman powers: (as Reptyl) Reptilian alien heritage, (as Reptyl Prime) Genetic mutation

PARAPHERNALIA

Costume specifications: (as Reptyl) Body armor and space suit of alien materials, (as Reptyl Prime) None
Personal weaponry: (as Reptyl) Ray-pistol, sword, (as Reptyl Prime) None
Special weaponry: (as Reptyl) Various, as needed, (as Reptyl Prime) None
Other accessories: None
Transportation: (as Reptyl) Starships, (as Reptyl Prime) Flight under own power
Design and manufacture of paraphernalia: Unnamed technicians employed by Reptyl

BIBLIOGRAPHY

First appearance: SILVER SURFER Vol. 3 #11
Origin issue: Reptyl's origin is as yet unrevealed.
Significant issues: SILVER SURFER Vol. 3 #11-12 (sheltered Contemplator II from Galactus's vengeance, captured Silver Surfer and Nova II, battled escaped Nova II, forced to release Silver Surfer, partially devoured Contemplator II); SILVER SURFER Vol. 3 #19 (set Firelord and Starfox against Silver Surfer and Nova II); SILVER SURFER ANNUAL #2 (abducted Lady Karlot and stole her treasure); SILVER SURFER Vol. 3 #27 (exchanged his crew with the Stranger for Empress S'byll, formed an alliance); SILVER SURFER Vol. 3 #28 (battled and seemingly killed the Super-Skrull); SILVER SURFER Vol. 3 #29 (led Skrull fleet against the Kree fleet, almost killed by Clumsy Foulup); FANTASTIC FOUR ANNUAL #24 (attacked by Super-Skrull, cast adrift in space); SILVER SURFER Vol. 3 #57 (metamorphosed into Reptyl Prime); SILVER SURFER Vol. 3 #63 (attacked Kree spacecraft); SILVER SURFER Vol. 3 #65 (battled Silver Surfer, escaped)

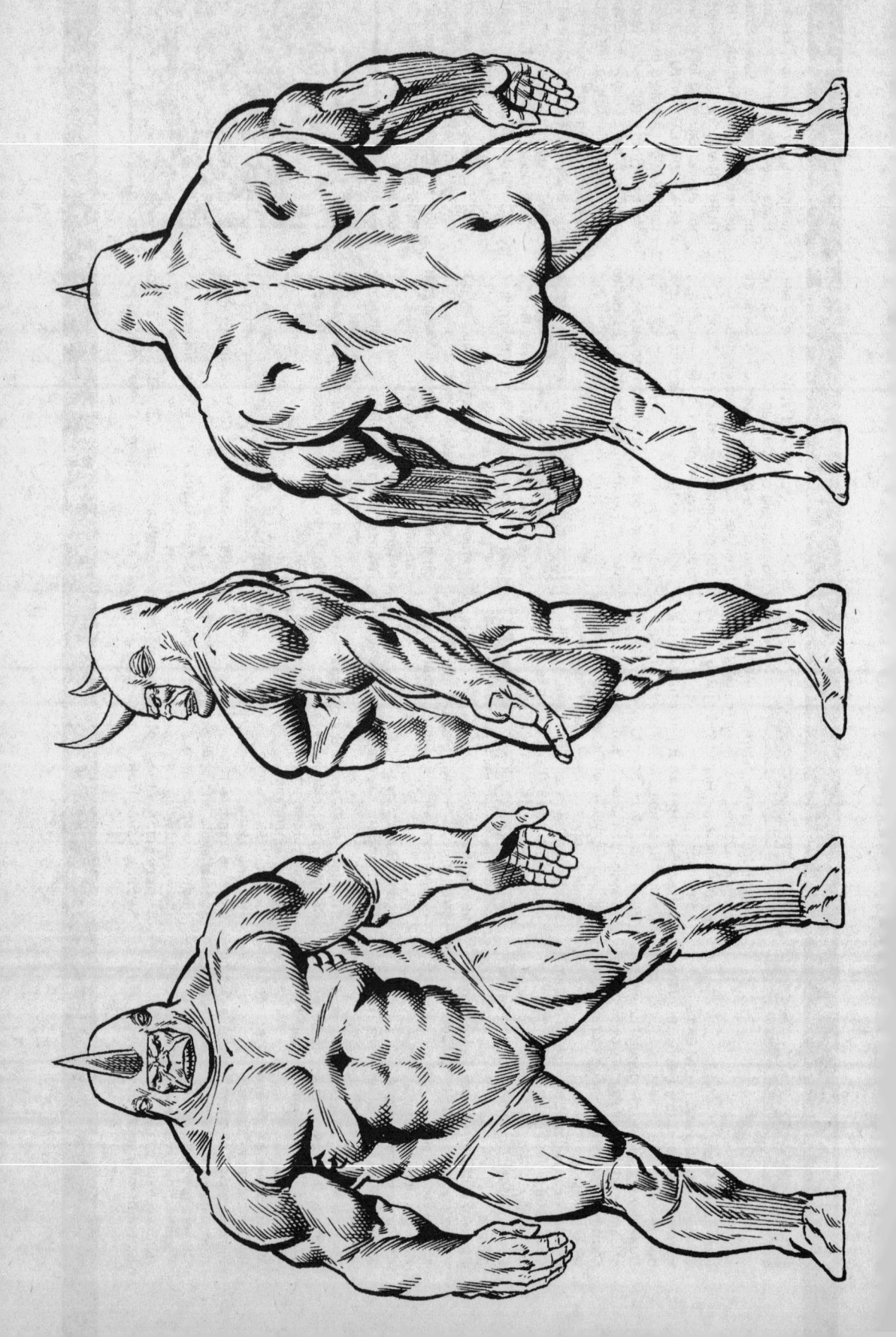

RHINO

RHINO

BIOGRAPHICAL DATA

Real name: Unrevealed
Other current aliases: None
Former aliases: None known
Dual identity: Known to legal authorities
Current occupation: Professional criminal
Former occupation: Unrevealed
Citizenship: United States of America
Legal status: Criminal record in the U.S.
Place of birth: Unrevealed
Marital status: Single
Known relatives: None
Known confidants: Thing, Silver Surfer, (formerly), Hydro-Man, Speed Demon, Dr. Goulding
Known allies: Justin Hammer, Boomerang, Leila Davis, (formerly) Leader, Igor and Georgi, Abomination, Sinister Syndicate (Beetle, Hydro-Man, Speed Demon), the Emissaries of Evil II (Egghead, Cobalt Man, Solarr), Moonstone II, Blackout I, Electro, Blacklash, Dr. Delia Childress, AIM, Kingpin
Major enemies: Spider-Man, Hulk, Doc Samson, Iron Man, Avengers, Beetle, Hydro-Man, Speed Demon, Kingpin, Miracle Man, Silver Sable, Sandman
Usual base of operations: Mobile
Former bases of operations: None
Current group membership: Justin Hammer's costumed mercenaries
Former group membership: Emissaries of Evil II, Sinister Syndicate
Extent of education: Unrevealed, probable high school dropout

PHYSICAL DESCRIPTION

Height: 6' 5"
Weight: 710 lbs.
Eyes: Brown
Hair: Brown
Other distinguishing features: None

POWERS AND ABILITIES

Intelligence: Normal
Strength: Superhuman Class 90
Speed: Superhuman
Stamina: Superhuman
Durability: Superhuman
Agility: Normal
Reflexes: Normal
Fighting skills: Good hand-to-hand combatant, no formal training
Special skills and abilities: None aside from those listed above
Superhuman physical powers: None
Superhuman mental powers: None
Special limitations: For a time the Rhino was unable to remove his costume because it had partly melted and hardened around his skin. (The Rhino erroneously believed it had been surgically attached to his skin.)
Source of superhuman powers: Mutagenic chemical and radiation treatments, including gamma ray bombardment

PARAPHERNALIA

Costume specifications: Thick polymer mat analogous to a rhinoceros hide, covering entire body except for his face (with sealable seams for waste elimination). Costume is highly impervious to damage, and temperature extremes. Two horns made of same material, project from forehead area of costume.
Personal weaponry: None
Special weaponry: None
Other accessories: None
Transportation: Conventional
Design and manufacture of paraphernalia: Originally, an unnamed team of scientists allied with Igor and Georgi; later, the Leader, and later still, an unnamed team of scientists employed by Justin Hammer

BIBLIOGRAPHY

First appearance: AMAZING SPIDER-MAN #41
Origin issue: AMAZING SPIDER-MAN #43
Significant issues: AMAZING SPIDER-MAN #41, 43 (first fought Spider-Man, who thwarted his attempted abduction of John Jameson; escaped captivity, defeated by Spider-Man who used acid to destroy his costume); INCREDIBLE HULK #104 (given superhuman strength and new costume by spies Igor and Georgi, assigned to abduct Bruce Banner, battled Hulk, injured in explosion of fuel truck, fell into state of shock); INCREDIBLE HULK #124 (revived by Leader, who further increased his strength and restored his costume, aided Leader in preventing the wedding of Bruce Banner to Betty Ross, rendered comatose by explosion of Leader's escape craft); INCREDIBLE HULK #157-159 (revived by Leader, who took mental control of him and used him to fight Hulk, traveled into outer space; regained control of his mind, fell to Counter-Earth, battled Hulk there, returned to Earth in spacecraft); INCREDIBLE HULK #171 (teamed with Abomination to fight Hulk); DEFENDERS #42-43 (joined Egghead's Emmisaries of Evil; defeated by Red Rajah, who mentally possessed Doctor Strange); INCREDIBLE HULK #218 (first fought Doc Samson); MARVEL TEAM-UP #102 (allied with AIM agent Delia Childress, battled Spider-Man and Doc Samson); AVENGERS #236-237 (joined in unsuccessful mass escape attempt from Project: Pegasus, fought Spider-Man and Avengers); THING #24 (agreed to participate in experiment to remove his costume; freed by Miracle Man, who hypnotized him into fighting the Thing; persuaded by Thing to return to Project: Pegasus); AMAZING SPIDER-MAN #280-281 (first appeared in new costume and as member of Sinister Syndicate, fought Spider-Man, Silver Sable and Sandman); DEADLY FOES OF SPIDER-MAN #1 (again worked with Sinister Syndicate, quit to undergo treatments to remove costume by Dr. Goulding, fought Beetle when latter killed Goulding, finally had costume removed, had Justin Hammer commission new costume for him)

RICTOR™

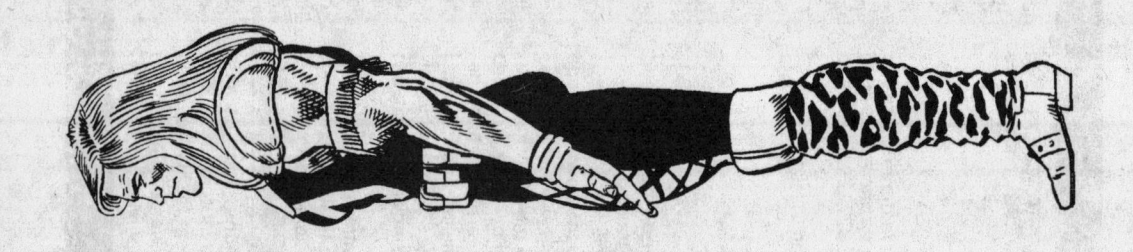

RICTOR

BIOGRAPHICAL DATA

Real name: J. E. "Ric" Richter
Other current aliases: None
Former aliases: (as Genoshan slave) Unit 2347
Dual identity: Publicly known
Current occupation: Adventurer, commando
Former occupation: (alleged) Soldier in unidentified Central American army, later X-Factor I trainee
Citizenship: Unrevealed, presumably Mexican
Legal status: No known criminal record
Place of birth: Unrevealed, presumably Mexico
Marital status: Single
Known relatives: None
Known confidants: Wolfsbane, Boomer, X-Force
Known allies: X-Force, Cameron Cheney, (former) X-Factor I, X-Terminators II, Weapon PRIME
Major enemies: The Right, Cameron Hodge, Sabretooth, Stryfe, Mutant Liberation Front, Caliban, Gideon II, Externals, Hela, N'astirh and demons of Otherplace, Deadpool, (former) Cable, X-Force, Genoshans
Usual base of operations: Camp Verde, Arizona
Former bases of operations: X-Factor's ship, New York City; X-Men Mansion, Salem Center, New York State
Current group membership: X-Force
Former group membership: Trainee of X-Factor I, X-Terminators II, New Mutants, Weapon PRIME
Extent of education: High school level

PHYSICAL DESCRIPTION

Height: 5' 9"
Weight: 145 lbs.
Eyes: Brown
Hair: Brown
Other distinguishing features: None

POWERS AND ABILITIES

Intelligence: Normal
Strength: Normal
Speed: Normal
Stamina: Normal
Durability: Normal
Agility: Normal
Reflexes: Athlete
Fighting skills: Fair hand-to-hand combat, coached in unarmed combat in X-Force
Special skills and abilities: None known
Superhuman physical powers: Ability to generate powerful waves of vibrations which can produce effects resembling those of earthquakes. Rictor is immune to the harmful effects of the vibrations he creates.
Superhuman mental powers: None
Special limitations: The limits of Rictor's superhuman power are as yet unrevealed.
Source of superhuman powers: Genetic mutation

PARAPHERNALIA

Costume specifications: Alien fabric
Personal weaponry: None
Special weaponry: None
Other accessories: None
Transportation: X-Force land and air vehicles
Design and manufacture of paraphernalia: (costume) Boomer using Shi'ar clothes synthesizer

BIBLIOGRAPHY

First appearance: X-FACTOR #17
Origin issue: Rictor's origin is as yet unrevealed.
Significant issues: X-FACTOR #17-18 (captured by the Right and used by them to create havoc in San Francisco, was freed by X-Factor I and became their trainee); X-TERMINATORS #1-4/NEW MUTANTS #73 (as member of X-Terminators II contended with N'Astirh and his demons during "Inferno" attack on New York); NEW MUTANTS #77-80, 83-86 (joined and went to Asgard with New Mutants, battled Hela); NEW MUTANTS #90-91 (fought Caliban, was severely injured by Sabretooth, was rescued by Cable and New Mutants); NEW MUTANTS #93-94 (alongside New Mutants, assisted Cable in fighting Stryfe and Mutant Liberation Front); NEW MUTANTS #95-97/UNCANNY X-MEN #270-272/X-FACTOR #60, 62 (captured and briefly enslaved in Genosha); NEW MUTANTS #98 (left New Mutants to try to bring Wolfsbane back from Genosha); X-FORCE #10 (agreed to join Weapon PRIME to capture Cable); X-FORCE #11-13 (alongside Weapon PRIME, fought Cable and X-Force, was defeated by X-Force); X-FORCE #15 (joined X-Force, aided them in saving Sunspot from Gideon); UNCANNY X-MEN #294-295/X-FACTOR #84/X-FORCE #16-17/X-MEN Vol. 2 #14 (alongside X-Force, was captured by X-Men and X-Factor II); X-FORCE #21 (alongside X-Force, battled War Machine aboard Graymalkin ["Ship"]); X-FORCE #24 (alongside X-Force, rescued captive X-Force members from Gideon II and Externals)

RINGER™

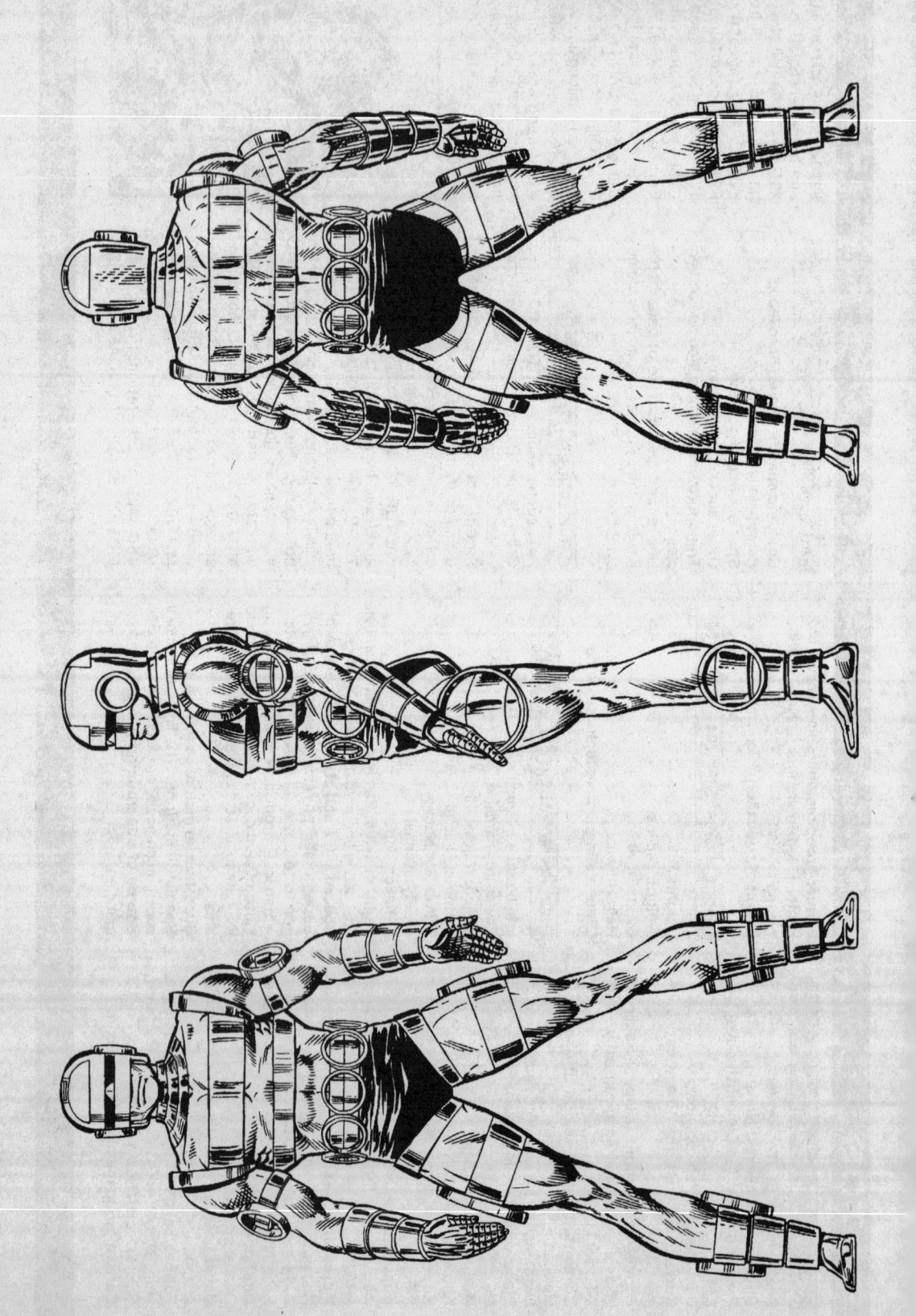

RINGER

BIOGRAPHICAL DATA

Real name: (I) Anthony "Tony" Davis, (II) Unrevealed
Other current aliases: (II) None known
Aliases at time of death: (I) None
Former aliases : (I) None
Dual identity: (I) Publicly known, (II) Secret
Current occupation: (II) Professional criminal
Occupation at time of death: (I) Professional criminal
Former occupations: (both) Unrevealed
Citizenship: (both) United States of America
Legal status: (both) Criminal record in the U.S.
Place of birth: (both) Unrevealed
Place of death: (I) "The Bar With No Name," Medina County, Ohio
Cause of death: (I) Shot by Scourge using explosive bullets
Marital status: (I) Married, (II) Unrevealed
Known relatives: (I) Leila Davis (wife), (II) None
Known confidants: (I) Leila Davis, (II) None
Known allies: (I) The Tinkerer, (II) Killer Shrike, Coachwhip, Justin Hammer, Blacklash, Barrier
Major enemies: (I) Nighthawk II (deceased), Spider-Man, the Beetle, Scourge, (II) Moon Knight, Thunderbolt II, the Pantheon (Agamemnon, Ulysses, Achilles)
Usual base of operations: (II) Los Angeles area
Base of operations at time of death: (I) American Midwest
Former bases of operations: (both) New York City area
Current group membership: (II) Employee of Justin Hammer
Group membership at time of death: (I) None
Former group membership: (both) None
Extent of education: (both) Unrevealed

PHYSICAL DESCRIPTION

Height: (I) 5' 8", (II) 5' 9"
Weight: (I) 145 lbs. (II) 160 lbs.
Eyes: (both) Brown
Hair: (I) Black (later dyed Blond as a disguise, (II) Black
Other distinguishing features: (both) None

POWERS AND ABILITIES

Intelligence: (I) Above normal, (II) Normal
Strength: (both) Normal
Speed: (both) Normal
Stamina: (both) Normal
Durability: (both) Normal
Agility: (both) Normal
Reflexes: (both) Normal
Fighting skills: (both) Minimal
Special skills: (I) Skilled inventor and engineer, (II) None known
Superhuman physical powers: (both) None
Superhuman mental powers: (both) None
Special limitations: (both) None
Source of superhuman powers: (both) Inapplicable

PARAPHERNALIA

Costume specifications: (both) Body armor of an unknown composition
Personal weaponry: (both) Various types of rings projected from devices on his wrists, including explosive rings, freezing rings, and constricting rings
Special weaponry: (both) A series of interlocking rings used as a ladder, a lasso, or a whip; particulate-matter condensers, which can transform solid ring weapons from soot and smog in the air
Other accessories: (both) None
Transportation: (I) Conventional, (II) An anti-gravity platform
Design and manufacture of paraphernalia: (design) Anthony Davis, (manufacture) the Tinkerer

BIBLIOGRAPHY

First appearance: (I) DEFENDERS #51; (II) MOON KNIGHT Vol. 3 #10
Origin issue: Neither Ringer's origin is as yet unrevealed.

Significant issues: DEFENDERS #51 (I: attempted robbery of building owned by Kyle Richmond, defeated by Nighthawk II); SPECTACULAR SPIDER-MAN #58 (I: had new costume built by the Tinkerer, coerced by the Beetle into battling Spider-Man, defeated by Spider-Man); CAPTAIN AMERICA #319 (I: attended meeting of costumed criminals at the "Bar With No Name", murdered by Scourge); MOON KNIGHT Vol. 3 #10 (II: during events of "Acts of Vengeance," made first public appearance, alongside Killer Shrike and Coachwhip, battled Moon Knight); INCREDIBLE HULK ANNUAL #17 (II: employed by Justin Hammer; alongside Blacklash and Barrier, attempted to trick Thunderbolt II into stealing experimental aircraft plans, foiled by the Pantheon)

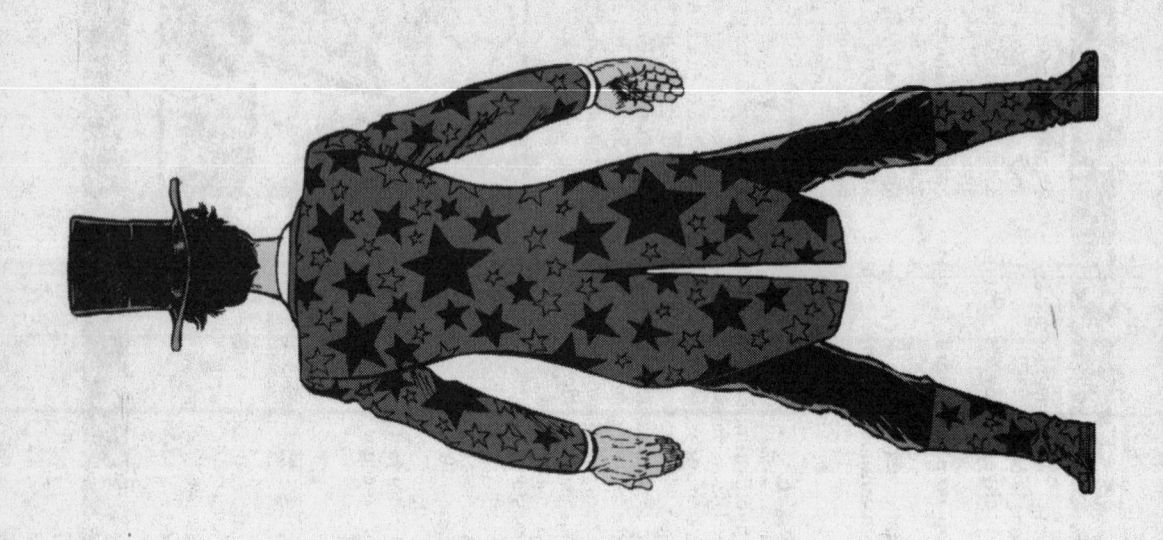

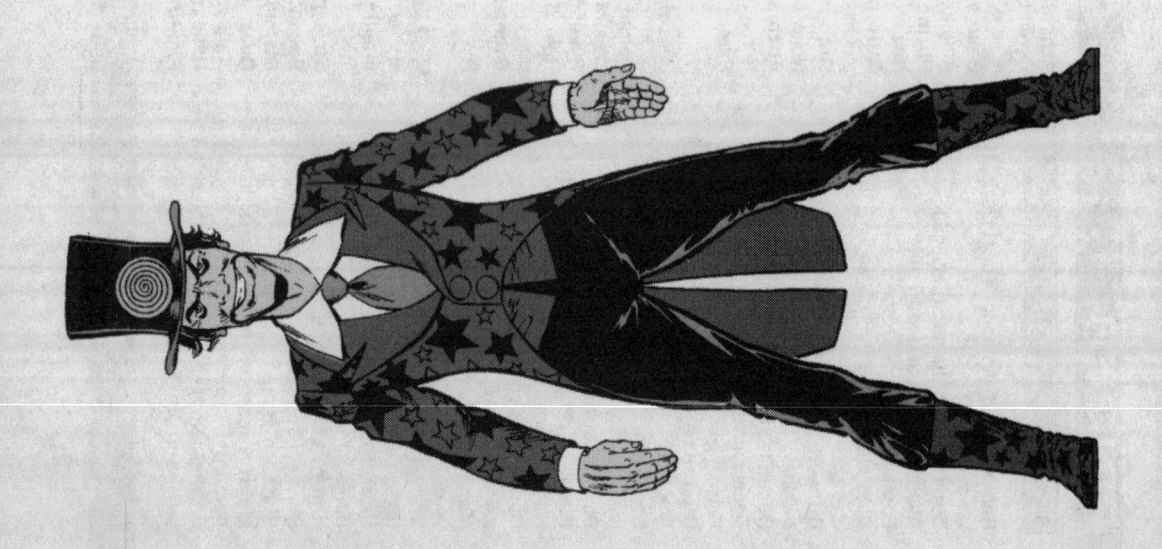

RINGMASTER™

RINGMASTER

BIOGRAPHICAL DATA

Real name: Maynard Tiboldt
Other current aliases: None
Former aliases : Mr. Thraller, and various other aliases to conceal his identity from his customers
Dual identity: Publicly known
Current occupation: Convict
Former occupation: Professional criminal; manager, director, and ringmaster of a small traveling circus
Citizenship: Austria (former); United States America (naturalized)
Legal status: Criminal record in the United States
Place of birth: Vienna, Austria
Marital status: Single
Known relatives: Fritz Tiboldt (father, alias Ringmaster I, deceased), Lola (mother, deceased)
Known confidants: None
Known allies: Circus of Crime (Clown, Human Cannonball, Ernesto and Luigi Gambonno, Princess Python, Strongman, Live Wire, Fire-Eater, Blackwing, Teena, et al), Doc Samson
Major enemies: The Hulk, Spider-Man, Daredevil, the Avengers, Thor
Usual base of operations: Incarcerated at unnamed state penitentiary
Former bases of operations: Mobile throughout the United States
Current group membership: None
Former group membership: Leader of the Circus of Crime
Extent of education: Unrevealed

PHYSICAL DESCRIPTION

Height: 6' 1"
Weight: 189 lbs.
Eyes: Green
Hair: Grey-black
Other distinguishing features: None

POWERS AND ABILITIES

Intelligence: Normal
Strength: Normal
Speed: Normal
Stamina: Normal
Durability: Normal
Agility: Normal
Reflexes: Normal
Fighting skills: Fair hand-to-hand combatant, moderately proficient acrobat
Special skills and abilities: Skilled hypnotist, self-taught electrical expert
Superhuman physical powers: None
Superhuman mental powers: None
Special limitations: Sufficiently strong-willed individuals are able to resist the Ringmaster's hypnotism if they cannot see the whirling pattern on his hat and the reflective stars on his costume, e.g. Daredevil, who is blind.
Source of superhuman powers: Inapplicable

PARAPHERNALIA

Costume specifications: Traditional ringmaster's attire
Personal weaponry: The Ringmaster's hat contains a small portable version of the nullatron, a mind-control device which amplifies his natural hypnotic talent, enabling him to mesmerize huge crowds of people simultaneously.
Special weaponry: None
Other accessories: None
Transportation: Various

Design and manufacture of paraphernalia: The original nullatron was designed by unknown scientists in Nazi-occupied lands during World War II and used by the Red Skull against the Invaders in 1942. The version in the Ringmaster's hat has been specially modified by him for his own uses

BIBLIOGRAPHY

First appearance: (Ringmaster I, historical) CAPTAIN AMERICA COMICS #5, (Ringmaster I, modern) CAPTAIN AMERICA #112, (Ringmaster II) INCREDIBLE HULK Vol. 1 #3
Origin issue: MARVEL TWO-IN-ONE #76
Significant issues: INCREDIBLE HULK Vol. 1 #3 (hypnotized and robbed crowds attending circus performances, enslaved Hulk, defeated by the Hulk under the control of Rick Jones); AMAZING SPIDER-MAN #16 (hypnotized and robbed crowds attending circus performance in New York, fought Spider-Man and Daredevil); AMAZING SPIDER-MAN #22 (abandoned Circus of Crime, who became Masters of Menace, attempted to steal their loot after their capture by Spider-Man, captured by police); AVENGERS #22 (attempted to enlist Avengers Hawkeye, Quicksilver and Scarlet Witch as circus performers, defeated by them); AVENGERS #60 (schemed to blow up Avengers Mansion during the wedding of Yellowjacket I and the Wasp; fought the Avengers); THOR #173 (enlisted a mind-controlled Ulik as an accomplice, defeated by Thor); DAREDEVIL #118 (with Blackwing, battled Daredevil); POWER MAN #24-25 (battled Power Man and Black Goliath); SUPER-VILLAIN TEAM-UP #8-9 (helped Namor the Sub-Mariner and the Shroud secretly enter Laveria); INCREDIBLE HULK Vol. 2 #217 (captured the sea-nymph Meriam, fought the Hulk); HOWARD THE DUCK #25-27 (enlisted Howard the Duck as an unwilling accomplice, defeated by Howard and Iris Raritan); MARVEL TWO-IN-ONE #76 (battled the Thing, Ice man, and Giant-Man II); INCREDIBLE HULK Vol. 2 #292 (pitted a mind-controlled Hulk against Dragon Man); SENSATIONAL SHE-HULK #1 (hired by the Headmen to test She-Hulk's strength and invulnerability); POWER PACK #59 (attempted to go straight, helped Circus of Crime escape from police after battling Power Pack); INCREDIBLE HULK Vol. 2 #377 (released from prison in Doc Samson's custody, helped Samson cure Bruce Banner's multiple personality, thus creating he new Hulk)

RINTRAH™

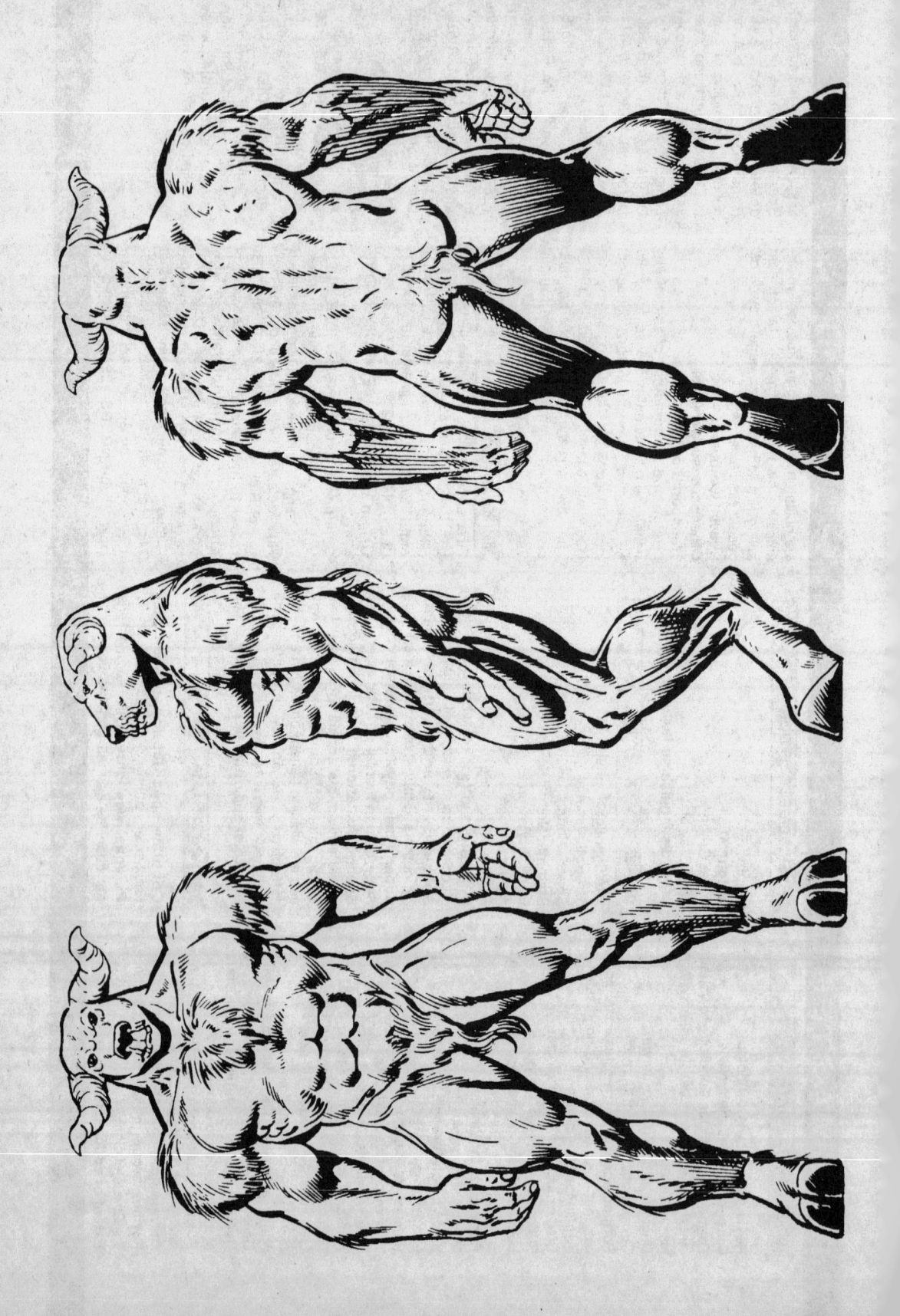

RINTRAH

BIOGRAPHICAL DATA

Real name: Rintrah
Other current aliases: None
Former aliases: None
Dual identity: None
Current occupation: Apprentice sorcerer to Doctor Stephen Strange
Former occupation: Apprentice sorcerer to Enitharmon the Weaver
Citizenship: R'Vaal
Legal status: None on Earth
Place of birth: Otherdimensional planet of R'Vaal
Marital status: Presumed single
Known relatives: None
Known confidants: Doctor Strange, Topaz, Sara Wolfe, Wong
Known allies: Doctor Strange, Clea, Topaz, Enitharmon the Weaver, Jack Russell (Werewolf), Ghost Rider II
Major enemies: Urthona, Enchantress
Usual base of operations: Dr. Strange's townhouse, Greenwich Village, Manhattan
Former bases of operations: Sanctum of Enitharmon the Weaver
Current group membership: None
Former group membership: None
Extent of education: Rudimentary knowledge of sorcery, due to training by Enitharmon the Weaver and Doctor Stephen Strange

PHYSICAL DESCRIPTION

Height: 8'
Weight: 800 lbs.
Eyes: Brown
Hair: Green
Other distinguishing features: Rintrah resembles an Earth bull with hands and the ability to walk erect; he also has green blood

POWERS AND ABILITIES

Intelligence: Above normal
Strength: Enhanced human
Speed: Athlete
Stamina: Enhanced human
Durability: Enhanced human
Agility: Enhanced human
Reflexes: Enhanced human
Fighting skills: Moderate hand-to-hand combat ability, relies on strength rather than skill
Special skills and abilities: Rudimentary knowledge of and the ability to wield magic, can cast spells enabling him to disguise his own appearance and that of other persons near him
Superhuman physical powers: Superhuman strength, stamina, and resistance to injury
Superhuman mental powers: None
Special limitations: None
Source of superhuman powers: Training in sorcery; Rintrah's superhuman physical powers are due to his being a member of an otherdimensional alien race

PARAPHERNALIA

Costume specifications: None
Personal weaponry: None
Special weaponry: None
Other accessories: None
Transportation: None
Design and manufacture of paraphernalia: Inapplicable

BIBLIOGRAPHY

First appearance: (shadow and voice only) DOCTOR STRANGE Vol. 2 #80, (fully seen) DOCTOR STRANGE Vol. 2 #81
Origin issue: Rintrah's origin is as yet unrevealed.
Significant issues: DOCTOR STRANGE Vol. 2 #80 (met Doctor Strange); DOCTOR STRANGE Vol. 2 #81 (Strange's spirit took possession of Rintrah's body to battle Urhona); STRANGE TALES Vol. 3 #4-5 (accompanied Doctor Strange to Kamar-Taj); STRANGE TALES Vol. 3 #17 (returned to apprenticeship with Enitharmon the Weaver); DOCTOR STRANGE Vol. 3 #5 (became Doctor Strange's apprentice) DOCTOR STRANGE Vol. 3 #12 (impersonated Doctor Strange to oppose Enchantress); MARVEL COMICS PRESENTS #44 (accidentally magically turned garbage into monster)

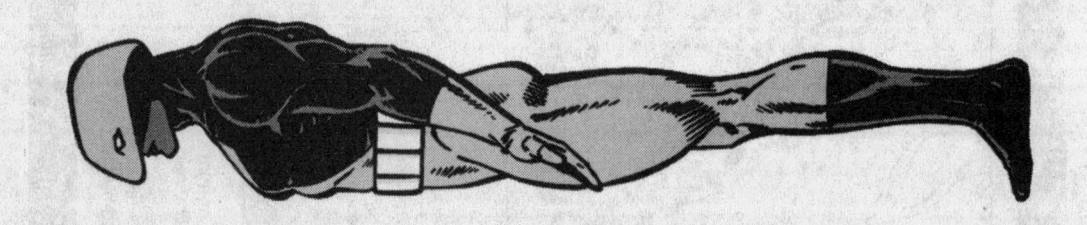

ROCK PYTHON

ROCK PYTHON

BIOGRAPHICAL DATA

Real name: M'Gula
Other current aliases: Michael Gula
Former aliases: None
Dual identity: Secret
Current occupation: Professional criminal
Former occupation: Unrevealed
Citizenship: Expatriated citizen of Rudyarda, South Africa
Legal status: Criminal record in Rudyarda, Gambia
Place of birth: Viceroy, Rudyarda
Marital status: Single
Known relatives: None
Known confidants: Boomslang, Cottonmouth
Known allies: The Serpent Society
Major enemies: The Viper, Captain America, Falcon, Battle Star, Nomad
Usual base of operations: Serpent Society headquarters, New York City
Former bases of operations: Mobile throughout Africa and America
Current group membership: The Serpent Society
Former group membership: Unrevealed
Extent of education: Attended vocational school

PHYSICAL DESCRIPTION

Height: 6'2"
Weight: 192 lbs.
Eyes: Brown
Hair: Brown
Other distinguishing features: None

POWERS AND ABILITIES

Intelligence: Normal
Strength: Enhanced human
Speed: Athlete
Stamina: Enhanced human
Durability: Superhuman
Agility: Normal
Reflexes: Normal
Fighting skills: Streetfighting techniques
Special skills and abilities: None
Superhuman physical powers: Rock Python's major attribute is his rock-hard skin, and muscle tissue, and bones. His body is impervious to high caliber arms fire, explosions up to at least 1000 pounds of TNT, heat up to at least 500° Fahrenheit, and impacts equivalent to a 200 foot fall.
Superhuman mental powers: None
Special limitations: None
Source of superhuman powers: Unrevealed

PARAPHERNALIA

Costume specifications: Synthetic stretch fabric, leather boots and a leather cartridge belt containing his personal weaponry
Personal weaponry: Rock Python carries various gimmick "snake eggs", 2 inch diameter spheroids containing various substances such as smoke bombs, acids, plastic explosives, and explosive-launched inch wide, razor-sharp steel alloy ribbon designed to ensnare opponents' legs like bolas, approximately 25 feet in length.
Special weaponry: None
Other accessories: Like all Serpent Society members, Rock Python wears a subcutaneous homing device at the base of his skull, enabling headquarters to know where he is at all times.
Transportation: Serpent Saucer
Design and manufacture of paraphernalia: Advanced Idea Mechanics

BIBLIOGRAPHY

First appearance: (cameo) CAPTAIN AMERICA #341, (full) CAPTAIN AMERICA #342
Origin issue: Rock Python's origin has yet to be revealed.
Significant issues: CAPTAIN AMERICA #342 (aided Viper in her attempted takeover of the Serpent Society, battled Nomad); CAPTAIN AMERICA #355 (revealed to be trying out for Serpent Society membership, tried to steal Falcon's uniform, battled Falcon and Battle Star); X-MEN ANNUAL #13 (as a member of the Serpent Society, encountered Rogue, Colossus, Havok); CAPTAIN AMERICA #381-382 (battled Captain America)

ROCKET RACCOON

ROCKET RACCOON

BIOGRAPHICAL DATA

Real name: Rocket Raccoon
Other current aliases: None
Former aliases: None known
Dual Identity: None
Current occupation: Interplanetary explorer
Former occupation: Chief law officer ("ranger") of Halfworld
Citizenship: Halfworld
Legal status: No criminal record
Place of birth: Halfworld, Keystone Quadrant star system
Marital status: Single
Known relatives: None
Known confidants: Lylla, Wal Russ
Known allies: Hulk, Keystone Quadrant Kops, Blackjack O'Hare, Uncle Pycko
Major enemies: Judson Jakes, Lord Dyvyne, Killer Clowns, Drakillars
Usual base of operations: Starship Ship
Former bases of operations: Cuckoo's Nest, Halfworld; starship Rakk 'n' Ruin
Current group membership: None
Former group membership: None
Extent of education: Unrevealed

PHYSICAL DESCRIPTION

Height: 4'
Weight: Unrevealed
Eyes: Blue
Hair: Brown and white
Other distinguishing features: Rocket Raccoon resembles an Earth raccoon, but normally stands and walks on his hind feet and can manipulate his hands as well as an Earth human.

POWERS AND ABILITIES

Intelligence: Above normal
Strength: Normal (for his size)
Speed: Normal
Stamina: Athlete
Durability: Athlete
Agility: Athlete
Reflexes: Athlete
Fighting skills: Excellent hand-to-hand combatant, with no distinct fighting style
Special skills and abilities: Accomplished starship pilot, excellent marksman
Superhuman physical powers: None. His sense of smell and eyesight are more acute than human
Superhuman mental powers: None
Special limitations: None
Source of superhuman powers: None

PARAPHERNALIA

Costume specifications: Alien materials
Personal weaponry: Two laser pistols
Special weaponry: Access to highly advanced unspecified weaponry
Other accessories: None
Transportation: Formerly the starship Rakk 'n' Ruin, now the starship Ship
Design and manufacture of paraphernalia: The robots

BIBLIOGRAPHY

First appearance: MARVEL PREVIEW #7
Origin issue: ROCKET RACCOON #4
Significant issues: HULK #271 (Judson Jakes tried to steal Halfworld Bible, thwarted by Rocket and the Hulk); ROCKET RACCOON #1 (Lord Dyvyne abducted Lylla, Jakes began Toy War); ROCKET RACCOON #2 (Toy War continued, Blackjack O'Hare teamed up with Rocket, Rocket reunited with Lylla); ROCKET RACCOON #3 (Rakk 'n' Ruin destroyed, Judson Jakes and Lord Dyvyne teamed up to kill Rocket Raccoon); ROCKET RACCOON #4 (Cured the Loon-ies, Judson Jakes and Lord Dyvyne apparently killed, Rocket and the animals and the robots left Halfworld); QUASAR #16 (revealed to have been a laboratory subject on the Stranger's planet, escaped captivity there)

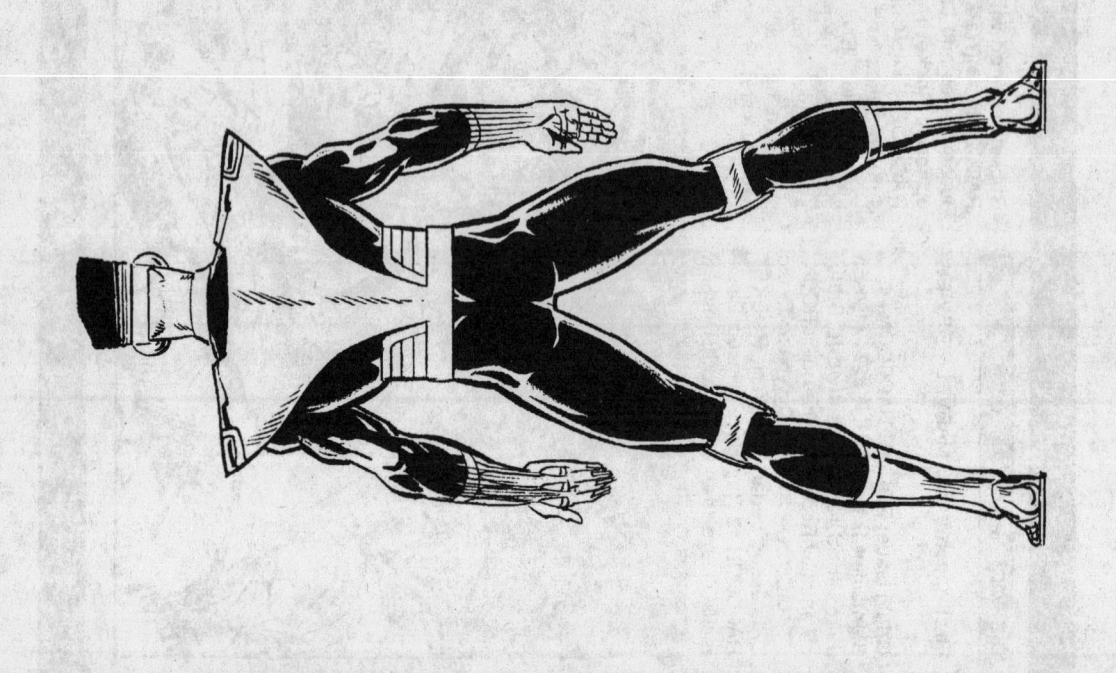

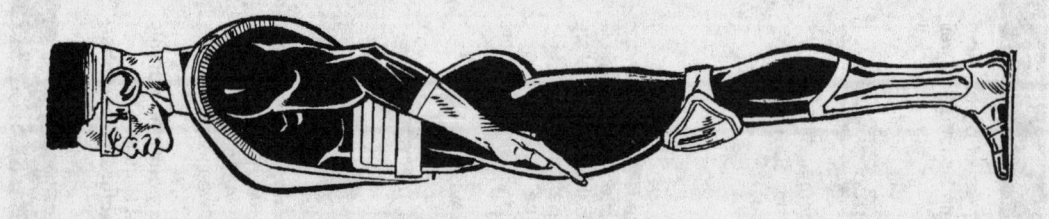

ROCKET RACER

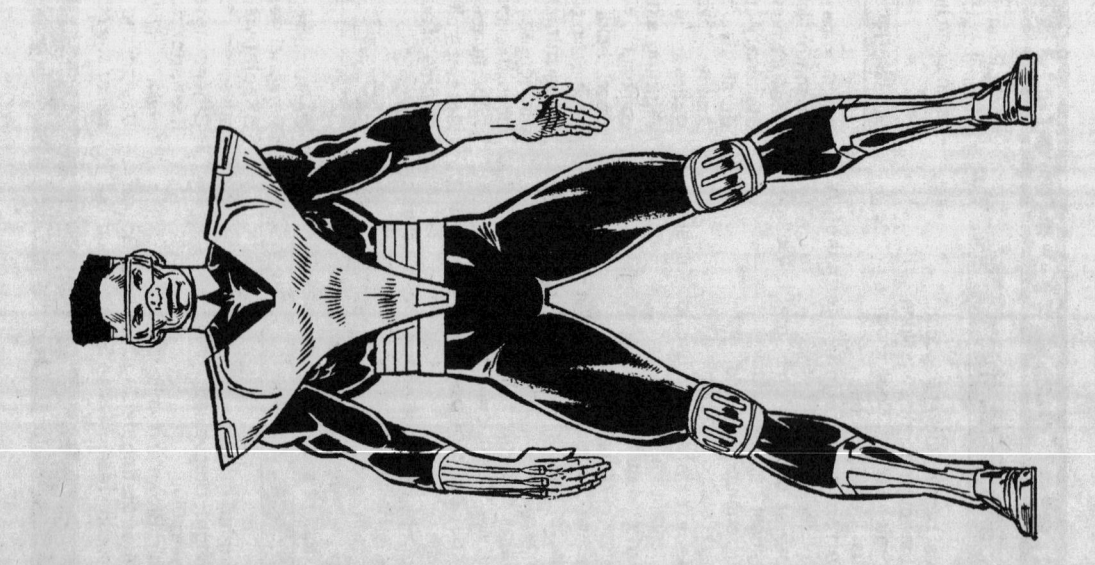

ROCKET RACER

BIOGRAPHICAL DATA

Real name: Robert Farrell
Other current aliases: None
Former aliases: None
Dual identity: Known to legal authorities
Current occupation: Student, inventor, occasional crimefighter and freelance operative for Silver Sable International
Former occupation: Burglar
Legal status: Criminal record in the U.S.
Citizenship: United States of America
Place of birth: Brooklyn, New York
Marital status: Single
Known relatives: Emma Johnson Farrell (mother), unnamed father (whereabouts unknown), three unnamed brothers, and three unnamed sisters
Known confidants: Spider-Man, Silver Sable
Known allies: The Prowler, Puma, Sandman, Will o' the Wisp
Major enemies: Big Wheel (deceased), the Bounty Hunter, Skinhead, the Space Phantom, Speed Demon
Usual base of operations: New York City
Former bases of operations: Same
Current group membership: The Outlaws
Former group membership: None
Extent of education: College student

PHYSICAL DESCRIPTION

Height: 5' 10"
Weight: 160 lbs.
Eyes: Brown
Hair: Black
Other distinguishing features: None

POWERS AND ABILITIES

Intelligence: Gifted
Strength: Normal
Speed: Normal
Stamina: Normal
Durability: Normal
Agility: Athlete
Reflexes: Athlete
Fighting skills: Moderate experience in streetfighting techniques
Special skills and abilities: None
Superhuman physical powers: None
Superhuman mental powers: None
Special limitations: None
Source of superhuman powers: None

PARAPHERNALIA

Costume specifications: Stretch fabric covered with appropriate padding
Personal weaponry: Gauntlets furnished with explosive mini-rockets
Special weaponry: None
Other accessories: None
Transportation: A cybernetically controlled, rocket-powered magnetic skateboard
Design and manufacture of paraphernalia: Robert Farrell; the Tinkerer

BIBLIOGRAPHY

First appearance: AMAZING SPIDER-MAN #172
Origin issue: SPECTACULAR SPIDER-MAN #104
Significant issues: AMAZING SPIDER-MAN #172 (first encountered Spider-Man); AMAZING SPIDER-MAN #182-183 (Tinkerer redesigned skateboard; fought Spider-Man and the Big Wheel); SPECTACULAR SPIDER-MAN #104 (saved by Spider-Man from the Bounty Hunter); WEB OF SPIDER-MAN #50 (attempted to prove Spider-Man innocent of a crime; first encountered Silver Sable and the Outlaws); WEB OF SPIDER-MAN #56-57 (joined forces with Spider-Man to stop the white supremecist, Skinhead); SPECTACULAR SPIDER-MAN ANNUAL #10 (hired by Silver Sable International to prevent two youths from stealing the victims' weapons at the Bar with No Name, the site of the Scourge massacre); MARVEL TALES #242 (again hired by Sable to stop the Speed Demon); SPECTACULAR SPIDER-MAN #169-170 (joined Spider-Man and the Outlaws against the Avengers and the Space Phantom); EXCALIBUR #36 (hired along with the Outlaws to retrieve a Symkarian nuclear device in England); MARVEL TALES #250 (hired by Sable to stop a runaway subway maintenance robot); AMAZING SPIDER-MAN ANNUAL #25, SPECTACULAR SPIDER-MAN ANNUAL #11, WEB OF SPIDER-MAN ANNUAL #7 (formally joined the Outlaws to rescue the kidnapped daughter of a Canadian official)

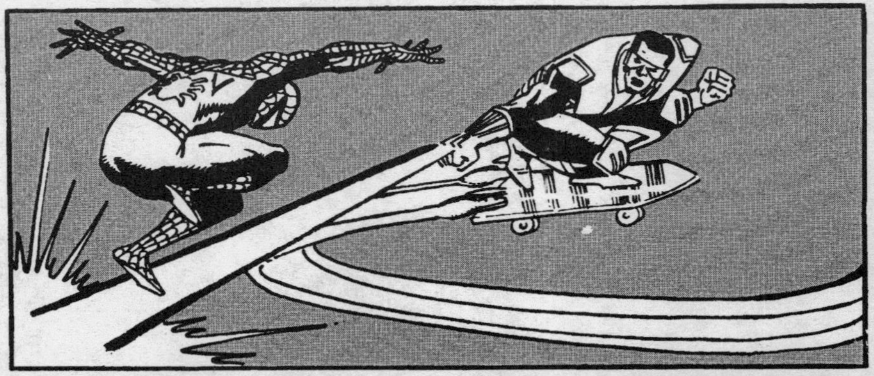

ROGUE

ROGUE

BIOGRAPHICAL DATA

Real name: Unrevealed
Other current aliases: None
Former aliases: Dr. Kellogg, (when her "Carol Danvers" personality was dominant), Carol Danvers, Ace
Dual identity: Secret
Current occupation: Adventurer
Former occupation: Terrorist
Citizenship: United States of America
Legal status: No criminal record, formerly sought by SHIELD on a charge of murder (for which she was framed); charges dropped
Place of birth: Caldecott County, Mississippi
Marital status: Single
Known relatives: Raven Darkholme (alias Mystique, unofficial foster mother)
Known confidants: X-Men, (formerly) Magneto, Mystique, Destiny II
Known allies: X-Men, Alpha Flight, Ka-Zar, Nick Fury, (formerly) Magneto, New Mutants, Brotherhood of Evil Mutants II
Major enemies: Magneto, Juggernaut, Master Mold, Wipeout, Genoshan government, Henry Peter Gyrich, Zaladane, (formerly) Dazzler, Avengers
Usual base of operations: Professor Xavier's School for Gifted Youngsters, Salem Center, Westchester County, New York State
Former bases of operations: X-Men headquarters, Australian outback
Current group membership: X-Men
Former group membership: Brotherhood of Evil Mutants II
Extent of education: College-level courses at Professor Xavier's school

PHYSICAL DESCRIPTION

Height: 5' 8"
Weight: 120 lbs
Eyes: Green
Hair: Brown with a bleached white streak
Other distinguishing features: None

POWERS AND ABILITIES

Intelligence: Normal
Strength: Superhuman Class 50
Speed: Unrevealed
Flight Speed: Subsonic
Stamina: Superhuman
Durability: Superhuman
Agility: Enhanced human
Reflexes: Enhanced human
Fighting skills: Good hand-to-hand combatant, received coaching from Wolverine
Special skills and abilities: Rogue could formerly draw upon the combat and espionage training of Carol Danvers by duplicate of Danvers', to dominate her conscious mind.
Superhuman physical powers: Aside from those mentioned above, the superhuman ability to absorb the memories, knowledge, talents, personality, and physical abilities (whether superhuman or not) of another human being (or members of some sentient alien races) through physical contact of her skin with the skin of that person (some times she also duplicates in herself gross physical characteristics of her victim). The victim's abilities and memories are absorbed for a one second to 60 second ratio of contact. The victim loses those abilities and memories for exactly the amount of time that Rogue possesses them. She has also permanently absorbed certain superhuman powers from Ms. Marvel I.
Superhuman mental powers: Psychic "seventh sense" that enables her to anticipate an enemy's move subconsciously during battle. When she possessed Carol Danvers' psyche, her "double" consciousness made her highly resistant to telepathic probes; it is not known if she still possesses this resistance.
Special limitations: Rogue cannot touch another human being without absorbing their memories, abilities, and superhuman powers (if any) and rendering them unconscious. Remnants of the personalities of victims whose memories she has absorbed remain buried in her subconscious indefinitely. Certain powerful beings have proven resistant to Rogue's power.
Source of superhuman powers: Genetic mutation, absorption of superhuman powers of Ms. Marvel I.

PARAPHERNALIA

Costume specifications: Synthetic stretch fabric
Personal weaponry: None
Special weaponry: None
Other accessories: None
Transportation: X-Men Blackbird jet, flight under own power
Design and manufacture of paraphernalia: Unrevealed

BIBLIOGRAPHY

First appearance: AVENGERS ANNUAL #10
Origin issue: (partially) UNCANNY X-MEN #185
Significant issues: AVENGERS ANNUAL #10 (battled Avengers as member of Brotherhood of Evil Mutants II, revealed that she had permanently absorbed Ms. Marvel I's memories and powers); DAZZLER #22, 24, 28 (with Mystique and Destiny II, attacked Angel and Dazzler, overpowered by Dazzler; defeated Dazzler but was herself defeated by Power Man II and Iron Fist, fled; defeated by Dazzler); UNCANNY X-MEN #171-172 (asked for admission to the X-Men to learn how to control her powers, was accepted, clashed with Carol Danvers as Binary; teamed with Wolverine in Japan); UNCANNY X-MEN #182 (invaded SHIELD Helicarrier to rescue Michael Rossi, irst fell under domination of Danvers' persona, was framed for murder of a SHIELD agent)

ROMA

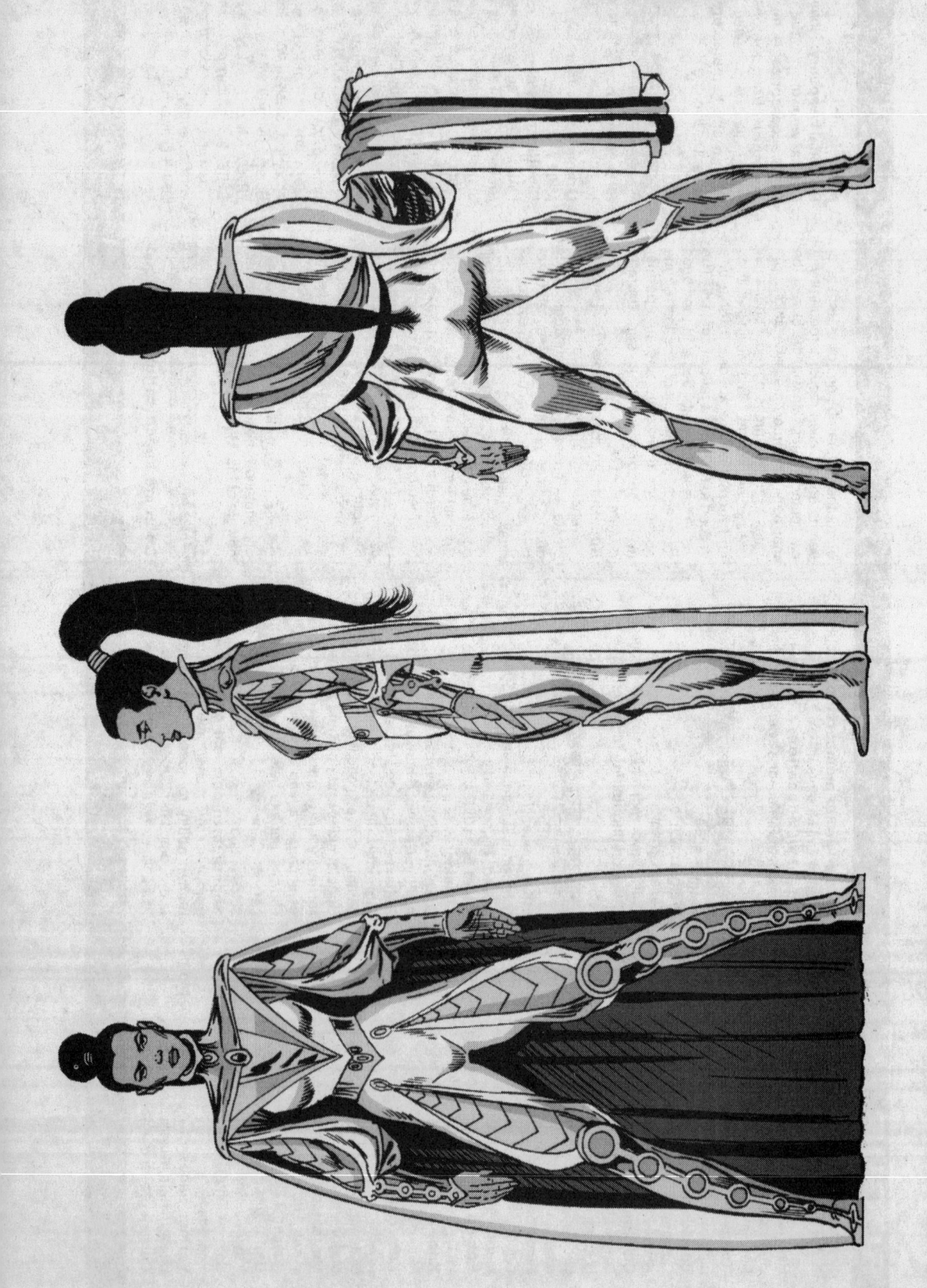

ROMA

BIOGRAPHICAL DATA

Real name: Roma
Other current aliases: The Goddess of the Northern Skies
Former aliases: None known
Dual identity: None; the general populace of earth is unaware of Roma's existence.
Current occupation: Guardian of the multiverse
Former occupation: None known
Citizenship: Otherworld
Legal status: No criminal record
Place of birth: Otherworld
Marital status: Single
Known relatives: Merlyn (father)
Known allies: Captain Britain, Meggan, Saturnyne, Excalibur
Known allies: Captain Britain, Opal Luna Saturnyne, Excalibur, X-Men, Captain UK
Major enemies: Adversary
Usual base of operations: The Starlight Citadel, Otherworld
Former bases of operations: None known
Current group membership: Superior to Captain Britain and his otherdimensional counterparts
Former group membership: None known
Extent of education: Extensively educated in sorcery

PHYSICAL DESCRIPTION

Height: 6'3"
Weight: 175 lbs.
Eyes: Variable (have appeared as green or brown)
Hair: Variable (have appeared as black or brown)
Other distinguishing features: Pointed ears

POWERS AND ABILITIES

Intelligence: Above normal
Strength: Normal
Speed: Normal
Stamina: Normal
Durability: Normal
Agility: Normal
Reflexes: Normal
Fighting skills: Minimal hand-to-hand combatant, relies on sorcery in battle
Special skills and abilities: Extensive knowledge of sorcery rivaling that of her father Merlyn
Superhuman physical powers: Roma has extraordinary prowess in manipulating magical energies for a wide variety of effects. She is virtually immortal.
Superhuman mental powers: Telepathy
Special limitations: None known
Source of superhuman powers: Member of the extradimensional race of Otherworld, highly trained in the mystical arts

PARAPHERNALIA

Costume specifications: Unknown fabrics of Otherworld
Personal weaponry: None known
Special weaponry: None known
Other accessories: None known
Transportation: Various mystical means
Design and manufacture of paraphernalia: Otherworld craftsmen

BIBLIOGRAPHY

First appearance: (UK) CAPTAIN BRITAIN Vol. 1 #1, (US) MARVEL TEAM-UP #65
Origin issue: Roma's origin is as yet unrevealed.
Significant issues: CAPTAIN BRITAIN Vol. 1 #1 (with Merlyn, granted Captain Britain his powers); CAPTAIN BRITAIN Vol. 2 #4-6 (as the successor to the seemingly deceased Merlyn, observed Captain Britain from Otherplace); CAPTAIN BRITAIN Vol. 2 #14 (brought Captain UK to an alternate Earth and reunited her with her husband); UNCANNY X-MEN #225 (held prisoner by the Adversary in her Starlight Citadel, made contact with X-Men's Colossus); UNCANNY X-MEN #227 (rescued by X-Men and Forge, restored dead X-Men to life); UNCANNY X-MEN #229 (cast a spell making the X-Men undetectable by mechanical or technological means, gave X-Men guardianship of the mystical "Siege Perilous"); EXCALIBUR #25 (warned Galactus not to slay Phoenix II); EXCALIBUR #49 (discovered that Merlyn was still alive); EXCALIBUR #50 (persuaded Excalibur to destroy Merlyn's tower in multiversal energy matrix, prevented Merlyn from killing Excalibur)
Note: All CAPTAIN BRITAIN Vol. 2 stories listed above were reprinted in the U.S. in the CAPTAIN BRITAIN trade paperback.

RONAN™

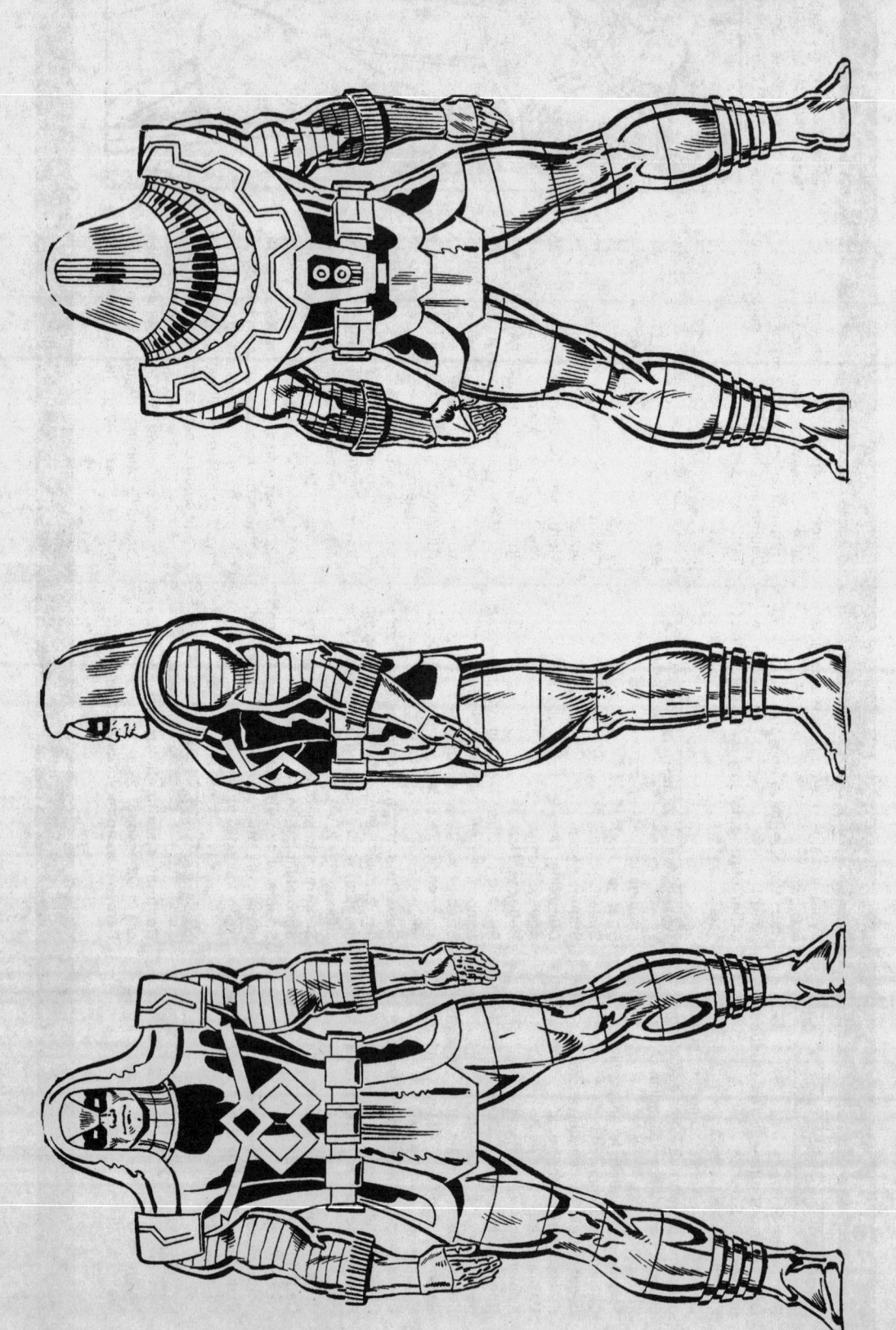

RONAN THE ACCUSER

BIOGRAPHICAL DATA

Real name: Ronan
Other current aliases: None
Former aliases: None
Dual identity: None, the general populace of Earth is unaware that Ronan is an extraterrestrial
Current occupation: Supreme public accuser of the Kree Empire
Former occupation: Unrevealed
Citizenship: Kree Empire
Legal status: No criminal record at present; charges of treason against the Kree Empire dropped
Place of birth: The planet Hala, Pama system, the planet Kree-Lar, Turanal system, Kree Empire, Greater Magellanic Cloud
Marital status: Unrevealed
Known relatives: None
Known confidants: None
Known allies: Zarek, the Supreme Intelligence, Nenora
Major enemies: The Fantastic Four, Captain Mar-Vell (deceased)
Usual base of operations: Citadel of Judgment, the planet Kree-Lar, Turanal system, Kree Empire, Greater Magellanic Cloud
Former bases of operations: Unrevealed
Current group membership: Leader of the Kree Accusers, member of the Supreme Council of the central government of the Kree Empire
Former group membership: Partner of Imperial Minister Zarek in the conspiracy against the Kree Supreme Intelligence
Extent of education: Unrevealed

PHYSICAL DESCRIPTION

Height: 7'5"
Weight: 480 lbs.
Eyes: Blue
Hair: Unrevealed
Other distinguishing features: Like all genetically pure members of the Kree race, Ronan's skin is blue.

POWERS AND ABILITIES

Intelligence: Above normal
Strength: (without augmentation from armor) Enhanced human, (augmented by armor) Superhuman Class 75
Speed: Enhanced human
Stamina: Enhanced human
Durability: Enhanced human
Agility: Enhanced human
Reflexes: Enhanced human
Fighting skills: Kree military combat training
Special skills and abilities: Extensive knowledge of the legal code of the Kree Empire
Superhuman physical powers: None; Ronan's physical attributes are normal for a member of the Kree race
Superhuman mental powers: None
Special limitations: Like all members of his race, Ronan cannot breathe the atmosphere of worlds such as Earth, and must rely on a chemical "breathing formula" or artificial life support systems built into his armor.
Source of superhuman powers: None

PARAPHERNALIA

Costume specifications: Full body exo-skeleton, alien materials
Personal weaponry: Devices in his armor which enhance physical strength and create fields of invisibility; devices within gauntlets which generate sufficient coldness to place certain life forms into a state of suspended animation
Special weaponry: The Universal Weapon, a device which uses cosmic energy for a variety of effects according to the wielder's will, including the disintegration, rearrangement, and transmutation of matter, the projection of concussive energy, control over gravity, the creation of force fields and "time-motion displacement fields" and interstellar teleportation along hyperspatial passages. The upper limits of these capacities are as yet unknown.
Other accessories: None
Transportation: Various, including Kree starships, and interstellar teleportation through the use of the Universal Weapon
Design and manufacture of paraphernalia: Unidentified technicians of the Kree Empire

BIBLIOGRAPHY

First appearance: FANTASTIC FOUR #65
Origin issue: The exact details of Ronan's origin are as yet unrevealed.
Significant issues: FANTASTIC FOUR #65 (first sent to Earth by Supreme Intelligence to punish Fantastic Four; first battled Fantastic Four); CAPTAIN MARVEL #16 (partnered with Zarek to overthrow the Supreme Intelligence; first battled Captain Mar-Vell); AVENGERS #89 (imprisoned Supreme Intelligence; seized control of the Kree Empire) AVENGERS #97 (paralyzed by psionic powers of Rick Jones; control of Kree Empire reverts to Supreme Intelligence); CAPTAIN MARVEL #41 (mentally dominated by Supreme Intelligence; battled Captain Mar-Vell); CAPTAIN MARVEL #49 (lost sanity); MS. MARVEL #19 (sanity restored by Supreme Intelligence; battled Ms. Marvel and Captain Mar-Vell; returned to former position as Supreme Accuser); SILVER SURFER Vol. 2 #13 (ordered by Kree empress Nenora to execute Silver Surfer); SILVER SURFER Vol. 2 #14 (executed Skrull duplicate of the Silver Surfer)

RUNNER

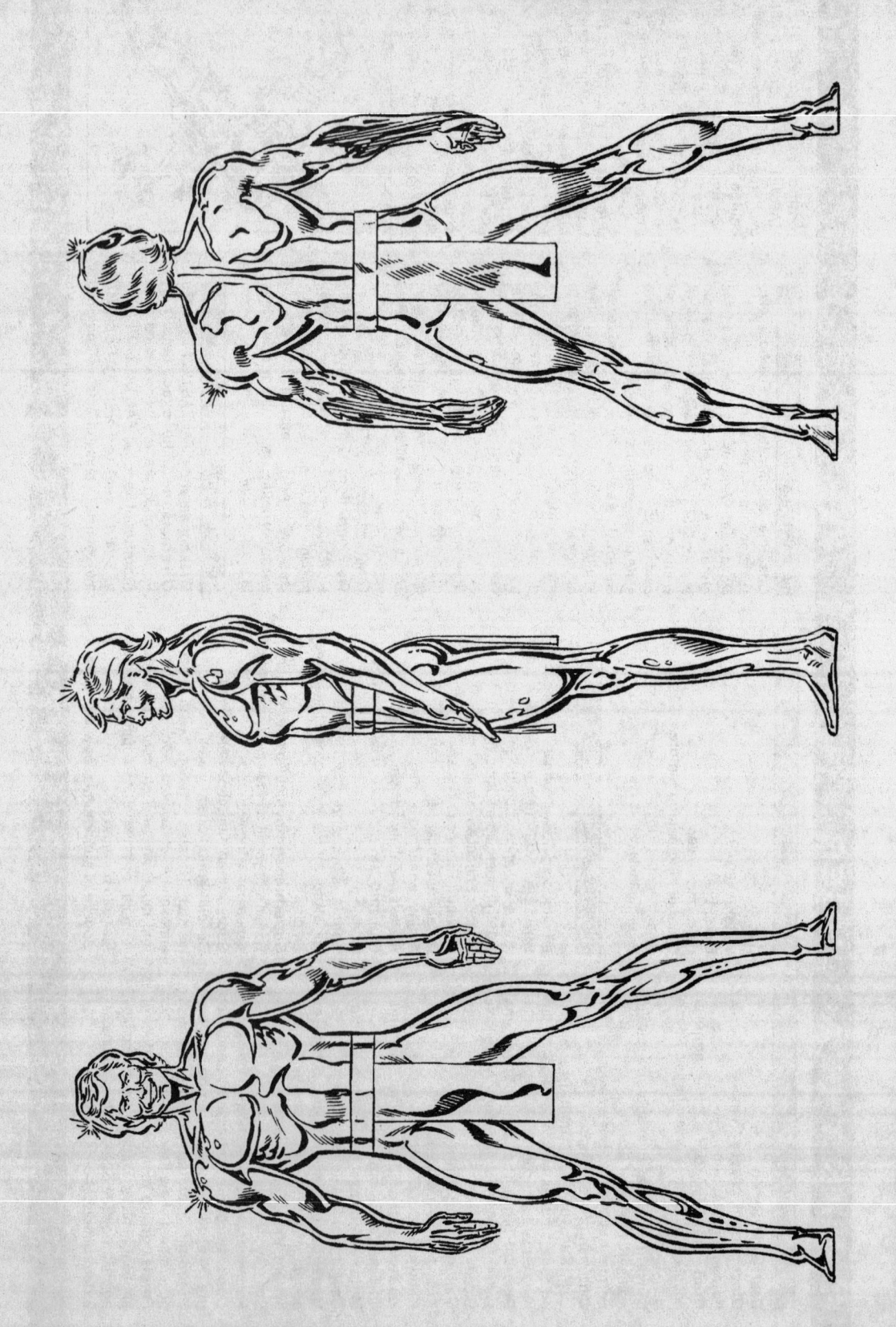

RUNNER

BIOGRAPHICAL DATA

Real name: Unrevealed
Other current aliases: None
Former aliases: None
Dual identity: None
Current occupation: Traveler, explorer
Former occupation: Unrevealed
Citizenship: None
Legal status: None
Place of birth: Unrevealed
Marital status: Unrevealed, presumed single
Known relatives: None
Known confidants: None
Known allies: Elders of the Universe, In-Betweener
Major enemies: Galactus, the Silver Surfer, Death
Usual base of operations: Mobile throughout the universe
Former bases of operations: Unrevealed
Current group membership: Elders of the Universe
Former group membership: Unrevealed
Extent of education: Unrevealed

PHYSICAL DESCRIPTION

Height: 7'
Weight: 325 lbs.
Eyes: Gold
Hair: Gold
Other distinguishing features: Metallic gold skin

POWERS AND ABILITIES

Intelligence: Above normal
Strength: Superhuman Class 10
Speed: Orbital velocity
Flight speed: Warp speed
Stamina: Immeasurable
Durability: Totally indestructible
Agility: Superhuman
Reflexes: Metahuman
Fighting skills: None
Special skills and abilities: Unrevealed
Superhuman physical powers: The Runner possesses a cosmic-enhanced life force which grants him a variety of superhuman traits, including augmentation of his physical attributes and senses, a virtually immortal body, immunity to aging and disease, and imperviousness to conventional injury. Also, the Runner can utilize his cosmic life force for a variety of effects, including the projection of energy blasts, transformation and rearrangement of matter on a planetary scale. Currently due to his machinations against Death, he cannot die.
Superhuman mental powers: The ability to stimulate the pleasure centers of beings around him, causing them to "feel good" in his presence (this attribute may not be under his conscious control)
Special limitations: None
Source of superhuman powers: Manipulation of cosmic energy; how the Runner acquired this ability is unrevealed

PARAPHERNALIA

Costume specifications: Alien materials
Personal weaponry: None
Special weaponry: None
Other accessories: None
Transportation: Running, travel through hyper-space under his own power
Design and manufacture of paraphernalia: Inapplicable

BIBLIOGRAPHY

First appearance: DEFENDERS #143
Origin issue: The Runner's origin is as yet unrevealed.
Significant issues: GIANT-SIZE DEFENDERS #143 (encountered Moondragon when she first left Titan years ago); SILVER SURFER Vol. 3 #3-4 (defeated Silver Surfer in combat; participated in ten other Elders' plot to kill Galactus); SILVER SURFER Vol. 3 #9 (battled Galactus and Silver Surfer); SILVER SURFER Vol. 3 #10 (converted to energy for consumption by Galactus); SILVER SURFER Vol. 3 #17 (along with other Elders devoured by Galactus, caused Galactus "cosmic indigestion" from within; escaped from Galactus); SILVER SURFER Vol. 3 #19 (teleported to parts unknown by Galactus); QUASAR #19 (sponsored race between Earth-dwelling possessors of superhuman speed including Makkari, Quicksilver, Whizzer, Speed Demon, Captain Marvel, Super-Sabre, and Black Racer, declared extradimensional "Buried Alien" winner, took him to "galactic marathon"); THANOS QUEST #2 (battled Thanos, defeated and reverted to infancy, forfeited his Infinity Gem and was subsequently used as a pawn in Thanos's conflict with the Collector, restored to adulthood and fought the Collector)

SABRA™

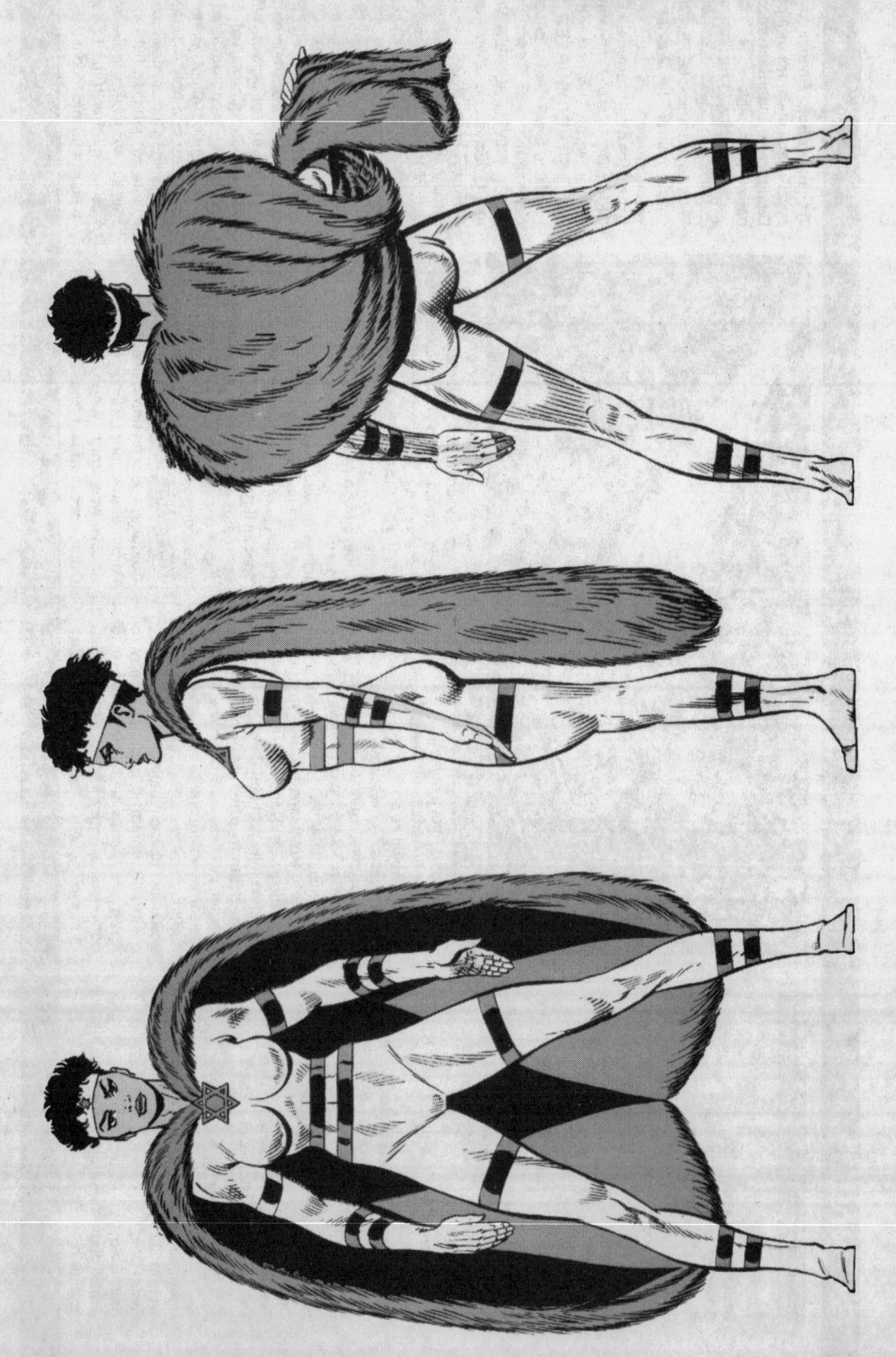

SABRA

BIOGRAPHICAL DATA

Real name: Ruth Bat-Seraph
Other current aliases: "Sabra" is the Israeli word for both a native-born Israeli and a sweet prickly pear.
Former aliases: None known
Dual identity: Secret; known to certain Israeli authorities
Current occupation: Police officer, government agent
Former occupation: None known
Citizenship: Israel
Legal status: No criminal record
Place of birth: Near Jerusalem, Israel
Marital status: Currently single
Known relatives: Son (name unrevealed, deceased)
Known confidants: None
Known allies: Israeli defense and intelligence operatives (the Mossad)
Major enemies: Terrorists
Usual base of operations: Jerusalem, Israel
Former bases of operations: Tel Aviv, Israel; special Israeli government kibbutz, location unrevealed
Current group membership: Israeli "Super-Agent" program
Former group membership: None
Extent of education: Unrevealed, presumably college graduate

PHYSICAL DESCRIPTION

Height: 5' 11"
Weight: 240 lbs.
Eyes: Brown
Hair: Brown
Other distinguishing features: None

POWERS AND ABILITIES

Intelligence: Normal
Strength: Superhuman Class 50
Speed: Enhanced human
Flight speed: Subsonic (via cape)
Stamina: Superhuman
Durability: Superhuman regenerative
Agility: Enhanced human
Reflexes: Enhanced human
Fighting skills: Excellent hand-to-hand combatant, trained in armed and unarmed combat by the Mossad
Special skills and abilities: Trained in police methods and skills and in anti-terrorist techniques
Superhuman physical powers: Aside from the above listed attributes, None
Superhuman mental powers: None
Special limitations: None known
Source of superhuman powers: Unrevealed possibly genetic mutation

PARAPHERNALIA

Costume specifications: Synthetic stretch fabric
Personal weaponry: Neuronic-frequency stunners built into her two wrist bracelets that shoot "energy-quills," small bundles of low-density plasma (like ball lightning), that travel just below the speed of sound, that paralyze the nervous system of any organic being almost instantaneously. The average human being will remain unconscious for about 1 to 2 hours.
Special weaponry: None known
Other accessories: A cape that contains a secret Israeli gravity-polarization device, which allows her to neutralize gravity's effect on her mass, and a tight array of four electric micro-turbines which impel air for sufficient thrust for inertialess mass to fly at speeds of up to 320 miles per hour. She wears special pressure reduction valve nose-filters to allow her to breathe at high speeds and high altitudes. The cape also contains a wafer-thin computer system which processes her mental commands received by the circuitry in her tiara. The cape also has an optical navigation device which functions as an auto-pilot.
Transportation: Flight via cape
Design and manufacture of paraphernalia: Unrevealed

BIBLIOGRAPHY

First appearance: (cameo) INCREDIBLE HULK #250, INCREDIBLE HULK #256
Origin issue: Sabra's origin is as yet unrevealed.
Significant issues: INCREDIBLE HULK #256 (first fought Hulk); MARVEL SUPER HERO CONTEST OF THE CHAMPIONS #1-4 (chosen as pawn of Death in latter's game against Grandmaster, met Iron Man and Arabian Knight, battled She-Hulk and Captain Britain); INCREDIBLE HULK #279 (appeared at Hulk amnesty ceremony in Washington D.C.); INCREDIBLE HULK #386-387 (fought Hulk, encountered Achilles of the Pantheon)

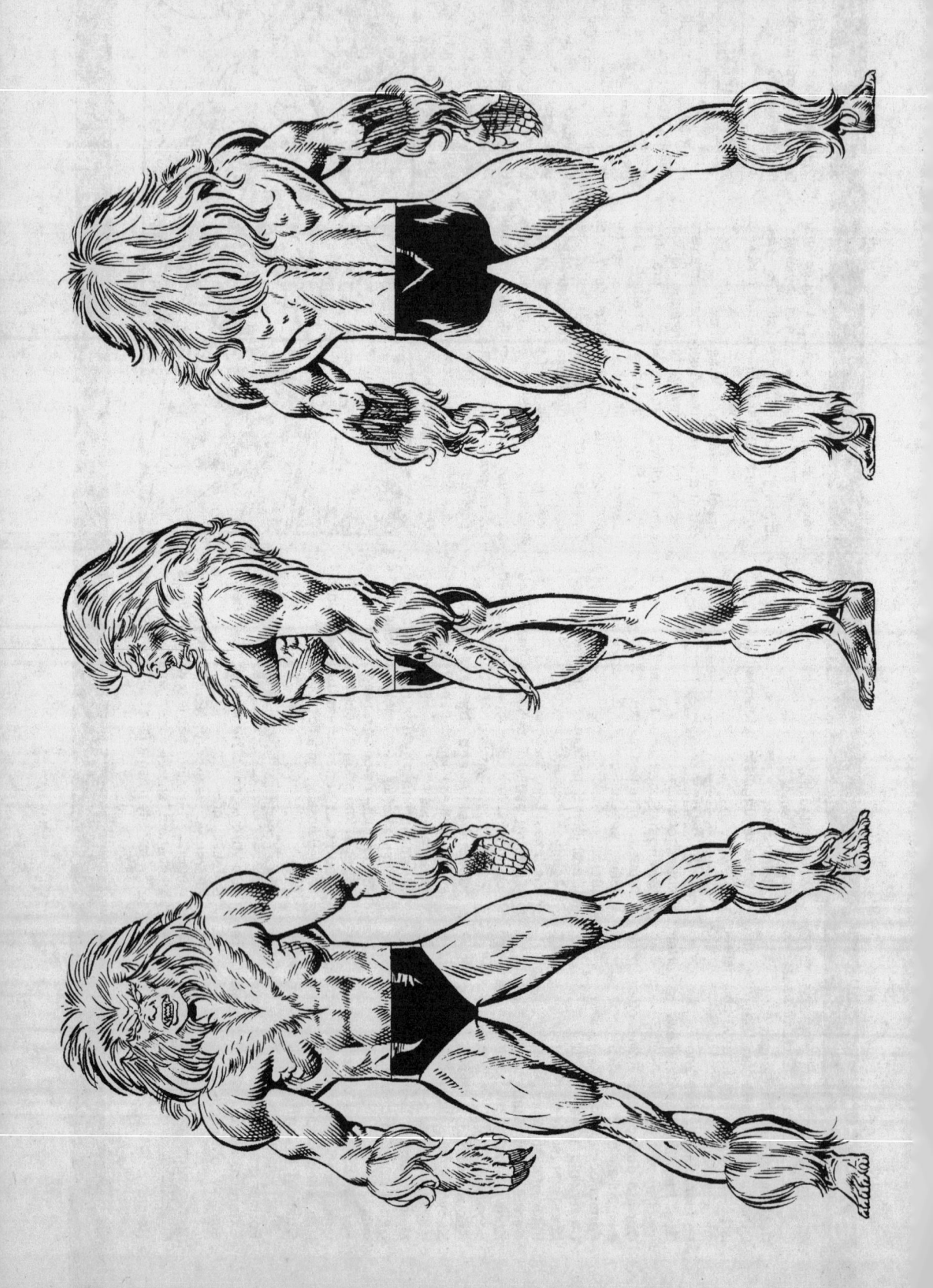

SABRETOOTH

SABRETOOTH

BIOGRAPHICAL DATA

Real name: Unrevealed
Other current aliases: None known
Former aliases: Slasher, (possibly) El Tigre
Dual identity: Secret
Current occupation: Mercenary assassin
Former occupation: (possibly) Government agent
Citizenship: Unrevealed
Legal status: International criminal record
Place of birth: Unrevealed
Marital status: Unrevealed, presumed single
Known relatives: None
Known confidants: Constrictor, Foreigner
Known allies: Foreigner, Constrictor, Mister Sinister, Marauders, (possibly, formerly) Wolverine, Mastodon
Major enemies: Wolverine, X-Men, Iron Fist, Power Man II, Misty Knight, Colleen Wing, Spider-Man, Black Cat, Werewolf, Cable, Caliban, Archangel, Psylocke
Usual base of operations: Mobile
Former bases of operations: Unrevealed
Current group membership: None
Former group membership: Marauders
Extent of education: Unrevealed

PHYSICAL DESCRIPTION

Height: 6'6"
Weight: 275 lbs.
Eyes: Amber
Hair: Blond
Other distinguishing features: Large, pointed, animal-like canine teeth and clawed hands and feet

POWERS AND ABILITIES

Intelligence: Normal
Strength: Enhanced human
Speed: Athlete
Stamina: Metahuman
Durability: Superhuman regenerative (possibly greater)
Agility: Enhanced human
Reflexes: Enhanced human
Fighting skills: Excellent hand-to-hand combatant, trained by the Foreigner and others
Special skills and abilities: Extra-ordinary hunter and tracker
Superhuman physical powers: "Fast healing" ability enabling him to regenerate damaged or destroyed areas of his cellular structure. This grants him virtual immunity to poisons and most drugs, and limited immunity to the fatigue poisons generated by his own body. He ages at an unusually slow rate. Sabretooth possesses superhumanly acute senses of sight, smell, taste, and hearing. He also has claws on each hand and foot strong enough to rend substances as durable as bone.
Superhuman mental powers: None
Special limitations: None
Source of superhuman powers: Unrevealed, presumed genetic mutation

PARAPHERNALIA

Costume specifications: Ordinary fabric
Personal weaponry: None
Special weaponry: None
Other accessories: None
Transportation: Conventional
Design and manufacture of paraphernalia: Inapplicable

BIBLIOGRAPHY

First appearance: IRON FIST #14
Origin issue: Sabretooth's origin is as yet unrevealed.
Significant issues: IRON FIST #14 (first clashed with Iron Fist); POWER MAN AND IRON FIST #66 (first appearance as Constrictor's partner, fought Iron Fist, Misty Knight, and Colleen Wing); POWER MAN AND IRON FIST #78 (still Constrictor's partner, committed series of murders as "Slasher," attacked Misty Knight); POWER MAN AND IRON FIST #84 (still Constrictor's partner, attacked Harmony Young, defeated by Power Man II); SPECTACULAR SPIDER-MAN #116, 119 (reunited with Foreigner, attempted to attack Black Cat, defeated by Spider-Man; defeated by Black Cat in combat); X-FACTOR #10/THOR #374/UNCANNY X-MEN #212-213 (as member of Marauders, participated in "mutant massacre" of Morlocks; battled Wolverine); DAREDEVIL #238 (fought Daredevil); CLASSIC X-MEN #10 (recounted first battle with Wolverine after latter joined the X-Men); UNCANNY X-MEN #219, 221-222 (with Marauders, joined in attack on Polaris; battled Wolverine during Marauders attempt to capture Madelyne Pryor); UNCANNY X-MEN #240, 243 (with Marauders, fought X-Men; attacked and defeated by Psylocke); WOLVERINE #10 (hunted Wolverine in Madripoor; recounted alleged first battle with Wolverine after murdering Wolverine's lover, Silver Fox, which may be false); X-FACTOR #51-53 (hunted Morlock Mole, battled Archangel); NEW MUTANTS #90-91 (attacked Rictor, battled Caliban, clashed with Cable); WOLVERINE #41, 45-46 (battled Wolverine, claimed to be his father; attacked Wolverine in Times Square, fought Hunter In Darkness, underwent hallucination about the "Project"); MARVEL COMICS PRESENTS #98 (battled Werewolf)

Note: In WOLVERINE #48-49, Wolverine experienced memories in which he and Sabretooth were partners as American secret agents; the validity of these memories is as yet unrevealed.

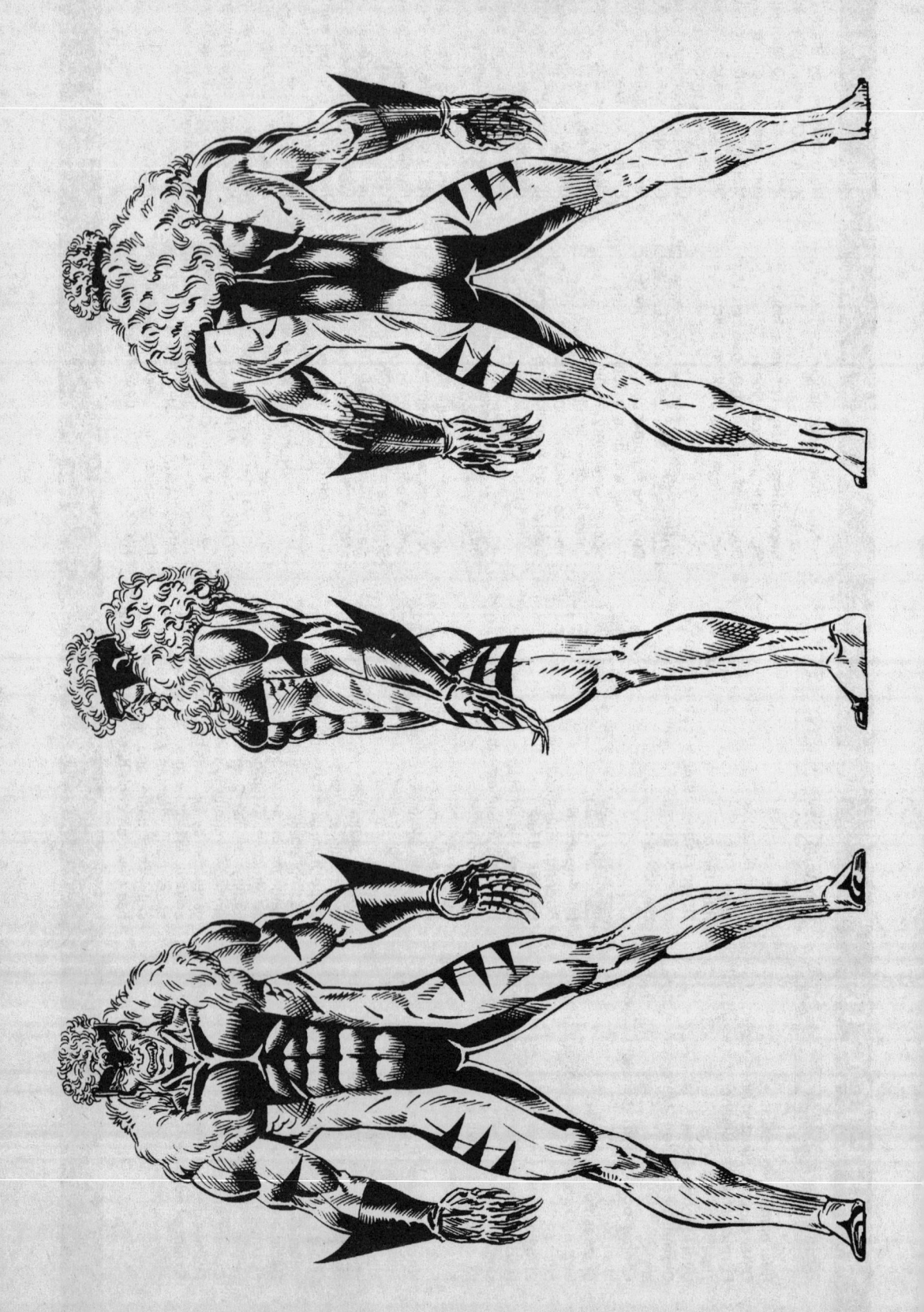

SABRETOOTH™

SABRETOOTH

BIOGRAPHICAL DATA

Real name: (possibly) Creed (rest of name unrevealed)
Other current aliases: None known
Former aliases: Slasher, El Tigre
Dual identity: Secret
Current occupation: Mercenary assassin
Former occupation: CIA agent
Citizenship: Unrevealed
Legal status: International criminal record
Place of birth: Unrevealed
Marital status: Unrevealed, presumed single
Known relatives: None
Known confidants: Constrictor, Foreigner
Known allies: Foreigner, Constrictor, Mister Sinister, Marauders, (former) Wolverine, Maverick, John Wraith, Mastodon, Silver Fox
Major enemies: Wolverine, X-Men, Iron Fist, Power Man II, Misty Knight, Colleen Wing, Spider-Man, Black Cat, Werewolf, Cable, Caliban, Archangel, Psylocke, Omega Red, Maverick, Shiva program, Psi-Borg II (Aldo Ferro, Il Topo Siciliano)
Usual base of operations: Mobile
Former bases of operations: Unrevealed
Current group membership: None
Former group membership: Weapon X Project team, Marauders
Extent of education: Unrevealed

PHYSICAL DESCRIPTION

Height: 6' 6"
Weight: 275 lbs.
Eyes: Amber
Hair: Blond
Other distinguishing features: Large, pointed, animal-like canine teeth and clawed hands and feet

POWERS AND ABILITIES

Intelligence: Normal
Strength: Enhanced human
Speed: Athlete
Stamina: Metahuman
Durability: Superhuman regenerative (possibly greater)
Agility: Enhanced human
Reflexes: Enhanced human
Fighting skills: Excellent hand-to-hand combatant, trained by the Foreigner, CIA, and others
Special skills and abilities: Extraordinary hunter and tracker
Superhuman physical powers: "Fast healing" ability enabling him to regenerate damaged or destroyed areas of his cellular structure. This grants him virtual immunity to poisons and most drugs, and limited immunity to the fatigue poisons generated by his own body. He ages at an unusually slow rate due to his "age suppression factor". Sabretooth possesses superhumanly acute senses of sight, smell, taste, and hearing. He also has claws on each hand and foot strong enough to rend substances as durable as bone.
Superhuman mental powers: None
Special limitations: None
Source of superhuman powers: Unrevealed, presumed genetic mutation

PARAPHERNALIA

Costume specifications: Ordinary fabric
Personal weaponry: None
Special weaponry: None
Other accessories: None
Transportation: Conventional
Design and manufacture of paraphernalia: Inapplicable

BIBLIOGRAPHY

First appearance: IRON FIST #14
Origin issue: Sabretooth's origin is as yet unrevealed.
Significant issues: IRON FIST #14 (first fought Iron Fist); POWER MAN AND IRON FIST #66 (first appearance as Constrictor's partner, fought Iron Fist, Misty Knight, and Colleen Wing); POWER MAN AND IRON FIST #78 (with Constrictor, committed series of murders as "Slasher," attacked Misty Knight); POWER MAN AND IRON FIST #84 (with Constrictor, attacked Harmony Young, defeated by Power Man II); SPECTACULAR SPIDER-MAN #116, 119 (reunited with Foreigner, attempted to attack Black Cat, defeated by Spider-Man; defeated by Black Cat in combat); X-FACTOR #10/THOR #374/UNCANNY X-MEN #212-213 (as member of Marauders, participated in "mutant massacre" of Morlocks; battled Wolverine); CLASSIC X-MEN #10 (recounted first battle with Wolverine after latter joined the X-Men); UNCANNY X-MEN #219, 221-222 (with Marauders, joined in attack on Polaris; battled Wolverine during Marauders attempt to capture Madelyne Pryor); UNCANNY X-MEN #240, 243 (with Marauders, fought X-Men; attacked and defeated by Psylocke); WOLVERINE #10 (hunted Wolverine in Madripoor; recounted alleged first battle with Wolverine after murdering Wolverine's lover, Silver Fox.); X-FACTOR #51-53 (hunted Morlock Mole, battled Archangel); NEW MUTANTS #90-91 (attacked Rictor, battled Caliban, clashed with Cable); WOLVERINE #41, 45-46 (battled Wolverine, claimed to be his father; attacked Wolverine in Times Square, fought Hunter In Darkness, underwent hallucination about the "Project"); WOLVERINE #48-49 (Wolverine experienced memory in which he and Sabretooth were partners as CIA agents); X-MEN Vol. 2 #5-7 (Wolverine experienced memory of Sabretooth killing Janice Hollenbeck during his mission to rescue her, beginning their feud; allied with Fenris and Matsuo Tsurayaba); WOLVERINE #60-61 (fought Shiva robot; flashback to missions in Vietnam and Cuba with Wolverine and John Wraith); WOLVERINE #62-64 (discovered Silver Fox was alive, Wolverine, Maverick, Silver Fox, and John Wraith, fought Psi-Borg II, was apparently consumed by Psi-Borg II)

SANDMAN

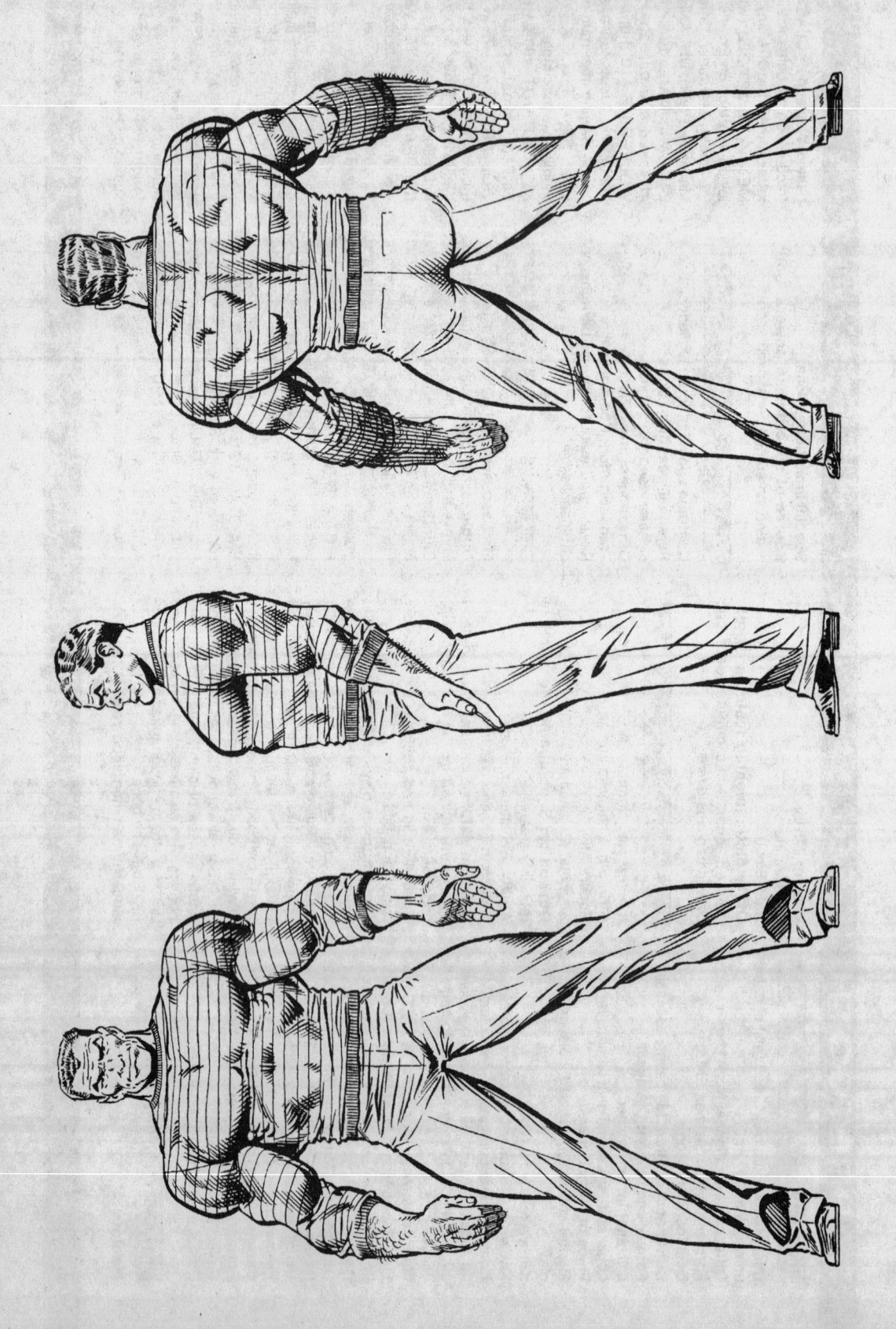

SANDMAN

BIOGRAPHICAL DATA

Real name: William Baker
Other current aliases: None
Former aliases: Flint Marko, Sylvester Mann
Dual identity: Publicly known
Current occupation: Agent of Silver Sable International, reserve member of the Avengers
Former occupation: Professional criminal
Citizenship: United States of America
Legal status: Criminal record in the U.S., pardoned
Place of birth: Queens, New York
Marital status: Divorced
Known relatives: Mrs. Baker (mother)
Known confidants: The Thing
Known allies: The Thing, Spider-Man, Silver Sable, the Outlaws, Le Peregrine, the Avengers, (former) The Sinister Six I, the Enforcers, the Frightful Four, Blastaar, the Mandarin, Baron Brimstone, Hydro-Man
Major enemies: Hydro-Man, the Sinister Syndicate, the Enforcers, Sinister Six II, the Wizard, the Trapster, (former) Spider-Man, the Fantastic Four, the Hulk
Usual base of operations: New York area
Former base of operations: Mobile
Current group membership: The Outlaws, operative for Silver Sable
Former group membership: The Avengers (reserves), the Sinister Six, the Frightful Four, leader of the Enforcers
Extent of education: Unrevealed

PHYSICAL DESCRIPTION

Height: 6' 1"
Weight: (in human form) 240 lbs. (at maximum density and normal mass) 450 lbs.
Eyes: Brown
Hair: Brown
Other distinguishing features: In his sand-form Sandman is composed entirely of a malleable sand-like substance.

POWERS AND ABILITIES

Intelligence: Normal
Strength: Superhuman Class 90
Speed: Normal
Stamina: Enhanced human
Durability: Metahuman regenerative
Agility: Athlete
Reflexes: Peak human
Fighting skills: Basic streetfighting techniques
Special skills and abilities: Unrevealed
Superhuman physical powers: In addition to the superhuman attributes listed above, Sandman has the ability to transform into a malleable sand-like substance which can be hardened, dispersed, or shaped according to his will. He can increase her size and mass to an unknown extent when in sand-form by incorporating sand grains in his vicinity into his body.
Superhuman mental powers: Ability to control his body and parts thereof while his head is not solid and his mind exists only in astral form
Special limitations: Temperatures of 3,400° F. can fuse his sand-like body into glass
Source of superhuman powers: Accidental radiation bombardment

PARAPHERNALIA

Costume specifications: Unstable molecules
Personal weaponry: None
Special weaponry: None
Other accessories: (former) A costume whose belt contained chemicals which could be mixed with sand for various effects
Transportation: Various
Design and manufacture of paraphernalia: (former costume) the Wizard

BIBLIOGRAPHY

First appearance: AMAZING SPIDER-MAN #4
Origin issue: AMAZING SPIDER-MAN #4, MARVEL TWO-IN-ONE #86
Significant issues: AMAZING SPIDER-MAN #4 (gained superhuman powers, battled Spider-Man, defeated); AMAZING SPIDER-MAN ANNUAL #1 (joined the Sinister Six, defeated by Spider-Man); AMAZING SPIDER-MAN #19 (alongside Enforcers, captured Human Torch II, defeated by Spider-Man and Human Torch); FANTASTIC FOUR #36 (with the Wizard, Paste Pot Pete, and Medusa, formed Frightful Four, defeated the Fantastic Four); FANTASTIC FOUR #61-62 (donned new costume, battled Fantastic Four); teamed with Blastaar, defeated by the Fantastic Four); INCREDIBLE HULK Vol. 2 #113-114 (first battled Hulk; with Mandarin, battled Hulk again); WONDER MAN Vol. 1 #1 (contracted cancer, took over medical research center, battled Wonder Man, cured of cancer by radiation); AMAZING SPIDER-MAN #217-218 (teamed with Hydro-Man to battle Spider-Man, merged with Hydro-Man as giant mud-creature); MARVEL TWO-IN-ONE #86 (with Hydro-Man, returned to normal, resolved to go straight, became friends with the Thing); MARVEL TEAM-UP #138 (began boarding with the Cassadas, teamed with Spider-Man against the Enforcers); AMAZING SPIDER-MAN #280-281 (teamed with Spider-Man and Silver Sable against the Sinister Syndicate, hired by Silver Sable as a freelance agent); AMAZING SPIDER-MAN #334, 338-339 (coerced by Dr. Octopus into rejoining Sinister Six; turned against Sinister Six; turned to glass by Doctor Octopus, saved by Spider-Man) AVENGERS #329 (received presidential pardon and joined the Avengers)

SASQUATCH

SASQUATCH

BIOGRAPHICAL DATA

Real name: Walter Langkowski
Other current aliases: None
Former aliases: Box III, Wanda Langkowski
Dual identity: Secret
Current Occupation: Adventurer
Former occupation: Professor of physics, professor of biophysics
Citizenship: Canada
Legal status: No criminal record
Place of birth: Vancouver, British Columbia, Canada
Marital status: Divorced
Known relatives: Veronica Langkowski (ex-wife)
Known confidants: Aurora, James MacDonald Hudson (Vindicator I, deceased), Heather Hudson (Guardian II)
Known allies: Alpha Flight, the X-Men, the Avengers, the Fantastic Four, the Hulk, Namor the Sub-Mariner, Dr. Strange, X-Factor II
Major enemies: The Master of the World, the Great Beasts, the Super-Skrull, Gilded Lily (deceased), Omega Flight, Loki, the Dreamqueen, Llan the Sorceror
Usual base of operations: Alpha Flight headquarters, Department H, Toronto, Ontario, Canada
Former bases of operations: Alpha Flight headquarters, Tamarind Island, British Columbia, Canada; Maison Alpha, Edmonton, Canada; Parliament building, Ottawa, Canada
Current group membership: Alpha Flight
Former group membership: Beta Flight I, Gamma Flight I
Extent of education: Ph.D. in physics

PHYSICAL DESCRIPTION

Height: 6'4", (as Sasquatch) 10'
Weight: 245 lbs., (as Sasquatch) 2000 lbs.
Eyes: Blue, (as Sasquatch) Red
Hair: Blonde, (as Sasquatch) Orange
Other distinguishing features: Body covered in thick orange fur, anthropoid ape-like physique, clawed hands and feet

POWERS AND ABILITIES

Intelligence: Genius
Strength: Athlete, (as Sasquatch) Superhuman Class 90
Speed: Athlete, (as Sasquatch) Enhanced human
Stamina: Athlete, (as Sasquatch) Metahuman
Durability: Athlete, (as Sasquatch) Metahuman
Agility: Athlete
Reflexes: Athlete
Fighting skills: Skilled hand-to-hand combatant
Special skills and abilities: Extensive knowledge of physics, expert on effects of radiation on human physiology, talented football player
Superhuman physical powers: Aside from the above listed attributes, none
Superhuman mental powers: None
Special limitations: As Langkowski, he is near-sighted, and wears glasses
Source of superhuman powers: Formerly, gamma-radiation experiment which unleashed energy freeing Tanaraq, one of the Great Beasts, which transformed and possessed Langkowski; currently, mind transferred to body of the late Snowbird, a shape-changing demi-goddess who had taken on the form of Sasquatch.

PARAPHERNALIA

Costume specifications: Inapplicable
Personal weaponry: None
Special weaponry: None
Other accessories: None
Transportation: Alpha Flight omni-jet
Design and manufacture of paraphernalia: Stark Enterprises

BIBLIOGRAPHY

First appearance: (as Sasquatch) X-MEN #120; (as Box II) ALPHA FLIGHT #24; (as Wanda Langkowski/white Sasquatch) ALPHA FLIGHT #45
Origin issue: ALPHA FLIGHT #11, 23
Significant issues: X-MEN #120-121 (with Alpha Flight, battled the X-Men in attempt to capture Wolverine); INCREDIBLE HULK ANNUAL #8 (battled the Hulk); INCREDIBLE HULK Vol. 2 #272 (alongside the Hulk, battled Wendigo III); ALPHA FLIGHT #1 (alongside Alpha Flight, battled Tundra); ALPHA FLIGHT #4 (with Alpha Flight, Namor, and the Invisible Woman, first encountered the Master of the World); ALPHA FLIGHT #9-10 (battled the Super-Skrull); ALPHA FLIGHT #12 (with Alpha Flight, battled Omega Flight); ROM #56-58 (alongside Rom and Alpha Flight, battled Dire Wraiths); X-MEN AND ALPHA FLIGHT #1-2 (with Alpha Flight, went on mission with X-Men; clashed with Loki); ALPHA FLIGHT #23-24 (Sasquatch form revealed as incarnation of Tanaraq, killed in battle by Snowbird; Langkowski's body destroyed, spirit animated Box robot); ALPHA FLIGHT #28-29 (spirit lost in attempt to take possession of the body of the Hulk); ALPHA FLIGHT #45 (spirit animated Snowbird's body as white Sasquatch and Wanda Langkowski); ALPHA FLIGHT #68 (transformed back to Walter Langkowski by Snowbird's spirit); ALPHA FLIGHT #71-75 (with Alpha Flight, first battled Llan the Sorcerer); AVENGERS #320-324 (with Alpha Flight, alongside the Avengers, and the People's Protectorate, battled Atlantean army, the Peace Corps, and the Combine); ALPHA FLIGHT #97-100 (alongside Alpha Flight, defended Her against the Consortium)

SATANA

SATANA

BIOGRAPHICAL DATA

Real name: Satana Hellstrom
Aliases at time of death: The Devil's Daughter
Former aliases: Judith Camber
Dual identity: None; the general populace of Earth was unaware of Satana's demonic parentage
Occupation at time of death: Succubus
Former occupation: None
Citizenship: United States of America
Legal status: No criminal record
Place of birth: Greentown, Massachusetts
Place of death: New York City
Cause of death: Stabbed by the demon Basilisk using a mystical blade
Marital status: (as Satana) Single, (as Judith Camber) Widowed
Known relatives: (as Satana) "Satan" (Mephisto, father), Victoria Wingate Hellstrom (mother, deceased), Daimon Hellstrom (Hellstorm, brother), Patsy Walker-Hellstrom (Hellcat, sister-in-law), (as Judith Camber) Gene Camber (husband), Paul Camber (son) Ruth Camber (daughter) (all deceased)
Known confidants: None
Known allies: Exiter (her cat familiar, deceased), Ruth Cummins (deceased), Zannarath (deceased), Michael Heron (deceased), Dr. Strange, Clea, Spider-Man
Major enemies: "Satan," the Basilisk II, the Four, Daimon Hellstrom (as Son of Satan), the N'garai, the Camarilla of the N'garai (Brian Abelard, Alejandro Fuerrega, Sharron McKay, Dennis St. Croix, Roberta Lancer, all deceased)
Base of operations at time of death: Mobile
Former bases of operations: "Hell"
Group membership at time of death: None
Former group membership: None
Extent of education: Schooled by "Satan" in the use of her demonic powers

PHYSICAL DESCRIPTION

Height: 5' 7 1/2"
Weight: 120 lbs.
Eyes: Black with red highlights
Hair: Red with white streak
Other distinguishing features: Incredibly long eyebrows which extend above her head in the semblance of a devil's horns

POWERS AND ABILITIES

Intelligence: Above normal
Strength: Superhuman Class 10
Speed: Enhanced human
Flight speed: Hover only
Stamina: Enhanced human
Durability: Enhanced human
Agility: Peak human
Reflexes: Peak human
Fighting skills: Minimal
Special skills and abilities: Extensive knowledge of black magical lore
Superhuman physical powers: Ability to manipulate magical forces for a variety of effects, including interdimensional teleportation, levitation, and projection of concussive bolts of mystical energy in the form of "soulfire"; as a succubus, able to extract and feed upon the psychic energy of human souls; ability to contain the Basilisk, powerful demon, within her spirit and to release it to do her bidding and then return within herself
Superhuman mental powers: Limited ability to control minds psionically
Special limitations: For a time, Satana had to extract and feed upon the psychic energy of human souls periodically in order to survive.
Source of superhuman powers: Some inherited from her father, some granted her by him, some due to her transformation into a succubus, some from manipulation of the forces of magic

PARAPHERNALIA

Costume specifications: Alien fabric
Personal weaponry: None
Special weaponry: None
Other accessories: None
Transportation: Levitation, interdimensional teleportation
Design and manufacture of paraphernalia: Inapplicable

BIBLIOGRAPHY

First appearance: VAMPIRE TALES #2
Origin issue: MARVEL SPOTLIGHT Vol. 1 #13
Significant issues: MARVEL SPOTLIGHT Vol. 1 #13 (birth and childhood recounted); VAMPIRE TALES #2-3 (returned to Earth as a succubus, stalked victims in New York; in Los Angeles, befriended Satanist Ruth Cummins; avenged Ruth's death by destroying Darkos Edge and Harry Gotham); HAUNT OF HORROR #2, 4 (battled the Four, a mystic cabal); HAUNT OF HORROR #5 (confronted her father who was disguised as Miles Gorney, defied him by saving Michael Heron's soul from him); MARVEL SPOTLIGHT Vol. 1 #24 (seemingly destroyed by Daimon Hellstrom, defeated the demoness Kthara); MARVEL PREVIEW #7 (transformed by the Camarilla of the N'garai into a human, Judith Camber; restored to normal; destroyed the Camarilla); MARVEL TEAM-UP #81 (aided Spider-Man against Doctor Strange, who had been transformed into a werewolf; sacrificed her life to cure Strange of lycanthropy)

SATANNISH

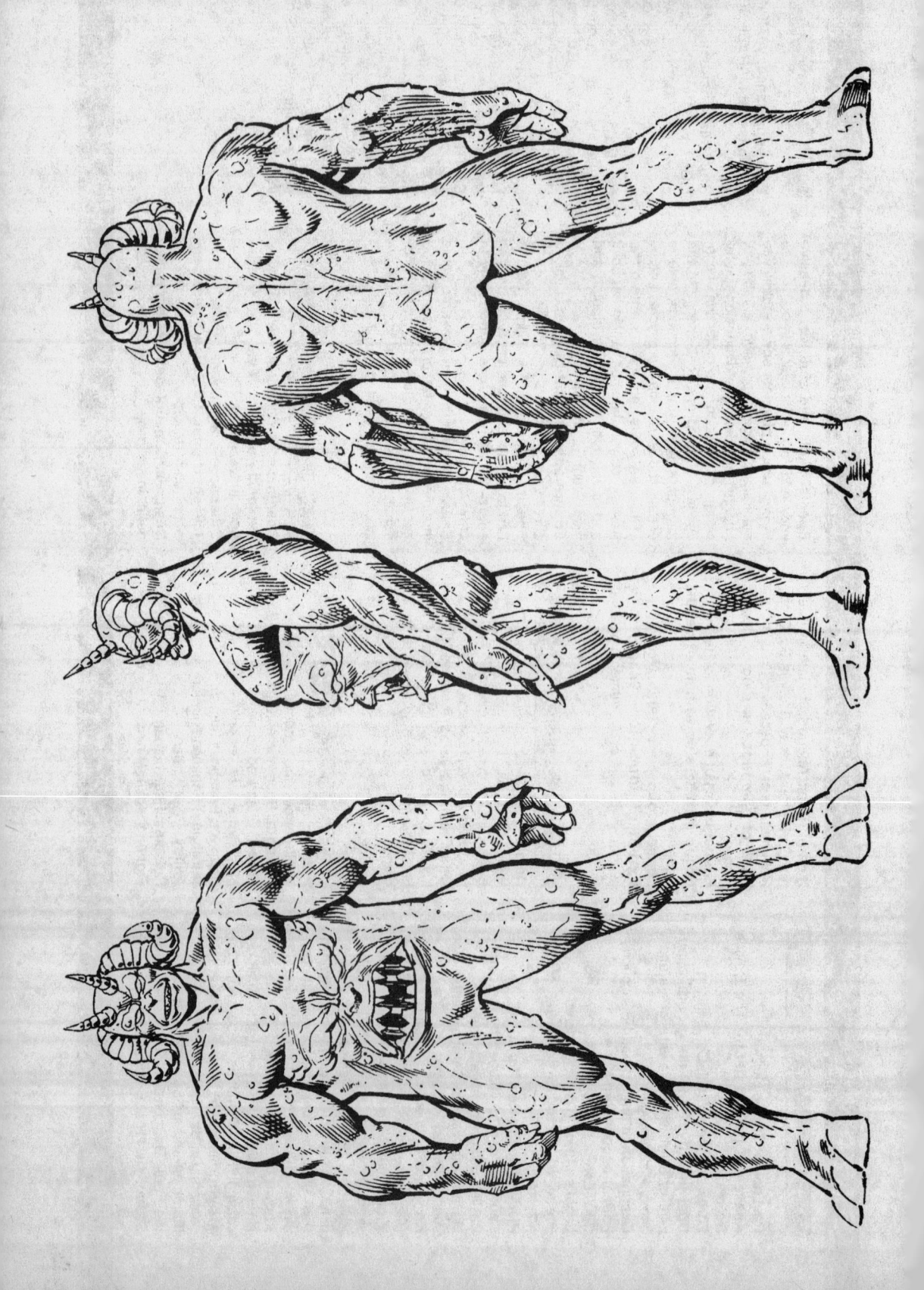

SATANNISH

BIOGRAPHICAL DATA

Real name: Unrevealed
Other current aliases: His names are legion.
Former aliases: Unrevealed
Dual identity: None; Satannish's existence is unknown to the general populace of Earth
Current occupation: Embodiment of evil
Former occupation: None
Citizenship: None
Legal status: Inapplicable
Place of origin: Unrevealed
Marital status: Unrevealed
Known relatives: None
Known confidants: None
Known allies: None
Major enemies: Doctor Strange, Mephisto
Usual base of operations: Unnamed extradimensional realm
Former bases of operations: Unrevealed
Current group membership: None
Former group membership: None
Extent of education: Unknown

PHYSICAL DESCRIPTION

Height: Variable
Weight: Variable
Eyes: Variable
Hair: Variable
Other distinguishing features: Satannish is a demonic being of vast supernatural power who adopts a variety of physical forms as needed. The guise he most often employs around human sorcerers is that of a green-skinned, horned being with a second face in his stomach.

POWERS AND ABILITIES

Intelligence: Immeasurable
Strength: Incalculable
Speed: Unrevealed
Stamina: Immeasurable
Durability: Totally indestructible
Agility: Unrevealed
Reflexes: Unrevealed
Fighting skills: None
Special skills and abilities: Unrevealed
Superhuman physical powers: Satannish is more akin to a supernatural force of nature than a being; as such he possesses virtually unlimited mystic power which can be used for a variety of effects, including (but not limited to) interdimensional teleportation, manipulation of time, space, and matter, size transformations, casting bolts of mystic energy as destructive force, demonic possession, and physical strength and durability
Superhuman mental powers: Unrevealed
Special limitations: Satannish's ability to manifest in the dimension of Earth is, in some unknown way limited by mystic factors, and he frequently makes use of pawns native to Earth for his purposes
Source of superhuman powers: Satannish is a being of pure mystical energy

PARAPHERNALIA

Costume specifications: None
Personal weaponry: None
Special weaponry: None
Other accessories: None
Transportation: Interdimensional teleportation
Design and manufacture of paraphernalia: Inapplicable

BIBLIOGRAPHY

First appearance: DOCTOR STRANGE Vol. 1 #174
Origin issue: DOCTOR STRANGE Vol. 3 #8
Significant issues: DOCTOR STRANGE Vol. 1 #174 (struck a pact with human sorcerer Lord Nekron; first encountered Doctor Strange); DEFENDERS ANNUAL #2 (made bargain with human sorceror Asmodeus; encountered Defenders); DOCTOR STRANGE Vol. 3 #5-8 (bargained with Baron Mordo during "Faust Gambit" incident; battled Mephisto in New York City, merged with Mephisto as a result of Doctor Strange's spell); DOCTOR STRANGE Vol. 3 #30 (revealed to have hidden in the shadow of Mephista, daughter of Mephisto, in order to be taken into Mephisto's domain, battled Mephisto, Mephista, and Doctor Strange, vanquished when Strange mystically connected Mephisto's and his life essences)

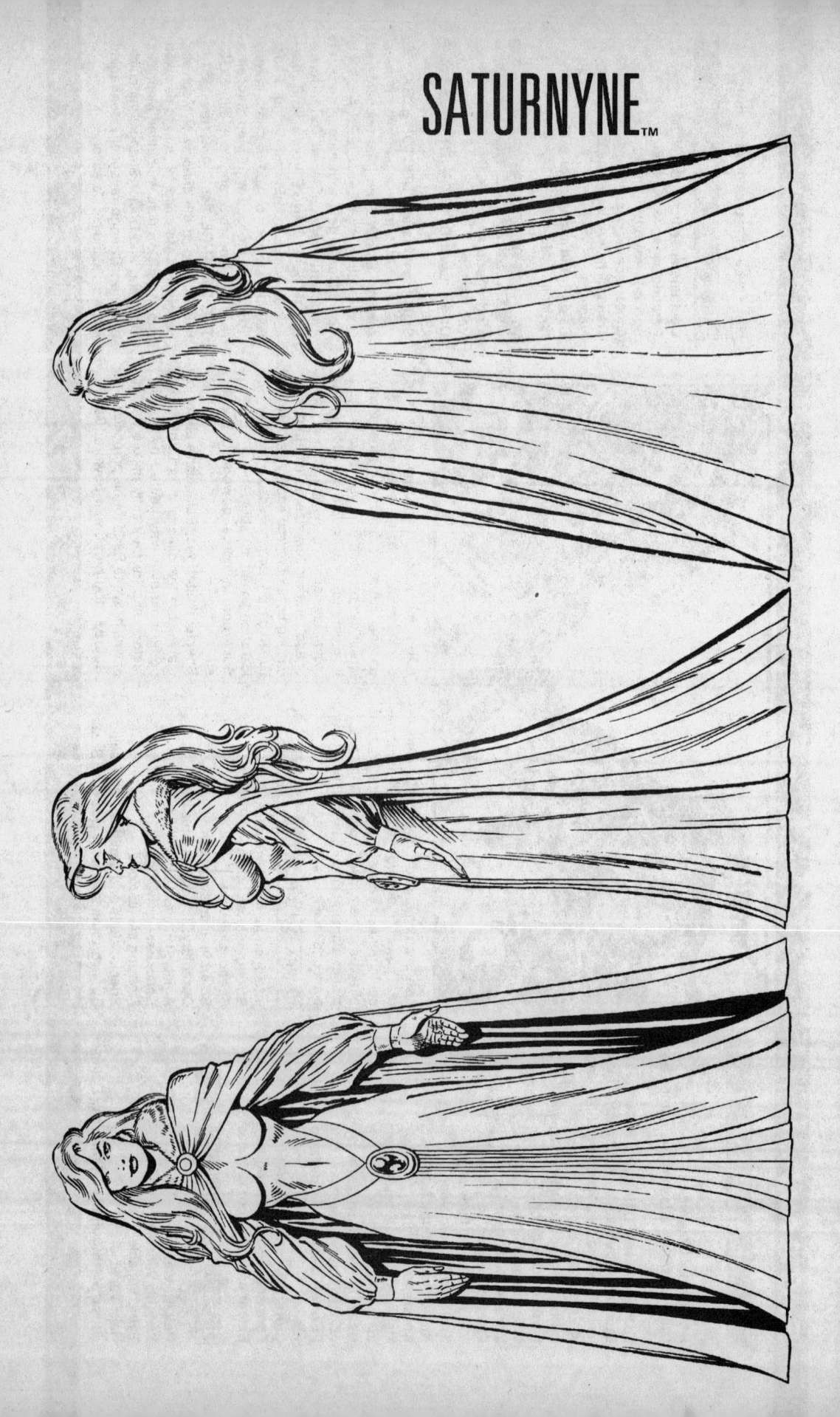

SATURNYNE

SATURNYNE

BIOGRAPHICAL DATA

Real name: Opal Luna Saturnyne
Other current aliases: Her Royal Whyness
Former aliases: None
Dual identity: None; the general populace of Earth is unaware of Saturnyne's existence
Current occupation: Omniversal Majestrix (responsible for the maintenance of order and reality in this sector of creation), agent of Roma
Former occupation: None known
Citizenship: Unrevealed
Legal status: Unrevealed on Earth
Place of birth: Unrevealed, said to be from "Earth 9"
Marital status: Unrevealed, presumed single
Known relatives: None
Known confidants: None
Known allies: Roma, Captain Britain, Technet, Horatio Cringebottom, Avant Gards, Captain UK, Dimensional Development Court, (former) Special Executive, Jackdaw I, Dimples
Major enemies: Mandragon, Status Crew, Sir James "Mad Jim" Jaspers, the Fury
Usual base of operations: Mobile throughout many dimensions
Former bases of operations: Braddock Manor, England; Earth 9
Current group membership: None
Former group membership: None

Extent of education: Unrevealed

PHYSICAL DESCRIPTION

Height: 5' 9"
Weight: 140 lbs.
Eyes: Blue
Hair: Blond
Other distinguishing features: None

POWERS AND ABILITIES

Intelligence: Above normal
Strength: Athlete
Speed: Athlete
Stamina: Athlete
Durability: Athlete
Agility: Athlete
Reflexes: Athlete
Fighting skills: Good hand-to-hand combatant
Special skills and abilities: Cunning strategist
Superhuman physical powers: None
Superhuman mental powers: None
Special limitations: None
Source of superhuman powers: None

PARAPHERNALIA

Costume specifications: Unrevealed
Personal weaponry: None
Special weaponry: None
Other accessories: Psychecom crystals (which carry holographic messages)
Transportation: Space and dimension warp technologies
Design and manufacture of paraphernalia: Unrevealed

BIBLIOGRAPHY

First appearance: (Opal Luna Saturnyne, US) CAPTAIN BRITAIN SPECIAL EDITION #1, (Opal Lun Sat-Yr9, UK) CAPTAIN BRITAIN Vol. 2 #2, (US) EXCALIBUR #5, (Queen Mother) EXCALIBUR #13

Origin issue: Saturnyne's origin is as yet unrevealed

Significant issues: CAPTAIN BRITAIN Vol. 2 #1 (first meeting with Captain Britain recounted); CAPTAIN BRITAIN Vol. 2 #2 (Opul Lun Sat-Yr9 sent Technet to retrieve Kaptain Briton); CAPTAIN BRITAIN Vol. 2 #6 (Opul Lun Sat-Yr9 first met Captain Britain); CAPTAIN BRITAIN Vol. 2 #14 (Opul Lun Sat-Yr9 overthrown by Captain UK); EXCALIBUR SPECIAL EDITION #1 (appeared in hologram, stated that she had authorized Technet to capture Phoenix II for being a "threat to reality"); EXCALIBUR #4 (Opul Lun Sat-Yr9 confronted Courtney Ross, one incinerated the other, survivor claimed to be Ross); EXCALIBUR #9, 11 (seeming Ross challenged Nigel Frobisher to high stakes card game at London Hellfire Club, won; Frobisher agreed to serve seeming Ross, who ordered him to engage Technet to rescue Jamie Braddock from Doc Croc); EXCALIBUR #13-14 (Queen Mother encountered Captain Britain and Excalibur, revealed to have arranged meeting of her son Prince William and Shadowcat's extradimensional counterpart Princess Katherine; Queen Mother present at betrothal of William and Katherine); EXCALIBUR #21 (seeming Ross took Kitty Pryde under her guidance); EXCALIBUR #24 (Opal Luna Saturnyne met Phoenix II but did not capture her); EXCALIBUR #32, 34 (seeming Ross enrolled Kitty Pryde in St. Searle's School for Young Ladies; seeming Ross arranged deal to save St. Searle's from bankruptcy); EXCALIBUR #42, 44 (Opal Luna Saturnyne appeared in hologram, rescinded warrant for Phoenix II, indefinitely extended Technet's exile on Earth; delivered message from Roma asking the other Captain Britains to free Excalibur's Captain Britain)

Note: Apparently each alternate reality has its own counterpart of Saturnyne. Opal Luna Saturnyne is the Omniversal Majestrix of the universe to which Captain Britain is native. Three other known counterparts of Saturnyne have appeared. One is the Queen Mother of Great Britain of an alternate Earth, and appears to be older than Opal Luna Saturnyne. Another, Opul Lun Sat-Yr9 was the Mastrix of the fascist Empire of True Briton. Still another, Sat'neen, is a rebel sorceress on an alternate Earth.

SAURON™

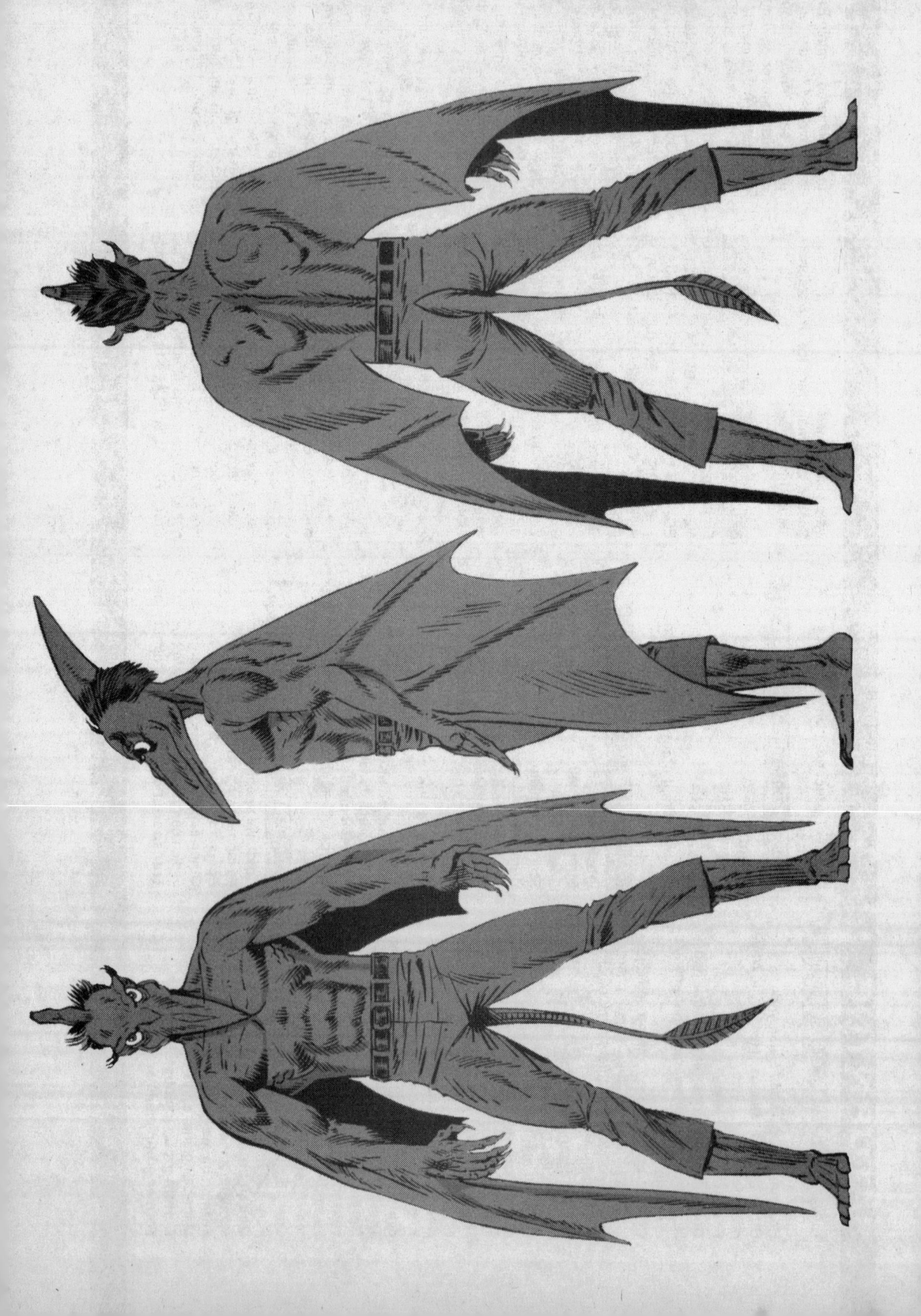

SAURON

BIOGRAPHICAL DATA

Real name: Dr. Karl Lykos
Other current aliases: None
Former aliases: None known
Dual identity: None; the general populace of Earth is unaware that Lykos was Sauron, and did not know Sauron existed.
Current occupation: (as Sauron) Would-be conqueror
Former occupation: (as Lykos) Geneticist, hypnotherapist
Citizenship: United States of America
Legal status: No criminal record
Place of birth: Unrevealed
Marital status: Single
Known relatives: None
Known confidants: Tanya Andersson (possibly deceased)
Known allies: (as Sauron) Zaladane, Savage Land Mutates, Brotherhood of Evil Mutants V (Toad, Blob, Pyro, Phantasia), (as Lykos) Professor Charles Xavier, X-Men, Ka-Zar
Major enemies: (as Sauron) X-Men, X-Force, Ka-Zar, (as Lykos) Savage Land Mutates, Toad, Blob
Usual base of operations: Unrevealed
Former bases of operations: New York City; Savage Land
Current group membership: Brotherhood of Evil Mutants V
Former group membership: Savage Land Mutates
Extent of education: M.D., Ph. D.s in genetics and psychology

PHYSICAL DESCRIPTION

Height: 7'
Weight: 200 lbs
Eyes: Red, (as Lykos) Brown
Hair: None, (as Lykos) Brown
Other distinguishing features: Lykos's Sauron form resembles a large crested pterodactyl extinct except in the Savage Land. Unlike true pterodactyls, Sauron has a toothed beak and a basically humanoid build, with legs as long as a human being's. Sauron has a wingspread of twelve feet, and razor-sharp claws.

POWERS AND ABILITIES

Intelligence: Above normal
Strength: Superhuman Class 10, (as Lykos) Normal
Speed: (as Lykos) Normal
Flight speed: (as Sauron) Natural winged flight
Stamina: (as Sauron) Unrevealed, (as Lykos) Normal
Durability: Superhuman, (as Lykos) Normal
Agility: Superhuman, (as Lykos) Normal
Reflexes: Superhuman, (as Lykos) Normal
Fighting skills: No hand-to-hand combat training, relied on strength and savagery
Special skills and abilities: Accomplished medical doctor, geneticist, and psychotherapist employing hypnotism
Superhuman physical powers: Aside from the above listed attributes, Sauron has the ability, in both his forms, to drain the life force from living victims into his body.
Superhuman mental powers: The ability to hypnotize victims by making eye contact with them and thereby induce hallucinations.
Special limitations: Sauron has to absorb the life energies from living victims to sustain his life; he would revert to human form if he didn't regularly absorb the life force from superhuman beings
Source of superhuman powers: Mutation through infection with genetic virus by mutant pterodactyls; usually transforms into Sauron through absorbing energies from superhuman mutants. (The Toad's technology transformed him into Sauron by draining life energy from Tanya Andersson, who is apparently not superhuman.

PARAPHERNALIA

Costume specifications: Conventional attire
Personal weaponry: None
Special weaponry: None
Other accessories: Sauron has made use of advanced technology created by Brainchild of the Savage Land Mutates
Transportation: Flight under own power
Design and manufacture of paraphernalia: Brainchild

BIBLIOGRAPHY

First appearance: (as Lykos) X-MEN Vol. 1 #59, (as Sauron) X-MEN Vol. 1 #60
Origin issue: X-MEN Vol. 1 #60
Significant issues: X-MEN Vol. 1 #59-61 (first transformed into Sauron, first fought X-Men, returned to human form, attempted suicide in Tierra del Fuego); UNCANNY X-MEN #114-115 (attacked Storm in Savage Land, reverted to Sauron, battled X-Men, returned to human form); MARVEL FANFARE #2-4 (reunited with Tanya in Savage Land, reverted to Sauron, teamed with Zaladane and Savage Land Mutates, captured X-Men, defeated by them, cured by Professor X); X-FORCE #5-11 (transformed back into Sauron by Toad through draining Tanya Andersson's life force, joined Toad's new Brotherhood of Evil Mutants, alongside them battled X-Force, slew Cannonball who later revived, was apparently shot dead by Cable, apparent corpse thrown by Cable to Morlocks); X-FACTOR #82 (revealed to have survived gunshot wound; battled X-Factor)

SAVAGE STEEL

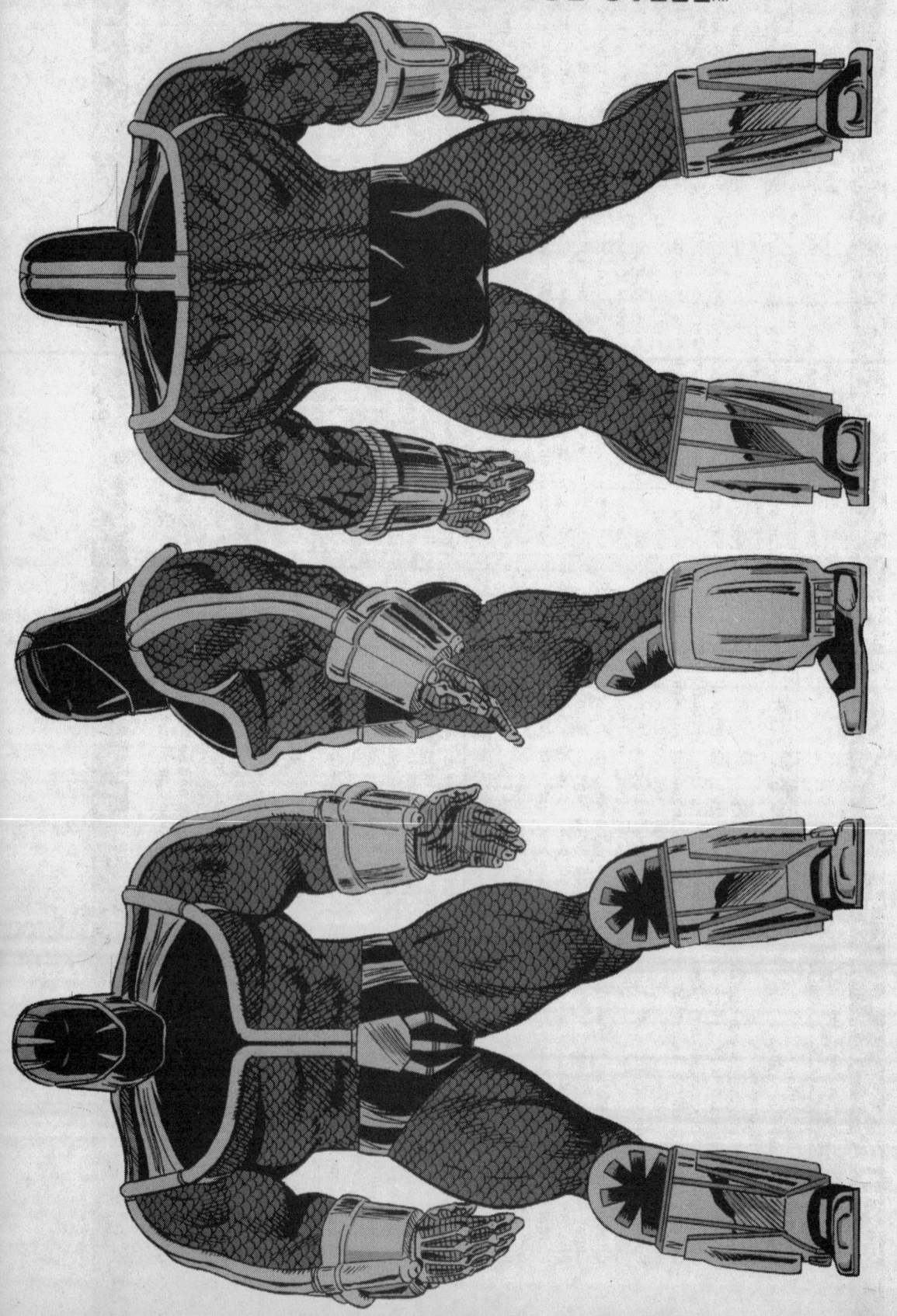

SAVAGE STEEL

BIOGRAPHICAL DATA

Real name: (I) Various members of the Cabal took turns wearing the Savage Steel armor, including Paul Trent and former members Harry Lennox, Johnny Leone, and Jimmy Zafar, (II) Arthur Vale, (III) James "Jimmy" Zafar
Other current aliases: (all) None
Former aliases : (all) None
Dual identity: (I, II) Known to the authorities, (III) Secret
Current occupation: (I) (Lennox, Leone) Unrevealed, (others) convicts, (II) Unrevealed, (III) Vigilante
Former occupations: (I) (Lennox) Private investigator, police officer, (others) police officers, (II) Police van driver, (III) Police officer
Citizenship: (all) United States of America
Legal status: (I) (Lennox, Leone) Criminal records in the United States, (others) Criminal records in the United States, (II, III) Criminal record
Place of birth: (all) Unrevealed, presumably New York City
Marital status: (I) Various, (II, III) Single
Known relatives: (all) None
Known confidants: (I) Mike Powell, (II) None, (III) (former) The Cabal, Mike Powell
Known allies: (I) The Cabal, (II) None, (III) Darkhawk, (former) The Cabal
Major enemies: (I) Darkhawk, the Punisher, Phillipe Bazin, (II) Iron Man I, Darkhawk
Usual base of operations: (III) New York area
Former bases of operations: (I, III) An abandoned service station at the corner of Allen and Delancey Streets on Manhattan's Lower East Side, (II) New York area
Current group membership: (III) None
Former group membership: (I, III) The Cabal, (II) None
Extent of education: (I, III) High school graduates, police academy graduates, (II) High school graduate

PHYSICAL DESCRIPTION

Height: (I) Various, (II) 5' 10", (III) 6' 1" (with armor) 7'
Weight: (I) Various, (II) 175 lbs., (III) 210 lbs., (with armor) 620 lbs.
Eyes: (I) Various, (II) Blue, (III) Brown
Hair: (I) Various, (II) Brown, (III) Black
Other distinguishing features: (all) None

POWERS AND ABILITIES

Intelligence: (all) Normal
Strength: (all) Normal, (with armor) Superhuman Class 75
Speed: (all) Normal
Flight Speed: Natural winged flight
Stamina: (all) Normal
Durability: (all) Normal
Agility: (all) Normal
Reflexes: (all) Normal
Fighting skills: (I, III) Police training in hand-to-hand combat, (II) None
Special skills: (I) (Lennox) Trained detective and marksman, (others) Trained marksmen, (II) None, (III) Trained marksman
Superhuman physical powers: (all) None
Superhuman mental powers: (all) None
Special limitations: (all) None
Source of superhuman powers: (all) Inapplicable

PARAPHERNALIA

Costume specifications: Armored battlesuit which serves as exoskeleton greatly amplifying user's strength
Personal weaponry: Hand-blasters firing multi-directional high-frequency electrical bolts
Special weaponry: Gas grenades, flares, sonic weaponry, targeting computer
Other accessories: Self-contained air supply for one hour
Transportation: flight via boot jets
Design and manufacture of paraphernalia: Tony Stark, modified by former Stane International engineers Stu, Tim, and Jane (last names unrevealed)

BIBLIOGRAPHY

First appearance: (I) DARKHAWK #4, (II) DARKHAWK ANNUAL #1, (III) (as Zafar) DARKHAWK #3, (as Savage Steel) DARKHAWK ANNUAL #2
Origin issue: (I) DARKHAWK #15, (II) DARKHAWK ANNUAL #1, (III) DARKHAWK ANNUAL #2
Significant issues: DARKHAWK #4 (I: battled Darkhawk, killed drug dealers); DARKHAWK #9 (I: tried to kill the Punisher; battled Punisher, Darkhawk, and weapons dealers); DARKHAWK #12 (I: attacked Phillippe Bazin during his trial, revealed as Harry Lennox); DARKHAWK #15 (I: how the Cabal created the Savage Steel identity revealed, Cabal defeated by Darkhawk, most members taken into custody); DARKHAWK ANNUAL #1 (II: stole armor, adopted Savage Steel identity, attempted to gain new weaponry, defeated by Iron Man I, armor deactivated); DARKHAWK ANNUAL #1 (III: as Zafar, rescued imprisoned Vale and Lennox from Cabal, faked their deaths and his own; with Vale and Lennox from Cabal, faked their deaths and his own; with Vale, Lennox, and Leone, joined Witness Relocation Program); DARKHAWK ANNUAL #2 (as Zafar, stole rebuilt armor from renegade Stane technicians, adopted Savage Steel identity); DARKHAWK #32 (with Darkhawk, battled terrorists)

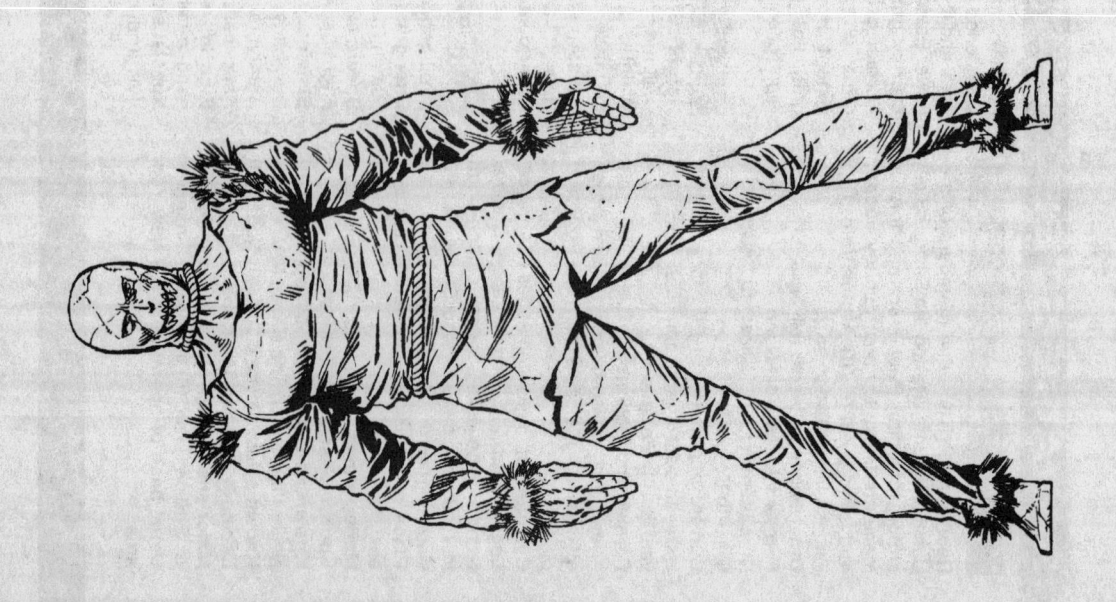

SCARECROW

SCARECROW

BIOGRAPHICAL DATA

Real name: Ebenezer Laughton
Other current aliases: None
Former aliases: Umberto the Uncanny
Dual identity: Publicly known
Current occupation: Serial killer, operative for the Firm
Former occupation: Carnival performer, professional thief, criminal operative for Count Nefaria and the Cowled Commander
Citizenship: United States of America
Legal status: Criminal record
Place of birth: Rhineback, New York
Marital status: Single
Known relatives: Ralph (brother)
Known confidants: None
Known allies: The Firm, (former) Count Lucino Nefaria (deceased), Unicorn I (deceased), Eel I (deceased), Porcupine (deceased), Plantman, Cowled Commander
Major enemies: Captain America, Ghost Rider II, Iron Man, X-Men, Falcon
Usual base of operations: New York City
Former base of operations: Mobile in Eastern United States
Current group membership: The Firm
Former group membership: Operative of the Nefaria "family" of the Maggia, operative for the Cowled Commander
Extent of education: High school dropout

PHYSICAL DESCRIPTION

Height: 6'
Weight: 165 lbs.
Eyes: Brown
Hair: Blond
Other distinguishing features: None

POWERS AND ABILITIES

Intelligence: Normal
Strength: Superhuman Class 10
Speed: Enhanced human
Stamina: Superhuman
Durability: Superhuman regenerative
Agility: Superhuman
Reflexes: Superhuman
Fighting skills: Formidable hand-to-hand combatant, no known combat training
Special skills and abilities: The Scarecrow has trained himself to have the agility of a professional contortionist, to be able to escape from conventional locks and chains, and to perform various acrobatic stunts. He is also a master at training birds.
Superhuman physical powers: Aside from the above listed attributes, the Scarecrow's body produces a mutated pheromone that affects the adrenal glands of people and higher animals (even crows) within twenty feet of him, causing a sensory overload which triggers a panic attack. The same pheromone affects the Scarecrow's own adrenal system, giving superhuman strength and stamina. Through unknown means the Scarecrow can now survive and quickly recover from various kinds of injuries that would be fatal to normal human beings.
Superhuman mental powers: None
Special limitations: Criminally insane
Source of superhuman powers: Surgical implants given to him by doctors employed by the Firm

PARAPHERNALIA

Costume specifications: Conventional fabrics
Personal weaponry: A pitchfork
Special weaponry: None
Other accessories: The Scarecrow is assisted in his crimes by crows whom he has trained to perform a variety of actions in response to his hand gestures and tones of voice. At his command the crows will attack and kill the victims he designates. The crows have been trained to attack anyone who rushes at the Scarecrow or points a gun at him. They are trained to carry off jewels, valuables, and anything else at which the Scarecrow points.
Transportation: Conventional means
Design and manufacture of paraphernalia: Unrevealed

BIBLIOGRAPHY

First appearance: TALES OF SUSPENSE #51
Origin issue: TALES OF SUSPENSE #51
Significant issues: TALES OF SUSPENSE #51 (became Scarecrow, defeated by Iron Man); X-MEN Vol. 1 #22-23 (participated in Count Nefaria's attempt to hold Washington, D.C. for ransom, battled X-Men); CAPTAIN AMERICA #158-159 (worked for the Cowled Commander, defeated by Captain America and the Falcon); CAPTAIN AMERICA ANNUAL #6 (clashed with Captain America); CAPTAIN AMERICA #279-280 (now insane, began murdering supporters of Coalition for an Upstanding America, disrupted a telethon, was defeated by Captain America); GHOST RIDER Vol. 2 #7 (embarked on series of murders, first battled Ghost Rider II, was impaled on own pitchfork, was carried off by the Firm); GHOST RIDER/CAPTAIN AMERICA: FEAR (received surgical implants, carried out more killings, abducted Stacy Dolan, fought Captain America and Ghost Rider II, survived being shot and impaled, was enlisted by Mr. Stern for the Firm)

SCARLET WITCH

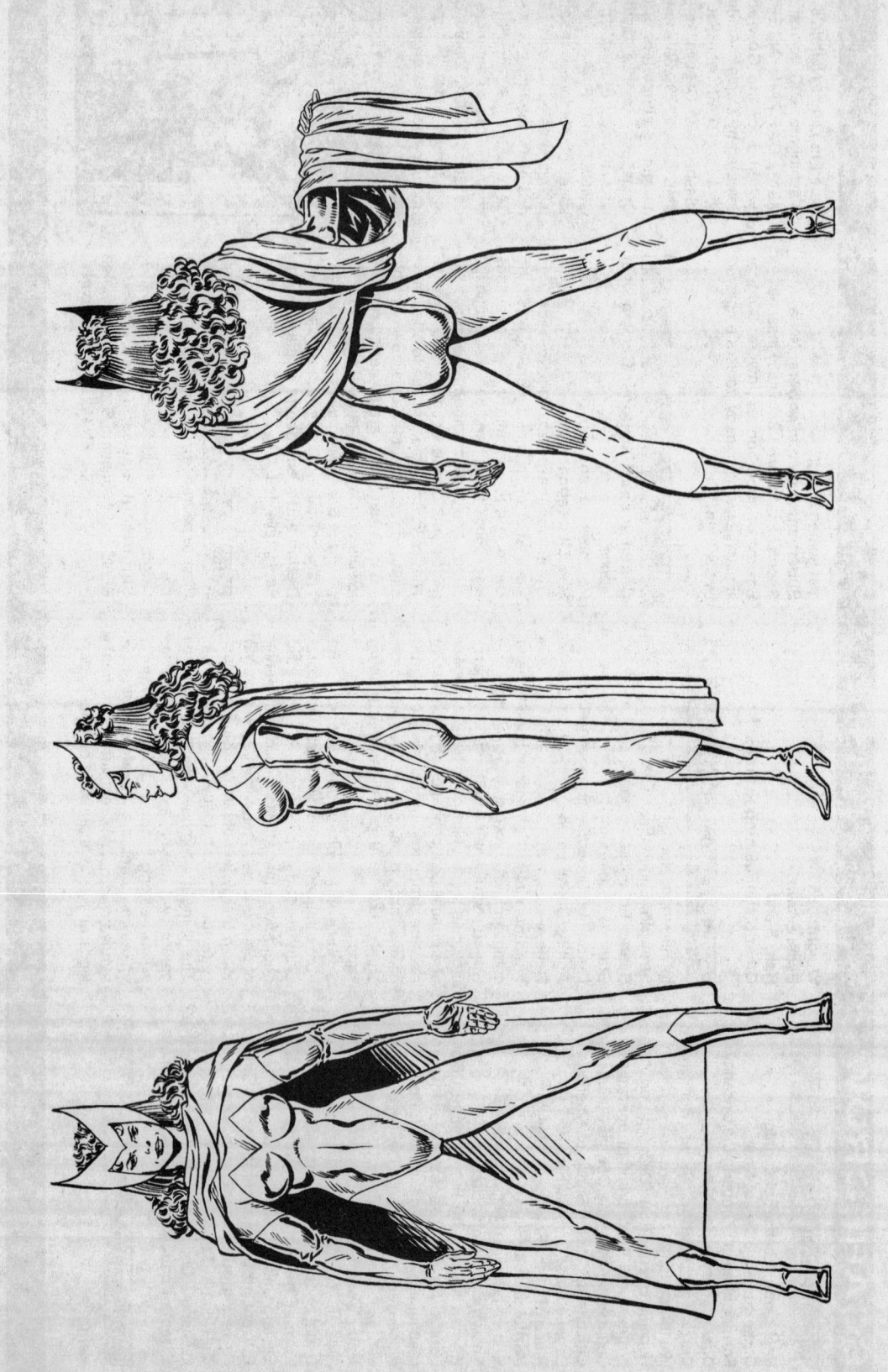

SCARLET WITCH

BIOGRAPHICAL DATA

Real name: Wanda Maximoff
Other current aliases: None
Former aliases: Wanda Frank, Wanda Magnus
Dual identity: Publicly known
Current occupation: Adventurer
Former occupation: Housewife, parent, witchcraft tutor
Citizenship: Former citizen of Transia, naturalized citizen of the United States
Legal status: No criminal record
Place of birth: Wundagore Mountain, Transia, Europe
Marital status: Separated
Known relatives: Vision (estranged husband), Pietro Maximoff (brother, alias Quicksilver), Magnus (father, alias Magneto), Magda (mother, presumed deceased), Django Maximoff (adoptive father, deceased), Marya Maximoff (adoptive mother, deceased), Crystal (sister-in-law), Luna (niece)
Known confidants: The Vision, Quicksilver
Known allies: The Avengers, Agatha Harkness, the Fantastic Four, the Inhumans
Major enemies: Magneto, the Toad, Dormammu, Immortus, Chthon, Set
Usual base of operations: Avengers West Coast Compound, Los Angeles, California
Former bases of operations: Mobile throughout Europe; Avengers Mansion, New York City; Leonia, New Jersey
Current group membership: Avengers West Coast
Former group membership: Brotherhood of Evil Mutants I, Avengers, Lady Liberators
Extent of education: Unrevealed

PHYSICAL DESCRIPTION

Height: 5' 7"
Weight: 130 lbs.
Eyes: Blue
Hair: Auburn
Other distinguishing features: None

POWERS AND ABILITIES

Intelligence: Normal
Strength: Normal
Speed: Normal
Stamina: Athlete
Durability: Normal
Agility: Normal
Reflexes: Athlete
Fighting skills: Basic Avengers hand-to-hand combat training
Special skills and abilities: Trained in sorcery by Agatha Harkness
Superhuman physical powers: None
Superhuman mental powers: Ability to affect probability fields to cause occurrence of various unlikely phenomena, including spontaneous combustion of flammable objects, rapid rust or decay of organic or inorganic materials, deflection of objects in flight, disruption of energy transmissions or fields
Special limitations: "Hex"-power has a 20% unreliability factor; range of hex limited by line of sight
Source of superhuman powers: Genetic mutation (control amplified through study of sorcery)

PARAPHERNALIA

Costume specifications: Synthetic stretch fabric
Personal weaponry: None
Special weaponry: None
Other accessories: None
Transportation: Avengers Quinjet
Design and manufacture of paraphernalia: Tony Stark

BIBLIOGRAPHY

First appearance: X-MEN #4
Origin issue: AVENGERS #187
Significant issues: X-MEN #4-7, 11 (as part of Magneto's Brotherhood of Evil Mutants, battled the original X-Men); AVENGERS #16 (with Quicksilver, joined the Avengers); AVENGERS #91 (fell in love with Vision); AVENGERS #108-109 (began romance with Vision); AVENGERS #118 (defeated Dormammu in climax of Avengers/Defenders clash); GIANT-SIZE AVENGERS #1 (Robert Frank, the Whizzer, alleged to be father); AVENGERS #128 (began study of sorcery under tutelage of Agatha Harkness); GIANT-SIZE AVENGERS #4 (captured by Dormammu, rescued by Vision, married Vision); AVENGERS #147-149 (alongside Avengers, defeated menace of the Serpent Crown); MARVEL TWO-IN-ONE #66 (with Thing and Stingray, halted menace of Serpent Crown); AVENGERS #185-187 (returned to Transia with brother and adoptive father, learned origins and that Whizzer not true father, temporarily possessed by demon Chthon); MARVEL TEAM-UP ANNUAL #5 (with Spider-Man, Thing, Dr. Strange, and Quasar, used Cosmic Cube to overcome Serpent Crown); VISION AND THE SCARLET WITCH Vol. 1 #4 (learned Magneto is true father); VISION AND THE SCARLET WITCH Vol. 2 #3 (magically conceived twin children); VISION AND THE SCARLET WITCH Vol. 2 #12 (seemingly gave birth to twin sons); WEST COAST AVENGERS Vol. 2 #34 (with Vision, joined Avengers West Coast); AVENGERS WEST COAST #51-52 ("children" abducted by Master Pandemonium, revealed as imaginary creations of her magic and willpower, formed from portions of Mephisto's being, returned to their original state); AVENGERS ANNUAL #18/AVENGERS WEST COAST ANNUAL #4/FANTASTIC FOUR ANNUAL #22 (during Atlantean invasion, captured by Ghaur and Lyra as one of the seven "brides" of Set, freed by Fantastic Four and Avengers); AVENGERS WEST COAST #55-57 (lost sanity, turned against Avengers, rejoined Magneto); AVENGERS WEST COAST #60-62 (captured by Immortus, rescued by Avengers, restored to sanity)

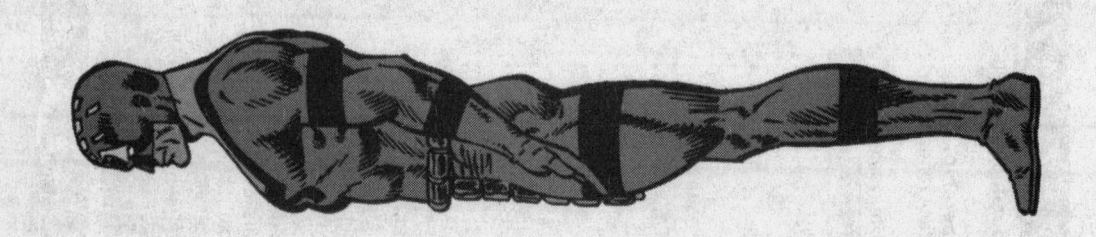

SCORPIO

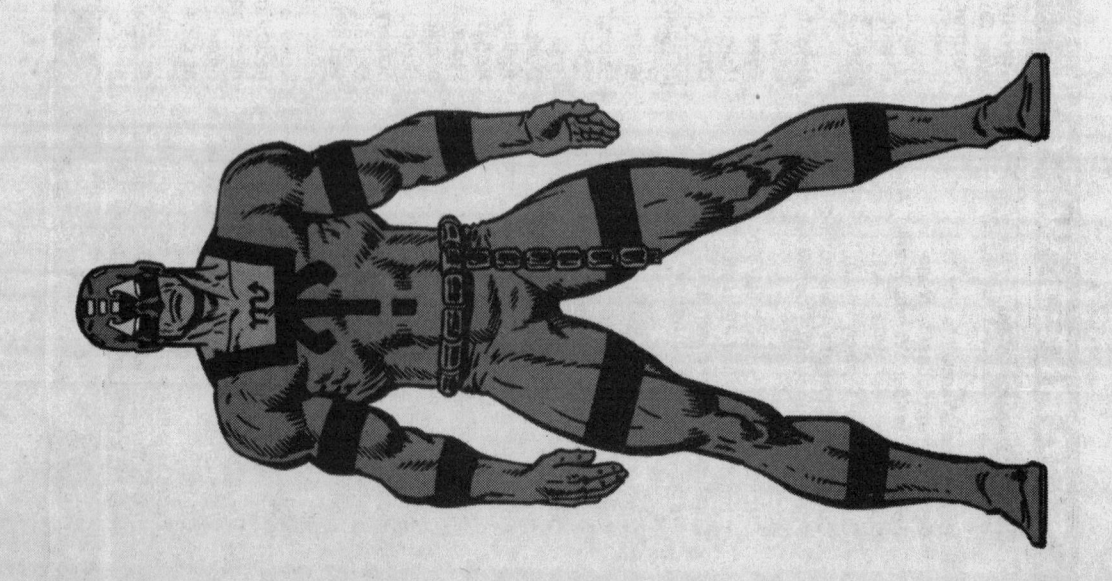

SCORPIO

BIOGRAPHICAL DATA

Real name: Jacob "Jake" Fury
Aliases at time of death: None
Former aliases: Flip Mason, Count Julio Scarlotti, Jacques LaPoint, Nick Fury
Dual identity: Known only to his brother
Occupation at time of death: Spy, terrorist, criminal
Former occupation: Soldier
Citizenship: United States of America
Legal status: No criminal record, wanted for questioning by SHIELD, legally dead
Place of birth: New York City
Place of death: Belleville, New Jersey
Cause of death: Self-inflicted gunshot wound
Marital status: Single
Known relatives: Nick Fury (brother), Jack Fury (father, deceased), Dawn Fury (sister), Mikel Fury (nephew)
Known confidants: Nick Fury Life Model Decoy
Known allies: Zodiac (Leo, Gemini, Virgo, Sagittarius, Aquarius, Capricorn, Taurus, Libra, Cancer, Pisces, Aries)
Major enemies: Nick Fury, the Defenders
Base of operations at time of death: Belleville, New Jersey
Former bases of operations: New Orleans, Louisiana; Las Vegas, Nevada
Group membership at time of death: Leader of the LMD Zodiac
Former group membership: Zodiac
Extent of education: College graduate

PHYSICAL DESCRIPTION

Height: 5' 10"
Weight: 185 lbs.
Eyes: Blue
Hair: Brown
Other distinguishing features: None

POWERS AND ABILITIES

Intelligence: Genius
Strength: Normal, (enhanced by Zodiac Key) Peak human
Speed: Normal, (enhanced by Zodiac Key) Athlete
Stamina: Normal, (enhanced by Zodiac Key) Peak human
Durability: Normal, (enhanced by Zodiac Key) Peak human
Agility: Athlete
Reflexes: Athlete
Fighting skills: Army basic training, above average knowledge of hand-to-hand combat, streetfighting techniques
Special skills and abilities: None
Superhuman physical powers: The Zodiac Key enabled Scorpio to transform his body into sentient water for brief periods of time.
Superhuman mental powers: None
Special limitations: Scorpio is totally dependent upon the Zodiac Key in order to maintain his superhuman powers. He did not have to be in physical contact with it to wield it.
Source of superhuman powers: The Zodiac Key is a power object of otherdimensional origin that taps an unidentified extradimensional energy for a variety of effects, including concussive force, electricity, magnetism, teleportation, physical transformation, etc. The Zodiac Key possesses sentience of a sort.
Note: After Jake Fury's death, the Zodiac Key employed his Theater of Genetics laboratory to create an android of Jake Fury. This Scorpio android, along with most of the other twelve Zodiac androids, still exists.

PARAPHERNALIA

Costume specifications: Synthetic stretch fabric
Personal weaponry: Zodiac Key
Special weaponry: None
Other accessories: Various
Transportation: Various hovercrafts
Design and manufacture of paraphernalia: (Zodiac Key) Unknown. (transportation and lab equipment) Unrevealed, possibly the Advanced Idea Mechanics

BIBLIOGRAPHY

First appearance: (as Jacob Fury) SGT. FURY AND HIS HOWLING COMMANDOS #68. (as Scorpio) NICK FURY, AGENT OF SHIELD Vol.1 #1
Origin issue: SGT. FURY AND HIS HOWLING COMMANDOS #68
Significant issues: SGT. FURY AND HIS HOWLING COMMANDOS #68 (background and resentment of brother revealed); NICK FURY, AGENT OF SHIELD Vol.1 #1 (battled brother at Las Vegas SHIELD base); NICK FURY, AGENT OF SHIELD Vol.1 #5 (battled brother in Manhattan, disguised self as Nick Fury to infiltrate New York SHIELD base, identity discovered by brother); AVENGERS #72 (Nick Fury undercover as Scorpio, took brother's place in Zodiac, battled the Avengers); AVENGERS #120-122 (disguised as own successor, Jacques LaPoint, played minor role in Zodiac's attempt to kill all Manhattan residents born under the sign of Gemini); DEFENDERS #46 (attempted to kidnap Kyle Richmond, battled Defenders); DEFENDERS #48-50 (constructed android Zodiac members to serve him, plan thwarted by the Defenders, committed suicide in despair); WEST COAST AVENGERS #26-28 (android Scorpio created by Zodiac Key, massacred human Zodiac organization, took over criminal operations, battled West Coast Avengers, defeated when teleported to dimension of Key's origin, abandoned there); WOLVERINE NICK FURY GRAPHIC NOVEL (man claiming to be son of Jake Fury appeared as new Scorpio, revealed to be Nick Fury's son, acquired the Zodiac Key, battled Wolverine and Nick Fury, taken into SHIELD custody for treatment of brainwashing)

Note: Accounts vary as to whether Jake Fury was the original Scorpio.

SCORPION

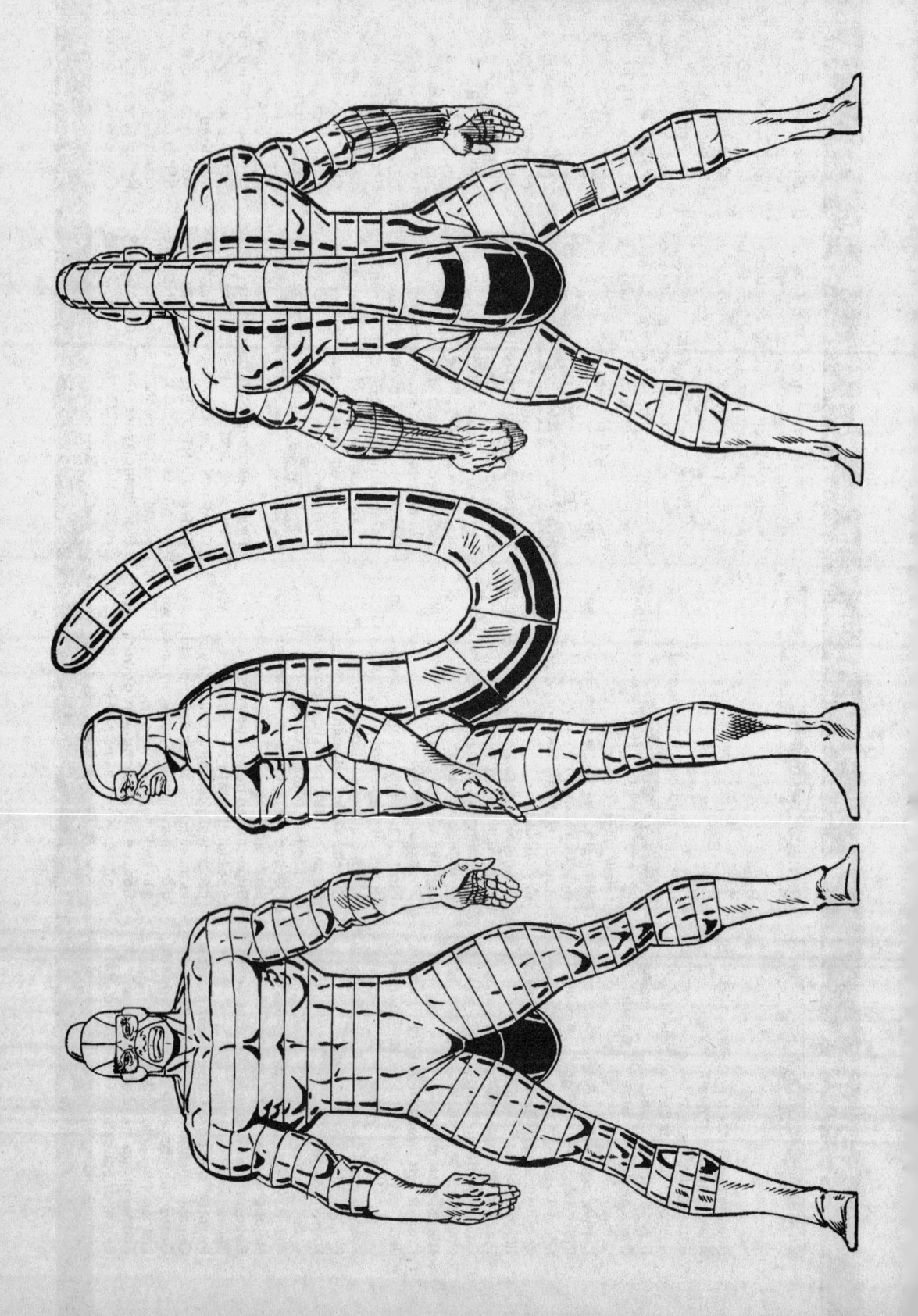

SCORPION

BIOGRAPHICAL DATA

Real name: Macdonald "Mac" Gargan
Other current aliases: None
Former aliases: None
Dual identity: Secret
Current occupation: Professional criminal
Former occupation: Private detective
Citizenship: United States of America
Legal status: Criminal record in the U.S.
Place of birth: Unrevealed
Marital status: Single
Known relatives: None
Known confidants: Mr. Hyde
Known allies: Masters of Evil III (Egghead, Whirlwind, Moonstone II, Tiger Shark)
Major enemies: Spider-Man
Usual ase of operations: Mobile
Former bases of operations: New York City
Current group membership: None
Former group membership: Masters of Evil III
Extent of education: College dropout

PHYSICAL DESCRIPTION

Height: 6' 2"
Weight: 220 lb
Eyes: Brown
Hair: Brown, (as Scorpion) Bald
Other distinguishing features: None

POWERS AND ABILITIES

Intelligence: Normal
Strength: Superhuman Class 25
Speed: Superhuman
Stamina: Superhuman
Durability: Superhuman
Agility: Superhuman
Reflexes: Superhuman
Fighting skills: Basic streetfighting and hand-to-hand combat techniques
Special skills and abilities: Although criminally insane, the Scorpion retains his deductive reasoning from his career as a private investigator.
Superhuman physical powers: Aside from the above listed attributes, none
Superhuman mental powers: None
Special limitations: The Scorpion once believed he was trapped inside his costume.
Source of superhuman powers: Chemical and radiological treatments which produced mutagenic alterations

PARAPHERNALIA

Costume specifications: Full-body battlesuit composed of two layers of light steel mesh separated by a thin layer of insulated rubber
Personal weaponry: A cybernetically controlled, seven-foot mechanical tail with a tool steel articulated framework with twelve segments, which can whip at speeds of over 100 feet per second. The tail has a low-density plasma projector and a spike at its tip which can squirt acid
Special weaponry: None
Other accessories: None
Transportation: The Scorpion can use his tail as an extra leg, or he can coil it behind him to spring himself a distance of at least 30 feet
Design and manufacture of paraphernalia: Phineas Mason (the Tinkerer); later modified by Justin Hammer

BIBLIOGRAPHY

First appearance: AMAZING SPIDER-MAN #20
Origin issue: AMAZING SPIDER-MAN #20
Significant issues: AMAZING SPIDER-MAN #20 (transformed into the Scorpion by Dr. Finley Stillwell with funds provided by J. Jonah Jameson to battle Spider-Man; defeated by Spider-Man); AMAZING SPIDER-MAN #29 (Spider-Man prevented him from killing JAmeson by turning him into a freak); CAPTAIN AMERICA #122 (hired by spy ring to follow SHIELD agent Sharon Carter; defeated by Captain America); DAREDEVIL #82 (acquired by Mr. Kline, who created android duplicates of the Scorpion and Mr. Hyde to dispatch against Daredevil); CAPTAIN AMERICA #122 (launched a campaign of terror with Mr. Hyde against SHIELD agents; defeated by Captain America and the Falcon); MS. MARVEL #1-2 (revenge attempt against Jameson thwarted by Ms. Marvel); SPECTACULAR SPIDER-MAN #21 (his sanity deteriorating, he mistakenly believed he could not remove his costume, until Spider-Man proved otherwise); MARVEL TEAM-UP #106 (formed an extortion racket to sabotage the *Daily Bugle*; thwarted by Spider-Man and Captain America); AVENGERS #222 (freed from prison by agents of Egghead, who wanted him as a members of the Masters of Evil III; defeated by the Avengers); AMAZING SPIDER-MAN #251 (Jameson publicly confessed his role in Scorpion's creation); AMAZING SPIDER-MAN ANNUAL #18 (kidnaped Jameson's son and bride at Jameson's wedding); AMAZING SPIDER-MAN #318-319 (battlesuit modified by Justin Hammer, who hired him to kidnap a war hero; double-crossed Hammer, who hired Blacklash and Rhino to subdue him); ALPHA FLIGHT #79-80 (attempted to enter Canada to avoid the Super Powers Registration Act, but repelled by Alpha Flight); AMAZING SPIDER-MAN #342-343 (hired by the Chameleon to kill a de-powered Spider-Man but defeated by the Black Cat)

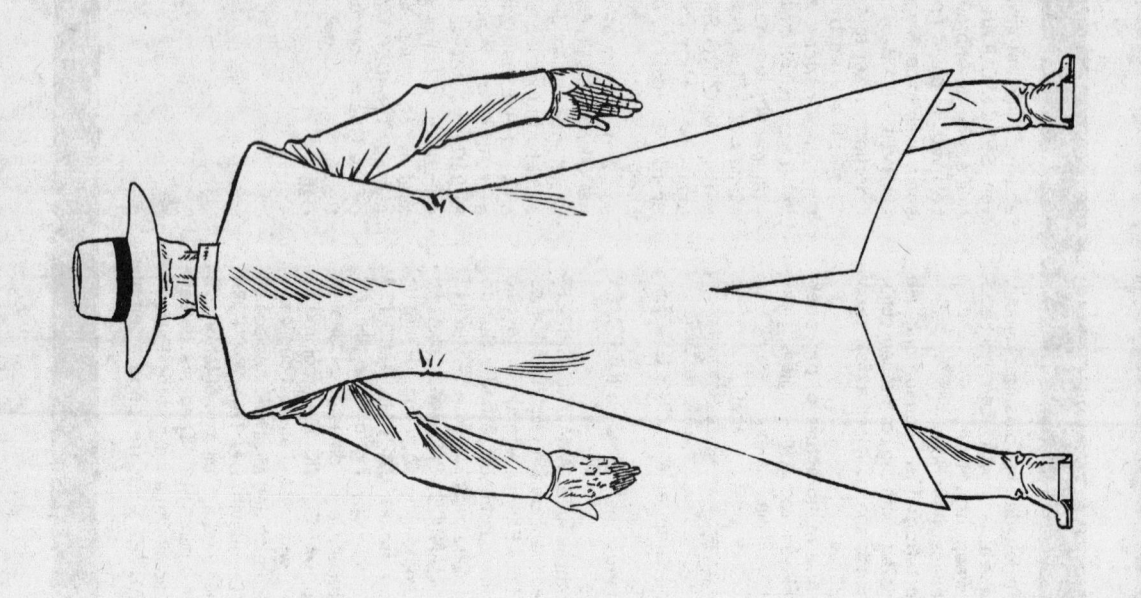

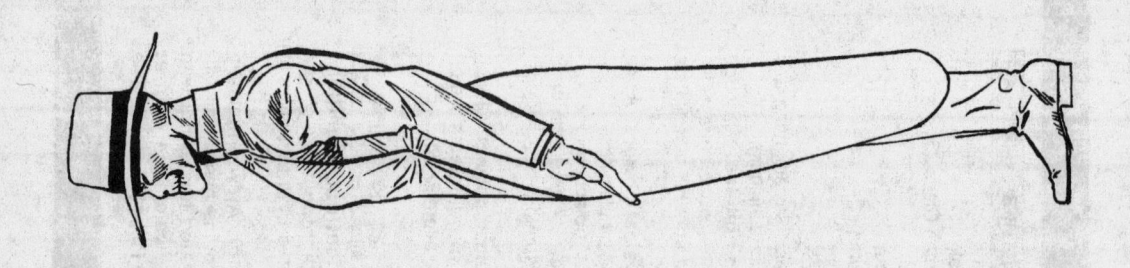

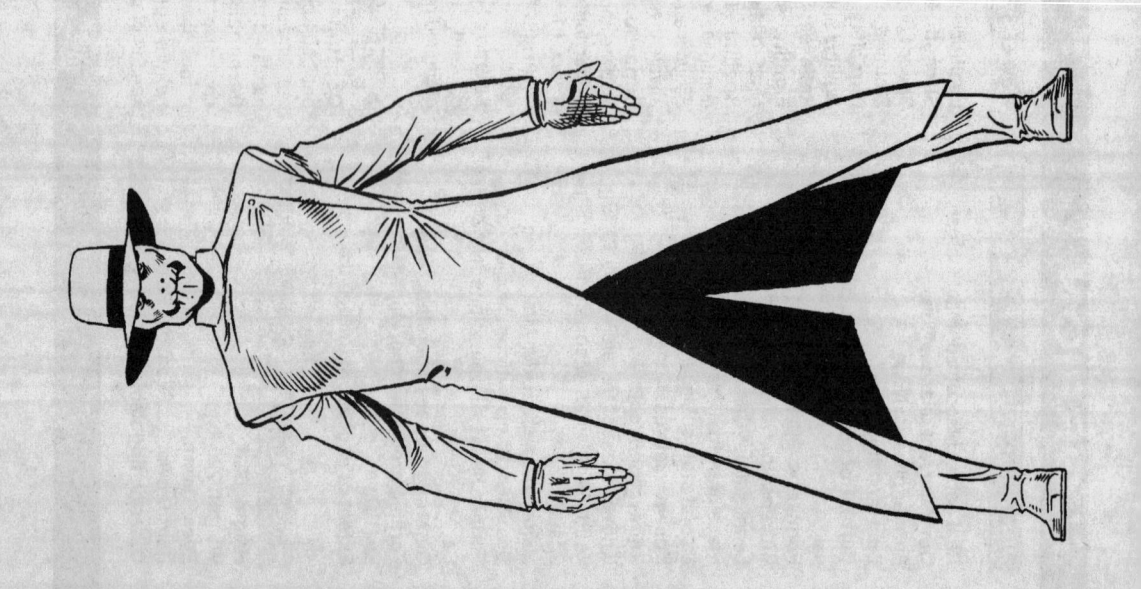

SCOURGE

SCOURGE

ORGANIZATION

Purpose: The elimination of the criminal element through assassination

Modus operandi: The use of subterfuge to get close to targets, then elimination by whatever lethal means are possible

Extent of operations: Nationwide, perhaps worldwide

Relationship to conventional authorities: Unrevealed, Scourge is generally believed to be a single individual, rather than an organized group

Base of operations: Southern California estate of Angel I

Former bases of operations: Mobile

Major funding: The personal fortune of the elderly millionaire who claims to have been the 1940's costumed hero Angel I

Known enemies: Captain America, USAgent, Dr. Karl Malus, Red Skull, (former) Enforcer, Miracle Man, Hate-Monger III, Megatek, Melter, Titania I, Basilisk I, Hammer, Anvil, Fly, Death Adder, Blue Streak, Wraith, Bird-Man II, Turner D. Century, Cheetah, Commander Kraken, Cyclone, Firebrand I, Grappler, Hellrazor, Hijacker, Jaguar, Letha, Mind-Wave, Mirage I, Rapier, Ringer I, Shellshock, Steeplejack II, Vamp, Red Skull II (all deceased)

Known allies: (former) Red Skull

MEMBERSHIP

Number of active members: Unrevealed

Number of reserve members: Unrevealed

Organizational structure: Behind the scenes direction by Angel I, under him, several individual Scourge agents capable of autonomous action

Known officers: Angel I, Domino I (deceased)

Known current members: Unrevealed

Known former members: Scourge I, Scourge II, Scourge III, Scourge IV (all deceased), Scourge V (Priscilla Lyons, Vagabond), Scourge VI (Caprice), Scourge VII (Bloodstain; deceased)

Known special agents: None

Membership requirements: Must be legal adult willing to submit to thorough investigation of personal background and swear an oath of loyalty to the principals of the Scourge organization

HISTORY

Founder: Angel I

Other leaders: None known

Previous purpose or goals: None known

Major campaigns or accomplishments: Massacre of villains at "Bar With No Name", deaths of various super-villains, death of Scourges I-IV before they could reveal the existence of the organization

Major setbacks: Death of Scourges I-IV, failure to kill Power Broker, betrayal of Scourge V to USAgent, death of Bloodstain, death of Domino I

TECHNOLOGY AND PARAPHERNALIA

Level of technology: Standard

Transportation: Conventional vehicles

Standard uniforms: All-white coat and hat, skull-like mask

Standard weaponry: .50 cal Thompson machine gun with sawed-off barrel and stock using special purpose 5-round magazine. Each .50 cal round is equipped with an acceleration activated, delay-triggered explosive shell

Standard accessories: Radio devices for communication with Domino I, makeup and costumes for disguise

BIBLIOGRAPHY

First appearance: (Scourge I) IRON MAN #194; (Scourge II) AMAZING SPIDER-MAN #277; (identified as Scourge II) CAPTAIN AMERICA #320; (Scourge III, disguised) CAPTAIN AMERICA #347; (Scourge III, in costume) CAPTAIN AMERICA #351 (Scourge II killed Watchdog); CAPTAIN AMERICA #358-364 (Scourge II captured by USAgent and killed by Scourge IV); CAPTAIN AMERICA #394 (Scourge III eliminated by Red Skull); USAGENT #1-4 (Priscilla Lyons, as Scourge V, was unable to bring herself to kill Matador; Lyons thus was targeted by other Scourges; Lyons sought help of USAgent; USAgent captured Scourge IV; Scourge VI killed Scourge IV; Scourge VI captured by USAgent; USAgent confronted Angel I and Domino I; Bloodstain killed in combat) (Scourge I killed Enforcer); THING #24 (Scourge I killed Miracle Man); SECRET WARS II #2 (Scourge I killed Hate-Monger II); AVENGERS #263 (Scourge I killed Titania I); THING #33 (Scourge I killed Titania I); FANTASTIC FOUR #289 (Scourge I killed Basilisk I); MARVEL FANFARE #29 (Scourge II killed Hammer and Anvil); AMAZING SPIDER-MAN #276 (Scourge I killed the Fly); CAPTAIN AMERICA #318 (Scourge I killed Death Adder and Blue Streak); AMAZING SPIDER-MAN #277 (Scourge I killed Wraith); CAPTAIN AMERICA #319 (Scourge I killed all costume villains at the "Bar With No Name"); CAPTAIN AMERICA #320 (Scourge I unmasked, defeated by Captain America, slain by Scourge II); CAPTAIN AMERICA #347 (renegade Scourge III killed Red Skull II on behalf of the Red Skull I); CAPTAIN AMERICA #350 (Scourge III attempted to kill Captain America VI [USAgent] for Red Skull); CAPTAIN AMERICA #351 (Scourge II killed Watchdog); CAPTAIN AMERICA #358-364 (Scourge II captured by USAgent and killed by Scourge IV); CAPTAIN AMERICA #362; (Scourge IV, seen) USAGENT #1; (Scourge V, as Lyons) CAPTAIN AMERICA #325; (Scourge V, as Vagabond) CAPTAIN AMERICA #336; (Scourge V) USAGENT #1; (Scourge VI, as Caprice) USAGENT #2; (Scourge VI) USAGENT #4; (Scourge VII, as Bloodstain) USAGENT #2; (Scourge VII) USAGENT #4

Origin issue: USAGENT #4

Significant issues: IRON MAN #194

SCRATCH, NICHOLAS™

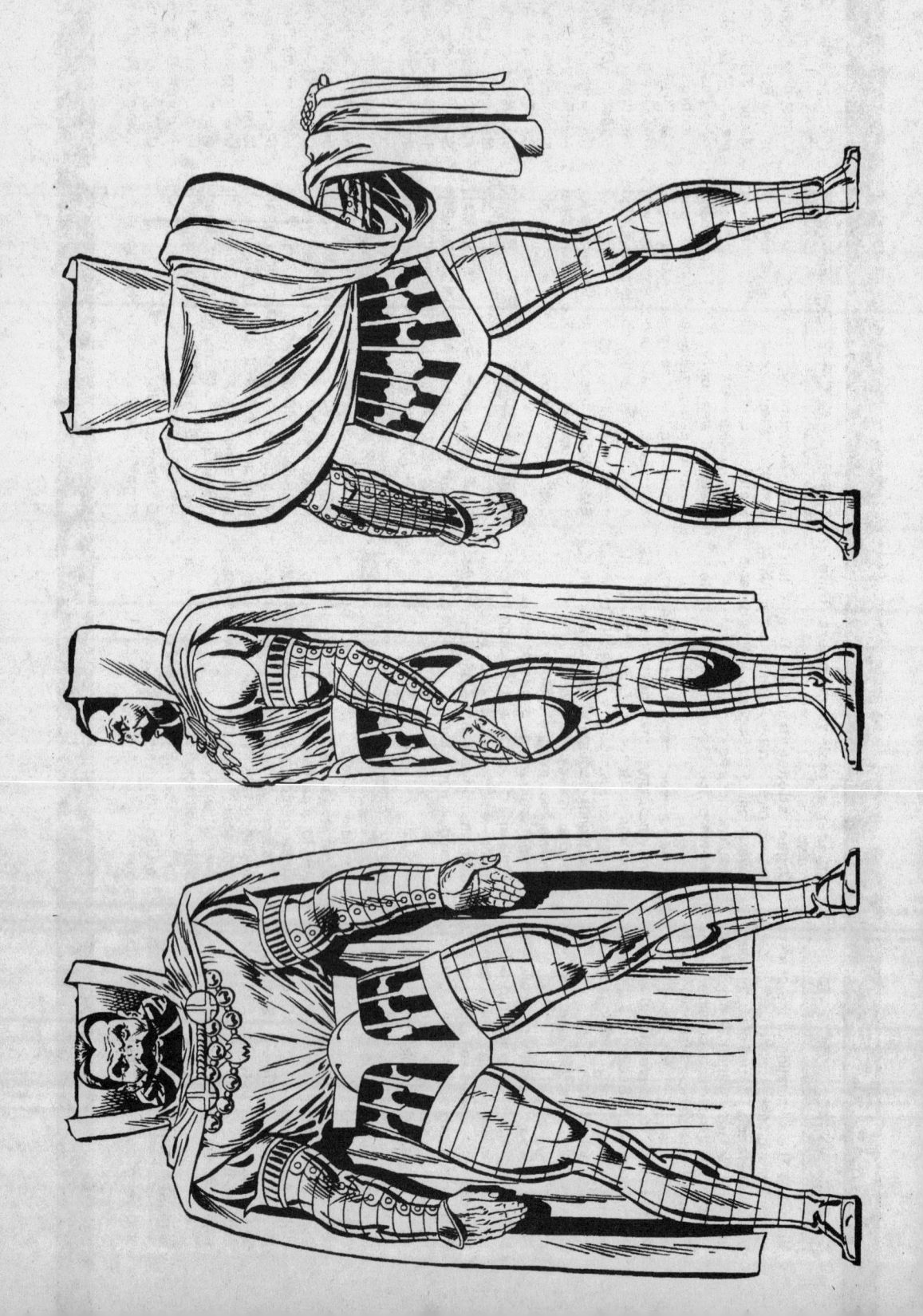

SCRATCH, NICHOLAS

BIOGRAPHICAL DATA

Real name: Nicholas Scratch (as far as is known)
Other current aliases: None
Former aliases: None known
Dual identity: None; Scratch's existence is unknown to the general populace of Earth
Current occupation: Unrevealed
Former occupation: Warlock, leader of New Salem
Citizenship: New, Salem (the United States government is unaware of New Salem's existence)
Legal status: No official criminal record; however, he has been exiled by the populace of the community of New Salem, Colorado, which considers itself an independent nation
Place of birth: New Salem, Colorado
Marital status: Married previously, currently unrevealed
Known relatives: Agatha Harkness (mother), Brutacus, Hydron, Thornn, Vakume (sons, presumed deceased), Gazelle, Reptilla, Vertigo I (daughters, presumed deceased)
Known confidants: None
Known allies: (formerly) Salem's Seven, witches and warlocks of New Salem
Major enemies: Agatha Harkness, the Fantastic Four, Gabriel the Devil-Hunter, Franklin Richards (Tattletale); (former) witches and warlocks of New Salem
Usual base of operations: Unrevealed
Former bases of operations: New Salem, Colorado; the Dark Realm pocket dimension
Current group membership: None
Former group membership: Witches and warlocks of New Salem
Extent of education: Extensive training in witchcraft

PHYSICAL DESCRIPTION

Height: 6'3"
Weight: 220 lbs.
Eyes: Blue
Hair: Black with white streaks in beard
Other distinguishing features: None

POWERS AND ABILITIES

Intelligence: Normal
Strength: Normal
Speed: Normal
Stamina: Normal
Durability: Normal
Agility: Normal
Reflexes: Normal
Fighting skills: Unrevealed
Special skills and abilities: Vast knowledge of magical lore
Superhuman physical powers: Nicholas Scratch formerly had the ability to manipulate magical forces for a number of effects, including teleportation, energy projection, animation and control of inanimate objects, and the tapping of extradimensional energy by invoking entities or objects of power existing in dimensions tangential to Earth's through the recitation of spells
Superhuman mental powers: Formerly, mesmerism, thought-casting, illusion-casting, mental-probing, and the ability to possess others minds
Special limitations: Nicholas Scratch was deprived of his supernatural powers by a spell cast by Agatha Harkness
Source of superhuman powers: Manipulation of the forces of magic

PARAPHERNALIA

Costume specifications: Ordinary fabric
Personal weaponry: None
Special weaponry: The "Satan Staff," a mystical power object that served as a focus for Scratch's magical powers, although he could employ them without the staff. Using the staff, he could direct the combined magical powers of the entire community of New Salem when they allowed him to do so.
Other accessories: None
Transportation: Interdimensional teleportation
Design and manufacture of paraphernalia: Unrevealed

BIBLIOGRAPHY

First appearance: FANTASTIC FOUR #185
Origin issue: Nicholas Scratch's origin is as yet unrevealed
Significant issues: FANTASTIC FOUR #185-186 (as leader of New Salem, captured Fantastic Four, Agatha Harkness, and Franklin Richards; had Agatha Harkness condemned to death for treason to New Salem, Harkness rescued by the Fantastic Four, New Salemites turned against Scratch and exiled him to the Dark Realm); FANTASTIC FOUR ANNUAL #14 (from Dark Realm, restored Salem's Seven's powers and took mental control of Fantastic Four, attempted world conquest, thwarted and confined to Dark Realm by Agatha Harkness); FANTASTIC FOUR #222-223 (from Dark Realm, took mental possession of Franklin Richards; had Salem's Seven take over New Salem, was defeated by Agatha Harkness and Gabriel, Devil-Hunter, Scratch's powers removed by Harkness, leaving him as normal human being)

Note: Nicholas Scratch's whereabouts at the time of the apparent destruction of all of New Salem's witches and warlocks, in VISION AND THE SCARLET WITCH Vol. 2 #3, remain unrevealed.

SCREAMING MIMI.

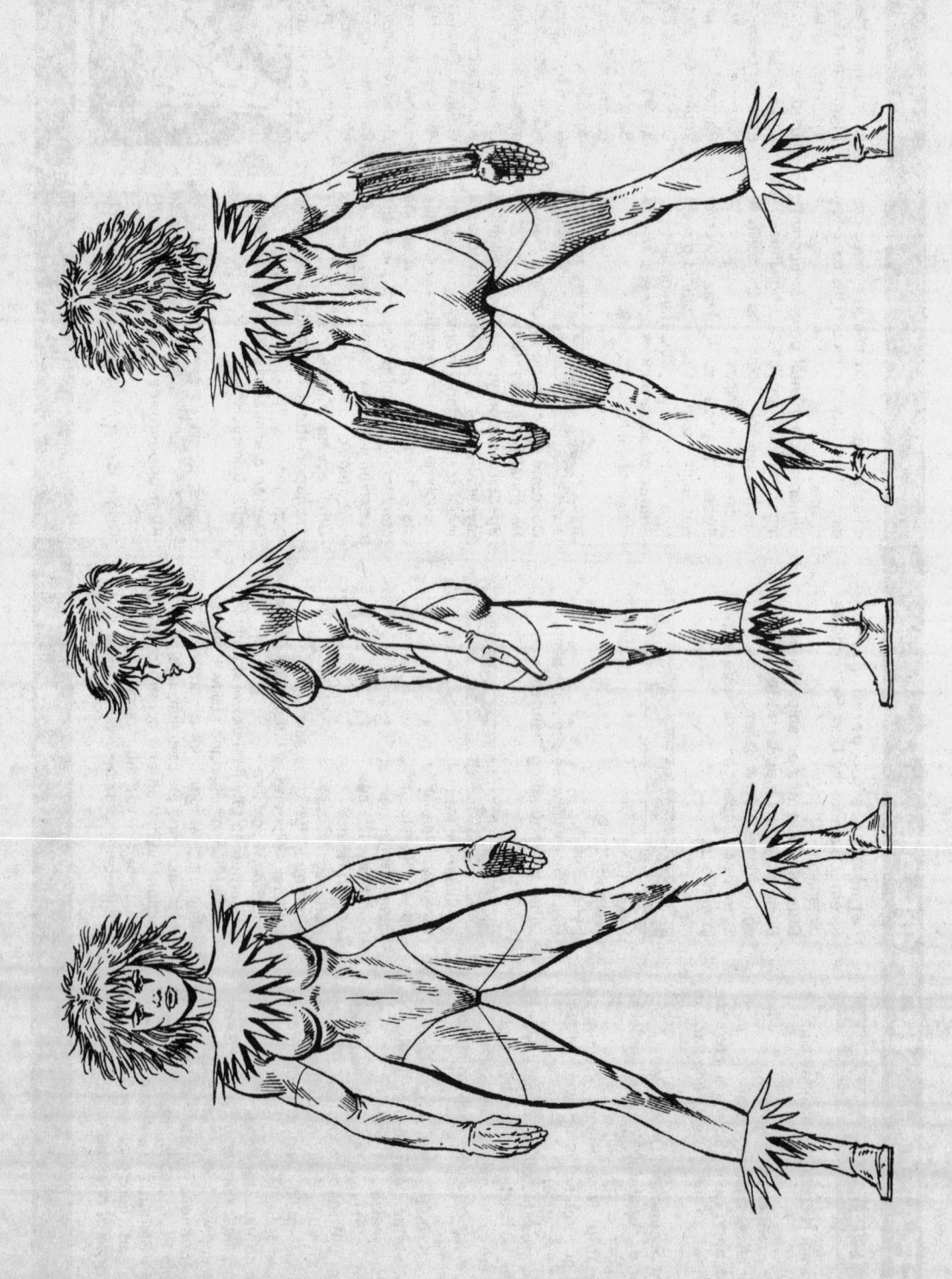

SCREAMING MIMI

BIOGRAPHICAL DATA

Real name: Mimi Schwartz
Other current aliases: None
Former aliases: None
Dual identity: Known to the U.S. legal authorities
Current Occupation: Professional criminal
Former occupation: Aspiring singer, mercenary
Citizenship: United States of America
Legal status: Criminal record in the U.S.
Place of birth: Boise, Idaho
Marital status: Single
Known relatives: None
Known confidants: Angar the Screamer
Known allies: The original Grapplers (Titania I [deceased], Letha I [deceased], Poundcakes), Auntie Freeze
Major enemies: The Thing, Dazzler, Quasar, Giant-Man II, Captain America, Hawkeye, Mockingbird
Usual base of operations: Mobile
Former bases of operations: Roxxon Coompany headquarters, New Jersey
Current group membership: None
Former group membership: The Grapplers, Unlimited Class Wrestling Federation
Extent of education: High school graduate

PHYSICAL DESCRIPTION

Height: 5'5"
Weight: 145 lbs
Eyes: Green
Hair: Blonde (dyed white)
Other distinguishing features: Slight build

POWERS AND ABILITIES

Intelligence: Normal
Strength: Enhanced human
Speed: Enhanced human; (vocal cords) superhuman
Stamina: Enhanced human; (vocal cords) superhuman
Durability: Enhanced human
Agility: Enhanced human
Reflexes: Enhanced human
Fighting skills: Extensively skilled hand-to-hand combatant using wrestling techniques, trained by Titania I
Special skills and abilities: Mimi has perfect pitch, the ability to hear in her mind the correct frequency for every musical note on the scale.
Superhuman physical powers: Aside from the above listed attributes, Mimi has the ability to scream with great volume and for a variety of effects. She is capable of emitting a sound equivalent in decibels to the noise of a jet engine passing 5 feet from one's ear. Every note on the scale she screams induces a different effect upon those who hear it. Low C causes low level anxiety and shortness of breath, D causes high level anxiety and panic attacks, E causes dizziness and vertigo, F causes nausea and stomach cramping, G causes severe headaches and fatigue, A causes blindness, B causes euphoria and eventual stupor, and high C causes the listener to visually hallucinate. By rapid oscillation between two notes she can combine effects. In addition, she can produce certain vocal effects in harmony with Angar the Screamer, such as specific sustained illusions. Her nervous system is immune to her own vocal powers.
Superhuman mental powers: None
Special limitations: Were she to use her vocal powers at full volume for an hour without resting, fatigue and hoarseness would impair her performance and effectiveness considerably.
Source of superhuman powers: Vocal cords were bionically altered and enhanced by technicians in the employ of Roxxon; her physical attributes were augmented by the Power Brokers special process, though she could not be fully augmented to the usual superhuman levels.

PARAPHERNALIA

Costume specifications: Synthetic stretch fabric
Personal weaponry: None
Special weaponry: None
Other accessories: None
Transportation: Conventional vehicles
Design and manufacture of paraphernalia: Roxxon technicians

BIBLIOGRAPHY

First appearance: MARVEL TWO-IN-ONE #54
Origin issue: Screaming Mimi's origin is as yet unrevealed.
Significant issues: MARVEL TWO-IN-ONE #54 (alongside Grapplers, fought Thundra in a wrestling ring); MARVEL TWO-IN-ONE #56 (led by Thundra into Project: Pegasus to smuggle in Nth Projector for Roxxon Oil Company, battled Quasar and Giant-Man II); DAZZLER #13 (alongside Grapplers, victimized Dazzler while in Ryker's Island prison); MARVEL TWO-IN-ONE #96 (alongside Grapplers, attempted to attack the Thing while he was in the hospital, battled Captain America); THING #33 (among the female wrestlers of the Unlimited Class Wrestling Federation, participated in a mass attack upon the Thing); AVENGERS SPOTLIGHT #28 (teamed with Angar the Screamer, impersonated Hawkeye and Mockingbird, battled them); CAPTAIN AMERICA #389-390 (among the various female superhumans aboard Superia's cruiseship, battled Captain America and Paladin)

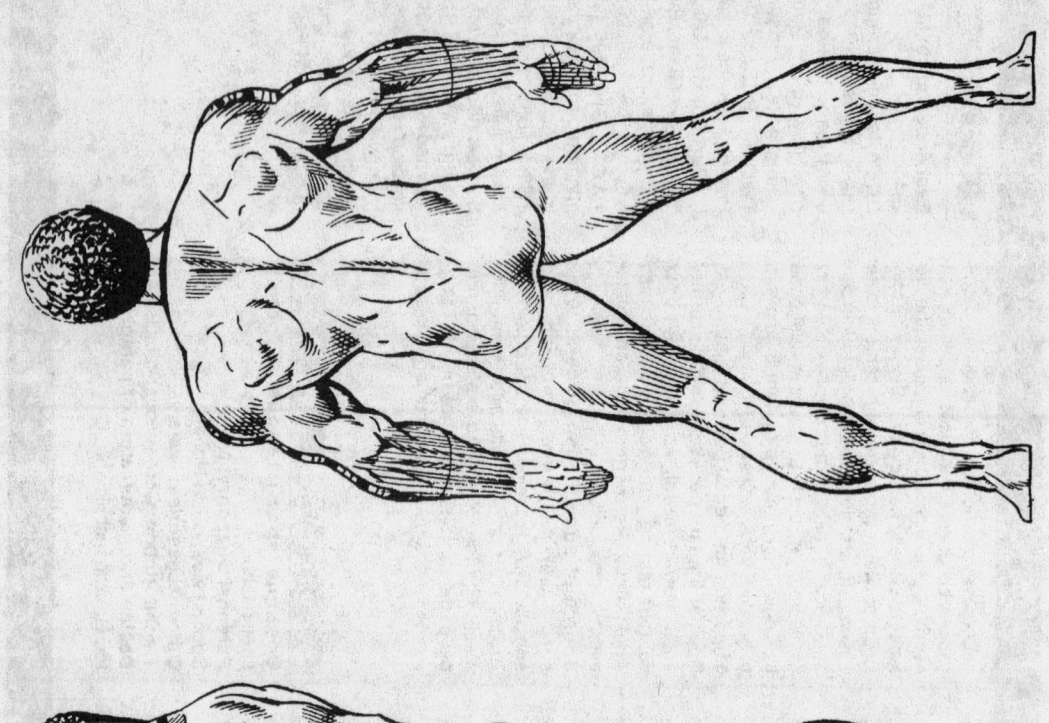

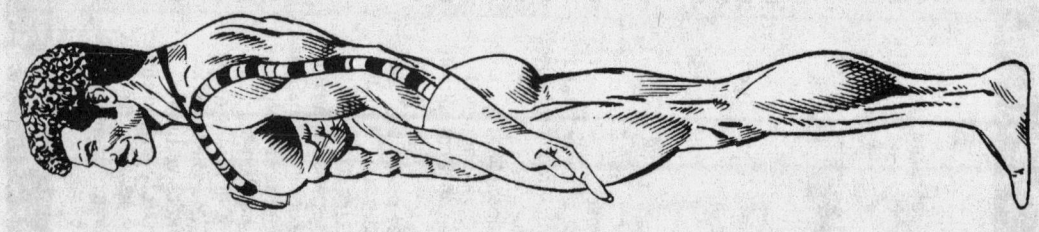

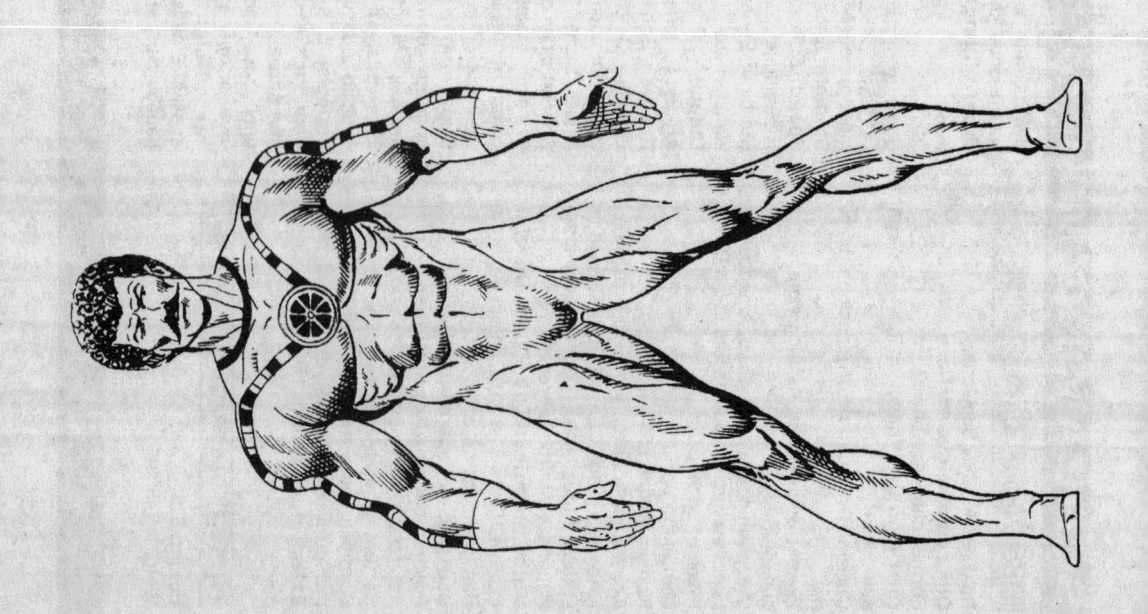

SEÑOR MUERTE™

SENOR MUERTE

BIOGRAPHICAL DATA

Real names: (Suerte/Muerte I) Ramon Garcia, (Suerte II) Jaime Garcia, (Muerte II) Philip Garcia
Other current aliases: (Suerte II) Mr. Luck, (Muerte II) Mr. Death
Former aliases: (I) Mr. Luck, Mr. Death, (Muerte II) Ramon Garcia
Dual Identity: (all) Publicly known
Occupation at time of death: (I) Owner of a chain of gambling casinos
Current occupation: (Suerte II, Muerte II) Convicts
Former occupation: (Suerte II) Professional gambler, thief, co-owner of gambling casinos, (Muerte II) Professional assassin, co-owner of gambling casinos
Citizenship: (all) Puerto Rico
Legal status: (all) Criminal records in the United States and Europe
Place of birth: (both) Hatillo, Puerto Rico
Place of death: (I) New York City
Cause of death: (I) Electrocuted by his own device while battling Luke Cage
Marital status: (all) Single
Known relatives: (I) Jaime Garcia, Philip Garcia (brothers), (Suerte II, Muerte II) Ramon Garcia (brother, deceased)
Known confidants: (all) None
Known allies: (I) None, (Suerte II) (former) Living Monolith, (Muerte II) (former) Tarantula I (deceased)
Major enemies: (I) Luke Cage, (Suerte II) Luke Cage, Iron Fist, (Muerte II) Captain America, Luke Cage, Iron Fist

Usual base of operations: (Suerte II, Muerte II) Mobile with casinos in Europe, Chicago, Las Vegas, and New York City
Base of operations at time of death: (all) None
Former base of operations: (all) None
Current group membership: (all) None
Former group membership: (all) None
Extent of education: (all) Unrevealed

Superhuman physical powers: (all) None
Superhuman mental powers: (all) None
Special limitations: (all) None
Source of superhuman powers: (all) Inapplicable

PARAPHERNALIA

Costume specifications: (I as Suerte) Conventional, (as Muerte) Synthetic stretch fabric containing circuitry enabling him to charge one hand or the other with electric current of 10,000 volts and to hurl bolts of electricity over short distances; (Suerte II) Conventional attire; (Muerte II) Sometimes wore a duplicate of his late brother's costume with the same properties, sometimes wore a blank-featured face-mask which could be reshaped to resemble a death's head, usually wore a coat and vest with specially designed pockets for carrying concealed weapons
Personal weaponry: (I, Suerte II) None, (Muerte II) An assortment of knives, high-powered handguns, hand grenades, and flame-throwers concealed in special pockets in his coat and vest
Special weaponry: (all) None
Other accessories: (I) A private casino equipped with booby-trapped devices, including a giant roulette wheel, razor-edged playing cards, poker chips, and giant dice
Transportation: (all) Conventional Design and manufacture of paraphernalia: Unrevealed

BIBLIOGRAPHY

First appearance: (I) HERO FOR HIRE #10; (Suerte II) POWER MAN/IRON FIST #56, (Muerte II) CAPTAIN AMERICA #224
Origin issue: (I) HERO FOR HIRE #10; (Suerte II, Muerte II) POWER MAN/IRON FIST #63
Significant issues: HERO FOR HIRE #5-6 (Suerte/Muerte I: behind the scenes sent men to kill Frank Jenks and Luke Cage); HERO FOR HIRE #10-11 (Suerte/Muerte I: attempted to kill Luke Cage, murdered rival casino owner, battled Cage, electrocuted); CAPTAIN AMERICA #224 (Muerte II: posed as his deceased brother; alongside Tarantula I, murdered government agent Ken Astor, attempted to hijack military convoy, battled Captain America); POWER MAN/IRON FIST #56 (Suerte II: attempted theft of Tutankhamen artifacts from museum, battled Cage and Iron Fist); POWER MAN/IRON FIST #63-64 (Suerte II, Muerte II: gambling operations disrupted by Cage and Iron Fist, set death-traps for Cage and Iron Fist, defeated by Cage and Iron Fist)

PHYSICAL DESCRIPTION

Height: (I, Muerte II) 6' 2", (Suerte II) 6' 1"
Weight: (I, Muerte II) 195 lbs., (Suerte II) 190 lbs.
Eyes: (both) Brown
Hair: (both) Brown
Other distinguishing features: (I, Muerte II) Moustache

POWERS AND ABILITIES

Intelligence: (all) Normal
Strength: (all) Athlete
Speed: (all) Athlete
Stamina: (all) Athlete
Durability: (all) Athlete
Agility: (all) Athlete
Reflexes: (all) Athlete
Fighting skills: (all) Average hand-to-hand combatant using basic streetfighting techniques, (Muerte II) Highly skilled in the use of knives, firearms, and explosives
Special skills and abilities: (all) Talented gamblers, highly skilled businessmen, (Suerte II) Expert thief, (Muerte II) Expert assassin

SERSI™

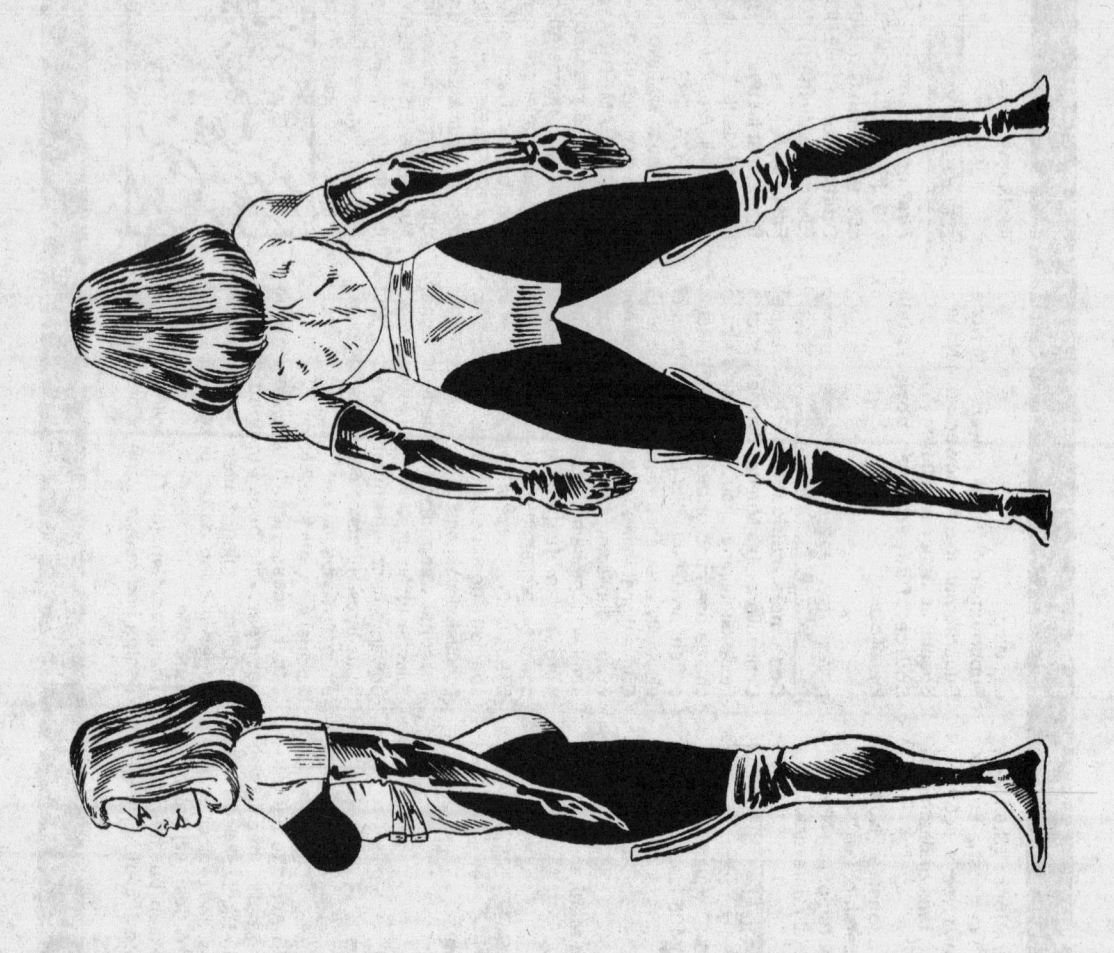

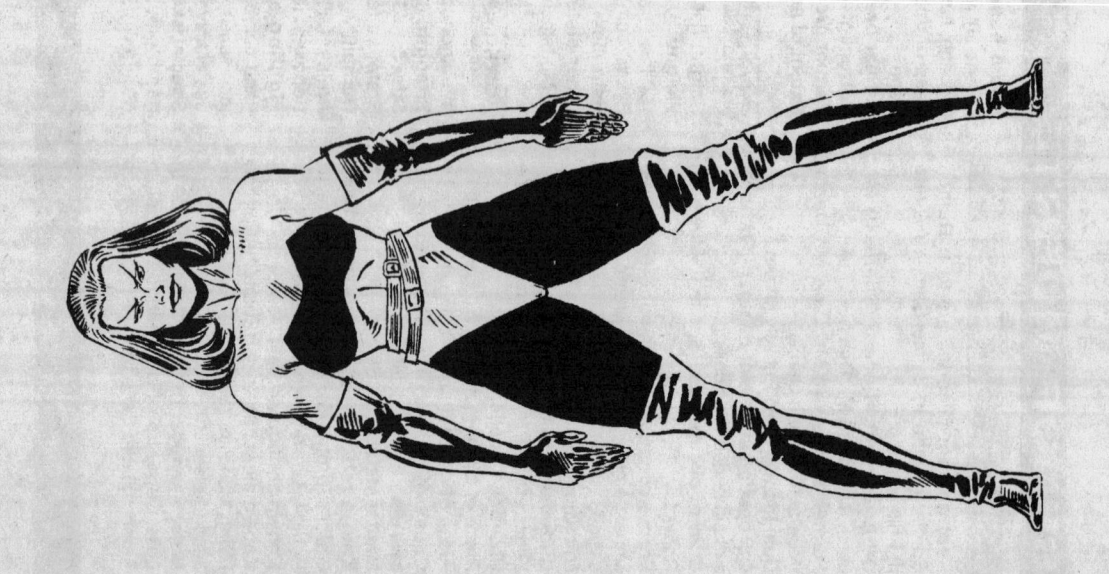

SERSI

BIOGRAPHICAL DATA

Real name: Sersi
Other current aliases: None
Former aliases: Circe, Sylvia Sersi
Dual identity: None; the fact that Sersi is an Eternal has been publicly revealed but is generally disbelieved by the Earth's populace.
Current occupation: Adventurer
Former occupation: Dancer, actress, stage magician, hedonist
Citizenship: Olympia, Greece, capital city of the Eternals of Earth; naturalized citizen of the United States
Legal status: No criminal record
Place of birth: Olympia, Greece
Marital status: Unrevealed, but unmarried at present
Known relatives: Helios (father), Perse (mother)
Known confidants: Dr. Samuel Holden, Black Knight III, (former) Odysseus (deceased), Thane Ector (deceased), Dave Chatterton (deceased)
Known allies: The Eternals of Earth, the Avengers, Karkas, Ransak the Reject, Captain America, Thor I, Iron Man II, Spider-Man, Alpha Flight
Major enemies: Ghaur, Brother Tode (deceased), Deviants, Dromedan, Maelstrom, Blastaar, Nebula, Collector, Kang, Lyra, Grim Reaper, (former) Odysseus (deceased), Thane Ector (deceased), Sybil Dorn (deceased), Kro
Usual base of operations: New York City
Former bases of operations: (in ancient times) The Greek island of Aegaea
Current group membership: Avengers, Eternals of Earth
Former group membership: None known
Extent of education: Unrevealed

PHYSICAL DESCRIPTION

Height: 5' 9"
Weight: 140 lbs.
Eyes: Blue
Hair: Black
Other distinguishing features: None

POWERS AND ABILITIES

Intelligence: Gifted
Strength: Superhuman Class 25 (can supplement her physical strength by psionically levitating heavy objects)
Speed: Enhanced human
Flight speed: Supersonic
Stamina: Metahuman
Durability: Metahuman regenerative
Agility: Superhuman
Reflexes: Superhuman
Fighting skills: Fair hand-to-hand combatant, relies on her superhuman powers in combat
Special skills and abilities: As a trained dancer who has perfected her art over centuries, aided by her superhuman physique, Sersi has extraordinary athletic ability.
Superhuman physical powers: Aside from the above listed attributes, Sersi possesses the ability to manipulate cosmic energy to augment her life force, granting her virtual invulnerability and immortality, the ability to project cosmic energy from her eyes or hands in the form of heat, light, or concussive force and possibly other powers.
Superhuman mental powers: Sersi's psionic ability to rearrange molecular structure of objects is far greater than that of any other Eternal. Also possesses total mental control over her physical form, granting virtual invulnerability and immortality; ability to levitate herself and thus fly at superhuman speed; ability to cast illusions to disguise her appearance and that of others from the perceptions of normal human beings; ability to teleport herself and others with her.
Special limitations: The limits on Sersi's molecular rearrangement powers are as yet unrevealed. Like other Eternals, Sersi finds their method of self-teleportation physically unpleasant and uses this power sparingly.
Source of superhuman powers: Member of the race of superhumans known as the Eternals

PARAPHERNALIA

Costume specifications: Materials of unknown composition
Personal weaponry: None
Special weaponry: None
Other accessories: None
Transportation: Self-levitation, self-teleportation, or Eternal or Avengers vehicles
Design and manufacture of paraphernalia: Eternal craftsmen

BIBLIOGRAPHY

First appearance: (as Circe) STRANGE TALES Vol. 1 #109, (as Sersi) ETERNALS Vol. 1 #3
Origin issue: Sersi's origin is as yet unrevealed.
Significant issues: STRANGE TALES Vol. 1 #109 (revealed to have imprisoned imps in Pandora's Box in ancient times); ETERNALS Vol. 1 #3-5 (battled Deviants in New York City); ETERNALS Vol. 1 #6 (publicly revealed herself to be an Eternal); THOR #284-289 (met and became ally of Thor I); THOR #291-292 (participated in battle between Olympian gods and Eternals); AVENGERS #246-248 (her party in New York invaded by Delphan Brothers; chosen by Uni-Mind to stay on Earth); ETERNALS Vol. 2 #1-12 (battled Ghaur alongside Eternals, Thor, and West Coast Avengers); AVENGERS #308-310 (traveled into Negative Zone with Avengers to find Blastaar, seemingly killed by Blastaar, returned to life); AVENGERS #314-318 (joined Avengers, helped them defeat Nebula); AVENGERS #334-339 (captured by Thane Ector, fought Sybil Dorn, became his ally); AVENGERS #358-359 (slew murderer Anskar on Arkon's world)

SETH™

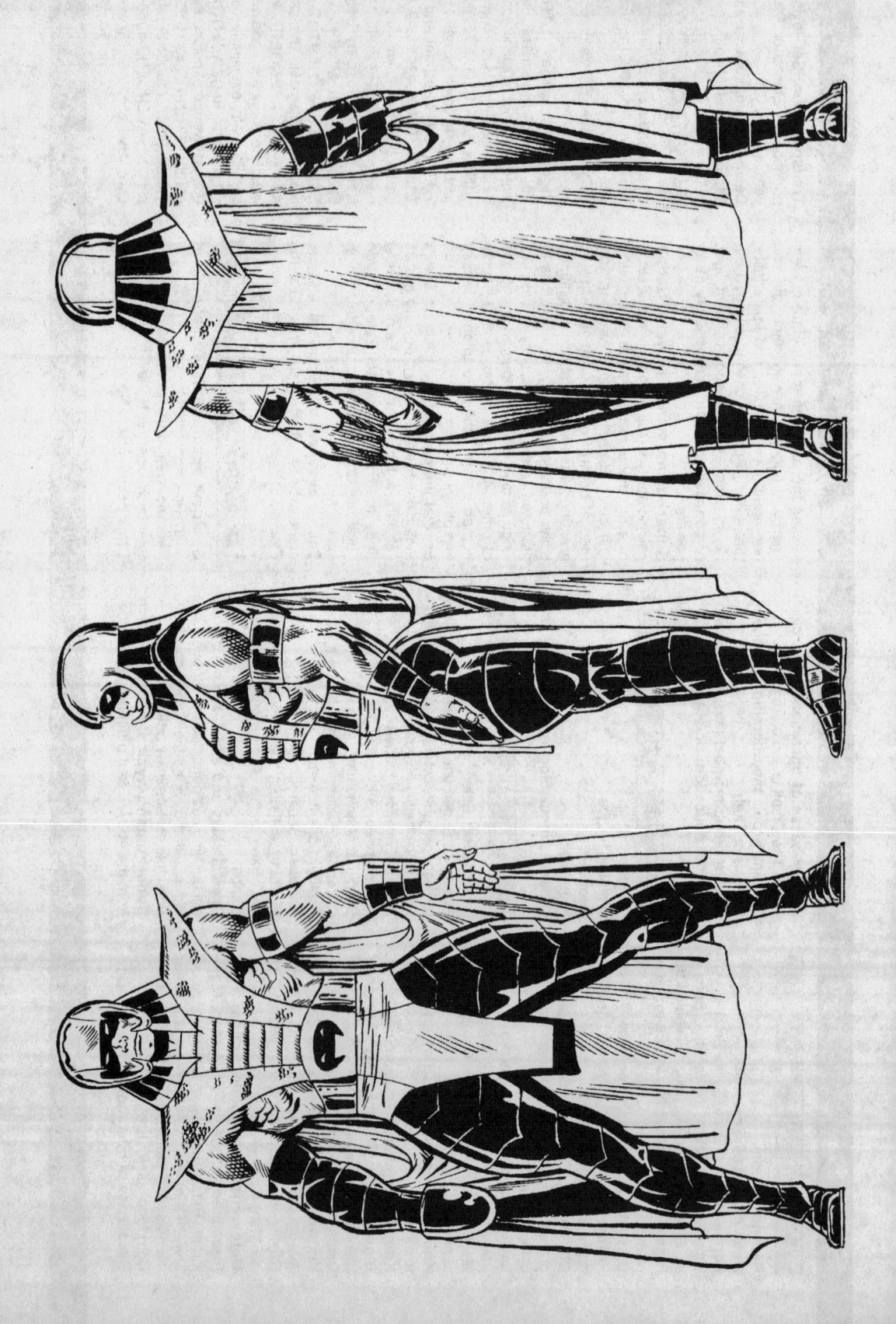

SETH

BIOGRAPHICAL DATA

Real name: Seth
Other current aliases: The Serpent God, Lord of the Unliving
Former aliases: None known
Dual identity: None; the general populace of Earth is unaware of Seth's existence except as a mythological character
Current occupation: Egyptian god of evil and death
Former occupation: Unrevealed
Citizenship: Celestial Heliopolis
Legal status: No criminal record
Place of birth: Unrevealed
Marital status: Separated
Known relatives: Nephtys (wife), Osiris (stepfather), Isis (mother), Horus (brother)
Known confidants: None
Known allies: The Devourer, Cheops (former) Earth Force
Major enemies: Thor, Odin, Gods of Heliopolis
Usual base of operations: Heliopolis
Former bases of operations: Unrevealed
Current group membership: Gods of Heliopolis
Former group membership: None
Extent of education: Unrevealed

PHYSICAL DESCRIPTION

Height: 6' 4"
Weight: 395 lbs.
Eyes: Brown
Hair: Red
Other distinguishing features: Seth's right hand is missing. He usually wears a metal cup over it.

POWERS AND ABILITIES

Intelligence: Above normal
Strength: Superhuman Class 75
Speed: Enhanced human
Stamina: Metahuman
Durability: Superhuman regenerative
Agility: Superhuman
Reflexes: Superhuman
Fighting skills: Unrevealed
Special skills and abilities: Extensive knowledge of necromancy
Superhuman physical powers: In addition to the above listed physical abilities, Seth possesses the power to project destructive force from his hand, to mesmerize others with a glance, and to cast various mystical spells for a variety of effects
Superhuman mental powers: Unrevealed
Special limitations: None
Source of superhuman powers: Seth is a member of the race of superhumans known as the Egyptian gods of Heliopolis. His power is augmented by manipulation of the forces of magic.

PARAPHERNALIA

Costume specifications: Heliopolitan materials
Personal weaponry: None
Special weaponry: None
Other accessories: None
Transportation: Various, including interdimensional teleportation
Design and manufacture of paraphernalia: Inapplicable

BIBLIOGRAPHY

First appearance: THOR #240
Origin issue: Seth's origin is as yet unrevealed.
Significant issues: THOR #240-241 (dismembered Osiris, defeated Horus, imprisoned family in pyramid for three thousand years, upon their freedom attacked them, Thor, and Odin with skeletal horsemen, defeated when energy projected through Odin's axe severed his right hand, flung into space); MARVEL TWO-IN-ONE #22-23 (attacked Thor in guise of Donald Blake, brought skeletal army to Earth to battle Thor and Thing, imprisoned Horus in Heliopolis, summoned monstrous Devourer, apparently surrendered when Devourer went on rampage); THOR #386 (plotted to invade Asgard); THOR #390 (directed invasion force to attack Asgard); THOR #395-397 (endowed three humans with superhuman powers to become his mortal allies, the Earth Force; attempted to gain the soul of Hogun the Grim; commanded second wave assault on Asgard); THOR #398-399 (revealed to have captured Odin and stolen powers of Egyptian gods; successfully conquered Asgard; battled Balder); THOR #400 (battled Earth Force, Odin, Hogun, Black Knight; transformed into huge serpent, dwindled into nothingness when Black Knight's ensorcelled body ripped through his jaws)
Note: Seth is not to be confused with Set the Elder God.

SHADOWCAT

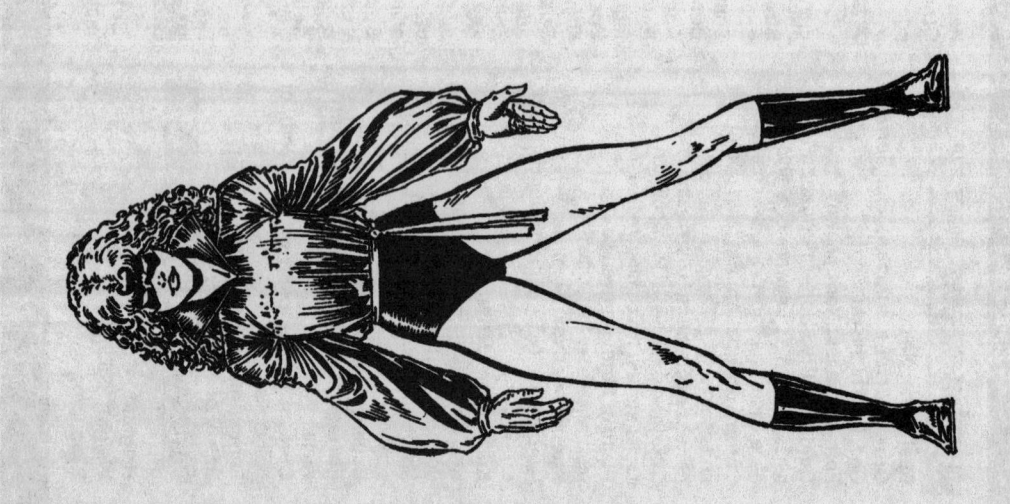

SHADOWCAT

BIOGRAPHICAL DATA

Real name: Katherine "Kitty" Pryde
Other current aliases: None
Former aliases: Ariel, Sprite
Dual identity: Secret
Current occupation: Adventurer, student
Former occupation: None
Citizenship: United States of America
Legal status: Minor, no criminal record
Place of birth: Deerfield, Illinois
Marital status: Single
Known relatives: Carmen Pryde (father), Theresa Pryde (mother), Samuel Prydeman (grandfather, deceased), Chava Rosanoff (great-aunt, deceased)
Known confidants: Storm, Illyana Rasputin, Lockheed, Phoebe Huntsman, Courtney Ross
Known allies: Excalibur, the X-Men, Wolverine, Fantastic Four, Illyana Rasputin, Lockheed, students at St. Searle
Major enemies: White Queen, Ogun, Shadow King
Usual base of operations: Excalibur's lighthouse off the coast of Britain
Former bases of operations: Professor Xavier's School for Gifted Youngsters, Salem Center, Westchester County, New York; Moira MacTaggart's Mutant Research Centre, Muir Island, Scotland
Current group membership: Excalibur
Former group membership: The X-Men
Extent of education: Now taking university-level courses

PHYSICAL DESCRIPTION

Height: 5' 6"
Weight: 110 lbs. (when fully solid)
Eyes: Brown
Hair: Brown
Other distinguishing features: None

POWERS AND ABILITIES

Intelligence: Genius
Strength: Athlete
Speed: Athlete
Stamina: Athlete
Durability: Athlete
Agility: Peak human
Reflexes: Athlete
Fighting skills: Moderate expertise of the martial arts of the Japanese ninja and samurai
Special skills and abilities: Shadowcat is highly talented in the design and use of computer hardware. She is a competent beginning driver of automobiles, a skilled pilot of piston and jet engine aircraft, and a competent pilot of certain advanced interstellar vehicles. She has been in ballet and modern dance. She speaks fluent English, Japanese, Russian, and royal and standard languages of the alien Shi'Ar, and has moderate expertise in Gaelic, Hebrew, and German.
Superhuman physical powers: Ability to pass through solid matter ("phase") by altering the vibratory rates of her atoms. The phasing process disrupts the flow of electricity in any object through which she passes. Shadowcat can extend her phasing effect to her own clothing or any other object with mass up to that of a small truck, as long as she remains in physical contact with it. Using her phasing ability Shadowcat can walk on air.
Superhuman mental powers: None
Special limitations: At present Shadowcat cam only become fully solid and maintain her solidity through a conscious act of will. Shadowcat is also slightly nearsighted
Source of superhuman powers: Genetic mutation.

PARAPHERNALIA

Costume specifications: Synthetic stretch fabric and leather
Personal weaponry: None
Special weaponry: None
Other accessories: None
Transportation: Various
Design and manufacture of paraphernalia: Inapplicable

BIBLIOGRAPHY

First appearance: X-MEN #129
Origin issue: X-MEN #129
Significant issues: X-MEN #129 (X-Men and White Queen both attempted to recruit her for their respective schools); X-MEN #130 (first met Cyclops, Phoenix I, Nightcrawler), X-MEN #131 (helped rescue X-Men from Hellfire Club); X-MEN #138 (joined X-Men); X-MEN #139 (assumed costumed identity of Sprite II), X-MEN #141-142 (Kitty's adult self rrom an alternate future took possession of her body in the present to help X-Men thwart assassination of Senator Robert Kelly by second Brotherhood of Evil Mutants); X-MEN #143 (singlehandedly defeated N'Garai demon); X-MEN #151-152 (briefly attended White Queen's Massachusetts Academy); X-MEN #166 (first met alien dragon Lockheed on another planet); X-MEN #168 (reunited with Lockheed on Earth); X-MEN #177-179 (abducted by Morlocks, nearly forced to wed Caliban); NEW MUTANTS #15-17 (abducted by White Queen, rescued by New Mutants); X-MEN #183 (ended romantic relationship with Colossus); KITTY PRYDE AND WOLVERINE #1-6 (brainwashed by Ogun into becoming ninja assassin, sent to attack Wolverine, assumed new costumed identity of Shadowcat); X-MEN #211 (injured by Harpoon's energy spear in massacre of the Morlocks, could not regain solidity); FANTASTIC FOUR VS. THE X-MEN #1-4 (cured by efforts of Doctor Doom and Mister Fantastic, but can now only maintain solidity through an act of conscious will); EXCALIBUR SPECIAL EDITION #1 (became founding member of Excalibur); EXCALIBUR #33 (began studies at St. Searle's school for girls in Britain)

SHALLA BAL

SHALLA BAL

BIOGRAPHICAL DATA

Real name: Shalla Bal
Other current aliases: None
Former aliases: Helena
Dual identity: None; the general populace of Earth is unaware of Shalla Bal's existence
Current occupation: Empress of Zenn-La
Former occupation: Unrevealed
Citizenship: Zenn-La
Legal status: No criminal record
Place of birth: Planet Zenn-La, Deneb System, Milky Way Galaxy
Marital status: Single
Known relatives: Anddar Bal (father)
Known confidants: The Silver Surfer (Norrin Radd)
Known allies: The Silver Surfer, Empress S'byll, the Cotati
Major enemies: Galactus, Doctor Doom, Mephisto, the Elders of the Universe, Nenora, Enslavers, Kree, Obliterator
Usual base of operations: Planet Zenn-La, Deneb System, Milky Way Galaxy
Former bases of operations: Latveria
Current group membership: None
Former group membership: None
Extent of education: Unrevealed

PHYSICAL DESCRIPTION

Height: 5' 9"
Weight: 125 lbs.
Eyes: Blue
Hair: Black
Other distinguishing features: None

POWERS AND ABILITIES

Intelligence: Normal
Strength: Normal
Speed: Normal
Stamina: Normal
Durability: Normal
Agility: Normal
Reflexes: Normal
Fighting skills: Minimal
Special skills and abilities: Accomplished in administering government
Superhuman physical powers: Zenn-Lavians have extraordinarily long life spans. Hence, Shalla Bal has lived for centuries although she is still physically a young woman. Shalla Bal was once able to restore life to Zenn-La's ecosphere due to a fragment of the Silver Surfer's cosmic power that he placed within her. Apparently she can still cause plant life to grow wherever she walks.
Superhuman mental powers: None
Special limitations: None
Source of superhuman powers: (long life span) Member of a race of aliens known as Zenn-Lavians, (plant growth ability) A portion of the Silver Surfer's power cosmic

PARAPHERNALIA

Costume specifications: Unidentified Zenn-La fabrics
Personal weaponry: None
Special weaponry: None
Other accessories: None
Transportation: Zenn-La's imperial starships and other modes of transport
Design and manufacture of paraphernalia: Unrevealed

BIBLIOGRAPHY

First appearance: SILVER SURFER Vol. 1 #1
Origin issue: SILVER SURFER Vol. 1 #1
Significant issues: SILVER SURFER Vol. 1 #1 (recounted how Shalla Bal was separated from her lover Norrin Radd when he became the Silver Surfer); SILVER SURFER Vol. 1 #3 (first used as a pawn by Mephisto against the Silver Surfer); FANTASTIC FOUR #155-157 (transported by Mephisto to Latveria and caused by him to believe she was a Latverian peasant named Helena); SILVER SURFER Vol. 2 #1 (escaped destruction of Zenn-La's ecosphere by Galactus, was abducted to earth by Mephisto, received portion of Silver Surfer's power cosmic, returned to Zenn-La and used this power to restore its ecosphere); SILVER SURFER Vol. 3 #2 (first appeared as Empress of Zenn-La); SILVER SURFER Vol. 3 #7 (told by Silver Surfer their romance was over); SILVER SURFER Vol. 3 #8-9 (held hostage with mantis by Elders, was rescued by Silver Surfer); SILVER SURFER Vol. 3 #20 (met Kree leader Nenora); SILVER SURFER Vol. 3 #21 (asked Silver Surfer to protect Zenn-La from Obliterator); SILVER SURFER Vol. 3 #25-31 (made alliance with Skrull Empress S'byll against Kree, informed by Cotati that Nenora was a disguised Skrull, was captured by Nenora's Kree Sentry, freed by Cotati, told S'byll and Surfer about Nenora's true nature, returned to Zenn-La by Surfer); SILVER SURFER: THE ENSLAVERS (taken captive by the Enslavers, was reunited with Surfer); SILVER SURFER Vol. 3 #50 (flashback showed Shalla Bal telling Norrin Radd about his father's suicide); SILVER SURFER Vol. 3 #57 (flashback to Shalla Bal's first meeting with Norrin Radd when they were children); SILVER SURFER: HOMECOMING (abducted with planet Zenn-La by the Great One, was reunited with Silver Surfer, disintegrated along with Great One's construct pocket universe); SILVER SURFER/WARLOCK: RESURRECTION #1-4 (Silver Surfer sought to return her to life)

SHANG-CHI

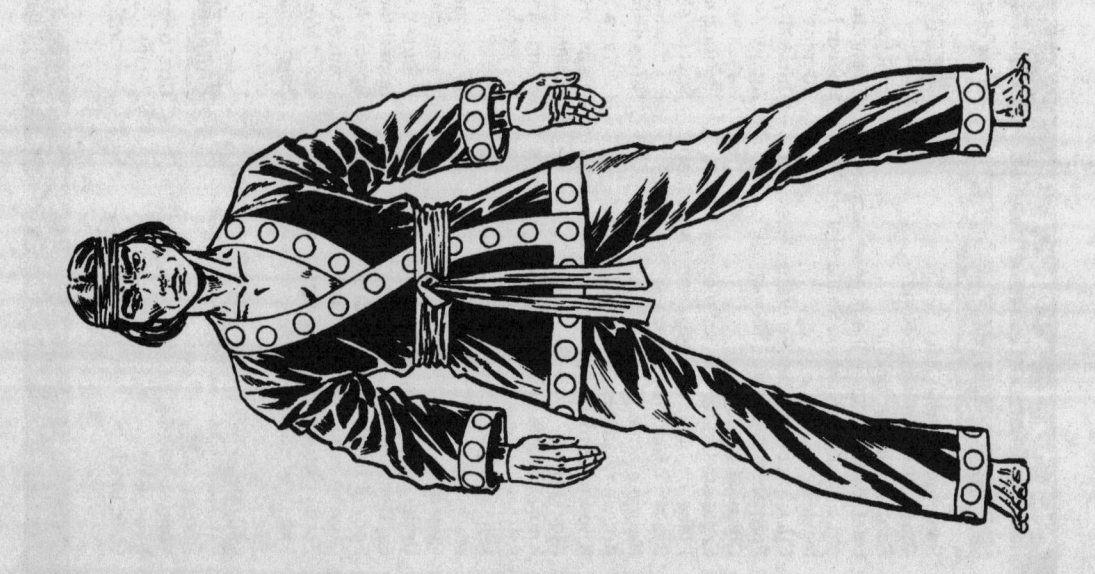

SHANG-CHI

BIOGRAPHICAL DATA

Real name: Shang-Chi
Other current aliases: Master of Kung Fu
Former aliases: None
Dual identity: None
Current occupation: Adventurer, secret agent
Former occupation: Fisherman
Citizenship: People's Republic of China
Legal status: No criminal record
Place of birth: Hunan province, People's Republic of China
Marital status: Single
Known relatives: Fu Manchu (father, deceased), mother (name unrevealed), Fah Lo Suee (half-sister)
Known confidants: Leiko Wu
Known allies: Sir Denis Nayland Smith, Dr. Petrie, Black Jack Tarr, Clive Reston, Leiko Wu, Shen Kui (the Cat)
Major enemies: Fu Manchu (deceased), Fah Lo Suee, Shadow-Stalker, Razor-Fist, Pavane, Shock-Wave, Skullcrusher, Zaran
Usual base of operations: Freelance Restorations, Stormhaven Castle, Scotland
Former bases of operations: MI-6 headquarters, London, England
Current group membership: Freelance Restorations
Former group membership: MI-6
Extent of education: Unrevealed

PHYSICAL DESCRIPTION

Height: 5' 10"
Weight: 175 lbs.
Eyes: Brown
Hair: Black
Other distinguishing features: None

POWERS AND ABILITIES

Intelligence: Above normal
Strength: Athlete
Stamina: Athlete
Durability: Athlete
Agility: Peak human
Reflexes: Peak human
Fighting skills: Greatest living practitioner of Kung Fu, expert at related martial arts
Special skills: Highly trained in arts of concentration and meditation, expert with various hand-weapons including bo, nunchakus, and shuriken
Superhuman physical powers: None
Superhuman mental powers: None
Special limitations: None
Source of superhuman powers: None

PARAPHERNALIA

Costume specifications: Ordinary fabric
Personal weaponry: None
Special weaponry: None
Other accessories: None
Transportation: Various vehicles supplied by Freelance Restorations
Design and manufacture of paraphernalia: Inapplicable

BIBLIOGRAPHY

First appearance: SPECIAL MARVEL EDITION #15
Origin issue: SPECIAL MARVEL EDITION #15
Significant issues: SPECIAL MARVEL EDITION #15 (raised and trained in martial arts by father, Fu Manchu, and his instructors; sent on mission to murder Dr. Petrie, first met Sir Denis Nayland Smith, learned Fu Manchu was evil, became Fu Manchu's enemy); SPECIAL MARVEL EDITION #16 (battled Midnight); MASTER OF KUNG FU #17 (first met Black Jack Tarr); MASTER OF KUNG FU #18 (became Smith's ally, opposed Fu Manchu, battled Si-Fan assassins); MASTER OF KUNG FU #19 (encountered Man-Thing); GIANT-SIZE SPIDER-MAN #2 (first met Spider-Man); GIANT-SIZE MASTER OF KUNG FU #3 (first met Clive Reston, battled Shadow-Stalker and Fu Manchu's Phansigar followers, rescued Dr. Petrie from Fu Manchu); MASTER OF KUNG FU #26 (first opposed Fah Lo Suee); MASTER OF KUNG FU #29-31 (opposed Carlton Velcro, first battled Razor-Fist and Pavane); MASTER OF KUNG FU #33 (first met Leiko Wu); MASTER OF KUNG FU #34-35 (opposed Mordillo and Brynocki); MASTER OF KUNG FU #38-39 (first encountered Cat); MASTER OF KUNG FU ANNUAL #1 (first met Iron Fist); MASTER OF KUNG FU #42-43 (first battled Shock-Wave); MASTER OF KUNG FU #45-50 (with Smith, Tarr, Reston, and Wu, opposed Fu Manchu); MASTER OF KUNG FU #51 (with Tarr, Reston, and Wu, quit MI-6); DEADLY HANDS OF KUNG FU #31 (teamed with Iron Fist, White Tiger, and Jack of Hearts against the Corporation); MARVEL TWO-IN-ONE #29 (first met the Thing; battled HYDRA); MASTER OF KUNG FU #59-60 (involved in game between Doctor Doom and the Prime Mover); MASTER OF KUNG FU #61 (first battled Skullcrusher); MASTER OF KUNG FU #77-79 (first battled Zaran); MARVEL TEAM-UP #84-85 (teamed with Spider-Man, Black Widow, and Nick Fury against Viper, Boomerang, and Silver Samurai); MASTER OF KUNG FU #83-89 (opposed Fu Manchu and Fah Lo Suee); MASTER OF KUNG FU #94 (with Smith, Tarr, Reston, and Wu, formed Freelance Restorations Ltd.); MASTER OF KUNG FU #118 (witnessed death of Fu Manchu); ROM #38-39 (teamed with Rom against Dire Wraiths); MASTER OF KUNG FU #125 (quit Freelance Restorations, forsook life as an adventurer; retired to remote Yang-Yin, China, as a fisherman); MARVEL COMICS PRESENTS #1-8 (returned from China; rejoined Tarr, Reston, and Wu; rescued Wu from terrorists; dosed with slow acting poison); MASTER OF KUNG FU: BLEEDING BLACK (cured of poison's effects by Fu Manchu's elixir vitae)

SHAPE

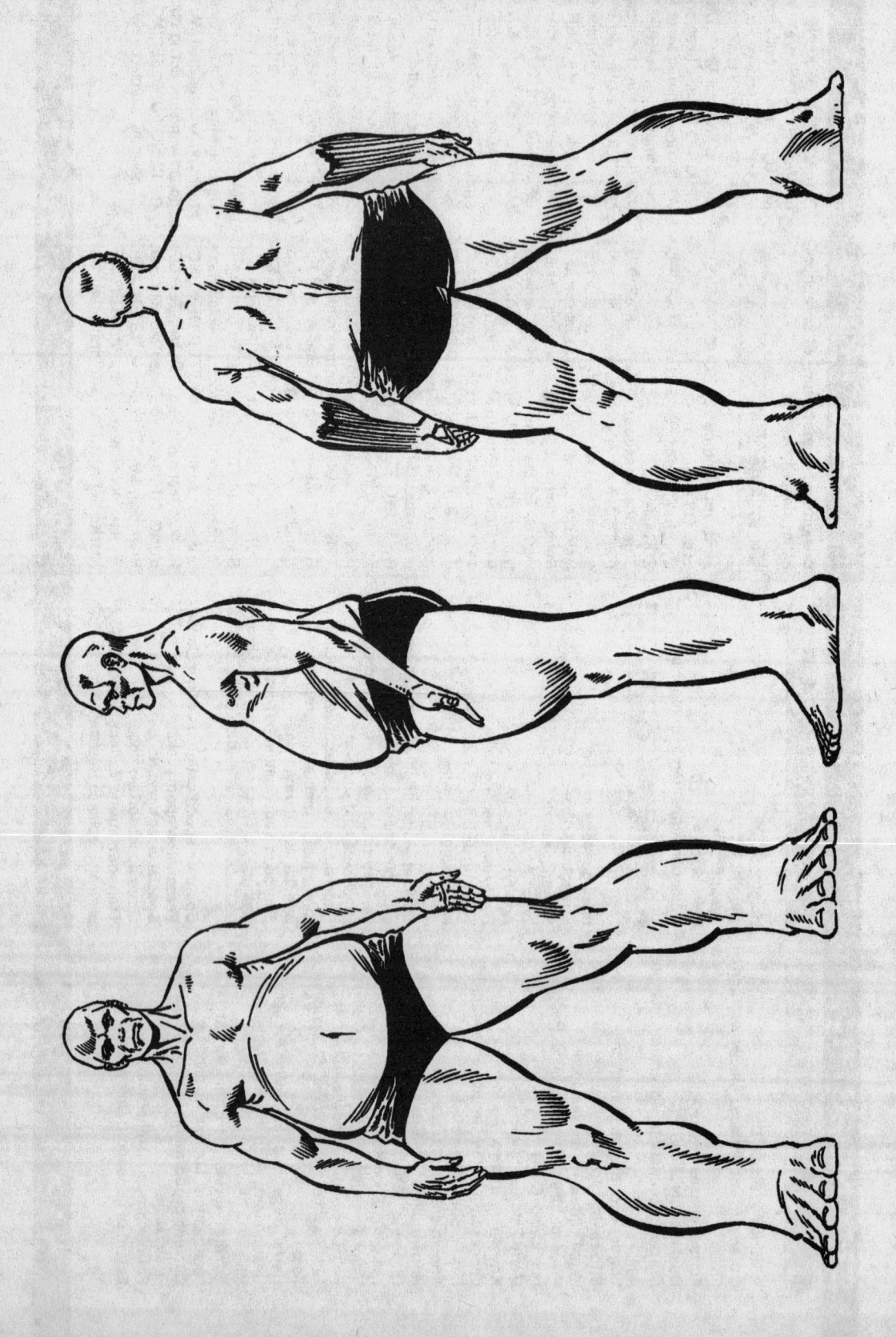

SHAPE

BIOGRAPHICAL DATA

Real name: Raleigh Lund
Other current aliases: None
Former aliases: None
Dual Identity: Publicly known to the citizens of the United States of America, on the alternate Earth of the Squadron Supreme
Occupation at time of death: Public crusader, adventurer, babysitter
Former occupation: Criminal
Citizenship: United States of America, on the alternate Earth of the Squadron Supreme
Legal status: Criminal record pardoned when he underwent behavior modification
Place of birth: Simak, Lowengard, U.S.A.
Marital status: Single
Known relatives: None
Known confidants: Arcanna Jones, Drusilla Jones
Known allies: (current) Squadron Supreme (Hyperion, Dr. Spectrum, Whizzer, Power Princess, Moonstone II, Skylark, Haywire); (former) Institute of Evil (Dr. Decibel, Foxfire, Quagmire, Ape X, Lamprey)
Major enemies: Master Menace, the Redeemers
Usual base of operations: Project: Pegasus, Mt. Athena, New York
Former bases of operations: Squadron City
Current group membership: Squadron Supreme
Former group membership: Institute of Evil
Extent of education: Special education drop-out

PHYSICAL DESCRIPTION

Height: 5' 9"
Weight: 255 lbs
Eyes: Blue
Hair: Bald
Other distinguishing features: The Shape is totally hairless and has approximately 200 pounds of body mass that he can shift from one area of his body to another. When he is relaxed it settles in his legs and lower body.

POWERS AND ABILITIES

Intelligence: Below normal
Strength: Enhanced human
Speed: Normal
Stamina: Athlete
Durability: Superhuman
Agility: Normal
Reflexes: Athlete
Fighting skills: Moderate knowledge of hand-to-hand combat incorporating ability to shift mass from one part of his body to another
Special skills and abilities: A natural affinity for children
Superhuman physical powers: The Shape's entire body is extremely rubbery and malleable. He can shift up to 80% of his physical mass from one part of his body to another at will, thus altering his entire shape. He can use this mass to elongate, compress, or enlarge various parts of his body, or form non-humanoid shapes such as hammer-shaped fists or a trampoline-shaped torso. His bones stretch to a maximum of five times their ordinary length. His body tissue can resist extreme temperatures and pressures, burning, lacerations, ballistic penetration, and impacts, without sustaining injury. The Shape has a high physical pain threshold.
Superhuman mental powers: None
Special limitations: The Shape's low intelligence prevents him from thinking of more creative uses for his shifting body mass. He is not invulnerable: certain extreme physical injuries are beyond his ability to resist.
Source of superhuman powers: Unrevealed

PARAPHERNALIA

Costume specifications: Synthetic stretch fabric
Personal weaponry: None
Special weaponry: None
Other accessories: None
Transportation: (former) Squadron jets
Design and manufacture of paraphernalia: Tom Thumb.

BIBLIOGRAPHY

First appearance: SQUADRON SUPREME #5
Origin issue: Shape's origin has yet to be revealed.
Significant issues: SQUADRON SUPREME #5 (battled Squadron as member of Institute of Evil); SQUADRON SUPREME #6 (underwent behavior modification, joined the Squadron); SQUADRON SUPREME #8 (helped supervise the manufacturing of force field belts); SQUADRON SUPREME #9 (babysat for Arcanna Jones' three children); SQUADRON SUPREME #12 (behavior modification reversed, but sided with Squadron against Nighthawk and the Redeemers, helped get pregnant Arcanna to delivery room); SQUADRON SUPREME GRAPHIC NOVEL (accompanied Squadron in futile struggle against the Nth Man); QUASAR #13 (traveled to Earth, Shape and Haywire mentally coerced by the Over-Mind to prevent Quasar from following the starship in which the Over-Mind had kidnaped the Squadron Supreme)

SHAPER OF WORLDS™

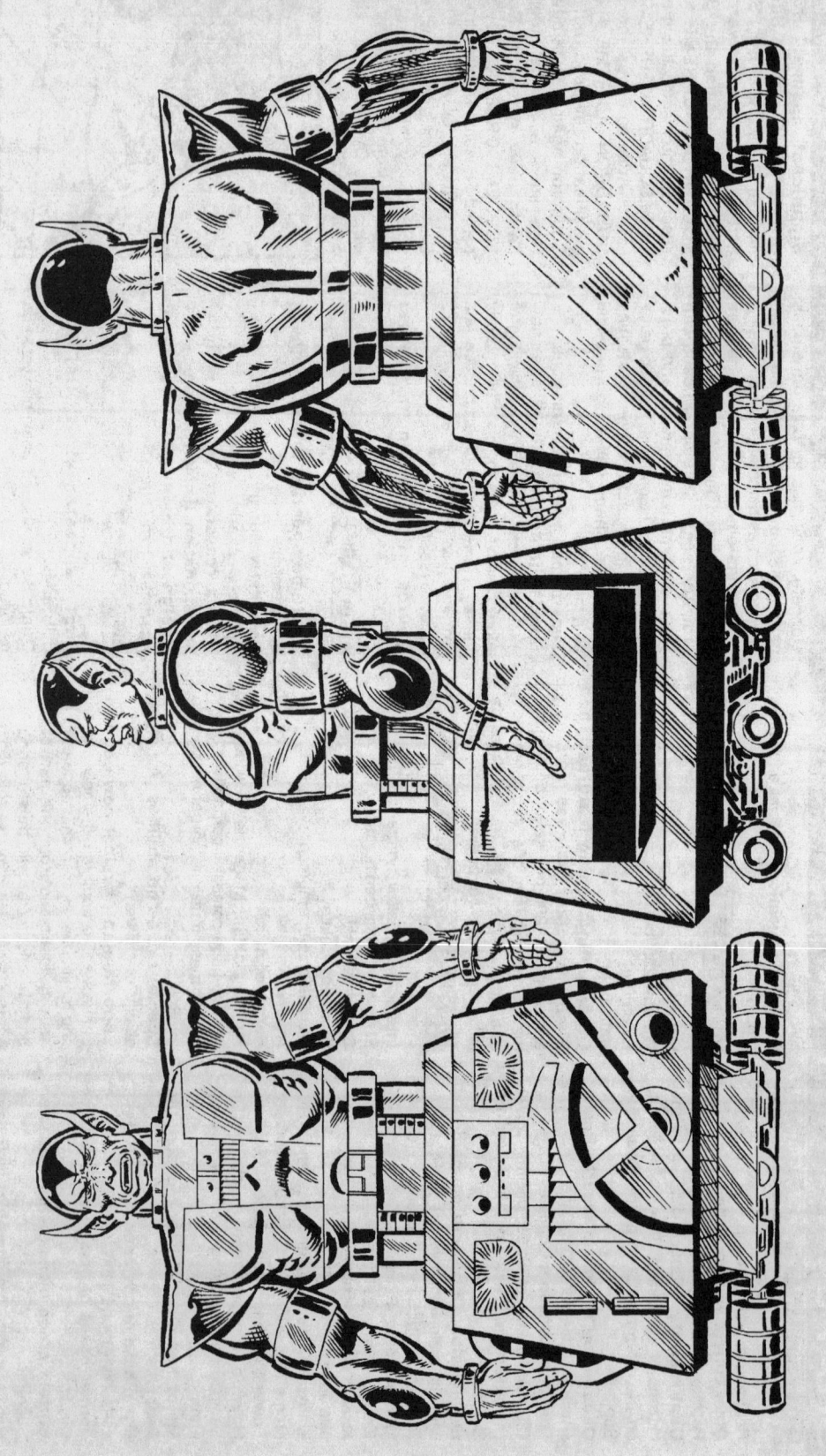

SHAPER OF WORLDS

BIOGRAPHICAL DATA

Real name: Unknown, perhaps inapplicable
Other current aliases: None
Former aliases: Skrull Cosmic Cube
Dual identity: None; the general populace of Earth is unaware of the Shaper of World's existence
Current occupation: Reality manipulator
Former occupation: Inapplicable
Citizenship: Inapplicable
Legal status: Unknown
Place of birth: Unnamed planet of the Skrull Empire, Andromeda Galaxy
Marital status: Unrevealed, possibly inapplicable
Known relatives: Kubik (formerly Earth Cosmic Cube), Kosmos (formerly the Beyonder)
Known confidants: None
Known allies: Glorian (apprentice), Kubik, Kree Supreme Intelligence
Major enemies: None
Usual base of operations: The known universe
Former bases of operations: The Skrull Empire, Andromeda Galaxy
Current group membership: None
Former group membership: None
Extent of education: Inapplicable

PHYSICAL DESCRIPTION

Height: 18'
Weight: 5.6 tons
Eyes: Blue
Hair: None
Other distinguishing features: The Shaper's torso from the waist down is a metallic trustrum with tractor treads for apparent mobility

POWERS AND ABILITIES

Intelligence: Immeasurable, but lacking in creative imagination
Strength: Unrevealed, possibly immeasurable
Flight speed: Warp speed
Stamina: Godlike
Durability: Unrevealed, possibly totally indestructible
Agility: Below normal
Reflexes: Peak human
Fighting skills: None
Special skills and abilities: None
Superhuman physical powers: Unknown, but potentially incalculable
Superhuman mental powers: Ability to restructure finite pockets of reality and to alter molecular configuration of persons and objects, intergalactic and interdimensional teleportation, empathic perception
Special limitations: Lacking a creative imagination, the Shaper must use the mind of another sentient being as a template for his transformations of worlds
Source of superhuman powers: Alien matter-energy construct

PARAPHERNALIA

Costume specifications: Alien materials
Personal weaponry: None
Special weaponry: None
Other accessories: None
Transportation: Teleportation
Design and manufacture of paraphernalia: Inapplicable

BIBLIOGRAPHY

First appearance: INCREDIBLE HULK #155
Origin issue: CAPTAIN AMERICA ANNUAL #7
Significant issues: INCREDIBLE HULK #155 (on unnamed extradimensional micro-world, created "world" based on Nazi-dominated 1940s Earth from mind of ex-Nazi scientist Otto Kronstieg; "world" destroyed by intervention of the Hulk); FANTASTIC FOUR #136-137 (on Earth, created "world" based on 1950s American popular culture from the mind of ex-henchman "Slugger" Johnson; "world" destroyed by intervention of Fantastic Four; took Thomas Gideon as his apprentice); INCREDIBLE HULK #190-191 (on unnamed planetoid, created "paradise world" based on his fondest dreams from mind of Hulk; captured by Toad Men of planet Tribbit; rescued by Hulk and Glorian (Thomas Gideon); "paradise world" destroyed when Hulk realized it's unreality); INCREDIBLE HULK #267 (transformation of Thomas Gideon into Glorian revealed; witnessed Glorian's attempt to create "world" based on dreams of inhabitants of a small town ruined by accidental intervention of Hulk); CAPTAIN AMERICA ANNUAL #7 [origin as a Skrull Cosmic Cube recounted; sent by Kree Supreme Intelligence to guide evolution of Earth Cosmic Cube into sentient being; encountered Captain America and Aquarian); FANTASTIC FOUR #319 (with Kubik [formerly Earth Cosmic Cube], encountered Fantastic Four and Doctor Doom in the universe of the Beyonder; recounted Beyonder's true origin as part of the same force that created the Molecule Man; witnessed transformation of Beyonder and Molecule Man into a Cosmic Cube [later known as Kosmos]); INCREDIBLE HULK #355-356 (allowed Glorian to return to Earth to use his powers to help Hulk achieve nobility); INCREDIBLE HULK #359 (saved Hulk and Glorian from Mephisto, in guise of Cloot)

SHAPESHIFTER™

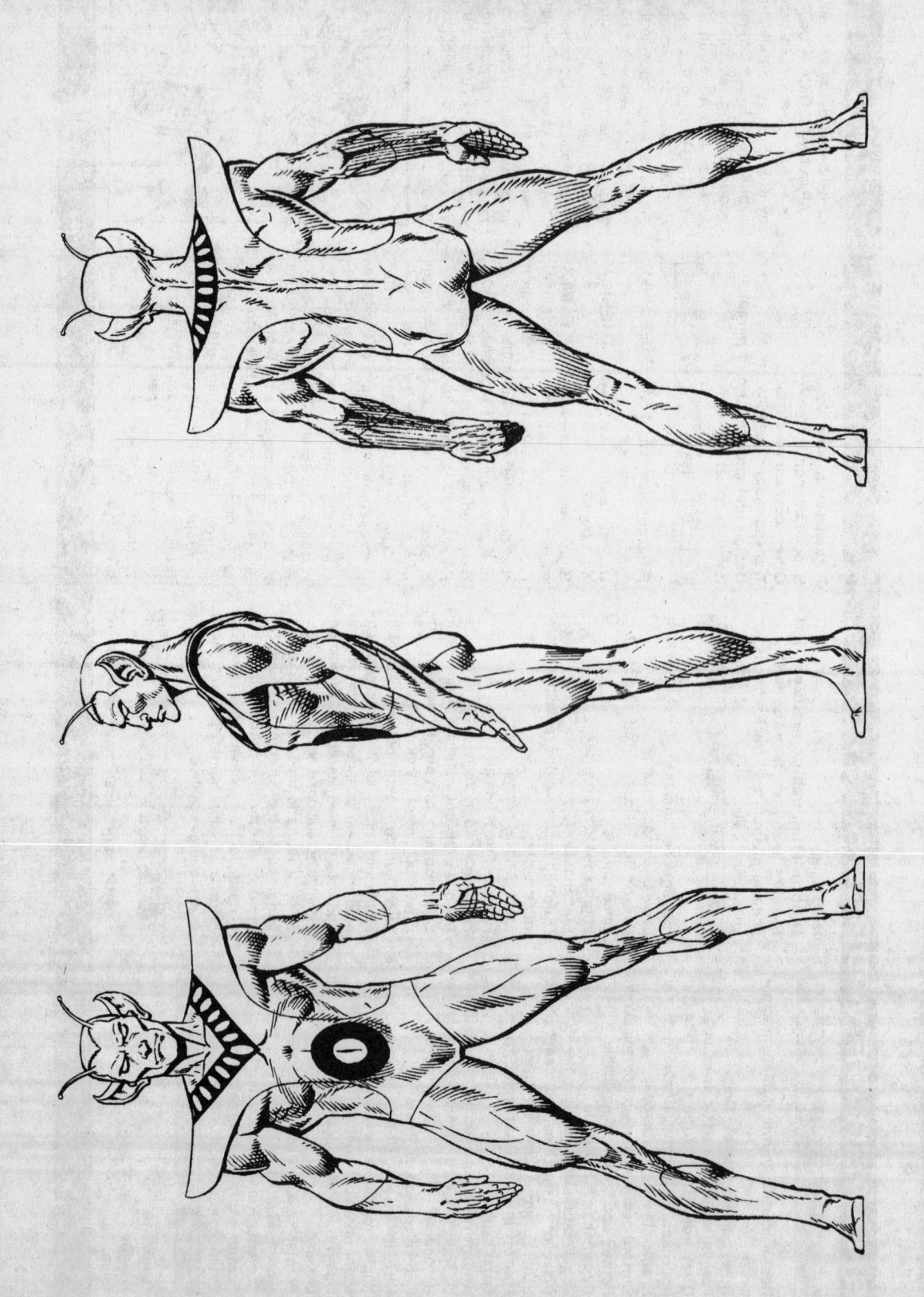

SHAPESHIFTER

BIOGRAPHICAL DATA

Real name: Unrevealed
Other current aliases: Shift
Former aliases: Hobgoblin I
Note: Shapeshifter is not to be confused with the various costumed criminals named Hobgoblin who have battled Spider-Man.)
Dual identity: None; the general populace of Earth is unaware of Shapeshifter's existence
Current occupation: Warrior serving in the Royal Elite of Shi'ar Imperial Guard
Former occupation: None known
Citizenship: Shi'ar Empire
Legal status: No criminal record in the Shi'ar Empire
Place of birth: Unrevealed location in the Shi'ar Galaxy (the identity of the alien race to which Titan belongs is unrevealed)
Marital status: Unrevealed
Known relatives: None
Known confidants: None
Known allies: Imperial Guard, Lilandra, (formerly) D'Ken, Deathbird
Note: The Imperial Guard serves whoever is ruler of the Shi'ar Empire; hence, at different times they have served D'Ken, Lilandra and Deathbird.
Major enemies: (formerly) Lilandra, X-Men, the Kree, the Avengers, Excalibur, the Starjammers
Usual base of operations: Chandilar (Shi'ar Throneworld), Shi'ar Empire
Former bases of operations: Unrevealed
Current group membership: Royal Elite, Shi'ar Imperial Guard
Former group membership: None
Extent of education: Unrevealed

PHYSICAL DESCRIPTION

Height: (normal form) 6' 1"
Weight: (normal form) 165 lbs.
Eyes: Variable
Hair: Variable, usually none in normal form
Other distinguishing features: In his normal form, Shapeshifter has two antennae on his head, which serve no known purpose, pointed ears, and purple skin.

POWERS AND ABILITIES

Intelligence: Normal
Strength: Variable
Speed: Variable
Stamina: Variable
Durability: Variable
Agility: Variable
Reflexes: Variable
Fighting skills: Fair hand-to-hand combatant, trained by Shi'ar Imperial Guard
Special skills and abilities: Excellent actor
Superhuman physical powers: Shapeshifter has the ability to change his shape, size, and physical appearance at will. He can even change his mass by drawing additional mass from another dimension or dispatching unnecessary mass into the same dimension. Apparently he can take on the physical abilities of any living creature whose physical appearance he imitates.
Superhuman mental powers: Shapeshifter's ability to duplicate the physical abilities of creatures may involve psionic scanning of the beings he imitates. Shapeshifter can also alter the appearance of his costume at will, possibly through psionic means.
Special limitations: None known
Source of superhuman powers: Unrevealed

PARAPHERNALIA

Costume specifications: Shi'ar fabrics mimicking the properties of unstable molecules, which allow them to affected by Shapeshifter's shape-changing powers.
Personal weaponry: None known
Special weaponry: None known
Other accessories: None known
Transportation: Shi'ar starships, small Imperial Guard anti-gravity device which allow flight
Design and manufacture of paraphernalia: Shi'ar scientists and technicians

BIBLIOGRAPHY

First appearance: X-MEN Vol. 1 #107
Origin issue: Shapeshifter's origin is as yet unrevealed.
Significant issues: X-MEN Vol. 1 #107-108 (joined in Imperial Guard's battle on behalf of Emperor D'Ken on nameless Shi'ar Empire planet; attacked the X-Men); X-MEN SPOTLIGHT ON: STARJAMMERS #2 (on Deathbird's behalf, joined Imperial Guard members in battle against Excalibur and Starjammers); AVENGERS #345 (impersonated Shi'ar Commander during Kree-Shi'ar War, persuaded Shi'ar praetor to attack Avengers), AVENGERS WEST COAST #81 (impersonated Doctor Minerva in order to capture Captain Atlas).
Note: It has been postulated that Shapeshifter is, in actuality, a member of the Skrull race, but this has not been proven conclusively.

SHATTERSTAR

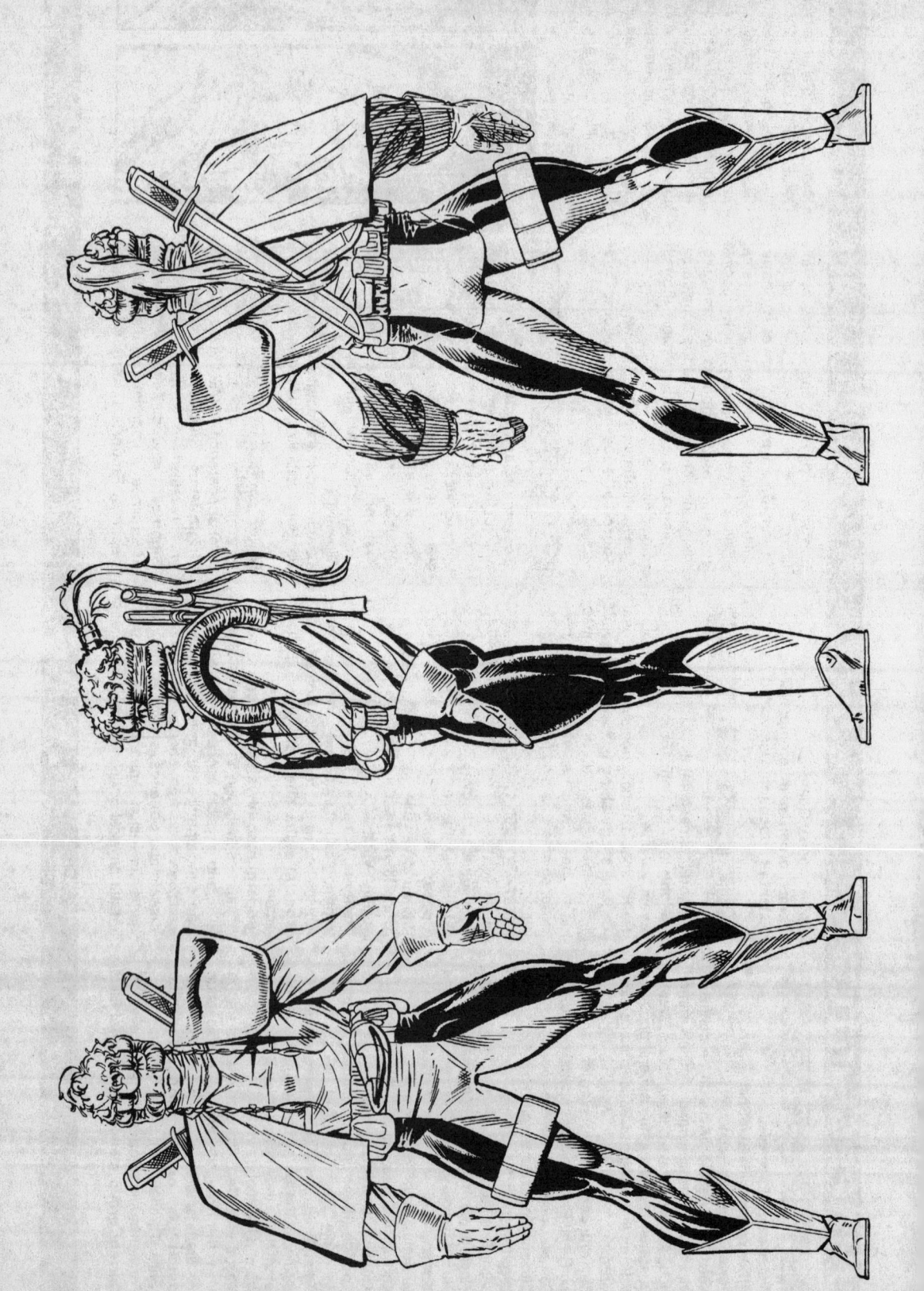

SHATTERSTAR II

BIOGRAPHICAL DATA

Real name: Unrevealed
Other current aliases: None
Former aliases: None known
Dual identity: None; the general populace of Earth is unaware that Shatterstar is an extradimensional being
Current occupation: Adventurer
Former occupation: Arena warrior, rebel
Citizenship: Mojo's dimension, 100 years in the future
Legal status: None on Earth, wanted for acts of rebellion against the Imperial Protectorate on his homeworld
Place of birth: Unidentified location in an alternate future of Mojo's dimension
Marital status: Single
Known relatives: None
Known confidants: None
Known allies: X-Force (Cable, Domino, Cannonball, Boom-Boom, Feral, Warpath, Siryn) Arize, the Cadre Alliance, the New Warriors, X-Factor I, the X-Men, Spider-Man
Major enemies: Mojo V, Spiral, the Imperial Protectorate, the Alliance of Evil, Harness, Proteus, Stryfe, Mutant Liberation Front, Reaper, Black Tom Cassidy, Juggernaut, Brotherhood of Evil Mutants III
Usual base of operations: X-Force headquarters
Former bases of operations: "The Wildways," Mojo's dimension; Professor Xavier's School for Gifted Youngsters, Salem Center, Westchester County, New York State
Current group membership: X-Force
Former group membership: The Cadre Alliance
Extent of education: Unrevealed

PHYSICAL DESCRIPTION

Height: 6'3"
Weight: 95 lbs.
Eyes: White no visible pupils
Hair: Red-blonde
Other distinguishing features: Black starburst design over left eye, three fingers and an opposable thumb on each hand, hair worn in a long queue and twin braids

POWERS AND ABILITIES

Intelligence: Above normal
Strength: Enhanced human
Speed: Enhanced human
Stamina: Enhanced human
Durability: Enhanced human regenerative
Agility: Enhanced human
Reflexes: Enhanced human
Fighting skills: Extensive training in many forms of martial arts and interpersonal combat of his homeworld, master swordsman
Special skills and abilities: Expert military strategist
Superhuman physical powers: Aside from the above listed attributes, none
Superhuman mental powers: None known
Special limitations: None known
Source of superhuman powers: Genetic engineering

PARAPHERNALIA

Costume specifications: Body armor composed of alien materials
Personal weaponry: Two 2 1/2 foot single-edged swords with spiked handguards
Special weaponry: Unrevealed additional weapons in belt pouches
Other accessories: Unrevealed additional devices in belt pouches
Transportation: Interdimensional teleportation unit (currently in disrepair), various X-Force airships and vehicles
Design and manufacture of paraphernalia: Unrevealed weaponsmiths and technicians of his homeworld

BIBLIOGRAPHY

First appearance: NEW MUTANTS #99
Origin issue: NEW MUTANTS #100, X-FORCE ANNUAL #1
Significant issues: NEW MUTANTS #100 (sent by Arize to Earth seeking the X-Men to help overthrow Mojo; battled Cable, Domino, and New Mutants; aided against Imperial Protectorate by New Mutants; joined X-Force); NEW MUTANTS ANNUAL #7 (with X-Force, battled Alliance of Evil, first encountered New Warriors); NEW WARRIORS ANNUAL #1 (battled Night Thrasher and Silhouette); X-MEN ANNUAL #15 (with X-Force, New Warriors, and Moira MacTaggart's "X-Men," battled Harness); X-FACTOR ANNUAL #6 (with X-Force, New Warriors, "X-Men," and X-Factor, battled Proteus); X-FORCE #1 (with X-Force, attacked Mutant Liberation Front base, battled Reaper); X-FORCE #3-4/SPIDER-MAN #16 (with X-Force and Spider-Man, battled Black Tom Cassidy and Juggernaut); X-FORCE #6-8 (with X-Force, battled Brotherhood of Evil Mutants III); X-FORCE ANNUAL #1 (with X-Force, returned to home dimension to help Arize against Mojo)

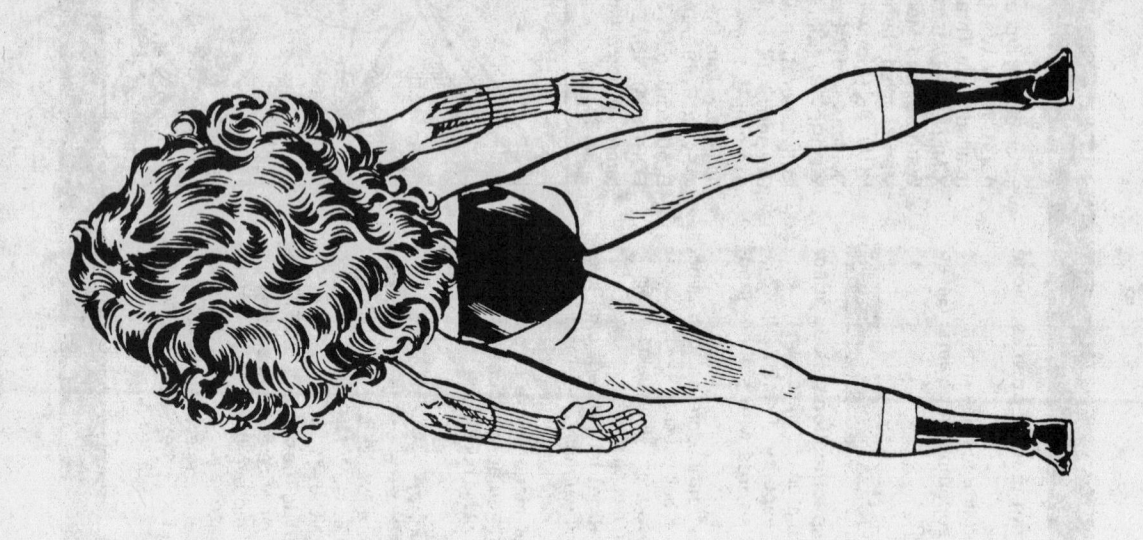

SHE-HULK

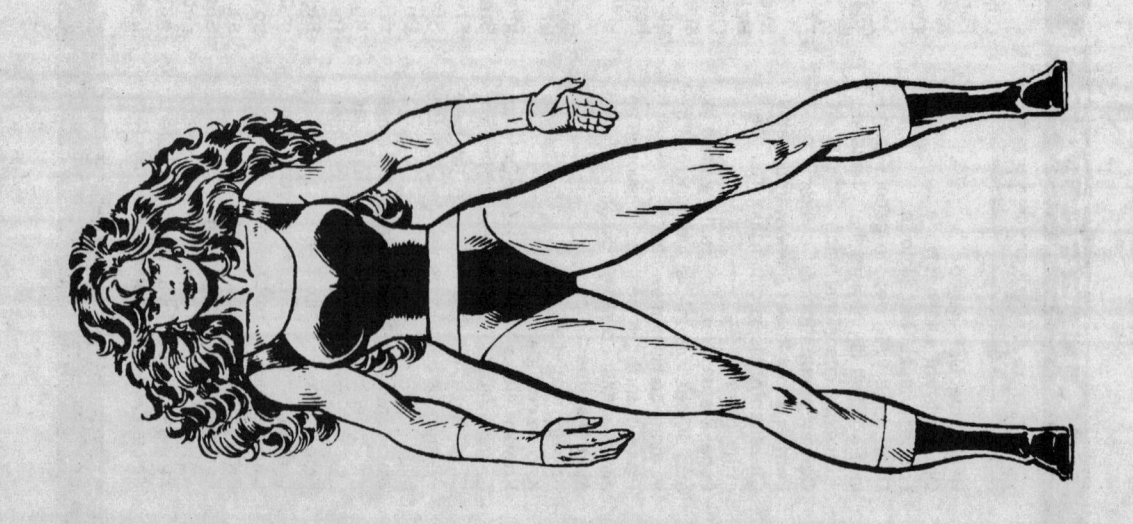

SHE-HULK

BIOGRAPHICAL DATA

Real name: Jennifer Walters
Other current aliases: None
Former aliases: None
Dual identity: Publicly known
Current occupation: Attorney, assistant District Attorney (working for New York City district attorney Blake Tower), adventurer
Former occupation: Criminal defense lawyer
Citizenship: United States of America
Legal status: No criminal record
Place of birth: Los Angeles, California
Marital status: Single
Known relatives: William Morris Walters (father), Elaine Walters (mother, deceased), Robert Bruce Banner (cousin), Betty Ross Banner (cousin by marriage), Brian Banner (uncle, apparently deceased), Rebecca Banner (aunt, apparently deceased), Mrs. Drake (aunt, apparently deceased)
Known confidants: Lousie Mason, Wyatt Wingfoot, Dan "Zapper" Ridge, Richard Rory
Known allies: The Avengers, Fantastic Four, Spider-Man
Major enemies: Titania, the Headmen, Xemnu the Titan, Doctor Bong, Spragg, Ring-master, Mahkizmo
Usual base of operations: New York City
Former bases of operations: Los Angeles, California; Baxter Building and Four Freedoms Plaza, New York City
Current group membership: The Avengers
Former group membership: Fantastic Four
Extent of education: Degree in Law

PHYSICAL DESCRIPTION

Height: 6' 7"
Weight: 650 lbs.
Eyes: Green
Hair: Green
Other distinguishing features: Green skin

POWERS AND ABILITIES

Intelligence: Above normal
Strength: Superhuman Class 90
Speed: Enhanced human
Stamina: Superhuman
Durability: Metahuman
Agility: Enhanced human
Reflexes: Enhanced human
Fighting skills: Good hand-to-hand combat ability, relies on strength rather than skill
Special skills and abilities: None
Superhuman physical powers: Superhuman strength, stamina, and durability, high resistance to disease and temperature extremes
Superhuman mental powers: None
Special limitations: Can no longer revert to original human form
Source of superhuman powers: Mutagenic effect of transfusion of gamma-irradiated blood from her cousin Bruce Banner (the Hulk)

PARAPHERNALIA

Costume specifications: Conventional attire or synthetic stretch fabric
Personal weaponry: None
Special weaponry: None
Other accessories: None
Transportation: Modified 1959 Dodge automobile equipped with technology enabling flight in Earth's atmosphere and in outer space for limited distances; car incapable of interstellar flight
Design and manufacture of paraphernalia: Al, alien ally of Ulysses Solomon Archer

BIBLIOGRAPHY

First appearance: SAVAGE SHE-HULK #1
Origin issue: SAVAGE SHE-HULK #1
Significant issues: SAVAGE SHE-HULK #1 (shot by operatives of gangsters Nick Trask, received blood transfusion from Bruce Banner, first became She-Hulk); SAVAGE SHE-HULK #11-12 (defended Dr. Michael Morbius in his trial for his vampiric killings); AVENGERS #221 (joined Avengers); MARVEL SUPER HEROES SECRET WARS #1 (transported to Battleworld by Beyonder); MARVEL SUPERHEROES SECRET WARS #7 (began feud with Titania); FANTASTIC FOUR #265 (returned to Earth as member of Fantastic Four); MARVEL GRAPHIC NOVEL #18: SENSATIONAL SHE-HULK (radiation prevented her from changing back to human form); SOLO AVENGERS #14 (appeared before Supreme Court, battled Titania); SENSATIONAL SHE-HULK #1 (hypnotized by Ringmaster into becoming a performer in his circus, bat-tled the Headmen); SENSATIONAL SHE-HULK #3 (with Spider-Man defeated the Headmen); SENSATIONAL SHE-HULK #4 (met Louise Mason, went to work for Blake Tower); SENSATIONAL SHE-HULK #5 (battled Doctor Bong); SENSATIONAL SHE-HULK #6-7 (first contended against Xemnu the Titan); SENSATIONAL SHE-HULK #8 (encountered Nick St. Christopher); SENSATIONAL SHE-HULK #31 (encountered Spragg)

SHE-HULK
IN ACTION

ART: KEITH POLLARD/JOSEF RUBINSTEIN

SHE-HULK'S SUPPORTING CAST

LOUISE "WEEZIE" MASON
Current occupation: Legal secretary and executive assistant
Relationship: Friend
First appearance: ALL-SELECT COMICS #11, BLONDE PHANTOM #1, (modern) SENSATIONAL SHE-HULK #2

WYATT WINGFOOT
Current occupation: American Indian rights activist, chief of Keewazi
Relationship: Boyfriend
First appearance: FANTASTIC FOUR #50

ULYSSES SOLOMON ARCHER
Current occupation: Space trucker
Relationship: Friend
First appearance: U.S. ONE #1

MORRIS WALTERS
Current occupation: Sheriff
Relationship: Father
First appearance: SAVAGE SHE-HULK #2

BLAKE TOWER
Current occupation: District Attorney
Relationship: Business associate
First appearance: DAREDEVIL #124

GARTH
Current occupation: housekeeper
Relationship: Manservant
First appearance: SENSATIONAL SHE-HULK #34

RICHARD RORY
Current occupation: Independently wealthy
Relationship: Friend
First appearance: MAN-THING Vol. 1 #2

DAN "ZAPPER" RIDGE
Current occupation: Independently wealthy
Relationship: Ex-boyfriend, friend
First appearance: SAVAGE SHE-HULK #2

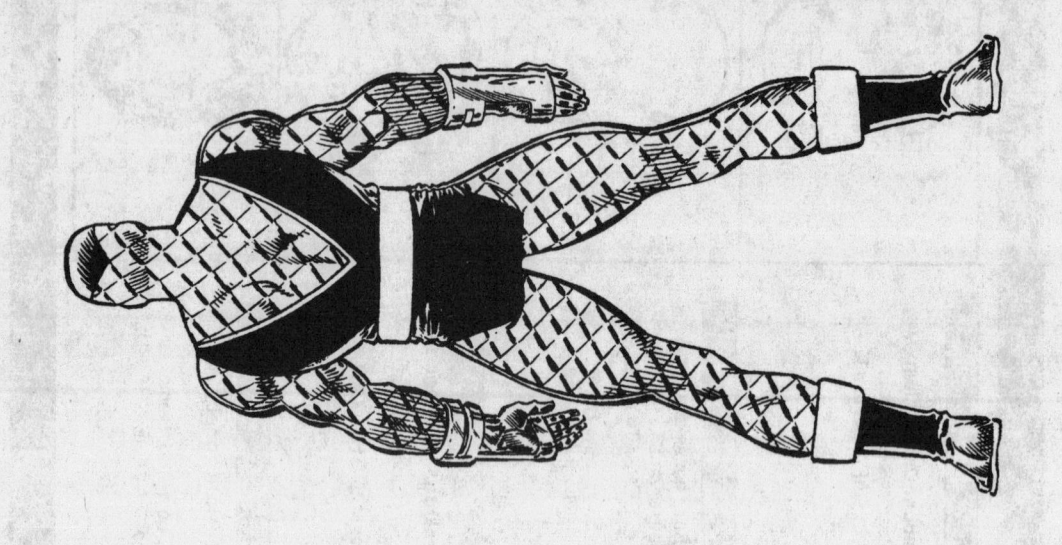

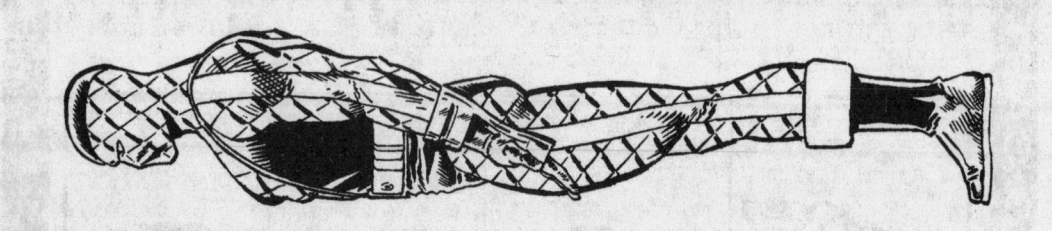

SHOCKER

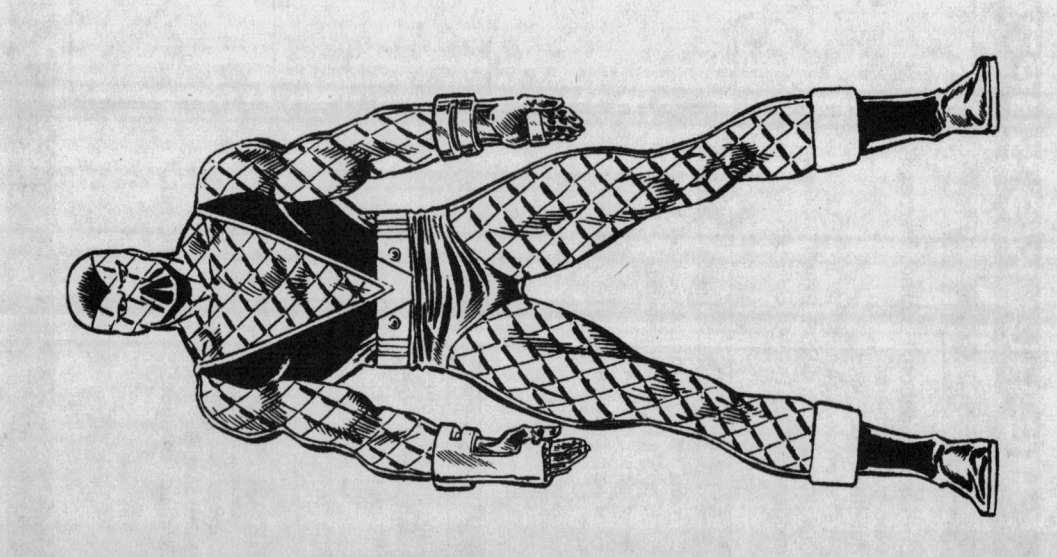

SHOCKER

BIOGRAPHICAL DATA

Real name: Herman Schultz
Other current aliases: None
Former aliases: None
Dual Identity: Publicly known
Current occupation: Burglar, hired assassin
Former occupation: Burglar
Citizenship: United States of America
Legal status: Criminal record in the United States
Place of birth: New York City
Marital status: Single
Known relatives: None
Known confidants: None
Known allies: (Masters of Evil III) Egghead, Radioactive Man, Tiger Shark, Moonstone, the Beetle; Chameleon, Hammerhead
Major enemies: Spider-Man, the Avengers, Electro
Usual base of operations: New York City
Former bases of operations: None
Current group membership: Masters of Evil III
Former group membership: None
Extent of education: High school dropout

PHYSICAL DESCRIPTION

Height: 5'9"
Weight: 175 lbs.
Eyes: Brown
Hair: Brown
Other distinguishing features: None

POWERS AND ABILITIES

Intelligence: Normal
Strength: Normal
Speed: Normal
Stamina: Normal
Durability: Normal
Agility: Normal
Reflexes: Normal
Fighting skills: Basic familiarity with streetfighting techniques
Special skills and abilities: Aptitude for working with tools
Superhuman physical powers: None
Superhuman mental powers: None
Special limitations: None

Source of superhuman powers: Inapplicable

PARAPHERNALIA

Costume specifications: Foam-lined synthetic fabric which absorbs all vibrations and establishes a vibrational shield which deflects normal blows and allows him to slip from any grasp.
Personal weaponry: Vibro-shock units triggered by a pump-action compressed air mechanism, creating a series of rapid-succession high-pressure air blasts that result in a series of powerful impacts. Thrown from a distance, they create destructive vibrations that can crumble solid concrete and cause extensive damage to the human body and it's internal organs
Special weaponry: None
Other accessories: None
Transportation: Various
Design and manufacture of paraphernalia: Herman Schultz

BIBLIOGRAPHY

First appearance: AMAZING SPIDER-MAN #46
Origin issue: AMAZING SPIDER-MAN #46
Significant issues: AMAZING SPIDER-MAN #46 (first encountered Spider-Man); AMAZING SPIDER-MAN #72 (stole ancient stone tablet earlier stolen by the Kingpin); AMAZING SPIDER-MAN #151 (attempted to extort one million dollars from New York City by severing selected cable junctions beneath the streets); AVENGERS #228 (joined Egghead's Masters of Evil III to incriminate Dr. Henry Pym, then on trial for treason; battled the Avengers); WEB OF SPIDER-MAN #10 (hired by Nazi war criminal Baron Von Lundt to kill Dominic Fortune; built vibro-shock units into entire uniform); SPECTACULAR SPIDER-MAN #157 (hired by the Chameleon and Hammerhead to induce Electro to join their organization); AMAZING SPIDER-MAN #335 (attempted to steal thousands of charity dollars at the celebrity fund raiser for the New York Public Library)

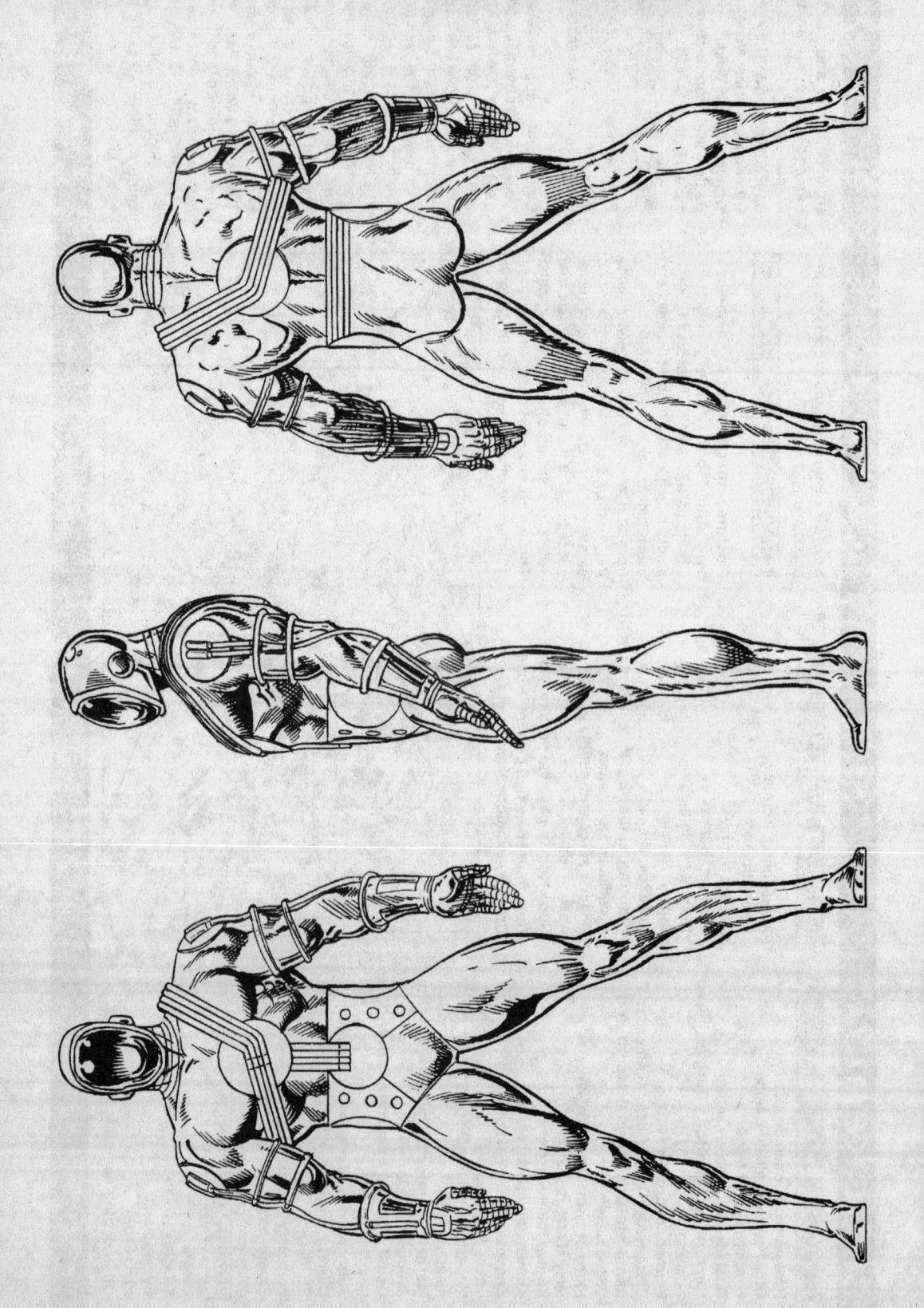

SHOCKWAVE

SHOCKWAVE

BIOGRAPHICAL DATA

Real name: Lancaster Sneed
Other current aliases: None
Former aliases: None
Dual Identity: Publicly known
Current occupation: Professional criminal, mercenary
Former occupation: British intelligence agent, carnival performer
Citizenship: United Kingdom
Legal status: Criminal record in the United kingdom and the United States
Place of birth: Newcastle-on-Tyne, England
Marital status: Single
Known relatives: Sir Denis Nayland Smith (uncle)
Known confidants: None
Known allies: Zaran I, Razor-Fist II, (former) Fah Lo Suee, Sir Herbert Griswold (Tarrant, deceased), Fu Manchu (presumed deceased), Brynocki (deceased), SHIELD Deltoids
Major enemies: Shang Chi, Sir Denis Nayland Smith, Dr. Petrie, Black Jack Tarr, Clive Reston, Leiko Wu, James Larner (deceased), Avengers West Coast, Captain America
Usual base of operations: Mobile
Former bases of operations: Mobile
Current group membership: None
Former group membership: Agent of MI-6; employee of Oriental Expiditers Limited, the Golden Dagger Sect, Fah Lo Suee, Fu Manchu, and SHIELD Deltoid conspiracy; partner of Zaran I and Razor Fist II
Extent of education: College

PHYSICAL DESCRIPTION

Height: 5'11"
Weight: 170 lbs., (in armor) 182 lbs.
Eyes: Green
Hair: Black, formerly red-brown
Other distinguishing features: Scarred facial features

POWERS AND ABILITIES

Intelligence: Normal
Strength: Enhanced human
Speed: Peak human
Stamina: Enhanced human
Durability: Enhanced human
Agility: Peak human
Reflexes: Peak human
Fighting skills: Master of various martial arts, especially karate; trained in armed and unarmed combat by British military intelligence
Special skills and abilities: Expert on electrical devices, skilled in demolitions work
Superhuman physical powers: Aside from the above listed attributes, none.
Superhuman mental powers: None
Special limitations: Sneed has a history of mental instability
Source of superhuman powers: Body surgically rebuilt using metal plates behalf of SHIELD Deltoids, defeated by Iron Man I, escaped); CAPTAIN AMERICA #411-413 (attended AIM Weapons Exposition; alongside other costumed criminals, battled Captain America

PARAPHERNALIA

Costume specifications: Exoskeleton body armor equipped with apparatus generating electrical shocks on contact
Personal weaponry: None
Special weaponry: None
Other accessories: None
Transportation: Conventional means
Design and manufacture of paraphernalia: Lancaster Sneed

BIBLIOGRAPHY

First appearance: MASTER OF KUNG FU #42
Origin issue: (related) MASTER OF KUNG FU #42, (depicted) MASTER OF KUNG FU #75
Significant issues: MASTER OF KUNG FU #42 (revealed as former MI-6 agent turned mercenary; conspired to kill Nayland Smith and Black Jack Tarr, first battled Shang Chi); MASTER OF KUNG FU #43 (revealed as Nayland Smith's nephew, defeated by Shang Chi); MASTER OF KUNG FU #72 (brainwashed by MI-6, attacked Nayland Smith, battled Clive Reston and Shang Chi); MASTER OF KUNG FU #73-75 (alongside Brynocki, battled Shang Chi and Leiko Wu on Mordillo Island; alongside Shang Chi, Leiko Wu, and Black Jack Tarr, battled Brynocki and his robots); WEST COAST AVENGERS Vol. 2 #11 (alongside Zaran I and Razor-Fist II, attacked West Coast Avengers on

SHOTGUN™

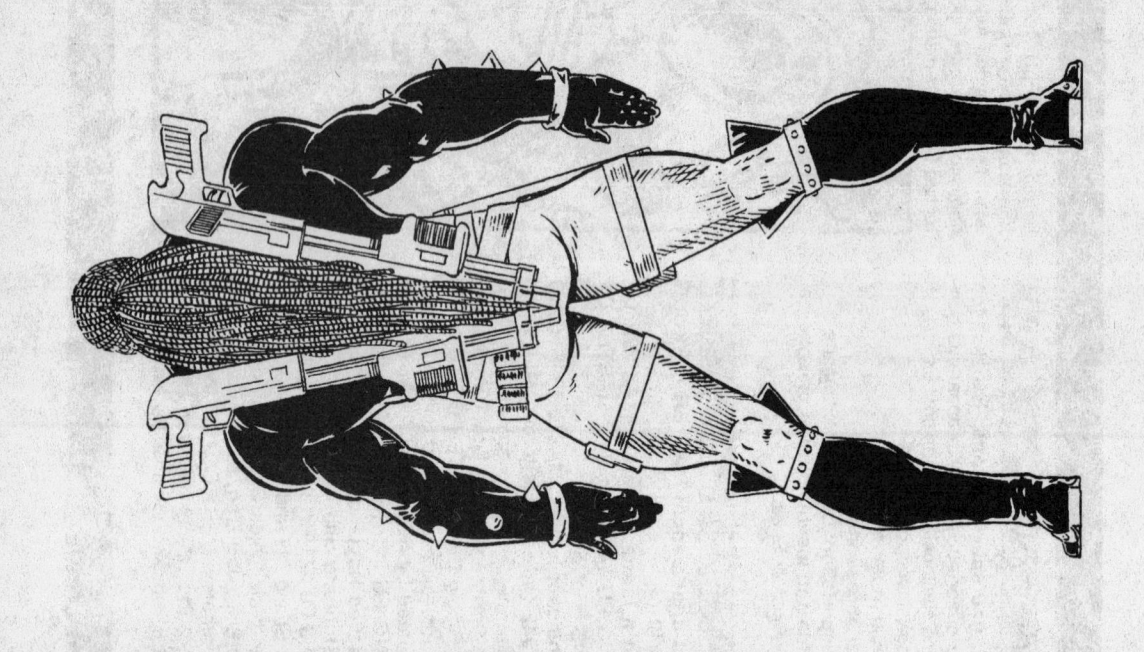

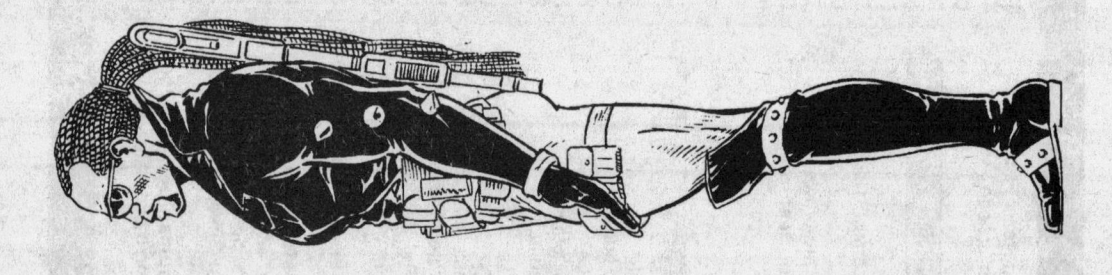

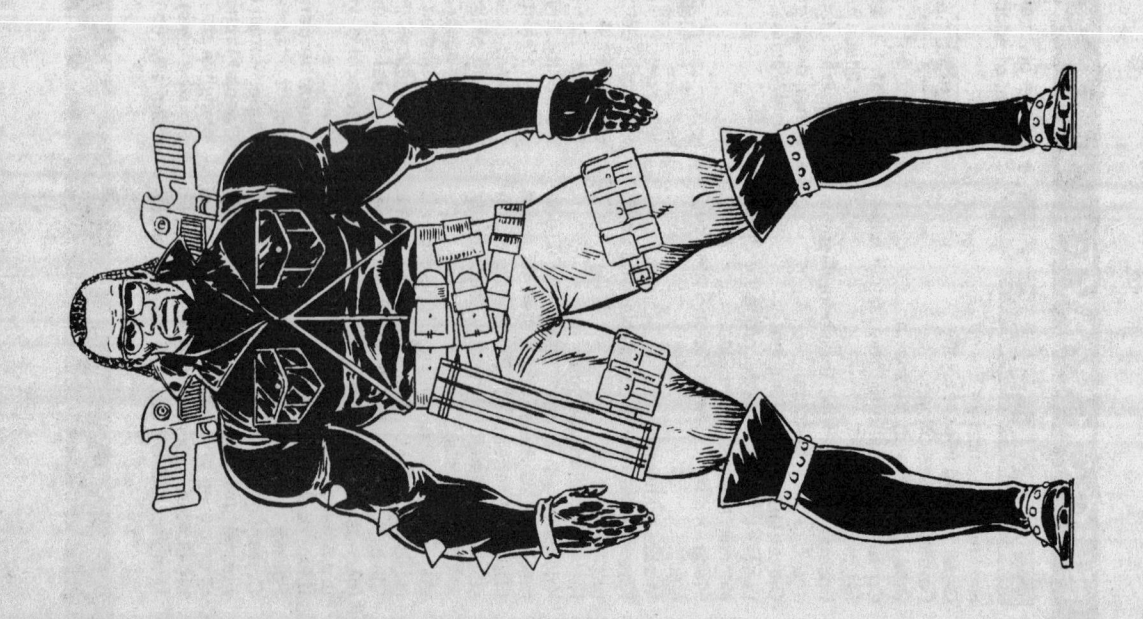

SHOTGUN II

BIOGRAPHICAL DATA

Real names: Unrevealed
Other current aliases: None
Former aliases: None known
Dual identity: Secret
Current occupation: Assassin
Former occupation: Soldier
Citizenship: United States of America
Legal status: No criminal record
Place of birth: Unrevealed
Marital status: Presumed single
Known relatives: None
Known confidants: None
Known allies: The Punisher, "Skip" Ash, the Central Intelligence Agency
Major enemies: Daredevil, Number Nine, the Carbone family, (former) Brandy Ash (deceased)
Usual base of operations: Mobile
Former bases of operations: Unrevealed
Current group membership: None
Former group membership: United States Army
Extent of education: Unrevealed

PHYSICAL DESCRIPTION

Height: 6' 4"
Weight: 240 lbs.
Eyes: Brown
Hair: Brown
Other distinguishing features: None

POWERS AND ABILITIES

Intelligence: Normal
Strength: Athlete
Speed: Athlete
Stamina: Athlete
Durability: Athlete
Agility: Athlete
Reflexes: Athlete
Fighting skills: Highly experienced hand-to-hand combat.
Special skills: Expert marksman with most known firearms
Superhuman physical powers: None
Superhuman mental powers: None
Special limitations: None
Source of superhuman powers: Inapplicable

PARAPHERNALIA

Costume specifications: Body armor (kevlar)
Personal weaponry: High-powered recoilless rifle firing a variety of explosive, concussive, combustible, and disintegrative ammunition
Special weaponry: Various, as needed
Other accessories: Various, as needed
Transportation: Specially-designed one-man tank
Design and manufacture of paraphernalia: Unnamed Central Intelligence Agency weaponry research and development personnel

BIBLIOGRAPHY

First appearance: DAREDEVIL #272
Origin issue: Shotgun's origin is as yet unrevealed.
Significant issues: DAREDEVIL #272-273 (sent by the CIA and Skip Ash to retrieve Number 9, battled Daredevil); PUNISHER WAR ZONE #4-6 (alongside the Punisher, battled the Carbone family)
Note: Shotgun II is not be confused with Zeke Sallinger, a member of the Harriers.

SHROUD™

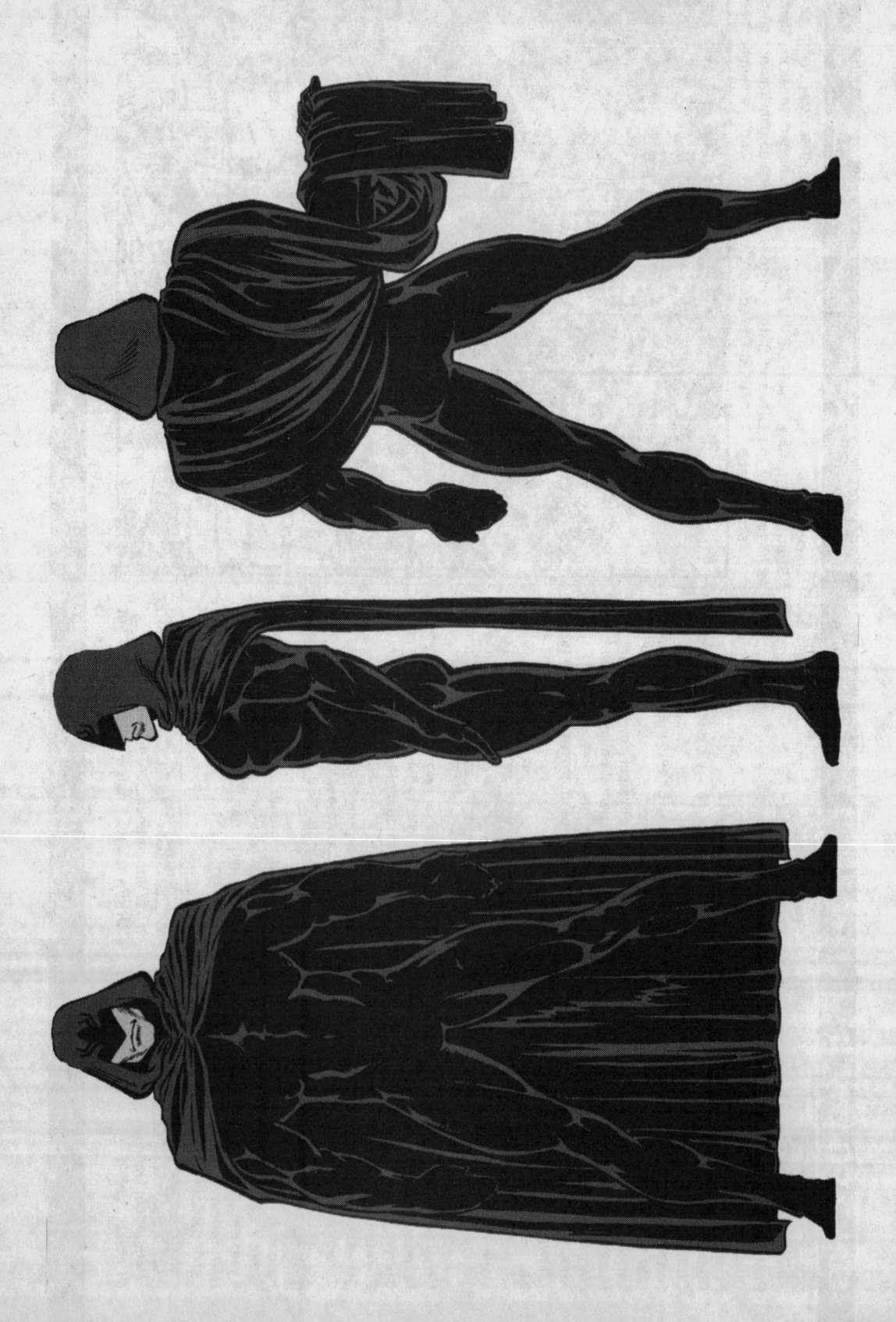

SHROUD

BIOGRAPHICAL DATA

Real name: Unknown
Other current aliases: Master of Darkness
Former aliases: None known
Dual Identity: Secret
Current occupation: Crimefighter masquerading as criminal gang leader
Former occupation: Unrevealed
Citizenship: United States of America
Legal status: No known criminal record, wanted by the police for questioning
Place of birth: Unrevealed
Marital status: Single
Known relatives: None
Known confidants: Werewolf
Known allies: Captain America, Cat and Mouse, Spider-Woman I, Spider-Man, the Night Shift (Werewolf, Dansen Macabre, Brothers Grimm II, Gypsy Moth, Tatterdemalion, Misfit, Needle, Digger, Ticktock)
Major enemies: The Cult of Kali, Doctor Doom, Red Skull, organized crime figures
Usual base of operations: Several bases in Los Angeles, California, including the Tower of Shadows
Former bases of operations: Temple of the Cult of Kali; Cat's Jazz Club, Los Angeles
Current group membership: Leader of the Night Shift
Former group membership: None
Extent of education: College degree in law and criminology

PHYSICAL DESCRIPTION

Height: 6'2"
Weight: 220 lbs.
Eyes: Pale blue
Hair: Reddish-blonde
Other distinguishing features: The Shroud has the image of the goddess Kali imprinted in livid scar tissue on his face from nose to hairline and from cheek to cheek; hence, he rarely removes his mask

POWERS AND ABILITIES

Intelligence: Above normal
Strength: Athlete
Speed: Athlete
Stamina: Athlete
Durability: Athlete
Agility: Peak human
Reflexes: Peak human
Fighting skills: Master of an unnamed Oriental martial art
Special skills and abilities: Adept acrobat
Superhuman physical powers: None
Superhuman mental powers: Mystical extrasensory perception (replaces his eyesight), which allows him to "see" through walls and through his own darkness; ability to create aperture into dimension of darkness and to project gas-like substance of darkness dimension into Earth for his own use.
Special limitations: The Shroud is blind. Loss of concentration can disrupt his power to summon and control darkness.
Source of superhuman powers: Extrasensory power: blinded in mystic ceremony by the Cult of Kali; Darkness power: exposure to bombardment of Red Skull's hypno-ray triggered latent power.
Note: While the Shroud's power of darkness may be a mystical ability like his extrasensory perception, since two other beings known to possess similar powers, Cloak and Darkstar, are mutants, it is possible that the Shroud too is a mutant whose latent power was triggered by the Red Skull's hypno-ray.

PARAPHERNALIA

Costume specifications: Synthetic stretch fabric
Personal weaponry: Explosive "bombarangs"
Special weaponry: None
Other accessories: None
Transportation: Personal one-man aircraft
Design and manufacture of paraphernalia: The Shroud

BIBLIOGRAPHY

First appearance: SUPER-VILLAIN TEAM-UP #5
Origin issue: SUPER-VILLAIN TEAM-UP #7
Significant issues: SUPER-VILLAIN TEAM-UP #5 (encountered the Human Torch); SUPER-VILLAIN TEAM-UP #6-10 (invaded Latveria; recounted his origin to Namor the Sub-Mariner; secretly entered Latveria disguised as members of the Ringmaster's Circus of Crime; joined Prince Rudolfo's revolution against Doctor Doom); SUPER-VILLAIN TEAM-UP #11-12 (assisted Doctor Doom and Captain America against the Red Skull, gained superhuman power of darkness); SPIDER-WOMAN I; battled the Cult of Kali); MARVEL TEAM-UP PREVIEW #21 (took on Cat and Mouse as his aides), MARVEL TEAM-UP #94 (teamed with Spider-Man against Dansen Macabre); AVENGERS #240-241 (aided the Avengers and Doctor Strange against Morgan Le Fey, helped restore former Spider-Woman I's astral self to her body); WEST COAST AVENGERS Vol. 1 #1 (refused Hawkeye's offer to join the West Coast Avengers); DOCTOR STRANGE Vol. 2 #67 (assisted Jessica Drew against crooks); WEST COAST AVENGERS Vol. 1 #3-4 (assisted West Coast Avengers against Graviton and the Blank); CAPTAIN AMERICA #330-331 (with the Night Shift, teamed with Captain America against the Power Broker and his augmented mutates); SOLO AVENGERS #3 (tested Moon Knight to take over as leader of Night Shift); WEST COAST AVENGERS Vol. 2 #29 (refused Taurus's offer to join new Zodiac); SOLO AVENGERS #9 (teamed with Hawkeye against gang leader Speedo); WEST COAST AVENGERS Vol. 2 #40 (stopped battle between Night Shift and West Coast Avengers)

SIDEWINDER

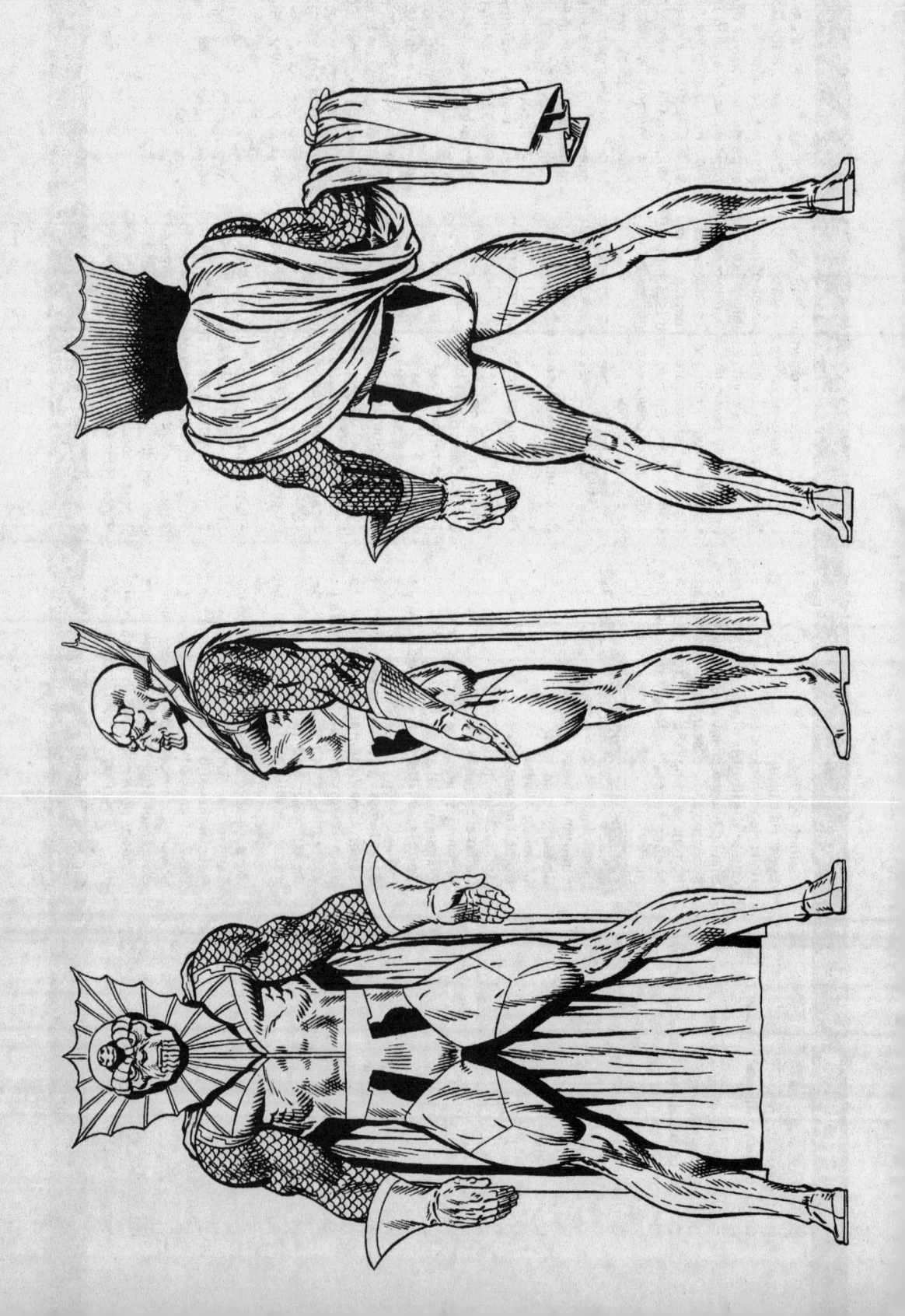

SIDEWINDER

BIOGRAPHICAL DATA

Real name: Seth Voelker
Other current aliases: None
Former aliases: None
Dual identity: Secret
Current occupation: Retired professional criminal
Former occupation: College professor, financial analyst, professional criminal
Citizenship: United States of America
Legal status: No criminal record
Place of birth: Kenosha, Wisconsin
Marital status: Single
Known relatives: None
Known confidants: None
Known allies: (former) The Serpent Society (Anaconda, Asp, Black Mamba, Bushmaster, Cobra, Cottonmouth, Diamondback, Death Adder [deceased], Rattler)
Major enemies: Captain America, Constrictor, the Serpent Society (King Cobra, Anaconda, Black Racer, Boomslang, Bushmaster, Coachwhip, Copperhead, Cottonmouth, Fer-de-Lance, Puff Adder, Rattler, Rock Python)
Usual base of operations: Mobile
Former bases of operations: Serpent Citadel, upstate New York
Current group membership: None
Former group membership: Serpent Squad II (Anaconda, Black Mamba, Death Adder, [deceased]); The Serpent Society
Extent of education: Advanced degree in economics

PHYSICAL DESCRIPTION

Height: 5' 9"
Weight: 180 lbs.
Eyes: Blue
Hair: Black, balding
Other distinguishing features: None

POWERS AND ABILITIES

Intelligence: Above normal
Strength: Normal
Speed: Normal
Stamina: Normal
Durability: Normal
Agility: Normal
Reflexes: Normal
Fighting skills: No experience at hand-to-hand combat
Special skills and abilities: Skilled financial expert, business planner, and strategist
Superhuman physical powers: None
Superhuman mental powers: None
Special limitations: None
Source of superhuman powers: None

PARAPHERNALIA

Costume specifications: Synthetic stretch fabric
Personal weaponry: None
Special weaponry: None
Other accessories: None
Transportation: Sidewinder's cloak contains electronic circuitry that enables him to open an aperture into another dimension. Sidewinder activates the cloak mentally through a device surgically implanted in his body, enabling him to travel "sideways" through interdimensional space, taking with him whatever and whomever he drapes his cloak over.
Design and manufacture of paraphernalia: Scientists at the Brand Corporation's mutagenics laboratory

BIBLIOGRAPHY

First appearance: MARVEL TWO-IN-ONE #64
Origin issue: Sidewinder's origin is as yet unrevealed.
Significant issues: MARVEL TWO-IN-ONE #64-65 (assigned by Roxxon Oil to lead Serpent Squad III to retrieve the Serpent Crown, battled Thing and Stingray, Triton, and the Scarlet Witch); CAPTAIN AMERICA #308-311, 313 (organized the Serpent Society, conducted initiation tests, contacted potential clients; dispatched Society to kill Modok on behalf of AIM); CAPTAIN AMERICA #315 (dispatched the Serpent Society against Captain America, freed them from prison after their capture); CAPTAIN AMERICA #319 (dispatched Society to hunt down the Scourge who had murdered Death Adder); CAPTAIN AMERICA #338 (rescued Black Racer, Copperhead, Fer-de-Lance, and Puff Adder from jail, enlisted them in the Serpent Society); CAPTAIN AMERICA #341-342 (poisoned by Viper II in her attempt to take over the Serpent Society, rescued by Diamondback); CAPTAIN AMERICA #345 (freed Diamondback and Nomad from Commission custody); X-MEN ANNUAL #13 (with Diamondback, stole artifact from Mister Jip on behalf of clients Ghaur and Llyra); CAPTAIN AMERICA #380-381 (rescued Diamondback from execution by Serpent Society, fled King Cobra's reprisals); CAPTAIN AMERICA ANNUAL #10 (unsuccessfully attempted to make peace with King Cobra by freeing him from the Vault)

SIEGE™

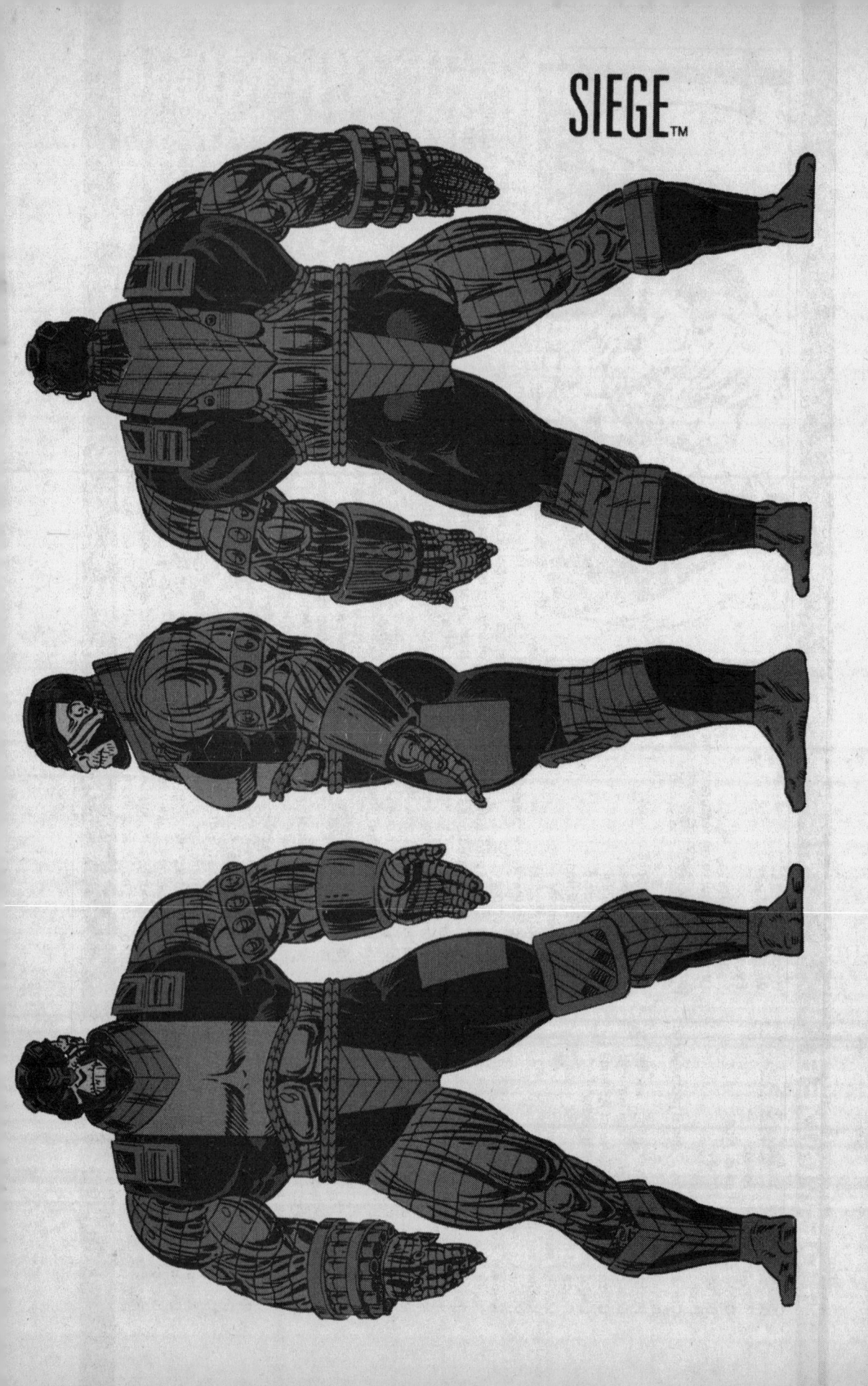

SIEGE

BIOGRAPHICAL DATA

Real name: John Kelly
Other current aliases: None
Former aliases: (as Kelly) Deathlok II
Dual identity: Secret
Current occupation: Mercenary
Former occupation: Professional soldier, police officer, scientific guinea pig
Citizenship: United States of America
Legal status: No criminal record, legally dead
Place of birth: Unrevealed
Marital status: Divorced
Known relatives: Karen Kelly (ex-wife), Sara Kelly (daughter), Biohazard (reanimated remains of his human brain)
Known confidants: (former) Harlan Ryker, Karen Kelly
Known allies: Deathlok III, Coldblood, Silver Sable, Wild Pack, Next Wave, Knights of Wundagore, Daredevil, Nick Fury, Godwulf (former) Harlan Ryker, Cybertek
Major enemies: Harlan Ryker, Mainframe, Ben Jacobs, Cyberwarriors, Genesis Coalition, Timestream, Venom, Demolisher
Usual base of operations: Mobile
Former bases of operations: Bronx, New York
Current group membership: Freelance operative for Silver Sable Inc. and SHIELD
Former group membership: (as Deathlok II) Cybertek, (as Kelly) New York Police Department, United States Marine Corps.
Extent of education: High school graduate

PHYSICAL DESCRIPTION

Height: 8'
Weight: 950 lbs.
Eyes: Red
Hair: (as Kelly) Blond; (as Siege) None
Other distinguishing features: Siege possesses a massive cyborg body. The left half of his face is in a semi-decomposed state. The right half of his face is in an armored cybernetic implant.

POWERS AND ABILITIES

Intelligence: Normal
Strength: Superhuman Class 100
Speed: Superhuman
Flight speed: Supersonic
Stamina: Superhuman
Durability: Superhuman
Agility: Enhanced human
Reflexes: Enhanced human
Fighting skills: Excellent hand-to-hand combatant with extensive combat training
Special skills and abilities: None
Superhuman physical powers: Aside from the above listed attributes, Siege's cyborg body possesses a built-in gatling assembly on his right forearm capable of discharging 100 low-yield plasma bursts per second. His right forearm contains a built-in plasma cannon capable of significantly more powerful discharges. Siege's built-in database is capable of a myriad of functions, including long-range surveillance and tracking systems and self-diagnostic and repair functions. At present, Siege does not know how to access all of his body's abilities.
Superhuman mental powers: As Kelly's personality has been encoded into the Siege cyborg in machine language, Siege is impervious to mental scans.
Special limitations: Siege's simplified digestive system can only absorb a liquid nutrient formula. He cannot digest ordinary food. Siege cannot feel any tactile sensations.
Source of superhuman powers: Mental patterns encoded into cyborg body

PARAPHERNALIA

Costume specifications: Woven metalmesh body suit of considerable durability
Personal weaponry: None
Special weaponry: None
Other accessories: None
Transportation: Flight under own power
Design and manufacture of paraphernalia: Former Cybertek scientists including Ben Jacobs, Stanley Cross, Dr. Hu, Dr. Fox, and Dr. Borruso

BIBLIOGRAPHY

First appearance: (as Deathlok II) MARVEL COMICS PRESENTS #62, (as Siege) DEATHLOK Vol.2 #19
Origin issue: MARVEL COMICS PRESENTS #62, DEATHLOK Vol. 2 #14, 17, 19
Significant issues: MARVEL COMICS PRESENTS #62 (as John Kelly, body rebuilt into the Deathlok cyborg; brain electrocuted by Deathlok's onboard computer); DEATHLOK Vol. 2 #12-15 (brain mutated into the creature Biohazard); DEATHLOK Vol. 2 #17 (brain patterns accessed by Deathlok III); DEATHLOK Vol. 2 #19 (brain patterns downloaded into Siege cyborg; with Deathlok III, Silver Sable and the Wild Pack, battled Mainframe, Ben Jacobs, and Cyberwarriors); DEATHLOK Vol. 2 #20-21 (with Deathlok III and Coldblood, battled Harlan Ryker, Mainframe, Ben Jacobs, and Cyberwarriors); SILVER SABLE #11-12 (with Silver Sable, Wild Pack, Next Wave, and Knights of Wundagore, battled Genesis Coalition and Cyberwarriors); DEATHLOK ANNUAL #2 (defeated airstrike on U.S. troops by hostile foreign power in the mideast); DEATHLOK Vol. 2 #27-28 (with Deathlok III, battled Timestream and his mercenaries in Australia); DAREDEVIL #322-323 (alongside Daredevil, battled Venom and the Hand); DEATHLOK #31-34 (with Deathlok and Godwulf, battled Timestream, Demolisher and Luther Manning in the past)

Note: The remains of John Kelly's original body have been incorporated into the framework of the Deathlok cyborg. The remains of his brain were mutated into the horrific creature called Biohazard.

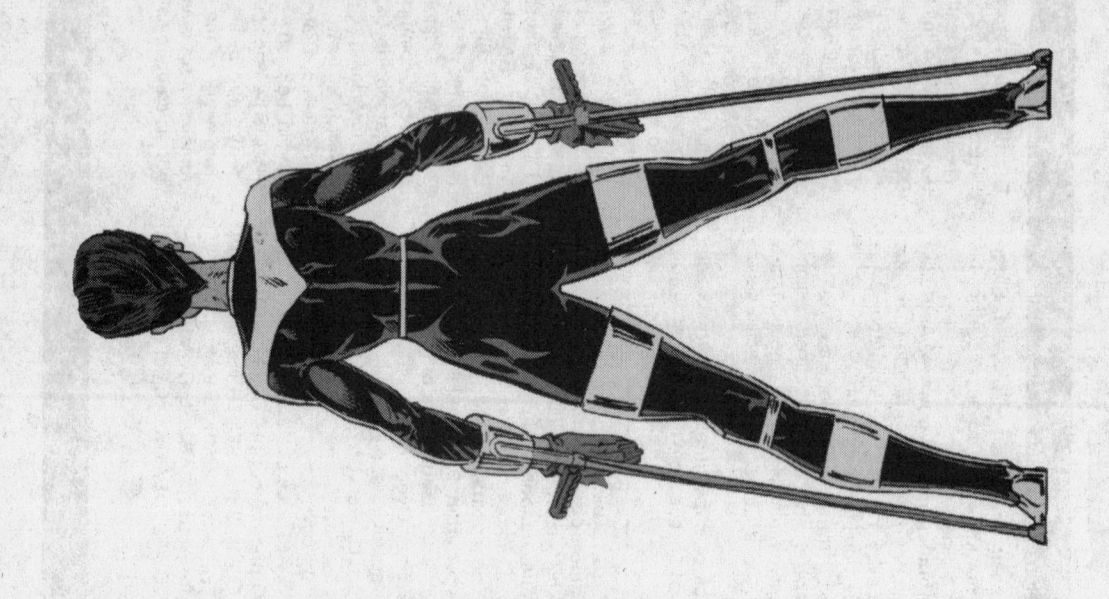

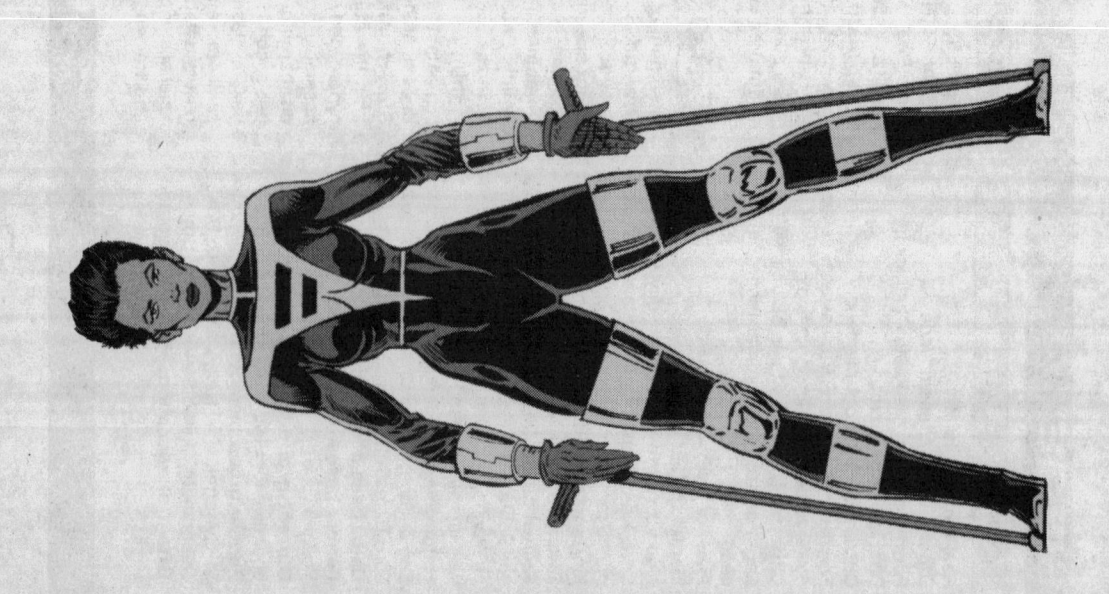

SILHOUETTE™

SILHOUETTE

BIOGRAPHICAL DATA

Real name: Silhouette Chord
Note: Silhouette is the English translation of her Cambodian name.
Other Current aliases: None
Former aliases: None known
Dual identity: Publicly known
Current occupation: Adventurer
Former occupation: Vigilante
Citizenship: United States of America
Legal status: No criminal record
Place of birth: New York City
Marital status: Single
Known relatives: Tai (grandmother), Andrew Chord (father), Miyami Chord (mother, deceased), Midnight's Fire (brother)
Known confidants: Night Thrasher, New Warriors, Father Janes, (former) Midnight's Fire
Known allies: Night Thrasher, New Warriors, Darkhawk, Spider-Man, Daredevil, (former) Midnight's Fire, the Concrete Carrion Gang
Major enemies: Tai, Sphinx I, Terrax, Gideon II, Psionex, (former) Bengal, Punisher, White Queen, Hellions (deceased)
Usual base of operations: New York City
Former base of operations: None
Current group membership: The New Warriors
Former group membership: The Concrete Carrion Gang
Extent of education: Unrevealed

PHYSICAL DESCRIPTION

Height: 5'6"
Weight: 105 lbs.
Eyes: Formerly brown, now white
Hair: Black
Other distinguishing features: Scars on back due to injuries from gunfire

POWERS AND ABILITIES

Intelligence: Normal
Strength: Enhanced human
Speed: Enhanced human (handicapped by crippled legs)
Stamina: Enhanced human
Durability: Enhanced human
Agility: Enhanced human
Reflexes: Enhanced human
Fighting skills: Superb hand-to-hand combatant, master of an unspecified martial art
Special skills and abilities: None known
Superhuman physical powers: Aside from the above listed attributes, Silhouette possesses the ability to teleport herself over short distances on Earth by traveling through the Darkforce dimension. She can "melt" into any shadow or area of darkness, thus entering the Darkforce dimension, and then reemerge on Earth through another shadow or area of darkness. Also possesses enhanced sensory perception abilities.
Superhuman mental powers: None
Special limitations: Legs are crippled due to injuries inflicted by gunfire. Can only teleport herself and any inanimate matter composed of unstable molecules.
Source of superhuman powers: Genetic heritage developed through many generations of selective breeding.

PARAPHERNALIA

Costume specifications: Unstable molecules
Personal weaponry: Crutches that are equipped with tasers that can emit electrical charges to stun an adversary, they also contain anesthetic needles, "smoke gas," and metal firing pellets
Special weaponry: None
Other accessories: Wears metal braces on her legs for aid in walking
Transportation: Teleportation by her own power or New Warriors vehicles
Design and manufacture of paraphernalia: (costume) Based on patents by Reed Richards; (crutches and braces) Taylor Foundation subsidiaries

BIBLIOGRAPHY

First appearance: NEW WARRIORS #2
Origin issue: NEW WARRIORS #2, 23-24
Significant issues: NEW WARRIORS #2 (worked with Midnight's Fire and Night Thrasher to fight criminal gangs, began romance with Night Thrasher, crippled by police gunfire, turned against Midnight's Fire); NEW WARRIORS #7-9 (fought Bengal, sought aid from New Warriors, revealed "shadow-melting" power to Night Thrasher; attacked by Punisher; made peace with Punisher); NEW WARRIORS #10 (with New Warriors, battled White Queen and the Hellions); NEW WARRIORS #15 (first clashed with Psionex); NEW WARRIORS #16-17 (with New Warriors and Fantastic Four, battled Terrax); NEW WARRIORS #18 (helped Night Thrasher investigate corruption in Taylor Foundation, witnessed Chord's suicide attempt); NEW WARRIORS #19 (with New Warriors, captured by Gideon II); NEW WARRIORS ANNUAL #2 (with New Warriors, first battled Sphinx I, allowed by Reed Richards to keep her unstable molecule costume)

SILVER DAGGER

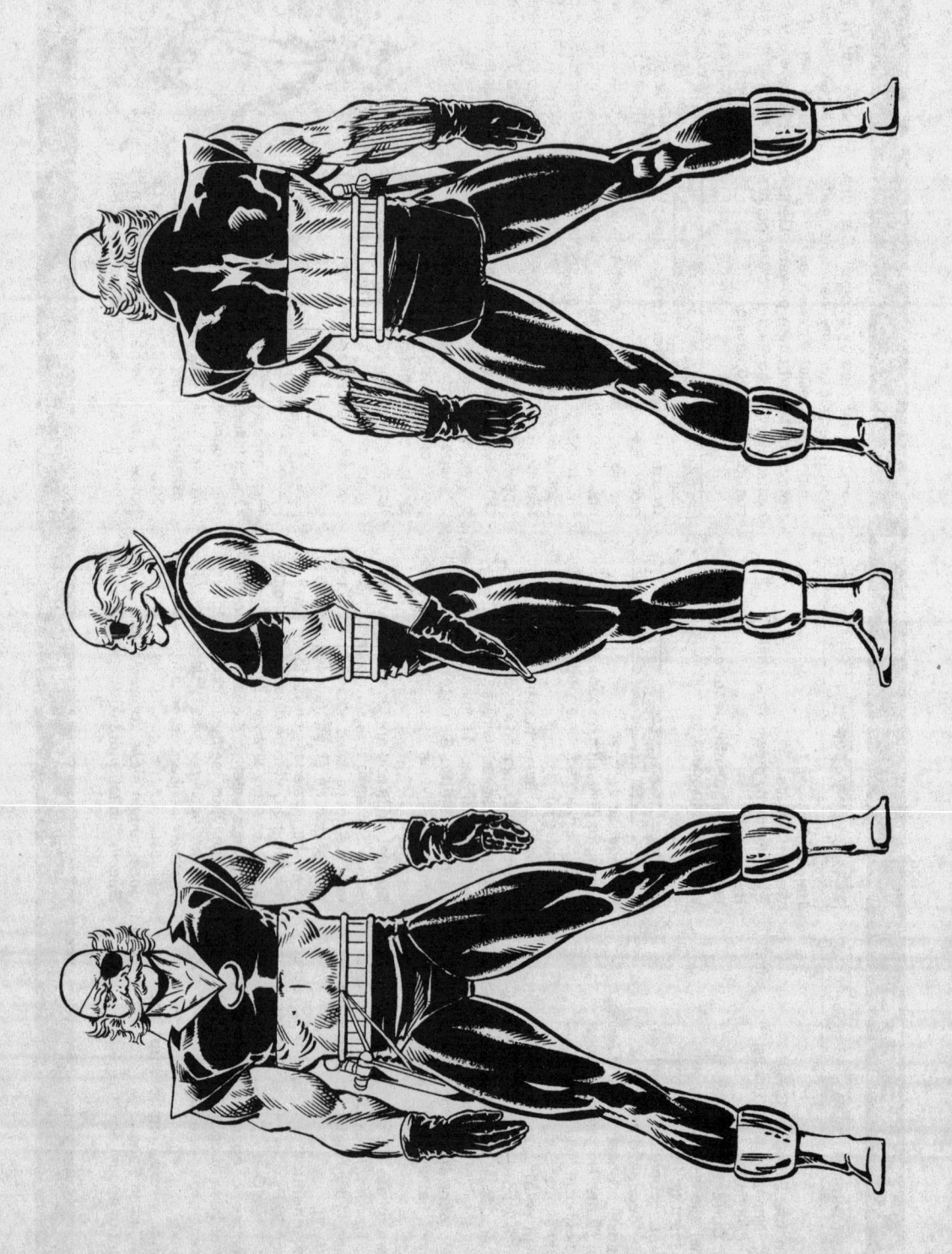

SILVER DAGGER

BIOGRAPHICAL DATA

Real name: Isaiah Curwen
Other current aliases: None
Former aliases: None
Dual Identity: Secret
Current occupation: Executioner of the wicked; evangelist
Former occupation: Cardinal in the Catholic Church
Citizenship: Unrevealed
Legal status: No criminal record
Place of birth: Unrevealed
Marital status: Single
Known relatives: None
Known confidants: None
Known allies: The Sword of the Lord
Major enemies: Dr. Strange, Werewolf by Night
Usual base of operations: Mobile
Former bases of operations: Vatican City, Italy
Current group membership: Leader of the Sword of the Lord
Former group membership: The Catholic Church (excommunicated)
Extent of education: D.d., PhD. in theology from a Jesuit college

PHYSICAL DESCRIPTION

Height: 6'
Weight: 220 lbs.
Eyes: (right) Black; (left) Silver
Hair: White (balding on top)
Other distinguishing features: Silver Dagger usually wears an eyepatch over his left eye.

POWERS AND ABILITIES

Intelligence: Gifted
Strength: Athlete
Speed: Athlete
Stamina: Athlete
Durability: Athlete
Agility: Athlete
Reflexes: Athlete
Fighting skills: Basic hand-to-hand combat skills, some akido, judo, and boxing
Special skills and abilities: Extensive knowledge of Christian theology, particularly of the apocalyptic sect he himself has created; some knowledge of magic and sorcery; ability to hurl bladed weapons with a high degree of accuracy; familiarity with a variety of automatic weapons. Plus a high degree of skill for strategy and tactics as used in commando-style low intensity conflict, and guerrilla warfare techniques. Also, he is an exceptionally charismatic personality, possessing powers of persuasion which border on superhuman, especially when addressing large groups of people
Superhuman physical powers: Silver Dagger formerly employed his knowledge of sorcery for a variety of effects; he has since repudiated all use of cast magic as "Satanic". Silver Dagger's left eye is now the original Eye of Agamatto and can project silver beams of mystical force.
Superhuman mental powers: None
Special limitations: None
Source of superhuman powers: The Eye of Agamatto

PARAPHERNALIA

Costume specifications: Leather bodysuit; rear of belt has a number of holders for throwing daggers
Personal weaponry: Specially-crafted 9" silver throwing daggers which have been dipped in holy water for enhanced effectiveness against supernatural creatures
Special weaponry: None
Other accessories: Silver Dagger and his team of zealot commandos have been known to make use of a variety of automatic weapons which have been modified to fire silver bullets, as well as sophisticated communications devices and other items used for stealth combat
Transportation: Various
Design and manufacture of paraphernalia: Unrevealed

BIBLIOGRAPHY

First appearance: DOCTOR STRANGE Vol. 2 #1
Origin issue: DOCTOR STRANGE Vol. 2 #5
Significant issues: DOCTOR STRANGE Vol. 2 #1-2, 4-5 (broke into Dr. Strange's sanctum, attempted to slay him with dagger, believing him to be demon-spawn, imprisoned and attempted brainwashing of Clea; trapped in dimension of Agamatto); MARVEL TEAM-UP #76-77 (conquered the dimension within the Orb of Agamatto; battled Dr. Strange, Spider-Man, Ms. Marvel, and Marie Leveau, stabbed by Leveau, returned to dimension of Agamatto); DOCTOR STRANGE Vol. 3 #7 (surrendered left eye to Agamatto, who awarded it to Dr. Strange); MARVEL COMICS PRESENTS #55-59 (attempted to slay the Werewolf by Night; with troops, battled the werewolf motorcycle gang, the Braineaters, bitten by the Werewolf, left at mercy of his own troops, eye inexplicably restored); DOCTOR STRANGE Vol. 3 #30 (escaped from Agamatto's dimension and own troops explained; battled Dr. Strange using own eye of Agamatto for first time, taken into custody by Agamatto again)

SILVER SABLE

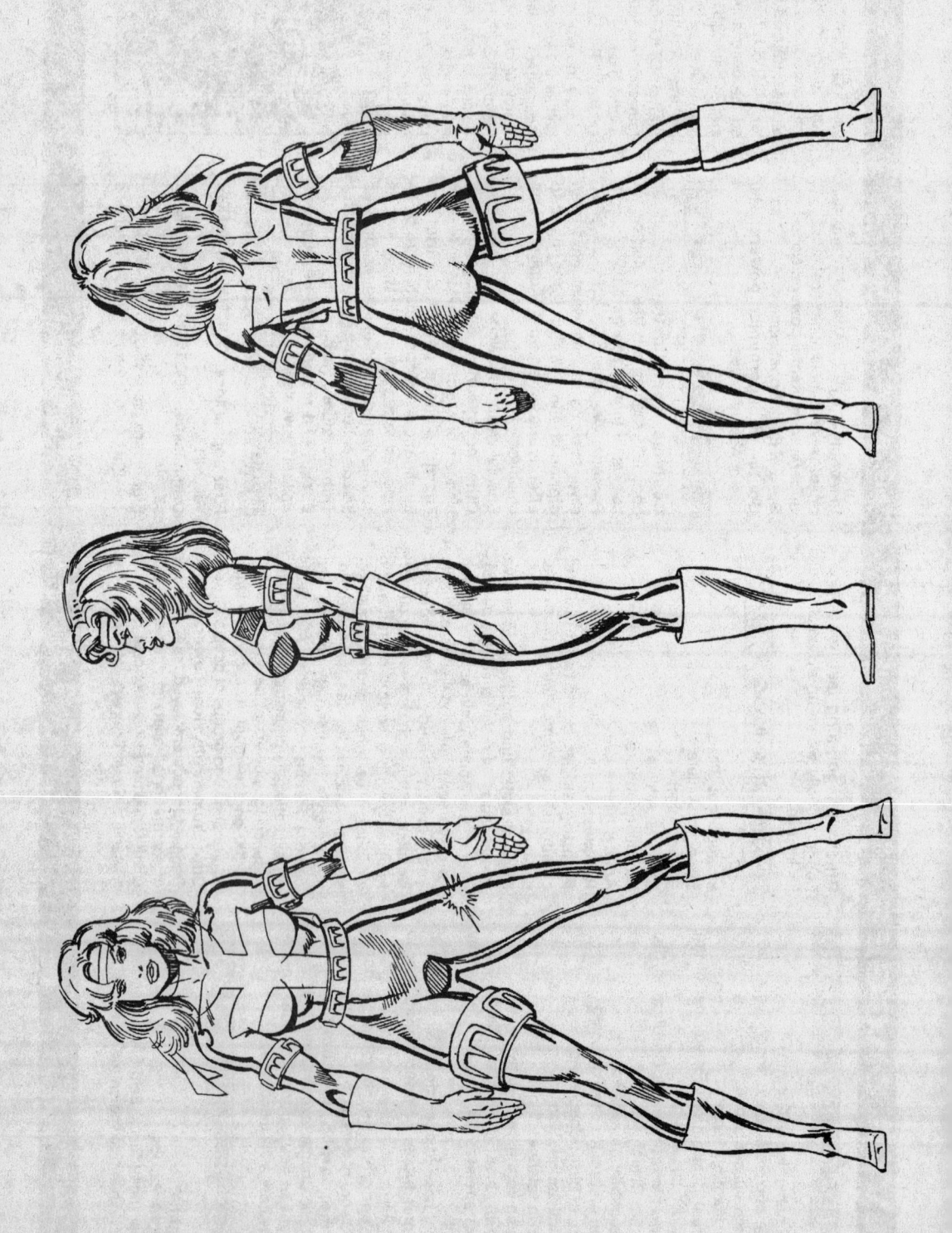

SILVER SABLE

BIOGRAPHICAL DATA

Real name: Unrevealed
Other current aliases: None
Former aliases: None
Dual identity: None
Current Occupation: Leader of the Wild Pack mercenary group
Former occupation: None
Legal status: No criminal record
Place of birth: Symkaria
Citizenship: Symkaria
Marital status: Divorced
Known relatives: Mortimer (uncle), the Foreigner (ex-husband), Anna (niece)
Known confidants: None
Known allies: Spider-Man, Sandman, Paladin, Prowler, Puma, Rocket Racer, Will O' the Wisp
Major enemies: The Foreigner, Hobgoblin, The Sinister Syndicate
Usual base of operations: The Symkarian Embassy, New York City
Former bases of operations: Symkaria
Current group membership: Wild Pack, Silver Sable International
Former group membership: The Outlaws
Extent of education: College graduate

PHYSICAL DESCRIPTION

Height: 5'5"
Weight: 125 lbs
Eyes: Blue
Hair: Silver
Other distinguishing features: None

POWERS AND ABILITIES

Intelligence: Above average
Strength: Athlete
Speed: Athlete
Stamina: Athlete
Durability: Athlete
Agility: Peak human
Reflexes: Athlete
Fighting skills: Formidable hand-to-hand combatant; skilled in various martial arts, expert markswoman, swordswoman and gymnast.
Special skills and abilities: Strong leadership abilities
Superhuman physical powers: None
Superhuman mental powers: None
Special limitations: None
Source of superhuman powers: Inapplicable

PARAPHERNALIA

Costume specifications: Synthetic stretch fabric lined with kevlar throughout the torso.
Personal weaponry: Katana (samurai sword), chia (three-pronged half-moon throwing projectiles), derringer
Special weaponry: Silver Sable has the latest technology and equipment at her disposal.
Other accessories: Various, as needed
Transportation: Limousine, stealthcraft
Design and manufacture of paraphernalia: Silver Sable International

BIBLIOGRAPHY

First appearance: AMAZING SPIDER-MAN #265
Origin issue: WEB OF SPIDER-MAN ANNUAL #5
Significant issues: AMAZING SPIDER-MAN #265 (hunted the Black Fox to recover valuable gems stolen by the thief; inadvertently thwarted by Spider-Man); AMAZING SPIDER-MAN #279-281 (hired by a South African republic to neutralize the international terrorist Jack O'Lantern; enlisted Spider-Man's aid against the Sinister Syndicate; formed alliance with Sandman); AMAZING SPIDER-MAN #320-325 (joined forces with Spider-Man, Paladin, Solo, and Captain America to track down Sabretooth and the Red Skull, who masterminded a plot to pit the United States in a war with Symkaria); WEB OF SPIDER-MAN #50 (hired Spider-Man to steal incriminating documents from a Maggia money launderer; first encountered the Outlaws); WEB OF SPIDER-MAN ANNUAL #5 (intelligence mission in Iraq resulted in death of a Wild Pack member; denied compensation to the slain man's family due to his negligence); SPECTACULAR SPIDER-MAN ANNUAL #10 (devised an initiation test for the Prowler and taught him a lesson in humility); EXCALIBUR #36 (hired the Outlaws to retrieve a Symkarian nuclear device in England); AMAZING SPIDER-MAN ANNUAL #25/ SPECTACULAR SPIDER-MAN ANNUAL #11/WEB OF SPIDER-MAN ANNUAL #7 (hired the Outlaws to rescue the kidnaped daughter of a Canadian official); SILVER SABLE #1 (with help of Spider-Man, Sandman, and the Wild Pack, rescued her niece from a kidnaping by HYDRA), SILVER SABLE #4-5 (encountered Doctor Doom doppelganger)

SILVER SAMURAI

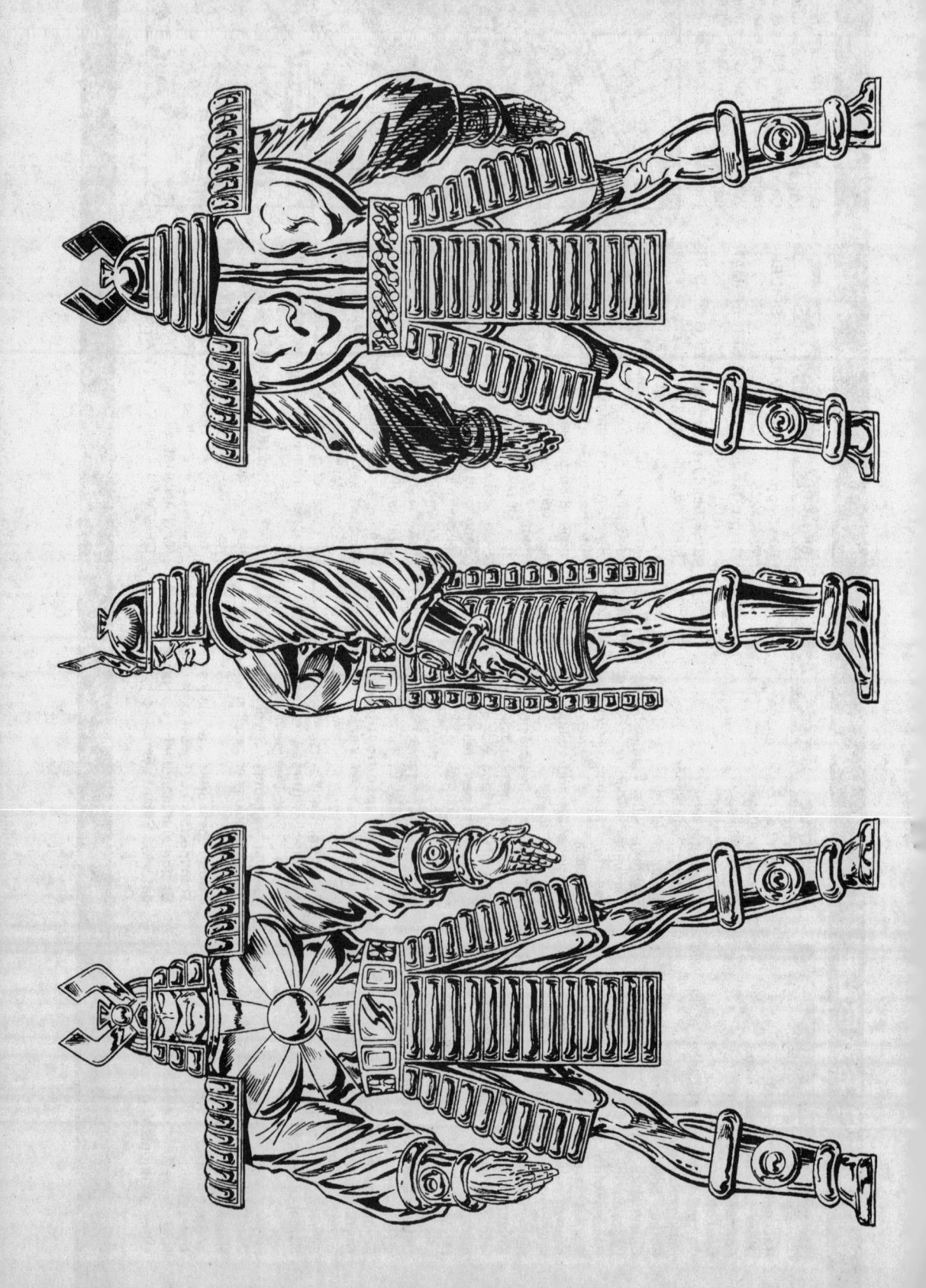

SILVER SAMURAI

BIOGRAPHICAL DATA

Real name: Kenuichio Harada
Other current aliases: None
Former aliases: Unrevealed
Dual identity: Known to the international law enforcement agencies
Current occupation: Oyabun (leader) of Clan Yashida
Former occupation: Martial arts student, Professional criminal
Citizenship: Unrevealed
Legal status: International criminal record
Place of birth: Unrevealed
Marital status: Single
Known relatives: Shingen Harada (father, deceased), Mariko Yashida (half-sister, deceased), Shiro Yashida (Sunfire, deceased), Tomo Yashida (cousin, deceased), Saburo Yashida (cousin, deceased)
Known confidants: Viper II
Known allies: Viper II, Boomerang, Lindsay McCabe, (former) Mandrill (deceased), Nekra (deceased), Black Spectre I
Major enemies: Daredevil, Black Widow, Shanna the She-Chi, Spider-Man, Nick Fury, Shang-Chi, Spider-Woman I, the New Mutants, the X-Men, Yukio, Wolverine
Usual base of operations: Mobile
Former bases of operations: Unrevealed
Current group membership: None
Former group membership: None
Extent of education: College graduate

PHYSICAL DESCRIPTION

Height: 6'6"
Weight: 250 lbs., (with armor) 310 lbs.
Eyes: Brown
Hair: Black
Other distinguishing features: None

POWERS AND ABILITIES

Intelligence: Normal
Strength: Athlete
Speed: Athlete
Stamina: Athlete
Durability: Athlete
Agility: Athlete
Reflexes: Athlete
Fighting skills: Master of *Kenjutsu* (samurai sword [katana]), highly skilled martial artist
Special skills and abilities: Expert in history and customs of the samurai class (Bushido)
Superhuman physical powers: Ability to generate a form of energy, presumably a tachyon field, with which he surrounds his sword, enabling it to slice through any known substance except adamantium
Superhuman mental powers: None
Special limitations: None
Source of superhuman powers: Genetic mutation

PARAPHERNALIA

Costume specifications: Lightweight steel alloy body armor
Personal weaponry: Katana (long sword)
Special weaponry: Shuriken (throwing stars) and other samurai weaponry
Other accessories: None
Transportation: Teleportational ring
Design and manufacture of paraphernalia: (armor) Unrevealed, (weaponry) Kenuicho Harada, (teleportation ring) Viper II

BIBLIOGRAPHY

First appearance: DAREDEVIL #111
Origin issue: UNCANNY X-MEN #173
Significant issues: DAREDEVIL #111 (employed by Mandrill and Black Spectre I); MARVEL TEAM-UP #57 (employed by Viper II, battled Spider-Man and Black Widow); MARVEL TEAM-UP #74 (recovered Viper II's teleport ring, battled Spider-Man, encountered the original Not-Ready-For-Prime-Time Players); MARVEL TEAM-UP #83-85 (alongside Viper II and Boomerang, battled Spider-Man, Nick Fury, Shang Chi, and Black Widow on orriginal SHIELD Helicarrier); SPIDER-WOMAN #42-43 (alongside Viper II, attempted to kidnap Michael Kramer, battled Spider-Woman I); NEW MUTANTS #5-6 (alongside Viper II, attempted theft of cavourite crystal, battled New Mutants); UNCANNY X-MEN Vol. 2 #172-174 (alongside Viper II, battled X-Men and Yukio); WOLVERINE Vol. 2 #2-3 (attempted to possess the Black Blade, battled Wolverine, aided Lindsay McCabe and O'Donnell, rescued Wolverine and Jessica Drew from cultists); CABLE #2 (revealed to have become head of Clan Yashida upon the death of Lady Mariko)

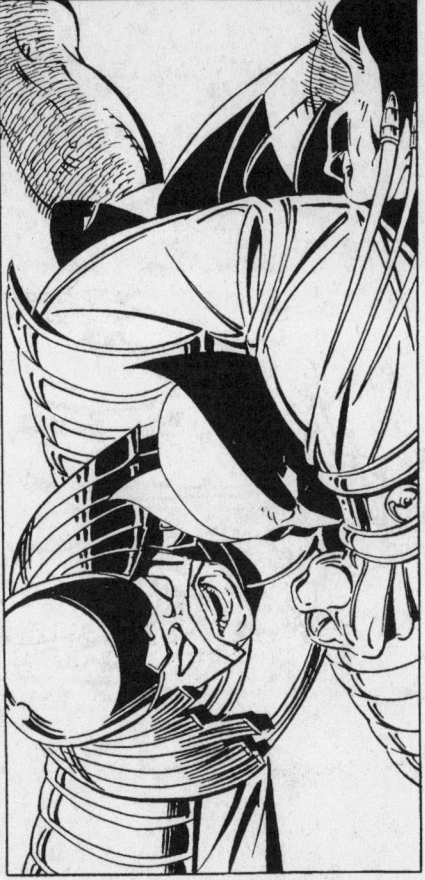

SILVER SURFER

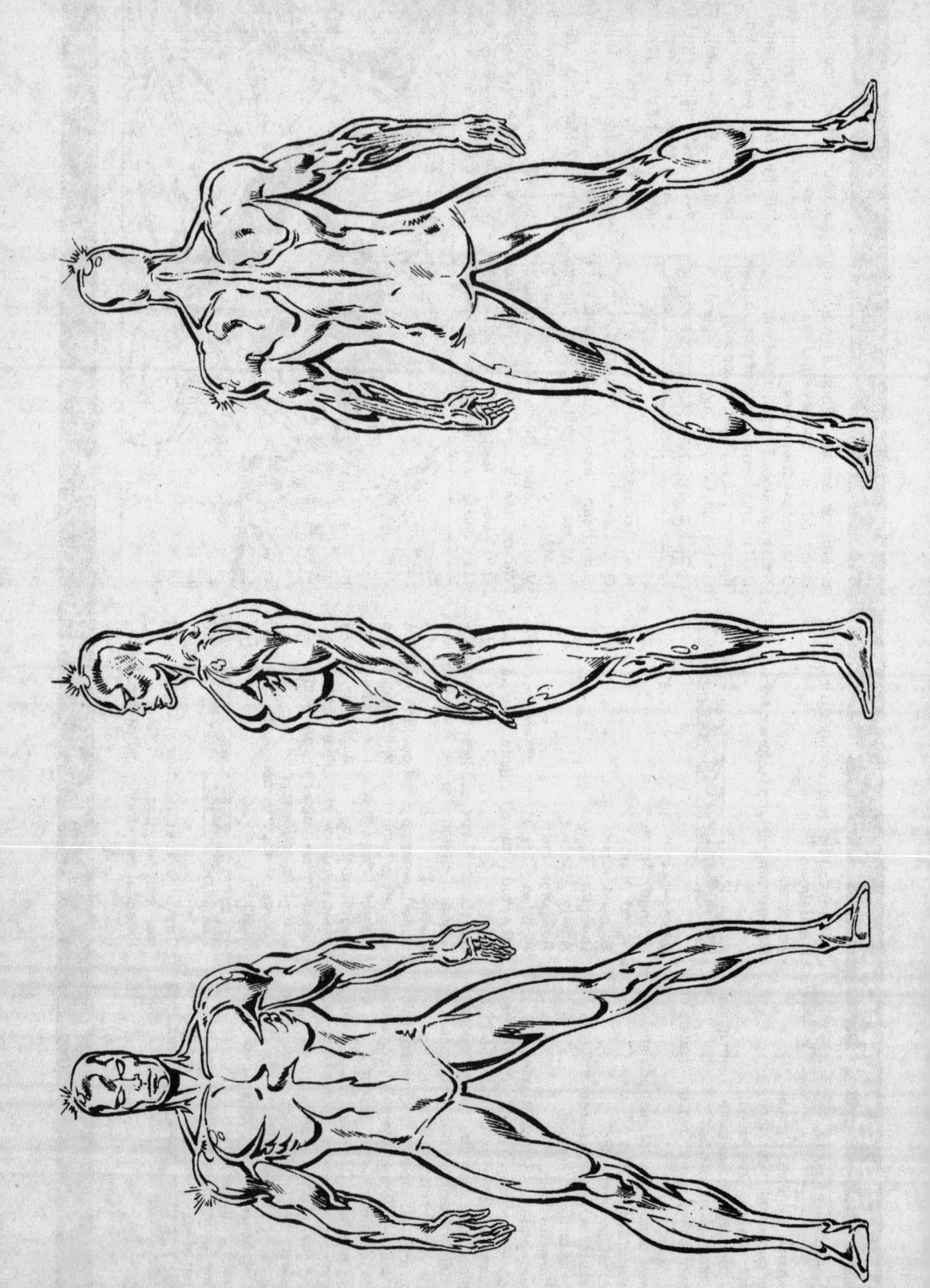

SILVER SURFER

BIOGRAPHICAL DATA

Real name: Norrin Radd
Other current aliases: None
Former aliases: None
Dual identity: None; existence unknown to the general populace of Earth
Current occupation: Wanderer, adventurer
Former occupation: Scholar, herald of Galactus
Citizenship: The planet Zenn-La
Legal status: No criminal record
Place of birth: The planet Zenn-La, Deneb System, Milky Way Galaxy
Marital status: Single
Known relatives: Jartarn Radd (father deceased), Elmar (mother, deceased)
Known confidants: (former) Shalla Bal, Mantis, Nova II
Known allies: Fantastic Four, the Defenders, the Avengers, Mentor, Starfox, Drax the Destroyer, Adam Warlock
Major enemies: (former) Galactus; Mephisto, Elders of the Universe, Thanos
Usual base of operations: Mobile throughout the universe
Former bases of operations: The planet Zenn-La, the planet Earth
Current group membership: None
Former group membership: The Defenders
Extent of education: Unrevealed

PHYSICAL DESCRIPTION

Height: 6'4"
Weight: Unknown
Eyes: (as Norrin Radd) Blue, (as Silver Surfer) White
Hair: (as Norrin Radd) None, except black eyebrows, (as Silver Surfer) None
Other distinguishing features: The Silver Surfer's skin is apparently a flexible metallic silvery material.

POWERS AND ABILITIES

Intelligence: Above normal
Strength: Superhuman Class 100
Flight speed: Warp speed
Stamina: Godlike
Durability: Godlike
Agility: Enhanced human
Reflexes: Enhanced human
Fighting skills: Average hand-to-hand combatant, relies wholly on cosmic energy powers
Special skills and abilities: Some knowledge of advanced alien technology of planet Zenn-La
Superhuman physical powers: Aside from the above listed attributes, the Silver Surfer has the ability to manipulate cosmic energy for a variety of effects, including projection of bolts of cosmic force, erection of force shields, molecular reconstruction and creation of objects, healing, augmentation of strength to superhuman levels; flight at near-light speeds through hyperinterstellar space and through hyperspace; near total physical invulnerability, ability to exist without food, sleep, or oxygen in space'
Superhuman mental powers: Mental command of his surfboard; ability to sense concentrations of energy, including life energies of living beings
Special limitations: None
Source of superhuman powers: Physical transformation by cosmic power of Galactus

PARAPHERNALIA

Costume specifications: None
Personal weaponry: None
Special weaponry: None
Other accessories: None
Transportation: "Surfboard" (possesses similar cosmic-powered attributes to Silver Surfer)
Design and manufacture of paraphernalia: Galactus

BIBLIOGRAPHY

First appearance: FANTASTIC FOUR #48
Origin issue: SILVER SURFER Vol. 1 #1
Significant issues: FANTASTIC FOUR #48-50 (first came to Earth as herald of Galactus, encountered Fantastic Four and Alicia Masters, turned against Galactus and battled him, exiled to Earth by Galactus); FANTASTIC FOUR #57-61 (cosmic power stolen by Doctor Doom, who used it to defeat Fantastic Four; recovered cosmic power after Doom disabled by Galactus's barrier); FANTASTIC FOUR #72 (attempted to bring about world peace by giving mankind a common enemy in himself, battled Fantastic Four, powers drained by "Sonic Shark" weapon); FANTASTIC FOUR #74-77 (entered a "microworld," pursued by Dr. Doom into turning against Fantastic Four); TOMB OF DRACULA #50 (encountered Dracula); SILVER SURFER Vol. 2 #1 (temporarily freed from Earth, discovered devastation of Zenn-La by Galactus, battled Mephisto, gave Shalla Bal cosmic power to replenish plant life on Zenn-La); DEFENDERS #112-114 (alongside Defenders, journeyed to parallel Earth of Squadron Supreme, battled Null and Over-Mind); FANTASTIC FOUR #260 (aided Fantastic Four against Terrax); AVENGERS #266 (helped Molecule Man restore the damage done to Earth by the Beyonder); SILVER SURFER Vol. 3 #1 (freed from Earth, first met Nova II, encountered the Champion); SILVER SURFER Vol. 3 #4 (first met Mantis, encountered the Elders of the Universe); SILVER SURFER Vol. 3 #34 (first encountered Thanos); SILVER SURFER Vol. 3 #46 (first met Adam Warlock); INFINITY GAUNTLET #1 (alongside other heroes, battled Thanos)

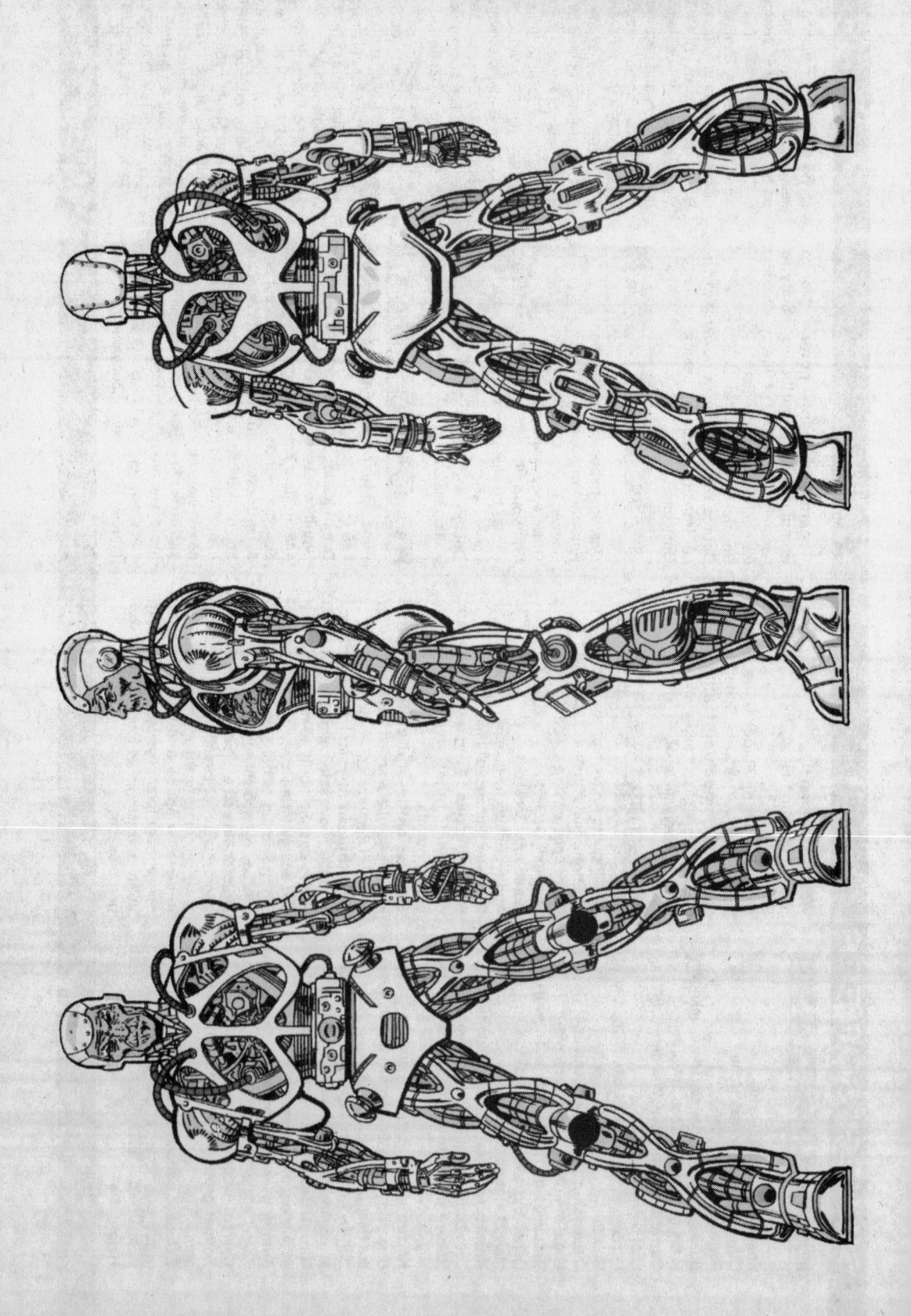

SILVERMANE™

SILVERMANE

BIOGRAPHICAL DATA

Real name: Silvio Manfredi
Other current aliases: None
Former aliases: Supreme Hydra
Dual Identity: None
Current occupation: Criminal organizer and mastermind
Former occupation: Racketeer
Citizenship: Former citizen of Italy, now naturalized citizen of the United States of America
Legal status: Criminal record, legally deceased
Place of birth: Palermo, Sicily
Marital status: Widowed
Known relatives: Caterina (wife, deceased), Joseph ("Joe Silvermane," Blackwing, son)
Known confidants: None
Known allies: Caeser "Big C" Cicero, Dominic Tyrone (the Rapier)
Major enemies: Spider-Man, the Lizard, the Green Goblin III, the Rapier, the Kingpin, Cloak and Dagger
Usual base of operations: New York City
Former bases of operations: None
Current group membership: None
Former group membership: The Maggia, HYDRA
Extent of education: High school graduate

PHYSICAL DESCRIPTION

Height: 6'2", (as cyborg) 7'
Weight: 195 lbs., (as cyborg) 440 lbs.
Eyes: Blue
Hair: Silver, (as cyborg) None
Other distinguishing features: Silvermane's brain, vital organs, and head have been transplanted into a robotic body.

POWERS AND ABILITIES

Intelligence: Normal
Strength: Normal, (as cyborg) Superhuman Class 25
Speed: Normal, (as cyborg) Athlete
Stamina: Normal, (as cyborg) Peak human
Durability: Normal, (as cyborg) Enhanced human
Agility: Normal
Reflexes: Normal
Fighting skills: Superb hand-to-hand combatant
Special skills and abilities: Excellent marksman, brilliant strategist and organizer
Superhuman physical powers: Aside from the above, Silvermane's senses have been enhanced to superhuman levels
Superhuman mental powers: None
Special limitations: Silvermane's organic body parts are those of a frail 80 year old man, and are hence quite vulnerable.
Source of superhuman powers: Cyborg materials, design, and construction

PARAPHERNALIA

Costume specifications: None
Personal weaponry: Various handguns and Thompson .50 caliber machine gun
Special weaponry: None
Other accessories: None known
Transportation: Conventional means
Design and manufacture of paraphernalia: Maggia-funded researchers

BIBLIOGRAPHY

First appearance: AMAZING SPIDER-MAN #73
Origin Issue: SPECTACULAR SPIDER-MAN ANNUAL #2, SPECTACULAR SPIDER-MAN #70
Significant Issues: AMAZING SPIDER-MAN #73-75 (forced Dr. Curtis Connors to prepare a mystical youth serum from and ancient clay tablet; first crossed paths with Spider-Man and the Lizard; drank the serum which caused him to grow increasingly younger until he reached the point before the age of birth); DAREDEVIL #120-123 (revealed that he mystically aged to his forties; assumed the mantle of Supreme Hydra; defeated by Daredevil, Nick Fury, and SHIELD); AMAZING SPIDER-MAN #177-180 (attempted to unite all of New York's gangs under his leadership, but was opposed by the Green Goblin III; survived a fall from a great height during a confrontation between him, the Goblin and Spider-Man); AMAZING SPIDER-MAN #197 (attempted to assassinate an amnesiac Kingpin); SPECTACULAR SPIDER-MAN ANNUAL #2 (his former partner, Dominic Tyrone, assumed the identity of the Rapier and sought vengeance against Silvermane's betrayal by attempting to slay him); SPECTACULAR SPIDER MAN #69-70 (his injuries resulted in undoing the effects of the rejuvenation serum; though bedridden, he continued to run his criminal empire until Dagger nearly killed him; transformed into a cyborg); SPECTACULAR SPIDER MAN #94-96 (the Kingpin gained control of his cyborg body until Dagger restored his life energy to him); AMAZING SPIDER MAN #284 (cyborg body severely damaged by Jack O' Lantern I during gang war between Hammerhead and Kingpin); WEB OF SPIDER-MAN #79-80 (used remote-controlled android doppelganger to battle Spider-Man in attempt to drain his radioactive blood to mobilize a new stronger cyborg body); DEATHLOK #8-9 (confronted Deathlok and the Punisher while setting up a major drug operation outside a grammar school)

SIRYN™

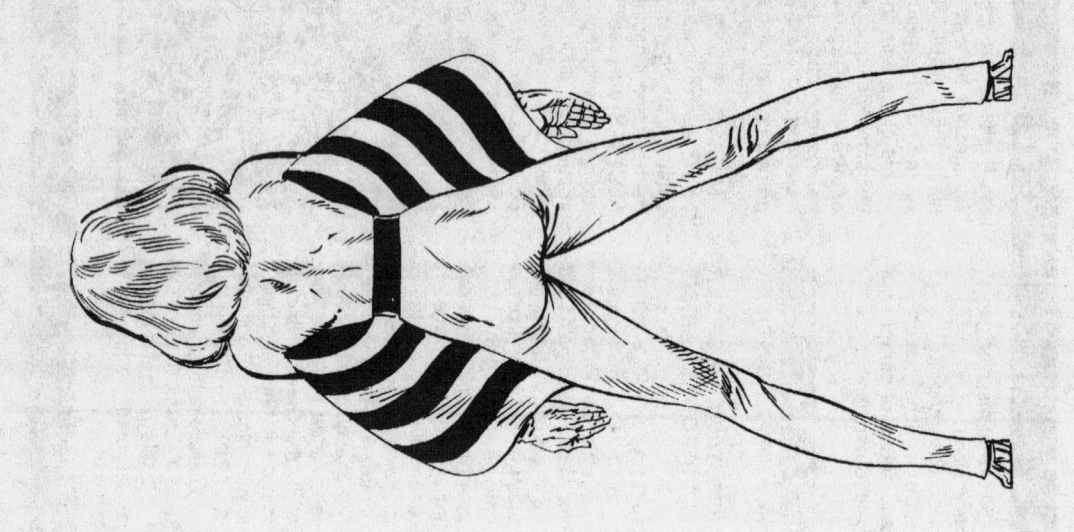

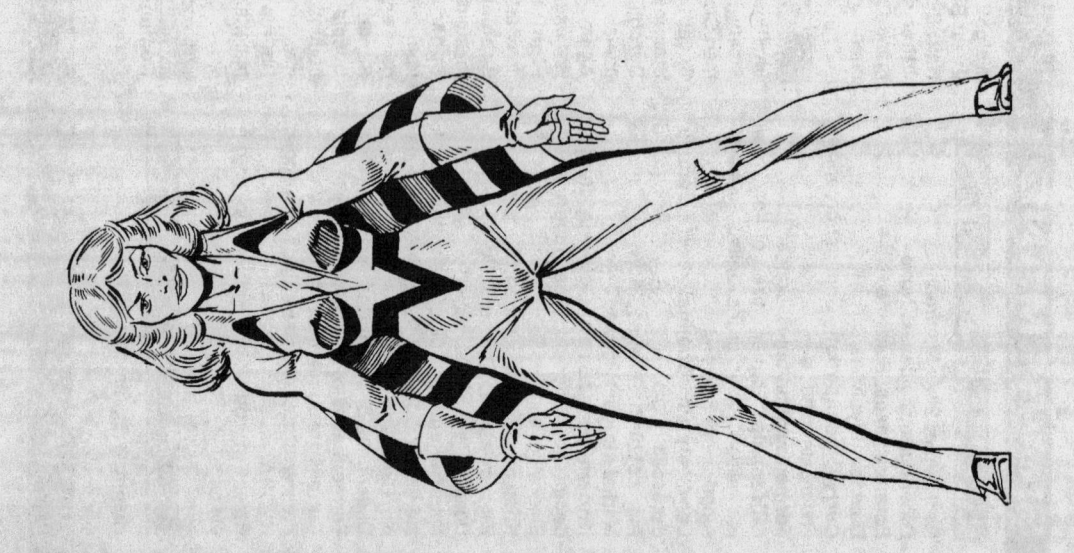

SIRYN

BIOGRAPHICAL DATA

Real name: Theresa Rourke
Other current aliases: None
Former aliases: None
Dual identity: Secret
Current occupation: Adventurer
Former occupation: Criminal (coerced pawn of Black Tom Cassidy and the Juggernaut)
Citizenship: Ireland
Legal status: No known criminal record
Place of birth: Cassidy Keep, County Mayo, Ireland
Marital status: Single
Known relatives: Sean Cassidy (alias Banshee, father), Maeve Rourke Cassidy (mother, deceased), Black Tom Cassidy (uncle)
Known confidants: Sean Cassidy, Moira MacTaggart
Known allies: (former) Black Tom Cassidy, Juggernaut; (current) the Fallen Angels, the X-Men, X-Force
Major enemies: Unipar
Usual base of operations: X-Force headquarters
Former bases of operations: Cassidy Keep, County Mayo, Ireland; Fallen Angels headquarters (the Beat Street Club), New York City; Muir Island, Scotland
Current group membership: X-Force
Former group membership: Former ally of Black Tom Cassidy and Juggernaut; the Fallen Angels

PHYSICAL DESCRIPTION

Height: 5'6"
Weight: 112 lbs.
Eyes: Blue
Hair: Reddish blonde
Other distinguishing features: None

POWERS AND ABILITIES

Intelligence: Normal
Strength: Athlete
Speed: Athlete
Flight speed: Speed of sound
Stamina: Athlete
Durability: Normal
Agility: Normal
Reflexes: Athlete
Fighting skills: Minimal hand-to-hand combat skills
Special skills: None known
Superhuman physical powers: Ability to create various sonic effects with her vocal cords, including producing a "sonic lance" (a concussive sonic blast) and propelling herself through the air at superhuman speed; ability to detect objects through sonar; superhumanly tough vocal cords and interiors of mouth and throat, highly resistant to injuries from sonic vibrations
Superhuman mental powers: Psionic powers to create force field that protects her only against her own sonic vibrations to assist her ability to fly, and to help direct her sonic powers
Special limitations: None known
Source of superhuman powers: Genetic mutation

PARAPHERNALIA

Costume specifications: Friction-proof materials
Personal weaponry: None
Special weaponry: None
Other accessories: None
Transportation: Flight under own power
Design and manufacture of paraphernalia: Unrevealed

BIBLIOGRAPHY

First appearance: SPIDER-WOMAN #37
Origin issue: The details of Siryn's origin are as yet unrevealed.
Significant issues: SPIDER-WOMAN #37 (coerced by Black Tom and Juggernaut to aid them in theft of vibranium in San Francisco, first battled Spider-Woman I); SPIDER-WOMAN #38 (defeated by Spider-Woman I, cleared of involuntary criminality by Black Tom Cassidy); X-MEN #148 (united with her father Sean Cassidy); FALLEN ANGELS #1 (left Muir Island for the United States); FALLEN ANGELS #2 (began search with Madrox for runaway New Mutants Sunspot and Warlock III); FALLEN ANGELS #3 (found Sunspot and Fallen Angels); FALLEN ANGELS #4 (transported with Fallen Angels to Devil Dinosaurs' planet); FALLEN ANGELS #6 (travelled to the "Coconut Grove," home planet of Ariel II); FALLEN ANGELS #7 (superhuman powers neutralized; made captive by Unipar of "Coconut Grove" planet); FALLEN ANGELS #8 (regained use of superhuman powers and freedom, returned to Earth, decided to remain in Fallen Angels to help reform their criminal members); X-MEN #278 (on Muir Island, under mental control of the Shadow King); X-MEN #280 (freed from the Shadow King's control)

Extent of education: High school level

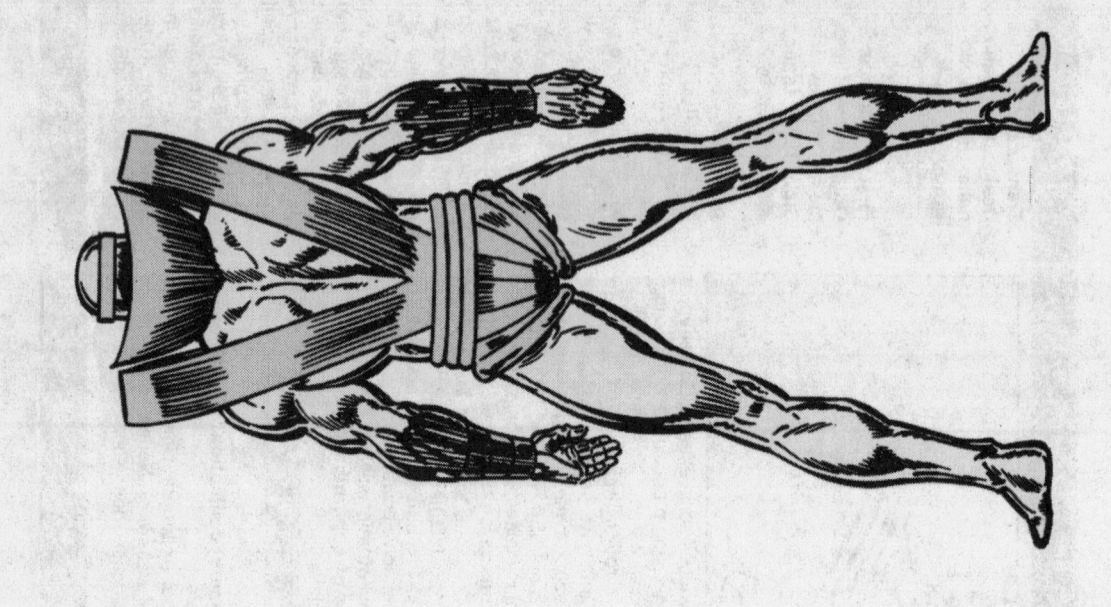

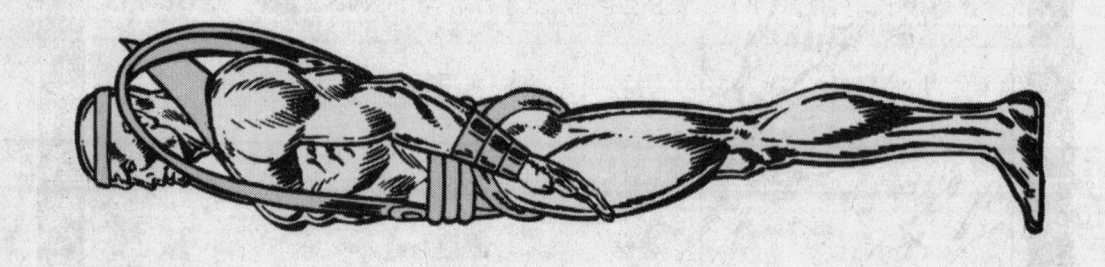

SISE-NEG

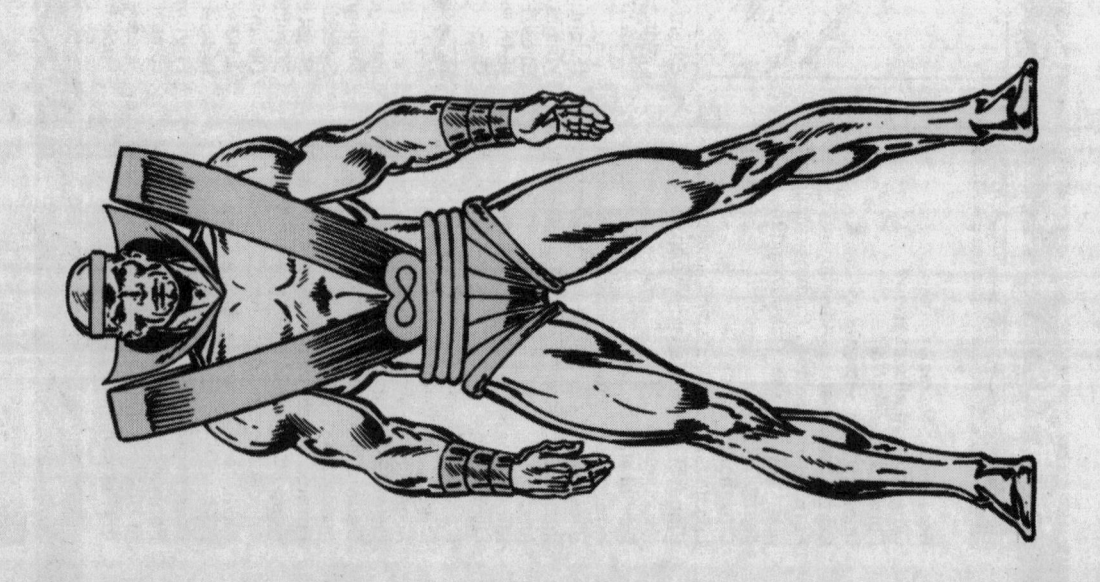

SISE-NEG

BIOGRAPHICAL DATA

Real name: Sise-Neg
Other current aliases: Genesis
Former aliases: Cagliostro
Dual identity: None; Sise-Neg's existence is unknown to the general populace of 20th century Earth
Current occupation: Sorcerer
Former occupation: Unrevealed
Citizenship: Unrevealed
Legal status: Unrevealed
Place of birth: Unrevealed
Marital status: Unrevealed
Known relatives: None
Known confidants: None
Known allies: None
Major enemies: Doctor Strange
Usual base of operations: Somewhere on 31st century Earth
Former bases of operations: 18th century Paris
Current group membership: None
Former group membership: None
Extent of education: Unrevealed

PHYSICAL DESCRIPTION

Height: 6' 1"
Weight: 225 lbs.
Eyes: Green
Hair: None
Other distinguishing features: None

POWERS AND ABILITIES

Intelligence: Gifted
Strength: Normal
Speed: Normal
Stamina: Normal
Durability: Normal
Agility: Normal
Reflexes: Normal
Fighting skills: No evidence of any knowledge of hand-to-hand combat
Special skills and abilities: Vast knowledge of the manipulation of magic
Superhuman physical powers: Virtually unlimited ability to manipulate the forces of magic for a variety of effects, including interdimensional teleportation, size transformations, time travel, matter transmutations, concussive force-bolts, energy/matter constructs, etc.
Superhuman mental powers: Telepathy
Special limitations: None
Source of superhuman powers: Absorption of all the magical energy in the entire universe

PARAPHERNALIA

Costume specifications: Unrevealed
Personal weaponry: None
Special weaponry: None
Other accessories: None
Transportation: Teleportation
Design and manufacture of paraphernalia: Inapplicable

BIBLIOGRAPHY

First appearance: MARVEL PREMIERE #13
Origin issue: MARVEL PREMIERE #13
Significant issues: MARVEL PREMIERE #13 (first encountered Dr. Strange in guise of sorcerer Cagliostro in 18th century Paris while Strange searched for Baron Mordo); MARVEL PREMIERE #14 (became godlike in magical power, time traveled to dawn of the universe with intention to recreate universe in own image, decided instead to "re-create" it as it was)

Note: It is unclear what Sise-Neg meant by "re-creating" the universe when it appeared as if he did nothing but allow creation to take its natural course.

SKIDS™

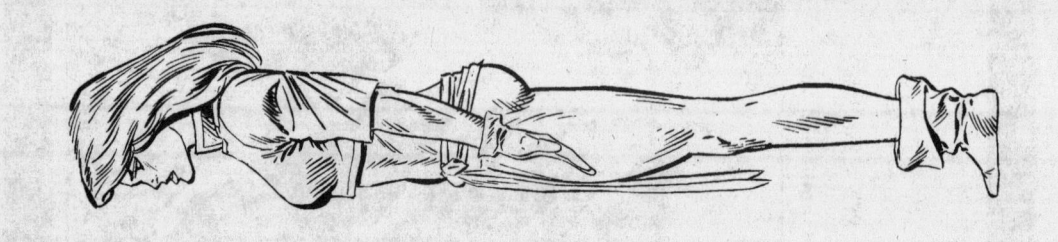

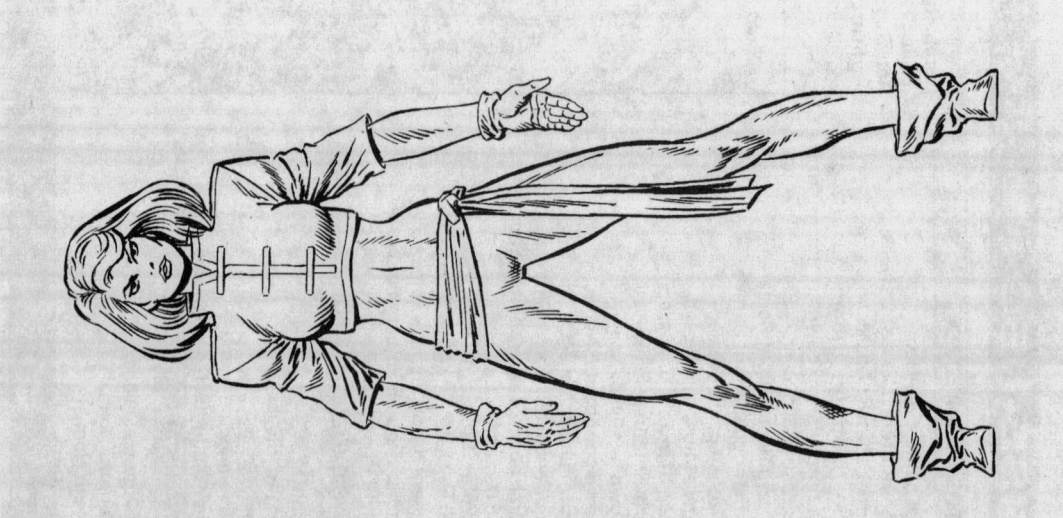

SKIDS

BIOGRAPHICAL DATA

Real name: Sally Blevins
Other current aliases: None
Former aliases: None
Dual identity: Publicly known
Current occupation: Unrevealed
Former occupation: X-Factor trainee
Citizenship: United States of America
Legal status: Outlaw, wanted by federal authorities, presumably still a minor
Place of birth: Unrevealed
Marital status: Single
Known relatives: Bill Blevins (father), Matilda Blevins (mother)
Known confidants: Rusty Collins
Known allies: X-Factor, New Mutants, X-Terminators, Mutant Liberation Front
Major enemies: Freedom Force, Nitro, Vulture, the Right, N'astirh
Usual base of operations: Unrevealed
Former bases of operations: X-Factor's ship, New York City; the Morlock tunnels, New York City area
Current group membership: Unrevealed, possibly Mutant Liberation Front
Former group membership: Morlocks, X-Factor trainee, New Mutants, X-Terminators
Extent of education: Unrevealed, presumed high school dropout, received further education at X-Factor headquarters

PHYSICAL DESCRIPTION

Height: 5'5"
Weight: 115 lbs.
Eyes: Blue
Hair: Blond
Other distinguishing features: None

POWERS AND ABILITIES

Intelligence: Normal
Strength: Normal
Speed: Athlete
Stamina: Normal
Durability: Normal
Agility: Athlete
Reflexes: Athlete
Fighting skills: Moderate skill at hand-to-hand combat from X-Factor

Special skills and abilities: None known
Superhuman physical powers: Ability to create protective frictionless force field around herself and others
Superhuman mental powers: None
Special limitations: None; formerly could not deactivate force field
Source of superhuman powers: Genetic mutation

PARAPHERNALIA

Costume specifications: Synthetic stretch fabric
Personal weaponry: None
Special weaponry: None
Other accessories: None
Transportation: None
Design and manufacture of paraphernalia: Inapplicable

BIBLIOGRAPHY

First appearance: X-FACTOR #7
Origin issue: X-FACTOR #16
Significant issues: X-FACTOR #8 (pursued by Freedom Force, became friend to Rusty Collins, first encounter with X-Factor); X-FACTOR #16 (origin revealed, Skids and Rusty began learning how to control their powers); X-TERMINATORS #1-4, NEW MUTANTS #72-74 (became founding member of second "X-Terminators" team, fought against N'astirh and other demons during "Inferno" invasion of New York City); NEW MUTANTS #76 (aided New Mutants and Namor the Sub-Mariner against undersea monster); NEW MUTANTS #78 (learned that Freedom Force planned to turn over abducted mutant children to federal government for exploitation); NEW MUTANTS #80 (with Rusty, captured by Freedom Force); NEW MUTANTS #85 (freed from prison cell by Rusty Collins to help him stop criminals Vulture and Nitro); NEW MUTANTS #86 (with Rusty Collins, escaped federal prison; defeated Nitro, but was injured; recaptured by Freedom Force); NEW MUTANTS #87 (with Rusty Collins, freed from imprisonment by Mutant Liberation Front)

SKRULLS™

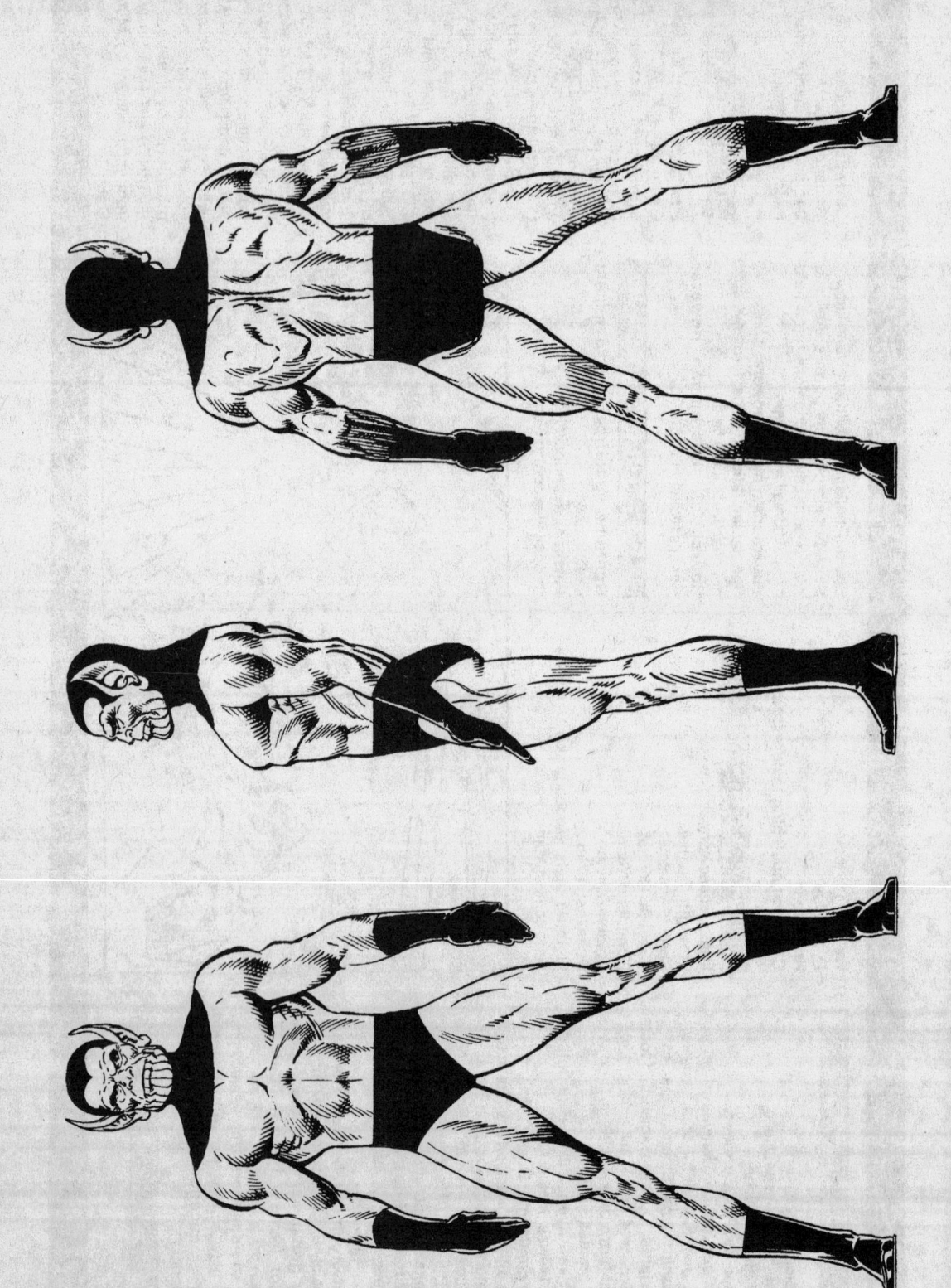

SKRULLS

HOME WORLD

Origin World: Skrullos, Drox System, Andromeda Galaxy
Habitat: Semi-tropical, 65% covered by water
Gravity: 1.05 Earth
Atmosphere: .70 nitrogen, .25 oxygen, .04 carbon dioxide, .01 rare gases
Note: The Skrull Empire extends throughout most of the Andromeda Galaxy and into neighboring galaxies. The Skrull Imperial Throneworld moved to planet Tarnax IV 100,000 years ago, but the planet was recently destroyed by Galactus.

PHYSICAL CHARACTERISTICS

Type: Reptilian/humanoid
Eyes: Two (usually red or green)
Note: Skrulls' eyes are incapable of as subtle visual perceptions as those of Earth humans, e.g. Skrulls once mistook samples of drawn artwork for photographs
Fingers: Five, including opposable thumb
Skin color: Green
Note: One text incorrectly depicts Skrulls as yellow
Average height: 5'5" (range 4'6" to 6'4")
Special adaptations: Genetic and molecular instability, genetic diversity, due to Celestial experimentation creating Skrull "Deviants" (now the only surviving Skrulls)
Unusual physical characteristics: Large pointed ears, furrowed chins
Superhumanoid powers: Physical malleability. Skrulls have the ability to change size, shape, and color at will, taking on the appearance but not the characteristics of other beings and objects within a volume range of .75 to 1.5 times the Skrull's original volume
Intelligence: Normal
Strength: Normal
Speed: Normal
Stamina: Normal
Durability: Normal
Agility: Normal
Reflexes: Normal

SOCIETY

Population: 30 billion (throughout empire; the population of Throneworld was 7 billion at time of destruction)
Government: Monarchy (succession disrupted by destruction of Throneworld, death of surviving royal family members, and ensuing civil wars)
Technology level: Advanced warp-drive starships, nuclear power and weapons
Cultural traits: Imperialistic, militaristic
Leaders: S'byll (current empress), Dorrek I (emperor, deceased), Dorrek II (emperor, deceased), R'Kill (empress, deceased), Anelle (princess, deceased), Karant Kiar (prelate), Gorth (planetary governor, deceased), K'targh (starfleet commander, deceased), Morrat (warlord, deceased)
Names of other representatives: K'irt (Super-Skrull), Paibok (Power-Skrull), Xalxar (starship pilot), Raksor (warrior), Skragg (mercenary), De'Lila (renegade), Nenora (espionage agent), Lyja (Lazerfist, espionage agent)
Major allies: The Ciegrimites, the Guna, the Kallusians, the Krylorians, the Morani, the Pheragots, the Queega, the Tektons, the Yirbek
Major enemies: The Dire Wraiths (destroyed), the Kree, 3-D Man, the Fantastic Four, Galactus, the Silver Surfer, Captain Mar-Vell (deceased), Torgo, the Avengers, Rick Jones, the Champions of Xandar, the Xandarians, Firelord, Kree, Avengers, Spider-Man, Nebula I, Reptyl, the Hulk, the X-Men, the Starjammers, the Shi'ar, the Shi'ar Imperial Guard, the Badoon, the Druffs, the Willameanis, the Xartans, the Z'Nox

BIBLIOGRAPHY

First appearance: FANTASTIC FOUR #2
Origin issue: SILVER SURFER Vol. 3 #5
Significant issues: ROM #50 (revealed to have been experimented on by the Celestials, thus creating the Dire Wraiths); AVENGERS #133 (first encounter with the Kree revealed; Skrull party killed by Kree, thus beginning Kree-Skrull Wars); CAPTAIN AMERICA ANNUAL #7 (revealed to have created the first Cosmic Cube, which became the Shaper of Worlds); MARVEL PREMIERE #35-37 (in 1958, attempted to sabotage Earth's space program, battled 3-D Man, set Cold Warrior against 3-D Man); FANTASTIC FOUR #2 (first fought Fantastic Four); FANTASTIC FOUR #18 (sent Super-Skrull to battle Fantastic Four); FANTASTIC FOUR #32 (had Super-Skrull pose as Dr. Franklin Storm and battle Fantastic Four as the Invincible Man, caused death of Dr. Storm); FANTASTIC FOUR #37 (Skrull Throneworld invaded by Fantastic Four to avenge Dr. Storm's death); CAPTAIN MARVEL #2-3 (sent Super-Skrull to battle Captain Mar-Vell); FANTASTIC FOUR #89-93 (abducted the Thing as contestant in the Skrull Games); AVENGERS #91-97 (war with the Kree revealed; battled Kree, Avengers, and Captain Mar-Vell; conflict ended by Rick Jones and Kree Supreme Intelligence); FANTASTIC FOUR #173-174 (revealed to have conquered medieval planet and abandoned it after its inhabitants perished); FANTASTIC FOUR #204-206/NOVA #25 (attacked the Xandarians, battled Fantastic Four and the Champions of Xandar) FANTASTIC FOUR #209 (Emperor Dorrek assassinated by Empress R'kill); FANTASTIC FOUR ANNUAL #15 (Skrull Prime Ten battled Fantastic Four and Captain Mar-Vell); UNCANNY X-MEN #137 (sent representative to witness the fate of Phoenix II); AVENGERS #209 (lone Skrull poisoned Vera Gantor to force Avengers to seek Resurrection Stone on his behalf); ROM #24 (battled Rom and the Champions of Xandar); MARVEL GRAPHIC NOVEL #1 (sent General Zedrao to give dying Captain Mar-Vell the Royal Skrull Medal of Honor)

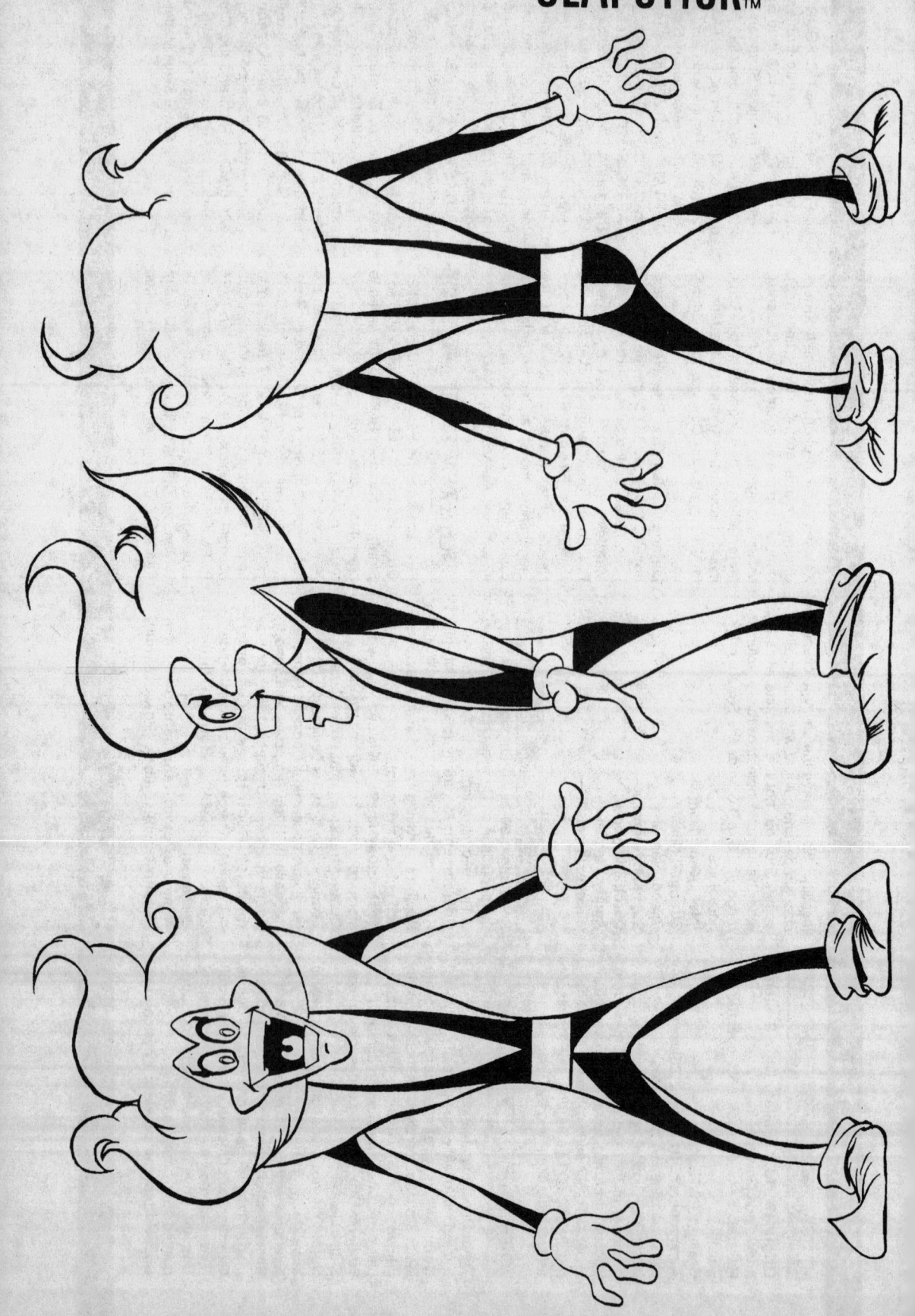

SLAPSTICK™

SLAPSTICK

BIOGRAPHICAL DATA

Real name: Steven Harmon
Other current aliases: None
Former aliases: None
Dual identity: Secret
Current occupation: High school student
Former occupation: Junior high school student
Citizenship: United States of America
Legal status: No criminal record
Place of birth: New York City
Marital status: Single
Known relatives: Unnamed parents
Known confidants: Mike Peterson
Known allies: Spider-Man, Daredevil, Ghost Rider II, Speedball
Major enemies: Clowns of Dimension X, the Overkiller, Dr. Denton, Teddy, the Neutron Bum
Usual base of operations: New York City area
Former bases of operations: None
Current group membership: None
Former group membership: None
Extent of education: Currently in high school

PHYSICAL DESCRIPTION

Height: Variable, (as Harmon) 5'7"
Weight: Variable, (as Harmon) 145 lbs.
Eyes: Blue pupils, yellow irises, (as Harmon) Blue
Hair: Purple, (as Harmon) Blond
Other distinguishing features: (as Slapstick) Chalk-white skin, disproportionately large head, (as Harmon) None

POWERS AND ABILITIES

Intelligence: Normal
Strength: Variable up to Enhanced human
Speed: Variable up to Enhanced human
Stamina: Variable up to Enhanced human
Durability: Metahuman
Agility: Metahuman
Reflexes: Superhuman
Fighting skills: None
Special skills and abilities: Experienced practical joker, highly developed bizarre sense of humor
Superhuman physical powers: Aside from the above listed attributes, virtually unlimited physical malleability, in the manner of an animated cartoon character
Superhuman mental powers: None
Special limitations: None known
Source of superhuman powers: Exposure to unknown alien device

PARAPHERNALIA

Costume specifications: Alien materials
Personal weaponry: Sub-space materializer gloves (enable Harmon to transform into Slapstick and to transport objects with the gloves' sub-space field)
Special weaponry: Various devices stored in the sub-space field of his gloves
Other accessories: None
Transportation: Conventional
Design and manufacture of paraphernalia: Unrevealed

BIBLIOGRAPHY

First appearance: SLAPSTICK #1
Origin issue: SLAPSTICK #1
Significant issues: SLAPSTICK #1 (gained superhuman powers, stopped invasion of Earth by extradimensional clowns); SLAPSTICK #2 (battled the Overkiller, encountered Spider-Man); SLAPSTICK #3 (battled Dr. Denton and Teddy, rescued Barbara Halsey); SLAPSTICK #4 (battled the Neutron Bum; encountered Daredevil, Ghost Rider II, Speedball, the Fantastic Four, the Avengers, the New Warriors)

SLEEPER

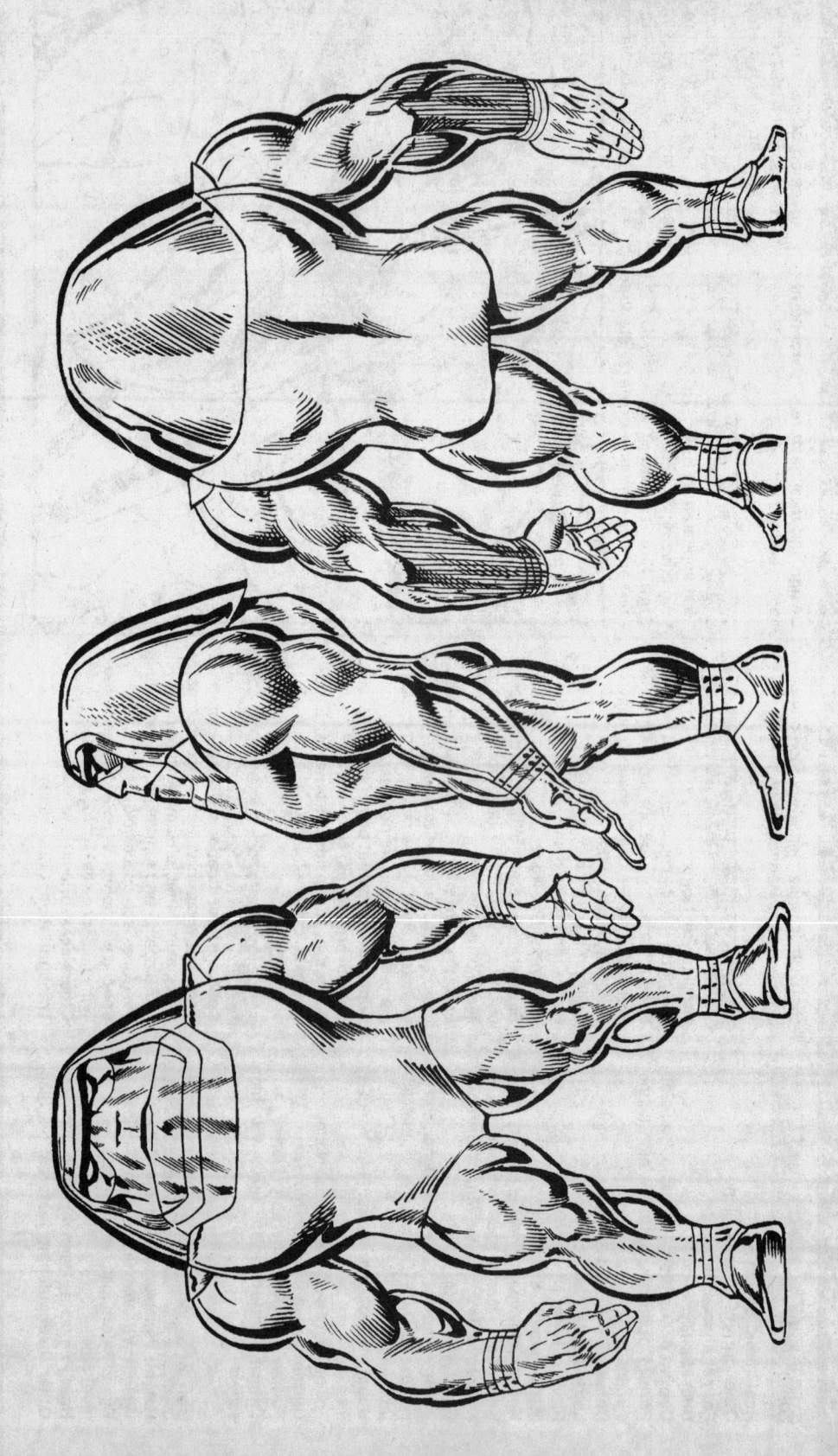

SLEEPER

BIOGRAPHICAL DATA

Real name: Sleeper
Other current aliases: The Fourth Sleeper
Former aliases: SL-4
Dual identity: Inapplicable
Current occupation: Henchman to the Red Skull
Former occupation: Agent of destruction
Citizenship: Inapplicable
Legal status: Property of Johann Schmidt, alias John Smith, the Red Skull
Place of construction: Berlin, Germany
Marital status: Inapplicable
Known relatives: Inapplicable
Known confidants: Inapplicable
Known allies: Red Skull, the Skeleton Crew (Machinesmith, Crossbones, Mother Night, the Voice)
Major enemies: Captain America
Usual base of operations: The Smith Building, Washington D.C.
Former bases of operations: Berlin, Germany; the Red Skull's hidden isle; somewhere in Massachusetts; Avengers Island
Current group membership: Skeleton Crew
Former group membership: None
Extent of programming: Capacity for limited self-motivated activity

PHYSICAL DESCRIPTION

Height: 6' 4"
Weight: 1064 lbs.
Eyes: None
Hair: None
Other distinguishing features: Overly massive head and disproportionately long arms

POWERS AND ABILITIES

Intelligence: Artificial, limited
Strength: Superhuman Class 10
Speed: Normal
Stamina: Metahuman
Durability: Demi-godlike
Agility: Normal
Reflexes: Superhuman
Fighting skills: Programmed to be moderately proficient at hand-to-hand combat

Special skills and abilities: None
Superhuman physical powers: Originally the Sleeper could alter its density from its natural tempered steel form to total intangibility. The circuits that controlled this function have burned out and have not been replaced. The Sleeper originally could also generate "volcanic" thermal energy and project it through its face-plate. This function has also apparently been eradicated.
Superhuman mental powers: None
Special limitations: The vibration of a certain "sonic crystal" caused the Sleeper's tangibility control to malfunction
Source of superhuman powers: Robotic materials, design, and construction

PARAPHERNALIA

Costume specifications: None
Personal weaponry: Repulsor-ray blasters mounted in eyesockets
Special weaponry: None currently
Other accessories: None
Transportation: Generally travels in the Red Skull's jet-copter
Design and manufacture of paraphernalia: AIM

BIBLIOGRAPHY

First appearance: STRANGE TALES #115
Origin issue: CAPTAIN AMERICA #101
Significant issues: CAPTAIN AMERICA #101-102 (crypt entombed within retrieved from sea, activated by Red Skull for first time since World War II, destroyed seacoast smelting factory, rendered intangible by "sonic crystal"); CAPTAIN AMERICA #354 (restored to tangibility by Machinesmith, used as "Trojan horse" to gain entrance onto Avengers Island in order to liberate the various robots incarcerated there, thwarted by Captain America); CAPTAIN AMERICA #368 (damage to it repaired by Machinesmith); CAPTAIN AMERICA #369 (animated by Machinesmith to join Skeleton Crew in search of the missing Red Skull, battled Hellfire Club mercenaries and Black Queen); CAPTAIN AMERICA #370 (replicas of five Sleeper robots pitted against Captain America and Diamondback)

SLEEPWALKER

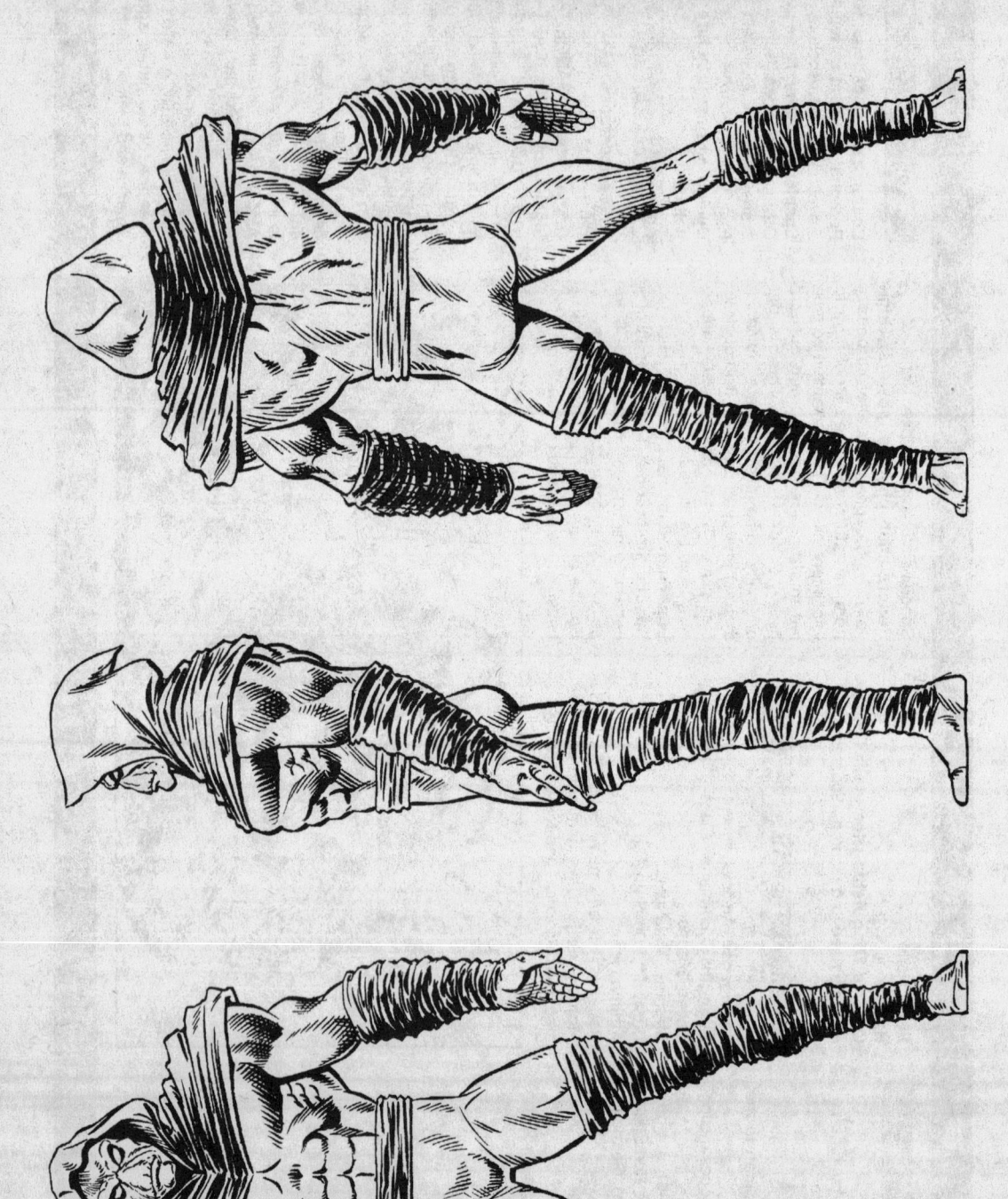

SLEEPWALKER

BIOGRAPHICAL DATA

Real names: Unrevealed
Other current aliases: None
Former aliases: None known
Dual identity: None; the general populace of Earth is unaware of Sleepwalker's existence within Rick Sheridan's mind.
Current occupation: Crimefighter
Former occupations: Uncertain; either a defender of the Mindscape as a member of the guardian Sleepwalker race (as he claims), or a scout for the dimension conquering Mindspawn race (as others claim)
Citizenship: The Mindscape (a dimension bordering on the minds of all intelligent beings)
Legal status: No criminal record
Place of birth: An unspecified location within the Mindscape (probable)
Marital status: Single
Known relatives: None known
Known confidants: Richard "Rick" Sheridan, Ricky (an imaginary younger version of Rick that exists only in Rick's mind)
Known allies: Spider-Man, Darkhawk, Deathlok III, Ghost Rider II, the Hulk, the Fantastic Four, Portal
Major enemies: Cobweb, 8-Ball, Bookworm, the Chain Gang, Lullaby, Tolliver Smith, the Office of Insufficient Evidence, Nightmare, Spectra, the Thought Police, Mr. Jyn, Hobgoblin II, the Brotherhood of Evil Mutants
Usual base of operations: New York City area and Rick Sheridan's mind
Former bases of operations: The Mindscape
Current group membership: Sleepwalkers (as he claims), or Mindspawn (as others claim)
Former group membership: Unrevealed
Extent of education: Unrevealed

PHYSICAL DESCRIPTION

Height: 5'7"
Weight: Unrevealed
Eyes: Red, faceted
Hair: None
Other distinguishing features: Light green skin, no nose

POWERS AND ABILITIES

Intelligence: Above normal
Strength: Superhuman Class 10
Speed: Enhanced human
Flight speed: Directed motion hovering
Stamina: Enhanced human
Durability: Superhuman
Agility: Enhanced human
Reflexes: Enhanced human
Fighting skills: Expert in the combat use of his powers
Special skills and abilities: Skilled tracker
Superhuman physical powers: Aside from the above listed attributes, Sleepwalker has superhuman visual acuity that allows him to see wavelength colors invisible to human eyes, projection of crude images of what he's seen from his eyes, the ability to project warp-beams from his eyes, which can alter the shape of physical matter
Superhuman mental powers: A mental link with the human Rick Sheridan that facilitates Sleepwalker's entry into Rick's mind
Special limitations: Sleepwalker claims he is sworn never to enter another being's mind, and never to use his warp-beams directly on another being. He gradually weakens the longer he is away from the mental plane. Prolonged stay on Earth can lead to death. The greater the distance he levitates above Earth, the greater his loss of strength. His ability to use his warp-beam diminishes as he uses it. The greater the intensity of its usage, the faster it is used up. His warp-beam power is replenished by rest.
Source of superhuman powers: Unrevealed

PARAPHERNALIA

Costume specifications: Alien materials
Personal weaponry: Imaginator (an amulet capable of teleporting Sleepwalker and targets into, out of, and to different locations within the Mindscape)
Note: Sleepwalker's Imaginator is currently lost within the mind of Rick Sheridan
Special weaponry: None
Other accessories: None
Transportation: Self-levitation
Design and manufacture of paraphernalia: Unrevealed

BIBLIOGRAPHY

First appearance: SLEEPWALKER #1
Origin issue: SLEEPWALKER #3
Significant issues: SLEEPWALKER #1 (first emerged from Rick Sheridan's mind, battled gang of thieves); SLEEPWALKER #3 (revealed to have battled Cobweb and become trapped in Rick Sheridan's mind; battled dream-images of Avengers, Fantastic Four, X-Factor, and X-Men); SLEEPWALKER #5-6 (with Spider-Man, battled Kingpin and Crimewave II); SLEEPWALKER #7/QUASAR #27 (with Darkhawk, Deathlok III, Moon Knight, and the Squadron Supreme, attempted to stop Eon's body from invading Earth's Universe; battled Chain Gang); SLEEPWALKER #12 (fought Nightmare); SLEEPWALKER #13-16 (battled Spectra; alongside Mr. Fantastic and the Thing, battled the Thought Police); DARKHAWK #20/SLEEPWALKER #17 (alongside Darkhawk and Spider-Man, saved Portal from the Brotherhood of Evil Mutants); SLEEPWALKER #18 (battled evil duplicates of Beast, Daredevil, and Firestar); SLEEPWALKER #19-24 (exchanged bodies with Rick Sheridan; battled Cobweb, Chain Gang, 8-Ball, and Hobgoblin II); SLEEPWALKER #25 (revealed to be the lead scout for the Mindspawn, an invasion force from the Mindscape intent on conquering Earth)

SLITHER

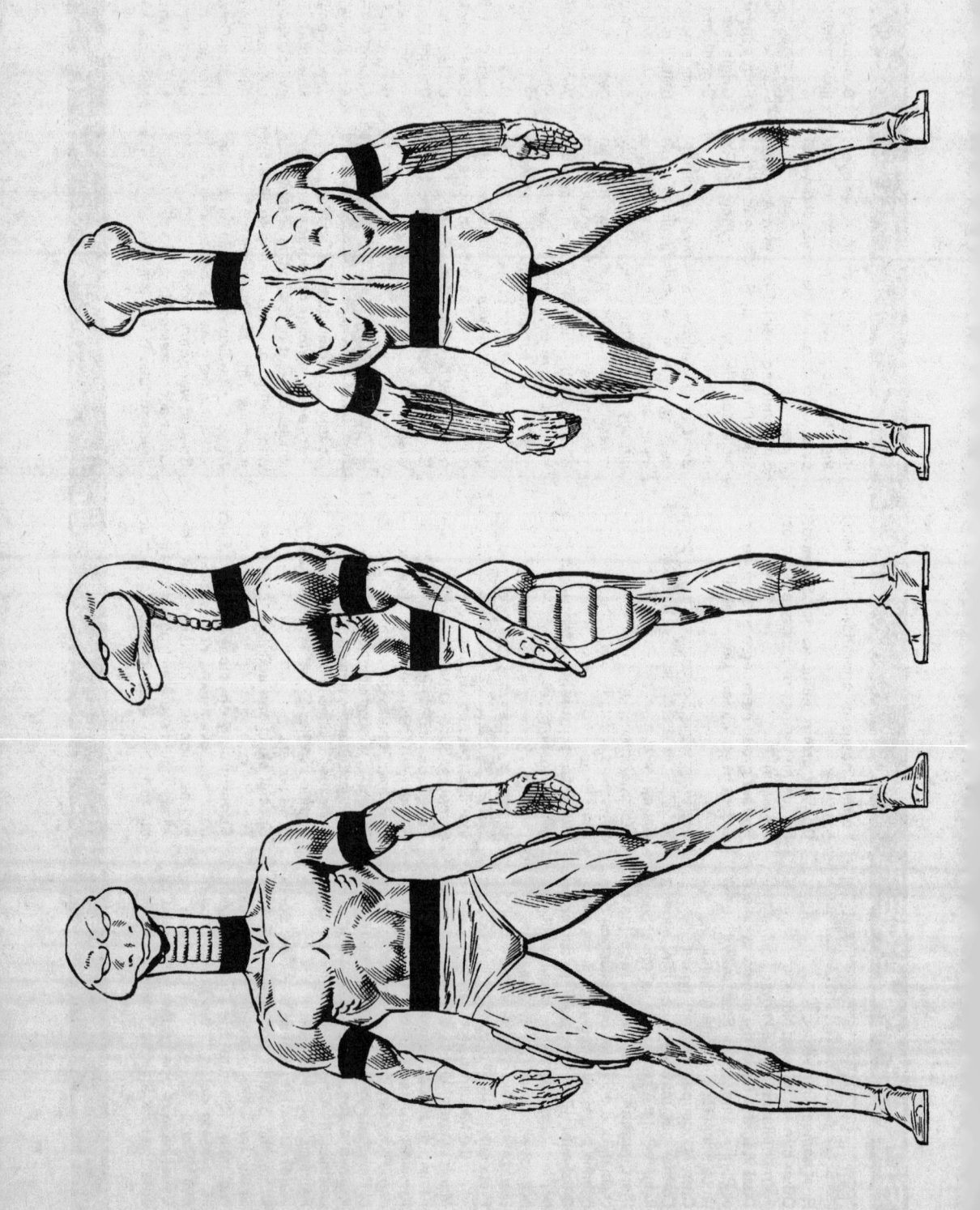

SLITHER

BIOGRAPHICAL DATA

Real name: Aaron Salomon
Other current aliases: None
Former aliases: None known
Dual identity: Known to the United States legal authorities
Current Occupation: Terrorist
Former occupation: Mercenary
Citizenship: Unrevealed
Legal status: Criminal record in the U.S.
Place of birth: Unrevealed
Marital status: Unrevealed
Known relatives: None
Known confidants: Viper II
Known allies: Viper II, (former) Mutant Force, Magneto, Mandrill, Mad Dog, Professor Power, Secret Empire III
Major enemies: Captain America, Defenders, Hulk, Nomad
Usual base of operations: Mobile
Former bases of operations: Mobile
Current group membership: Viper II's terrorist organization
Former group membership: Brotherhood of Evil Mutants II, Mutant Force, Serpent Society (under Viper II)
Extent of education: Unrevealed

PHYSICAL DESCRIPTION

Height: 6'9"
Weight: 210 lbs
Eyes: Green
Hair: None
Other distinguishing features: Slither's head resembles that of a snake, and his long neck resembles part of a snake's body. Although the rest of his body is humanoid in shape, he has green scaled skin like a reptile's. He speaks with a pronounced hiss. He often crouches or crawls rather than standing or walking erect.

POWERS AND ABILITIES

Intelligence: Normal
Strength: Unrevealed, possibly enhanced human
Speed: Normal
Stamina: Unrevealed, possibly enhanced human
Durability: Unrevealed, possibly enhanced human
Agility: Enhanced human
Reflexes: Enhanced human
Fighting skills: Fair hand-to-hand combatant; favorite combat tactic is to wrap his body around an opponent's as a snake can, and constrict himself, exerting suffocating pressure upon his victim.
Special skills and abilities: None
Superhuman physical powers: Aside from the above listed attributes, Slither has an extraordinarily flexible body, like a snake's
Superhuman mental powers: None
Special limitations: Emotional dependence on Viper II
Source of superhuman powers: Genetic mutation

PARAPHERNALIA

Costume specifications: Synthetic stretch fabric
Personal weaponry: None
Special weaponry: None
Other accessories: None
Transportation: Conventional means
Design and manufacture of paraphernalia: Inapplicable

BIBLIOGRAPHY

First appearance: CAPTAIN AMERICA ANNUAL #4
Origin issue: Slither's origin is as yet unrevealed.
Significant issues: CAPTAIN AMERICA ANNUAL #4 (recruited by Magneto into Brotherhood of Evil Mutants II, battled Captain America); DEFENDERS #78-80 (as Mutant Force member, employed by Mandrill in his scheme to take over the U.S., battled Valkyrie, Wasp Hellcat, Nighthawk II, and Yellowjacket I); DEFENDERS #83 (alongside Mutant Force, recruited into U.S. government service, battled Hulk); DEFENDERS #87 (testified with rest of Mutant Force against Defenders before a special government tribunal); DEFENDERS #125 (with Mutant Force and Mad Dog, invaded Patsy Walker's wedding, defeated by Beast); DEFENDERS #126, 128-130 (with rest of Mutant Force, employed by Professor Power's Secret Empire III, battled Defenders, defeated by them); CAPTAIN AMERICA #342-344 (aided Viper II's takeover of Serpent Society, fought Captain America, defeated and captured by Nomad)

SLUG™

SLUG

BIOGRAPHICAL DATA

Real name: Ulysses X. Lugman
Other current aliases: None
Former aliases: None
Dual identity: Publicly known
Current Occupation: Drug kingpin, criminal organizer, president and owner of several legal businesses
Former occupation: Unrevealed
Legal status: Suspected of various criminal acts, but never tried and convicted
Citizenship: United States of America
Place of birth: Miami, Florida
Marital status: Single
Known relatives: None
Known confidants: None
Known allies: Various underlings
Major enemies: Nomad, Poison, Captain America
Usual base of operations: A yacht usually outside the port of Miami, Florida
Former bases of operations: Same
Current group membership: None
Former group membership: None
Extent of education: Unrevealed

PHYSICAL DESCRIPTION

Height: 6' 8"
Weight: 1068 lbs.
Eyes: Blue
Hair: White
Other distinguishing features: He has an extremely long torso, making his arms and legs appear stunted.

POWERS AND ABILITIES

Intelligence: Gifted
Strength: Normal
Speed: Below normal
Stamina: Below normal
Durability: Peak human
Agility: Below normal
Reflexes: Normal
Fighting skills: Minimal skill at hand-to-hand combat. He has on occasion suffocated his opponents in the folds of his flesh.
Special skills and abilities: The Slug is a master strategist with a keen mind for business and the ability to lead through intimidation and reward. The Slug's high percentage of fat enables him float effortlessly in water. His metabolism grants him limited immunity to drugs and poisons.
Superhuman physical powers: None
Superhuman mental powers: None
Special limitations: The Slug has extremely light-sensitive eyes, causing him to wear shaded eyeglasses virtually all the time. The Slug is extraordinarily obese, so much so that he is unable to support his own weight by standing and is unable to move his body mass under his own power; he needs to consume vast quantities of food and liquid everyday, he eats during most of his waking moments.
Source of superhuman powers: None

PARAPHERNALIA

Costume specifications: Normal attire custom tailored
Personal weaponry: None
Special weaponry: Conventional firearms
Other accessories: None
Transportation: A custom-designed electric wheelchair/forklift with tank-treads
Design and manufacture of paraphernalia: Unrevealed

BIBLIOGRAPHY

First appearance: CAPTAIN AMERICA #325
Origin issue: The Slug's origin is as yet unrevealed.
Significant issues: CAPTAIN AMERICA #325 (learned to be Kingpin's Miami drug connection, organization infiltrated by Nomad, battled Nomad and Captain America, yacht sunk by Nomad); WEB OF SPIDER-MAN ANNUAL #4 (conferred with Kingpin about disruption in drug supply caused by the High Evolutionary's agents); MARVEL COMICS PRESENTS #61-66 (agreed to eliminate investment counselor Joe Trinity for employee Dallas Kerr, encountered transformed Trinity and Poison)

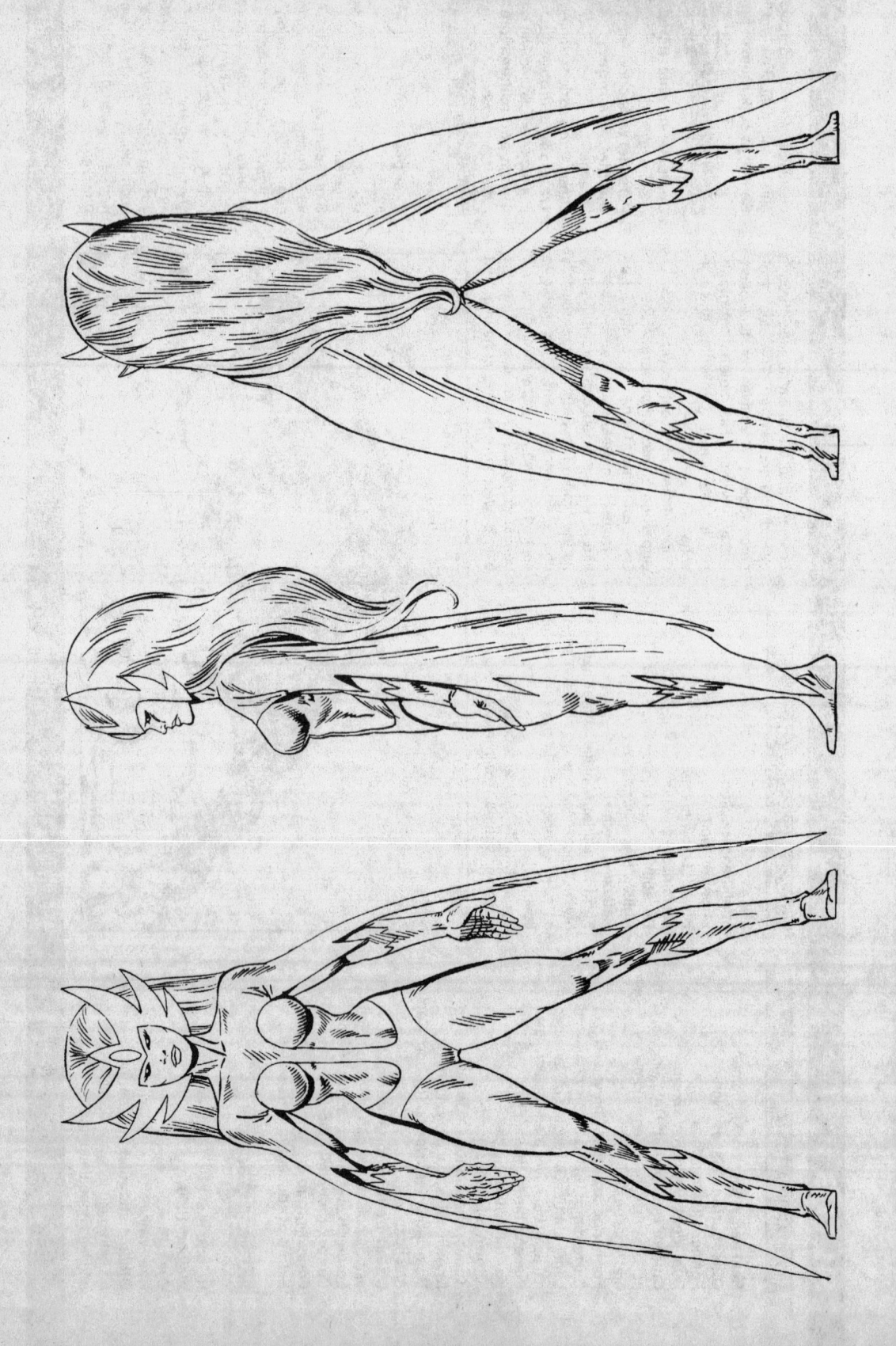

SNOWBIRD

SNOWBIRD

BIOGRAPHICAL DATA

Real name: Narya
Other aliases at time of death: Anne McKenzie Thompson
Former aliases: None known
Dual identity: Secret, the general populace of Earth is unaware that Snowbird is a goddess
Current occupation: Goddess
Former occupation: Adventurer, Records Officer of the Royal Canadian Mounted Police at Yellowknife, Northwest Territories, Canada
Legal status: No criminal record
Place of birth: Near Resolute Bay, Northwest Territories, Canada
Place of death: A mine in Burial Butte, a town in the Canadian Klondike
Cause of death: Slain by a plasma burst discharged by Vindicator II to prevent Pestilence II from taking possession of Snowbird's body
Marital status: Married
Known relatives: Hodiak (grandfather), Nelvanna (mother), Richard Lawrence Easton (father), Michael Twoyoungmen (Shaman, foster father), Douglas Thompson (husband, physically deceased), Unnamed son (physically deceased)
Known confidants: Douglas Thompson, Michael Twoyoungmen
Known allies: Alpha Flight, Wolverine, X-Men, Nelvanna, Hodiak, Turoq the Shaper
Major enemies: Pestilence II, the Great Beasts, Loki
Base of operations at time of death: The other dimensional realm of the Native American gods of Arctic Canada ("Paradise")
Former bases of operations: Canada, especially Alpha Flight headquarters, Tamarind Island, British Columbia, Maison Alpha, and Yellowknife Northwest Territories
Group membership at time of death: The Native American gods of Arctic Canada
Former group membership: Alpha Flight
Extent of education: Tutored by Michael Twoyoungmen; trained as an RCMP colonel

PHYSICAL DESCRIPTION

Height: 5' 10"
Weight: 108 lbs.
Eyes: (as Snowbird) White, (as Anne McKenzie) Blue
Hair: Pale blond (in her animal and Sasquatch forms her fur was white.)
Note: The measurements listed are those possessed by Snowbird in her normal mortal humanoid form and in her Anne McKenzie form.
Other distinguishing features: Snowbird's "real" face on her physical form looked inhuman; she used her shape-changing powers to make it look more human (as Snowbird) or entirely human (as McKenzie).

POWERS AND ABILITIES

Intelligence: Normal
Strength: Superhuman Class 10, (in Sasquatch form) Superhuman Class 90
Speed: Peak human, (in Sasquatch form) Enhanced human
Flight speed: Natural winged flight
Stamina: Superhuman, (in Sasquatch form) Metahuman
Durability: Superhuman, (in Sasquatch form) Metahuman
Agility: Superhuman, (in Sasquatch form) Metahuman
Reflexes: Superhuman, (in Sasquatch form) Metahuman
Fighting skills: Fair hand-to-hand combatant, coached by Puck and Wolverine, but preferred using her other powers in combat
Special skills and abilities: None known
Superhuman physical powers: Aside from the above listed attributes, Snowbird was a metamorph who possessed the superhuman ability to assume any form of any Arctic Canadian animal as well as that of a human being (but presumably only if the human was female. Her shape-changing powers also affected her clothing. When she took the form of an animal whose mass and volume were less than that of a human being, she became a human sized version of that animal. When she took the form of an animal whose mass and volume were greater than that of a human being, she gained additional mass, which she shed upon return to human form. Upon taking the form of an animal, she also gained that animal's special abilities. She also had the power of flight. Snowbird grew to adulthood with unusual rapidity, and went through an entire pregnancy in two weeks.
Superhuman mental powers: Mystical senses enabling her to detect magical energies. Limited postcognitive abilities enabling her to envision an event that took place up to six hours in the past in her present immediate vicinity. She could also generate a "healing glow"
Special limitations: Snowbird could not change from one animal form directly into another without great strain. Her personality became overlaid with the traits and instinctual patterns of the animal she became as long as she remained in that form. Snowbird's life force was bound to the country of Canada, and she could only live healthfully in Canada.
Source of superhuman powers: Member of the race of superhumans known as the gods of the Native Americans of Arctic Canada

PARAPHERNALIA

Costume specifications: Conventional fabrics
Personal weaponry: None
Special weaponry: None
Other accessories: None
Transportation: Flight under own power
Design and manufacture of paraphernalia: Unrevealed

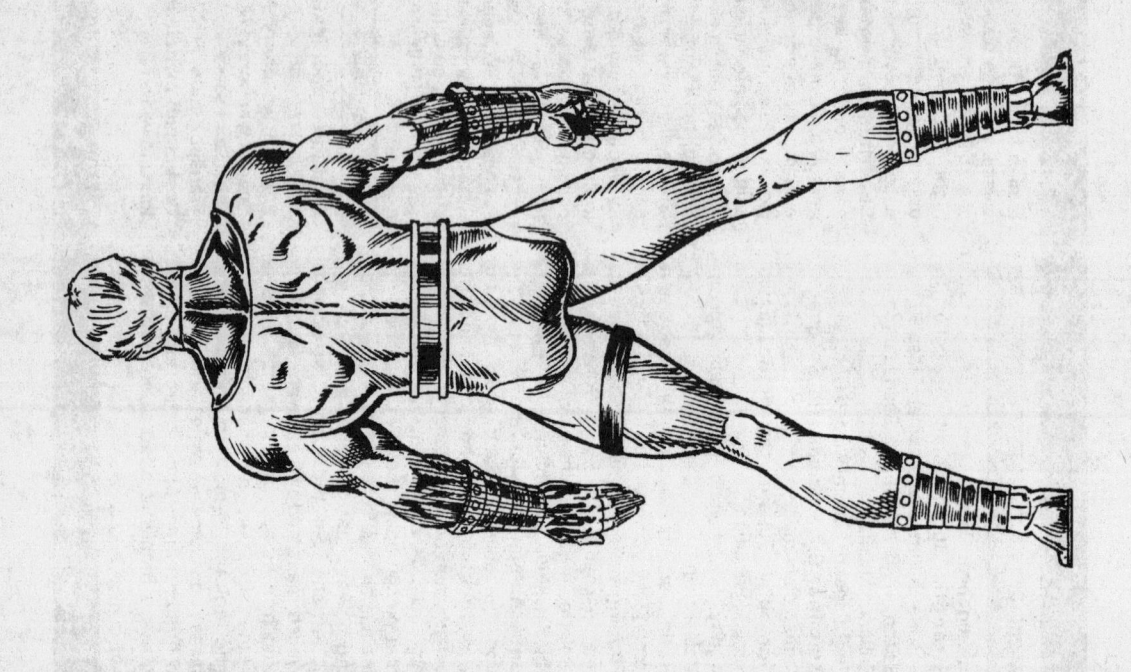

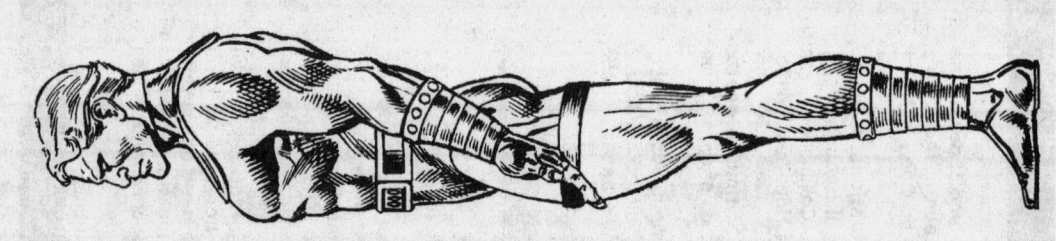

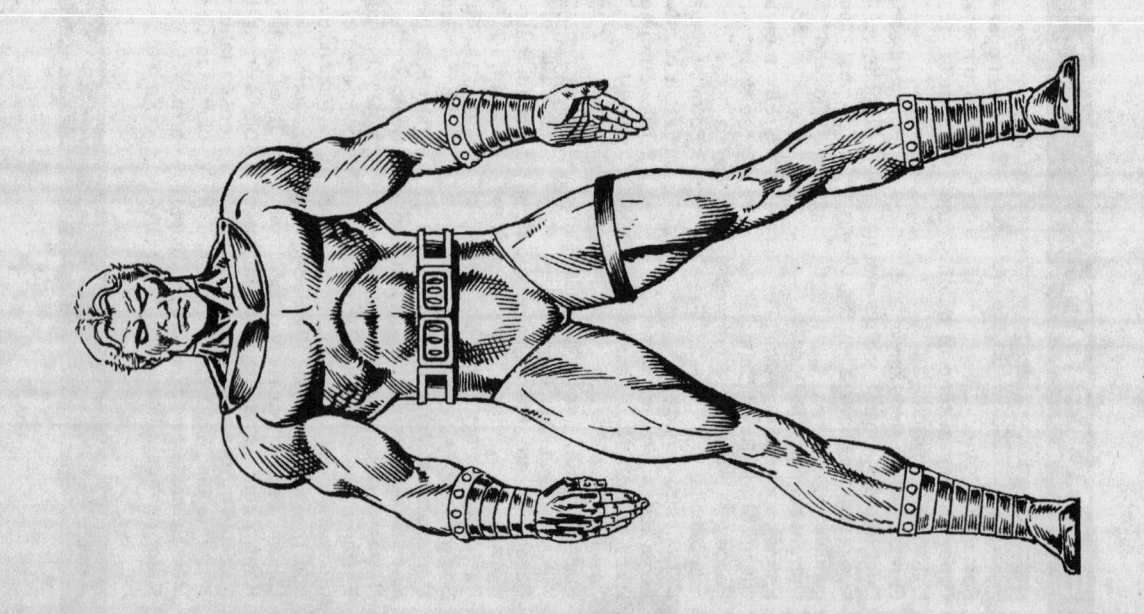

SNOWBLIND

SNOWBLIND

BIOGRAPHICAL DATA

Real name: Unrevealed
Other aliases at time of death: None
Former aliases: None known
Dual identity: Known to the legal authorities
Occupation at time of death: Businessman dealing in narcotics, sometimes assassin
Former occupation: Assassin
Citizenship: United States of America
Legal status: Held in police custody at time of demise.
Place of birth: Unrevealed
Place of death: Manhattan
Cause of death: Lifeforce drained by Deathwatch
Marital status: Unrevealed
Known relatives: None
Known confidants: None
Known allies: Captain Gene Hoffman (NYPD), (former) Deathwatch (deceased), Francesca Tofield
Major enemies: Ghost Rider II, Deathwatch (deceased), Hag, Troll, Lieutenant Michael Badalino (NYPD)
Base of operations at time of death: an unspecified brownstone in Brooklyn Heights, New York
Former base of operations: None known
Group membership at time of death: Headed own narcotics distribution organization
Former group membership: None known
Extent of education: Unrevealed

PHYSICAL DESCRIPTION

Height: 6' 1"
Weight: 190 lbs.
Eyes: No visible irises
Hair: White
Other distinguishing features: None

POWERS AND ABILITIES

Intelligence: Normal
Strength: Normal, (enhanced) Superhuman Class 10
Speed: Athlete, (enhanced) Enhanced human
Stamina: Athlete, (enhanced) Enhanced human
Durability: Athlete, (enhanced) Enhanced human
Agility: Athlete, (enhanced) Enhanced human
Reflexes: Athlete, (enhanced) Enhanced human
Fighting skills: Highly skilled hand-to-hand combatant
Special skills and abilities: Trained in assassination techniques
Superhuman physical powers: Aside from the above listed attributes, the ability to project a "white field" of light in which only he can see, but normal human beings cannot. Ghost Rider II can see within this field unless Snowblind turned part of it back upon himself. Snowblind's physical attributes increased within this field of light
Superhuman mental powers: None
Special limitations: Snowblind is blind except within his "white field"
Source of superhuman powers: Unrevealed

PARAPHERNALIA

Costume specifications: Conventional fabric
Personal weaponry: Conventional firearms
Special weaponry: None
Other accessories: None
Transportation: Conventional means
Design and manufacture of paraphernalia: Commercial manufacturers

BIBLIOGRAPHY

First appearance: GHOST RIDER Vol. 2 #13
Origin issue: Snowblind's origin is as yet unrevealed.
Significant issues: GHOST RIDER Vol. 2 #13 (first battled Ghost Rider II); GHOST RIDER Vol. 2 #21 (defeated in combat by Ghost Rider II, shot by Lieutenant Michael Badalino); GHOST RIDER Vol. 2 #23 (held in hospital under police guard, confronted by Ghost Rider II, revealed that Deathwatch was not human); GHOST RIDER Vol. 2 #24 (captured and killed by Deathwatch, Hag, and Troll)

SOLO™

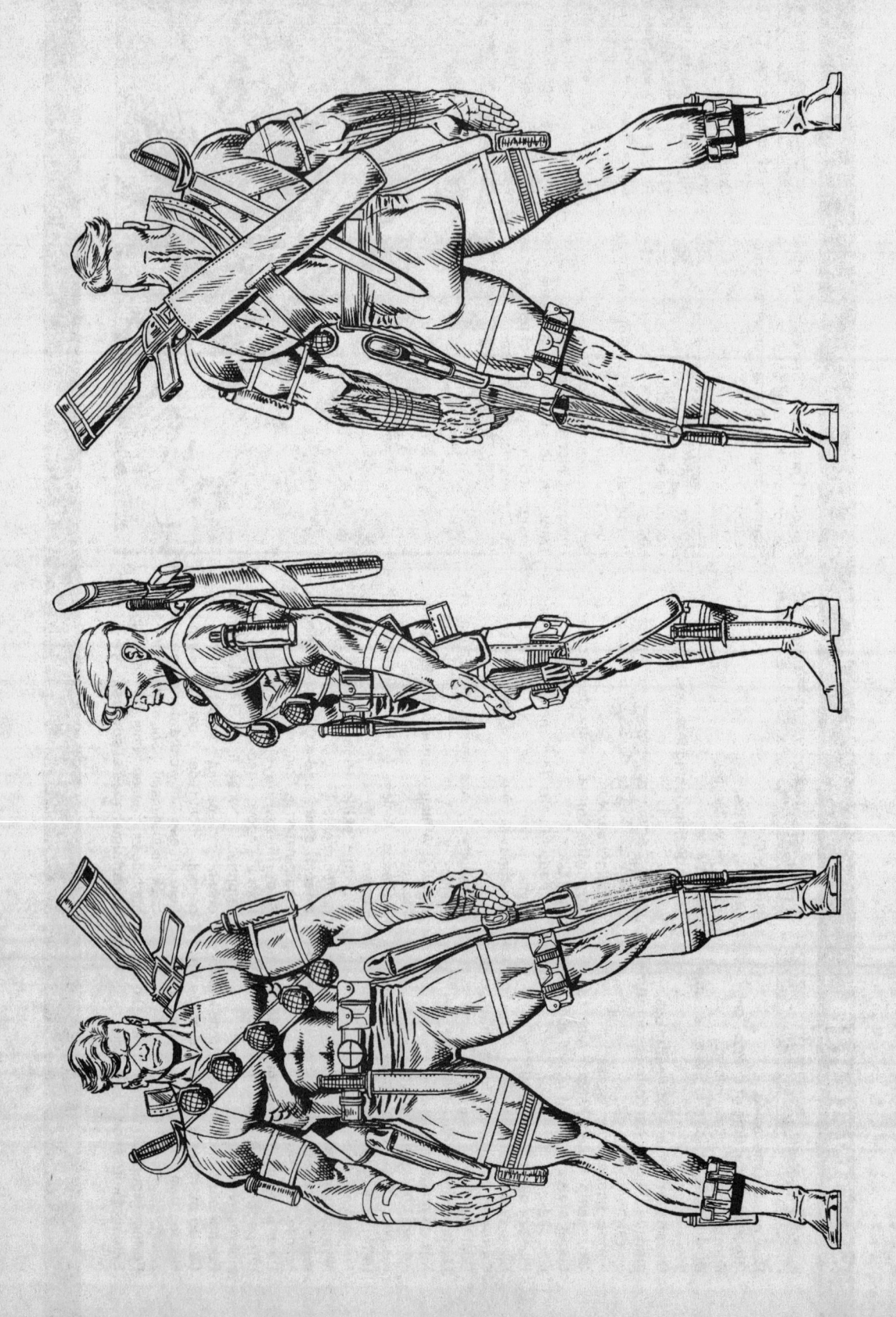

SOLO

BIOGRAPHICAL DATA

Real names: Unrevealed
Other current aliases: None known
Former aliases: None known
Dual identity: Secret
Current occupation: Counter-terrorist
Former occupation: Unrevealed
Citizenship: Solo has renounced his citizenship to any country
Legal status: Unrevealed
Place of birth: Unrevealed
Marital status: Unrevealed
Known relatives: None
Known confidants: None
Known allies: Spider-Man, Silver Sable, Captain America, Black Cat
Major enemies: Major Toler Weil, ULTIMATUM, La Tarantula, ARES, Deathstorm, all terrorists
Usual base of operations: Global
Former bases of operations: West Germany
Current group membership: None
Former group membership: None known
Extent of education: Unrevealed

PHYSICAL DESCRIPTION

Height: 6'
Weight: 200 lbs.
Eyes: Brown
Hair: Red-brown
Other distinguishing features: None

POWERS AND ABILITIES

Intelligence: Gifted
Strength: Athlete
Speed: Athlete
Stamina: Athlete
Durability: Athlete
Agility: Athlete
Reflexes: Athlete
Fighting skills: Mastery of many forms of hand-to-hand combat.
Special skills: Highly adept in the use of conventional weapons and firearms
Superhuman physical powers: Ability to teleport short distances
Superhuman mental powers: None
Special limitations: There appears to be a limit to the distance and the amount of time between Solo's teleports.
Source of superhuman powers: Unrevealed

PARAPHERNALIA

Costume specifications: Bullet-proof quilted kevlar with pouches to hold weapons and ammunition.
Personal weaponry: An arsenal of portable conventional weaponry, including sub-machine guns, automatic rifles, automatic pistols, hand grenades, combat knives, etc.
Special weaponry: None
Other accessories: Ninja climbing claws
Transportation: Teleportation
Design and manufacture of paraphernalia: Unrevealed

BIBLIOGRAPHY

First appearance: WEB OF SPIDER-MAN #19
Origin issue: Solo's origin is as yet unrevealed.
Significant issues: WEB OF SPIDER-MAN #19 (teleported inside a foreign embassy in West Germany and killed all the terrorists); AMAZING SPIDER-MAN #323 (foiled ULTIMATUM's plot to destroy the Arc de Triomph in Paris); AMAZING SPIDER-MAN #324 (shot ULTIMATUM terrorists who were trying to destroy Ellis Island, joined forces with Spider-Man to capture ULTIMATUM's commanding officer); AMAZING SPIDER-MAN ANNUAL #24 (outside Barcelona, Spain, assassinated Toro Mendoza, leader of the Cascan Sepratists); SPIDER-MAN #20-23 (tricked by Mysterio into thinking that he had killed the Sinister Six); MARVEL COMIC PRESENTS #88 (fought La Tarantula); AMAZING SPIDER-MAN ANNUAL #26 (defeated a Sicilian crime syndicate); AMAZING SPIDER-MAN #367 (joined forces with Spider-Man against agents of the Taskmaster and the Red Skull); MARVEL COMIC PRESENTS #124 (rematch with La Tarantula, each combatant wrongly believed he had killed the other); AMAZING SPIDER-MAN ANNUAL #27 (joined forces with Black Cat against the terrorist organization called ARES, stopped their money laundering operation, encountered their leader Deathstorm who revealed he had ties with Solo's past); SHIELD #44-45 (joined forces with Nick Fury against the Viper)

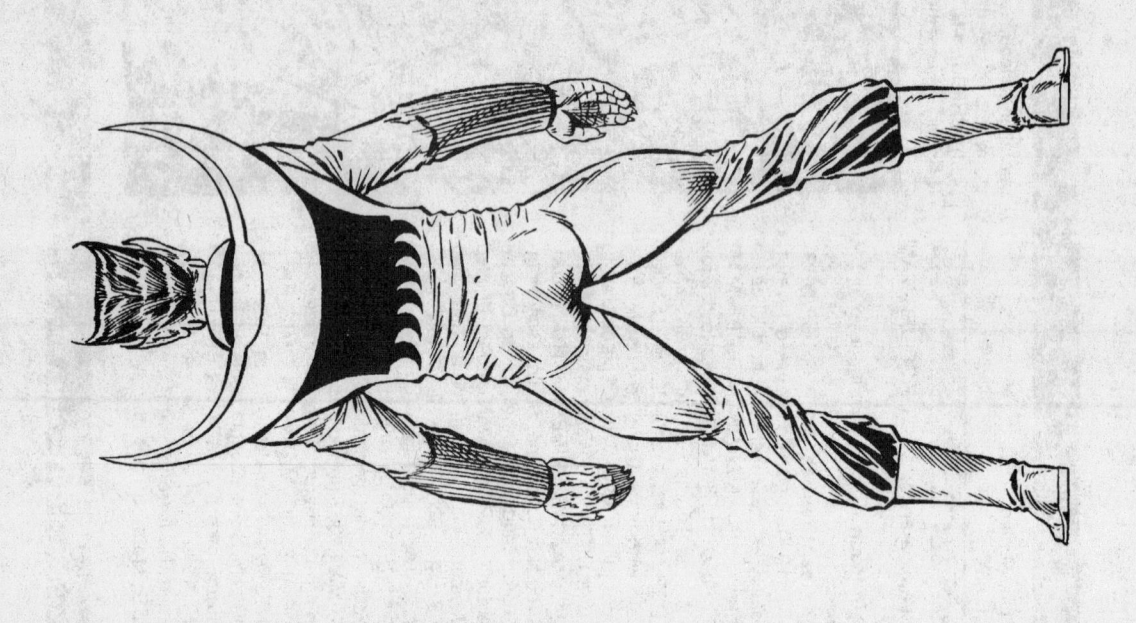

SPACE PHANTOM™

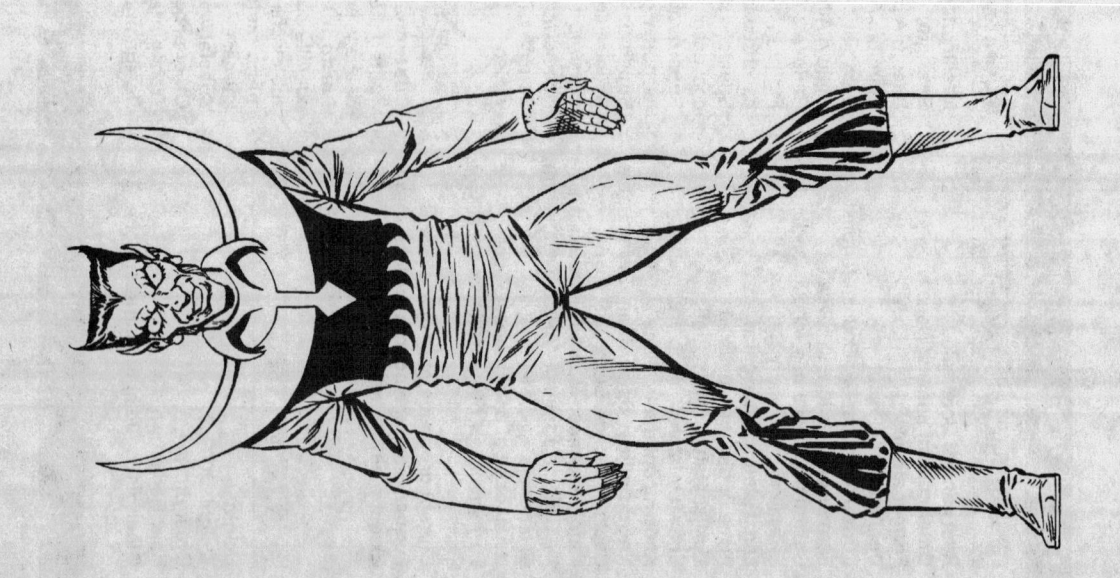

SPACE PHANTOM

BIOGRAPHICAL DATA

Real name: Unrevealed
Other current aliases: None
Former aliases: None
Dual identity: None; the general populace of Earth is unaware of the Space Phantom's existence
Current occupation: Servant of Immortus
Former occupations: Military strategist
Citizenship: The planet Phantus
Legal status: None
Place of birth: Planet Phantus, Phalbo system, Milky Way Galaxy
Marital status: Single
Known relatives: None
Known confidants: None
Known allies: Immortus, the Grim Reaper, HYDRA
Major enemies: The Avengers
Usual base of operations: Unknown location in the transtemporal realm of Limbo
Former bases of operations: The planet Phantus
Current group membership: None
Former group membership: Soldier of the army of Phantus; leader of a segment of HYDRA while impersonating Madame Hydra I (Viper)
Extent of education: Unrevealed

PHYSICAL DESCRIPTION

Height: 6' 8"
Weight: 215 lbs.
Eyes: Blue
Hair: Red
Other distinguishing features: Like all members of his race, the Space Phantom has webbed hands and feet.

POWERS AND ABILITIES

Intelligence: Above normal
Strength: Variable; normal to superhuman Class 100
Flight speed: Variable; normal to warp speed
Stamina: Variable; normal to immeasureable
Durability: Variable; normal to godlike
Agility: Variable; normal to metahuman
Reflexes: Variable; normal to metahuman
Fighting skills: Variable
Special skills: Knowledge of sophisticated alien technology far in advance of present day Earth; advanced knowledge of tie and time travel
Superhuman physical powers: Ability to assume the appearance and powers of virtually any single mortal being. At the point that he assumes the being's likeness, the model is automatically shunted to Limbo, and materializes exactly where he/she was when "shunted." The Space Phantom has no difficulty imitating a number of people in rapid succession, nor does there appear to be a time limit on the period in which he can imitate someone.
Superhuman mental powers: None
Special limitations: The Space Phantom appears to not be able to duplicate beings who possesses magical enchantments (such as Thor); when he attempts to duplicate such a being he is himself shunted into Limbo.
Source of superhuman powers: Bestowed upon him by Immortus

PARAPHERNALIA

Costume specifications: Alien materials
Personal weaponry: None
Special weaponry: None
Other accessories: None
Transportation: Various
Design and manufacture of paraphernalia: Inapplicable

BIBLIOGRAPHY

First appearance: AVENGERS #2
Origin issue: THOR #281
Significant issues: AVENGERS #2 (first appeared on Earth, battled Avengers, shunted back to Limbo when he attempted to mimic Thor); AVENGERS #106-108 (allied with Grim Reaper; impersonated Madame Hydra, and commanded a division of HYDRA in that identity, battled Avengers, shunted back into Limbo when he attempted to mimic Rick Jones who was then linked to Captain Mar-Vell); GIANT-SIZE AVENGERS #4 (compelled by Immortus to impersonate Mantis to deceive Kang); THOR #281-282 (attempted to trick Thor into freeing the planet Phantus from Limbo; allied with Thor to save Phantus); ROM #19 (encountered Rom in Limbo); AVENGERS #268 (encountered Avengers in Limbo); SPECTACULAR SPIDER-MAN #168-170 (used as pawn by the Young God Calculus in scheme pitting Spider-Man against the Avengers)

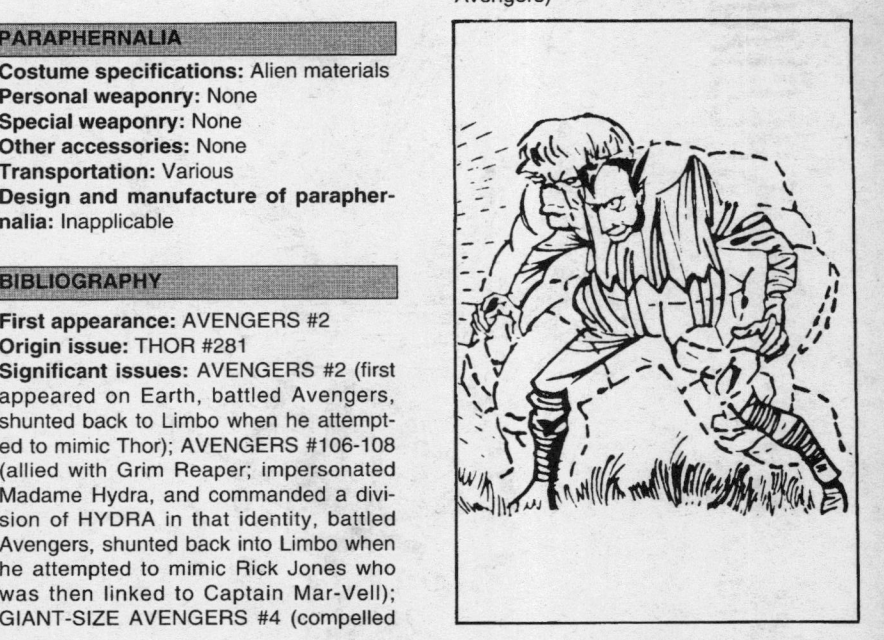

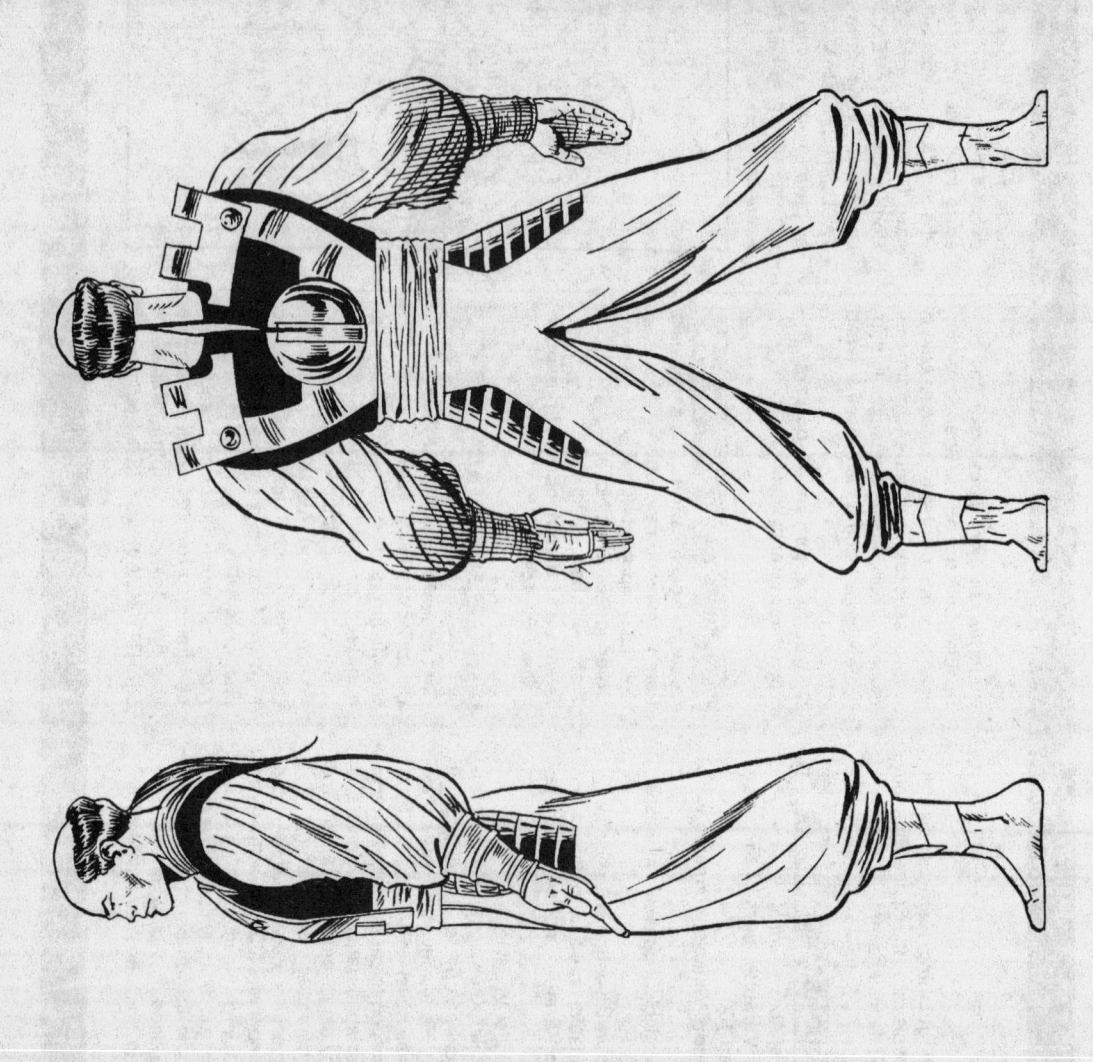

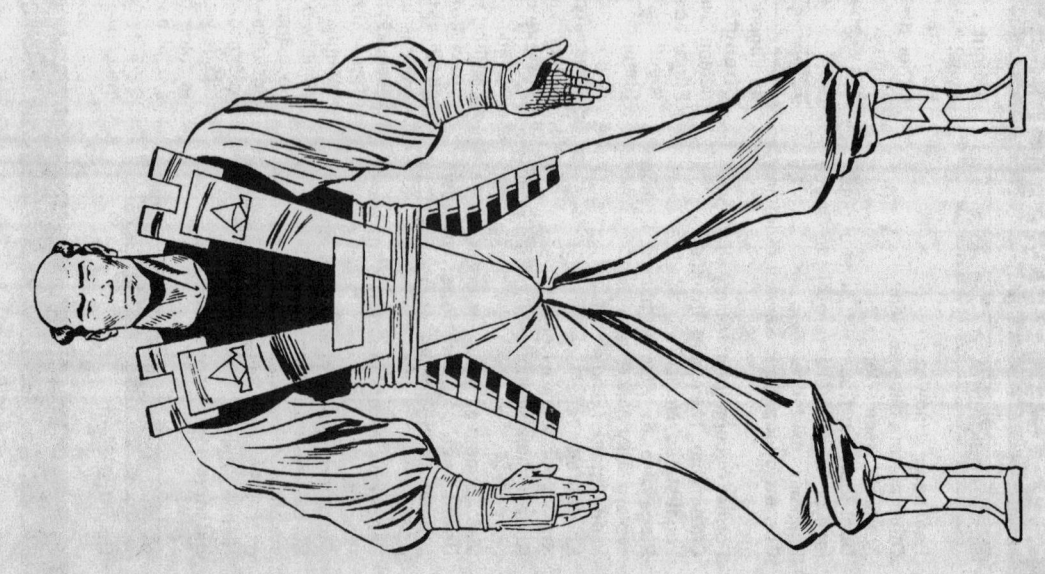

SPECIALIST™

SPECIALIST

BIOGRAPHICAL DATA

Real name: Unrevealed
Other current aliases: None
Former aliases: None known
Dual identity: Secret; known to the Stark/Fujikawa executive board
Current occupation: Assassin, field operative for Stark/Fujikawa Corporation
Former occupation: Unrevealed
Citizenship: Japan, circa 2099
Legal status: No known criminal record
Place of birth: Osaka, Japan, circa 2099
Marital status: Presumed single
Known relatives: None
Known confidants: None
Known allies: Stark/Fujikawa Corporation, Tyler Stone
Major enemies: Spider-Man 2099, Tyler Stone
Usual base of operations: Mobile
Former bases of operations: Unrevealed
Current group membership: Stark/Fujikawa Corporation
Former group membership: None known
Extent of education: Unrevealed

PHYSICAL DESCRIPTION

Height: 6' 4"
Weight: 235 lbs.
Eyes: Brown
Hair: Black
Other distinguishing features: None

POWERS AND ABILITIES

Intelligence: Normal
Strength: Peak human
Speed: Athlete
Stamina: Athlete
Durability: Athlete
Agility: Peak human
Reflexes: Peak human
Fighting skills: Expert martial artist, trained as a samurai warrior; highly proficient with various martial arts weaponry of the 21st Century
Special skills and abilities: Skilled hovercraft pilot
Superhuman physical powers: None
Superhuman mental powers: None
Special limitations: None
Source of superhuman powers: Inapplicable

PARAPHERNALIA

Costume specifications: Unrevealed bulletproof fabric insulated against electric shock and body armor of unknown materials
Personal weaponry: A 4' samurai sword capable of slicing through solid steel
Special weaponry: Shurikens, nunchakus
Other accessories: None
Transportation: One-man hovercraft
Design and manufacture of paraphernalia: Unnamed Stark/Fujikawa technicians

BIBLIOGRAPHY

First appearance: SPIDER-MAN 2099 #4
Origin issue: The Specialist's origin is as yet unrevealed.
Significant issues: SPIDER-MAN 2099 #4 (at behest of Tyler Stone, captured Kasey Nash in order to lure Spider-Man 2099 into battle); SPIDER-MAN 2099 #5 (battled Spider-Man 2099, throat slit in battle)

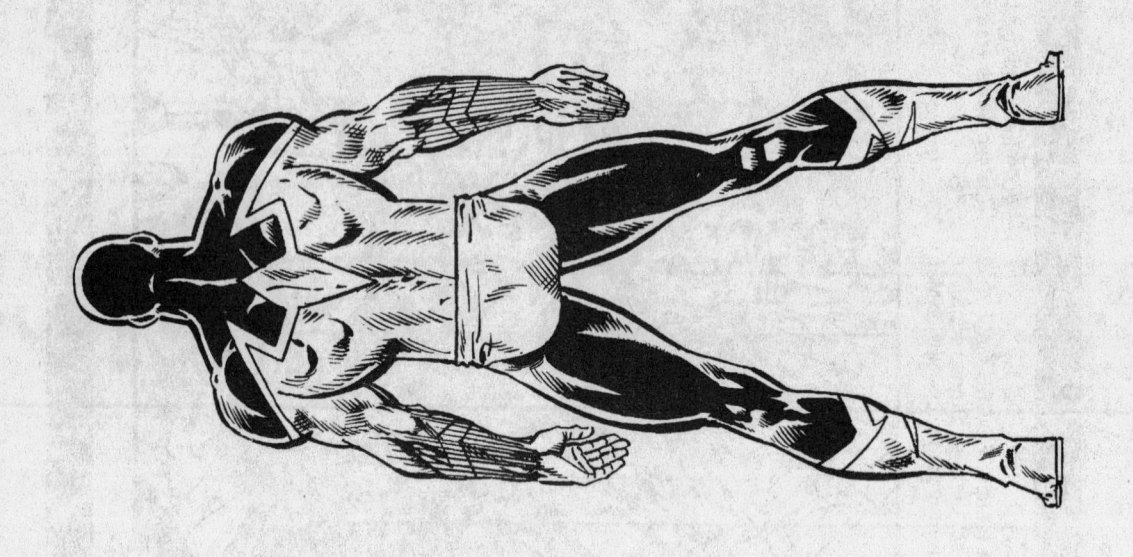

SPEED DEMON

SPEED DEMON

BIOGRAPHICAL DATA

Real name: James Sanders
Other current aliases: None
Former aliases: Whizzer II, Harvey James
Dual identity: Known to the United States government
Current occupation: Professional criminal
Former occupation: Pharmaceutical chemist
Citizenship: United States of America
Legal status: Criminal record in the United States
Place of birth: New York, New York
Marital status: Single
Known relatives: None
Known confidants: None
Known allies: (former) Squadron Sinister (Hyperion I, Doctor Spectrum I, Nighthawk I), Nebulon, Grandmaster, (current) Sinister Syndicate (Beetle, Rhino, Hydro-Man, Boomerang), Hobgoblin II (as Jack O'Lantern)
Major enemies: Hawkeye (as Goliath II), the Defenders, Spider-Man, Silver Surfer, Sandman, the Avengers
Usual base of operations: New York area
Former bases of operations: Unrevealed
Current group membership: Sinister Syndicate
Former group membership: Squadron Sinister

Extent of education: Master's degree in chemistry

PHYSICAL DESCRIPTION

Height: 5' 11"
Weight: 175 lbs.
Eyes: Brown
Hair: Gray
Other distinguishing features: None

POWERS AND ABILITIES

Intelligence: Above normal
Strength: Peak human
Speed: Subsonic
Stamina: Superhuman
Durability: Enhanced human
Agility: Athlete
Reflexes: Superhuman
Fighting skills: Extensive experience in streetfighting techniques utilizing his superhuman speed
Special skills and abilities: Expertise in chemistry
Superhuman physical powers: Superhuman speed and reflexes, can create cyclones by running in circles, can run up walls and across water
Superhuman mental powers: None
Special limitations: His metabolism requires air, food, and water; deprivation of any of these will diminish his speed and endurance
Source of superhuman powers: Mutagenic chemicals concocted under the Grandmaster's mental guidance

PARAPHERNALIA

Costume specifications: Synthetic stretch fabric
Personal weaponry: None
Special weaponry: None
Other accessories: None

Transportation: Travels about on foot
Design and manufacture of paraphernalia: Inapplicable

BIBLIOGRAPHY

First appearance: (as Whizzer II) AVENGERS #70, (as Speed Demon) AMAZING SPIDER-MAN #222
Origin issue: Speed Demon's full origin has yet to be depicted.
Significant issues: AVENGERS #70 (recruited by Grandmaster as part of his Squadron Sinister, given superhuman powers to imitate those of the Squadron Supreme's Whizzer, battled Goliath II); DEFENDERS #13-14 (took part in Squadron's negotiations with Nebulon to sell him the Earth, assisted him in scheme to melt the polar ice, battled the Defenders); GIANT-SIZE DEFENDERS #4 (attacked by the Defenders); AVENGERS ANNUAL #8 (memory restored, battled Captain America, Hawkeye, and Scarlet Witch); AMAZING SPIDER-MAN #222 (assumed new identity, set out upon crime spree, battled Spider-Man); AMAZING SPIDER-MAN #280-281 (hired by Jack O'Lantern to battle Spider-Man and Silver Sable as one of the Sinister Syndicate, also battled Sandman); QUASAR #17 (participated in the Runner's marathon to the moon to determine fastest being on Earth, lost); DEADLY FOES OF SPIDER-MAN #1 (participated in Sinister Syndicate's crime spree, vied with Boomerang for Leila Davis's affections)

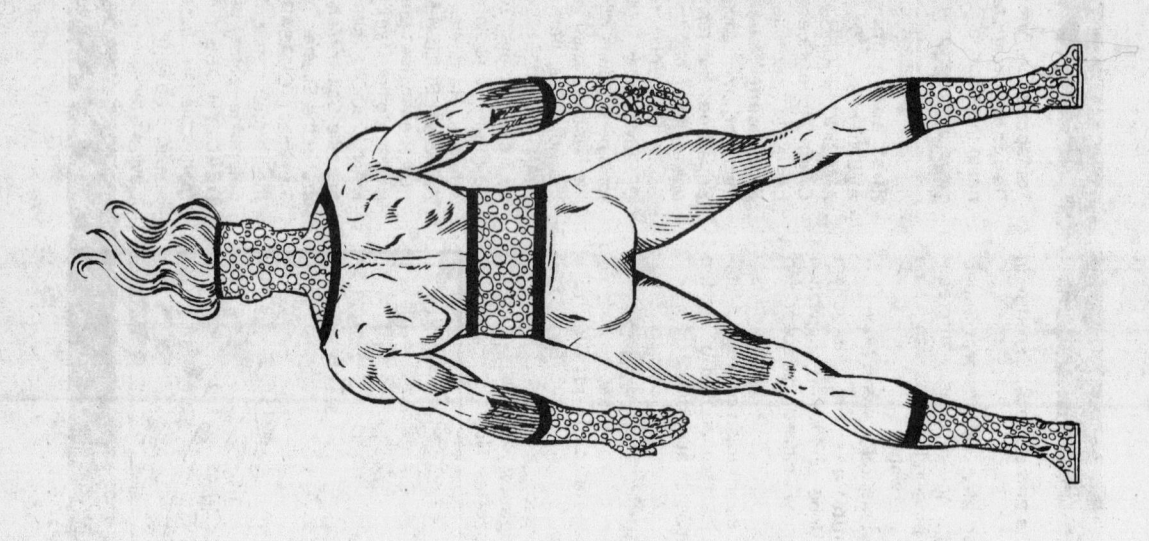

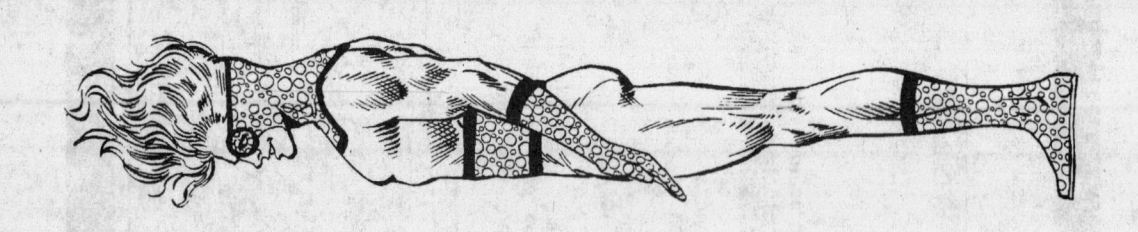

SPEEDBALL

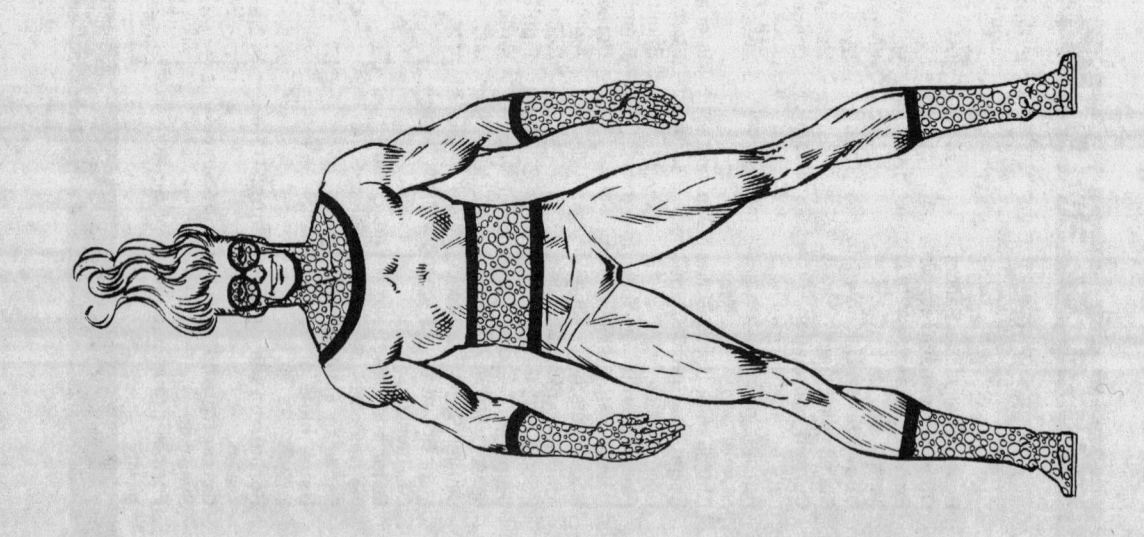

SPEEDBALL

BIOGRAPHICAL DATA

Real name: Robert "Robbie" Baldwin
Other Current aliases: The Masked Marvel
Former aliases: None
Dual identity: Secret
Current occupation: Adventurer, student, engineering intern
Former occupation: Part-time laboratory worker
Citizenship: United States of America
Legal status: Criminal record, still a minor
Place of birth: Springdale, Connecticut
Marital status: Single
Known relatives: Justin Baldwin (father), Madeline Naylor Baldwin (mother)
Known confidants: New Warriors, Madeline Naylor Baldwin, Niels the cat
Known allies: New Warriors, Spider-Man, Daredevil, Fantastic Four, Thor I
Major enemies: Terrax, Psionex, Force of nature, Gideon, White Queen, Basher, Bonehead Gang, Bug-Eyed Voice, Feathered Felon, Graffiti Guerillas, Harlequin Hit Men, Jolly Roger, Sticker, Two Legged Rat
Usual base of operations: New York City; Springdale, Connecticut
Former base of operations: None
Current group membership: The New Warriors
Former group membership: None
Extent of education: Current high school student

PHYSICAL DESCRIPTION

Height: 5' 6", (as Speedball) 5' 10"
Weight: 133 lbs., (as Speedball) 170 lbs.
Eyes: Blue
Hair: Blond
Other distinguishing features: When Speedball uses his superhuman powers, his voices alters in an unknown fashion and solid force bubbles of residue kinetic field energy appear on his body and, when he bounces, in his wake.

POWERS AND ABILITIES

Intelligence: Normal
Strength: Normal
Speed: Normal (however, his superhuman power can cause him to bounce at a great speed dependent on the amount of kinetic energy directed against him
Stamina: Normal
Durability: Metahuman
Agility: Normal
Reflexes: Normal
Fighting skills: Average hand-to-hand combatant, relies on superhuman powers in combat, received some training from New Warriors
Special skills and abilities: None known
Superhuman physical powers: Aside from the above listed attributes, Speedball possesses the superhuman ability to create a kinetic force field of unknown energy around himself which absorbs all kinetic energy directed against him and reflects it with even greater force against whatever object with which he is in contact.. Hence, if he struck a wall, he would travel at a greater velocity in the opposite direction. While bouncing, he is immune to any kind of harm caused by physical contact. Speedball's power activates automatically when any physical contact occurs above a low level that has not yet been precisely determined. When Speedball's kinetic field activates, his body increases in height and mass (drawn from extradimensional source); he reverts to his normal size and mass on deactivating the field
Superhuman mental powers: None
Special limitations: Control over his superhuman powers is increasing; questions are arising as to whether or not Robbie Baldwin is still fully human
Source of superhuman powers: Mutagenic effects of irradiation by unknown form of energy

PARAPHERNALIA

Costume specifications: Normal clothing that transforms into his costume for unknown reasons when his superhuman power is activated. The costume transforms back into normal clothing when he stops using his superhuman powers.
Personal weaponry: None
Special weaponry: None
Other accessories: None
Transportation: Bouncing under own power or New Warriors aircraft
Design and manufacture of paraphernalia: Unrevealed

BIBLIOGRAPHY

First appearance: AMAZING SPIDER-MAN ANNUAL #22
Origin issue: SPEEDBALL #1
Significant issues: SPEEDBALL #1 (gained superhuman powers and masked identity); AMAZING SPIDER-MAN ANNUAL #22 (first met Spider-Man and Daredevil); NEW WARRIORS #1 (joined New Warriors, first battled Terrax); THOR #411-412 (with New Warriors, aided Thor I in battle against Juggernaut); NEW WARRIORS #4 (with New Warriors, first battled Psionex); NEW WARRIORS #7 (revealed double identity to New Warriors); NEW WARRIORS #9 (with New Warriors, first battled Force of Nature, revealed double identity to his mother); NEW WARRIORS #10 (with New Warriors, battled White Queen and the Hellions); NEW WARRIORS #14 (met Darkhawk); FANTASTIC FOUR #356 (with New Warriors, manipulated by Puppet Master into battling Fantastic Four); NEW WARRIORS #15-17 (with New Warriors and Fantastic Four, battled Terrax); NEW WARRIORS #19 (with New Warriors, captured by Gideon); NEW WARRIORS ANNUAL #2 (superhuman research done by Sphinx raised questions regarding the make up of Speedball's kinetic field)

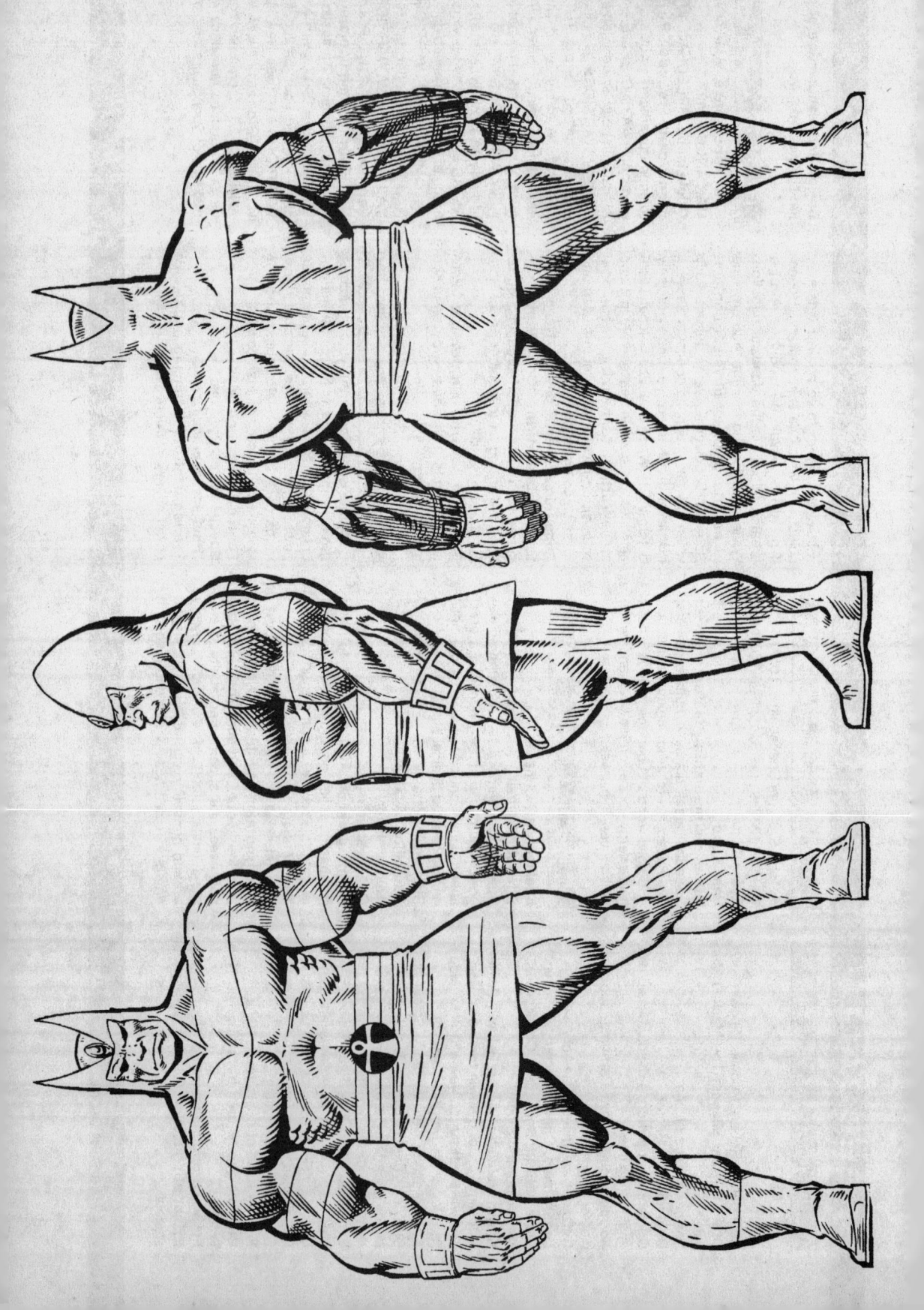

SPHINX

SPHINX I

BIOGRAPHICAL DATA

Real name: Unrevealed
Other current aliases: The Dreaded One
Former aliases: None
Dual identity: Secret
Current occupation: Wizard in the Egyptian Pharaoh's court, later conqueror
Citizenship: None, formerly citizen of ancient Egypt
Legal status: None
Place of birth: Somewhere in Egypt
Marital status: Single (at least in recent years)
Known relatives: None
Known confidants: Sayge (Veritas)
Known allies: Thraxon (Inhuman)
Major enemies: Nova I, Fantastic Four, Thing, Inhumans Royal Family, Black Bolt, Galactus, Puppet Master, Comet, Condor, Crimebuster, Diamondhead, Powerhouse, Doctor Sun, Kur
Usual base of operations: A mobile flying pyramid, formerly located in Egypt
Former bases of operations: Pyramid of Knowledge, upstate New York
Current group membership: None
Former group membership: None
Extent of education: Training in sorcery by ancient Egyptian wizards

PHYSICAL DESCRIPTION

Height: 7'2"
Weight: 450 lbs
Eyes: Red
Hair: Bald
Other distinguishing features: None

POWERS AND ABILITIES

Intelligence: Above normal
Strength: Superhuman Class 90
Flight speed: Unrevealed
Speed: Peak human
Stamina: Demi-godlike
Durability: Demi-godlike
Agility: Superhuman
Reflexes: Superhuman
Fighting skills: None, relied on superhuman strength and other powers rather than skill
Special skills and abilities: Knowledge of ancient Egyptian sorcery
Superhuman physical powers: Aside from the above listed attributes, Sphinx had virtual immortality.
Superhuman mental powers: Ability to manipulate mystical and cosmic energies, telepathic abilities including the ability to control or probe the minds of others and ability to induce hallucinations, ability to project beams of concussive force, heat, or light and to levitate or teleport himself and other persons or objects
Special limitations: Dependent on mystical Ka Stone for his superhuman powers
Source of superhuman powers: Genetic mutation, the Ka Stone, and other sources

PARAPHERNALIA

Personal weaponry: Ka stone
Special weaponry: None
Other accessories: None
Transportation: Levitation and teleportation
Design and manufacture of paraphernalia: Unrevealed

Costume specifications: Ordinary fabric

BIBLIOGRAPHY

First appearance: NOVA #6
Origin issue: NOVA #7
Significant issues: NOVA #6-7 (revealed that he must learn the answer to an undisclosed question before he can fulfill his desire to die, embarked on his campaign against Nova I; revealed he was once Egyptian wizard who competed in test of power against Moses, attempted to destroy Nova I, Condor, Diamondhead, and Powerhouse); NOVA #10-11 (defeated Condor, Diamondhead, and Powerhouse; battled Nova, departed after being impressed by Nova's bravery); FANTASTIC FOUR ANNUAL #12 (battled Fantastic Four and Inhumans Royal Family, defeated by Black Bolt); NOVA #24 (took mental control of Nova I, brought Nova I, Comet, Crimebuster, Diamondhead, Powerhouse aboard Nova-Prime starship); NOVA #25 (flashback to encounter with Quasimodo; used Nova-Prime starship to journey to planet Xandar, took Nova I, Doctor Sun, and others with him; battled Nova I, Doctor Sun, Comet, and Diamondhead; battled Skrull starships); FANTASTIC FOUR #208, 212-213 (learned information from living computers of Xandar that enabled him to gain vast cosmic powers and grow enormously in size; confronted by Galactus; battled and defeated by Galactus who returned him to his original human form, crushed Ka stone, and sent him back to ancient Egypt, supposedly entrapped in a "time loop" in which he will eternally relive his life), MARVEL TWO-IN-ONE #91 (escape from "time loop" revealed, attempted to recreate the Ka Stone, restoration process interrupted by Thing, leaving Ka Stone incomplete); THING #34 (Ka Stone revealed to be disintegrating; battled Thing; taken control of by Puppet Master who caused him to crush Ka Stone; aged rapidly and crumbled to dust); DOCTOR STRANGE Vol. 2 #27 (revealed to have been a mutant who was manipulated by the alien Caretakers from Arcturus until he turned against them)

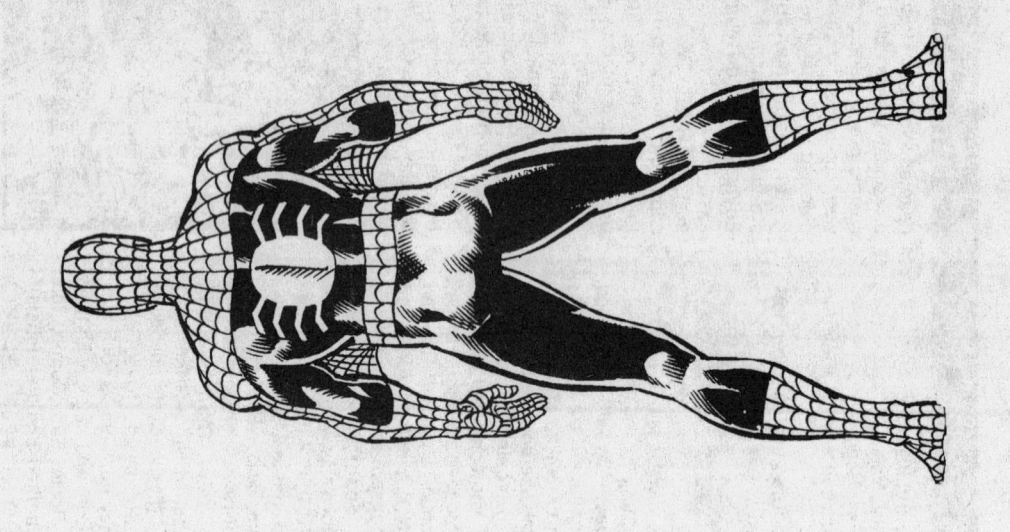

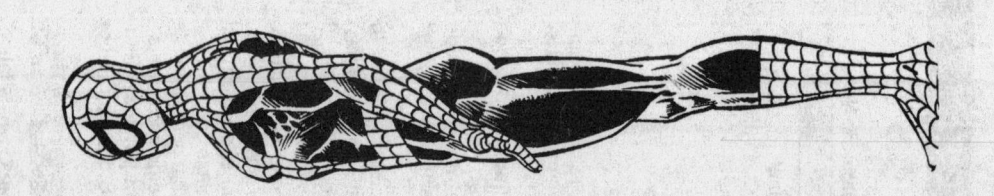

SPIDER-MAN

SPIDER-MAN

BIOGRAPHICAL DATA

Real name: Peter Parker
Other current aliases: None
Former aliases: None
Dual identity: Secret
Current occupation: Adventurer, freelance photographer, student
Former occupation: Wrestler, performer
Citizenship: United States of America
Legal status: No criminal record
Place of birth: Queens, New York
Marital status: Married
Known relatives: Mary Jane Watson-Parker (wife); Mary Parker (mother, deceased); Richard Parker (father, deceased); Benjamin Parker (uncle, deceased); May Parker (aunt); Gayle Watson (father-in-law); Tommy Byrnes, Byrnes (sister-in-law); Kevin Byrnes (nephews)
Known confidants: Mary Jane Watson-Parker, Harry Osborne
Known allies: The Human Torch, Daredevil, the Black Cat
Major enemies: The Chameleon, Doctor Octopus, Electro, Hobgoblin, Kingpin, Kraven, Lizard, Mysterio, Scorpion, Venom, Vulture
Usual base of operations: Manhattan
Former bases of operations: None
Current group membership: None
Former group membership: The Avengers
Extent of education: Graduate school student

PHYSICAL DESCRIPTION

Height: 5' 10"
Weight: 165 lbs.
Eyes: Hazel
Hair: Brown
Other distinguishing features: None

POWERS AND ABILITIES

Intelligence: Gifted
Strength: Superhuman Class 10
Speed: Superhuman
Stamina: Superhuman
Durability: Enhanced human
Agility: Superhuman
Reflexes: Superhuman
Fighting skills: No specific style, but a combination of his skills, agility, strength, and equilibrium
Special skills and abilities: Inventive
Superhuman physical powers: Superhuman strength, reflexes, agility, and equilibrium; premonitional "spider-sense" warning him of immediate danger to his person and able to detect signal from his spider-tracer; the ability to adhere to most surfaces with his hands and feet
Superhuman mental powers: None
Special limitations: None
Source of superhuman powers: Venom from the bite of radioactive spider
Note: Spider-Man briefly possessed the powers of Captain Universe in addition to his own

PARAPHERNALIA

Costume specifications: Synthetic stretch fabric
Personal weaponry: Web-shooters
Special weaponry: None
Other accessories: Miniature tracking devices ("spider-tracers"), miniature belt spotlight
Transportation: Web-lines emitted from web-shooters
Design and manufacture of paraphernalia: Peter Parker

BIBLIOGRAPHY

First appearance: AMAZING FANTASY #15
Origin issue: AMAZING FANTASY #15
Significant issues: AMAZING SPIDER-MAN #1 (met Fantastic Four; fought first costumed foe, the Chameleon); AMAZING SPIDER-MAN #2 (hired by the Daily Bugle, first confronted the Vulture); AMAZING SPIDER-MAN #3 (first fought Doctor Octopus); AMAZING SPIDER-MAN #6 (first fought the Lizard); AMAZING SPIDER-MAN #9 (first fought Electro); AMAZING SPIDER-MAN #13 (first fought Mysterio); AMAZING SPIDER-MAN ANNUAL #1 (first fought the Sinister Six); AMAZING SPIDER-MAN #15 (first fought Kraven the Hunter); AMAZING SPIDER-MAN #20 (first fought the Scorpion); AMAZING SPIDER-MAN #28 (graduated high school); AMAZING SPIDER-MAN #42 (met Mary Jane Watson); AMAZING SPIDER-MAN #50 (first fought the Kingpin); AMAZING SPIDER-MAN ANNUAL #5 (cleared dead parents' names); AMAZING SPIDER-MAN #100-102 (grew and lost four extra arms); AMAZING SPIDER-MAN #121 (death of Gwen Stacy); AMAZING SPIDER-MAN #122 (death of original Green Goblin); AMAZING SPIDER-MAN #129 (first fought the Punisher); AMAZING SPIDER-MAN #136 (Harry Osborn became the second Green Goblin); AMAZING SPIDER-MAN #183 (Mary Jane refused Peter Parker's first proposal of marriage); AMAZING SPIDER-MAN #185 (graduated from college); AMAZING SPIDER-MAN #194 (first confronted the Black Cat); AMAZING SPIDER-MAN #200 (final showdown with the burglar who killed his uncle); AMAZING SPIDER-MAN #238 (first fought the Hobgoblin); SECRET WARS #8 (received alien costume); AMAZING SPIDER-MAN #257 (Mary Jane revealed she knows Peter Parker is Spider-Man); WEB OF SPIDER-MAN #1 (rid himself of the alien costume); AMAZING SPIDER-MAN ANNUAL #21 (marriage to Mary Jane); AMAZING SPIDER-MAN #300 (first fought Venom); AMAZING SPIDER-MAN #304 (Peter Parker's book, Webs, published); AMAZING SPIDER-MAN #310 (returned to graduate school for PhD. in biochemistry); SPECTACULAR SPIDER-MAN #158 (became temporarily endowed with Captain Universe powers)

SPIDER-MAN IN ACTION

ART: ALEX SAVIUK/JOE RUBINSTEIN

SPIDER-MAN'S SUPPORTING CAST

LANCE BANNON
Current occupation: Freelance photographer for the *Daily Bugle*
Relationship: Rival/competitor of Peter Parker's for freelance assignments
First appearance: AMAZING SPIDER-MAN #208

KATHERINE "KATE" CUSHING
Current occupation: City Editor for the *Daily Bugle*
Relationship: Peter Parker's supervisor
First appearance: AMAZING SPIDER-MAN #270

JEAN DeWOLFF
Occupation at time of death: Captain, 37th Precinct, Manhattan, New York Police Department
Relationship: Ally of Spider-Man
First appearance: MARVEL TEAM-UP #39

GLORIA "GLORY" GRANT
Current occupation: Secretary of J. Jonah Jameson
Relationship: Good friend and former neighbor of Peter Parker, but bears a deep hatred of Spider-Man
First appearance: AMAZING SPIDER-MAN #140

FELICIA HARDY (BLACK CAT)
Current occupation: Part-time cat-burglar, adventurer
Relationship: Former lover of Spider-Man; currently close friend and confidant
First appearance: AMAZING SPIDER-MAN #194

J. JONAH JAMESON
Current occupation: Publisher of the *Daily Bugle*
Relationship: Employer of Peter Parker, but bears a deep animosity towards Spider-Man
First appearance: AMAZING SPIDER-MAN #1

BETTY BRANT-LEEDS
Current occupation: Secretary to Katherine Cushing
Relationship: Peter Parker's first girlfriend; currently good friends
First appearance: AMAZING SPIDER-MAN #4

JOY MERCADO
Current occupation: Reporter for *Now Magazine*
Relationship: Formerly assigned to national and international assignments with Peter Parker
First appearance: SPECTACULAR SPIDER-MAN ANNUAL #5

SPIDER-MAN'S® WEB-SHOOTERS™

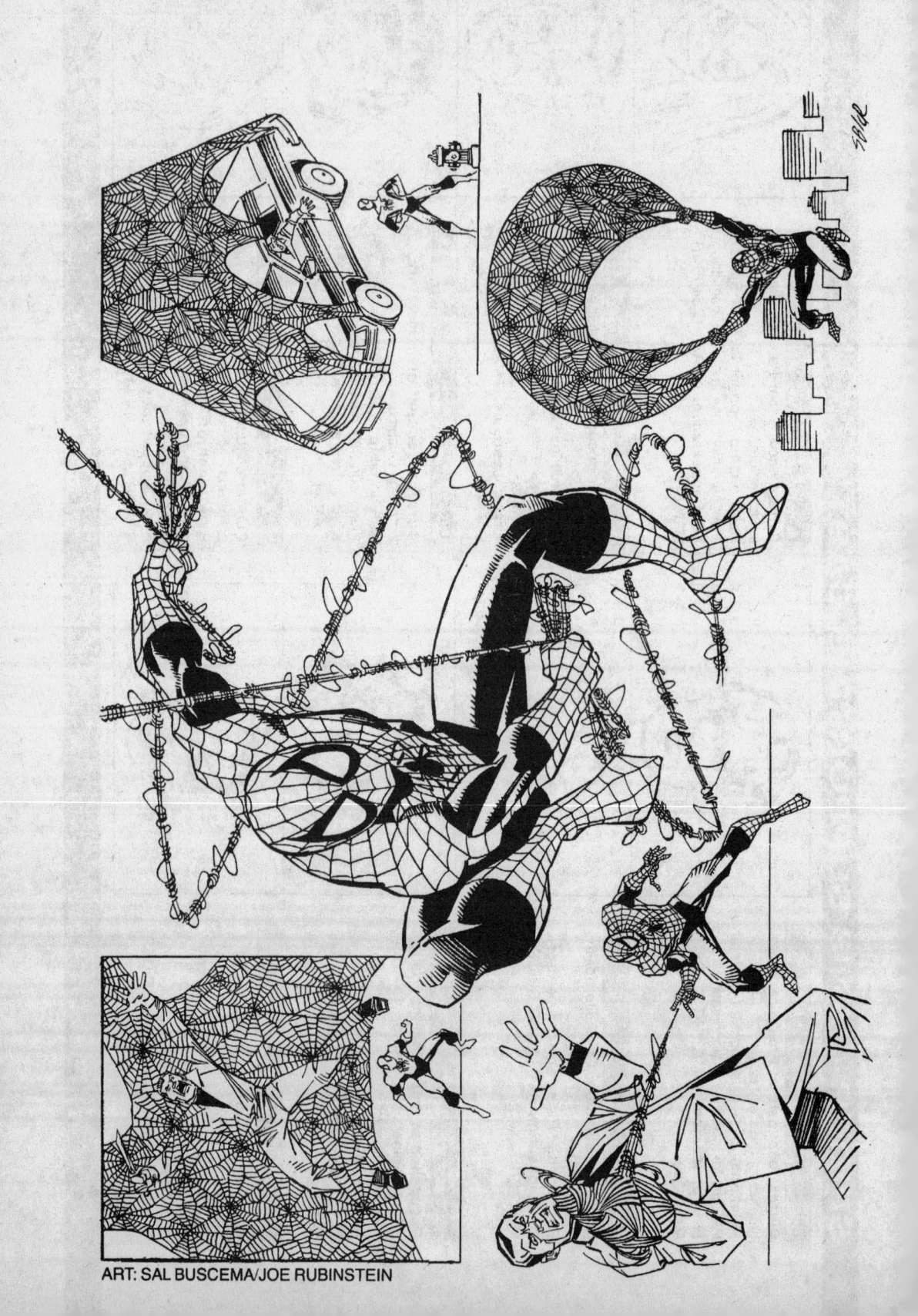

ART: SAL BUSCEMA/JOE RUBINSTEIN

SPIDER-MAN'S SUPPORTING CAST

ELIZABETH "LIZ" ALLEN

Current occupation: Major shareholder of *Osborn Industries, Inc.*
Relationship: One-time rival for Peter Parker's affections; current wife of his best friend, Harry Osborn
First appearance: AMAZING SPIDER-MAN #4

HAROLD "HARRY" OSBORN

Current occupation: Owner and president of *Osborn Industries, Inc.* Sometimes assumes the costumed identity of Green Goblin
Relationship: Peter Parker's best friend and confidant
First appearance: AMAZING SPIDER-MAN #31

BENJAMIN "BEN" PARKER

Occupation at time of death: Former carnival barker; later occupation unrevealed; retired at time of death
Relationship: Peter Parker's uncle
First appearance: AMAZING FANTASY #15
Final appearance: AMAZING FANTASY #15

MAY REILLY PARKER

Current occupation: Landlady
Relationship: Peter Parker's aunt
First appearance: AMAZING FANTASY #15

JOE "ROBBIE" ROBERTSON

Current occupation: Editor-in-Chief of the *Daily Bugle*
Relationship: Peter Parker's employer and friend
First appearance: AMAZING SPIDER-MAN #51

GWENDOLYNE "GWEN" STACY

Occupation at time of death: Student
Relationship: Girlfriend of Peter Parker
First appearance: AMAZING SPIDER-MAN #31

EUGENE "FLASH" THOMPSON

Current occupation: Boxer
Relationship: Best friend of Peter Parker
First appearance: AMAZING FANTASY #15

MARY JANE WATSON-PARKER

Current occupation: Model, soap opera actress
Relationship: Peter Parker's wife and confidante
First appearance: AMAZING SPIDER-MAN #42

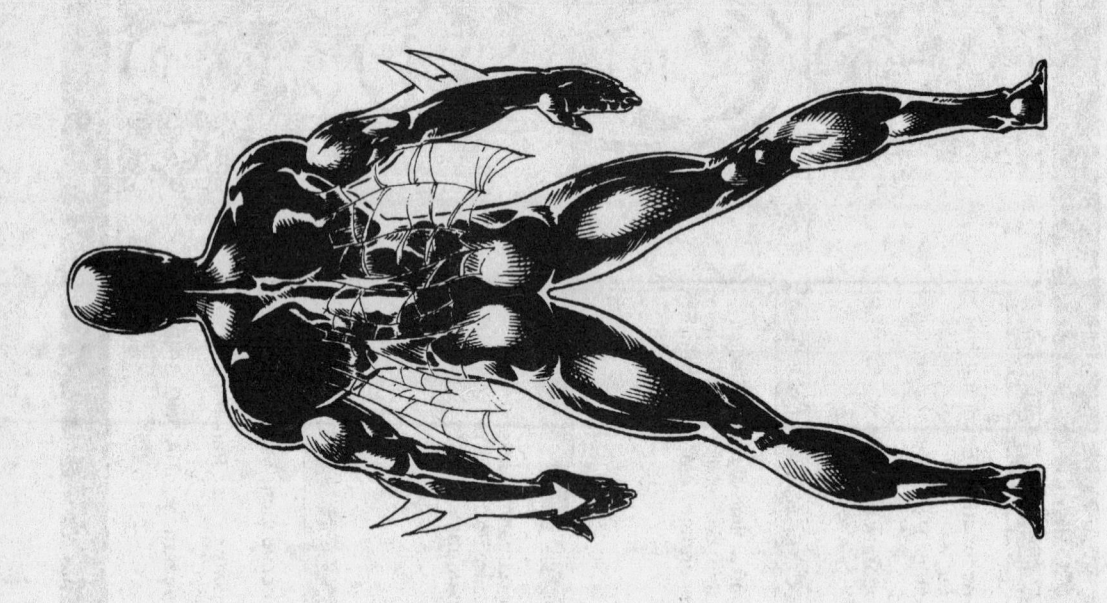

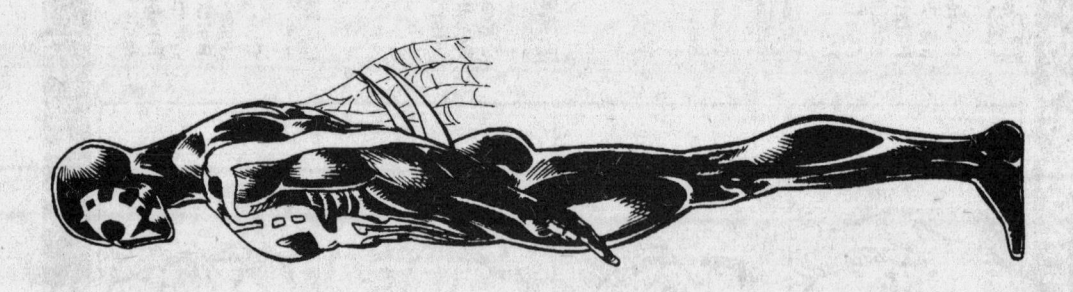

SPIDER-MAN 2099

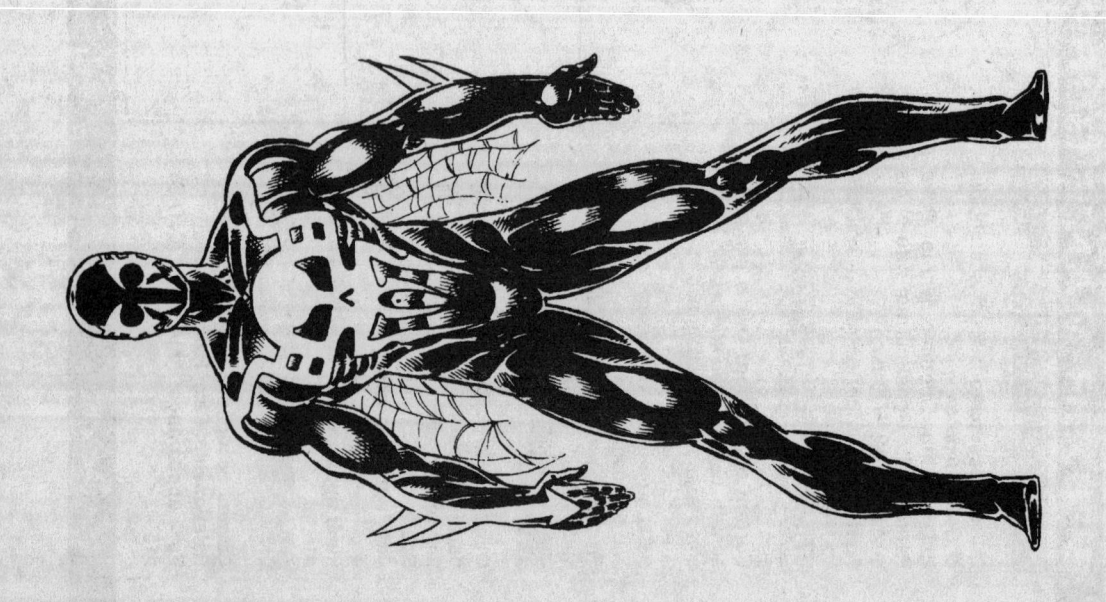

SPIDER-MAN 2099

BIOGRAPHICAL DATA

Real name: Miguel O'Hara
Other current aliases: None
Former aliases: None
Dual identity: Secret
Current occupation: Geneticist
Former occupation: College student
Citizenship: United States of America, circa 2099
Legal status: No criminal record
Place of birth: New York City, circa late 21st Century
Marital status: Single
Known relatives: Gabriel O'Hara (brother), unnamed father (deceased)
Known confidants: Gabriel O'Hara
Known allies: (as O'Hara) Dana D'Angelo, Kasey Nash
(as Spider-Man 2099)
Major enemies: Tyler Stone, Aaron Delgato, Venture, the Specialist, Rico Estevez, Vulture 2099, the Freakers, Mutagen, Thanatos
Usual base of operations: New York City, circa 2099
Former bases of operations: None
Current group membership: None
Former group membership: None
Extent of education: Advanced degree in genetics

PHYSICAL DESCRIPTION

Height: 5' 10"
Weight: 170 lbs.
Eyes: Brown
Hair: Brown
Other distinguishing features: Pronounced canine teeth (fangs), retractable talons on fingers and toes, spinerettes in forearms

POWERS AND ABILITIES

Intelligence: Gifted
Strength: Superhuman Class 10
Speed: Superhuman
Stamina: Superhuman
Durability: Enhanced human
Agility: Superhuman
Reflexes: Superhuman
Fighting skills: Minimal
Special skills and abilities: Highly skilled geneticist
Superhuman physical powers: Aside from the above listed attributes, the ability to adhere to most surfaces using talons on his hands and feet, the ability to rend substances up to and including cinderblock using his talons, the ability to fire webbing-like substance from spinerettes in his forearms; enhanced fast-healing metabolism; enhanced sensory acuity, including the ability to see in pitch darkness
Superhuman mental powers: None
Special limitations: None
Source of superhuman powers: Genetic imprinting with spider DNA

PARAPHERNALIA

Costume specifications: Unstable molecular fabric
Personal weaponry: None
Special weaponry: None
Other accessories: None
Transportation: None
Design and manufacture of paraphernalia: Miguel O'Hara

BIBLIOGRAPHY

First appearance: AMAZING SPIDER-MAN #365
Origin issue: SPIDER-MAN 2099 #1
Significant issues: SPIDER-MAN 2099 #1 (addicted to Rapture drug by Tyler Stone in attempt to force his compliance, attempted to restore normal genetic structure using experimental genetic engineering equipment, experiment ruined by Aaron Delgato, gained superhuman powers); SPIDER-MAN 2099 #2-3 (first encountered Thorites, battled Venture); SPIDER-MAN 2099 #4-5 (battled the Specialist); SPIDER-MAN 2099 #6-8 (encountered Freakers, battled Vulture 2099); 2099 UNLIMITED #1 (battled Mutagen); SPIDER-MAN 2099 #9 (battled Tyler Stone, Alchemax, and Stark-Fujikawa); SPIDER-MAN 2099 #11 (first encountered Thanatos)

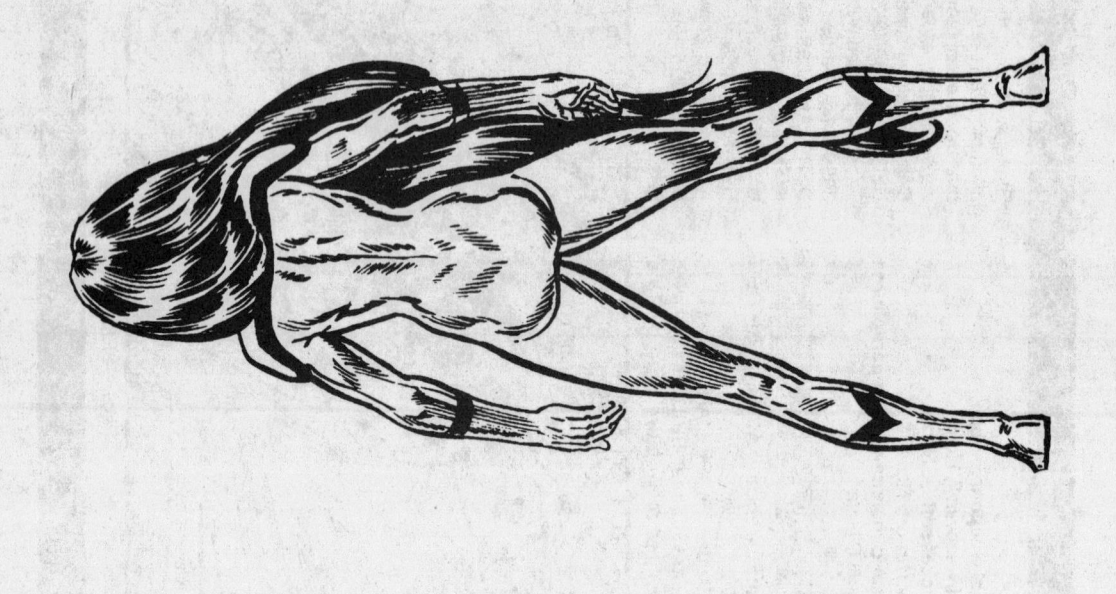

SPIDER-WOMAN

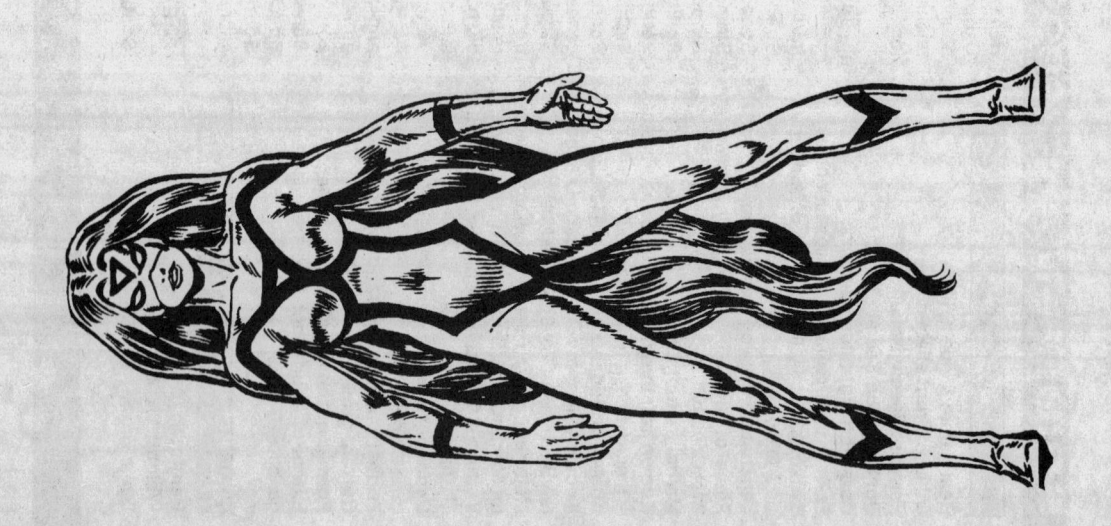

SPIDER-WOMAN I

BIOGRAPHICAL DATA

Real name: Jessica Drew
Other current aliases: None
Former aliases: Arachne
Dual identity: Secret; Jessica Drew does not currently use her Spider-Woman identity
Current occupation: Private investigator
Former occupation: HYDRA agent, adventurer
Citizenship: United States of America (naturalized)
Legal status: No criminal record
Place of birth: London, England
Marital status: Single
Known relatives: Jonathan Drew (father, deceased), Merriam Drew (mother, deceased)
Known confidants: Lindsay McCabe
Known allies: (current) Wolverine, (former) the High Evolutionary, Bova, Modred the Mystic, Jerry Hunt, Magnus the Magician, Nick Fury, the Shroud, Jack Russell, Scott McDowell, David Ishima, Sabrina Morrel
Major enemies: Morgan Le Fay, Gypsy Moth, original Brothers Grimm, Viper II
Usual base of operations: Madripoor
Former bases of operations: Wundagore, Transia; London, England; Los Angeles, California; San Francisco, California
Current group membership: None
Former group membership: None
Extent of education: High school equivalency courses in Wundagore;* espionage training in HYDRA; vocational training in undercover detective work

PHYSICAL DESCRIPTION

Height: 5' 10"
Weight: 133 lbs.
Eyes: Green
Hair: (natural) Light auburn; dyed jet black
Other distinguishing features: None

POWERS AND ABILITIES

Intelligence: Normal
Strength: Superhuman Class 10
Speed: Peak human
Stamina: Peak human
Durability: Peak human
Agility: Athlete
Reflexes: Peak human
Fighting skills: Extensive combat training by HYDRA
Special skills and abilities: Espionage and detective skills
Superhuman physical powers: Besides superhuman strength, Jessica Drew has the ability to stick to walls by excreting an unknown adhesive substance from her palms and soles. Her body also exudes a high concentration of pheromones eliciting pleasure in most men and fear in most women. Her body used to generate and project a form of bioelectricity ("venom-blast") but this ability was removed by Dr. Strange. Her body once also possessed an immunity to poisons and radiation.
Superhuman mental powers: None
Special limitations: None
Source of superhuman powers: A combination of special serum derived from spider blood and a certain radiation treatment

PARAPHERNALIA

Costume specifications: Ordinary fabric
Personal weaponry: Walther PPK handgun
Special weaponry: As needed
Other accessories: None
Transportation: Various
Design and manufacture of paraphernalia: Inapplicable

BIBLIOGRAPHY

First appearance: MARVEL SPOTLIGHT #32
Origin issue: MARVEL SPOTLIGHT #32, SPIDER-WOMAN #1
Significant issues: MARVEL SPOTLIGHT #32 (as HYDRA agent, battled Nick Fury and SHIELD, quit HYDRA, responsible for fatal crash of HYDRA head Otto Vermis); MARVEL TWO-IN-ONE #30-32 (captured and brainwashed by HYDRA, sent to attack the Thing); MARVEL TWO-IN-ONE #33 (battled magical elements alongside the Thing and Modred the Mystic); SPIDER-WOMAN #1 (true origin recounted); SPIDER-WOMAN #2 (battled Excalibur, agent of Morgan Le Fey, met Magnus the Magician); SPIDER-WOMAN #3 (moved to Los Angeles with Magnus); SPIDER-WOMAN #5-6 (encountered Morgan Le Fey's ghost); SPIDER-WOMAN #7 (tracked down her father's murderers); SPIDER-WOMAN #13-16 (alongside the Shroud, battled Nekra and the Cult of Kali, learned of pheromone secretions); SPIDER-WOMAN #20 (encountered Spider-Man); SPIDER-WOMAN #21 (began partnership with criminologist Scott McDowell); SPIDER-WOMAN #37-38 (moved to San Francisco, battled Siryn, Black Tom Cassidy, Juggernaut, alongside X-Men; became licensed private investigator); SPIDER-WOMAN #41 (battled Morgan Le Fey); SPIDER-WOMAN #42-44 (battled Viper II and Silver Samurai; Viper II attempted to convince her the she was her mother; Viper II shown to be pawn of Chthon, betrayed Chthon rather than hurt Drew); CAPTAIN AMERICA #281 (battled Viper II, who believed Drew had brainwashed her into believing that she was Drew's mother); MARVEL TWO-IN-ONE #85 (gave up immunity powers to save Giant-Man II); SPIDER-WOMAN #50 (traveled in astral form with Magnus to Sixth Century England to free friends' souls from Morgan Le Fey; body died while gone from it); AVENGERS #240-241 (Avengers and Dr. Strange traveled to astral plane to battle Morgan Le Fey and reunite Drew's spirit with her body, bioelectric powers eliminated, abandoned Spider-Woman identity); WOLVERINE #2 (ensorceled by Black Blade, battled Wolverine)

SPIDER-WOMAN II

SPIDER-WOMAN II

BIOGRAPHICAL DATA

Real name: Julia Carpenter
Other current aliases: None
Former aliases: None
Dual identity: Secret; known to certain government officials
Current occupation: Adventurer
Former occupation: Government agent
Citizenship: United States of America
Legal status: No criminal record
Place of birth: Denver, Colorado
Marital status: Divorced
Known relatives: Rachel Carpenter (daughter), Larry Carpenter (estranged husband)
Known confidants: None
Known allies: Avengers West Coast, Valerie Cooper
Major enemies: The Seekers, the Wrecker, Mystique
Usual base of operations: Los Angeles, California
Former bases of operations: Denver, Colorado
Current group membership: Avengers West Coast
Former group membership: Freedom Force
Extent of education: High school graduate

PHYSICAL DESCRIPTION

Height: 5' 9"
Weight: 140 lbs.
Eyes: Blue
Hair: Reddish blond
Other distinguishing features: None

POWERS AND ABILITIES

Intelligence: Normal
Strength: Superhuman Class 10
Speed: Enhanced human
Stamina: Athlete
Durability: Enhanced human
Agility: Athlete
Reflexes: Athlete
Fighting skills: Moderate experience but intensive training in hand-to-hand combat
Special skills and abilities: Unrevealed
Superhuman physical powers: See above
Superhuman mental powers: Spider-Woman possesses the ability to spin a "psi-web" of psionic energy beween two surfaces. This web, once solidified, possesses sufficient tensile strength to support a 10 ton weight. It remains in effect for up to approximately 1 hour. She can also project and release sufficient psionic energy through her hands and feet to enable her to walk on walls and ceilings.
Special limitations: Spider-Woman finds that physical gesturing aids her in the weaving of her psionic webs.
Source of superhuman powers: Unrevealed

PARAPHERNALIA

Costume specifications: Synthetic stretch fabric
Personal weaponry: None
Other accessories: None
Transportation: Various, now Avengers quinjets
Design and manufacture of paraphernalia: (Quinjets) Stark Enterprises

BIBLIOGRAPHY

First appearance: MARVEL SUPER HEROES SECRET WARS #6-7
Origin issue: Spider Woman's origin is as yet unrevealed.
Significant issues: SECRET WARS #6-12 (allied herself with the superhuman champions, battled Absorbing Man, Doctor Doom, Hulk, killed and resurrected by Doom with the power of the Beyonder); AVENGERS ANNUAL #15 (as member of Freedom Force, battled the Avengers, helped bring them into custody at the Vault, had change of heart, went to the Vault to aid the Avengers, battled Guardsmen); IRON MAN #214 (alongside Iron Man, battled renegade AIM agents named Seekers who sought to capture her for the reward, reassigned by government agent Valerie Cooper to undercover solo work); SPECTACULAR SPIDER-MAN #125-126 (alongside Spider-Man, battled the Wrecking Crew as a government assignment); AVENGERS WEST COAST #70-74 (battled the Pacific Overlords alongside the Avengers, fought USAgent); AVENGERS WEST COAST #75 (joined the Avengers)

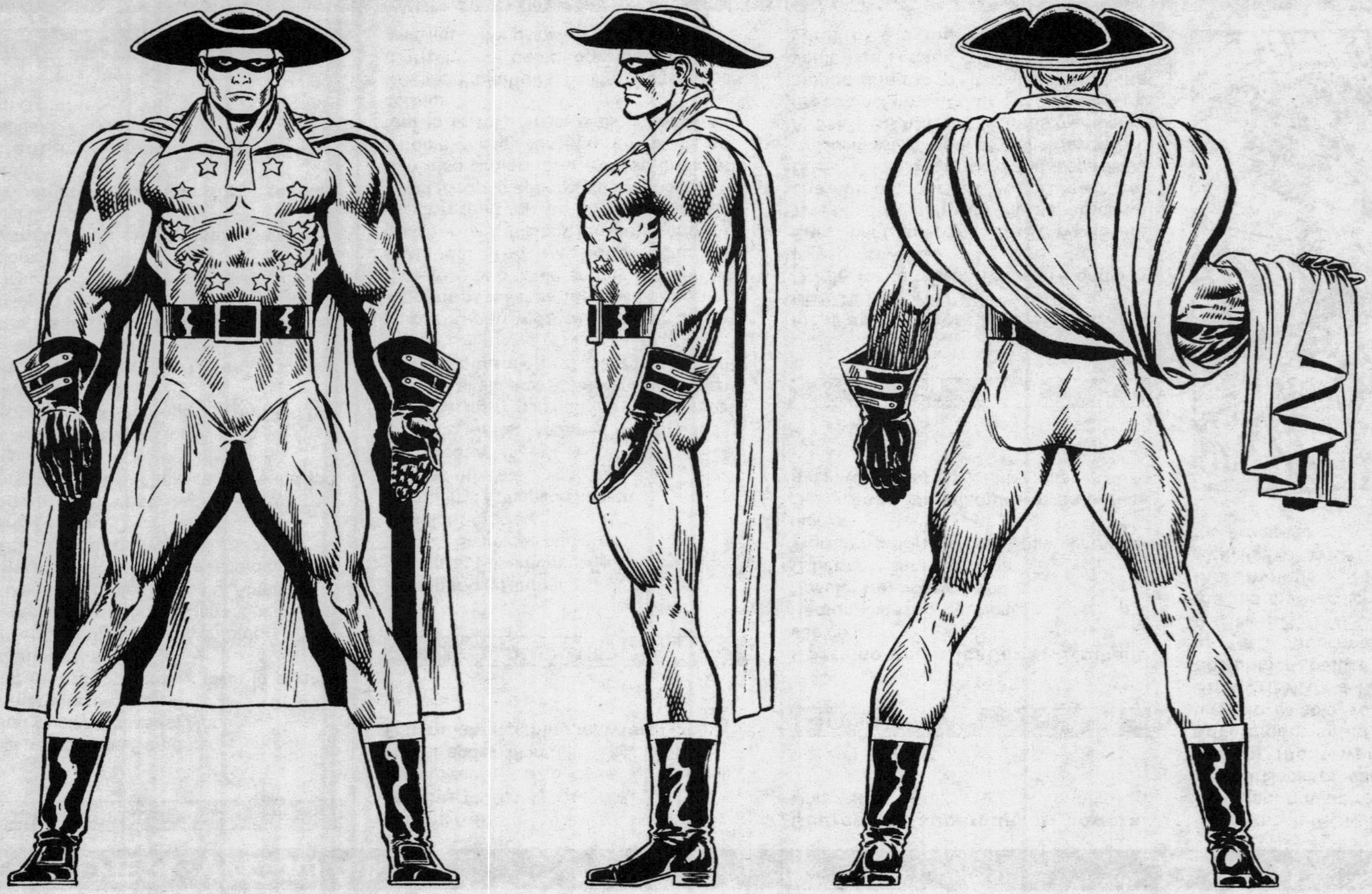

SPIRIT OF 76

SPIRIT OF '76

BIOGRAPHICAL DATA

Real name: William Nasland
Aliases at time of death: Captain America II
Former aliases: None
Dual identity: Known to certain U.S. government officials and to his teammates in the Invaders/All-Winners Squad
Occupation at time of death: Adventurer
Former occupation: Unrevealed
Citizenship: United States of America
Legal status: No criminal record
Place of birth: Philadelphia, Pennsylvania
Place of death: Boston, Massechussetts
Cause of death: Crushed to death by one of Adam II's robots
Marital status: Presumed single
Known relatives: None
Known confidants: Bucky II (Fred Davis)
Known allies: (as Spirit of '16) The Crusaders (Dyna-Mite [later Destroyer II], Ghost Girl, Thunderfist, Tommy Lightning, Captain Wings), (as Captain America II) the Invaders/All-Winners Squad (Bucky II, Human Torch I, Toro, Namor the Sub-Mariner, Whizzer I, Miss America), Blonde Phantom
Major enemies: (as Spirit of '16) Nazi and Japanese agents, (as Captain America II) Nazi agents, Japanese armed forces, Ibisa, Adam II
Base of operations at time of death: Mobile
Former bases of operations: Philadelphia, Pennsylvania; London, England
Group membership at time of death: All-Winners Squad
Former group membership: Crusaders, Invaders
Extent of education: Unrevealed

PHYSICAL DESCRIPTION

Height: 6'2"
Weight: 215 lb
Eyes: Blue
Hair: Black
Other distinguishing features: None

POWERS AND ABILITIES

Intelligence: Normal
Strength: Athlete
Speed: Athlete
Stamina: Athlete
Durability: Athlete
Agility: Athlete
Reflexes: Athlete
Fighting skills: Superb hand-to-hand combatant
Special skills and abilities: Unrevealed
Superhuman physical powers: None
Superhuman mental powers: None
Special limitations: None
Source of superhuman powers: Inapplicable

PARAPHERNALIA

Costume specifications: (as Spirit of '76) Ordinary fabric with a cloak of an unknown bulletproof and fireproof material, (as Captain America II) Ordinary fabric
Personal weaponry: (as Spirit of '76) None, (as Captain America II) A steel shield, approximately 2.5 feet in diameter
Special weaponry: None
Other accessories: None
Transportation: (as Spirit of '76) Conventional, (as Captain America II) Conventional or the Sub-Mariner's Atlantean flagship
Design and manufacture of paraphernalia: (Spirit of '76 cloak) William Nasland, (Captain America II's shield) U.S. government after a design by Steve Rogers

BIBLIOGRAPHY

First appearance: (as Spirit of '76) INVADERS #14, (as Captain America II) WHAT IF Vol. 1 #4
Origin issue: (as Spirit of '76) Origin is as yet unrevealed, (as Captain America II) WHAT IF Vol. 1 #4
Significant issues: INVADERS #14-15 (as Spirit of '76, alongside the Crusaders, tricked into battling the Invaders); WHAT IF Vol. 1 #4 (chosen by President Truman to replace Captain America I after his apparent death); NAMOR ANNUAL #1 (alongside Namor the Sub-Mariner and the Red Guardian I, stopped Nazi plot to destroy the Potsdam Conference) ALL-WINNERS COMICS #19 (alongside All-Winners Squad, battled Ibisa); SHE-HULK Vol. 2 #22 (alongside All-Winners Squad and Blonde Phantom, fought to prevent criminal attempt to steal atomic bomb, encountered time-traveling She-Hulk); WHAT IF Vol. 1 #4 (alongside All-Winners Squad, battled Adam II, killed in action, replaced by the Patriot as Captain America III); CAPTAIN AMERICA ANNUAL #6 (brought through time by the Contemplator to battle Adam II of an alternate alongside Captain America I, III, and IV)

SPIRIT OF VENGEANCE

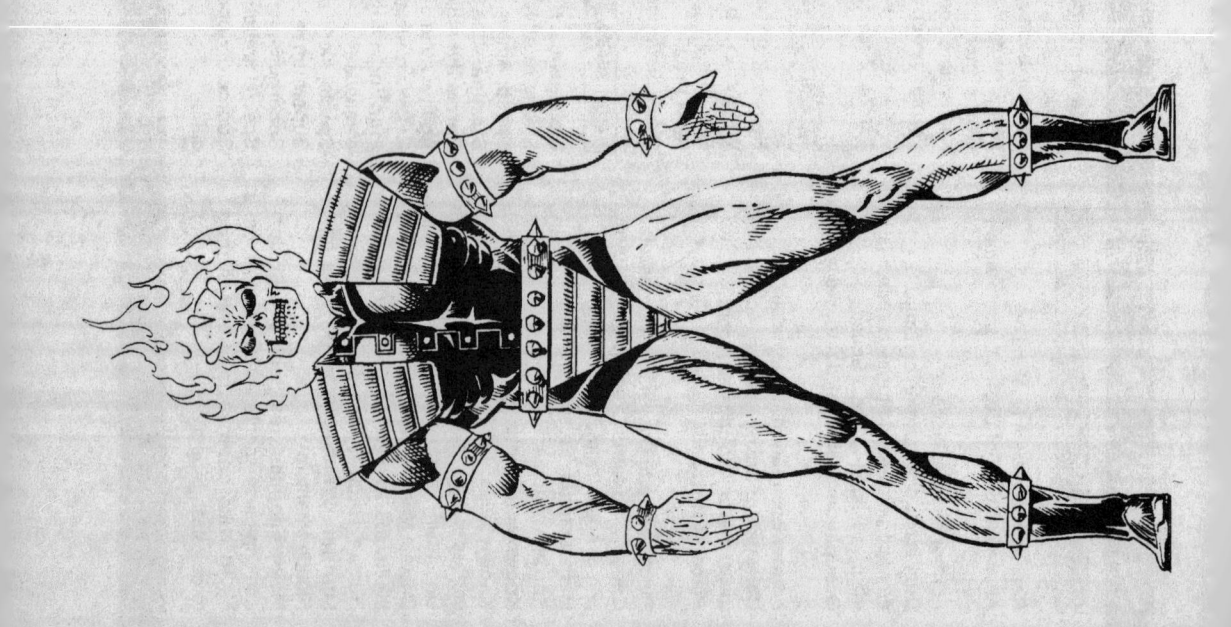

SPIRIT OF VENGEANCE

BIOGRAPHICAL DATA

Real name: Wileaydus Autolycus
Other current aliases: The Flaming Demon
Former aliases: None
Dual identity: Secret; the general populace of 20th Century Earth is unaware of existence of the Spirit of Vengeance.
Current occupation: Freedom fighter, adventurer
Former occupation: Priest
Citizenship: Planet Sarka, Tilnast System, Milky Way Galaxy, circa 3015 A.D.
Legal status: No criminal record
Place of birth: An unknown location on the planet Sarka
Marital status: Single
Known relatives: None
Known confidants: None
Known allies: The Guardians of the Galaxy, the Galactic Guardians, Krugarr
Major enemies: The Universal Church of Truth, Korvac, the Intimidators, Bubonicus, Dormammu
Usual base of operations: Mobile throughout known space aboard the starship *Icarus*
Former bases of operations: Planet Sarka
Current group membership: Galactic Guardians
Former group membership: Guardian of the Galaxy (reserve member)
Extent of education: Advanced degree in theology

PHYSICAL DESCRIPTION

Height: 6' 2", (as Autolycus) 5' 10"
Weight: Unrevealed, (as Autolycus) 180lbs.
Eyes: Flaming red, (as Autolycus) Blue
Hair: None, (as Autolycus) Blue-black
Other distinguishing features: (as Autolycus) Blue skin, (as Spirit of Vengeance) Head resembling a flaming skull

POWERS AND ABILITIES

Intelligence: Normal
Strength: Superhuman Class 10
Speed: Enhanced human
Stamina: Immeasurable
Durability: Godlike
Agility: Athlete
Reflexes: Enhanced human
Fighting skills: Untrained but formidable hand-to-hand combatant
Special skills and abilities: Experienced priest
Superhuman physical powers: The ability to mystically transform into a being with the above listed attributes, who can project "soulfire" or "hellfire" (fire-like mystical energy) for various effects, including bursts of flame painful to victims through physical stimulation of the life force rather than burning; he can create his "Death-Cycle"
Superhuman mental powers: None known
Special limitations: The extent of Spirit of Vengeance's superhuman powers is as yet unrevealed
Source of superhuman powers: Unrevealed

PARAPHERNALIA

Costume specifications: Body armor of alien materials
Personal weaponry: None
Special weaponry: None
Other accessories: None
Transportation: Death-Cycle (a flying motorcycle-like vehicle created of "hellfire" and capable of traversing airless space); the starship *Icarus*
Design and manufacture of paraphernalia: Unrevealed

BIBLIOGRAPHY

First appearance: (as Autolycus) GUARDIANS OF THE GALAXY #12; (as Spirit of Vengeance) GUARDIANS OF THE GALAXY #13
Origin issue: The Spirit of Vengeance's origin is as yet unrevealed.
Significant issues: GUARDIANS OF THE GALAXY #12 (mistakenly thought the Guardians of the Galaxy were the Black Knights of the Universal Church of Truth); GUARDIANS OF THE GALAXY #13-14 (battled Guardians of the Galaxy, realized his error, aided them against Universal Church of Truth, killed Grand Inquisitor II, given Guardian's star); GUARDIANS OF THE GALAXY ANNUAL #1 (helped to form the Galactic Guardians, fought Korvac and his Intimidators); GUARDIANS OF THE GALAXY #35 (with Galactic Guardians, fought Bubonicus); GUARDIANS OF THE GALAXY #36-37 (with Galactic Guardians, Guardians of the Galaxy, Krugarr, and Ancient One II [Dr. Strange], battled Dormammu)

SPITFIRE

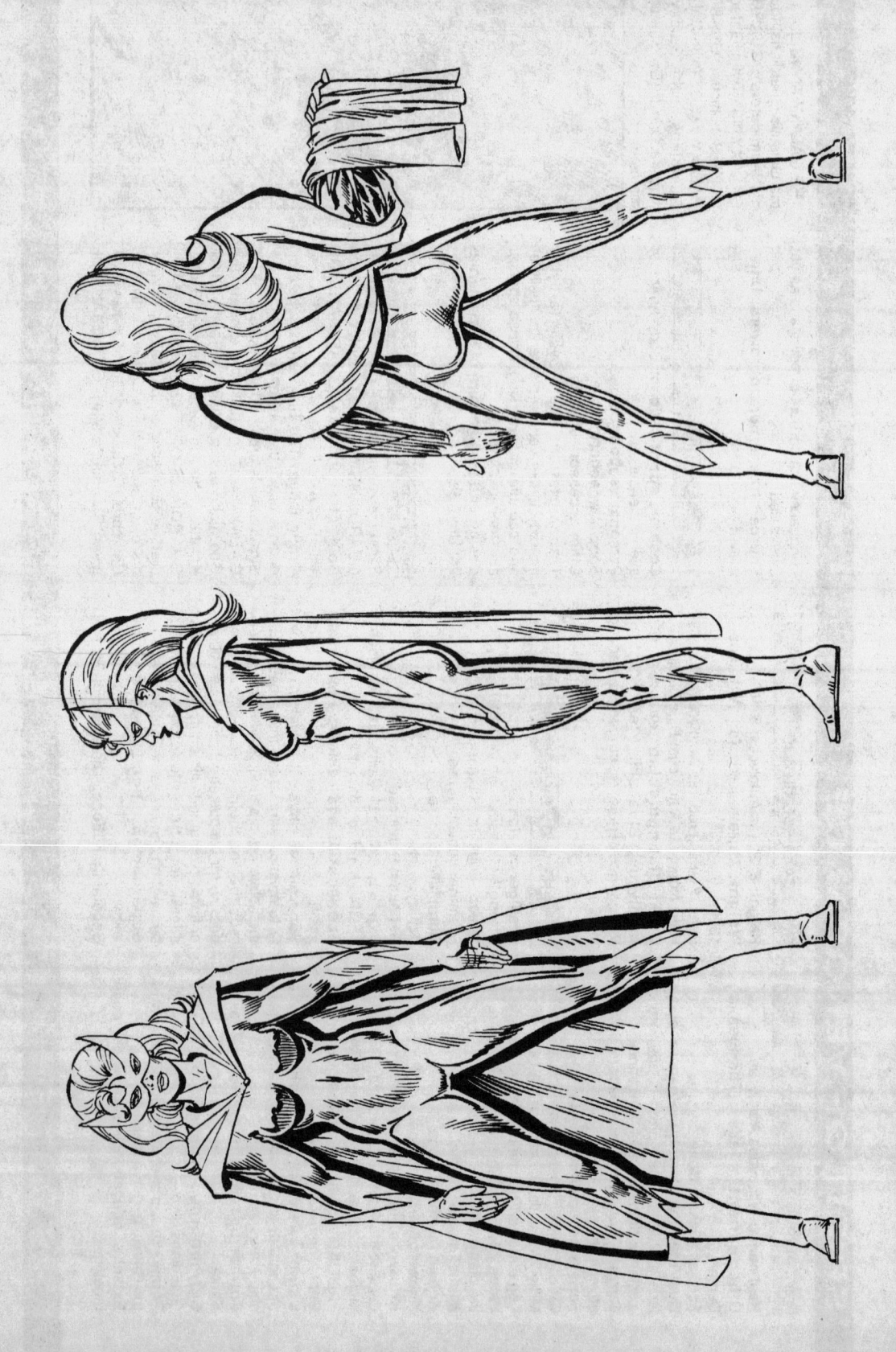

SPITFIRE

BIOGRAPHICAL DATA

Real name: Jacqueline "Jackie" Falsworth Crichton (Lady Crichton)
Other current aliases: None
Former aliases: None
Dual identity: Publicly known, but secret during World War II
Current occupation: Chief-Executive-Officer, Falsworth Industries
Former occupation: Adventurer, special agent for United Kingdom and Allied Forces during World War II, former member of the United Kingdom's Home Guard
Citizenship: United Kingdom
Legal status: No criminal record
Place of birth: Maidstone, England
Marital status: Widowed
Known relatives: Lord William Falsworth (grandfather, deceased), Lord Montgomery Falsworth (alias Union Jack I, father, deceased), John Falsworth (alias Baron Blood I, uncle, deceased), Brian Falsworth (alias Union Jack II, brother, deceased), Lord Crichton (husband, deceased), Kenneth Crichton (son)
Known confidants: Captain America, Human Torch I, Sub-Mariner, Namorita, Union Jack III
Known allies: Invaders, Namorita, Union Jack III
Major enemies: Baron Blood I, Master Man I, Warrior Woman, Adolf Hitler
Usual base of operations: Falsworth Manor, Little Storping-on-the-Thames, near London, England; New York City
Former bases of operations: (as Invader) Big Ben tower; Houses of Parliament, London, England
Current group membership: None
Former group membership: Invaders
Extent of education: College

PHYSICAL DESCRIPTION

Height: 5'4"
Weight: 110 lbs.
Eyes: Blue
Hair: Blonde
Other distinguishing features: Due to a second transfusion of artificial blood from the original Human Torch, Spitfire today has the body of a teenage girl, although she is chronologically many decades older; her hair is still white from age, but it is turning blonde again.

POWERS AND ABILITIES

Intelligence: Normal
Strength: Athlete, Superhuman (leg press only)
Speed: Subsonic
Stamina: Enhanced human
Durability: Enhanced human
Agility: Peak human
Reflexes: Enhanced human
Fighting skills: Exceptional hand-to-hand combatant (during World War II) utilizing her ability to move at superhuman speeds, due to training by Union Jack I and Captain America; currently out of practice
Special skills and abilities: Trained airplane pilot
Superhuman physical powers: Superhuman speed and reflexes, can create cyclones by running in circles, can run up walls and across water.
Superhuman mental powers: None
Special limitations: None
Source of superhuman powers: Mutagenic reaction to vampiric bite by Baron Blood I and transfusion of artificial blood from the Human Torch I

PARAPHERNALIA

Costume specifications: Synthetic stretch fabric chemically treated for protection from friction and other hazards of superhuman speed
Personal weaponry: None
Special weaponry: None
Other accessories: None
Transportation: British DKOI aircraft, circa 1940
Design and manufacture of paraphernalia: Unrevealed

BIBLIOGRAPHY

First appearance: (as Jackie) INVADERS #7, (as Spitfire without name or costume) INVADERS #11, (with name and costume) INVADERS #12
Origin issue: (as Spitfire) INVADERS #11
Significant issues: INVADERS #7 (first met Invaders, rescued by Human Torch I from Baron Blood); INVADERS #9 (revealed to have been bitten by Baron Blood, abducted by him, rescued by Captain America); INVADERS #11 (received transfusion of artificial blood from Human Torch I, endowed with superhuman speed, saved Human Torch from Blue Bullet); INVADERS #12 (adopted costume and name of Spitfire, went on first mission with Invaders); INVADERS #18-21 (with Invaders, parachuted into Nazi Germany; captured by Nazis, was about to be executed when rescued by Union Jack II; battled Warrior Woman; escaped from Germany with Invaders); INVADERS #30 (with Invaders, fought Teutonic Knight, helped prevent assassination of Winston Churchill by Baron Von Strucker); INVADERS #34 (alongside Invaders, clashed with Master Man, freed Mighty Destroyer from captivity); INVADERS #41 (returned to active duty with the Invaders); CAPTAIN AMERICA #253-254 (reunited with Captain America for first time since World War II, present during his final battle with Baron Blood I); MARVEL SUPER-HEROES WINTER SPECIAL Vol. 2 #4 (used superhuman speed for the first time in a decade to overcome criminal); NAMOR THE SUB-MARINER #12 (aided Namorita and Union Jack III in rescuing Namor from Master Man I and Warrior Woman, shot in overpowering Nazi, received blood transfusion from Human Torch I, causing her to revert to physical adolescence)

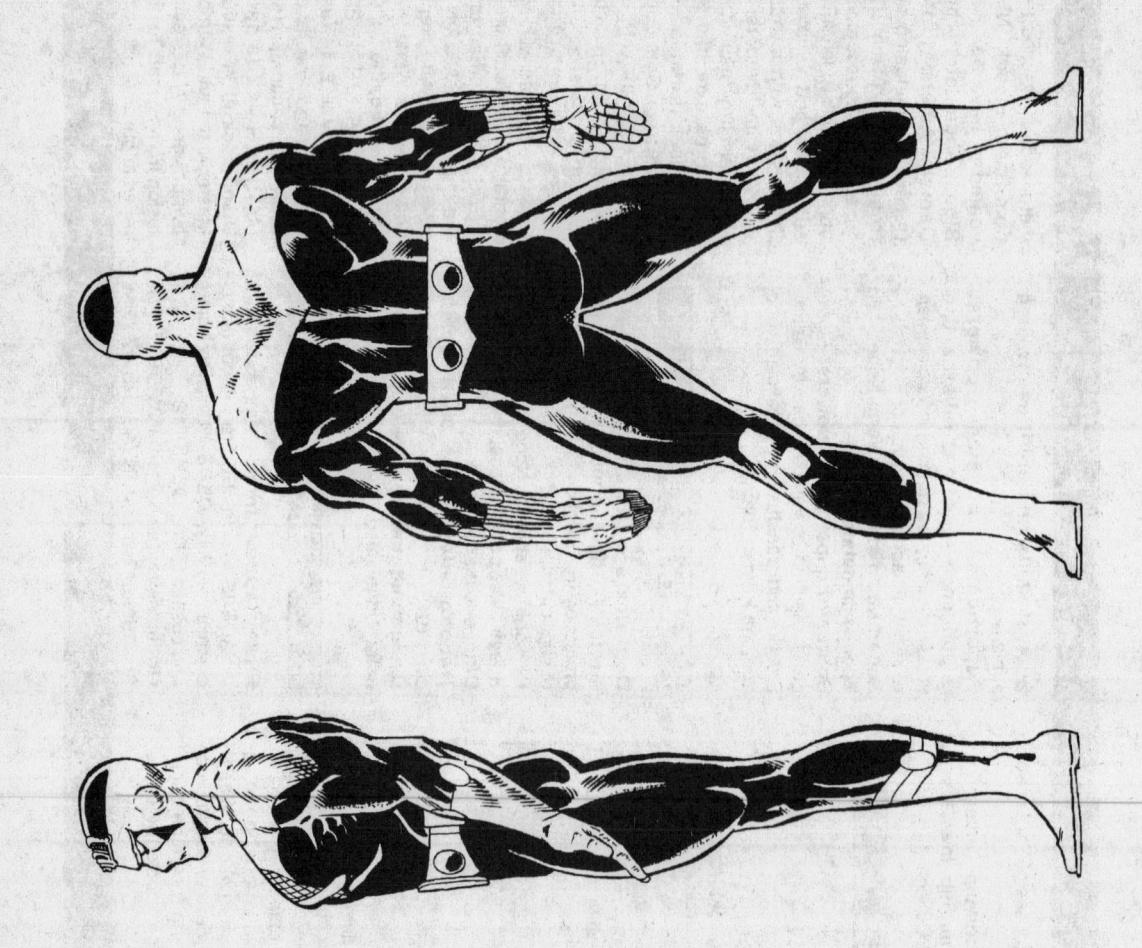

SPYMASTER™

SPYMASTER

BIOGRAPHICAL DATA

Real name: (both) Unrevealed
Other current aliases: (II) None
Former aliases : (I) Ted Calloway, Jake Jordan, Anthony Stark, Harmon Taylor, others presumably, (II) Number One, Santa Claus
Dual Identity: (both) Secret
Current occupation: (II) Industrial spy and saboteur, assassin
Occupation at time of death: (I) Industrial spy and saboteur, assassin
Former occupations: (I) Boxer, (II) Unrevealed
Citizenship: (both) Presumably United States of America
Legal status: (both) No known criminal record
Place of birth: (both) Unrevealed
Place of death: (I) Los Angeles, California
Cause of death: (I) Used the Ghost's intangibility device to pass through a wall, when the Ghost removed the device, it caused Spymaster I to rematerialize partially inside the wall
Marital status: (both) Unrevealed
Known relatives: (both) None
Known confidants: (both) Unrevealed
Known allies: (I) Espionage Elite, Zodiac I, Buck Richlen, Val Adair, Justin Hammer, Madame Masque I, AIM, Roxxon Oil, (II) Taskmaster, Justin Hammer
Major enemies: (I) Iron Man I, Ghost, James Rhodes, Happy Hogan, Daredevil, industrial spy and saboteur, master of disguise superb actor, highly agile and athletic, greatly skilled in the uses of virtually any kind of gun
Superhuman physical powers: (both) None
Superhuman mental powers: (both) None
Special limitations: (both) None known
Source of superhuman powers: (both) Inapplicable

PARAPHERNALIA

Costume specifications: Bulletproof kevlar battlesuit containing various pockets for holding weaponry
Personal weaponry: (both) various conventional weaponry
Special weaponry: Spymaster I used various special devices including, devices in his gloves and mask that projected concussive energy blasts, small, powerful hovering electromagnets, incendiary missiles, "razor-discs" that could pierce Iron Man's armor, devices that enabled him to absorb Iron Man I's repulsor energy, stun-guns, and sleep inducing "somnu-gas." Both Spymaster's have employed electronically amplified nun-chakas that can damage Iron Man's armor. Presumably Spymaster II has much of his predecessor's arsenal.
Other accessories: (both) None known
Transportation: (I) Formerly flight, via boot jets; flew an advanced model hoverjet that could operate automatically according to pre-programmed instructions, used a device in his belt buckle to summon hoverjet; (II) None known
Design and manufacture of paraphernalia: (I) Partly, Justin Hammer's scientists, (II) Justin Hammer's scientists

BIBLIOGRAPHY

First appearance: (I) IRON MAN #33; (II) IRON MAN #254
Origin issue: (I) Spymaster I's origin is as yet unrevealed; (II) IRON MAN #254
Significant issues: IRON MAN # 33-34, 35, DAREDEVIL #73, IRON MAN #36 (I) (with his Espionage Elite, assigned by Zodiac I to steal information from Stark Industries, thwarted by Iron Man I; assigned by Zodiac I to capture Daredevil but failed; aided Aquarius I, Capricorn I and Sagittarius I in attempt to steal Zodiac Key from Stark; transported to otherdimensional realm of Brotherhood of the Ankh; returned to Earth and escaped); IRON MAN #113, 115-117 (assigned by renegade SHIELD agents to assassinate Tony Stark, failed); IRON MAN #138-139 (employed by Madame Masque I to steal prototype energizer link, abducted Bethany Cabe); IRON MAN #220 (assigned by Roxxon to assassinate Ghost, was killed by Ghost instead); IRON MAN #255 (new Spymaster appointed by Taskmaster for Justin Hammer; first battled Iron Man)

(II) Iron Man I
Usual base of operations: (I) Mobile [at time of death], (II) Presumably mobile
Former bases of operations: (I) None known, (II) Taskmaster's Academy, Apple Valley, California
Current group membership: (I) None (at time of death), (II) Employee of Justin Hammer
Former group membership: (I) Espionage Elite, (II) Taskmaster's Academy
Extent of education: (both) Unrevealed

PHYSICAL DESCRIPTION

Height: (I) 6', (II) 5' 11"
Weight: (I) 195 lbs., (II) 190 lbs.
Eyes: (I) Blue, (II) Brown
Hair: (I) Blond, (II) Unrevealed
Other distinguishing features: None

POWERS AND ABILITIES

Intelligence: (both) Normal
Strength: (both) Athlete
Speed: (both) Athlete
Stamina: (both) Athlete
Durability: (both) Athlete
Agility: (both) Athlete
Reflexes: (both) Athlete
Fighting skills: (I) Excellent hand-to-hand combatant, formal training in boxing and various martial arts, (II) Excellent hand-to-hand combatant, trained at Taskmaster's Academy
Special skills: (both) Extraordinary

SQUADRON SUPREME

SQUADRON SUPREME

ORGANIZATION

Full name: Squadron Supreme (since surrendering control of the government of "Other-Earth's" United States, the members now refer to the team simply as the Squadron)

Purpose: Originally, to preserve the security of Other-Earth (aka Earth-S, an alternate world in another dimension) against superhuman threats of earthly or alien origin that are too powerful to be overcome by any single superhuman adventurer. Currently, the Squadron is based on "mainstream" Earth and intervenes against superhuman threats there only on unusual occasions; their primary goal is to find a means of returning to Other-Earth.

Modus operandi: Team responds to crisis alerts worldwide, with special emphasis on the United States, from their Other-Earth headquarters. Currently, while based on "mainstream" Earth, the Squadron performs certain missions for Project: Pegasus.

Extent of operations: While based on Other-Earth, the Squadron was primarily concerned with the United States, but also operated worldwide and in outer space when necessary

Relationship to conventional authorities: Cooperated with United States government on Other-Earth, became virtual government operatives when the Other-Earth United States was dominated by the Serpent Cartel and Over-Mind, later assumed overall control of the United States government with the cooperation of President Jules Gardner. Currently the Squadron cooperates with the "mainstream" Earth's United States energy research agency, Project: Pegasus.

Base of operations: Project: Pegasus, upstate New York of "mainstream" Earth

Former bases of operations: Rocket Central (Squadron satellite) orbiting Other-Earth; Squadron Mountain Headquarters in Moreland, United States of Other-Earth; Squadron City, Great American Desert, United States of Other-Earth

Major funding: Currently receiving room and board at Project Pegasus on "mainstream" Earth; formerly received funding from Kyle Richmond (Nighthawk I)

Known enemies: Master Menace, Scarlet Centurion, Over-Mind, Null the Living Darkness, Serpent Cartel, Brain-Child, Deathurge, (former) Nth Man I, Institute of Evil (Ape-X, Doctor Decibel, Foxfire, Lamprey, Quagmire, Shape), Nighthawk's Redeemers, Avengers

Known allies: Avengers, Defenders, Silver Surfer, Professor Imam, Quasar, Doctor Strange

MEMBERSHIP

Number of active members: 8
Number of reserve members: 0
Organizational structure: Team is composed of a designated leader and an unrestricted number of other active members, all of whom have either superhuman or extraordinary skills.

Known officers: Hyperion I (leader)

Known current members: Hyperion I, Power Princess, Whizzer II, Doctor Spectrum I, Moonglow II (Arcanna), Haywire, Shape, Skylark (Lady Lark)

Known former members: Nighthawk I, Amphibian, Blue Eagle (Cap'n Hawk, American Eagle I), Golden Archer (Black Archer), Nuke I, Tom Thumb, Ape-X, Doctor Decibel, Foxfire, Lamprey, Inertia, Redstone, Thermite (all deceased); Moonglow I, Quagmire

Known special agents: None

Membership requirements: Must be a recognized adult costumed adventurer

HISTORY

Founder: Hyperion I, Nighthawk I, Power Princess, Whizzer II, Doctor Spectrum I, Amphibian, the Skrull

Other leaders: Power Princess (leader during Hyperion's blindness)

Previous purpose or goals: Squadron assumed control of government of United States of Other-Earth in order to remake the nation into a virtual utopia by eliminating such problems as hunger, disease, and crime.

Major campaigns or accomplishments: Repeatedly thwarted attempts by Scarlet Centurion to conquer 20th Century Other-Earth; repeatedly foiled criminal Institute of Evil; defeated Brain-Child; overthrew Serpent Cartel's domination of federal government; halted world takeover by Over-Mind and Null the Living Darkness; established relations with Avengers and Defenders; reversed economic and technological collapse of Other-Earth United States within one year through "Utopia Program," which eliminated hunger, imposed strict gun controls, and instituted "behavior modification" of criminals; helped defeat Deathurge and Maelstrom's attempted destruction of "mainstream" Earth

Major setbacks: Most members fell under mental domination of Serpent Cartel; most members mentally enslaved by Over-Mind and used by him to devastate much of Other-Earth; resignations of Nighthawk II and Amphibian, expulsion of Golden Archer; blinding of Hyperion I; defeat by Nighthawk's Redeemers; deaths of Nighthawk I, Blue Eagle, Nuke I, Tom Thumb, Foxfire, Inertia, Redstone, Thermite; exile to "mainstream" Earth; members mentally enslaved by Over-Mind and forced to help him against the Stranger

TECHNOLOGY AND PARAPHERNALIA

Level of technology: Highly advanced, mostly invented by Tom Thumb
Transportation: Various advanced air and spacecraft, designed by Tom Thumb
Standard uniforms: None
Standard weaponry: None
Standard accessories: Communications equipment devised by Tom Thumb

STALLIOR™

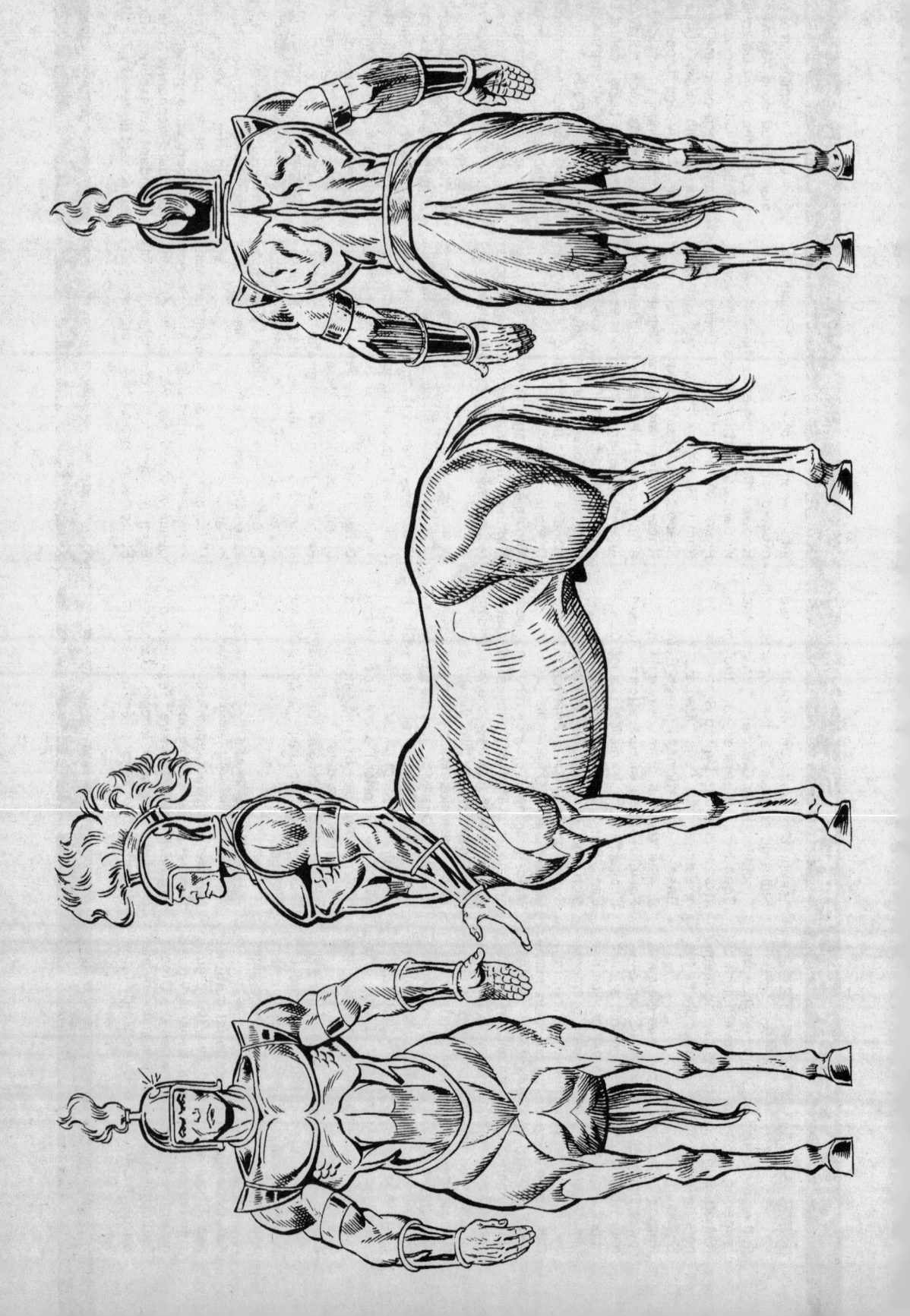

STALLIOR

BIOGRAPHICAL DATA

Real name: Unrevealed
Other current aliases: None
Former aliases: None
Dual identity: None; Stallior's existence is unknown to the general populace of Earth
Current occupation: Insurrectionist
Former occupation: Guardsman
Citizenship: Attilan
Legal status: Criminal record for treason
Place of birth: Island of Attilan, Atlantic Ocean
Marital status: Single
Known relatives: Chiron (brother), Centaurius (cousin)
Known confidants: None
Known allies: Maximus, "Evil Inhumans" (Aireo [later Skybreaker], Falcona, Leonus, Timberius, Nebulo)
Major enemies: Inhumans royal family, Fantastic Four, the Hulk
Usual base of operations: Attilan
Former bases of operations: City of Attilan, Himalayan Mountain Range, China; Island of Attilan, Atlantic Ocean
Current group membership: "Evil Inhumans"
Former group membership: None
Extent of education: Unrevealed

PHYSICAL DESCRIPTION

Height: 8' 2"
Weight: 1420 lbs.
Eyes: Brown
Hair: Black
Other distinguishing features: Stallior resembles a centaur of mythology

POWERS AND ABILITIES

Intelligence: Normal
Strength: Enhanced human, (legs only) Superhuman Class 10
Stamina: Enhanced human
Durability: Enhanced human
Agility: Enhanced human
Reflexes: Enhanced human
Fighting skills: Inhuman militia training in hand-to-hand and armed combat
Special skills and abilities: None known
Superhuman physical powers: Aside from the above listed, none
Superhuman mental powers: None
Special limitations: Like all Inhumans, Stallior's immune system is weaker than that of an average human
Source of superhuman powers: Genetically superior Inhuman physiology enhanced and mutated by Terrigen Mist

PARAPHERNALIA

Costume specifications: Helmet and body armor covering humanoid portion of his torso only
Personal weaponry: Ball and 5' chain, circular shield approximately 2' in diameter
Special weaponry: Various as needed
Other accessories: None
Transportation: Usually on hoof
Design and manufacture of paraphernalia: Unidentified Inhuman technicians

BIBLIOGRAPHY

First appearance: INCREDIBLE HULK ANNUAL #1
Origin issue: Stallior's origin is as yet unrevealed.
Significant issues: INCREDIBLE HULK ANNUAL #1 (alongside the "Evil Inhumans," found guilty of treason and banished to "the Un-Place", alongside Maximus and "Evil Inhumans," battled the Hulk and the Inhumans' Royal Family); FANTASTIC FOUR #83 (alongside Maximus and "Evil Inhumans", battled Fantastic Four and Inhumans' Royal Family); INCREDIBLE HULK #119-120 (alongside Maximus and "Evil Inhumans", battled Hulk and U.S. army); SILVER SURFER Vol. 1 #18 (alongside Inhumans, battled Silver Surfer); INHUMANS #5-6 (alongside Maximus and "Evil Inhumans," battled Royal Family); MARVEL FAN-FARE #14 (alongside Royal Family attempted to capture Quicksilver during Aireo's crime spree)

STARBOLT™

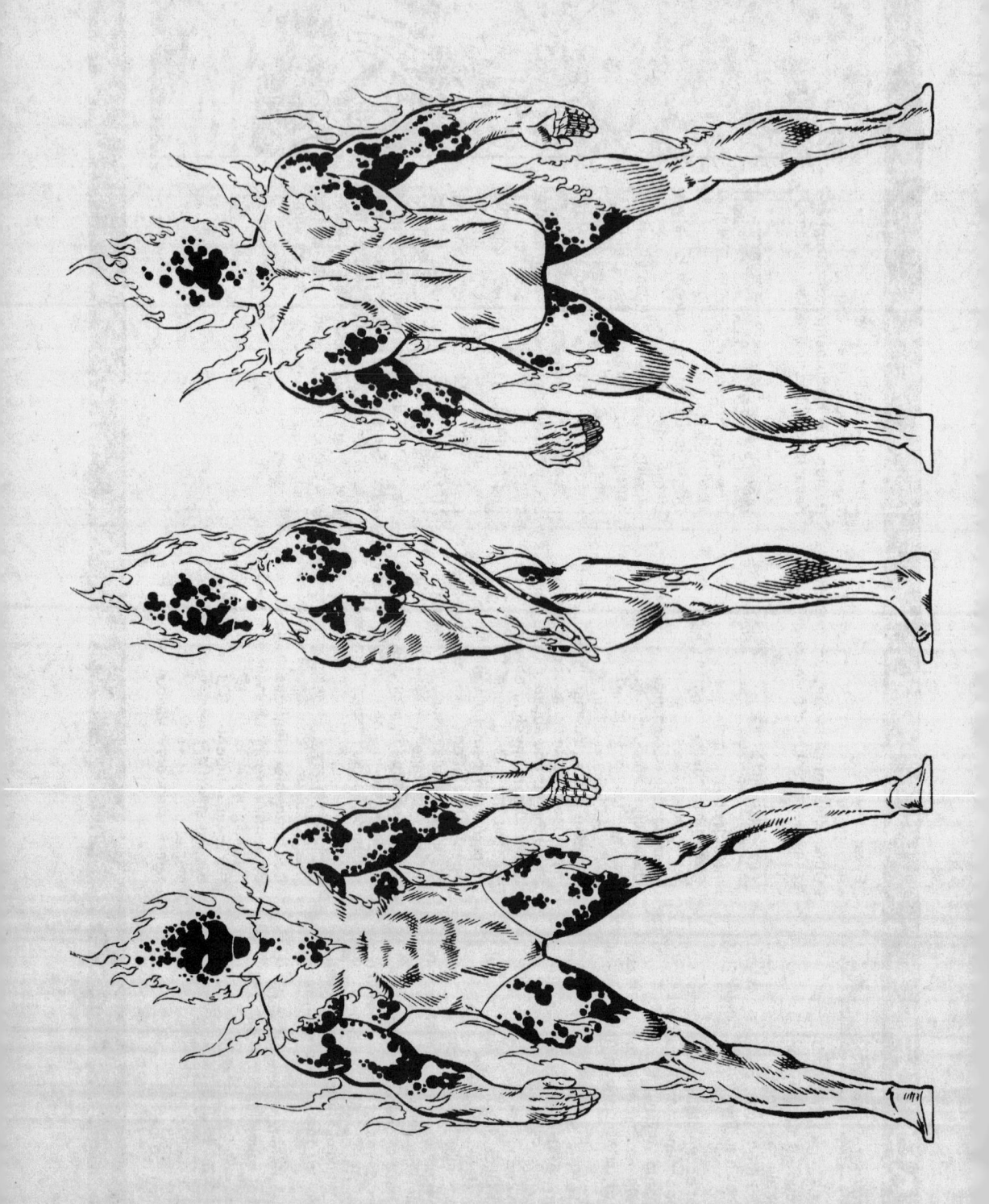

STARBOLT

BIOGRAPHICAL DATA

Real name: Unrevealed
Other current aliases: Bolt
Former aliases: None known
Dual identity: None, the general populace of Earth is unaware of Starbolt's existence
Current occupation: Warrior serving in the Royal Elite of Shi'ar Imperial Guard
Former occupation: None known
Citizenship: Shi'ar Empire
Legal status: No criminal record in the Shi'ar Empire
Place of birth: Unrevealed location in the Shi'ar Galaxy (the identity of the alien race to which Starbolt belongs is unrevealed)
Marital status: Unrevealed
Known relatives: None
Known confidants: None
Known allies: Imperial Guard, Starjammers, the X-Men, (formerly) D'Ken, Deathbird
Note: The Imperial Guard serves whoever is ruler of the Shi'ar Empire; hence, at different times they have served D'Ken, Lilandra, and Deathbird.
Major enemies: The Brood, Skrulls, (formerly) Deathbird, Quasar, Kismet, the Kree
Usual base of operations: Chandilar (Shi'ar Throneworld), Shi'ar Empire
Former bases of operations: None known
Current group membership: Royal Elite, Shi'ar Imperial Guard
Former group membership: None
Extent of education: Unrevealed

PHYSICAL DESCRIPTION

Height: 5' 11"
Weight: Unrevealed
Eyes: Unrevealed
Hair: Unrevealed
Other distinguishing features: Starbolt's head is perpetually engulfed in a plume of unknown energy that resembles flames.

POWERS AND ABILITIES

Intelligence: Normal
Strength: Athlete
Speed: Athlete
Flight speed: Subsonic
Stamina: Athlete
Durability: Athlete
Agility: Athlete
Reflexes: Athlete
Fighting skills: Good hand-to-hand combatant, trained by Shi'ar Imperial Guard
Special skills and abilities: None known
Superhuman physical powers: Starbolt can create an unknown form of energy, producing heat and light, resembling flames from all portions of his body without harm to himself; he can fire bolts of this energy from his hands; Starbolt can survive unprotected in the vacuum of outer space. Starbolt's "flames" do not require the presence of oxygen, and can exist in the vacuum of space.
Superhuman mental powers: Ability to fly through self-levitation
Special limitations: None known
Source of superhuman powers: Unrevealed, powers presumed to be natural attributes of his race

PARAPHERNALIA

Costume specifications: Shi'ar fabrics mimicking the properties of unstable molecules, making them resistant to intense heat
Personal weaponry: None known
Special weaponry: None known
Other accessories: None known
Transportation: Shi'ar starships, flight under own power
Design and manufacture of paraphernalia: Shi'ar scientists and technicians

BIBLIOGRAPHY

First appearance: X-MEN Vol. 1 #107
Origin issue: Starbolt's origin is as yet unrevealed.
Significant issues: X-MEN Vol. 1 #107 (joined in Imperial Guardsmen's battle on behalf of Emperor D'Ken on nameless Shi'ar Empire planet; attacked Wolverine); UNCANNY X-MEN #137 (fought X-Men during Shi'ar trial by combat over life of Phoenix I); UNCANNY X-MEN #157-158 (on mission to find Lilandra, joined other Imperial Guardsmen, Nightcrawler, and Kitty Pryde in battling Shi'ar Lord Samedar's renegade Imperial Guardsmen, was captured, freed on Lilandra's command); UNCANNY X-MEN #275 (on Deathbird's behalf, assisted other Imperial Guardsmen in battle against X-Men and Starjammers); QUASAR #33 (battled Quasar and Her [Kismet] in space during Kree-Shi'ar War, was defeated and captured by Quasar)

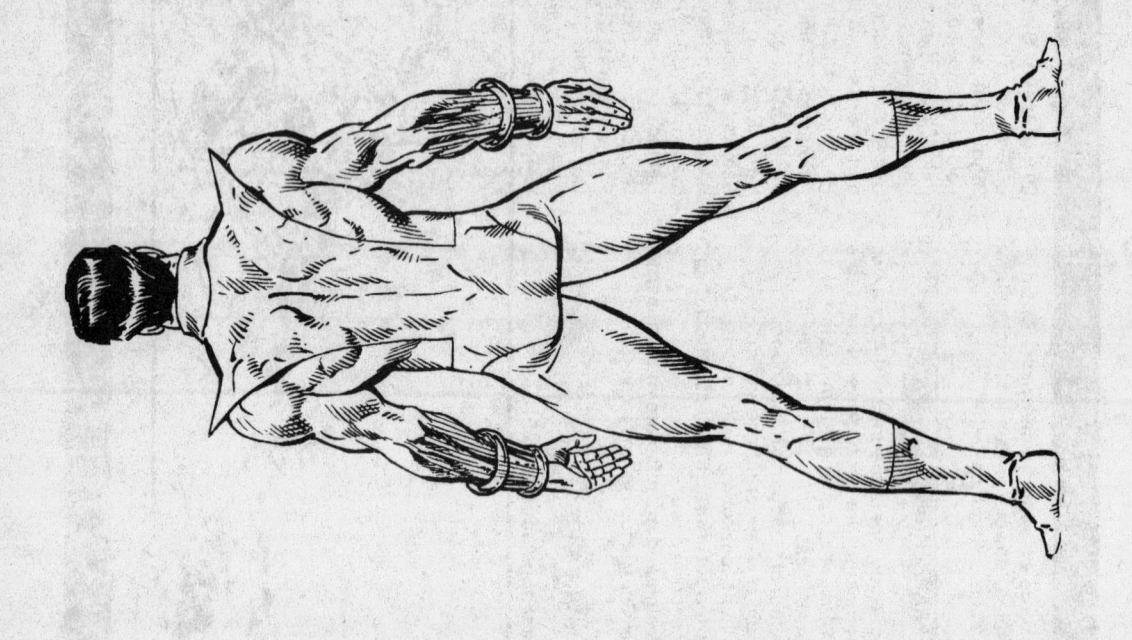

STARFOX

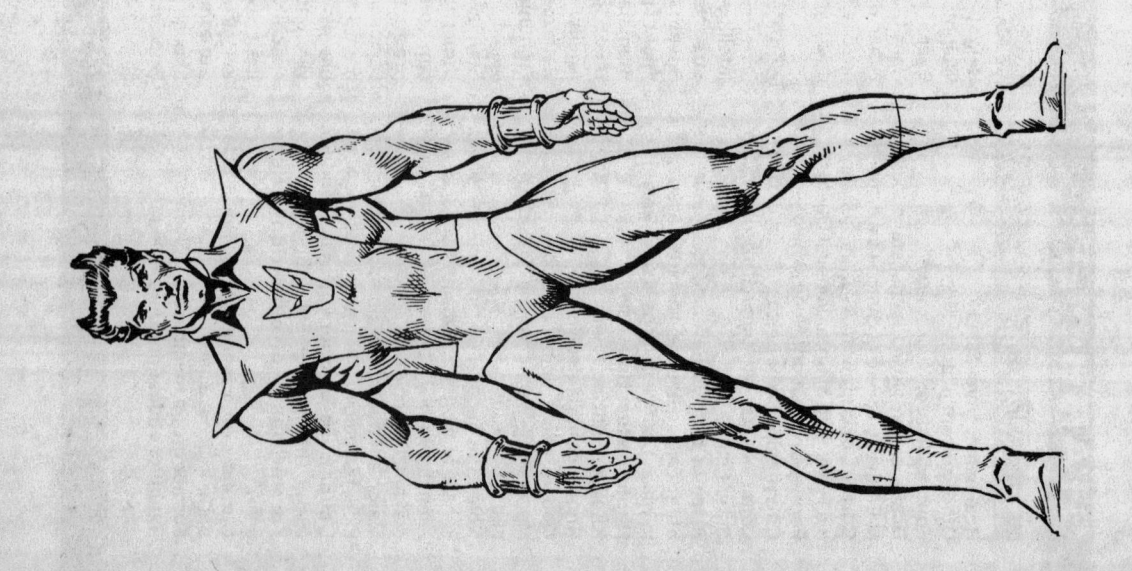

STARFOX

BIOGRAPHICAL DATA

Real name: Eros
Other current aliases: None
Former aliases: Unknown
Dual identity: None; the general populace of Earth is unaware that Starfox is an Eternal from Titan.
Current occupation: Adventurer, womanizer
Former occupation: Same
Citizenship: Citizen of Titan
Legal status: No criminal record on Earth or Titan
Place of birth: Titan, moon of Saturn
Marital status: Single
Known relatives: Alars (alias Mentor; father); Sui-san (mother, deceased); Thanos (brother); Zuras (uncle, deceased), Thena (cousin); Kronos (grandfather, discorporated); Nebula (alleged grandniece)
Known confidants: Captain Mar-Vell (deceased)
Known allies: The Avengers, Firelord, Elysius, Heater Delight
Major enemies: Thanos, Nebula
Usual base of operations: Outer space
Former bases of operations: New York, New York
Current group membership: None
Former group membership: The Avengers
Extent of education: Unrevealed

PHYSICAL DESCRIPTION

Height: 6'1"
Weight: 190 lbs.
Eyes: Blue
Hair: Red
Other distinguishing features: None

POWERS AND ABILITIES

Intelligence: Above normal
Strength: Superhuman Class 10
Speed: Enhanced human
Flight speed: Supersonic
Stamina: Superhuman
Durability: Enhanced human
Agility: Peak human
Reflexes: Peak human
Fighting skills: Limited knowledge of basic hand-to-hand combat
Special skills and abilities: Limited mastery of 500 alien languages
Superhuman physical powers: Strength, stamina, longevity, immunity to terrestrial diseases
Superhuman mental powers: Psionic stimulation of the pleasure centers of the brains of beings within 25 feet of himself; the ability to fly by mentally manipulating cosmic energy
Special limitations: Starfox's mental powers do not work on beings whose brains do not have pleasure centers.
Source of superhuman powers: Starfox is a member of the long-lived offshoot of humanity called the Eternals. His psionic powers are possessed to some degree by all Eternals, but he developed them in his own unique manner.

PARAPHERNALIA

Costume specifications: Alien materials
Personal weaponry: None
Special weaponry: None
Other accessories: None
Transportation: Self-flight, use of faster-than-light Titanian cruiser
Design and manufacture of paraphernalia: Unrevealed Titanian technicians

BIBLIOGRAPHY

First appearance: (cameo) IRON MAN #55, (full) CAPTAIN MARVEL #27
Origin issue: CAPTAIN MARVEL #29
Significant issues: CAPTAIN MARVEL #27 (met Captain Mar-Vell, battled Thanos's minions); CAPTAIN MARVEL #29 (held captive by Thanos, Thanos's killing of mother revealed); CAPTAIN MARVEL #31 (freed from captivity, met Iron Man, Moondragon); WARLOCK #12 (met Pip the Troll, relationship with Heater Delight revealed); CAPTAIN MARVEL #58 (held captive by Isaac); CAPTAIN MARVEL #61 (freed); CAPTAIN MARVEL GRAPHIC NOVEL (present when Mar-Vell died from cancer, promised to look after Elysius for Mar-Vell); AVENGERS #230 (left Titan, Elysius for Earth); AVENGERS #231 (arrived on Earth); AVENGERS #232 (made an Avengers trainee, given codename "Starfox" by Wasp, went on first mission); AVENGERS #238 (helped resuscitate the Vision with the help of Isaac); AVENGERS #243 (made full Avenger); AVENGERS #246-247 (first meeting with Earth Eternals); AVENGERS #248 (revealed pleasure-stimulating powers to assembled Avengers); MARVEL TEAM-UP #143 (traveled to another dimension with Spider-Man); AVENGERS #260 (battled Nebula, learned of her claim to be Thanos's granddaughter); AVENGERS #261 (left Avengers with Firelord to pursue Nebula); AVENGERS WEST COAST #48 (left Nebula); AVENGERS #316 (held captive by Nebula, freed self); AVENGERS #317-318 (assisted Avengers and the Stranger against Nebula)

STARHAWK

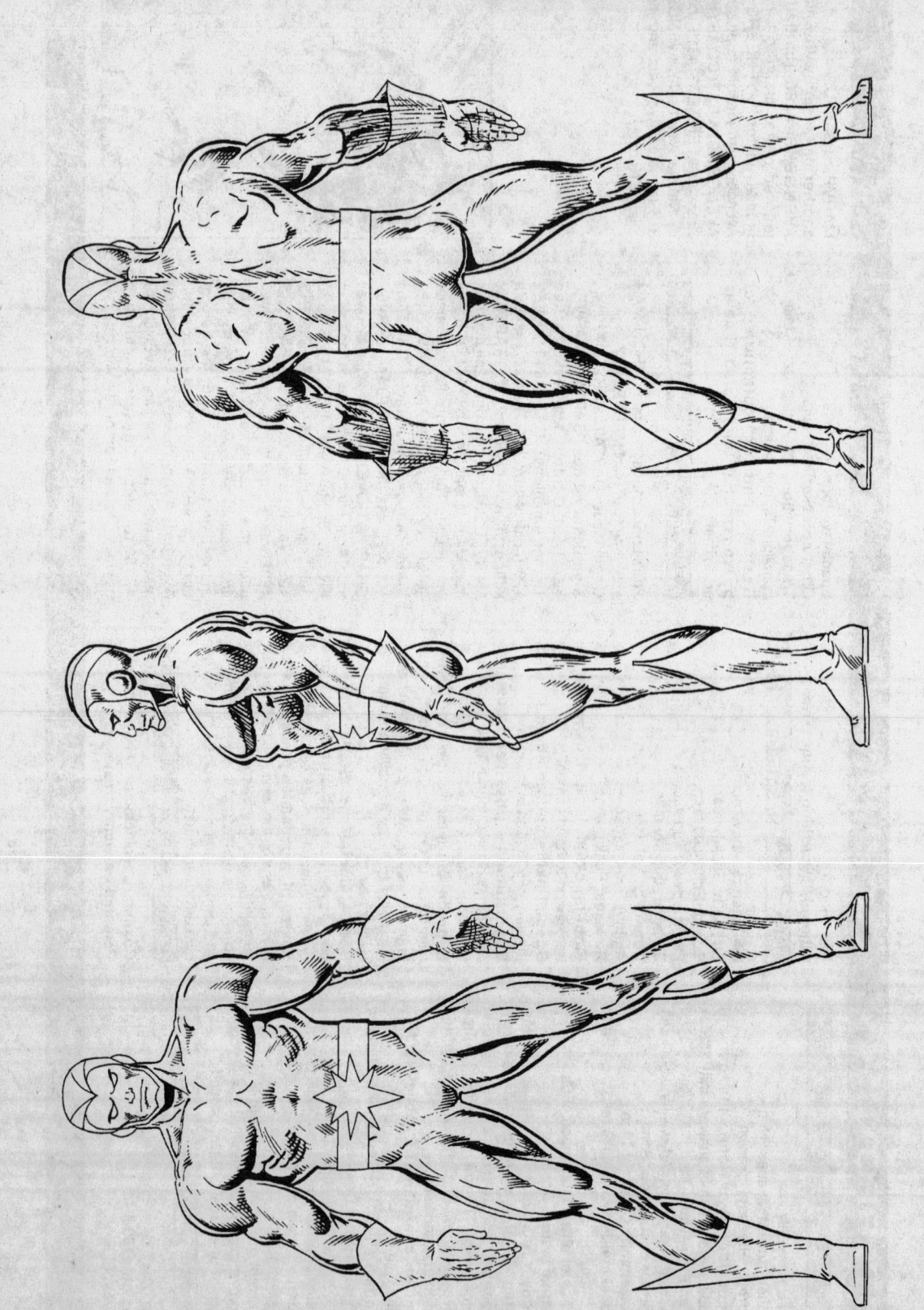

STARHAWK I

BIOGRAPHICAL DATA

Real name: Stakar
Other current aliases: "One Who Knows," "Giver of Light"
Former aliases: None
Dual identity: Known to his fellow Guardians of the Galaxy
Current occupation: Adventurer, protector
Former occupation: Unrevealed
Citizenship: Planet Arcturus IV, 31st Century A.D.
Legal status: No criminal record
Place of birth: Planet Arcturus IV, Arctrus System, Milky Way Galaxy, circa 31st Century A.D. in an alternate future
Marital status: Separated
Known relatives: Ogord (adoptive father), Salaan, (adoptive mother), Aleta (estranged wife, adoptive sister), Tara, Sita (daughters, deceased), John (son, deceased)
Known confidants: None
Known allies: The Guardians of the Galaxy, the Defenders, the Avengers, the Fantastic Four, Spider-Man, Moondragon, Her (Kismet), the High Evolutionary, Dargo, Keeper, Firelord, Krugarr, Mainframe, Giraud, Silver Surfer, Dr. Strange, the Spirit of Vengeance
Major enemies: The Brotherhood of the Badoon Empire, the Reavers of Arcturus, Korvac, the Minions of Menace, the Stark, Force II, Malevolence, Rancor
Usual base of operations: Mobile throughout the Milky Way Galaxy aboard the starship *Captain America II*, former Avengers sub-basements, New York City
Former bases of operations: Mobile throughout the Earth solar system aboard the starship *Captain America I*, space station *Drydock*, and the starship *Freedom's Lady*
Current group membership: Guardians of the Galaxy (Major Victory, Charlie-27, Martinex, Yondu, Nikki, Starhawk, Aleta, Replica, Talon)
Former group membership: Avengers (honorary)
Extent of education: Unrevealed

Special skills and abilities: Knowledge of archaeology of planet Arcturus IV, extensive knowledge of various civilizations throughout the Milky Way Galaxy
Superhuman physical powers: Aside from the above listed attribute, Starhawk possesses an extremely long lifespan; immunity to most known diseases and radiation sickness; manipulation of light to create concussive force blasts, heat, and solid-light constructs; ability to fly by tapping anti-gravitons
Superhuman mental powers: Extrasensory sensitivity to energy patterns and fluctuations
Special limitations: None
Source of superhuman powers: Stakar is a mutant member of the alien race of the planet Arcturus IV who was merged into a composite being with his adoptive sister Aleta by an alien energy device.

PHYSICAL DESCRIPTION

Height: 6' 4"
Weight: 450 lbs.
Eyes: White, no visible pupils or irises
Hair: Red blond
Other distinguishing features: None

POWERS AND ABILITIES

Intelligence: Gifted
Strength: Superhuman Class 10
Speed: Peak human
Flight speed: Sub-light speed
Stamina: Enhanced human
Durability: Enhanced human
Agility: Enhanced human
Reflexes: Superhuman
Fighting skills: Unskilled hand-to-hand combatant

PARAPHERNALIA

Costume specifications: Alien materials, including retracting transparent facemask and life support system and retractable solar wind collector wings
Personal weaponry: None
Special weaponry: None
Other accessories: None
Transportation: Flight under own power, or the starship *Captain America II*
Design and manufacture of paraphernalia: Unrevealed

BIBLIOGRAPHY

First appearance: DEFENDERS #27
Origin issue: MARVEL PRESENTS #9-10
Significant issues: DEFENDERS #27 (first met the Guardians of the Galaxy and the Defenders; aided in the defeat of the Badoon invasion force); MARVEL PRESENTS #3-7 (joined Guardians of the Galaxy on space mission, helped defeat the Topographical Man); MARVEL PRESENTS #9-11 (revealed how Stakar and Aleta had first merged into composite being as Starhawk, helped battle the Reavers of Arcturus); THOR ANNUAL #6 (teamed with time-travelling Thor, battled Korvac and his Minions of Menace); AVENGERS #167-168, 170, 173, 175-177 (traveled to present alongside fellow Guardians, assisted Avengers in battle against Korvac); FANTASTIC FOUR ANNUAL #24/THOR ANNUAL #16/SILVER SURFER ANNUAL #4/GUARDIANS OF THE GALAXY ANNUAL #1 (alongside the Guardians, Fantastic Four, Dargo, and Keeper, battled manifestations of Korvac's power in various eras); GUARDIANS OF THE GALAXY #1-4 (in 3017 A.D., went on quest to find the lost shield of Captain America; battled Taserface and the Stark; defeated the Stark); GUARDIANS OF THE GALAXY #32-33 (sent back in time by Aleta to begin his life cycle again)

STARHAWK™

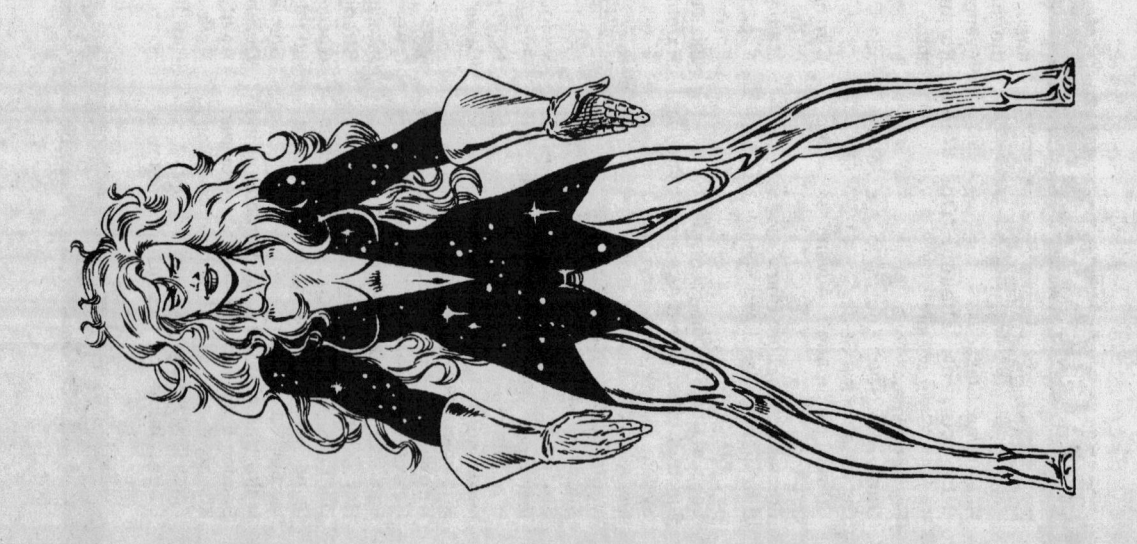

STARHAWK II

BIOGRAPHICAL DATA

Real name: Aleta
Other current aliases: None
Former aliases: Stakar, "One Who Knows," "Giver of Light"
Dual identity: Known to her fellow Guardians of the Galaxy
Current occupation: Adventurer, protector
Former occupation: Unrevealed
Legal status: No criminal record
Citizenship: Planet Arcturus IV, 31st Century A.D.
Place of birth: Planet Arcturus IV, Arcturus System, Milky Way Galaxy, circa 31st Century A.D. in an alternate future
Marital status: Separated
Known relatives: Ogord (adoptive father), Salaan, (adoptive mother), Stakar (estranged husband, adoptive brother), Tara, Sita (daughters, deceased), John (son, deceased)
Known confidants: None
Known allies: The Guardians of the Galaxy, the Defenders, the Avengers, the Fantastic Four, Spider-Man, Moondragon, Her (Kismet), the High Evolutionary, Dargo, Keeper, Firelord, Krugarr, Mainframe, Giraud, Silver Surfer, Dr. Strange, the Spirit of Vengeance
Major enemies: The Brotherhood of the Badoon Empire, the Reavers of Arcturus, Korvac, the Minions of Menace, the Stark, Force II, Malevolence, Rancor
Usual base of operations: Mobile throughout the Milky Way Galaxy aboard the starship *Captain America II* in the 31st century
Former bases of operations: Mobile throughout the Earth solar system aboard the starships *Captain America I* and *Freedom's Lady* (in the 31st century), space station *Drydock* (in the 20th century)
Current group membership: Guardians of the Galaxy (Major Victory, Charlie-27, Martinex, Yondu, Nikki, Starhawk, Aleta, Replica, Talon)
Former group membership: Avengers (honorary)
Extent of education: Unrevealed

PHYSICAL DESCRIPTION

Height: 5' 11"
Weight: 120 lbs.
Eyes: White, no visible pupils or irises
Hair: Blond
Other distinguishing features: None

POWERS AND ABILITIES

Intelligence: Gifted
Strength: Superhuman Class 10
Speed: Peak human
Flight speed: Warp speed
Stamina: Enhanced human
Durability: Enhanced human
Agility: Enhanced human
Reflexes: Superhuman
Fighting skills: Unskilled hand-to-hand combatant

Special skills and abilities: Knowledge of archaeology of planet Arcturus IV, extensive knowledge of various civilizations throughout the Milky Way Galaxy
Superhuman physical powers: Aside from the above listed attribute, Starhawk possesses an extremely long lifespan; immunity to most known diseases and radiation sickness; manipulation of light to create concussive force blasts, heat, and solid-light constructs; ability to fly by tapping anti-gravitons
Superhuman mental powers: Extrasensory sensitivity to energy patterns and fluctuations
Special limitations: None
Source of superhuman powers: Aleta is a mutant member of the alien race of the planet Arcturus IV who was merged into a composite being with his adoptive sister Stakar by an alien energy device. Though no longer merged with Stakar, she retains the powers granted to her through their merging.

PARAPHERNALIA

Costume specifications: Alien materials.
Personal weaponry: None
Special weaponry: None
Other accessories: None
Transportation: Flight under own power, or the starship *Captain America II*
Design and manufacture of paraphernalia: Unrevealed

BIBLIOGRAPHY

First appearance: DEFENDERS #27
Origin issue: MARVEL PRESENTS #9-10
Significant issues: DEFENDERS #27 (first met the Guardians of the Galaxy and the Defenders; aided in the defeat of the Badoon invasion force); MARVEL PRESENTS #3-7 (joined Guardians of the Galaxy on space mission, helped defeat the Topographical Man); MARVEL PRESENTS #9-11 (revealed how Stakar and Aleta had first merged into composite being as Starhawk, helped battle the Reavers of Arcturus); THOR ANNUAL #6 (teamed with time-travelling Thor, battled Korvac and his Minions of Menace); AVENGERS #167-168, 170, 173, 175-177 (traveled to present alongside fellow Guardians, assisted Avengers in battle against Korvac); FANTASTIC FOUR ANNUAL #24/THOR ANNUAL #16/SILVER SURFER ANNUAL #4/GUARDIANS OF THE GALAXY ANNUAL #1 (alongside the Guardians, Fantastic Four, Dargo, and Keeper, battled manifestations of Korvac's power in various eras); GUARDIANS OF THE GALAXY #1-4 (in 3017 A.D., went on quest to find the lost shield of Captain America; battled Taserface and the Stark; defeated the Stark); GUARDIANS OF THE GALAXY #32-33 (defeated and expelled Stakar's consciousness from her being, sent Stakar back in time to begin his life cycle again)

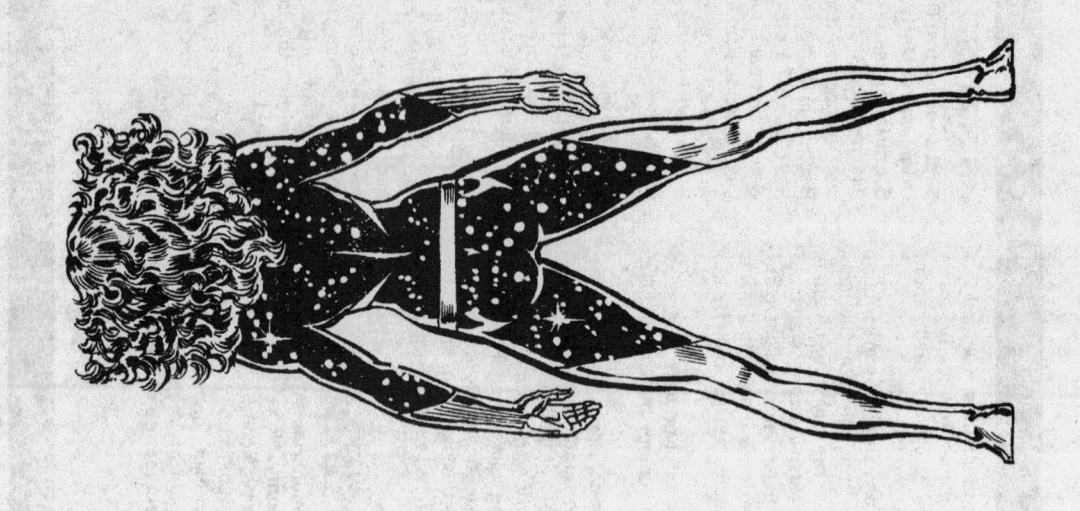

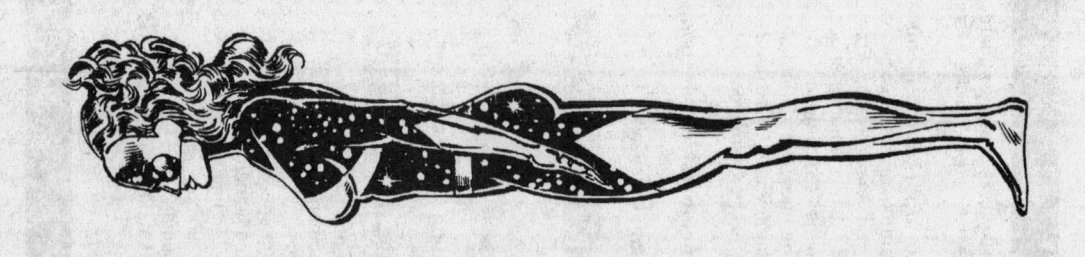

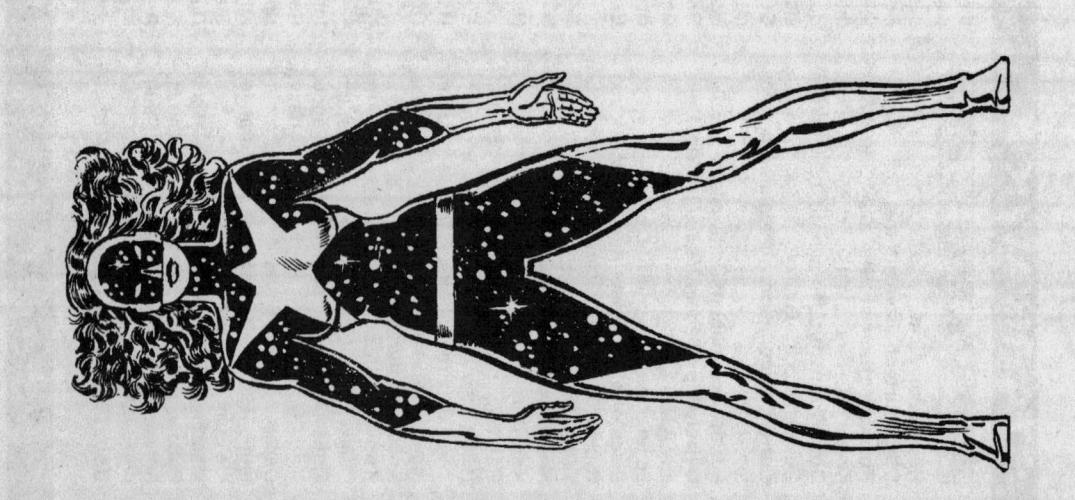

STARLIGHT™

STARLIGHT

BIOGRAPHICAL DATA

Real name: Tania Belinsky
Other current aliases: Zvezda Syvet ("Starlight" in Russian)
Former aliases: Red Guardian II
Dual identity: Secret
Current occupation: Cosmic companion, wanderer
Former occupation: Dissident champion, adventurer
Citizenship: Soviet Union
Legal status: No criminal record, wanted by the Soviet authorities
Place of birth: Leningrad, Union of Soviet Socialist Republic
Marital status: Single
Known relatives: Dr. Andrei Belinsky (father)
Known confidants: None
Known allies: Sergei Krylov, the Presence, (former) the Defenders-
Major enemies: Soviet Super-Soldiers, the Stranger, Quasar
Usual base of operations: Mobile
Former bases of operations: Moscow, U.S.S.R., New York City
Current group membership: None
Former group membership: Defenders (unoffical)
Extent of education: PhD. in medicine

PHYSICAL DESCRIPTION

Height: 5' 9"
Weight: 125 lbs.
Eyes: Blue
Hair: Black
Other distinguishing features: None

POWERS AND ABILITIES

Intelligence: Gifted
Strength: Superhuman Class 10
Speed: Peak human
Flight speed: Supersonic
Stamina: Superhuman
Durability: Superhuman
Agility: Athlete
Reflexes: Peak human
Fighting skills: Extensive experience in hand-to-hand combat
Special skills: Skilled at neurosurgery and medicine
Superhuman physical powers: Superhuman strength, the generation of nuclear energy for flight and projecting of radiation blasts
Superhuman mental powers: None
Special limitations: Starlight gives off low levels of nuclear radiation at all times, putting normal human beings to associate with her for any length of time at risk
Source of superhuman powers: Mutation from cobalt radiation

PARAPHERNALIA

Costume specifications: Alien materials/ synthetic stretch fabric
Personal weaponry: None
Special weaponry: None
Other accessories: None
Transportation: Flight, under own power
Design and manufacture of paraphernalia: Inapplicable

BIBLIOGRAPHY

First appearance: (as Red Guardian II) DEFENDERS #35, (as Starlight) QUASAR #19
Origin issue: Starlight's full origin is as yet unrevealed.
Significant issues: DEFENDERS #35 (as Dr. Belinsky, traveled to the U.S. at behest of Doctor Strange to perform brain transplant); DEFENDERS #36 (battled Plant Man simulacrum alongside Doctor Strange); DEFENDERS #37-38 (teleported to other dimension alongside Power Man and Doctor Strange, battled Eel and Porcupine); DEFENDERS #40 (battled unnamed masked Soviet); DEFENDERS #44-45 (teamed with Valkyrie and Hellcat to battle Dr. Strange as the Red Rajah and Nighthawk, Hulk, and Power Man); DEFENDERS #52 (brought to lab complex of Sergei, met the Presence); DEFENDERS #53 (mentally dominated by Sergei, forced to undergo nuclear transformation); DEFENDERS #55 (battled the Defenders alongside the presence, seperated from him); DEFENDERS #65 (assigned to investigate Presence's reappearance, battled giant amoeba, reunited with Presence); INCREDIBLE HULK #258-259 (alongside the Presence, encountered Hulk, Darkstar, Crimson Dynamo, Vanguard, Ursa Major, and Professor Phobos, left Earth with the Presence); QUASAR #16 (revealed to be laboratory subjects of the Stranger); QUASAR #19-20 (as Starlight, returned to Earth with Presence and Jack of Hearts, battled Quasar and Fantastic Four, aided Presence in his attempt to kill Eon); MARVEL COMICS PRESENTS #70 (battled Darkstar and Black Widow)

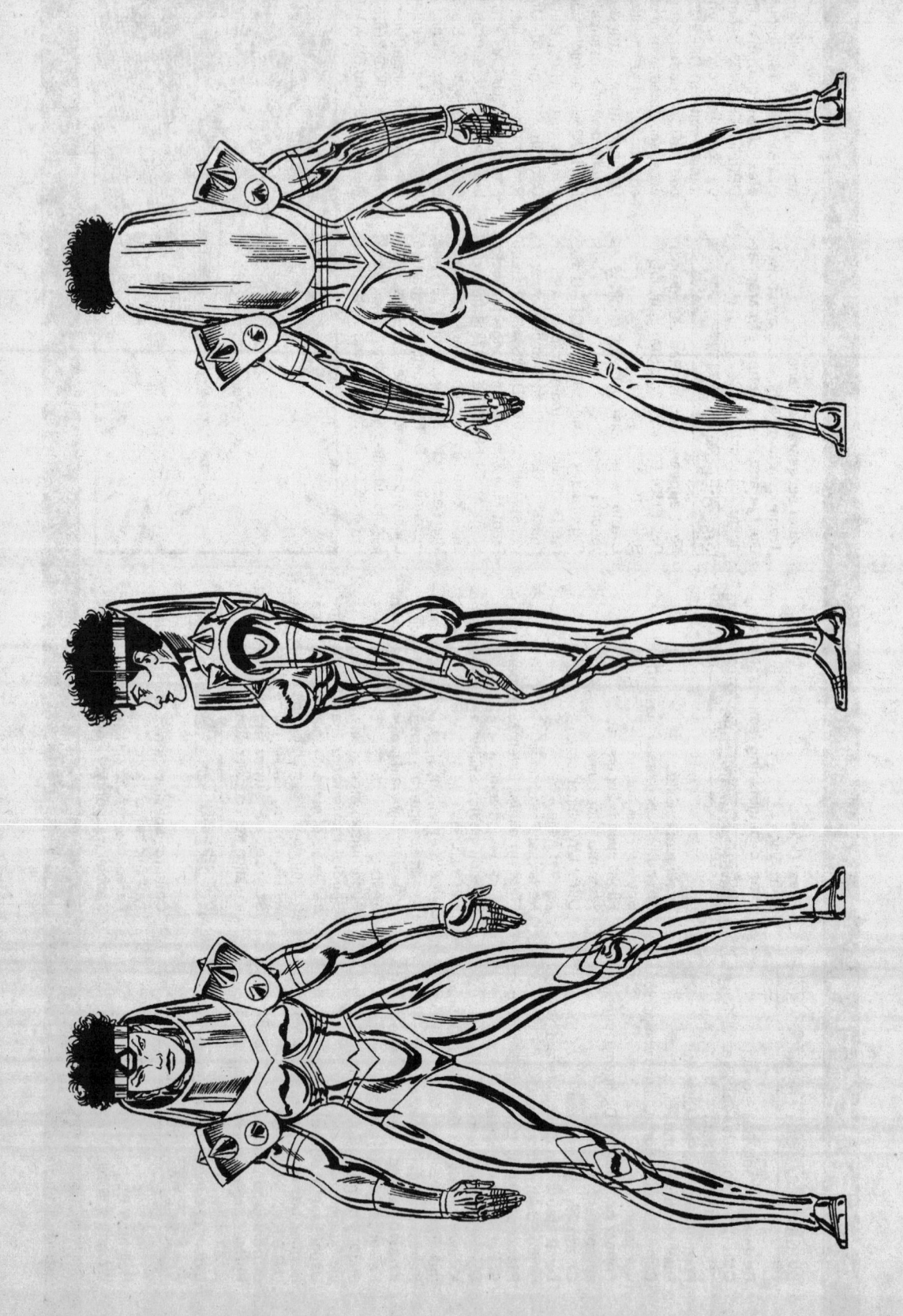

STELLARIS™

STELLARIS

BIOGRAPHICAL DATA

Real name: Unrevealed
Other current aliases: The Celestial Slayer
Former aliases: None known
Dual identity: None; the general populace of Earth is unaware that Stellaris is an extraterrestrial
Current occupation: Seeker of vengeance
Former occupation: Unrevealed
Citizenship: Unrevealed
Legal status: Wanted as an outlaw on Earth
Place of birth: An unidentified planet
Marital status: Unrevealed
Known relatives: None
Known confidants: None
Known allies: Nobilus
Major enemies: Celestials, Thor I, Thor II (Eric Masterson), Thor III (Dargo Ktor), Hercules, Captain America, Quasar, Avengers, High Evolutionary
Usual base of operations: Mobile throughout known space, currently on Earth
Former bases of operations: An unidentified planet
Current group membership: None
Former group membership: None known
Extent of education: Unrevealed

PHYSICAL DESCRIPTION

Height: 5'6"
Weight: 130 lbs.
Eyes: Blue
Hair: Brown
Other distinguishing features: None

POWERS AND ABILITIES

Intelligence: Normal
Strength: Athlete
Speed: Athlete
Flight speed: Warp speed (in battlesuit)
Stamina: Athlete
Durability: Athlete
Agility: Athlete
Reflexes: Athlete
Fighting skills: Skilled in her native world's equivalent of streetfighting techniques
Special skills and abilities: Unrevealed
Superhuman physical powers: None
Superhuman mental powers: None
Special limitations: None
Source of superhuman powers: Inapplicable

PARAPHERNALIA

Costume specifications: A suit of "living armor" of unknown composition that resembles the armor worn by Celestials. She can mentally will the armor to reshape itself to her specifications, and even cause it to increase or decrease in size and mass. Hence, she can cause the armor to become much larger and more massive than herself, cause it instead to resemble a form-fitting jumpsuit, or even cause it to take on the appearance of normal terrestrial clothing. Stellaris can also will the armor to form a vast array of weaponry and vehicles. Examples so far observed include armament that fires blasts of concussive energy and intense heat and a "sonic shatter-pistol." She can cause part of her battlesuit to become an advanced skycycle or even to become a vehicle resembling a normal Earth motorcycle that can nevertheless fly through the air. Stellaris's battlesuit is said to contain power on the level of the Silver Surfer's. The battlesuit contains an array of sensor devices. It also contains a self-destruct system that will cause the battlesuit to implode, releasing enough concussive force to destroy a planet.
Personal weaponry: See Costume specifications
Special weaponry: See Costume specifications
Other accessories: None known
Transportation: Atmospheric flight and interstellar travel via battlesuit
Design and manufacture of paraphernalia: Unrevealed

BIBLIOGRAPHY

First appearance: (helmet concealing face) THOR #419, (face revealed) THOR #421
Origin issue: Stellaris's origin is as yet unrevealed.
Significant issues: THOR #419 (tracked Replicoid to Earth and killed him); THOR #420 (first battled Thor I, Captain America, and Quasar); THOR #421 (fought Hercules, defeated by Thor I, allowed to escape when she threatened to destroy Earth); THOR #422 (secretly entered High Evolutionary's starship *New Wundagore*, freed Nobilus);THOR #423 (escaped with Nobilus, sought to kill Red Celestial in Black Galaxy); THOR #424 (set off enormous explosion to destroy Celestial that instead served to complete the birthing of a new Celestial); THOR #438-439 (recovered, returned to Earth to kill Thor I, fought Thor II and Thor III, decided to "relax" on Earth for a while)

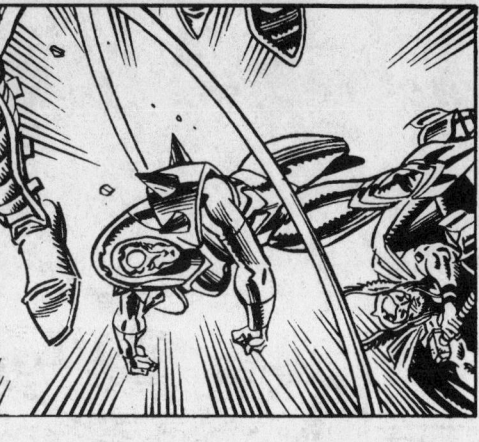

STILT-MAN ™

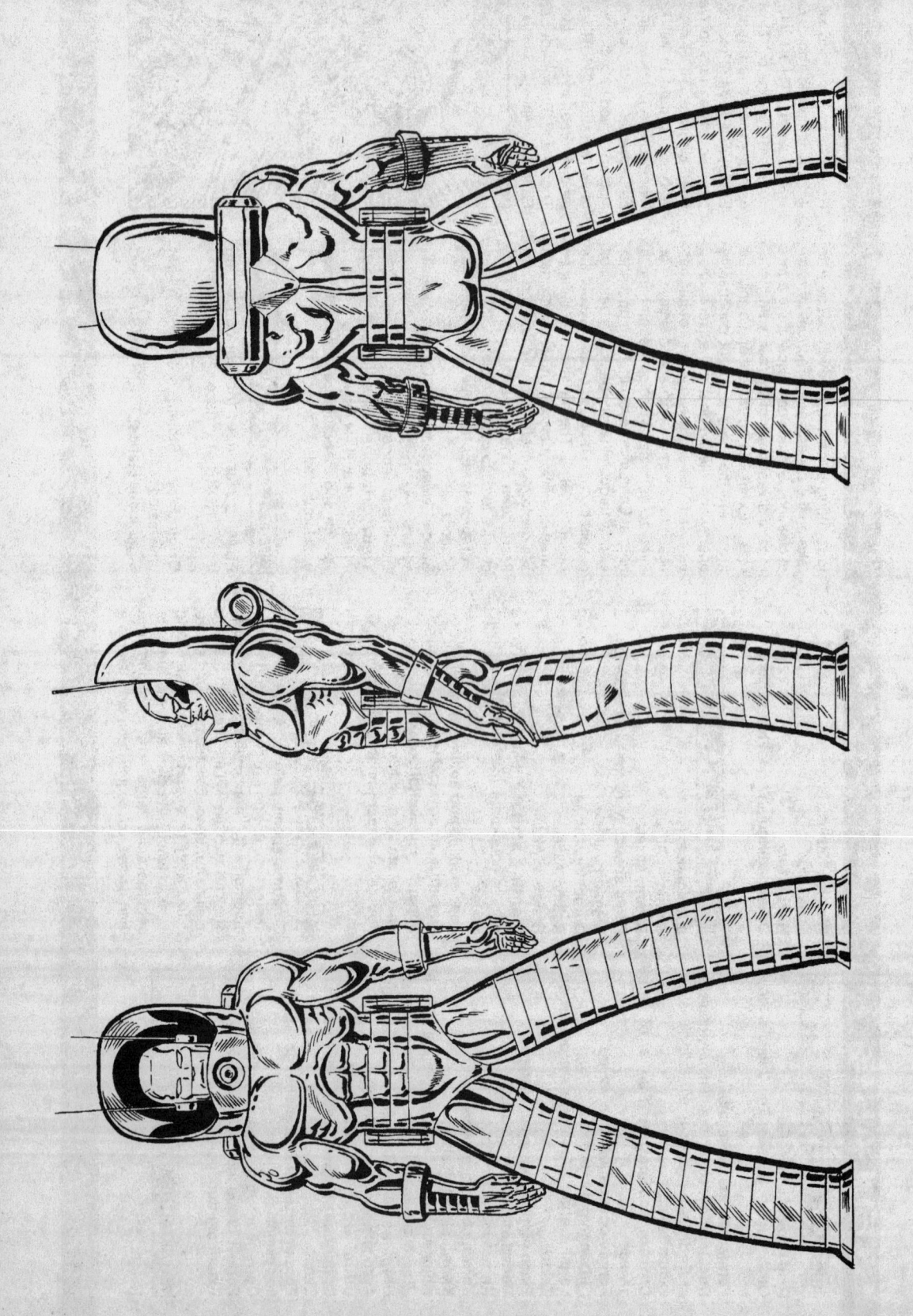

STILT-MAN

BIOGRAPHICAL DATA

Real name: Wilbur Day
Other current aliases: None
Former aliases: None
Dual identity: Publicly known
Current occupation: Professional criminal
Former occupation: Scientist, inventor, and engineer
Citizenship: United States of America
Legal status: Criminal record
Place of birth: New York, New York
Marital status: Single
Known relatives: None
Known confidants: None
Known allies: Masked Marauder, Emissaries of Evil I (Electro, Matador, Gladiator, Leap-Frog), Blastaar
Major enemies: Daredevil, Captain America, Falcon, Thor, Spider-Man
Usual base of operations: Mobile
Former base of operations: New York City area
Current group membership: None
Former group membership: Emissaries of Evil I
Extent of education: Degrees in physics and mechanical engineering

PHYSICAL DESCRIPTION

Height: 5'11" (with battlesuit) 292'
Weight: 150 lbs., (with battlesuit) 400 lbs.
Eyes: Blue
Hair: Gray
Other distinguishing features: None

POWERS AND ABILITIES

Intelligence: Normal
Strength: Normal; (in battlesuit) Enhanced human
Speed: Normal
Stamina: Normal
Durability: Normal
Agility: Normal
Reflexes: Normal
Fighting skills: None
Special skills and abilities: Moderately talented disguise artist
Superhuman physical powers: None
Superhuman mental powers: None
Special limitations: None
Source of superhuman powers: Inapplicable

PARAPHERNALIA

Costume specifications: Body armor
Personal weaponry: Hydraulic "stilts"
Special weaponry: Gas grenades, charged-particle beam blaster, vacuum device
Other accessories: Various devices stolen from the Trapster
Transportation: Hydraulic "stilts"
Design and manufacture of paraphernalia: Carl Kaxton (hydraulic ram device), Wilbur Day (hydraulic stilts, battlesuit, weaponry), Peter Petruski (additional weaponry)

BIBLIOGRAPHY

First appearance: DAREDEVIL #8
Origin issue: DAREDEVIL #8
Significant issues: DAREDEVIL #8 (stole design for hydraulic device from employer Carl Kaxton and used it to create hydraulic stilts and armored battlesuit for use in robberies, battled Daredevil, seemingly shrunk into nothingness when accidentally hit by experimental molecular condenser ray); DAREDEVIL #26 (return from limbo-like "microverse" recounted, attempted to help Leap-Frog escape from custody, defeated by Daredevil); DAREDEVIL #27 (teamed with Masked Marauder in attempt to trap Daredevil, battled Spider-Man, defeated by Daredevil); DAREDEVIL ANNUAL #1 (escape from Daredevil aided by Electro recounted; teamed with Electro, Matador, Leap-Frog, and Gladiator as, Emmisaries of Evil I; battled Daredevil); DAREDEVIL #48 (hired by mobsters to kill district attorney candidate Foggy Nelson, battled Daredevil); DAREDEVIL #67 (disguised as Stunt-Master, attacked Daredevil on Hollywood movie set); DAREDEVIL #102 (in San Francisco, kidnaped Carl Kaxton and daughter to force him to recreate molecular condenser; battled by Daredevil and Black Widow); CAPTAIN AMERICA #191 (hired by Los Angeles mobsters to kill the Falcon; stole various weapons and devices from the Trapster); BLACK GOLIATH #4 (robbed Los Angeles bank, battled Black Goliath, teleported Black Goliath and companions to alien planet using Z-ray weapon); CHAMPIONS #11-12 (attacked Black Goliath at Champions headquarters in search of alien power-source, battled Champions, Z-ray weapon destroyed by Darkstar, escaped Champions); THOR #269 (freed from prison by Blastaar and F.A.U.S.T., given new battlesuit constructed of secondary Adamantium with additional weaponry, stole radioactive isotopes, battled Thor, battlesuit confiscated); DAREDEVIL #186 (hired to kidnap assistant District Attorney Maxine Lavender; waylaid in civilian identity by Turk, a small-time hood, who stole his battlesuit; Turk, wearing battlesuit, defeated by Daredevil); AMAZING SPIDER-MAN #237 (sought to regain reputation by defeating Spider-Man; turned automated Cordco factory against Spider-Man; when Spider-Man saved his life, returned favor by not taking opportunity to kill him); IRON MAN #225 (armor disabled by Iron Man during "Armor Wars"); SENSATIONAL SHE-HULK #4 (attempted to kill District Attorney Blake Tower for sending him to prison, captured by She-Hulk); FANTASTIC FOUR #336 (among villains assembled by Doctor Doom to battle Fantastic Four in Washington D.C. during "Acts of Vengeance"); AVENGERS ANNUAL #19 (among villains who attempted to attack the Avengers at site of their reconstructed mansion, foiled by construction workers)

STINGRAY ™

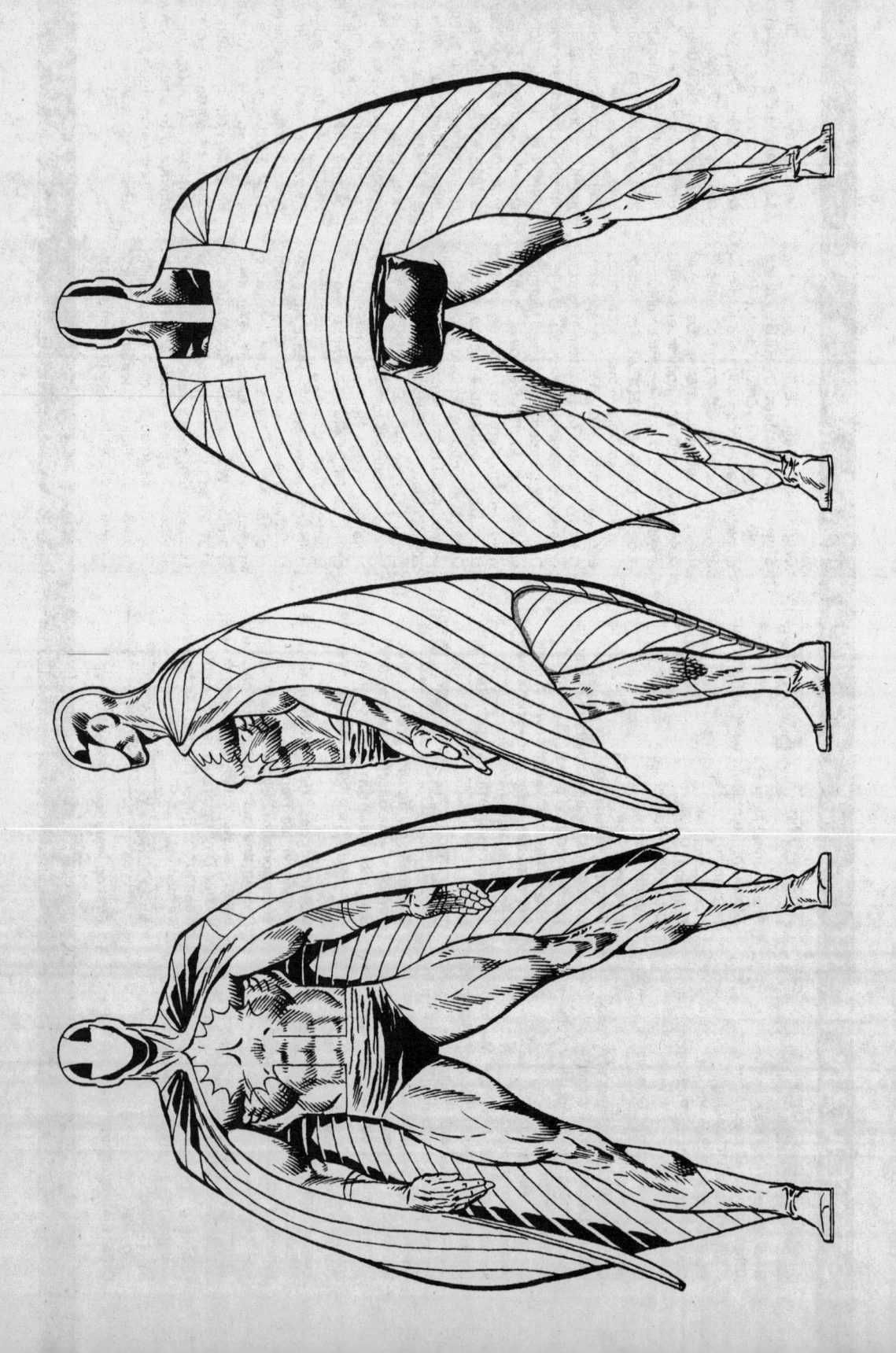

STINGRAY

BIOGRAPHICAL DATA

Real name: Walter Newell
Other current aliases: None
Former aliases: None
Dual identity: Publicly known
Current occupation: Oceanographer, adventurer
Former occupation: Inventor
Citizenship: United States of America
Legal status: No criminal record
Place of birth: Gloucester, Massachusetts
Marital status: Married
Known relatives: Diane Arliss Newell (wife), Todd Arliss (Tiger Shark, brother-in-law)
Known confidants: Diane Newell
Known allies: Namor the Sub-Mariner, Triton, the Thing, the Avengers
Major enemies: Tiger Shark, the Plunderer, Attuma, Llyra, Serpent Squad II, Heavy Metal
Usual base of operations: New York City
Former base of operations: Hydrobase, Atlantic Ocean (later became Avengers Island)
Current group membership: Avengers East Coast (honorary member, reservist); Avengers support crew)
Former group membership: None
Extent of education: Ph.D. in oceanography

PHYSICAL DESCRIPTION

Height: 6' 3"
Weight: 200 lbs.
Eyes: Hazel
Hair: Brown
Other distinguishing features: None

POWERS AND ABILITIES

Intelligence: Gifted
Strength: Normal, (in armor) Superhuman Class 25
Speed: Normal, (in armor) Peak human
Flight speed: Directed motion hovering
Water speed: Normal, (in armor) Superhuman
Stamina: Normal, (in armor) Peak human
Durability: Normal, (in armor) Enhanced human
Agility: Normal, (in armor) Athlete
Reflexes: Normal, (in armor) Athlete
Fighting skills: Fair hand-to-hand combatant
Special skills and abilities: Experienced oceanographer, skilled inventor of experimental oceanographic equipment
Superhuman physical powers: None
Superhuman mental powers: None
Special limitations: None
Source of superhuman powers: Inapplicable

PARAPHERNALIA

Costume specifications: Armored exoskeleton suit of superhard artificial cartilage designed mainly for underwater use (equipped with oxygen-diffusing system providing breathable air almost indefinitely)
Personal weaponry: Electrical discharge device built into exoskeleton (able to project bolts of up to 20,000 volts through air or water)
Special weaponry: None
Other accessories: None
Transportation: Flight for short distances or swimming via exoskeleton
Design and manufacture of paraphernalia: Walter Newell

BIBLIOGRAPHY

First appearance: (as Newell) TALES TO ASTONISH #95, (as Stingray) SUB-MARINER #19
Origin issue: SUB-MARINER #19
Significant issues: TALES TO ASTONISH #95 (as Newell, first encountered Namor the Sub-Mariner and Lady Dorma, supervised construction of undersea city later destroyed by the Plunderer); SUB-MARINER #16 (as Newell, aided Namor and Dorma against Tiger Shark); SUB-MARINER #19 (created Stingray suit, battled Namor at behest of federal agents); SUB-MARINER #31 (alongside Namor and Triton, battled Attuma); SUB-MARINER #39, 41-45 (as Newell, with Diane Arliss, aided Namor's search for his father, Leonard McKenzie); SUB-MARINER #46-47 (helped Namor battled Llyra and Tiger Shark, witnessed death of Leonard McKenzie; attended his funeral); INCREDIBLE HULK Vol. 2 #221 (battled Hulk); DEFENDERS #62-64 (attended Defenders membership rally, battled assembled criminals); MARVEL TWO-IN-ONE #64-66 (alongside Thing, Triton, and Scarlet Witch, battled Serpent Squad II and Roxxon Oil); MARVEL TWO-IN-ONE #71 (alongside Thing, Gorgon, and Karnak, battled Maelstrom's Minions); MARVEL TWO-IN-ONE #74 (marriage to Diane Arliss revealed, attended the Fantastic Four's Christmas party); AVENGERS #262 (as Newell, offered the Avengers use of Hydrobase as a base for their quinjets); AVENGERS #289 (helped defend Avengers Island against Heavy Metal, battled Machine Man and the Super-Adaptoid); IRON MAN #226 (during "Armor Wars," was mistakenly attacked by Iron Man I); QUASAR #5 (helped Quasar salvage equipment from sunken Avengers Island); AVENGERS SPOTLIGHT #27 (defeated by the Mad Thinker's "Awesome" Android); MARVEL COMICS PRESENTS #53-56 (battled Tiger Shark); AVENGERS #319-324 (aided Avengers, Alpha Flight, and the People's Protectorate against the Atlantean army, the Peace Corpse, and the Combine); NAMOR ANNUAL #1 (alongside Namor, battled Doradian forces during the "Subterranean Wars")

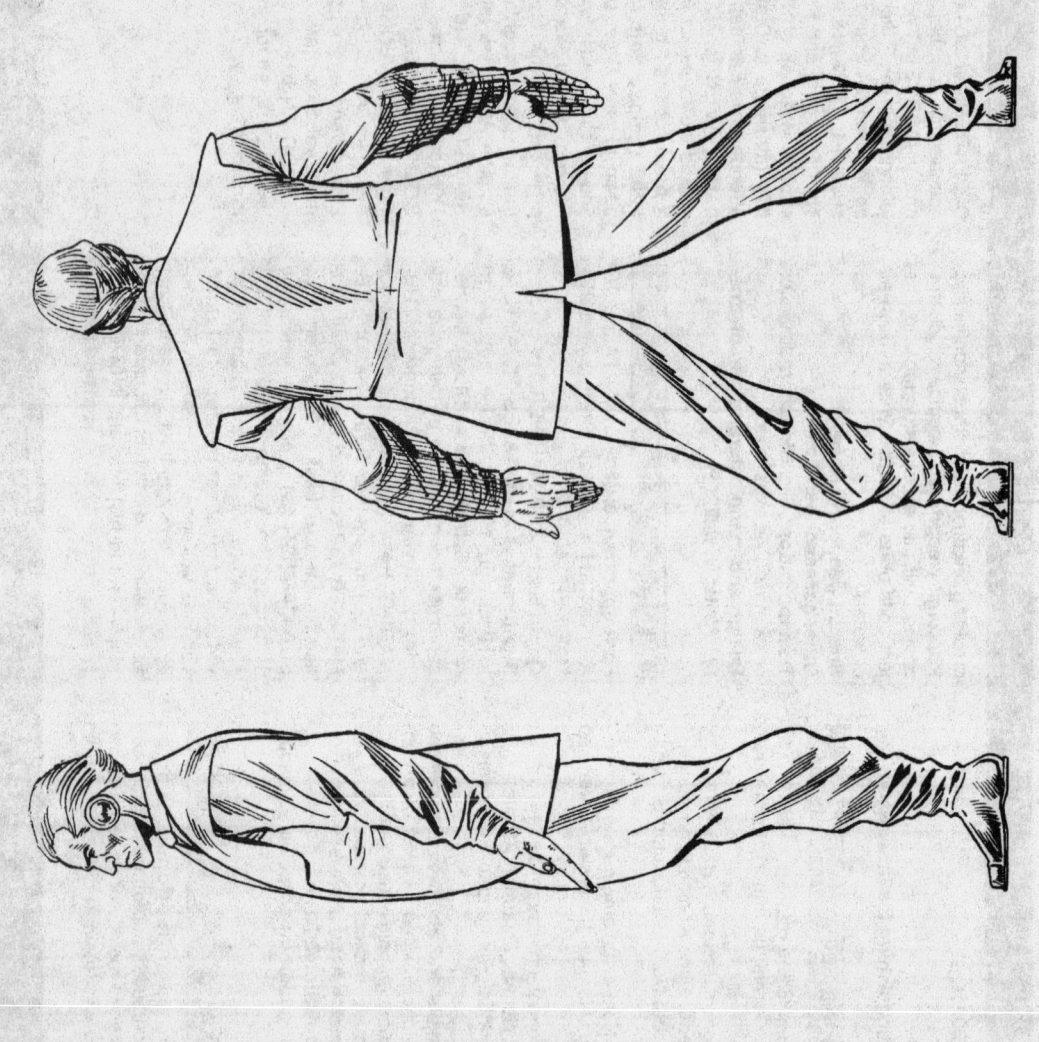

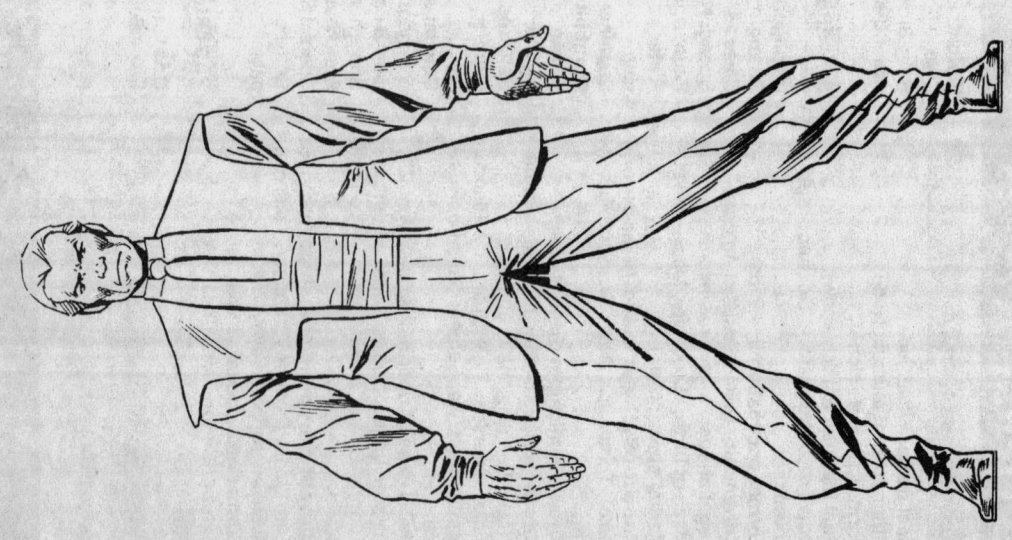

TYLER STONE™

STONE, TYLER

BIOGRAPHICAL DATA

Real name: Tyler Stone
Other current aliases: None
Former aliases: None
Dual identity: None
Current occupation: Head of New York branch of Alchemax
Former occupation: Unrevealed
Citizenship: United States of America, circa 2099
Legal status: No criminal record
Place of birth: Unrevealed
Marital status: Unrevealed
Known relatives: Kron Stone (son), unnamed father (deceased)
Known confidants: None
Known allies: Venture, the Public Eye, the Watchdogs
Major enemies: Spider-Man 2099, Roxxon, Stark-Fujikawa, Synthia, Rico Estevez, Thanatos
Usual base of operations: Alchemax headquarters, New York City, circa 2099
Former bases of operations: Unrevealed
Current group membership: Alchemax Corporation
Former group membership: Unrevealed
Extent of education: Advanced degree in Business administration

PHYSICAL DESCRIPTION

Height: 6'
Weight: 185 lbs.
Eyes: Blue
Hair: Blond
Other distinguishing features: None

POWERS AND ABILITIES

Intelligence: Gifted
Strength: Normal
Speed: Normal
Stamina: Normal
Durability: Normal
Agility: Normal
Reflexes: Normal
Fighting skills: Unrevealed
Special skills and abilities: Accomplished business administrator, skilled planner
Superhuman physical powers: None
Superhuman mental powers: None
Special limitations: None
Source of superhuman powers: Inapplicable

PARAPHERNALIA

Costume specifications: Conventional fabric circa 2099
Personal weaponry: None
Special weaponry: None
Other accessories: Various, as needed
Transportation: Conventional 21st century vehicles and aircraft
Design and manufacture of paraphernalia: Commercial manufacturers

BIBLIOGRAPHY

First appearance: SPIDER-MAN 2099 #1
Origin issue: Tyler Stone's origin is as yet unrevealed.
Significant issues: SPIDER-MAN 2099 #1 (addicted Miguel O'Hara to Rapture drug to force his compliance); SPIDER-MAN 2099 #2-3 (hired Venture, to capture Spider-Man 2099); SPIDER-MAN 2099 #4-5 (set the Specialist against Spider-Man 2099); SPIDER-MAN 2099 #6 (fired Public Eye Sgt. Rico Estevez, reported failure of his plans to Alchemax CEO); SPIDER-MAN 2099 #7 (conferred with Mr. Hikaru of Stark-Fujikawa); SPIDER-MAN 2099 #8 (conferred with Dana D'Angelo); SPIDER-MAN 2099 #9 (plotted against Spider-Man 2099 and Stark-Fujikawa); SPIDER-MAN 2099 #11 (first encountered Thanatos)

STORM™

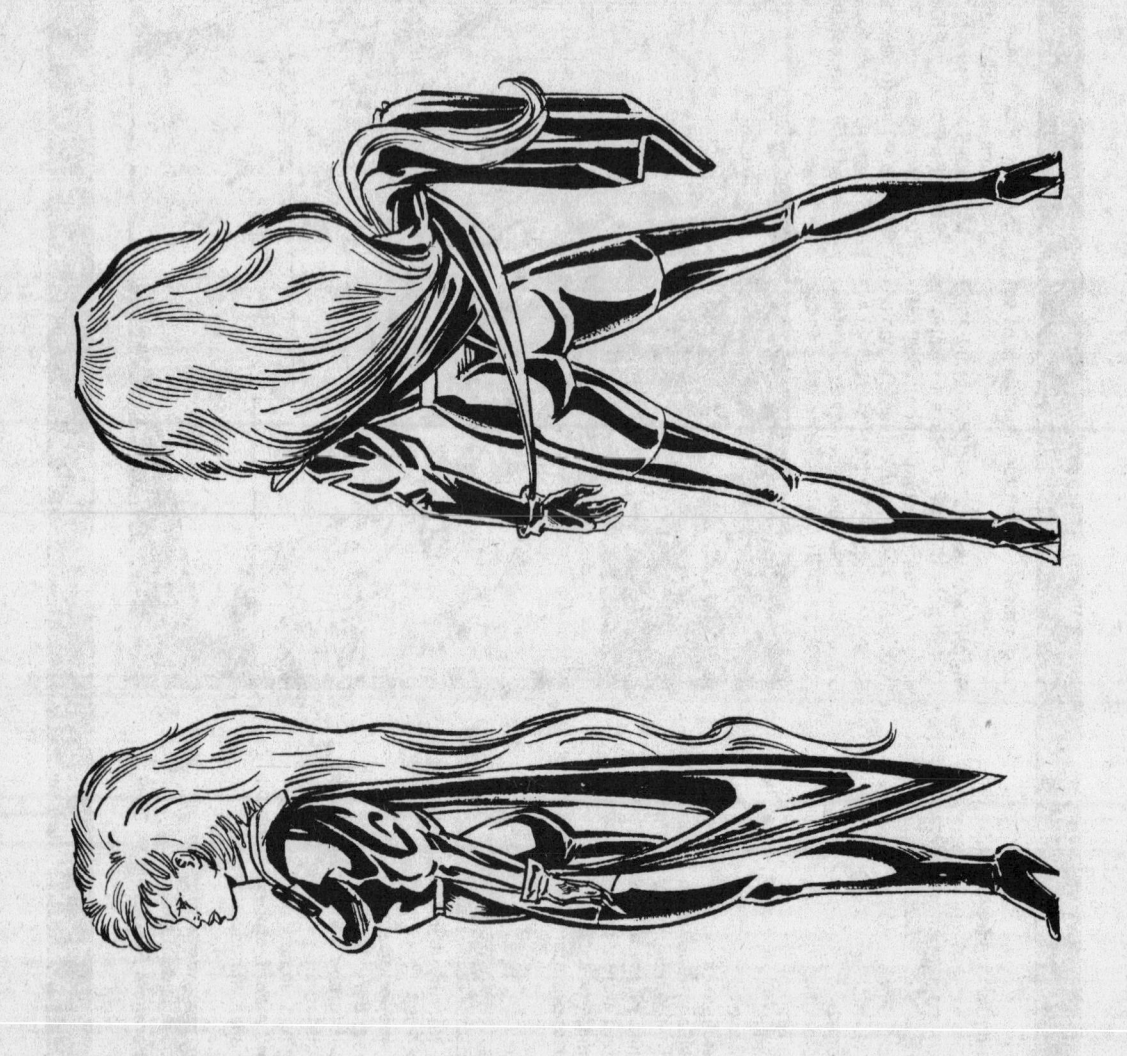

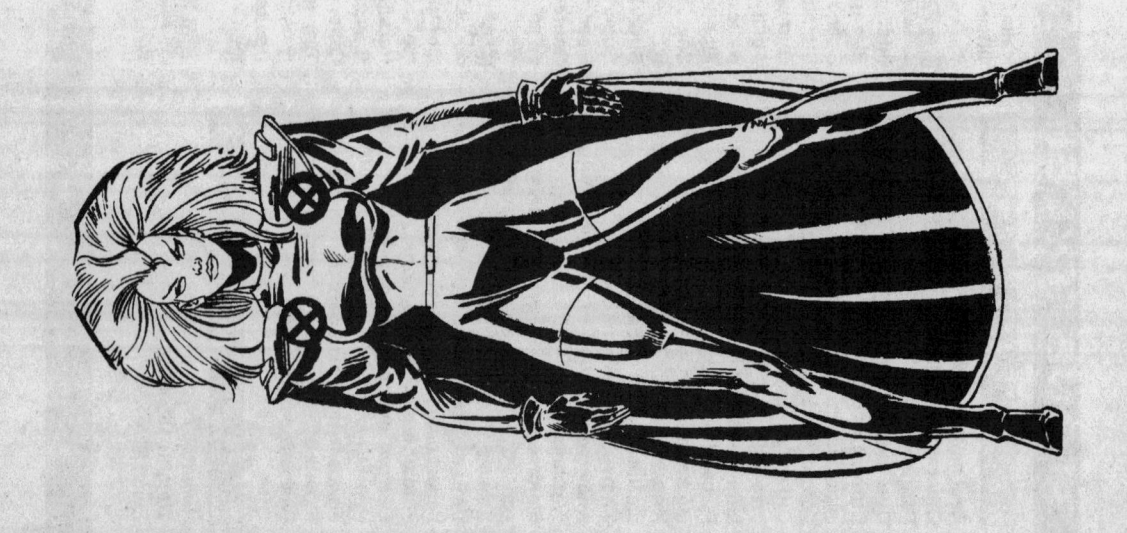

STORM

BIOGRAPHICAL DATA

Real name: Ororo Munroe
Other current aliases: None
Former aliases: (in Kenya and Tanzania) "Beautiful Windrider"
Dual identity: Secret
Current occupation: Adventurer
Former occupation: Thief, "goddess" to an African tribe
Citizenship: United States of America
Legal status: No criminal record in the United States. (She probably has a record as a juvenile offender in Egypt, but not under her true name.)
Place of birth: New York City
Marital status: Single
Known relatives: David Munroe (father, deceased), N'Dare Munroe (mother, deceased), Ashake (ancestor, deceased)
Known confidants: Forge, Wolverine, Marvel Girl (Jean Grey), Shadowcat (Kitty Pryde), Colossus, Nightcrawler, Callisto, Gambit, Black Panther
Known allies: X-Men, New Mutants, Black Panther
Major enemies: Shadow King (Amahl Farouk), Genoshan government, Henry Peter Gyrich, the White Queen
Usual base of operations: Professor Xavier's School for Gifted Youngsters, Salem Center, Westchester County, New York State
Former bases of operations: Cairo, Egypt; X-Men Headquarters in Australian outback
Current group membership: X-Men
Former group membership: Leader of the Morlocks
Extent of education: College level courses taken at Professor Xavier's School for Gifted Youngsters

PHYSICAL DESCRIPTION

Height: 5' 11"
Weight: 127 lbs
Eyes: Blue
Hair: White
Other distinguishing features: None

POWERS AND ABILITIES

Intelligence: Above normal
Strength: Athlete
Speed: Athlete
Flight Speed: Subsonic (when propelled by winds)
Stamina: Athlete
Durability: Athlete
Agility: Athlete
Reflexes: Athlete
Fighting skills: Excellent hand-to-hand combatant, trained by Wolverine
Special skills and abilities: Extraordinary ability at picking locks, excellent marksman with handguns
Superhuman physical powers: Limited immunity to extreme heat and cold
Superhuman mental powers: Psionic ability to control the weather over limited areas; ability to fly by creating winds strong enough to support her weight
Special limitations: Psionic powers over weather are affected by her emotions
Source of superhuman powers: Genetic mutation

PARAPHERNALIA

Costume specifications: Synthetic stretch fabric
Personal weaponry: None
Special weaponry: None
Other accessories: Carries lockpicks
Transportation: Flies by riding winds summoned by her superhuman powers, also travels in X-Men Blackbird jet
Design and manufacture of paraphernalia: Unrevealed

BIBLIOGRAPHY

First appearance: GIANT-SIZE X-MEN #1
Origin issue: GIANT-SIZE X-MEN #1, X-MEN Vol. 1 #102, MARVEL TEAM-UP #100
Significant issues: GIANT-SIZE X-MEN #1 (acted as "goddess" to African tribe, recruited into X-Men by Professor X, given the name "Storm"); X-MEN #102 (suffered major claustrophobic attack, origin revealed); X-MEN Vol. 1 #113 (freed X-Men from captivity by Magneto); UNCANNY X-MEN #117 (recounted childhood meeting with Professor X); UNCANNY X-MEN #129 (captured by White Queen); UNCANNY X-MEN #135-137 (clash with Dark Phoenix); UNCANNY X-MEN #138 (became deputy leader of X-Men); MARVEL TEAM-UP #100 (revealed how Ororo first met Black Panther); UNCANNY X-MEN #147 (became "Rogue Storm"), UNCANNY X-MEN #151 (switched bodies with White Queen); UNCANNY X-MEN #159 (attacked by Dracula); UNCANNY X-MEN #170 (defeated Callisto, becoming new leader of the Morlocks); UNCANNY X-MEN #185 (deprived of superhuman powers by gun designed by Forge and fired by Henry Peter Gyrich); UNCANNY X-MEN #186 (first met and fell in love with Forge); UNCANNY X-MEN #187-188 (helped Forge battle Dire Wraiths); NEW MUTANTS #32-34 (aided New Mutants against Shadow King Amahl Farouk); NEW MUTANTS SPECIAL EDITION #1 X-MEN ANNUAL #9 (journeyed to Asgard, briefly enslaved by Loki); UNCANNY X-MEN #196 (nearly killed by Andreas von Strucker); UNCANNY X-MEN #201 (defeated Cyclops in competition to become X-Men's leader); UNCANNY X-MEN #224 (reunited with Forge); UNCANNY X-MEN #225 (regained superhuman powers); UNCANNY X-MEN #227 (died in giving life force to defeat Adversary, resurrected by Roma); UNCANNY X-MEN #253 (reverted to childhood by Nanny); UNCANNY X-MEN #267 (first met Gambit), UNCANNY X-MEN #270-272 (returned to adulthood, enslaved by Genoshans, regained free will and escaped captivity)

STRANGER

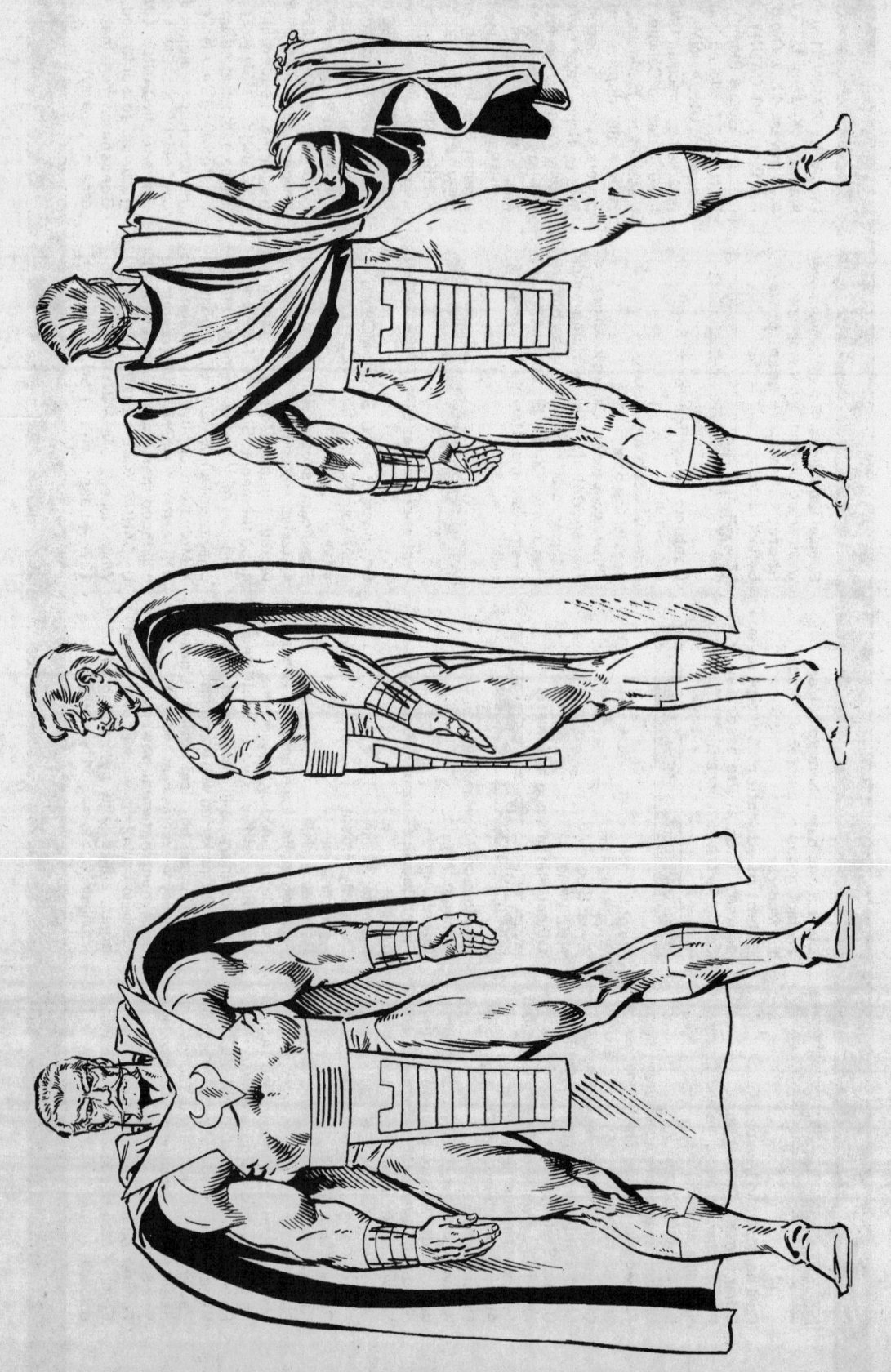

STRANGER

BIOGRAPHICAL DATA

Real name: Unrevealed
Other current aliases: None
Former aliases: None
Dual identity: None; the general populace of Earth is unaware of the Stranger's existence
Current occupation: Experimental scientist, surveyor of worlds, vivisectionist
Former occupation: Unrevealed
Citizenship: Unrevealed
Legal status: None
Place of birth: Unrevealed
Marital status: Unrevealed
Known relatives: None
Known confidants: None
Known allies: None
Major enemies: The X-Men, Over-Mind, Jakar, various other laboratory subjects
Usual base of operations: "Stranger's World", location unrevealed; unnamed starship for collecting laboratory specimens
Former bases of operations: Unrevealed
Current group membership: None
Former group membership: None
Extent of education: Unrevealed

PHYSICAL DESCRIPTION

Height: Variable (6' to 36')
Weight: Variable (0 to approximately 10 tons)
Eyes: Black
Hair: White
Other distinguishing features: A moustache

POWERS AND ABILITIES

Intelligence: Immeasurable
Strength: Incalculable
Land speed: Superhuman
Flight speed: Beyond light speed
Stamina: Godlike
Durability: Godlike
Agility: Normal
Reflexes: Athlete
Fighting skills: None
Special skills and abilities: Scientific knowledge beyond the understanding of humanity
Superhuman physical powers: The ability to manipulate cosmic and psionic forces for a variety of effects, including projection of cosmic energy as a concussive force, molecular manipulation of matter, conversion of matter to energy for faster than light travel, creation of force shields, levitation, and the enhancement of his own strength, speed, endurance, and size. The full range of the Stranger's abilities have yet to be catalogued and the precise limits of his known abilities are unmeasured.
Superhuman mental powers: The ability to mentally manipulate cosmic energy to reshape matter
Special limitations: None
Source of superhuman powers: Unrevealed

PARAPHERNALIA

Costume specifications: Alien materials
Personal weaponry: None
Special weaponry: None
Other accessories: None
Transportation: Conversion of body to unknown energy which travels at faster-than-light speeds; interdimensional teleportation; a huge starship which serves as his mobile base and specimen-transport craft.
Design and manufacture of paraphernalia: Unrevealed

BIBLIOGRAPHY

First appearance: X-MEN #11
Origin issue: The Stranger's true origin is unrevealed; a false origin was recounted in FANTASTIC FOUR #116.
Significant issues: X-MEN #11 (first appearance on Earth; encountered X-Men and Magneto's Brotherhood of Evil Mutants; abducted Magneto and Toad); X-MEN #18 (recaptured Magneto and Toad); TALES TO ASTONISH #89 (attempted to use Hulk to destroy Earth); AVENGERS #47 (first appearance of laboratory world, as Magneto escapes from same); SILVER SURFER Vol. 1 #5 (recanted desire for Earth's destruction); FANTASTIC FOUR #116 (battled Over-Mind); THOR #178 (laboratory world visited by Thor who set specimens free, battled the Stranger and the Abomination); CHAMPIONS #12 (prevented destruction of Earth by Doomsday Bomb); MARVEL TEAM-UP #55 (battled Gardener for possession of a Soul Gem); MARVEL TWO-IN-ONE ANNUAL #5 (battled Pluto); SILVER SURFER Vol. 2 #31 (encountered Living Tribunal, who insisted that the Stranger has an unrevealed higher purpose in the cosmic scheme of things which the Stranger denies); AVENGERS #315-316 (joined Avengers in battle against Nebula's quest for the Infinity Union); QUASAR #14 (investigated Watcher "suicide plague", exposition of laboratory world); QUASAR #15 (battled Over-Mind; approached by Watchers for aid in halting lethal information virus)

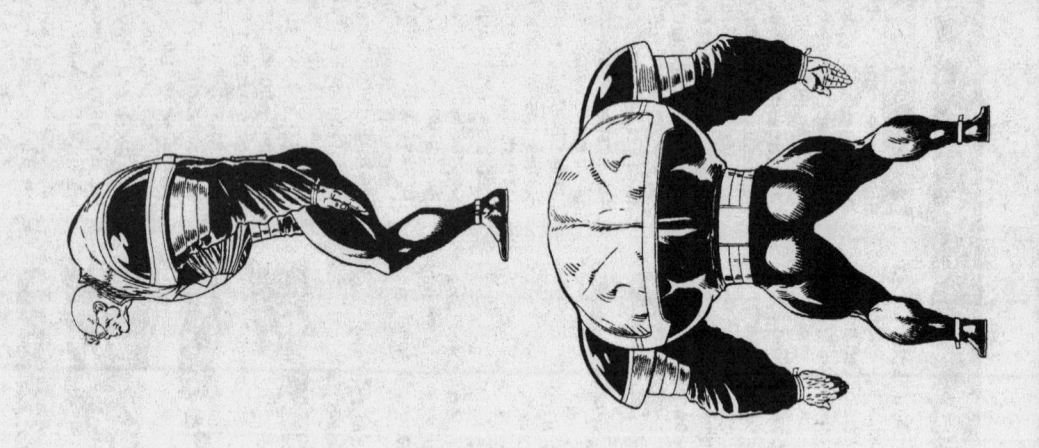

STRONG GUY ™

STRONG GUY

BIOGRAPHICAL DATA

Real name: Guido Carosella
Other current aliases: None
Former aliases: None
Dual identity: Publicly known
Current occupation: Government operative
Former occupation: Bodyguard
Citizenship: United States of America
Legal status: No criminal record
Place of birth: Unrevealed
Marital status: Single
Known relatives: Mr. and Mrs. Carosella (parents, deceased)
Known confidants: Wolfsbane, Polaris, Havok, Lila Cheney, Babette (masseuse)
Known allies: X-Factor II, X-Men, Dazzler, Lila Cheney, Dr. Valerie Cooper
Major enemies: Shadow King, Mister Sinister, Slab, Nasty Boys, Brotherhood of Evil Mutants V (Toad, Sauron, Blob, Pyro, Phantazia), Mutant Liberation Front, Cyber, Hell's Belles
Usual base of operations: X-Factor headquarters, Embassy Row, Washington, D.C.
Former bases of operations: Lila Cheney's home, Malibu California
Current group membership: X-Factor II
Former group membership: None
Extent of education: Bachelor of Arts in drama from New York University

PHYSICAL DESCRIPTION

Height: 7'
Weight: 750 lbs.
Eyes: Blue
Hair: White/blond
Other distinguishing features: An unusual percentage of body mass is concentrated in Guido's upper half of his body near sighted and wears corrective lenses.
Source of superhuman powers: Genetic mutation

PARAPHERNALIA

Costume specifications: Standard X-Factor uniform made of synthetic stretch fabric and lightweight body armor. Costume is insulated against extremes of heat and cold.
Personal weaponry: None
Special weaponry: None
Other accessories: None
Transportation: U.S. government vehicles
Design and manufacture of paraphernalia: U.S. government

POWERS AND ABILITIES

Intelligence: Gifted
Strength: Superhuman Class 50; can range upwards to an unknown limit through absorption of kinetic energy
Speed: Normal
Stamina: Superhuman
Durability: Metahuman
Agility: Normal
Reflexes: Normal
Fighting skills: Formidable hand-to-hand combatant, relies on streetfighting techniques
Special skills and abilities: Talented musical comedy actor and stand-up comedian
Superhuman physical powers: Aside from the above listed attributes, Strong Guy has the ability to absorb kinetic energy and to use it to enhance his physical strength up to an unknown level.
Superhuman mental powers: None
Special limitations: Strong Guy cannot long store the kinetic energy he absorbs and must physically expend it within 90 seconds. Otherwise, the energy will physically distort his body permanently. Strong Guy is in constant physical pain. He is

BIBLIOGRAPHY

First appearance: (as Guido) NEW MUTANTS #29, (as Strong Guy) X-FACTOR #72
Origin issue: Strong Guy's origin is as yet unrevealed.
Significant issues: NEW MUTANTS #29 (worked as bodyguard for Lila Cheney, met Cannonball II, and Magik); UNCANNY X-MEN #259-260 (found Dazzler near Lila Cheney's Malibu house, helped rescue Dazzler from drowning); UNCANNY X-MEN #270, 273-274 (found injured Lila Cheney when she teleported back to Malibu; accompanied Cheney to seek help from X-Men); UNCANNY X-MEN #278, 280 (came under mental control of the Shadow King); X-FACTOR #71-72 (joined X-Factor; adopted Strong Guy name); X-FACTOR #74-75 (fought Slab, unintentionally toppled Washington Monument, with X-Factor battled Nasty Boys); INCREDIBLE HULK #290-292, X-FACTOR #76 (with X-Factor, aided American-supported Trans-Sabal government in war against rebels, fought Hulk); X-FACTOR #77-78 (with X-Factor, clashed with Mutant Liberation Front); X-FACTOR #80-81 (with X-Factor, fought Cyber and Hell's Belles, poisoned by Cyber, recovered); X-FACTOR #82 (with X-Factor, fought Brotherhood of Evil Mutants); INFINITY WAR #1-6 (participated in Earth super heroes' war against Magus I)

STRYFE™

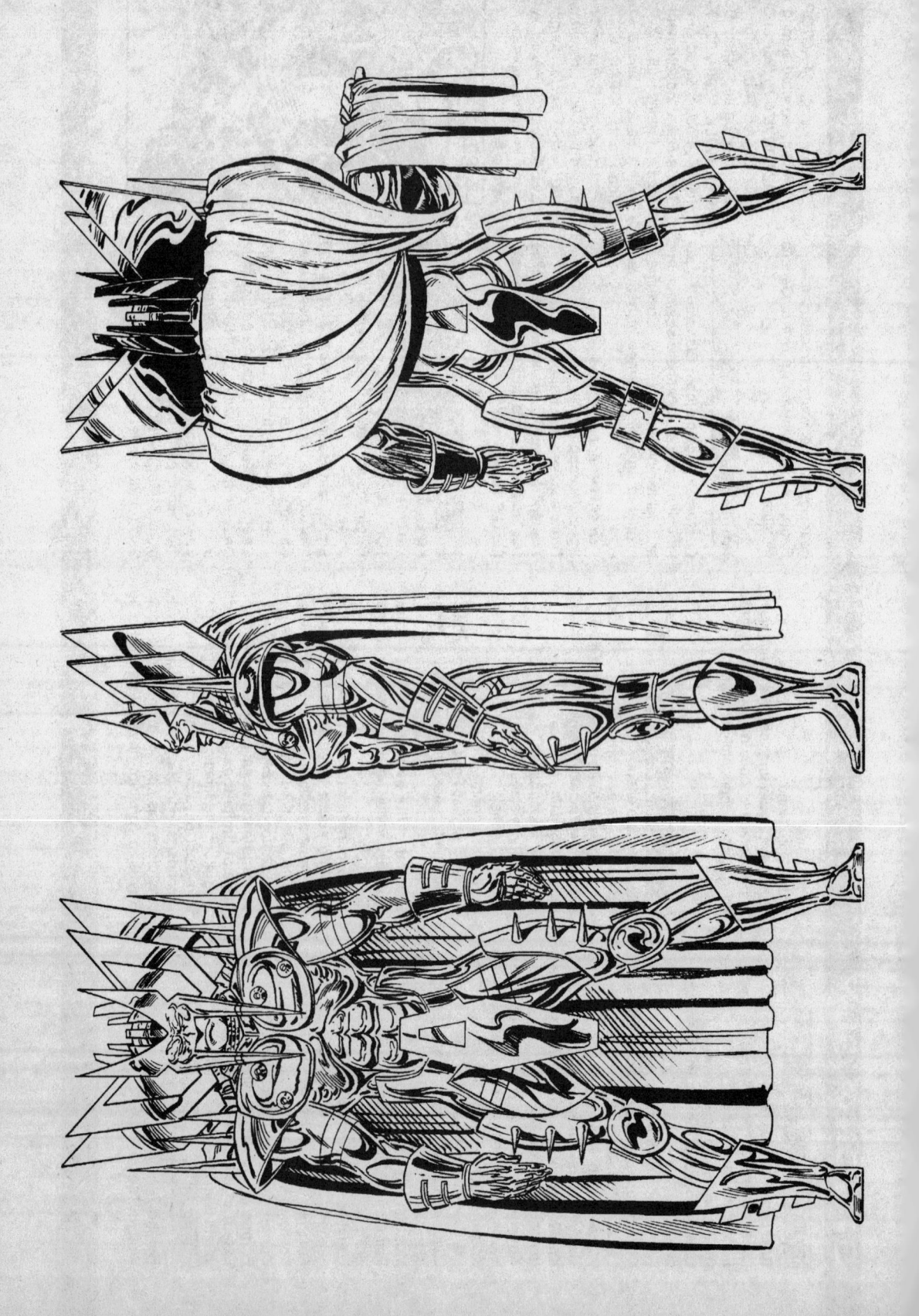

STRYFE

BIOGRAPHICAL DATA

Real name: Unrevealed
Other aliases at time of apparent death: None known
Former aliases: Once impersonated Cable
Dual identity: Secret
Occupation at time of apparent death: Terrorist leader
Former occupation: Anarchist and terrorist rebel in Nor-Am Pact region circa 3783-3806 A.D. in an alternate future
Citizenship: Nor-Am Pact region circa 3783-3806 A.D. in an alternate future
Legal status: None in present-day Earth
Place of birth: Presumably Nor-Am Pact region circa 3783-3806 A.D. in an alternate future
Place of apparent death: The moon
Causer of apparent death: Detonation of self-destruct system by Cable
Marital status: Presumed single
Known relatives: None
Known confidants: None
Known allies: Mutant Liberation Front (Dragoness, Forearm, Kamikaze, Reaper, Strobe, Sumo, Thumbelina, Wildside, Zero), Dark Riders (Foxbat, Gauntlet, Harddrive, Psynapse, Tusk), Mister Sinister, General Nguyen Ngoc
Major enemies: Cable, Apocalypse, Professor X, Cyclops, Marvel Girl, X-Force, X-Factor II, Weapon X II (Kane), Sabretooth, Sunfire, (former) Dark Riders, High Lords of New Canaan, Clan Chosen
Base of operations at time of apparent death: Various bases worldwide
Former bases of operations: Various bases worldwide, including Arkansas, Japan, and Antarctica
Group membership at time of apparent death: Leader of the Mutant Liberation Front, leader of the Dark Riders
Former group membership: None known
Extent of education: Unrevealed

PHYSICAL DESCRIPTION

Height: 6'8"
Weight: 350 lbs.
Eyes: Blue
Hair: White
Other distinguishing features: Stryfe is known to have bionic eyes and may have other bionic parts and systems.

POWERS AND ABILITIES

Intelligence: Superhuman
Strength: Superhuman Class 10
Speed: Enhanced human
Stamina: Enhanced human
Durability: Enhanced human
Agility: Enhanced human
Reflexes: Enhanced human
Fighting skills: Extensive training in military combat techniques and the martial arts, master marksman with firearms
Special skills and abilities: Cunning terrorist strategist.
Superhuman physical powers: Stryfe is believed to be a mutant whose physical abilities and intelligence are enhanced above the normal human levels.
Superhuman mental powers: Vast telekinetic abilities, sufficient to block the use of Cyclops and Marvel Girl's superhuman powers. Uses his telekinesis to levitate himself.
Special limitations: None known
Source of superhuman powers: Genetic mutation, cyborg body parts

PARAPHERNALIA

Costume specifications: Battle armor of unknown composition that is highly impervious to damage
Personal weaponry: Wields a blade capable of harming Apocalypse
Special weaponry: Various advanced weaponry from the 39th Century A.D. of his alternate future
Other accessories: Various advanced technology from the 39th Century A.D. of his alternate future, including time-vortex field generator
Transportation: Teleportation through Zero's superhuman powers, self-levitation through his own telekinetic powers
Design and manufacture of paraphernalia: Unrevealed

BIBLIOGRAPHY

First appearance: NEW MUTANTS #87
Origin issue: X-FORCE #17
Significant issues: NEW MUTANTS #87 (ordered Mutant Liberation Front to capture Rusty Collins and Skids); NEW MUTANTS #93-94 (in Japan fought Cable and first clashed with New Mutants, thwarted in attempt to poison water supplies of major cities); NEW MUTANTS #100 (face revealed); X-FORCE #1 (abandoned Antarctic Mutant Liberation Front base during invasion by X-Force); X-FACTOR #77-78 (had Mutant Liberation Front free captive mutants Hairbag and Slab, turned them over to Mister Sinister, ordered MLF attack on clinic); X-FORCE #9-10 (confronted and defeated Kane [Weapon X II]); X-MEN Vol. 2 #13 (declared enmity for Apocalypse); CABLE #1-2 (battled Cable, who learned Stryfe was his double); UNCANNY X-MEN #294 (posing as Cable, made assassination attempt on Professor X); X-FORCE #16 (confronted his captives Cyclops and Marvel Girl); X-MEN Vol. 2 #15 (bested Dark Riders, confronted Apocalypse); X-FORCE #17 (wounded Apocalypse, became leader of the Dark Riders); X-FORCE #18 (seemingly killed during combat with Cable on moon when Cable's self-destruct device detonated)

SUNDER

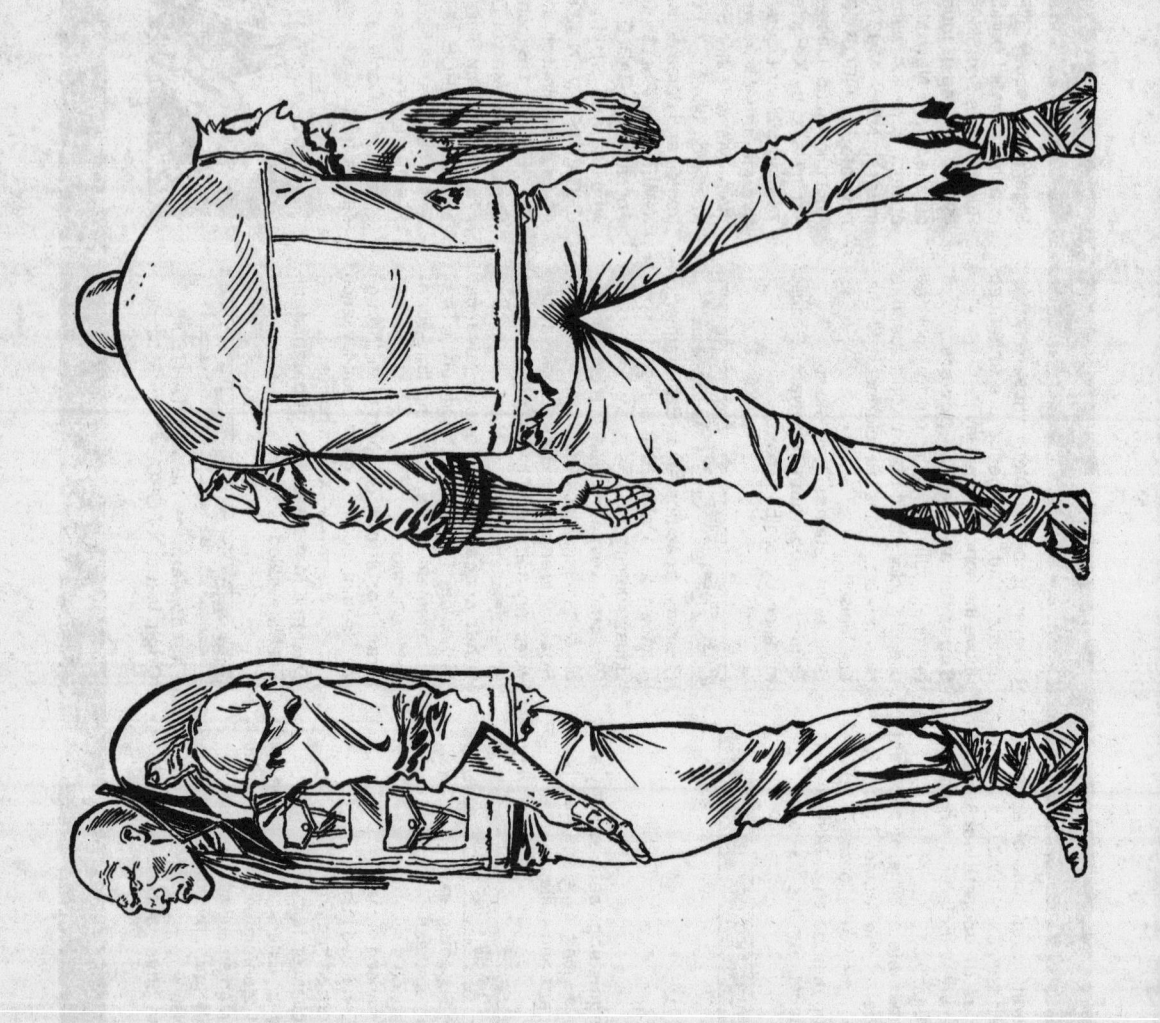

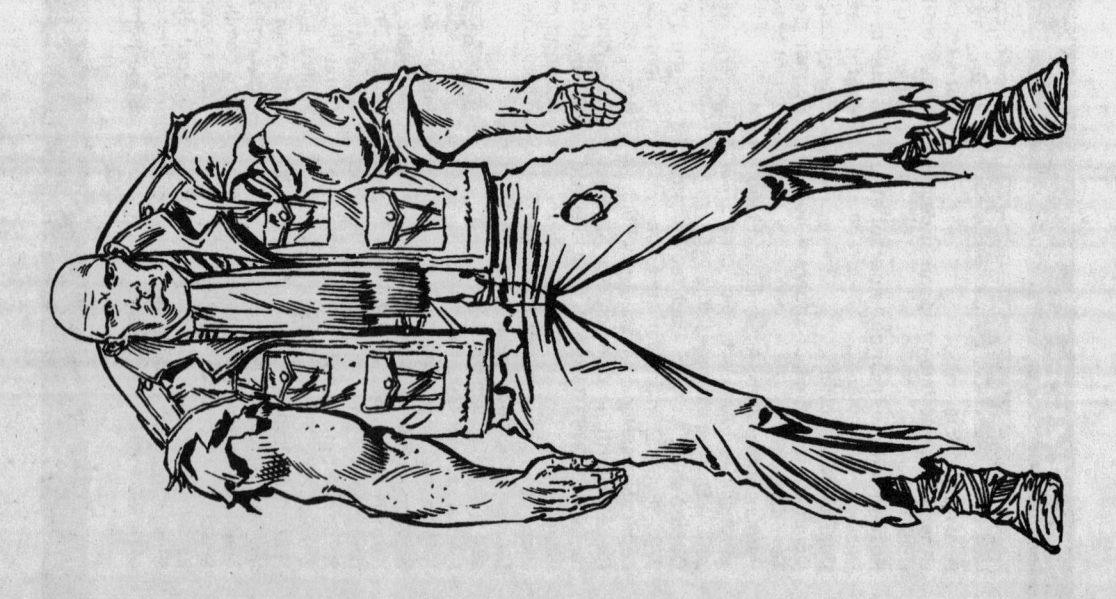

SUNDER

BIOGRAPHICAL DATA

Real name: Unrevealed
Other aliases at time of death: None known
Former aliases: None known
Dual identity: Sunder abandoned whatever identity he may once have had in the human world
Occupation at time of death: Adventurer
Former occupation: Aide to Callisto
Citizenship: Presumably United States
Legal status: United States legal authorities are unaware of Sunder's existence among the Morlocks; any previous identity he may have had in human society is presumed dead
Place of birth: Unrevealed
Place of death: Muir Island
Cause of death: Bullet wound in the back
Marital status: Presumed single
Known relatives: None known
Known confidants at time of death: Callisto
Known allies: Callisto, other Morlocks, the X-Men
Major enemies: The Marauders, the Reavers
Usual base of operations: Muir Island, off the cost of Scotland
Former bases of operations: The Alley and other tunnels beneath the surface of the New York City area
Group membership at time of death: Morlocks; Sunder also joined the team of X-Men organized by Moira MacTaggert that battled the Reavers
Former group membership: None
Extent of education: Unrevealed

PHYSICAL DESCRIPTION

Height: 7'1"
Weight: 245 lbs.
Eyes: Blue
Hair: Bald
Other distinguishing features: None

POWERS AND ABILITIES

Intelligence: Normal
Strength: Superhuman Class 75
Speed: Unrevealed, probably Peak human
Stamina: Superhuman
Durability: Superhuman
Agility: Unrevealed, probably Athlete
Reflexes: Unrevealed, probably Athlete
Fighting skills: Sunder is an untrained but formidable hand-to-hand combatant
Special skills and abilities: None
Superhuman physical powers: Superhuman strength
Superhuman mental powers: None
Special limitations: None
Source of superhuman powers: Mutation

PARAPHERNALIA

Costume specifications: Conventional materials, although he wore a specially designed X-Man uniform consisting of light body armor in his battle against the Reavers
Personal weaponry: None
Special weaponry: None
Other accessories: None
Transportation: Various
Design and manufacture of paraphernalia: Inapplicable

BIBLIOGRAPHY

First appearance: X-MEN #169
Origin issue: Sunder's origin is as yet unrevealed
Significant issues: X-MEN #169 (kidnaped Angel to the realm of the Morlocks for Callisto); X-MEN #178-179 (aided Callisto in abducting Kitty Pryde and attempting to force Pryde to marry the Morlock Caliban); X-MEN #190 (served wizard Kulan Gath when latter took over Manhattan); X-MEN #254 (shot in the back by Prettyboy while aiding Moira MacTaggart's new team of X-Men in battle against the Reavers)

SUNFIRE

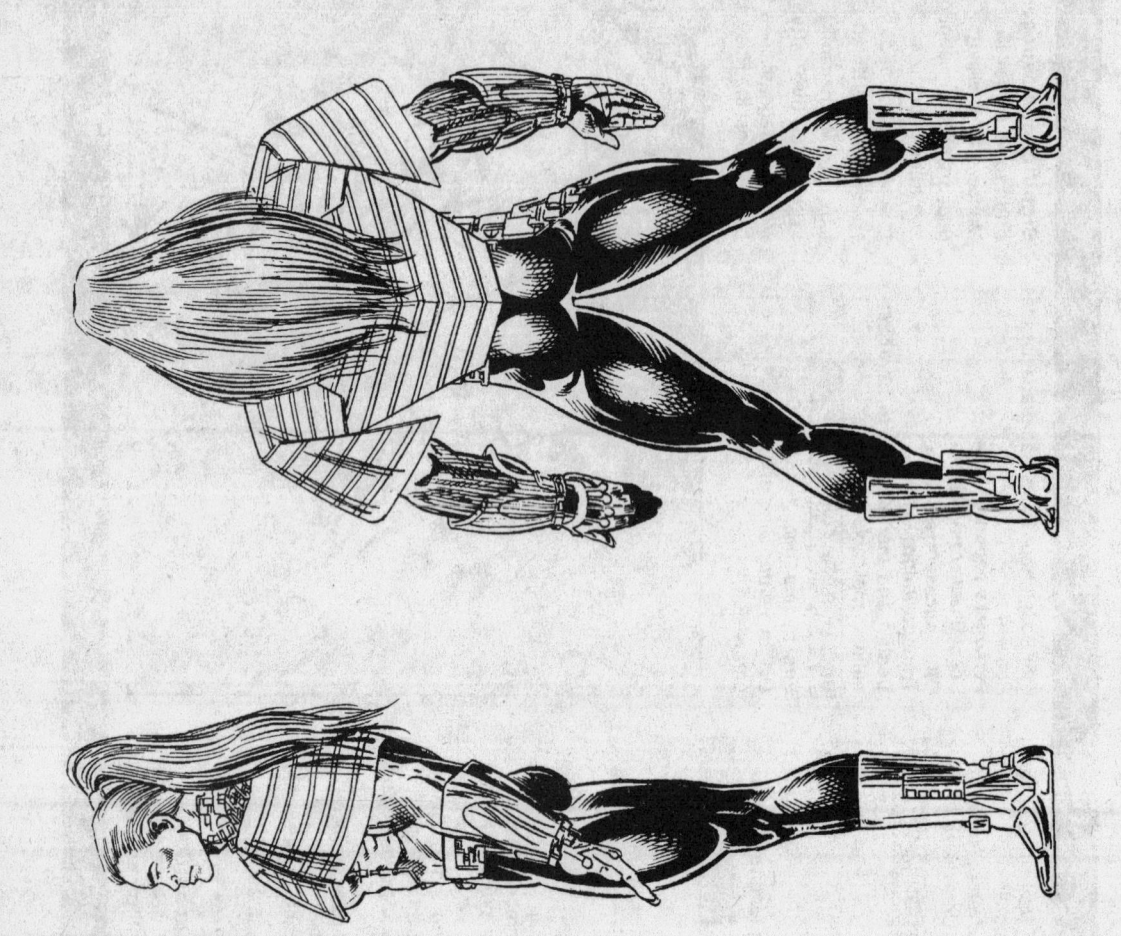

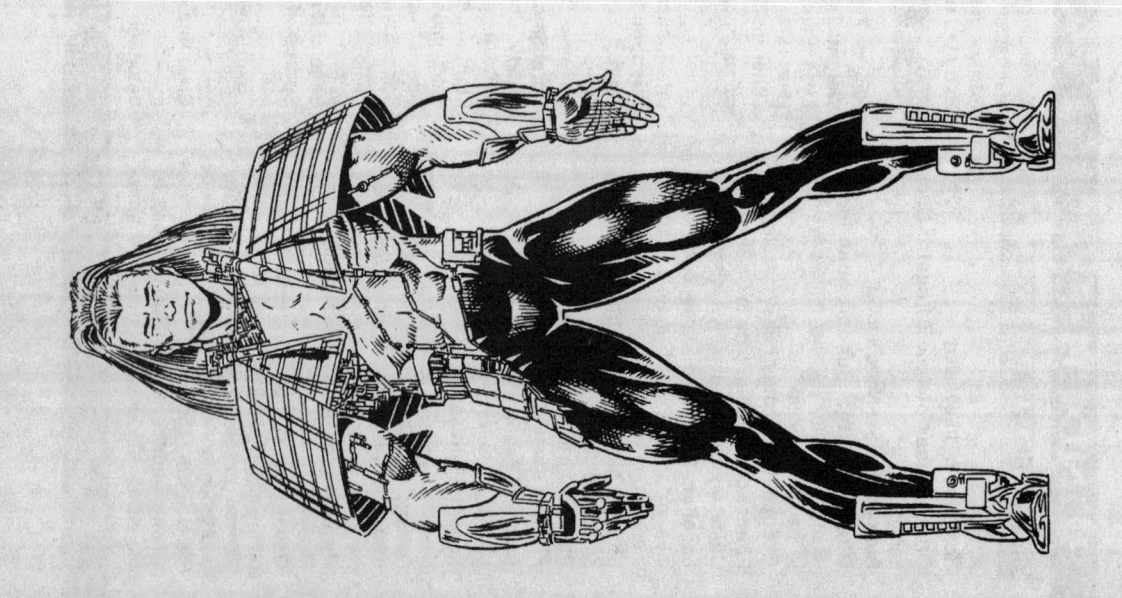

SUNFIRE

BIOGRAPHICAL DATA

Real name: Shiro Yoshida
Other current aliases: None
Former aliases: None
Dual identity: Secret; known to the upper echelons of the Japanese government
Current occupation: Adventurer
Former occupation: Student
Citizenship: Japan
Legal status: No criminal record
Place of birth: Agarashima, Japan
Marital status: Single
Known relatives: Saburo Yoshida (father, deceased), unnamed mother (deceased), Tomo Yoshida (uncle, deceased), Shingen Harada (first cousin, once removed, deceased), Mariko Yashida (second cousin, deceased), Keniuchio Harada (Silver Samurai, second half-cousin)
Known confidants: None
Known allies: The X-Men, Iron Man I, Namor the Sub-Mariner, Captain America, Cable, the New Mutants, Avengers West Coast
Major enemies: The Mandarin, Ultimo, Krakoa, Moses Magnum, Mutant Liberation Front, Dr. Demonicus, the Pacific Overlords, the Corruptor, Deadline, the Hand
Usual base of operations: Yoshida ancestral home, Tokyo, Japan
Former bases of operations: None
Current group membership: None
Former group membership: The X-Men, Pacific Overlords
Extent of education: College graduate

PHYSICAL DESCRIPTION

Height: 5' 10"
Weight: 175 lbs.
Eyes: Dark brown
Hair: Black
Other distinguishing features: None

POWERS AND ABILITIES

Intelligence: Normal
Strength: Peak human
Speed: Athlete
Flight speed: Artificial winged flight
Stamina: Athlete
Durability: Athlete
Agility: Athlete
Reflexes: Athlete
Fighting skills: Trained in karate and Japanese Samurai swordsmanship, kendo; expert in combat use of his superhuman powers
Special skills and abilities: None known
Superhuman physical powers: Ability to ionize matter into fiery plasma state and to utilize this heat energy for flight propulsion and energy release in the form of heat blasts and concussive force blasts
Superhuman mental powers: Ability to form psionic force field while using his plasma as protection from heat and radiation, both of his own generation and from outside sources
Special limitations: None
Source of superhuman powers: Genetic mutation

PARAPHERNALIA

Costume specifications: Synthetic stretch fabric made from unstable molecules
Personal weaponry: None
Special weaponry: None
Other accessories: None
Transportation: Flight under own power
Design and manufacture of paraphernalia: Unrevealed

BIBLIOGRAPHY

First appearance: X-MEN Vol. 1 #64
Origin issue: X-MEN Vol. 1 #64
Significant issues: X-MEN Vol. 1 #64 (at behest of his uncle Tomo, attacked United Nations and U.S. Capitol Building, battled the original X-Men; turned against Tomo and killed him when Tomo killed his father); SUB-MARINER #52-54 (battled Namor the Sub-Mariner, alongside Namor, battled Dragon-Lord I); IRON MAN #68-70 (battled Iron Man I, abducted by the Mandarin to power one of his machines; alongside Iron Man I, battled Ultimo); GIANT-SIZE X-MEN #1 (joined the new X-Men from Krakoa); X-MEN Vol. 1 #94 (quit X-Men); IRON MAN #98-99 (battled Iron Man I and Guardsman II); X-MEN Vol. 1 #118-119 (with X-Men, battled Moses Magnum); MARVEL SUPER-HERO CONTEST OF CHAMPIONS #1-3 (among heroes summoned by the Grandmaster, battled Darkstar); UNCANNY X-MEN #181 (with X-Men, battled alien dragon); NEW MUTANTS #93-94 (alongside Cable, Wolverine, and the New Mutants, battled Stryfe, and the MLF); MARVEL COMICS PRESENTS #32 (battled the Corruptor and Deadline); AVENGERS WEST COAST #71 (hypnotized by Dr. Demonicus; alongside Pele, battled Hawkeye, Namor, and Spider-Woman II); UNCANNY X-MEN #284-286 (received new armor, with X-Men, battled the inhabitants of the Void); WOLVERINE #55-56 (alongside Gambit, battled the Hand)

SUNSPOT ™

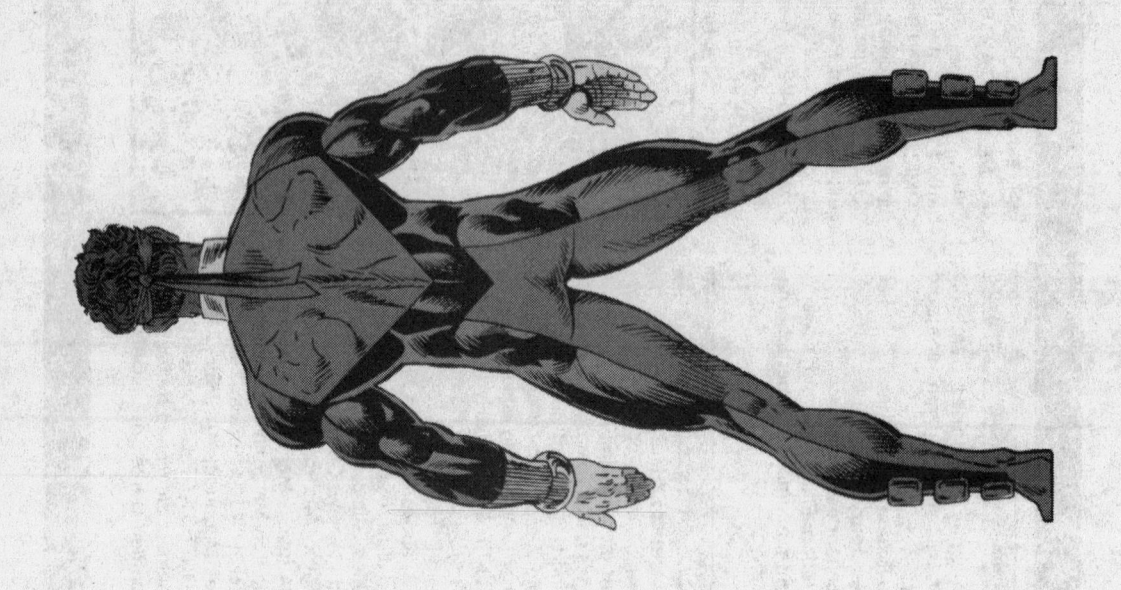

SUNSPOT

BIOGRAPHICAL DATA

Real name: Roberto Da Costa
Other current aliases: None
Former aliases: None
Dual identity: Secret
Current occupation: Adventurer, commando, CEO of Da Costa Corporation
Former occupation: Student
Citizenship: Brazil
Legal status: No criminal record
Place of birth: Rio de Janeiro
Marital status: Single
Known relatives: Emmanuel Da Costa (father, deceased), Nina Da Costa (mother)
Known confidants: Juliana Sandoval (deceased), Cannonball, Nina Da Costa, X-Force, Cable, (former) Gideon II, New Mutants, Magneto, Gosamyr
Known allies: X-Force, Cable, Lila Cheney, (former) the New Mutants, the X-Men, X-Factor I, X-Terminators II, Magneto, Fallen Angels, Cloak & Dagger, Hellions, Gosamyr
Major enemies: Gideon II, Externals, Stryfe, Mutant Liberation Front, Shadow King (Amahl Farouk), Black Tom Cassidy, Juggernaut, Arianna, Jankos, Friends of Humanity, Hela, The Right, (former) White Queen, Hellions, Freedom Force
Usual base of operations: Camp Verde Reservation, Arizona
Former bases of operations: Professor Xavier's School for Gifted Youngsters, Salem Center, Westchester County, Upstate New York; Beat Street Club, New York City; X-Force headquarters, Adirondack Mountains, New York
Current group membership: X-Force
Former group membership: New Mutants, Fallen Angels, Gladiators, Hellions
Extent of education: High school level

PHYSICAL DESCRIPTION

Height: (on first joining the New Mutants) 5', (currently) 5'8"
Weight: (on first joining the New Mutants) 130 lbs., (currently) 170 lbs.
Eyes: Brown
Hair: Black
Other distinguishing features: When utilizing his strength at superhuman levels, Sunspot and sometimes all or part of his clothing turn pure black.

POWERS AND ABILITIES

Intelligence: Normal
Strength: Athlete, (enhanced) Superhuman Class 10
Speed: Athlete
Stamina: Athlete, (enhanced) Enhanced human
Durability: Athlete, (enhanced) Enhanced human
Agility: Athlete
Reflexes: Athlete
Fighting skills: Good hand-to-hand combatant, trained at Xavier's School and later by Cable, also trained in swordsmanship by Gladiators
Special skills and abilities: Good aircraft pilot, excellent soccer player
Superhuman physical powers: Ability to absorb solar energy and convert it for use as physical strength. His physical resistance to impact also increases somewhat when he employs superhuman strength. For unknown reasons small black spots appear in the air around Sunspot when he utilizes superhuman strength. Although Sunspot can absorb energy from stars and reflected solar energy from the moon, the amounts that reach him on Earth are too miniscule todd significantly to his power. Recently Sunspot has developed the ability to project concussive energy blasts from his hands
Superhuman mental powers: None
Special limitations: When not in direct sunlight, Sunspot can exhaust his superhuman strength by using up the stores of energy within his body
Source of superhuman powers: Genetic mutation

PARAPHERNALIA

Costume specifications: Synthetic stretch fabric
Personal weaponry: None
Special weaponry: None
Other accessories: None
Transportation: X-Force vehicles and vehicles provided by his late father's companies
Design and manufacture of paraphernalia: (costume) Boomer using Shi'ar clothes synthesizer

BIBLIOGRAPHY

First appearance: MARVEL GRAPHIC NOVEL #4
Origin issue: MARVEL GRAPHIC NOVEL #4
Significant issues: MARVEL GRAPHIC NOVEL #4 (first discovered own mutant powers, witnessed his girlfriend Juliana Sandoval's murder, joined New Mutants); MARVEL TEAM-UP ANNUAL #6 (injected with variation of drug that helped create Cloak and Dagger, briefly became monster); NEW MUTANTS #9-11 (was reunited with parents; with New Mutants, visited Nova Roma); NEW MUTANTS #16-17 (first encountered White Queen and Hellions); NEW MUTANTS #29-31 (was abducted and forced to serve as one of the Gladiators); NEW MUTANTS SPECIAL EDITION #1/UNCANNY X-MEN ANNUAL #9 (visited Asgard); FALLEN ANGELS #1-8 (left New Mutants, joined Fallen Angels); NEW MUTANTS #50 (alongside New Mutants, fought Magus II); NEW MUTANTS #60 (battled Cameron Hodge and the Right); NEW MUTANTS #65 (alongside New Mutants, battled Freedom Force); NEW MUTANTS #68 (fell in love with Gosamyr)

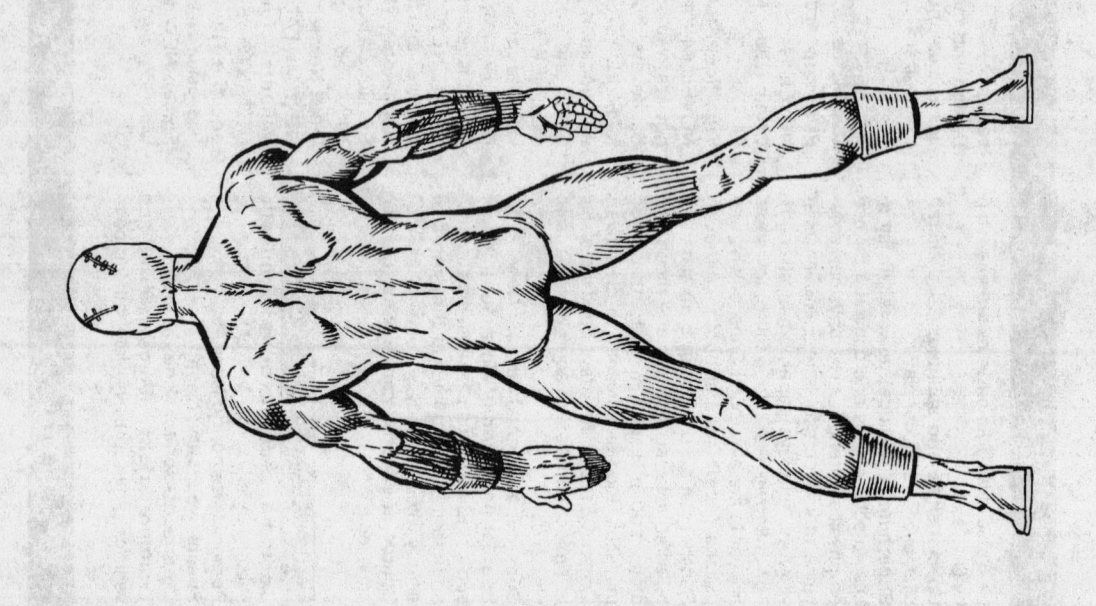

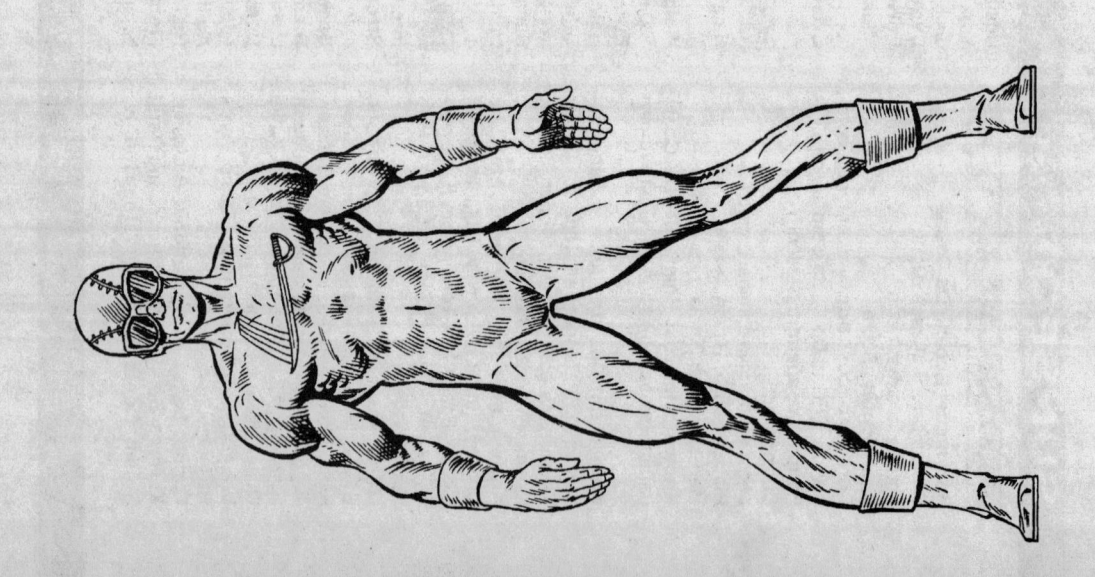

SUPER-SABRE™

SUPER SABRE

BIOGRAPHICAL DATA

Real name: Martin Fletcher
Other aliases at time of death: None known
Former aliases: None known
Dual identity: Secret, known to the United States government
Occupation at time of death: Special operative for federal government
Former occupation: Vigilante
Citizenship: United States of America
Legal status: No criminal record, pardoned by the federal government for past crimes
Place of birth: Undisclosed location in Massachusetts
Place of death: Kuwait City, Kuwait
Cause of death: Decapitation by "cutting wind" of Aminedi of Desert Storm
Marital status: Single
Known relatives: None
Known confidants at time of death: Crimson Commando, Stonewall
Known allies: Freedom Force
Major enemies: Storm, Cable, X-Men, X-Factor I, New Mutants, Desert Storm
Usual base of operations: Freedom Force headquarters, the Pentagon, Arlington, Virginia
Former bases of operations: Unnamed "hometown" in Massachusetts, later Adirondack State Park, New York State
Group membership at time of death: Freedom Force
Former group membership: Partner of Crimson Commando and Stonewall
Extent of education: Unrevealed, at least high school level

PHYSICAL DESCRIPTION

Height: 5'8"
Weight: 145 lbs.
Eyes: Unrevealed
Hair: White
Other distinguishing features: None

POWERS AND ABILITIES

Intelligence: Normal
Strength: Peak human
Speed: Supersonic (finger snapping), subsonic (running)
Stamina: Superhuman
Durability: Enhanced human
Agility: Athlete
Reflexes: Superhuman
Fighting skills: Good hand-to-hand combatant utilizing a unique style that exploits his superhuman speed, trained by Crimson Commando
Special skills and abilities: None known
Superhuman physical powers: Along with the above listed attributes, Super Sabre could create a "micro-sonic boom" by snapping his fingers, create wall of air by pressure by moving his arms at superhuman speed, run up walls and across water.
Superhuman mental powers: None
Special limitations: His metabolism required air, food, and water; deprivation of any of these would diminish his speed and endurance, physical abilities weakened with age but much less so than a normal human being of his advanced age
Source of superhuman powers: Unrevealed

PARAPHERNALIA

Costume specifications: Synthetic stretch fabric treated to be highly resistant to damage from friction heat and other hazards of superhuman speed; helmet contains visor that protects eyes from hazards of moving at superhuman speed
Personal weaponry: None
Special weaponry: None
Other accessories: None
Transportation: Freedom Force aircraft
Design and manufacture of paraphernalia: United States government

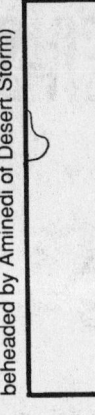

BIBLIOGRAPHY

First appearance: UNCANNY X-MEN #215
Origin issue: UNCANNY X-MEN #215
Significant issues: UNCANNY X-MEN #215-216 (alongside Crimson Commando and Stonewall, captured Storm and drug dealer Patricia Morrison, set out to hunt both to their deaths; seemingly killed in avalanche while fighting Storm); UNCANNY X-MEN #223, 225-227 (publicly reappeared, offered to join Freedom Force; alongside Freedom Force, battled X-Men in Dallas; battled cavemen transported to Dallas by time-waves created by Adversary; witnessed temporary deaths of X-Men, witnessed Forge's return to Dallas); NEW MUTANTS #65 (with Freedom Force, fought New Mutants in Dallas); X-FACTOR #30-31 (alongside Freedom Force, confronted Cyclops and Marvel Girl; defeated by Marvel Girl); NEW MUTANTS #78 (attempted to apprehend Rusty Collins, thwarted by Skids); NEW MUTANTS #88-89 (alongside Freedom Force, attempted to capture Cable who escaped from federal custody); QUASAR #78 (competed and lost in Runner's race to determine fastest human being on Earth); NEW MUTANTS ANNUAL #7 (sent with rest of Freedom Force to rescue or kill physicist Reinhold Kurtzmann, beheaded by Aminedi of Desert Storm)

SUPER-SKRULL

SUPER-SKRULL

BIOGRAPHICAL DATA

Real name: Kl'rt
Other current aliases: None
Former aliases: Invincible Man, Dr. Franklin Storm, Carol Danvers, the Thing, Bobby Wright/Captain Hero, Daniel Rand/Iron Fist
Dual identity: Publicly known to the Skrulls
Current occupation: Warrior
Former occupation: Unrevealed
Citizenship: Skrull Empire
Legal status: Former exile, now exonerated
Place of birth: Planet Tarnax IV (now destroyed), Tarnax System, Andromeda Galaxy
Marital status: Single
Known relatives: None
Known confidants: None
Known allies: The Skrulls, Empress S'byll, (former) Emperor Dorrek (deceased), Thanos, Master Khan, the Silver Surfer
Major enemies: The Fantastic Four, Thor I, Captain Mar-Vell (deceased), the Kree, the Avengers, Rick Jones, Red Wolf III, Spider-Man, Ms. Marvel I (Binary), Sasquatch, the Silver Surfer, the Eternals, the Stranger, Reptyl, the Hulk, Iron Fist, Namor the Sub-Mariner, Namorita, Ka-Zar, Misty Knight, Quasar, Kismet
Usual base of operations: Mobile throughout known space
Former base of operations: Mobile throughout the Skrull Empire
Current group membership: None
Former group membership: None
Extent of education: Graduate of the Skrullian military academy

PHYSICAL DESCRIPTION

Height: 6'
Weight: 625 lbs.
Eyes: Green
Hair: None
Other distinguishing features: Green skin, large pointed ears, furrowed chin

POWERS AND ABILITIES

Intelligence: Normal
Strength: Superhuman Class 10, (augmented by energy beam) Superhuman Class 25
Speed: Enhanced human
Flight speed: Supersonic
Stamina: Superhuman
Durability: Superhuman
Agility: Metahuman
Reflexes: Peak human
Fighting skills: Expert in all forms of armed and unarmed combat known to the Skrulls, highly trained in combat uses of his superhuman powers
Special skills and abilities: Trained starship pilot, skilled impersonator
Superhuman physical powers: The Super-Skrull possesses the combined superhuman abilities of the Fantastic Four, including a heightened degree of physical malleability (a trait common to all Skrulls), the above listed attributes, the ability to envelop himself in fiery plasma and to utilize this heat energy for various effects, including flight, formation of fiery shapes, and energy release in the form of heat blasts, "nova flame bursts," and concussive force blasts.
Superhuman mental powers: The Super-Skrull possesses the ability to project a potent hypnotic force from his eyes, plus the combined superhuman mental powers of the Fantastic Four, including the ability to control ambient heat energy in his immediate environment allowing his to take control of flames not of his own generation and to absorb heat from outside sources, the ability to render himself amd others invisible and the creation of invisible force fields
Special limitations: None
Source of superhuman powers: (physical malleability) Deviant Skrull heritage, (additional powers) bionic re-engineering by Skrull scientists
Note: The Super-Skrull's powers have been further augmented at times by exposure to a broadcast energy beam from the Skrull homeworld.

PARAPHERNALIA

Costume specifications: Alien materials
Personal weaponry: None
Special weaponry: None
Other accessories: None
Transportation: Skrull starship
Design and manufacture of paraphernalia: Unnamed Skrull technicians

BIBLIOGRAPHY

First appearance: FANTASTIC FOUR #18
Origin issue: FANTASTIC FOUR #18
Significant issues: FANTASTIC FOUR #18 (granted superhuman powers, sent to Earth, battled the Fantastic Four); FANTASTIC FOUR #32 (as Invincible Man, fought the Fantastic Four, returned to Skrull homeworld in exchange for Franklin Storm); FANTASTIC FOUR ANNUAL #3 (among villains summoned by Doctor Doom to attack Reed and Sue Richards wedding); THOR #142 (fought Thor I); CAPTAIN MARVEL #2-3 (sent to battle Captain Mar-Vell); AVENGERS #92-94 (during first Kree-Skrull War, captured Captain Mar-Vell, Quicksilver, and Scarlet Witch); CAPTAIN MARVEL #25-27 (alongside Skragg, sent by Thanos to capture Rick Jones, battled Captain Mar-Vell and the Thing); MARVEL TEAM-UP #61-62 (battled Spider-Man, Human Torch II and Ms. Marvel I; became trapped in the Van Allen Radiation Belt); ALPHA FLIGHT #9-10 (temporarily freed from Van Allen Belt, revealed to have contracted cancer, battled Sasquatch); NAMOR THE SUB-MARINER #25 (revealed to have been magically freed from the Van Allen Belt and cured of cancer by Master Khan)

SUPREME INTELLIGENCE

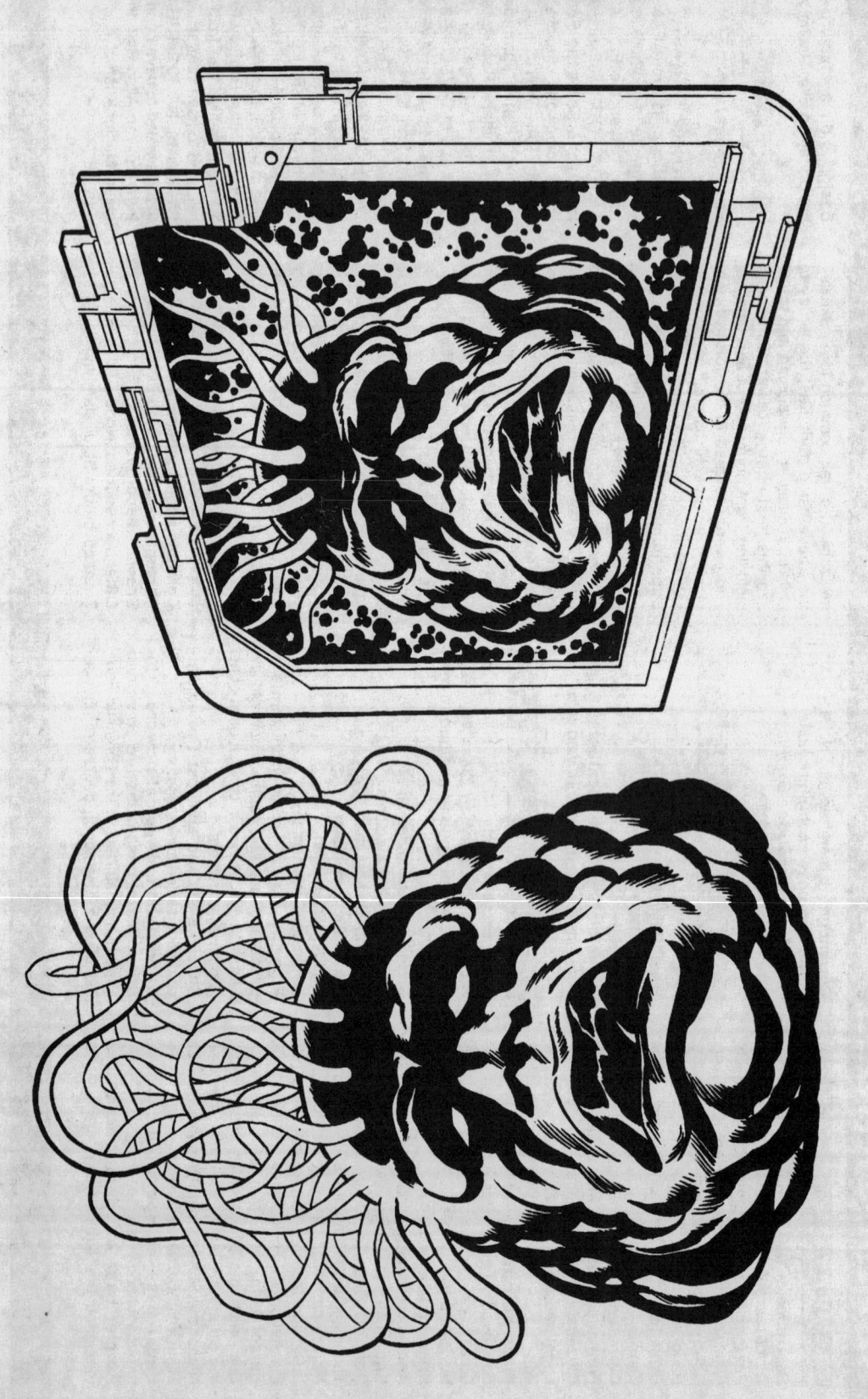

SUPREME INTELLIGENCE

BIOGRAPHICAL DATA

Real name: Inapplicable
Other current aliases: None
Former aliases: None
Dual Identity: Inapplicable
Current occupation: Ruler of the Kree Empire
Former occupation: Inapplicable
Citizenship: Inapplicable
Legal status: Inapplicable
Place of construction: The planet Kree-Lar
Marital status: Inapplicable
Known relatives: Inapplicable
Known confidants: Inapplicable
Known allies: None
Major enemies: The Skrull Empire, Captain Marvel I (deceased), Silver Surfer, the Avengers
Usual base of operations: The planet Kree-Lar
Former bases of operations: None
Current group membership: Government of the Kree Empire
Former group membership: None
Extent of programming: Inapplicable

PHYSICAL DESCRIPTION

Height: (of primary monitor display) 40'
Weight: (of entire unit) Unrevealed
Eyes: (of holographic display) Yellow
Hair: (of holographic display) None
Other distinguishing features: The Supreme Intelligence is a vast cybernetic/organic computer system composed of 5,000 cubic meters of computer circuitry incorporating the disembodied brains of the greatest statesmen and philosophers in Kree history, preserved cryogenically; this aggregation of brains creates a single collective intelligence able to use the vast information storage and processing capabilities of the computer system in a creative way; when wishing to interact with it, the Kree address it within it's terminal chamber, where a holographic image is projected on a gigantic monitor screen

Source of superhuman powers: The Supreme Intelligence is a vast cybernetic/organic computer system composed of computer circuitry incorporating the disembodied brains of the greatest statesmen and philosophers in Kree history

PARAPHERNALIA

Costume specifications: Inapplicable
Personal weaponry: None
Special weaponry: None
Other accessories: The Supreme Intelligence has access to the total resources of the Kree Empire
Transportation: Inapplicable
Design and manufacture of paraphernalia: Unrevealed Kree technicians

BIBLIOGRAPHY

First appearance: FANTASTIC FOUR #64
Origin issue: The details of the Supreme Intelligence's origin are as yet unrevealed
Significant issues: FANTASTIC FOUR #64 (sent Ronan the Accuser to execute Fantastic Four); CAPTAIN MARVEL #16 (discovered treachery of Zarek and Ronan; honored Captain Mar-Vell with new uniform); AVENGERS #89 (deposed as leader of Kree Empire by Ronan); AVENGERS #96 (revealed to have mentally influenced Rick Jones, and U.S. Alien Activities Commission from behind the scenes in plot to regain power); AVENGERS #97 (stimulated Rick Jones's psionic potential to end Earth-vicinity campaign in Kree-Skrull War, revealed that Kree race had reached evolutionary dead-end; regained leadership of Kree Empire); CAPTAIN MARVEL #41 (mentally dominated Ronan, used same as pawn in battle against Rick Jones and Captain Marvel); CAPTAIN MARVEL #46 (attempted to absorb minds of Rick Jones and Captain Marvel; employed remote-controlled androids as housing for consciousness); SILVER SURFER Vol. 2 #6 (plotted new campaign in Kree-Skrull War); SILVER SURFER Vol. 2 #7 (acquired Soul Gem; absorbed soul of Silver Surfer); SILVER SURFER Vol. 2 #8 (lost sanity when Surfer's soul escaped from him with Soul Gem); SILVER SURFER Vol. 2 #29 (Contemplator began restructuring Supreme Intelligence's scrambled conciousness); SILVER SURFER Vol. 2 #30 (taken over by mind of Contemplator); SILVER SURFER Vol. 2 #31 (liberated from the Contemplator's control by Cotati wizard; under Cotati's influence, appointed "Clumsy Foulup" supreme Kree Leader)

POWERS AND ABILITIES

Intelligence: Immeasurable
Strength: Inapplicable
Speed: Inapplicable
Flight speed: Inapplicable
Stamina: Inapplicable
Durability: Inapplicable
Agility: Inapplicable
Reflexes: Inapplicable
Fighting skills: None
Special skills and abilities: Vast knowledge, far surpassing that of present day Earth
Superhuman physical powers: None; occasionally employs remote controlled androids as surrogate bodies; the attributes of these androids are all metahuman
Superhuman mental powers: Information storage and processing abilities far above that of the human brain
Special limitations: The Supreme Intelligence is stationary

SUPREMOR™

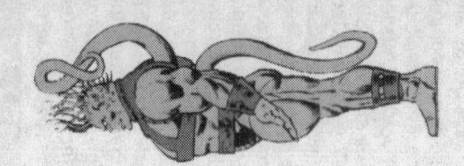

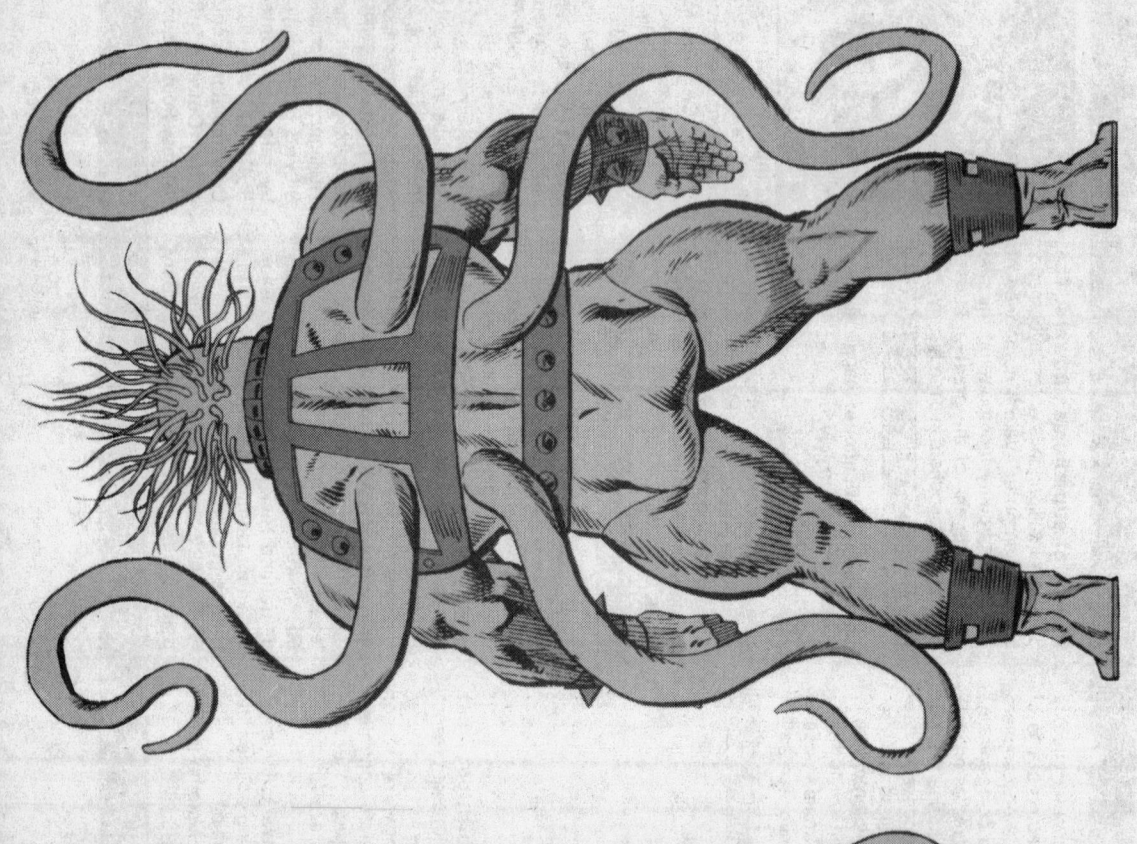

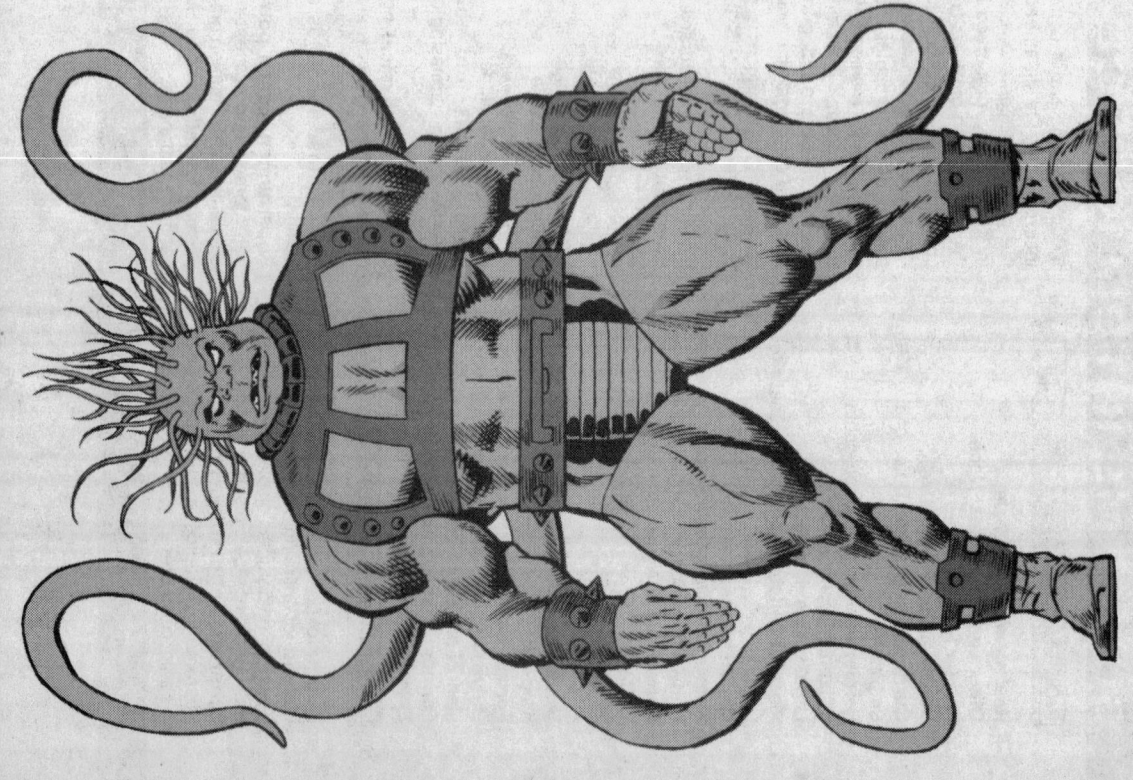

SUPREMOR

BIOGRAPHICAL DATA

Real name: Supremor
Note: The name "Supremor" has formerly been used to refer to the Kree Supreme Intelligence. Currently the name "Supremor" is applied to one of a number of androids created to resemble the Supreme Intelligence.
Other current aliases: None
Former aliases: None
Dual identity: None; the general populace of Earth is unaware of Supremor's existence.
Current occupation: Presumably none
Former occupation: Warrior, leader of the Kree Starforce
Citizenship: Inapplicable
Legal status: Property of the Kree Supreme Intelligence, now impounded by Shi'ar Majestrix Lilandra
Place of construction: Harfax (city-state on Kree throneworld Hala)
Marital status: Inapplicable
Known relatives: Inapplicable
Known confidants: Supreme Intelligence
Known allies: The Kree Supreme Intelligence, the Starforce (Captain Atlas, Doctor Minerva, Ronan the Accuser, Korath the Pursuer, Shatterax, Ultimus)
Major enemies: The Shi'ar Imperial Guard (especially Hussar and Titan), the Avengers (especially Sersi), (former) Captain Mar-Vell
Usual base of operations: Now imprisoned (and presumably deactivated) on Chandilar (Shi'ar throneworld)
Former bases of operations: Hala
Current group membership: None
Former group membership: Starforce
Extent of education: Inapplicable

PHYSICAL DESCRIPTION

Height: 8' 2"
Weight: Unrevealed
Eyes: No visible pupils or irises
Hair: None
Other distinguishing features: Supremor is a semi-humanoid android whose head resemble the holographic image of the Kree Supreme Intelligence. Supremor has green artificial skin, four tentacles that emerge from his back, and numerous long thin tendrils emerging from his head.

POWERS AND ABILITIES

Intelligence: Immeasurable
Strength: Unrevealed; possibly incalculable; said to possess the "collective strength of the greatest Kree warriors"
Speed: Superhuman
Stamina: Metahuman
Durability: Metahuman
Agility: Metahuman
Reflexes: Metahuman
Fighting skills: Highly formidable had-to-hand combatant, utilizes Kree methods of armed and unarmed combat, drawing upon knowledge of great Kree warriors contained in Supreme Intelligence's memory
Special skills and abilities: Can draw upon vast knowledge held by Supreme Intelligence
Superhuman physical powers: Aside from those listed above, Supremor has the ability to leap great distances, project unknown energy as concussive bolts from his hands (Supremor did not display this ability during his most recent activation)
Superhuman mental powers: Can greatly extend the tendrils from his head to contact a victim and assimilate his or her intellect and memories, which are then transmitted to the Supreme Intelligence
Special limitations: Presumably cannot function if the Supreme Intelligence is deactivated or destroyed
Source of superhuman powers: Kree technology augmented by the Supreme Intelligence's life force.

PARAPHERNALIA

Costume specifications: Kree fabrics
Personal weaponry: None
Special weaponry: None
Other accessories: None
Transportation: Teleportation devices
Design and manufacture of paraphernalia: Unidentified Kree technicians

BIBLIOGRAPHY

First appearance: CAPTAIN MARVEL #46
Origin issue: Supremor's origin is as yet unrevealed.
Significant issues: CAPTAIN MARVEL #46 (Supremor robots employed by Supreme Intelligence to battle Captain Mar-Vell); CAPTAIN AMERICA #398-399 (reactivated by Supreme Intelligence to serve as first member Kree Starforce; met Shatterax, Korath, and Ultimus on Hala); AVENGERS #346 (alongside Starforce, battled the Avengers, was bested by Sersi); THOR #446/AVENGERS WEST COAST #82 (alongside Starforce, invaded Shi'ar Empire to assassinate Lilandra, battled another contingent of Avengers and Shi'ar Imperial Guard, bested Imperial Guard's Titan, defeated by Hussar and Living Lightning; held prisoner with other members of Starforce on Shi'ar throneworld)

SURTUR

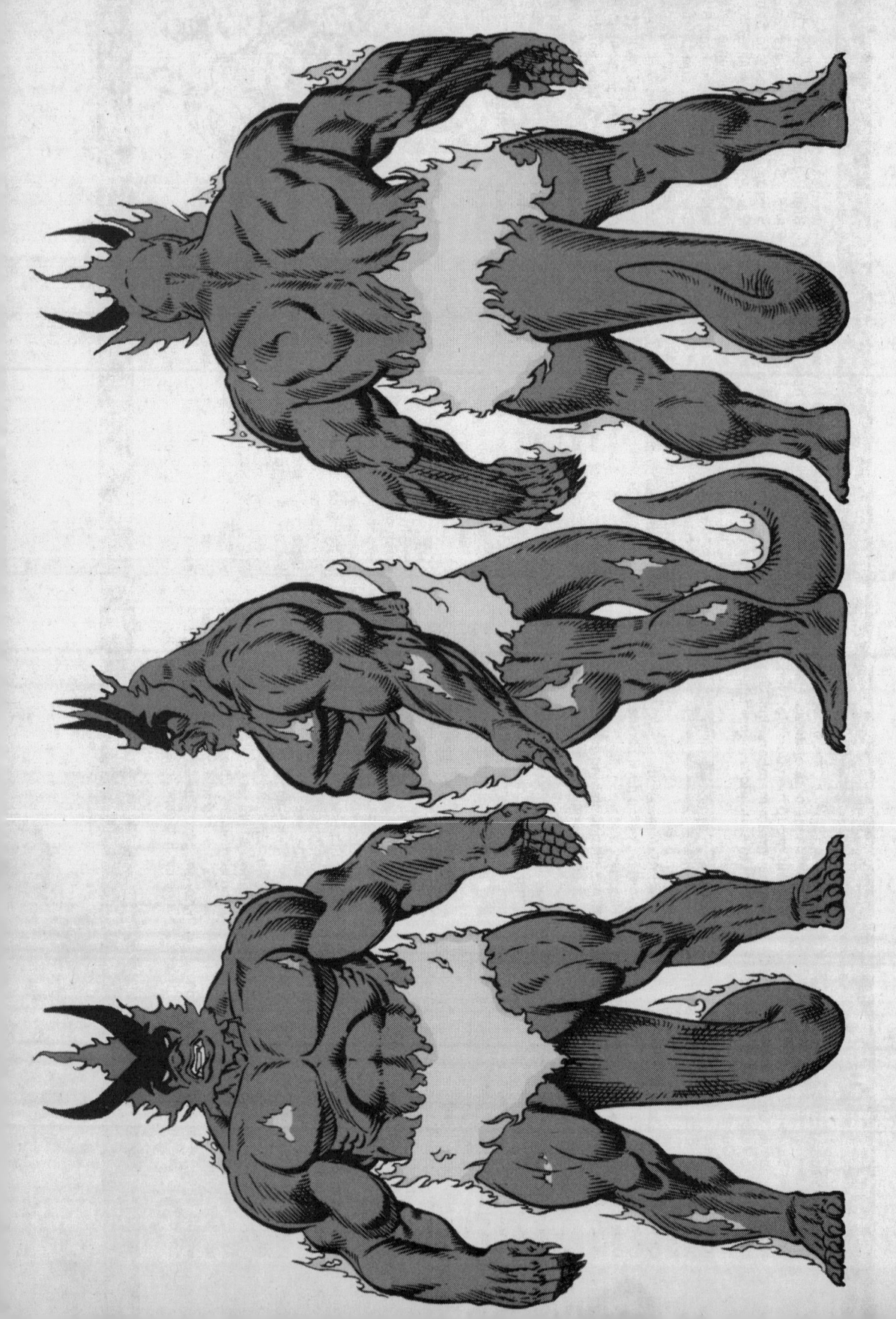

SURTUR

BIOGRAPHICAL DATA

Real name: Surtur
Other current aliases: None
Former aliases: None
Dual identity: None; the general populace of Earth is unaware of Surtur's existence except as a mythological character.
Current occupation: Monarch of Muspelheim, destroyer
Former occupation: None
Citizenship: Realm of Muspelheim, dimension of Asgard
Legal status: Ruler of Muspelheim
Place of creation: Unrevealed, possibly Muspelheim
Marital status: Presumed single
Known relatives: None
Known confidants: None
Known allies: Ymir, Malekith (deceased), Hela
Major enemies: Odin, Thor, gods of Asgard
Usual base of operations: Dimension of Asgard
Former bases of operations: None
Current group membership: None
Former group membership: None
Extent of education: Unrevealed

PHYSICAL DESCRIPTION

Height: Over 1000'
Weight: Unrevealed
Eyes: No visible pupils
Hair: None
Other distinguishing features: Red skin, horns, prehensile tail, body continually sheathed in flame

POWERS AND ABILITIES

Intelligence: Immeasurable
Strength: Incalculable
Speed: Superhuman
Flight speed: Warp speed
Stamina: Immeasurable
Durability: Godlike
Agility: Superhuman
Reflexes: Superhuman

Fighting skills: Master warrior and swordsman, but relies mostly on other powers
Special skills and abilities: Vast knowledge of ancient and arcane wisdom
Superhuman physical powers: Aside from the above listed attributes, Surtur has the ability to manipulate cosmic energy for various effects, including projection of concussive force, generation of intense heat and flame, levitation, molecular manipulation of himself, interdimensional teleportation, and virtual immortality
Superhuman mental powers: Unrevealed
Special limitations: Vulnerable to intense cold, can be imprisoned by certain magical spells or by other beings wielding cosmic energy powers equalling his own
Source of superhuman powers: Manipulations of cosmic energy

PARAPHERNALIA

Costume specifications: None
Personal weaponry: Twilight, also known as the Sword of Doom
Special weaponry: None
Other accessories: None
Transportation: Interdimensional teleportation
Design and manufacture of paraphernalia: Surtur

BIBLIOGRAPHY

First appearance: JOURNEY INTO MYSTERY #97

Origin issue: Surtur's origin is as yet unrevealed

Significant issues: JOURNEY INTO MYSTERY #97 (existence revealed); JOURNEY INTO MYSTERY #99 (battle with Villi, Ve, and Odin and entrapment in Muspelheim at an unknown time in the past recounted); JOURNEY INTO MYSTERY #104 (in modern times, freed by Loki, alongside Skagg the Storm giant, battled thor, Odin and Balder on Earth; imprisoned on an asteroid); AVENGERS #61 (with Ymir the Frost Giant, freed by Sons of Satannish, battled Dr. Strange, Black Knight III, and the Avengers on Earth, returned to Muspelheim); THOR #175-177 (attacked Asgard during Loki's reign, defeated Thor and Asgardian forces, imprisoned by Thor); THOR #337 (escaped Muspelheim through Burning Galaxy); THOR #341-342 (summoned Malekith to attack Earth; killed Odin's raven Huginn); AVENGERS #249/THOR #350 (sent demonic legions to battle Beta Ray Bill, Fantastic Four, Avengers and Asgardian forces on Earth); THOR #351-352 (attacked Asgard); THOR #353 (battled Odin, Thor, and Loki in Asgard; trapped in Muspelheim); THOR #399-400 (escaped Muspelheim through dimension of Death, battled Thor, essence absorbed by Odin); THOR #418 (took possession of Odin, imprisoned Grand Vizier); THOR #425 (battled Ymir in attempt to cause Ragnarok, defeated by Thor wielding Odin's power, imprisoned in Sea of Eternal Night)

SWORDSMAN

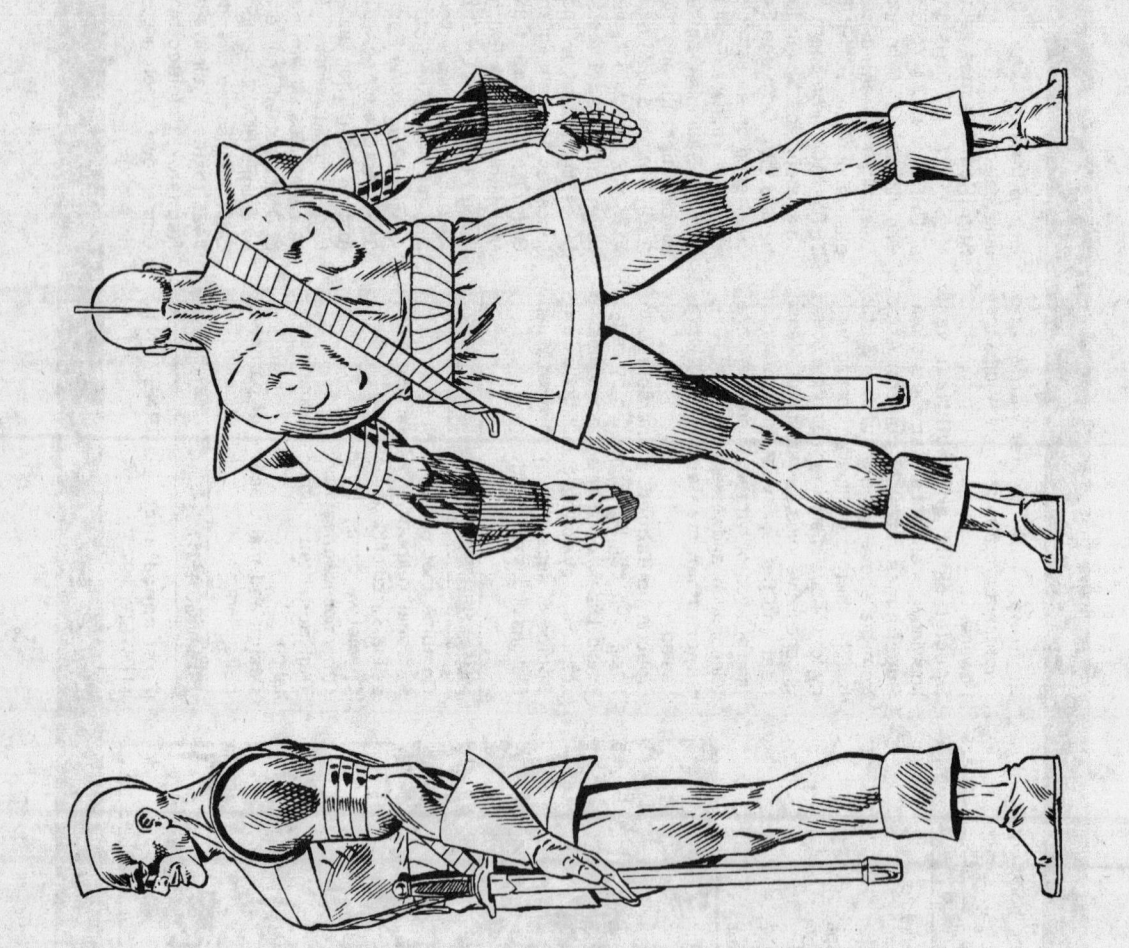

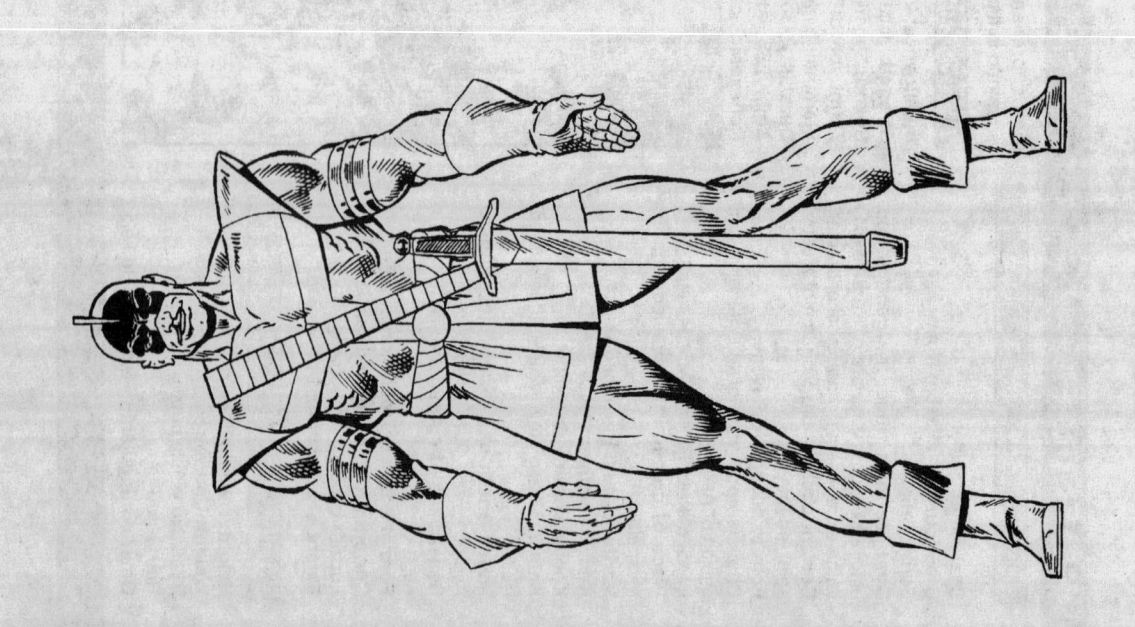

SWORDSMAN I

BIOGRAPHICAL DATA

Real name: Jacques Duquesne
Aliases at time of death: None known
Former aliases: None
Dual identity: Secret, known to Avengers and certain FBI officials
Occupation at time of death: Adventurer
Former occupation: Mercenary, professional criminal, carnival performer
Citizenship: France
Legal status: International criminal record, given a special government pardon in the United States for his services to the Avengers
Place of birth: Unrevealed, presumably France or Sin-Cong
Place of death: Forbidden City, Beijing, People's Republic of China
Cause of death: Struck by lethal energy bolt fired by Kang
Marital status: Unrevealed, presumed single
Known relatives: Crimson Cavalier (alleged relative, presumed deceased), Armand Duquesne (father, deceased)
Known confidants: Mantis
Known allies: Mantis, the Avengers, Pharaoh Rama-Tut; (former) Wong-Chu and the revolutionaries of Sin-Cong, Mandarin, Power Man I, Black Widow, Batroc, Living Laser, Egghead (deceased), Grim Reaper (deceased), Monsieur Khrull
Major enemies: Kang; (former) Wong-Chu, Captain America, Hawkeye, the Avengers

Base of operations at time of death: Avengers Mansion, New York City
Former base of operations: Mobile
Group membership at time of death: The Avengers
Former group membership: The revolutionaries of Sin-Cong; Lethal Legion I
Extent of education: Secondary school

PHYSICAL DESCRIPTION

Height: 6' 4"
Weight: 250 lbs.
Eyes: Blue
Hair: Black
Other distinguishing features: None

POWERS AND ABILITIES

Intelligence: Normal
Strength: Athlete
Speed: Athlete
Stamina: Athlete
Durability: Athlete
Agility: Athlete
Reflexes: Peak human
Fighting skills: Master in the uses of bladed weapons, especially swords. Highly adept at unarmed combat.
Special skills and abilities: Cunning criminal strategist
Superhuman physical powers: None
Superhuman mental powers: None
Special limitations: Recovered alcoholic
Source of superhuman powers: None

PARAPHERNALIA

Costume specifications: Conventional fabric
Personal weaponry: Sword equipped by Mandarin with devices adapted from alien Makluan technology. By pressing one of the buttons on the sword's hilt, the Swordsman could project a concussive force beam, a disintegrating ray, a large jet of flame, electrical energy in a form resembling lightning, or a stream of nerve gas that induced temporary unconsciousness.
Special weaponry: Various throwing knives and daggers as needed
Other accessories: None
Transportation: Avengers quinjet
Design and manufacture of paraphernalia: Unrevealed

BIBLIOGRAPHY

First appearance: AVENGERS #19
Origin issue: AVENGERS SPOTLIGHT #22
Significant issues: AVENGERS #19 (first fought Avengers); AVENGERS #20 (received weapons in sword from Mandarin, joined Avengers as double agent for Mandarin, betrayed Mandarin but was driven from team by Avengers); AVENGERS #29-30 (under Black Widow's leadership, first teamed with Power Man I and fought Avengers); TALES OF SUSPENSE #88 (with Power Man I, fought Captain America as pawns of the Red Skull); AVENGERS ANNUAL #1 (participated in Mandarin's attempt at world conquest); CAPTAIN AMERICA #105 (battled Captain America as a member of Batroc's Brigade); AVENGERS #65 (employed by Egghead, battled Hawkeye in latter's Goliath II persona); AVENGERS #78-79 (with Power Man I, joined Lethal Legion I); AVENGERS #100 (briefly rejoined Avengers in war against Ares in Olympus); AVENGERS #112 (first appeared with Mantis); AVENGERS #114 (rejoined Avengers); AVENGERS #116-118, DEFENDERS #9-10 (participated in Avengers-Defenders war); AVENGERS #129, GIANT-SIZE AVENGERS #2 (tracked captive Avengers to Kang's pyramid lair, confronted Rama-Tut; killed by Kang while shielding Mantis)

Note: The Swordsman's corpse was reanimated by the eldest alien Cotati on Earth, which infused at least a portion of its own consciousness into it. The Swordsman's resurrected body appeared in AVENGERS #131-135 and GIANT-SIZE AVENGERS #4, and after battling the Avengers crumbled to dust in WEST COAST AVENGERS #39

TALISMAN™

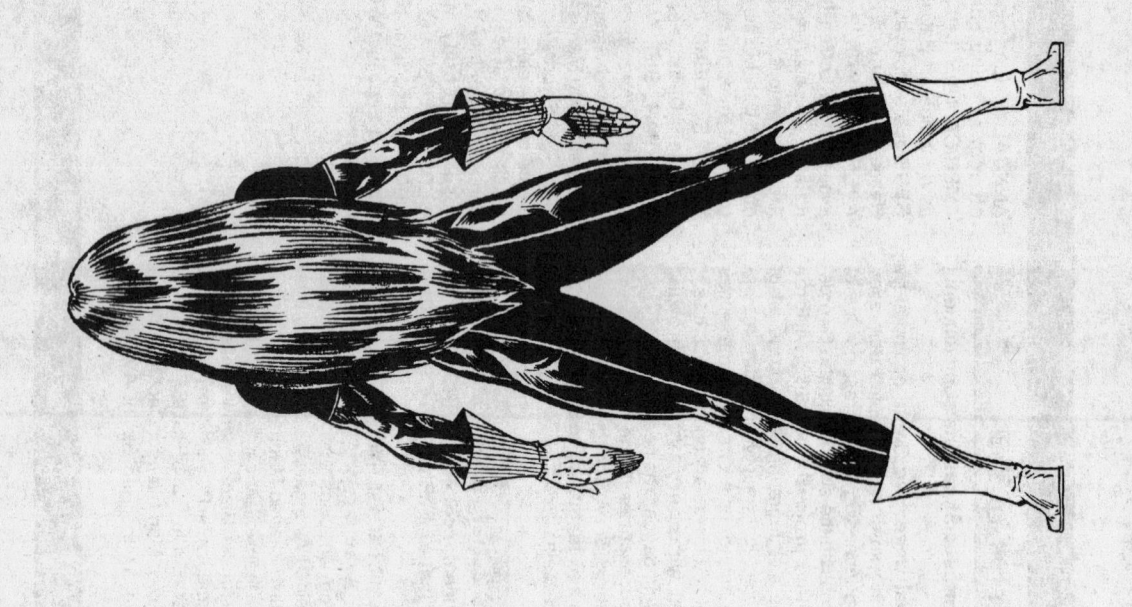

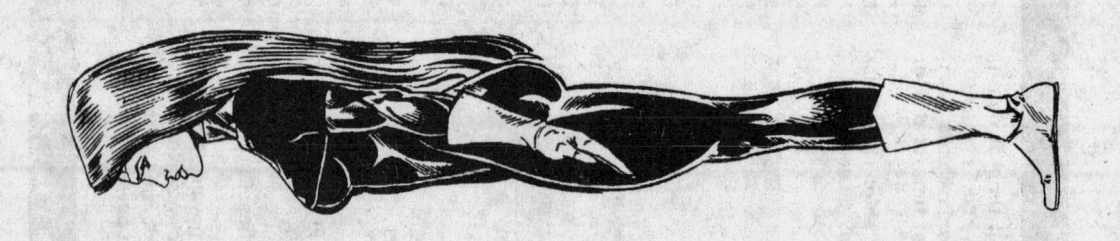

TALISMAN II

BIOGRAPHICAL DATA

Real name: Elizabeth Twoyoungmen
Other current aliases: The Binder of Spirits, the Breaker of Dark Spells, the Promised One
Former aliases: Nahita (in past incarnation)
Dual identity: Publicly known
Current Occupation: Special operative of the Canadian government, assigned to Beta Flight
Former occupation: Art student
Citizenship: Canada
Legal status: No criminal record
Place of birth: Calgary, Alberta, Canada
Marital status: Single
Known relatives: Michael Twoyoungmen (Shaman, father); Kathryn Twoyoungmen (mother, deceased), unnamed great-grandfather (deceased)
Known confidants: Shaman, Heather Hudson
Known allies: Beta Flight, Alpha Flight, Shaman, Doctor Strange, (in past incarnation) Tribe of the Moon
Major enemies: Llan the Sorceror, Ska'r, Pestilence III, Dreamqueen, Ranaq the Devourer, Omega Flight II, (former) Omega Flight I
Usual base of operations: Alpha Flight headquarters, Toronto, Canada
Former bases of operations: Alpha Flight headquarters, Tamarind Island, British Columbia, Canada; Montreal University, Montreal, Canada; Maison Alpha, Edmonton, Canada
Current group membership: Beta Flight
Former group membership: Alpha Flight, (in past incarnation) Tribe of the Moon
Extent of education: College (interrupted)

PHYSICAL DESCRIPTION

Height: 5' 8"
Weight: 132 lbs
Eyes: Brown
Hair: Black
Other distinguishing features: None

POWERS AND ABILITIES

Intelligence: Normal
Strength: Normal
Speed: Normal
Flight speed: Directed motion hovering
Stamina: Normal
Durability: Normal
Agility: Normal
Reflexes: Normal
Fighting skills: Average hand-to-hand combatant, trained in some unarmed combat by Alpha and Beta Flight
Special skills and abilities: Considerable knowledge of the mystic arts of the Sarcee Indians
Superhuman physical powers: Ability to tap into mystical forces and to manipulate them for a wide variety of effects
Superhuman mental powers: Ability to command spirits of the natural world of Canada to do her bidding, ability to perceive various mystical phenomena
Special limitations: Cannot remove her tiara (the "circlet of enchantment") without enduring great pain
Source of superhuman powers: Descent from forty generations of Sarcee shamans, ability to manipulate magic greatly amplified by the circlet of enchantment

PARAPHERNALIA

Costume specifications: Mystically created
Personal weaponry: None
Special weaponry: None
Other accessories: The "circlet of enchantment" (tiara) which enables her to utilize her full mystical potential
Transportation: Flight via mystical levitation; mystical ability to open interdimensional portals; vehicles supplied by the Canadian government
Design and manufacture of paraphernalia: Unrevealed

BIBLIOGRAPHY

First appearance: (as Twoyoungmen) ALPHA FLIGHT #5, (as Talisman) ALPHA FLIGHT #19
Origin issue: ALPHA FLIGHT #5, 19, 83
Significant issues: ALPHA FLIGHT #5 (revealed how, as a child, blamed her father for her mother's death); ALPHA FLIGHT #14 (saw apparition of Ranaq); ALPHA FLIGHT #18-19 (mystical powers triggered by Ranaq, defeated Ranaq, on Shaman's instructions donned tiara and became Talisman); ALPHA FLIGHT #24 (alongside Alpha Flight, fought Great Beasts); ALPHA FLIGHT #26-28 (captured by Omega Flight I, became trapped in the void within Shaman's mystic pouch, rescued by Beyonder, quit Alpha Flight); ALPHA FLIGHT #35, 37-38 (presided over testing of Shaman; captured by Pestilence III, who removed her tiara; tiara was donned by Shaman, who thus became Talisman III, Elizabeth was reconciled with him); ALPHA FLIGHT #67-70 (sent dream by Snowbird about Dream Queen, learned she still had her powers; took back tiara, became Talisman again; aided Alpha Flight against Dream Queen); ALPHA FLIGHT #71-72 (first fought Llan the Sorceror); ALPHA FLIGHT #74-75 (with Alpha Flight, fought illusory "super heroes" on Dream Queen's world); ALPHA FLIGHT #76 (exorcised demon serving Llan from child); ALPHA FLIGHT #81-82 (brought together Aurora, Purple Girl, Laura Dean, and Goblyn to find Northstar); ALPHA FLIGHT #83 (spirit traveled back in time to learn about her past incarnation as Nahita and her first defeat of Llan); ALPHA FLIGHT #85-86 (defeated Llan with the aid of Dr. Strange and Alpha and Gamma Flights); ALPHA FLIGHT #110, 112 (attacked and injured by Omega Flight II, forced to release the Ska'r; directed Gamma Flight in defeating the Ska'r, joined new Beta Flight)

TALON ™

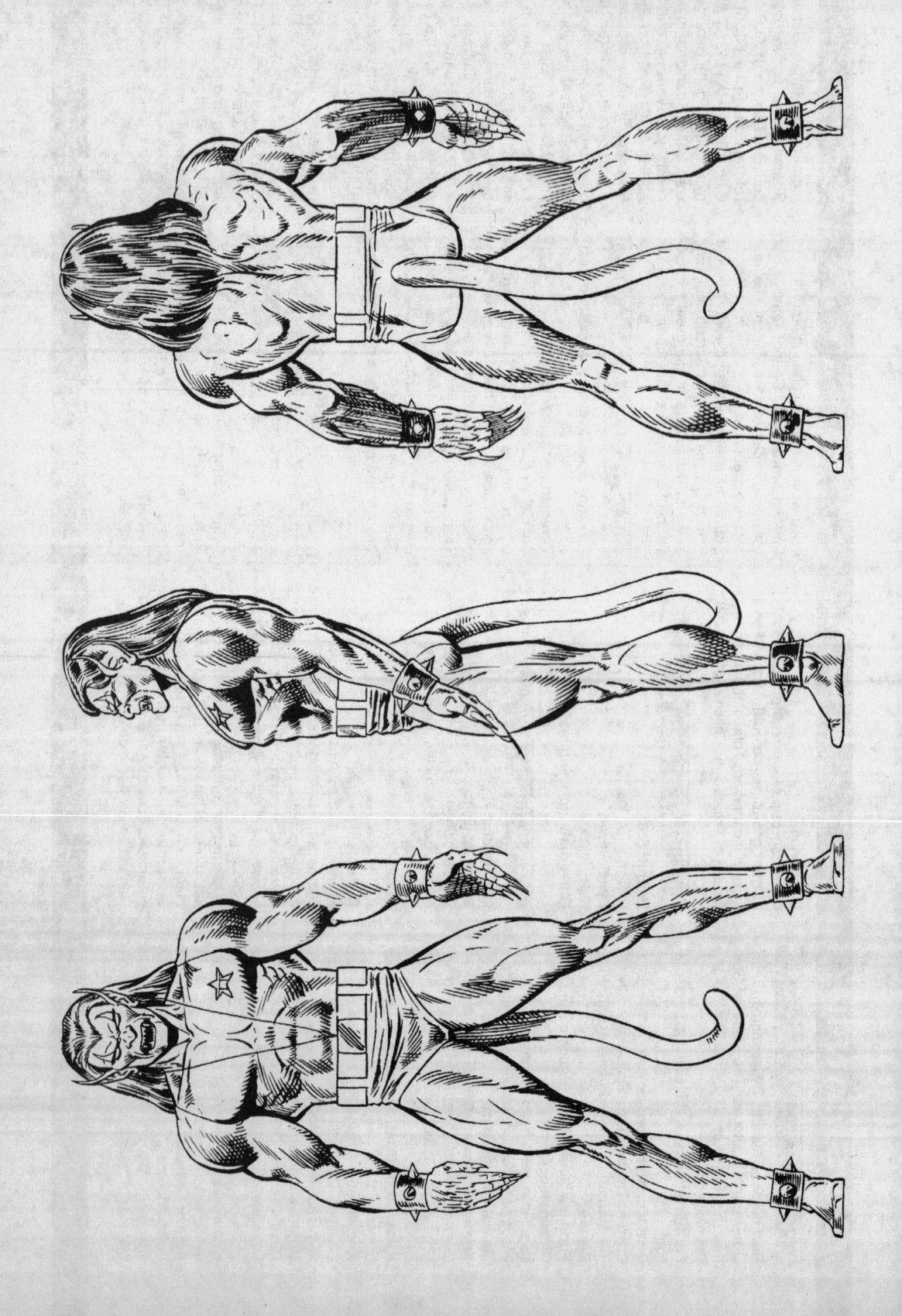

TALON

BIOGRAPHICAL DATA

Real name: Unrevealed
Other current aliases: None
Former aliases: None
Dual identity: None; the general populace of 20th Century Earth is unaware of Talon's existence.
Current occupation: Adventurer
Former occupation: Student of the mystic arts, apprentice to Krugarr
Citizenship: City of Attilan, the blue area of Earth's moon
Legal status: No criminal record
Place of birth: City of Attilan, the blue area of Earth's moon, circa 31st Century A.D. in an alternate future
Marital status: Single
Known relatives: None
Known confidants: None
Known allies: The Guardians of the Galaxy, Krugarr, Dr. Strange, Commandeers, Silver Surfer, Firelord, the Inhumans
Major enemies: The Punishers, Rancor, Galactus, The Brotherhood of the Badoon Empire
Usual base of operations: Mobile throughout the Milky Way Galaxy aboard the starship Captain America II, New York City area circa 31st Century A.D.
Former bases of operations: Inhumans reservation beneath City of Attilan
Current group membership: Guardians of the Galaxy
Former group membership: None
Extent of education: Unrevealed

PHYSICAL DESCRIPTION

Height: 5'8"
Weight: 165 lbs.
Eyes: Green
Hair: Black
Other distinguishing features: Orange fur-covered body, razor-sharp talons on hands and feet, pointed ears, pronounced canine teeth, 3 1/2' prehensile tail

POWERS AND ABILITIES

Intelligence: Normal
Strength: Superhuman Class 10
Speed: Enhanced human
Stamina: Enhanced human
Durability: Enhanced human
Agility: Enhanced human
Reflexes: Enhanced human
Fighting skills: Highly skilled hand-to-hand combatant
Special skills and abilities: Olympic-level acrobat and gymnast, limited knowledge of magical lore
Superhuman physical powers: Aside from the above listed attribute, Talon possesses razor-sharp talons on hands and feet which can be detached and hurled as weapons, then regrow instantly; limited ability to manipulate the forces of magic for a number of effects, as yet unrevealed
Superhuman mental powers: Unrevealed, if any
Special limitations: Like all Inhumans, Talon's immune system is probably weaker than that of an average human.
Source of superhuman powers: Genetically superior Inhuman physiology, possibly exposed to the mutagenic Terrigen Mist

PARAPHERNALIA

Costume specifications: Alien materials
Personal weaponry: None
Special weaponry: None
Other accessories: None
Transportation: The starship Captain America II
Design and manufacture of paraphernalia: Unrevealed

BIBLIOGRAPHY

First appearance: GUARDIANS OF THE GALAXY #18
Origin issue: GUARDIANS OF THE GALAXY #27
Significant issues: GUARDIANS OF THE GALAXY #18-20 (deflected shot fired at Vance Astro, sent Krugarr to save Vance's life: alongside the Guardians of the Galaxy and the Commandeers, battled the Punishers; joined the Guardians); GUARDIANS OF THE GALAXY #21-23 (alongside the Guardians, battled Rancor and her lieutenants); GUARDIANS OF THE GALAXY #24-25 (alongside the Guardians, Silver Surfer, and Firelord, battled Galactus); GUARDIANS OF THE GALAXY #26 (with Nikki, learned the origin of the Guardians); GUARDIANS OF THE GALAXY #27 (alongside the Guardians, journeyed to the 20th Century; developed Gral's Disease, revealed to be an Inhuman, first encountered 20th Century Inhumans); GUARDIANS OF THE GALAXY #28-29 (alongside the Guardians, battled Masters of Evil V); GUARDIANS OF THE GALAXY #30-33 (alongside Charlie-27 and Nikki, attacked the Badoon homeworld)

TAMARA RAHN

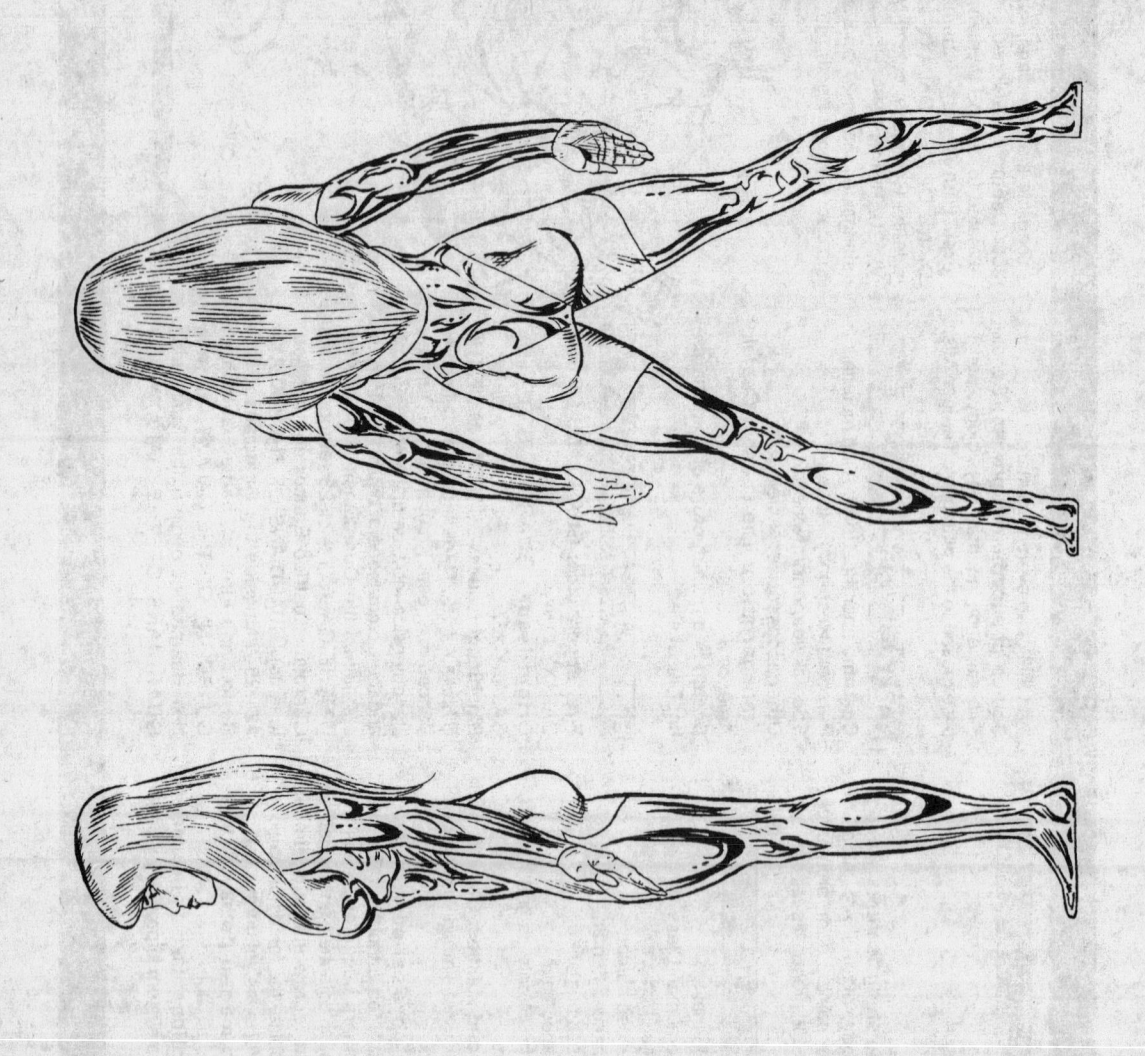

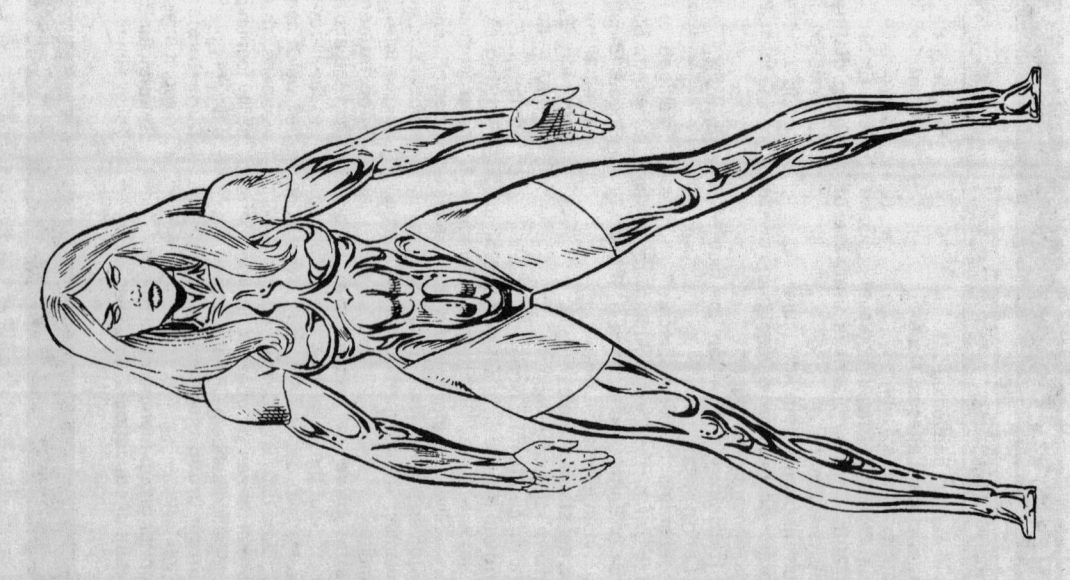

RAHN, TAMARA

BIOGRAPHICAL DATA

Real name: Tamara Rahn
Other current aliases: None
Former aliases: Tamara of the Sisterhood
Dual identity: None; the general populace of earth is unaware of Tamara Rahn's existence.
Current occupation: Unrevealed
Former occupation: Unrevealed
Citizenship: Atlantis, (formerly) Planet Laab
Legal status: No criminal record
Place of birth: Planet Laab (now destroyed)
Marital status: Single
Known relatives: None
Known confidants: Namor the Sub-Mariner, Namorita
Known allies: Namor the Sub-Mariner, Namorita, Lord Vashti, the Atlanteans, Avengers, Tiger Shark, (former) Doctor Doom
Major enemies: Attuma, the Faceless Ones, the Nereid, Suma-Ket, (former) Namor, Lord Vashti, the Atlanteans, Dr. hydro (deceased), Dr. Dorcas (deceased), Tiger Shark
Usual base of operations: Atlantis, mobile in Atlantic Ocean
Former bases of operations: Planet Laab, Hydro-Base
Current group membership: None
Former group membership: None
Extent of education: Unrevealed

PHYSICAL DESCRIPTION

Height: 5' 4"
Weight: 245 lbs.
Eyes: Red
Hair: Blonde
Other distinguishing features: Red skin, gills

POWERS AND ABILITIES

Intelligence: Normal
Strength: (on Laab) Enhanced human, (on Earth) Superhuman Class 25, (in water) Superhuman Class 50
Speed: Peak human
Water speed: Superhuman
Stamina: Athlete, (in water) Superhuman
Durability: Superhuman
Agility: Peak human, (in water) Superhuman
Reflexes: Athlete, (in water) Superhuman
Fighting skills: Excellent hand-to-hand combatant, trained in Atlantean forms of armed and unarmed combat
Special skills and abilities: Speaks English, Atlantean, and Lemurian; highly skilled business executive
Superhuman physical powers: Aside from the above listed attributes, the ability to survive underwater for indefinite periods, and specially developed vision which gives him the ability to see clearly in the murky depths of the ocean.
Superhuman mental powers: None
Special limitations: Inability to breathe out of water for more than a few minutes without artificial aid
Source of superhuman powers: Alien physiology

PARAPHERNALIA

Costume specifications: Atlantean materials
Personal weaponry: None
Special weaponry: None
Other accessories: None
Transportation: Swimming.
Design and manufacture of paraphernalia: Inapplicable

BIBLIOGRAPHY

First appearance: SUB-MARINER #58
Origin issue: Tamara Rahn's origin is as yet unrevealed.
Significant issues: SUB-MARINER #56 (behind the scenes, arrived on Earth as a stowaway on her people's spacecraft, witnessed deaths of her race at the hands of the Atlanteans); SUB-MARINER #58 (sought vengeance against the Atlanteans, foiled by namor the Sub-Mariner, forgiven and befriended by Namor and Vashti, made honorary Atlantean citizen); SUB-MARINER #59-60 (captured by surface men, freed during Atlantean invasion); SUB-MARINER #62 (with Namor the Sub-Mariner and Namorita, freed the Hydro-base amphibians from Dr. Hydro); SUPER-VILLAIN TEAM-UP #3 (with Namorita and Hydrobase amphibians, held captive by Dr. Dorcas, Tiger Shark, and Attuma; freed by Namor and Dr. Doom); SUPER-VILLAIN TEAM-UP #9/AVENGERS #155-156 (alongside the Avengers, Namor, and Dr. Doom, battled Attuma); NAMOR THE SUB-MARINER #34 (helped Tiger Shark battle the Faceless Ones); NAMOR THE SUB-MARINER #35 (brought Tiger Shark to Atlantis); NAMOR THE SUB-MARINER #36 (saved Tiger Shark from the Nereid); NAMOR THE SUB-MARINER #37-40 (alongside Namor, Tiger Shark, and Atlanteans, battled Suma-Ket)

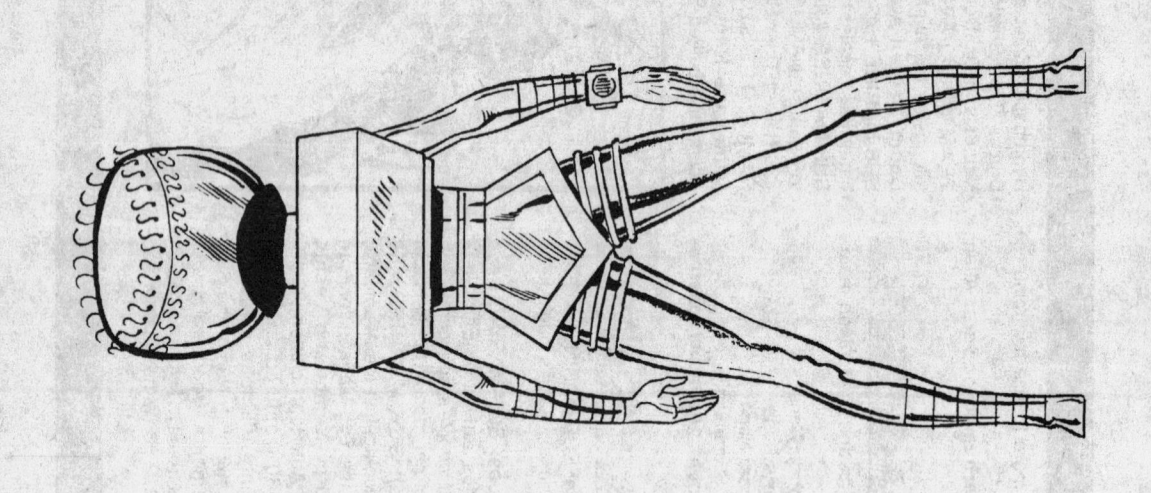

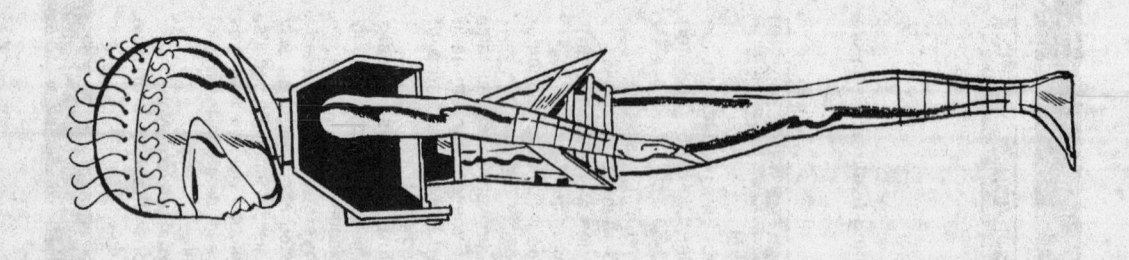

TANA NILE

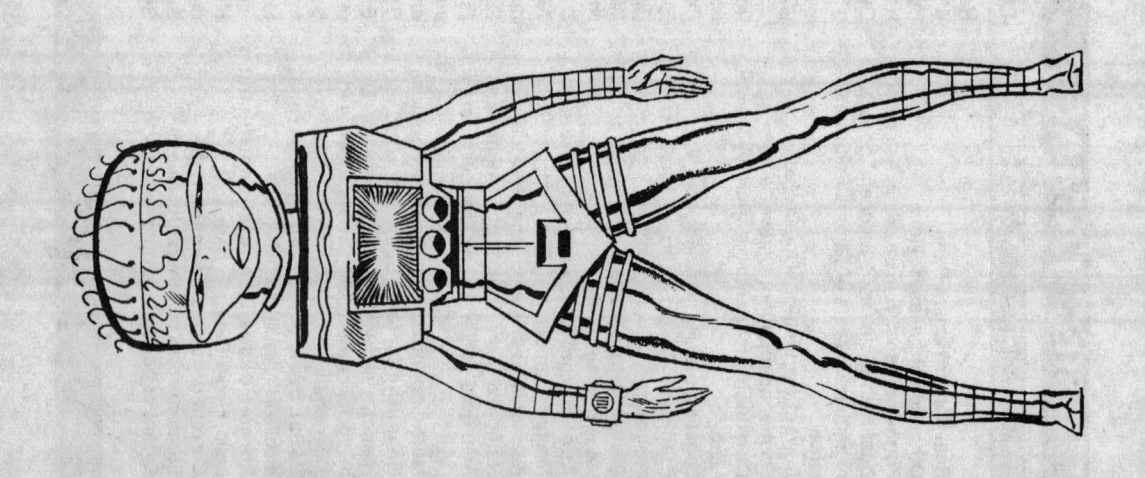

TANA NILE

BIOGRAPHICAL DATA

Real name: Tana Nile
Other current aliases: None known
Former aliases: None known
Dual identity: Tana Nile adopts human form when on Earth, and the general populace of Earth is unaware that she is an alien.
Current occupation: Colonizer
Former occupation: None known
Citizenship: Rigel
Legal status: None on Earth, no criminal record on Rigel
Place of birth: Rigel-3
Marital status: Single (as far as is known, but apparently engaged to Grand Commissioner of Rigel)
Known relatives: None
Known confidants: Silas Grant
Known allies: Thor, Balder, Sif, Hildegarde, Silas Grant
Major enemies: (formerly) Thor, (currently) Ego-Prime
Usual base of operations: Command Planet Rigel II
Former bases of operations: Rigel-3, New York City, Blackworld
Current group membership: Colonizers of Rigel
Former group membership: None
Extent of education: Equivalent of graduate school education on Rigel-3

PHYSICAL DESCRIPTION

Height: 5' 4"
Weight: 110 lbs.
Eyes: Blue
Hair: Black
Other distinguishing features: None

POWERS AND ABILITIES

Intelligence: Normal
Strength: (usually) Normal, (with increased density) Superhuman Class 10
Speed: Normal
Stamina: Normal
Durability: (usually) Normal, (with increased density) Superhuman
Agility: Normal
Reflexes: Normal
Fighting skills: Good hand to hand combatant, trained in Rigellian martial arts
Special skills and abilities: Highly skilled in infiltration of alien races and in terraforming planets
Superhuman physical powers: Ability to increase her own density at will, increasing her strength and resistance to physical injury
Superhuman mental powers: Psionic ability to control the mind of another humanoid or to override another humanoid's control of his or her voluntary muscles (through "mind thrust")
Special limitations: None known
Source of superhuman powers: Alien attributes of the of the Rigellian race

PARAPHERNALIA

Costume specifications: Body armor of unknown composition, includes devices enabling Tana Nile to rearrange the molecular structure of her body and clothing in order to disguise herself as an Earthwoman
Personal weaponry: "Stasis gun" that can project concussive energy or intense heat
Special weaponry: None
Other accessories: Solar beam communicator device, worn on wrist, permitting instantaneous communication between Earth and Rigel via hyperspace transmission
Transportation: Warp-drive starships
Design and manufacture of paraphernalia: Rigellian technology

BIBLIOGRAPHY

First appearance: (disguised as Earthwoman); THOR #129, (in true form) THOR #130
Origin issue: Tana Nile's origin is as yet unrevealed.
Significant issues: THOR #129 (first appeared in human form as Jane Foster's roommate); THOR #130 (took control of Jane Foster's will, first appeared in true Rigellian form); THOR #133 (attempted to take control of Earth, was ordered by Rigellians to cease attempt to colonize Earth); THOR #134 (left Earth to be given new assignment, was told that the High Commissioner of Rigel had chosen her to be his wife); THOR #160 (encountered Thor during his second journey into the Black Galaxy); THOR #198 (encountered Sif, Hildegarde, and sailor Silas Grant on Blackworld planet while she fought Ego-Prime); THOR #201 (revealed that Ego-Prime was a slab that she had removed from Ego the Living Planet and had taken to Blackworld in order to transform it into a habitable world, but that Ego-Prime had proved to be uncontrollable; Blackworld destroyed in nuclear war; Tana Nile and allies arrive on Earth, pursued by Ego-Prime); THOR #202-203 (aided by Silas Grant in clashes with Ego-Prime's monsters); THOR #204 (assumed human form in order to live on Earth); THOR #211 (aided Thor in battling trolls); THOR #212 (first visited Asgard); THOR #213 (captured by Sssthgar, freed by Thor, released Odin, Hogun, and Fandral from captivity); THOR #214 (accompanied Thor to Dark Nebula to help rescue Sif and Karnilla); THOR #217 (returned to Asgard); THOR #218 (accompanied Thor to Rigel-3, witnessed destruction of Rigel-3 by Rhunians, reunited with Grand Commissioner); THOR #220 (accompanied Thor to Rhun); THOR #221 (bade farewell to Thor, Silas Grant announces he will stay with his "good friend" Tana)

TARANTULA

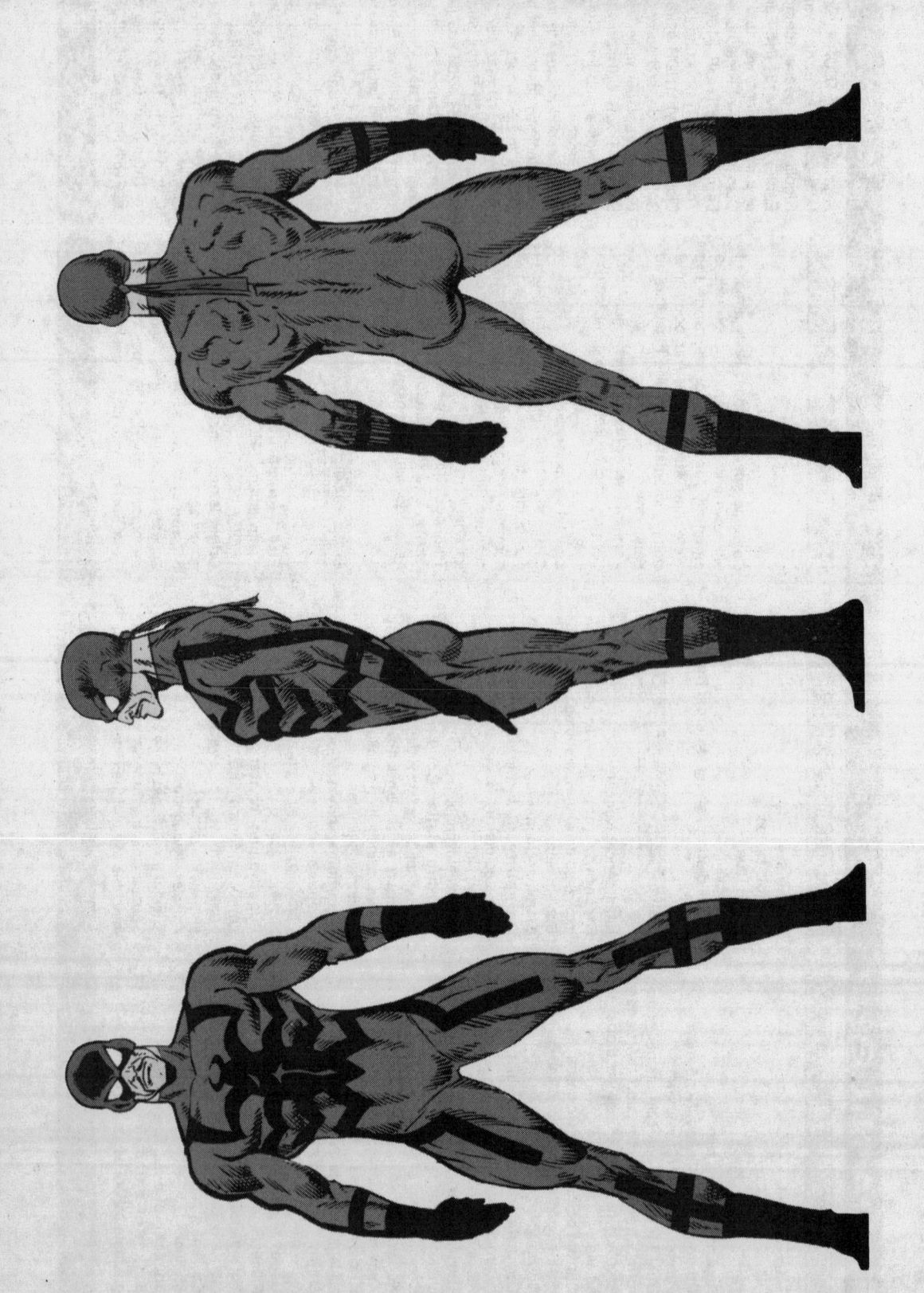

TARANTULA

BIOGRAPHICAL DATA

Real names: (I) Anton Miguel Rodriguez, (II) Luis Alvarez

Other current aliases: (II) La Tarantula

Former aliases: (I) Mr. Valdez, (II) El Arana

Dual identities: (I) Publicly known, (II) Known to certain officials in Delvadia and the United States

Occupation at time of death: (I) Professional criminal

Current occupation: (II) Special operative of the Delvadian government, mercenary

Former occupations: (I) Revolutionary terrorist, government operative, (II) Captain in the Delvadian army

Citizenship: (both) Delvadia, a small South American republic

Legal status: (I) International criminal record, (II) Criminal record in the U.S.

Place of births: (I) Somewhere in Delvadia, (II) San Palo, Delvadia

Place of death: (I) New York City

Cause of death: (I) Suicide by jumping off a building into a hail of police gunfire while in a mutated state

Marital status: (both) Single

Known relatives: (I) Hidalgo Rodriguez (brother); (II) None

Known confidants: (both) None

Known allies: (I) Lightmaster, Kraven, the Jackal and Senor Suerte II, (II) Captain America VI, the Punisher, the Chameleon, the Scorpion, the Femme Fatales

Major enemies: (I) Spider-Man, the Punisher, Captain America, the Will O' The Wisp; (II) Spider-Man, the Black Cat, Batroc the Leaper

Usual base of operations: (I) New York City, (II) Mobile

Former bases of operations: (I) Delvadia; Miami Beach, Florida; (II) Delvadia; New York City

Current group membership: (both) None

Former group membership: (I) Employee of the Brand Corporation, (II) Captain in the Delvadian militia

Extent of education: (both) Educated in military school

PHYSICAL DESCRIPTION

Height: (I) 6'1", (II) 6'2"
Weight: (I) 185 lbs, (II) 190 lbs.
Eyes: (I) Brown, (II) Blue
Hair: (both) Black
Other distinguishing features: None

POWERS AND ABILITIES

Intelligence: (both) Normal
Strength: (I) Athlete; (II) Peak human
Speed: (I) Normal, (in his prime) Athlete; (II) Normal
Stamina: (I) Athlete; (II) Peak human
Durability: (both) Athlete
Agility: (I) Athlete; (II) Peak human
Reflexes: (I) Athlete; (II) Peak human
Fighting skills: (both) Excellent hand-to-hand combatants, skilled in various martial arts, but particularly in kick-boxing.

Special skills: (both) None known

Superhuman physical powers: (I) Mutated into a giant spider, the Tarantula possessed Superhuman Class 10 strength and could spin webbing as a real spider can, (II) None

Superhuman mental powers: (both) None

Special limitations: (both) None

Source of superhuman powers: (I) The Brand Corporation's mutagenic serum, (II) Dr. Karl Mendoza's formula

PARAPHERNALIA

Costume specifications: Synthetic stretch fabric

Personal weaponry: Retractable blades in boots, and retractable spikes in gloves, anointed with harmful or lethal drugs and poisons

Special weaponry: Both Tarantulas armed themselves at times with standard firearms.

Other accessories: None

Transportation: Conventional

Design and manufacture of paraphernalia: Delvadian government

BIBLIOGRAPHY

First appearance: (I) AMAZING SPIDER-MAN #134; (II) WEB OF SPIDER-MAN #35

Origin issue: AMAZING SPIDER-MAN #135; (II) WEB OF SPIDER-MAN #36

Significant issues: AMAZING SPIDER-MAN #134-135 (I: hijacked a Hudson River dayliner to rob the passengers and hold them for ransom; plan disrupted by Spider-Man and the Punisher); AMAZING SPIDER-MAN #147-148 (escaped prison with help of the Jackal, who sought revenge on Spider-Man; defeated by Spider-Man); SPECTACULAR SPIDER-MAN #1-2 (hired by Lightmaster to assist Kraven the Hunter in commiting various kidnapings and murders; again thwarted by Spider-Man); CAPTAIN AMERICA #224 (joined forces with Senor Suerte II to steal "Mad-bombs" and use them for extortion; defeated by Captain America); AMAZING SPIDER-MAN #233-236 (hired by Brand Corporation to silence an informer, thwarted by Spider-Man; injected with Mutagenic serum to grant him superhuman powers, but the Will O' The Wisp affected the process transforming Tarantula into a humanoid spider; battled Will O' The Wisp and Spider-Man, fell into Jamaica Bay; survived plunge, but continued to mutate, battled Spider atop building, horrified at what he had become, committed suicide); WEB OF SPIDER-MAN #35-36 (Luis Alvarez chosen to be Tarantula II by Delvadian government officials, underwent mutagenic treatment); SPECTACULAR SPIDER-MAN #137 (sent to the United States by Delvadian government to eliminate political refugees from that country and to avenge the original Tarantula by killing Spider-Man, defeated by him); PUNISHER #68-72 (battled Punisher, Batroc)

TASKMASTER

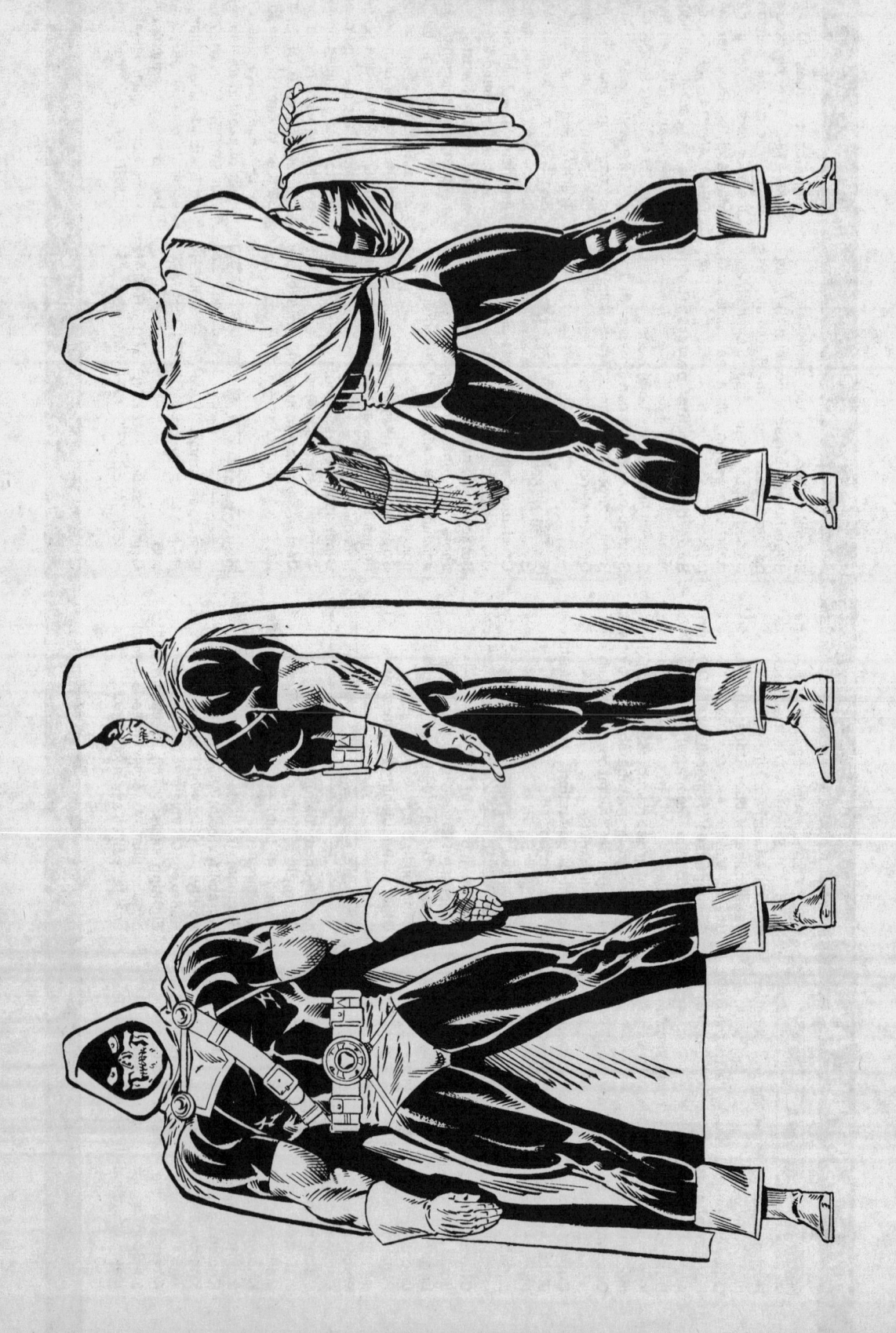

TASKMASTER

BIOGRAPHICAL DATA

Real name: Unrevealed
Other current aliases: None
Former aliases: None
Dual identity: Known to the authorities
Current occupation: Professional criminal, combat instructor
Former occupation: Unrevealed
Citizenship: United States of America
Legal status: Criminal record in the United States
Place of birth: Bronx, New York
Marital status: Unrevealed
Known relatives: None
Known confidants: None
Known allies: Black Abbott, Justin Hammer (employers)
Major enemies: The Avengers, Ant-Man II, Spider-Man, Hawkeye, the Thing, Nomad III, Daredevil, the Punisher
Usual base of operations: Mobile
Former bases of operations: The Solomon Institute for the Criminally Insane, Southampton, Long Island; a warehouse on Manhattan's Lower West Side; the Carson Carnival of Traveling Wonders; a traveling circus; a derelict graveyard in Brooklyn; an estate in Apple Valley, California
Current group membership: None
Former group membership: None
Extent of education: Unrevealed

PHYSICAL DESCRIPTION

Height: 6'2"
Weight: 220 lbs.
Eyes: Unrevealed
Hair: Unrevealed
Other distinguishing features: None

POWERS AND ABILITIES

Intelligence: Gifted
Strength: Athlete
Speed: Athlete
Stamina: Athlete
Durability: Athlete
Agility: Athlete
Reflexes: Athlete
Fighting skills: Skilled in all present-day and many historical martial arts, boxing, wrestling, swordsmanship, archery, marksmanship, gymnastics and aerial acrobatics
Special skills and abilities: "Photographic reflexes" enable him to duplicate without practice the physical movements of others
Superhuman physical powers: None
Superhuman mental powers: None
Special limitations: None
Source of superhuman powers: None

PARAPHERNALIA

Costume specifications: Leather and synthetic stretch fabric
Personal weaponry: A throwing shield, a multi-purpose billy club, a bow and trick arrows, a .45 caliber Colt automatic, and a 36-inch sword
Special weaponry: None
Other accessories: None
Transportation: Various
Design and manufacture of paraphernalia: Unrevealed

BIBLIOGRAPHY

First appearance: AVENGERS #195
Origin issue: AVENGERS #196
Significant issues: AVENGERS #195 (revealed to have set up series of criminal training academies, including one using Solomon Institute for the Criminally Insane as a front; captured Yellowjacket, Wasp, and Ant-Man II when they invaded the premises); AVENGERS #196 (origin recounted; discovered "photographic reflex" ability, decided to use it for crime as a trainer of criminal henchmen; battled the Avengers, who exposed his front operation; escaped); MARVEL TEAM-UP #103 (established new training academy in Manhattan, battled Spider-Man and Ant-Man II, escaped); AVENGERS #222 (used traveling carnival as mobile base, battled Hawkeye and Ant-Man II, escaped); MARVEL TEAM-UP #146 (trained henchmen for the Black Abbott; alongside Black Abbott, battled Spider-Man and Nomad III; escaped); THE THING #26 (used another circus as base, battled the Thing and Vance (Marvel Boy) Astrovik, captured by the U.S. Secret Service); CAPTAIN AMERICA #334 (used by governmental Commission on Superhuman Activities to train John Walker in use of Captain America's shield); AMAZING SPIDER-MAN #308 (having escaped the authorities, set up base in derelict graveyard in Brooklyn, battled Spider-Man, escaped); DAREDEVIL #292-293 (competed in contest against Tombstone, battled Daredevil and Punisher)

TATTERDEMALION™

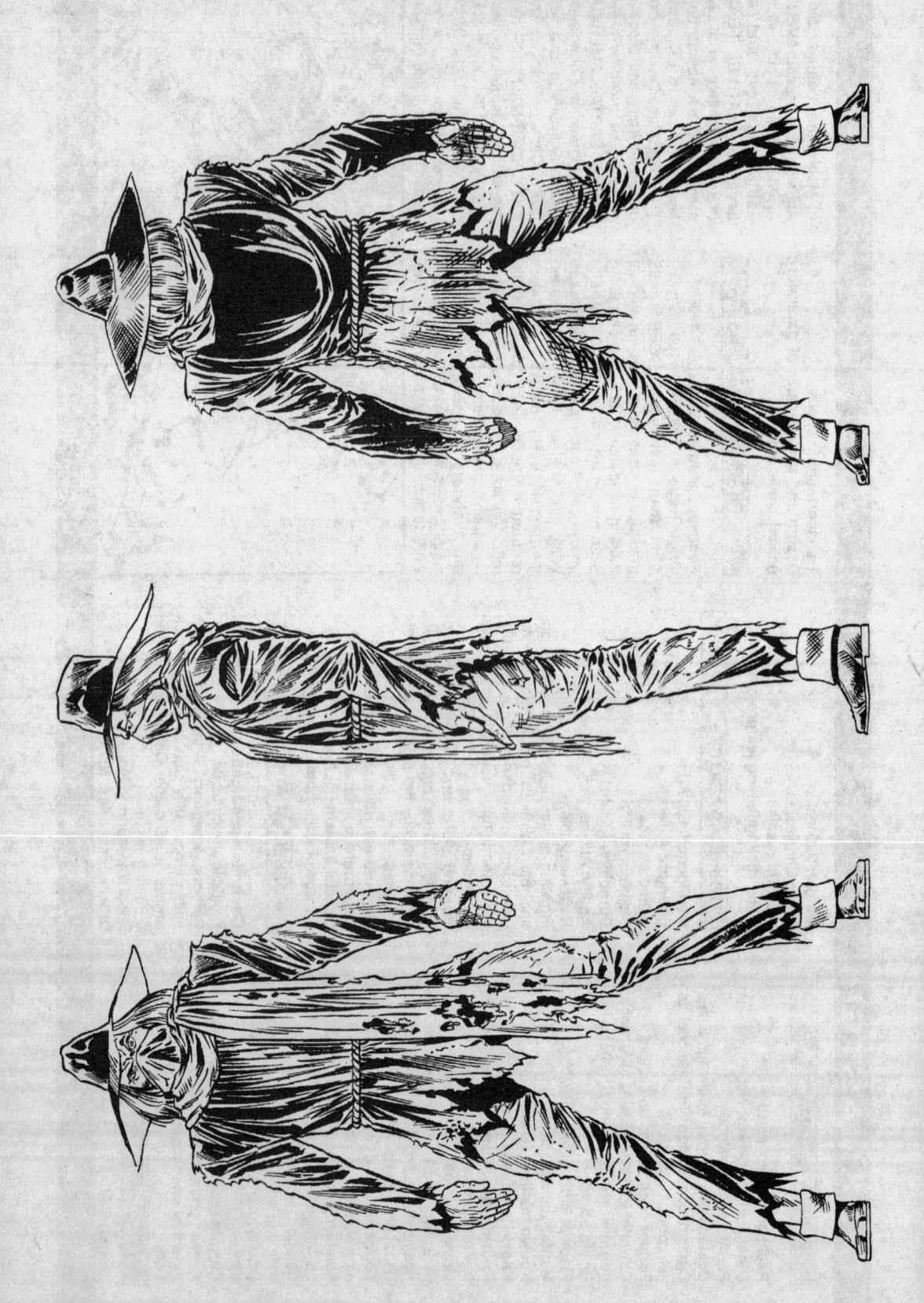

TATTERDEMALION

BIOGRAPHICAL DATA

Real name: Arnold Paffenroth
Other current aliases: None
Former aliases: Michael Wyatt
Dual identity: Secret
Current occupation: Professional criminal
Former occupation: Tap-dancer, actor
Citizenship: United States of America
Legal status: Criminal record in the U.S.
Place of birth: Las Vegas, Nevada
Marital status: Divorced
Known relatives: None
Known confidants: None
Known allies: The Night Shift (Shroud, Werewolf, Dansen Macabre, Gypsy Moth, Brothers Grimm II, Misfit, Needle, Digger, Ticktock), Hangman II, Satannish
Major enemies: Spider-Man, Dazzler, Ghost Rider I, Locksmith, Dazzler, Avengers West Coast, (formerly) Werewolf, Ticktock
Usual base of operations: Several bases in Los Angeles, California
Former bases of operations: Las Vegas, Nevada
Current group membership: The Night Shift
Former group membership: None
Extent of education: High school graduate

PHYSICAL DESCRIPTION

Height: 5' 9"
Weight: 165 lbs.
Eyes: Blue
Hair: Brown
Other distinguishing features: Due to his lack of hygienic habits, the Tatterdemalion emits a harsh offensive odor at all times.

POWERS AND ABILITIES

Intelligence: Below normal
Strength: Athlete, (enhanced by Satannish) Peak human
Speed: Athlete, (enhanced by Satannish) Peak human
Stamina: Athlete, (enhanced by Satannish) Peak human
Durability: Athlete, (enhanced by Satannish) Peak human
Agility: Athlete, (enhanced by Satannish) Peak human
Reflexes: Athlete, (enhanced by Satannish) Peak human
Fighting skills: Good hand-to-hand combatant
Special skills and abilities: Expert tap-dancer
Superhuman physical powers: None
Superhuman mental powers: None
Special limitations: The Tatterdemalion is mentally disturbed.
Source of superhuman powers: Inapplicable

PARAPHERNALIA

Costume specifications: Kevlar body armor under several layers of ordinary fabric, coated with special greasy substance which makes him difficult to hold (enhanced by Satannish), the Tatterdemalion's greasy coating now renders him impossible to hold)
Personal weaponry: Specially designed gloves treated with solvent which dissolves paper and fabrics (enhanced by Satannish, the Tatterdemalion's solvent is now strong enough to pain the normally invulnerable Wonder Man), long weighted scarf (enhanced by Satannish, the Tatterdemalion's scarf is now strong enough to be used to choke Wonder Man)
Special weaponry: Cloak containing chloroform gas capsules
Other accessories: None
Transportation: Usually on foot
Design and manufacture of paraphernalia: Unknown designers employed by the Committee

BIBLIOGRAPHY

First appearance: (unnamed) WEREWOLF BY NIGHT #9, (named) MARVEL TEAM-UP #93
Origin issue: DAZZLER #36
Significant issues: WEREWOLF BY NIGHT #9 (with an army of derelicts, hired by Sidney Sarnak on behalf of the Committee; battled Werewolf); MARVEL TEAM-UP #93 (outfitted by the Committee, began attacking the wealthy, battled Werewolf and Spider-Man); GHOST RIDER Vol. 2 #55 (battled Werewolf and Ghost Rider I); SPIDER-WOMAN #50 (with other superhuman adventurers and criminals, imprisoned by Locksmith, freed by Spider-Woman I); DAZZLER #36 (attempted to stimulate career of Julia Walker, his former dance partner, by terrorism; battled Dazzler); CAPTAIN AMERICA #330-331 (joined the Night Shift, teamed with Captain America against the Power Broker and his augmented mutates); SOLO AVENGERS #3 (alongside Night Shift, tested Moon Knight to take over as leader of Night Shift); WEST COAST AVENGERS Vol. 2 #40 (alongside Night Shift, battled West Coast Avengers); AVENGERS WEST COAST #76-79 (alongside Night Shift, Hangman II, and Satannish, battled Avengers West Coast; abilities enhanced by Satannish's black magic)

TAURUS

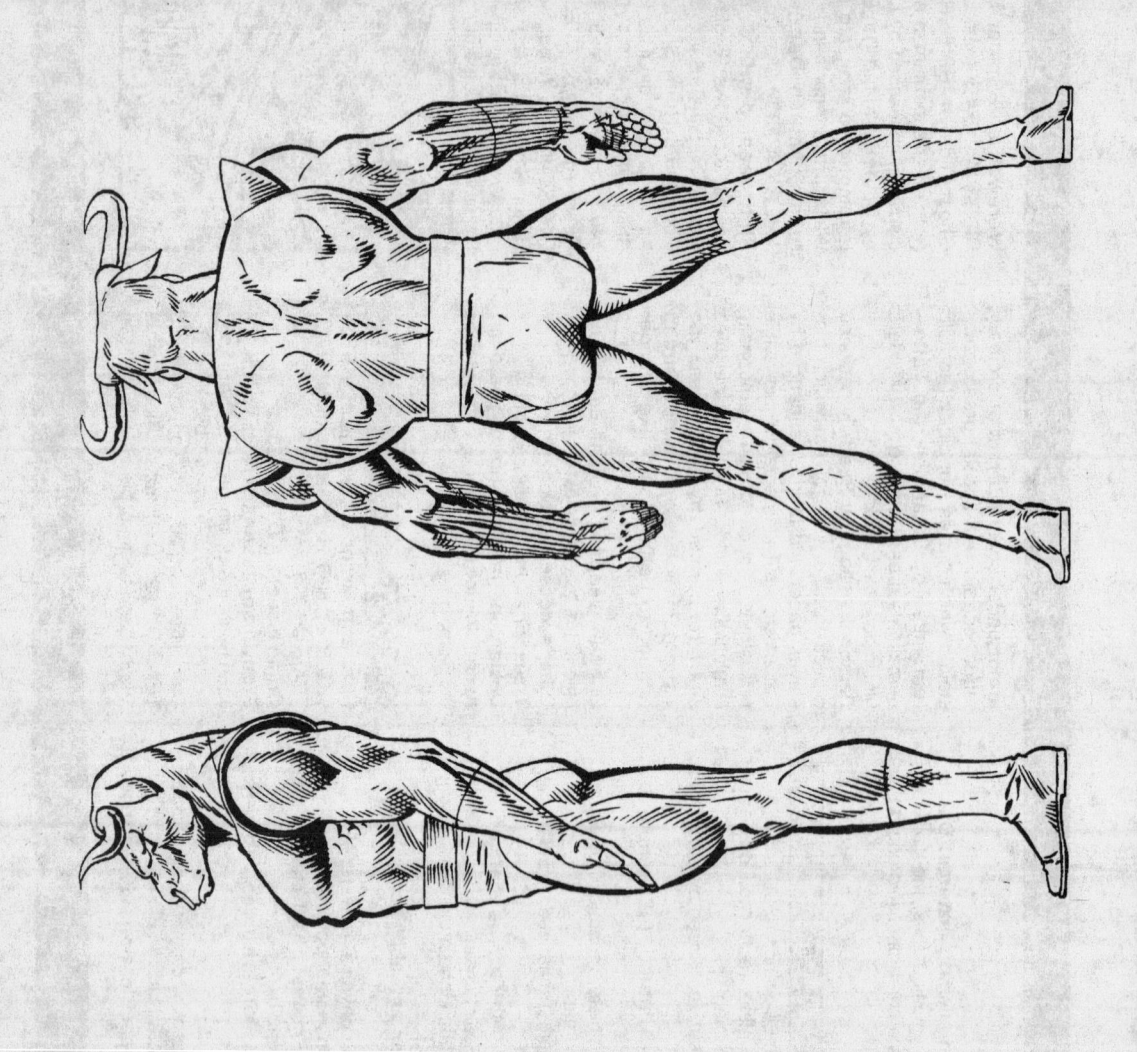

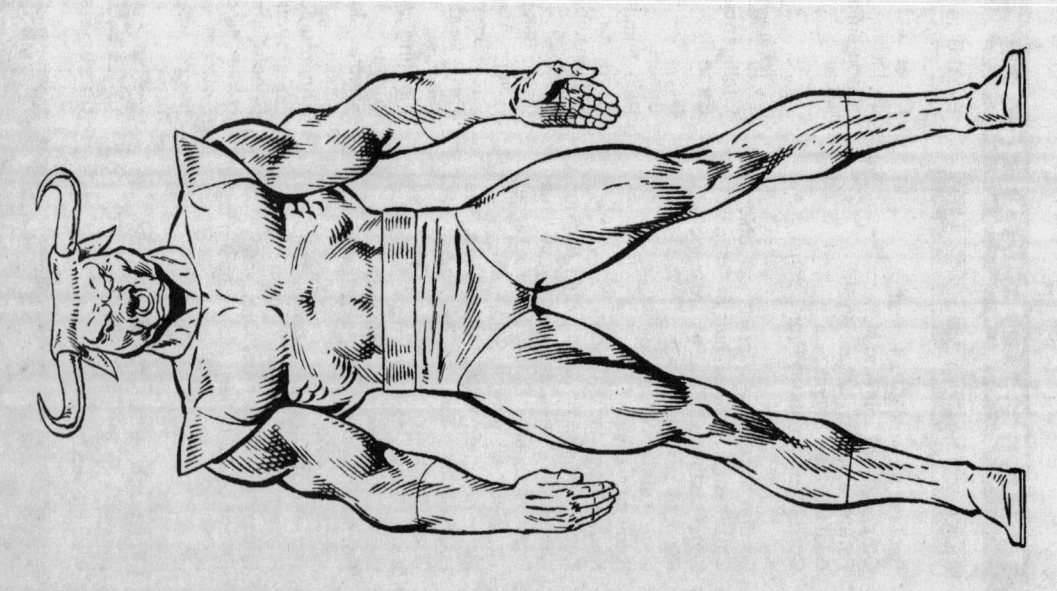

TAURUS

BIOGRAPHICAL DATA

Real name: Cornelius van Lunt
Aliases at time of death: None
Former aliases: None
Dual identity: Publicly known
Occupation at time of death: Professional criminal mastermind
Former occupation: Multimillionaire businessman
Citizenship: United States of America
Legal status: Criminal record in the United States
Place of birth: Unrevealed
Place of death: Just outside of Los Angeles, California
Cause of death: Plane crash following battle with Moon Knight
Marital status: Single
Known relatives: None
Known confidants: None
Known allies: Zodiac I (Aries, Gemini, Cancer, Leo, Virgo, Libra, Scorpio, Sagittarius, Capricorn, Aquarius, Pisces, Aries II, Aquarius II, all deceased)
Major enemies: The Avengers, Daredevil, Moon Knight, Zodiac II (deactivated)
Base of operations at time of death: New York City
Former bases of operations: None
Group membership at time of death: None
Former group membership: Zodiac I
Extent of education: Degree in business administration, extensive knowledge of astrology

PHYSICAL DESCRIPTION

Height: 6' 2"
Weight: 260 lbs.
Eyes: Brown
Hair: Black, balding
Other distinguishing features: None

POWERS AND ABILITIES

Intelligence: Above normal
Strength: Athlete
Stamina: Athlete
Durability: Normal
Agility: Normal
Reflexes: Normal
Fighting skills: Average hand-to-hand combatant; personal fighting style involved bull-like charges at opponents with lowered horns
Special skills and abilities: Skilled businessman, organizer, strategist, knowledgeable amateur astrologer
Superhuman physical powers: None
Superhuman mental powers: None
Special limitations: None
Source of superhuman powers: None

PARAPHERNALIA

Costume specifications: Synthetic stretch fabric and leather, reinforced with kevlar; armored helmet with horns constructed of unknown hard material
Personal weaponry: Star-Blazer handgun (fired intense blasts of stellar energy)
Special accessories: Star-Blazer cannon (larger, more powerful version of the Star-Blazer handgun)
Transportation: Starship/Star Blazer and various other aircraft
Design and manufacture of paraphernalia: Cornelius van Lunt (Taurus costume), Darren Bentley (Star-Blazer), unknown Zodiac technicians (Starship)

BIBLIOGRAPHY

First appearance: (as Taurus) AVENGERS #72, (as van Lunt) AVENGERS #77
Origin issue: Taurus's origin is as yet unrevealed
Significant issues: AVENGERS #72 (alongside Zodiac, summoned by Nick Fury disguised as Scorpio, battled the Avengers, escaped); AVENGERS #77 (as van Lunt, attempted hostile takeover of Stark Industries as part of plan to make Avengers his employees); AVENGERS #80-81 (as van Lunt, had Will (Red Wolf) Talltree's parents murdered to gain their land, opposed by Red Wolf II and Avengers, believed to have drowned); AVENGERS #120-122 (with Zodiac, schemed to kill all New York residents born under the sign of Gemini with Star-Blazer weapon, foiled by Avengers, defeated rebellion within Zodiac, captured by Avengers with all other Zodiac leaders, identity exposed); AVENGERS #124 (jailed, allowed Avengers to use his Star-Blazer weapon against the Star-Stalker); IRON MAN #183-184 (attempted to compete against the Maggia, who sent the android Taurus of Zodiac II to wreck his headquarters; hired Iron Man II, who defeated Taurus II; deduced Iron Man's James Rhodes identity, sent Aries II and Aquarius II in an unsuccessful attempt to assassinate him); WEST COAST AVENGERS #26-29 (witnessed the massacre of all other Zodiac leaders by Scorpio's android Zodiac, aided Avengers West Coast in defeating Zodiac II, escaped, attempted to enlist the Shroud in a new Zodiac, battled Moon Knight, killed in plane crash)

TERMINATRIX™

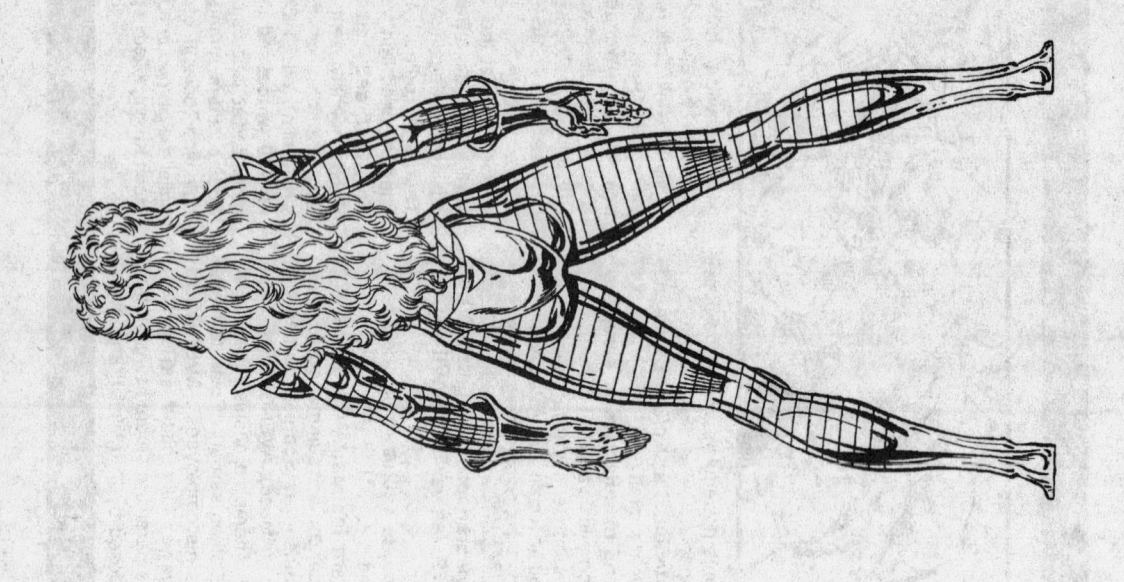

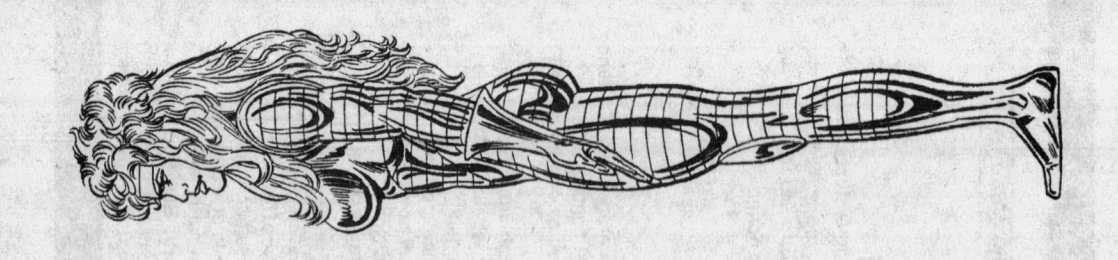

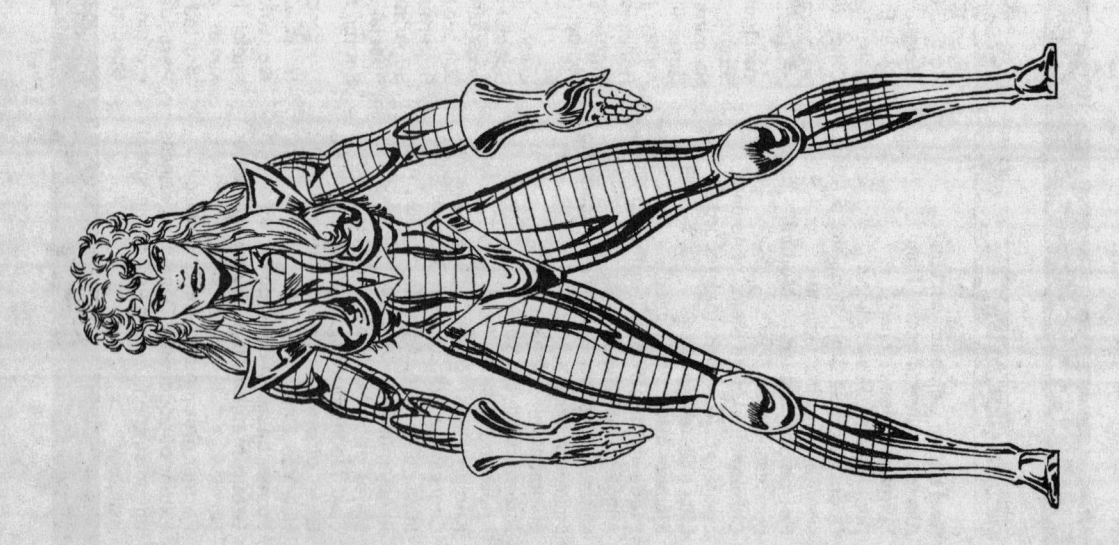

TERMINATRIX

BIOGRAPHICAL DATA

Real name: Ravonna
Other current aliases: None
Former aliases: Nebula, Kang-Nebula, Hecate, Temptress
Dual identities: Secret
Current occupation: Ruler of Chronopolis, conqueror
Former occupation: Princess, subversive, assassin
Citizenship: An unrevealed kingdom in an alternate future of 41st Century Earth
Legal status: No criminal record, wanted by the Council of Kangs
Place of birth: An unrevealed kingdom in an alternate future of 41st Century Earth
Marital status: Single
Known relatives: Carelius (father, deceased)
Known confidants: None
Known allies: Grandmaster, the Anachronauts, (former) Doctor Druid, various lieutenant Kangs
Major enemies: Kang, the Council of Kangs, the Avengers, Doctor Druid, the Fantastic Four
Usual base of operations: Chronopolis
Former bases of operations: An unrevealed kingdom in an alternate future of 41st Century Earth; mobile throughout the various timelines and time periods
Current group membership: Head of the Anachronauts
Former group membership: The Council of Kangs

Extent of education: Advanced schooling in the arts and sciences of the 41st Century

PHYSICAL DESCRIPTION

Height: 5'8"
Weight: 142 lbs.
Eyes: (as Ravonna) Brown, (as Nebula/Terminatrix) Blue
Hair: (as Ravonna) Brunette, (as Nebula) Blonde
Other distinguishing features: Terminatrix possesses shape-shifting technology, enabling her to alter her appearance at will

POWERS AND ABILITIES

Intelligence: Gifted
Strength: Athlete
Speed: Enhanced human
Stamina: Peak human
Durability: Superhuman
Agility: Enhanced human
Reflexes: Enhanced human
Fighting skills: Formidable hand-to-hand combatant, mastery of various types of exotic weaponry
Special skills and abilities: Mastery of a vast array of futuristic technology
Superhuman physical powers: Aside from the above listed, none
Superhuman mental powers: None
Special limitations: None
Source of superhuman powers: Unrevealed

PARAPHERNALIA

Costume specifications: Body armor of an unknown composition
Personal weaponry: Vibro-knives, concussion blasters
Special weaponry: Various as needed
Other accessories: Various as needed
Transportation: Various as needed
Design and manufacture of paraphernalia: Numerous unrevealed sources

BIBLIOGRAPHY

First appearance: (as Ravonna) AVENGERS #23, (as Nebula) AVENGERS #293, (as Temptress) FANTASTIC FOUR ANNUAL #25, (as Terminatrix) AVENGERS ANNUAL #21
Origin issue: AVENGERS ANNUAL #21
Significant issues: AVENGERS #23-24 (first met Kang when he attempted to annex her time era into his empire, fell in love with him, shielded him from renegade's assassination attempt, fell into death-like coma); AVENGERS #69-71 (while she was in suspended animation, Kang played the Grandmaster in tournament of champions in order to gain the power to free Ravonna, but after winning Kang chose to try to kill the Avengers instead, losing his chance to save her); AVENGERS #267-269 (temporal counterpart of Ravonna revealed to be a consort of Kang, later learned to be confederate of Immortus in his scheme to defeat Kang); AVENGERS ANNUAL #21 (in Flashback, revealed Ravonna was rescued by the Grandmaster, was embittered at Kang for not saving her when he had the chance, vowed to wreak vengeance on him); AVENGERS #291-297 (appeared to Doctor Druid in visions in a scheme to enlist his aid in acquiring deadliest weapon in the omniverse; assuming the guise of Avengers foe Nebula, attempted to infiltrate the Council of Cross-Time Kangs; completed her mental subjugation of Doctor Druid, directed him to takeover leadership of Avengers; used Druid to help her ensorcel the Avengers to accompany her to the center of a timestorm to retrieve the great weapon; thwarted by Avengers and three Cross-Time Kangs, fell into timestorm with Druid); FANTASTIC FOUR #337-341 (as Nebula, attempted to enlist aid of Fantastic Four to free her; appeared in a vision to Human Torch II, mind-controlled Invisible Woman; attempted to steal the Ultimate Nullifier but thwarted by the Fantastic Four); AVENGERS SPOTLIGHT #37 (escaped the timestorm to Lincoln, Nebraska in 1961, thwarted by a rejuvenated Doctor Druid); CAPTAIN AMERICA ANNUAL #11/THOR ANNUAL #17/AVENGERS ANNUAL #11/FANTASTIC FOUR ANNUAL #21 (vainly attempted to enthrall Doctor Druid; convinced Druid to help her investigate Kang's 20th Century stronghold; as Temptress, met Fantastic Four, used their time-sled to enter Chronopolis; defeated prime Kang in personal duel)

TERMINUS™

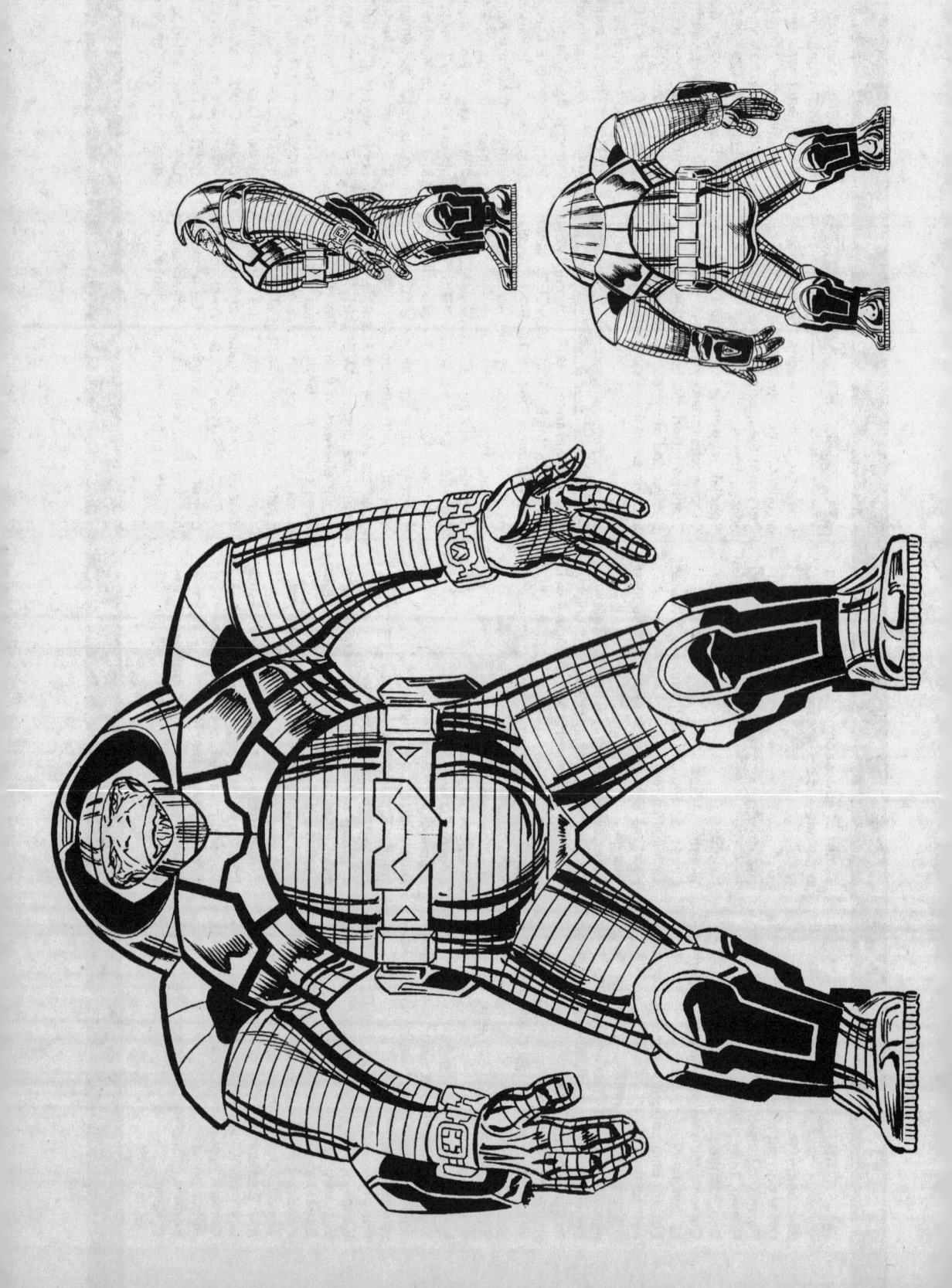

TERMINUS

BIOGRAPHICAL DATA

Real name: Terminus
Aliases at time of death: Terminex, Terminator, Terminoid, Ulterminus
Former aliases: Termini
Dual identity: None
Occupation at time of death: Destroyer
Former occupation: Inapplicable
Citizenship: Inapplicable
Legal status: Inapplicable
Place of birth: (original Terminus) An unnamed planet, (Stage-5 Terminus) Earth
Place of death: An unidentified location in outer space near Earth's solar system
Cause of death: Forced to use himself as energy source, imploded, creating a black hole into which he disappeared
Marital status: Inapplicable
Known relatives: Inapplicable
Known confidants: None
Known allies: None
Major enemies: Fantastic Four, Avengers, X-Men, High Evolutionary
Base of operations at time of death: Mobile on Earth
Former base of operations: Mobile throughout the universe, later abandoned Deviant caverns in Subterranea
Group membership at time of death: None
Former group membership: None
Extent of education: Inapplicable; apparently Terminus's original ancestral Termini-microbes were genetically programmed to devastate all inhabited worlds spared by the Celestials, and Terminus inherited this programming.

PHYSICAL DESCRIPTION

Height: (first form) 150', (Stage-5 Terminus) 300', growing rapidly to 500'
Weight: Unrevealed
Eyes: No visible pupils or irises
Hair: Unrevealed, if any
Other distinguishing features: Terminus is a living being composed of organic metal who is descended from genetically engineered "termini-molecules". Over subsequent ages the "termini-microbes" evolved into larger, more complex beings, many of which finally merged into the creature known as Terminus. Terminus's body contained human-sized insect-like "antibodies" and metallic "leeches" that attacked anything that invaded Terminus's body. While based in Earth's Subterranea, Terminus genetically engineered new Termini-microbes, which rapidly evolved through various stages known as Termini. The "second stage" Termini gestate inside Earth animals, take the form of organic metal versions of those animals, and would increase their size by consuming metal. The "third stage" Termini were roughly humanoid in shape and ten feet in height. These Termini merged into a single "fourth stage" being that resembled Terminus, but with a tail instead of a lance. The original Terminus consumed this second being, which gestated inside the original Terminus and then absorbed the latter's body mass within itself. The resulting creature, the "Stage-5 Terminus," resembled the first Terminus but was twice as tall and massive and possessed four arms.

POWERS AND ABILITIES

Intelligence: Normal
Strength: Incalculable
Speed: Enhanced human
Flight speed: (lance) Warp speed
Stamina: Immeasurable
Durability: Metahuman regenerative
Agility: Below normal
Reflexes: Normal
Fighting skills: No combat training, relied on brute force
Special skills and abilities: Genetic engineering used to create further Termini-microbes
Superhuman physical powers: Aside from the above listed attributes, Terminus had the ability to absorb and discharge vast amounts of energy through his lance.
Superhuman mental powers: Can mentally summon his lance to him when separated from him even over vast distances
Special limitations: "First stage" Termini can be destroyed by intense cold, while "second stage" Termini can be destroyed by intense heat. The adult Terminus is dependent on his lance for propulsion through the air or outer space and for draining the energy he requires for survival from outside sources.
Source of superhuman powers: Genetic engineering by the unnamed alien race that created the first Termini-microbes, evolution over subsequent ages

PARAPHERNALIA

Costume specifications: Inapplicable
Personal weaponry: Terminus's lance is apparently composed of the same organic metal as his body, can regenerate itself when damaged, and is 240 feet in length. The lance can discharge vast amounts of atomic energy, enough to tear open the crust of a planet. This energy manifests itself both as concussive force and as intense heat. Terminus can use the lance to create an "atomic storm" that surrounds his body while he moves without harming it. Terminus uses the lance to drain energy and materials from outside sources. Apparently the energy the lance discharges comes from Terminus's own body.
Special weaponry: None
Other accessories: None
Transportation: Flight under own power, through the use of his lance
Design and manufacture of paraphernalia: Inapplicable

BIBLIOGRAPHY

First appearance: FANTASTIC FOUR #269
Origin issue: THOR ANNUAL #15

TERRAX

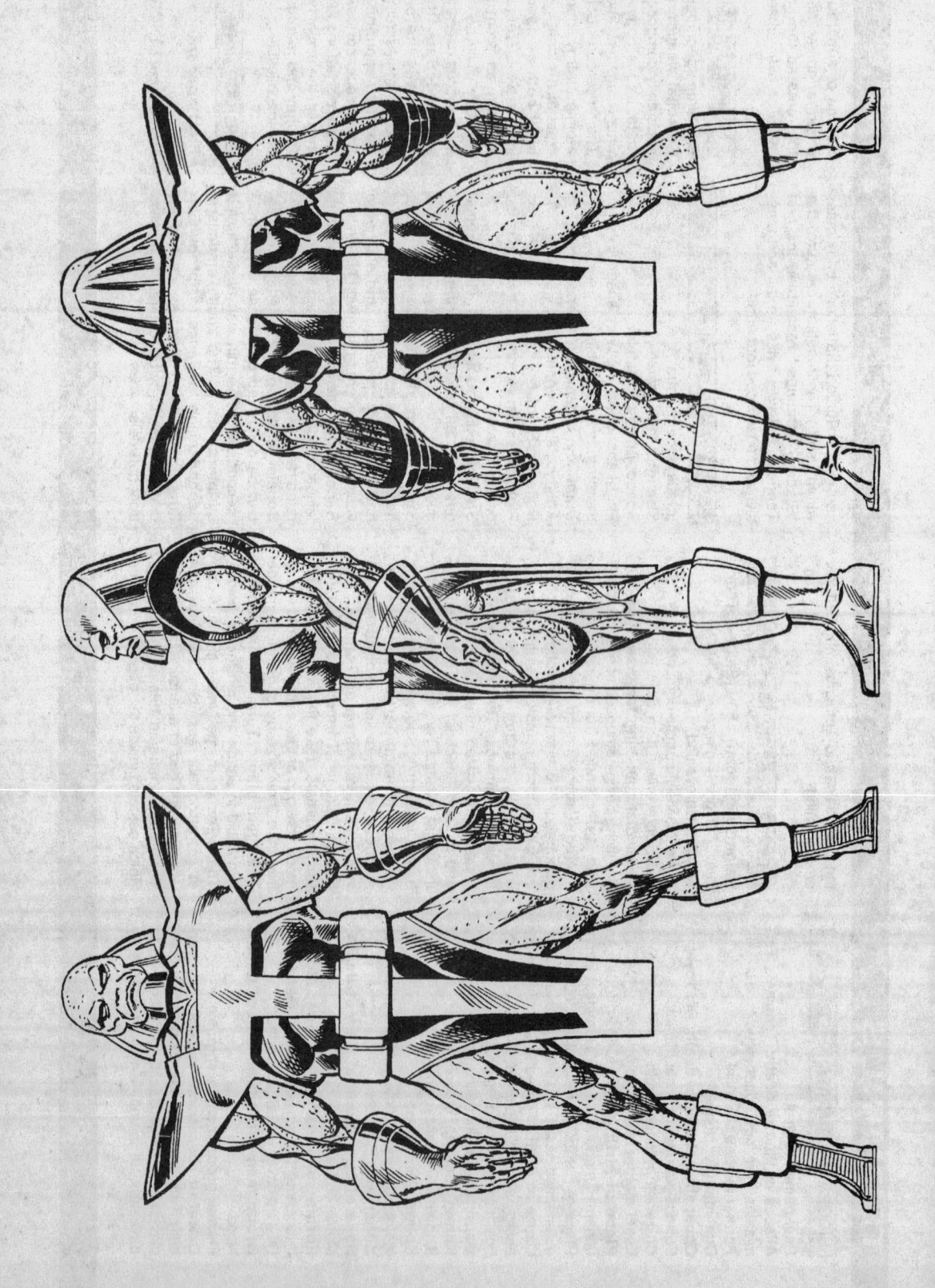

TERRAX

BIOGRAPHICAL DATA

Real name: Tyros
Other current aliases: Tyros the Terrible, Terrax the Tamer
Former aliases: None
Dual identity: None, most of the general populace of Earth is unaware of Terrax's existence
Current occupation: Would-be conqueror, destroyer
Former occupation: Dictator, herald of Galactus
Citizenship: City-state of Lanlak, Birj (a moon of the gas-giant planet Marman)
Legal status: No criminal record
Place of birth: City-state of Lanlak, Birj (also translated as Terran)
Marital status: Unrevealed
Known relatives: None
Known confidants: None
Known allies: (former) Galactus, Doctor Doom
Major enemies: Fantastic Four, Dazzler, Rom, Galactus, Doctor Doom, Silver Surfer, New Warriors
Usual base of operations: Planet Pluraris IV
Former bases of operations: City-state of Lanlak, Birj; mobile throughout the known universe
Current group membership: None
Former group membership: Herald of Galactus, Legion of the Unliving II
Extent of education: Unrevealed

PHYSICAL DESCRIPTION

Height: 6'6"
Weight: 2,750 lbs.
Eyes: Grey
Hair: (as Tyros) Bald with black fringe and beard, (as Terrax) None
Other distinguishing features: (as Terrax) Rock-like outer coating, growth of unknown composition replacing his hair

POWERS AND ABILITIES

Intelligence: Normal
Strength: Superhuman Class 75, potentially Superhuman Class 100
Speed: Athlete
Flight speed: Orbital Velocity, (formerly) Warp speed
Stamina: Godlike
Durability: Godlike
Agility: Enhanced human
Reflexes: Enhanced human
Fighting skills: Good hand-to-hand combatant, relies on his cosmic powers in battle
Special skills and abilities: None known
Superhuman physical powers: Aside from the above listed attributes, Terrax can manipulate cosmic energy for various effects, including projection of energy bolts of cosmic force, augmentation of his strength to greater superhuman levels, survive unprotected in the vacuum of outer space without need of oxygen, food or sleep; as sentient energy, the ability to take over another living beings as a host body.
Superhuman mental powers: Ability to manipulate molecules of rock and earth for a variety of effects, including moving asteroids, meteors, and planetary masses at high speeds (dependent on their size and distance from Terrax), affecting tectonic plates to cause earthquakes and create chasms, and levitating large land masses miles into the air
Special limitations: After his recreation as a being of sentient energy, Terrax required constant contact with a planet's surface in order to sustain his physical form by ground soil replenishment. Following his resurrection using Genetech officer Harmon Furmintz as a host body, this restriction does not apply; however, Terrax no longer has the capability to traverse interplanetary space.
Source of superhuman powers: Genetic mutation of his alien physiology augmented by physical transformation by cosmic power of Galactus

PARAPHERNALIA

Costume specifications: Alien materials
Personal weaponry: A cosmic axe with a 5' handle and a 2' blade, able to emanate waves of destructive force sufficiently powerful to rend a tear in Galactus's ship and to create highly impervious force shields
Special weaponry: None
Other accessories: (as Tyros) An anti-gravity sky-sled
Transportation: Flight under own power
Design and manufacture of paraphernalia: Galactus, (sky-sled) Doctor Doom

BIBLIOGRAPHY

First appearance: FANTASTIC FOUR #211
Origin issue: FANTASTIC FOUR #211
Significant issues: FANTASTIC FOUR #211, 213 (captured by Fantastic Four at behest of Galactus, transformed by Galactus into his herald; attacked Fantastic Four; defeated by Human Torch II); DAZZLER #10-11 (fled from Galactus, retrieved by Dazzler at Galactus's behest); ROM #26-27 (led Galactus to planet Galador, battled Rom and other spaceknights); FANTASTIC FOUR #242-243 (levitated Manhattan into space to force Fantastic Four to battle Galactus, attacked Galactus, stripped of cosmic powers, fell from top of World Trade Center); FANTASTIC FOUR #258-260 (as Tyros, re-energized with cosmic power by Doctor Doom, battled Fantastic Four, turned against Doom, consumed by cosmic power in battle with Silver Surfer); AVENGERS ANNUAL #16 (resurrected as member of Legion of the Unliving II, battled Iron Man I); NEW WARRIORS #1 (accidentally revived as sentient energy by Genetech's AIELAC unit, battled New Warriors, destroyed); NEW WARRIORS #15-17 (used Harmon Furmintz as host body; battled New Warriors and Fantastic Four; exiled by Silver Surfer to Pluraris IV)

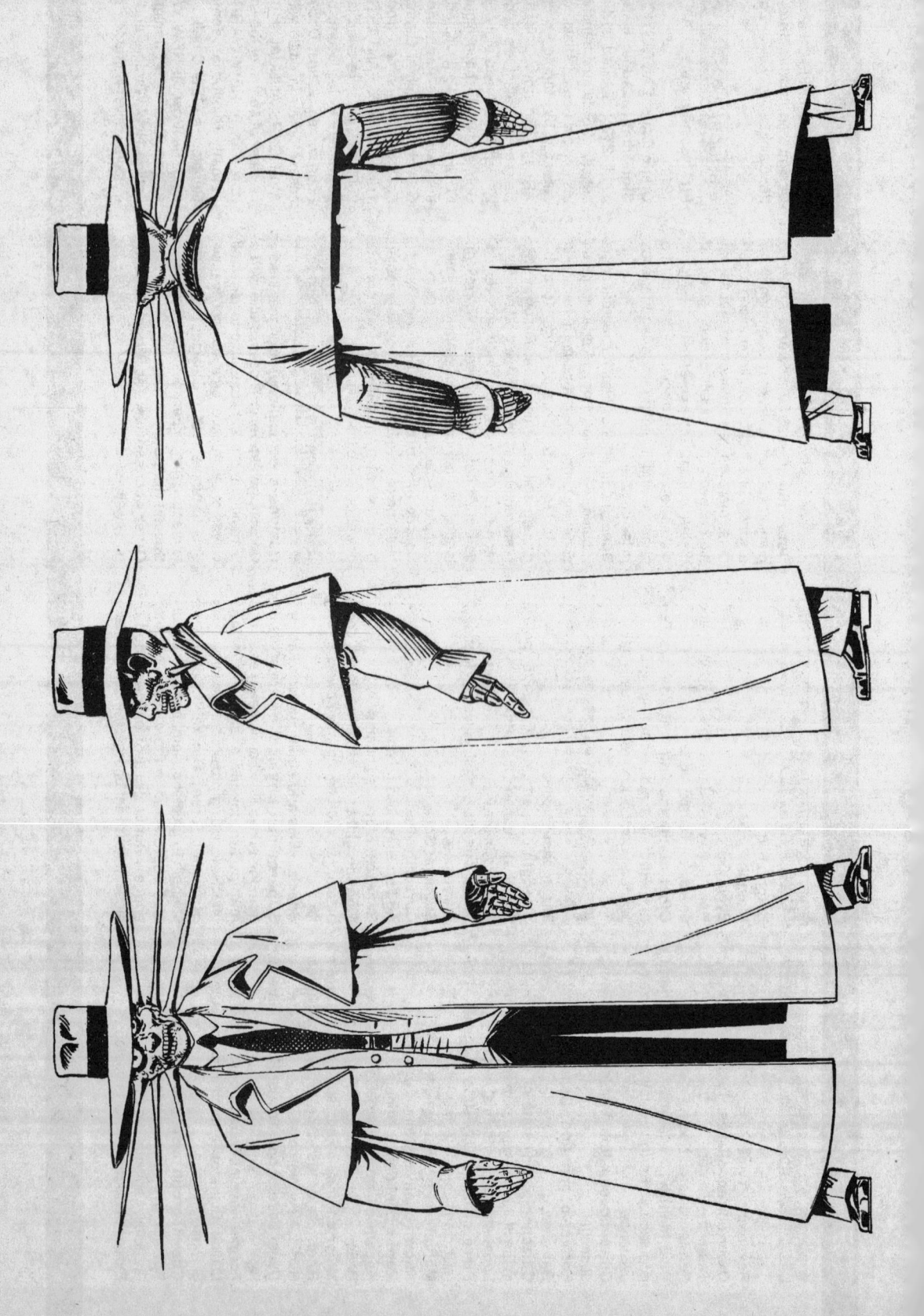

TERROR, INC.

TERROR INC.

BIOGRAPHICAL DATA

Real name: Unrevealed
Other current aliases: Terror
Former aliases: None known
Dual Identity: Secret
Current occupation: Assassin for hire
Former occupation: Unrevealed
Citizenship: Unrevealed
Legal status: Unrevealed
Place of birth: Unrevealed
Marital status: Unrevealed, currently single
Known relatives: None
Known confidants: None
Known allies: Alexis Primo, Rekrab, Hellfire, Wolverine, Jubilee
Major enemies: Beelzeboul, Vulkanus, Doctor Strange, the Punisher; (former) Roger Barbatos (deceased)
Usual base of operations: Mobile throughout the United States and Europe
Former bases of operations: Unrevealed
Current group membership: None
Former group membership: None known
Extent of education: Unrevealed

PHYSICAL DESCRIPTION

Height: Variable, usually 6' 2"
Weight: Variable, usually 170 lbs.
Eyes: Variable
Hair: None
Other distinguishing features: Terror has three 10" projections of unknown composition extending from either side of his face, greenish yellow skin, pronounced sharpened canine teeth, and a face resembling a nearly naked skull without lips or eyelids. He also has a metal glove encasing the hermetically sealed hand of a deceased lover. Since Terror has the ability to replace parts of his body's component parts, most of his vital statistics are subject to constant change.

POWERS AND ABILITIES

Intelligence: Above normal
Strength: Variable, at minimum Athlete
Speed: Variable, at minimum Athlete
Stamina: Variable, at minimum Athlete
Durability: Superhuman regenerative
Agility: Variable, at minimum Athlete
Reflexes: Variable, at minimum Athlete
Fighting skills: Experienced hand-to-hand combatant, gains additional fighting skills from "borrowed" body parts
Special skills and abilities: Expert marksman with most weapons, accomplished businessman, gains varied additional skills from "borrowed" body parts
Superhuman physical powers: Ability to replace parts of his body (hand, feet, arms, legs, eyes, ears, nose, etc.) with those of other organisms, thus taking on skills or abilities of the person or being to whom the "borrowed" part belonged, in addition to experiencing sights, sounds, or sensations which they once experienced; Terror can also remove from other beings and add to his body additional parts which he himself does not normally possess, such as wings or a prehensile tail.
Superhuman mental powers: None
Special limitations: None known
Source of superhuman powers: Unrevealed

PARAPHERNALIA

Costume specifications: Conventional fabric
Personal weaponry: Standard handguns
Special weaponry: Various firearms as needed
Other accessories: Various body parts specially preserved for future use
Transportation: Conventional
Design and manufacture of paraphernalia: Commercial manufacturers

BIBLIOGRAPHY

First appearance: TERROR INC. #1
Origin issue: Terror's origin is as yet unrevealed.
Significant issues: TERROR INC. #1-5 (turned over Mikal Drakonmegas to his demonic father, Beelzeboul, in return for Beelzeboul's contract with Roger Barbatos which had protected Barbatos from Terror's previous attempts to assassinate him; turned against Beelzeboul and saved Drakonmegas; destroyed contract, thus retroactively killing Barbatos); DAREDEVIL #305 (met with mob leader Deragon regarding planned criminal summit in Las Vegas); WOLVERINE #58-59 (aided Wolverine and Jubilee against Monkeywrench and Pick Axis); TERROR INC. #6 (first encountered the Punisher)

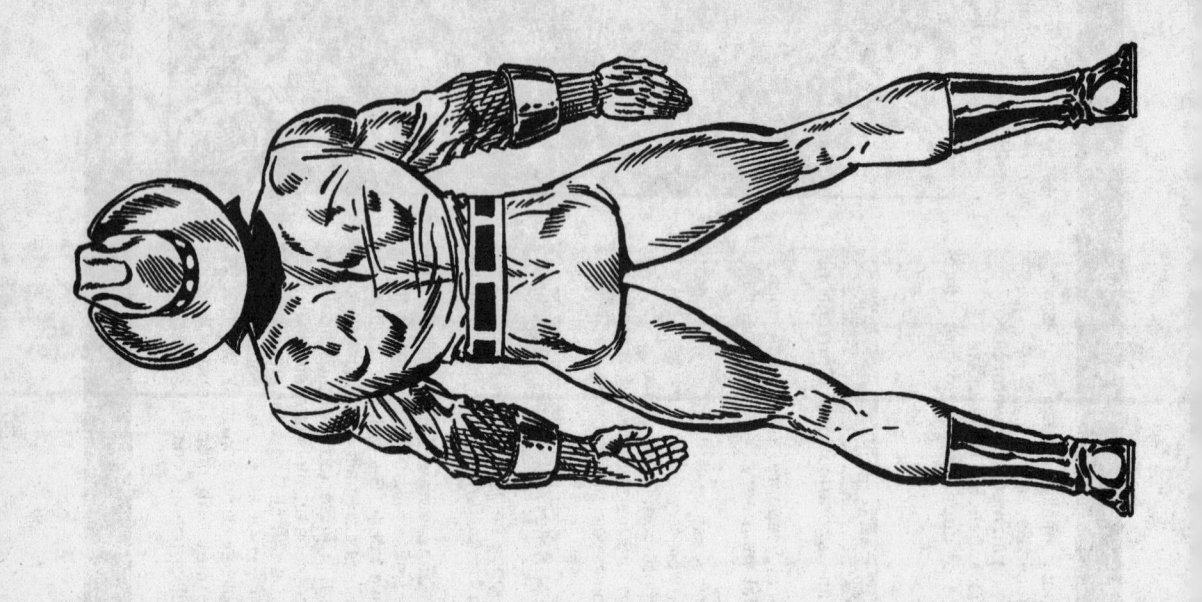

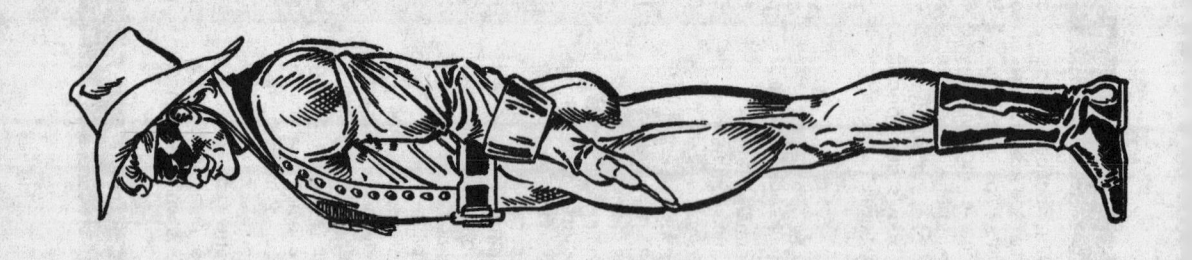

TEXAS TWISTER

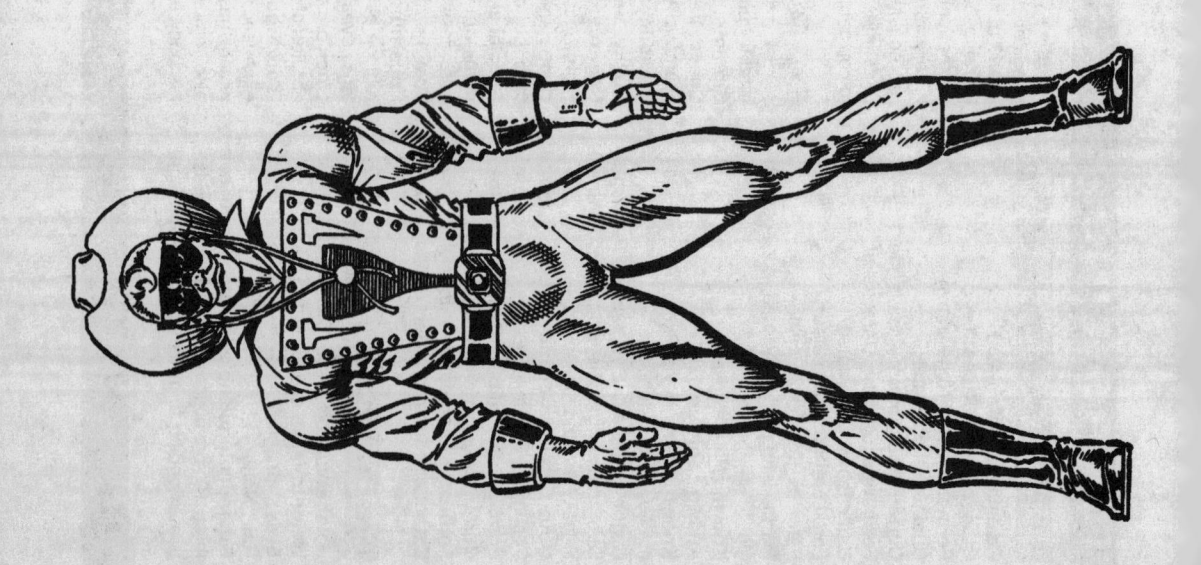

TEXAS TWISTER

BIOGRAPHICAL DATA

Real name: Drew Daniels
Other current aliases: None
Former aliases: None
Dual identity: Secret
Current occupation: Rodeo performer, adventurer
Former occupation: Cattle hand
Citizenship: United States of America
Legal status: No criminal record
Place of birth: Amarillo, Texas
Marital status: Single
Known relatives: None
Known confidants: Victoria Star (Shooting Star)
Known allies: The Falcon, Marvel Man (now known as Quasar), Nick Fury, the Rangers (Red Wolf, Phantom Rider, Firebird)
Major enemies: The Corrupter, the demon Riglevio
Usual base of operations: Mobile throughout the American Southwest
Former bases of operations: SHIELD headquarters, New York City
Current group membership: The Rangers
Former group membership: SHIELD
Extent of education: High school graduate

PHYSICAL DESCRIPTION

Height: 6'5"
Weight: 245 lbs.
Eyes: Blue
Hair: Red
Other distinguishing features: None

POWERS AND ABILITIES

Intelligence: Normal
Strength: Athlete
Speed: Athlete
Air speed: Natural winged flight limit
Stamina: Superhuman
Durability: Enhanced human
Agility: Athlete
Reflexes: Superhuman

Fighting skills: SHIELD unarmed combat training
Special skills and abilities: Expert horse rider, lasso thrower, sharpshooter
Superhuman physical powers: Various abilities enabling him to withstand the rigors of motion inside a tornado, such as denser skin to prevent unwanted heat loss, friction burns, and particle abrasions, enhanced eyesight, and a high degree of resistance to dizziness and motion sickness
Superhuman mental powers: The telekinetic ability to accelerate air within a radius of 100 feet from his body, thereby creating a tornado-like mass of swirling wind around him. The largest tornado he can create is approximately 200 feet in diameter, the smallest is approximately 2 inches in diameter. The approximate wind speed he can create is about 225 miles per hour. Such a wind swirling about his body is capable of lifting him off the ground and supporting him in midair. He can control the size of the tornado at will and also project its center to a point outside of his body.
Special limitations: Mental fatigue will eventually impair performance.
Source of superhuman powers: Bombardment by radioactive particles during a tornado

PARAPHERNALIA

Costume specifications: Leather and natural stretch fabric
Personal weaponry: None
Special weaponry: None
Other accessories: None
Transportation: Usually travels under his own power
Design and manufacture of paraphernalia: Inapplicable

BIBLIOGRAPHY

First appearance: FANTASTIC FOUR #177
Origin issue: FANTASTIC FOUR #177
Significant issues: FANTASTIC FOUR #177 (tried out for the Frightful Four, turned down membership when he heard the nature of their activities); CAPTAIN AMERICA #217 (tried out for the Super-Agent program of SHIELD, sparred with Captain America); CAPTAIN AMERICA #229 (sparred with Captain America again, quit the Super-Agents); INCREDIBLE HULK #265 (battled Hulk, rescued Rick Jones from the Corrupter, helped form the Rangers); WEST COAST AVENGERS #8 (alongside the Rangers, battled West Coast Avengers under the influence of the demon Riglevio possessing Shooting Star); SOLO AVENGERS #18 (exorcised the demon from Shooting Star, became possessed by it, Hawkeye and Shooting Star coaxed the demon out)

THANOS™

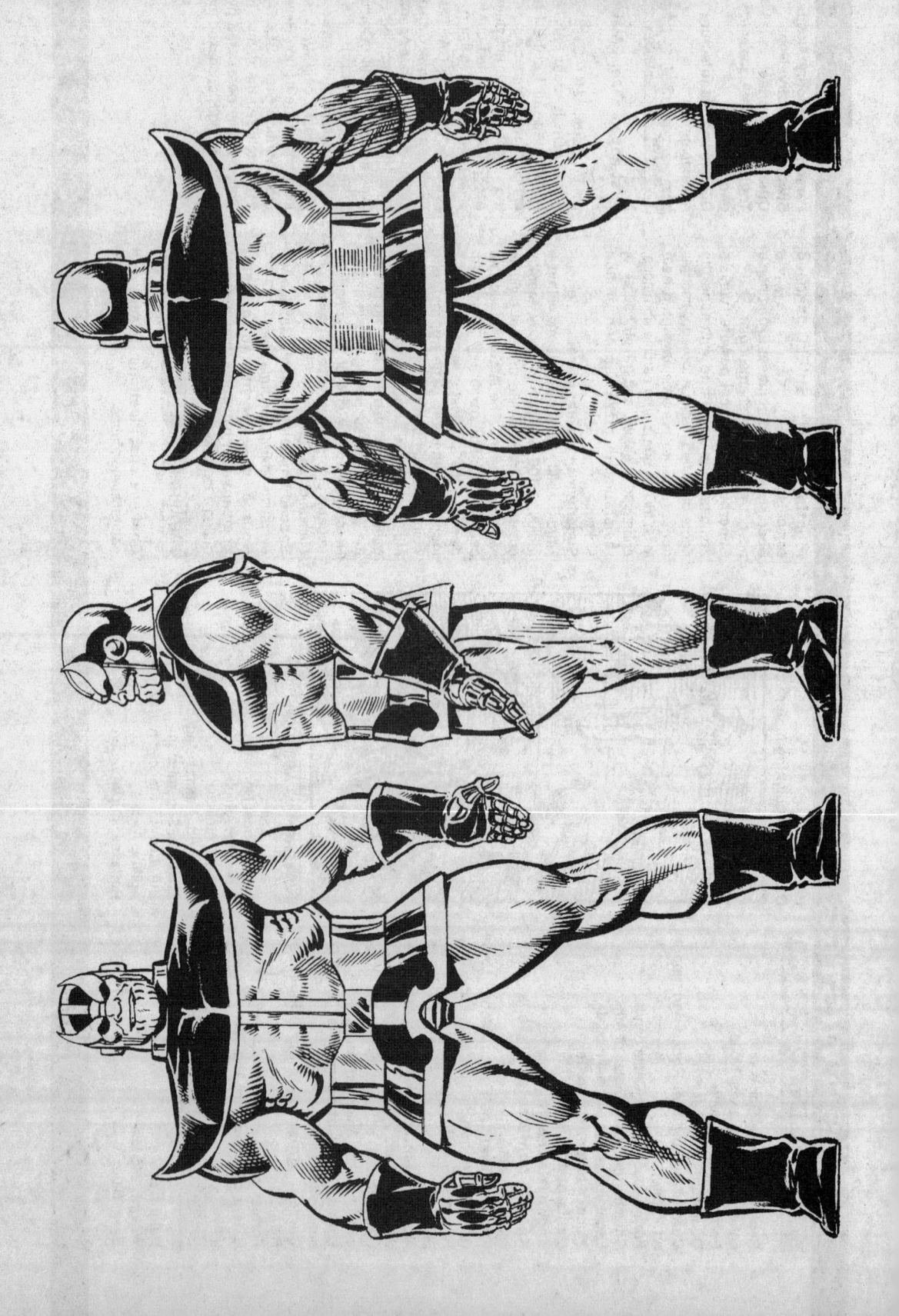

THANOS

BIOGRAPHICAL DATA

Real name: Thanos
Other current aliases: None
Former aliases: None
Dual identity: None
Current occupation: Worshiper of Death
Former occupation: Conqueror
Citizenship: Titan, moon of Saturn
Legal status: None
Place of birth: Titan
Marital status: Single
Known relatives: Alars (alias Mentor, father), Eros (alias Starfox, brother), Sui-San (mother, deceased), Zuras (uncle, deceased), Cybele (sister-in-law), Thena (niece), Nebula (alleged granddaughter)
Known confidants: None
Known allies: The Controller, the Super-Skrull, the Blood Brothers, Adam Warlock, Death
Major enemies: Captain Marvel, Adam Warlock, the Silver Surfer, the Avengers
Usual base of operations: Mobile throughout the universe
Former bases of operations: The starship *Sanctuary II*
Current group membership: Elders of the Universe
Former group membership: Commander of an army of galactic mercenaries
Extent of education: Unrevealed

PHYSICAL DESCRIPTION

Height: 6' 7"
Weight: 985 lbs.
Eyes: Red, no visible pupils
Hair: None
Other distinguishing features: Greyish-purple skin

POWERS AND ABILITIES

Intelligence: Superhuman intellect
Strength: Superhuman Class 100
Speed: Enhanced human
Stamina: Demi-godlike
Durability: Godlike
Agility: Enhanced human
Reflexes: Enhanced human
Note: With the Infinity Gauntlet, all of Thanos's attributes, except for his intelligence, are at their maximum levels.
Fighting skills: Although Thanos has generally eschewed physical combat, he has demonstrated formidable hand-to-hand fighting skills.
Special skills and abilities: Vast knowledge of science, metaphysics, and the occult.
Superhuman physical powers: Besides the above listed attributes, Thanos possesses various superhuman powers, including the capacity to tap, transform, and direct vast quantities of cosmic energy for destructive force.
Superhuman mental powers: Thanos has demonstrated psionic abilities, including telepathy, the limits of which are as yet unknown.
Special limitations: None
Source of superhuman powers: Thanos is a mutant member of the race of superhumans known as Eternals, who has augmented his innate abilities through bionic and mystical techniques.

PARAPHERNALIA

Costume specifications: Alien materials
Personal weaponry: None
Special weaponry: Thanos once gained possession of the Cosmic Cube, and used it for his own purposes; presently, he possesses a gauntlet which incorporates six Infinity Gems, each one of which grants him total mastery over six basic aspects of existence: Time, Space, Power, Mind, Reality, and Soul, making him virtually omnipotent.
Other accessories: Various exotic extraterrestrial devices, as needed
Transportation: A throne-like chair capable of teleportation and faster-than-light travel; the starship *Sanctuary II*
Design and manufacture of paraphernalia: Unrevealed

BIBLIOGRAPHY

First appearance: IRON MAN #55
Origin issue: CAPTAIN MARVEL #29 (partial)
Significant issues: IRON MAN #55 (employed the Blood Brothers against Iron Man and Drax the Destroyer); CAPTAIN MARVEL #25-33 (employed Super-Skrull and Kragg in plan to capture Captain Mar-Vell; battled Drax the Destroyer; gained possession of the Cosmic Cube; battled Mar-Vell and the Avengers; tapped into power of Cosmic Cube to gain control over all reality in order to woo Death; lost omnipotence when Mar-Vell gained possession of Cosmic Cube); WARLOCK #9-11 (allied himself with Adam Warlock against Magus; used time probe to make it possible for Adam Warlock to prevent his future self from becoming the Magus); AVENGERS ANNUAL #7 (attempted to use six Infinity Gems to destroy every star in the universe as a gift for Death; battled the Avengers, Captain Mar-Vell and Adam Warlock); MARVEL TWO-IN-ONE ANNUAL #2 (attempted to use Warlock's Soul Gem to destroy Earth's sun; body transformed into stone by spirit of Adam Warlock); DEATH OF CAPTAIN MARVEL GRAPHIC NOVEL (Thanos's spirit accompanied Mar-Vell's soul into realm of Death); SILVER SURFER #34-35, 38 (reanimated by Death, first encountered Silver Surfer; denied Nebula's claim to being his granddaughter, tricked Surfer into thinking him dead); THANOS QUEST #1-2 (acquired the Infinity Gems from the various Elders of the Universe who possessed them; used the Gems to become omnipotent); SILVER SURFER #45 (used Soul Gem to steal the souls of Silver Surfer and Drax the Destroyer); INFINITY GAUNTLET #1-6 (attempted to employ the limitless powers of the six Infinity Gems to become supreme being of the universe as part of bid to win the heart of the personification of Death)

THENA™

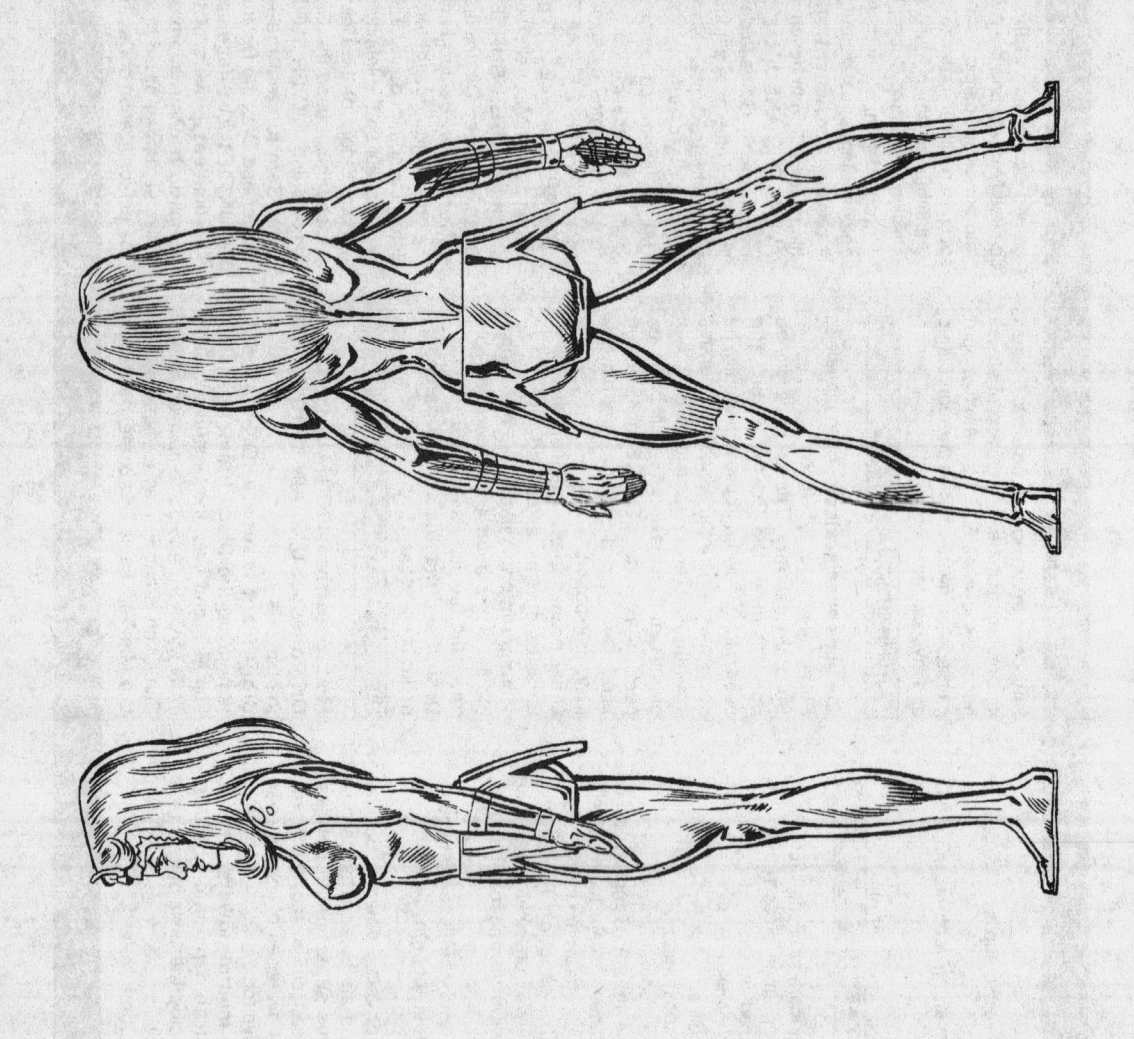

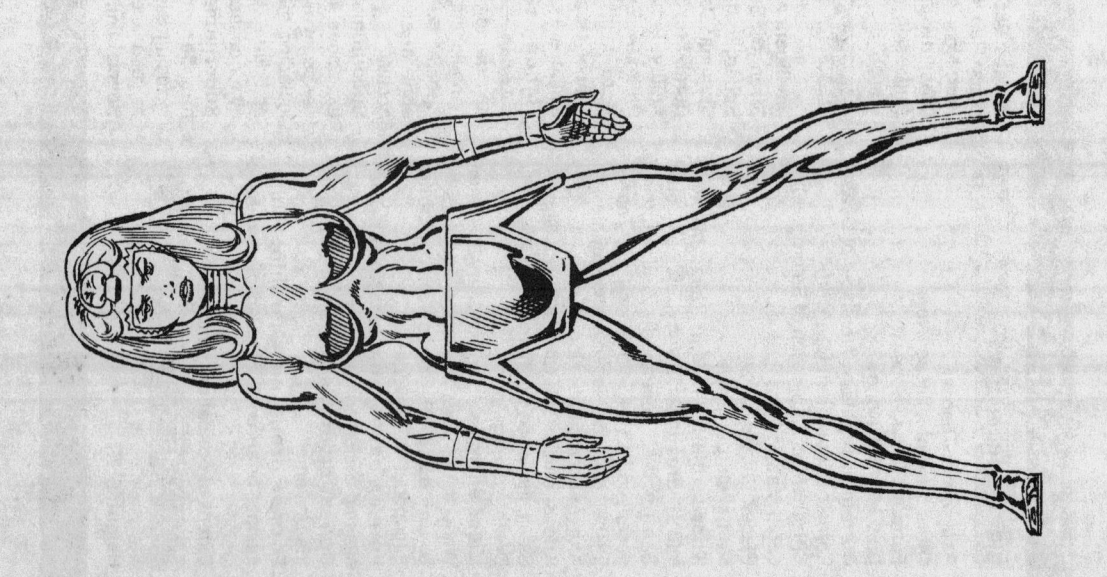

THENA

BIOGRAPHICAL DATA

Real name: Thena (changed by royal decree from her original name, Azura)
Other current aliases: None known
Former aliases: Thena has often been mistaken for the Olympian goddess Athena
Dual identity: None; the fact that Thena is an Eternal has been publicly revealed, but is generally disbelieved by Earth's populace.
Current occupation: Scholar, warrior, advisor to Prime Eternal
Former occupation: Prime Eternal (leader of the Eternals of Earth)
Citizenship: Olympia, Greece, capital city of the Eternals of Earth
Legal status: No criminal record; former exile from Eternal sanctuaries
Place of birth: Olympia, Greece
Marital status: Single
Known relatives: Zuras (father, deceased), Cybele (mother), Deborah Ritter (daughter), Donald Ritter (son)
Known confidants: Cybele, Karkas, Ransak the Reject, (sometimes) Warlord Kro, Sersi, (former) Zuras
Known allies: The Eternals of Earth (especially Ikaris, Sersi, Makkari), Karkas, Ransak the Reject, Thor I, Avengers
Major enemies: Ghaur, Brother Tode (deceased), Deviants, Zakka, Tutinax, Maelstrom, Blastaar, Dr. Daniel Damian (deceased)
Usual base of operations: New York City
Former bases of operations: Olympia
Current group membership: Eternals of Earth
Former group membership: The Eternals of Olympia
Extent of education: Has studied under the greatest Eternal and human scholars throughout her lifetime

PHYSICAL DESCRIPTION

Height: 5' 10"
Weight: 160 lbs.
Eyes: Blue
Hair: Blond
Other distinguishing features: None

POWERS AND ABILITIES

Intelligence: Gifted
Strength: Superhuman Class 25 (can supplement her physical strength by psionically levitating heavy objects)
Speed: Supersonic
Stamina: Metahuman
Durability: Metahuman regenerative
Agility: Superhuman
Reflexes: Superhuman
Fighting skills: Formidable hand-to-hand combatant, with extensive training in unarmed combat and the use of many ancient and Eternal high-tech weaponry
Special skills and abilities: Highly educated in numerous areas of Eternal and human knowledge
Superhuman physical powers: Aside from the above listed attributes, Thena possesses the ability to manipulate cosmic energy to augment her life force, granting her virtual invulnerability and immortality; the ability to project cosmic energy from his eyes or hands in the form of heat, light, or concussive force and possibly other powers.
Superhuman mental powers: Total mental control over his physical form, granting virtual invulnerability and immortality; ability to levitate herself and thus fly at superhuman speed; psionic ability to rearrange molecular structure of objects; ability to cast illusions to disguise her appearance and that of other s from the perceptions of normal human beings; ability to teleport her self ands others with her; ability to initiate formation of the Uni-Mind
Special limitations: None
Source of superhuman powers: Member of the race of superhumans known as the Eternals

PARAPHERNALIA

Costume specifications: Body armor of unknown composition
Personal weaponry: Bow that fires arrows that release "cold energy," energy spear that surrounds victims with ring of intense heat and light or bombards them with anti-gravitons
Special weaponry: None
Other accessories: None
Transportation: Self-levitation, self-teleportation, or various Eternal vehicles
Design and manufacture of paraphernalia: Eternal armorers and technicians

BIBLIOGRAPHY

First appearance: ETERNALS Vol. 1 #5
Origin issue: Thena's origin is as yet unrevealed.
Significant issues: ETERNALS Vol. 1 #5-6 (battled Deviants in New York City to help rescue Sersi, reunited with Kro, publicly revealed herself to be an Eternal); ETERNALS Vol. 1 #8-12 (visited Deviant Lemuria with Kro, took Karkas and Reject under her protection, participated in the Uni-Mind); ETERNALS ANNUAL #1 (with Karkas and Reject, battled Zakka, and Tuitinax); THOR #285-289 (met and became ally of Thor); THOR #291-292 (battled Athena of Olympus, during battle between Olympian gods and Eternals); AVENGERS #246-248 (formed Uni-Mind, battled Maelstrom alongside the Avengers, chosen by Uni-Mind to stay on Earth); ETERNALS Vol. 2 #1-12 (became Prime Eternal, fell under mental domination of Kro; thwarted other Eternal's efforts against him, deposed by Ikaris as Prime Eternal and banished; captured with Kro by Ghaur, freed from Kro's brain mine; battled Ghaur alongside Eternals, Thor, and West Coast Avengers); ETERNALS: THE HEROD FACTOR #1 (revealed her first meeting with Kro, how they fell in love and she became pregnant; reunited with her children and Kro)

THIN MAN ™

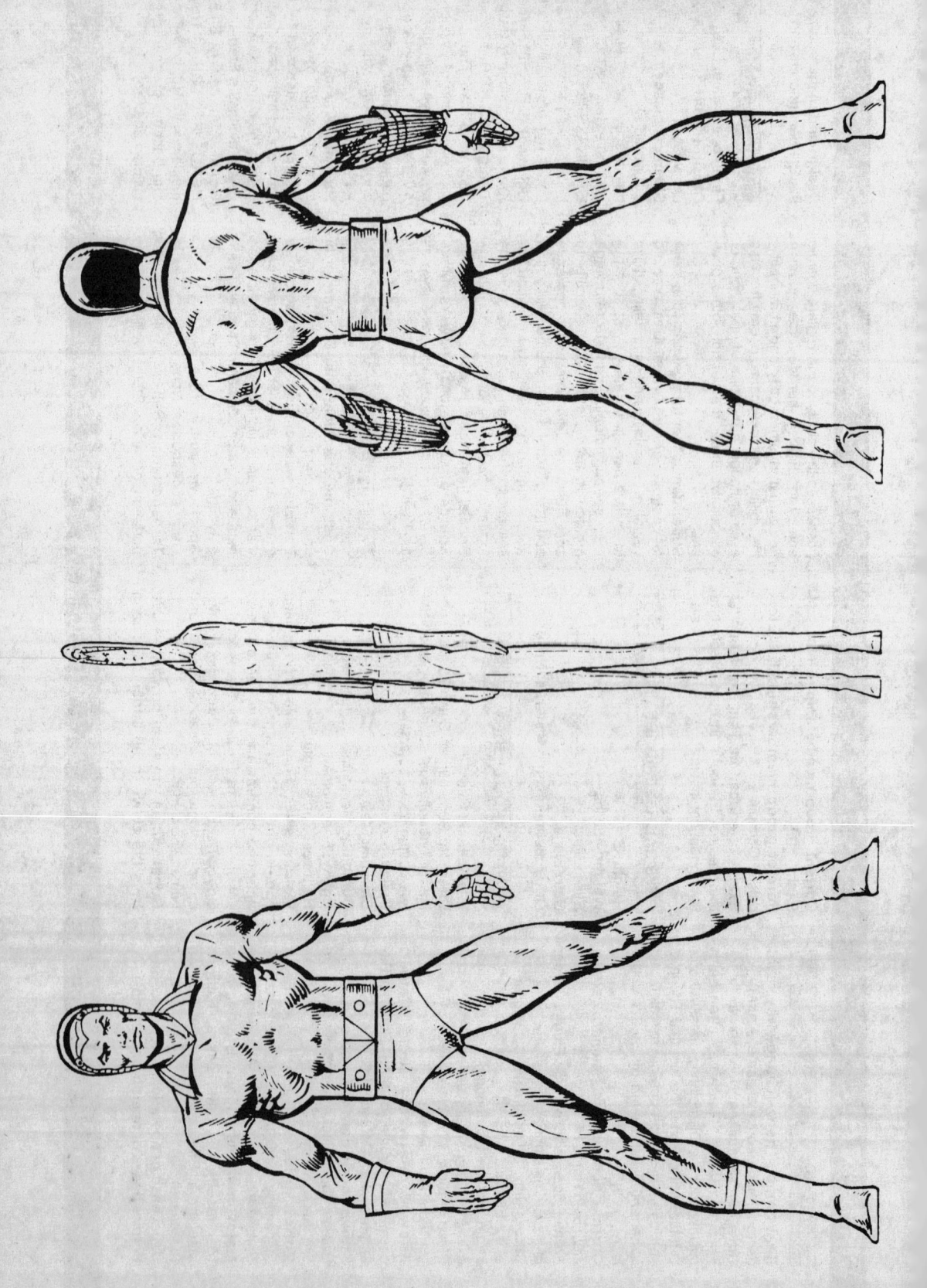

THIN MAN

BIOGRAPHICAL DATA

Real name: Dr. Bruce Dickson
Other current aliases: None
Former aliases: None
Dual identity: Secret (at least in the 1940s), known to the United States government
Current occupation: Unrevealed
Former occupation: Scientist, adventurer
Citizenship: United States of America
Legal status: No criminal record
Place of birth: Unrevealed
Marital status: Unrevealed
Known relatives: None
Known confidants: Olalla
Known allies: The Liberty Legion, the Invaders, the Thing, Chief of Elders of Kahalia
Major enemies: The Red Skull, Iron Cross, Master Man, U-Man, Skyshark, Nazis
Usual base of operations: Unknown
Former bases of operations: Liberty Legion headquarters, New York City
Current group membership: None
Former group membership: The Liberty Legion
Extent of education: Ph. D in undisclosed area of science

PHYSICAL DESCRIPTION

Height: 6'
Weight: 170 lbs.
Eyes: Blue
Hair: Blond
Other distinguishing features: None

POWERS AND ABILITIES

Intelligence: Above normal
Strength: Athlete
Speed: Athlete
Stamina: Athlete
Durability: Peak human
Agility: Athlete
Reflexes: Athlete
Fighting skills: The Thin Man is a good hand-to-hand combatant who has received coaching from the Patriot and Miss America.
Special skills and abilities: Accomplished airplane pilot
Superhuman physical powers: Ability to convert the mass of his entire body into highly malleable state at will, enabling him to stretch, deform, expand, or compress all or any part of his body into any shape. He most often uses his power to elongate portions of his body, such as his arms, or to flatten his body to the thinness of an average sheet of typing paper, enabling him to pass under a shut door. The limits on the Thin Man's powers are unknown. He can absorb the impact of a projectile shot at him or of any concussive force, within certain unknown limits, by deforming his body. When underwater he can resist intense water pressure to a superhuman extent for a period of minutes.
Superhuman mental powers: None
Special limitations: None
Source of superhuman powers: Unknown scientific process developed by the people of Kahalia

PARAPHERNALIA

Costume specifications: Costume is made of an unknown Kahalian fabric that stretches and contracts in size as he does
Personal weaponry: None
Special weaponry: None
Other accessories: None
Transportation: Various
Design and manufacture of paraphernalia: Unknown

BIBLIOGRAPHY

First appearance: (historical) MYSTIC COMICS #4, (modern) MARVEL PREMIERE #29
Origin issue: MYSTIC COMICS #4, MARVEL PREMIERE #29
Significant issues: MARVEL PREMIERE #29 (joined the Liberty Legion); INVADERS #6 (Liberty Legion began battling Nazis in USA); MARVEL PREMIERE #30 (with Liberty Legion, battled Invaders, who were hypnotically controlled by Red Skull); MARVEL TWO-IN-ONE ANNUAL #1/MARVEL TWO-IN-ONE #20 (Thing travelled back in time to 1942 aided Liberty Leg:on in battling Master Man, U-Man, and Skyshark); INVADERS #35-37 (Liberty Legion battled Iron Cross)

THING

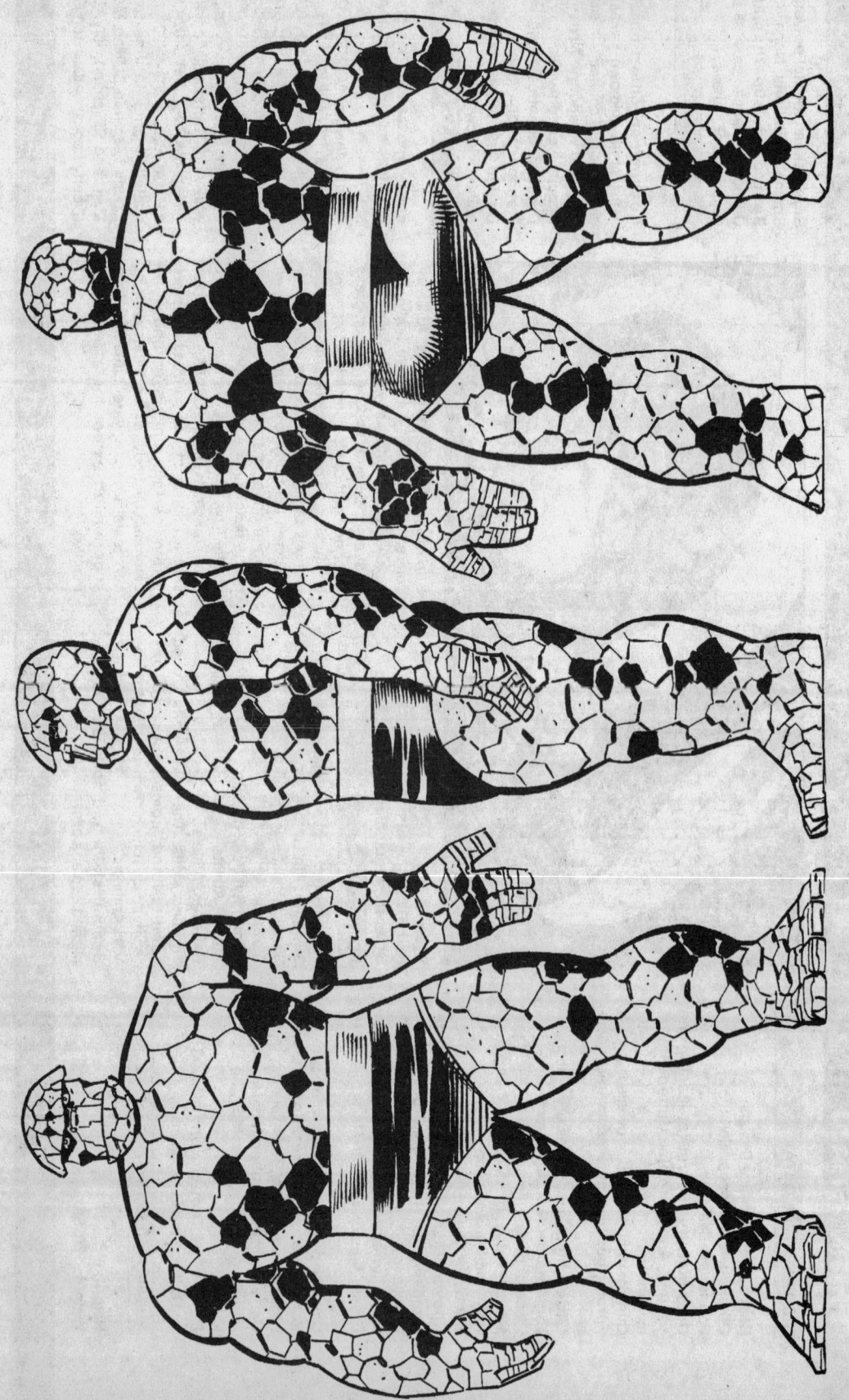

THING

BIOGRAPHICAL DATA

Real name: Benjamin Jacob Grimm
Other current aliases: None
Former aliases: Blackbeard the pirate
Dual identity: Publicly known
Current occupation: Adventurer
Former occupation: Test pilot, movie actor, professional motorcycle stunt rider, professional wrestler
Citizenship: United States of America
Legal status: No criminal record
Place of birth: New York City
Marital status: Single
Known relatives: Daniel Grimm, Elsie Grimm (parents, deceased), Daniel Jacob Grimm (brother, deceased), Jacob "Jake" Grimm (uncle), Alyce Grimm (aunt, deceased), Petunia "Penny" Grimm (uncle), Franklin Benjamin Grimm (godson)
Known confidants: Alicia Masters, Reed Richards, Johnny Storm, Sharon Ventura (Ms. MArvel II), Jacob Grimm, Petunia Grimm, Dennis Dunphy (Demolition-Man), Sandman, She-Hulk, Wyatt Wingfoot, Alynn Cambers, (former) Alyce Grimm, Daniel Jacob Grimm, Desmond Pitt (Darkoth)
Known allies: Mister Fantastic Invisible Woman, Human Torch II, She-Hulk, Ms. Marvel II, MArvel Boy II, Aquarian (Wundarr), Crystal, Medusa, Avengers, Black Panther, Daredevil, Doctor Strange, Inhumans, Nick Fury, Quasar, Sandman, Silver Surfer, Spider-Man, X-Men, Agatha Harkness, Impossible Man, Torgo, (former) Diablo, Frightful Four, Mole Man, (occasional) Thundra, Yancy Street Gang
Major enemies: Doctor Doom, Frightful Four, Galactus, Mad Thinker, Puppet master, Skrulls, Diablo, Rama-Tut, Red Ghost, Terrible Trio, (former) Hulk, Namor the Sub-Mariner, Sphinx I
Usual base of operations: Four Freedoms Plaza, New York City
Former bases of operations: Baxter Building, New York City; Central City, California; Unlimited Class Wrestling Federation headquarters, Los Angeles, California; Avengers Compound, Malibu, California
Current group membership: Fantastic Four, Avengers (reservist)
Former group membership: Avengers West Coast, Thunderiders, Unlimited Class Wrestling Federation, former leader of the Yancy Street Gang
Extent of education: College graduate

PHYSICAL DESCRIPTION

Height: 6'
Weight: 500 lbs.
Eyes: Blue
Hair: None, (in human form) Brown
Other distinguishing features: Body is covered with a orange, flexible, rock-like hide. He has no apparent neck. He has only four fingers, including the thumb, on each hand and four toes on each foot. He has no outer ear structure.

POWERS AND ABILITIES

Intelligence: Normal
Strength: Superhuman Class 90
Speed: Enhanced human
Stamina: Superhuman
Durability: Superhuman
Agility: Normal
Reflexes: Peak human
Fighting skills: Excellent hand-to-hand combatant, trained in boxing and wrestling
Special skills and abilities: Brilliant aircraft pilot
Superhuman physical powers: Aside from the above listed, none
Superhuman mental powers: None
Special limitations: None
Source of superhuman powers: Mutagenic effect due to exposure to cosmic radiation

PARAPHERNALIA

Costume specifications: Synthetic stretch fabric made of "unstable molecules," making them unusually resistant to damage
Personal weaponry: None
Special weaponry: None
Other accessories: During periods when he has reverted to human form, Ben has worn a robotic suit resembling his Thing form which enhances his strength to levels approaching the Thing's superhuman strength.
Transportation: Fantasti-Car, Pogo Plane, Skrull-design starship, and other land and air vehicles owned by the Fantastic Four; Ben also rides motorcycles.
Design and manufacture of paraphernalia: Reed Richards

BIBLIOGRAPHY

First appearance: FANTASTIC FOUR #1
Origin issue: FANTASTIC FOUR #1, FANTASTIC FOUR ANNUAL #1-2, THING #1
Significant issues: FANTASTIC FOUR #1 (first became Thing, joined Fantastic Four, first clashed with Mole Man); FANTASTIC FOUR #8 (first met Alicia Masters); FANTASTIC FOUR #12 (first fought Hulk); FANTASTIC FOUR ANNUAL #2 (recounted how he first met Reed Richards and Victor von Doom); FANTASTIC FOUR #38-40 (first reverted to human form; restored to Thing form to battle Doctor Doom); THING #1 (recounted how, as a youth, he led Yancy Street Gang); FANTASTIC FOUR #307 (became leader of Fantastic Four); FANTASTIC FOUR #310 (further mutated by cosmic radiation); FANTASTIC FOUR #326-327 (reverted to human form; returned leadership of FF to Reed Rich-ards); FANTASTIC FOUR #350 (turned self back into Thing out of love for Ms. Marvel II)

THOR

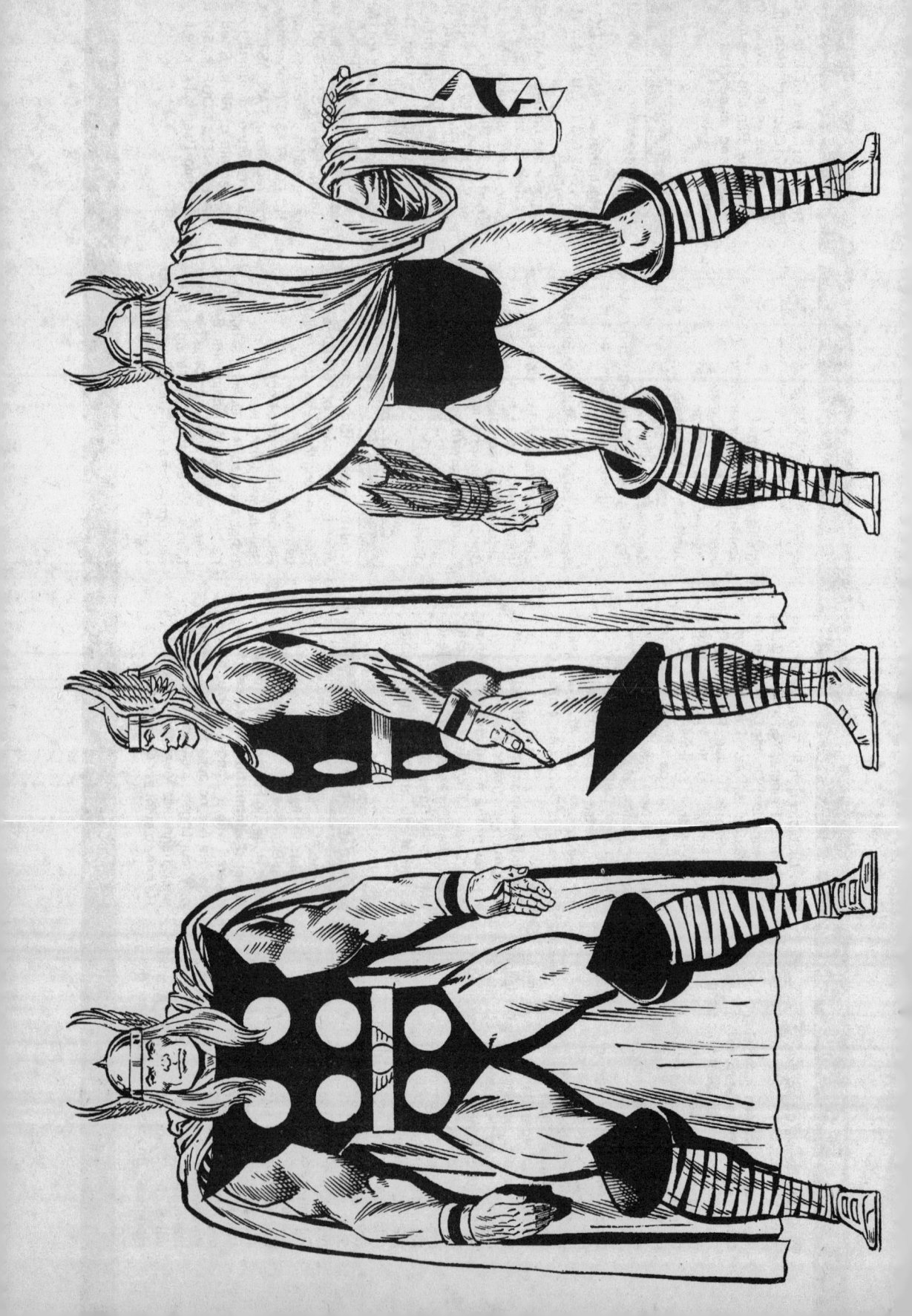

THOR

BIOGRAPHICAL DATA

Real name: Thor
Other current aliases: The God of Thunder
Former aliases: Donner, Dr. Donald Blake, Sigurd Jarlson, Eric Masterson
Note: According to one account, Thor also had previous aliases as the mythological characters Sigmund and Siegfried.
Dual identity: Thor's identity as Blake, Jarlson, and Masterson are secret. The general populace of Earth knows of Thor's existence, but most do not believe he is the god of Norse mythology.
Current occupation: Warrior god of thunder, protector of Earth
Former occupation: (as Blake) Physician, surgeon, (as Jarlson) Construction worker, (as Masterson) Architect
Citizenship: Prince of Asgard, honorary citizen of the United States
Legal status: No criminal record
Place of birth: A cave somewhere in Norway
Marital status: (as Thor, Blake, and Jarlson) Single, (as Masterson) Divorced
Known relatives: (as Thor) Odin (father) Gaea (mother), Frigga (adoptive mother), Loki (adoptive brother), Vidar (half-brother), Buri (alias Tiwaz, paternal great-grandfather, presumably deceased), Bolthorn (maternal great-grandfather, presumably deceased), Bor (grandfather, presumably deceased), Bestla (grandmother, presumably deceased), Vili, Ve (uncles, presumably deceased), Sigyn (former sister-in-law, Hela (alleged niece), Jormungand (Midgard Serpent, alleged nephew, deceased)
Known confidants: Balder, Sif, Hercules, Captain America, Iron Man, Warriors Three (Fandral, Volstagg, Hogun), Jane Foster-Kincaid
Known allies: Gods of Asgard, Avengers, Beta Ray Bill/Thor, Thor III, Einherjar, Tana Nile, Earth Force, Leir
Major enemies: Loki, Absorbing Man, Hela, Jormungand, Enchantress, Mephisto, Seth, Mister Hyde, Ymir, Surtur, Grey Gargoyle, Mangog
Usual base of operations: Dimension of Asgard, New York City
Former bases of operations: (as Thor) Scandinavian Coast, (as Blake) Chicago, Illinois
Current group membership: Avengers, Gods of Asgard
Former group membership: None
Extent of education: (as Blake) Medical school, earned M.D.

PHYSICAL DESCRIPTION

Height: 6' 6"
Weight: 640 lbs.
Eyes: Blue
Hair: Blond
Other distinguishing features: None

POWERS AND ABILITIES

Intelligence: Above normal
Strength: Superhuman Class 100
Speed: Superhuman
Flight speed: Unrevealed, possibly escape velocity
Stamina: Godlike
Durability: Metahuman
Agility: Superhuman
Reflexes: Superhuman
Fighting skills: Trained in Asgardian arts of war, highly skilled hand-to-hand combatant, proficient with most Asgardian weaponry, high skilled in the use of his hammer
Special skills and abilities: Due to his life as Don Blake, Thor possesses considerable knowledge and expertise in medicine.
Superhuman physical powers: Aside from the above listed attributes, an extremely long life span and immunity to all Earthly diseases.
Superhuman mental powers: None
Special limitations: Due to Odin's enchantment, while in Earth's dimension, Thor would revert to his mortal form if separated from his hammer for over sixty seconds
Source of superhuman powers: Thor is a hybrid member of the race of superhumans known as Asgardians and his mother Gaea

PARAPHERNALIA

Costume specifications: Asgardian materials
Personal weaponry: The enchanted hammer Mjolnir, made of mystic uru metal, which is nearly indestructible, and given the following enchantments by Odin. First, no living being, unless he/she be worthy, can lift the hammer. Second, it will return to the exact spot from which it was thrown. Third, it enables the wielder to control the elements of storm and to project forms of mystical energy. Fourth, it enables the wielder to open trans-dimensional portals. Fifth, it enables Thor to transform himself into mortal form (Blake or Masterson). Sixth, it enables the wielder to fly
Special weaponry: Enchanted belt of strength that doubles Thor's physical attributes when he wears it, but physically drains him after wearing it
Other accessories: A suit of Asgardian battle armor or a pair of strong iron gauntlets
Transportation: Interdimensional teleportation, or flight using Mjolnir; a chariot-like vehicle pulled by two large enchanted goats, Toothgnasher and Toothgrinder
Design and manufacture of paraphernalia: (Mjolnir) Brokk and Eitri, (battle armor) Thor

THOR

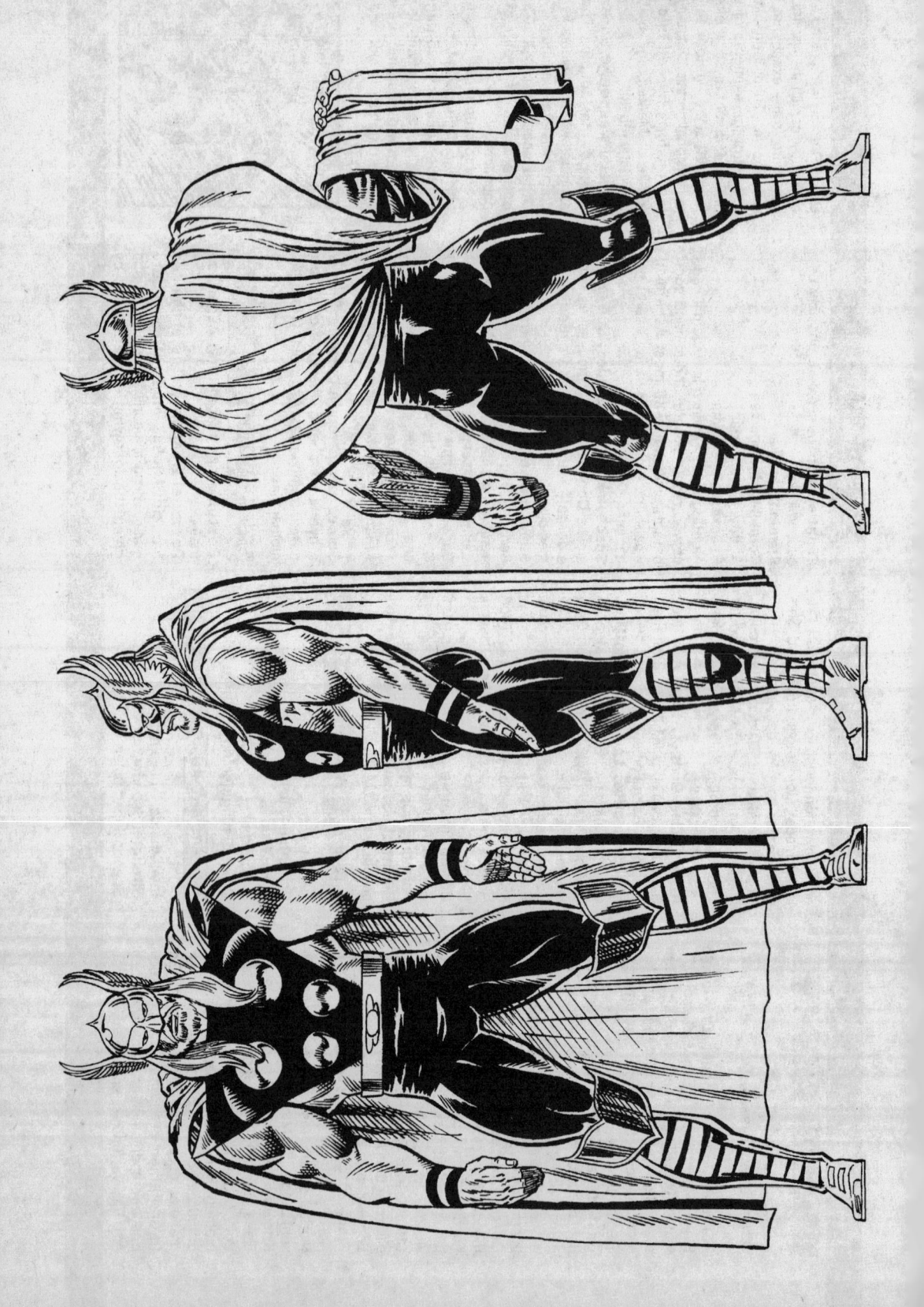

THOR II

BIOGRAPHICAL DATA

Real name: Eric Kevin Masterson
Other current aliases: The God of Thunder
Former aliases: None
Dual identity: Secret
Current occupation: (as Thor) Adventurer, (as Masterson) Architect
Former occupation: None known
Citizenship: United States of America
Legal status: No criminal record
Place of birth: Unrevealed
Marital status: Divorced
Known relatives: Marcy Masterson Steele (wife, divorced), Kevin Masterson (son)
Known confidants: Thor I, Susan Austin, Jackie Lukus, Jerry Sapristi, Hercules, Captain America, (former) Marcy Masterson
Known allies: Thor I, Balder, Sif, Warriors Three (Fandral, Volstagg, Hogun), Hercules, Captain America, Avengers, Beta Ray Bill/Thor, Thor III (Dargo Ktor), Doctor Strange, Silver Surfer, Adam Warlock
Major enemies: Loki, Mongoose, Annihilus, Absorbing Man, Titania II, Enchantress, Stellaris, Zarrko the Tomorrow Man, Mephisto, Arnim Zola, Doughboy, Thanos
Usual base of operations: New York City
Former bases of operations: None known
Current group membership: Avengers (East Coast)
Former group membership: "Thor Corps" (Beta Ray Bill, Thor III)

Extent of education: Masters degree in architecture

PHYSICAL DESCRIPTION

Height: 5'10", (as Thor II) 6'6"
Weight: 160 lbs., (as Thor II) 640 lbs.
Eyes: Blue
Hair: Blond
Other distinguishing features: None

POWERS AND ABILITIES

Intelligence: Above normal
Strength: Superhuman Class 100
Speed: Superhuman
Flight speed: Unrevealed, possibly escape velocity
Stamina: Godlike
Durability: Metahuman
Agility: Superhuman
Reflexes: Superhuman
Fighting skills: Formidable hand-to-hand combatant, relies on sheer strength; no combat training apart from recent coaching by Captain America
Special skills and abilities: Highly skilled architect
Superhuman physical powers: Aside from the above listed attributes, an extremely long life span and immunity to all Earthly diseases.
Superhuman mental powers: None
Special limitations: Due to Odin's enchantment, while in Earth's dimension, Thor II would revert to his mortal form if separated from his hammer for over sixty seconds
Source of superhuman powers: Asgardian sorcery that granted him the powers of Thor I

PARAPHERNALIA

Costume specifications: Asgardian materials
Personal weaponry: The enchanted hammer Mjolnir, made of mystic uru metal, which is nearly indestructible, and given the following enchantments by Odin. First, no living being, unless he/she be worthy, can lift the hammer. Second, it will return to the exact spot from which it was thrown. Third, it enables the wielder to control the elements of storm and to project forms of mystical energy. Fourth, it enables the wielder to open trans-dimensional portals. Fifth, it enables Thor to transform himself into his mortal form. Sixth, it enables the wielder to fly.
Special weaponry: None
Other accessories: None
Transportation: Interdimensional teleportation or flight using Mjolnir
Design and manufacture of paraphernalia: (Mjolnir) Brokk and Eitri (Asgardian dwarves)

BIBLIOGRAPHY

First appearance: (as Masterson) THOR #391, (merged with Thor I) THOR #408, (as Thor II) THOR #432
Origin issue: THOR #408, THOR #432
Significant issues: THOR #391-392 (first met Thor I, was injured by falling girders, taken to hospital by Thor I; now on crutches, attacked by Quicksand, saved by Thor I); THOR #405-408 (abducted by Mongoose; accompanied Thor I to Black Galaxy, first met Hercules, merged with Thor I by Odin to save Eric's life); THOR #421 (gave up custody of son to ex-wife); THOR #423 (separated from Thor I by Red Celestial); THOR #425 (saved Thor I's life, merged with him again); THOR #431-432 (son Kevin captured by Ulik for Loki; Thor I freed Kevin and seemingly slew Loki in battle, Heimdall separated Thor I from Masterson, banished Thor I, transformed Masterson into Thor II); THOR #433 (first met Enchantress as Leena Moran, battled Ulik); THOR #434-435 (revealed double identity to Captain America, first visited Asgard, fought Warriors Three, Balder, Heimdall, Sif, while trying to discover whereabouts of Thor I; helped rescue sleeping Odin from Annihilus); THOR #436 (battled Absorbing Man and Titania II, let them go free); THOR #437 (manipulated by Enchantress and Hercules into fighting Quasar); THOR #438 (learned Marcy and Bobby Steele intended to adopt Kevin, battled Stellaris); THOR #439-441 (teamed with Beta Ray Bill and Thor II against Zarrko and Loki); THOR #442-443 (recovered uru hammer from Mephisto)

3-D MAN

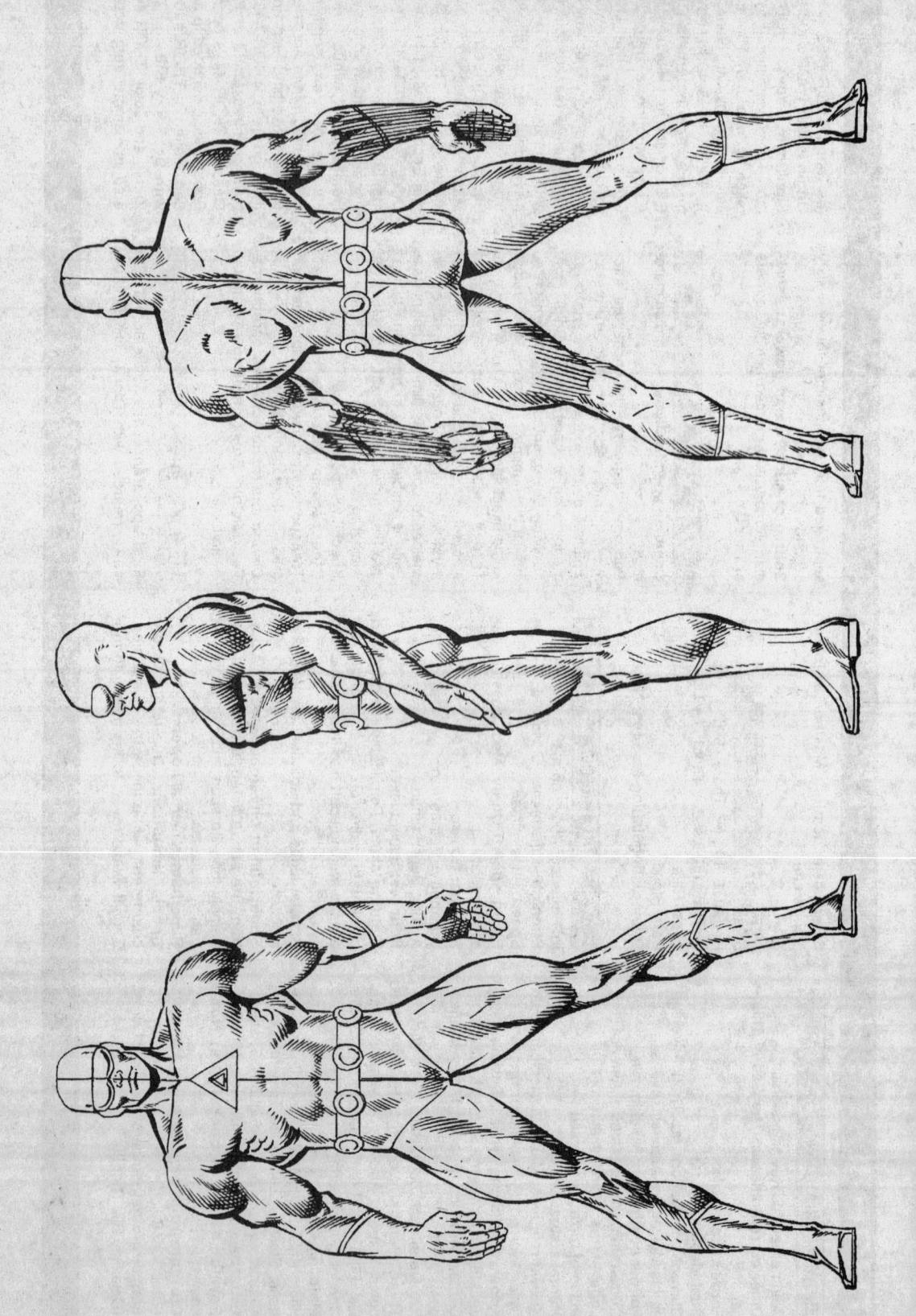

3-D MAN

BIOGRAPHICAL DATA

Real name: Charles "Chuck" Chandler and Harold "Hal" Chandler (brothers)
Other current aliases: None
Former aliases: None
Dual identity: Secret
Current occupation: (Hal) Research scientist
Former occupation: (Chuck) Test pilot, (Hal) Student
Citizenship: United States of America
Legal status: No criminal record (Chuck has been declared legally deceased)
Place of birth: Los Angeles, California
Marital status: (Hal) Married
Known relatives: (Hal) Peggy Clark-Chandler (wife), Chuck Chandler II, Hal Chandler, Jr. (sons), unnamed parents
Known confidants: Peggy Chandler, Chuck Chandler II, Hal Chandler, Jr.
Known allies: The 1950s Avengers (Marvel Boy I (deceased), Venus, Gorilla-Man, the Human Robot, James Woo (deceased), Namora (deceased), Jann of the Jungle
Major enemies: The Skrulls, Fritz Von Voltzman (nee Karl von Horstbaden, presumed deceased), the Great Video, Skull-Face, Electro I, Cold Warrior, Yellow Claw
Usual base of operations: Los Angeles, California
Former bases of operations: Los Alamos, New Mexico
Current group membership: None
Former group membership: The 1950s Avengers
Extent of education: College graduate

PHYSICAL DESCRIPTION

Height: (Chuck and 3-D Man) 6' 2", (Hal) 5' 10"
Weight: (Chuck and 3-D Man) 200 lbs., (Hal) 170 lbs.
Eyes: (Chuck and Hal) Blue, (3-D Man) Unrevealed
Hair: (Chuck and Hal) Reddish blonde, (3-D Man) Unrevealed
Other distinguishing features: Hal requires eyeglasses and crutches to walk

POWERS AND ABILITIES

Intelligence: Above normal
Strength: Enhanced human
Speed: Enhanced human
Stamina: Peak human
Durability: Peak human
Agility: Peak human
Reflexes: Peak human
Fighting skills: Good hand-to-hand combatant
Special skills and abilities: (Chuck) expert pilot, talented football player, (Hal) Experienced scientific researcher
Superhuman physical powers: As reflected in the above listed attributes, the 3-D Man possesses approximately threes times the physical attributes and sensory acuity of the average human male
Superhuman mental powers: Limited quasi-telepathic ability to perceive the distinctive aura of the Skrull race, even when a Skrull has assumed another form; telepathic link with Hal Chandler, who becomes comatose when the 3-D Man is active (the 3-D Man's consciousness is apparently a synthesis of Chuck and Hal's mind's, with Chuck's usually dominant)
Special limitations: Hal is astigmatic, and requires glasses; a poliomyelitis victim as a child, he now requires crutches to walk; 3-D Man can only remain in three-dimensional reality for 3 hours at a time before returning to two-dimensional existence
Source of superhuman powers: Exposure to unknown radiation in explosion of Skrull starship

PARAPHERNALIA

Costume specifications: A specially designed NASA flight suit (circa late 1950s), altered in appearance and bonded to his skin
Personal weaponry: None
Special weaponry: None
Other accessories: None
Transportation: Conventional
Design and manufacture of paraphernalia: Inapplicable

BIBLIOGRAPHY

First appearance: MARVEL PREMIERE #35
Origin issue: MARVEL PREMIERE #35
Significant issues: MARVEL PREMIERE #35 (as Chuck Chandler, test-piloted XF-13 rocket-plane, encountered Skrull invaders, affected by radiation in explosion of Skrull ship, believed killed but actually transformed into two-dimensional being capable of being summoned into three-dimensional existence by his brother Hal; as 3-D Man, battled Skrull agents); MARVEL PREMIERE #36 (battled Skrull infiltrators); MARVEL PREMIERE #37 (battled the Cold Warrior); WHAT IF Vol. 1 #9 (exploits with 1950s Avengers recounted, battled Yellow Claw and superhuman minions, team asked to disband by President Dwight D. Eisenhower); INCREDIBLE HULK Vol. 2 #251 (reappeared for the first time in many years, encountered the Hulk, revealed his existence to Hal Chandler's family, returned to two-dimensional reality); MARVEL SUPER-HERO CONTEST OF THE CHAMPIONS #1 (alongside many other heroes, summoned by the Grandmaster)

THUNDERBALL

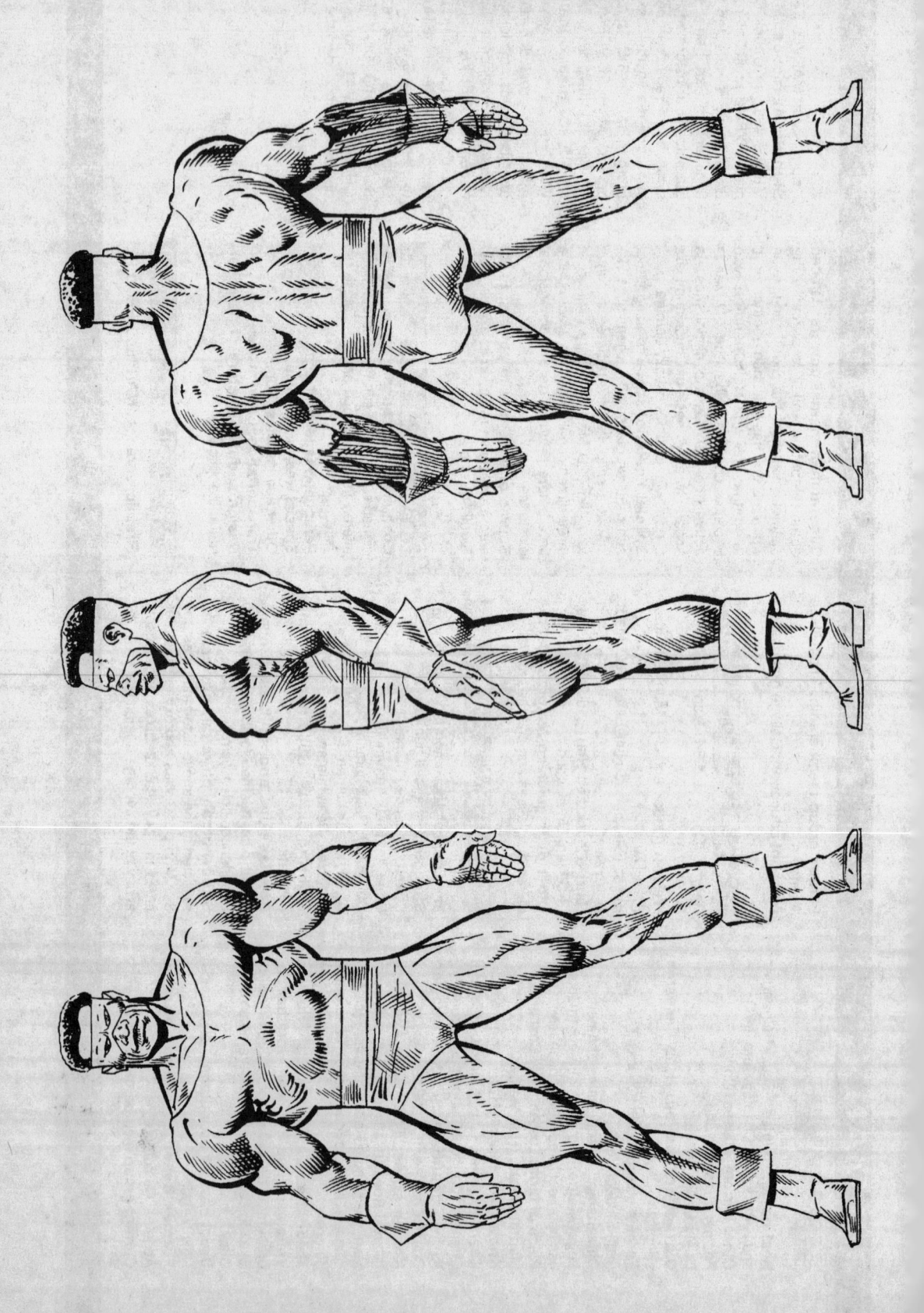

THUNDERBALL

BIOGRAPHICAL DATA

Real name: Eliot Franklin
Other current aliases: None
Former aliases: None
Dual identity: Known to the authorities
Current occupation: Professional criminal
Former occupation: Physicist and engineer
Citizenship: United States of America
Legal status: Criminal record in the U.S.
Place of birth: Buffalo, New York
Marital status: Single
Known relatives: None
Known confidants: None
Known allies: The Wrecking Crew (Wrecker, Piledriver, Bulldozer); Masters of Evil IV (Baron Zemo II, Tiger Shark, Mr. Hyde, Goliath IV, the Fixer, Moonstone II, Blackout I, Yellowjacket II, Absorbing Man, Titania II, Screaming Mimi, Grey Gargoyle), Electro, Ironclad, Midnight II, Secret Empire IV
Major enemies: Thor, the Avengers, Hercules, Spider-Man, Venom
Usual base of operations: New York City
Former bases of operations: None
Current group membership: None
Former group membership: The Wrecking Crew, Masters of Evil IV, the Secret Empire IV
Extent of education: Ph.D. in physics

PHYSICAL DESCRIPTION

Height: 6'6"
Weight: 225 lbs., (enhanced) 350 lbs.
Eyes: Brown
Hair: Black
Other distinguishing features: None

POWERS AND ABILITIES

Intelligence: Gifted
Strength: Superhuman Class 10
Speed: Normal
Stamina: Enhanced human
Durability: Superhuman
Agility: Normal
Reflexes: Normal
Fighting skills: Experienced streetfighter
Special skills and abilities: Gifted physicist, experienced planner and tactician
Superhuman physical powers: Aside from the above listed attributes, none
Superhuman mental powers: None
Special limitations: None
Source of superhuman powers: Asgardian magic

PARAPHERNALIA

Costume specifications: Synthetic stretch fabric
Personal weaponry: A virtually indestructable wrecking ball attached to a four foot-long chain
Special weaponry: An energized wrecking ball capable of projecting electrical energy bolts and an energized exoskeleton suit (used when not in possession of his regular wrecking ball and superhuman powers)
Other accessories: None
Transportation: (with Wrecking Crew) Magical teleportation through the Wrecker's crowbar; (with Secret Empire) Various air and land vehicles
Design and manufacture of paraphernalia: (energized wrecking ball and exoskeleton suit) Eliot Franklin

BIBLIOGRAPHY

First appearance: DEFENDERS #17
Origin issue: DEFENDERS #18
Significant issues: DEFENDERS #17-19 (gained superhuman powers, battled Defenders alongside Wrecking Crew while attempting to locate Gamma Bomb); IRON FIST #11-12 (battled Captain America and Iron Fist alongside the Wrecking Crew while trying to lure Thor into battle); THOR #304 (battled Thor alongside the Wrecking Crew); IRON MAN #171 (battled Iron Man II); MARVEL SUPER-HEROES SECRET WARS #1-12 (taken to the Beyonder's Battleworld with the rest of the Wrecking Crew and various other criminals, battled the Avengers, X-Men, Fantastic Four, and others); SPECTACULAR SPIDER-MAN #125-126 (battled Spider-Man and Spider Woman II alongside the Wrecking Crew while attempting to acquire the means to blackmail the federal government; fought with Wrecker for control over Norn power, defeated by Spider-Man and Spider-Woman II); AVENGERS #273-277 (joined the Masters of Evil IV alongside the Wrecking Crew, took over Avengers Mansion, defeated Hercules, drained of powers by Thor); FANTASTIC FOUR #355 (protected from Wrecker's vengeance by the Thing); THE VAULT GRAPHIC NOVEL (alongside other superhuman criminals, attempted escape from the Vault, battled Avengers and Freedom Force; battled Venom for leadership of the convicts, helped Iron Man and Dr. Pym disarm bomb which would have destroyed the Vault); FANTASTIC FOUR #335 (among villains assembled by Doctor Doom to battle the Fantastic Four during the "Acts of Vengeance"); THOR #418: 426-428 (with Wrecking Crew, freed Wrecker and Ulik from police custody; battled Hercules and Thor; battled Thor, Excalibur, and Code: Blue); AMAZING SPIDER-MAN #353-358 (freed from police custody by Midnight II, joined forces with Secret Empire IV, battled Spider-Man, Darkhawk, Punisher, Moon Knight, Nova, and Night Thrasher)

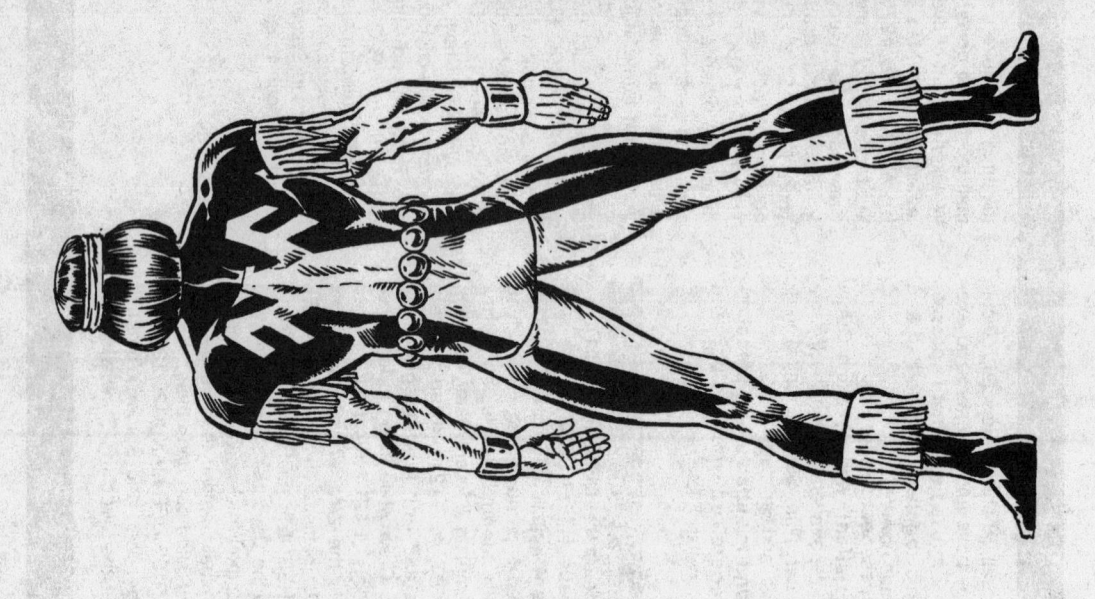

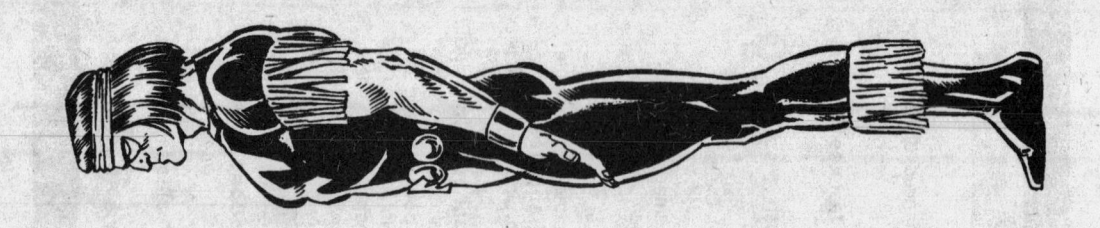

THUNDERBIRD

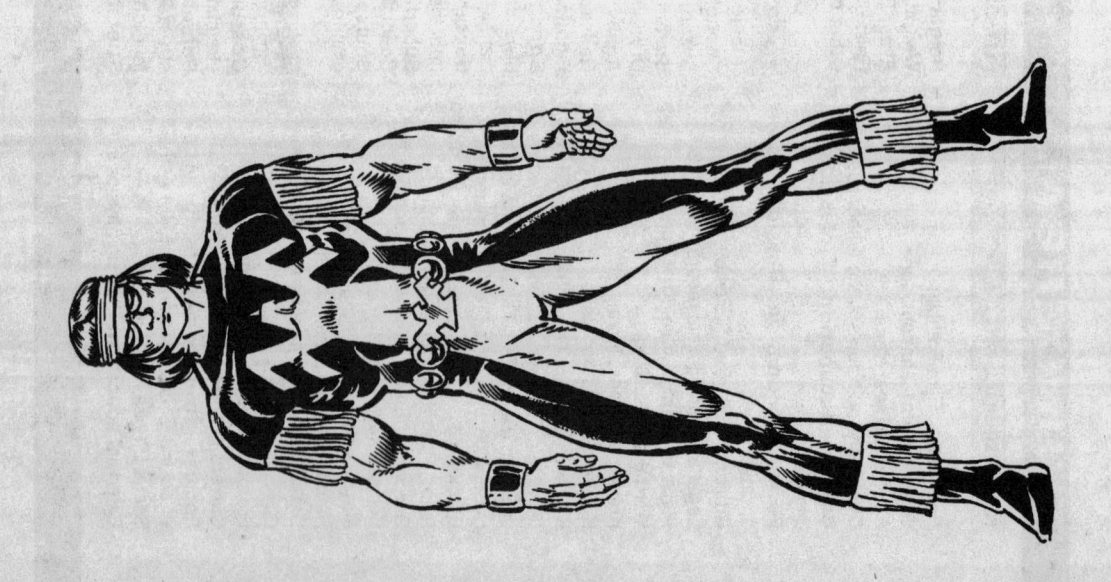

THUNDERBIRD

BIOGRAPHICAL DATA

Real name: John Proudstar
Aliases at time of death: None
Dual identity: Secret
Occupation at time of death: Adventurer
Former occupation: Corporal in the United States Marines
Citizenship: United States of America
Legal status: No criminal record
Place of birth: Apache reservation at Camp Verde, Arizona
Place of death: Valhalla Base, Colorado
Cause of death: Airplane crash
Marital status: Single
Known relatives: Neal Proudstar (father), Maria Proudstar (mother), James Proudstar (brother, alias Warpath)
Known confidants: None
Known allies: The X-Men
Major enemies: Count Nefaria
Usual base of operations: Professor Xavier's School for Gifted Youngsters, Westchster, New York
Former bases of operations: Camp Verde, Arizona
Group membership at time of death: The X-Men
Former group membership: None
Extent of education: High school drop-out

PHYSICAL DESCRIPTION

Height: 6' 1 1/2"
Weight: 225 lbs.
Eyes: Brown
Hair: Black

Other distinguishing features: None

POWERS AND ABILITIES

Intelligence: Normal
Strength: Superhuman Class 10
Speed: Peak human
Stamina: Enhanced human
Durability: Peak human
Agility: Peak human
Reflexes: Enhanced human

Fighting skills: Military training, in hand to hand combat
Special skills and abilities: None
Superhuman physical powers: Superhuman strength, speed, stamina, and durability due to dense musculature
Superhuman mental powers: None
Special limitations: None
Source of superhuman powers: Mutation

PARAPHERNALIA

Costume specifications: Synthetic stretch fabric
Personal weaponry: None
Special weaponry: None
Other accessories: None
Transportation: X-Men jet, the Blackbird
Design and manufacture of paraphernalia: Inapplicable

BIBLIOGRAPHY

First appearance: GIANT-SIZE X-MEN #1
Origin issue: CLASSIC X-MEN #3
Significant issues: GIANT-SIZE X-MEN #1 (recruited by Professor Xavier to rescue the original X-Men from Krakoa the mutant island); X-MEN #94 (accompanied X-Men to Valhalla Base to combat Count Nefaria); X-MEN #95 (battled the Ani-Men, died disabling jet Count Nefaria used as his means of escape)

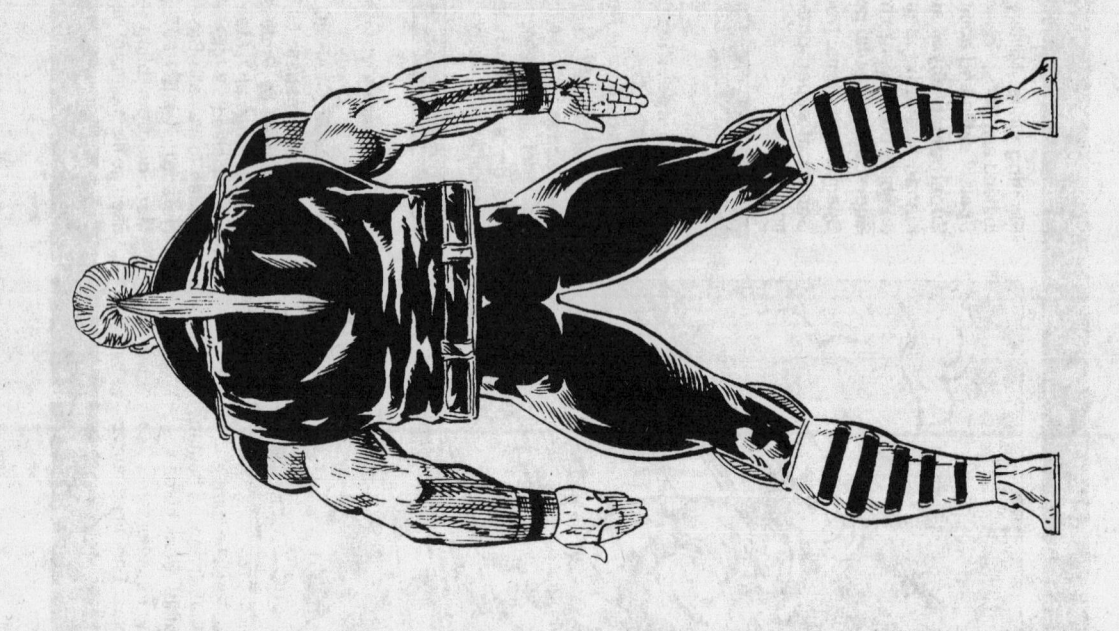

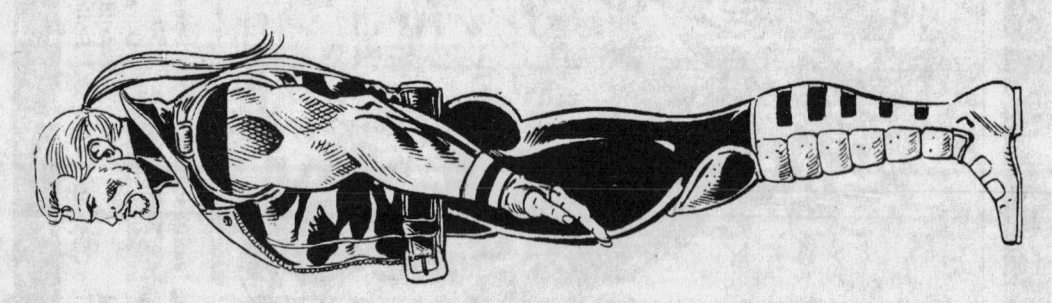

THUNDERSTRIKE

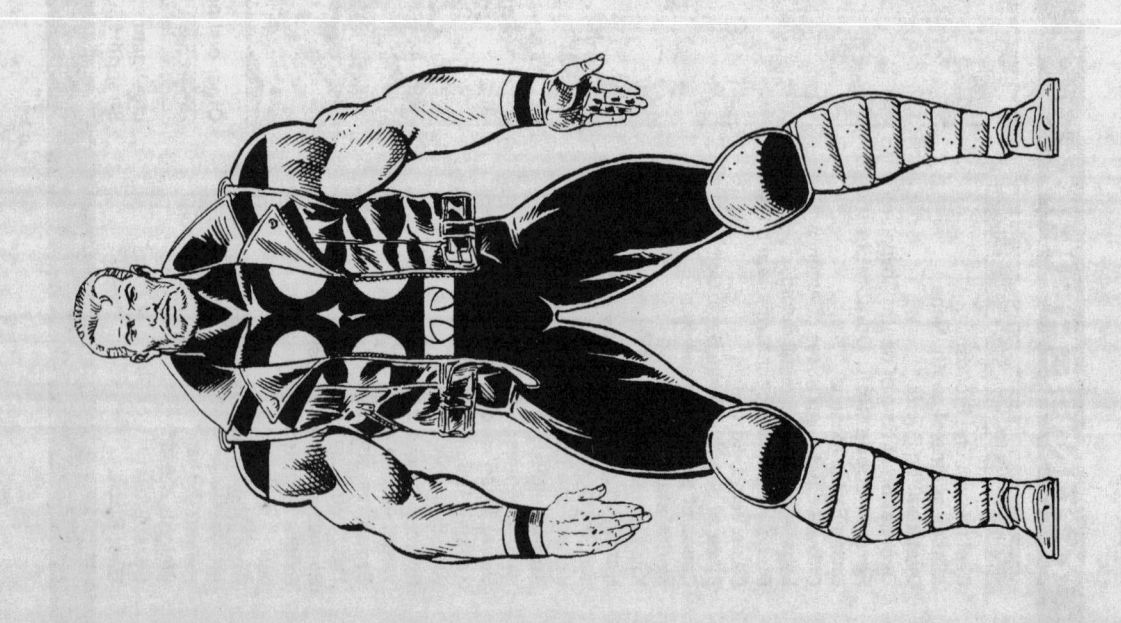

THUNDERSTRIKE

BIOGRAPHICAL DATA

Real name: Eric Kevin Masterson
Other current aliases: None
Former aliases: Thor II
Dual identity: Secret
Current occupation: (as Thunderstrike) Adventurer, crimefighter, (as Masterson) Architect
Former occupation: None known
Citizenship: United States of America
Legal status: No criminal record
Place of birth: Unrevealed
Marital status: Divorced
Known relatives: Marcy Masterson Steele (wife, divorced), Kevin Masterson (son), Unnamed parents
Known confidants: Thor I, Susan Austin, Jackie Lukus, Samantha Joyce, Jerry Sapristi, Hercules, Captain America, (former) Marcy Masterson
Known allies: Thor I, Balder, Sif, Warriors Three (Fandral, Volstagg, Hogun), Hercules, Captain America, Avengers, Beta Ray Bill/Thor, Thor III (Dargo Ktor), Quasar, Code: Blue, Odin, Doctor Strange, Silver Surfer, Adam Warlock
Major enemies: Loki, Mongoose, Bloodaxe, Annihilus, Absorbing Man, Titania II, Enchantress, Stellaris, Zarrko the Tomorrow Man, Mephisto, Arnim Zola, Doughboy, Possessor, Carjack, (former) Thanos
Usual base of operations: New York City
Former bases of operations: None known
Current group membership: Avengers (East Coast)
Former group membership: "Thor Corps" (Beta Ray Bill, Thor III)
Extent of education: Masters degree in architecture

PHYSICAL DESCRIPTION

Height: 5' 10", (as Thunderstrike) 6' 6"
Weight: 160 lbs., (as Thunderstrike) 640 lbs.
Eyes: Blue
Hair: Blond
Other distinguishing features: None

POWERS AND ABILITIES

Intelligence: Above normal
Strength: Superhuman Class 50
Speed: Superhuman
Flight speed: Unrevealed, possibly escape velocity
Stamina: Superhuman
Durability: Superhuman
Agility: Superhuman
Reflexes: Superhuman
Fighting skills: Formidable hand-to-hand combatant, received some combat training from Captain America
Special skills and abilities: Highly skilled architect
Superhuman physical powers: Aside from the above listed attributes, none
Superhuman mental powers: None
Special limitations: As Masterson, nearsighted and wears glasses
Source of superhuman powers: Asgardian sorcery

PARAPHERNALIA

Costume specifications: Asgardian materials, leather jacket made on Earth
Personal weaponry: The enchanted mace Thunderstrike, made of mystic uru metal, which is nearly indestructible, and given the following enchantments by Odin. By stamping the mace Thunderstrike can revert to his mortal human form, dressed in whichever clothes he last wore in that form, while the mace transforms into a wooden cane. By stamping the cane Eric Masterson turns back into his Thunderstrike form, bearded and garbed in his Thunderstrike costume, while the cane again becomes the mace. By throwing the mace and gripping its strap, Thunderstrike can fly. He can use the mace to project powerful concussive blasts of mystical energy. The mace magically enables him to survive the adverse conditions of outer space, including its lack of oxygen.
Special weaponry: None known
Other accessories: None known
Transportation: Flight using Thunderstrike
Design and manufacture of paraphernalia: (Thunderstrike) Brokk and Eitri (Asgardian dwarves)

BIBLIOGRAPHY

First appearance: (as Masterson) THOR #391, (merged with Thor I) THOR #408, (as Thor II) THOR #432, (as Thunderstrike) QUASAR #47
Origin issue: THOR #408, 432, 459, THUNDERSTRIKE #1
Significant issues: THOR #391-392 (first met Thor I, was injured by falling girders, taken to hospital by Thor I; now on crutches, attacked by Quicksand, saved by Thor I); THOR #405-408 (abducted by Mongoose; accompanied Thor I to Black Galaxy, first met Hercules; mortally wounded by Mongoose, merged with Thor I by Odin to save Eric's life); THOR #421 (gave up custody of son to ex-wife); THOR #423 (separated from Thor I by Red Celestial); THOR #425 (saved Thor I's life, merged with him again); THOR #431-432 (son Kevin captured by Ulik for Loki; Thor I freed Kevin and seemingly slew Loki in battle, Heimdall separated Thor I from Masterson, banished Thor I, transformed Masterson into Thor II); THOR #433 (first met Enchantress as Leena Moran, battled Ulik); THOR #434-435 (revealed double identity to Captain America, first visited Asgard, fought Warriors Three, Balder, Heimdall, Sif, while trying to discover whereabouts of Thor I; helped rescue sleeping Odin from Annihilus); THOR #439-441 (teamed with Beta Ray Bill and Thor II against Zarrko and Loki); THOR #459 (given the enchanted mace Thunderstrike by Thor and Odin); THUNDERSTRIKE #1 (adopted the name Thunderstrike, battled Bloodaxe and Carjack)

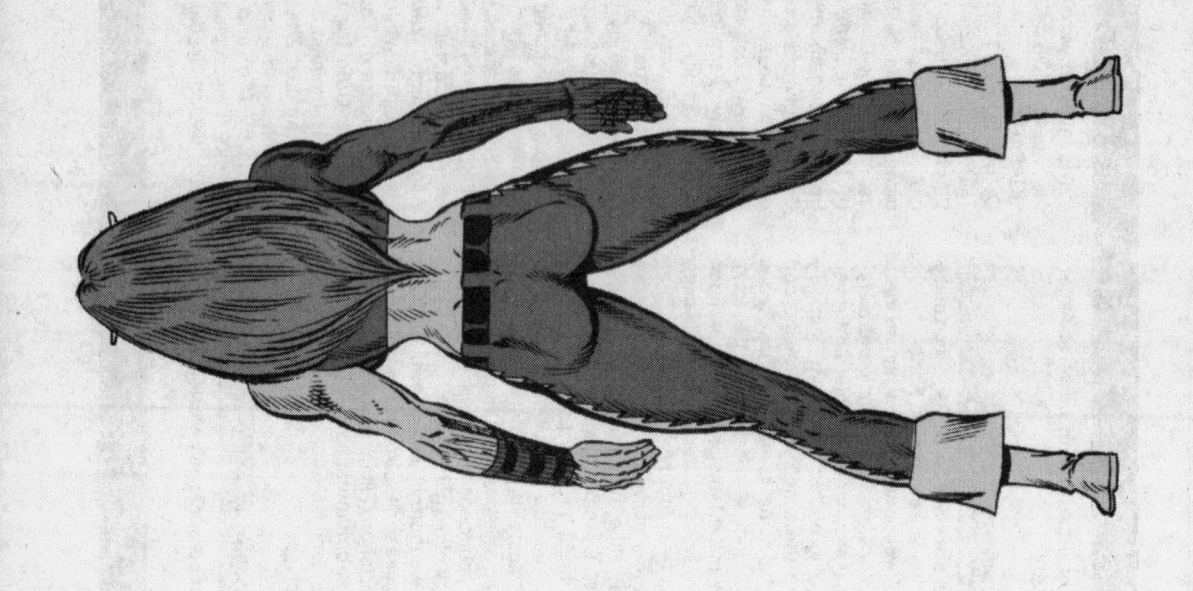

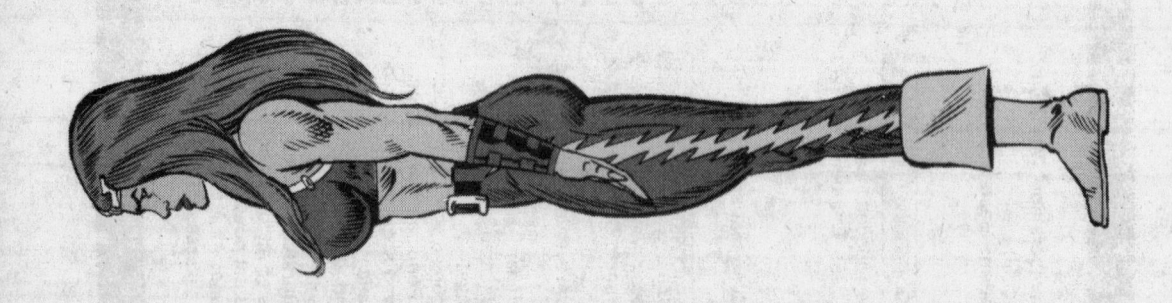

THUNDRA

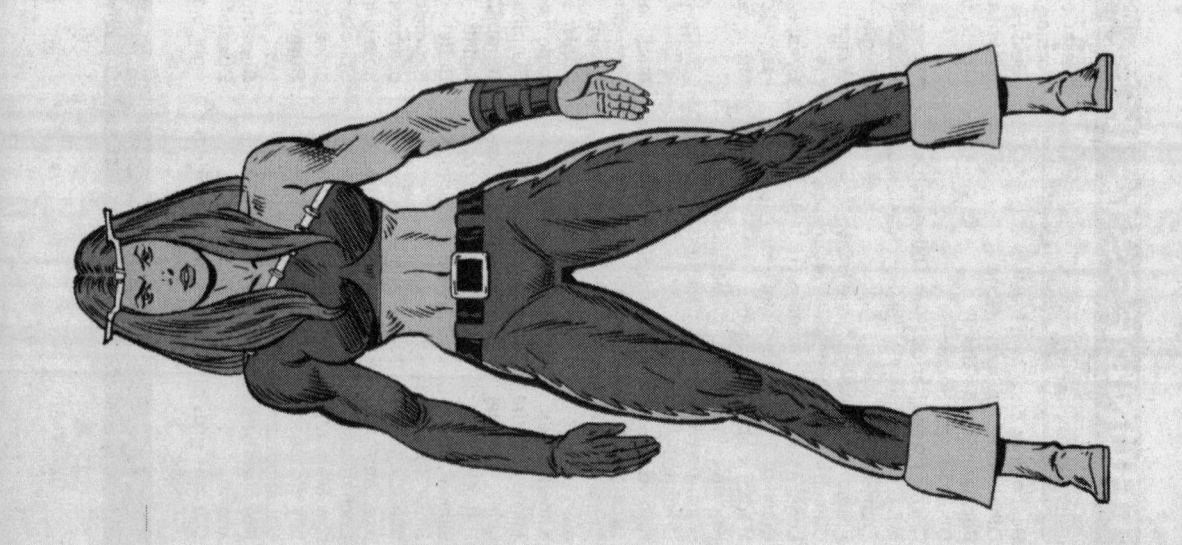

THUNDRA

BIOGRAPHICAL DATA

Real name: Thundra
Other current aliases: None
Former aliases: None
Dual identity: None
Current occupation: Empress of Femizonia
Former occupation: Warrior, professional wrestler
Citizenship: United Sisterhood Republic of an alternate future 23rd Century Earth
Legal status: No criminal record
Place of birth: Greater Milago, Midwestern Republic, United Sisterhood Republic
Marital status: Single
Known relatives: None
Known confidants: Ben Grimm (the Thing)
Known allies: Fantastic Four
Major enemies: Mahkizmo
Usual base of operations: United Sisterhood Republic, in an alternate future of the 23rd Century
Former bases of operations: New York area, 20th Century
Current group membership: Empress of the Femizons
Former group membership: Frightful Four (Wizard, Trapster, Sandman), the Grapplers (Letha [deceased], Screaming Mimi, Titania I [deceased], Poundcakes)
Extent of education: Unrevealed

PHYSICAL DESCRIPTION

Height: 7' 2"
Weight: 250 lbs.
Eyes: Green
Hair: Red
Other distinguishing features: None

POWERS AND ABILITIES

Intelligence: Above normal
Strength: Superhuman Class 75
Speed: Peak human
Stamina: Peak human
Durability: Superhuman
Agility: Peak human
Reflexes: Peak human
Fighting skills: Extensive training in hand-to-hand and military combat techniques of the 23rd Century; experienced swordswoman, seasoned combat veteran
Special skills and abilities: Intensive pain-management training
Superhuman physical powers: Aside from the above listed attributes, none
Superhuman mental powers: None
Special limitations: None
Source of superhuman powers: Genetic engineering

PARAPHERNALIA

Costume specifications: Synthetic stretch fabric and leather
Personal weaponry: A three-foot linked chain
Special weaponry: None
Other accessories: None
Transportation: Various
Design and manufacture of paraphernalia: Inapplicable

BIBLIOGRAPHY

First appearance: FANTASTIC FOUR #129
Origin issue: FANTASTIC FOUR #151
Significant issues: FANTASTIC FOUR #129-130 (joined Frightful Four, battled Fantastic Four); FANTASTIC FOUR #133 (battled the Thing in personal combat, quit the Frightful Four); GIANT-SIZE SUPER-STARS #1 (battled the Hulk, who was possessing the Thing's body); FANTASTIC FOUR #148 (assisted Fantastic Four against Frightful Four); FANTASTIC FOUR #149 (assisted Fantastic Four against Namor the Sub-Mariner); FANTASTIC FOUR #151-153 (time travel from 23rd Century Femizonia, an alternate future ruled by women, to prevent formation of Machus, an alternate future ruled by men revealed; alongside Fantastic Four, battled Mahkizmo, remained in 20th Century after dimensional interface of Femizonia and Machus); FANTASTIC FOUR #177-178 (assisted Fantastic Four and Tigra, against Frightful Four); FANTASTIC FOUR #179-183 (assisted Fantastic Four, Tigra, and Impossible Man, against Brute, Mad Thinker, and Annihilus); MARVEL TWO-IN-ONE #53-55 (met wrestling promoter Herkimer Oglethorpe, became professional wrestler); MARVEL TWO-IN-ONE #56 (alongside the Grapplers, employed by Roxxon to smuggle Nth Projector out of Project Pegasus, battled the Thing); MARVEL TWO-IN-ONE #58 (alongside the Thing, Quasar, Giant-Man II, and Aquarian, fought the Nth Man); AVENGERS ANNUAL #8 (encountered Hyperion II and the Avengers, battled Ms. Marvel I); MARVEL TWO-IN-ONE #67 (with Hyperion II, stole the Nth Projector from the Nth Command; returned to alternate Femizonia which did not interface with Machus); FANTASTIC FOUR #303 (revealed as Empress of Femizonia, teamed with Thing to battle Machan rebels); AVENGERS WEST COAST #75 (abducted the Avengers and Fantastic Four to the future to enlist their aid in defending Femizonia from the extradimensional Arkon and his warriors from Polemachus, fought Arkon in personal combat, became romantically inclined toward him)

TIGER SHARK

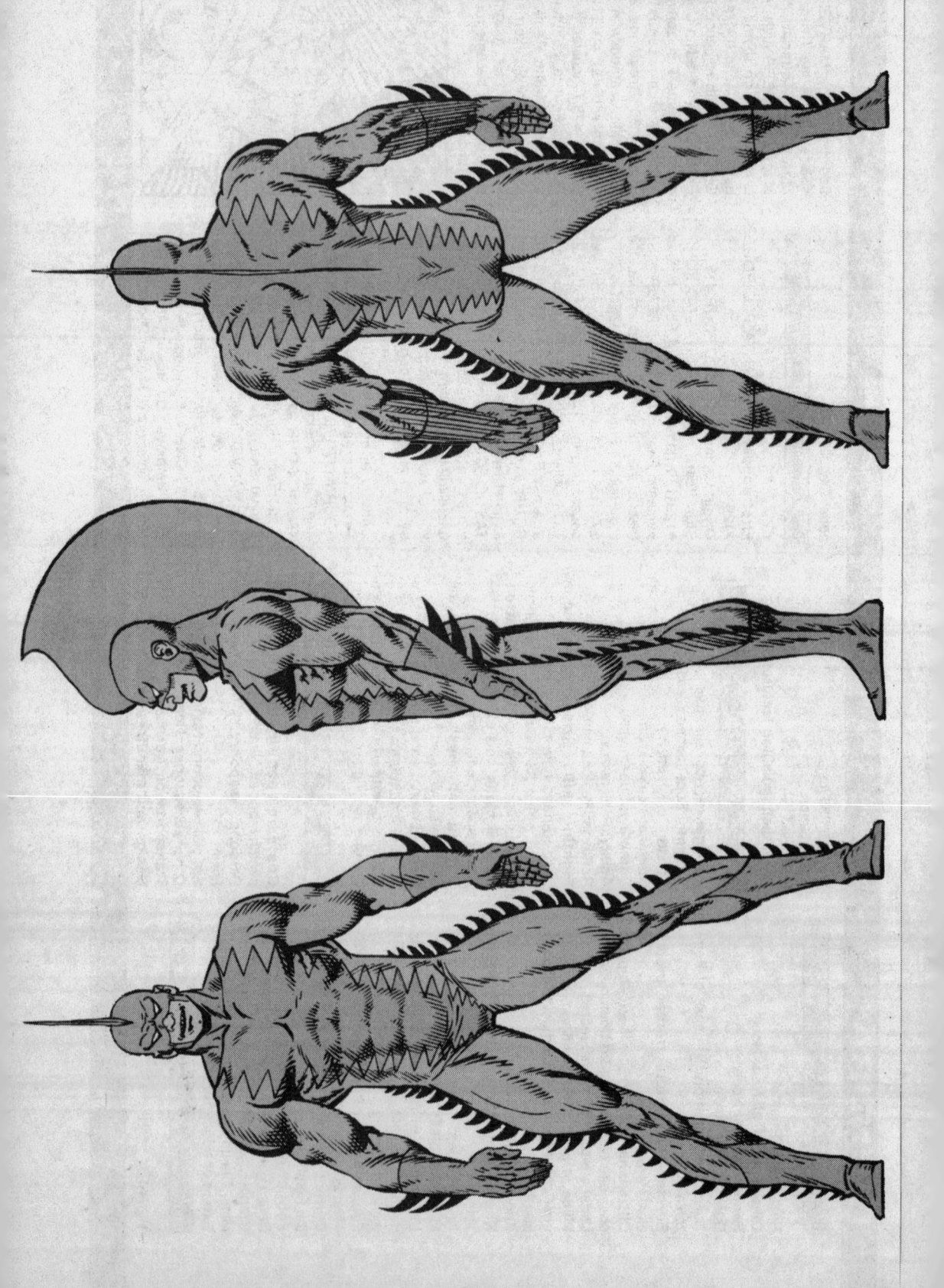

TIGER SHARK

BIOGRAPHICAL DATA

Real name: Todd Arliss
Other current aliases: None
Former aliases: None
Dual identity: Publicly known
Current occupation: Professional criminal
Former occupation: Athlete (swimmer)
Citizenship: United States of America
Legal status: Criminal record in the U.S.
Place of birth: Pasadena, California
Marital status: Single
Known relatives: Diane Arliss Newell (sister), Walter Arliss (aka Stingray, brother-in-law)
Known confidants: None
Known allies: Dr. Lemuel Dorcas, Llyra, Attuma, Masters of Evil III (Egghead, Radioactive Man, Scorpion, Moonstone II, Shocker, Beetle, Whirlwind), Masters of Evil IV (Baron Zemo II, Moonstone II, Whirlwind, Mr. Hyde, Absorbing Man, Titania, Screaming Mimi, Grey Gargoyle, Yellowjacket II, Goliath IV, Blackout I, Fixer, Wrecker, Bulldozer, Piledriver, Thunderball)
Major enemies: Namor the Sub-Mariner, the Avengers, Stingray
Usual base of operations: Mobile
Former bases of operations: Atlantic Ocean
Current group membership: None
Former group membership: Masters of Evil III and IV
Education: Unrevealed

PHYSICAL DESCRIPTION

Height: 6' 1"
Weight: 450 lbs.
Eyes: Grey
Hair: Brown
Other distinguishing features: Tiger Shark has gills on his cheeks and razor-sharp pointed teeth

POWERS AND ABILITIES

Intelligence: Normal
Strength: (on land) Superhuman Class 50, (in water) Superhuman Class 75
Speed: Enhanced human
Water speed: Superhuman
Stamina: (on land) Enhanced human, (in water) Superhuman
Durability: (on land) Enhanced human, (in water) Superhuman
Agility: (on land) Peak human, (in water) Superhuman
Reflexes: (on land) Peak human, (in water) Superhuman
Fighting skills: Minimal experience at hand-to-hand combat; relies on brute strength and shark-like tenacity in battle
Special skills and abilities: Todd Arliss was an Olympic champion swimmer before he acquired superhuman powers.
Superhuman physical powers: Besides the above listed attributes, Tiger Shark has the ability to survive indefinitely underwater
Superhuman mental powers: None
Special limitations: Tiger Shark must be immersed in water to achieve his full strength. On land, he must wear his special costume to retain his strength.
Source of superhuman power: Genetic engineering process adapting abilities of tiger sharks and Namor the Sub-Mariner

PARAPHERNALIA

Costume specifications: Waterproof synthetic stretch fabric; contains a water circulation system which bathes him with a thin layer of water whenever he is on land.
Personal weaponry: None
Special weaponry: None
Other accessories: None
Transportation: Swimming under own power
Design and manufacture of paraphernalia: Dr. Lemuel Dorcas

BIBLIOGRAPHY

First appearance: SUB-MARINER #5
Origin issue: SUB-MARINER #5
Significant issues: SUB-MARINER #5-6 (gained superhuman powers in experiment by Dr. Dorcas to cure his injured back, defeated by Namor the Sub-Mariner, taken to Atlantis for possible cure for his condition); SUB-MARINER #9 (escaped from Atlantis during rebellion caused by the Serpent Crown); SUB-MARINER #16 (encountered the People of the Mist in the Sargasso Sea, battled Namor); SUB-MARINER #24 (battled Orka in undersea crevice); SUB-MARINER #43-46 (allied with Llyra, battled Namor and Stingray; killed Namor's father, Leonard MacKenzie); INCREDIBLE HULK Vol. 2 #160 (battled Hulk at Niagara Falls); MARVEL TEAM-UP #14 (allied with Dr. Lemuel Dorcas, battled Namor and Spider-Man); SUPER-VILLAIN TEAM-UP #1-3 (allied with Dr. Dorcas and Attuma, battled Namor and Doctor Doom; imprisoned on Hydrobase); MS. MARVEL #15-16 (escaped Hydrobase, abducted Namorita, battled Ms. Marvel I); AVENGERS #222 (joined Masters of Evil III; battled Avengers); AVENGERS #228-229 (alongside Masters of Evil III, aided Egghead's scheme to ruin Henry Pym, defeated by Pym and Avengers); AVENGERS #273-277 (joined Baron Zemo II's Master of Evil IV, invaded Avengers Mansion, battled Hercules, escaped when the Avengers retook the mansion); WEST COAST AVENGERS #16 (alongside Whirlwind, captured by Tigra and Hellcat; imprisoned in the Vault); MARVEL COMICS PRESENTS #53-56 (feigned illness to escape the Vault, battled Stingray, later helped Stingray rescue his sister); WOLVERINE #19-20 (during events of "Acts of Vengeance," battled Wolverine and La Bandera in Tierra Verde); MARVEL COMICS PRESENTS #77 (captured by Dr. Barnabas Lucian Cross, rescued by Namor)

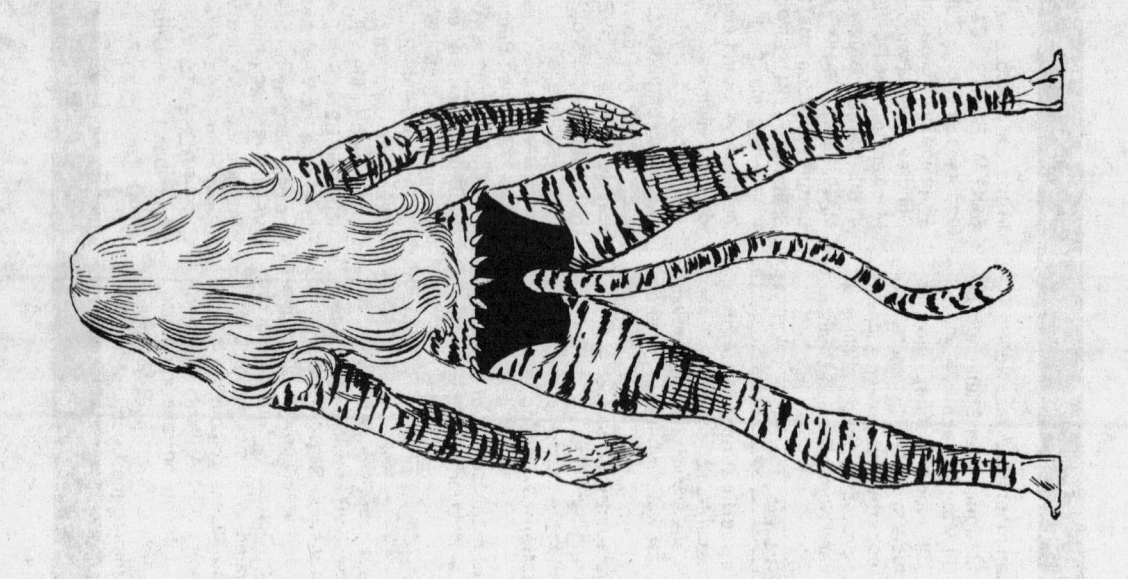

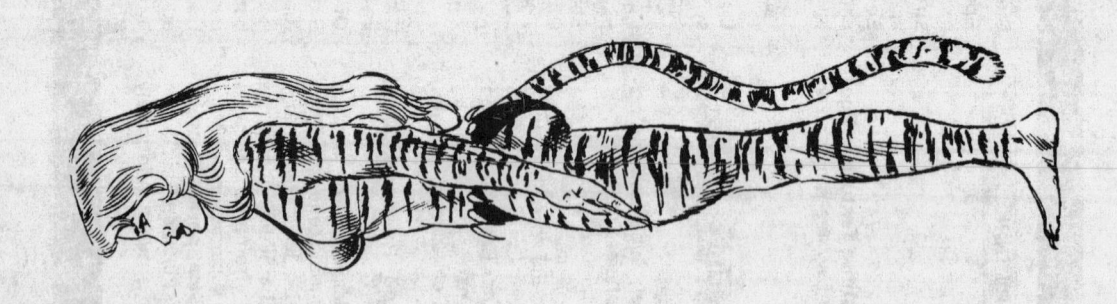

TIGRA

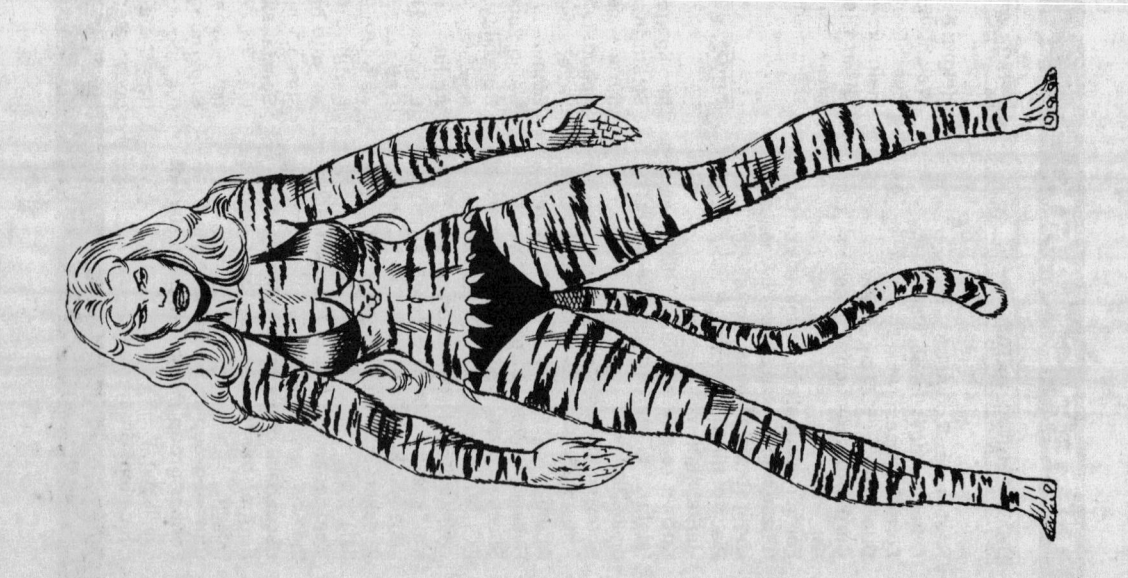

TIGRA

BIOGRAPHICAL DATA

Real name: Greer Grant Nelson
Other current aliases: Werecat, Werewoman
Former aliases: The Cat II
Dual identity: Publically known
Current Occupation: Adventurer
Former occupation: Laboratory assistant, model, private investigator
Citizenship: United States of America
Legal status: No criminal record
Place of birth: Chicago, Illinois
Marital status: Widowed
Known relatives: William Nelson (husband, deceased)
Known confidants: Mockingbird, Thing, Wonder Man, (former) Dr. Joanne MArie Tumulo
Known allies: Avengers West Coast, Avengers East, Hellcat, Spider-Man, Agatha Harkness, the Fantastic Four, the Shroud, Jessica Drew, Hellstorm, Ebony
Major enemies: Tabur, HYDRA, Master Pandemonium, Graviton, Ultron, Allatou, Dominus, Scorpio I, Zodiac II, (former) Malcolm Donalbain, Kraven the Hunter, Werewolf, Molecule Man, unnamed king of the Cat People (deceased)
Usual base of operations: Avengers Compound, Palos Verdes, California (currently on leave in the Australian outback)
Former bases of operations: Chicago, Illinois; Avengers Mansion, New York City; San Francisco, California
Current group membership: Avengers West Coast (currently on leave)
Former group membership: Avengers East
Extent of education: Bachelor of science degree

PHYSICAL DESCRIPTION

Height: 5' 10"
Weight: 180 lbs
Eyes: Green
Hair: Orange fur with black stripes, (in human form) Black
Other distinguishing features: In her superhuman form Tigra possesses a tail, unusually sharp canine teeth, vertically slitted catlike pupils and irises, claws on her hands and feet, and pointed ears.

POWERS AND ABILITIES

Intelligence: Normal
Strength: Superhuman Class 10
Speed: Superhuman
Stamina: Superhuman
Durability: Superhuman
Agility: Superhuman
Reflexes: Superhuman
Fighting skills: Excellent hand-to-hand combatant; received Avengers training in unarmed combat by Captain America
Special skills and abilities: Extraordinarily adept athlete and gymnast. Her superhuman sense of smell makes her a superb tracker.
Superhuman physical powers: Aside from the above listed attributes, Tigra possesses superhumanly acute senses of smell, hearing, and vision including night vision
Superhuman mental powers: None
Special limitations: Tigra formerly possessed a "cat-soul" (in addition to her human soul) that eventually caused her to become savage and bestial in behavior and appearance
Source of superhuman powers: Combination of science, magic, and mental energy utilized by Dr. Joanne Marie Tumulo and other Cat People

PARAPHERNALIA

Costume specifications: Black bikini made of synthetic stretch fabric
Personal weaponry: None
Special weaponry: None
Other accessories: Wears a mystical amulet that enables her to transform into her original human form or into her Tigra form at will; Avengers ID card (contains mini-radio)
Transportation: Avengers Quinjet
Design and manufacture of paraphernalia: (Quinjet) Tony Stark

BIBLIOGRAPHY

First appearance: (as the Cat) THE CAT #1, (as Tigra) GIANT-SIZE CREATURES #1
Origin issue: (as the Cat) THE CAT #1 (as Tigra) GIANT-SIZE CREATURES #1
Significant issues: THE CAT #1 (became costumed crimefighter known as the Cat) GIANT-SIZE CREATURES #1 (was transformed into Tigra, first encountered Werewolf); MARVEL CHILLERS #4 (first battled Kraven the Hunter); MARVEL TEAM-UP #67 (teamed with Spider-Man against Kraven); AVENGERS #211 (joined Avengers); UNCANNY X-MEN #155-156 (aided X-Men against Deathbird); AVENGERS #215-216 (alongside Avengers, battled Molecule Man, quit Avengers); WEST COAST AVENGERS Vol. 1 #1 (helped formed West Coast Avengers); WEST COAST AVENGERS Vol. 1 #3-4 (alongside West Coast Avengers fought Graviton, became close friend of Wonder Man); WEST COAST AVENGERS Vol. 2 #1 (began flirtation with Henry Pym); WEST COAST AVENGERS Vol. 2 #3 (was defeated by Kraven and rescued by Mockingbird); WEST COAST AVENGERS Vol. 2 #4-5 (sought help from Avengers in overcoming "cat" side of her personality, which caused her to try to become the lover of both Wonder Man and Henry Pym, fought Werewolf); WEST COAST AVENGERS Vol. 2 #6-7 (was transported with West Coast Avengers by Balkatar to realm of Cat People, was asked by their king to slay Master Pandemonium); WEST COAST AVENGERS Vol. 2 #9 (failed to kill Master Pandemonium); WEST COAST AVENGERS Vol. 2 #12-13 (captured by Graviton, freed Avengers from him)

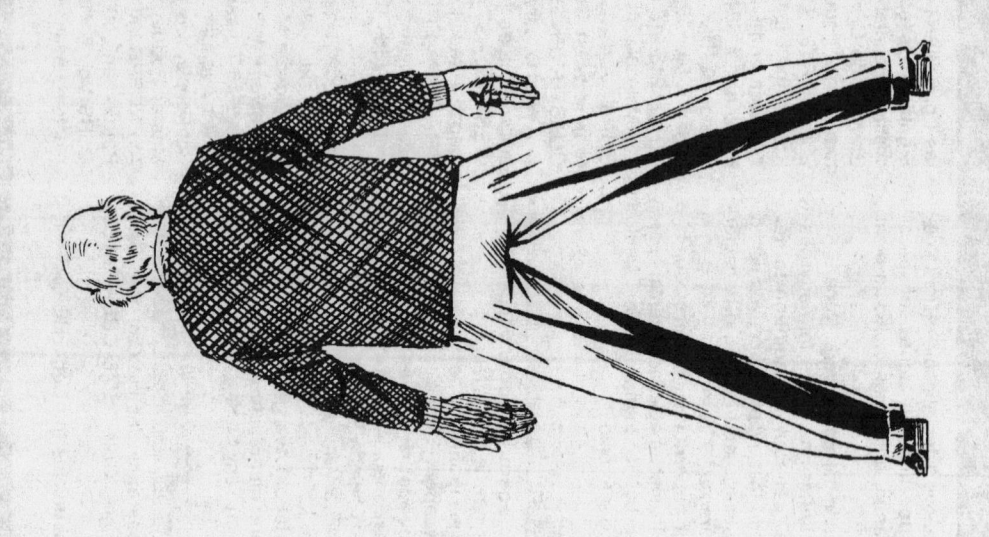

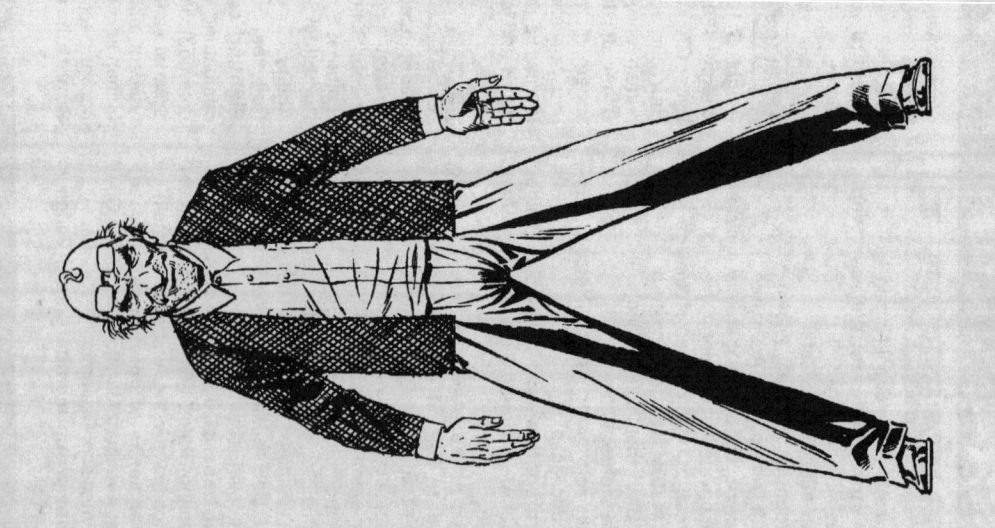

TINKERER™

TINKERER

BIOGRAPHICAL DATA

Real name: Phineas Mason
Other current aliases: None
Former aliases: Unknown
Dual identity: Publicly known
Current occupation: Inventor and technician serving the underworld
Former occupation: Unknown
Citizenship: Presumably the United States of America
Legal status: No known criminal record
Place of birth: Unrevealed
Marital status: Unknown
Known relatives: Richard "Rick" Mason (alias the Agent, son)
Known confidants: Toy (a robot assistant)
Known allies: Justin Hammer
Major enemies: Spider-Man
Usual base of operations: New York City
Former bases of operations: Unrevealed
Current group membership: None
Former group membership: None
Extent of education: Unknown, presumably at least a college graduate

PHYSICAL DESCRIPTION

Height: 5' 8"
Weight: 170 lbs.
Eyes: Gray
Hair: White
Other distinguishing features: None

POWERS AND ABILITIES

Intelligence: Genius
Strength: Below normal
Speed: Below normal
Stamina: Below normal
Durability: Below normal
Agility: Below normal
Reflexes: Below normal
Fighting skills: None
Special skills and abilities: Extensive knowledge in a wide variety of scientific disciplines; a high degree of expertise in the design and manufacture of inventive weapons and devices derived from pre-existing technologies
Superhuman physical powers: None
Superhuman mental powers: None
Special limitations: The Tinkerer's advanced age limits his physical abilities.
Source of superhuman powers: None

PARAPHERNALIA

Costume specifications: Conventional attire
Personal weaponry: None
Special weaponry: None
Other accessories: A wide variety of scientific and technological devices as needed
Transportation: Conventional vehicles
Design and manufacture of paraphernalia: Phineas Mason

BIBLIOGRAPHY

First appearance: AMAZING SPIDER-MAN #2
Origin issue: The Tinkerer's origin is as yet unrevealed.
Significant issues: AMAZING SPIDER-MAN #2 (first encountered Spider-Man, fooled Spider-Man into thinking he was an alien), AMAZING SPIDER-MAN #20 (created the Scorpion's tail), AMAZING SPIDER-MAN #160 (hired by the Kingpin to rebuild the Spider-Mobile to destroy Spider-Man), AMAZING SPIDER-MAN #182 (redesigned Rocket Racer's rocket-powered skateboard), AMAZING SPIDER-MAN #183 (designed an armed wheel-shaped vehicle called the Big Wheel), INCREDIBLE HULK #238 (repaired the Goldbug's bug-ship), SPECTACULAR SPIDER-MAN #53 (robbed loan companies by using remote-controlled toys until stopped by Spider-Man), CAPTAIN AMERICA #324 (provided Whirlwind with improved armor and weaponry), THE AGENT GRAPHIC NOVEL (provided his freelance operative son, Rick, with information about a South American coup), CAPTAIN AMERICA #369 (provided Diamondback with new throwing diamonds)

TITAN™

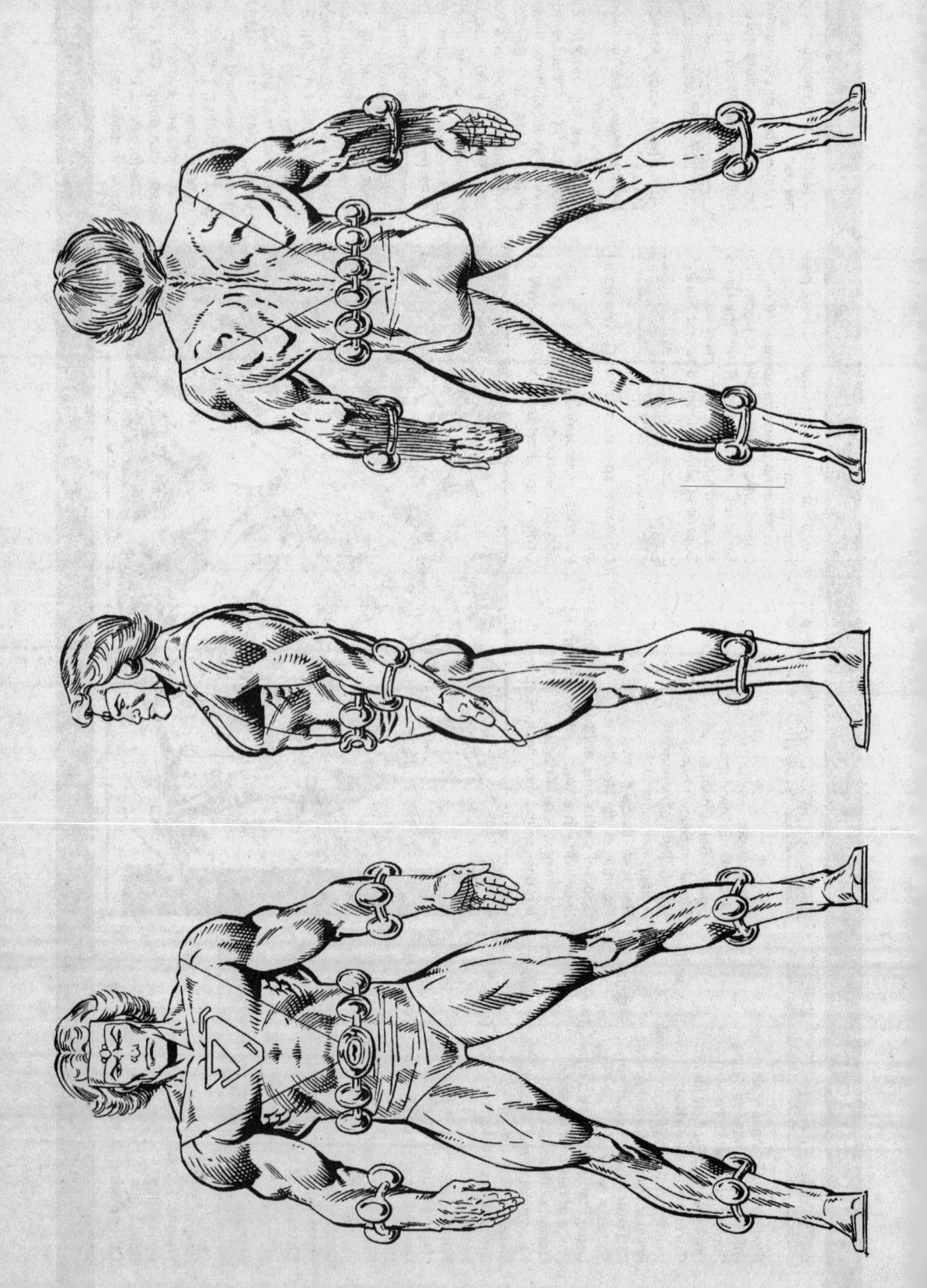

TITAN

BIOGRAPHICAL DATA

Real name: Unrevealed
Other current aliases: None
Former aliases: None known
Dual identity: None; the general populace of Earth is unaware of Titan's existence
Current occupation: Warrior serving in the Royal Elite of Shi'ar Imperial Guard
Former occupation: None known
Citizenship: Shi'ar Empire
Legal status: No criminal record in the Shi'ar Empire
Place of birth: Unrevealed location in the Shi'ar Galaxy (the identity of the alien race to which Titan belongs is unrevealed)
Marital status: Unrevealed
Known relatives: None
Known confidants: None
Known allies: Imperial Guard, Starjammers, the X-Men, (formerly) D'Ken, Deathbird
Note: The Imperial Guard serves whoever is ruler of the Shi'ar Empire; hence, at different times they have served D'Ken, Lilandra and Deathbird.
Major enemies: The Brood, Skrulls, Excalibur, (formerly) Deathbird, the Avengers, the Kree
Usual base of operations: Chandilar (Shi'ar Throneworld), Shi'ar Empire
Former bases of operations: None known
Current group membership: Royal Elite, Shi'ar Imperial Guard
Former group membership: None

Extent of education: Unrevealed

PHYSICAL DESCRIPTION

Height: (normal size) 6', (maximum potential height unrevealed)
Weight: (normal size) 195 lbs., (maximum potential weight unrevealed)
Eyes: Brown
Hair: Brown
Other distinguishing features: None

POWERS AND ABILITIES

Intelligence: Normal
Strength: (normal size) Athlete, (at known maximum height) Unrevealed
Speed: Athlete
Stamina: (normal size) Athlete, (at known maximum height) Superhuman
Durability: (normal size) Athlete, (at known maximum height) Superhuman
Agility: Athlete
Reflexes: Athlete
Fighting skills: Good hand-to-hand combatant, trained by Shi'ar Imperial Guard
Special skills and abilities: None known
Superhuman physical powers: Aside from the above listed attributes, Titan has the ability to increase his size and mass at will from his normal of 6' to an unknown limit (at least 40') and decrease his size back to normal height. Titan's extra mass is drawn psionically from an extradimensional source, to which it returns as he decreases in size. His weight increases as a cube (factor multiplied by itself three times) as he grows in height
Superhuman mental powers: None
Special limitations: None known
Source of superhuman powers: Unrevealed

PARAPHERNALIA

Costume specifications: Shi'ar fabrics mimicking the properties of unstable molecules, making them able to expand and contract as Titan changes size
Personal weaponry: None known
Special weaponry: None known
Other accessories: None known
Transportation: Shi'ar starships, small Imperial Guard anti-gravity device which allow flight
Design and manufacture of paraphernalia: Shi'ar scientists and technicians

BIBLIOGRAPHY

First appearance: X-MEN Vol. 1 #107
Origin issue: Titan's origin is as yet unrevealed.
Significant issues: X-MEN Vol. 1 #107-108 (joined in Imperial Guard's battle on behalf of Emperor D'Ken on nameless Shi'ar Empire planet; attacked the X-Men); X-MEN SPOTLIGHT ON: STARJAMMERS #2 (on Deathbird's behalf, joined Imperial Guard members in battle against Excalibur and Starjammers; fought Captain Britain); UNCANNY X-MEN #275 (on Deathbird's behalf, assisted other Imperial Guardsmen in battle against X-Men and Starjammers, was defeated by them); THOR #446 (battled Supremor to defend Lilandra during Kree-Shi'ar War), AVENGERS WEST COAST #82 (joined in Imperial Guard's battle with Avengers on Chandilar during Kree-Shi'ar War, defeated by Scarlet Witch)

TITANIA

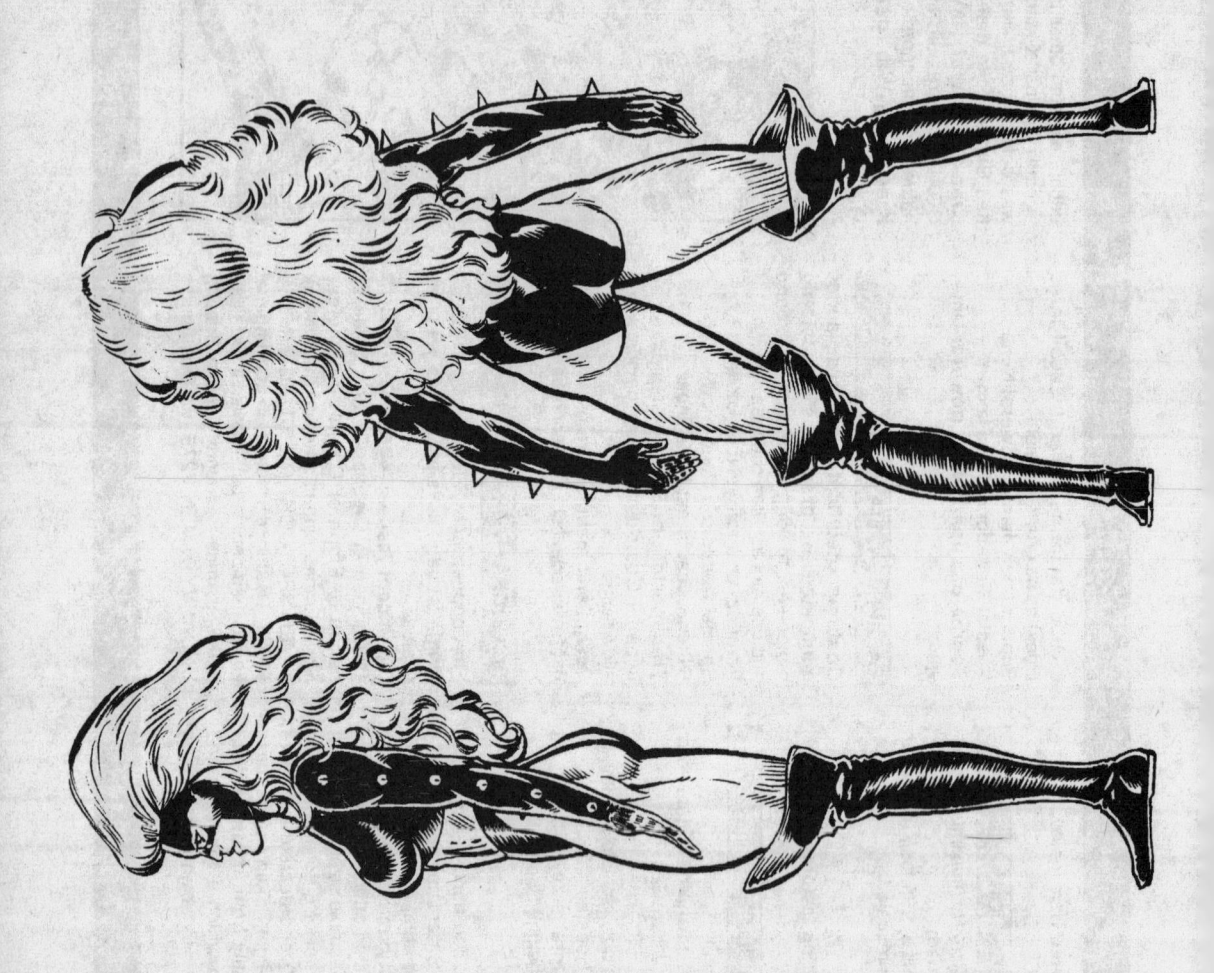

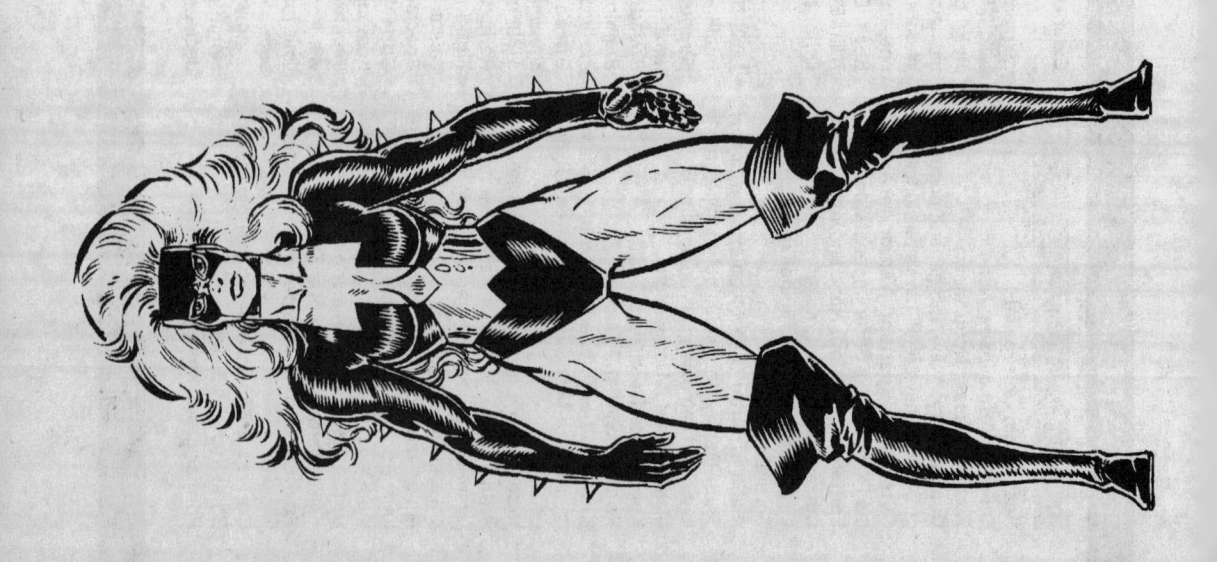

TITANIA

BIOGRAPHICAL DATA

Real name: Mary "Skeeter" MacPherran
Other current aliases: None
Former aliases: None
Dual identity: Known to the authorities
Current occupation: Professional criminal
Former occupation: Unrevealed
Citizenship: United States of America
Legal status: Criminal record in the U.S.
Place of birth: Denver, Colorado
Marital status: Single
Known relatives: None
Known confidants: Volcana, Absorbing Man
Known allies: Doctor Doom, Baron Zemo II, Frightful Four (Wizard, Hydro-Man, Klaw), Goliath, Brothers Grimm, Graviton, Trapster
Major enemies: She-Hulk, Spider-Man, the Avengers
Usual base of operations: Mobile
Former bases of operations: Denver, Colorado; New York City
Current group membership: None
Former group membership: Masters of Evil IV, Frightful Four
Extent of education: High school graduate

PHYSICAL DESCRIPTION

Height: 6'6"
Weight: 545 lbs.
Eyes: Blue
Hair: Reddish blonde
Other distinguishing features: None

POWERS AND ABILITIES

Intelligence: Normal
Strength: Superhuman Class 90
Speed: Enhanced human
Stamina: Metahuman
Durability: Metahuman
Agility: Athlete
Reflexes: Athlete
Fighting skills: Extensive experience in streetfighting techniques
Special skills and abilities: None
Superhuman physical powers: Superhuman strength, stamina, and durability
Superhuman mental powers: None
Special limitations: None
Source of superhuman powers: Cellular augmentation through radiation

PARAPHERNALIA

Costume specifications: Synthetic stretch fabric
Personal weaponry: None
Special weaponry: None
Other accessories: None
Transportation: Various
Design and manufacture of paraphernalia: Inapplicable

BIBLIOGRAPHY

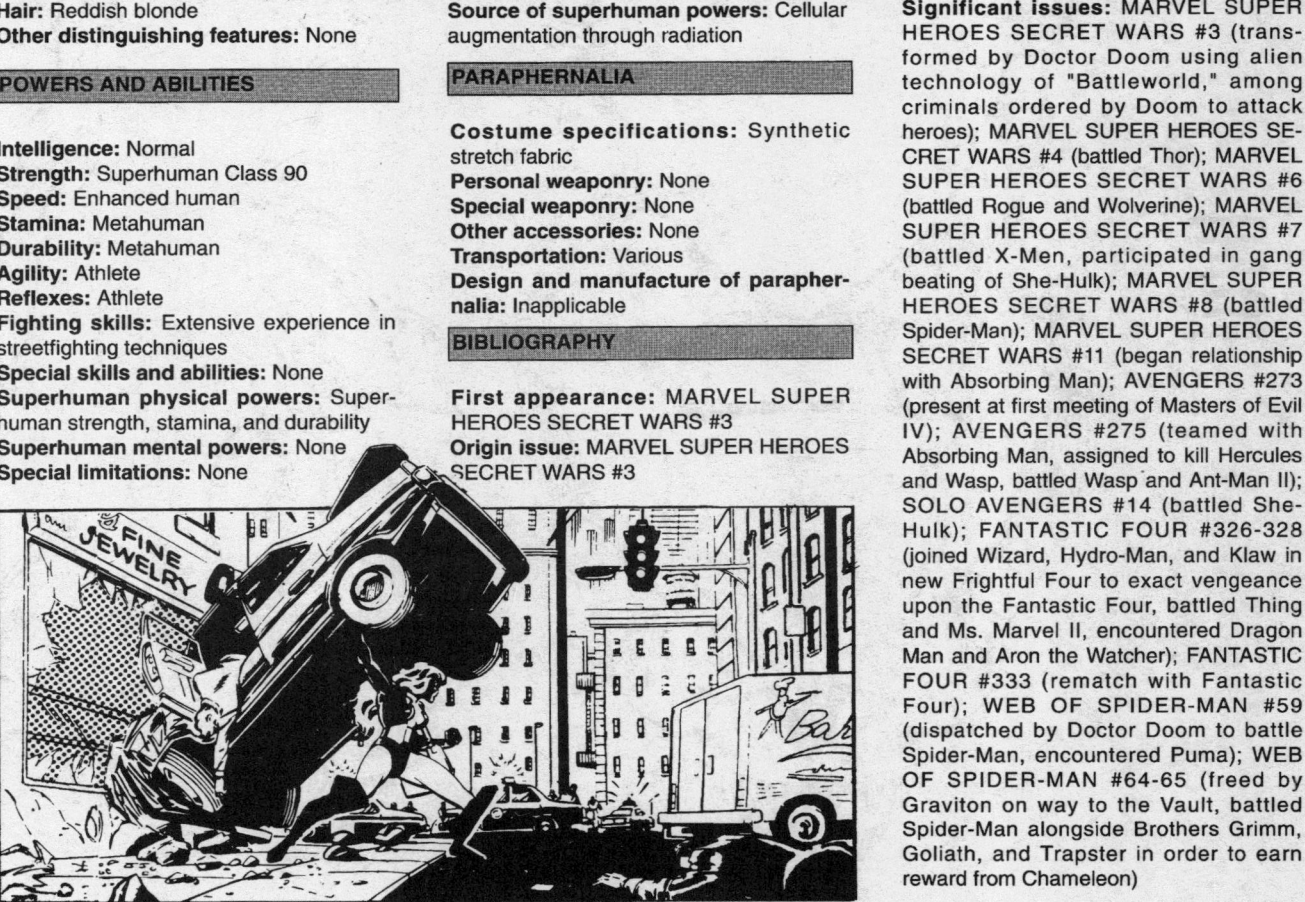

First appearance: MARVEL SUPER HEROES SECRET WARS #3
Origin issue: MARVEL SUPER HEROES SECRET WARS #3
Significant issues: MARVEL SUPER HEROES SECRET WARS #3 (transformed by Doctor Doom using alien technology of "Battleworld," among criminals ordered by Doom to attack heroes); MARVEL SUPER HEROES SECRET WARS #4 (battled Thor); MARVEL SUPER HEROES SECRET WARS #6 (battled Rogue and Wolverine); MARVEL SUPER HEROES SECRET WARS #7 (battled X-Men, participated in gang beating of She-Hulk); MARVEL SUPER HEROES SECRET WARS #8 (battled Spider-Man); MARVEL SUPER HEROES SECRET WARS #11 (began relationship with Absorbing Man); AVENGERS #273 (present at first meeting of Masters of Evil IV); AVENGERS #275 (teamed with Absorbing Man, assigned to kill Hercules and Wasp, battled Wasp and Ant-Man II); SOLO AVENGERS #14 (battled She-Hulk); FANTASTIC FOUR #326-328 (joined Wizard, Hydro-Man, and Klaw in new Frightful Four to exact vengeance upon the Fantastic Four, battled Thing and Ms. Marvel II, encountered Dragon Man and Aron the Watcher); FANTASTIC FOUR #333 (rematch with Fantastic Four); WEB OF SPIDER-MAN #59 (dispatched by Doctor Doom to battle Spider-Man, encountered Puma); WEB OF SPIDER-MAN #64-65 (freed by Graviton on way to the Vault, battled Spider-Man alongside Brothers Grimm, Goliath, and Trapster in order to earn reward from Chameleon)

TOAD™

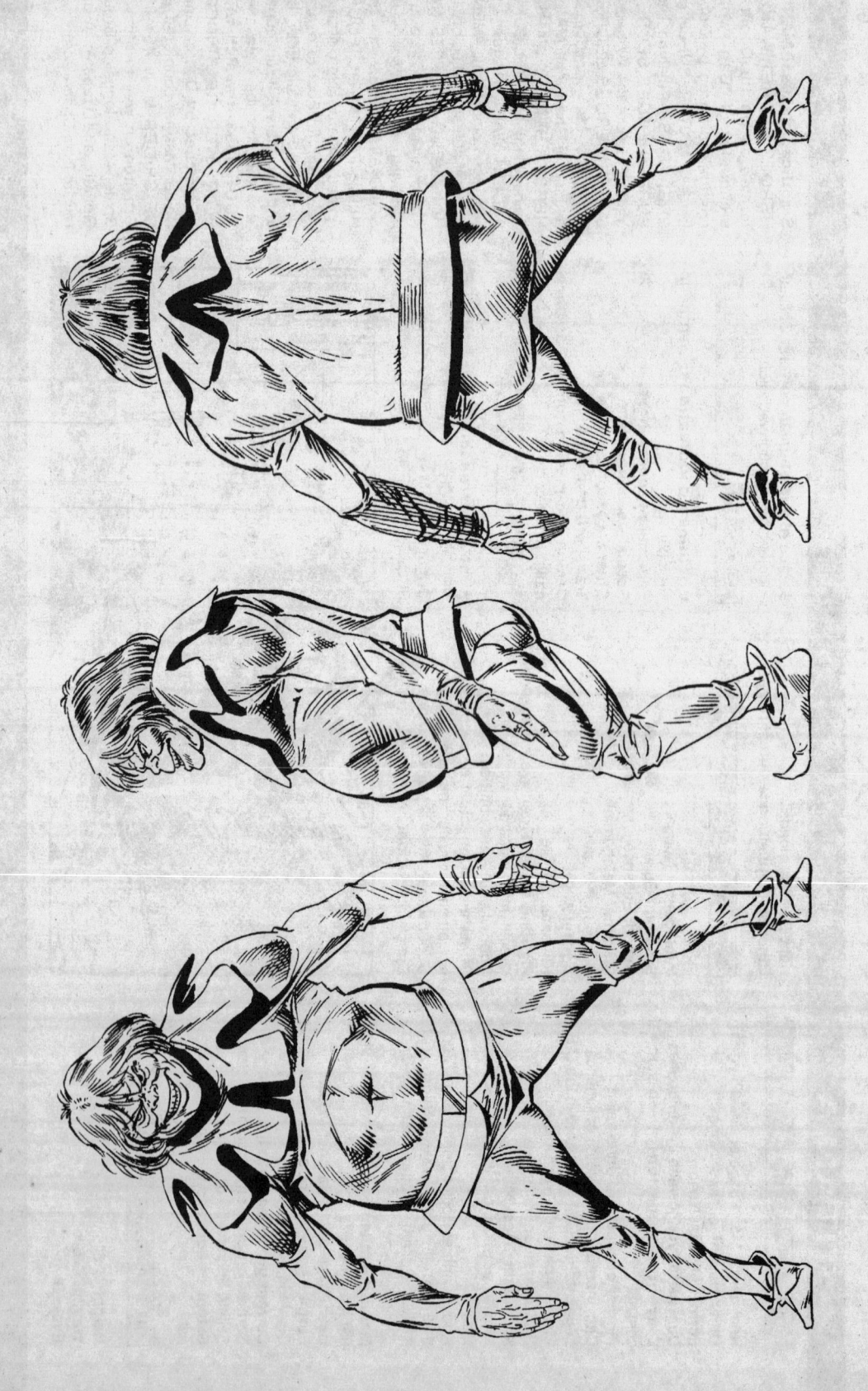

TOAD

BIOGRAPHICAL DATA

Real name: Mortimer Toynbee
Other current aliases: None known
Former aliases: The Terrible Toad-King, also impersonated the Stranger
Dual identity: Publicly known
Current occupation: Subversive
Former occupation: Caretaker of amusement park, adventurer
Citizenship: United Kingdom
Legal status: Criminal record
Place of birth: York, England
Marital status: Single
Known relatives: None
Known confidants: (former) Scarlet Witch, Quicksilver, Spider-Man
Known allies: Brotherhood of Evil Mutants V (Sauron, Blob, Pyro, Phantazia), Gideon, (former) Magneto, Brotherhood of Evil Mutants I (Mastermind, Quicksilver, Scarlet Witch, Blob), Frog-Man II, Spider-Kid
Major enemies: X-Men, Magneto, X-Force, X-Factor II, Darkhawk, Quicksilver, Vision, Scarlet Witch, Avengers, Spider-Man, Doctor Doom, Sleepwalker, Portal
Usual base of operations: Unrevealed
Former bases of operations: Asteroid M, other bases used by Magneto, Polemachus, castle in upstate New York
Current group membership: Brotherhood of Evil Mutants V
Former group membership: Brotherhood of Evil Mutants I, Misfits
Extent of education: Unrevealed

PHYSICAL DESCRIPTION

Height: 5' 8"
Weight: 260 lbs.
Eyes: Brown
Hair: Brown
Other distinguishing features: None

POWERS AND ABILITIES

Intelligence: Normal
Strength: (upper torso) Enhanced human, (lower torso and legs) Superhuman Class 10
Speed: (leaping) Enhanced human
Stamina: Superhuman
Durability: Enhanced human
Agility: Enhanced human
Reflexes: Enhanced human
Fighting skills: Highly formidable in kickboxing despite lack of formal training
Special skills and abilities: Considerable knowledge of advanced technology due to his studies of machinery in the possession of Arcade, Arkon, Magneto, and the Stranger.
Superhuman physical powers: Aside from the above listed attributes, the Toad can reach an altitude of 24 feet and cover a distance on the ground of 36 feet in a single leap. The Toad has an unusually flexible spine, enabling him to crouch continually without damage. Can produce a sticky resin-like substance from his hands
Superhuman mental powers: None
Special limitations: None
Source of superhuman powers: Genetic mutation

PARAPHERNALIA

Costume specifications: Conventional fabrics
Personal weaponry: In the past the Toad has employed a robotic suit of battle armor containing an exoskeleton that greatly amplifies his strength. The battlesuit emits a pulse of ball lightning when he hits a target. The suit is also equipped with thermoblasters, poison gas projectors, and a self-teleportation device. The Toad has also used a strength amplifying "exoskeleton" composed of pure energy
Special weaponry: The Toad possesses alien technology that he stole from the Stranger's world and can utilize it to create synthozoid robots, among other uses
Other accessories: None
Transportation: Starship built on Arkon's world; alien teleportation technology
Design and manufacture of paraphernalia: Arcade, alien technicians

BIBLIOGRAPHY

First appearance: X-MEN Vol. 1 #4
Origin issue: The Toad's origin is as yet unrevealed.
Significant issues: X-MEN Vol. 1 #4-7 (as member of the Brotherhood of Evil Mutants I, aided Magneto in repeated clashed with the X-Men); X-MEN Vol. 1 #11 (abducted with Magneto from Earth by Stranger); X-MEN Vol. 1 #18 (abandoned on Stranger's world by escaping Magneto); AVENGERS #47-49 (returned to Earth with Magneto); X-MEN Vol. 1 #43-45 (aided Magneto against the X-Men); AVENGERS #53 (rebelled against Magneto, fled his lair with Quicksilver and Scarlet Witch); X-MEN Vol. 1 #59-60 (captured by Sentinels, freed by X-Men); AVENGERS #75 (captured with Quicksilver and Scarlet Witch); AVENGERS #137-139 (used stranger's alien technology to menace Avengers); MARVEL TWO-IN-ONE #68 (attempted to kill Angel in castle outfitted with traps by Arcade, instead turned castle into amusement park); AMAZING SPIDER-MAN #266 (ejected from castle by Doctor Doom, became suicidal, was befriended by Spider-Man, teamed with Frog-Man II and Spider-Kid as Misfits); VISION AND SCARLET WITCH Vol. 2 #6-7, 11 (sought repeatedly to abduct Scarlet Witch, was thwarted by Quicksilver, Vision, and Scarlet Witch); NEW MUTANTS ANNUAL #7, UNCANNY X-MEN ANNUAL #15, X-FACTOR ANNUAL #6 (played "game" with Gideon, sought to enlist Proteus in new Brotherhood); X-FORCE #5-7 (organized Brotherhood of Evil Mutants V, transformed Karl Lykos back into Sauron, with Brotherhood battled X-Force); X-FACTOR #82 (with Brotherhood, first battled X-Factor II); DARKHAWK #19-20 (with Brotherhood V, fought Darkhawk, Sleepwalker, and Portal)

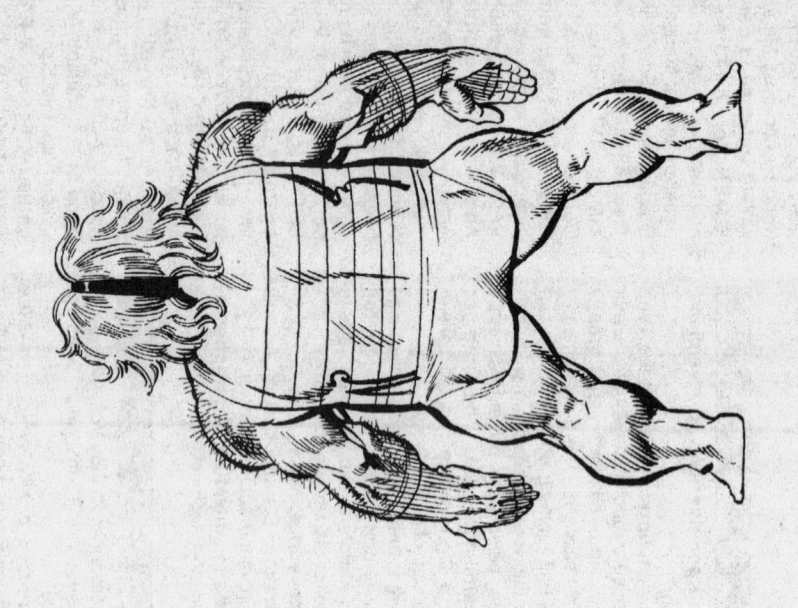

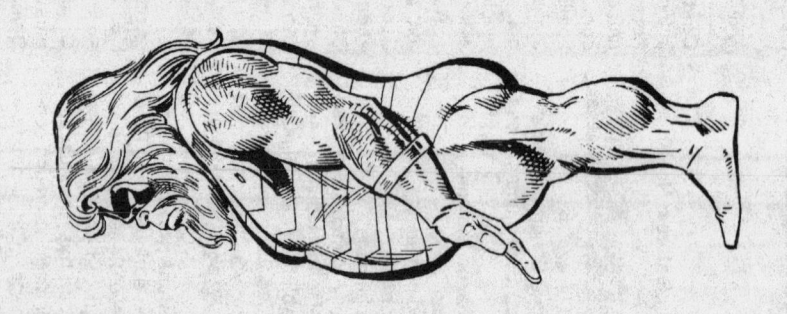

TOM THUMB

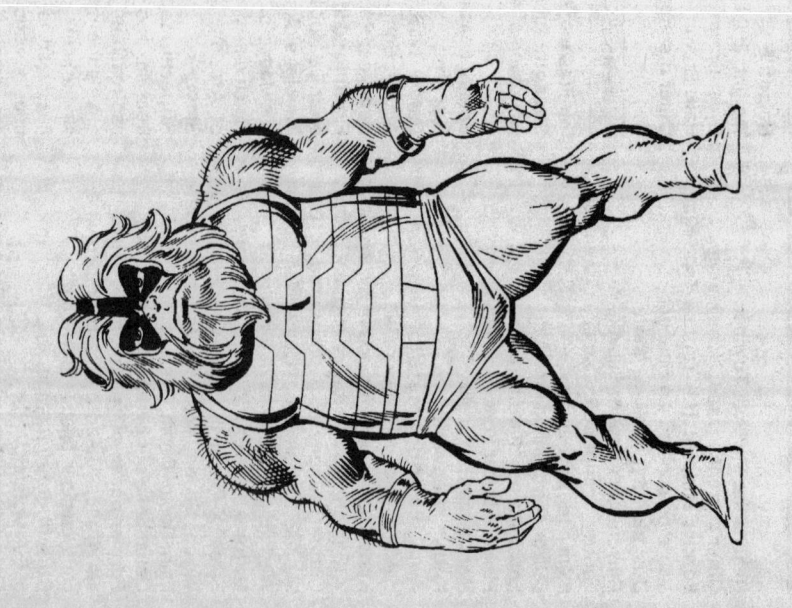

TOM THUMB

BIOGRAPHICAL DATA

Real name: Thomas Thompson
Aliases at time of death: None
Former aliases: None
Dual identity: Publicly known on the Squadron Supreme's Earth ("Other-Earth"/Earth-S)
Occupation at time of death: Scientist, inventor, adventurer
Former occupation: None
Citizenship: United States of "Other-Earth"
Legal status: No criminal record
Place of birth: Melzburg, Danteana
Place of death: Squadron City, Great American Desert
Cause of death: Cancer
Marital status: Single
Known relatives: None
Known confidants: AIDA, Ape X
Known allies: The Squadron Supreme, Defenders, (former) Serpent Cartel
Major enemies: Scarlet Centurion, Iron Moth, the Over-Mind, Null the Living Darkness, Institute of Evil, Nuke I
Base of operations at time of death: TTTech Laboratories, Squadron City, Great American Desert
Former base of operations: Rocket Central (Squadron Supreme's space station, orbiting Other-Earth), Squadron mountain headquarters, Moreland
Group membership at time of death: The Squadron Supreme
Former group membership: None

Extent of education: Ph. Ds in mathematics, physics, and electrical engineering

PHYSICAL DESCRIPTION

Height: 3' 7"
Weight: 95 lbs.
Eyes: Blue
Hair: Grey
Other distinguishing features: Tom Thumb was a dwarf due to an abnormality of the pituitary gland.

POWERS AND ABILITIES

Intelligence: Extraordinary genius
Strength: Below normal
Speed: Below normal
Stamina: Normal
Durability: Normal
Agility: Normal
Reflexes: Normal
Fighting skills: Average hand-to-hand combatant, but highly adept at manipulating various advanced weaponry of his own design
Special skills and abilities: Expert and innovator in a wide range of scientific and technological fields, including computer science, medicine, psychology, force field technology, and spacecraft design; possessed total recall and great physical dexterity
Superhuman physical powers: None
Superhuman mental powers: None
Special limitations: Physical limitations due to dwarfish size and build
Source of superhuman powers: None

PARAPHERNALIA

Costume specifications: Conventional fabrics
Personal weaponry: Tom Thumb used a one-man flying vehicle that was equipped with various advanced weaponry, including guns firing concussive energy blasts.
Special weaponry: Various, as needed
Other accessories: AIDA (Artificially Intelligent Data Analyzer), a highly advanced computer with a human-like personality and sentience; the Behavior Modification Machine, which could alter the personalities and thinking processes of human beings; the Hibernaculum, a means of storing a human body in suspended animation; and the Transtemporal Somaprojector, a means of time travel. He also invented and wore a personal force field belt, which projected a protective field of energy about the wearer that could even deflect bullets.
Transportation: One-man vehicle propelled by small jets
Design and manufacture of paraphernalia: Tom Thumb

BIBLIOGRAPHY

First appearance: AVENGERS #85
Origin issue: SQUADRON SUPREME #10
Significant issues: AVENGERS #85-86 (first encountered Avengers; with Squadron Supreme and Avengers, battled Brain-Child II); AVENGERS #148-149 (with Squadron, battled Avengers on behalf of Serpent Cartel, then turned against Cartel); DEFENDERS #112-114 (alongside other Squadron members, mind-controlled by the Over-Mind; used along with other members as pawns in Over-Mind's conquest of "Other-Earth," freed by the Defenders; battled and defeated Over-Mind and Null the Living Darkness); SQUADRON SUPREME #1 (alongside the Squadron Supreme, assumed control of the government of United States of "Other-Earth", publicly revealed true identity); SQUADRON SUPREME #2 (asked by Nuke I to find cure for his parents' cancer, failed, learned he himself had terminal cancer, refused to kill Hyperion I in exchange for cure from Scarlet Centurion, Nuke I swore vengeance on Thumb); SQUADRON SUPREME #3 (completed Behavior Modification Machine); SQUADRON SUPREME #5-6 (captured by Institute of Evil; voted to expel Golden Archer II from the Squadron); SQUADRON SUPREME #9-10 (stole Scarlet Centurion's "panacea potion", discovered it was ineffective to cure his cancer, died; placed in Hibernaculum in the hope that he could someday be resurrected)

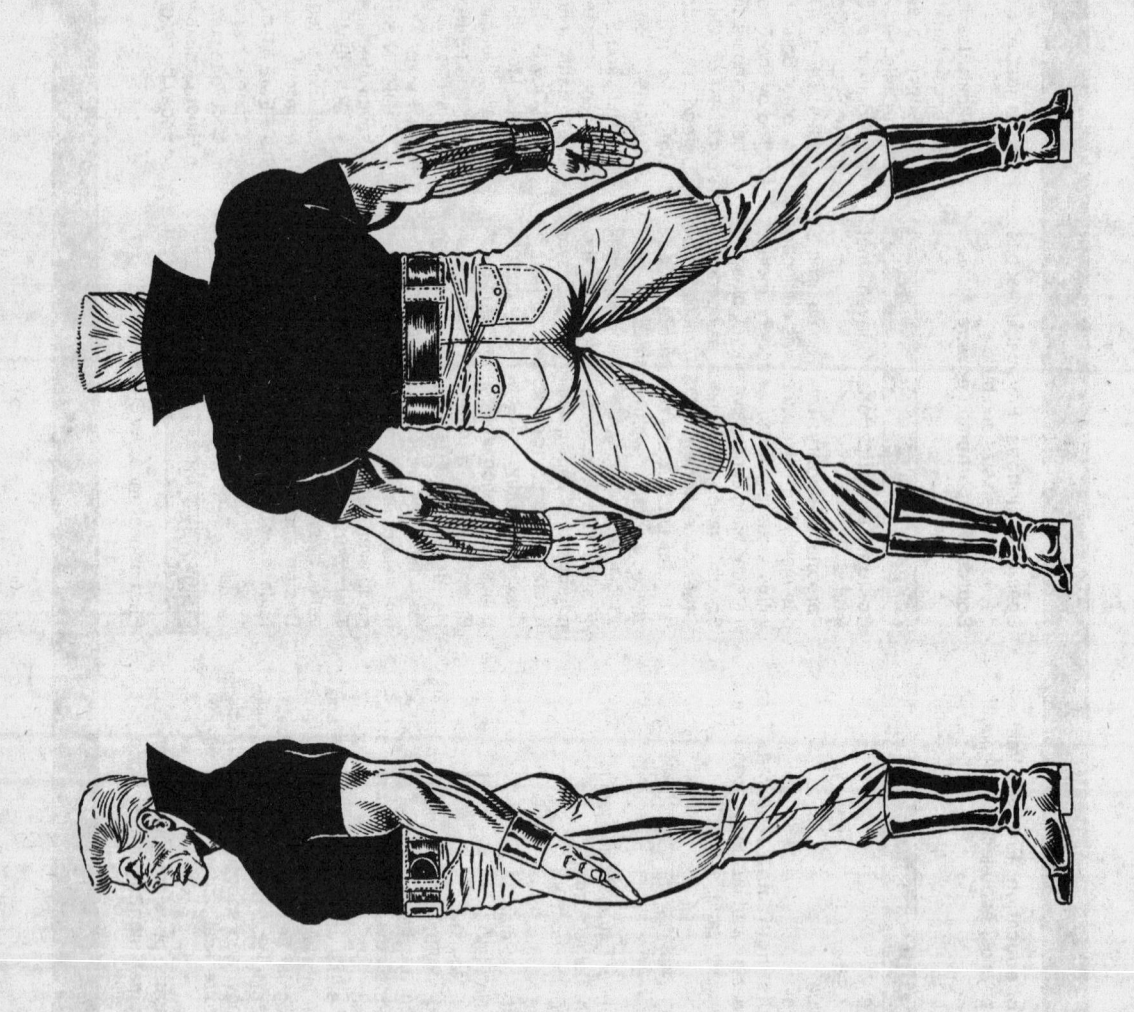

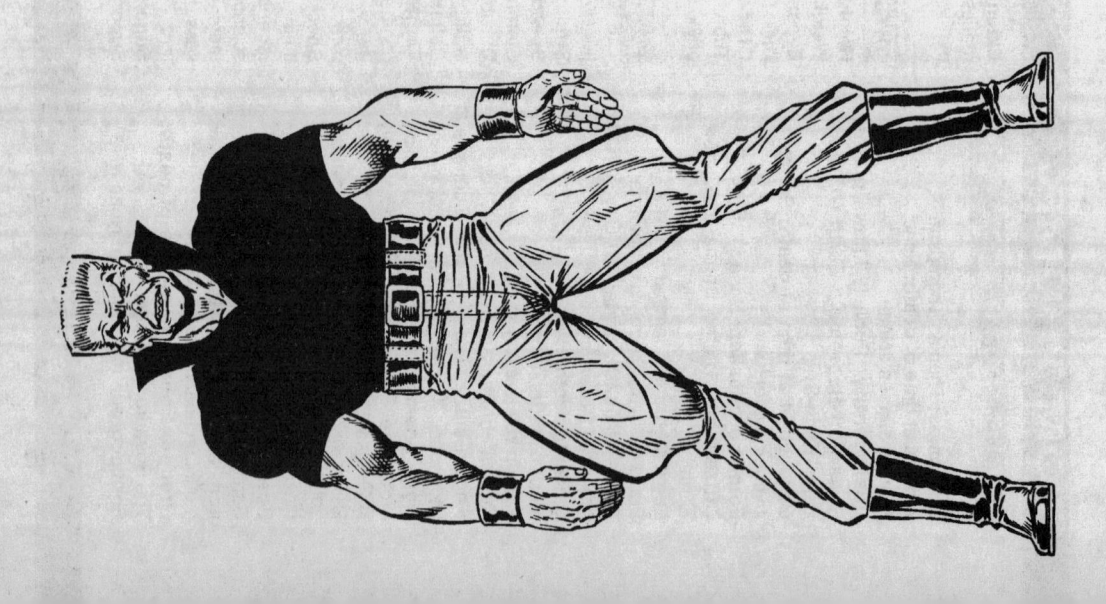

TOMBSTONE ™

TOMBSTONE

BIOGRAPHICAL DATA

Real name: Lonnie Thompson Lincoln
Other current aliases: None
Former aliases: None known
Dual identity: Publicly known
Current occupation: Hitman
Former occupation: None
Citizenship: United States of America
Legal status: Criminal record in the U.S.
Place of birth: Harlem, New York City
Marital status: Single
Known relatives: None
Known confidants: Joe Robertson
Known allies: None
Major enemies: Spider-Man, the Punisher, Daredevil, Joe Robertson
Usual base of operations: New York City
Former bases of operations: Philadelphia, Pennsylvania
Current group membership: None
Former group membership: Employed by the Kingpin and the Arranger, employed by the Chameleon and Hammerhead, employed by the Hand
Extent of education: High school dropout

PHYSICAL DESCRIPTION

Height: 6'7"
Weight: 215 lbs.
Eyes: Pink
Hair: White
Other distinguishing features: Tombstone is an albino, lacking all pigmentation in his skin, hair, and eyes. He has also filed all his teeth into razor-sharp points.

POWERS AND ABILITIES

Intelligence: Below normal
Strength: Enhanced human
Speed: Enhanced human
Stamina: Enhanced human
Durability: Enhanced human
Agility: Athlete
Reflexes: Enhanced human
Fighting skills: Skilled streetfighting hand-to-hand combatant, which he combines with superhuman strength to create a unique fighting style.
Special skills and abilities: Adept in the use of conventional firearms
Superhuman physical powers: Aside from the above listed attributes, none
Superhuman mental powers: None
Special limitations: Like all albinos, Tombstone is sensitive to the sun
Source of superhuman powers: Mutagenic reaction to an experimental preservative gas absorbed into his bloodstream

PARAPHERNALIA

Costume specifications: Ordinary fabric
Personal weaponry: None
Special weaponry: None
Other accessories: None
Transportation: Conventional
Design and manufacture of paraphernalia: Inapplicable

BIBLIOGRAPHY

First appearance: WEB OF SPIDER-MAN #36
Origin issue: SPECTACULAR SPIDER-MAN #139
Significant issues: WEB OF SPIDER-MAN #36 (returned to New York as Kingpin's hitman); SPECTACULAR SPIDER-MAN #137 (threatened Joe Robertson to remain silent about a murder Tombstone committed years ago); WEB OF SPIDER-MAN #38 (threw Hobgoblin out the Arranger's window); SPECTACULAR SPIDER-MAN #138 (kidnaped mutant known as the Persuader for the Arranger), SPECTACULAR SPIDER-MAN #139 (confronted an armed Joe Robertson and broke his spine); SPECTACULAR SPIDER-MAN #142 (first encountered Spider-Man in Atlanta, Georgia; defeated and sent to Philadelphia State Penitentiary); SPECTACULAR SPIDER-MAN #150, 153, 155, 157, 161 (obtained transfer to Lewisburg State Penitentiary where Joe Robertson was incarcerated; killed Robertson's befriended bodyguard, Bruiser; captured Spider-Man during a prison break and nearly beat him to death before Robertson stopped him, escaped with Robertson down the Susquehanna River; taken in by an Amish farmer, stabbed with a pitchfork by Robertson who escaped him, joined criminal organization headed by Hammerhead and Chameleon; saved Robertson from the Hobgoblin so that he could kill Robertson himself); WEB OF SPIDER-MAN #66-68 (encountered Robertson at the Osborn Chemical Plant, who shot him and trapped him in an airtight test chamber which contained a gas that granted him superhuman powers; called off his vendetta against Robertson in gratitude); DAREDEVIL #292-293 (defeated by Daredevil and the Punisher while competing against the Taskmaster in a real game of Assassin sponsored by the Hand)

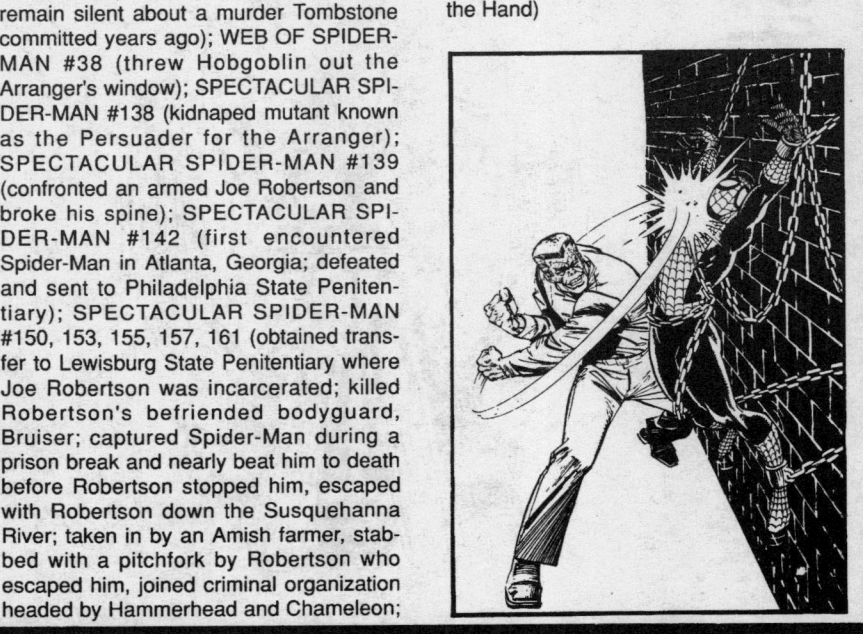

TRAPSTER

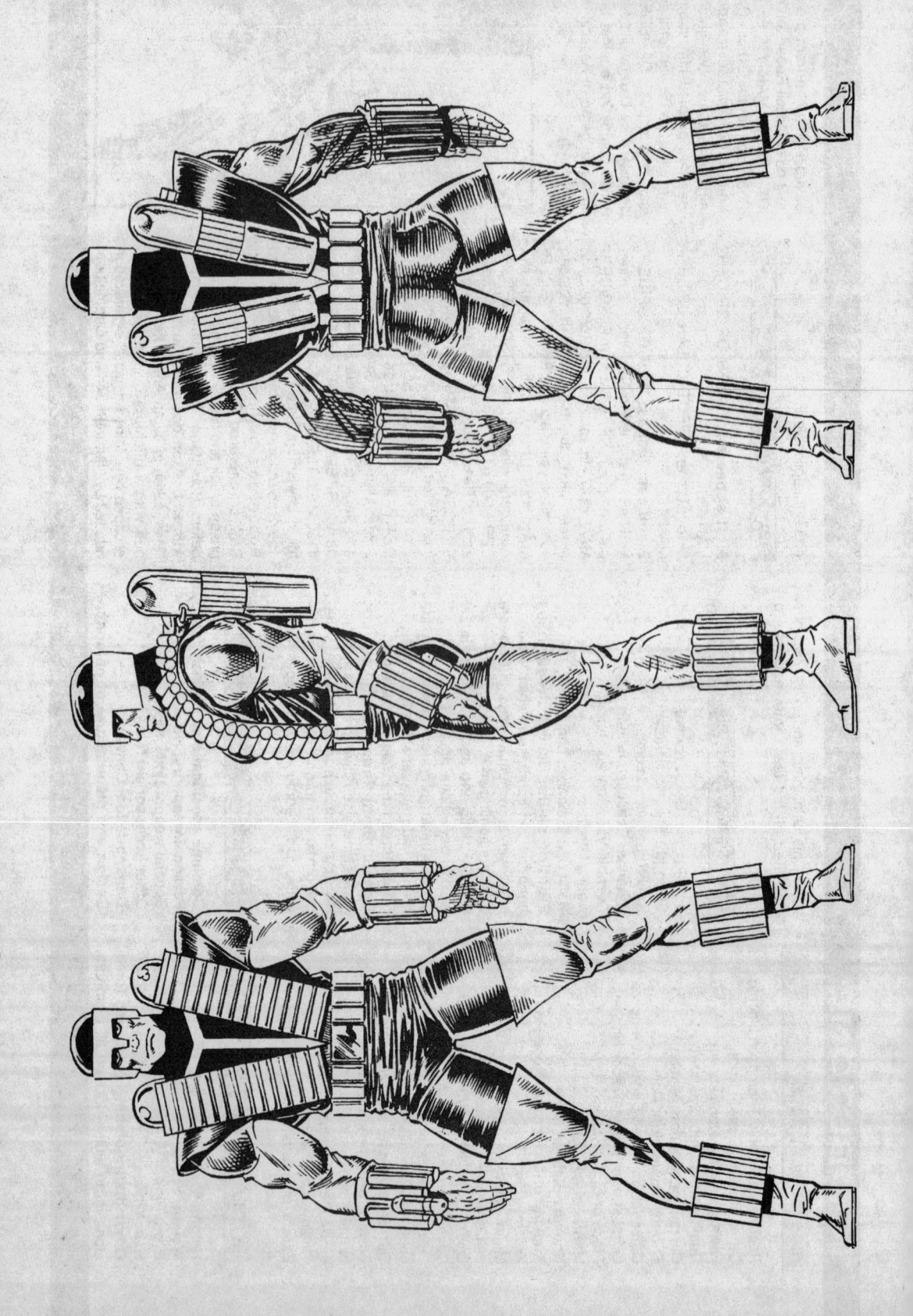

TRAPSTER I & II

BIOGRAPHICAL DATA

Real name: (I) Peter Petruski; (II) Lawrence "Larry" Curtiss
Other current aliases: (both) None
Former aliases: (I) Paste-Pot Pete, (II) None known
Dual identity: (I) Publicly known, (II) Known only to certain officers of Roxxon Oil Company
Current occupation: (I) Professional criminal; (II) Assistant head of security for Roxxon Oil Company
Former occupation: (I) Research chemist, (II) Unrevealed
Citizenship: (both) United States of America
Legal status: (I) Criminal record in the U.S., (II) No criminal record
Place of birth: (I) Gary, Indiana; (II) Concord, New Hampshire
Marital status: (I) Single, (II) Unrevealed
Known relatives: (both) None
Known confidants: (I) The Wizard, Catherine Polumbo, (former) Sandman; (II) None
Known allies: (I) The Wizard, the Tinkerer, (former) Sandman, Medusa, the Red Skull, Thundra, Brute, Electro, Llyra, Whirlwind, Graviton, Brothers Grimm II, Goliath IV, Titania II, (II) None
Major enemies: (I) The Fantastic Four, Daredevil, Captain America, Medusa, Spider-Man, Thundra, Ghost Rider I, Stilt-Man, Tigra, the Chameleon, Sandman, Trapster II, (II) Iron Man I, James Rhodes, Trapster I
Base of operations at time of death: (I) Mobile, (II) Roxxon Oil corporate headquarters
Former bases of operations: (I) Various
Current group membership: (I) Frightful Four, (II) Roxxon Oil
Former group membership: (both) None
Extent of education: (I) College degree in chemistry, (II) Unrevealed

PHYSICAL DESCRIPTION

Height: (I) 5' 10", (II) 5' 9"
Weight: (I) 160 lbs, (II) 155 lbs.
Eyes: (both) Brown
Hair: (both) Brown
Other distinguishing features: (both) None

POWERS AND ABILITIES

Intelligence: (I) Above normal, (II) Normal
Strength: (both) Normal
Speed: (both) Normal
Stamina: (both) Normal
Durability: (both) Normal
Agility: (both) Normal
Reflexes: (both) Normal
Fighting skills: (both) Minimal, depends on weaponry in combat
Special skills and abilities: (I) Expert chemist, skilled marksman, talented disguise artist, (II) Skilled marksman
Superhuman physical powers: (both) None
Superhuman mental powers: (both) None
Special limitations: (both) None
Source of superhuman powers: (both) Inapplicable

PARAPHERNALIA

Costume specifications: (both) Synthetic stretch fabric equipped with storage canisters for paste and lubricant, and adhesive-rigged boots and gloves to enable walking up walls
Personal weaponry: (both) Paste-shooters (worn on wrists, discharge powerful fireproof chemically inert adhesive paste or powerful lubricant), (I) (former) Paste-gun (discharged powerful adhesive paste)
Special weaponry: (I) Various mechanical traps (used to restrain or entangle adversaries), (II) Heat-seeking mini-missiles equipped with concussion charges, glue missiles (fired from paste-shooters)
Other accessories: (I) Anti-gravity discs, explosive caps, ultrasound transmitters, (II) Unrevealed
Transportation: (I) Anti-gravity platform or conventional vehicles, (II) Conventional vehicles
Design and manufacture of paraphernalia: (I) (paste, lubricant, weaponry) Peter Petruski, (anti-gravity discs and platform, some accessories) the Wizard, (some accessories) the Tinkerer

BIBLIOGRAPHY

First appearance: (I) (as Paste-Pot Pete) STRANGE TALES Vol. 1 #104, (as Trapster I) FANTASTIC FOUR #38 (I: IRON MAN ANNUAL #12
Origin issues: (I) STRANGE TALES Vol. 1 #104; (II) Trapster II's origin is as yet unrevealed.
Significant issues: STRANGE TALES Vol. 1 #104 (I: created super-adhesive paste-gun, battled Human Torch II); STRANGE TALES Vol. 1 #110 (I: alongside the Wizard, battled Human Torch II); AVENGERS #6 (I: provided Avengers with solvent to dissolve Baron Zemo I's Adhesive-X, paroled from prison); STRANGE TALES Vol. 1 #124 (I: adopted new costume and weaponry, battled Human Torch II and the Thing); FANTASTIC FOUR #36 (I: with Wizard, Sandman, and Medusa, formed the Frightful Four, battled the Fantastic Four); FANTASTIC FOUR #38 (I: adopted Trapster nom de crime and new weaponry; with Frightful Four, defeated the Fantastic Four); JOURNEY INTO MYSTERY #116 (I: chance near-encounter with Balder prevented Frightful Four's takeover of Fantastic Four headquarters); FANTASTIC FOUR #41-43 (I: with Frightful Four, battled Fantastic Four); DAREDEVIL #35-36 (I: battled Daredevil); CAPTAIN AMERICA #108 (I: hired by the Red Skull to acquire information from Sharon Carter, battled Captain America); MARVEL SUPER-HEROES Vol. 2 #15 (I: alongside Wizard and Sandman, battled Medusa); FANTASTIC FOUR #94 (I: with Wizard, Sandman, and Medusa as the Frightful Four, battled the Fantastic Four)

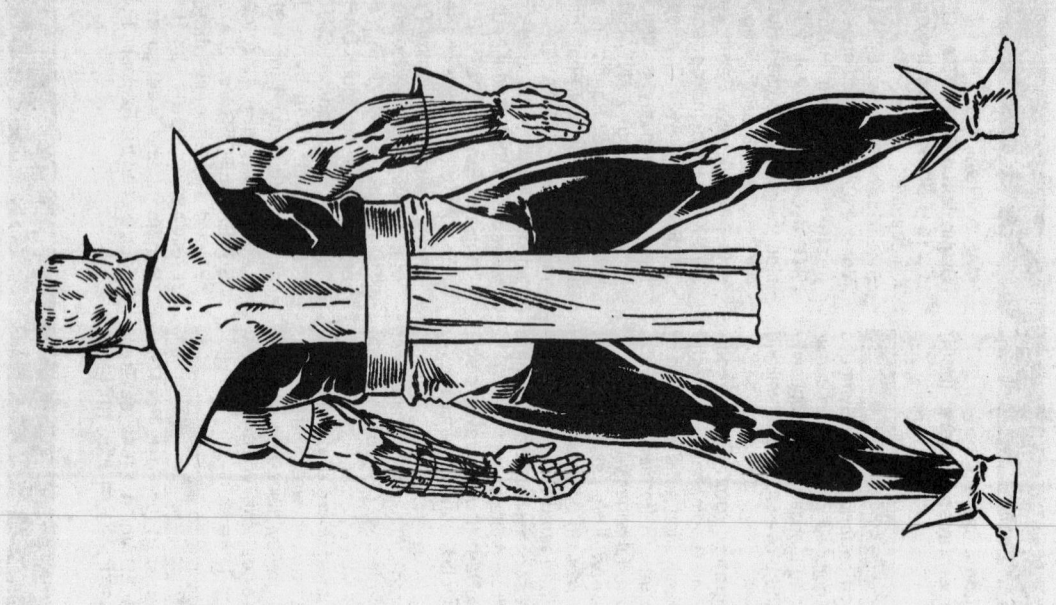

TRICKSHOT

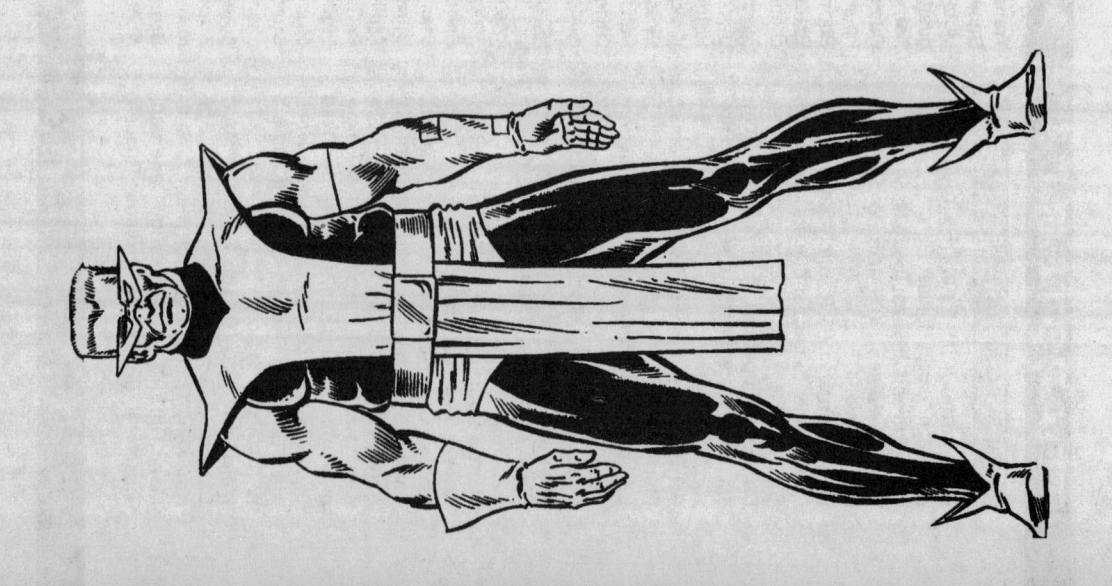

TRICKSHOT

BIOGRAPHICAL DATA

Real name: Unrevealed
Other current aliases: Unrevealed
Former aliases: Unrevealed
Dual identity: Secret
Current occupation: Assassin, professional criminal
Former occupation: Circus performer
Citizenship: United States of America
Legal status: International criminal record
Place of birth: Unrevealed
Marital status: Presumed single
Known relatives: None
Known confidants: None
Known allies: None
Major enemies: Hawkeye
Usual base of operations: Mobile
Former bases of operations: Carson Carnival of Traveling Wonders
Current group membership: None
Former group membership: None
Extent of education: High school dropout

PHYSICAL DESCRIPTION

Height: 6'2"
Weight: 287 lbs.
Eyes: Brown
Hair: Brown
Other distinguishing features: None

POWERS AND ABILITIES

Intelligence: Normal
Strength: Normal human level
Speed: Normal human level
Stamina: Below normal
Durability: Normal
Agility: Below normal
Reflexes: Athlete
Fighting skills: Basic streetfighting techniques
Special skills and abilities: Extremely well-honed archery skills.
Superhuman physical powers: None
Superhuman mental powers: None
Special limitations: Trickshot's weight and medical condition reduce his ability to function at peak performance levels for extended periods of time.
Source of superhuman powers: None

PARAPHERNALIA

Costume specifications: Synthetic stretch fabric
Personal weaponry: Hunter's bow
Special weaponry: A wide variety of "trick" arrows, such as smoke bombs, bola arrows, 360 degree arrows, and many others.
Other accessories: Unrevealed
Transportation: Various
Design and manufacture of paraphernalia: Unrevealed

BIBLIOGRAPHY

First appearance: SOLO AVENGERS #1
Origin issue: Trickshot's origin is as yet unrevealed.
Significant issues: SOLO AVENGERS #2 (training of Hawkeye revealed); SOLO AVENGERS #5 (revealed to have terminal cancer); AVENGERS SPOTLIGHT #24 (aided Hawkeye against Knickknack); AVENGERS SPOTLIGHT #25 (aided Hawkeye and Mockingbird against Crossfire, Brothers Grimm, Mad Dog, Bobcat, Razorfist, and Death-Throws; cancer revealed to be in remission)

TRITON

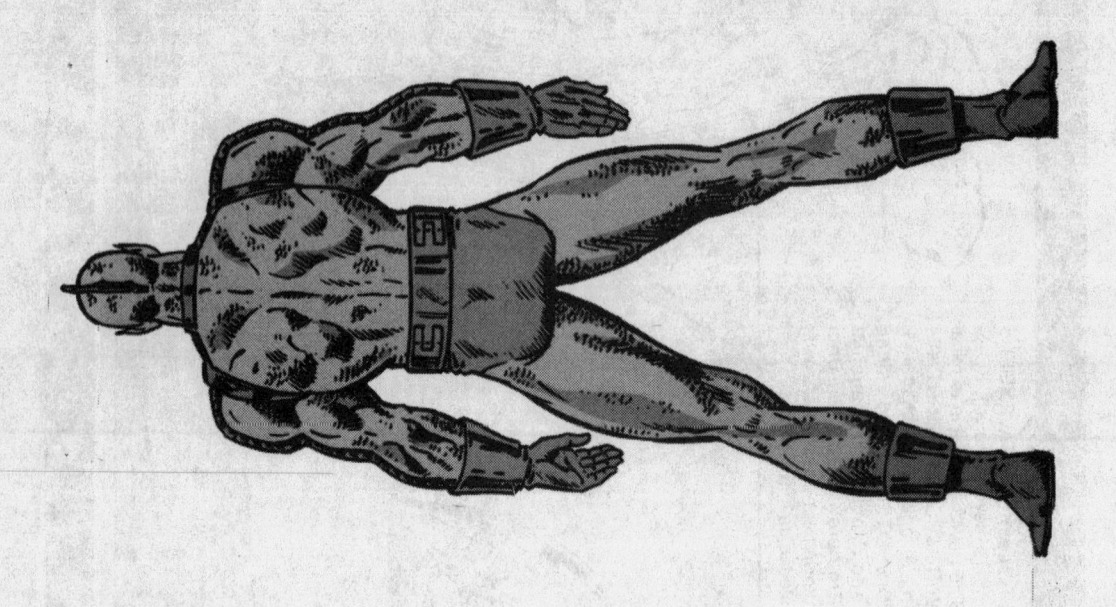

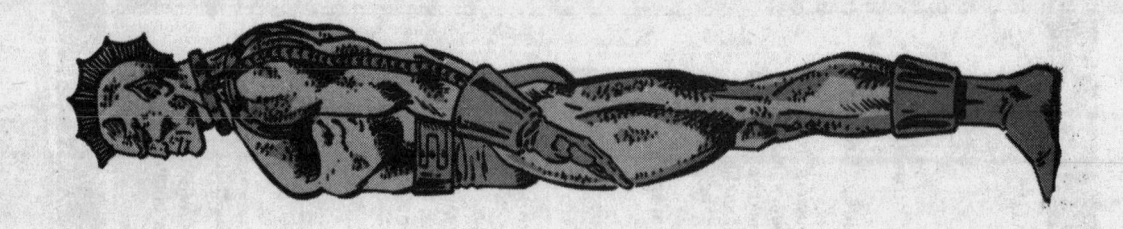

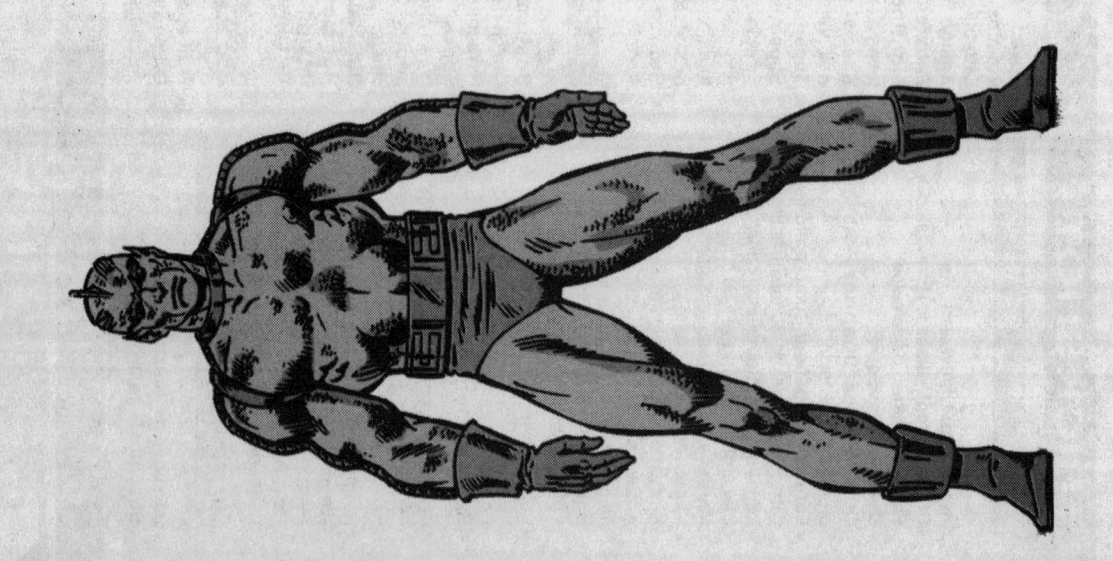

TRITON

BIOGRAPHICAL DATA

Real name: Unrevealed
Other current aliases: None
Former aliases: None
Dual identity: None; Triton's existence is not well known to the general populace of Earth
Current occupation: Scout
Former occupation: Unrevealed
Citizenship: Attilan
Legal status: No criminal record
Place of birth: Island of Attilan, Atlantic Ocean
Marital status: Single
Known relatives: Mander (father), Azur (mother), Karnak (brother), Gorgon, Black Bolt, Maximus, Medusa, Crystal (cousins)
Known confidants: None
Known allies: The Sub-Mariner, the Fantastic Four
Major enemies: Maximus
Usual base of operations: City of Attilan, Blue Area, Earth's Moon
Former bases of operations: Island of Attilan, Atlantic Ocean; City of Attilan, the Himalayan Mountain Range, China
Current group membership: The Royal Family of the Inhumans
Former group membership: None
Extent of education: Unrevealed

PHYSICAL DESCRIPTION

Height: 6' 1"
Weight: 210 lbs.
Eyes: Green
Hair: None
Other distinguishing features: Scaly, greenish skin, a small dorsal fin running from the base of the skull to the forehead, membranous fins extending from temples, webbing between toes and between fingers

POWERS AND ABILITIES

Intelligence: Normal
Strength: Enhanced human
Speed: (on land) Below normal, (in water) Superhuman
Stamina: (on land) Below normal, (in water) Enhanced human
Durability: Enhanced human
Agility: (on land) Below normal, (in water) Enhanced human
Reflexes: Enhanced human
Fighting skills: Basic Inhuman royal militia training
Special skills and abilities: Unrevealed
Superhuman physical powers: Superhuman strength, ability to survive underwater indefinitely, ability to withstand temperature and pressure of ocean depths
Superhuman mental powers: None
Special limitations: Triton cannot exist out of water without artificial aids
Source of superhuman powers: Artificially mutated by Terrigen mist

PARAPHERNALIA

Costume specifications: When on land, Triton employs a water circulation system consisting of lengths of plastic tubing which run along his torso and limbs, maintaining a constant mist of water and providing a supply of fresh water to his gills
Personal weaponry: None
Special weaponry: None
Other accessories: None
Transportation: Various, most often swimming under own power
Design and manufacture of paraphernalia: Maximus

BIBLIOGRAPHY

First appearance: FANTASTIC FOUR #45
Origin issue: Triton's origin is as yet unrevealed
Significant issues: FANTASTIC FOUR #45 (first encountered Fantastic Four); FANTASTIC FOUR #54 (acquired artificial life support system which enabled him to exist out of water); FANTASTIC FOUR #69 (first left Great Refuge); FANTASTIC FOUR #59-61 (freed from "negative zone" barrier, along with rest of Inhumans); FANTASTIC FOUR #62 (aided Fantastic Four in battle against Blastaar); SUB-MARINER #2 (first met Sub-Mariner; battled Plantman's Leviathan); FANTASTIC FOUR #82-83 (aided Inhuman Royal Family in defeating Maximus's attempt to overthrow Great Refuge); AMAZING ADVENTURES #2 (singlehandedly captured Maximus); AMAZING ADVENTURES #3-4 (battled the Mandarin alongside Royal Family); AVENGERS #95 (traveled to New York to warn Avengers of Inhumans' involvement in Kree-Skrull War); FANTASTIC FOUR #150 (attended wedding of Quicksilver and Crystal; joined in battle with Ultron-7); INHUMANS #1-2 (battled Blastaar and Kree Kaproids); INHUMANS #3-4 (traveled to New York City with Royal Family seeking aid for earthquake-threatened Attilan; battled Shatterstar); INHUMANS #5 (imprisoned by Maximus); INHUMANS #6 (aided Inhuman Royal Family in defeat of Maximus and evil Inhumans); INHUMANS #7-8 (left Earth with Inhuman Royal Family to prevent Kree subjugation of Inhumans; battled various aliens); INHUMANS #10 (battled Kree agents); INHUMANS #11 (returned to Earth; battled Kree agent, Pursuer); INHUMANS #12 (battled Hulk alongside Royal Family); FANTASTIC FOUR #240 (participated in Inhuman exodus when Attilan was relocated to Earth's Moon); AVENGERS ANNUAL #12 (grappled with the Avengers under Maximus's mind control); MARVEL GRAPHIC NOVEL: THE INHUMANS (accompanied Medusa to Earth when she fled Attilan to avoid compulsory abortion by order of Genetic Council); MARVEL COMICS PRESENTS #28 (battled mutated aquatic life caused by toxic waste)

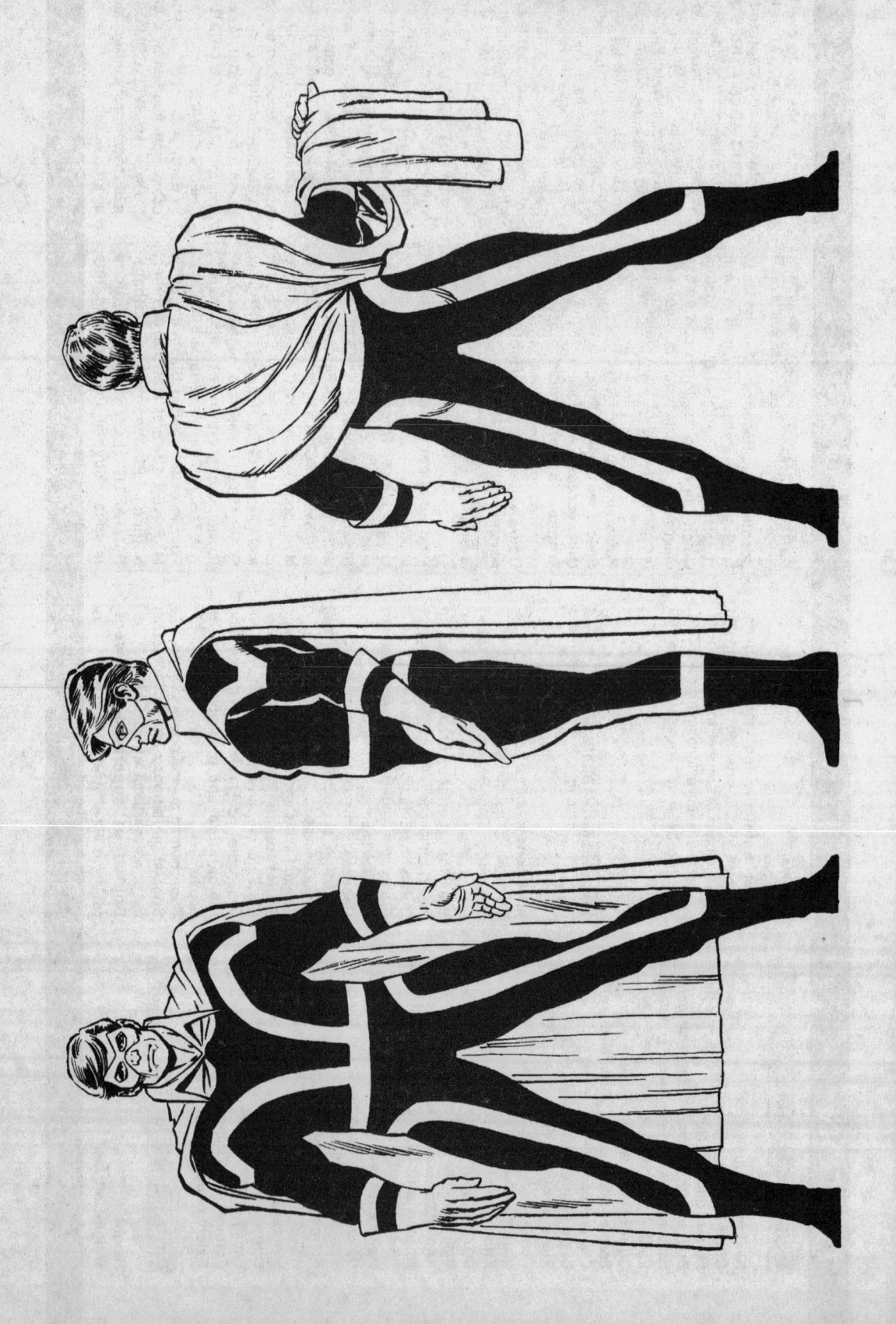

TRUMP

TRUMP

BIOGRAPHICAL DATA

Real name: Carlton Sanders
Other current aliases: None
Former aliases: None
Dual identity: Known to the authorities
Current occupation: Professional criminal
Former occupation: Children's television host, magician, illusionist
Citizenship: United States of America
Legal status: Criminal record in the U.S.
Place of birth: Bartlesville, Oklahoma
Marital status: Single
Known relatives: None
Known confidants: None
Known allies: (former) Stymie Schmidt
Major enemies: Daredevil
Usual base of operations: Mobile
Former base of operations: Tulsa, Oklahoma
Current group membership: None
Former group membership: None
Extent of education: College degree in drama; extensively studied clowning, illusions, bridge, and stage magic

PHYSICAL DESCRIPTION

Height: 6'
Weight: 242 lbs.
Eyes: Blue
Hair: Brown
Other distinguishing features: None

POWERS AND ABILITIES

Intelligence: Above average
Strength: Normal
Speed: Normal
Stamina: Athlete
Durability: Normal
Agility: Normal
Reflexes: Athlete
Fighting skills: Fair hand-to-hand combatant; generally avoids physical confrontation and employs weaponry when necessary
Special skills and abilities: Expert at sleight-of-hand, skilled marksman
Superhuman physical powers: None
Superhuman mental powers: None
Special limitations: None
Source of superhuman powers: Inapplicable

PARAPHERNALIA

Costume specifications: Synthetic stretch fabric
Personal weaponry: Cane which shoots pellets from one end, has a taser (electrical "stun-tip") at the other; a cape containing pouches with various tricks including decks of cards, nylon ribbons, metal rings, handcuffs, scarves, etc.; gloves with pockets containing a garrote and razor blades; boots with hollow heels containing various lockpicking and escape tools
Special weaponry: Various conventional handguns
Other accessories: Trained pigeons, tame rabbits
Transportation: Conventional means
Design and manufacture of paraphernalia: Various novelty companies

BIBLIOGRAPHY

First appearance: DAREDEVIL #203
Origin issue: The Trump's origin is as yet unrevealed
Significant issues: DAREDEVIL #203 (while in Manhattan, attempted to steal a shipment of guns for unnamed clients in the southwest, encountered and captured by Daredevil); CAPTAIN AMERICA #371 (interrupted stage performance at Manhattan comedy club attended by Steve Rogers and Rachel Leighton to practice new illusions, unknowingly thwarted by Black Mamba); CAPTAIN AMERICA #411 (among the various costumed criminals at AIM's Weapons Expo)

TURBO™

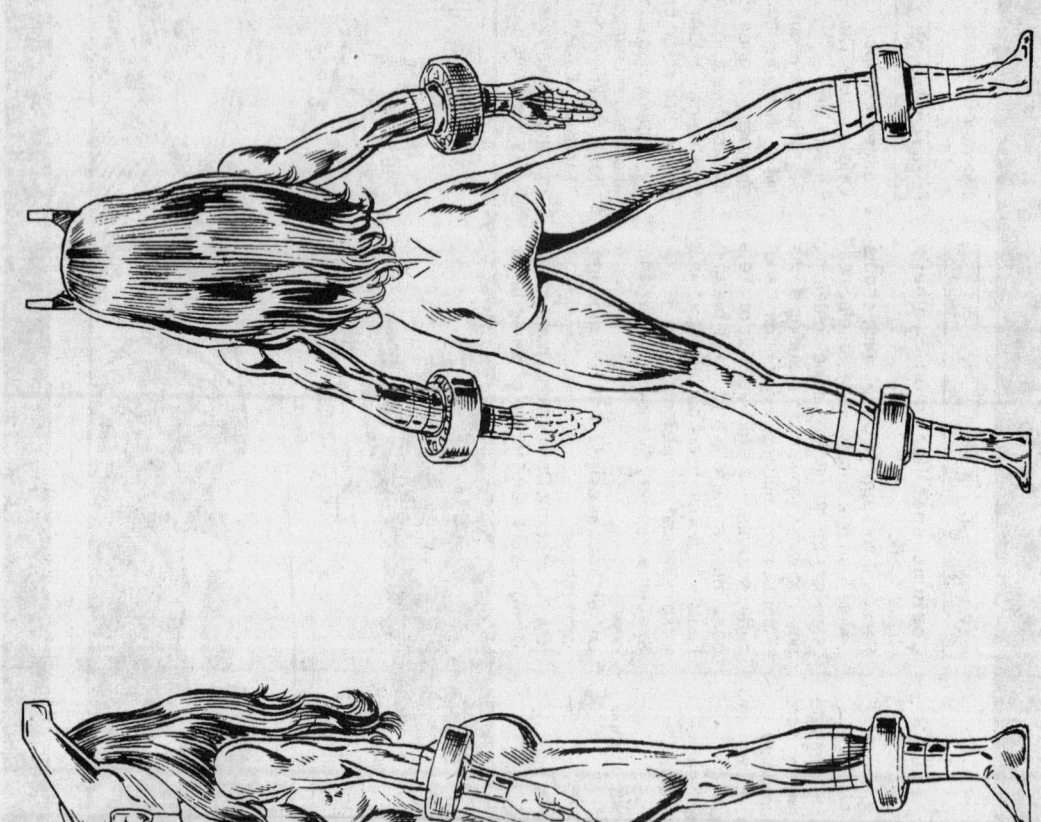

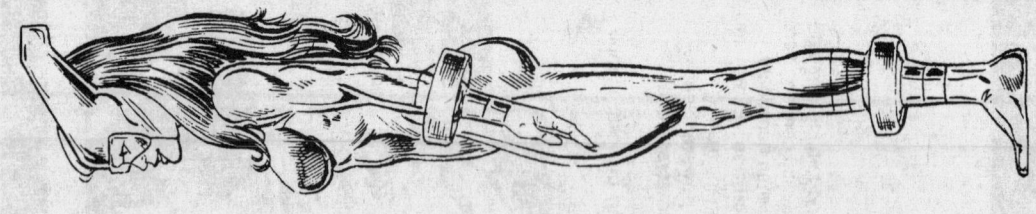

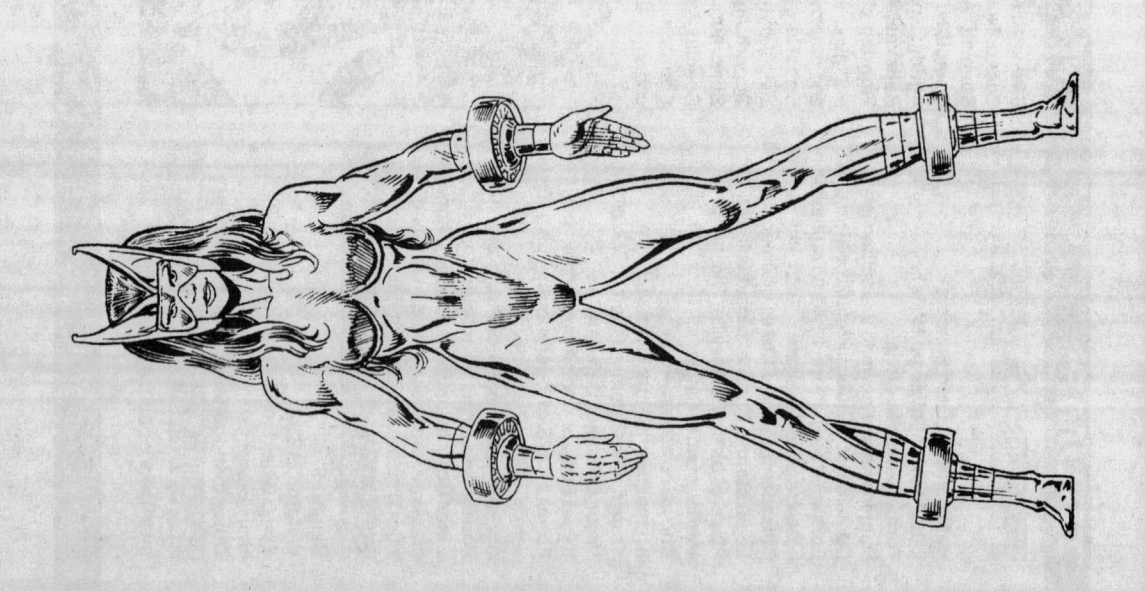

TURBO

BIOGRAPHICAL DATA

Real name: (I) Michiko "Mickey" Musashi, (II) Michael Brent "Mike" Jeffries

Note: Musashi and Jeffries share the use of the Turbo (Torpedo) costume, and hence share the Turbo identity

Other current aliases: (both) None

Former aliases : (both) None

Dual identity: (both) Secret

Current occupation: (I) Sophomore English and journalism college student, adventurer, (II) Freshman engineering college student, adventurer

Former occupation: (both) None known

Citizenship: (both) United States of America

Legal status: (both) No criminal records, still minors

Place of birth: (I) Hartford, Connecticut, (II) Westbrook, West Virginia

Marital status: (both) Single

Known relatives: (both) None

Known confidants: Michael Jefferies (Turbo II), the New Warriors, (II) Michiko Musashi (Turbo I), Nova I, the New Warriors

Known allies: (both) Nova I, The New Warriors, (II) Spider-Man, Avengers, the Thing, Darkhawk

Major enemies: (both) Cardinal, Air Control (Killer Shrike, Sparrow, Tanager), Weapon Y, (I) Sea Urchin, (II) (former) Darkling

Usual base of operations: (both) Long Island University, Hempstead, New York

Former bases of operations: (both, as Turbo) None

Current group membership: (both) Allies of the New Warriors

Former group membership: (both) None

Extent of education: (both) College students

PHYSICAL DESCRIPTION

Height: (I) 5'6", (II) 5'9 1/2"
Weight: (I) 120 lbs., (II) 155 lbs.
Eyes: (I) Brown, (II) Blue
Hair: (I) Black, (II) Brown
Other distinguishing features: None

POWERS AND ABILITIES

Intelligence: (both) Normal
Strength: (both) Normal
Speed: (both) Normal
Stamina: (both) Normal
Durability: (both) Normal
Agility: (I) Athlete, (II) Below normal
Reflexes: (both) Normal
Fighting skills: (both) No unarmed combat experience or training, rely on the new Turbo (Torpedo) suit in combat, receiving coaching in use of suit from Nova I
Special skills and abilities: (I) None known, (II) Comic book fan and collector with considerable knowledge about superheroes and super-villains
Superhuman physical powers: (both) None
Superhuman mental powers: (both) None
Special limitations: The efficiency with which a wearer can use the Turbo (Torpedo) suit depends on the degree to which his or her brain pattern interacts with its technology. Turbo I can use the suit at 46% efficiency while Turbo II uses it at 29% efficiency. The helmet and suit are useless without one another.
Source of superhuman powers: (both) Inapplicable

PARAPHERNALIA

Costume specifications: Turbo I and II use the helmet and battlesuit previously worn by Torpedo II and III (both now deceased). The suit is equipped with small nuclear-powered jet turbo units located at the wrists and ankles that generate high speed winds. Turbo I can project wide wind gusts up to 50 mph over 500 ft. range and narrow gusts up to 100 mph over a 200 ft. range. Turbo II can project wide wind gusts up to 40 mph over 300 ft. range and narrow gusts up to 75 mph over a 100 ft. range. The Turbo jets enable Turbo I to fly at a top speed of approximately 5000 mph for 6 hours and Turbo II to fly at a top speed of approximately 2500 mph for 6 hours. The jets enable the wearer to project pulsed concussive force blasts nicknamed "hyperpunches." Turbo I's double hyperpunch is equal to a blow of Superhuman Class 100, while Turbo II's double hyperpunch is equal to a blow of Superhuman Class 75. Turbo I and Turbo II can regulate their hyperpunches so as to strike a person without causing serious injury. Assisted by the power of the turbo jets, Turbo I can lift 20 tons and Turbo II can lift 10 tons. The suit projects a force field that can disperse radiation directed against it and protects the wearer against the adverse effects of motion at high speeds; The force field also enables the wearer to breathe when moving at high speeds. The helmet enables the wearer to control the suit cybernetically.

Personal weaponry: None
Special weaponry: None
Other accessories: None
Transportation: Flight via Turbo (Torpedo) suit
Design and manufacture of paraphernalia: Michael Stivak (Torpedo II, deceased) employing both Earth and Dire Wraith technology

BIBLIOGRAPHY

First appearance: (I) NEW WARRIORS #28, (II) (first mentioned as Jeffries) NEW WARRIORS #28, (first seen) NEW WARRIORS #33
Origin issue: AVENGERS #328
Significant issues: NEW WARRIORS #28 (Turbo I first met and teamed with new Warriors, captured Sea Urchin); NEW WARRIORS #33-34/NEW WARRIORS ANNUAL #3 (Turbo II, alongside New Warriors, battled Darkling)

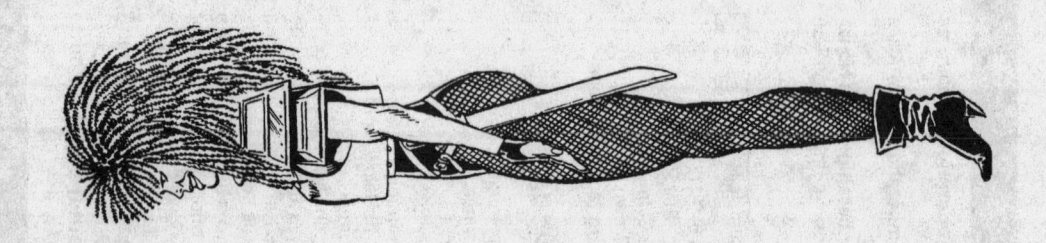

TYPHOID

TYPHOID

BIOGRAPHICAL DATA

Real name: Mary (last name unrevealed)
Other current aliases: None
Former aliases: Unrevealed
Dual identity: Known to U.S. legal and psychiatric authorities
Former aliases: Unrevealed
Current occupation: Professional criminal
Former occupation: Actress, teacher
Citizenship: United States of America
Legal status: No criminal record
Place of birth: Unrevealed
Marital status: Single
Known relatives: None
Known confidants: None
Known allies: Bullet, Bushwacker, Ammo, Wild Boys, Kingpin
Major enemies: Daredevil
Usual base of operations: New York City
Former bases of operations: Chicago
Current group membership: Kingpin's operatives
Former group membership: None
Extent of education: Unrevealed

PHYSICAL DESCRIPTION

Height: 5'10"
Weight: 140 lbs.
Eyes: Brown
Hair: Brown
Other distinguishing features: Typhoid usually wears white make-up on the right side of her face.

POWERS AND ABILITIES

Intelligence: Above normal
Strength: Athlete
Speed: Athlete
Stamina: Athlete
Durability: Athlete
Agility: Athlete
Reflexes: Peak human
Fighting skills: Basic hand-to-hand combat, some Judo
Special skills and abilities: Exceptional skill in wielding and throwing bladed weapons.
Superhuman physical powers: None
Superhuman mental powers: Limited telekinesis (able to levitate objects up to approximately 10 lbs.), pyrokinesis (able to cause spontaneous combustion within line of sight), psionic hypnosis
Special limitations: Typhoid is a victim of Multiple Personality Disorder; both her physical and mental abilities are linked to her Typhoid persona. Certain individuals are mentally resistant to her hypnotic powers.
Source of superhuman powers: Unrevealed

PARAPHERNALIA

Costume specifications: Leather jacket with metal shoulder pads, mesh stockings, leather boots, leotard
Personal weaponry: A variety of machetes and smaller knives
Special weaponry: None
Other accessories: None
Transportation: Various
Design and manufacture of paraphernalia: Unrevealed

BIBLIOGRAPHY

First appearance: DAREDEVIL #254
Origin issue: DAREDEVIL #254
Significant issues: DAREDEVIL #254 (first met Matt Murdock; origin revealed; hired assassin by Kingpin); DAREDEVIL #255 (first battled Daredevil; romance with Matt Murdock); DAREDEVIL #256 (temporarily reverted to Mary personality); DAREDEVIL #257 (reverted back to "Typhoid" personality; romanced Kingpin); DAREDEVIL #258 (hired Bullet, Bushwacker, Ammo, and the Wild Boys to attack Daredevil); DAREDEVIL #260 (led Bullet, Bushwacker, Ammo, and the Wild Boys against Daredevil); POWER PACK #53 (sent by Doctor Doom to learn secrets of Kymelian technology from Power Pack) CAPTAIN AMERICA #373 (revealed to be in Kingpin's employ once again; met Bullseye); CAPTAIN AMERICA #376 (helped thwart attempt on Kingpin's life by Crossbones)

TYR™

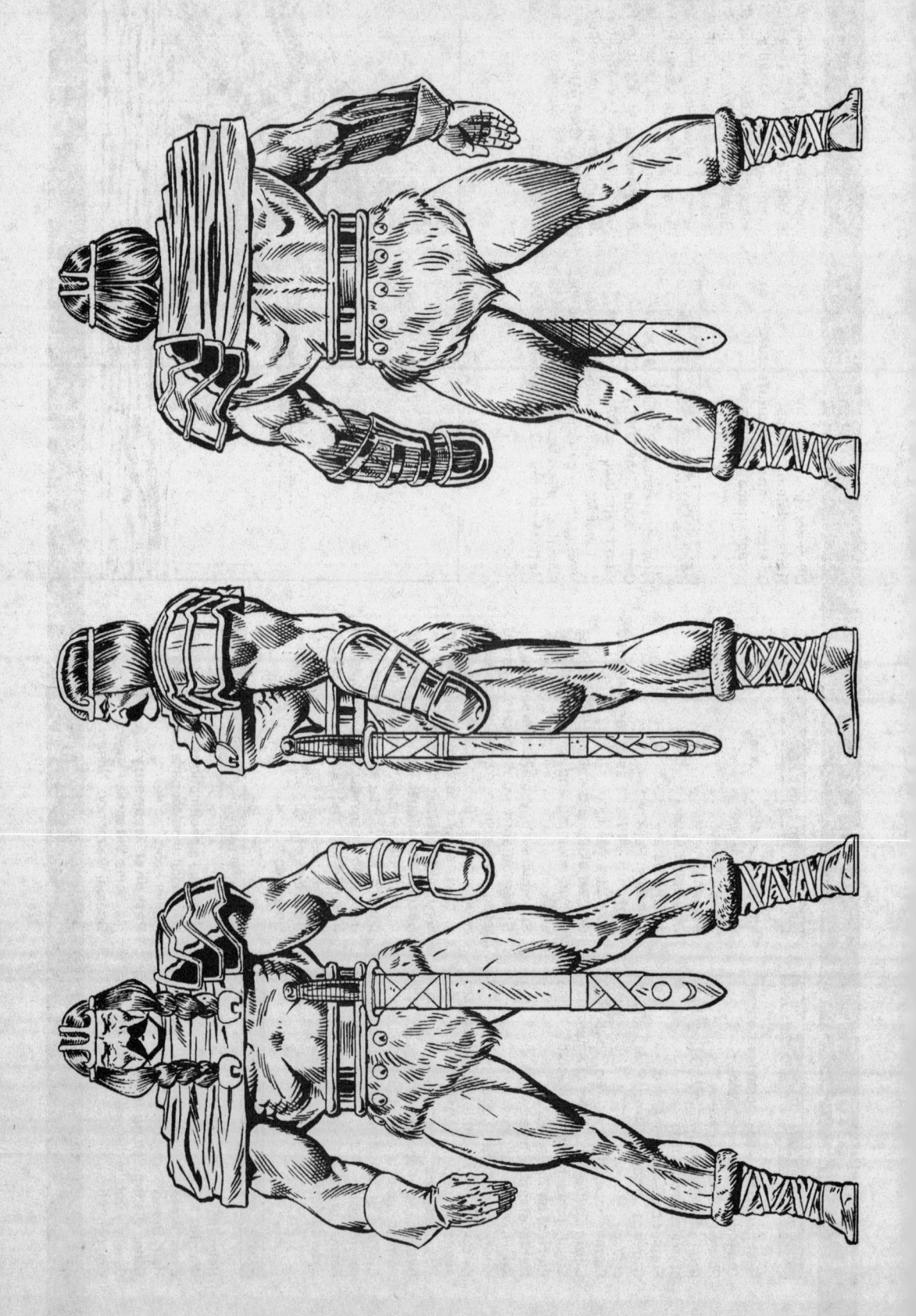

TYR

BIOGRAPHICAL DATA

Real name: Tyr
Other current aliases: None
Former aliases: None
Dual identity: None; the general populace of Earth knows of Tyr's existence, but most do not believe he is a god of Norse mythology.
Current occupation: God of war
Former occupation: None
Citizenship: Realm of Asgard
Legal status: No criminal record
Place of birth: Presumably Asgard
Marital status: Single
Known relatives: None
Known confidants: None
Known allies: (former) Loki
Major enemies: (former) Thor, Odin; (current) Surtur
Usual base of operations: Dimension of Asgard
Former bases of operations: None
Current group membership: Gods of Asgard
Former group membership: None
Extent of education: Unrevealed

PHYSICAL DESCRIPTION

Height: 6'7"
Weight: 510 lbs.
Eyes: Blue
Hair: Black
Other distinguishing features: Tyr is missing his left hand which is covered by a metal cup.

POWERS AND ABILITIES

Intelligence: Normal
Strength: Superhuman Class 50
Speed: Superhuman
Stamina: Superhuman
Durability: Superhuman
Agility: Superhuman
Reflexes: Superhuman
Fighting skills: Trained in Asgardian arts of war, highly skilled hand-to-hand combatant, proficient with all Asgardian weaponry
Special skills and abilities: None known
Superhuman physical powers: Aside from the above listed attributes, Tyr has an extremely long life span and immunity to all Earthly diseases.
Superhuman mental powers: None
Special limitations: Tyr's left hand is missing, having been bitten off by the wolf-god Fenris.
Note: According to Norse mythology, it was Tyr's right hand that was lost, but in the Asgard of the Marvel Universe, he lacks his left.
Source of superhuman powers: Tyr is a member of the race of superhumans known as Asgardians

PARAPHERNALIA

Costume specifications: Asgardian materials
Personal weaponry: Sword
Special weaponry: Shield
Other accessories: Tyr once stole the Mace of of the Myth-Wars, a weapon once wielded by Odin and possessing powers similar to Thor's hammer Mjolnir.
Transportation: Horse, Interdimensional teleportation via the Mace of the Myth-Wars
Design and manufacture of paraphernalia: Forges of Asgard

BIBLIOGRAPHY

First appearance: JOURNEY INTO MYSTERY #85
Origin issue: Tyr's origin is as yet unrevealed.
Significant issues: JOURNEY INTO MYSTERY #85 (first appearance among Asgardians); THOR #275 (battled with Asgardian forces against false Ragnarok); THOR #302 (lost friendly wager to Thor); THOR #324-327 (allied with Loki against Odin, captured the goddess Idunn and the Golden Apples of Immortality, unleashed the Midgard Serpent on Earth; with the enemies of Asgard, followed Odin and the other gods to Earth, betrayed by Loki, defeated by Odin); THOR #350-352, 359 (alongside Beta Ray Bill, the Avengers, the Fantastic Four, and Asgardian forces, battled Surtur's demons on Earth; returned to Asgard)
Note: Tyr is not to be confused with Tyr of the Blinding Blade, an inhabitant of the World with a Thousand Galaxies who appeared in THOR ANNUAL #2.

TYRANNUS

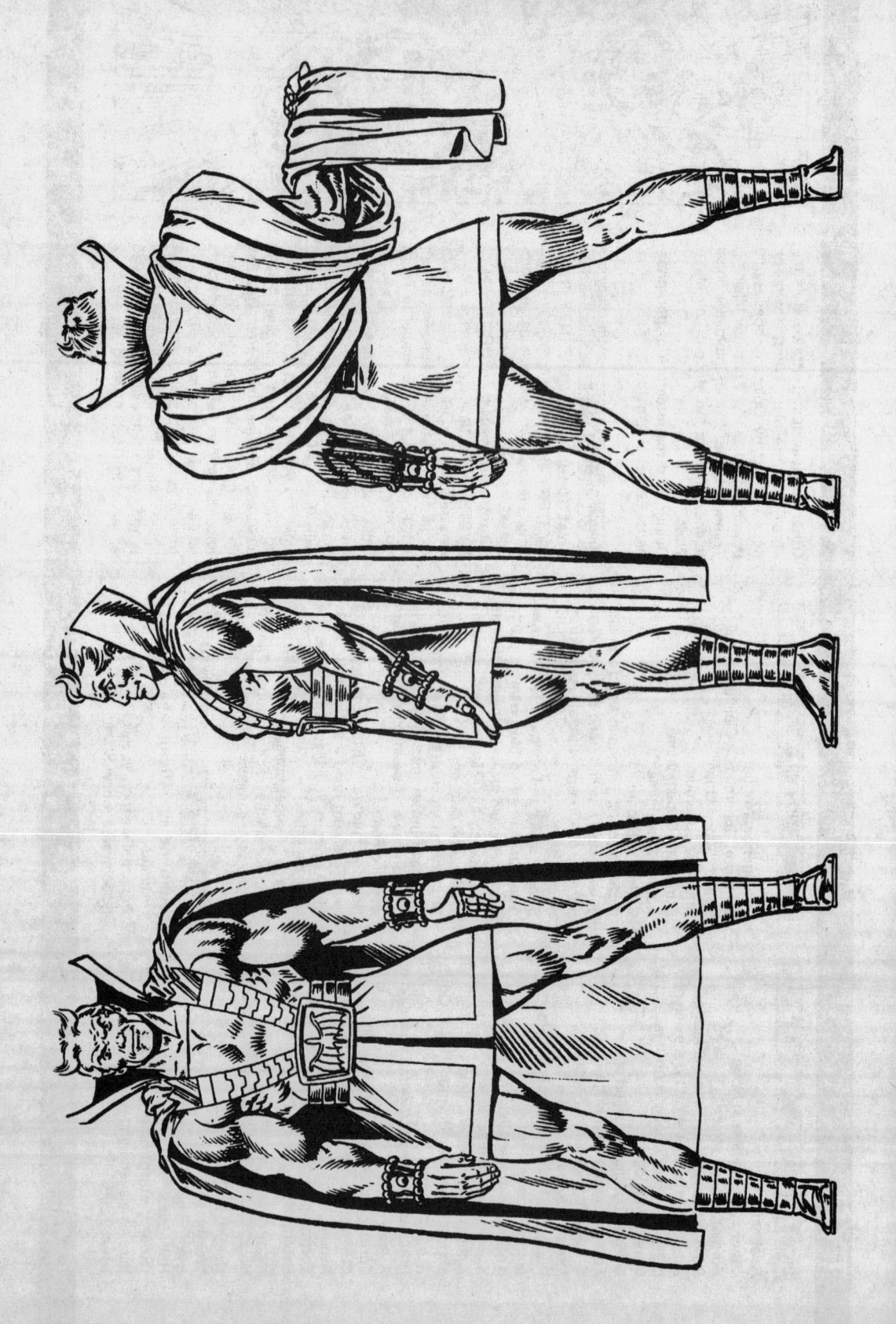

TYRANNUS

BIOGRAPHICAL DATA

Real name: Unrevealed
Other current aliases: None
Former aliases: Des, Dr. Tyrone, Abomination
Dual identity: None. Tyrannus's existence is not known to the general population of Earth
Current occupation: Emperor of the Tyrannoid subterraneans, aspiring conqueror
Former occupation: None
Citizenship: Roman Empire
Legal status: No criminal record
Place of birth: Unrevealed, presumably Rome, Italy
Marital status: Unrevealed, now unmarried
Known relatives: None, but presumably a descendant of other Roman emperors
Known confidants: None
Known allies: Tyrannoid subterraneans, (formerly) Ghaur, Llyra, Viper II, Hulk, Kala, Prince Rey of El Dorado, Keeper of the Flame of El Dorado
Major enemies: Merlin, the Mole Man, Kala, Hulk, X-Men, Fantastic Four, Spider-Man, Daredevil, Dr. Strange, Viper II
Usual base of operations: Subterranea
Former bases of operations: El Dorado, ancient Rome
Current group membership: None
Former group membership: None
Extent of education: Presumably educated by the finest teachers of the final years of the Roman Empire

PHYSICAL DESCRIPTION

Height: 6' 2"
Weight: 225 lbs.
Eyes: Light brown
Hair: Blond
Other distinguishing features: None

POWERS AND ABILITIES

Intelligence: Extraordinary genius
Strength: Athlete
Speed: Athlete
Stamina: Athlete
Durability: Athlete
Agility: Athlete
Reflexes: Athlete
Fighting skills: Excellent hand-to-hand combatant, trained in swordsmanship and other combat skills
Special skills and abilities: Mastery of advanced technology of the Deviants which he found in Subterranea, upon which he has made further advances; limited knowledge of sorcery
Superhuman physical powers: Superhuman longevity and youth
Superhuman mental powers: Various psionic abilities, including telepathy, mind control of others, and the ability to drain the life force of others
Special limitations: Dependent on "fountain of youth" in Subterranea to maintain his youth and immortality
Source of superhuman powers: Cobalt "Flame of Life" in El Dorado, "fountain of youth" in Subterranea

PARAPHERNALIA

Costume specifications: Clothing of ancient Roman Empire, including battle armor and helmet
Personal weaponry: Ancient Roman weaponry (e.g., swords, spears)
Special weaponry: Guns projecting various types of radiation, other advanced technological weaponry
Other accessories: None
Transportation: Teleportation devices, flying vehicles, gigantic earth-borers
Design and manufacture of paraphernalia: Designed by Tyrannus based on Deviant technology and his own innovations, manufactured by Subterraneans under his supervision

BIBLIOGRAPHY

First appearance: INCREDIBLE HULK Vol. 1 #5
Origin issue: Tyrannus's origin is as yet unrevealed.
Significant issues: INCREDIBLE HULK Vol. 1 #5 (first battled Hulk); TALES TO ASTONISH #80-81 (reverted to old man when Mole Man captured "fountain of youth," used Hulk as pawn against Mole Man and recaptured fountain); X-MEN #34 (forced scientist Ralph Roberts to design gigantic robot for him to use in his war against the Mole Man; defeated by the X-Men); INCREDIBLE HULK Vol. 2 #127 (used Hulk and robot Mogul as slaves in war against Mole Man); FANTASTIC FOUR #127-128 (secretly allied with Kala against Mole Man); NOVA #5 (projected consciousness into Subterranean, who attacked New York City but was thwarted by Nova I); INCREDIBLE HULK Vol. 2 #240 (in guise of aged Des, ally of Prince Rey and the Keeper of the Flame of El Dorado, captured Hulk); INCREDIBLE HULK Vol. 2 #241 (Des restored to youthfulness, killed Rey and Keeper); INCREDIBLE HULK Vol. 2 #242 (merged with Cobalt "Flame of Life" of El Dorado); INCREDIBLE HULK Vol. 2 #243 (defeated by Hulk and ascended into outer space, still in form of cobalt flame); INCREDIBLE HULK ANNUAL #15 (life force took possession of Abomination's body); WEST COAST AVENGERS #25 (in Abomination's body, battled Wonder Man); SOLO AVENGERS #12 (in Abomination's body, battled Hawkeye); AMAZING SPIDER-MAN ANNUAL #23 (freed by Ghaur and Llyra from Abomination's body and restored to human form; adopted guise of Dr. Tyrone); SPECTACULAR SPIDER-MAN ANNUAL #9 (as Dr. Tyrone, transformed alcoholics and drug addicts into serpent men; enslaved Spider-Man); DAREDEVIL ANNUAL #4 (battled Daredevil and Dr. Strange, attempted to bring Set to Earth, but was attacked by Viper II and swallowed by serpent demon)

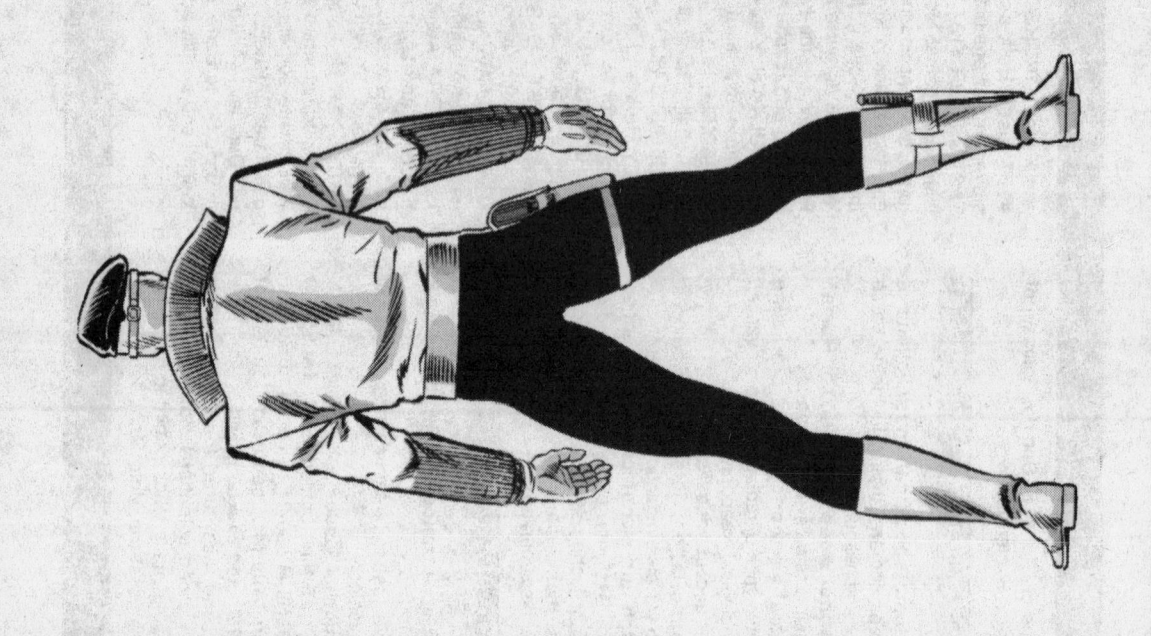

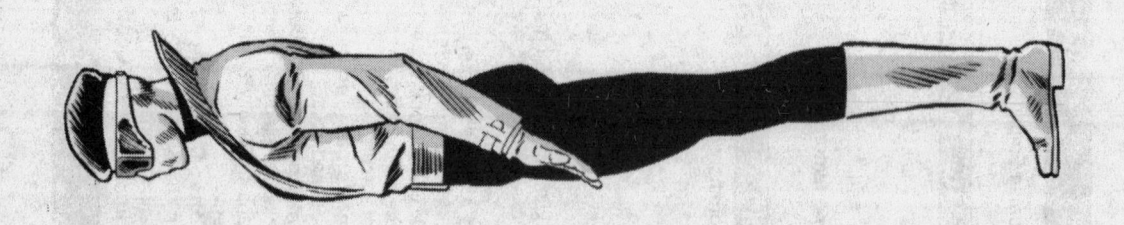

ULTIMATUM™

ULTIMATUM

ORGANIZATION

Full Name: Underground Liberated Totally Integrated Mobile Army to Unite Mankind

Purpose: To unite mankind by abolishing the concept of nationalism and bringing about the end of all nations, thereby making possible the establishment of a world government

Modus operandi: Terrorist activity against governments and institutions and symbols representing nationalism, supplying arms to subversives

Extent of operations: Worldwide, primarily in Western Europe and the United States

Relationship to conventional authorities: Outlawed by the United Nations, sought by SHIELD, NATO, Interpol, and other law enforcement agencies

Base of operations: Unrevealed

Former bases of operations: Former HYDRA base in the Swiss Alps, base in unrevealed location above the Arctic Circle, ski lodge on Symkarian-Latverian border

Major funding: (formerly) Red Skull, (currently) Unrevealed

Known enemies: Captain America, Solo, Spider-Man, Moon Knight, Punisher, Demolition-Man, Silver Sable, Paladin, SHIELD

Known allies: (formerly) Red Skull, Prime Minister Limka of Symkaria, Life Foundation

MEMBERSHIP

Number of active members: Unrevealed
Number of reserve members: Unrevealed

Organizational structure: Flag-Smasher's title: Supreme Commander, various regional leaders, rest of organization apparently organized along military lines (e.g. Weil's rank as "major")

Known officers: Flag-Smasher (leader)
Known current members: Dimitri (last name unrevealed), Luft, Rivvik
Known former members: Major Weil, Vladimir Krantz, Basil (deceased)

Known special agents: Anarchy (Note: Sabretooth, though not a member of ULTIMATUM, was hired by the organization to assassinate Symkarian Prime Minister Limka.)

Membership requirements: Must be an adult who professes a belief in ULTIMATUM's one world philosophy; background in the military or as a soldier of fortune is preferred

HISTORY

Founder: Flag-Smasher

Other leaders: Major Toler Weil (former regional leader in Europe)

Previous purpose or goals: (during Flag-Smasher's absence) To subvert existing governments or foment wars to destabilize such governments in order to make possible their domination by the Red Skull

Major campaigns or accomplishments: Hijacked American airliner and took its passengers as hostages to exchange for surrender of Captain America; attempted to destroy the world's technology through an electromagnetic pulse; assassinated fiancee of King Stefan of Symkaria and Symkarian Prime Minister Limka and attempted to start war between Symkaria and the United States; attempted to blow up Ellis Island; attempted to distribute arms to subversive elements in the United States to create nationwide chaos

Major setbacks: Swiss base Captured by Captain America and SHIELD, Arctic base destroyed (and electromagnetic pulse generator) by D-Man on order of Captain America, failed to assassinate King Stefan of Symkaria, exposure and defeated attempt of ULTIMATUM to cause war between United States and Symkaria failed in attempt to destroy Arc de Triomphe and Ellis Island, major arms stockpile captured by Punisher and Moon Knight

Note: Although Flag-Smasher was the founder of ULTIMATUM, its initial funding secretly came from Red Skull, who used its activities to create political chaos benefitting his own fascist ends. Upon Flag-Smasher's discovery of the Red Skull's involvement, the Skull had other ULTIMATUM leaders who were loyal to him stage a successful coup against Flag-Smasher through its Symkarian campaign. Presumably the ULTIMATUM rank and file were never aware of the Red Skull's control of the organization. Following the Symkarian debacle, Flag-Smasher regained control of ULTIMATUM and purged the organization of members known to be loyal to the Red Skull.

TECHNOLOGY AND PARAPHERNALIA

Level of technology: As highly advanced as any on Earth

Transportation: Various, including submarines, jets-propelled skis for flight by individual members, and teleportation devices

Standard uniforms: White or black berets, white masks covering entire face, goggles, white jackets, black shirts, white or black pants, white gloves and boots

Standard weaponry: Automatic firearms

Standard accessories: Jet-skis with electromagnetic grips and fuel tanks (worn on back), grappling hooks and hook thrusters

BIBLIOGRAPHY

First appearance: CAPTAIN AMERICA #321
Origin issue: ULTIMATUM's origin is as yet unrevealed

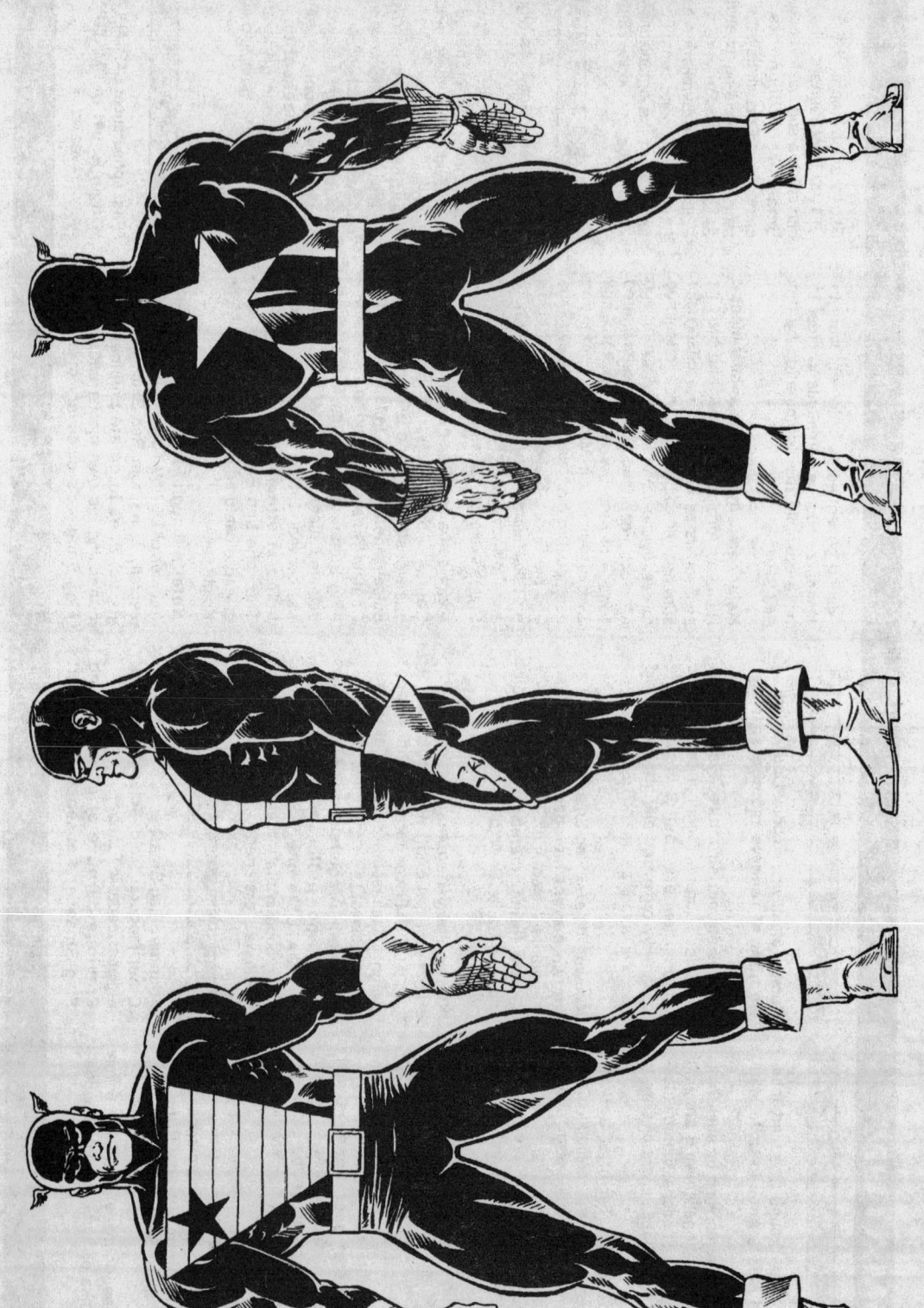

U.S. AGENT

U.S.AGENT

BIOGRAPHICAL DATA

Real name: John F. Walker
Other current aliases: Jack Daniels
Former aliases: Super-Patriot II, Captain America VI
Dual Identity: (as Captain America VI) Publicly known; (as Super-Patriot II and U.S.Agent) Secret, known to the Commission on Superhuman Activities
Current occupation: Adventurer, U.S. government operative
Former occupation: Soldier
Citizenship: United States of America
Legal status: No criminal record
Place of birth: Custer's Grove, Georgia
Marital status: Single
Known relatives: Caleb Walker, Emily Walker (parents, deceased), Michael Walker (brother, deceased), Kate Tollifson (sister)
Known confidants: Battle Star (Lemar Hoskins), (former) Jerome Johnson, Hector Lennox
Known allies: Battle Star, Avengers West Coast, Commission on Superhuman Activities; (former) Ethan Thurm, the Buckies (Bold Urban Commandos), Valerie Cooper, Freedom Force
Major enemies: Power Broker, Dr. Karl Malus, the Watchdogs, the Red Skull, Flag-Smasher, ULTIMATUM, Right-Winger, Left Winger, Ethan Thurm, Scourge
Usual base of operations: Commission on Superhuman Activities headquarters, Washington D.C.; Avengers Compound, Los Angeles, California
Former bases of operations: Special Powers Compound, Fort Meade, Maryland; mobile
Current group membership: Commission on Superhuman Activities, Avengers West Coast
Former group membership: Partner of Battle Star
Extent of education: High school graduate

PHYSICAL DESCRIPTION

Height: 6' 4"
Weight: 270 lbs.
Eyes: Blue
Hair: Blond
Other distinguishing features: None

POWERS AND ABILITIES

Intelligence: Normal
Strength: Superhuman Class 10
Speed: Enhanced human
Stamina: Superhuman
Durability: Superhuman
Agility: Superhuman
Reflexes: Superhuman
Fighting skills: Excellent hand-to-hand combatant, received rigorous training in unarmed combat and the use of his shield in a style similar to Captain America I from Taskmaster
Special skills and abilities: Highly trained in gymnastics and acrobatics
Superhuman physical powers: Aside from the above listed attributes, none.
Superhuman mental powers: None
Special limitations: None
Source of superhuman powers: Augmentation of his physical attributes by Dr. Karl Malus on behalf of the Power Broker

PARAPHERNALIA

Costume specifications: Synthetic stretch bulletproof fabric
Personal weaponry: Carries a nearly indestructible vibranium shield, approximately 2.5' in diameter, painted red, white, and black
Special weaponry: None
Other accessories: An official Avengers I.D. card which contains a microminiature communications device
Transportation: Avengers Quinjet
Design and manufacture of paraphernalia: (costume) Dennis Dunphy, (shield and quinjet) Tony Stark

BIBLIOGRAPHY

First appearance: (as Super-Patriot II) CAPTAIN AMERICA #323, (as Captain America VI) CAPTAIN AMERICA #333, (as U.S.Agent) WEST COAST AVENGERS Vol. 2 #44
Origin issue: CAPTAIN AMERICA 380-381
Significant issues: CAPTAIN AMERICA #323, (as Super-Patriot II) staged fake battle with the Buckies for publicity, challenged Captain America's role as symbol of America); CAPTAIN AMERICA #327 (revealed to be working with the Buckies, battled Captain America); CAPTAIN AMERICA #333-335 (chosen by the Commission to become Captain America VI, partnered with Bucky V [Battle Star]; trained by Freedom Force, Guardsmen, and Taskmaster; went on first mission, fought Watchdogs); CAPTAIN AMERICA #341 (publicly announced he was a replacement, battled Right-Winger and Left-Winger); CAPTAIN AMERICA #345 (killed a group of Watchdogs after they killed his parents); AMERICA #347 (battled Left-Winger and Right-Winger); CAPTAIN AMERICA #348-349 (captured by Flag-Smasher; rescued by original Captain America, Battle Star, and D-Man); CAPTAIN AMERICA #350-351 (battled Red Skull and original Captain America, gave up role as Captain America VI, helped fake his own assassination); CAPTAIN AMERICA #354 (renamed U.S.Agent, battled Iron Monger III in test for the commission); WEST COAST AVENGERS Vol. 2 #44-45 (joined the West Coast Avengers under the orders of the Commission); CAPTAIN AMERICA #376-378 (rescued Battle Star from the Power Broker, reconciled with Battle Star, learned that his memories had been altered and that his parents were dead)

UATU THE WATCHER

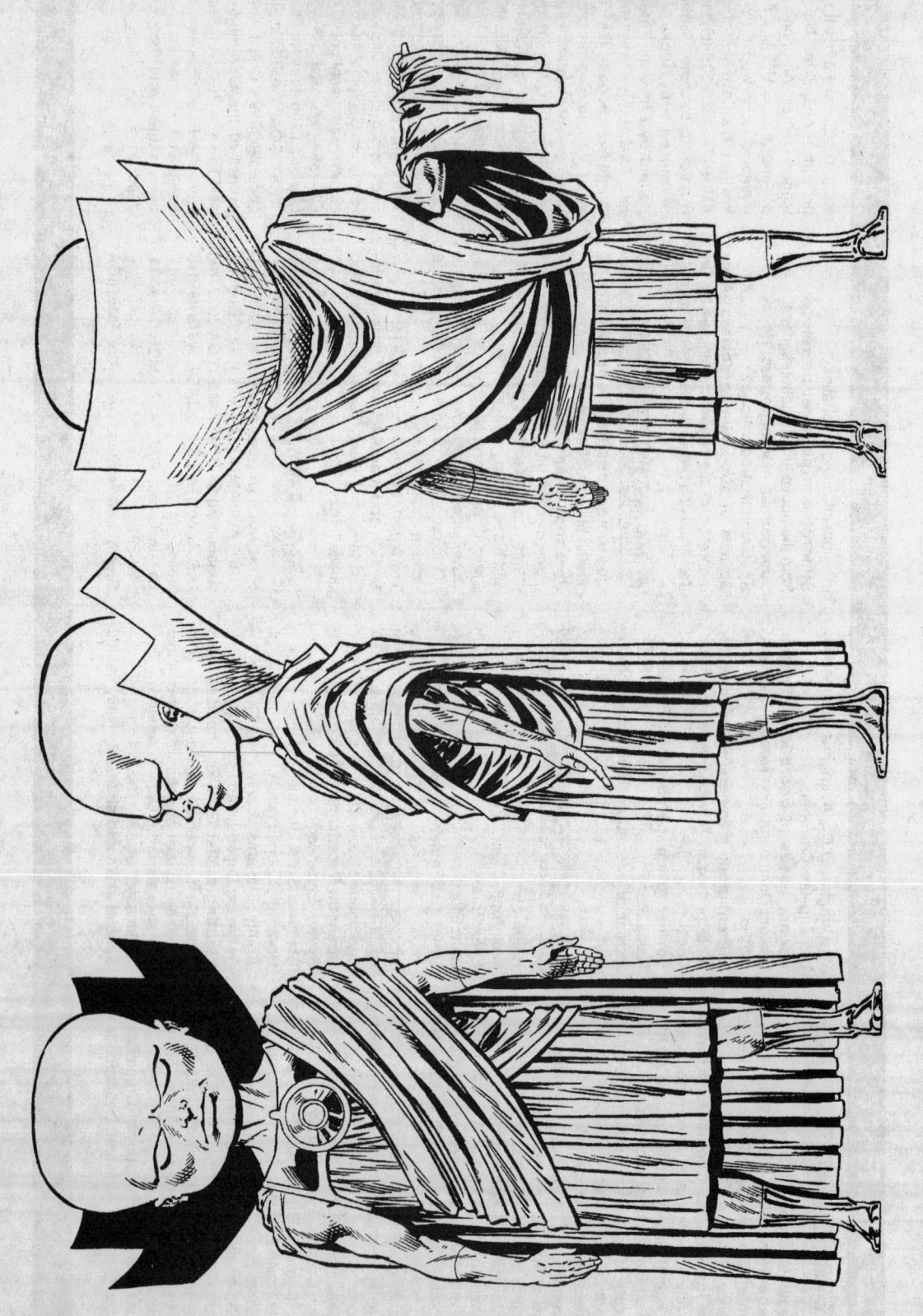

UATU THE WATCHER

BIOGRAPHICAL DATA

Real name: Uatu
Other current aliases: The Watcher
Former aliases: None known
Dual identity: None; the general populace of Earth is unaware of the Watchers existence (he erases memories of himself from most people who see him)
Current occupation: Observer
Former occupation: Altruist
Citizenship: Watchers' homeworld
Legal status: Found guilty by the Watchers' High Tribunal of intervention in the affairs of Earth humanity, released under his own cognizance
Place of birth: Watchers' homeworld
Marital status: Single
Known relatives: Ikor (father)
Known confidants: Fantastic Four
Known allies: Fantastic Four, Avengers, Quasar, Spider-Man, Recorder, Timekeepers, (sometimes) Celestials, Epoch, Eternity, Galactus, In-Betweener, Lord Chaos, Master Hate, Master Order, Mistress Love, Stranger
Major enemies: Maelstrom
Usual base of operations: Blue Area of Earth's Moon
Former base of operations: Watchers' homeworld
Current group membership: Watchers
Former group membership: None
Extent of education: Highly extensive in his youth on his homeworld; Uatu has devoted himself to the study of Earth's sentient beings for millions of years; in recent years he has undertaken the study of the Earths of alternate realities

PHYSICAL DESCRIPTION

Height: Variable
Weight: Variable
Eyes: No visible irises
Hair: None
Other distinguishing features: Unusually large head in comparison with those of Earth humans

POWERS AND ABILITIES

Intelligence: Immeasurable
Strength: Potentially incalculable (Watchers can augment their strength if they choose to, however they tend to minimize their physical activities)
Speed: Potentially orbital velocity (Watchers can augment their speed if they choose to, however they tend to minimize their physical activities)
Flight speed: Warp speed
Stamina: Immeasurable
Durability: Godlike
Agility: Metahuman
Reflexes: Metahuman
Fighting skills: Minimal; does not engage in hand-to-hand combat
Special skills and abilities: Extraordinary knowledge of the history of Earth's sentient beings on "mainstream" Earth and numerous alternate Earths
Superhuman physical powers: Apart from those listed above, Uatu can convert his body to a form of unknown energy (while retaining his sentience) for travel through hyperspace and then return to physical form. Possesses virtual immortality (bolstered by treatment with "delta-rays")
Superhuman mental powers: Vast psionic abilities including telepathy and energy-manipulation powers. Can psionically alter his appearance at will. Apparently possesses intelligence far more complex than a human being's, enabling him to monitor activities throughout Earth's solar system simultaneously
Special limitations: Watchers can die by losing the will to live.
Source of superhuman powers: Member of the Watcher's race, psionic powers further developed through training

PARAPHERNALIA

Costume specifications: Alien materials
Personal weaponry: None
Special weaponry: Uatu's home on the Blue Area of the Moon contains a large array of alien weaponry.
Other accessories: With permission of the Timekeepers, Uatu possesses a portal through which he can observe alternate realities. Uatu's home also contains an enormous array of artifacts and technology
Transportation: Flight under own power
Design and manufacture of paraphernalia: Various alien races throughout the universe

BIBLIOGRAPHY

First appearance: FANTASTIC FOUR #13, (name Uatu revealed) CAPTAIN MARVEL Vol. 1 #39
Origin issue: TALES OF SUSPENSE #53
Significant issues: FANTASTIC FOUR #13 (first encountered Fantastic Four and Red Ghost on the moon); FANTASTIC FOUR #20 (warned Fantastic Four about Molecule Man I, took him into custody); TALES OF SUSPENSE #53 (revealed how Uatu and Ikor persuaded Watchers to aid other races, how their gift of nuclear energy to Prosilicans led to disaster, how the Watchers devised their code of non-interference); FANTASTIC FOUR ANNUAL #3 (enabled Mister Fantastic to find device to defeat horde of enemies); FANTASTIC FOUR #48-50 (aided Fantastic Four in repelling Galactus from Earth); AVENGERS SPECIAL #2 (witnessed Avengers' battle against Scarlet Centurion); AVENGERS #118 (witnessed Avengers and defenders battle against Dormammu and Loki); CAPTAIN MARVEL Vol. 1 #39 (placed on trial by other Watchers); WHAT IF Vol. 1 #1 (first known observation of an alternate Earth); UNCANNY X-MEN #137 (witnessed physical demise of Phoenix I); QUASAR #30 (enlisted Quasar's aid in gathering renegade Living Lasers)

ULIK

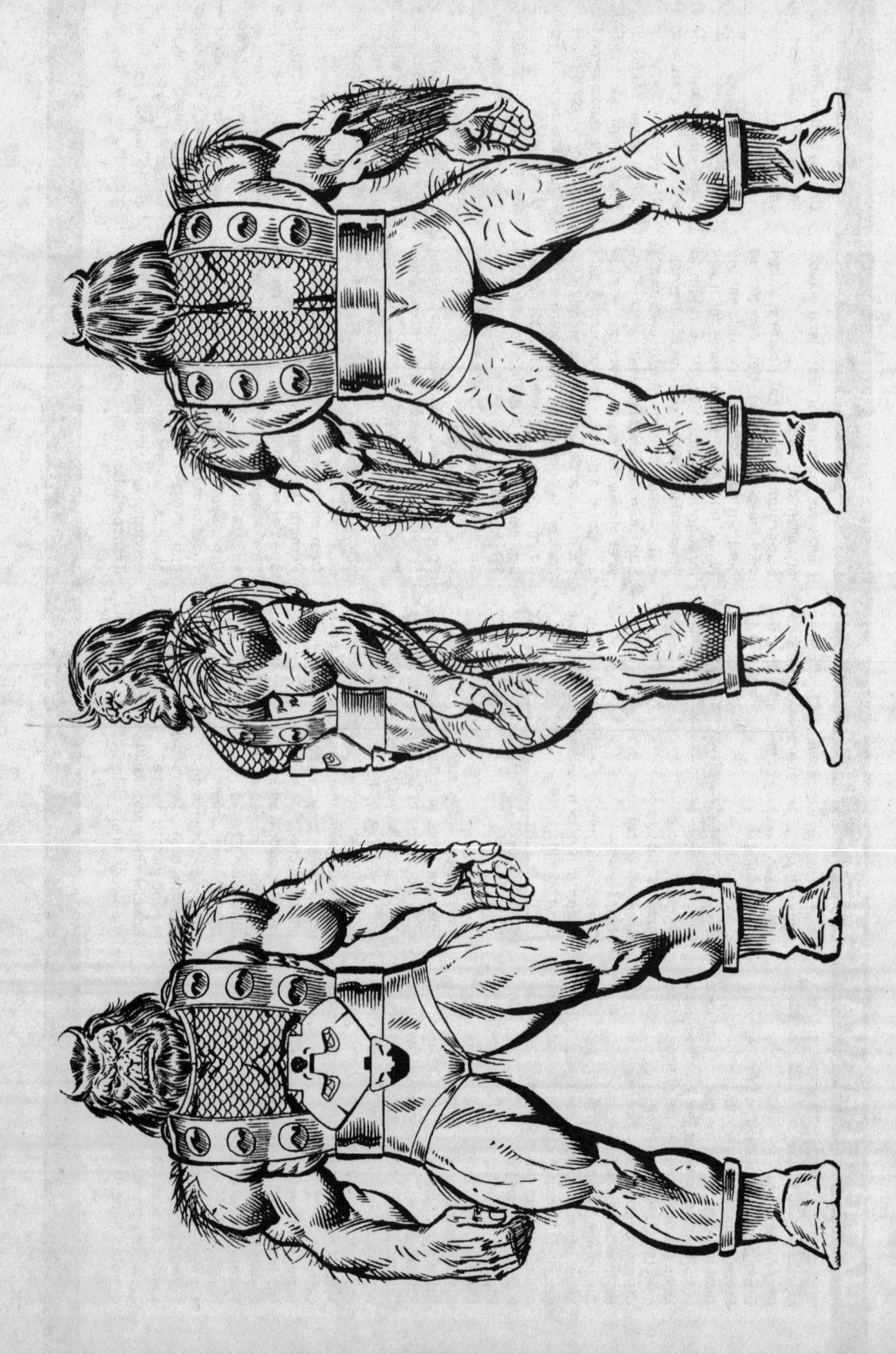

ULIK

BIOGRAPHICAL DATA

Real name: Ulik
Other current aliases: None
Former aliases: None
Dual identity: None; the general populace of Earth is unaware of Ulik's existence
Current occupation: Warrior
Former occupation: Unrevealed
Citizenship: The Domain of Trolls
Legal status: No criminal record
Place of birth: Domain of Trolls, Nornheim, dimension of Asgard
Marital status: Single
Known relatives: Horth (brother, reported deceased)
Known confidants: Inapplicable
Known allies: Geirrodur (former), Loki, the Enchantress
Major enemies: Thor, the gods of Asgard
Usual base of operations: Domain of Trolls, dimension of Asgard
Former bases of operations: None
Current group membership: Rock Trolls of the dimension of Asgard
Former group membership: None

PHYSICAL DESCRIPTION

Extent of education: Unrevealed
Height: 6'4"
Weight: 780 lbs.
Eyes: Brown
Hair: Orange-Brown
Other distinguishing features: Ulik is an ape-like humanoid with a hairy orange leather-like hide and two-toed feet

POWERS AND ABILITIES

Intelligence: Normal
Strength: Superhuman Class 90
Speed: Enhanced human
Stamina: Superhuman
Durability: Metahuman
Agility: Enhanced human
Reflexes: Enhanced human
Fighting skills: Extensive experience in hand-to-hand combat
Special skills and abilities: Unrevealed
Superhuman physical powers: Superhuman strength, speed, and durability; ability to into the infrared range of the spectrum, which allows him to see in near-total darkness
Superhuman mental powers: None known
Special limitations: None known
Source of superhuman powers: Well above average development of traits common to his species

PARAPHERNALIA

Costume specifications: Alien materials
Personal weaponry: A variety of weapons common to Asgardian Rock Trolls, including "pounders", metal bands forged of an unknown alloy and worn over the hands like brass knuckles, as well as a sword and mace
Special weaponry: None
Other accessories: None
Transportation: An "ultra-drill," a vehicle which can bore through solid ground
Design and manufacture of paraphernalia: The weaponsmiths of the Rock Trolls

BIBLIOGRAPHY

First appearance: THOR #137
Origin issue: The details of Ulik's background is as yet unrevealed.
Significant issues: THOR #137-139 (joined Rock Trolls in war against gods of Asgard; attempted to steal Thor's uru hammer on behalf of Rock Trolls, battled Thor); THOR #210-211 (allied with Geirrodur against Thor); THOR #237-239 (kidnaped Jane Foster as means of forcing Thor to aid him in his plot to gain vengeance against Geirrodur and Zotaar); THOR #252 (battled Thor for possession of mystic artifact called the ruby Eye); THOR ANNUAL #13 (brother Horth captured by Mephisto; battled Thor at Mephisto's request in order to free Horth); THOR #413-414 (employed on Earth by Loki as hireling, given amulet to enhance power, battled Hercules, Thor, shot in eye by Detective Marcus Stone, causing temporary defeat); THOR #427 (back in Loki's employ on Earth); THOR #430 (ambushed the Wrecker); THOR #431 (battled Thor to prevent him from entering Loki's headquarters on Earth)

ULTIMO

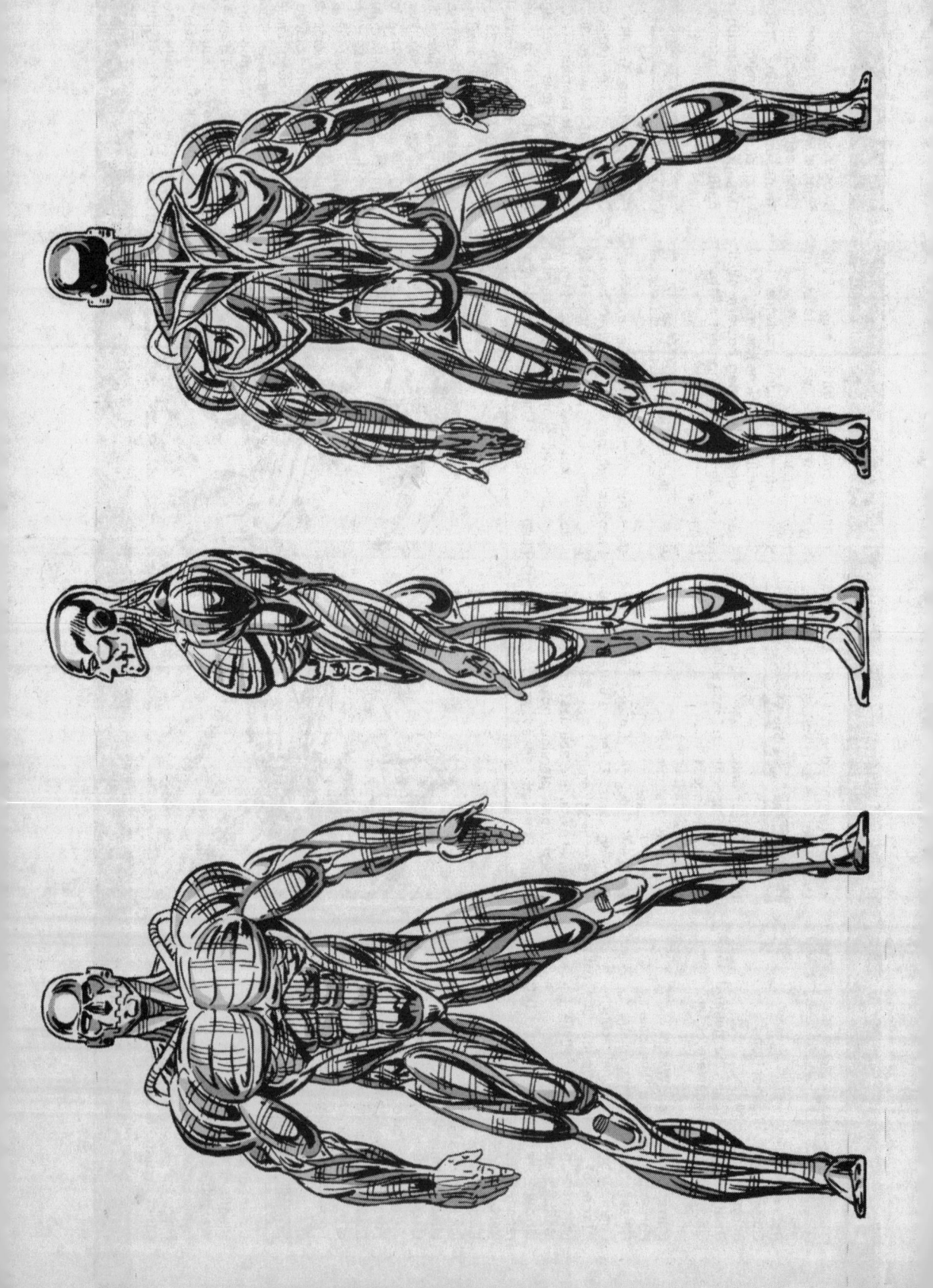

ULTIMO

BIOGRAPHICAL DATA

Real name: Ultimo
Other current aliases: The Living Holocaust
Former aliases: None
Dual identity: None
Current occupation: Combat instrument
Former occupation: None
Citizenship: Inapplicable
Legal status: Inapplicable
Place of creation: Unknown. Ultimo was found by the Mandarin in a long-dormant volcano in the vicinity of the "Palace of the Star Dragon" in the "Valley of the Spirits", somewhere in the People's Republic of China
Marital status: Inapplicable
Known relatives: Inapplicable
Known confidants: Inapplicable
Known allies: Mandarin, (former) Living Laser, the Swordsman I (deceased), Power Man I, (Goliath III), the Enchantress, the Executioner I (deceased)
Major enemies: Iron Man I, Thor I, Hawkeye, the Avengers, the Yellow Claw, Sunfire, War Machine, Iron Legion
Usual base of operations: Mobile
Former bases of operations: Same as above
Current group membership: None
Former group membership: The Mandarin's unnamed grouping of Avengers foes
Extent of programming: No capacity for self-motivated activity; dependent on programming or commands of its programmer.

PHYSICAL DESCRIPTION

Height: 100'
Weight: Unrevealed
Eyes: Yellow
Hair: None
Other distinguishing features: Formerly had a blue skinlike epidermis

POWERS AND ABILITIES

Intelligence: Non-sentient (equivalent)
Strength: Superhuman Class 100
Speed: Enhanced human
Stamina: Metahuman
Durability: Demigodlike
Agility: Enhanced human
Reflexes: Enhanced human
Fighting skills: Programmed for combat use of its superhuman powers
Special skills and abilities: None
Superhuman physical powers: Aside from the above listed attributes, the ability to fire beams of powerful concussive force or beams capable of disintegrating matter from its eyes
Superhuman mental powers: None
Special limitations: None
Source of superhuman powers: Artificial construction

PARAPHERNALIA

Costume specifications: Alien materials
Personal weaponry: None
Special weaponry: None
Other accessories: None
Transportation: usually on foot
Design and manufacture of paraphernalia: Unknown

BIBLIOGRAPHY

First appearance: (in shadow) TALES OF SUSPENSE #76, (fully seen) TALES OF SUSPENSE #77
Origin issue: TALES OF SUSPENSE #77
Significant issues: TALES OF SUSPENSE #76-78 (first battled Iron Man); AVENGERS ANNUAL #1 (sent by Mandarin to assist the Living Laser, battled Thor and Hawkeye); IRON MAN #69-70 (sent by Mandarin to attack Yellow Claw and Loc Do, battled Iron Man and Sunfire); IRON MAN #95-96 (sent by Mandarin to attack Washington D.C., battled Iron Man); IRON MAN #298-300 (caused earthquakes in California, battled Iron Man, War Machine, Iron Legion)

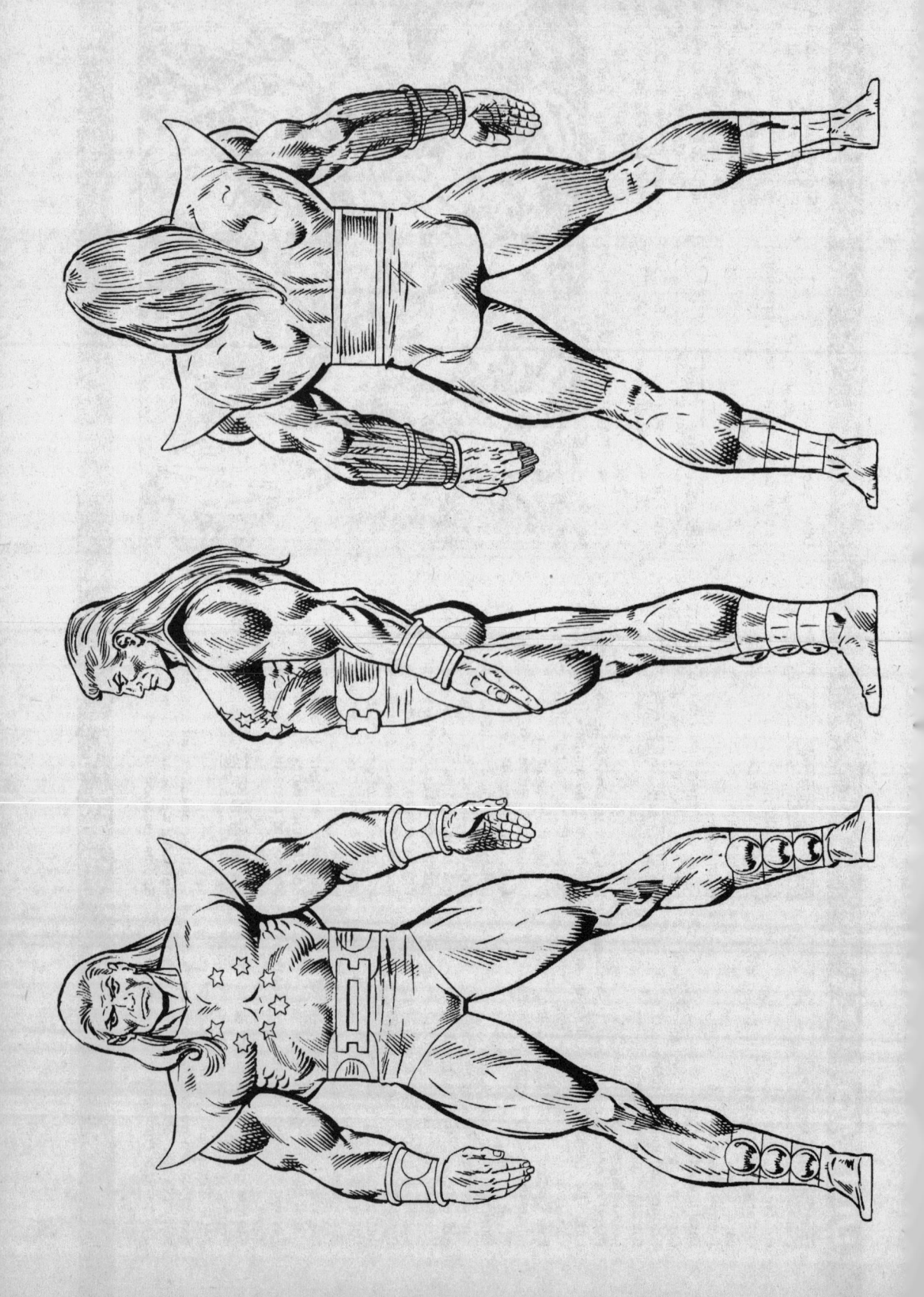

ULTIMUS

ULTIMUS

BIOGRAPHICAL DATA

Real name: Unrevealed
Other current aliases: None
Former aliases: The Demon Druid
Dual identity: None; the general populace of Earth is unaware of Ultimus's existence.
Current occupation: Warrior
Former occupation: Unrevealed
Citizenship: An unnamed alien planet
Legal status: No criminal record
Place of birth: An unnamed alien planet
Marital status: Unrevealed, presumed single
Known relatives: None
Known confidants: None
Known allies: The Kree Supreme Intelligence, the Starforce (Captain Atlas, Doctor Minerva, Ronan the Accuser, Korath the Pursuer, Shatterax, Supremor)
Major enemies: Thor, Excalibur, the Avengers, the Shi'ar Imperial Guard
Usual base of operations: The Kree Empire
Former bases of operations: Mobile
Current group membership: Starforce
Former group membership: None
Extent of education: Unrevealed

PHYSICAL DESCRIPTION

Height: 8'6"
Weight: 680 lbs.
Eyes: White with no visible pupils
Hair: Silver-white with black eyebrows
Other distinguishing features: Blue skin

POWERS AND ABILITIES

Intelligence: Normal
Strength: Superhuman Class 90
Speed: Superhuman
Flight speed: Unrevealed, possibly hover only
Stamina: Superhuman
Durability: Metahuman
Agility: Superhuman
Reflexes: Superhuman
Fighting skills: Good had-to-hand combatant
Special skills and abilities: Unrevealed
Superhuman physical powers: Aside from those listed above, Ultimus has the ability to manipulate cosmic energy to augment his life force, granting him great longevity and regenerative abilities, the projection of cosmic energy as concussive bolts from his hands, the ability to project an invisible force field about his body varying from a radius of one-inch to several yards, the ability to fly by harnessing anti-gravitons, and possibly other powers
Superhuman mental powers: A homing instinct enabling him to locate a particular site, such as Stonehenge
Special limitations: None known
Source of superhuman powers: Ultimus is believed to be a Kree Eternal, a genetic offshoot of the humanoid blue-skinned Kree

PARAPHERNALIA

Costume specifications: Alien fabric
Personal weaponry: None
Special weaponry: None
Other accessories: None
Transportation: Teleportation
Design and manufacture of paraphernalia: Inapplicable

BIBLIOGRAPHY

First appearance: THOR #209
Origin issue: Ultimus's origin is as yet unrevealed.
Significant issues: THOR #209 (accidentally awakened from 3,000 years in subterranean suspended animation on Earth; as the Demon Druid, battled Thor in England, reached Stonehenge and launched himself into space); EXCALIBUR #20 (reappeared in Scotland, encountered Excalibur, created nuclear facsimile of Stonehenge which opened teleportational gateway to his homeworld); WONDER MAN #7 (contacted on an unnamed planet in the Kree Galaxy and recruited by the Supreme Intelligence to aid in the Kree-Shi'ar War); CAPTAIN AMERICA #399 (traveled to Hala, met Shatterax, Korath, and Supremor for the first time); AVENGERS #346 (alongside Starforce, battled the Avengers, witnessed the assassination of Ael-Dan and Dar-Benn by Deathbird); THOR #446/AVENGERS WEST COAST #82 (alongside Starforce, arrived in Shi'ar Empire to assassinate Lilandra, battled another contingent of Avengers and Shi'ar Imperial Guard); AVENGERS #347 (returned to Hala alongside Lilandra, Starforce, and Imperial Guard after detonation of the nega-bomb to help Kree rebuild under Shi'ar rule); QUASAR #35 (alongside Starforce and Deathbird, encountered Quasar, Her, and Makkari on Hala)

ULTRON

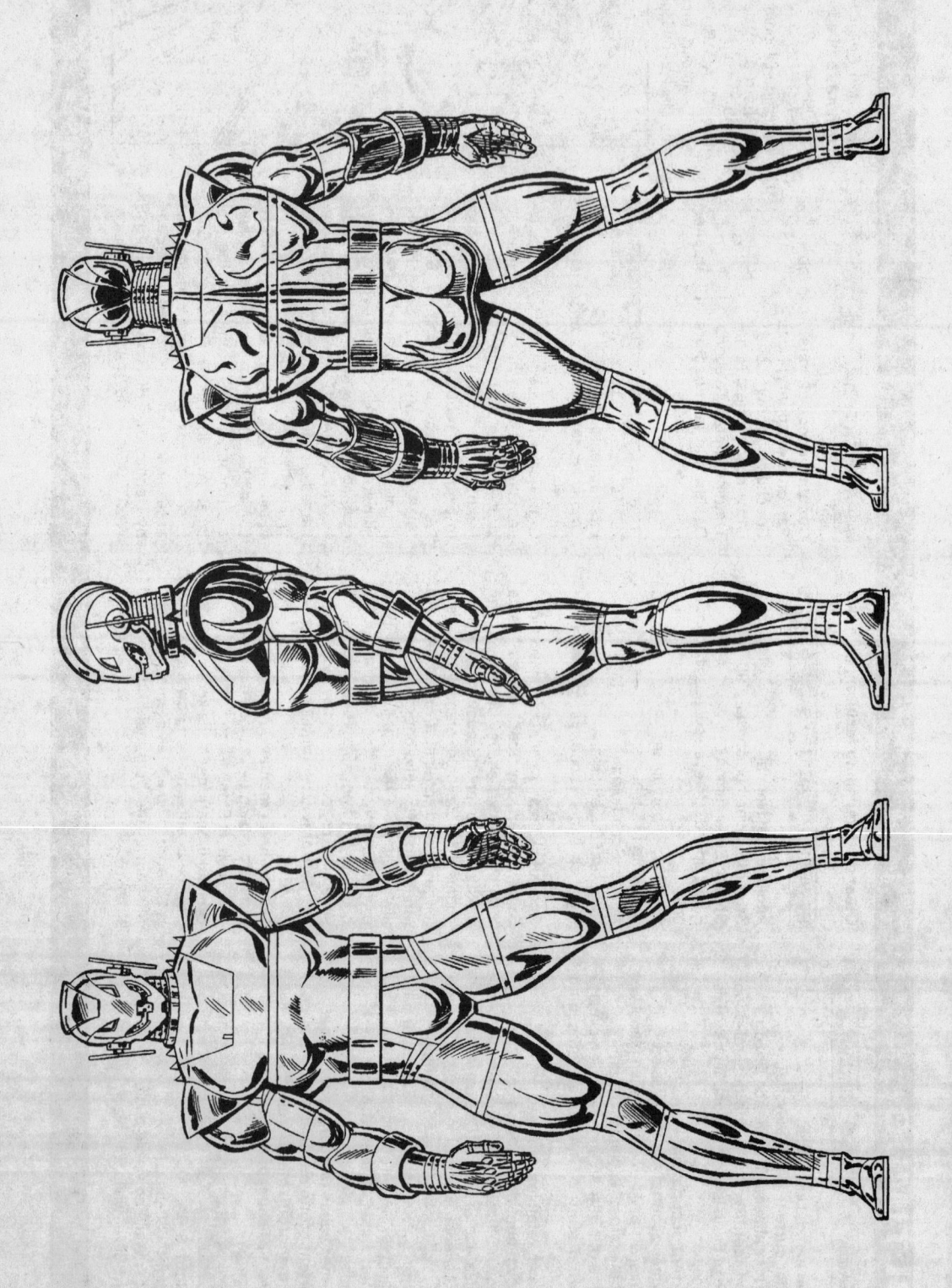

ULTRON

BIOGRAPHICAL DATA

Real name: Ultron
Other current aliases: None
Former aliases: Crimson Cowl, Ultron-5, Ultron-6, Ultron-7, Ultron-11, Ultron-12, Ultron-Mark 12, Ultron-13
Dual identity: None
Current occupation: Would-be conqueror, enslaver of men
Former occupations: None
Citizenship: Inapplicable
Legal status: Undetermined
Place of creation: Cresskill, New Jersey
Creator/programmer: (Ultron-1) Dr. Henry Pym, (Ultron-2, et al.) self-construct
Marital status: Inapplicable
Known relatives: Inapplicable
Known confidants: None
Known allies: (former) Masters of Evil II (Melter (deceased), Radioactive Man, Klaw, Whirlwind), Vision, Maximus, Jocasta, Lethal Legion II (Grim Reaper (deceased), Nekra (deceased), Man-Ape, Black Talon II, Goliath IV), Kingpin
Major enemies: Dr. Pym, the Wasp, the Vision, the Avengers, the Fantastic Four, the Inhumans, Wonder Man, Jocasta, Machine Man, Dr. Doom, Daredevil, Spider-Man, Kingpin, Sunturion, Mechadoom (deceased)
Usual base of operations: Mobile
Former bases of operations: Various
Current group membership: None
Former group membership: Leader of the Masters of Evil II, co-leader of the Lethal Legion II
Extent of programming: Capacity for creative intelligence and self-repair

PHYSICAL DESCRIPTION

Height: 6'
Weight: 950 lbs.
Optical imaging sensors: Red
Hair: None
Other distinguishing features: Body constructed of adamantium, giving it a shiny metallic appearance. Its head is less humanoid in appearance than its body, having inhuman features and eyes and ears (optical and audial sensors) not resembling those of human beings. Ultron has occasionally reformed itself with a humanoid appearance above the waist and the appearance of a complex machine, including tractor beam apparatus for flight, below the waist.

POWERS AND ABILITIES

Intelligence: Genius (3.2 terabyte memory capacity)
Strength: Superhuman Class 25
Speed: Superhuman
Flight speed: Subsonic
Stamina: Superhuman
Durability: Demi-godlike
Agility: Normal
Reflexes: Superhuman
Fighting skills: Average hand-to-hand combatant, relies mainly on built-in weaponry and indestructible construction
Special skills: Expert roboticist, master planner and strategist
Superhuman physical powers: Aside from the above listed attributes, Ultron has the ability to project concussive blasts of energy from its optical sensors and hands, the ability to convert electromagnetic radiation into electrical energy for use or storage, and the ability to alter its own structure using a built-in molecular rearranger.
Superhuman mental powers: Superhuman cybernetic analytical capabilities, ability to process information and make calculations with superhuman speed and accuracy; an encephalo-beam can beam subliminal commands into susceptible human brains); a program transmitter (can project entire memory/personality system into duplicate robotic bodies or other computer systems)
Special limitations: Ultron's adamantium body can only be reshaped using the Molecular Rearranger. Despite its immense memory capacity, Ultron's knowledge is limited in some respects by the extent of its programming. Also, its behavior is solely motivated by an irrational hatred of its creator and all human beings. Were Ultron a living being, it would be certifiably insane.
Source of superhuman powers: Robotic materials, design, and construction; adamantium composition

PARAPHERNALIA

Costume specifications: None
Personal weaponry: Enchephalo-beam, concussion blasters, tractor beams, energy absorbers
Special weaponry: Various, as needed
Other accessories: Various, as needed
Transportation: Flight under own power
Design and manufacture of paraphernalia: Ultron

BIBLIOGRAPHY

First appearance: (as Crimson Cowl) AVENGERS #54, (as Ultron-5) AVENGERS #55, (as Ultron-6) AVENGERS #58, (as Ultron-7) AVENGERS #127, (as Ultron-8) AVENGERS #161, (as Ultron-9) AVENGERS #202, (as Ultron-10) MARVEL TWO-IN-ONE #92, (as Ultron-11) MARVEL SUPERHEROES SECRET WARS #1, (as Ultron-12) WEST COAST AVENGERS Vol. 2 #1, (as Ultron Mark 12) WEST COAST AVENGERS #6, (as Ultron-13) DAREDEVIL #275
Origin issue: AVENGERS #58
Significant issues: AVENGERS #54-55 (organized and led Masters of Evil II against the Avengers); AVENGERS #57-58 (created the Vision, set him against Avengers, defeated when Vision turned against him); AVENGERS #66-68 (recreated with adamantium body); AVENGERS #127/FANTASTIC FOUR #150 (recreated by Maximus with body of android Omega; battled Avengers, Inhumans, and Fantastic Four; defeated by Franklin Richards)

U-MAN

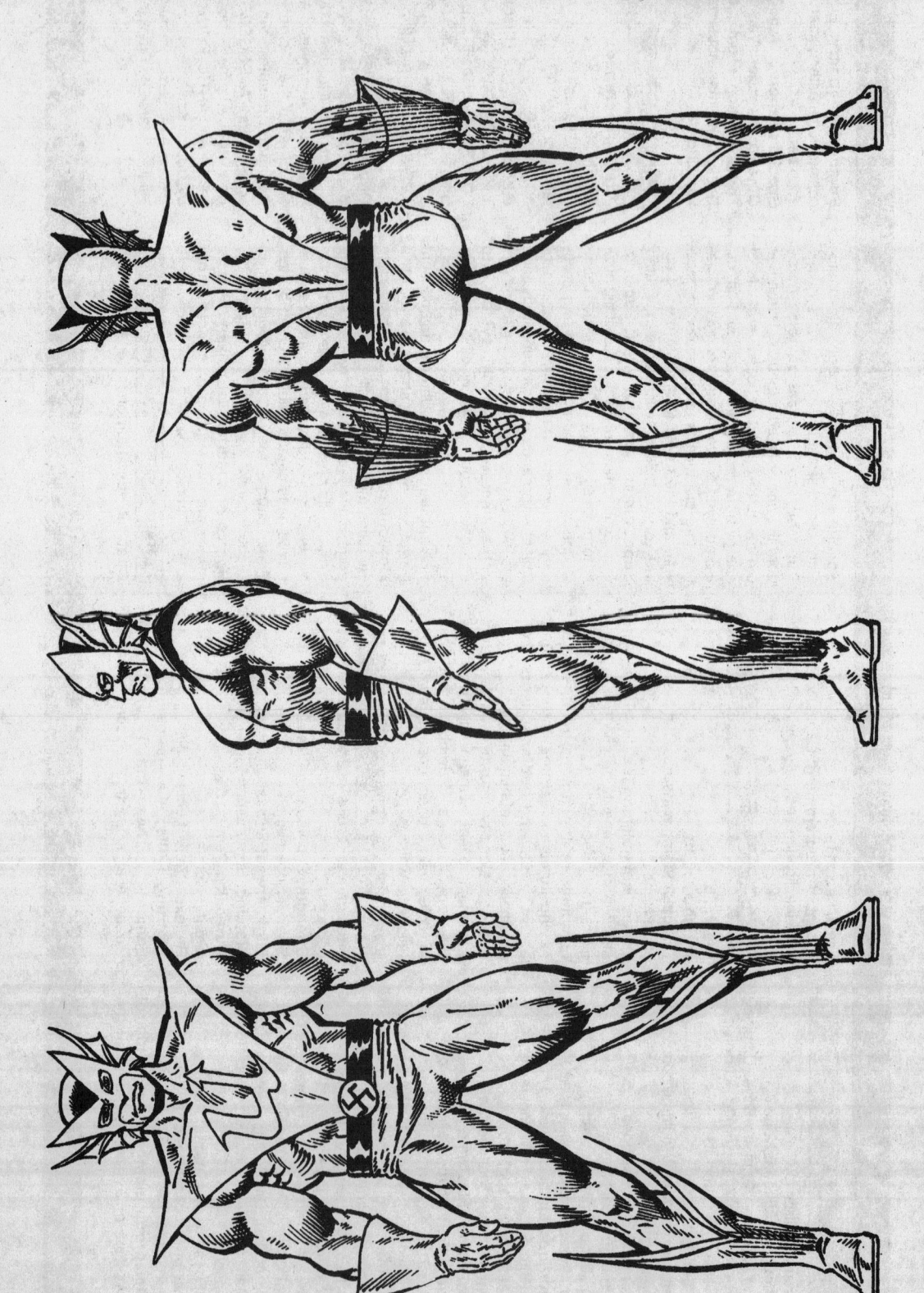

U-MAN

BIOGRAPHICAL DATA

Real name: Meranno
Other current aliases: None
Former aliases: None
Dual identity: None
Current occupation: Warrior
Former occupation: Scientist
Citizenship: The Kingdom of Lemuria
Legal status: Criminal record, officially pardoned by Attuma
Place of birth: Unrevealed
Marital status: Single
Known relatives: None
Known confidants: None
Known allies: Super-Axis (Baron Blood I, Master Man, Warrior Woman, Lady Lotus)
Major enemies: The Invaders, Namor the Sub-Mariner, the Avengers
Usual base of operations: Atlantic Ocean
Former bases of operations: Atlantic Ocean
Current group membership: The Royal Atlantean Militia
Former group membership: Super-Axis
Extent of education: Unrevealed

PHYSICAL DESCRIPTION

Height: 7'
Weight: 450 lbs.
Eyes: Blue
Hair: Blond, later gray
Other distinguishing features: Blue skin

POWERS AND ABILITIES

Intelligence: Normal
Strength: Superhuman Class 50
Water speed: Superhuman
Stamina: (in water) Superhuman, (on land) Athlete
Durability: Superhuman
Agility: (in water) Enhanced human, (on land) Athlete
Reflexes: (in water) Enhanced human, (on land) Athlete
Fighting skills: Atlantean warrior training
Special skills and abilities: Extensive knowledge of biochemistry
Superhuman physical powers: Superhuman strength and durability; ability to survive underwater for indefinite periods, ability to see clearly in the murky depths
Superhuman mental powers: None
Special limitations: Although U-Man is capable of surviving out of water far longer than an average Atlantean, he cannot do so indefinitely; the exact length of time he can survive on land is unknown, but it is longer than 20 minutes
Source of superhuman powers: Enhancement of the racial characteristics of the evolutionary offshoot of the human race called *Homo Mermanus*, through a combination of advanced Atlantean science and Nazi technology

PARAPHERNALIA

Costume specifications: Atlantean materials
Personal weaponry: None
Special weaponry: None
Other accessories: None
Transportation: Various, Usually swimming under own power also Atlantean warships
Design and manufacture of paraphernalia: Unidentified Atlantean technicians

BIBLIOGRAPHY

First appearance: INVADERS #3
Origin issue: INVADERS #4
Significant issues: INVADERS #3 (alliance with Nazi Germany announced to world); INVADERS #4 (first battled Invaders); INVADERS #37 (mentally dominated by Lady Lotus); INVADERS #38 (commanded by Lady Lotus to battle Kid Commandos and kidnap Golden Girl); INVADERS #39 (commanded by Lady Lotus to battle Invaders); INVADERS #41 (joined Nazi superhuman team, Super-Axis); AVENGERS ANNUAL #18 (participated in Atlantean attack on the surface world); AVENGERS #318-324 (joined with Atlantean militia in temporary alliance with the Avengers, Alpha Flight, and the People's Protectorate to prevent nuclear holocaust)

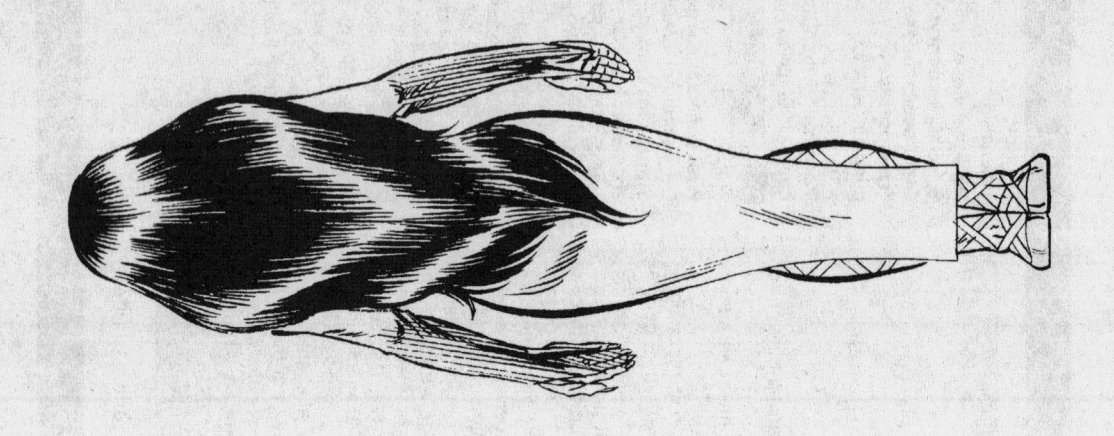

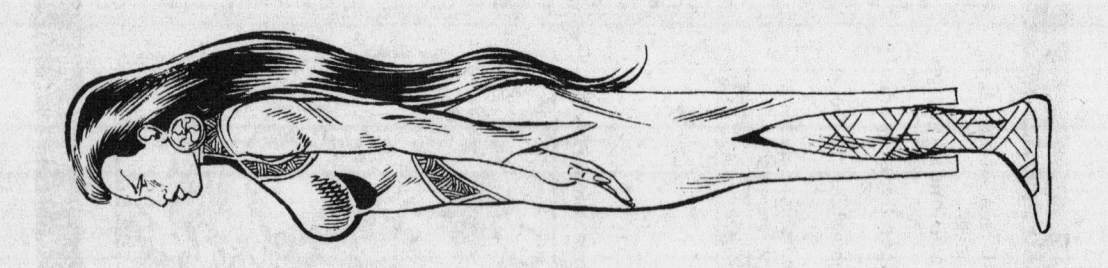

UMAR

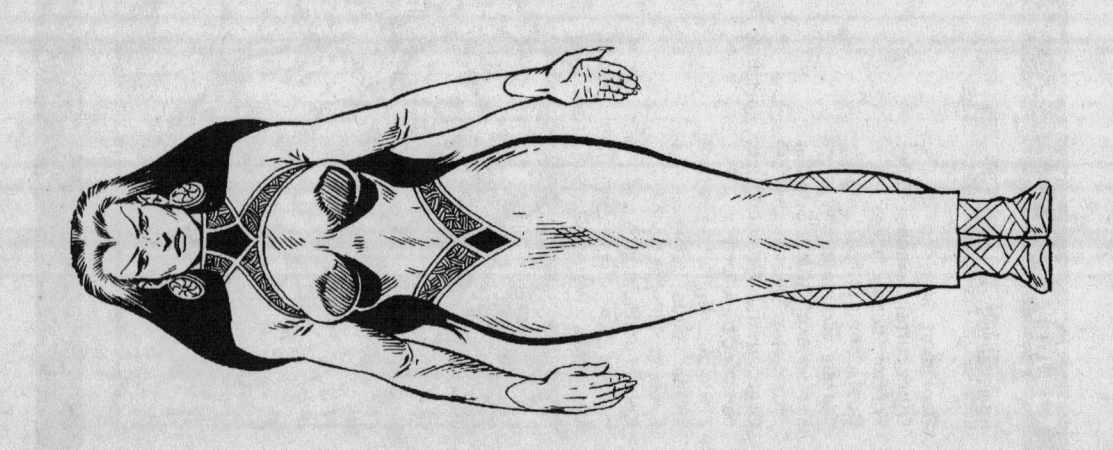

UMAR

BIOGRAPHICAL DATA

Real name: Umar
Other current aliases: Umar the Unrelenting
Former aliases: None
Dual identity: None; the general populace of Earth is unaware of Umar's existence.
Current occupation: Ruler of the Dark Dimension
Former occupation: Unrevealed
Citizenship: The Dark Dimension
Legal status: Exiled citizen of the dimension of Faltine, citizen of the Dark Dimension
Place of birth: The Faltine Dimension
Marital status: Married
Known relatives: Sinifer (father); Clea (daughter); Dr. Strange (son-in-law), Baron Mordo (consort)
Note: Umar once told Orini, Clea's natural father, that her own mother had been human, but this was likely a fabrication on her part, since Faltinians, as energy-beings, would seem to reproduce asexually. Sinifer is presumably the sole parent of Umar and Dormammu. Accounts also vary as to whether Dormammu and Umar are twins or whether Dormammu is the elder sibling.
Known confidants: None
Known allies: (former) Dormammu, Orini (current) Baron Mordo
Major enemies: Doctor Strange, Clea, the Mindless Ones, Gaea, Vision, Scarlet Witch, Agatha Harkness
Usual base of operations: The Dark Dimension
Former bases of operations: The Faltine Dimension
Current group membership: None
Former group membership: None
Extent of education: Unrevealed

PHYSICAL DESCRIPTION

Height: 5' 11"
Weight: 200 lbs.
Eyes: Green
Hair: Black
Other distinguishing features: As ruler of the Dark Dimension, Umar's head is surrounded by a plume of mystic fire, the flames of regency.

POWERS AND ABILITIES

Intelligence: Gifted
Strength: Enhanced human
Speed: Enhanced human
Stamina: Enhanced human
Durability: Metahuman
Agility: Enhanced human
Reflexes: Enhanced human
Fighting skills: None
Special skills and abilities: Vast knowledge of magical lore
Superhuman physical powers: Ability to manipulate the forces of magic for a variety of effects, including interdimensional teleportation, size transformations, time travel, transmutations, energy manifestations such as powerful concussive blasts, magically constructed animate beings, etc.
Superhuman mental powers: Telepathy, illusion-casting, limited mind-control
Special limitations: None
Source of superhuman powers: Manipulation of the forces of magic

PARAPHERNALIA

Costume specifications: Unknown
Personal weaponry: None
Special weaponry: None
Other accessories: None
Transportation: Usually interdimensional teleportation
Design and manufacture of paraphernalia: Inapplicable

BIBLIOGRAPHY

First appearance: STRANGE TALES Vol. 1 #150
Origin issue: DOCTOR STRANGE Vol. 2 #71, DOCTOR STRANGE Vol. 3 #22
Significant issues: STRANGE TALES Vol. 1 #150 (freed from her imprisonment by Dormammu, stopped invasion of the Dark Dimension by the Mindless Ones, became ruler of the dark Dimension); STRANGE TALES Vol. 1 #151-155 (battled Dr. Strange, encountered Veritas [aka Sayge]); STRANGE TALES Vol. 1 #156 (invaded Earth dimension, battled the Ancient One, forced to flee by Zom); DR. STRANGE Vol. 1 #173 (freed Dr. Strange, enabling him to defeat Dormam-mu); DR. STRANGE Vol. 2 #6´ (attacked Dr. Strange and Clea on Earth; transported essence of Dormammu to Earth's core, where he reformed); DR. STRANGE Vol. 2 #7 (with Orini, defeated Dr. Strange on Dormammu's behalf); GIANT-SIZE AVENGERS #4 (with Dormammu battled Scarlet Witch, Vision, and Agatha Harkness); DR. STRANGE Vol. 2 #9 (her seduction of Orini resulting in the birth of Clea recounted; stole Dormammu's powers, battled Dr. Strange and Clea; defeated when Gaea caused Dormammu's power to return to him); THOR ANNUAL #9 (battled Thor in attempt to disrupt chess match between Odin and Dormammu); DR. STRANGE Vol. 2 #68 (intervened in Dr. Strange's battle with a deranged Black Knight); DR. STRANGE Vol. 2 #69 (conjured a sea serpent and water elementals to attack Dr. Strange and Black Knight on Earth); DR. STRANGE Vol. 2 #71 (origin recounted); DR. STRANGE Vol. 2 #72 (secret of Clea's parentage revealed to her and Dr. Strange); DR. STRANGE Vol. 2 #73 (deposed as ruler of Dark Dimension by Clea); DR. STRANGE Vol. 2 #74 (with Orini, banished to alien dimension by Dr. Strange and Clea); DR. STRANGE Vol. 3 #22 (freed from banishment by Dormammu, battled him, defeated, saved from destruction by Dr. Strange and Clea); DR. STRANGE Vol. 3 #24 (with Dr. Strange, Clea, and Baron Mordo, defeated Dormammu; resumed rule of Dark Dimension)

UNICORN™

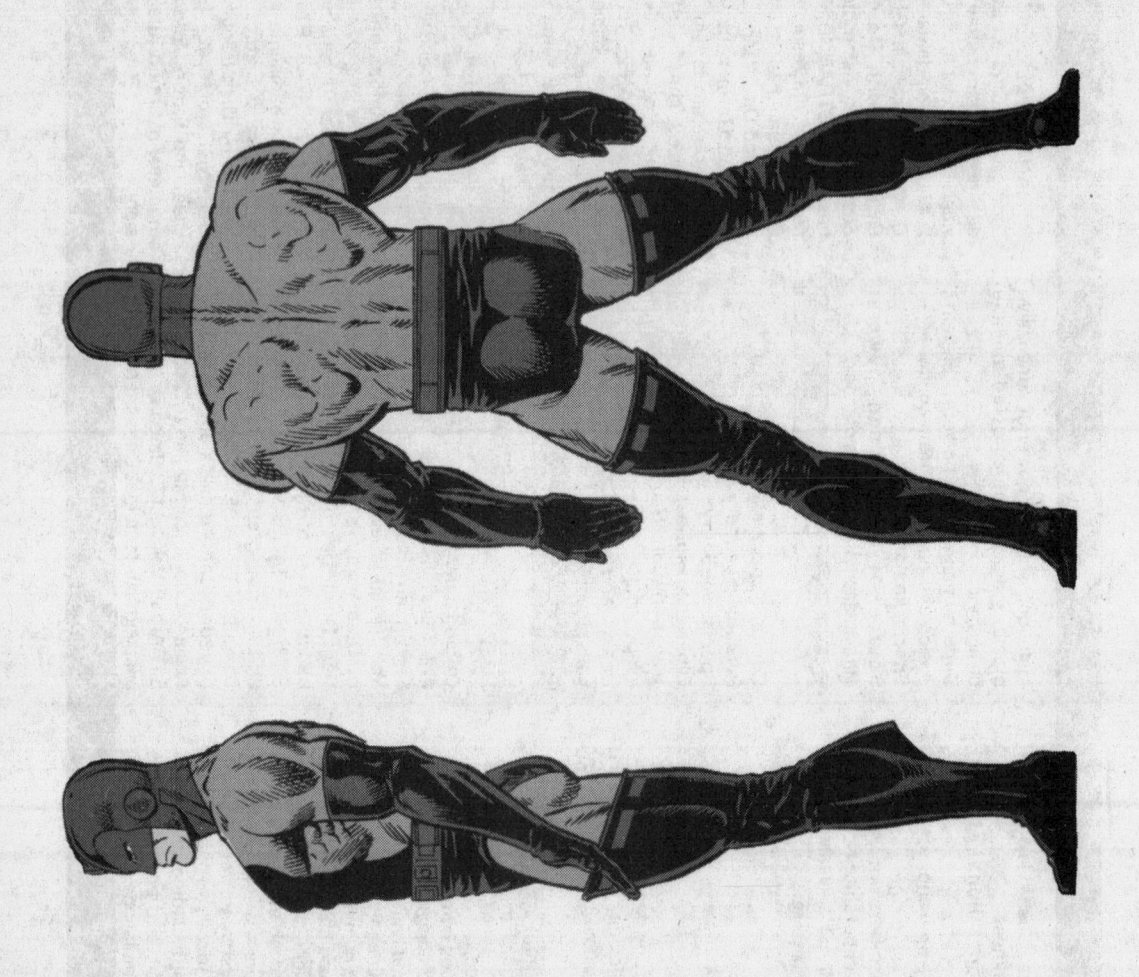

UNICORN I

BIOGRAPHICAL DATA

Real name: Milos Masaryk
Aliases at time of death: None
Former aliases: None known
Dual identity: Known to the United States legal authorities
Occupation at time of death: Professional criminal and mercenary
Former occupation: Intelligence operative
Citizenship: Czechoslovakia
Legal status: Criminal record in the U.S.
Place of birth: Bratislava, Czechoslovakia
Place of death: Atlantic Ocean off New York City area
Cause of death: Drowning
Marital status: Presumed single
Known relatives: None
Known confidants: Titanium Man I
Known allies: Count Luchino Nefaria (deceased), Eel I (deceased), Plantman, Porcupine (deceased), Scarecrow I, Red Ghost, Mandarin, Titanium Man I, Professor Anton Vanko (Crimson Dynamo I, deceased)
Major enemies: Iron Man I, X-Men, Red Ghost, Mandarin
Base of operations at time of death: Mobile
Former base of operations: KGB headquarters, Moscow
Group membership at time of death: None
Former group membership: KGB, Magia (Nefaria "family")
Extent of education: College degree

PHYSICAL DESCRIPTION

Height: 6'2"
Weight: 220 lbs.
Eyes: Blue
Hair: Red
Other distinguishing features: None

POWERS AND ABILITIES

Intelligence: Normal (deteriorated over time due to cellular deterioration)
Strength: Superhuman Class 25
Speed: Enhanced human
Stamina: Superhuman
Durability: Metahuman
Agility: Enhanced human
Reflexes: Enhanced human
Fighting skills: Formidable hand-to-hand combatant, received training in armed and unarmed combat by the KGB, highly proficient in the use of conventional firearms
Special skills and abilities: Fluent in English and Russian, KGB training in intelligence techniques
Superhuman physical powers: Aside from the above listed attributes, none
Superhuman mental powers: None
Special limitations: The process endowing the Unicorn with superhuman powers caused accelerated cellular deterioration, which eventually severely affected his sanity and physical health
Source of superhuman powers: Mutagenic radiation treatments

PARAPHERNALIA

Costume specifications: Body armor of unknown composition
Personal weaponry: Helmet equipped with an energy projector that can project concussive energy blasts (electron or neutron beams), lasers, and microwave energy. Power supply is an array of nuclear-powered thermo-electric cells in Unicorn's belt
Special weaponry: None
Other accessories: None
Transportation: Flight via rocket belt enabling him to travel at speeds up to 180 miles per hour
Design and manufacture of paraphernalia: (design) Professor Anton Vanko and other Soviet scientists, (manufacture) Soviet technicians

BIBLIOGRAPHY

First appearance: TALES OF SUSPENSE #56
Origin Issue: TALES OF SUSPENSE #56
Significant issues: TALES OF SUSPENSE #56 (first battled Iron Man when caught spying on Stark Industries); FANTASTIC FOUR ANNUAL #3 (among criminals that attacked wedding of Reed Richards and Susan Storm); X-MEN Vol. 1 #22-23 (aided Count Nefaria in attack on Washington, D.C.; battled X-Men); IRON MAN #4 (gained superhuman strength but began undergoing rapid cellular deterioration; attempted to extort money from U.S. Congress, thwarted by Iron Man); IRON MAN #15-16 (teamed with Red Ghost against Iron Man); IRON MAN #57-58 (enslaved by Mandarin, Mandarin's consciousness entrapped in Unicorn's body); IRON MAN #68 (Mandarin's mind freed from Unicorn's body); IRON MAN #113-115 (began undergoing mental deterioration, allied himself with Titanium Man I; captured by Iron Man); IRON MAN #154 (accidentally freed, now insane, had final battle with Iron Man, walked into ocean to his death)

UNI-MIND ™

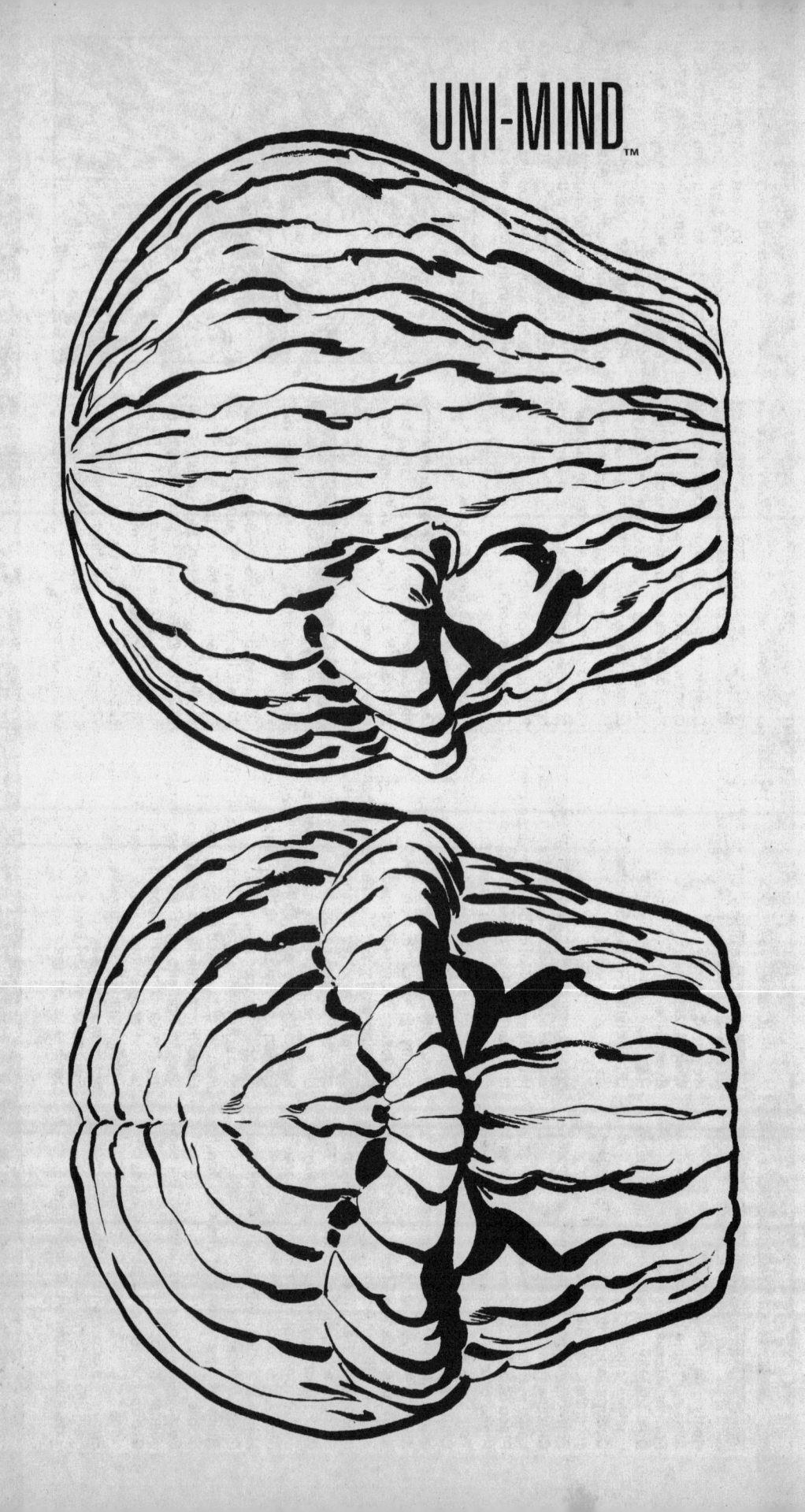

UNI-MIND

BIOGRAPHICAL DATA

Real name: Inapplicable; the Uni-Mind is a physical manifestation of a group intelligence composed of several hundred beings of the genetic offshoot of humanity, the Eternals
Other current aliases: None
Former aliases: None
Dual identity: Inapplicable; the general populace of Earth is unaware of the Uni-Mind's existence
Current occupation: Voyager, explorer
Former occupation: Ambassador
Citizenship: The majority of the Uni-Mind's constituents are citizens of the Eternal city of Olympia
Legal status: Inapplicable
Place of origin: Olympia
Marital status: Inapplicable
Known relatives: Inapplicable
Known confidants: Inapplicable
Known allies: Eternals of Earth
Major enemies: Deviant Empire, the Celestials
Usual base of operations: Mobile throughout the Galaxy
Former bases of operations: Earth vicinity
Current group membership: The Uni-Mind is a group unto itself.
Former group membership: None
Extent of education: The composite knowledge and experience of all its constituent beings

PHYSICAL DESCRIPTION

Height: 30'
Weight: Unrevealed
Eyes: White
Hair: None
Other distinguishing features: The Uni-Mind is a collective being composed of cosmic and psionic energy which manifests itself as a gigantic brain-like organism

POWERS AND ABILITIES

Intelligence: Immeasurable
Strength: Inapplicable
Flight speed: Warp speed
Stamina: Immeasurable
Durability: Godlike
Agility: Inapplicable
Reflexes: Inapplicable
Fighting skills: No physical abilities

Special skills and abilities: The composite knowledge, skills, abilities, and experience of all its constituent beings
Superhuman physical powers: None
Superhuman mental powers: The Uni-Mind is a collective being which is created by a significant number of Eternals merging their physical and mental beings together into one organism, as such it possesses vast psionic abilities across a wide range of mental talents, including levitation, psychokinesis, telepathy, the ability to project mental bolts of force, the ability to travel through the vacuum of space unharmed and intellectual powers of information processing and problem-solving far beyond human understanding.
Special limitations: Superior cosmic powers, such as those possessed by Celestials, are capable of unbinding the collective form of the Uni-Mind, breaking it down into its constituent beings
Source of superhuman powers: The collective psionic and cosmic powers of several hundred Eternals

PARAPHERNALIA

Costume specifications: None
Personal weaponry: None
Special weaponry: None
Other accessories: None
Transportation: Self-levitation
Design and manufacture of paraphernalia: Inapplicable

BIBLIOGRAPHY

First appearance: ETERNALS Vol. 1 #12
Origin issue: WHAT IF Vol. 1 #25
Significant issues: ETERNALS Vol. 1 #12 (Zuras summoned all of Earth's Eternals in an attempt to communicate with Celestials); ETERNALS Vol. 1 #14 (Zuras dissolved the Uni-Mind, its mission unfulfilled); WHAT IF Vol. 1 #25 (following death of their father Kronos, Zuras and Alars initiate first Uni-Mind ritual in order to determine who shall lead Eternals of Titanos, Zuras selected, Alars left Earth); AVENGERS #247-248 (majority of Earth's Eternals merged into Uni-Mind; transformed majority of Earth's Deviants into a stone block and cast it into outer space; Uni-Mind then left for outer space, leaving behind a handful of Eternals); ETERNALS Vol. 2 #12 (recounted defeat of the Deviant priest-lord Ghaur)

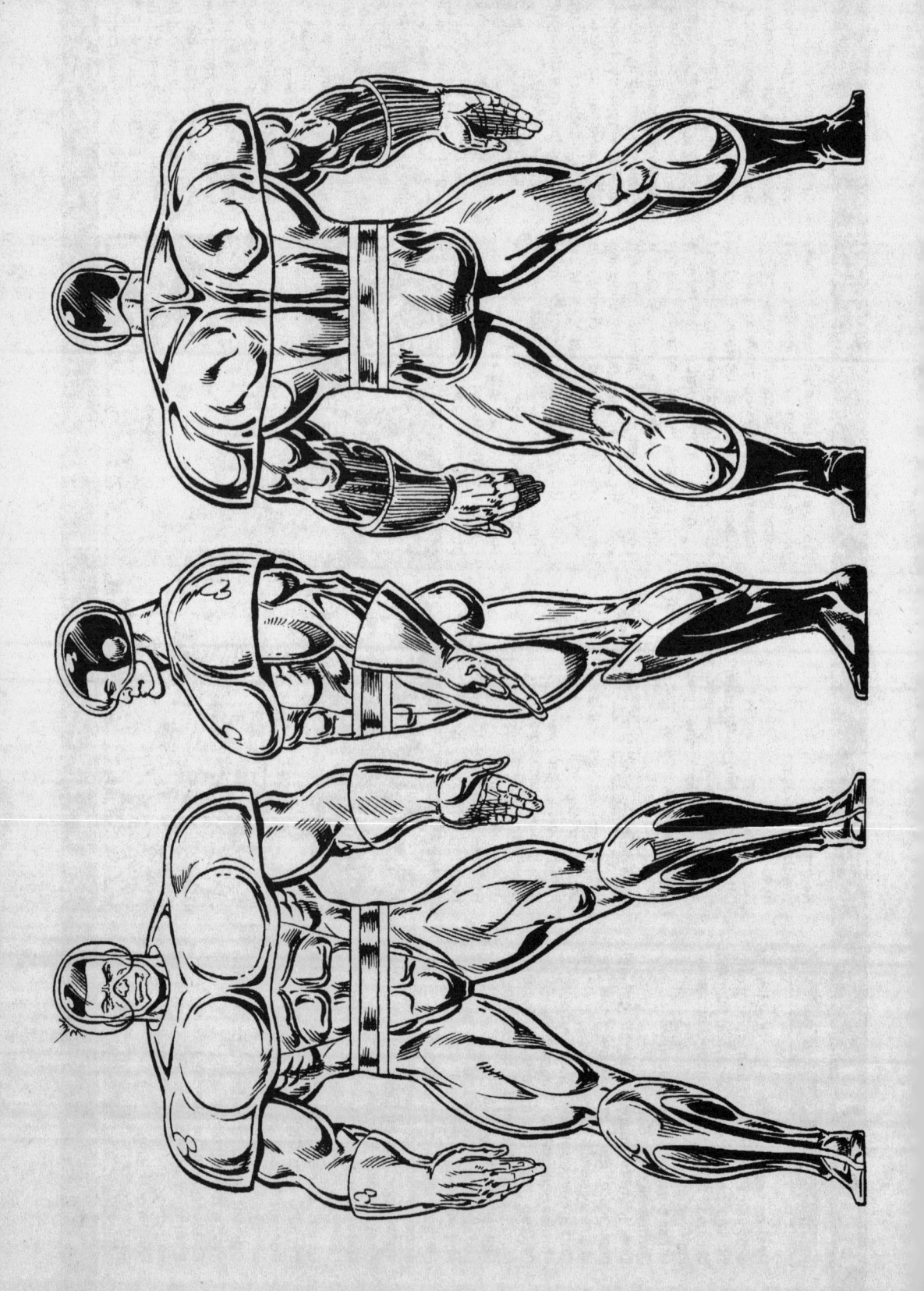

UNION JACK™

UNION JACK III

BIOGRAPHICAL DATA

Real name: Joseph "Joe" Chapman
Other current aliases: None
Former aliases: None
Dual Identity: Secret
Current occupation: Adventurer
Former occupation: Art student
Citizenship: United Kingdom
Legal status: No criminal record
Place of birth: Manchester, England
Marital status: Single
Known relatives: None
Known confidants: Kenneth Crichton, Captain America, Spitfire, Captain Britain, Dai Thomas, Kate McClellan, Ben Gallagher (deceased), Peter Hunter (Albion), Iron Man I, James Rhodes (War Machine)
Known allies: Captain America, Spitfire, Namor the Sub-Mariner, Namorita, Captain Britain, Knights of Pendragon (Dai Thomas, Kate McClellan, Ben Gallagher [deceased], Peter Hunter [Albion], Adam Crown, Francesca Lexley Grace, Breeze James, "Sir Gawain" [robot] Green Knight, Iron Man I, Black Panther, Mr. Fantastic, Invisible Woman, Black Knight III, Jim Rhodes (War Machine), Arrakhyl, Spider-Man
Major enemies: Master Man I, Warrior Woman, Master Man II, the Bane, the Red Lords, Mys-TECH, Magpie, the Warheads; (former) Baron Blood I (deceased), Francesca Lexley Grace, Colin "Dolph" Snewing (deceased), the Omni Corporation
Usual base of operations: Camelaird Farm, Wiltshire, England; the Green Chapel, dimension Avalon
Former bases of operations: Mobile within England
Current group membership: Knights of Pendragon
Former group membership: None
Extent of education: College degree in art

sense the presence of agents of the Bane and to recognize them as such despite disguises, access to knowledge of past incarnations of the Pendragon
Special limitations: None known
Source of superhuman powers: Possession by the spirit of the Pendragon (in this case, Sir Lancelot)

PARAPHERNALIA

Costume specifications: A suit of magical/cybernetic exoskeleton armor composed of unknown materials
Personal weaponry: A 6' striking staff of unknown materials
Special weaponry: A steel dagger with a 6" blade, a Webley .455 caliber pistol, a 1 1/2" diameter shield of unknown materials
Other accessories: None
Transportation: Beryl (a computerized motorcycle-like vehicle equipped with extensive information databanks, recording memory files, radiation detectors, tracking sensors, atuomated navigation system, medical analysis instruments, remote guidance system, and the capacity for interdimensional travel)
Design and manufacture of paraphernalia: (dagger and pistol) Commercial manufacturers, (other paraphernalia) The Green Chapel, dimension of Avalon

PHYSICAL DESCRIPTION

Height: 6' 4", (in armor) 6' 6"
Weight: 238 lbs., (in armor) 285 lbs.
Eyes: Blue
Hair: Reddish blond
Other distinguishing features: None

POWERS AND ABILITIES

Intelligence: Normal
Strength: Enhanced human, (in armor) Superhuman Class 10
Speed: Enhanced human
Stamina: Peak human
Durability: Peak human
Agility: Peak human
Reflexes: Peak human
Fighting skills: Experienced hand-to-hand combatant, expert wrestler
Special skills and abilities: Superb athlete
Superhuman physical powers: Aside from the above listed attributes, superhuman sensory acuity
Superhuman mental powers: Ability to

BIBLIOGRAPHY

First appearance: (as Chapman) CAPTAIN AMERICA #253, (as Union Jack III) CAPTAIN AMERICA #254
Origin issue: CAPTAIN AMERICA #254
Significant issues: CAPTAIN AMERICA #253-254 (first encountered Captain America; disguised as Union Jack I, helped Captain America battle Baron Blood I); NAMOR THE SUB-MARINER #12 (aided Namorita and Spitfire in rescuing Namor from Master Man I and Warrior Woman); KNIGHT OF PENDRAGON Vol. 1 #7 (possessed by Pendragon spirit and healed of injuries, appeared at Kate McClellan's London apartment); KNIGHT OF PENDRAGON Vol. 1 #8 (adopted new costume; alongside Captain Britain, encountered a Bane-possessed Cam McClellan); KNIGHT OF PENDRAGON Vol. 1 #10 (alongside Captain Britain and Kate McClellan, battled minions of the Bane, conferred with Kate McClellan, Ben Gallagher, and Peter Hunter; with them, attacked by the Bane in Kent); KNIGHT OF PENDRAGON Vol. 1 #11-12 (first encountered Iron Man I; with Iron Man I, Captain Britain, and Knights of Pendragon, battled the Bane, freed Cam McClellan; established Pendragon base at Camelaird Farm); KNIGHT OF PENDRAGON Vol. 1 #14-15 (alongside Kate McClellan, Ben Gallagher, Mr. Fantastic, Invisible Woman, and Black Panther, battled the Bane in Africa; alongside Black Panther, battled Bane ninjas and transformed Dolph in Hong Kong; killed by Dolph); KNIGHT OF PENDRAGON Vol. 1 #17-18 (together with other Pendragons, resurrected)

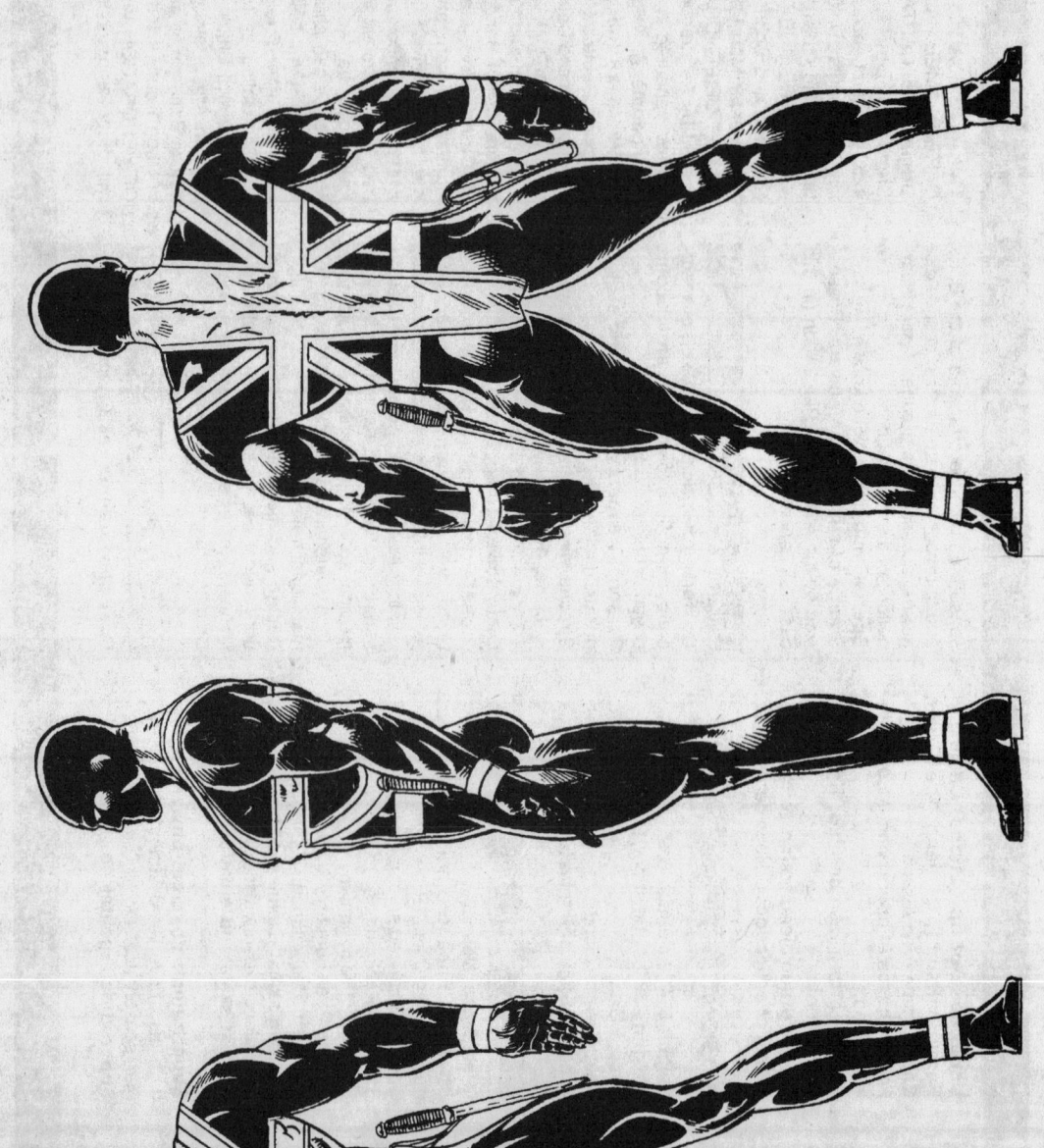

UNION JACK ™

UNION JACK I & II

BIOGRAPHICAL DATA

Real name: (I) James Montgomery, Lord Falsworth; (II) Brian Falsworth
Aliases at time of death: (both) None
Former aliases: (I) None, (II) The Mighty Destroyer I
Dual identity: (both) Secret
Occupation at time of death: (I) Country squire, retired; (II) Unrevealed
Former occupation: (both) Adventurers, British government operatives
Citizenship: (both) United Kingdom
Legal status: (both) No criminal record
Place of birth: (both) Falsworth Manor, in a village to the north of London, England
Place of death: (I) Falsworth Manor, (II) A road somewhere in Britain
Cause of death: (I) Heart failure due to old age, (II) Killed in an automobile accident
Marital status: (I) Widower, (II) Unrevealed
Known relatives: (I) Lord Falsworth (father, deceased), Lady Falsworth (wife, deceased), John Falsworth (Baron Blood I, brother, deceased), Jacqueline Falsworth Crichton (Spitfire, daughter), Brian Falsworth (Union Jack II, son, deceased), Lord Crichton (son-in-law, deceased), Kenneth Crichton (grandson); (II) Lord Falsworth (grandfather, deceased), Montgomery, Lord Falsworth (Union Jack I, father, deceased), Lady Falsworth (mother, deceased), John Falsworth (Baron Blood I, uncle, deceased), Jacqueline Falsworth Crichton (Spitfire, sister), Lord Crichton (brother-in-law, deceased), Kenneth Crichton (nephew)
Known confidants: (both) Spitfire, the Invaders
Known allies: (I) Freedom's Five (Phantom Eagle [deceased], Crimson Cavalier, Sir Steel, Silver Squire [all presumed deceased], the Invaders (Captain America I, Bucky I [deceased], Human Torch I, Toro [deceased], Namor the Sub-Mariner, Spitfire), (II) The Invaders, the Mighty Destroyer II
Major enemies: (I) Baron Blood I, (II) Adolf Hitler (deceased), Master Man I (deceased), Warrior Woman, Scarlet Scarab I, Teutonic Knight, Baron Strucker, Baron Blood I (deceased)
Base of operations at time of death: (both) Falsworth Manor, England
Former bases of operations: (both) None
Group membership at time of death: (both) None
Former group membership: (I) Freedom's Five, the Invaders; (II) the Invaders
Extent of education: (both) College graduates

PHYSICAL DESCRIPTION

Height: (I) 6' 1", (II) 6'
Weight: (I) 240 lbs., (II) 235 lbs.
Eyes: (I) Blue, (II) Brown
Hair: (I) Black, later white, (II) Brown
Other distinguishing features: None

POWERS AND ABILITIES

Intelligence: (both) Above normal
Strength: (I) Athlete, (II) Peak human
Speed: (I) Athlete, (II) Peak human
Stamina: (I) Athlete, (II) Peak human
Durability: (I) Athlete, (II) Peak human
Agility: (I) Athlete, (II) Peak human
Reflexes: (I) Athlete, (II) Peak human
Fighting skills: (both) Highly trained in armed and unarmed combat
Special skills and abilities: (both) Superb athletes
Superhuman physical powers: (both) (I) None, (II) Aside from the above listed attributes, the ability to discharge bolts of electricity from his hands
Superhuman mental powers: (both) None
Special limitations: (both) None
Source of superhuman powers: (I) Inapplicable, (II) Ingestion of a variant of the super-soldier formula, (electrical powers) body energized by lightning strike
Note: The above listed attributes apply to both men as they were in their prime. Union Jack I was confined to a wheelchair as of 1942 and was debilitated by extreme old age at the time of his death. Union Jack II had probably lost the abilities given him by the variant Super-Soldier Formula, as well as his electrical powers, before his death

PARAPHERNALIA

Costume specifications: (both) Bulletproof fabric
Personal weaponry: (both) A 6" steel dagger and a Webley .455 caliber pistol
Special weaponry: None
Other accessories: None
Transportation: Conventional vehicles
Design and manufacture of paraphernalia: Commercial manufacturers

BIBLIOGRAPHY

First appearance: (I) INVADERS Vol. 1 #7, (II) (as Mighty Destroyer I) INVADERS Vol. 1 #18, (as Union Jack II) INVADERS Vol. 1 #19
Origin issue: (I) INVADERS Vol. 1 #7, (II) INVADERS Vol. 1 #19-21
Significant issues: INVADERS Vol. 1 #7-9 (I: revealed to have been a member of Freedom's Five during World War I; alongside the Invaders, battled Baron Blood I; joined the Invaders, legs crushed under a boulder by Baron Blood I); INVADERS Vol. 1 #11 (I: quit the Invaders); INVADERS Vol. 1 #18-21 (I: alongside Spitfire and Dyna-Mite, parachuted into Nazi Germany in search of Brian Falsworth, captured by Nazis, rescued by Union Jack II); CAPTAIN AMERICA #253-254 (I: contacted Captain America to combat Baron Blood I, died of heart failure); INVADERS Vol. 1 #18-21 (II: revealed to have been imprisoned by Nazis and to have taken a variant of the Super-Soldier Formula, becoming the Mighty Destroyer I; as Mighty Destroyer I, alongside Captain America, battled Nazi soldiers, rescued Lord Falsworth and Dyna-Mite, adopted Union Jack II identity, alongside Invaders, fought Master Man I)

UNUS™

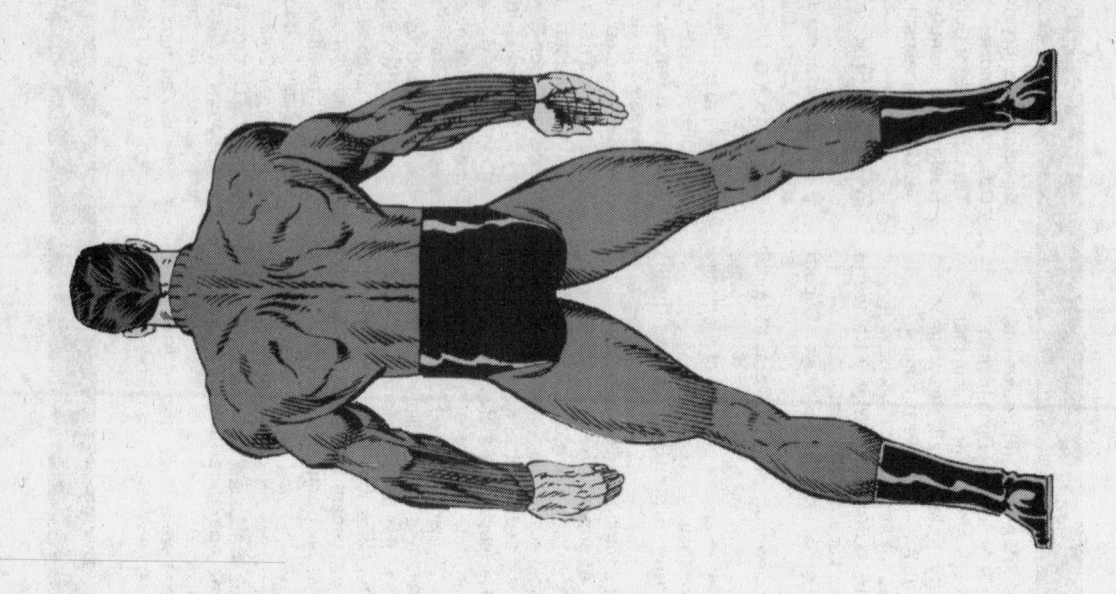

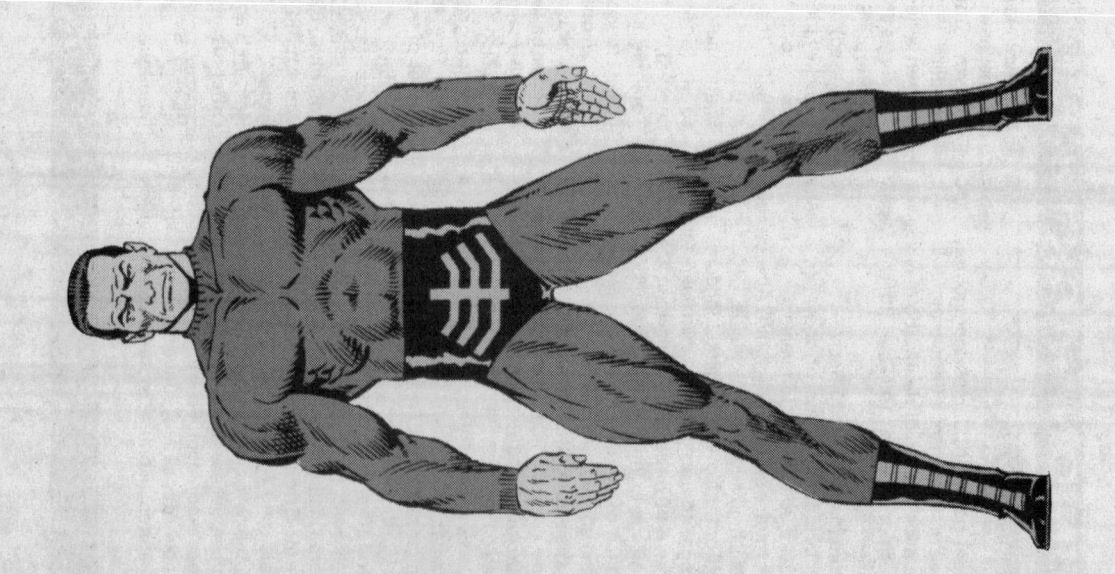

UNUS

BIOGRAPHICAL DATA

Real name: Angelo Unuscione, legally changed in United States to Gunther Bain
Other aliases at time of apparent death: The Untouchable
Former aliases: None
Dual identity: Publicly known
Occupation at time of apparent death: Professional criminal
Former occupation: Wrestler, subversive
Citizenship: Former citizen of Italy, naturalized citizen of the United States of America
Legal status: Criminal record in the U.S.
Place of birth: Milan, Italy
Place of apparent death: Unspecified location in New York City
Cause of apparent death: Suffocation within his own force field
Marital status: Unrevealed
Known relatives: None
Known confidants: Blob
Known allies: Blob, (former) Mastermind, Lorelei I, Vanisher, Factor Three, Magneto
Major enemies: X-Men, Hulk, Power Man II (Cage), Iron Fist, Doc Samson, Mutant Master, Secret Empire II, Sentinels
Base of operations at time of death: Mobile
Former bases of operations: Factor Three headquarters, somewhere in Eastern Europe
Group membership at time of death: None
Former group membership: Factor Three, agent of the Secret Empire II, Brotherhood of Evil Mutants II

Extent of education: Presumably high school dropout

PHYSICAL DESCRIPTION

Height: 6'1"
Weight: 220 lbs
Eyes: Blue
Hair: Black
Other distinguishing features: None

POWERS AND ABILITIES

Intelligence: Normal
Strength: Athlete
Speed: Athlete
Flight speed: Athlete
Stamina: Athlete
Durability: Athlete
Agility: Athlete
Reflexes: Athlete
Fighting skills: Expert wrestler
Special skills and abilities: None known
Superhuman physical powers: None
Superhuman mental powers: The ability to generate a field of invisible psionic energy around his body. The field acts to deflect objects and even energy beams, and can withstand great concussive force. Normally Unus can control the force field at will. Normally, certain types of radiant energy, such as sunlight, can pass through the field, as do air and sound waves (at least within certain unknown limits).
Special limitations: Formerly vulnerable to Beast's ray gun that augmented his force field power beyond his control; in recent years Unus's power again became uncontrollable due to unknown reasons, finally repelling air molecules. (The field dispersed upon Unus's apparent demise.)
Source of superhuman powers: Genetic mutation

PARAPHERNALIA

Costume specifications: Conventional fabric
Personal weaponry: Sometimes carried baseball bat, which, when encased in his force field, can deliver blows with superhuman force
Special weaponry: None
Other accessories: None
Transportation: Conventional means
Design and manufacture of paraphernalia: Inapplicable

BIBLIOGRAPHY

First appearance: X-MEN Vol. 1 #8
Origin issue: X-MEN Vol. 1 #8
Significant issues: X-MEN Vol. 1 #8 (sought to join Brotherhood of Evil Mutants I, turned criminal, first battled X-Men, force field power increased by Beast beyond Unus's ability to control it, promised to reform, normal power level restored by Beast); X-MEN Vol. 1 #20 (first teamed with Blob, posed as X-Man to frame X-Men as criminals); X-MEN Vol. 1 #37-39 (joined Factor Three conspiracy to conquer Earth, aided X-Men against Mutant Master when latter was exposed as extraterrestrial); X-MEN Vol. 1 #59-60 (captured by Sentinels); AMAZING ADVENTURES #12-13 (teamed with Blob and Mastermind as Secret Empire II agents, defeated by Beast); CAPTAIN AMERICA AND THE FALCON #174 (held prisoner by the Secret Empire II); DEFENDERS #15-16 (joined Magneto's Brotherhood of Evil Mutants II, battled Defenders, reverted to infancy by Alpha the Ultimate Mutant); CHAMPIONS #17 (reverted to adulthood, teamed with Vanisher, Blob, and Mastermind against the Champions); INCREDIBLE HULK ANNUAL #11 (battled Doc Samson); POWER MAN AND IRON FIST #90 (embarked on New York crime spree, defeated by Iron Fist and Power Man); MARVEL FANFARE #7 (force field power became nearly uncontrollable, field smashed by Hulk); SPECTACULAR SPIDER-MAN #91 (force field again beyond Unus's control, apparently died of suffocation within force field)

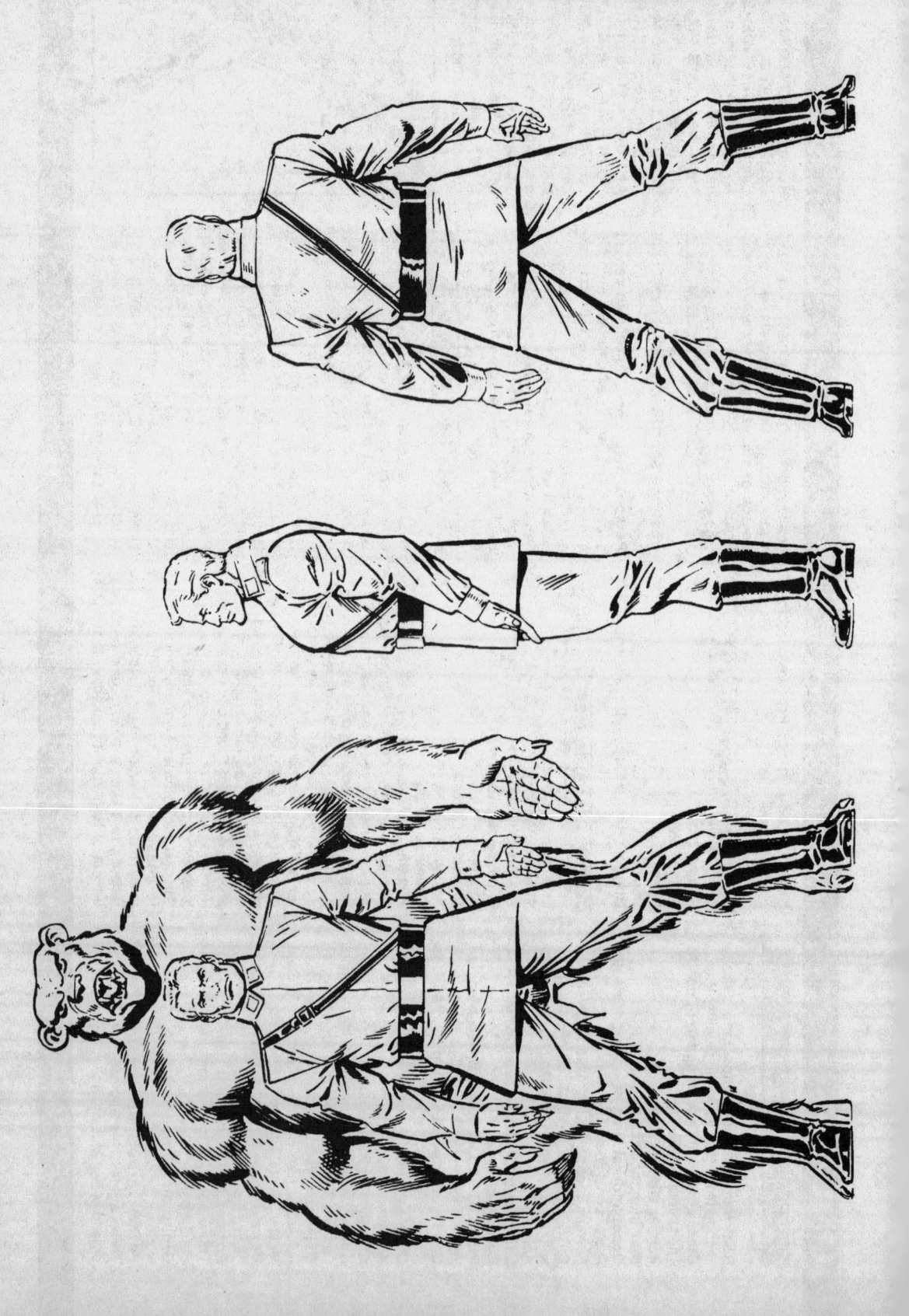

URSA MAJOR

URSA MAJOR

BIOGRAPHICAL DATA

Real name: Mikhail (Uriokovitch) Ursus
Other current aliases: None
Former aliases: None
Dual identity: Publicly known
Current occupation: None
Former occupation: Soviet government agent
Citizenship: Union of Soviet Socialist Republics
Legal status: No criminal record in the U.S.S.R.
Place of birth: Blagoveshchensk, U.S.S.R.
Marital status: Single
Known relatives: None
Known confidants: Vanguard, Darkstar
Known allies: Crimson Dynamo III
Major enemies: The People's Protectorate
Usual base of operations: None
Former bases of operations: Khystym, U.S.S.R.
Current group membership: The Soviet Super-Soldiers
Former group membership: None
Extent of education: Graduate of Professor Phobos's mutant training school

PHYSICAL DESCRIPTION

Height: 6' 3", (transformed) 7' 5"
Weight: 255 lbs., (transformed) 955 lbs.
Eyes: Brown
Hair: Brown

Other distinguishing features: When transformed Ursa Major resembles a large humanoid grizzly bear.

POWERS AND ABILITIES

Intelligence: Normal
Strength: Athlete, (transformed) Superhuman Class 25
Speed: Peak human
Stamina: Peak human
Durability: Peak human
Agility: Athlete
Reflexes: Athlete
Fighting skills: Trained by the Soviet Military, trained in the use of his powers by Professor Phobos
Special skills: Unrevealed
Superhuman physical powers: Ursa Major can change into a large humanoid grizzly bear while retaining his human intelligence
Superhuman mental powers: None
Special limitations: If Ursa Major remains in his bear form for over six hours, he begins to lose control over his human intelligence.
Source of superhuman powers: Genetic mutation

PARAPHERNALIA

Costume specifications: Conventional materials
Personal weaponry: None
Special weaponry: None
Other accessories: None
Transportation: Unrevealed
Design and manufacture of paraphernalia: Inapplicable

BIBLIOGRAPHY

First appearance: INCREDIBLE HULK #258
Origin issue: INCREDIBLE HULK #258
Significant issues: INCREDIBLE HULK #258-259 (joined Soviet Super-Soldiers, dispatched with them to Khystym to stop the Presence, encountered the Hulk, discovered teacher Pieter Phobos was true threat, opposed him); MARVEL SUPER HEROES CONTEST OF THE CHAMPIONS #1 (battled Red Ghost alongside Soviet Super-Soldiers); X-MEN VS. THE AVENGERS #1-3 (with Soviet Super-Soldiers, dispatched to capture Magneto, battled X-Men and Avengers); CAPTAIN AMERICA #352 (with Vanguard and Darkstar, attempted to defect to the United States, beaten comatose by the Supreme Soviets [later called the People's Protectorate])

VALINOR™

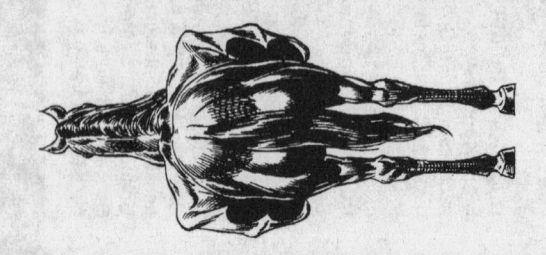

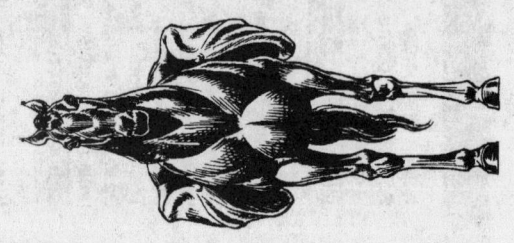

VALINOR

BIOGRAPHICAL DATA

Real name: Valinor
Other current aliases: None
Former aliases: None
Dual identity: Inapplicable
Current occupation: Steed of the Blood Wraith
Former occupation: Steed of the Black Knight III
Citizenship: Inapplicable
Legal status: Property of Sean Dolan (Blood Wraith)
Place of birth: Extradimensional realm of Avalon
Marital status: Inapplicable
Known relatives: None
Known confidants: Inapplicable
Known allies: Sean Dolan (Blood Wraith), (former) Black Knight III, Amergin, Dr. Strange, the Avengers, Victoria Bentley Valkyrie, Captain Britain, Black Knight I (deceased)
Major enemies: Balor, the Fomor, Morgan Le Fey, Black Knight III, Mordred, the Dreadknight, Crusader II, Swordsman II
Usual base of operations: Unrevealed
Former base of operations: Extradimensional realm of Avalon; Castle Garrett, Great Britain; Castle Garrett, Washington, D.C.
Current group membership: None
Former group membership: None
Extent of education: Inapplicable

PHYSICAL DESCRIPTION

Height: 64" (at withers)
Weight: 1,200 lbs.
Eyes: Brown
Hair: Black
Other distinguishing features: Large bat-like wings with a 15' wingspan from wingtip to wingtip

POWERS AND ABILITIES

Intelligence: Above normal (equine)
Strength: Enhanced human
Speed: Enhanced human
Flight speed: Natural winged flight
Stamina: Superhuman
Durability: Peak human
Agility: Peak human
Reflexes: Peak human
Fighting skills: Experienced battle steed on land and aloft
Special skills and abilities: Excellent rapport with his master, Blood Wraith, enabling him to understand and obey complex commands
Superhuman physical powers: Aside from the above listed attributes, none
Superhuman mental powers: None
Special limitations: None
Source of superhuman powers: Magical enchantment by spell cast by Amergin, mage of Avalon; mystical rapport with the Ebony Blade.

PARAPHERNALIA

Costume specifications: None
Personal weaponry: None
Special weaponry: None
Other accessories: None
Transportation: Flight under own power
Design and manufacture of paraphernalia: Inapplicable

BIBLIOGRAPHY

First appearance: AVENGERS #226
Origin issue: Valinor's origin is as yet unrevealed.
Significant issues: AVENGERS #226 (in the 12th Century, carried the Black Knight II into battle against Balor and the Fomor alongside Avengers; accompanied Black Knight on his return to 20th Century Earth); DOCTOR STRANGE Vol. 2 #68 (fell ill due to spell that gave him his wings, cured by Doctor Strange but lost his wings in the process); BLACK KNIGHT Vol. 2 #1-4 (wings restored magically, carried Black Knight III possessed by the spirit of the Black Knight I into battle against Morgan Le Fey, Mordred, Dreadknight, Balor, and celtic demons alongside Victoria Bentley/Valkyrie, Captain Britain, Sean Dolan, and Doctor Strange); AVENGERS SPOTLIGHT #39 (carried Black Knight III into battle against Crusader II); AVENGERS #343 (carried Black Knight III into battle against Swordsman II and Magdelene, shot down by power beam, rescued by Thor II); AVENGERS ANNUAL #22 (came into the possession of Blood Wraith, carried Blood Wraith into battle against the Black Knight III and the Avengers)
Note: Valinor also carried the Black Knight and Captain Britain on various adventures chronicled in Marvel U.K. titles which took place between the Black Knight's return to the 20th Century in AVENGERS #226 and the events of DOCTOR STRANGE Vol. 2 #68.

VALKIN™

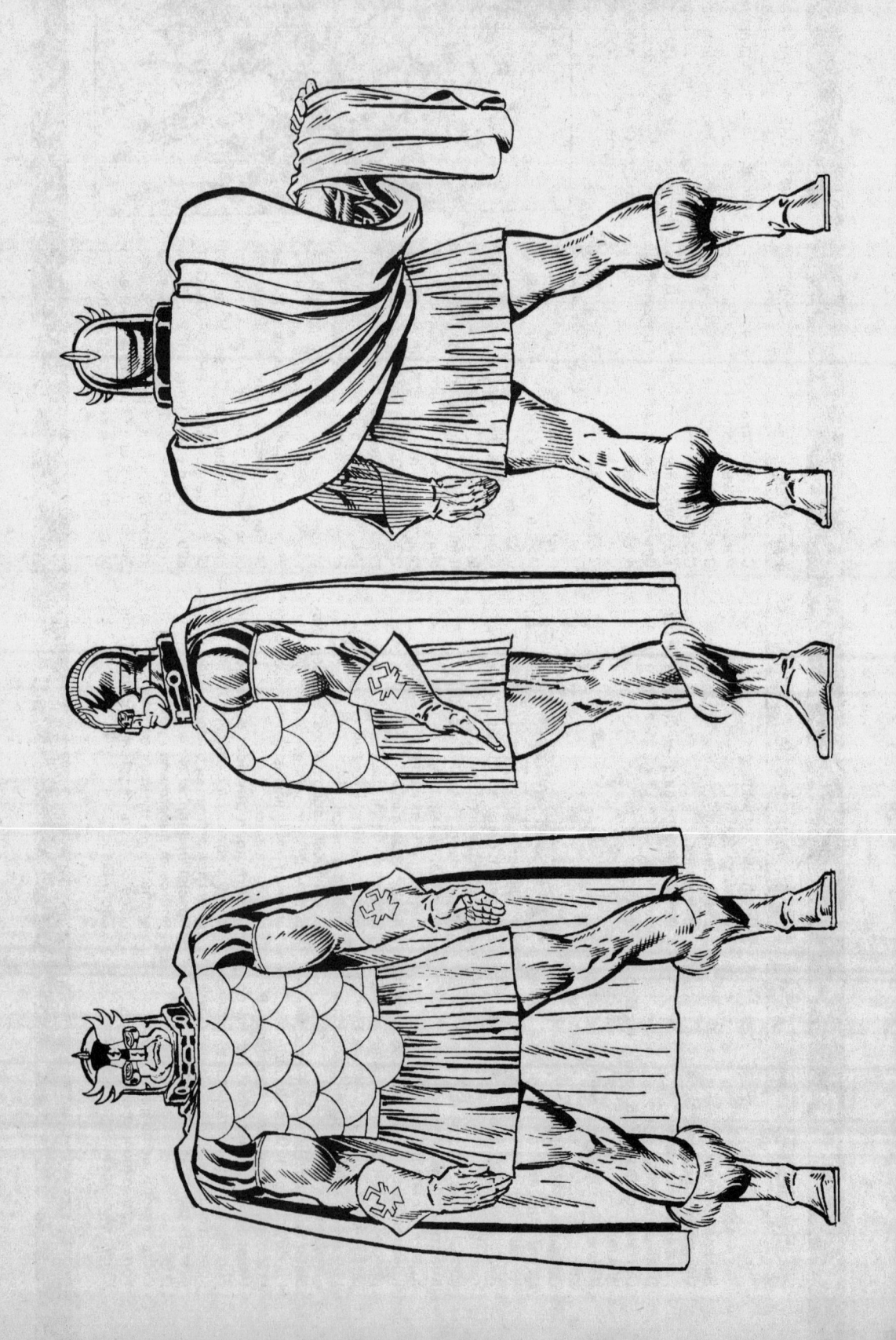

VALKIN

BIOGRAPHICAL DATA

Real name: Valkin
Other current aliases: None
Former aliases: General Vulcanin
Dual identity: Secret
Current occupation: Leader of Earth's Eternals
Former occupation: Leader of Polar Eternals; General in the Soviet army
Citizenship: (as Valkin) Polaria, (as Vulcanin) U.S.S.R.
Legal status: No criminal record
Place of birth: Unrevealed
Marital status: Married
Known relatives: Virako (brother, deceased), Druig (son), Ikaris (nephew, adopted son)
Known confidants: Ikaris, Virako, Aginar, Zarin
Known allies: Zuras, other Eternals
Major enemies: Deviants (especially Brother Tode and Kro)
Usual base of operations: Mobile in outer space within Uni-Mind
Former bases of operations: Polaria, Siberia
Current group membership: Polar Eternals, Eternals of Earth
Former group membership: None
Extent of education: Unrevealed

PHYSICAL DESCRIPTION

Height: 6' 1"
Weight: 290 lbs.
Eyes: Blue
Hair: Black
Other distinguishing features: None

POWERS AND ABILITIES

Intelligence: Above normal
Strength: Superhuman Class 50
Flight speed: Speed of sound
Stamina: Metahuman
Durability: Metahuman regenerative
Agility: Superhuman
Reflexes: Superhuman
Fighting skills: Unrevealed, presumably a good hand-to-hand combatant
Special skills and abilities: Brilliant military strategist, architect
Superhuman physical powers: Superhuman strength; virtual invulnerability; ability to project cosmic energy from eyes or hands in the form of heat, light, concussive force, or lightning-like electrical bolts
Superhuman mental powers: Total mental control over physical form, granting virtual immortality; ability to levitate himself and thereby fly at superhuman speed; low-level psychic abilities, enabling him to cast illusions disguising his appearance and to read the mind of anyone with lesser psychic ability; psionic ability to rearrange molecular structure of objects
Special limitations: None
Source of superhuman powers: Member of the race of superhumans known as the Eternals

PARAPHERNALIA

Costume specifications: None
Personal weaponry: None
Special weaponry: None
Other accessories: None
Transportation: Self-levitation, also Soviet aircraft
Design and manufacture of paraphernalia: Polar Eternals

BIBLIOGRAPHY

First appearance: ETERNALS Vol. 1 #11
Origin issue: Valkin's origin is as yet unrevealed.
Significant issues: ETERNALS Vol. 1 #11 (went to Olympia to participate in formation of Uni-Mind); THOR ANNUAL #7 (with other Eternals prepared for coming of Third Celestial Host of Celestials in South America, brother Virako died battling World-Worm, adopted Virako's son Ikaris); AVENGERS #248 (became leader of Eternals leaving Earth in the form of the Uni-Mind)

VAMP

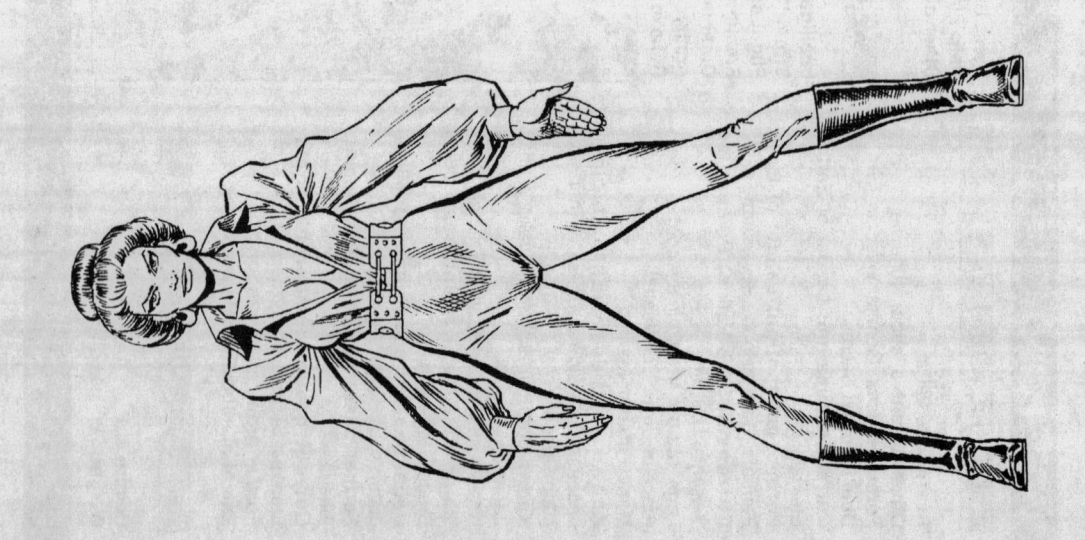

VAMP

BIOGRAPHICAL DATA

Real name: Unrevealed
Aliases at time of death: Animus
Former aliases: None known
Dual identity: Secret, known to the United States legal authorities
Occupation at time of death: Professional criminal
Former occupation: Secret agent
Citizenship: United States of America
Legal status: Criminal record in the U.S.
Place of birth: Unrevealed
Place of death: The "Bar With No Name," Medina County, Ohio
Cause of death: Shot with explosive bullets by Scourge
Marital status: Unrevealed
Known relatives: None
Confidants at time of death: Senator Eugene Stivak
Known allies: The Corporation, Blue Streak (deceased), Eugene Stivak (deceased), Curtiss Jackson (later Power Broker), Moonstone II
Major enemies: Captain America, Nick Fury, SHIELD, the Falcon, the Hulk, Marvel Man (later Quasar)
Base of operations at time of death: Mobile
Former bases of operations: SHIELD headquarters, New York City
Group membership at time of death: None
Former group membership: SHIELD "Super-Agents" (Blue Streak, Texas Twister, Marvel Man
Extent of education: Unrevealed

PHYSICAL DESCRIPTION

Height: 5' 6", (as Animus) 6' 5"
Weight: 125 lbs., (as Animus) 310 lbs.
Eyes: Violet, (as Animus) Black
Hair: Black, (as Animus) Bald
Other distinguishing features: (as Animus) Oversized cranium, inhuman features, no female sexual characteristics

POWERS AND ABILITIES

Intelligence: Normal
Strength: Athlete, (with absorbo-belt) up to Superhuman Class 10, (as Animus) Superhuman Class 25
Speed: Athlete
Stamina: Athlete
Durability: Athlete
Agility: Athlete
Reflexes: Athlete
Fighting skills: Excellent hand-to-hand combatant, black belt in judo
Special skills and abilities: None known
Superhuman physical powers: Aside from the above listed, none
Superhuman mental powers: Limited telepathic abilities, (as Animus) Ability to project psionic bolts of concussive force, ability to levitate and animate inanimate objects by telekinesis, ability to cause crystalline club-weapon to materialize
Special limitations: (as Animus) Inability to project psionic energy without remaining physically still, inability to withstand psionic backlash resulting from the destruction of her club
Source of superhuman powers: Presumably genetic engineering

PARAPHERNALIA

Costume specifications: Ordinary fabric
Personal weaponry: (as Animus) A huge crystalline club which served to store, focus, and project psionic energy
Special weaponry: None
Other accessories: (as Vamp) Absorbo-belt which enabled her to duplicate within herself the powers and skills of any opponent within certain limits
Transportation: Teleportation (effected by Corporation technology)
Design and manufacture of paraphernalia: (Absorbo-belt) Unnamed SHIELD scientists; (club) Unnamed Corporation scientists

BIBLIOGRAPHY

First appearance: (as Vamp) CAPTAIN AMERICA #217, (as Animus) CAPTAIN AMERICA #222
Origin issue: The Vamp's origin is as yet unrevealed
Significant issues: CAPTAIN AMERICA #217 (using absorbo-belt), joined SHIELD "Super-Agents"); CAPTAIN AMERICA #222-223 (as Animus, attacked Captain America with animated Volkswagen and Abraham Lincoln statue, battled Captain America, escaped); CAPTAIN AMERICA #229-230/INCREDIBLE HULK Vol. 2 #232/CAPTAIN AMERICA #231(revealed as double agent for the Corporation, revealed as Animus; with Moonstone II, Curtiss Jackson and Eugene Stivak, battled Captain America, Hulk, and Marvel Man; club destroyed by Hulk, causing her to fall into catatonic state; placed in custody and medical care of SHIELD; CAPTAIN AMERICA #319 (recovered, attended criminals' meeting at "Bar With No Name," shot and killed by Scourge)

VANGUARD

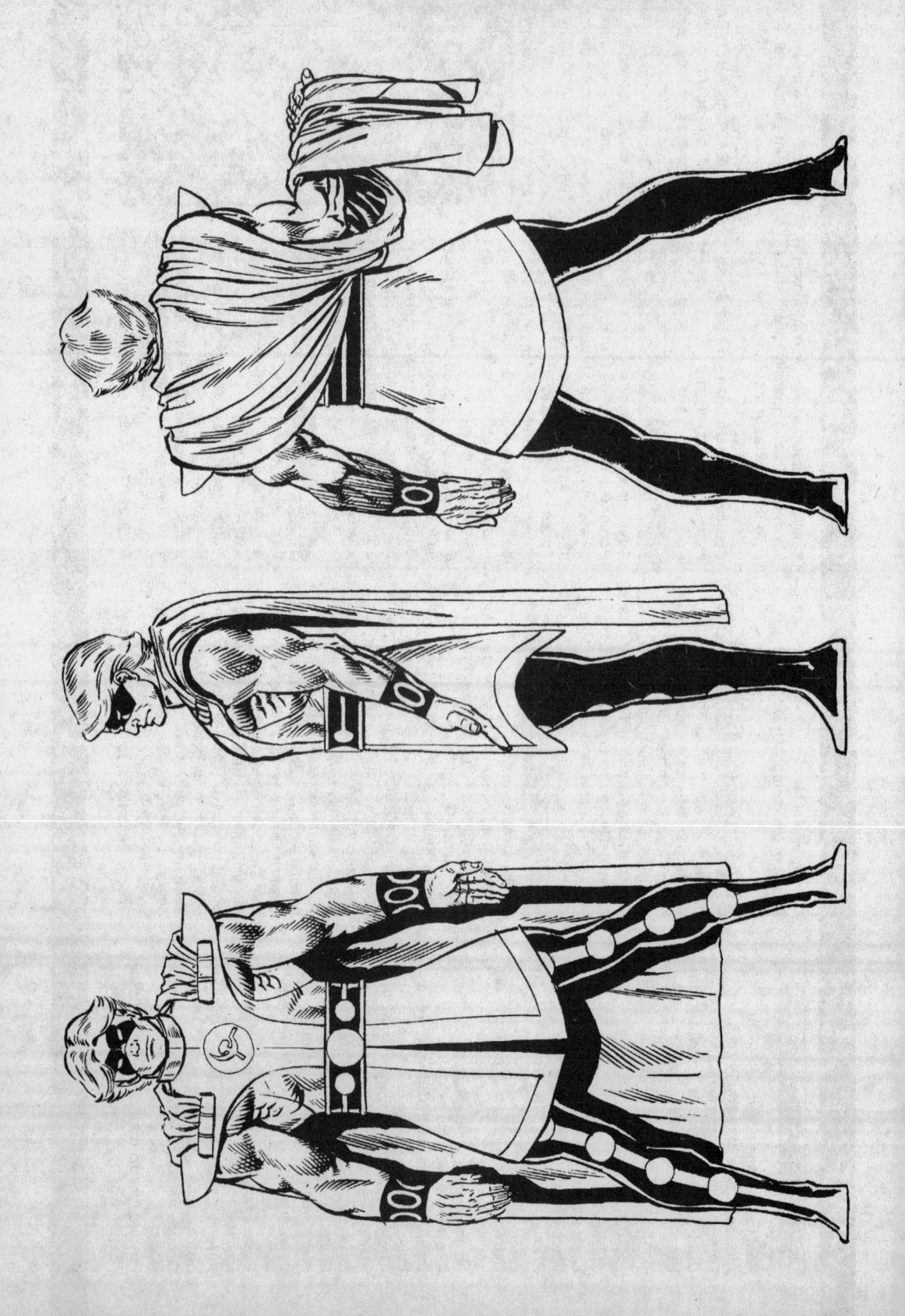

VANGUARD

BIOGRAPHICAL DATA

Real name: Nikolai Krylenko
Other current aliases: None
Former aliases: The Great Beast
Dual Identity: Known to officials of the American and Soviet Governments
Current occupation: Unknown
Former occupation: Adventurer, special operative of the Soviet government, soldier in Soviet army
Citizenship: USSR, seeking political asylum in the United States of America
Legal status: No criminal record, unofficially branded an outlaw by the Soviet government
Place of birth: Minsk, USSR
Marital status: Single
Known relatives: Sergei Krylov (alias, the Presence, father), Marya Krylov (mother, deceased), Laynia Petrovna (alias Darkstar, sister)
Known confidants: Darkstar, Ursa Major
Known allies: Darkstar, Ursa Major, Captain America, Iron Man, Jack of Hearts, Rom, Starshine II, Sergei the Presence, Starlight, (formerly) Gremlin II, Crimson Dynamo V
Major enemies: Dire Wraiths, Magneto, People's Protectorate, Professor Pieter Phobos, KGB, Crimson Dynamo V
Usual base of operations: Unknown
Former bases of operations: Khystym, Siberia
Current group membership: Soviet Super-Soldiers
Former group membership: None
Extent of education: College level

PHYSICAL DESCRIPTION

Height: 6' 3"
Weight: 230 lbs.
Eyes: Blue
Hair: Red
Other distinguishing features: None

POWERS AND ABILITIES

Intelligence: Normal
Strength: Athlete
Speed: Athlete
Stamina: Athlete
Durability: Athlete
Agility: Athlete
Reflexes: Athlete
Fighting skills: Good hand-to-hand combatant, with military training in armed and unarmed combat
Special skills and abilities: None known
Superhuman physical powers: Possesses force field that repels virtually all electromagnetic and kinetic energy
Superhuman mental powers: None
Special limitations: Strength of force field can be diminished by fatigue; ability to direct energy he repels is dependent on usage of his hammer and sickle
Source of superhuman powers: Genetic mutation

PARAPHERNALIA

Costume specifications: Contains body armor of unknown composition
Personal weaponry: Specially designed hammer and sickle, which, when crossed in front of his body, serve as an electronic "lens" enabling him to redirect any energy repelled by his natural force field; the hammer and sickle can also be used as practical weapons for throwing slicing or pounding; the hammer contains a computer and laser gyroscope which enable the hammer, when thrown, to return to its take-off point.
Special weaponry: None
Other accessories: None
Transportation: Darkstar's teleportational power
Design and manufacture of paraphernalia: Soviet government

BIBLIOGRAPHY

First appearance: IRON MAN #109
Origin issue: INCREDIBLE HULK #259
Significant issues: IRON MAN #109 (as member of Soviet Super-Soldiers, fought Iron Man and Jack of Hearts on moon); IRON MAN #112 (aided Iron Man, Jack of Hearts, and other Soviet Super Soldiers in battling renegade Rigellians led by Commander Arcturus); INCREDIBLE HULK #258 (sent with Darkstar and Ursa Major by KGB to defeat Sergei, the Presence; met Professor Phobos); INCREDIBLE HULK #259 (fought Sergei and Starlight, then known as Red Guardian II; learned that Sergei was his father and that Phobos had exploited the Soviet Super-Soldiers, aided in freeing Sergei and Starlight and defeating Phobos); CONTEST OF CHAMPIONS #1-3 (played active role as pawn in competition between Grandmaster and Death); ROM #45 (sent with other Soviet Super-Soldiers by Soviet government to Khystym to battle Gremlin, fought Rom and Starshine II); ROM #46 (allied with Rom and Starshine II, fought Dire Wraiths; became ally of Gremlin, took over Dire Wraith base in Khystym as new Soviet Super-Soldiers headquarters); X-MEN VS. AVENGERS #1-3 (agreed with other Soviet Super-Soldiers to help bring Magneto to justice, fought Avengers, turned against Crimson Dynamo V); CAPTAIN AMERICA #352 (with Darkstar and Ursa Major, arrived at Avengers Island, asked Captain America to help them seek political asylum in America, was beaten nearly to death by People's Protectorate, then known as Supreme Soviets); CAPTAIN AMERICA #353 (comatose subconscious minds of injured Vanguard, Darkstar, and Ursa Major formed "Great Beast" that attempted to drain life energies of People's Protectorate; Vanguard, Darkstar, and Ursa Major regained consciousness and began recovery from injuries)

VANISHER™

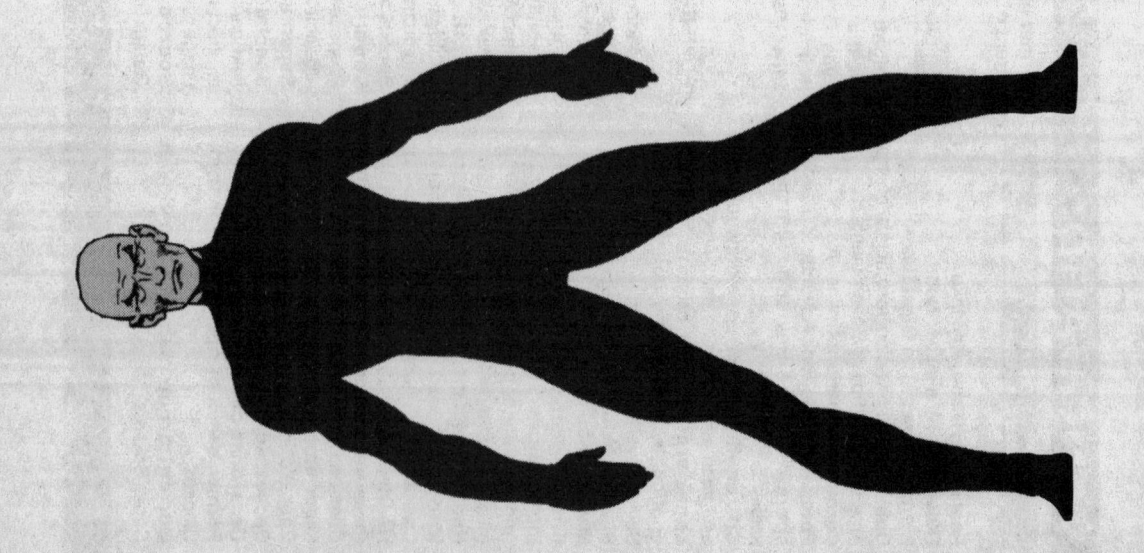

VANISHER

BIOGRAPHICAL DATA

Real name: Unrevealed
Other current aliases: None known
Former aliases: Telford Porter
Dual identity: Presumably known to the authorities
Current occupation: Professional criminal
Former occupation: Subversive
Citizenship: Unrevealed
Legal status: Criminal record
Place of birth: Unrevealed
Marital status: Unrevealed
Known relatives: None
Known confidants: None
Known allies: Enforcers, (former) Factor Three, Blob, Mastermind I, Unus, Fallen Angels
Major enemies: X-Men, Professor X, Nightcrawler, Spider-Man, Darkstar, (former) Champions of Los Angeles, Mutant Master, Darkling
Usual base of operations: New York City
Former bases of operations: Beat Street Club, New York City
Current group membership: Outer Circle of Enforcers II
Former group membership: Factor Three
Extent of education: Unrevealed

PHYSICAL DESCRIPTION

Height: 5'5"
Weight: 175 lbs.
Eyes: Green
Hair: Bald
Other distinguishing features: None

POWERS AND ABILITIES

Intelligence: Normal
Strength: Normal
Speed: Normal
Stamina: Normal
Durability: Normal
Agility: Normal
Reflexes: Normal
Fighting skills: Poor hand-to-hand combatant, no combat training
Special skills and abilities: Good knowledge of robotics and computers
Superhuman physical powers: None
Superhuman mental powers: Psionic ability to teleport himself, his clothes, and a certain amount of additional mass. Apparently the vanisher traverses the Darkforce Dimension when teleporting from one place on Earth to another. The Vanisher has an extrasensory ability theat prevents him from materializing part or all of his body within a solid object.
Special limitations: The limitations on the Vanisher's teleportational range or the amount of mass he can teleport with himself remain unrevealed. It is known that the Vanisher can go from southern California to New York State in a single teleport.
Source of superhuman powers: Genetic mutation

PARAPHERNALIA

Costume specifications: Conventional fabrics
Personal weaponry: Guns which shoot gas or fire energy beams
Special weaponry: The Vanisher once reprogrammed Sentinel robots to do his bidding.
Other accessories: None known
Transportation: Self teleportation
Design and manufacture of paraphernalia: Vanisher

BIBLIOGRAPHY

First appearance: X-MEN Vol. 1 #2
Origin issue: The Vanisher's origin is as yet unrevealed.
Significant issues: X-MEN Vol. 1 #2 (committed series of spectacular crimes, built large criminal organization, stole defense plans and attempted to extort millions of dollars from the United States government for their return, first battled X-Men, was rendered amnesiac by Professor X); X-MEN Vol. 1 #37-39 (joined in Factor Three's attempt at world conquest, but finally teamed with X-Men in defeating Mutant Master); X-MEN Vol. 1 #60 (was held prisoner by Sentinels, was released through X-Men's intervention); CHAMPIONS #17 (used reprogrammed Sentinels in attempt to defeat Champions of Los Angeles, was trapped in mid-teleportation by Darkstar); BIZARRE ADVENTURES #27 (traveled to another dimension with Nightcrawler, returned to Earth); FALLEN ANGELS #1-8 (acted as mentor in thievery to Fallen Angels); NEW WARRIORS #33-34/NEW WARRIORS ANNUAL #3 (fell under control of Darkling, used by him to attack New Warriors and other superheroes); WEB OF SPIDER-MAN #99-100 (alongside other members of the Outer Circle of Enforcers II, attacked Spider-Man; was defeated by him)

VECTOR

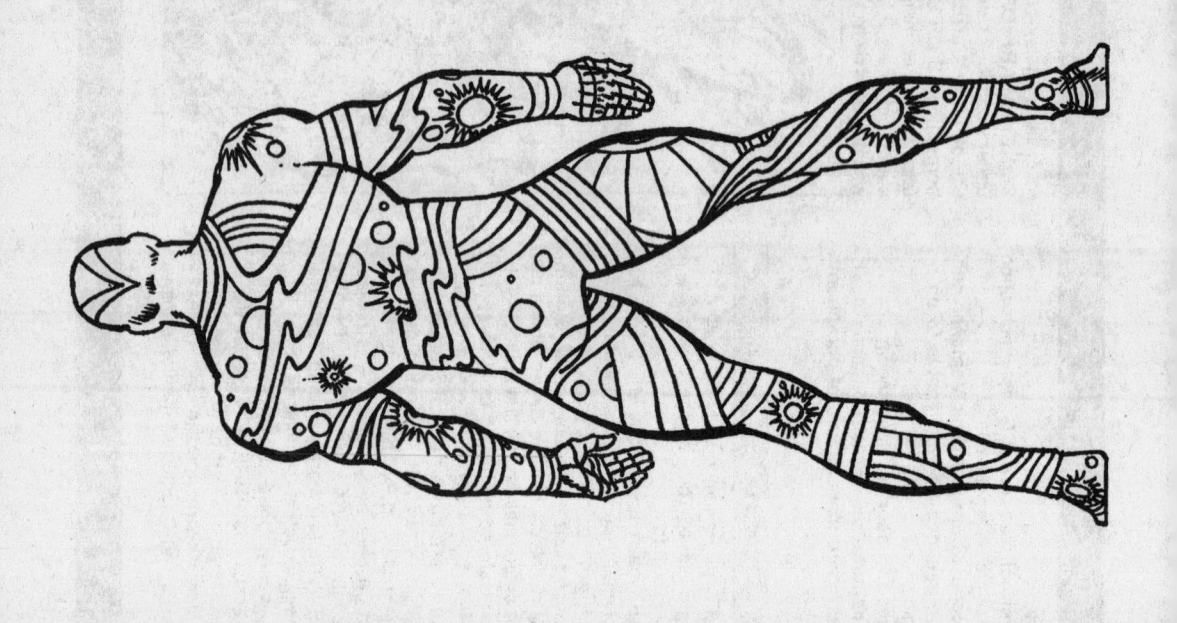

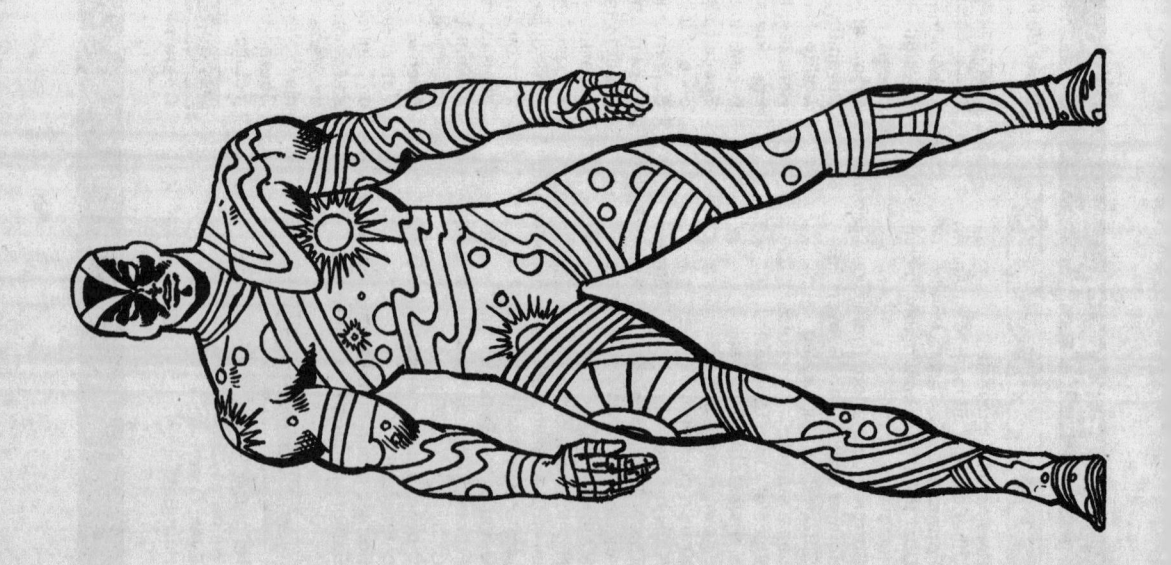

VECTOR

BIOGRAPHICAL DATA

Real name: Simon Utrecht
Other current aliases: None
Former aliases: None
Dual identity: Known to the authorities
Current occupation: Professional criminal
Former occupation: Industrialist
Citizenship: United States of America
Legal status: No criminal record
Place of birth: Unrevealed
Marital status: Single
Known relatives: None
Known confidants: None
Known allies: U-Foes (Vapor, X-Ray, Ironclad)
Major enemies: Hulk, Avengers
Usual base of operations: Mobile
Former bases of operations: None
Current group membership: U-Foes
Former group membership: None
Extent of education: College graduate

PHYSICAL DESCRIPTION

Height: 6'
Weight: 195 lbs.
Eyes: Brown, (as Vector) White
Hair: Grey, (as Vector) None
Other distinguishing features: Body covered with yellow filmy substance

POWERS AND ABILITIES

Intelligence: Above normal
Strength: Normal
Flight speed: Supersonic
Stamina: Normal
Durability: Normal
Agility: Normal
Reflexes: Normal
Fighting skills: None
Special skills and abilities: None
Superhuman physical powers: None
Superhuman mental powers: Ability to telekinetically propel matter away from himself, flight (via psychokinesis)
Special limitations: Influx of cosmic radiation can cause temporary loss of control of powers, as in deflecting the air around him, deflecting his own body from the Earth, being deflected into other dimensions; ability to deflect objects only ten times the the weight he can lift; cannot attract objects, only repel them
Source of superhuman powers: Exposure to cosmic radiation

PARAPHERNALIA

Costume specifications: Inapplicable
Personal weaponry: None
Special weaponry: None
Other accessories: None
Transportation: Flight (via psychokinesis)
Design and manufacture of paraphernalia: Inapplicable

BIBLIOGRAPHY

First appearance: INCREDIBLE HULK #254
Origin issue: INCREDIBLE HULK #254
Significant issues: INCREDIBLE HULK #254 (with his teammates, duplicated original rocket flight of Fantastic Four through cosmic ray belt and gained superhuman powers, battled Hulk, lost control of powers and deflected self into space); INCREDIBLE HULK #275 (rescued and returned to Earth by teammate X-Ray, reunited with U-Foes); INCREDIBLE HULK #276 (with U-Foes, defeated Hulk); INCREDIBLE HULK #277 (with U-Foes, exhibited captive Bruce Banner on national TV; freed by Rick Jones, Betty Ross, and alien Bereet, Banner transformed to Hulk and defeated U-Foes; Vector's hands crushed by Hulk); INCREDIBLE HULK #304 (with U-Foes, escaped special government prison, but accidentally "deflected" himself and teammates into crossroads dimension); INCREDIBLE HULK #305 (with U-Foes, battled Hulk in "crossroads" dimension, defeated Hulk with help of alien "Puffball Collective", trapped in dimension where he must constantly repel projectiles hurled by high winds to survive); AVENGERS #304 (escaped back to "Crossroads" dimension; learned to use psychokinetic powers for flight; with U-Foes, escaped back to Earth through dimensional warp unintentionally opened by mutant Charles Little Sky, battled Avengers and Puma, defeated by Thor); AVENGERS WEST COAST #53 (freed from Vault, the other U-Foes attacked Avengers West Coast, mistakenly believing they had killed Vector; Vector reappeared and led teammates in strategic retreat)

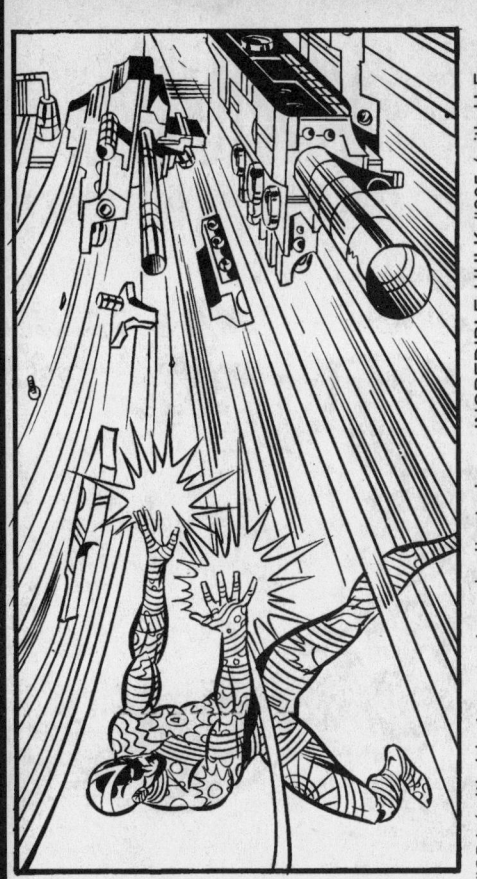

VENOM™

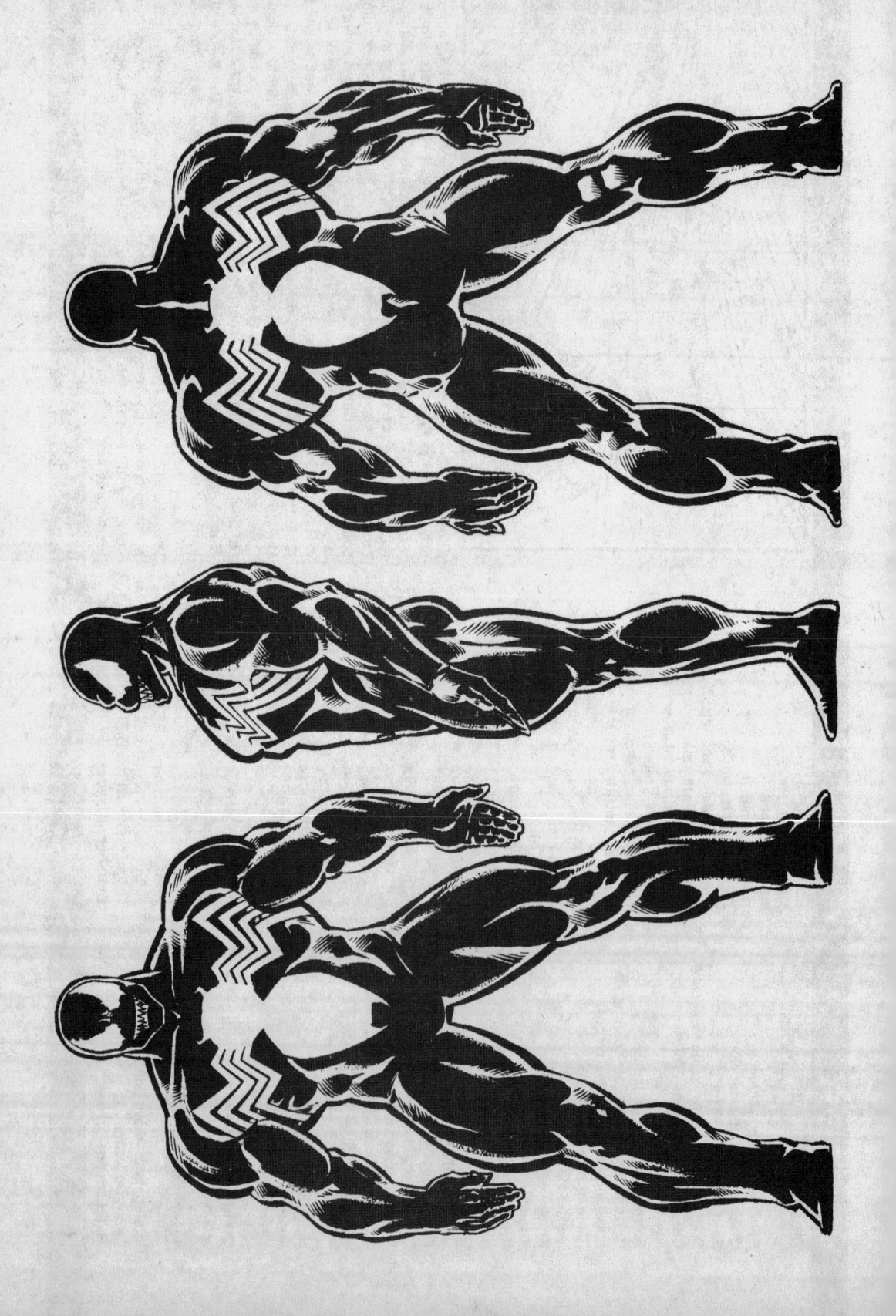

VENOM

BIOGRAPHICAL DATA

Real name: Edward "Eddie" Brock
Other current aliases: None
Former aliases: None
Dual identity: Known to local authorities
Current occupation: Convict
Former occupation: Journalist for the *Daily Globe*
Citizenship: United States of America
Legal status: Criminal record in the U.S.
Place of birth: New York City
Marital status: Single
Known relatives: None
Known confidants: None
Known allies: None
Major enemies: Spider-Man
Usual base of operations: New York City
Former bases of operations: The Vault, Colorado
Current group membership: None
Former group membership: The Associated Press
Extent of education: College graduate with Bachelor of Arts in journalism

PHYSICAL DESCRIPTION

Height: 6'3"
Weight: 260 lbs.
Eyes: Blue
Hair: Reddish blond
Other distinguishing features: As Venom, Brock has an elongated jaw, teeth, and tongue which are really constructs of the alien costume

POWERS AND ABILITIES

Intelligence: Normal
Strength: Superhuman Class 25
Speed: Superhuman
Stamina: Normal
Durability: Normal
Agility: Superhuman
Reflexes: Superhuman
Fighting skills: Moderate experience at hand-to-hand combat
Special skills and abilities: As a former journalist, Venom is highly skilled at deductive reasoning
Superhuman physical powers: In addition to the above listed physical abilities, Venom possesses the ability to adhere to most surfaces with his hands and feet and project a web-like substance from any part of his costume. The above attributes are conferred upon him by the costume. Without it, most of his attributes are normal.
Superhuman mental powers: Symbiotic relationship with his alien costume
Special limitations: Sensitivity to intense noise
Source of superhuman powers: Alien costume

PARAPHERNALIA

Costume specifications: Alien material made of tough, flexible fibers of organic polymers which have the ability to mimic any type of clothing whatsoever the costume in as yet unexplained manner dampens Spider-Man's Spider-sense.
Personal weaponry: None
Special weaponry: None
Other accessories: None
Transportation: Web-lines emitted from alien's substance
Design and manufacture of paraphernalia: Unrevealed

BIBLIOGRAPHY

First appearance: (as alien costume) SECRET WARS #8, (behind the scenes) WEB OF SPIDER-MAN #18, (actual appearance) AMAZING SPIDER-MAN #299

Origin issue: AMAZING SPIDER-MAN #300

Significant issues: SECRET WARS #8 (Spider-Man obtained alien costume); AMAZING SPIDER-MAN #258 (Spider-Man learned the costume is living, alien symbiote; separated himself from costume with "sonic blaster"); WEB OF SPIDER-MAN #1 (costume reattached to Spider-Man, who brought it to a bell tower to destroy it with intense sound; costume saved Spider-Man's life, then crawled away); WEB OF SPIDER-MAN #18 (Brock pushed Peter Parker in front of a moving subway without activating his spider-sense); AMAZING SPIDER-MAN #299 (Venom confronted Mary Jane Watson-Parker); AMAZING SPIDER-MAN #300 (battled Spider-Man for first time); AMAZING SPIDER-MAN #315 (escaped from Vault by mimicking a fallen guard); AMAZING SPIDER-MAN ANNUAL #25 (prevented the holdup of a truckstop on his way to New York); AMAZING SPIDER-MAN #316 (confronted the Black Cat; battled Spider-MAn in meat-packing plant); AMAZING SPIDER-MAN #317 (encountered Peter Parker as Eddie Brock at Parker's Aunt May's house; Spider-Man defeated him by tempting costume to reattach itself to him); QUASAR #6 (escaped from Vault during massive "Acts of Vengeance" breakout; returned by Quasar); THE VAULT GRAPHIC NOVEL (engineered failed prison break from the Vault, killed warden); AMAZING SPIDER-MAN #330-331 (faked suicide at the Vault by coating himself with a layer of synthetic skin generated by costume; escaped Vault from its morgue); AMAZING SPIDER-MAN #332 (saved a baby while battling Spider-Man); AMAZING SPIDER-MAN #333 (plague-inducing villain called Styx rendered alien costume comatose); AMAZING SPIDER-MAN #345 (alien costume reattached itself to Brock while in prison); AMAZING SPIDER-MAN #346 (trapped Spider-Man in a cryogenics chamber); AMAZING SPIDER-MAN #347 (transported Spider-Man to a deserted island, where Spider-Man faked his own death to convince Venom that his vendetta was over)

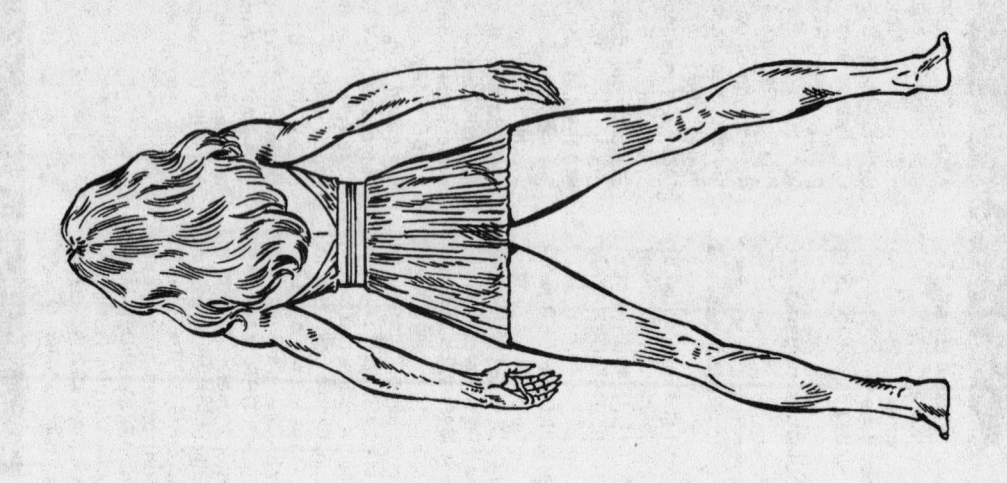

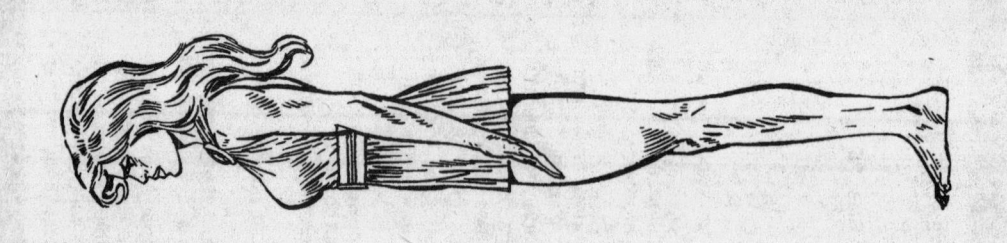

VENUS

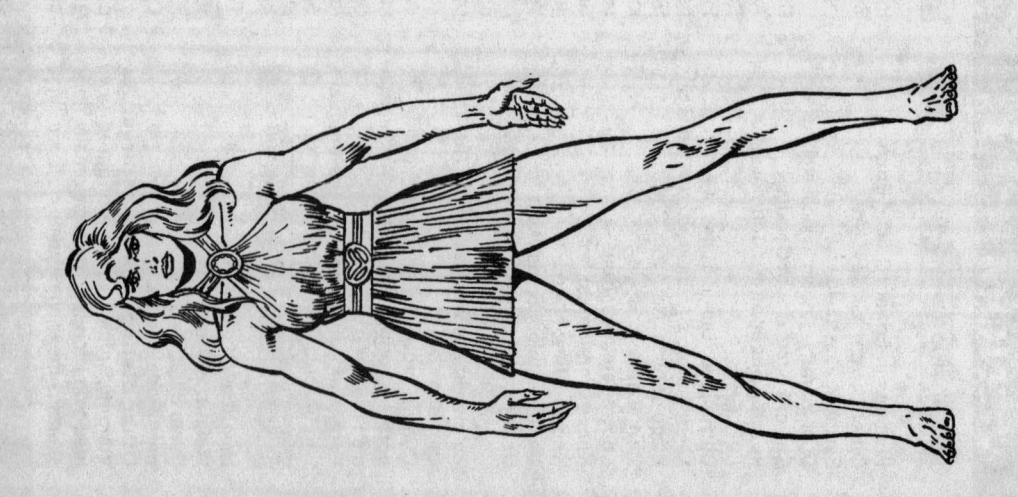

VENUS

BIOGRAPHICAL DATA

Real name: Aphrodite (Aphrodite is her original Greek name. Venus is her later Roman name.)
Other current aliases: Unrevealed
Former aliases: Victoria Nutley Starr
Dual Identity: The general populace of Earth is unaware of Venus's existence except as a mythological character
Current occupation: Goddess of love and beauty, occasional adventurer
Former occupation: Professor of humanities
Citizenship: Realm of Olympus
Legal status: No criminal record
Place of birth: Olympus
Marital status: Widowed
Known relatives: Zeus (father), Dione (mother), Hephaestus (former husband), Cupid (son)
Known confidants: Cupid
Known allies: Pantheon of Olympus, Namor the Sub-Mariner
Major enemies: Ares, Pluto, Hippolyta
Usual base of operations: Olympus
Former bases of operations: Los Angeles, California
Current group membership: Pantheon of Olympus
Former group membership: None
Extent of education: Unrevealed

PHYSICAL DESCRIPTION

Height: 5' 6"
Weight: 280 lbs. (Olympian tissue is denser than human tissue.)
Eyes: Blue
Hair: Blonde
Other distinguishing features: Venus is extraordinarily beautiful, perfectly proportioned, and possesses no physical flaws whatsoever. By the standards of western civilization of Earth, she is the epitome of female beauty and one of the most aesthetically perfect female beings in existence.

POWERS AND ABILITIES

Intelligence: Normal
Strength: Enhanced human
Speed: Enhanced human
Stamina: Metahuman
Durability: Metahuman
Agility: Superhuman
Reflexes: Superhuman
Fighting skills: Minimal ability at hand to hand combat
Special skills and abilities: Master of all the arts and sciences of physical love
Superhuman physical powers: The conventional attributes of an Olympian goddess; enhanced physical properties, extraordinary vitality, virtual immortality
Superhuman mental powers: None
Special limitations: None
Source of superhuman powers: Born a goddess

PARAPHERNALIA

Costume specifications: Conventional Romanesque attire
Personal weaponry: None
Special weaponry: None
Other accessories: A magical girdle named Cestus that enables wearer to ensorcel anyone to become a love-slave, and to neutralize or transform all weapons of war
Transportation: Various (usually chariots)
Design and manufacture of paraphernalia: Hephaestus

BIBLIOGRAPHY

First appearance: (historical) VENUS #1, (modern) SUB-MARINER #57
Origin issue: The exact details of Venus's origin have yet to be depicted.
Significant issues: SUB-MARINER #57 (on Earth disguised as a mortal on mission of peace, pursued by Ares, defended by Namor the Sub-Mariner, surrendered Cestus to Ares); CHAMPIONS #1-3 (commanded by Pluto to become the bride of Ares as part of Pluto's bid to overthrow Zeus, opposed them alongside the Champions, subdued Queen Hippolyta non-violently); AVENGERS #283-284 (aided the Avengers in their attempt to quell the rage of Zeus over Hercules's beating by mortals)

VERMIN™

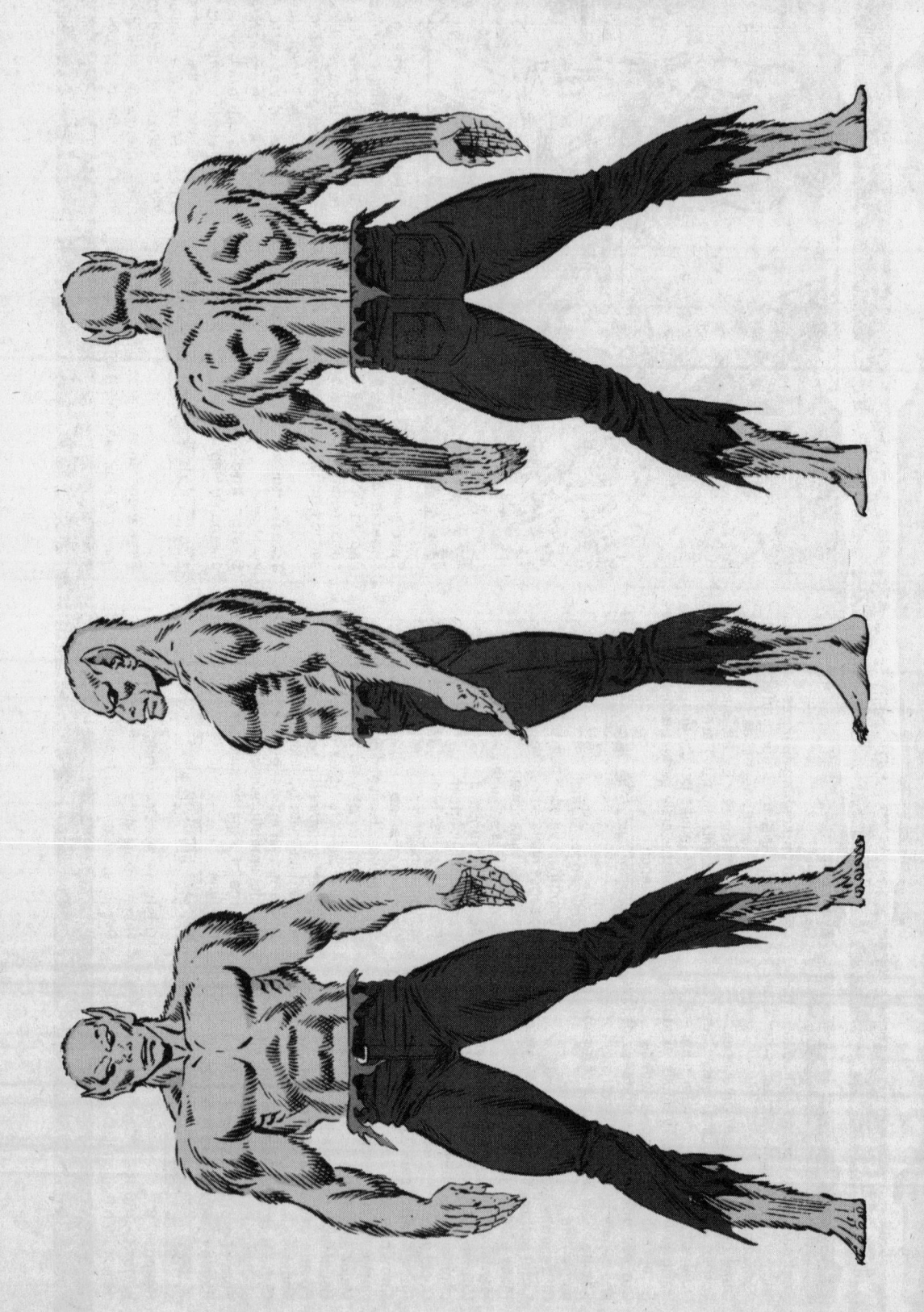

VERMIN

BIOGRAPHICAL DATA

Real name: Edward Whelan
Other current aliases: None
Former aliases: None
Dual identity: Secret
Current occupation: Unrevealed
Former occupation: Geneticist
Citizenship: United States of America
Legal status: Unrevealed
Place of birth: Unrevealed
Marital status: Single
Known relatives: Unnamed father and mother
Known confidants: Dr. Ashley Kafka
Known allies: (former) Arnim Zola, Baron Zemo II
Major enemies: Captain America, Baron Zemo II, Spider-Man
Usual base of operations: Mobile
Former bases of operations: Unrevealed
Current group membership: None
Former group membership: None
Extent of education: College graduate

PHYSICAL DESCRIPTION

Height: 6'
Weight: 220 lbs.
Eyes: Red, (human form) Brown
Hair: Brown, (human form) Black
Other distinguishing features: Vermin has inch-long claw-like fingernails, razor-sharp pointed teeth, and fur covering most of his body, giving him the appearance of a humanoid rat. Recently, Vermin has gained the ability to revert to human form at will.

POWERS AND ABILITIES

Intelligence: Learning impaired
Strength: Enhanced human
Speed: Peak human
Stamina: Peak human
Durability: Peak human
Agility: Peak human
Reflexes: Peak human
Fighting skills: Average hand-to-hand combatant, relies mainly on bestial ferocity.
Special skills and abilities: None known
Superhuman physical powers: Aside from the above listed attributes, Vermin has an extremely acute sense of smell, the ability to control rats and stray dogs within a radius of two miles (presumably hypersonic).
Superhuman mental powers: None
Special limitations: None
Source of superhuman powers: Experimental process designed by Arnim Zola

PARAPHERNALIA

Costume specifications: Conventional fabrics
Personal weaponry: None
Special weaponry: None
Other accessories: None
Transportation: Conventional means
Design and manufacture of paraphernalia: Inapplicable

BIBLIOGRAPHY

First appearance: CAPTAIN AMERICA #272
Origin issue: SPECTACULAR SPIDER-MAN #182
Significant issues: CAPTAIN AMERICA #272 (transformed into present form by Arnim Zola and Baron Zemo II, defeated by Captain America, turned over to SHIELD); CAPTAIN AMERICA #275-278 (escaped SHIELD, returned to service of Zola and Zemo, shackled by Zemo with Captain America in dungeon, battled mutates, escaped, wounded Zemo); MARVEL TEAM-UP #128 (battled Captain America and Spider-Man at street festival, captured); WEB OF SPIDER-MAN #31-32 /AMAZING SPIDER-MAN #293-294/ SPECTACULAR SPIDER-MAN #131-132 (kidnaped women off the streets into sewers, murdered and devoured them, defeated and captured by an insane Kraven the Hunter disguised as Spider-Man, forced by Kraven to battled the real Spider-Man, then allowed to escape, finally captured and turned over to the police by Spider-Man); SPECTACULAR SPIDER-MAN #178-184 (escaped asylum, attacked his parents at their home in Scarsdale, captured by Spider-Man and returned to psychiatric care; gained ability to temporarily revert to human form)

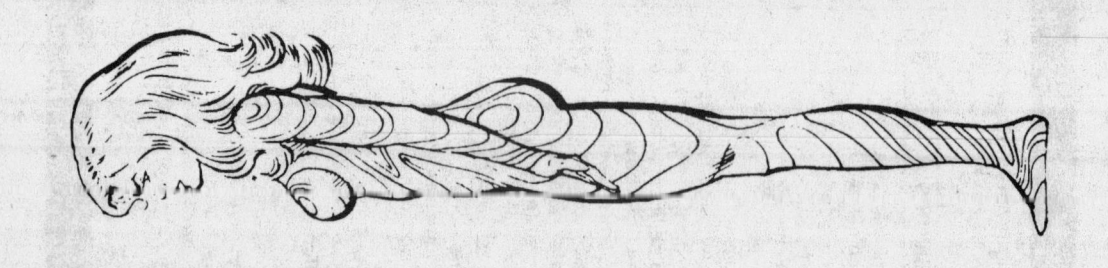

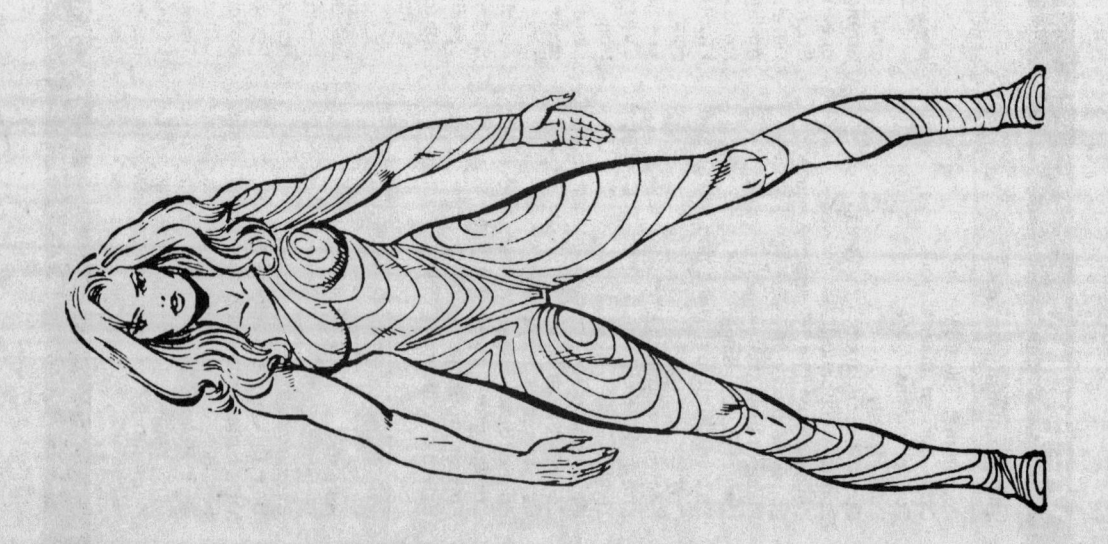

VERTIGO

VERTIGO

BIOGRAPHICAL DATA

Real name: Unrevealed
Other current aliases: None known
Former aliases: None known
Dual identity: Secret
Current occupation: Assassin
Former occupation: None
Citizenship: Unrevealed
Legal status: Unrevealed
Place of birth: The Savage Land
Marital status: Unrevealed, presumed single
Known relatives: None
Known confidants: None
Known allies: The Marauders (Harpoon, Scalphunter, Arclight, Sabretooth, Prism, Scrambler, Riptide); Savage Land Mutates (Brainchild, Amphibius, Gaza, Lupo, the Piper, Barbarus, Equilibrius)
Major enemies: The X-Men
Usual base of operations: Mobile
Former bases of operations: The Savage Land
Current group membership: The Marauders
Former group membership: The Savage Land Mutates
Extent of education: No formal education

PHYSICAL DESCRIPTION

Height: 5' 6"
Weight: 115 lbs.
Eyes: Blue
Hair: Silver
Other distinguishing features: None

POWERS AND ABILITIES

Intelligence: Normal
Strength: Normal
Speed: Normal
Flight speed: Normal
Stamina: Normal
Durability: Normal
Agility: Normal
Reflexes: Normal
Fighting skills: Poor hand-to-hand combat skills
Special skills: Ability to disorient another person's sense of balance, inducing vertigo and possibly unconsciousness
Superhuman physical powers: None
Superhuman mental powers: None
Special limitations: None

PARAPHERNALIA

Costume specifications: Synthetic stretch fabric
Personal weaponry: None
Special weaponry: None
Other accessories: None
Transportation: Unrevealed
Design and manufacture of paraphernalia: Inapplicable

BIBLIOGRAPHY

First appearance: MARVEL FANFARE #1

Origin issue: Vertigo's full origin is as yet unrevealed.
Significant issues: MARVEL FANFARE #1 (first battled X-Men); X-MEN #211 (revealed to be a Marauder); X-MEN #221 (with Marauders, attempted to kill Madelyne Pryor); X-MEN #241 (apparently killed in battle with X-Men)
Note: Vertigo II is not to be confused with Vertigo I of the Salem's Seven

VIBRO™

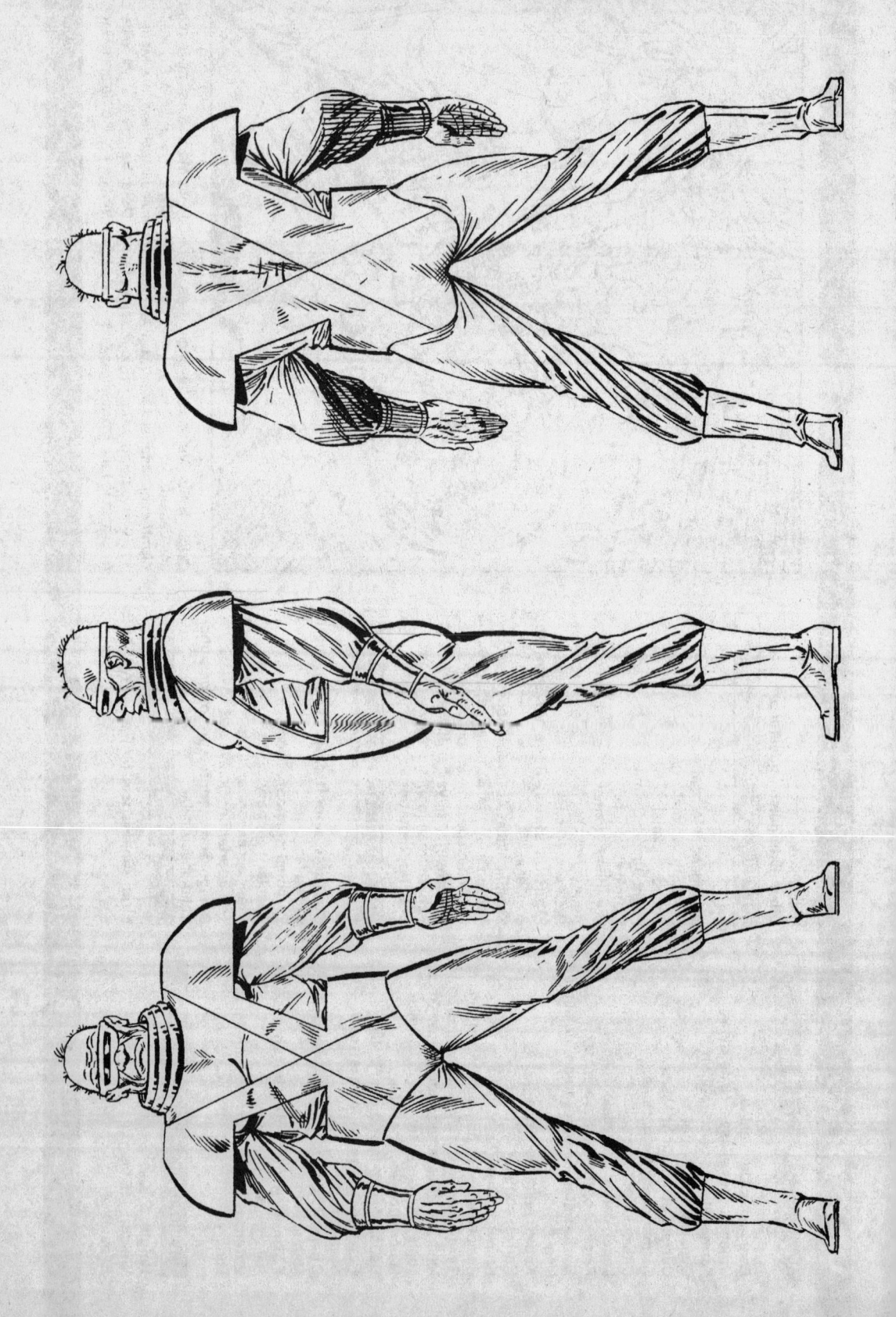

VIBRO

BIOGRAPHICAL DATA

Real name: Alton Francis Vibreaux
Other current aliases: None
Former aliases : None
Dual Identity: Publicly known
Current occupation: Environmental terrorist
Former occupations: Seismologist, engineer
Citizenship: United States of America
Legal status: Criminal record in the U.S.
Place of birth: Baton Rouge, Louisiana
Marital status: Single
Known relatives: None
Known confidants: None
Known allies: (former) The Griffin
Major enemies: Franklin Fortney, Iron Man II, Iron Man I, the Falcon, Nomad III, Avengers West Coast
Usual base of operations: San Andreas Fault area, California
Former bases of operations: Palmdale, California
Current group membership: None
Former group membership: None
Extent of education: Ph. D in geological engineering

PHYSICAL DESCRIPTION

Height: 5' 8"
Weight: 165 lbs.
Eyes: Blue
Hair: Black (nearly bald)
Other distinguishing features: Acute facial disfigurement, scalp and dental damage

POWERS AND ABILITIES

Intelligence: Gifted, (formerly) Below normal
Note: Due to traumatic accident in which he gained superhuman powers, Vibro suffered mental deficiencies for some time thereafter, from which he has now somewhat, if not fully recovered.
Strength: Normal
Speed: Normal
Flight speed: Subsonic
Stamina: Normal
Durability: Normal
Agility: Normal
Reflexes: Normal
Fighting skills: Minimal
Special skills: Expert in laser technology
Superhuman physical powers: Ability to generate high-level seismic vibrations and fire them from his hands as vibratory or concussive force, causing shockwaves, opening chasms, and/or generating earthquakes; ability to harness thrust of his vibratory force emissions for flight; ability to generate shields of vibratory force around himself; immunity to effects of his own powers
Superhuman mental powers: None
Special limitations: Mental derangement due to traumatic accident; powers decrease with relative distance from San Andreas Fault
Source of superhuman powers: Nuclear powered seismic energy-absorbing apparatus grafted to his body

PARAPHERNALIA

Costume specifications: Body armor of an unknown composition and synthetic stretch fabric
Personal weaponry: A nuclear-powered seismic energy-absorbing apparatus, now transformed into a vibrational energy generator, which was grafted itself to Vibro's body
Special weaponry: None
Other accessories: None
Transportation: Flight under his own power
Design and manufacture of paraphernalia: Alton Francis Vibreaux

BIBLIOGRAPHY

First appearance: IRON MAN #186
Origin issue: IRON MAN #186
Significant Issues: IRON MAN #187-187 (fell into San Andreas Fault during test of his experimental apparatus, gained superhuman powers, sought vengeance on employer Franklin Fortney, battled Iron Man II); IRON MAN #191-192 (battled Iron Man II; defeated by Tony Stark wearing original Iron Man armor); CAPTAIN AMERICA #304 (alongside the Griffin, attempted escape from the Vault; encountered the Falcon and Nomad III); AVENGERS WEST COAST #58 (caused massive earthquake in Los Angeles, battled Avengers West Coast); IRON MAN #267 (battled Iron Man I)

VIDAR

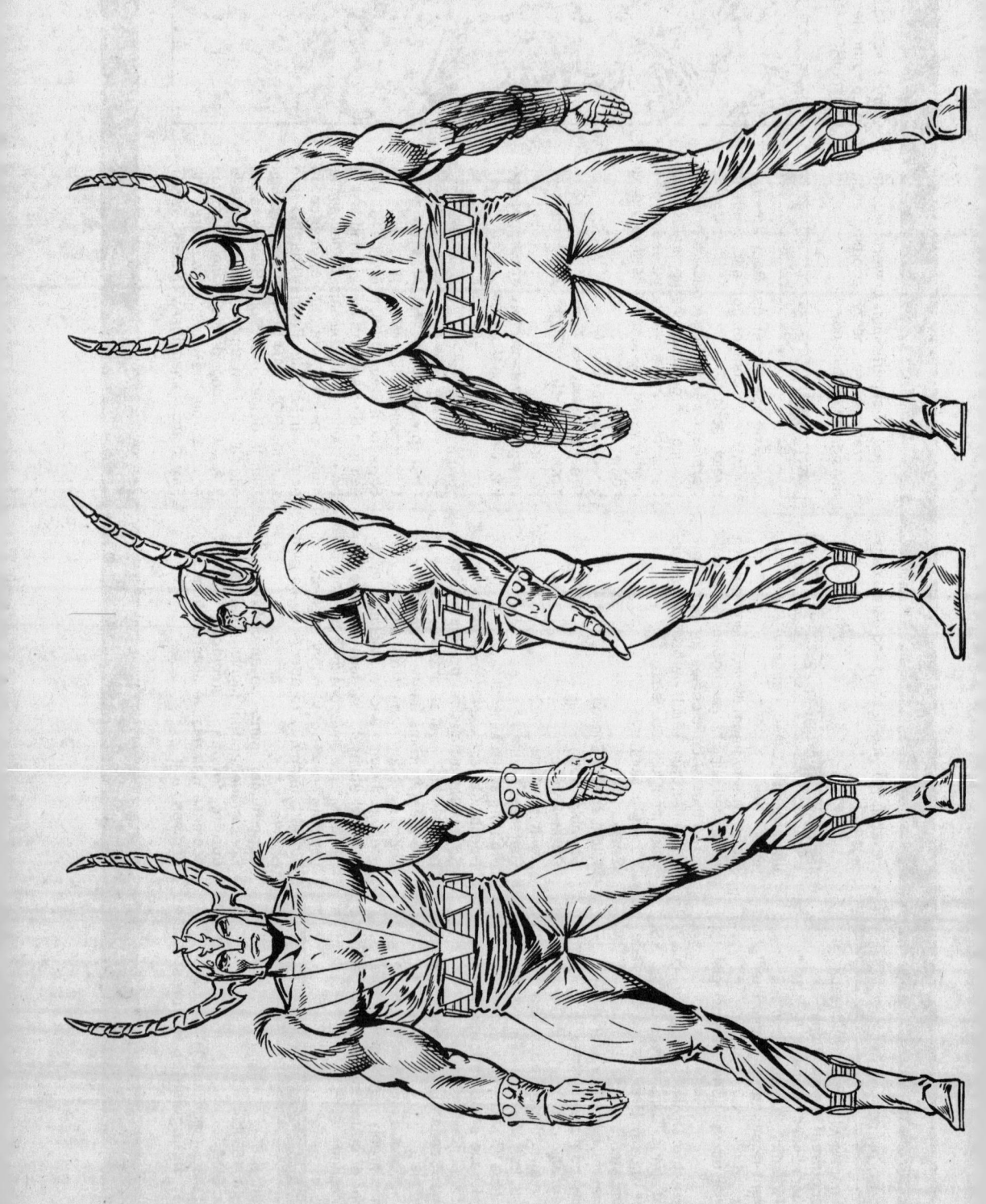

VIDAR

BIOGRAPHICAL DATA

Real name: Vidar
Other current aliases: None
Former aliases: None
Dual identity: None; the general populace of Earth is unaware of Vidar's existence except as a mythological character
Current occupation: Farmer, warrior
Former occupation: Huntsman
Citizenship: Realm of Asgard
Legal status: Citizen of Asgard
Place of birth: Unrevealed
Marital status: Widower
Known relatives: Odin (father), Grid (mother), Solveig (wife, deceased), Thor, Loki (half-brothers), Buri (Tiwaz, great-grandfather), Bor (grandfather), Vili, Ve (uncles)
Known confidants: None
Known allies: Gods of Asgard
Major enemies: The Storm giants, the Frost giants
Usual base of operations: A valley in the Asgardian Mountains
Former bases of operations: None
Current group membership: Gods of Asgard
Former group membership: None
Extent of education: Unrevealed

PHYSICAL DESCRIPTION

Height: 10'
Weight: 690 lbs.
Eyes: Blue
Hair: Blond
Other distinguishing features: None

POWERS AND ABILITIES

Intelligence: Normal
Strength: Superhuman Class 50
Speed: Superhuman
Stamina: Superhuman
Durability: Superhuman
Agility: Superhuman
Reflexes: Superhuman
Fighting skills: Expert with staff and sword
Special skills and abilities: None
Superhuman physical powers: Aside from the above listed attributes, Vidar has no other superhuman physical powers
Superhuman mental powers: None
Special limitations: None
Source of superhuman powers: Vidar is a member of the race of superhumans known as Asgardians; his great size is due to his physiology as the hybrid son of an Asgardian father and a Storm giant mother.

PARAPHERNALIA

Costume specifications: Asgardian materials
Personal weaponry: A six-foot staff (once imbued with by odin with power equal to that of Thor's hammer)
Special weaponry: None
Other accessories: None
Transportation: A flying chariot pulled by a giant ram
Design and manufacture of paraphernalia: Unrevealed

BIBLIOGRAPHY

First appearance: THOR ANNUAL #12
Origin issue: Vidar's origin is as yet unrevealed.
Significant issues: THOR ANNUAL #12 (alongside Thor, sought vengeance for the murder of his wife by Storm giants); MARVEL SUPER-HEROES Vol. 2 #5 (armed with Thor's power, fought as Asgard's champion against an alliance of the Storm Giants and Frost Giants)
Note: The original Vidar of Asgard appeared in THOR #293-294 in an account of how the original Asgard perished and how its nine survivors (including Vidar) gave birth to the present Odin, but this account may be apocryphal. In any case, this earlier Vidar was not the same person as the current Vidar.

VIPER™

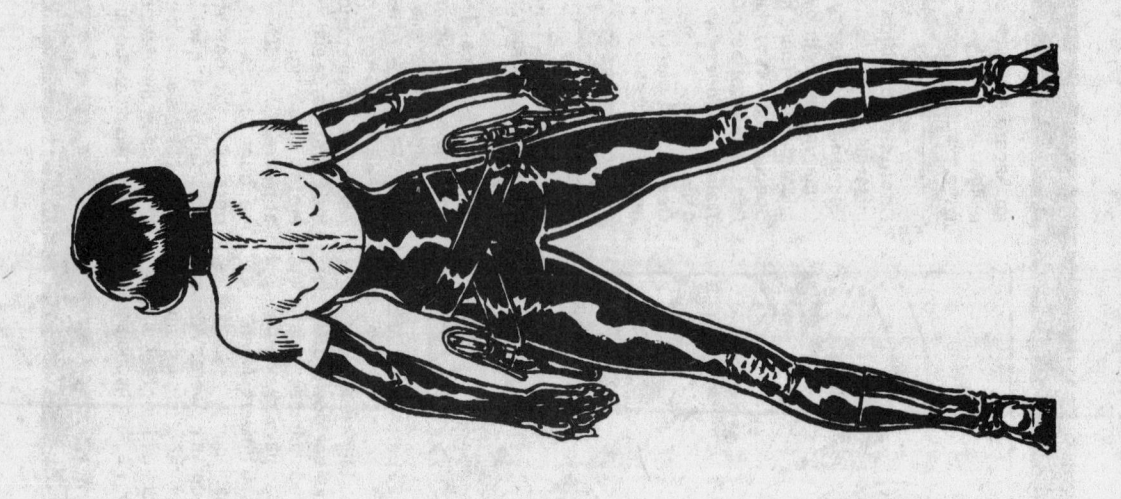

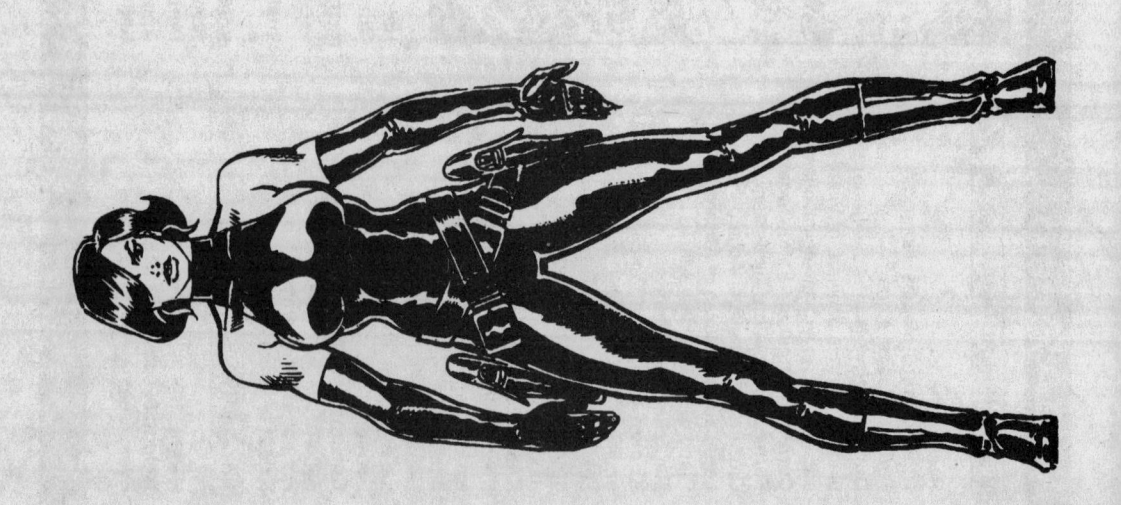

VIPER II

BIOGRAPHICAL DATA

Real name: Unrevealed
Other current aliases: None
Former aliases: Madame Hydra I, Mrs. Smith, Leona Hiss
Dual identity: The authorities have yet to determine her real name.
Current occupation: Terrorist, nihilist
Former occupation: Head of East Coast United States division of HYDRA
Citizenship: Unrevealed
Legal status: Criminal record in the U.S.
Place of birth: Somewhere in Eastern Europe
Marital status: Single
Known relatives: None
Known confidants: (former) Silver Samurai
Known allies: Slither, (former) the hordes of HYDRA, the Serpent Squad (Cobra, Eel, Princess Python), Warlord Krang, Ishiro Tagara, Boomerang, Constrictor
Major enemies: Captain America, Nomad III, Jessica Drew (Spider-Woman I), Nick Fury
Usual base of operations: Mobile
Former bases of operations: New York City; Big Sur, California; Hartsdale, Illinois
Current group membership: None
Former group membership: HYDRA, Serpent Squad I
Extent of education: Unrevealed

PHYSICAL DESCRIPTION

Height: 5' 9"
Weight: 141 lbs.
Eyes: Green
Hair: Black (tinted with green highlights)
Other distinguishing features: Scar tissue above and below her right eye, had caps put on her canines to make them sharp and elongated

POWERS AND ABILITIES

Intelligence: Above normal
Strength: Athlete
Speed: Athlete
Stamina: Athlete
Durability: Athlete
Agility: Athlete
Reflexes: Athlete
Fighting skills: Extensive training in hand-to-hand combat
Special skills and abilities: Extensive combat tactical experience
Superhuman physical powers: None. For a brief time Chthon replaced her right eye with a black orb capable of projecting persons into a magical dimension
Superhuman mental powers: None
Special limitations: None
Source of superhuman powers: None

PARAPHERNALIA

Costume specifications: Synthetic stretch fabric
Personal weaponry: Various ray pistols and conventional handguns; formerly possessed a teleportation ring
Special weaponry: Various as needed, including poison-tipped throwing darts, knives, whips
Other accessories: Inside the hollow caps of her teeth is a special poison to which she has an immunity.
Transportation: Various HYDRA vehicles, hover-sleds, teleportation ring
Design and manufacture of paraphernalia: Unrevealed

BIBLIOGRAPHY

First appearance: CAPTAIN AMERICA #110
Origin issue: CAPTAIN AMERICA #110
Significant issues: CAPTAIN AMERICA #110 (as Madame Hydra, fought and captured Captain America while trying to contaminate New York City's water supply); CAPTAIN AMERICA #111 (captured Rick Jones to bait trap for Captain America); CAPTAIN AMERICA #113 (subdued the Avengers with gas, battled Captain America); AVENGERS #107 (revealed that Space Phantom had exchanged places with her, current whereabouts undisclosed); CAPTAIN AMERICA #180-182 (murdered original Viper, assumed his name and leadership of Serpent Squad, kidnaped Roxxon president Hugh Jones in order to put him in thrall of the Serpent Crown, battled Nomad I and Namor the Sub-Mariner); MARVEL TEAM-UP #83-85 (took over SHIELD Helicarrier, planned to crash it into the Congress building, employed Boomerang and Silver Samurai as operatives, battled Spider-Man, Black Widow, Shang Chi, Nick Fury); SPIDER-WOMAN #42 (employed Silver Samurai as chief operative, attempted to kidnap Michael Kramer, a man carrying a fatal experimental disease, in order to release it on America, battled Spider-Woman I, became convinced that she was Spider-Woman's mother); SPIDER-WOMAN #44 (battled Spider-Woman, revealed herself to be pawn of Chthon for fifty years, saved Spider-Woman's life by defying Chthon); CAPTAIN AMERICA #281-283 (employing Constrictor as chief operative, captured Spider-Woman I, believing she was responsible for making her think they were related, captured Captain America, planned to release her new bubonic plague); NEW MUTANTS #5-6 (employing Silver Samurai, attempted to coerce Team America into stealing the cavourite crystal, battled New Mutants); CAPTAIN AMERICA #341-344 (with Slither, Copperhead, Puff Adder, Fer-De-Lance, and Black Racer as operatives, infiltrated Serpent Society in attempt to take it over, dispatched Cobra, Boomslang, and Copperhead to poison Washington D.C.'s water supply with snake mutagen, terrorized the White House and the President, battled Captain America); PUNISHER ANNUAL #2 (freed from prison by Tyrannus, used snake mutagen on drug addicts, battled the Punisher); DAREDEVIL ANNUAL #4 (battled Tyrannus)

VISHANTI™

VISHANTI

BIOGRAPHICAL DATA

Real names: Hoggoth, Oshtur, and Agamotto
Other current aliases: Hoggoth the Hoary, Lord of Hosts; Oshtur the Omnipotent, Lady of the Skies; Agamotto the All-Seeing, the Light of Truth
Former aliases: Unrevealed
Dual identities: Inapplicable, the general populace of Earth is unaware of the Vishanti's existence.
Current occupation: Mystical deities
Former occupations: (Hoggoth and Oshtur) Unrevealed, (Agamotto) First Sorceror Supreme of the Earth dimension
Citizenship: Inapplicable
Legal status: None
Place of birth: Unrevealed
Marital status: Unrevealed, possibly inapplicable
Known relatives: Unrevealed, possibly inapplicable
Known confidants: Unrevealed, besides one another
Known allies: The Ancient One, Doctor Strange, Eternity
Major enemies: Shuma-Gorath, Sligguth, Dormammu
Usual base of operations: Unknown extradimensional realms
Former bases of operations: (Hoggoth and Oshtur) Unrevealed, (Agamotto) the Earth dimension
Current group membership: The Vishanti
Former group membership: Unrevealed, if any
Extent of education: Unrevealed, possibly inapplicable

PHYSICAL DESCRIPTION

Height: Unrevealed, possibly inapplicable
Weight: Unrevealed, possibly inapplicable
Eyes: (Hoggoth) Blue, multi-faceted; (Oshtur) Blue-white, resembling stars; (Agamotto as lion or tiger) Red, resembling flames, (Agamotto as a caterpillar) Hazel
Hair: (Hoggoth) Sometimes silver, sometimes bald, (Oshtur) Usually auburn, (Agamotto as a lion) Golden brown, (Agamotto as a tiger) Orange with black markings, (Agamotto as a caterpillar) None
Other distinguishing features: (Hoggoth) Blue skin, pointed ears, (Oshtur) Green skin, (Agamotto as a lion or tiger) Golden skin, Image of an ankh on his brow, (Agamotto as a caterpillar) None
Note: The Vishanti have never appeared to any human, even those trained in the occult, in their true aspect, which no mortal mind could comprehend and remain sane, instead appearing in a variety of disguised physical forms. It is their most frequently adopted forms that the above statistics apply.

POWERS AND ABILITIES

Intelligence: Immeasurable
Strength: Incalculable
Speed: Unrevealed, perhaps inapplicable
Flight speed: Warp speed
Stamina: Immeasurable
Durability: Godlike
Agility: Unrevealed, perhaps inapplicable
Reflexes: Unrevealed, perhaps inapplicable
Fighting skills: Inapplicable
Special skills: Unrevealed, perhaps inapplicable
Superhuman physical powers: Vast ability to manipulate magical energies for virtually any purpose
Superhuman mental powers: Same as above
Special limitations: None known
Source of superhuman powers: Manipulation of the forces of magic

PARAPHERNALIA

Costume specifications: Inapplicable
Personal weaponry: Inapplicable
Special weaponry: Inapplicable
Other accessories: (Vishanti) The Book of the Vishanti, a treatise on magic compiled by the Vishanti, which besides containing countless spells and other mystic lore, is itself a powerful magical icon whose mere physical presence repulses spells hurled against it; attained by the Ancient One many years ago by time-traveling to ancient Babylonia, it is currently held by Doctor Strange; (Agamotto) the Orb of Agamotto, a large crystal orb which allows the user to view events of mystical significance occurring throughout his sphere of influence; the Eye of Agamotto, an amulet which allows the wearer to become his "third eye", allowing him to execute mystical mental probes of persons and objects; all of which were long ago presented to the Ancient One by Eternity and are currently possessed by Doctor Strange.
Transportation: Interdimensional teleportation, flight in astral form
Design and manufacture of paraphernalia: Inapplicable

BIBLIOGRAPHY

First appearance: (first invoked) STRANGE TALES Vol. 1 #115; (first appeared) MARVEL PREMIERE #5
Origin issue: Origins is as yet unrevealed
Significant issues: MARVEL PREMIERE #5 (Vishanti, summoned by Dr. Strange to aid him against Sligguth, the minion of Shuma-Gorath); FANTASTIC FOUR ANNUAL #23 (appeared to Kubik and Kosmos on their tour of the planes of existence); DR. STRANGE Vol. 2 #1-2, 4-5 (Agamotto, appeared Dr. Strange as a talking caterpillar in the world within his amulet, became the jailer of Silver Dagger after he was banished there)

VISION™

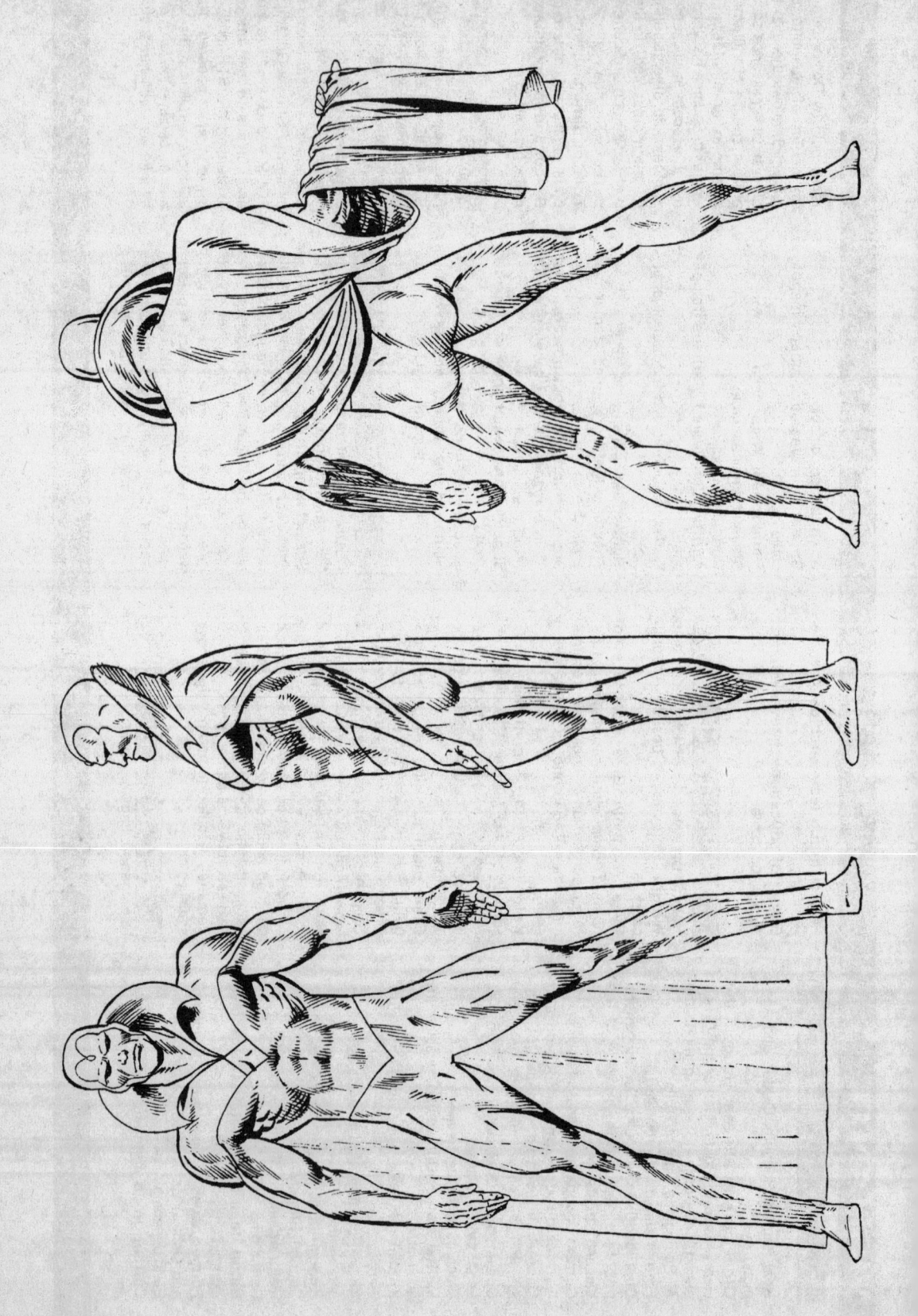

VISION II

BIOGRAPHICAL DATA

Real name: The Vision
Other current aliases: None
Former aliases: Victor Shade
Note: The Vision was formerly believed to have once been the original android Human Torch, who used the alias Jim Hammond. Also, the Vision was originally programmed with the brain patterns of Simon Williams (Wonder Man), and later reprogrammed with the brain patterns of the late Alex Lipton.
Dual identity: Currently none
Current occupation: Adventurer
Former occupations: Servant of Ultron
Citizenship: Unrevealed, presumably the Vision is considered a citizen of the United States of America, although this has never been legally contested.
Legal status: No criminal record
Place of creation: Unrevealed, presumably somewhere in New York City area
Marital status: Separated
Known relatives: Wanda Maximoff (Scarlet Witch, estranged wife), Magneto (father-in-law), Pietro Maximoff (Quicksilver, brother-in-law), Crystal Maximoff (sister-in-law), Luna Maximoff (niece), Simon Williams (Wonder Man, "brother"), Eric Williams (Grim Reaper, "brother", deceased), Martha Williams (adoptive mother), Thomas, William ("sons", now non-existent)
Known confidants: (former) Wanda Maximoff (Scarlet Witch), Dr. Miles Lipton (deceased)
Known allies: The Avengers, the Avengers West Coast, the Fantastic Four, Daredevil, Spider-Man, Dr. Strange, the Silver Surfer
Major enemies: Ultron, the Grim Reaper, Kang, Necrodamus, Quasimodo, the Mad Thinker, the Kree, the Skrulls
Usual base of operations: Avengers Mansion, New York City
Former bases of operations: Avengers West Coast Compound
Current group membership: Avengers
Former group membership: Avengers West Coast
Extent of programming: Capacity for creative intelligence and unlimited self-motivated activity, (formerly) capacity for human-like emotions

PHYSICAL DESCRIPTION

Height: 6'3"
Weight: (normal) 300 lbs., variable down to 0 lbs. and up to 90 tons
Eyes: Gold, (formerly) Red
Hair: None
Other distinguishing features: The Vision's entire body was once pale yellow and prior to that completely red, it is unclear whether his current red facial skin color is indicative of his entire body; he has audial receptors instead of ears, and a solar jewel mounted on his brow

POWERS AND ABILITIES

Intelligence: Above normal
Strength: Superhuman Class 75
Speed: Superhuman
Flight speed: Directed motion hovering
Stamina: Superhuman
Durability: Metahuman
Agility: Enhanced human
Reflexes: Superhuman
Fighting skills: Trained in unarmed combat by Captain America, expert in combat use of his superhuman powers
Special skills: Expert on his own construction and repair, highly skilled tactician and strategist
Superhuman physical powers: Aside from the above listed attributes, Vision has the ability to control his density by interfacing with an unknown dimension to/from which he can shunt or accrue mass, thus becoming either intangible or extraordinarily massive and diamond hard; he can partially materialize within another person, causing his victim extreme pain; the ability to fire beams of infrared and microwave radiation with temperatures from 500 to 30,000 degrees F. from his eyes
Superhuman mental powers: Superhuman analytical capabilities, ability to process information and make calculations with superhuman speed and accuracy
Special limitations: None
Source of superhuman powers: Design and construction of artificial materials as a synthetic being

PARAPHERNALIA

Costume specifications: Unknown materials incorporating unstable molecules
Personal weaponry: None
Special weaponry: None
Other accessories: Solar Jewel (absorbs ambient solar energy, converts it for use as an energy source, and expels excess energy in the form of infrared and microwave radiation)
Transportation: Flight under own power or Avengers Quinjet
Design and manufacture of paraphernalia: (original costume and solar jewel) Ultron, (second costume) Vision and Henry Pym, (new costume) Unrevealed, (quinjet) Tony Stark

BIBLIOGRAPHY

First appearance: AVENGERS #57
Origin issue: AVENGERS #58, 135; AVENGERS WEST COAST #50
Significant issues: AVENGERS #57 (sent by Ultron to lead Avengers into a trap, aided the Avengers against Ultron); AVENGERS #58 (learned how Ultron created him using Wonder Man's brain patterns, joined the Avengers); AVENGERS #66-68 (temporarily controlled by Ultron, rebuilt Ultron of adamantium, battled Avengers); AVENGERS #76 (first met the Scarlet Witch); AVENGERS #108-109 (began romance with Scarlet Witch)

VOICE™

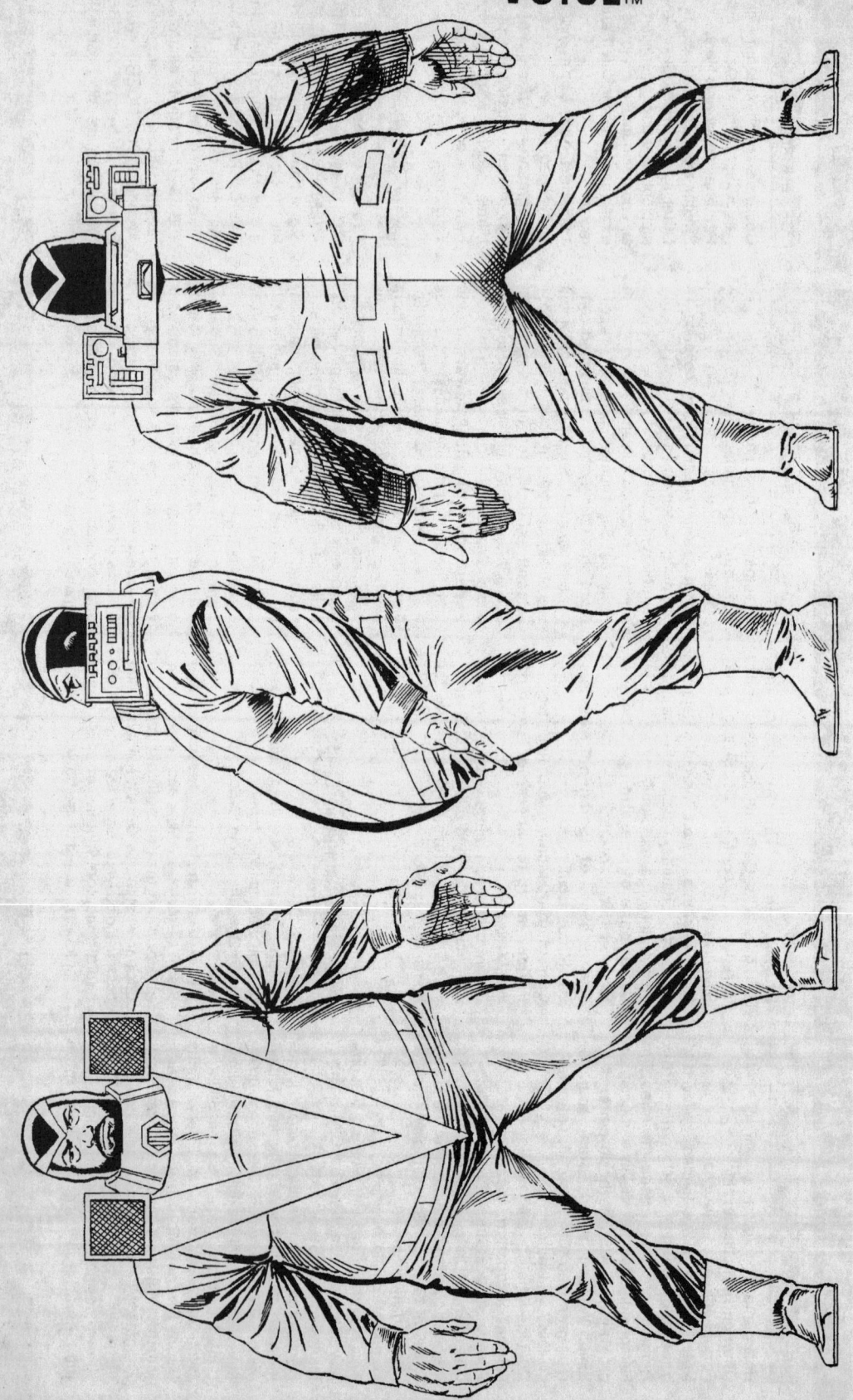

VOICE

BIOGRAPHICAL DATA

Real name: Jason Lorne Cragg
Other current aliases: None
Former aliases: The Voice of Truth, the man with the Voice of Doom
Dual identity: Publicly known
Current occupation: Professional criminal, agent of the Red Skull
Former occupation: Radio announcer, professional orator, Soviet agent
Citizenship: United States of America
Legal status: No known criminal record
Place of birth: Gary, Indiana
Marital status: Single
Known relatives: None
Known confidants: None
Known allies: The Red Skull, Crossbones, the Skeleton Crew, the Controller, (former) Madame X, El Toro, the Beasts of Berlin, the Scarlet Beetles, Quicksilver
Major enemies: Dr. Pym, Captain America, Avengers West Coast, Magneto, the Black Queen, the Hellfire Club
Usual base of operations: Mobile
Former bases of operations: New York City
Current group membership: None
Former group membership: Skeleton Crew
Extent of education: High school graduate

PHYSICAL DESCRIPTION

Height: 5'10"
Weight: 200 lbs.
Eyes: Brown
Hair: Brown
Other distinguishing features: None

POWERS AND ABILITIES

Intelligence: Normal
Strength: Normal
Speed: Normal
Stamina: Normal
Durability: Normal
Agility: Normal
Reflexes: Normal
Fighting skills: Minimal
Special skills and abilities: None known
Superhuman physical powers: Ability to cause anyone within the sound of his voice to believe he is speaking the truth and to obey his every command
Superhuman mental powers: None
Special limitations: None
Source of superhuman powers: Exposure to "ionized atom" radiation (possibly triggering latent mutant power); later microsurgery on tongue and vocal cords

PARAPHERNALIA

Costume specifications: Synthetic stretch fabric and body armor including neck brace supporting vocal amplifier
Personal weaponry: None
Special weaponry: None
Other accessories: A specially modified digital precision vocal amplifier worn atop shoulders supported by neck brace (enhances the power and range of the Voice's influence)
Transportation: Various vehicles and aircraft supplied by the Red Skull
Design and manufacture of paraphernalia: Unnamed technicians employed by the Red Skull

BIBLIOGRAPHY

First appearance: TALES TO ASTONISH Vol. 1 #42
Origin issue: TALES TO ASTONISH Vol. 1 #42
Significant issues: TALES TO ASTONISH Vol. 1 #42 (gained superhuman power, incited hate campaign against Ant-Man I, infected with laryngitis); WEST COAST AVENGERS Vol. 2 #36 (regained superhuman powers through microsurgery, became Soviet agent; alongside Quicksilver, forced the West Coast Avengers to battle Dr. Pym); WEST COAST AVENGERS Vol. 2 #37 (forced Mantis to battle West Coast Avengers, defeated by Hawkeye, sent to the Vault), CAPTAIN AMERICA #366 (with Crossbones, sent by the Red Skull to retrieve the Controller; alongside Crossbones and the Controller, battled Captain America); CAPTAIN AMERICA #369-370 (alongside the Skeleton Crew, searched for missing Red Skull; injured in battle with the Black Queen and Hellfire Club mercenaries)
Note: Jason Cragg is not to be confused with David Angar, alias Angar the Screamer, who once used the alias of the Voice.

VOLCANA

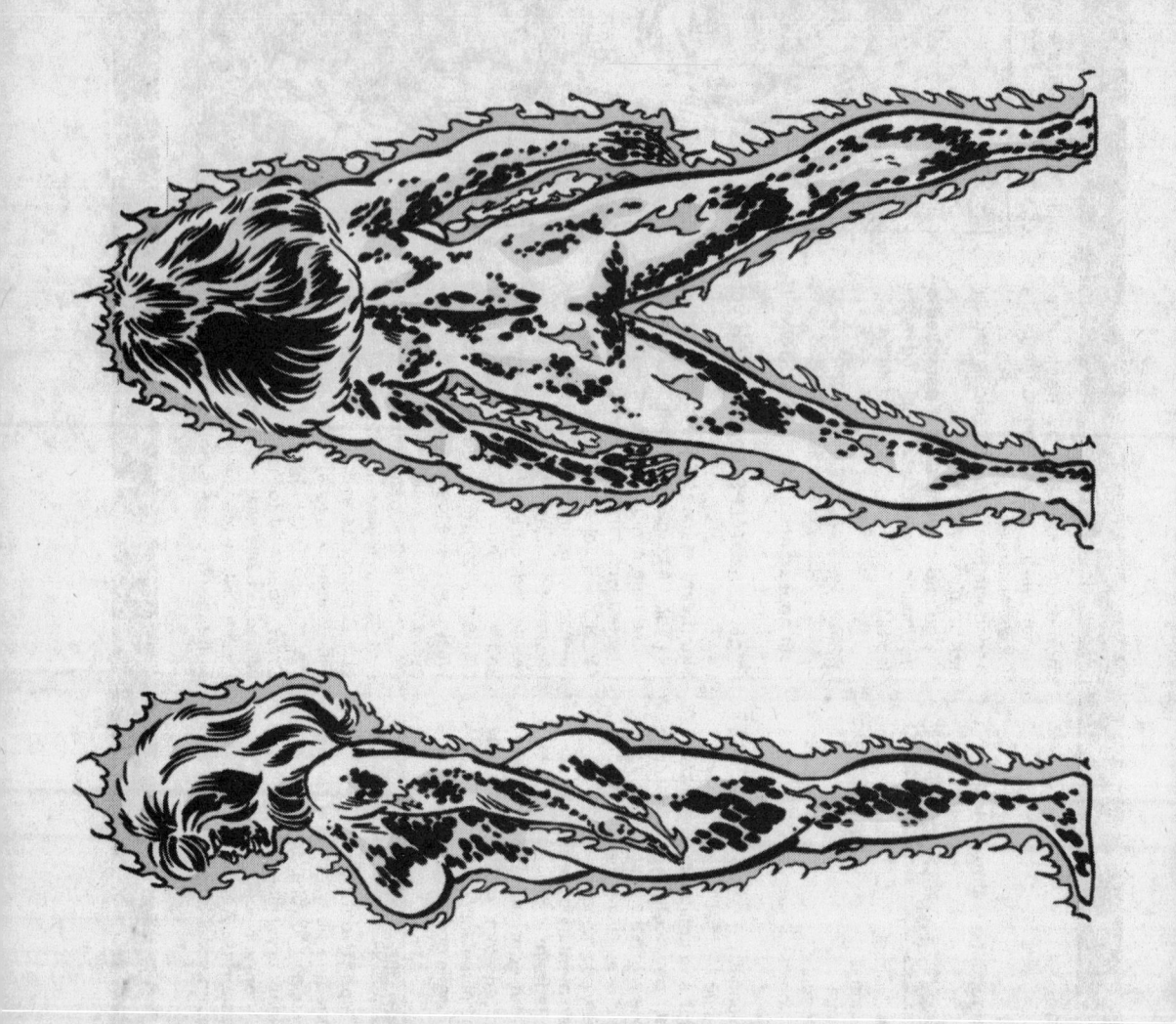

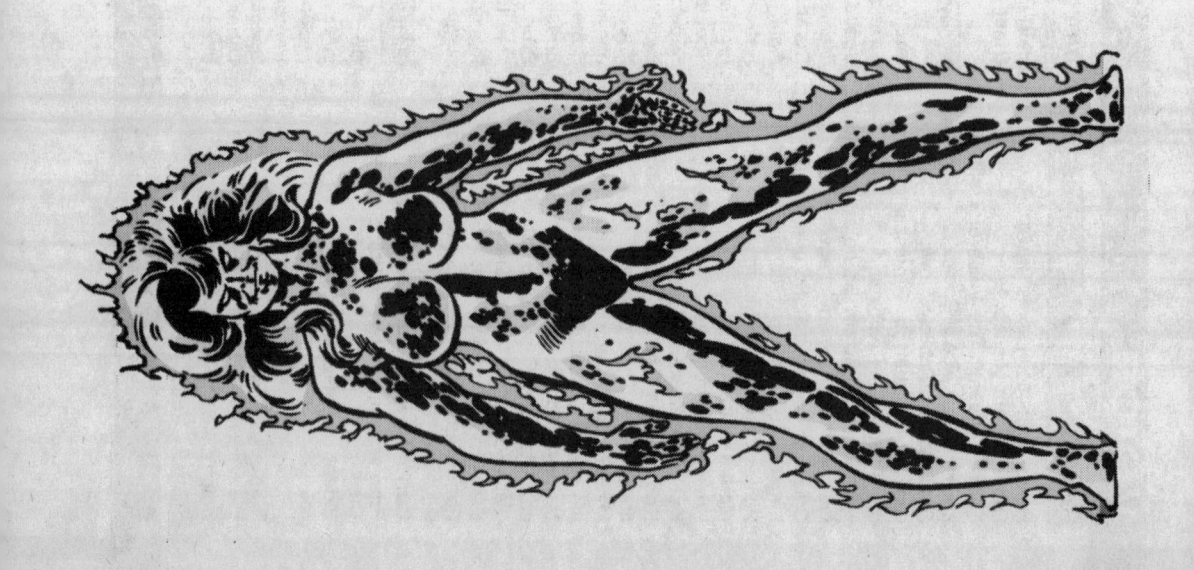

VOLCANA

BIOGRAPHICAL DATA

Real name: Marsha Rosenberg
Other current aliases: None
Former aliases: None
Dual identity: Secret
Current occupation: Day care center employee
Former occupation: Unrevealed
Citizenship: United States of America
Legal status: No criminal record
Place of birth: Denver, Colorado
Marital status: Single
Known relatives: None
Known confidants: Molecule Man
Known allies: (former) Dr. Doom, Ultron, Dr. Octopus, the Absorbing Man, the Enchantress, Kang, Wrecker, Piledriver, Thunderball, Bulldozer
Major enemies: The Enchantress
Usual base of operations: New York City
Former bases of operations: Unrevealed
Current group membership: None
Former group membership: None
Extent of education: High school graduate

PHYSICAL DESCRIPTION

Height: 6' 5"
Weight: 210 lbs.
Eyes: (in human form) Blue, (in plasma, stone, and ash forms) White with no pupils
Hair: (in human form) Black, (in plasma form) White, (in stone and ash form) Gray
Other distinguishing features: None

POWERS AND ABILITIES

Intelligence: Normal
Strength: (stone form) Superhuman Class 50
Speed: Normal
Stamina: Normal
Durability: (as Marsha) Normal, (as Volcana) Superhuman
Agility: Normal
Reflexes: Normal
Fighting skills: None
Special skills and abilities: None
Superhuman physical powers: The ability to convert her entire body into three distinct forms, 1) Plasma: highly charged particles which surround her in white-hot flame and is able to emit controlled bursts of thermal energy (in excess of 5000° Fahrenheit) up to 40 feet, 2) Stone: a volcanic rock (basalt) -like composition which still enables movement and grants her superhuman strength. 3) Ash: a volcanic ash (pumice) -like composition whose configuration she can shift, shape and control at will. She has normal human strength in this form.
Superhuman mental powers: None
Special limitations: Volcana cannot make partial transformations; she can possess the attributes of only one of her forms at a time. Monitoring devices subcutaneously implanted by Doctor Doom can be triggered to stimulate the aggression centers of her brain.
Source of superhuman powers: Genetic manipulation by highly advanced alien technology performed by Doctor Doom

Note: The alien technology that empowered her make her powers totally undetectable when she is in human form.

PARAPHERNALIA

Costume specifications: Volcana has no costume per se; however, Marsha Rosenberg's clothing is manufactured from unstable molecules; thus, it is not destroyed when she is in her plasma form.
Personal weaponry: None
Special weaponry: None
Other accessories: None
Transportation: Various
Design and manufacture of paraphernalia: Inapplicable

BIBLIOGRAPHY

First appearance: MARVEL SUPER HEROES SECRET WARS #3
Origin issue: MARVEL SUPER HEROES SECRET WARS #3
Significant issues: MARVEL SUPER HEROES SECRET WARS #3 (gained superhuman powers; allied herself with Doctor Doom and criminal faction, battled She-Hulk); MARVEL SUPER HEROES SECRET WARS #4 (befriended the Molecule Man); MARVEL SUPER HEROES SECRET WARS #6 (bargained with the Enchantress); MARVEL SUPER HEROES SECRET WARS #12 (battled Enchantress with intent to renege on bargain); SECRET WARS II #1 (took up residence on Earth with Owen Reece; hosted Beyonder upon his arrival on Earth); SECRET WARS II #8 (tricked Molecule Man into challenging the Beyonder); SECRET WARS II #9 (participated in defeat of the Beyonder); AVENGERS #265 (assisted Avengers in repairing damage to Earth's crust caused by Beyonder); FANTASTIC FOUR #319 (accompanied Molecule Man and Fantastic Four to Beyonder's universe; separated from Molecule Man); FANTASTIC FOUR ANNUAL #23 (battled Moonstone, first use of stone form); FANTASTIC FOUR ANNUAL #24 (battled Klaw, first use of ash form)

VOLSTAGG

VOLSTAGG

BIOGRAPHICAL DATA

Real name: Volstagg
Other current aliases: Volstagg the Enormous, Volstagg the Voluminous, the Lion of Asgard
Former aliases: None
Dual identity: None; the general populace of Earth is aware of Volstagg's existence but does not acknowledge his godhood.
Current occupation: Warrior of Asgard, parent, adventurer
Former occupation: Warrior, adventurer
Citizenship: Realm of Asgard
Legal status: No criminal record
Place of birth: Asgard
Marital status: Married
Known relatives: Hildegund (wife), Alaric, Rolfe (sons), Flosi, Gudrun, Gunnhild ["Hildy"] (daughters), Kevin, Mick (adopted sons)
Known confidants: Hogun, Fandral, Balder, Thor
Known allies: Fandral, Hogun, Thor, Balder, Odin, Sif, Heimdall, Beta Ray Bill
Major enemies: Loki, Fafnir, Surtur, Mangog, Ymir, Seth
Usual base of operations: Asgard
Former bases of operations: None
Current group membership: The Warriors Three (with Hogun and Fandral)
Former group membership: None
Extent of education: Unrevealed

PHYSICAL DESCRIPTION

Height: 6' 8"
Weight: 1,425 lbs.
Eyes: Blue
Hair: Red
Other distinguishing features: Volstagg is extremely obese.

POWERS AND ABILITIES

Intelligence: Normal
Strength: Superhuman Class 50
Speed: Athlete, (in his prime) Superhuman
Stamina: Superhuman
Durability: Superhuman
Agility: Athlete, (in his prime) Superhuman
Reflexes: Peak human, (in his prime) Superhuman
Fighting skills: Above average hand-to-hand combatant, swordsman, and horseman, (in his prime) superb hand-to-hand combatant, swordsman, and horseman; expert with quarterstaff
Special skills and abilities: Unrevealed
Superhuman physical powers: Aside from the above listed attributes, none
Superhuman mental powers: None
Special limitations: Volstagg's battle prowess is somewhat limited by his advanced age and tremendous girth. However, he can still use his sheer bulk to his advantage in combat.
Source of superhuman powers: Volstagg is a member of the race of superhumans known as Asgardians.

PARAPHERNALIA

Costume specifications: Asgardian fabric
Personal weaponry: Sword
Special weaponry: None, (in his prime) Quarterstaff
Other accessories: None
Transportation: Horse, Asgardian Starjammer
Design and manufacture of paraphernalia: Forges of Asgard

BIBLIOGRAPHY

First appearance: JOURNEY INTO MYSTERY #119
Origin issue: Volstagg's origin is as yet unrevealed.
Significant issues: (appears with the Warriors Three unless otherwise noted): JOURNEY INTO MYSTERY #119 (joined Thor's quest for the power that had cracked the Oversword of Asgard); JOURNEY INTO MYSTERY #124-125 (helped repel attack of Flying Trolls of Thryheim); THOR #129-131 (helped defeat the forces of Harokin); THOR #134-136 (battled the dragon Fafnir); THOR #137-145 (defeated Mogul of the Mystic Mountain); THOR #155-157 (helped defend Asgard against Mangog); THOR #169-170 (battled the Thermal Man); THOR #175-176 (among forces of Asgard defeated by Loki); THOR #177 (helped defend Asgard against Surtur); THOR #180-181 (helped Thor escape Mephisto); THOR #185-188 (entranced by Infinity, forced to battle Thor; battled Balder, Sif, and other Asgardians; freed from trance by Loki and Karnilla; joined life force to awaken Odin in time to defeat Infinity); THOR #195-198 (sent on quest by Odin, returned to help defend Asgard against Mangog); THOR #202-205 (battled Ego-Prime, exiled to Earth, abducted by Mephisto, freed by Thor); THOR #208-217 (with Thor and company, set out on quest to find missing Odin; battled Ssssthgar's slavers, Mercurio, and Xorr; defeated doppelgangers created by wizard Igron); THOR #242-245 (battled Zarrko the Tomorrow Man); MARVEL SPOTLIGHT Vol. 1 #30 (defeated diamond exchange robbers in New York); THOR #248-250 (helped depose usurpers Mangog and Igron); THOR #255-263 (again set out on quest to find missing Odin; battled Sporr, Grey Gargoyle, and Soul-Survivors); THOR #264-266 (defeated Executioner and Enchantress; battled Destroyer and Loki); THOR #274-278 (helped defend Asgard against Ragnarok); THOR #287-288 (battled Fafnir); MARVEL FANFARE #13 (rescued Mord); AVENGERS #249/THOR #350-352 (battled forces of Surtur on Earth); THOR #377-378 (overcome by mystery plague); THOR #393 (helped defend Asgard against the forces of Seth); MARVEL FANFARE #36 (went alone on quest to rescue Mord); THOR #404-406 (went on quest with Thor to seek Ulagg); AVENGERS #310 (helped Avengers battle Blastarr); THOR #421-426 (battled Ymir and Surtur); THOR #434 (attempted to prevent Thor II from entering Asgard)

VULTURE™

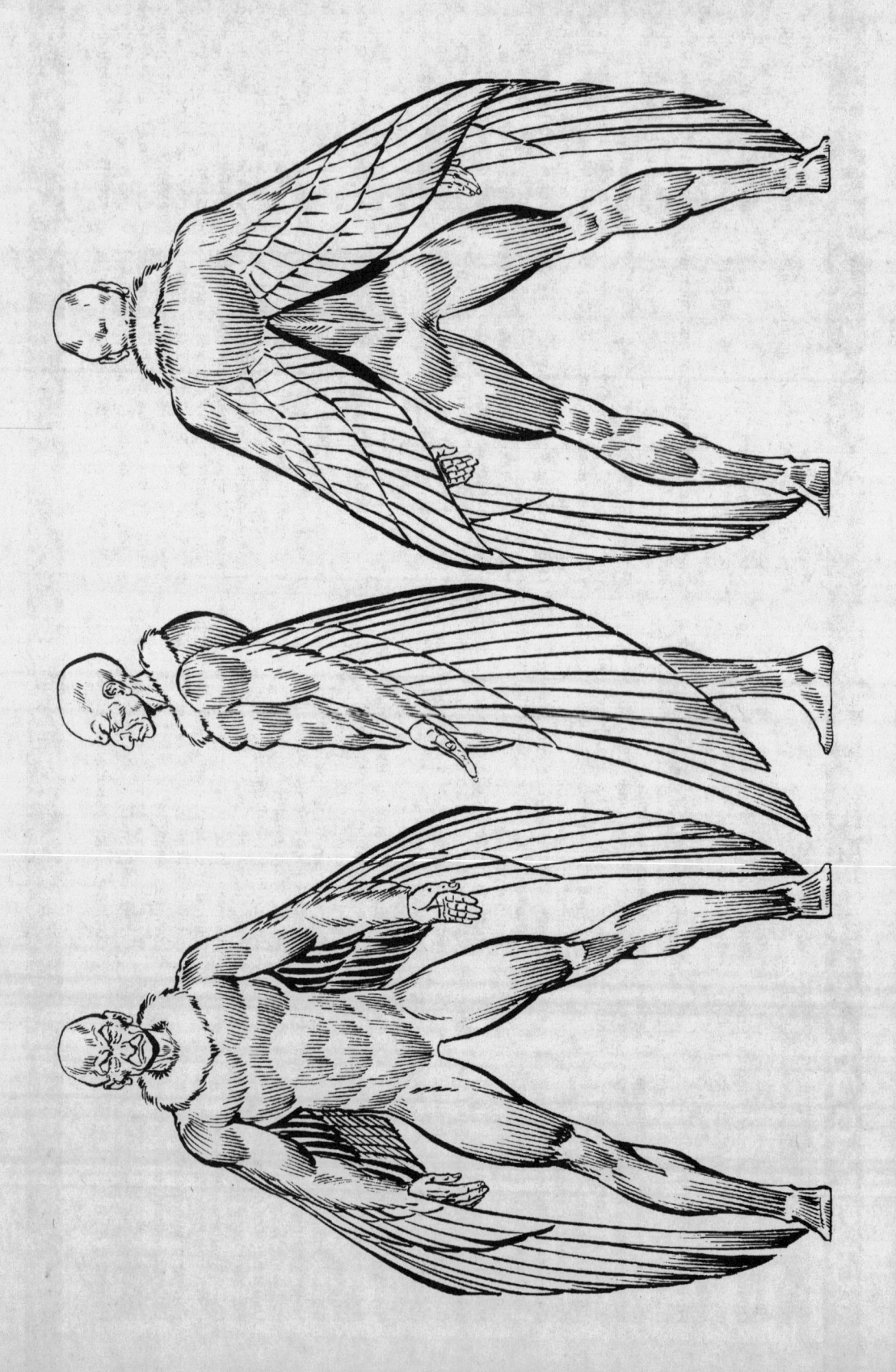

VULTURE

BIOGRAPHICAL DATA

Real name: Adrian Toomes
Other current aliases: None
Former aliases: None
Dual identity: Publicly known
Current occupation: Professional criminal
Former occupation: Electronics engineer
Citizenship: United States of America
Legal status: Criminal record in the United States
Place of birth: Staten Island, New York
Marital status: Widowed
Known relatives: Malachi Toomes (nephew, deceased)
Known confidants: None
Known allies: Sinister Six I (Doctor Octopus, Electro, Kraven, Mysterio, Sandman), Sinister Six II (Doctor Octopus, Electro, Hobgoblin, Mysterio, Sandman)
Major enemies: Spider-Man, Gregory Bestman, Blackie Drago, Mr. Morgan, the Vulturians
Usual base of operations: New York City
Former bases of operations: None
Current group membership: Sinister Six II
Former group membership: Sinister Six I
Extent of education: Master of Science degree in electrical engineering

PHYSICAL DESCRIPTION

Height: 5' 11"
Weight: 175 lbs.
Eyes: Hazel
Hair: Bald
Other distinguishing features: The Vulture's aged features, hunched body, bald head, and hooked nose make him resemble the bird of his namesake.

POWERS AND ABILITIES

Intelligence: Gifted
Strength: (without electromagnetic harness) Normal, (augmented by harness) Peak human
Speed: Natural winged flight limit
Stamina: (without electromagnetic harness) Normal, (augmented by harness) Peak human
Durability: Normal
Agility: Normal
Reflexes: Normal
Fighting skills: Minimal
Special skills and abilities: The Vulture is a brilliant electronics engineer with a great talent for invention
Superhuman physical powers: None
Superhuman mental powers: None
Special limitations: The Vulture is elderly and depends on his electromagnetic harness to augment his strength, vitality, and athletic prowess
Source of superhuman powers: None

PARAPHERNALIA

Costume specifications: Synthetic stretch fabric housing a tailored electromagnetic harness with bird-like wings attached beneath the arms.
Personal weaponry: Electromagnetic anti-graviton generator worn on his body as a harness enabling him to fly silently for periods up to 6 hours at a maximum altitude of 11,000 feet with precise maneuverability.
Special weaponry: None
Other accessories: None
Transportation: Flight via harness
Design and manufacture of paraphernalia: Adrian Toomes

BIBLIOGRAPHY

First appearance: AMAZING SPIDER-MAN #2
Origin issue: AMAZING SPIDER-MAN #2
Significant issues: AMAZING SPIDER-MAN #2 (first encountered Spider-Man during jewelry heist); AMAZING SPIDER-MAN #7 (modified harness, attempted to rob the Daily Bugle payroll); AMAZING SPIDER-MAN ANNUAL #1 (joined Doctor Octopus's first Sinister Six); AMAZING SPIDER-MAN #48 (believed himself to be dying in prison, revealed location of an extra Vulture outfit to cellmate Blackie Drago who became second Vulture); AMAZING SPIDER-MAN #49 (Drago, as the Vulture, teamed with Kraven against Spider-Man); AMAZING SPIDER-MAN #63 (Toomes defeated Drago); AMAZING SPIDER-MAN #64 (defeated Spider-Man in battle); AMAZING SPIDER-MAN #127-128 (Dr. Clifton Shallot mutated his body into form resembling Toome's, but possessing natural wings and flight capability); SPECTACULAR SPIDER-MAN #4-5 (humiliated racketeering mobster, Mr. Morgan, trying to rob the Vulture of his revenge); SPECTACULAR SPIDER-MAN #44-45 (arranged the murder of New York's top mobsters to become New York's new crimelord, battled Spider-Man); AMAZING SPIDER-MAN #224 (escaped prison, battled Spider-Man); AMAZING SPIDER-MAN #240-241 (came out of retirement to claim vengeance on Gregory Bestman, his former research partner who embezzled him out of the profits); WEB OF SPIDER-MAN #1-2 (confronted the Vulturians, a group of youths who stole his designs); WEB OF SPIDER-MAN #24 (became involved in Atlantic City casino racketeering to prepare for his own ostentatious funeral, but thwarted by the Hobgoblin); WEB OF SPIDER-MAN #45 (moved gambling operations to Las Vegas, where he attacked Snake Diamond in the middle of the desert for stealing his formula for a special embalming fluid); NEW MUTANTS #86 (confronted mutants Rusty Collins and Skids in an attempt to release Nitro); AMAZING SPIDER-MAN #336-339 (joined Doctor Octopus's new Sinister Six, killed Nathan Lubensky)

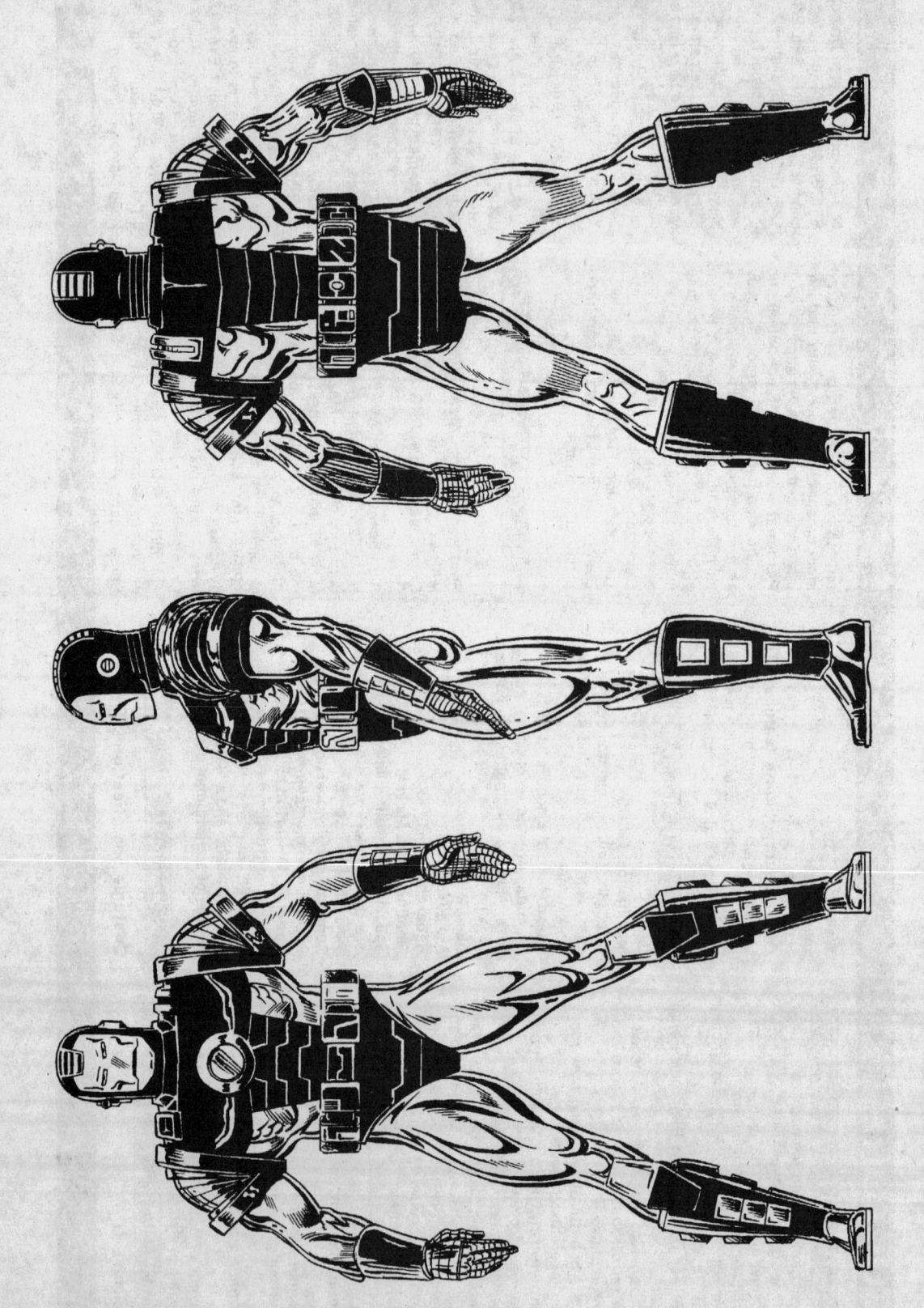

WAR MACHINE™

WAR MACHINE

BIOGRAPHICAL DATA

Real name: James R. Rhodes
Other current aliases: "Rhodey"
Former aliases: Iron Man IV
Dual identity: Secret
Current occupation: Adventurer
Former occupation: United States Marine, pilot, aviation engineer, co-owner of Circuits Maximus, president and CEO of Stark International
Legal status: Citizen of United States of America with no criminal record
Place of birth: Philadelphia, Pennsylvania
Marital status: Single
Known relatives: Unnamed mother
Known confidants: Tony Stark (Iron Man I), (former) Morley Erwin (deceased), Clytemnestra Erwin (deceased)
Known allies: Iron Man I, Avengers West Coast, Bethany Cabe, the Eternals, Shaman, Force I, Spider-Man, the Masters of Silence, Rae La Costa
Major enemies: Justin Hammer, Roxxon Oil, the Mandarin, the Maggia, AIM, the Ghost, the Dreadnoughts, the Beetle, Blacklash, Blizzard II, Boomerang, Spymaster II; (former) Madame Masque I (deceased), Spymaster I (deceased), Obadiah Stane (Iron-Monger I, deceased), Fin Fang Foom (presumed deceased)
Usual base of operations: Avengers West Coast Compound, Los Angeles California
Former bases of operations: Stark Enterprises complex, Silicon Valley, California; Stark International main plant, Long Island, New York; Circuits Maximus, Silicon Valley, California
Current group membership: Avengers West Coast
Former group membership: None
Extent of education: High school graduate, learned aviation engineering in the U.S. Marines

PHYSICAL DESCRIPTION

Height: 6' 1", (with armor) 6' 6"
Weight: 210 lbs., (with armor) 450 lbs.
Eyes: Brown
Hair: Brown
Other distinguishing features: None

POWERS AND ABILITIES

Intelligence: Above normal
Strength: Normal, (with armor) Superhuman Class 90
Speed: Athlete
Flight speed: (with armor) Supersonic
Stamina: Athlete
Durability: Athlete
Agility: Athlete
Reflexes: Athlete
Fighting skills: (as Rhodes) Trained in armed and unarmed combat as a U.S. Marine, (as Iron Man) experience in unique fighting style which takes advantage of his armor's specialized powers.
Special skills: Highly skilled athlete, superb aircraft pilot, expert marksman

Superhuman physical powers: None
Superhuman mental powers: None
Special limitations: None
Source of superhuman powers: Inapplicable

PARAPHERNALIA

Costume specifications: Armored battlesuit

Personal weaponry: War Machine's armor contains a powered exoskeleton greatly amplifying the user's strength. The suit contains various offensive weaponry, including repulsor rays (particle beams), uni-beam (includes visible light, infrared, ultraviolet, tractor, laser, and image inducer), and pulse bolts (plasma discharges); and defensive weaponry, including energy shield (laser absorption grid), electromagnetic pulse (energy-dampening field), and targeting computer

Special weaponry: Various, as needed, including shoulder-mounted gatling gun assembly, wrist-mounted laser blade, shoulder-mounted micro-rocket launcher and wrist-mounted particle beam discharger

Other accessories: Self contained air supply for 1.2 hours

Transportation: Flight, via electrically powered turbines in boots and jetpack

Design and manufacture of paraphernalia: Anthony Stark

BIBLIOGRAPHY

First appearance: (as Rhodes) IRON MAN #120, (as Iron Man IV) IRON MAN #170, (as War Machine) IRON MAN #284
Origin issue: (as Rhodes) IRON MAN #144, (as Iron Man IV) IRON MAN #170, (as War Machine) IRON MAN #284
Significant issues: IRON MAN #144 (as Rhodes, first encountered Iron Man I; alongside Iron Man I, attacked a Viet Cong rocket base; offered a job as pilot by Tony Stark); IRON MAN #169-170 (donned the Iron Man armor and became Iron Man IV, battled Magma Man when Tony Stark was incapacitated); WEST COAST AVENGERS Vol. 2 #1-4 (joined the West Coast Avengers; alongside them, battled Graviton and the Blank); IRON MAN #199-200 (injured in bomb blast by Obadiah Stane; forsook Iron Man identity); IRON MAN #284 (named CEO of Stark Enterprises and given War Machine armor)

Note: Jim Rhodes was the fourth Iron Man, counting as "official Iron Men" only Tony Stark and those who have worn the armor to substitute for him at his behest. Happy Hogan was Iron Man II and Eddie March was Iron Man III. Not counted are Michael O'Brien, who wore the armor for a good cause but without Stark's consent, Force I, who once wore the identity of Iron Man, "Weasel" Willis, a thief who once stole the armor, and the renegade Tony Stark LMD who once posed as both Stark and Iron Man.

WARLOCK, ADAM.

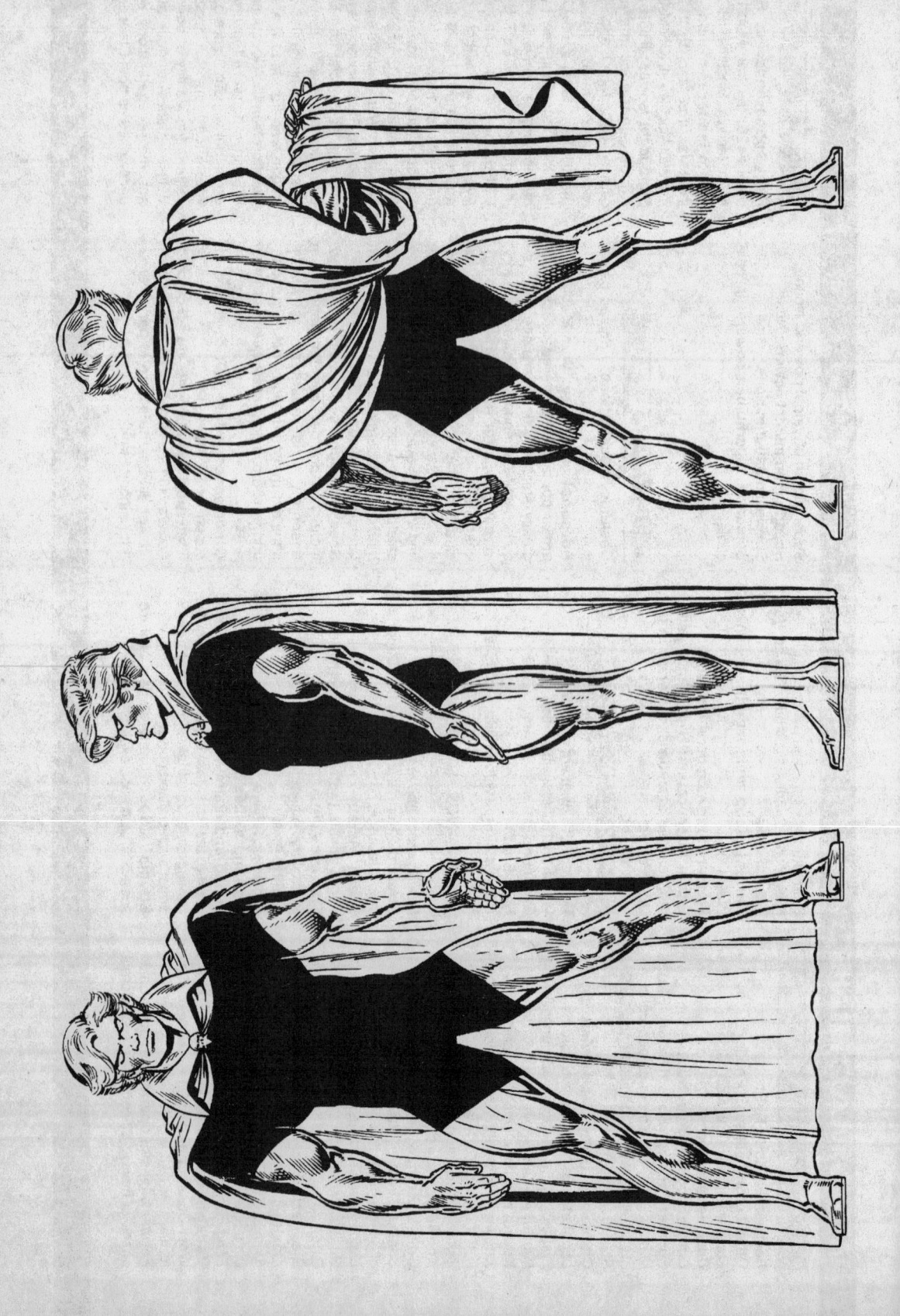

WARLOCK, ADAM

BIOGRAPHICAL DATA

Real name: Adam Warlock
Other current aliases: None
Former aliases: Him
Dual Identity: None
Current occupation: Unrevealed
Former occupation: Avenger, savior of worlds
Citizenship: None
Legal status: No criminal record
Place of creation: The Beehive, Shard Island, Atlantic Ocean
Marital status: Single
Known relatives: Her (genetic "twin")
Known confidants: Pip the Troll, Gamora
Known allies: High Evolutionary, the Avengers, Spider-Man, the Thing, Doctor Strange, Silver Surfer, Pip the Troll, Gamora, Drax the Destroyer, Thanos
Major enemies: Magus, Thanos, Star-Thief I, Man-Beast, Nebula
Usual base of operations: The known universe
Former bases of operations: The pocket universe within the Soul Gem; Counter-Earth
Current group membership: Infinity Watch
Former group membership: None
Extent of education: Self-taught

PHYSICAL DESCRIPTION

Height: 6' 2"
Weight: 240 lbs.
Eyes: Red, no visible whites
Hair: Gold
Other distinguishing features: Golden hued skin

POWERS AND ABILITIES

Intelligence: Above normal
Strength: Superhuman Class 10, (enhanced by cosmic energy) Superhuman Class 50
Flight speed: Supersonic, (enhanced by cosmic energy) Warp speed
Stamina: Enhanced human
Durability: Metahuman
Agility: Enhanced human
Reflexes: Enhanced human
Fighting skills: Minimal experience in hand-to-hand combat
Special skills and abilities: Accomplished self-taught philosopher
Superhuman physical powers: Aside from the above listed attributes, Warlock has the ability to manipulate cosmic for a variety of effects, including projection of concussive blasts. When he wore the Soul Gem, he was able to utilize it for an even wider variety of energy manipulations, including the absorption the life energy ("souls") of living organisms. The uses of the Infinity Gem now in his possession have yet to be revealed.
Superhuman mental powers: Telepathy and cosmic awareness
Special limitations: While he wore the Soul Gem, Warlock could not remove it, as it had secretly siphoned off the majority of his own life energy, and his his ability to manipulate cosmic energy was severely limited.
Source of superhuman powers: Warlock is an artificially-created being whose body has certain cosmic energy receptive cells.

PARAPHERNALIA

Costume specifications: Alien materials
Personal weaponry: None
Special weaponry: None
Other accessories: Formerly, Warlock possessed a green "Soul Gem" which adhered to his forehead and allowed him to manipulate various energies. This gem appeared to possesses a consciousness of its own, and demonstrated a vampiric hunger for the life energies of organic beings, and in later days the gem's personality repeatedly attempted to exert its influence over Adam Warlock's mind. When Warlock himself was absorbed by the gem, it was discovered to contain a pocket universe in which the gem's victims coexisted peacefully in a pastoral valley. Warlock later took control of all six Soul Gems, now called Infinity Gems, which he wore on the Infinity Gauntlet. He currently retains possession of one Infinity Gem.
Transportation: Flight under own power
Design and manufacture of paraphernalia: Inapplicable

BIBLIOGRAPHY

First appearance: FANTASTIC FOUR #66
Origin issue: FANTASTIC FOUR #66-67 (created by scientists of the Enclave; encountered Fantastic Four; left Earth); INCREDIBLE HULK #176-178 (allied with Hulk against Man-Beast; executed by Man-Beast; reborn in more powerful form, defeated Man-Beast; left Counter-Earth); STRANGE TALES #178-180 (first encountered his future self, the Magus, embarked on quest to destroy same); WARLOCK #9, 11, 15 (allied with Thanos against Magus; traveled to the future where he stole his own soul to prevent his metamorphosis into the Magus; attempted communication with Soul-Gem, resisted attempt at bodily possession by same); AVENGERS ANNUAL #7 (allied with Avengers and Captain Mar-Vell against Thanos; absorbed the souls of Gamora and Pip the Troll after they were mortally wounded by Thanos; soul stolen by temporally-displaced previous self); MARVEL TWO-IN-ONE ANNUAL #2 (soul temporarily released from Soul Gem, transformed Thanos into stone, returned to gem); INFINITY GAUNTLET #1-6 (left the Soul Gem; battled Thanos for possession of the Infinity Gems)

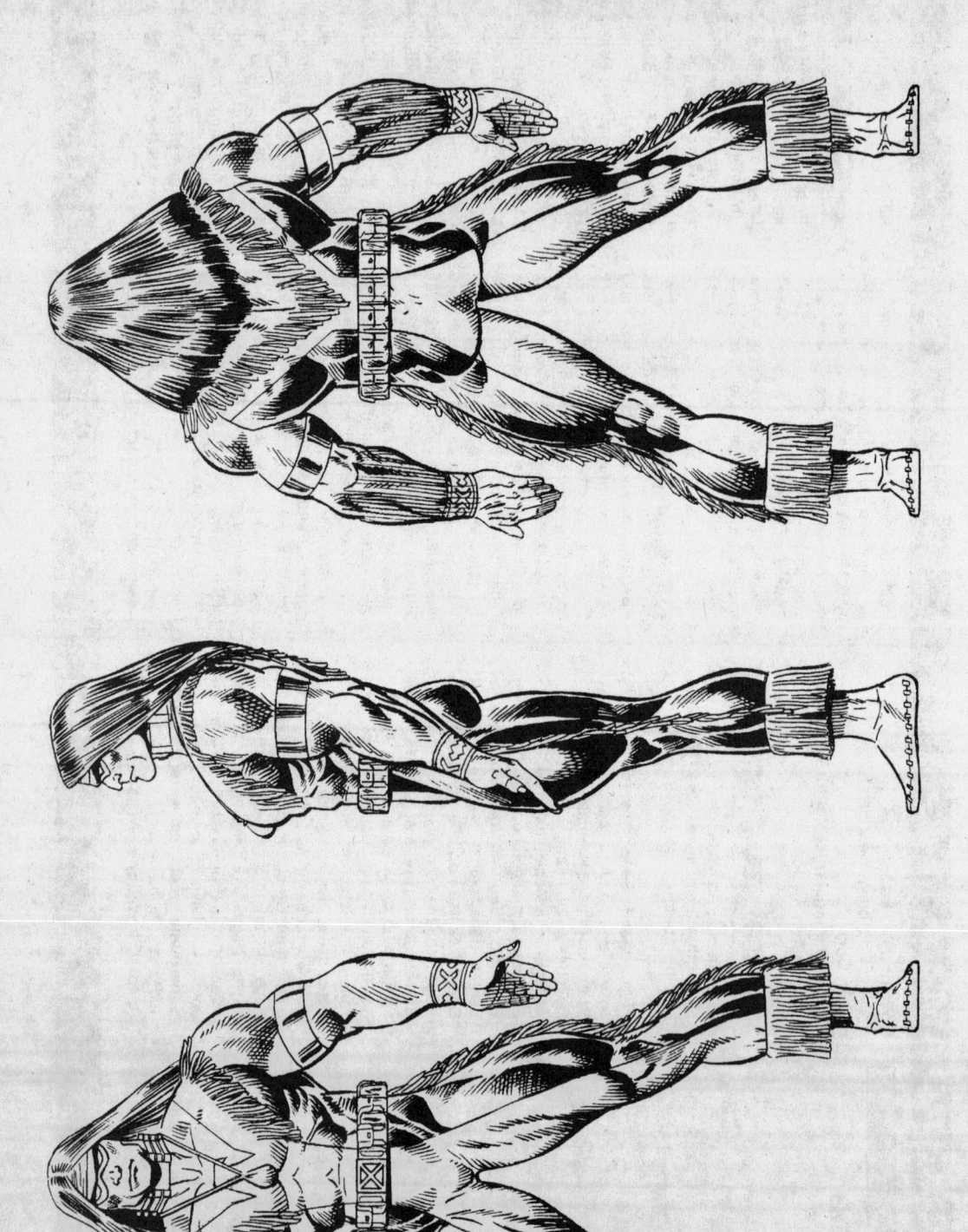

WARPATH

WARPATH

BIOGRAPHICAL DATA

Real name: James Proudstar
Other current aliases: None
Former aliases: Thunderbird II
Dual Identity: Secret
Current occupation: Adventurer
Former occupation: Student
Citizenship: United States of America
Legal status: No known criminal record, still a minor
Place of birth: Apache Reservation at Camp Verde, Arizona
Marital status: Single
Known relatives: Neal Proudstar (father, deceased), Maria Proudstar (mother, deceased), John Proudstar (Thunderbird I, brother, deceased)
Known confidants: X-Force, Magma, Firestar
Known allies: X-Force, Cable, (former) White Queen, Hellions, Hellfire Club, Firestar
Major enemies: Gideon, Externals, White Queen, Juggernaut, Stryfe, Mutant Liberation Front, Brotherhood of Evil Mutants V, Weapon PRIME, (former) X-Men, New Mutants
Usual base of operations: Camp Verde, Arizona
Former bases of operations: Apache Reservation at Camp Verde, Arizona; Massachusetts Academy, Berkshire Mountains, Massachusetts; Professor Xavier School for Gifted Youngsters, Salem Center, Westchester County, New York State; X-Force headquarters, Adirondack Mountains, upstate New York (Bolivar Trask's former Sentinels base)
Current group membership: X-Force
Former group membership: Hellions
Extent of education: Dropout from high school education at Massachusetts Academy

PHYSICAL DESCRIPTION

Height: 7' 2" (6' 1" in his first appearance, has since grown to adult height)
Weight: 350 lbs. (214 lbs. in his first appearance)
Eyes: Brown
Hair: Black
Other distinguishing features: None

POWERS AND ABILITIES

Intelligence: Normal
Strength: Superhuman Class 75 (with potential to reach Superhuman Class 90 when older)
Speed: Superhuman
Stamina: Superhuman
Durability: Superhuman
Agility: Superhuman
Reflexes: Superhuman
Fighting skills: Good hand-to-hand combatant, trained in unarmed combat by the White Queen and Cable
Special skills and abilities: Skilled hunter and tracker
Superhuman physical powers: Aside from the above listed attributes, none
Superhuman mental powers: None
Special limitations: None
Source of superhuman powers: Genetic mutation

PARAPHERNALIA

Costume specifications: Synthetic stretch fabric and soft body armor of unknown composition
Personal weaponry: None
Special weaponry: None
Other accessories: None
Transportation: X-Force land and air vehicles
Design and manufacture of paraphernalia: (costume) Boomer using Shi'ar clothes synthesizer, (vehicles) Cable

BIBLIOGRAPHY

First appearance: NEW MUTANTS #16
Origin issue: CLASSIC X-MEN #3
Significant issues: NEW MUTANTS #16-17 (alongside Hellions, first clashed with New Mutants); UNCANNY X-MEN #193 (sought vengeance on X-Men for Thunderbird I's death, failed, was reconciled with X-Men); NEW MUTANTS #99 (recruited into X-Force by Cable, populace of home village was massacred by Hellfire Club); X-FORCE #1 (alongside X-Force, first battled Mutant Liberation Front); X-FORCE #3-4 (alongside X-Force and Spider-Man, battled Juggernaut); X-FORCE #6-7, 9 (alongside X-Force, battled Brotherhood of Evil Mutants V); X-FORCE #13 (alongside X-Force, battled Weapon Prime); X-FORCE #15 (alongside X-Force, rescued Sunspot from Gideon); UNCANNY X-MEN #294-295/X-FACTOR #84/X-FORCE #16-19/X-MEN Vol. 2 #14 (alongside X-Force fought X-Men and X-Factor II, was taken prisoner with X-Force by X-Men and X-Factor II); NEW WARRIORS #31 (traveled to Nova Roma to tell Magma that most other Hellions were dead); X-FORCE #21, 23 (with Boomer and Siryn taken prisoner by Gideon and Externals; rescued by X-Force teammates)

WARSTAR™

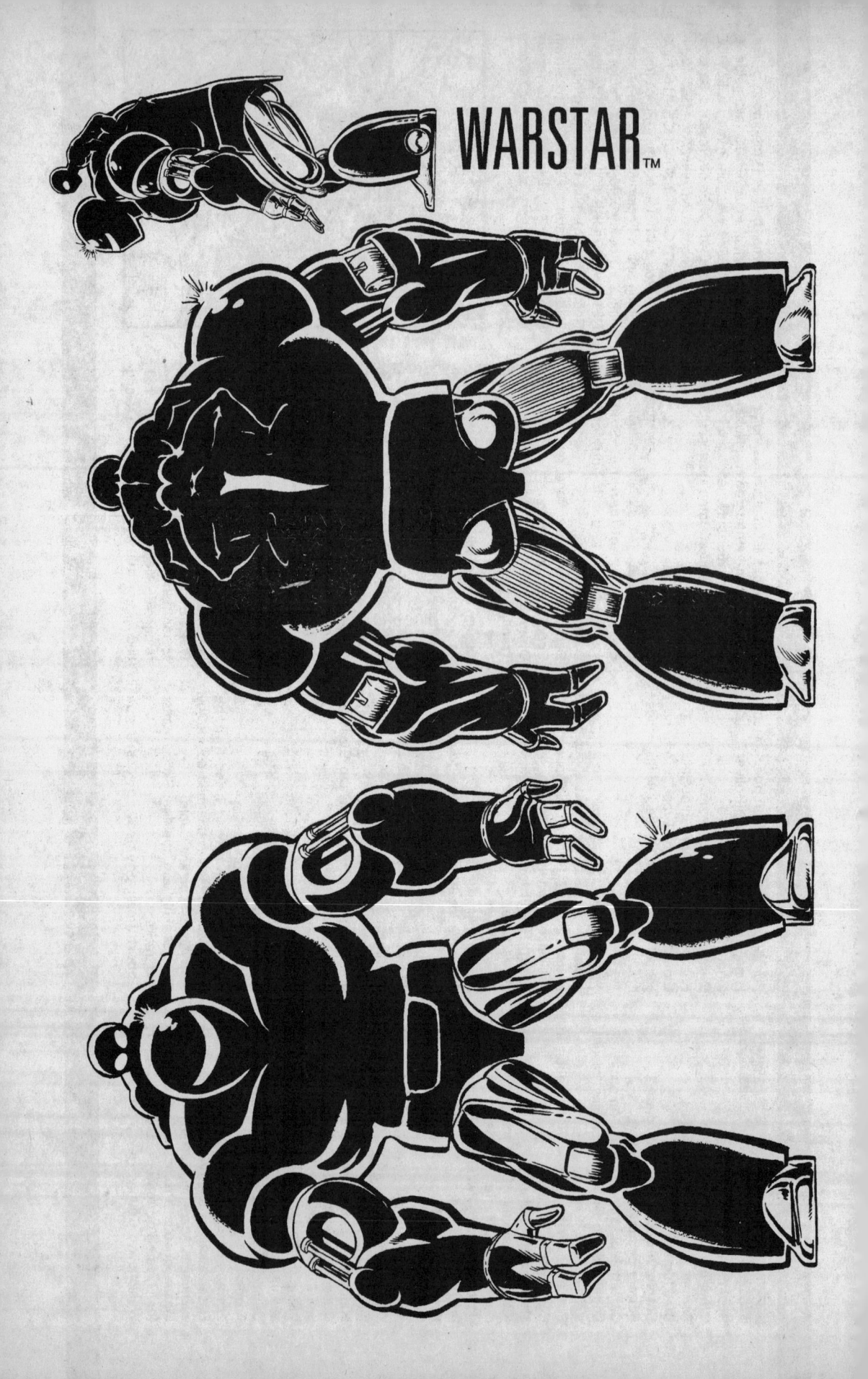

WARSTAR

BIOGRAPHICAL DATA

Real names: B'nee and C'cil
Other current aliases: None
Former aliases: None known
Dual identity: None, the general populace of Earth is unaware of Warstar's existence
Current occupation: Warriors serving in the Royal Elite of Shi'ar Imperial Guard
Former occupation: Warriors serving Shi'ar Lord Samedar
Citizenship: Shi'ar Empire
Legal status: Traitor to the Shi'ar Empire, apparently pardoned
Place of birth: Somewhere in the Shi'ar Empire
Marital status: Unrevealed, perhaps inapplicable
Known relatives: None
Known confidants: None
Known allies: Imperial Guard, Lilandra, the Brood, (formerly) Deathbird, Lord Samedar
Major enemies: (former) X-Men, Starjammers, Ch'od, Captain America, the Avengers
Usual base of operations: Chandilar (Aerie, Shi'ar Throneworld), Shi'ar Empire
Former bases of operations: None known
Current group membership: Royal Elite, Shi'ar Imperial Guard
Former group membership: Renegade Imperial Guard faction serving Lord Samedar
Extent of education: Unrevealed

PHYSICAL DESCRIPTION

Height: (B'nee) 5' 9", (C'cil) 14' 2"
Weight: (B'nee) 150 lbs., (C'cil) 975 lbs.
Eyes: (both) Green, no visible pupils or irises
Feathers: (both) None
Other distinguishing features: Warstar is actually a mechanoid symbiote of two separate beings, B'nee and C'cil. B'nee rides in a cavity in C'cil's back.

POWERS AND ABILITIES

Intelligence: (B'nee) Normal, (C'cil) Below normal
Strength: (B'nee) Enhanced human, (C'cil) Superhuman Class 90
Speed: (B'nee) Enhanced human, (C'cil) Enhanced human
Stamina: (B'nee) Enhanced human, (C'cil) Superhuman
Durability: (B'nee) Enhanced human, (C'cil) Superhuman
Agility: (B'nee) Enhanced human, (C'cil) Enhanced human
Reflexes: (B'nee) Enhanced human, (C'cil) Enhanced human
Fighting skills: Trained armed and unarmed combat by the Shi'ar Imperial Guard
Special skills and abilities: None known
Superhuman physical powers: Aside from the above listed attributes, B'nee can electrically shock an opponent with his touch
Superhuman mental powers: B'nee and C'cil appear to communicate through a means that may be telepathic.
Special limitations: B'nee and C'cil are empathically linked so that when B'nee feels pain, so does C'cil. Due to his low intellect, C'cil relies on B'nee to guide him in combat.
Source of superhuman powers: Unrevealed

PARAPHERNALIA

Costume specifications: Unrevealed
Personal weaponry: None
Special weaponry: None
Other accessories: None
Transportation: Shi'ar starships, small Imperial Guard anti-gravity device which allow flight
Design and manufacture of paraphernalia: Shi'ar scientists and technicians

BIBLIOGRAPHY

First appearance: UNCANNY X-MEN #137
Origin issue: Warstar's origin is as yet unrevealed.
Significant issues: UNCANNY X-MEN #137 (joined in Imperial Guard's trial by combat with the X-Men to decide fate of Phoenix); UNCANNY X-MEN #157 (served traitorous Lord Samedar, battled X-Men); X-MEN SPOTLIGHT ON: STARJAMMERS #2 (on Deathbird's behalf, battled Ch'od of the Starjammers); UNCANNY X-MEN #275 (back in Imperial Guard, now serving Deathbird; was defeated along with other Imperial Guardsmen by X-Men and Starjammers); CAPTAIN AMERICA #398 (fought Captain America in Arizona in attempt to abduct Rick Jones); AVENGERS WEST COAST #80 (battled Captain America, Iron Man, and Wonder Man during Kree-Shi'ar War); AVENGERS WEST COAST #81 (defeated by Gilgamesh and She-Hulk); QUASAR #33 (alongside Imperial Guard, confronted Quasar)

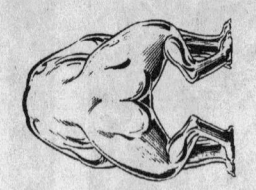

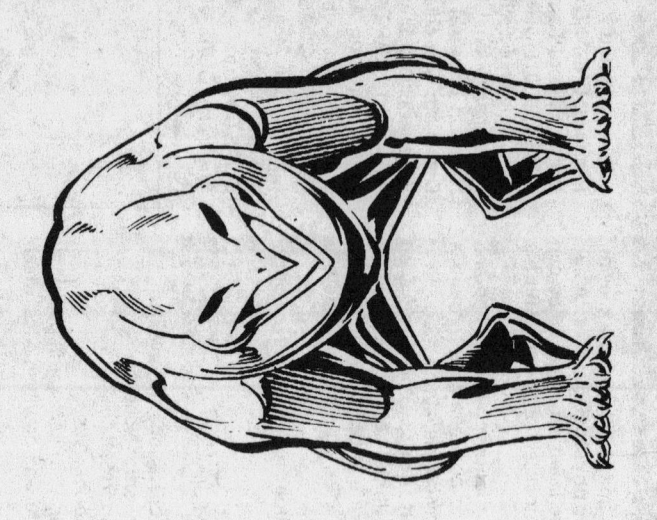

WARWOLVES

WARWOLVES

HOME WORLD

Native dimension: "Mojoverse"
Origin World: "Mojoworld"
Habitat: Temperate climate
Gravity: Same as Earth's
Atmosphere: Approximately same as Earth's

PHYSICAL CHARACTERISTICS

Type: Sentient canine/humanoid, created through genetic engineering by Mojo's scientists
Eyes: Two
Fingers: (front paws) Four, including opposable thumb
Toes: (hind feet) Three
Skin color: White
Average height: 6'
Special adaptations: Warwolves can stand erect on their hind legs or walk or run on all fours; their front paws can be used as hands or feet. Warwolves are immune to direct attack by psionic energy. Warwolves can track their prey by scent as earth canines do. Warwolves also possess remarkable leaping ability
Unusual physical characteristics: A group of Warwolves can merge into a single being while retaining their individual heads and psyches.. Warwolves have slick, smooth skins and have sharp claws on each paw.
Superhumanoid powers: Warwolves can drain life forces of their victims, causing the victim's skeletons and internal organs to discorporate, leaving behind their intact skins. After donning a victim's skin, a Warwolf will then change shape to match that of the victim. Warwolves can also mimic the voices of their victims or of other persons. A group of Warwolves can together psionically create an interdimensional portal

Intelligence: Normal
Strength: Enhanced human
Speed: Enhanced human
Stamina: Enhanced human
Durability: Superhuman regenerative
Agility: Enhanced human
Reflexes: Enhanced human

SOCIETY

Population: Unrevealed
Government: None, Warwolves serve Mojo
Technology level: None
Cultural traits: Ruthless hunters, strong sense of humor, fondness for televised entertainment
Leaders: None known among own race; apparently Warwolves were ruled by Mojo
Names of other representatives: Bowzer, Ducks, Jacko, Popsie, and Scarper
Major allies: Mojo
Major enemies: Excalibur, Gatecrasher's Technet

BIBLIOGRAPHY

First appearance: EXCALIBUR SPECIAL EDITION #1
Origin issue: The Warwolves origin is as yet unrevealed.
Significant issues: EXCALIBUR SPECIAL EDITION #1 (six Warwolves sent to London by Mojo to capture Rachel Summers [Phoenix III], fought Technet and Nightcrawler over her, two Warwolves were seemingly killed); EXCALIBUR #1-2 (remaining Warwolves on Earth abducted Shadowcat, who used her phasing power to merge with and control one of them, Warwolves defeated and captured by Excalibur, were imprisoned at London Zoo); EXCALIBUR #22 (human and animal rights groups sought to free Warwolves from London Zoo); EXCALIBUR #40-41 (two allegedly "dead" Warwolves teamed with four captives to impersonate X-Men; captured Rachel Summers; were forced through interdimensional portal by Excalibur, who rescued Summers)

WASP™

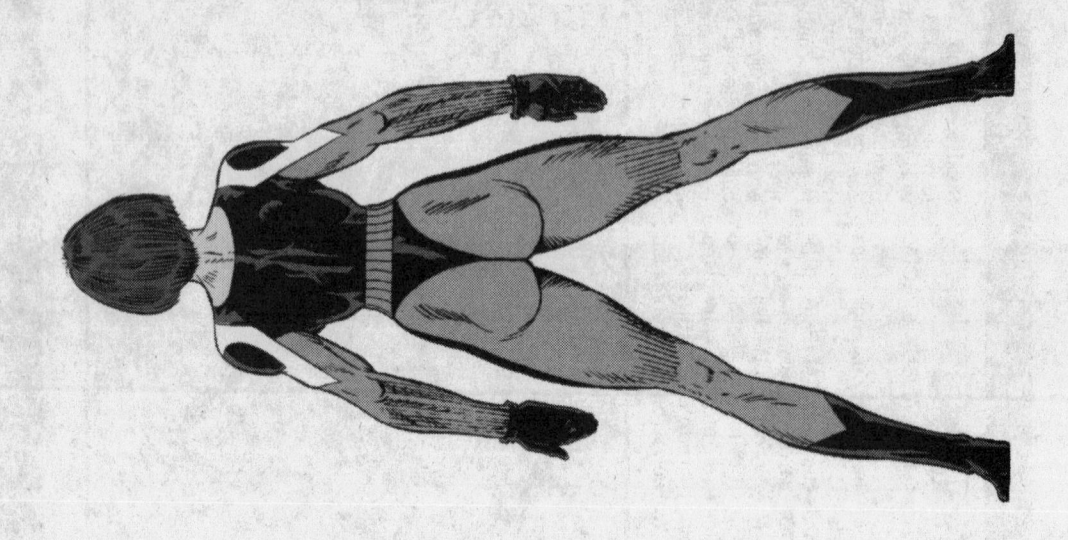

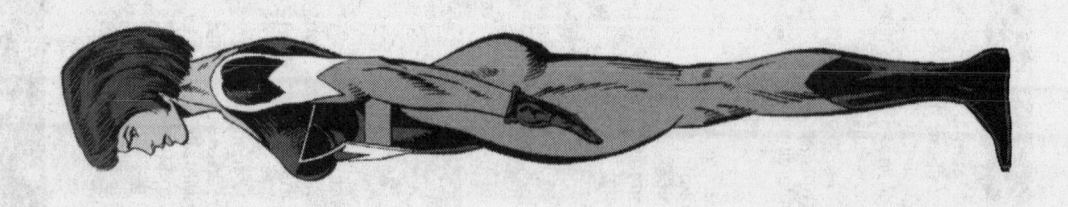

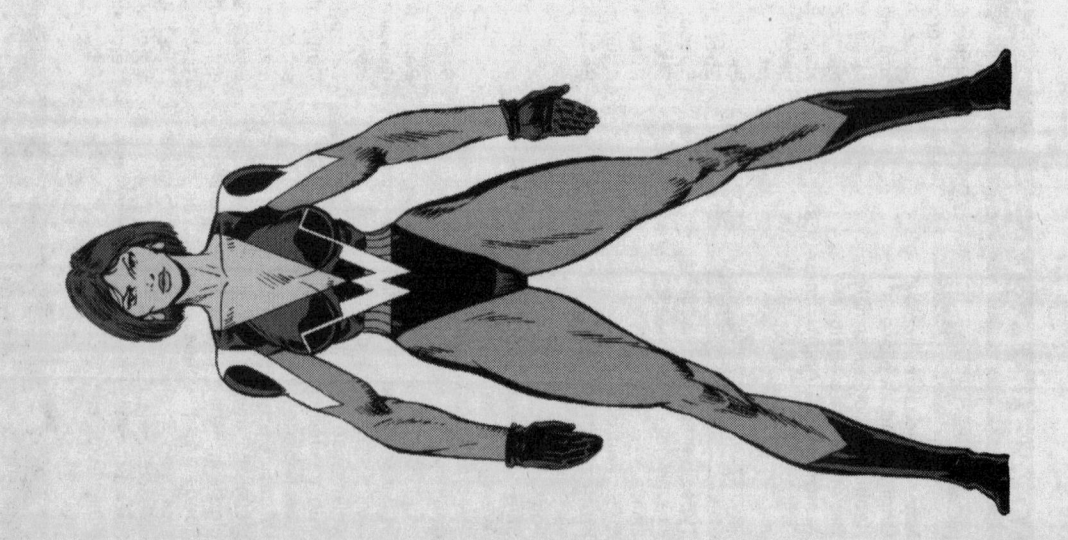

WASP

BIOGRAPHICAL DATA

Real name: Janet Van Dyne
Other Current aliases: None
Former aliases: Janet Pym
Dual identity: Publicly known
Current occupation: Adventurer, fashion designer, screenwriter, president of Van Dyne Industries, board member of Nevell Industries, independently wealthy socialite
Former occupation: Debutante
Citizenship: United States of America
Legal status: No criminal record
Place of birth: Cresskill, New Jersey
Marital status: Divorced
Known relatives: Vernon Van Dyne (father deceased), Henry J. Pym (ex-husband)
Known confidants: Henry Pym, Thor I, Iron Man I, Captain America, She-Hulk
Known allies: Dr. Pym, the Avengers, Avengers West Coast, the Fantastic Four, Paladin, Ant-Man II
Major enemies: Egghead (deceased), the Porcupine (deceased), Whirlwind (formerly Human Top II), Masters of Evil I, II, III, and IV, Kang, Immortus, Count Nefaria (deceased), the Collector, the Living Laser (deceased), Ultron, Dr. Nemesis
Usual base of operations: An apartment in Manhattan and an estate in Cresskill, New Jersey
Former base of operations: Avengers Mansion, New York City; Avengers Compound, Los Angeles
Current group membership: Avengers West Coast (reserve member)
Former group membership: Avengers, Lady Liberators
Extent of education: Unrevealed

PHYSICAL DESCRIPTION

Height: (normal) 5' 2"
Weight: (normal) 110 lbs.
Eyes: Blue
Hair: Auburn
Other distinguishing features: At a height of up to 4' 2", the Wasp possesses wings. She can also cause two tiny antennae to protrude from her temples.

POWERS AND ABILITIES

Intelligence: Above normal
Strength: Athlete, (at 1' height) Enhanced human, (at 1/2" height) Athlete
Speed: Athlete
Flight speed: Directed motion hovering
Stamina: Athlete
Durability: Athlete
Agility: Athlete
Reflexes: Athlete
Fighting skills: Trained in unarmed combat by Captain America and in combat utilizing her specialized powers by Henry Pym
Special skills and abilities: Gifted fashion designer, skilled amateur screenwriter, experienced leader and strategist
Superhuman physical powers: Aside from the above listed attributes, the Wasp has the ability to shrink in size up to 1/2" in height, and the ability to project bio-electric force bolts from her hands.
Superhuman mental powers: The Wasp can cause two tiny antennae to protrude from her temples, giving her the ability to communicate telepathically with insects. She rarely uses this ability, however.
Special limitations: None
Source of superhuman powers: Cellular implantation and later biochemical augmentation by Henry Pym, cellular mutation due to repeated exposure to Pym particles

PARAPHERNALIA

Costume specifications: Unstable molecules
Personal weaponry: None
Special weaponry: None
Other accessories: None
Transportation: Flight under own power, Avengers Quinjet
Design and manufacture of paraphernalia: (costumes) Janet Van Dyne, (quinjet) Tony Stark

BIBLIOGRAPHY

First appearance: TALES TO ASTONISH #44
Origin issue: TALES TO ASTONISH #44
Significant issues: TALES TO ASTONISH #44 (gained superhuman powers, became Henry Pym, alias Ant-Man I's partner); AVENGERS #1 (helped form the Avengers); AVENGERS #13-14 (wounded in battle against Count Nefaria); AVENGERS #16 (with Henry Pym, alias Giant-Man I, left Avengers); AVENGERS #28 (with Henry Pym, alias Goliath I, rejoined Avengers, first battled Collector); AVENGERS #60 (married Henry Pym, alias Yellowjacket I); AVENGERS #75 (with Yellowjacket I, left Avengers); MARVEL FEATURE Vol. 1 #6-10 (with Ant-Man I, temporarily trapped at insect size, battled Whirlwind, Para-Man, and Dr. Nemesis); AVENGERS #137 (with Yellowjacket I, rejoined Avengers); MARVEL TEAM-UP #59-60 (with Spider-Man and Yellowjacket I, battled Equinox; powers augmented by Yellowjacket I); AVENGERS #181 (rejoined Avengers without Pym); AVENGERS #214 (separated from Pym); AVENGERS #217 divorced Pym, became Avengers chairman; with Avengers, arrested Yellowjacket I); AVENGERS #243 (surrendered Avengers chairmanship to Vision); AVENGERS #28 (with Paladin, battled Baron Brimstone); AVENGERS #256 (resumed Avengers chairmanship); AVENGERS #278 (stepped down as chairman, left Avengers); WEST COAST AVENGERS Vol. 2 #32 (joined West Coast Avengers); SOLO AVENGERS #15 (battled Red Ronin); AVENGERS WEST COAST #69 (elected as regular member of Avengers West, but chose to become reserve member)

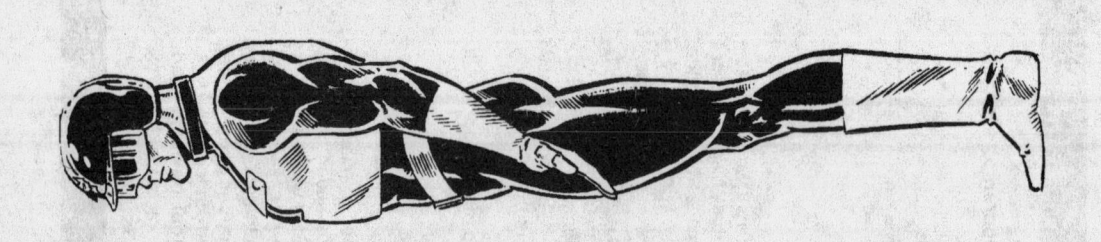

WATCHDOGS

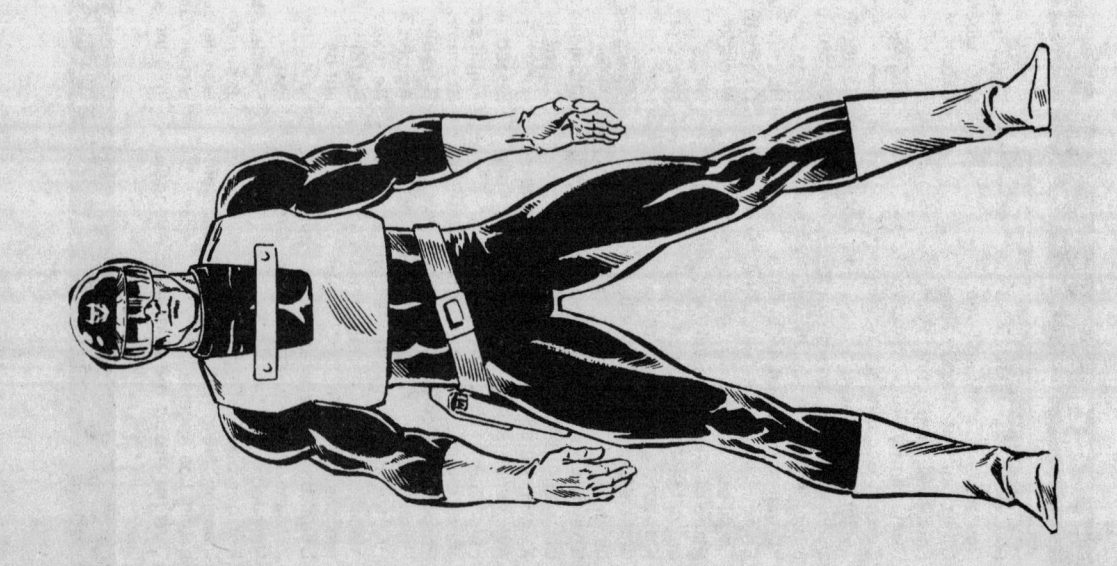

WATCHDOGS

ORGANIZATION

Purpose: To impose their conservative moral views on the general public; specifically to denounce pornography, obscenity, abortion, homosexuality, sex education, and the teaching of evolution

Modus Operandi: Terrorism, vandalism, arson, intimidation, violence

Extent of operations: Georgia, Alabama, Mississippi, Tennessee, West Virginia, Missouri, plus Washington D.C. and New York City

Relationship to conventional authorities: Ongoing investigation by the Federal Bureau of Investigation, outstanding warrants for the arrest of several certain Watchdog members

Base of operations: Unrevealed

Former bases of operations: Custer's Grove, Georgia

Major funding: Partial financing by Johann Schmidt (alias the Red Skull) through his dummy corporation, the Freedom Foundation, public contributions, other undisclosed financiers

Known enemies: USAgent, Battle Star

Known allies: None

MEMBERS

Number of active members: 500 (estimated)
Number of reserve members: 2000 (estimated)

Organizational structure: National leader is called Watchdog One or Top Dog. Each state ("realm") is governed by a Head Dog. Each realm has one or more operating units ("packs") which are led by Pack Leaders. Members call one another Dog-Brothers.

Known officers: None
Known current members: None
Known former members: None
Known special agents: None

Membership requirements: Must be an adult male over 21 with a valid gun permit willing to sign an affidavit in blood that he is not a homosexual, believes in the Bible and the Constitution, disavows all immoral acts, and is willing to use violence to oppose all activities, materials, institutions, and individuals which are deemed to undermine the morality and decency of the United States.

HISTORY

Founder: Unrevealed
Other leaders: Unknown
Previous purpose or goals: None

Major campaigns or accomplishments: The torching of 15 adult bookstores and 3 women's health clinics, the assassination of at least 5 "immoral" persons

Major setbacks: Constant pruning of the ranks by Federal and local authorities, John Walker (USAgent) busted 22 Watchdogs, killed 9, and wounded 16

TECHNOLOGY AND PARAPHERNALIA

Level of technology: Conventional, all weapons and paraphernalia purchased from legitimate retailers

Transportation: Various, no standard vehicle, members use their own ground vehicles, usually pick up trucks, vans, motorcycles, and recreational vehicles.

Standard uniforms: Synthetic stretch materials with kevlar vests and leather boots and accessories, hard plastic helmets

Standard weaponry: Conventional armament; American-manufactured handguns and rifles, Army surplus explosives

Standard accessories: Army surplus walkie-talkies, short-wave radios

BIBLIOGRAPHY

First appearance: CAPTAIN AMERICA #335
Origin issue: The origin of the Watchdogs has yet to be revealed.

Significant issues: CAPTAIN AMERICA #335 (major Watchdog pack torches an adult bookstore and women's health clinic, attempts to lynch alleged pornographer, and is busted by John Walker, the interim Captain America), CAPTAIN AMERICA #345 (Watchdogs hold Walker's parents captive in effort to get revenge upon him), CAPTAIN AMERICA #350 (the Red Skull employed a single Watchdog in his elite cadre of bodyguards)

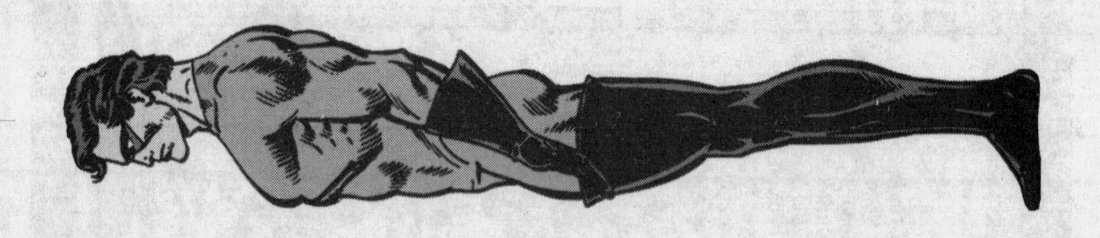

WATER WIZARD

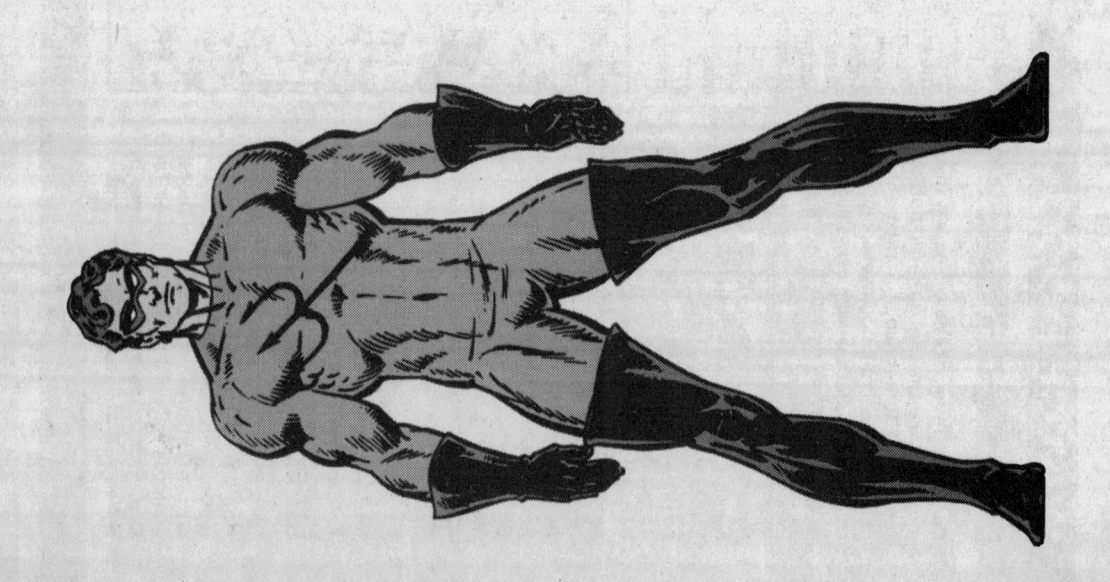

WATER WIZARD

BIOGRAPHICAL DATA

Real name: Peter Van Zante
Other current aliases: Aqueduct
Former aliases: None
Dual identity: Known to the authorities
Current occupation: Professional criminal
Former occupation: Soldier
Citizenship: United States of America
Legal status: Criminal record in America
Place of birth: Chicago, Illinois
Marital status: Single
Known relatives: None
Known confidants: None
Known allies: Enforcer (deceased), Moondark, Force of Nature
Major enemies: Ghost Rider I (Johnny Blaze), Arabian Knight, Justin Hammer
Usual base of operations: Mobile
Former bases of operations: Los Angeles, California; Chicago, Illinois
Current group membership: None
Former group membership: None
Extent of education: High school graduate

PHYSICAL DESCRIPTION

Height: 5'10"
Weight: 210 lbs.
Eyes: Brown
Hair: Brown
Other distinguishing features: None

POWERS AND ABILITIES

Intelligence: Normal
Strength: Normal
Speed: Normal
Stamina: Normal
Durability: Normal
Agility: Normal
Reflexes: Athlete
Fighting skills: Military training
Special skills and abilities: None
Superhuman physical powers: None
Superhuman mental powers: Water Wizard can psychokinetically control all forms of liquid within 500 feet of himself for a variety of effects including rainstorms, floods, and mobile animated water-creatures
Special limitations: Water Wizard cannot control the temperature of water or combine hydrogen and oxygen to create water.
Source of superhuman powers: Power surge in an experimental cell stimulator while out at sea

PARAPHERNALIA

Costume specifications: Synthetic waterproof stretch fabric
Personal weaponry: None
Special weaponry: None
Other accessories: None
Transportation: Different vehicles constructed from water
Design and manufacture of paraphernalia: Inapplicable

BIBLIOGRAPHY

First appearance: GHOST RIDER Vol.1 #23
Origin issue: GHOST RIDER Vol.1 #23
Significant issues: GHOST RIDER Vol.1 #23 (robbed brokerage house, contacted by the Enforcer, assigned to kill the original Ghost Rider, failed); GHOST RIDER Vol.1 #24 (salvaged the Enforcer's disintegration ring from San Diego Harbor, battled and was defeated by Ghost Rider); GHOST RIDER Vol.1 #59 (contacted by Moondark in Chicago, sent to battle Ghost Rider again, burned by Ghost Rider's mystical flames again, went into shock and was institutionalized; GHOST RIDER Vol.1 #61 (broken out of the institution by Ghost Rider to help drought-ridden town); GHOST RIDER Vol.1 #62 (traveled to Saudi Arabia, learned he could control other forms of liquid than water, battled the Arabian Knight and Ghost Rider); IRON MAN #126 (hired by Justin Hammer); IRON MAN #127 (ran away during battle with Iron Man earning Hammer's enmity); CAPTAIN AMERICA #320 (discovered the 17 victims of Scourge at the Bar With No Name, alerted Captain America for protection); FANTASTIC FOUR #336 (encountered Hydro-Man while attacking Four Freedoms Plaza); NEW WARRIORS #7-9 (first appearance as Aqueduct, member of Force of Nature, employed by Project: Earth to prevent rain forest razing, battled the New Warriors)

WEAPON X

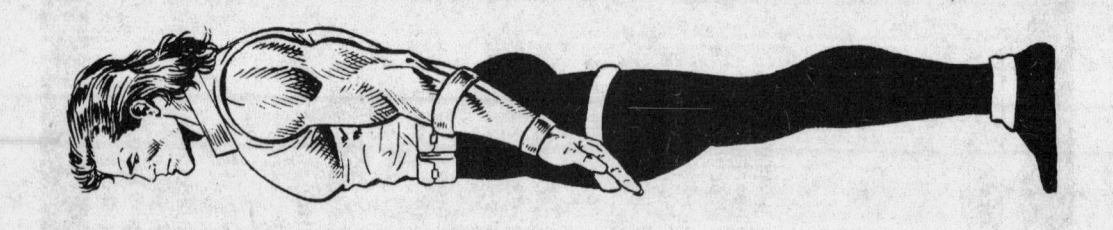

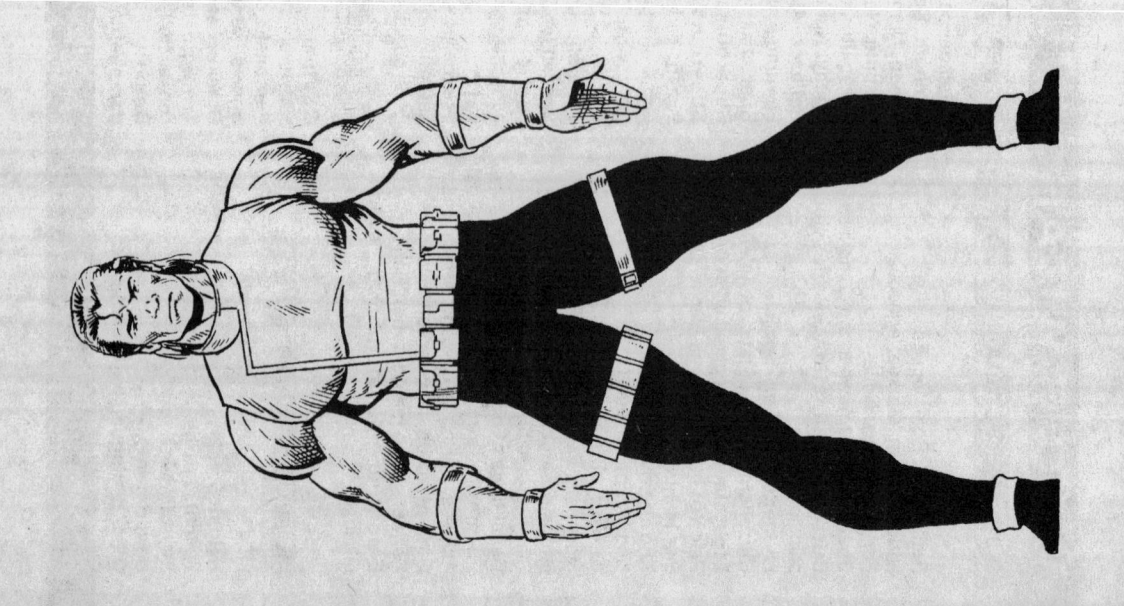

KANE (WEAPON X II)

BIOGRAPHICAL DATA

Real name: Garrison Kane
Other current aliases: None known
Former current aliases: Weapon X II
Dual identity: Known to Canadian government officials
Current occupation: Mercenary
Former occupation: Covert operative for Canadian government's Department K
Citizenship: Canada
Legal status: No known criminal record
Place of birth: Unrevealed
Marital status: Unrevealed
Known relatives: Unnamed parents (deceased)
Known confidants: Cable
Known allies: Cable, Dawnsilk, Hope, Tetherblood, Boak, Eleven, Col. George Washington Bridge, Hammer II, Domino II, Grizzly II, Wildheart, (former) Six Pack (Wild Pack II), Weapon PRIME
Major enemies: Stryfe, Mutant Liberation Front, Deadpool, Flatliners, Sinsear, Canaanites, HYDRA, (former) Cable
Usual base of operations: Damarus Cove Islands, south of Boothbay Harbor, Maine
Former bases of operations: Clan Chosen safehouse in Applecrust proper (Greenwich Village), New York City in the 40th Century A.D. of alternate future
Current group membership: None
Former group membership: Six Pack (Wild Pack II), Department K, Weapon PRIME, Clan Chosen rebel forces
Extent of education: Unrevealed

PHYSICAL DESCRIPTION

Height: 6'2"
Weight: (including bionic parts) 350 lbs.
Eyes: Blue
Hair: Black
Other distinguishing features: Bionic parts, including synthetic-organic metal arms, hands and shoulders constructed in an alternate 40th Century A.D.. The left and right sides of his torso have also been replaced by synthetic-organic metal parts, although the middle section is still organic. Ordinarily the metal parts of his body appear as flesh, but he can cause the metal to appear by willing a "synthorg transfer." Kane also has bionic legs and a bionic left eye.

POWERS AND ABILITIES

Intelligence: Normal
Strength: Superhuman Class 10
Speed: Enhanced human
Stamina: Enhanced human
Durability: Athlete
Agility: Enhanced human
Reflexes: Enhanced human
Fighting skills: Excellent hand-to-hand combatant, highly trained in armed and unarmed combat
Special skills and abilities: Extensive knowledge of the 40th Century A.D. of the alternate future in which Cable was based
Superhuman physical powers: Aside from the above listed attributes, Kane's artificial hands are detachable and can be shot from his arms. He can also fire plasma from his metal arms. The arms can also produce large organic metal shields for protection. He can see in the infrared portion of the spectrum and project holograms from his eyes. His bionic parts contain a wide variety of devices, most of which have yet to be identified. He can generate electricity from his metal parts to shock an assailant. The bionic parts are also self-repairing.
Superhuman mental powers: None
Special limitations: Claustrophobia
Source of superhuman powers: Bionics from late 20th Century, modified in Cable's 40th Century alternate future

PARAPHERNALIA

Costume specifications: Conventional fabrics
Personal weaponry: Formerly used various firearms, now mainly relies on weapons installed in his bionic body parts
Special weaponry: "Ion blade" that generates destructive energy
Other accessories: None known
Transportation: None; formerly used Cable's "bodyslide" teleportation technology
Design and manufacture of paraphernalia: Unrevealed

BIBLIOGRAPHY

First appearance: X-FORCE #2
Origin issue: Kane's origin is as yet unrevealed.
Significant issues: X-FORCE #2 (battled Deadpool, asked by G.W. Bridge to help capture Cable, refused to join Weapon PRIME; X-FORCE #7 (confronted Mutant Liberation Front); X-FORCE #8 (flashback to Wild Pack II's raid on HYDRA base ten years ago); X-FORCE #11-12 (served as member of Weapon PRIME in attack on Cable and X-Force); CABLE: BLOOD AND METAL #1-2 (flashbacks to Kane's participation in Wild Pack II mission in Iran and Six Pack's confrontations with Stryfe in Afghanistan and Uruguay, in present visited Hammer II and battled Cable in Switzerland; with Cable, fought Silver Samurai's ninjas in Japan and battled Stryfe and the Mutant Liberation Front in Mexico, brought by Cable to 40th Century A.D. to save Kane's life and give him new bionic arms); ALPHA FLIGHT #115-116 (met Weapon Omega, fought Rok); CABLE #1 (alongside Clan Chosen rebels battled Flatliners in 40th Century of alternate future, learned about Cable's past there, was reunited with Cable); CABLE #2 (returned to 20th Century with Cable); CABLE #3 (with Cable confronted G. W. Bridge in Switzerland); DEADPOOL #1 (embarked on search for Copycat, fought Deadpool); DEADPOOL #2 (captured by Sinsear)

WENDIGO™

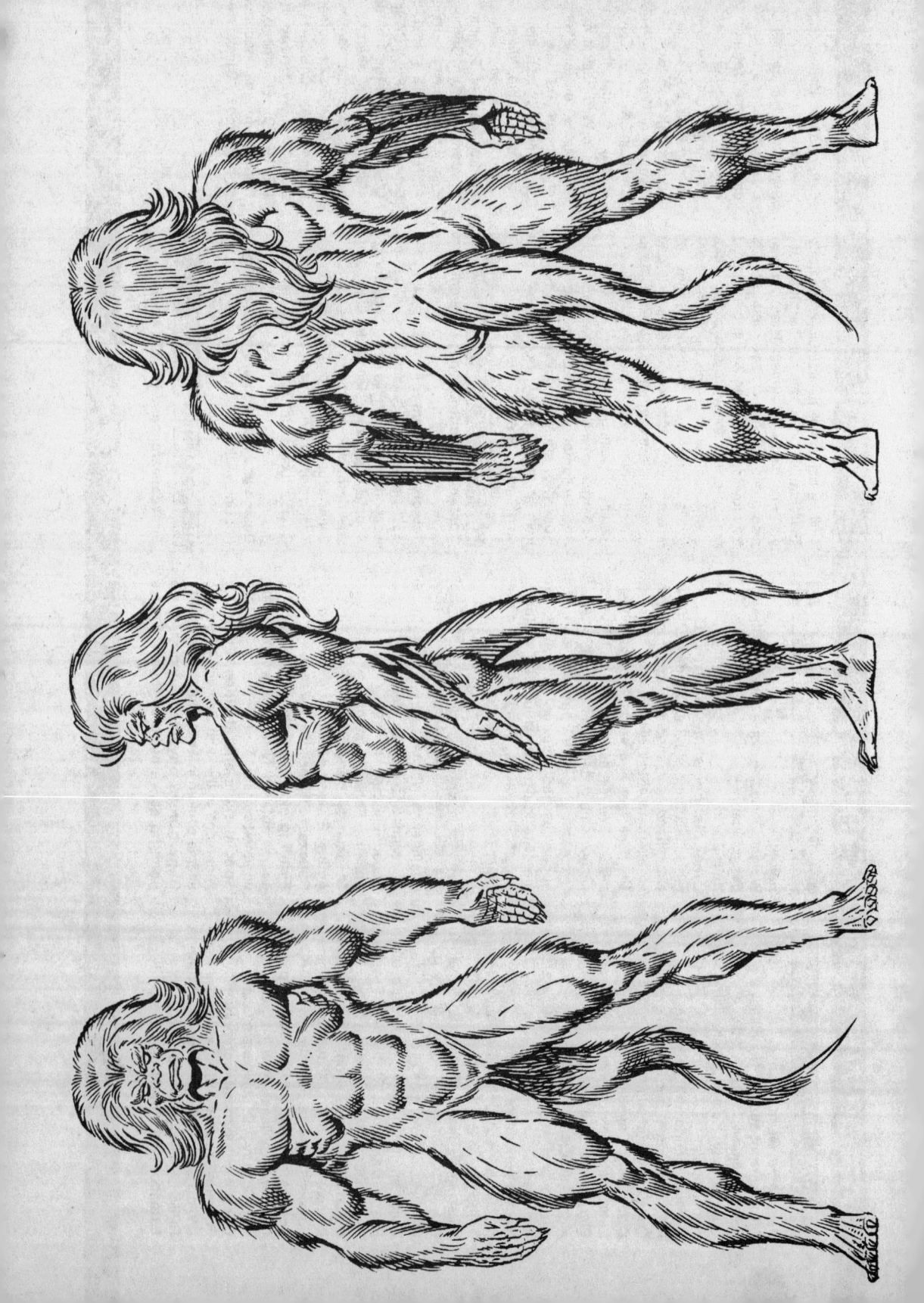

WENDIGO

BIOGRAPHICAL DATA

Real name: (I) Paul Cartier, (II) George Baptiste, (III) Francois Lartigue, (IV) Unrevealed
Other current aliases: (I-IV) None
Former aliases: (I-IV) None
Dual Identity: (I-IV) Secret
Current occupation: (I, IV) Unrevealed, (II) College professor, (III) Fur trapper
Former occupation: (I-IV) Unrevealed
Citizenship: (I-IV) Canada
Legal status: (I-IV) Criminal record in Canada
Place of birth: (I-IV) Unrevealed
Marital status: (I, II, III) Single, (IV) Unrevealed
Known relatives: (I) Marie Cartier (sister), (II, III, IV) None
Known confidants: (I-IV) None
Known allies: (I-IV) None
Major enemies: Hulk, Wolverine, Nightcrawler, Vindicator, Shaman, Snowbird (deceased), Sasquatch, Spider-Man
Usual base of operations: (I-IV) Canadian North Woods
Former bases of operations: (I-IV) None
Current group membership: (I-IV) None
Former group membership: (I-IV) None
Extent of education: (II) College graduate, (I, III, IV)

PHYSICAL DESCRIPTION

Height: (I) 5' 10", (II) 6', (III) 6' 1", (IV) Unrevealed; (I-IV as Wendigo) 9' 7"
Weight: (I) 175 lbs., (II) 190 lbs., (III) 200 lbs., (IV) Unrevealed; (I-IV as Wendigo) 1800 lbs.
Eyes: (I, II, III) Brown, (IV) Unrevealed; (I-IV as Wendigo) Red
Hair: (I, II, III) Brown, (IV) Unrevealed; (I-IV as Wendigo) White
Other distinguishing features: Covered with fur, clawed hands and feet, long tail, fang-like teeth

POWERS AND ABILITIES

Intelligence: (I-IV) Normal, (I-IV as Wendigo) Non-sentient
Strength: (I-IV) Normal, (I-IV as Wendigo) Superhuman Class 75
Speed: (I-IV) Normal, (I-IV as Wendigo) Enhanced human
Stamina: (I-IV) Normal, (I-IV as Wendigo) Metahuman
Durability: (I-IV) Normal, (I-IV as Wendigo) Demi-godlike
Agility: Normal
Reflexes: (I-IV) Normal, (I-IV as Wendigo) Athlete
Fighting skills: (I-IV) Unrevealed, (as Wendigo) No human combat techniques; battle in instinctive animal-like response and ferocity
Special skills and abilities: None
Superhuman physical powers: None aside from the above listed attributes
Superhuman mental powers: None
Special limitations: None
Source of superhuman powers: Transformation by ancient magical curse

PARAPHERNALIA

Costume specifications: None
Personal weaponry: None
Special weaponry: None
Other accessories: None
Transportation: Travel on foot
Design and manufacture of paraphernalia: Inapplicable

BIBLIOGRAPHY

First appearance: (I) INCREDIBLE HULK Vol. 2 #162, (II) INCREDIBLE HULK Vol. 2 #181, (III) INCREDIBLE HULK Vol. 2 #272, (IV) SPIDER-MAN #8
Origin issue: INCREDIBLE HULK Vol. 2 #162
Significant issues: (I) INCREDIBLE HULK Vol. 2 #162 (Paul Cartier transformed into the Wendigo, battled Hulk, escaped); (I) INCREDIBLE HULK Vol. 2 #180 (battled Hulk, encountered Wolverine); (I) INCREDIBLE HULK Vol. 2 #181 (battled Hulk and Wolverine, Paul Cartier cured as Georges Baptiste became Wendigo); MONSTERS UNLEASHED #9 (terrorized snowbound group); UNCANNY X-MEN #139-140 (battled Wolverine, Nightcrawler, and members of Alpha Flight; captured; cured by Shaman); (III) INCREDIBLE HULK Vol. 2 #272 (Francois Lartrigue transformed into Wendigo, battled Hulk and Sasquatch, captured; taken to be cured by Shaman); (IV) SPIDER-MAN #8-12 (unknown person transformed into Wendigo, wrongly suspected of terrorizing British Columbia town, encountered Spider-Man and Wolverine)

Note: A green creature also called the Wendigo once appeared during a blizzard in New York City, as seen in AMAZING SPIDER-MAN #277, but this creature was apparently unrelated to the Canadian Wendigo.

WEREWOLF

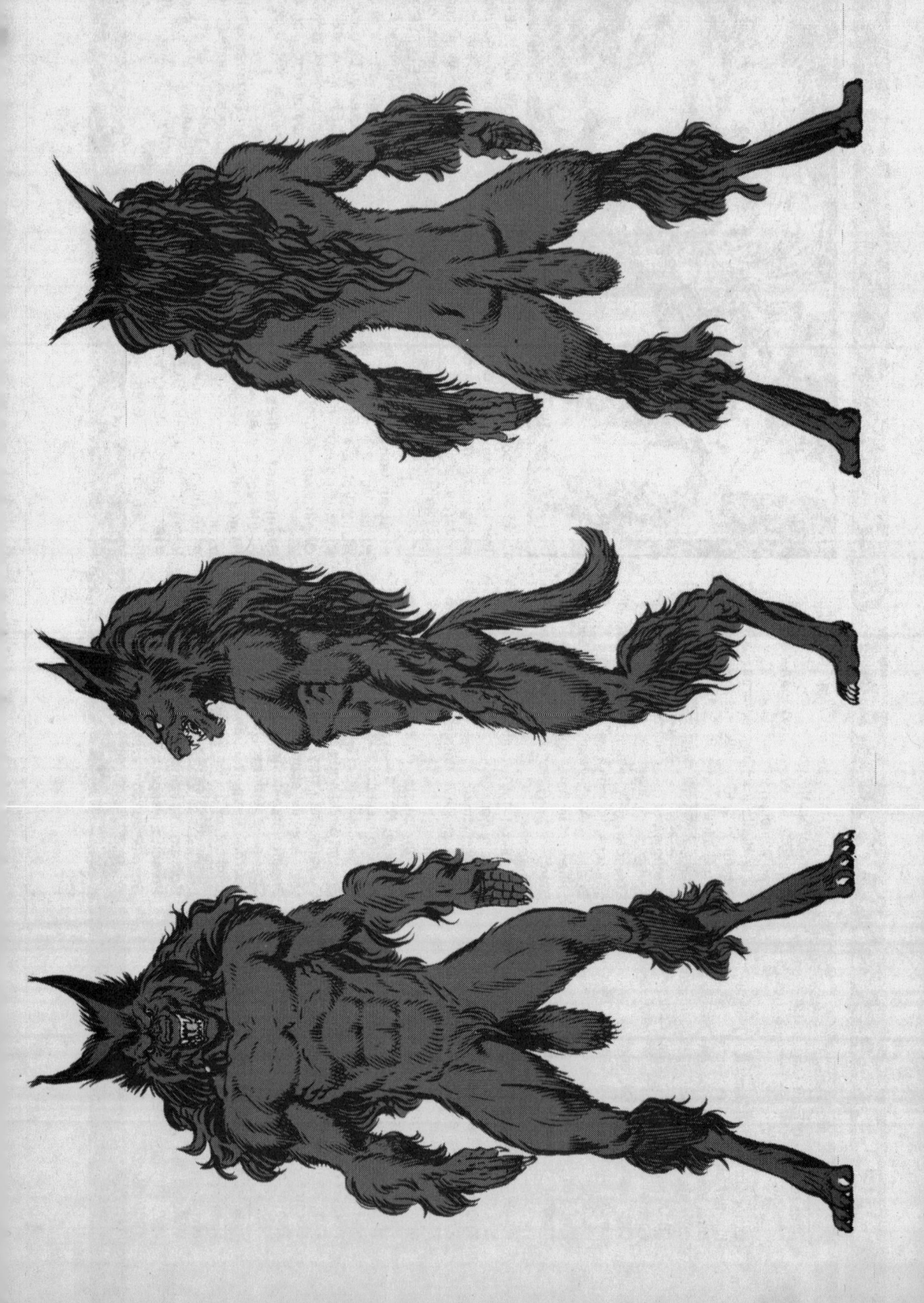

WEREWOLF

BIOGRAPHICAL DATA

Real name: Jacob Russoff (given name), Jack Russell (adopted name)
Other current aliases: None
Former aliases: None
Dual identity: Secret
Current occupation: Traveler
Former occupation: Unemployed
Citizenship: United States of America (naturalized)
Legal status: No criminal record
Place of birth: Medias, Transylvania
Marital status: Single
Known relatives: Gregory Russoff (father, deceased), Laura Russell (mother, deceased), Philip Russell (step-father), Lissa Russell (sister), Louisa Russoff (great great-grandmother, deceased), Grigori Russoff (great great great-grandfather, deceased)
Known confidants: Buck Cowan, Topaz, Michael Morbius, the Shroud
Known allies: The Night Shift (Shroud, Dansen Macabre, Brothers Grimm II, Gypsy Moth, Tatterdemalion, Misfit, Needle, Digger, Ticktock), Moon Knight
Major enemies: Silver Dagger, Hangman I, Doctor Glitternight, Dracula
Usual base of operations: Mobile
Former bases of operations: Los Angeles, California
Current group membership: None
Former group membership: The Night Shift
Extent of education: High school graduate

PHYSICAL DESCRIPTION

Height: 5' 10", (as werewolf) 6' 8"
Weight: 200 lbs., (as werewolf) 300 lbs.
Eyes: Blue, (as werewolf) Red
Hair: Red, (as werewolf) Reddish-brown with black and tan streaks
Other distinguishing features: None

POWERS AND ABILITIES

Intelligence: Above normal
Strength: Peak human, (as werewolf) Enhanced human
Speed: Peak human, (as werewolf) Enhanced human
Stamina: Peak human, (as werewolf) Enhanced human
Durability: Enhanced human, (as werewolf) Metahuman regenerative
Agility: Peak human, (as werewolf) Enhanced human
Reflexes: Peak human, (as werewolf) Enhanced human
Fighting skills: None
Special skills and abilities: Above average familiarity with the forces of magic

Superhuman physical powers: The ability to transform into a large powerful form which is a hybrid of human and wolf; in this form, he possesses the best qualities of both creatures, retaining his full human intellect and reasoning ability while gaining the proportionate physical advantages of a nearly seven-foot tall wolf. This transformation is painless and completely under his control at all times; he can transform his entire body or an isolated portion he chooses. In addition to the traits listed above in his werewolf form (and to a lesser extent in his human form), Jack Russell possesses superhumanly acute senses of hearing, smell, and taste, and can see beyond the spectrum of light visible to normal humans into both the ultraviolet and infrared ranges. His perceptions of infrared in particular is so acute that he can judge an individuals physical and mental state simply by observing the patterns of heat in that person's body. Also he cannot be killed by conventional means, though he can be severely wounded by such. He can fully recuperate from non-fatal wounds ten times faster than a normal human.

Superhuman mental powers: Unrevealed

Special limitations: Although at one time his transformations were governed by the lunar cycle, Russell has gained full mastery over his condition and is no longer limited in any way by lunar phases, enabling him to transform at any time of the day or night, with the two following modifiers: sunlight causes him minor irritation, and while his transformations are entirely voluntary he may experience an increased urge to transform during the full moon. Like all supernatural creatures, the Werewolf can be killed by weapons made of silver.

Source of superhuman powers: Descendant of mystically altered offshoot of man known as Lycanthropes

PARAPHERNALIA

Costume specifications: None
Personal weaponry: None
Special weaponry: None
Other accessories: None
Transportation: Motorcycle
Design and manufacture of paraphernalia: Commercial manufacturer

BIBLIOGRAPHY

First appearance: MARVEL SPOTLIGHT #2
Origin issue: MARVEL SPOTLIGHT #2
Significant issues: MARVEL SPOTLIGHT #2-3 (inherited the "curse" of lycanthropy, became werewolf; battled motorcycle gang, infected members with lycanthropy); WEREWOLF BY NIGHT #15 (battled Dracula); WEREWOLF BY NIGHT #41 (granted limited control over his transformation by Three Who Are All); SPIDER-WOMAN #32 (captured by Dr. Karl Malus, underwent scientific experiments; escaped and apprehended Malus with the aid of Spider-Woman I); WEST COAST AVENGERS Vol. 2 #5 (battled West Coast Avengers; revealed to be under the care of Michael Morbius); CAPTAIN AMERICA #330 (revealed to have become member of Night Shift); MARVEL COMICS PRESENTS #54-59 (battled Silver Dagger; Russell and Werewolf personae merged; powers altered)

WHIPLASH

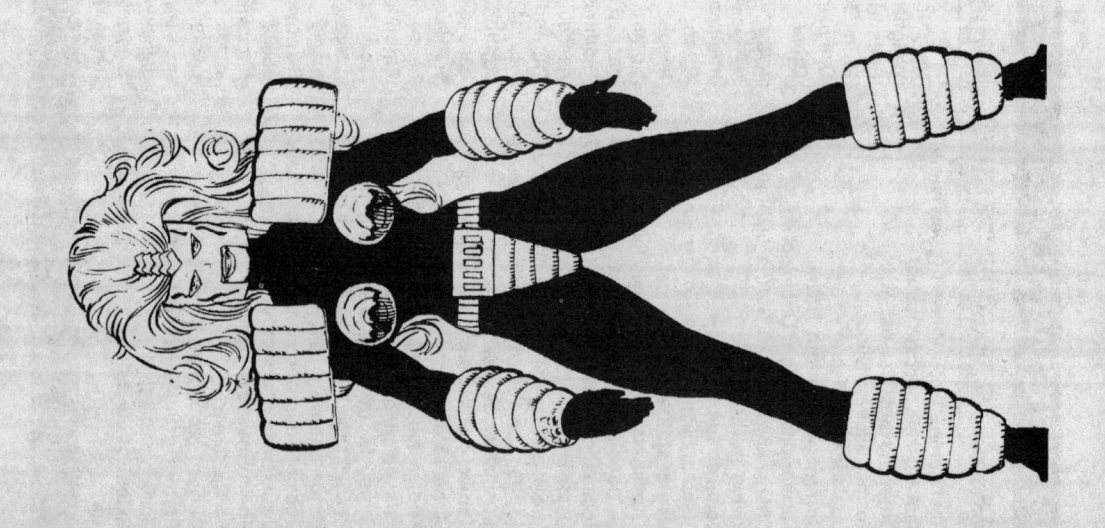

WHIPLASH II

BIOGRAPHICAL DATA

Real name: Unrevealed
Other current aliases: None
Former aliases : Unrevealed
Dual identity: Secret
Current occupation: Professional criminal
Former occupation: Unrevealed
Citizenship: Unrevealed
Legal status: Unrevealed
Place of birth: Unrevealed
Marital status: Unrevealed
Known relatives: None
Known confidants: Bloodlust
Known allies: Critical Mass, Femme Fatales (Bloodlust, Mindblast, Knockout)
Major enemies: Spider-Man, Wolverine, Black Cat
Usual base of operations: Mobile
Former bases of operations: Unrevealed
Current group membership: The Femme Fatales
Former group membership: Critical Mass's band of mutants
Extent of education: Unrevealed

PHYSICAL DESCRIPTION

Height: 5'10"
Weight: 142 lbs.
Eyes: Blue
Hair: Blonde
Other distinguishing features: None

POWERS AND ABILITIES

Intelligence: Normal
Strength: Peak human
Speed: Athlete
Stamina: Peak human
Durability: Athlete
Agility: Peak human
Reflexes: Athlete
Fighting skills: Extensive hand-to-hand combat experience
Special skills and abilities: Expertise at using whips
Superhuman physical powers: Unrevealed
Superhuman mental powers: None
Special limitations: None
Source of superhuman powers: Whiplash II was reputed to belong to a group composed of mutants. Whether she is a mutant or not and what her mutant abilities are are as yet unrevealed.

PARAPHERNALIA

Costume specifications: Synthetic stretch fabric laced with kevlar, leather shoulder padding and steel breastplates and mask
Personal weaponry: Two gauntlets containing three spring-loaded retractable omnium steel cables on each arm. Each cable can extend a maximum length of about 25 feet and contains needle-sharp adamantium barbs on the tips.
Special weaponry: None
Other accessories: Unrevealed
Transportation: Unrevealed
Design and manufacture of paraphernalia: Unrevealed

BIBLIOGRAPHY

First appearance: MARVEL COMICS PRESENTS #49
Origin issue: Whiplash II's origin is as yet unrevealed.
Significant issues: MARVEL COMICS PRESENTS #49-50 (alongside Critical Mass's mutant band, kidnaped "Mr. Beck" and daughter in order to coerce them to join their band, battled Spider-Man and Wolverine, disappeared after daughter's telekinetic explosion enabled her to get free); AMAZING SPIDER-MAN #340 (alongside Femme Fatales, hired by the Chameleon in the guise of Dr. Turner to battle Spider-Man to convince him to have the doctor further study his powers); AMAZING SPIDER-MAN #343 (alongside Femme Fatales, Scorpion, Tarantula, and Chameleon, battled Spider-Man and the Black Cat); CAPTAIN AMERICA #389-390 (among superhuman females aboard Superia's cruise-ship, attacked Captain America and Paladin en masse, traveled to Superia's Island to be one of her new "Femizons")

Note: Whiplash II should not be confused with Whiplash I (Mark Scarlotti) who is now known as Blacklash.

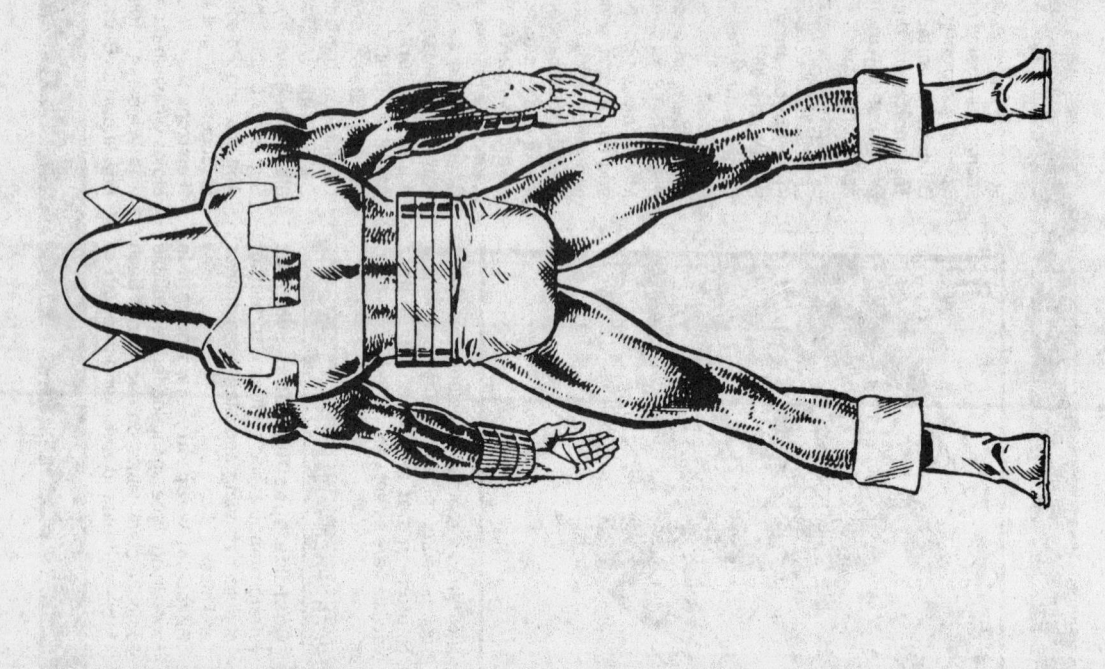

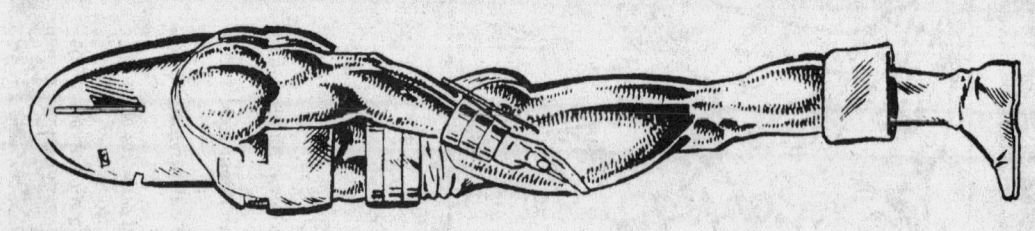

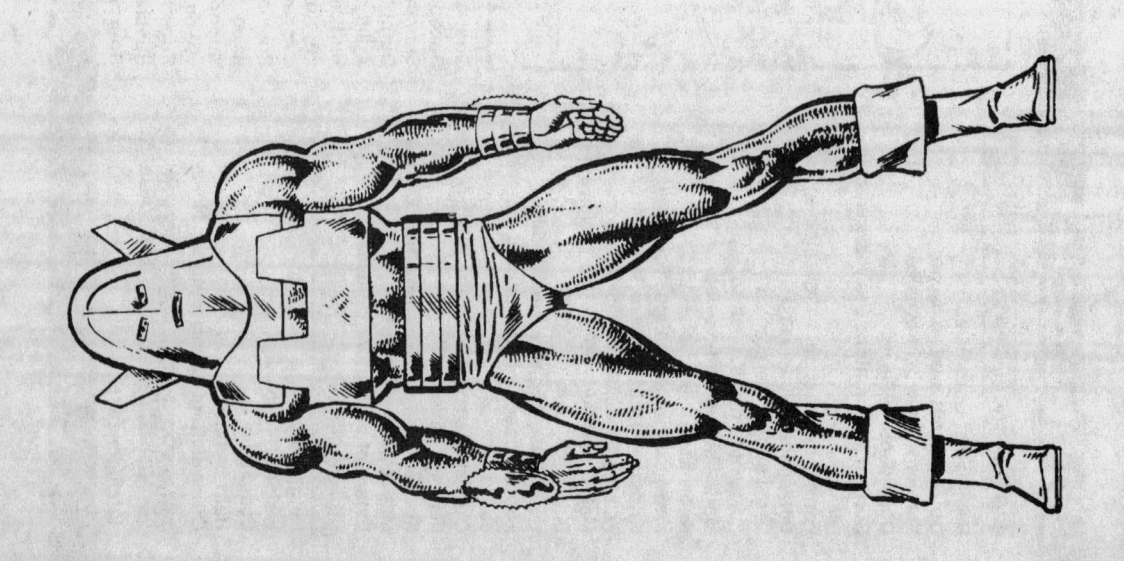

WHIRLWIND™

WHIRLWIND

BIOGRAPHICAL DATA

Real name: David Cannon
Other current aliases: None
Former aliases: Human Top
Dual identity: Publicly known
Current occupation: Professional criminal
Former occupation: Circus performer; professional wrestler; ice skating competitor
Citizenship: United States of America
Legal status: Criminal record
Place of birth: Kansas City, Missouri
Marital status: Single
Known relatives: None
Known confidants: None
Known allies: Batroc, Porcupine, Trapster, Lethal Legion (Count Nefaria), Power Man I, Living Laser), Masters of Evil II (Klaw, Radioactive Man, Melter), Masters of Evil III (Egghead, Radioactive Man, Scorpion, Moonstone, Tiger Shark), Masters of Evil IV (Tiger Shark)
Major enemies: The Avengers, Henry Pym
Usual base of operations: Mobile
Current group membership: None
Former group membership: Former member of the Masters of Evil II, III, IV; agent of Count Nefaria
Education: High school dropout

PHYSICAL DESCRIPTION

Height: 6'1"
Weight: 220 lbs.
Eyes: Blue
Hair: Brown
Other distinguishing features: None

POWERS AND ABILITIES

Intelligence: Normal
Strength: Enhanced human
Speed: Subsonic
Stamina: Enhanced human
Durability: Athlete
Agility: Metahuman
Reflexes: Metahuman
Fighting skills: Extensive experience at a unique style of combat that exploits his superhuman abilities
Special skills and abilities: Unrevealed
Superhuman physical powers: The ability to rotate his body around its lengthwise axis at speeds up to 400 revolutions per minute, without impairing his ability to see, speak or interact with his environment (for instance, pick up objects or change clothes); Although he can only rotate at subsonic speeds he can only travel up to 50 mph in a straight line for up to 30 minutes, or fly like a helicopter at speeds of up to 120 mph for up to 10 minutes at a time; the ability to focus air currents generated by his rotation into a jet stream powerful enough to blast a hole through a brick wall, as well as create a windscreen able to deflect matter as massive as a falling boulder; plus, the ability to create small tornadoes.
Superhuman mental powers: None
Special limitations: None
Source of superhuman power: Genetic mutation

PARAPHERNALIA

Costume specifications: Full body armor
Personal weaponry: Two 10 inch diameter hardened tool-steel sawblades mounted on metal bracelets and driven by two DC servo-motors each; activated by palm switches, each blade is capable of 1600 revolutions per minute; also, shuriken (throwing stars) and razor sharp jacks
Special weaponry: None
Other accessories: None
Design and manufacture of paraphernalia: The Tinkerer
Transportation: Various, often flight under own power

BIBLIOGRAPHY

First appearance: (as Human Top) TALES TO ASTONISH #50; (as Whirlwind) AVENGERS #46
Origin issue: TALES TO ASTONISH #50
Significant issues: TALES TO ASTONISH #50 (first battled Henry Pym [then known as Giant-Man] while pursuing career as a jewel thief); AVENGERS #46 (redesigned costume, adopted "Whirlwind" identity; also adopted identity of "Charles Mathews", chauffeur of Janet Van Dyne [the Wasp]); AVENGERS #54 (joined Masters of Evil II, participated in plot to destroy Avengers); AVENGERS #83 (joined Masters of Evil III, participated in Vermont battle against Avengers); CAPTAIN AMERICA #130 (with Batroc and Porcupine on mission for the Red Skull); AVENGERS #139 (discarded "Charles Mathews" identity after Henry Pym [then known as Yellowjacket] discovered his true identity; battled Pym); AVENGERS #164 (employed by Count Nefaria; joined Lethal Legion; powers temporarily enhanced); AVENGERS #222 (joined Masters of Evil III in plan to destroy Avengers; caused defeat of Masters by attacking prematurely); CAPTAIN AMERICA #324 (partnered with Trapster; obtained new battle armor and weapons from Tinkerer; battled Captain America in attempt to bolster criminal reputation); WEST COAST AVENGERS #16 (partnered with Tiger Shark; travelled to San Francisco to steal experimental "psycho-circuit"; battled Avengers West Coast)

WHITE BISHOP

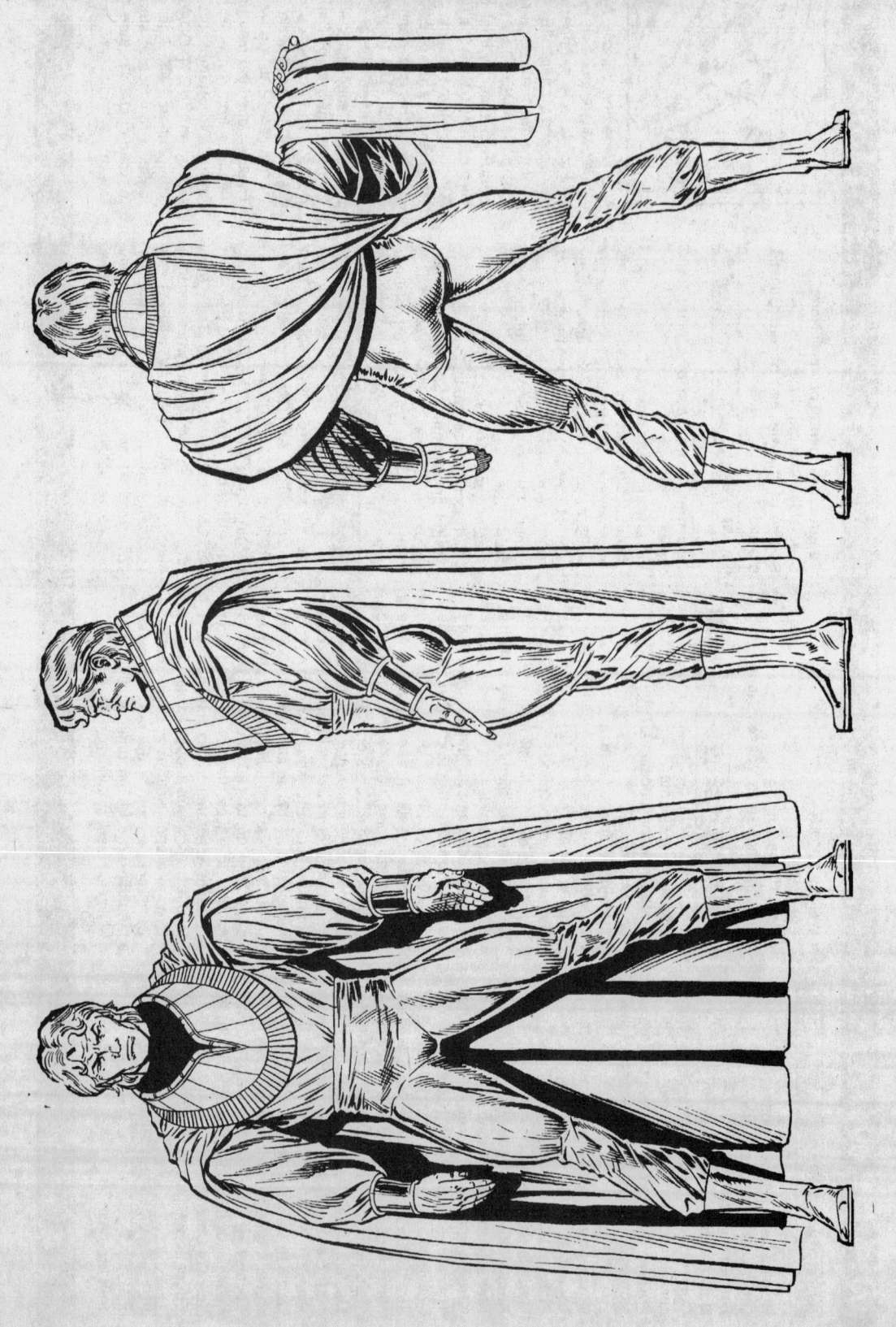

WHITE BISHOP

BIOGRAPHICAL DATA

Real name: Donald Pierce
Aliases at time of death: None
Former aliases: None
Dual identity: None; the general populace of Earth was unaware of Pierce's criminal activities
Occupation at time of death: Professional criminal and terrorist
Former occupation: CEO and principal shareholder of Pierce-Consolidated Mining
Citizenship: United States of America
Legal status: No criminal record
Place of birth: Philadelphia, Pennsylvania
Place of death: The Hellfire Club Mansion, New York City
Cause of death: Electrocuted by Sentinels sent by Trevor Fitzroy from the future
Marital status: Presumed single
Known relatives: None
Known confidants: None
Known allies: The Reavers (Cole, Macon, Reese, Pretty Boy, Bonebreaker, Skullbuster [all deceased], Cylla), (former) Inner Circle of Hellfire Club (Sebastian Shaw (legally deceased), Emma Frost (deceased), Harry Leland (deceased), Elsie Dee, Albert
Major enemies: The X-Men, the New Mutants, Wolverine, Freedom Force, Sebastian Shaw, Emma Frost, Trevor Fitzroy
Base of operations at time of death: The Reavers' Australian headquarters
Former bases of operations: The Hellfire Club Mansion, New York City; a mining and laboratory complex in Cameron, Kentucky
Group membership at time of death: Leader of the Reavers
Former group membership: The Hellfire Club Inner Circle
Extent of education: College graduate in geological engineering and business administration

PHYSICAL DESCRIPTION

Height: 6' 2"
Weight: 220 lbs.
Eyes: Blue
Hair: Blonde
Other distinguishing features: Donald Pierce was a cyborg with four artificial limbs.

POWERS AND ABILITIES

Intelligence: Above normal
Strength: Superhuman Class 10
Speed: Enhanced human
Stamina: Enhanced human
Durability: Enhanced human
Agility: Enhanced human
Reflexes: Enhanced human
Fighting skills: Fair hand-to-hand combatant; relies on his cyborg strength
Special skills and abilities: Accomplished strategist and business administrator
Superhuman physical powers: Aside from the above listed attributes, ability to generate shocking electrical current through cyborg limbs or to hurl electrical force over short distances
Superhuman mental powers: The ability to turn psionic assaults against attacker to a limited degree
Special limitations: None
Source of superhuman powers: Various as needed

PARAPHERNALIA

Costume specifications: (with the Hellfire Club) Conventional attire of the 18th Century; (with the Reavers) body armor
Personal weaponry: None
Special weaponry: Various as needed
Other accessories: None
Transportation: Teleportation via Gateway's powers
Design and manufacture of paraphernalia: Unrevealed

BIBLIOGRAPHY

First appearance: UNCANNY X-MEN #129
Origin issue: The White Bishop's origin is as yet unrevealed.
Significant issues: UNCANNY X-MEN #132-134 (with Mastermind and the Inner Circle of the Hellfire Club, battled the X-Men; defeated by Colossus); MARVEL GRAPHIC NOVEL #4 (with cyborgs Cole, Macon, and Reese, kidnaped Professor Xavier and Tessa in revenge plot against Hellfire Club and X-Men; defeated by the New Mutants; returned by Tessa to Hellfire Club and expelled from Inner Circle); UNCANNY X-MEN #251-253 (joined the Reavers, took back the Reavers' former base, captured and crucified Wolverine; tracked the escaped Wolverine and Jubilee); UNCANNY X-MEN #254-255 (with the Reavers, attacked Muir Island, battled Moira MacTaggart's "X-Men" and Freedom Force); UNCANNY X-MEN #262 (with Reavers, attacked Frost Techtonics plant in California); WOLVERINE Vol. 2 #37-39 (created androids Elsie Dee and Albert; sent them against Wolverine); UNCANNY X-MEN #281 (with Reavers, killed when attacked by Trevor Fitzroy's Sentinels)

WHITE QUEEN

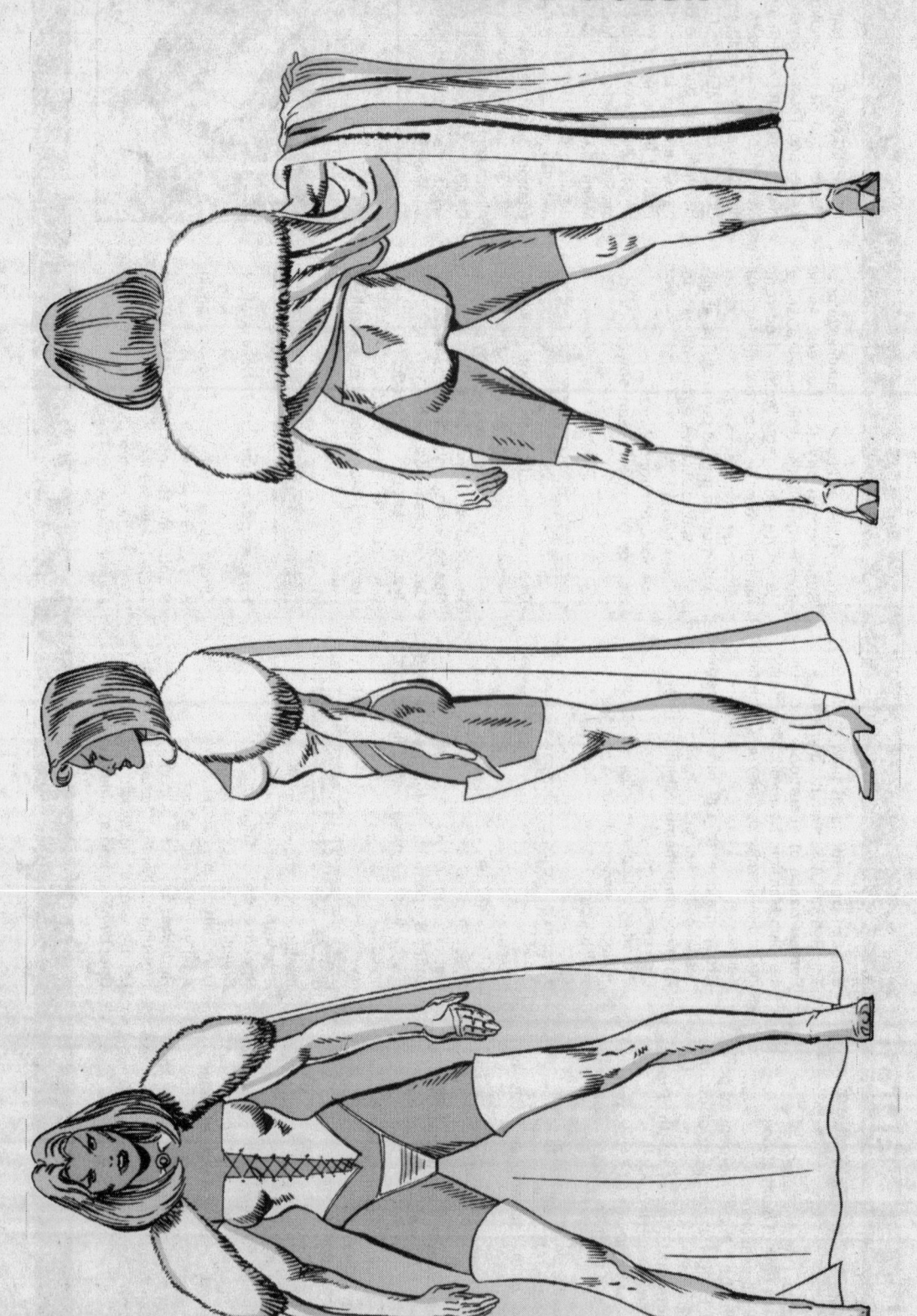

WHITE QUEEN

BIOGRAPHICAL DATA

Real name: Emma Frost
Other current aliases: None
Former aliases: Storm
Dual identity: Secret; the general populace is aware of the she is a leader in the Hellfire Club, but is unaware of her criminal activities
Current occupation: Chairman of the Board and CEO of Frost International, Chairman of the Board of Trustees and headmistress of Massachusetts Academy, Snow Valley, Massachusetts; subversive
Former occupation: Businesswoman
Citizenship: United States of America
Legal status: No criminal record
Place of birth: Boston, Massachusetts
Marital status: Single
Known relatives: None
Known confidants: (former) Sebastian Shaw (ex-Black King, deceased)
Known allies: (former) Inner Circle of Hellfire Club (Sebastian Shaw, Harry Leland, Friedrich von Roehm all deceased), Lourdes Chantel (deceased), the Hellions (most now deceased), Mastermind (deceased), Magneto, Black Queen II (Selene)
Major enemies: The X-Men, the New Mutants, Firestar, the New Warriors, Trevor Fitzroy, the Sentinels, (former) Mastermind (deceased), Donald Pierce (deceased), the Reavers (deceased), Edward Buckman (deceased), Paris Seville (deceased)
Usual base of operations: Boston, Massachusetts; Hellfire Club mansion, New York City; Massachusetts academy, Snow Valley, Massachusetts
Former bases of operations: Chicago, Illinois; Washington, D.C.
Current group membership: The Lords Cardinal of the Inner Circle of the Hellfire Club
Former group membership: Mentor of the Hellions
Extent of education: College degree in business administration

PHYSICAL DESCRIPTION

Height: 5' 10"
Weight: 144 lbs.
Eyes: Blue
Hair: Ash blonde
Other distinguishing features: None

POWERS AND ABILITIES

Intelligence: Gifted
Strength: Normal
Speed: Athlete
Stamina: Athlete
Durability: Athlete
Agility: Athlete
Reflexes: Athlete
Fighting skills: Some training in hand-to-hand combat
Special skills and abilities: Superb businesswoman, highly capable planner, expert in electronics, skilled inventor of electronic devices utilizing psionic energy
Superhuman physical powers: None
Superhuman mental powers: Telepathy, mind-control, mental sedation of unconscious victims, projection of psionic force bolts causing mental pain or unconsciousness, induction of mental pain by touch
Special limitations: None
Source of superhuman powers: Genetic mutation

PARAPHERNALIA

Costume specifications: Synthetic and ordinary fabric styled in a late 18th century English motif
Personal weaponry: None
Special weaponry: A gun-like device enabling her to exchange minds with another person
Other accessories: None
Transportation: Various vehicles of the Hellfire Club and Frost International
Design and manufacture of paraphernalia: Emma frost and Frost International

BIBLIOGRAPHY

First appearance: UNCANNY X-MEN #129
Origin issue: The White Queen's origin is as yet unrevealed.
Significant issues: CLASSIC X-MEN #7 (discovered plans of Edward Buckman and Steven Lang to destroy all mutants; alongside Sebastian Shaw, Lourdes Chantel, Harry Leland, battled Lang's Sentinels; alongside Shaw, killed Buckman and the Council of the Chosen, took control of the Hellfire Club); UNCANNY X-MEN #129-131 (attempted to recruit Kitty Pryde for massachusetts Academy; captured Storm, Colossus, and Wolverine; battled Phoenix); UNCANNY X-MEN #151-152 (exchanged bodies with Storm); UNCANNY X-MEN #169 (rendered temporarily catatonic by Mastermind); FIRESTAR #1-4 (recruited Firestar for Massachusetts Academy; organized and trained the Hellions; battled Firestar); UNCANNY X-MEN #180 (attempted to recruit Doug Ramsey for Massachusetts Academy, captured Kitty Pryde); NEW MUTANTS #15-17 (with Hellions, battled the New Mutants); NEW MUTANTS #38-40 (coerced Magneto into allowing New Mutants to join Massachusetts Academy); UNCANNY X-MEN #210 (with Shaw and Selene, invited Magneto to join Hellfire Club); NEW MUTANTS #56-57 (engineered contest between New Mutants and Hellions, recruited Magma for Massachusetts Academy): NEW MUTANTS #62 (had Empath accompany Magma to Nova Roma); NEW MUTANTS ANNUAL #4 (alongside Magneto, Shaw, and Selene, battled the High Evolutionary's forces to rescue Magma); NEW MUTANTS #69-71, 73 (helped Magneto search for missing New Mutants; alongside Magneto, Shaw, and Selene, encountered effects of Inferno); NEW MUTANTS #75 (alongside Magneto, Shaw, and Selene, battled New Mutants; voted to oust Shaw from Club);

WHITE TIGER

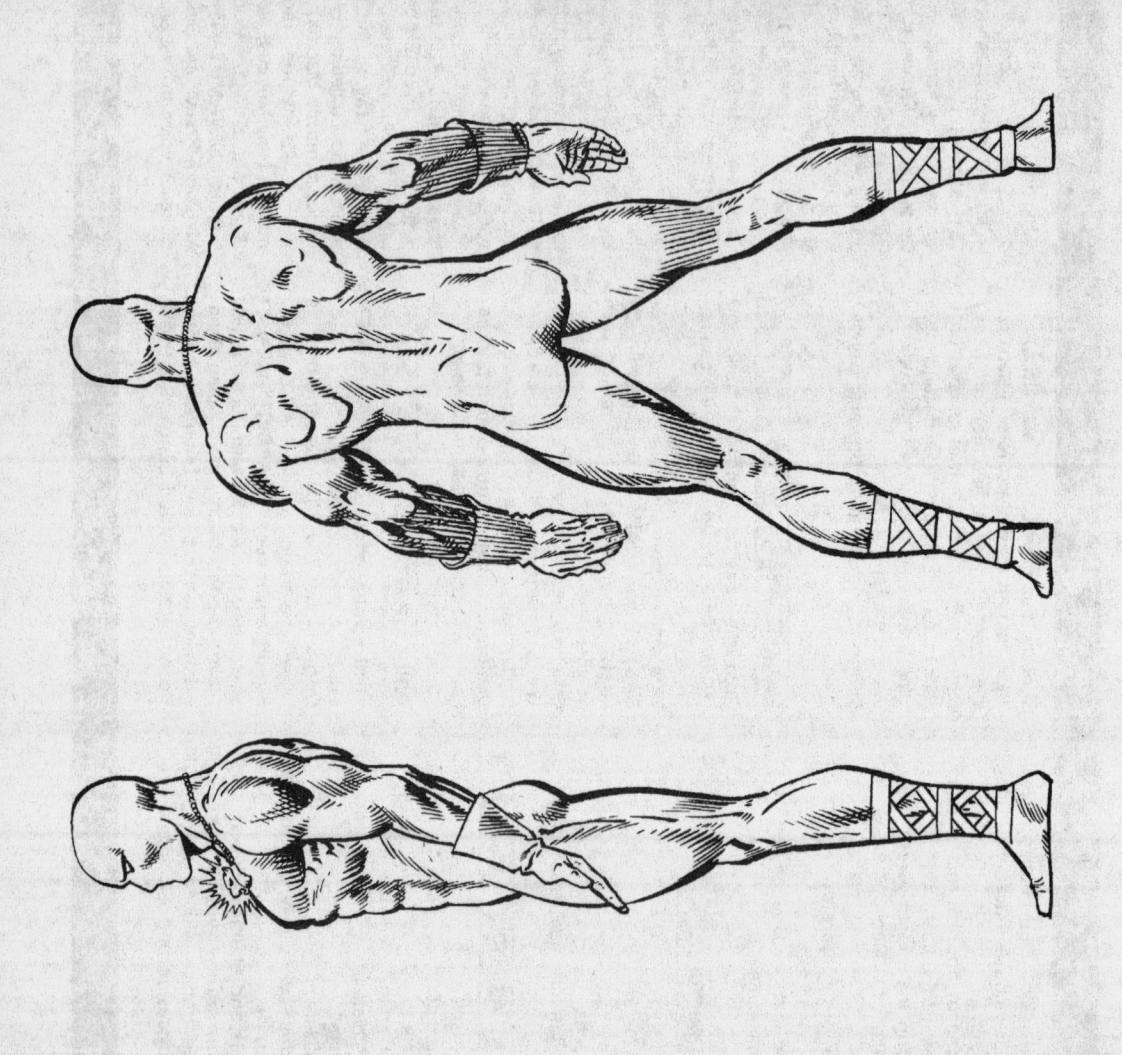

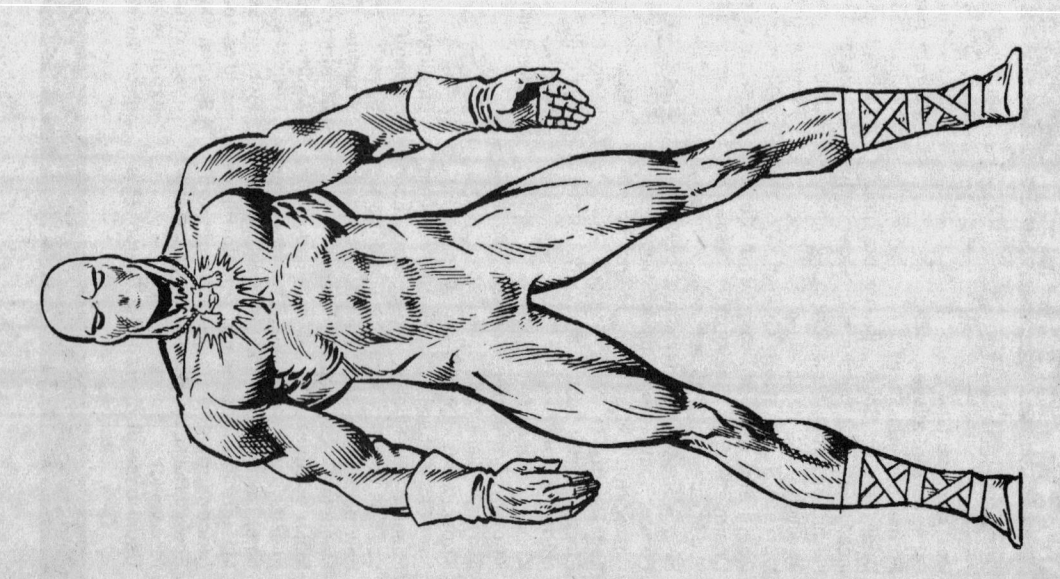

WHITE TIGER

BIOGRAPHICAL DATA

Real name: Hector Ayala
Other current aliases: None
Former aliases: White Tiger
Dual identity: Known to the public, costumed identity currently abandoned
Current occupation: College student
Former occupation: Unrevealed
Citizenship: United States of America
Legal status: No criminal record
Place of birth: San Juan, Puerto Rico
Marital status: Single
Known relatives: Nestor Ayala (father, deceased), Maria Ayala (mother, deceased), Filippe Ayala (brother, deceased), Awilda Ayala (sister, deceased)
Known confidants: Holly Gillis
Known allies: Detective Nathanial Byrd, Detective James D'Angelo, Jack of Hearts, Shang-Chi, Iron Fist, Spider-Man
Major enemies: Gideon Mace
Usual base of operations: New York City
Former bases of operations: None
Current group membership: None
Former group membership: None
Extent of education: Completed some college courses

PHYSICAL DESCRIPTION

Height: 6'
Weight: 190 lbs.
Eyes: Brown
Hair: Black
Other distinguishing features: None

POWERS AND ABILITIES

Intelligence: Above normal
Strength: (without amulet) Athlete, (with amulet) Enhanced human
Speed: (without amulet) Athlete, (with amulet) Enhanced human
Stamina: (without amulet) Athlete, (with amulet) Enhanced human
Durability: (without amulet) Athlete, (with amulet) Enhanced human
Agility: (without amulet) Athlete, (with amulet) Enhanced human
Reflexes: (without amulet) Athlete, (with amulet) Enhanced human
Fighting skills: Without his amulet, Hector Ayala had minimal experience in hand-to-hand combat. The amulet conferred on him the experience and abilities of a master martial artist.
Special skills and abilities: Unrevealed
Superhuman physical powers: See above
Superhuman mental powers: None
Special limitations: The White Tiger only possessed his enhanced abilities when wearing the three mystical tiger amulets.
Source of superhuman powers: The three mystical tiger amulets originally worn by the Sons of the Tiger (Abraham Brown, Bob Diamond, and Lin Sun)

PARAPHERNALIA

Costume specifications: Synthetic stretch fabric
Personal weaponry: None
Special weaponry: None
Other accessories: The three mystical tiger amulets (a head and two paws)
Transportation: Conventional transportation
Design and manufacture of paraphernalia: Unknown artisans from extradimensional K'un-Lun.
Note: The amulets are currently back in K'un-Lun, reunited with the jade tiger statue they were cut from.

BIBLIOGRAPHY

First appearance: DEADLY HANDS OF KUNG-FU #19
Origin issue: DEADLY HANDS OF KUNG-FU #19
Significant issues: DEADLY HANDS OF KUNG-FU #19 (discovered the tiger amulets thrown away by the Sons of the Tiger, transformed for the first time into the White Tiger), DEADLY HANDS OF KUNG-FU #20 (went into action for the first time against a street gang), DEADLY HANDS OF KUNG-FU #21 (battled the Prowler who believed him to be a murderer), DEADLY HANDS OF KUNG-FU #22-23 (battled the Jack of Hearts who also believed him to be behind his father's murder), DEADLY HANDS OF KUNG-FU #26 (fought off unnamed Corporation costumed assailants threatening his sister and Jack of Hearts), DEADLY HANDS OF KUNG-FU #31 (alongside Jack of Hearts, Shang-Chi, and Iron Fist, fought Stryke and other agents of the Corporation, learned his brother Filippo was attempting to find employment with Fu Manchu), DEADLY HANDS OF KUNG-FU #32 (encountered the Sons of the Tiger), SPECTACULAR SPIDER-MAN #9-10 (impersonated by Professor Vasquez, battled Spider-Man), SPECTACULAR SPIDER-MAN #25-31 (alongside Spider-Man and Daredevil, battled the Masked Marauder, Darter and Carrion), SPECTACULAR SPIDER-MAN #52 (gunned down by Gideon Mace, operated upon to remove the bullets, recovered, gave up the tiger amulets, moved out west with his girlfriend Holly Gillis

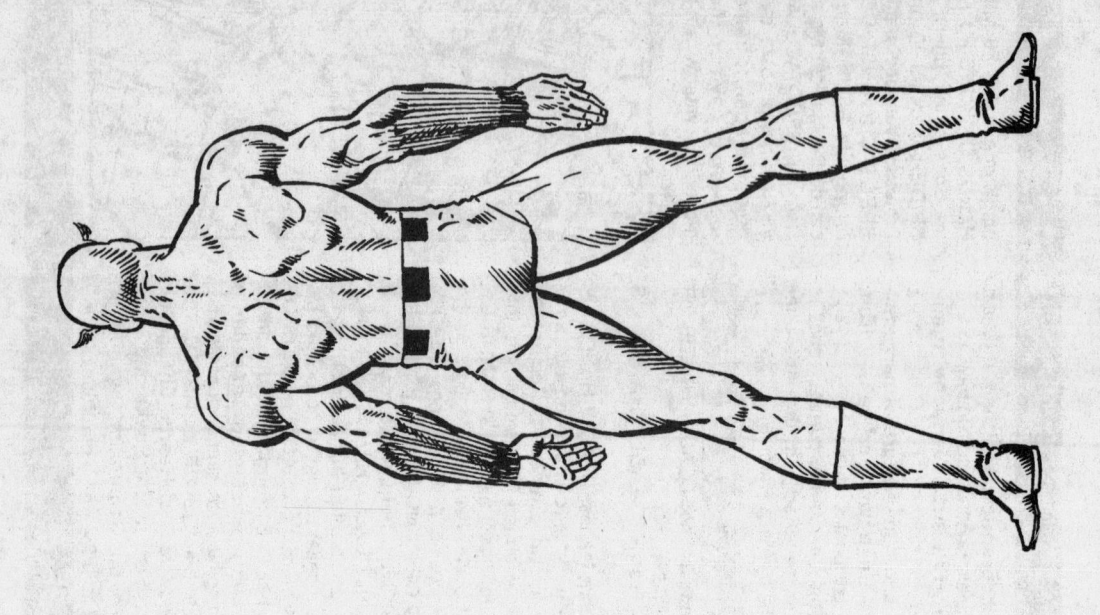

WHIZZER

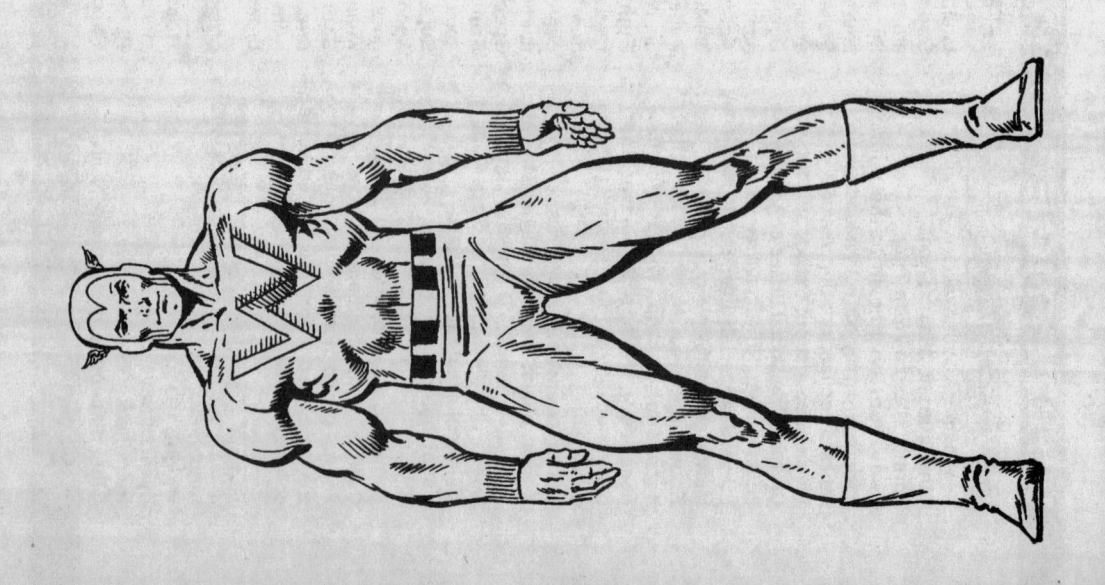

WHIZZER

BIOGRAPHICAL DATA

Real name: Robert L. Frank
Other aliases at time of death: None
Former aliases: None
Dual Identity: Known to the United States government
Occupation at time of death: Adventurer
Former occupation: Nuclear laboratory technician
Citizenship: United States of America
Legal status: No criminal record in the United States
Place of birth: St. Louis, Missouri
Place of death: New York City
Cause of death: Heart attack
Marital status: Widower
Known relatives: Dr. Emil Frank (father, deceased), Madeline Joyce Frank (wife, alias Miss America, wife, deceased), Robert Frank Jr. (alias Nuklo, son)
Known confidants at time of death: Madeline Joyce Frank (alias Miss America, wife, deceased)
Known allies: Captain America, the Invaders, the Liberty Legion, the All-Winners Squad, the Avengers
Major enemies: The Red Skull, Isbisa
Usual base of operations: New York City
Former bases of operations: New York City
Group membership at time of death: None
Former group membership: The Liberty Legion, the All-Winners Squad

Extent of education: High school graduate

PHYSICAL DESCRIPTION

Height: 5' 10"
Weight: 180 lbs.
Eyes: Brown
Hair: Brown, later gray
Other distinguishing features: None

POWERS AND ABILITIES

Intelligence: Normal
Strength: Enhanced human (leg press only)
Speed: Superhuman
Stamina: Enhanced human
Durability: Enhanced human
Agility: Peak human
Reflexes: Enhanced human
Fighting skills: A unique, self-taught fighting style which exploits the ability to move at superhuman speeds
Special skills and abilities: Unrevealed
Superhuman physical powers: Superhuman speed and reflexes, can create cyclones by running in circles, can run up walls and across water. In his prime he could attain speeds 50% faster than he could in middle age.
Superhuman mental powers: None
Special limitations: None

Source of superhuman powers: Mutagenic reaction to injection of mongoose blood

PARAPHERNALIA

Costume specifications: Ordinary fabric
Personal weaponry: None
Special weaponry: None
Other accessories: None
Transportation: Various, often on foot
Design and manufacture of paraphernalia: Inapplicable

BIBLIOGRAPHY

First appearance: (modern) GIANT-SIZE AVENGERS #1
Origin issue: MARVEL PREMIERE #29
Significant issues: GIANT-SIZE AVENGERS #1 (encountered Avengers, reunited with son Nuklo, suffered heart attack, learned erroneously that the Scarlet Witch and Quicksilver were his children), MARVEL PREMIERE #29-30 (career as 40's crimefighter recounted, joined the Liberty Legion); AVENGERS #153 (duped by Living Laser into battling the Avengers, suffered second heart attack); AVENGERS #155-156 (battled Atlanteans and Namor alongside Avengers); AVENGERS #165 (attacked Count Nefaria); VISION AND SCARLET WITCH Vol.1 #2 (suffered fatal heart attack while battling long-time foe Isbisa; son Nuklo cured of excessive radiation level, died still believing Quicksilver and Scarlet Witch were his children)

WHIZZER

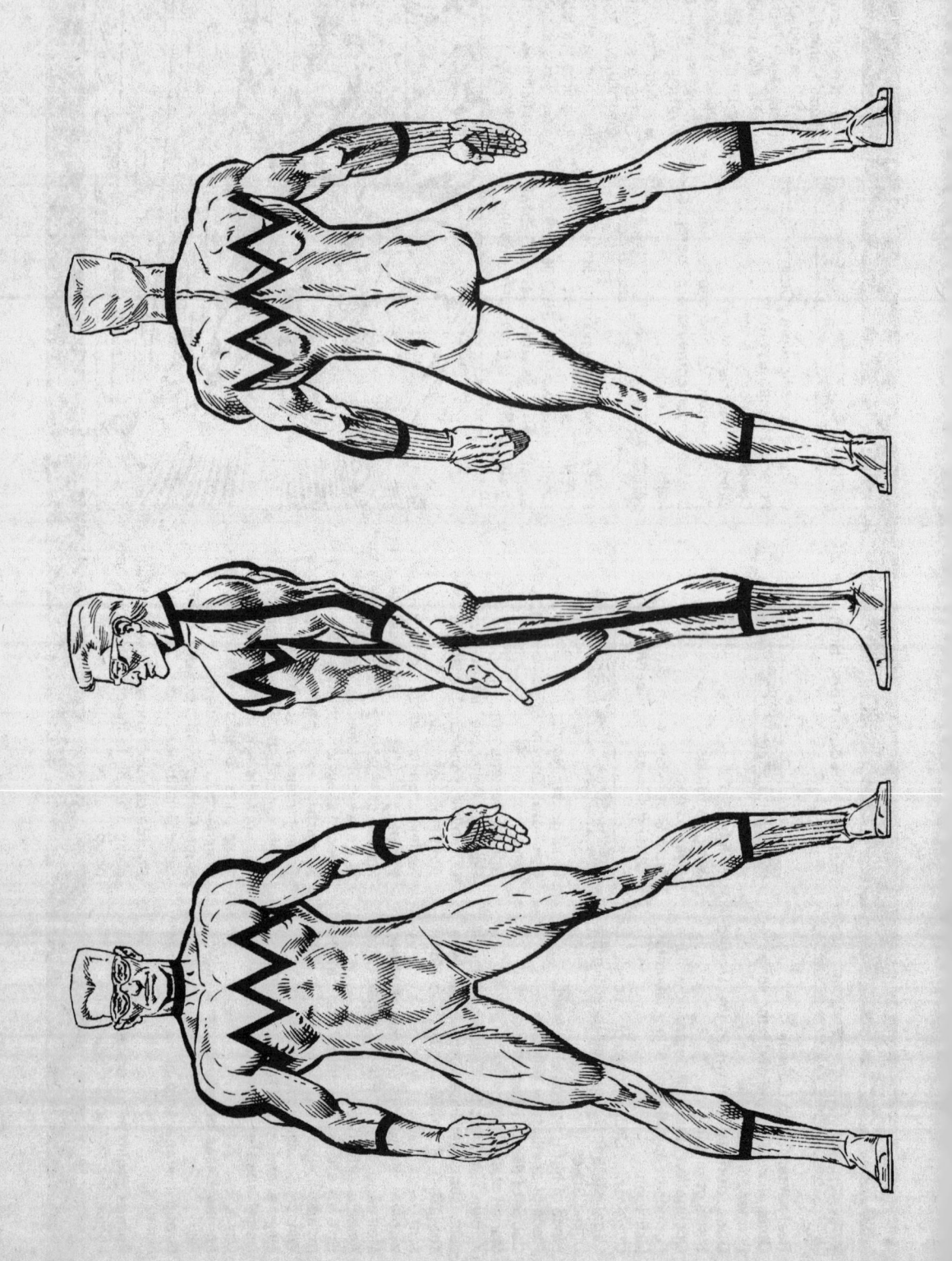

WHIZZER II

BIOGRAPHICAL DATA

Real name: Stanley Stewart
Current aliases: None
Former aliases: None known
Dual identity: Publicly known to the citizens of the United States of "Other-Earth" ("Earth-S")
Current occupation: Adventurer
Former occupation: Postman
Citizenship: United States of "Other-Earth" or "Earth-S"
Legal status: No criminal record
Place of birth: Unrevealed
Marital status: Married
Known relatives: Madeline (wife), Tina (daughter)
Known confidants: Madeline Stewart, Doctor Spectrum II, Arcanna Jones (Moonglow II), Phillip Jones
Known allies: The Squadron Supreme, Quasar, Avengers, Defenders, Doctor Strange
Major enemies: Scarlet Centurion, the Over-Mind, Null the Living Darkness, Bollix, the Rustler, (former) Institute of Evil, Master Menace, Nth Man I
Usual base of operations: Project: Pegasus, New York State
Former base of operations: Rocket Central (Squadron Supreme satellite); Squadron Mountain headquarters, Moreland; Squadron City, Great American Desert, United States of "Other-Earth"
Current group membership: The Squadron Supreme
Former group membership: None
Extent of education: Unrevealed, at least high school

PHYSICAL DESCRIPTION

Height: 5' 11"
Weight: 180 lbs.
Eyes: Blue
Hair: White-blond
Other distinguishing features: None

POWERS AND ABILITIES

Intelligence: Normal
Strength: (upper body) Athlete, (lower body and legs) Enhanced human
Speed: Subsonic
Stamina: Superhuman
Durability: Enhanced human
Agility: Athlete
Reflexes: Superhuman
Fighting skills: Good hand-to-hand combatant, coached by Nighthawk I, relies on speed rather than combat skills
Special skills and abilities: None known
Superhuman physical powers: Aside from the above listed attributes, the Whizzer can create cyclones by running in circles, can run up walls and across water, has limited immunity to the effects of friction
Superhuman mental powers: None
Special limitations: The Whizzer's body generates normal fatigue poisons. As a result, after using his superhuman speed powers extensively during the day, the Whizzer must lie in a deep sleep for approximately eight hours. He must also consume an unusually large amount of food due to the huge amounts of energy that superhumanly fast motion requires.
Source of superhuman powers: Mutagenic effects of fogbank of unknown nature.

PARAPHERNALIA

Costume specifications: Synthetic stretch fabric, treated to resist adverse effects of friction
Personal weaponry: None
Special weaponry: None
Other accessories: Wears goggles to help protect his eyes from the adverse effects of running at superhuman speed
Transportation: None, travels under own power; formerly sometimes used Squadron air vehicles
Design and manufacture of paraphernalia: Unrevealed

BIBLIOGRAPHY

First appearance: AVENGERS #85
Origin issue: (partial) SQUADRON SUPREME #9
Significant issues: AVENGERS #85-86 (first encountered Avengers; with Squadron Supreme and Avengers, battled Brain-Child II); AVENGERS #148-149 (with Squadron, battled the Avengers on behalf of Serpent Cartel, then turned against Cartel); DEFENDERS #112-114 (with Squadron, fell under mind control of the Over-Mind; freed by Defenders; battled alongside the Squadron and Defenders against the Over-Mind and Null the Living Darkness); SQUADRON SUPREME #1 (resolved with the Squadron to assume the government of the United States); SQUADRON SUPREME #5 (deserted Squadron when Institute of Evil captured his family, launched berserk attack on Institute); SQUADRON SUPREME #12 (defeated by Haywire during battle between Squadron and Redeemers); SQUADRON SUPREME: DEATH OF A UNIVERSE (with Squadron, attempted to save the universe from the expanding Nth Man); QUASAR #13-15 (with Squadron stranded on the Avengers' Earth, encountered Quasar, relocated to Project: Pegasus; fell under mental control of Over-Mind; regained will on the Stranger's laboratory world); QUASAR #17 (participated in Runner's race of superhumanly fast Earth people); QUASAR #19 (alongside Squadron Supreme in Dr. Strange's failed attempt to return them to their own Earth); QUASAR #25 (with Hyperion and Spectrum, battled Deathurge)

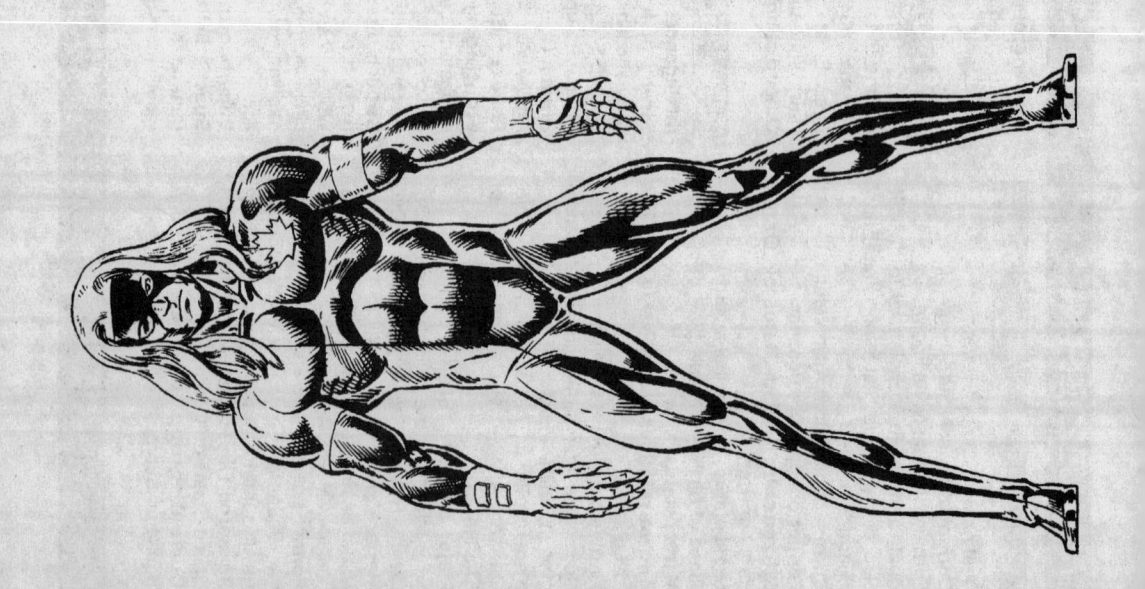

WILDHEART™

WILDHEART

BIOGRAPHICAL DATA

Real name: (allegedly) Kyle (last name unrevealed)
Other current aliases: None
Former aliases: Wild Child, Weapon Omega
Dual identity: Secret, known to certain Canadian government officials
Current Occupation: Special operative of the Canadian government, assigned to Alpha Flight
Former occupation: Professional criminal
Citizenship: Canada
Legal status: Criminal record in Canada and the U.S.
Place of birth: Unrevealed, presumably Canada
Marital status: Single
Known relatives: None
Known confidants: None
Known allies: Alpha Flight, Nemesis, Beta Flight, X-Factor II, Weapon X II (Kane), (former) Jerry Jaxon, Omega Flight I
Major enemies: Rok, Diablo, Wrecker, Wrecking Crew, Wyre, "Wild Child" doppelganger, (former) Wolverine, Alpha Flight
Usual base of operations: Alpha Flight headquarters, Toronto, Canada
Former bases of operations: Roxxon headquarters, New York City; later mobile
Current group membership: Alpha Flight
Former group membership: Gamma Flight I, Omega Flight I
Extent of education: Unrevealed

PHYSICAL DESCRIPTION

Height: 5' 8"
Weight: 135 lbs
Eyes: Green-blue
Hair: Blond
Other distinguishing features: Wildheart has long fingernails which can be used as claw-like weapons

POWERS AND ABILITIES

Intelligence: Normal
Strength: Athlete
Speed: Athlete
Stamina: Metahuman
Durability: Superhuman regenerative
Agility: Enhanced human
Reflexes: Enhanced human
Fighting skills: Superb hand-to-hand combatant, trained by Wolverine; in his bestial rages Wildheart relies more on sheer ferocity than fighting skill
Special skills and abilities: None known
Superhuman physical powers: Aside from the above listed attributes, possesses superhumanly acute senses.
Superhuman mental powers: None
Special limitations: The savage, bestial side of Wildheart's personality has been suppressed by an unknown drug, but his savage self still threatens to overwhelm his sanity at times.
Source of superhuman powers: Genetically engineered by Secret Empire scientists using DNA replicated from Wyre

PARAPHERNALIA

Costume specifications: Synthetic stretch fabric
Personal weaponry: None
Special weaponry: None
Other accessories: None
Transportation: Alpha Flight omni-jet, and other vehicles supplied by the Canadian government
Design and manufacture of paraphernalia: Stark Enterprises

BIBLIOGRAPHY

First appearance: (unidentified) ALPHA FLIGHT #1; (identified as Wild Child) ALPHA FLIGHT #11, (as Weapon Omega) ALPHA FLIGHT #102, (as Wildheart) ALPHA FLIGHT #118, (in Wildheart costume) ALPHA FLIGHT #19
Origin issue: ALPHA FLIGHT #118
Significant issues: ALPHA FLIGHT #1 (seen as member of Gamma Flight); ALPHA FLIGHT #11-13 (joined Omega Flight, alongside them, battled Alpha Flight); ALPHA FLIGHT #26-28 (alongside Omega Flight, battled Alpha Flight again in West Edmonton Mall, was defeated by Madison Jefferies); MARVEL COMICS PRESENTS #51-53 (embarked on series of killings, severely injured Heather Hudson, battled Wolverine); ALPHA FLIGHT #76 (first appeared as member of Gamma Flight II); ALPHA FLIGHT #84 (alongside Gamma Flight II, battled Alpha Flight); ALPHA FLIGHT #85-86 (aided Gamma and Alpha Flights against Llan the Sorcerer's forces); ALPHA FLIGHT #87 (went on a rampage, mauled Laura Dean, was captured by Wolverine); ALPHA FLIGHT #102-103 (cured of mental illness; as Weapon Omega alongside Alpha Flight, fought Diablo); ALPHA FLIGHT #104 (joined Alpha Flight's "Core Alpha"); ALPHA FLIGHT #107 (met X-Factor II); ALPHA FLIGHT #108 (prevented mind-controlled Omerta from assassinating Italy's head of State); ALPHA FLIGHT #111 (fought Wild Child doppelganger during Infinity War); ALPHA FLIGHT #114-115 (attacked by Alpha Flight); ALPHA FLIGHT #116 (searched for Nemesis, held prisoner with her by Rok, rescued by Weapon X II (Kane)); ALPHA FLIGHT #117-118 (defeated Wyre in personal combat; learned about his origin, renamed himself Wildheart); ALPHA FLIGHT #119 (aided Alpha Flight in combat against Wrecker)

WILL O' THE WISP

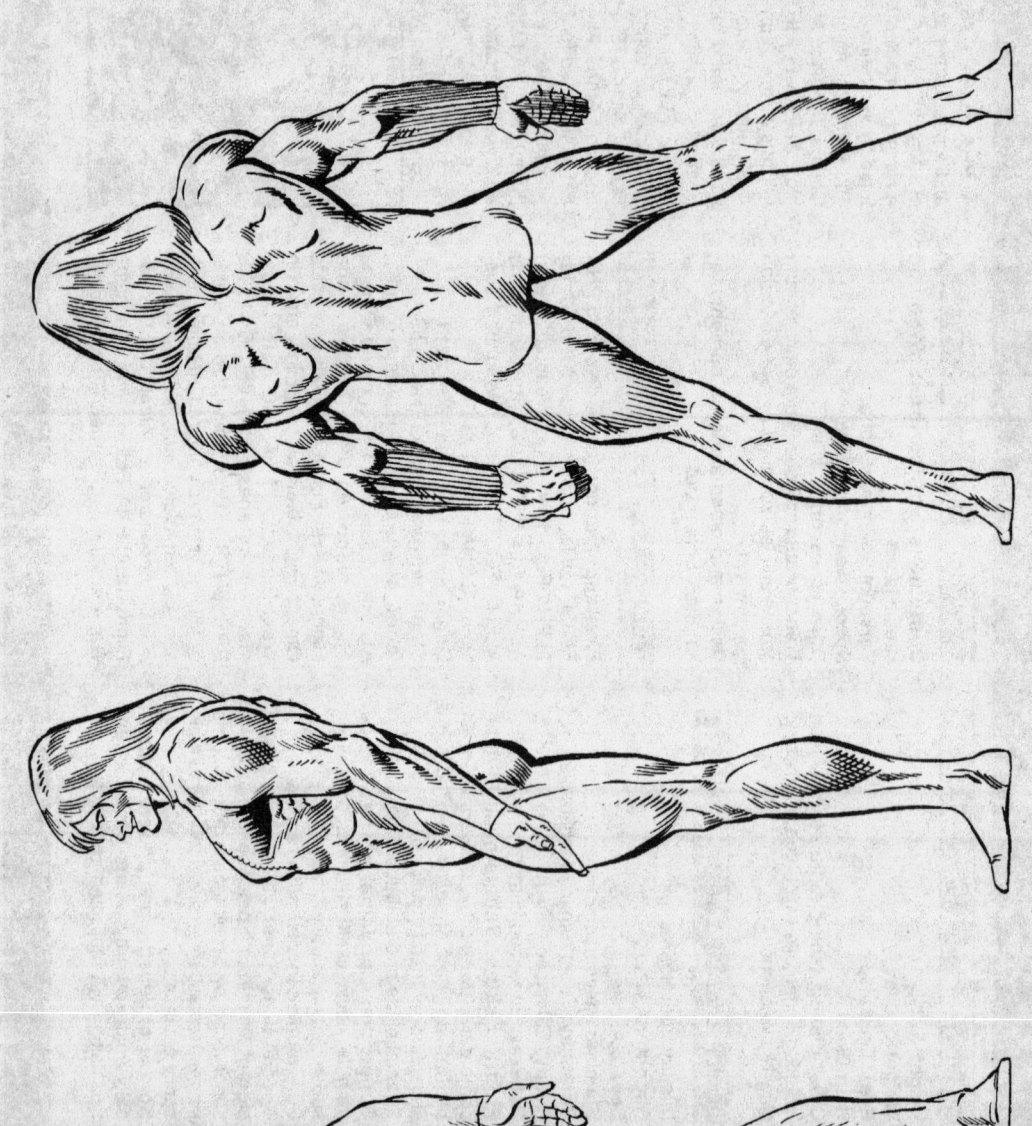

WILL O' THE WISP

BIOGRAPHICAL DATA

Real name: Jackson Arvad
Other Current aliases: The Wisp
Former aliases: None
Dual identity: Publicly known
Current occupation: Adventurer
Former occupation: Scientist
Citizenship: United States of America
Legal status: Criminal record in the U.S.
Place of birth: Scranton, Pennsylvania
Marital status: Single
Known relatives: None
Known confidants: None
Known allies: Spider-Man, Silver Sable, Sandman, Prowler, Puma, Rocket Racer
Major enemies: Jonas Harrow, James Melvin
Usual base of operations: Mobile
Former base of operations: New York City
Current group membership: The Outlaws
Former group membership: None
Extent of education: Masters of Science degree in electrical engineering

PHYSICAL DESCRIPTION

Height: 6' 1"
Weight: 195 lbs.
Eyes: White
Hair: Blond
Other distinguishing features: Will O' The Wisp can will the molecules of his body to oscillate at a small distance from his body, making him look like an ethereal glowing sphere.

POWERS AND ABILITIES

Intelligence: Above normal
Strength: Superhuman Class 25
Speed: Superhuman
Flight speed: Subsonic
Stamina: Peak human
Durability: Superhuman
Agility: Peak human
Reflexes: Enhanced human
Fighting skills: Minimal
Special skills and abilities: Brilliant scientist especially in the field of electromagnetics
Superhuman physical powers: Apart from those listed above, Will O' The Wisp has control over his body's electromagnetic particles, enabling him to vary the density of his body from intangibility to rock-solid.
Superhuman mental powers: Ability to mesmerize victims
Special limitations: None
Source of superhuman powers: Jackson Arvad and James Melvin's "magno-chamber"

PARAPHERNALIA

Costume specifications: Presumably unstable molecules
Personal weaponry: None
Special weaponry: None
Other accessories: None
Transportation: Flight under own power
Design and manufacture of paraphernalia: Unrevealed

BIBLIOGRAPHY

First appearance: AMAZING SPIDER-MAN #167
Origin issue: AMAZING SPIDER-MAN #235
Significant issues: AMAZING SPIDER-MAN #167-168 (forced by Jonas Harrow to carry out criminal activities; Spider-Man persuaded him to resist Harrow); SPECTACULAR SPIDER-MAN #57-58 (took control of Killer Shrike's battlesuit and kidnaped Dr. Marla Madison, who restored him to his corporeal form); AMAZING SPIDER-MAN #234-236 (forced his former partner, James Melvin, to expose the Brand Corporation's illicit activities to the news media); WEB OF SPIDER-MAN #50 (first encountered the Outlaws while hunting down Spider-Man in connection with a crime); AMAZING SPIDER-MAN ANNUAL #25/SPECTACULAR SPIDER-MAN ANNUAL #11/WEB OF SPIDER-MAN ANNUAL #7 (joined the Outlaws to rescue the kidnaped daughter of a Canadian official)

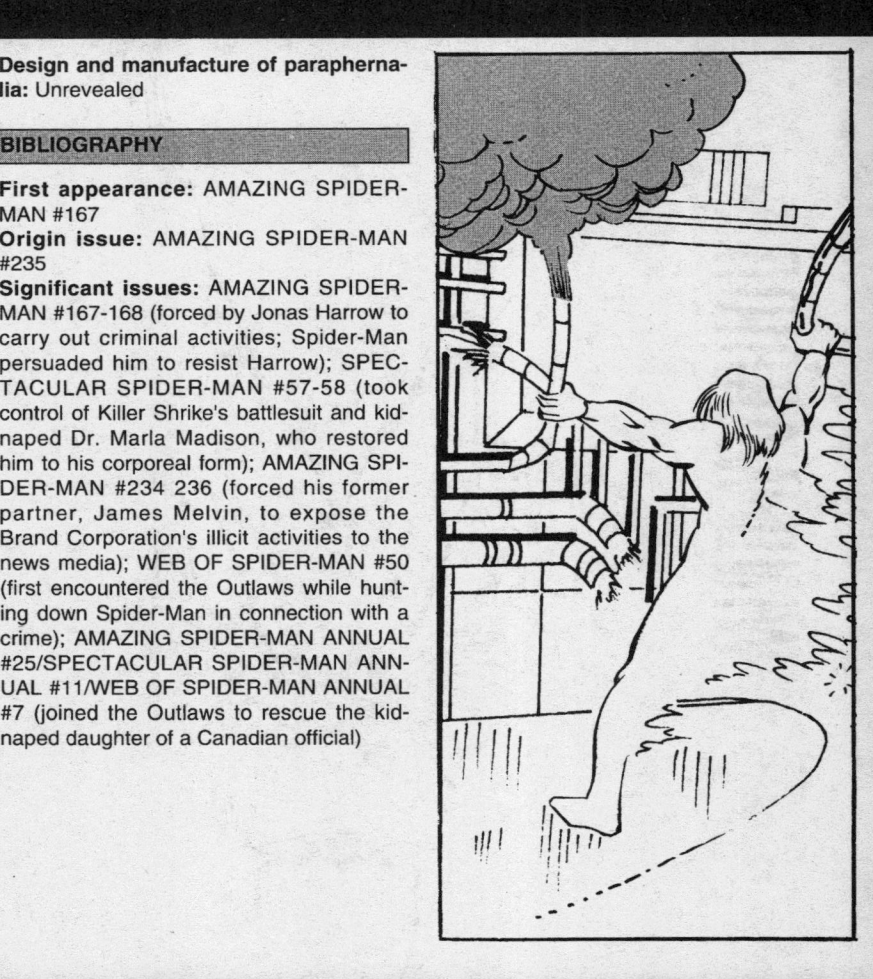

WIND WARRIOR

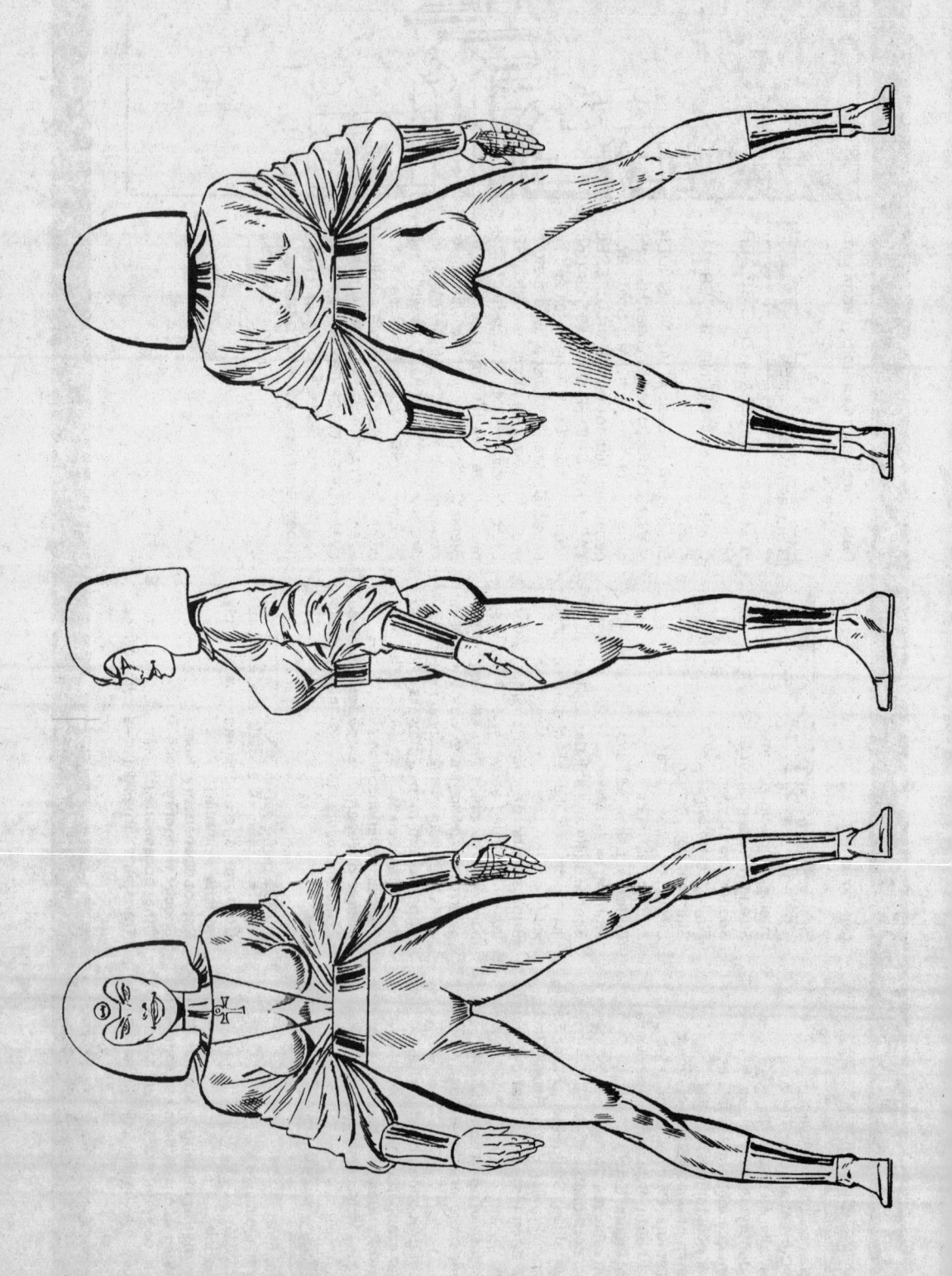

WIND WARRIOR

BIOGRAPHICAL DATA

Real name: Pamela Shaw
Other current aliases: None
Former aliases: None
Dual identity: Secret
Current occupation: Housewife
Former occupation: None
Citizenship: United States of America
Legal status: No criminal record
Place of birth: Unrevealed, presumably United States
Marital status: Separated
Known relatives: Mr. Shaw (estranged husband), unnamed child (deceased)
Known confidants: None
Known allies: Earth Force (Skyhawk, Earth Lord), Thor I, Hogun the Grim, Black Knight III, Gods of Heliopolis
Major enemies: Seth
Usual base of operations: New York City
Former bases of operations: None
Current group membership: Earth Force
Former group membership: None
Extent of education: Unrevealed

PHYSICAL DESCRIPTION

Height: 5' 2" (as Wind Warrior) 5' 11"
Weight: 112 lbs., (as Wind Warrior) 146 lbs.
Eyes: Brown
Hair: Auburn, (as Wind Warrior) Unrevealed
Other distinguishing features: None

POWERS AND ABILITIES

Intelligence: Normal
Strength: Superhuman Class 10
Speed: Enhanced human
Flight speed: Artificial winged flight
Stamina: Enhanced human
Durability: Enhanced human
Agility: Peak human
Reflexes: Peak human
Fighting skills: Minimal
Special skills and abilities: None known
Superhuman physical powers: Aside from the above listed attributes, Wind Warrior has the ability to transform her body to become winds and whirlwinds of strengths ranging up to tornado force, ability to fly by summoning winds strong enough to bear her aloft
Superhuman mental powers: None
Special limitations: None
Source of superhuman powers: Magically endowed by the Egyptian god Seth

PARAPHERNALIA

Costume specifications: Unspecified materials
Personal weaponry: None
Special weaponry: None
Other accessories: None
Transportation: None
Design and manufacture of paraphernalia: Unrevealed

BIBLIOGRAPHY

First appearance: THOR #395
Origin issue: THOR #395
Significant issues: THOR #395-399 (attempted suicide following death of her baby; healed and granted superhuman powers along with Skyhawk and Earth Lord by Seth, deceived by Seth into thinking Hogun was a menace, fought Thor and Hogun; reconciled with Thor and Hogun, transported to Seth's dimension, fought Seth's warriors; captured by Seth's forces, freed by Hogun); THOR #400 (confronted Seth, mortally injured, restored to life and returned to Earth by gods of Heliopolis); THOR ANNUAL #16 (prevented Earth Lord from endangering a baby by attacking Silver Sable and her Wild Pack who they mistook for kidnapers)

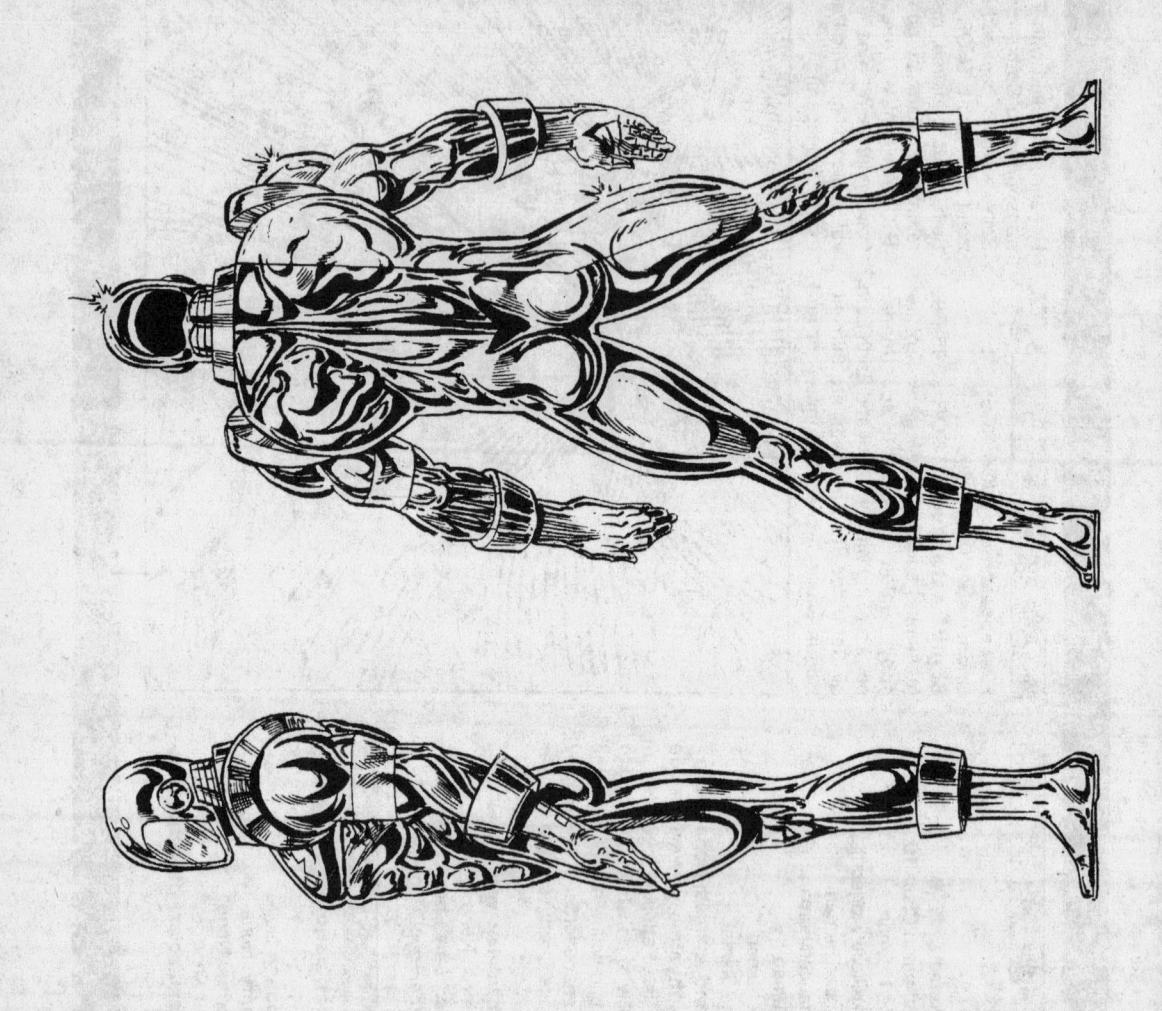

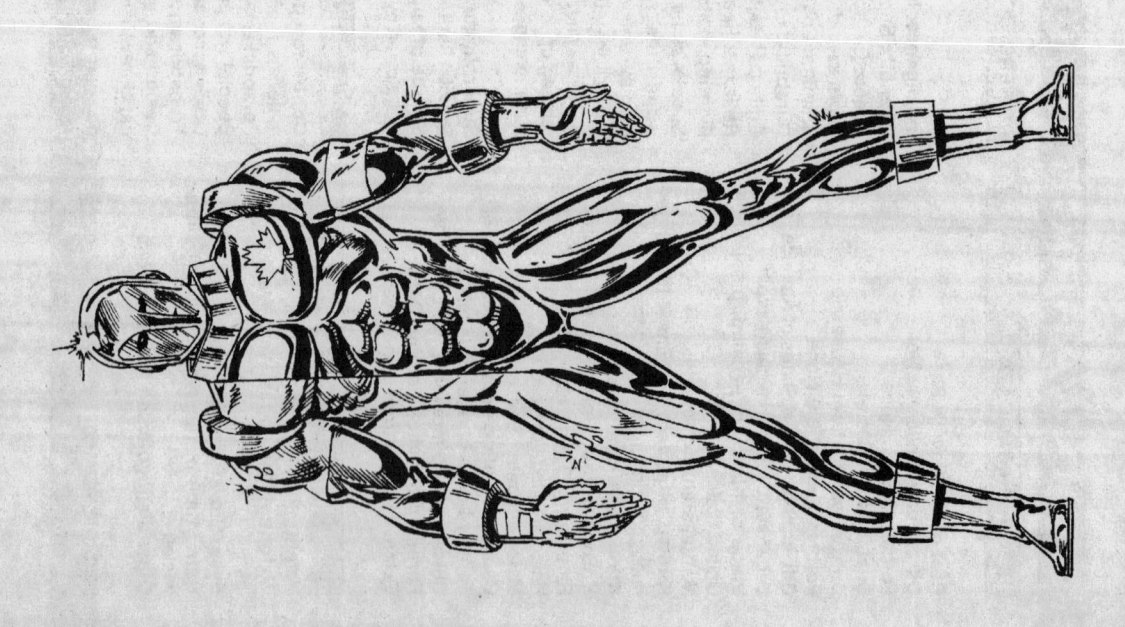

WINDSHEAR

WINDSHEAR

BIOGRAPHICAL DATA

Real name: Colin Ashworth Hume
Other current aliases: None
Former aliases: None known
Dual identity: Publicly known
Current occupation: Adventurer
Former occupation: Special operative for Roxxon Oil Corporation
Citizenship: Canada
Note: Colin Hume moved with his family to Great Britain when he was five years old and remained there until recently; however, as a child born in Canada of a British father and a Canadian mother, he is a Canadian citizen.
Legal status: No criminal record
Place of birth: Toronto, Ontario, Canada
Marital status: Presumed single
Known relatives: Franklin "Frank" Hume (father), Jaqueline Freeman Hume (mother), Martin Freeman (grandfather, deceased)
Known confidants: None
Known allies: Alpha Flight, Fantastic Four, Avengers, Kismet
Major enemies: Samuel Higgins, Headlok, the Master, the Consortium
Usual base of operations: Alpha Flight headquarters, Department H, Toronto, Ontario, Canada
Former bases of operations: Roxxon Oil, Super Human Division, United Kingdom Branch; Roxxon Energy Research Station, Denver, Colorado
Current group membership: Alpha Flight
Former group membership: Employee of Roxxon Oil
Extent of education: College Graduate

PHYSICAL DESCRIPTION

Height: 6'
Weight: 200 lbs.
Eyes: Brown
Hair: Black
Other distinguishing features: None

POWERS AND ABILITIES

Intelligence: Normal
Strength: Athlete, (in armor) Superhuman Class 10
Speed: Athlete
Flight speed: (in armor) Subsonic
Stamina: Athlete
Durability: Athlete, (in armor) Superhuman
Agility: Athlete
Reflexes: Athlete
Fighting skills: Average hand-to-hand combatant, relies on battlesuit in combat
Special skills and abilities: None known
Superhuman physical powers: Ability to create constructs of "hard-air" molecules, to project streams of "hard-air" molecules from hands as concussive force, and to utilize "hard-air" molecules for propulsion in flight
Superhuman mental powers: None
Special limitations: None
Source of superhuman powers: Genetic mutation

PARAPHERNALIA

Costume specifications: Battlesuit composed of unspecified materials
Personal weaponry: Turbojets built into armor enable Windshear to better control projection of "hard-air" molecules from gauntlets and propulsive force from boots. The battlesuit also affords the wearer increased strength and durability.
Special weaponry: None
Other accessories: Retractable protective tinted plexiglass faceplate, radio communicator built into helmet
Transportation: Flight via electrically powered turbines in boots and jetpack and "hard-air" molecule propulsion
Design and manufacture of paraphernalia: Unnamed Roxxon Oil technicians

BIBLIOGRAPHY

First appearance: ALPHA FLIGHT #87
Origin issue: Windshear's origin is as yet unrevealed.
Significant issues: ALPHA FLIGHT #87 (recruited from Britain to help battle machine-creature at Roxxon's Denver Energy Research Station, first met Box IV and Diamond Lil); ALPHA FLIGHT #88 (with Box IV and Diamond Lil), encountered "Muir Island X-Men", recruited Forge to help battle machine-creature; with Forge, discovered James McDonald Hudson at core of machine-creature); ALPHA FLIGHT #90 (quit Roxxon Oil); returned to Canada with Box IV, Diamond Lil, and Hudson; joined Alpha Flight as probationary member); ALPHA FLIGHT #94 (alongside Alpha Flight, the Thing and Human Torch II, battled Fantastic Four and Alpha Flight members controlled by Headlok); ALPHA FLIGHT #95 (background revealed, elected to full membership in Alpha Flight); ALPHA FLIGHT #96 (alongside Alpha Flight, battled oil spill and tanker fire); ALPHA FLIGHT #98-100 (alongside Alpha Flight, defended Kismet against the Consortium, first encountered the Avengers, Nova II, and Galactus); ALPHA FLIGHT #102 (appointed administrator of Alpha Flight)

WING, COLLEEN

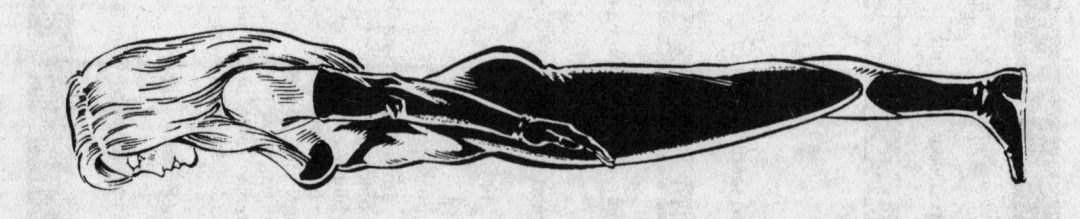

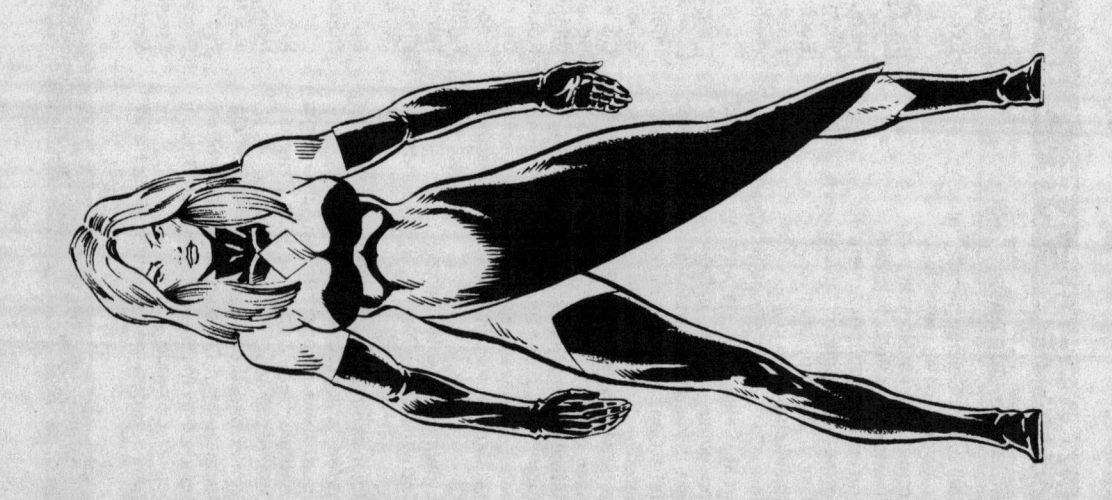

COLLEEN WING

BIOGRAPHICAL DATA

Real name: Colleen Wing
Other current aliases: None
Former aliases: None known
Dual identity: None
Current occupation: Private investigator for Nightwing Restorations
Former occupation: None
Citizenship: United States of America
Legal status: No criminal record
Place of birth: Unrevealed
Marital status: Single
Known relatives: Professor Lee Wing (father), Kenji Ozawa (grandfather, deceased)
Known confidants: Misty Knight, Professor Lee Wing, Danny Rand (alias Iron Fist), Bob Diamond
Known allies: Misty Knight, Iron Fist, Power Man, Sons of the Tiger, X-Men, Namor the Sub-Mariner, Spider-Man
Major enemies: Master Khan, Angar the Screamer, Emil Vachon, Constrictor, Sabretooth, Chemistro II, Chiantang, Super-Skrull
Usual base of operations: Nightwing Restorations offices, Manhattan
Former bases of operations: Mountains of northern Honshu, Japan
Current group membership: Partner of Misty Knight ("Daughters of the Dragon")
Former group membership: None
Extent of education: College graduate

PHYSICAL DESCRIPTION

Height: 5'9"
Weight: 135 lbs.
Eyes: Blue
Hair: Dark red
Other distinguishing features: None

POWERS AND ABILITIES

Intelligence: Above normal
Strength: Athlete
Speed: Athlete
Stamina: Athlete
Durability: Athlete
Agility: Athlete
Reflexes: Athlete
Fighting skills: Mastery of traditional combat skills of the Japanese samurai, including swordsmanship (kenjutsu)
Special skills and abilities: Excellent detective skills
Superhuman physical powers: None
Superhuman mental powers: None
Special limitations: None
Source of superhuman powers: Inapplicable

PARAPHERNALIA

Costume specifications: Modified from traditional Japanese designs
Personal weaponry: Katana (a traditional Japanese long sword)
Special weaponry: None
Other accessories: None
Transportation: Various
Design and manufacture of paraphernalia: Unrevealed

BIBLIOGRAPHY

First appearance: MARVEL PREMIERE #19
Origin issue: POWER MAN AND IRON FIST #70
Significant issues: MARVEL PREMIERE #19 (first met Iron Fist); MARVEL PREMIERE #22 (aided Iron Fist in battling Cult of Kara-Kai); IRON FIST #5-7 (captured by Master Khan and Angar the Screamer, who turned her and Misty Knight into mesmerized slaves; battled Iron Fist, who finally freed her from their mental control); DEADLY HANDS OF KUNG FU #32-33 (teamed with Misty in opposing agents of criminal Emil Vachon in Hong Kong); DEADLY HANDS OF KUNG FU #34 (captured by Emil Vachon, who turned her into heroin addict; rescued by Misty Knight, overcame addiction and took vengeance on Vachon); MARVEL TEAM-UP #64 (fought Davos, the second Steel Serpent; met Spider-Man); X-MEN #118-119 (aided X-Men and Sunfire in battling Moses Magnum in Japan); X-MEN #120-121 (accompanied X-Men to Canada); X-MEN #122 (made romantic overtures toward Cyclops); X-MEN #123-124 (was held prisoner by Arcade); POWER MAN AND IRON FIST #59 (first met Bob Diamond); POWER MAN AND IRON FIST #66 (battled Constrictor and Sabretooth); POWER MAN AND IRON FIST #70 (Professor Wing regained memory, Colleen's training in samurai skills by her grandfather revealed); POWER MAN AND IRON FIST #73 (began romance with Bob Diamond); POWER MAN AND IRON FIST #76 (shot by Warhawk); POWER MAN AND IRON FIST #84 (fought Constrictor); POWER MAN AND IRON FIST #93 (turned to glass by Chemistro II); POWER MAN AND IRON FIST #94 (restored to normal); POWER MAN AND IRON FIST #99 (fought Fera [now Ferocia]); POWER MAN AND IRON FIST #117 (temporarily ended friendship with Misty due to latter's romance with Tyrone King); POWER MAN AND IRON FIST #118 (transported to K'un-L'un); POWER MAN AND IRON FIST #122 (killed Chiantang the mystic dragon); POWER MAN AND IRON FIST #125 (attended funeral of impostor she believed to be Danny Rand); NAMOR THE SUB-MARINER #8 (saw second Danny Rand impostor on television); NAMOR THE SUB-MARINER #10 (confronted second Danny Rand impostor, actually the Super-Skrull); NAMOR THE SUB-MARINER #13 (was present at exhumation of corpse of first Danny Rand impostor)

WINGFOOT, WYATT™

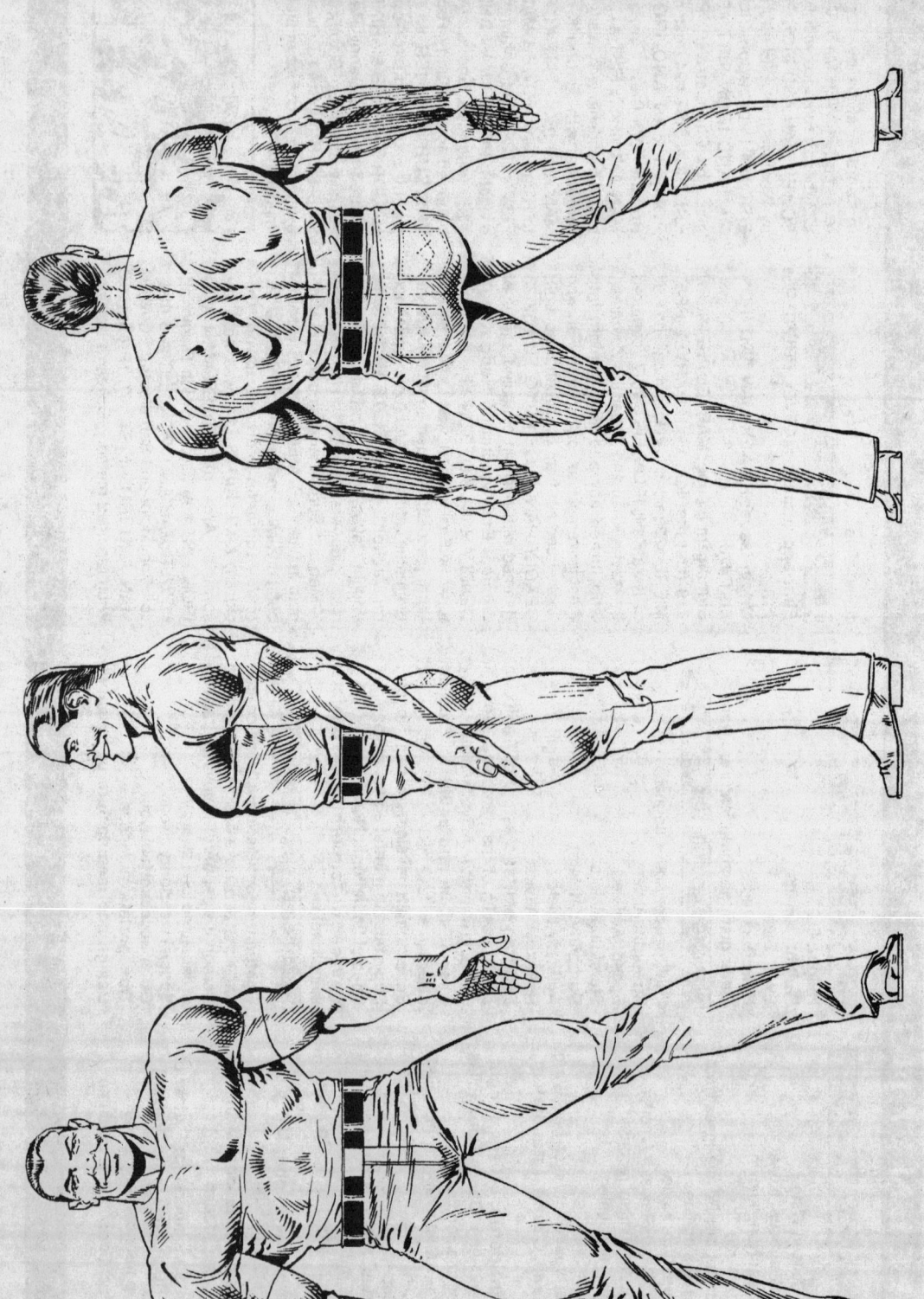

WINGFOOT, WYATT

BIOGRAPHICAL DATA

Real name: Wyatt Wingfoot
Other Current aliases: None
Former aliases: None known
Dual identity: None
Current occupation: Tribal chieftain, occasional adventurer
Former occupation: Student, teacher
Citizenship: United States of America
Legal status: No criminal record
Place of birth: Keewazi Reservation, Oklahoma
Marital status: Single
Known relatives: Will Wingfoot (father, deceased), Rain Falling West (sister), Silent Fox (grandfather, deceased), Roberta Elk Step (grandmother, deceased)
Known confidants: Jennifer Walters (She-Hulk), Johnny Storm (Human Torch II)
Known allies: She-Hulk, Fantastic Four, Black Panther, the Inhumans, Agatha Harkness, American Eagle, Ka-Zar, Shanna the She-Devil
Major enemies: Klaw, Doctor Doom, the Miracle Man (deceased), Annihilus, Terminus, Carlton Beatrice
Usual base of operations: Keewazi reservation, Oklahoma
Former base of operations: Baxter Building, New York City; Metro College, New York City
Current group membership: None
Former group membership: None
Extent of education: College Graduate

PHYSICAL DESCRIPTION

Height: 6' 5"
Weight: 260 lbs.
Eyes: Brown
Hair: Black
Other distinguishing features: None

POWERS AND ABILITIES

Intelligence: Normal
Strength: Athlete
Speed: Athlete
Stamina: Athlete
Durability: Athlete
Agility: Athlete
Reflexes: Athlete
Fighting skills: Excellent hand-to-hand combatant
Special skills and abilities: Superb athlete, highly skilled tracker, animal trainer, horseman, motorcyclist, and marksman
Superhuman physical powers: None
Superhuman mental powers: None
Special limitations: None known
Source of superhuman powers: Inapplicable

PARAPHERNALIA

Costume specifications: Conventional attire
Personal weaponry: None
Special weaponry: None
Other accessories: None
Transportation: Horseback, motorcycle, gyro-cruiser
Design and manufacture of paraphernalia: (gyro-cruiser) Wakanda Design Group

BIBLIOGRAPHY

First appearance: FANTASTIC FOUR #50
Origin issue: Wyatt Wingfoot's origin is as yet unrevealed.
Significant issues: FANTASTIC FOUR #50 (enrolled at Metro College, first met Johnny Storm); FANTASTIC FOUR #52-53 (accompanied the Fantastic Four to Wakanda, first met the Black Panther, helped the Fantastic Four against Klaw); FANTASTIC FOUR #54 (with Human Torch II, went on quest to rescue Inhumans from "Negative Zone" barrier, encountered Prester John); FANTASTIC FOUR #80 (alongside Fantastic Four and Keewazi Tribe, battled Tomazooma robot); FANTASTIC FOUR #138-139 (graduated college, alongside Fantastic Four, battled the Miracle Man); FANTASTIC FOUR #140-141 (alongside the Fantastic Four and Agatha Harkness, battled Annihilus); MARVEL TEAM-UP #18 (alongside the Human Torch II, encountered the Hulk, battled Blastaar); FANTASTIC FOUR #143-144 (alongside the Fantastic Four, battled Doctor Doom); MARVEL TWO-IN-ONE #8 (with his tribe, ensorcelled by the Miracle Man, rescued by the Thing and Ghost Rider I); MARVEL TEAM-UP #32 (with his tribe, possessed by the demon Dryminestes, restored to normal by Human Torch II and Daimon Hellstrom); FANTASTIC FOUR #192 (helped Human Torch II battle Texas Twister); MARVEL TWO-IN-ONE ANNUAL #6 (alongside the Thing, Ka-Zar, and American Eagle, battled Klaw); FANTASTIC FOUR #269-270 (first met She-Hulk, helped She-Hulk and Mr. Fantastic battle Terminus, postponed his investiture as chief of the Keewazi, returned to New York with Mr. Fantastic and She-Hulk); FANTASTIC FOUR #271-273 (alongside Fantastic Four, journeyed to alternate Earth, helped battle the Warlord); FANTASTIC FOUR #275 (began romance with She-Hulk; with She-Hulk, confronted publisher T.J.Vance); MARVEL GRAPHIC NOVEL #18: SHE-HULK (alongside She-Hulk, abducted by SHIELD I, menaced by intelligent cockroach colony, survived crash of SHIELD I Helicarrier); FANTASTIC FOUR #278-279 (alongside Fantastic Four, battled Doctor Doom II); FANTASTIC FOUR #293-295 (alongside Fantastic Four, investigated temporal zone surrounding Central City, California); FANTASTIC FOUR #300 (attended wedding of Johnny Storm and Alicia Masters [Lyja]); SHE-HULK: CEREMONY #1-2 (became engaged to She-Hulk; alongside She-Hulk, battled Carlton Beatrice; broke engagement) GUNS OF THE SAVAGE LAND GRAPHIC NOVEL (accompanied Ka-Zar and Shanna the She-Devil to the Savage Land)

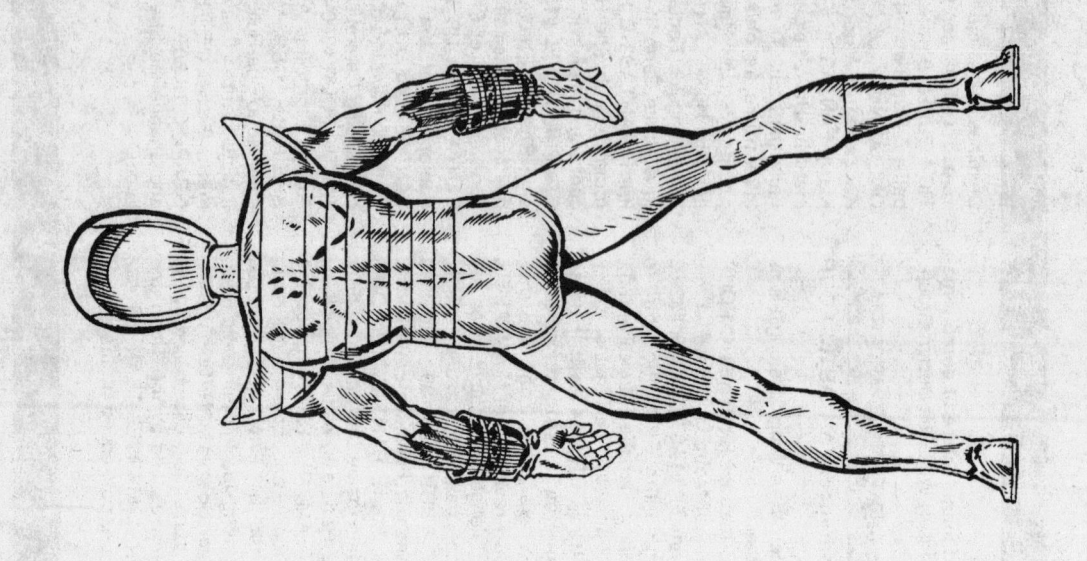

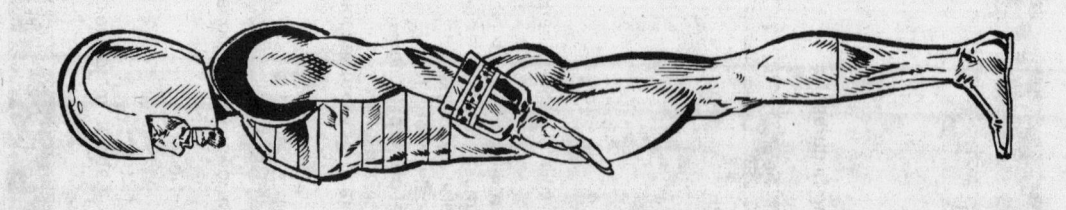

WIZARD

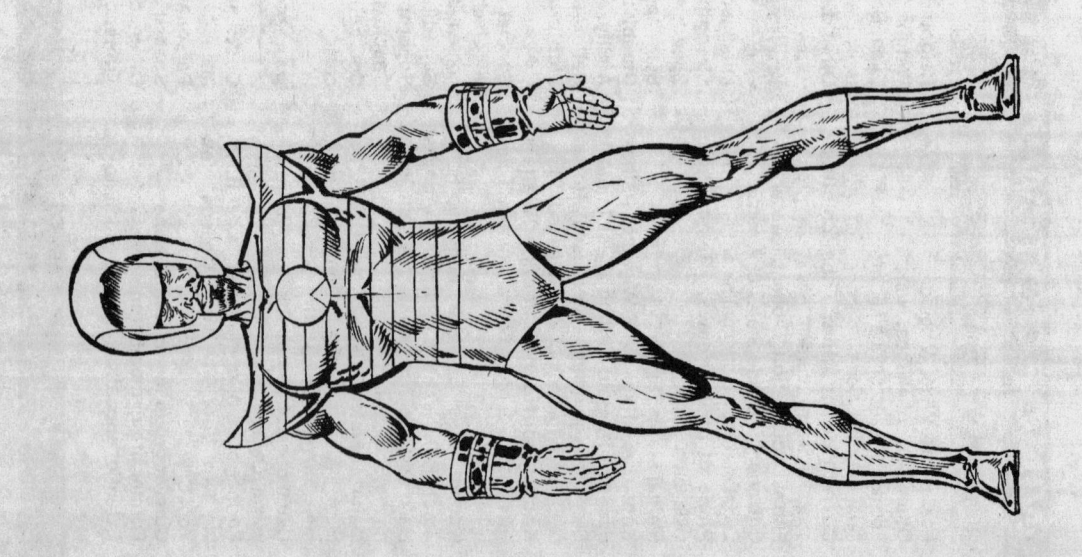

WIZARD

BIOGRAPHICAL DATA

Real name: Bentley Wittman
Other current aliases: None
Former aliases: The Wingless Wizard
Dual identity: Known to the authorities
Current occupation: Professional criminal
Former occupation: Inventor, stage magician, escape artist, chess champion
Citizenship: United States of America
Legal status: Criminal record in the U.S.
Place of birth: Unrevealed
Marital status: Single
Known relatives: None
Known confidants: None
Known allies: Frightful Four (Trapster, Sandman, Medusa, Thundra, Brute, Electro, Llyra, Hydro-Man, Klaw, Titania), Mysterio, Plantman, "Acts of Vengeance" prime movers (Loki, Kingpin, Doctor Doom, Magneto, Red Skull, Mandarin)
Major enemies: Fantastic Four, Spider-Man, the Avengers
Usual base of operations: New York area
Former bases of operations: Mobile; Long Island, New York
Current group membership: None
Former group membership: Frightful Four, "Acts of Vengeance" prime movers
Extent of education: Ph.Ds in several sciences

PHYSICAL DESCRIPTION

Height: 5' 8"
Weight: 150 lbs.
Eyes: Hazel
Hair: Dark brown
Other distinguishing features: Moustache and goatee

POWERS AND ABILITIES

Intelligence: Genius
Strength: Normal
Speed: Normal
Flight speed: Artificial winged flight
Stamina: Normal
Durability: Normal
Agility: Normal
Reflexes: Normal
Fighting skills: Minimal
Special skills and abilities: Scientist and engineer, stage magician, escape artist, master of disguise
Superhuman physical powers: None
Superhuman mental powers: None
Special limitations: None
Source of superhuman powers: None

PARAPHERNALIA

Costume specifications: Body armor
Personal weaponry: Anti-gravity discs, wonder-gloves
Special weaponry: Various
Other accessories: None
Transportation: Flight via anti-gravity discs
Design and manufacture of paraphernalia: The Wizard

BIBLIOGRAPHY

First appearance: STRANGE TALES #102
Origin issue: STRANGE TALES #102
Significant issues: STRANGE TALES #102 (captured and impersonated Human Torch II); STRANGE TALES #105 (rematch with Torch); STRANGE TALES #110 (with Paste-Pot Pete, battled Torch); STRANGE TALES #118 (captured Torch and Invisible Woman); FANTASTIC FOUR #36 (organized Frightful Four with Paste-Pot Pete, Sandman, and Medusa; battled Fantastic Four); FANTASTIC FOUR #38 (with Frightful Four, battled FF); FANTASTIC FOUR #41-43 (with Frightful Four, temporarily turned Thing against FF; battled FF); FANTASTIC FOUR #57 (engineered Sandman's escape from prison, provided him with design for new costume); MARVEL SUPER HEROES Vol. 1 #15 (with Trapster and Sandman, battled Medusa); AMAZING SPIDER-MAN ANNUAL #4 (teamed with Mysterio, battled Torch and Spider-Man); FANTASTIC FOUR #78 (battled FF); FANTASTIC FOUR #94 (with Frightful Four, battled FF); MARVEL TEAM-UP #2 (with Trapster and Sandman, invaded FF headquarters, encountered Annihilus); FANTASTIC FOUR #129-130 (replaced Medusa with Thundra in Frightful Four, battled FF and Medusa); FANTASTIC FOUR #133 (betrayed by Thundra); FANTASTIC FOUR #148 (with Trapster and Sandman, battled FF); FANTASTIC FOUR #176-178 (with Trapster and Sandman, captured FF; recruited Brute into Frightful Four); SPECTACULAR SPIDER-MAN #42/FANTASTIC FOUR #218 (with Frightful Four, captured Spider-Man, invaded FF headquarters); AMAZING SPIDER-MAN #213 (battled Spider-Man and Namor); AVENGERS #231-232 (provided Plantman with vehicle and equipment); AVENGERS #235 (attacked by Avengers); FANTASTIC FOUR #300 (with Mad Thinker and Puppet Master, attempted to disrupt wedding of Human Torch and Alicia Masters); FANTASTIC FOUR #301 (captured Thing and Franklin Richards in attempt to use them against FF); FANTASTIC FOUR #326-333 (formed new Frightful Four with Klaw, Hydro-Man, and Titania; invaded FF headquarters, sided with real FF against FF clones created by Aron the Watcher); AVENGERS SPOTLIGHT #26 (engineered mass break-out from the Vault); SPECTACULAR SPIDER-MAN #158/ AMAZING SPIDER-MAN #327/AVENGERS #312 (plotted "Acts of Vengeance" with other prime movers); SPECTACULAR SPIDER-MAN #159 (freed Brothers Grimm from prison, sent them against Spider-Man); AVENGERS #313 (with Mandarin, battled Avengers); AVENGERS WEST COAST #55 (inadvertently led Avengers to criminals' base); AMAZING SPIDER-MAN ANNUAL #24 (escaped Ryker's Island Prison); SPECTACULAR SPIDER-MAN ANNUAL #10 (with Trapster, defeated by reformed Sandman)

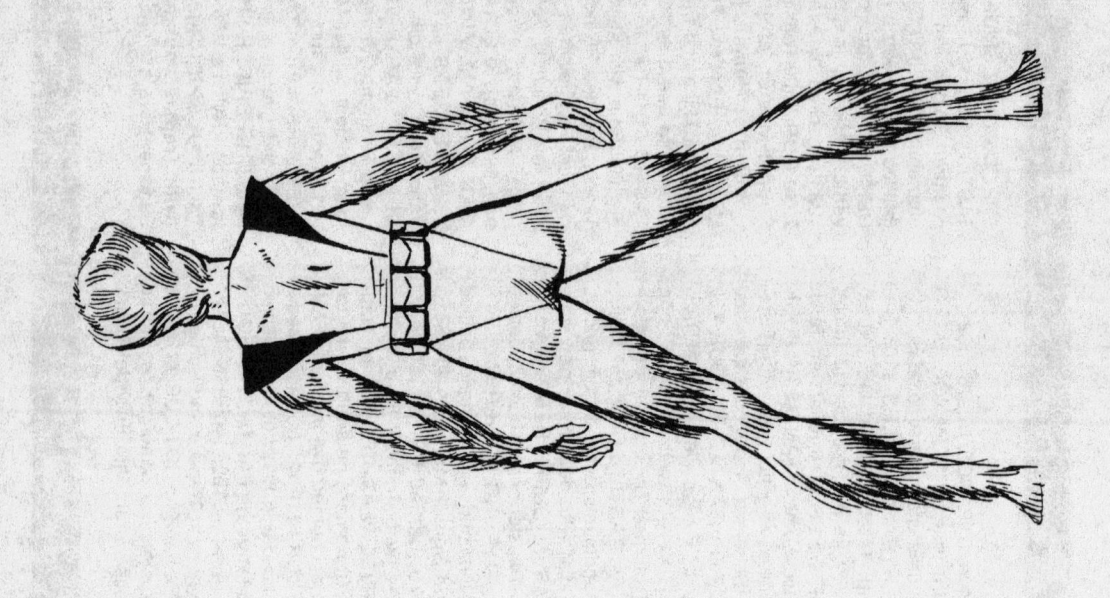

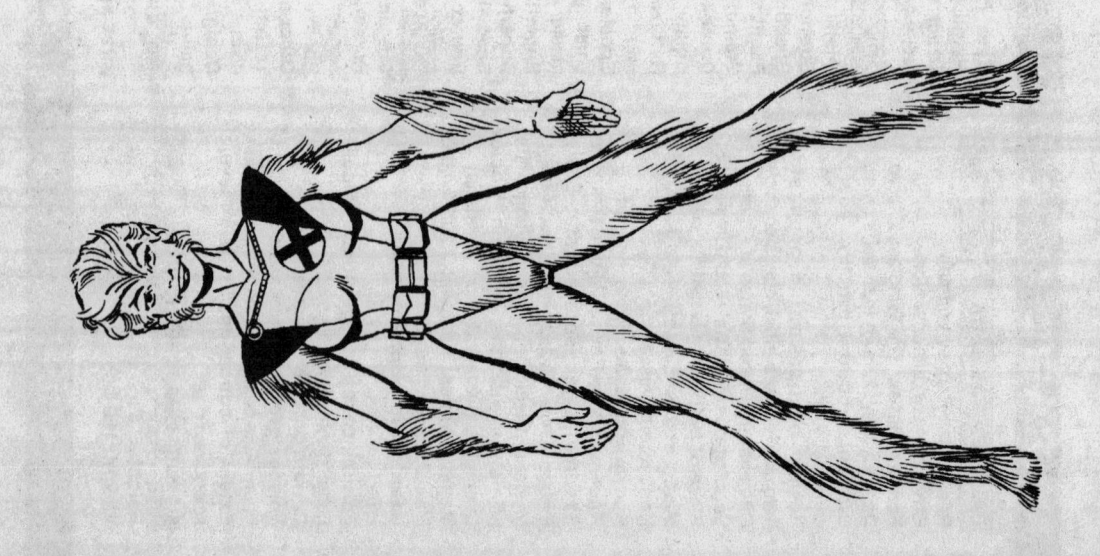

WOLFSBANE™

WOLFSBANE

BIOGRAPHICAL DATA

Real name: Rahne Sinclair
Other current aliases: None
Former aliases: Mutate #490 (in Genosha)
Dual identity: Known to the United States federal authorities
Current occupation: United States government special operative
Former occupation: Student, adventurer
Citizenship: United Kingdom, on special visa in the U.S.
Legal status: No criminal record, still a minor, ward of Moira MacTaggart
Place of birth: Unspecified location in Ross and Cromarty, Scotland
Marital status: Single
Known relatives: Montgomery Sinclair (father, deceased)
Known confidants: Moira MacTaggart, Sam Guthrie (Cannonball), Lorna Dane (Polaris), Rictor, Guido (Strong Guy), Professor X, (former) Cypher (deceased), Dani Moonstar, Magik, Magma, Magneto, Warlock III
Known allies: X-Factor II, Dr. Valerie Cooper, X-Men, Prince Hrimhari, (former) New Mutants, X-Factor I, Magneto, Catseye, Hellions
Major enemies: Cameron Hodge, Mister Sinister, Nasty Boys, Stryfe, Mutant Liberation Front, Shadow King, Hela, Enchantress, Ani-Mator, White Queen, Hellions, Reverend Craig, Genoshan Magistrates

Usual base of operations: X-Factor II headquarters, Embassy Row, Washington, D.C.
Former bases of operations: Professor Xavier's School for Gifted Youngsters, Salem Center, Westchester County, New York State; X-Factor I headquarters, New York City
Current group membership: X-Factor II
Former group membership: New Mutants, Hellions
Extent of education: Currently engaged in high school level studies

PHYSICAL DESCRIPTION

Height: 4' 10", (transitional form) 5' 2", (lupine) 32" at shoulder
Weight: 90 lbs., (transitional form) 120 lbs., (lupine) 140 lbs.
Eyes: Blue Green
Hair: Red, (transitional and lupine form) Reddish-brown
Other distinguishing features: Due to further artificial mutation induced in Genosha, Wolfsbane can reach a height of roughly 8' and weight over 400 lbs. in her transitional form and roughly 12' (when standing on her hind legs) and weight over 1000 lbs. in her "absolute" lupine form. The source of the additional mass is presumably extradimensional.

POWERS AND ABILITIES

Intelligence: Normal
Strength: Normal, (lupine) Enhanced human, ("absolute" lupine form) Superhuman Class 10
Speed: Normal, (lupine) Enhanced human
Stamina: Normal, (lupine) Enhanced human
Durability: Normal, (lupine) Enhanced human, ("absolute" lupine form) Superhuman
Agility: Normal, (lupine) Enhanced human
Reflexes: Normal, (lupine) Enhanced human
Fighting skills: Training in hand-to-hand combat at Xavier's School, by Xavier, Cable, and others
Special skills and abilities: None known
Superhuman physical powers: Aside from the above listed attributes, Wolfsbane has the ability to transform herself into a wolf at will, while retaining her human intelligence, or into a transitional form which combines human and lupine aspects; recently she has learned to enter different transitional forms which vary slightly in appearance. In her lupine form her senses are similar to those of a wolf's, but also superior to them. In lupine form she can see into the infrared and ultraviolet portions of the spectrum, thereby enabling her to perceive heat patterns and to see in the dark. In her lupine form she can also hear sounds and detect scents outside the normal human range. In her transitional form she is less agile than she is as a wolf, but stronger than she is human form. In her transitional form she can speak, use her forepaws as hands and easily stand erect, and at least some of her senses remain superhumanly acute.
Superhuman mental powers: In lupine form Wolfsbane can achieve a limited degree of telepathic communication with Dani Moonstar (Mirage II)
Special limitations: In lupine form Wolfsbane may have more understanding complex human concepts. The artificial mutation process Wolfsbane underwent causes her to act with animalistic savagery in her lupine and "absolute" forms
Source of superhuman powers: Genetic mutation with further mutation by the Genoshan Genegineer

PARAPHERNALIA

Costume specifications: Special uniform made of "unstable molecules" that converts to a collar in her non-human forms
Personal weaponry: None
Special weaponry: None
Other accessories: None
Transportation: Land and aircraft supplied by the U.S. Government
Design and manufacture of paraphernalia: (originally) Professor Xavier, (currently) U.S. government scientist

WOLVERINE

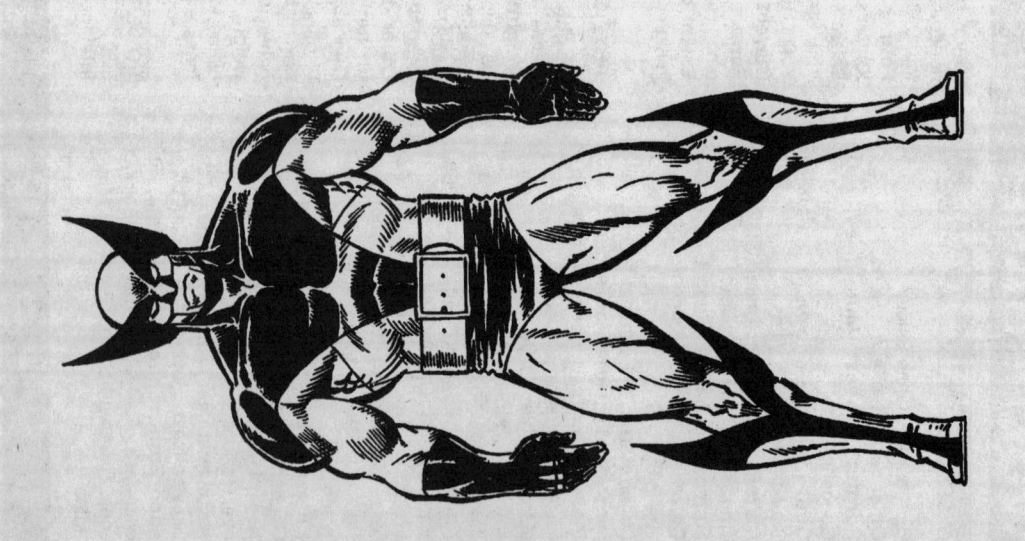

WOLVERINE

BIOGRAPHICAL DATA

Real name: Logan
Other current aliases: Patch
Former aliases: Weapon X
Dual identity: Secret
Current occupation: Adventurer
Former occupation: Soldier, secret agent, operative for Canadian government's Department H
Citizenship: Canada
Legal status: No known criminal record
Place of birth: Unrevealed
Marital status: Single
Known relatives: Akiko (adopted daughter)
Known confidants: Mariko Yashida
Known allies: The X-Men, X-Factor, Shadowcat, Alpha Flight, James and Heather Hudson, Tyger Tiger, Jessica Drew, Lindsay McCabe, Archie Corrigan, O'Donnell, Nick Fury, Carol Danvers, the Black Widow, Yukio
Major enemies: Sabretooth, Ogun, Lady Deathstrike, the Reavers, General Nguyen Ngoc Coy, Geist, Bloodscream, Cameron Hodge, Shadow King
Usual base of operations: Professor Xaviers' School For Gifted Youngsters, Salem Center, Westchester County, New York; the Princess Bar, Madripoor
Former bases of operations: The X-Men's Australian headquarters, Department H headquarters in Canada
Current group membership: The X-Men
Former group membership: Alpha Flight
Extent of education: Unrevealed

PHYSICAL DESCRIPTION

Height: 5' 3"
Weight: 195 lbs.
Eyes: Brown
Hair: Black
Other distinguishing features: Wolverine can project and retract three one-foot long Adamantium claws from the back of each hand.

POWERS AND ABILITIES

Intelligence: Above normal
Strength: Enhanced human
Speed: Athlete
Stamina: Metahuman
Durability: Superhuman regenerative
Agility: Enhanced human
Reflexes: Enhanced human
Fighting skills: Wolverine is familiar with and experienced in virtually every fighting style on Earth
Special skills and abilities: Wolverine speaks fluent English, Japanese, Russian, Chinese, Cheyenne, Lakota, and Spanish, and has some knowledge of French, Thai, and Vietnamese. He is an accomplished pilot.
Superhuman physical powers: Wolverine possesses a "fast healing" ability enabling him to regenerate damaged or destroyed areas of his cellular structure. This grants him virtual immunity to poisons and limited immunity to the fatigue poisons generated by his own body. It also retards his aging process. Wolverine possesses superhumanly acute senses of sight, smell, and hearing. Wolverine's skeleton has been artificially laced with molecules of Adamantium, rendering his bones virtually unbreakable. He has also been equipped with three Adamantium claws on each hand.
Superhuman mental powers: None
Special limitations: None known
Source of superhuman powers: Wolverine's healing ability and superhuman senses are the result of mutation. His Adamantium skeleton and claws were given to him by as yet unknown parties.

PARAPHERNALIA

Costume specifications: Synthetic stretch fabric
Personal weaponry: None
Special weaponry: None
Other accessories: None
Transportation: Blackbird jet
Design and manufacture of paraphernalia: Unnamed Shi'Ar technicians

BIBLIOGRAPHY

First appearance: INCREDIBLE HULK #180
Origin issue: Wolverine's origin is as yet unrevealed.
Significant issues: INCREDIBLE HULK #180-181 (as Weapon X first battled Hulk and Wendigo); GIANT-SIZE X-MEN #1 (joined the X-Men); X-MEN #109 (battled James Hudson); X-MEN #120-121 (captured by Alpha Flight); X-MEN #133 (invaded Hellfire Club's New York headquarters); X-MEN #138 (took first known trip into outer space); X-MEN #139-140 (made peace with Alpha Flight); X-MEN #162 (destroyed Brood alien that attempted to take over his body); WOLVERINE Vol. 1 #1-4 (killed Lord Shingen Harada, became engaged to Mariko), X-MEN #173 (under Mastermind's influence, Mariko called off her wedding to Wolverine); X-MEN #181 (rescued Akiko, promised to raise her as his daughter); KITTY AND WOLVERINE #1-6 (battled and killed Ogun, his former mentor); ALPHA FLIGHT #33-34 (first meeting of Wolverine with James and Heather Hudson revealed, first battled Lady Deathstrike); X-MEN ANNUAL #11 (saved universe from alien conqueror Horde); X-MEN #227 (died as part of spell to defeat the Adversary, but is resurrected by Roma); X-MEN #229 (first battled the Reavers); CLASSIC X-MEN #10 (first clash with Sabretooth after joining X-Men recounted); X-MEN #251 (crucified by the Reavers, freed himself, met Jubilee); X-MEN #268 (first meeting with Captain America and the future Black Widow during World War II recounted); NEW MUTANTS #93-94 (renewed feud with Cable, assisted Cable and New Mutants against Stryfe and Mutant Liberation Front); MARVEL COMICS PRESENTS #72-85 (how Wolverine got his Adamantium skeleton and claws recounted)

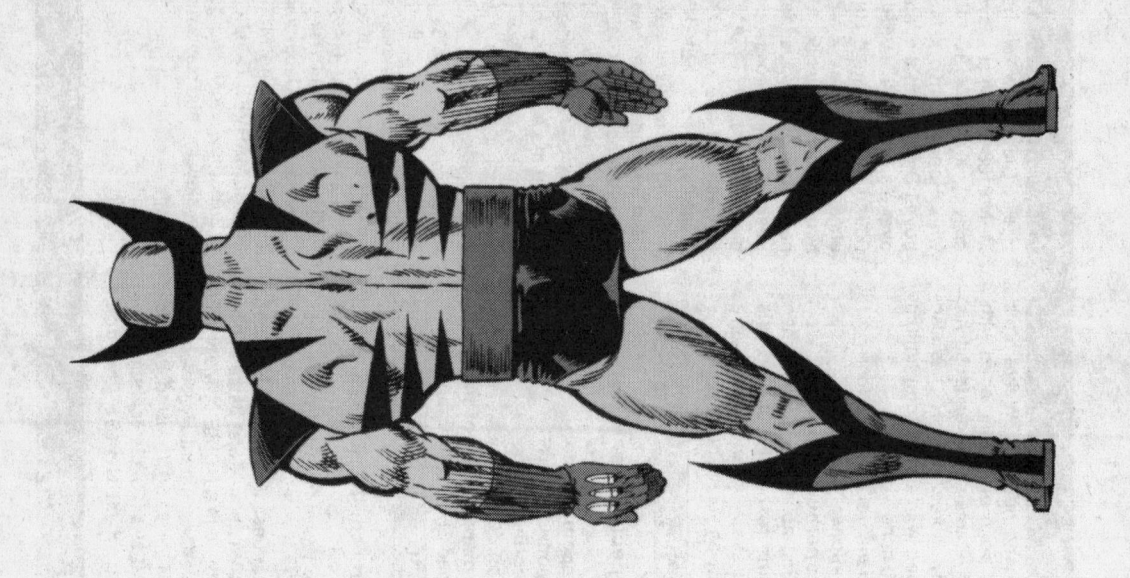

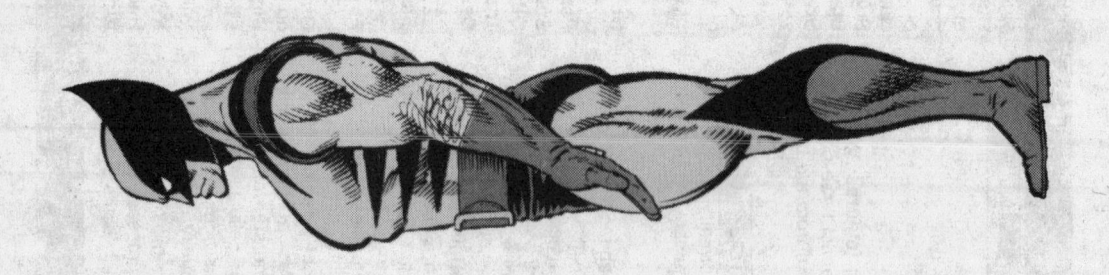

WOLVERINE

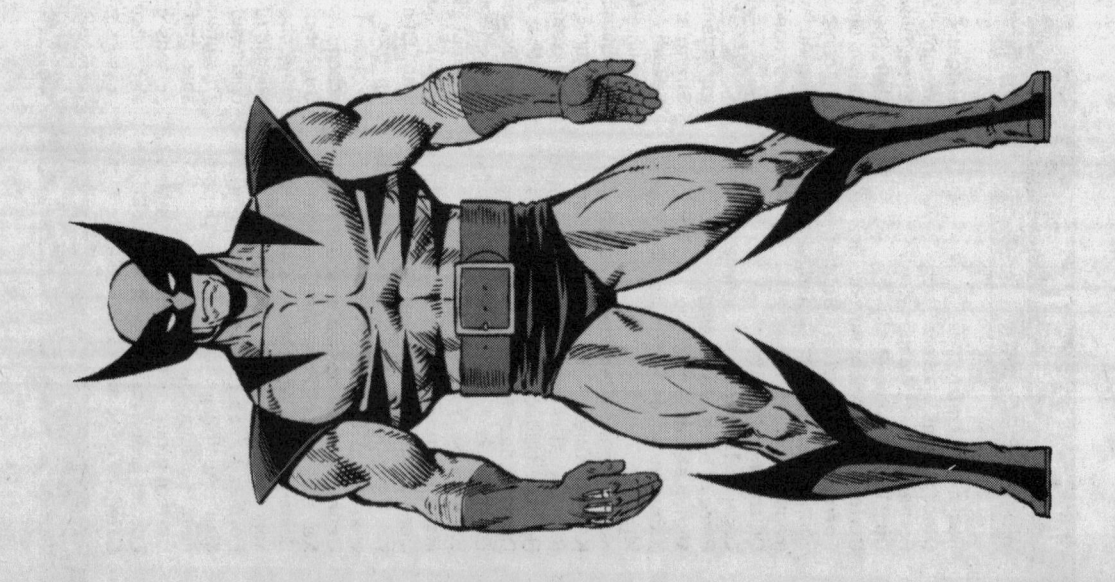

WOLVERINE

BIOGRAPHICAL DATA

Real name: Logan
Other current aliases: Patch
Former aliases: Weapon X
Dual identity: Secret
Current occupation: Adventurer
Former occupation: Soldier, secret agent, operative for Canadian government's Department H
Citizenship: Canada
Legal status: No known criminal record
Place of birth: Unrevealed
Marital status: Single
Known relatives: Akiko (adopted daughter)
Known confidants: Mariko Yashida
Known allies: The X-Men, X-Factor, Shadowcat, Alpha Flight, James and Heather Hudson, Tyger Tiger, Jessica Drew, Lindsay McCabe, Archie Corrigan, O'Donnell, Nick Fury, Carol Danvers, the Black Widow, Yukio, Maverick
Major enemies: Sabretooth, Ogun, Lady Deathstrike, the Reavers, General Nguyen Ngoc Coy, Geist, Bloodscream, Cameron Hodge, Shadow King, Omega Red
Usual base of operations: Professor Xaviers' School For Gifted Youngsters, Salem Center, Westchester County, New York; the Princess Bar, Madripoor
Former bases of operations: The X-Men's Australian headquarters, Department H headquarters in Canada
Current group membership: The X-Men
Former group membership: Alpha Flight
Extent of education: Unrevealed

PHYSICAL DESCRIPTION

Height: 5' 3"
Weight: 195 lbs.
Eyes: Brown
Hair: Black
Other distinguishing features: Wolverine can project and retract three one-foot long Adamantium claws from the back of each hand.

POWERS AND ABILITIES

Intelligence: Above normal
Strength: Enhanced human
Speed: Athlete
Stamina: Metahuman
Durability: Superhuman regenerative
Agility: Enhanced human
Reflexes: Enhanced human
Fighting skills: Wolverine is familiar with and experienced in virtually every fighting style on Earth
Special skills and abilities: Wolverine speaks fluent English, Japanese, Russian, Chinese, Cheyenne, Lakota, and Spanish, and has some knowledge of French, Thai, and Vietnamese. He is an accomplished pilot.
Superhuman physical powers: Wolverine possesses a "fast healing" ability enabling him to regenerate damaged or destroyed areas of his cellular structure. This grants him virtual immunity to poisons and limited immunity to the fatigue poisons generated by his own body. It also retards his aging process. Wolverine possesses superhumanly acute senses of sight, smell, and hearing. Wolverine's skeleton has been artificially laced with molecules of Adamantium, rendering his bones virtually unbreakable. He has also been equipped with three Adamantium claws on each hand.
Superhuman mental powers: None
Special limitations: None known
Source of superhuman powers: Wolverine's healing ability and superhuman senses are the result of mutation. His Adamantium skeleton and claws were given to him by as yet unknown parties.

PARAPHERNALIA

Costume specifications: Synthetic stretch fabric
Personal weaponry: None
Special weaponry: None
Other accessories: None
Transportation: Blackbird jet
Design and manufacture of paraphernalia: Unnamed Shi'ar technicians

BIBLIOGRAPHY

First appearance: INCREDIBLE HULK #180
Origin issue: Wolverine's origin is as yet unrevealed.
Significant issues: INCREDIBLE HULK #180-181 (as Weapon X first battled Hulk and Wendigo); GIANT-SIZE X-MEN #1 (quit Canada's Department H, joined the X-Men); WOLVERINE Vol. 1 #1-4 (killed Lord Shingen Harada, became engaged to Mariko), X-MEN #173 (under Mastermind's influence, Mariko called off her wedding to Wolverine); X-MEN #181 (rescued Akiko, promised to raise her as his daughter); KITTY AND WOLVERINE #1-6 (battled and killed Ogun, his former mentor); X-MEN #227 (died as part of spell to defeat the Adversary, but is resurrected by Roma); CLASSIC X-MEN #10 (first clash with Sabretooth after joining X-Men recounted); X-MEN #251 (crucified by the Reavers, freed himself, met Jubilee); X-MEN #268 (first meeting with Captain America and the future Black Widow during World War II recounted); NEW MUTANTS #93-94 (renewed feud with Cable, assisted Cable and New Mutants against Stryfe and Mutant Liberation Front); MARVEL COMICS PRESENTS #72-85 (how Wolverine got his Adamantium skeleton and claws recounted); WOLVERINE #50 (filial relationship with Sabretooth revealed to be memory implant, returned to original costume); X-MEN Vol. 2 #5-7 (recounted past relationship with Sabretooth)
Note: Recently, Wolverine has discovered that many of his memories were implanted during the time that he received his adamantium claws and skeleton; he has not yet discovered to what extent his memories have been tampered with.

WOLVERINE IN ACTION
ART: SAM KIETH

WOLVERINE'S SUPPORTING CAST

TIGER TYGER
Current occupation: Part owner of the *Princess Bar*
Relationship: Ally, former business partner
First appearance: UNCANNY X-MEN #226

PROFESSOR X
Current occupation: Head educator of Professor Charles Xavier's School for Gifted Youngsters
Relationship: Team leader
First appearance: X-MEN Vol. 1 #1

ELSIE DEE
Current occupation: Wanderer
Relationship: Construct originally designed to kill Wolverine, currently an ally
First appearance: WOLVERINE Vol. 2 #38

JUBILEE
Current occupation: Student member of the X-Men
Relationship: Teammate and friend
First appearance: UNCANNY X-MEN #244

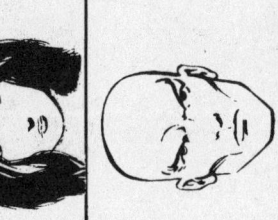

JEAN GREY
Current occupation: Member of the X-Men
Relationship: Teammate and confidant
First appearance: X-MEN Vol. 1 #1

SABRETOOTH
Current occupation: Assassin
Relationship: Alleged former espionage partner; determined to kill Wolverine. Believed himself to be Wolverine's father
First appearance: IRON FIST #14

JESSICA DREW
Current occupation: Private investigator
Relationship: Ally
First appearance: MARVEL SPOTLIGHT Vol. 1 #32

MARIKO YASHIDA
Current occupation: Head of clan Yashida in Tokyo, Japan
Relationship: Former fiancee of Wolverine
First appearance: UNCANNY X-MEN #118

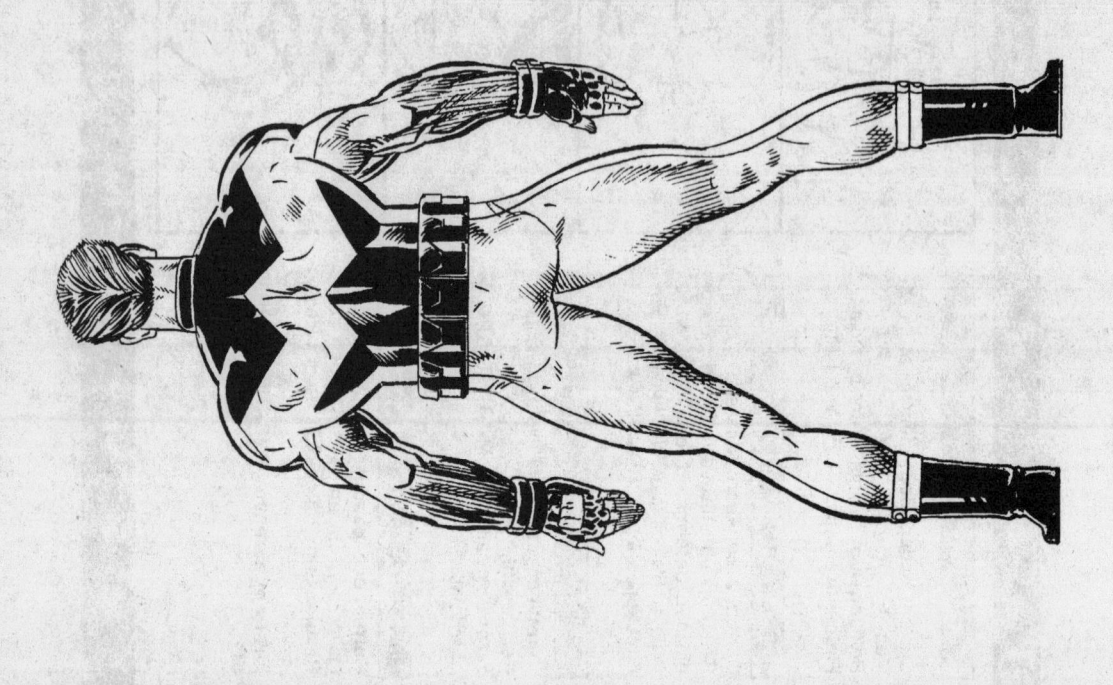

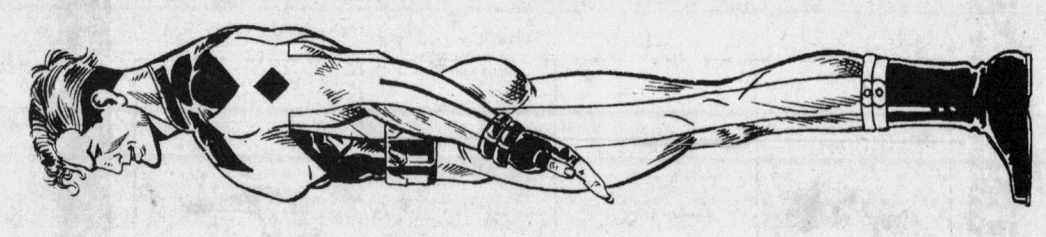

WONDER MAN

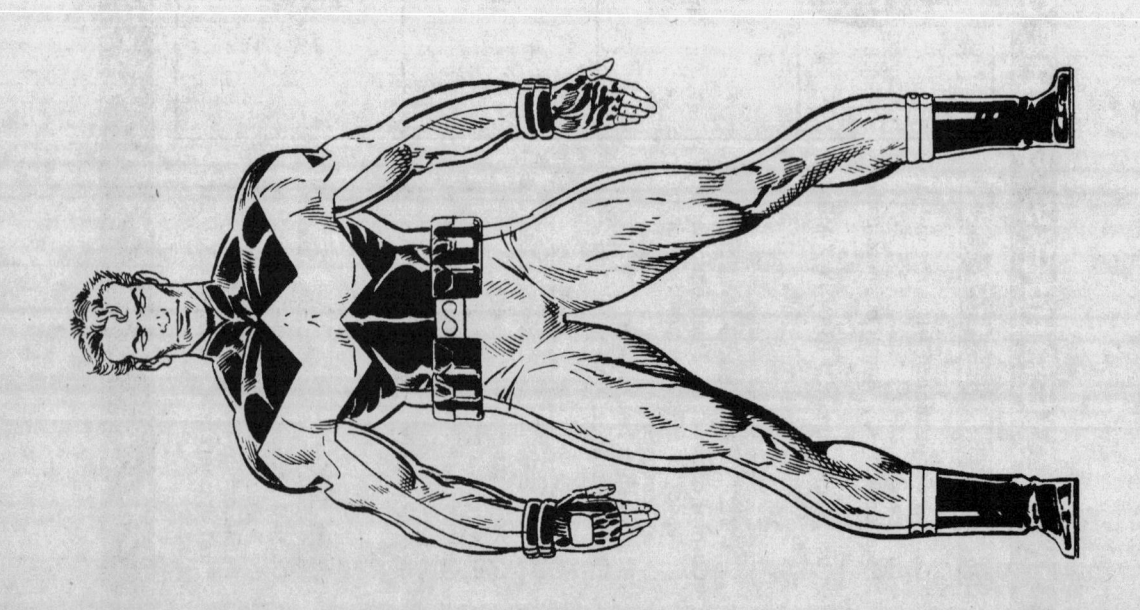

WONDER MAN

BIOGRAPHICAL DATA

Real name: Simon Williams
Other current aliases: None
Former aliases: Mr. Muscles
Dual identity: Publically known
Current Occupation: Adventurer, motion picture actor
Former occupation: Industrialist, security troubleshooter, television actor, stuntman
Citizenship: United States of America
Legal status: Criminal record in the U.S. for embezzlement, pardoned
Place of birth: Paterson, New Jersey
Marital status: Single
Known relatives: Sanford Williams (father, deceased), Martha Williams (mother), Eric Williams (Grim Reaper, brother, deceased), Vision ("brother"), Wanda Maximoff ("sister-in-law")
Known confidants: None
Known allies: Avengers West Coast, Ka-Zar, Avengers East, the Beast, Spider-Man, the Fantastic Four, (former) Masters of Evil I (Baron Zemo I [deceased], Enchantress, Executioner I [deceased])
Major enemies: Grim Reaper (deceased), Ultron, Goliath III, Lotus, Splice, Rampage, Armed Response, Angkor, the Enchantress, Graviton, Lethal Legion III, Master Pandemonium, Arkon, Immortus, the Maggia
Usual base of operations: Avengers Compound, Los Angeles, California
Former bases of operations: Avengers Mansion, New York City
Current group membership: Avengers West Coast
Former group membership: Masters of Evil I, Legion of the Unliving I, Avengers
Extent of education: Advanced degree in electrical engineering

PHYSICAL DESCRIPTION

Height: 6' 2"
Weight: 380 lbs
Eyes: Red (no visible irises; eyeballs permeated with shifting spots of ionic energy)
Hair: Grey (dyed black)
Other distinguishing features: Wonder Man's eyes glow a bright red unless he concentrates on making them appear normal.

POWERS AND ABILITIES

Intelligence: Normal
Strength: Superhuman Class 100
Speed: Superhuman
Stamina: Superhuman
Durability: Metahuman
Agility: Superhuman
Reflexes: Superhuman
Fighting skills: Exceptional hand-to-hand combatant; recieved Avengers training in unarmed combat by Captain America
Special skills and abilities: Trained electrical engineer, capable industrialist, experienced stuntman, talented actor
Superhuman physical powers: Aside from the above listed attributes, Wonder Man has the ability to exist indefinitely without air, food, or water, and he no longer ages
Superhuman mental powers: None
Special limitations: None
Source of superhuman powers: Chemical and radiation treatments with "ionic" energy by Baron Zemo I

PARAPHERNALIA

Costume specifications: Synthetic stretch fabric
Personal weaponry: None
Special weaponry: None
Other accessories: Avengers ID card (contains mini-radio)
Transportation: Leaping, Avengers Quinjet, (formerly) Flight via ionic jet flight-pack
Design and manufacture of paraphernalia: (Quinjet, flight-pack) Tony Stark

BIBLIOGRAPHY

First appearance: AVENGERS #9
Origin issue: AVENGERS #9
Significant issues: AVENGERS #9 (given superhuman powers by Baron Zemo I to help Masters of Evil I destroy the Avengers, instead aided Avengers against Zemo, seemingly died); AVENGERS #58 (his recorded brain patterns used as basis for the android's Vision's mind); AVENGERS #102 (body stolen by Grim Reaper); AVENGERS #131-132/GIANT-SIZE AVENGERS #3 (resurrected as one of Kang's Legion of the Unliving, battled Avengers); AVENGERS #151-153 (revived as zombie by Black Talon II at behest of Grim Reaper, battled Avengers); AVENGERS #154-156 (restored to true life, aided Avengers against Attuma and Dr. Doom); AVENGERS #158-159 (fought the Vision, helped Avengers battle Graviton); AVENGERS #160 (alongside Avengers, first fought Grim Reaper, revealed to have become a being of ionic energy); MARVEL PREMIERE #55 (invaded his former plant which had been taken over by the Maggia, fought Madame Masque I, and Dreadnought); WEST COAST AVENGERS Vol. 1 #1 (helped formed West Coast Avengers); EMPEROR DOOM (foiled Dr. Doom's plot to control world); MARVEL COMICS PRESENTS #38-45 (ensorcelled by the Enchantress, battled Avengers); WONDER MAN Vol. 2 #1 (battled Goliath III); WONDER MAN Vol. 2 #2 (battled Enchantress); WONDER MAN Vol. 2 #3 (first met would-be sidekick "Spider", battled Gamma-Burn, wrecked jet-pack); WONDER MAN Vol. 2 #4 (first battled Splice); AVENGERS WEST COAST #80-82/QUASAR #32-33/WONDER MAN Vol. 2 #7-9 (took part in the Kree-Shi'ar War; had his powers altered when he and the Vision failed to prevent the Shi'ar Nega-Bomb from detonating); WONDER MAN Vol. 2 #11-12 (battled Angkor); WONDER MAN #22-25 (journeyed to Hades, battled Mephisto, Blackheart, Enchantress, and Grim Reaper; learned he was immortal)

WONG™

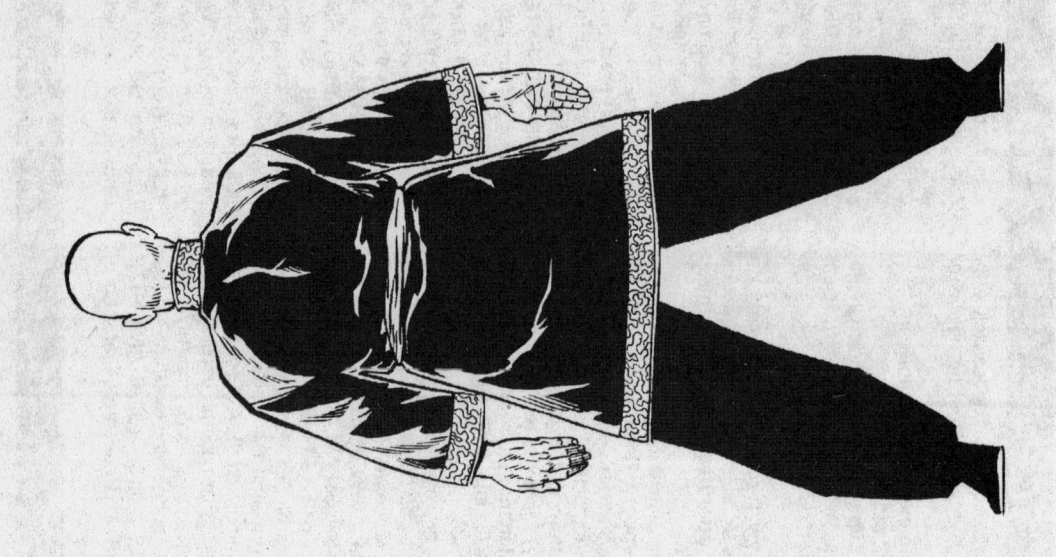

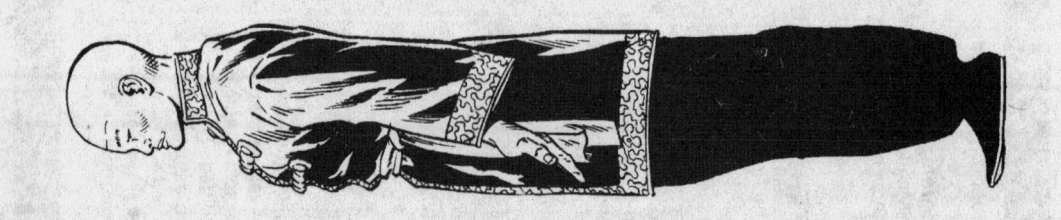

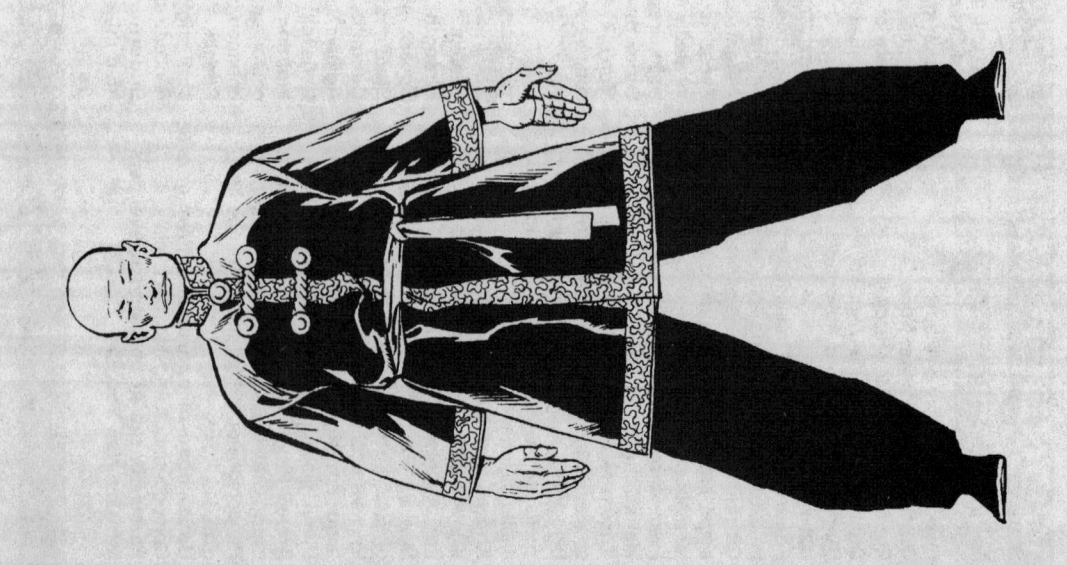

WONG

BIOGRAPHICAL DATA

Real name: Wong
Other current aliases: None
Former aliases: None
Dual Identity: None
Current occupation: Servant of Doctor Stephen Strange
Former occupation: Student of martial arts and mystic of Kamar-Taj, co-director of the Stephen Strange Memorial Institute
Citizenship: Kamar-Taj, Tibet; resident alien in the United States of America
Legal status: No criminal record
Place of birth: Kamar-Taj, Tibet
Marital status: Betrothed
Known relatives: Imei Chang (fiancee), Kan (ancestor, presumed deceased), Hamir (father)
Known confidants: Doctor Stephen Strange, Imei Chang, Sara Wolfe
Known allies: Doctor Strange, Clea, Rintrah, Topaz
Major enemies: Urthona, Dracula, Shialmar the Shadow Queen
Usual base of operations: Doctor Strange's townhouse, Greenwich Village, Manhattan, New York City
Former bases of operations: Kamar-Taj, Tibet
Current group membership: None
Former group membership: None
Extent of education: Unrevealed

PHYSICAL DESCRIPTION

Height: 5' 8"
Weight: 140 lbs.
Eyes: Brown
Hair: Blond (Wong now shaves his head)
Other distinguishing features: None

POWERS AND ABILITIES

Intelligence: Normal
Strength: Athlete
Speed: Athlete
Stamina: Athlete
Durability: Athlete
Agility: Athlete
Reflexes: Athlete
Fighting skills: Mastery of the martial arts of Kamar-Taj
Special skills and abilities: Unrevealed
Superhuman physical powers: None
Superhuman mental powers: None
Special limitations: None
Source of superhuman powers: Inapplicable

PARAPHERNALIA

Costume specifications: Conventional
Personal weaponry: None
Special weaponry: None
Other accessories: None
Transportation: Conventional
Design and manufacture of paraphernalia: Weavers of Kamar-Taj

BIBLIOGRAPHY

First appearance: STRANGE TALES Vol. 1 #110, (name revealed) STRANGE TALES Vol. 1 #147
Origin issue: DOCTOR STRANGE Vol. 2 #75
Significant issues: TOMB OF DRACULA #44, DR. STRANGE Vol. 2 #14 (turned into vampire by Dracula, restored to humanity by Doctor Strange); DR. STRANGE Vol. 2 #42-44 (abducted to Shadowqueen's dimension, rescued by Doctor Strange, aided Strange in defeating Shadowqueen); DOCTOR STRANGE Vol. 2 #45 (attacked by N'Garai demon); DR. STRANGE Vol. 2 #75 (Origin revealed); DR. STRANGE Vol. 2 #81 (severely injured by Urthona); STRANGE TALES Vol. 3 #3 (believed Doctor Strange was dead due to spell cast by Strange); STRANGE TALES Vol. 3 #17 (reunited with Doctor Strange, regained full memory of him, united with Imei Chang)

WOODGOD

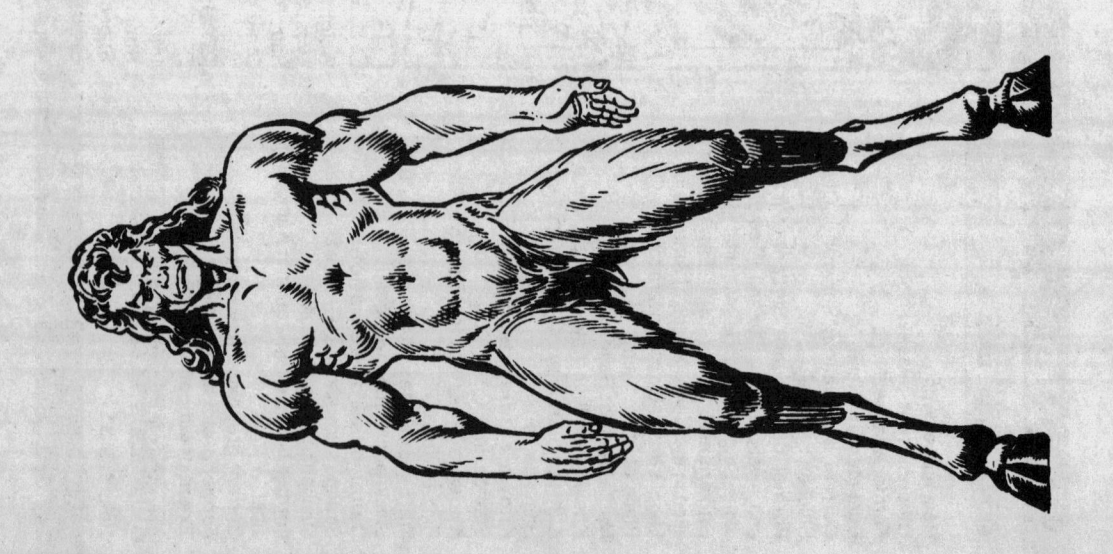

WOODGOD

BIOGRAPHICAL DATA

Real name: Woodgod
Other current aliases: None
Former aliases: None
Dual identity: Secret
Current occupation: Lawgiver of the Changelings
Former occupation: None
Citizenship: The Community of Changelings
Legal status: None
Place of birth: The Pace farm just outside Liberty, New Mexico
Marital status: Single
Known relatives: David Pace ("father," deceased), Ellen Pace ("mother," deceased)
Known confidants: None
Known allies: Hulk, Spider-Man
Major enemies: Colonel Del Tremens, citizens of Liberty, New Mexico, Leoninus
Usual base of operations: Community of Changelings in a valley in the Colorado Rocky Mountains
Former bases of operations: The Pace farm just outside Liberty, New Mexico
Current group membership: The Community of Changelings
Former group membership: None
Extent of education: Unrevealed

PHYSICAL DESCRIPTION

Height: 6'3"
Weight: 265 lbs.
Eyes: Red
Hair: Brown
Other distinguishing features: Woodgod resembles the Greek mythological half-man half-goat, forest-god Pan.

POWERS AND ABILITIES

Intelligence: Above normal
Strength: Superhuman Class 50
Speed: Enhanced human
Stamina: Enhanced human
Durability: Enhanced human
Agility: Enhanced human
Reflexes: Enhanced human
Fighting skills: None, relies on superhuman strength in combat
Special skills: Extensive knowledge of advanced techniques of genetic engineering
Superhuman physical powers: Aside from the above listed attributes, Woodgod has a superhuman resistance to chemical toxins
Superhuman mental powers: None
Special limitations: None
Source of superhuman powers: Woodgod is an artificial being created through advanced genetic engineering techniques.

PARAPHERNALIA

Costume specifications: None
Personal weaponry: None
Special weaponry: None
Other accessories: None
Transportation: Galloping under own power
Design and manufacture of paraphernalia: Inapplicable

BIBLIOGRAPHY

First appearance: MARVEL PREMIERE #31
Origin issue: MARVEL PREMIERE #31
Significant issues: MARVEL PREMIERE #31 (creation; death of "parents" David and Ellen Pace, battled Col. Del Tremens and the U.S. Army); MARVEL TEAM-UP #53-54 (battled Hulk and Spider-Man, allied with same to battle Col. Del Tremens and the U.S. army); HULK #251-252 (returned to Pace farm, used David Pace's notes and equipment to create Changelings; resisted coup by murderous Changeling Leoninus; established Changeling community in Colorado Rocky Mountains); QUASAR #14 (revealed to have become experimental subject of the Stranger on his laboratory world); QUASAR #20 (returned to Earth in Jack of Heart's caravan); MARVEL COMICS PRESENTS #76 (thwarted attempts by Leoninus and Roxxon to take control of Changelings' breeding patterns)

WORM.™

WORM

BIOGRAPHICAL DATA

Real name: Unrevealed
Other current aliases: None
Former aliases: None known
Dual Identity: The general populace of Earth is unaware of Worm's existence.
Current occupation: Warrior
Former occupation: Unrevealed
Citizenship: The Savage Land
Legal status: None
Place of birth: The Savage Land
Marital status: Unrevealed
Known relatives: None
Known confidants: None
Known allies: Zaladane, Savage Land Mutates
Major enemies: the X-Men, Ka-Zar, Shanna the She-Devil
Usual base of operations: The Savage Land
Former bases of operations: Same
Current group membership: The Savage Land Mutates
Former group membership: None known
Extent of education: No formal education

PHYSICAL DESCRIPTION

Height: 9' 4" (length)
Weight: 740 lbs.
Eyes: Red
Hair: Unrevealed, possibly none
Other distinguishing features: Worm resembles a huge serpent with a humanoid face, arms, and hands. He has no legs, and his hands are covered with suction cup-like pores. His skin is green and scaled like a reptile's.

POWERS AND ABILITIES

Intelligence: Normal
Strength: Unrevealed
Speed: Below normal
Stamina: Normal
Durability: Unrevealed
Agility: Below normal
Reflexes: Normal
Fighting skills: Unrevealed
Special skills: None known
Superhuman physical powers: Produces an unknown mucus-like secretion through the suction cup-like pores in his hands. Worm coats his victims with a transparent mucoid film composed of his secretion. This mucoid secretion slowly enters the victim's pores and adheres to his or her brain tissues. As time passes, a chemical in the secretion dulls the victim's control over his or her own thoughts and physical movements, rendering the victim submissive to Worm's commands. Worm's control over his victims can last indefinitely, unless the victim is exceptionally strong-willed. In that case, the victim can eventually fight off the effects of the chemical and regain control of his or her mind.
Superhuman mental powers: Worm apparently possesses psionic powers that play a role in his control over victims whose wills have been dulled by the chemical he secretes. He can empower another person (even one who otherwise lacks psionic powers) to take psionic control over particular victims of his chemical
Special limitations: Worm's ease of movement is restricted by his serpent-like lower body.
Source of superhuman powers: Possibly artificially induced mutation

PARAPHERNALIA

Costume specifications: Ordinary fabric
Personal weaponry: None
Special weaponry: None
Other accessories: None
Transportation: None
Design and manufacture of paraphernalia: Inapplicable

BIBLIOGRAPHY

First appearance: UNCANNY X-MEN #250
Origin issue: Worm's origin is as yet unrevealed.
Significant issues: X-MEN #250 (used his powers to amass an army of Savage Land natives to battle X-Men for Zaladane, took control of Colossus, Dazzler, and Polaris of the X-Men and Ka-Zar, all of whom fought the effects of his power, and defeated Zaladane, Worm and their forces); X-MEN #274-275 (with other Savage Land Mutates, aided Zaladane in battle against Magneto, Ka-Zar and allies, used his powers over most of Zaladane's army; transferred psionic control over his victims Shanna and Nereel to Brainchild, was captured by Ka-Zar and allies, powers temporarily absorbed by Rogue and used by her to restore his victims' free will)

WRAITH™

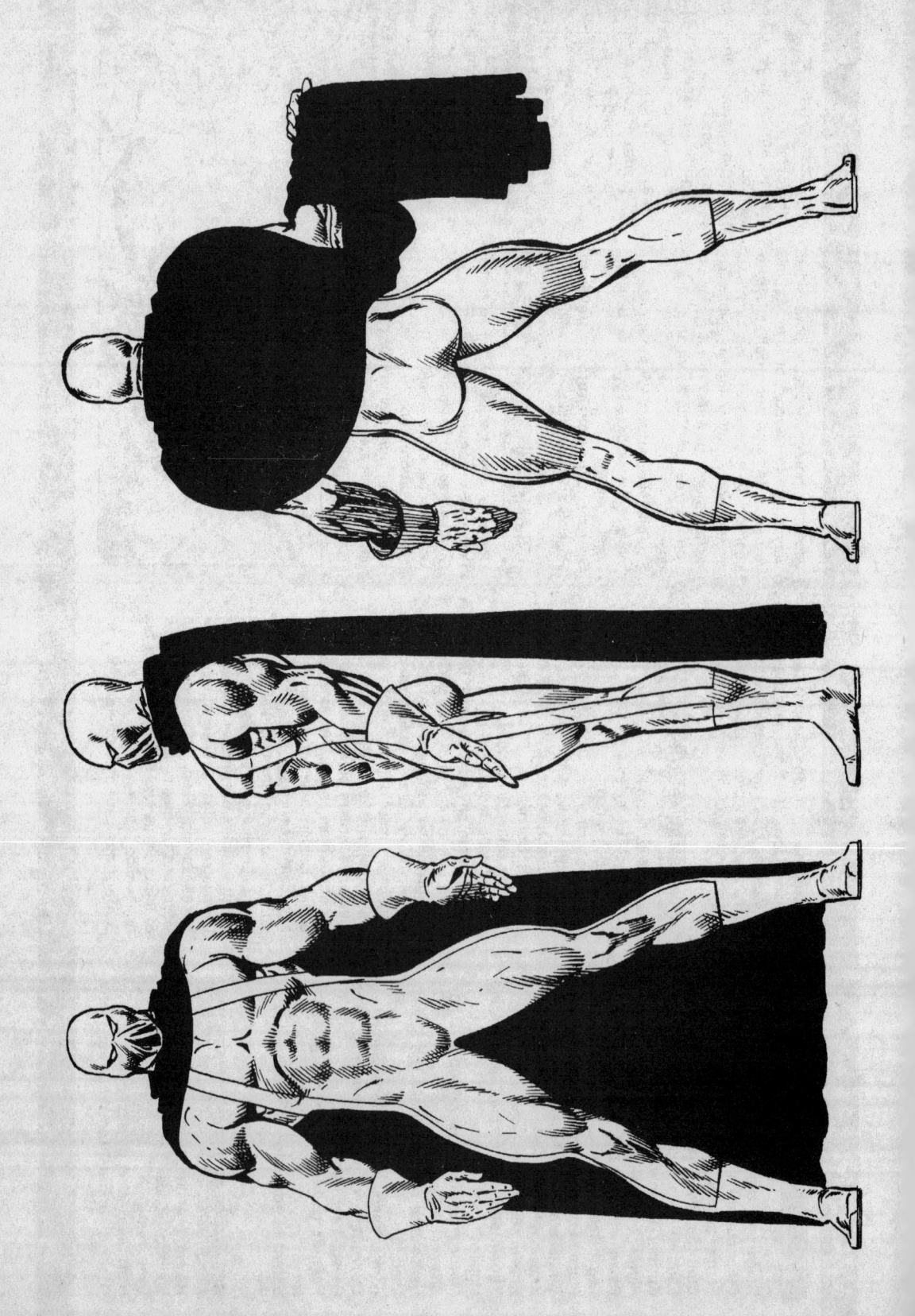

WRAITH

BIOGRAPHICAL DATA

Real name: Brian DeWolff
Other aliases at time of death: None known
Former aliases: None known
Dual identity: Secret, known to the legal authorities
Occupation at time of death: Adventurer
Former occupation: Policeman, vigilante
Citizenship: United States of America
Legal status: No criminal record
Place of birth: Unrevealed
Place of death: New York City
Cause of apparent death: Shot by Scourge
Marital status: Single
Known relatives: Phillip DeWolff (father), Celia DeWolff (mother, deceased), Jean DeWolff (sister, deceased)
Known confidants: Jean DeWolff (deceased)
Known allies: Iron Man I, Doctor Strange, Spider-Man, Jean DeWolff, Jack of Hearts, Guardsman II (Michael O'Brien), Jasper Sitwell, Eddie March, (former) Madame Masque I
Major enemies: Phillip DeWolff, Midas I, Scourge, Whiplash I, Maggia, (former) Spider-Man, Iron Man I, Doctor Strange
Base of operations at time of death: New York City
Former base of operations: None
Group membership at time of death: None
Former group membership: None
Extent of education: Graduate of New York City police academy

PHYSICAL DESCRIPTION

Height: 5'11"
Weight: 190 lbs.
Eyes: Blue
Hair: Reddish blond
Other distinguishing features: None

POWERS AND ABILITIES

Intelligence: Normal
Strength: Normal
Speed: Normal
Stamina: Normal
Durability: Normal
Agility: Normal
Reflexes: Normal
Fighting skills: Received police training in armed and unarmed combat
Special skills and abilities: None known
Superhuman physical powers: None
Superhuman mental powers: Psionic ability to control the mind of one other person at a time. Ability to cast illusions in the minds of one or more people simultaneously, thereby making reality appear to change or making himself seem invisible. Psionic ability to induce pain without causing his victim physical injury. Telekinetic ability to levitate matter. Telepathic ability to read minds. Psionic ability to affect Spider-Man's mind in such a way as to shield himself from detection by the latter's "spider-sense."
Special limitations: None known
Source of superhuman powers: Effect of energy from advanced technology procured by Philip DeWolff

PARAPHERNALIA

Costume specifications: Conventional fabrics
Personal weaponry: None
Special weaponry: None
Other accessories: None
Transportation: None
Design and manufacture of paraphernalia: Unrevealed

BIBLIOGRAPHY

First appearance: MARVEL TEAM-UP #48
Origin issue: MARVEL TEAM-UP #48-50 (was psionically controlled by his father Phillip, who used him to murder his enemies; clashed with Spider-Man, Iron Man I, Doctor Strange, and Jean DeWolff; was defeated by Spider-Man and Iron Man I); MARVEL TEAM-UP #51 (fell under mental possession by Phillip, Phillip was defeated by Doctor Strange and Iron Man I, Strange revived Wraith's own consciousness, was reunited with his sister Jean); IRON MAN #105-108 (teamed with Iron Man I, Jean DeWolff, and others in battling Midas); MARVEL TEAM-UP #72 (aided Spider-Man and Iron Man I against Whiplash and Maggia); AMAZING SPIDER-MAN #278 (driven mad with grief by Jean's death, intended to take vengeance on New York City police department, was assassinated by Scourge)

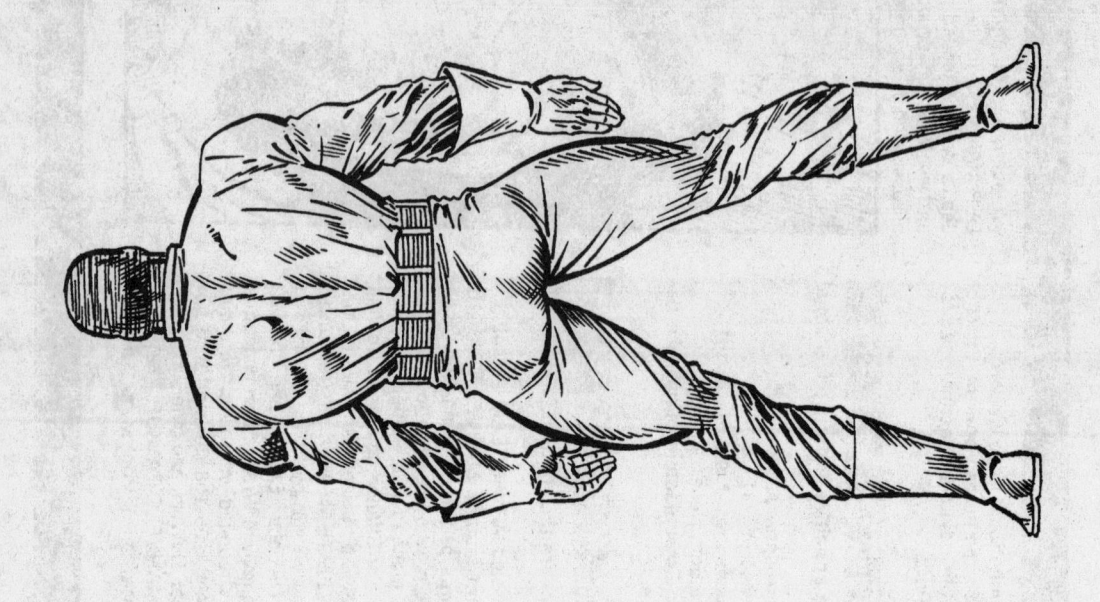

WRECKER

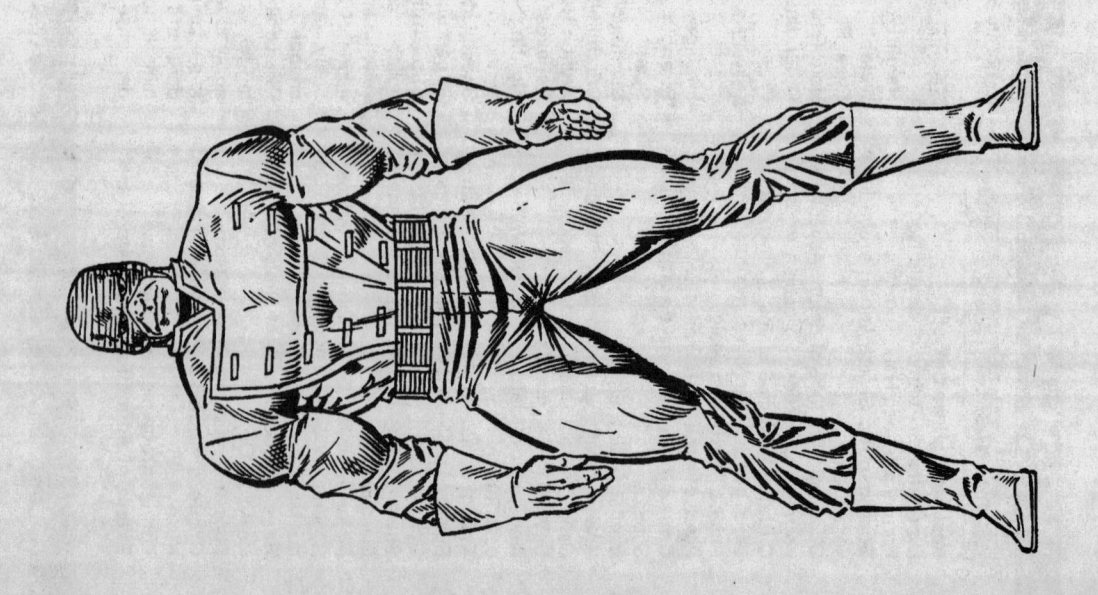

WRECKER

BIOGRAPHICAL DATA

Real name: Dirk Garthwaite
Other current aliases: None
Former aliases: None
Dual identity: None
Current occupation at time: Professional criminal
Former occupation: Manual laborer
Citizenship: United States of America
Legal status: Criminal record in the United States
Place of birth: New York City
Marital status: Single
Known relatives: Mother (name unrevealed, deceased)
Known confidants: None
Known allies: The Wrecking Crew (Thunderball, Piledriver, Bulldozer); Masters of Evil IV (Baron Zemo II, Tiger Shark, Mister Hyde, Goliath, the Fixer, Moonstone, Blackout, Yellowjacket, Absorbing Man, Titania); Ulik
Major enemies: Thor, the Avengers, Hercules
Usual base of operations: New York City
Former bases of operations: None
Current group membership: The Wrecking Crew
Former group membership: Masters of Evil IV
Extent of education: Unrevealed

PHYSICAL DESCRIPTION

Height: 6'3"
Weight: 320 lbs.
Eyes: Blue
Hair: Brown
Other distinguishing features: None

POWERS AND ABILITIES

Intelligence: Normal
Strength: Superhuman Class 50
Speed: Normal
Stamina: Superhuman
Durability: Metahuman
Agility: Normal
Reflexes: Normal
Fighting skills: High proficiency at streetfighting techniques
Special skills and abilities: None
Superhuman physical powers: Superhuman strength and durability
Superhuman mental powers: The Wrecker has established a mental link with his enchanted crowbar, enabling him to utilize it for a variety of effects, including storage of the mystic enchantment from which he gains his powers, mental domination of anyone who holds it, projection of an aura which can repel bullets
Special limitations: None
Source of superhuman powers: Mystical enchantment by the Asgardian Norn Queen Karnilla

PARAPHERNALIA

Costume specifications: Ordinary materials
Personal weaponry: A four foot-long cast iron crowbar which has become virtually indestructible due to mystic enchantment
Special weaponry: None
Transportation: Various
Design and manufacture of paraphernalia: Unrevealed

BIBLIOGRAPHY

First appearance: THOR #148
Origin issue: THOR #148
Significant issues: THOR #148-150 (accidentally given superhuman power by Karnilla intended for Loki, battled Thor, defeated by Sif animating the Destroyer); THOR #171 (escaped confinement, battled Thor who neutralized his superhuman powers); DEFENDERS #17-19 (origin of Wrecking Crew recounted, battled Dr. Strange, Nighthawk, Hulk, and Power Man alongside Wrecking Crew while attempting to locate Gamma Bomb); FANTASTIC FOUR #168 (manipulated by the Puppet Master into fighting the Fantastic Four and Power Man); IRON FIST #11-12 (battled Captain America and Iron Fist alongside the Wrecking Crew while trying to lure Thor into battle); THOR #305 (battled Thor alongside the Wrecking Crew in revenge attempt); SECRET WARS #1-12 (taken to the Beyonder's Battleworld with the rest of the Wrecking Crew and various other criminals, battled the Avengers, X-Men, Fantastic Four, and others); SPECTACULAR SPIDER-MAN #125-126 (battled Spider-Man and Spider Woman II alongside the Wrecking Crew while attempting to acquire the means to blackmail the federal government, fought with Thunderball for control over Norn power, mother died); AVENGERS #273-276 (joined the Masters of Evil IV alongside the Wrecking Crew, took over Avengers Mansion, battled Hercules); AVENGERS #277 (fought Captain America and the Wasp); IRON MAN #251 (attempted to kill Tony Stark, battled Iron Man); THOR #418 (teamed with Ulik and the Wrecking Crew, battled Hercules and Thor); THOR #426-428 (teamed with the Wrecking Crew, battled Thor, Excalibur, and Code: Blue); THOR #429 (battled Ghost Rider)

XEMNU

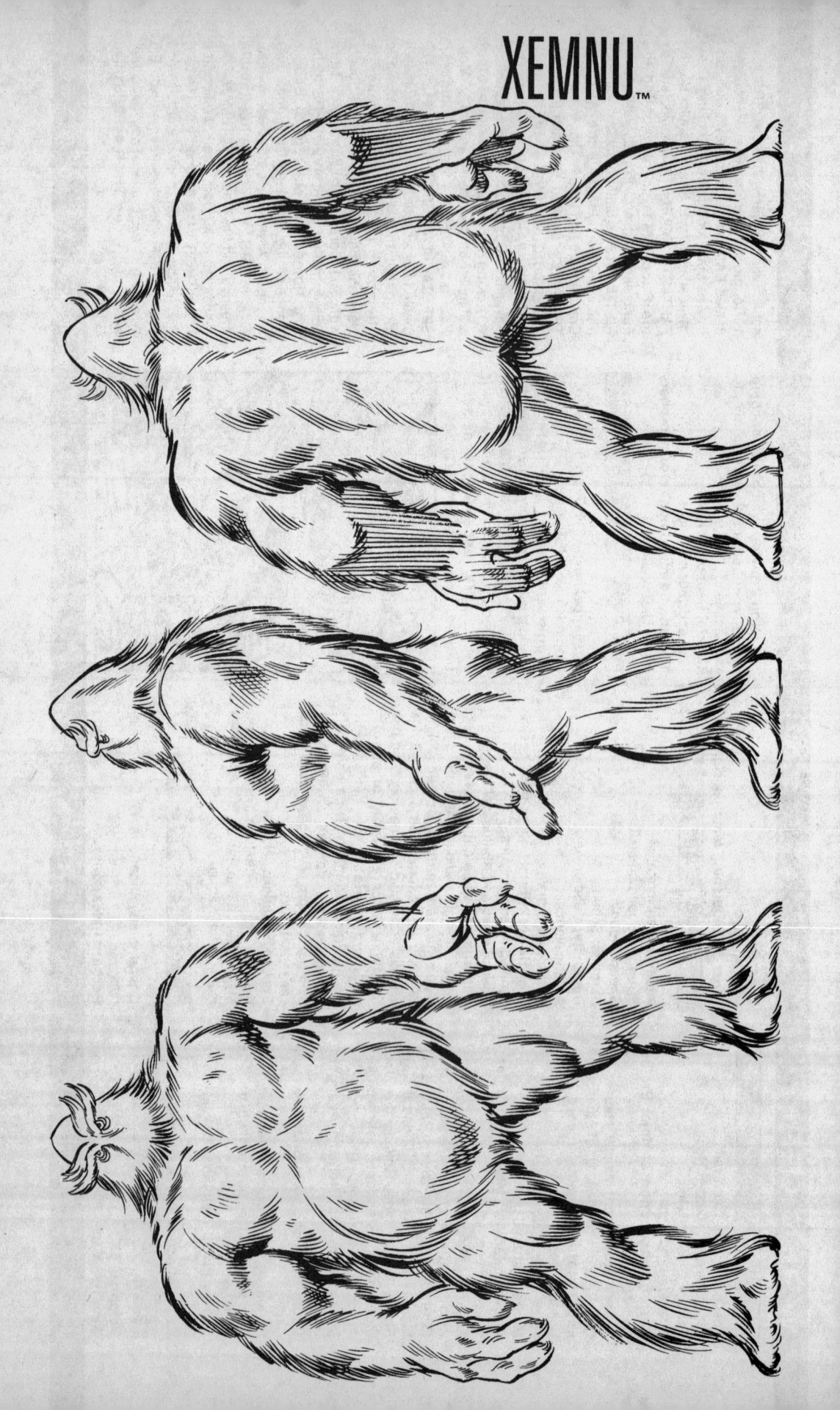

XEMNU

BIOGRAPHICAL DATA

Real name: Xemnu
Other current aliases: The Titan
Former aliases: The Hulk, Richmond Wagner, Amos Moses
Dual identity: The general populace of Earth believes Xemnu to be a fictional character in television programs
Current occupation: Would-be conqueror, teddy bear
Former occupation: Ruler of his home planet, television star
Citizenship: Unrevealed
Legal status: None on Earth, formerly convicted criminal on a prison world, currently property of Enilwen
Place of birth: Unidentified planet in another solar system
Marital status: Single
Known relatives: None
Known confidants: None
Known allies: None
Major enemies: The Hulk, She-Hulk, the Defenders, the Thing, Wonder Man, Joe Harper
Usual base of operations: Mobile
Former bases of operations: Plucketville, Queens, New York
Current group membership: None
Former group membership: None
Extent of education: Unknown, perhaps inapplicable

PHYSICAL DESCRIPTION

Height: 11', (originally) 20'
Weight: 1100 lbs., (originally) 2000 lbs.
Eyes: Red
Hair: White
Other distinguishing features: Xemnu is covered in white fur, and has only three fingers (including opposable thumb) on each hand.

POWERS AND ABILITIES

Intelligence: Gifted
Strength: Super-human Class 90
Speed: Enhanced human
Stamina: Superhuman
Durability: Superhuman
Agility: Normal
Reflexes: Normal
Fighting skills: Minimal hand-to-hand combat skills
Special skills: Advanced knowledge of genetics
Superhuman physical powers: Aside from the above listed attributes, Xemnu has no other physical powers
Superhuman mental powers: Telepathy, hypnosis, possession, can place mental blocks on others, can project psionic concussive blasts, levitation, animate unliving objects, can create "atmos-spheres", a protective sphere of psionic energy, which he can use to fly with himself within it
Special limitations: For unknown reasons the Hulk has become immune to Xemnu's psionic possession.
Source of superhuman powers: Alien genetic structure

PARAPHERNALIA

Costume specifications: Inapplicable
Personal weaponry: None
Special weaponry: Television, machine that turn humans into members of his species
Other accessories: None
Transportation: Atmos-spheres, starcraft
Design and manufacture of paraphernalia: Xavier's school

BIBLIOGRAPHY

First appearance: JOURNEY INTO MYSTERY #62
Origin issue: JOURNEY INTO MYSTERY #62
Significant issues: JOURNEY INTO MYSTERY #62 (escaped prison planet, fled to Earth, took hypnotic control of humankind, was thwarted by Joe Harper), MARVEL FEATURE #3 (took possession of the body of astronaut Richmond Wagner, attempted to abduct Earth children to repopulate his homeworld, battled Defenders, defeated by Hulk); DEFENDERS #12 (took possession of Amos Moses, attempted to kidnap townspeople of Plucketville to repopulate home world, thwarted by the Defenders); HULK ANNUAL #5 (created clones of alien monsters to attack Hulk, also battled Hulk himself, was defeated when dam burst); MARVEL TWO-IN-ONE #78 (attempted to hypnotize American public over television, took mental control of Wonder Man, used him to attack Thing, fled in starship); SHE-HULK #6 (kidnaped U.S. Archer in hopes of getting his unborn child from his wife); SHE-HULK #7 (attempted to turn She-Hulk into "She-Xemnu," captured and given to Enilwen, a teddy bear collector)

X-MEN
FIRST LINE-UP

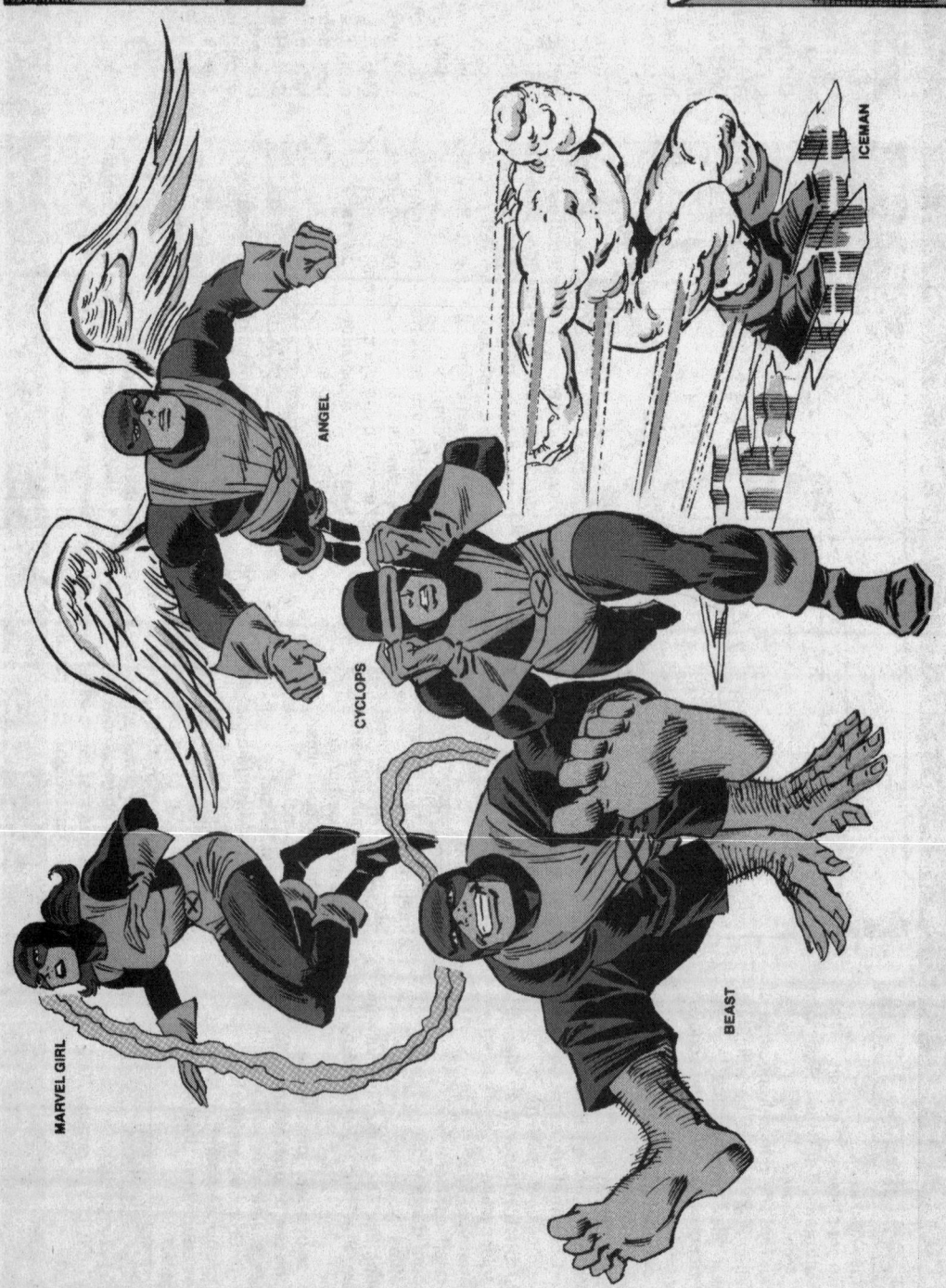

PROFESSOR X

MIMIC

ANGEL

ICEMAN

CYCLOPS

MARVEL GIRL

BEAST

X-MEN

ORGANIZATION

Purpose: To train superhuman mutants in the uses of their special powers, to defend "normal" humanity against attack by malevolent superhuman mutants, to assist superhuman mutants against oppression and persecution, and to promote peaceful relations between "normal" humans and mutants

Modus operandi: Team uses Cerebro technology to locate superhuman mutants, also responds to news of threats involving mutants

Extent of operations: Worldwide, have traveled to other solar systems and galaxies and otherdimensional worlds when necessary

Relationship to conventional authorities: Originally operated in cooperation with FBI (Agent Fred Duncan as liaison), for many years regarded as outlaws, now operates in unofficial cooperation with Dr. Valerie Cooper (of X-Factor II and the Commission on Superhuman Activities), and Col. Nick Fury of SHIELD

Base of operations: Professor Xavier's School for Gifted Youngsters, Salem Center, Westchester County, New York State

Former bases of operations: Mutant Research Center, Muir Island, Scotland; former Reavers base in Australian outback

Major funding: Charles Xavier's personal fortune

Known enemies: Magneto, Juggernaut, Sentinels, Apocalypse, Shadow King, Mastermind, Mister Sinister, Marauders, White Queen, Arcade, Brood, Fenris, Upstarts, Mojo, Sabretooth, Blob, Unus, Vanisher, Savage Land Mutates, Matsuo Tsurayaba, Omega Red, Adversary, (former) Brotherhood of Evil Mutants, I, III, IV, Count Nefaria (deceased), Factor Three, Garokk the Petrified Man (apparently deceased) Genoshan government and police force,Living Monolith, Lords Cardinal of the Hellfire Club, Lucifer (reported deceased), Reavers (mostly deceased), Zaladane (apparently deceased)

Known allies: Alpha Flight, Arkon, Avengers, Daredevil, Doctor Strange, Excalibur, Fantastic Four, Firestar, Nick Fury, Gateway, Ghost Rider II, Iron Fist, Ka-Zar, Misty Knight, Lilandra, Roma, Shanna the She-Devil, Spider-Man, Starjammers, Colleen Wing, X-Factor II, (former) New Mutants

Known officers: Professor Xavier (leader), Cyclops (deputy leader of Blue Team), Storm (deputy leader of Gold Team), Forge (assistant to Xavier)

Known current members: Professor Xavier (leader), Forge, (Blue Team), Beast, Cyclops, Gambit, Jubilee, Psylocke, Rogue, Wolverine, (Gold Team) Archangel, Bishop, Colossus, Jean Grey (Marvel Girl), Iceman, Storm

Known former members: Banshee, Changeling (deceased), Dazzler, Havok, Longshot, Magneto, Mimic, Nightcrawler, Phoenix I (deceased), Phoenix II, Polaris, Shadowcat, Sunfire, Thunderbird I (deceased)

Note: Moira Mactaggart organized a short-lived alternate X-Men team comprised of Banshee, Tom Corsi, Lorna Dane (Polaris), Forge, Sharon Friedlander, Legion (apparently deceased), Amanda Sefton, and Sunder (deceased)

Known special agents: Moira Mactaggart ("silent partner" of Xavier, head of Mutant Research Center), Tom Corsi (former general support), Sharon Friedlander, Stevie Hunter (athletic instructor), Madrox the Multiple Man (former assistant to Dr. Mactaggart), Madelyne Pryor-Summers (former pilot and communications officer, deceased)

Membership requirements: Must be a superhumanly powerful mutant, although there have been exceptions, such as Mimic and Longshot.

MEMBERSHIP

Number of active members: 15

Number of reserve members: None at present, although former members sometimes participate in missions.

Organizational structure: Team is currently composed of an overall leader, who usually remains at headquarters, and two subordinate teams, each with a deputy leader who directs combat activity in the field.

HISTORY

Founder: Professor Charles Xavier (Professor X)

Other leaders: Changeling, Storm, Cyclops, Mimic

Previous purpose or goals: Same as above

Major campaigns or accomplishments: Thwarted Magneto's takeover of Cape Citadel, foiled Vanisher's attempt to blackmail U.S. government, overthrew Magneto's dictatorship of San Marco, prevented destruction of the Universe by M'Krann Crystal

Major setbacks: Capture of Professor Xavier by Factor Three, break-up of team upon Xavier's apparent demise, team captured by Krakoa, death of Thunderbird I, apparent demise of X-Men in Savage Land

TECHNOLOGY AND PARAPHERNALIA

Level of technology: Extraordinarily advanced, including Shi'ar technology far in advance of Earth's.

Transportation: Blackbird jet, and conventional means

Standard uniforms: None

Standard weaponry: None

Standard accessories: None

BIBLIOGRAPHY

First appearance: X-MEN Vol. 1 #1
Origin issue: X-MEN Vol 1 #38-56

X-MEN
SECOND LINE-UP
ART: PAT OLLIFFE/JOSEF RUBINSTEIN

X-MEN MEMBERSHIP ROSTER

PROFESSOR X

Real name: Charles Xavier
Current status: Active
Membership record: X-MEN Vol. 1 #1-7, 9-33, 39, 65, 66, 94-110, 113; UNCANNY X-MEN #114, 117, 129, 131-133, 135-138, 139-145, 147-150, 151-158, 161-162, 164-165, 167-169, 171, 173-175, 177-181, 184-186, 188-193, 196, 199-200, 282-284, 286-289, 291-present; GIANT-SIZE X-MEN #1-5, 8-present; GIANT-SIZE X-MEN #1; UNCANNY X-MEN ANNUAL #1; UNCANNY X-MEN ANNUAL #16

Note: Professor X was the founder of the X-Men and has served as the team's overall leader and mentor for most of its history through the present

CYCLOPS

Real name: Scott Summers
Current status: Deputy leader, Blue Team
Membership record: X-MEN Vol. 1 #1-43, 45-46, 49-66, 94-102, 104-113; UNCANNY X-MEN #114-138, 150-159, 161-168, 170-175, 185, 197, 199-201, 288-291; X-MEN Vol. 2 #1-present; GIANT-SIZE X-MEN #1; X-MEN ANNUAL #1; UNCANNY X-MEN ANNUAL #3, 5, 9

Note: Cyclops was the first member to be recruited officially by Professor X. He became deputy leader of the X-Men early in the team's history and, other than a few leaves of absence, held it until he forfeited it to Storm. With the other original members he formed X-Factor, but recently returned to the X-Men

ICEMAN

Real name: Robert L. Drake
Current status: Active, Gold Team
Membership record: X-MEN Vol. 1 #1-43, 46, 49-66; UNCANNY X-MEN #145-146, 281-present; X-MEN Vol. 2 #1-3, 5; GIANT-SIZE X-MEN #1; UNCANNY X-MEN ANNUAL #16

Note: Iceman was the second official recruit into the X-Men. He later served as a member of the Champions of Los Angeles, the Defenders, and the original X-Factor, but has since returned to the X-Men

ARCHANGEL

Real name: Warren K. Worthington III
Current status: Active, Gold Team
Membership record: (as Angel) X-MEN Vol. 1 #1-27, 29-46, 49-66; GIANT-SIZE X-MEN #1; UNCANNY X-MEN #139-148; UNCANNY X-MEN ANNUAL #1; (as Archangel) UNCANNY X-MEN #281-289, 291-present; X-MEN Vol. 2 #1-3, 5

Note: As the Angel, Archangel was the third official recruit into the X-Men. He later served as a member of the Champions of Los Angeles, the Defenders, and the original X-Facto. During the his membership in X-Factor Apocalypse physically altered him into the being known as Archangel, who has since returned to the X-Men

BEAST

Real name: Henry P. McCoy
Current status: Active, Blue Team
Membership record: X-MEN Vol. 1 #1-43, 46, 49-66; GIANT-SIZE X-MEN #1 (as a member), X-MEN Vol. 1 #111-113; UNCANNY X-MEN #114, 134-137 (as a non-member ally); UNCANNY X-MEN #288; X-MEN Vol. 2 #1-3, 5-present

Note: The Beast was the fourth official recruit into the X-Men. He later served as a replacement for an injured Angel and even served briefly as deputy leader. He left the team when he temporarily lost his superhuman powers.

MARVEL GIRL

Real name: Jean Grey
Current status: Active, Gold Team
Membership record: X-MEN Vol. 1 #1-24, 27-43, 46, 49-66; UNCANNY X-MEN #281-present; X-MEN Vol. 2 #1-3, 8; GIANT-SIZE X-MEN #1; UNCANNY X-MEN ANNUAL #16 (as member); UNCANNY X-MEN Vol. 1 #97-100 (as non-member ally)

Note: Though she was the fifth official recruit into the X-Men, Jean Grey had actually been training under Xavier's tutelage since she was eleven. Although she quit the team, she became involved on an X-Men mission during which she was placed in suspended animation by the Phoenix Force, who then took on her identity and became known as Phoenix II. Years later, after the demise of Phoenix II, Jean was found and revived. She became a founding member of X-Factor. She has since rejoined the X-Men

MIMIC

Real name: Calvin Rankin
Current status: Inactive
Membership record: X-MEN Vol. 1 #27-29

Note: Originally an adversary of the X-Men, the Mimic later joined the team as a replacement for an injured Angel and even served briefly as deputy leader. He left the team when he temporarily lost his superhuman powers.

CHANGELING

Real name: Unrevealed
Current status: Deceased
Membership record: X-MEN Vol. 1 #40-42

Note: The Changeling was a former adversary of the X-Men. Discovering he was dying of cancer, he sought to reform. Professor Xavier persuaded him to use his shape-changing powers to impersonate him while Xavier went into seclusion to prepare to deal with the invading Z'Nox. Xavier imparted a small portion of his telepathic ability to him. The Changeling, as Xavier, died saving the world from being destroyed by the Subterranean Grotesk

X-MEN
THIRD LINE-UP

X-MEN MEMBERSHIP ROSTER

POLARIS

Real name: Lorna Dane
Current status: Inactive (active with X-Factor II)
Membership record: X-MEN Vol. 1 #49 (as Iceman's friend); GIANT-SIZE X-MEN #1, X-MEN Vol. 1 #94 (as a member), X-MEN Vol. 1 #50-51, 97 (as an antagonist), X-MEN Vol. 1 #52, 57-58, 60-61, UNCANNY X-MEN #125-129, 145-146, 158-159, 163, 173, 218, 249-250, 253 (as a non-member ally), UNCANNY X-MEN #219, 221-222, 239-241, 243 (as an antagonist possessed by Malice III), UNCANNY X-MEN #254-255, 257-258, 269, 280; UNCANNY X-MEN ANNUAL #15 (as a member of Moira MacTaggart's X-Men)
Note: Polaris first became met the X-Men when she was captured by Mesmero. She was recruited into the X-Men to aid in their battle against the alien Z'nox.

HAVOK

Real name: Alexander "Alex" Summers
Current status: Inactive (active with X-Factor II)
Membership record: X-MEN Vol. 1 #65-66, 94, GIANT-SIZE X-MEN #1, UNCANNY X-MEN #218-219, 221-227, 229-235, 237-243, 245-251 (as a member); X-MEN Vol. 1 #54-61, 105, 119, UNCANNY X-MEN #125-129, 145-146, 158-159, 163, 168, 173, 175 (as a non-member ally); X-MEN Vol. 1 #97 (as an antagonist), UNCANNY X-MEN #270-272 (as a brainwashed antagonist); UNCANNY X-MEN ANNUAL #11-13 (as a member)
Note: Havok first became involved with the X-Men when he was captured by the Living Pharaoh and then by the Sentinels. Professor X recruited Havok into the X-Men to aid in their battle against the alien Z'nox.

BANSHEE

Real name: Sean Cassidy
Current status: Inactive
Membership record: X-MEN Vol. 1 #94-UNCANNY X-MEN #129; X-MEN Vol. 2 #1-5; GIANT-SIZE X-MEN #1; UNCANNY X-MEN ANNUAL #3
Note: After Professor X freed him from the control of the subversive Factor Three, the Irish-born Banshee became the X-Men's ally against them. Xavier later recruited him into the new team of X-Men assembled for the Krakoa mission.

NIGHTCRAWLER

Real name: Kurt Wagner
Current status: Inactive (active with Excalibur)
Membership record: X-MEN Vol. 1 #94-UNCANNY X-MEN #170, 174-175, 177-181, 183, 186, 188-194, 196, 199-204, 206-213, 227; GIANT-SIZE X-MEN #1; UNCANNY X-MEN ANNUAL #3-10
Note: The German-born Nightcrawler was the first recruit into the new team of X-Men organized by Professor X to rescue the original X-Men from the Living Island Krakoa.

WOLVERINE

Real name: Logan
Current status: Active, Blue Team
Membership record: X-MEN Vol. 1 #94-UNCANNY X-MEN #168; UNCANNY X-MEN #172-176, 178-181, 183, 192-196, 199-203, 205, 207-216, 219-221, 223-230, 233-243, 245-246, 251-253, 257-258, 261, 268, 271-280; X-MEN Vol. 2 #1-present; GIANT-SIZE X-MEN #1; UNCANNY X-MEN ANNUAL #3-16; X-MEN ANNUAL VOL. 2 #1
Note: The Canadian Wolverine resigned from the team that would become known as Alpha Flight when Professor X asked him to join the new team of X-Men he organized for the Krakoa mission.

STORM

Real name: Ororo Munroe
Current status: Active, Deputy leader, Gold Team
Membership record: X-MEN Vol. 1 #94-UNCANNY X-MEN #175, 177-181, 183-194, 196-198, 201-203, 206, 208-210, 212-216, 219-227, 229-231, 233-239, 241-248, 253, 255, 257, 265-267, 270-278, 280-present; X-MEN Vol. 2 #1-3, 5, 8; GIANT-SIZE X-MEN #1; UNCANNY X-MEN ANNUAL #3-14
Note: Born in the United States, Storm grew up in Africa, where she was recruited by Professor Xavier for the new team of he had assembled for the Krakoa mission

SUNFIRE

Real name: Shiro Yashida
Current status: Inactive
Membership record: X-MEN Vol. 1 #64 (as an antagonist); GIANT-SIZE X-MEN #1, X-MEN Vol. 1 #94 (as a member); UNCANNY X-MEN #118-120, 284-286 (as a non-member ally)
Note: The only Japanese X-Man, Sunfire was recruited by Professor X to help save the original X-Men from Krakoa.

COLOSSUS

Real name: Piotr (Peter) Nikolaievich Rasputin
Current status: Active, Gold Team
Membership record: X-MEN Vol. 1 #94-UNCANNY X-MEN #175, 177-181, 183-184, 187-194, 196-197, 199-203, 206-213, 225-227, 229-241, 243-251 279-288, 290-present; X-MEN Vol. 2 #1, 3, 5 (as a member); UNCANNY X-MEN #259-260, 262-264 (as Peter Nicholas), UNCANNY X-MEN #277-278 (as an antagonist), GIANT-SIZE X-MEN #1; UNCANNY X-MEN ANNUAL #3-10, 12-13, 16
Note: A native of Russia, Colossus was recruited into the new X-Men team for the Krakoa mission.

X-MEN
FOURTH LINE-UP
ART: KIRK JARVINEN/JOSEF RUBINSTEIN

NIGHTCRAWLER

ROGUE

COLOSSUS

SPRITE

ANGEL

CYCLOPS

STORM

PROFESSOR X

WOLVERINE

X-MEN MEMBERSHIP ROSTER

THUNDERBIRD I

Real name: John Proudstar
Current status: Inactive (deceased)
Membership record: GIANT-SIZE X-MEN #1, X-MEN Vol. 1 #94-95
Note: An Apache from Arizona, Thunderbird was recruited by Professor X to join the new team of X-Men assembled for the Krakoa mission. Thunderbird became the second X-Man to die in action when he was killed in the explosion of Count Nefaria's skycraft during his second recorded mission with the team.

PHOENIX II

Real name: None, adopted persona of Jean Grey
Current status: Inactive (active as Phoenix III in Excalibur)
Membership record: X-MEN Vol. 1 #105-109 (as non-member ally), X-MEN Vol. 1 110-UNCANNY X-MEN #114, 117, 119, 122, 125-137 (as a member)
Note: The sentient cosmic entity known as the Phoenix Force created for itself a human body identical to that of Jean Grey (Marvel Girl), and took from her a portion of her consciousness. The X-Men believed that Phoenix was indeed Jean Grey and welcomed her back into their team. Mastermind used his powers to corrupt her psyche, triggering her change into the insane Dark Phoenix. Phoenix slew her human body rather than further menace the cosmos. The Phoenix Force later merged with Rachel Summers, the new Phoenix. The portion of Grey's consciousness within Phoenix infused itself into Madeline Pryor, and has since been restored to the psyche of Jean Grey herself.

SHADOWCAT

Real name: Katherine "Kitty" Pride
Current status: Inactive (active with Excalibur)
Membership record: UNCANNY X-MEN #129-131 (as a non-member ally), UNCANNY X-MEN #138-143, 145, 148-153, 155-175, 177-180, 183, 192-197, 199-203, 206-213, 227; UNCANNY X-MEN ANNUAL #4-10
Note: Joining at age thirteen, Kitty Pryde was the youngest person ever to become an X-Man. She remained a member continuously except for an unofficial leave she took in Japan, where she adopted the name Shadowcat. She took a leave of absence due to injuries sustained in battle with the Marauders during the massacre of the Morlocks. The leave became permanent when Shadowcat became a founding member of Excalibur.

ROGUE

Real name: Unrevealed
Current status: Active, Blue Team
Membership record: UNCANNY X-MEN #158 (as an antagonist); UNCANNY X-MEN #171-175, 178-179, 181-196, 199-203, 206-219, 221-247, 269, 274-275, 278-280; 294, UNCANNY X-MEN ANNUAL #7-13; X-MEN VOL. 2. #1-present, X-MEN ANNUAL Vol. 2 #1 (as member)
Note: Rogue originally encountered the X-Men as an enemy belonging to Mystique's Brotherhood of Evil Mutants. In desperate need of help in coping with her powers, she gained admission to the X-Men. She has remained a loyal active member ever since.

PHOENIX III

Real name: Rachel Summers
Current status: Inactive (active with Excalibur)
Membership record: UNCANNY X-MEN #141-142 (as a member of the X-Men in a future alternate reality); UNCANNY X-MEN #184 (as a non-member ally); UNCANNY X-MEN #188-192, 194-196, 199-203, 206-207, 209, UNCANNY X-MEN ANNUAL #8 (as member); UNCANNY X-MEN ANNUAL #14 (as member of Excalibur)
Note: Rachel Summers was originally a member of the X-Men of the future of an alternate reality in which mutants were confined to prison camps. She traveled back in time to "mainstream" reality where she joined its X-Men and became the new host of the Phoenix Force. After being transported to Mojoworld, she returned to Earth and helped form Excalibur.

MAGNETO

Real name: Magnus
Current status: Inactive (now an antagonist)
Membership record: X-MEN Vol. 1 #1, 4-7, 11, 17-18, 43-45, 62-63, 104, 111-113, UNCANNY X-MEN #125, 148-150 (as an antagonist), UNCANNY X-MEN #200-203, 210-213, 230, 269, UNCANNY X-MEN ANNUAL #10 (as a member); UNCANNY X-MEN #274-275, X-MEN Vol. 2 #1-3 (as an antagonist)
Note: For years Magneto was the X-Men's leading antagonist. However, Dr. Moira MacTaggart tampered with his mind while holding him captive. As a result, Magneto made his peace with the X-Men and even agreed to substitute for Professor Xavier during the latter's long sojourn with the Starjammers. Magneto has since returned to his war against "normal" humanity

PSYLOCKE

Real name: Betsy Braddock
Current status: Active, Blue Team
Membership record: UNCANNY X-MEN #211-212, UNCANNY X-MEN ANNUAL #10 (as a non-member ally); UNCANNY X-MEN #213-219, 221-230, 232-251, 255-258, 261, 268, 271-278, 280, UNCANNY X-MEN ANNUAL #11-14, X-MEN Vol. 2 #1-3, 5-12, 14-present, X-MEN ANNUAL Vol. 2 #1 (as a member)

X-MEN
FIFTH LINE-UP
ART: BRANDON PETERSON/JOSEF RUBINSTEIN

X-MEN MEMBERSHIP ROSTER

DAZZLER

Real name: Alison Blaire
Current status: Inactive
Membership record: UNCANNY X-MEN #130-131, 148, 213 (as non-member ally), UNCANNY X-MEN #214-219, 221-248, 250, UNCANNY X-MEN ANNUAL #11-13 (as member), UNCANNY X-MEN #259-260, X-MEN Vol. 2 #10-11 (as non-member ally)

Note: The Dazzler first encountered members of the X-Men during their initial clash with the Hellfire Club's Inner Circle. She then declined membership, preferring to continue her rock music career. After public exposure as a mutant, she finally joined the team. After traveling through the "Siege Perilous" she quit the team. She recently aided the X-Men and Longshot in overthrowing Mojo's rule over Longshot's dimension and remained with Longshot in his dimension.

LONGSHOT

Real name: None known
Current status: Inactive
Membership record: UNCANNY X-MEN #215-219, 221, 223-227, 229-237, 240-243, 245-247, UNCANNY X-MEN ANNUAL #10-13, X-MEN Vol. 2 #5-7, 10-11 (as a member)

Note: As an artificially created humanoid from another dimension, Longshot is one of the few X-Men who is not an Earth-born mutant. He joined the team upon arriving on Earth in an amnesiac state. Recently, he teamed with the X-Men in overthrowing the rule of Mojo in his native dimension.

DOCTOR MOIRA MACTAGGART

Real name: Dr. Moira MacTaggart
Current status: Inactive
Membership record: X-MEN Vol. 1 #96-98, 101, 104, 106, 109-110, UNCANNY X-MEN #119, 122, 125-129, 133, 135, 141-142, 146, 148, 150, 158-159, 161, 163, 165, 167, 175, 199, 212, 216-217, 227, 253, UNCANNY X-MEN ANNUAL #5, X-MEN Vol. 2 #1-4, 14-15 (as a non-member ally), UNCANNY X-MEN #254, 257-259, 269, 271, 273, 278, 280, UNCANNY X-MEN ANNUAL #15 (as leader of alternate team)

Note: Moira MacTaggart first met Charles Xavier when they were both graduate students, and they were romantically involved for a time. MacTaggart was Xavier's "silent partner" in founding the X-Men and was a major influence in the creation of the New Mutants. At present she remains a consultant to Xavier, based at her Mutant Research Center on Muir Island off the coast of Scotland.

TOM CORSI

Real name: Thomas Corsi
Current status: Inactive
Membership record: UNCANNY X-MEN #212, 278 (as a non-member ally), UNCANNY X-MEN #254 (as member of alternate team)

Note: Corsi was a policeman in the town of Salem Center, New York, where the X-Men are based. He and Sharon Friedlander were magically transformed into superhuman beings resembling Cheyenne Indians by a demonic bear. They went to work for Xavier as members of his support staff. Corsi now works at Moira MacTaggart's Mutant Research Center.

SHARON FRIEDLANDER

Real name: Sharon Friedlander
Current status: Inactive
Membership record: UNCANNY X-MEN #212, 278 (as a non-member ally), UNCANNY X-MEN #254 (as member of alternate team)

Note: Friedlander was a nurse who was magically transformed into superhuman beings resembling Cheyenne Indians by a demonic bear. She went to work for Xavier as a member of his support staff. Moira Mactaggart recruited her and Tom Corsi into her alternate team of X-Men. Friedlander now works at Moira MacTaggart's Mutant Research Center.

FORGE

Real name: Unrevealed
Current status: Inactive
Membership record: UNCANNY X-MEN #184 (unconnected with X-Men), UNCANNY X-MEN #185-188, 224, 226-227, 253, (as a non-member ally); UNCANNY X-MEN #254-255, 257-264, 270, 273-280 (as member of alternate team), UNCANNY X-MEN #282-284, 286-290, X-MEN Vol. 2 #1-3, 5, 8, X-MEN ANNUAL Vol. 2 #1 (as regular team member)

Note: Forge was an inventor working for the United States government who developed a "neutralizer" gun that could inhibit a mutant's use of their powers. Outraged when the neutralizer was used on Storm, he befriended and fell in love with her. He subsequently teamed with the X-Men against the Dire Wraiths and the Adversary. Moira MacTaggart inducted him into her alternate team of X-Men, and Forge later became an aide to Xavier in the main team.

LEGION

Real name: David Charles Haller
Current status: Inactive (deceased)
Membership record: UNCANNY X-MEN ANNUAL #254-255, 259, 269, 278, UNCANNY X-MEN ANNUAL #15 (as a member of alternate team)

Note: Legion was the illegitimate son of Charles Xavier and suffered from a multiple personality disorder. During a period of mental stability, he became a member of Moira MacTaggart's alternate team of X-Men. After falling under the possession of the Shadow King, Legion recently died.

X-MEN
SIXTH LINE-UP

ART: RICK LEONARDI/JOSEF RUBINSTEIN

STORM

ROGUE

MAGNETO

COLOSSUS

HAVOK

DAZZLER

PSYLOCKE

WOLVERINE

LONGSHOT

X-MEN MEMBERSHIP ROSTER

JUBILEE

Real name: Jubilation Lee
Current status: Active, Blue Team
Membership record: UNCANNY X-MEN #244, 248, 251-253, 257-258, 261, 268, 271-280, UNCANNY X-MEN ANNUAL #13-14 (as non-member ally), UNCANNY X-MEN #295, UNCANNY X-MEN ANNUAL #11-13, X-MEN Vol. 2 #4-14 (as member)
Note: An Asian-American orphan girl, Jubilee first encountered members of the X-Men at a Southern California shopping mall, and secretly followed them through a teleportational warp to their Australian headquarters. She lived at the base without the X-Men's knowledge until she aided Wolverine in his escape from the Reavers. Accompanying Wolverine in his subsequent travels, Jubilee became an unofficial member of the X-Men, and then an official member of the Blue Team after Professor Xavier's return from the Starjammers.

BISHOP

Real name: Bishop (first name unrevealed)
Current status: Active, Gold Team
Membership record: UNCANNY X-MEN #282-285 (as antagonist); UNCANNY X-MEN #287-present, UNCANNY X-MEN ANNUAL #16, X-MEN Vol. 2 #14-15 (as member)
Note: Bishop is a mutant native of an alternate 21st Century future in which he belonged to the XCE, a police organization whose members honor the memory of the X-Men. He traveled to the X-Men's time in pursuit of mutant outlaws from his own time period. Unable to return to his own time, Bishop was inducted into the X-Men by Professor Xavier.

GAMBIT

Real name: Remy LeBeau
Current status: Active, Blue Team
Membership record: UNCANNY X-MEN #266-267, 270, 272-280, 294-295, UNCANNY X-MEN ANNUAL #15 (as non-member ally), X-MEN Vol. 2 #1-present, X-MEN ANNUAL Vol. 2 #1 (as member)
Note: Gambit, a Cajun from New Orleans, encountered Storm after she had become separated from the X-Men and temporarily transformed into a child. He subsequently became an unofficial member of the X-Men, and then an official member of the Blue Team after Professor Xavier's return from the Starjammers.

X-MEN SUPPORTING CAST

AMOS FREDRICK "FRED" DUNCAN

Current occupation: FBI agent
Relationship: Former federal liaison with X-Men
First appearance: X-MEN Vol. 1 #2
Other appearances: X-MEN Vol. 1 #38-39, 46

JOHN GREY

Current occupation: College professor
Relationship: Father of Jean Grey (Marvel Girl)
First appearance: X-MEN Vol. 1 #5
Other appearances: X-MEN Vol. 1 #104-106, 108-109, UNCANNY X-MEN #136, 138, 145-146, 201, 240, 243

ELAINE GREY

Current occupation: Unrevealed
Relationship: Mother of Jean Grey (Marvel Girl)
First appearance: X-MEN Vol. 1 #5
Other appearances: X-MEN Vol. 1 #104-106, 108-109, UNCANNY X-MEN #136, 138, 145-146, 201, 240, 243

ZELDA (last name unrevealed)

Current occupation: (when last depicted) Waitress
Relationship: Girlfriend of Bobby Drake (Iceman)
First appearance: X-MEN Vol. 1 #7
Other appearances: X-MEN Vol. 1 #14, 19, 22, 27, 31-32, 41, 47

X-MEN
SEVENTH LINE-UP
ART: TOM MORGAN/JOSEF RUBINSTEIN

X-MEN'S SUPPORTING CAST

WARREN K. WORTHINGTON, JR.
Occupation at time of death: Chairman of the board of Worthington Industries
Relationship: Father of Warren Worthington III (Archangel)
First appearance: X-MEN Vol. 1 #14
Other appearances: X-MEN Vol. 1 #17-18, 54

KATHRYN WORTHINGTON
Occupation at time of death: Socialite
Relationship: Mother of Archangel
First appearance: X-MEN Vol. 1 #14
Other appearances: X-MEN Vol. 1 #17-18, 54

NORTON McCOY
Current occupation: Unrevealed, former atomic energy plant worker
Relationship: Father of Henry McCoy (Beast)
First appearance: X-MEN Vol. 1 #15
Other appearances: X-MEN Vol. 1 #49-50, 51-53

EDNA ANDREWS McCOY
Current occupation: Housewife
Relationship: Mother of Henry McCoy (Beast)
First appearance: X-MEN Vol. 1 #15
Other appearances: X-MEN Vol. 1 #49-50, 51-53

VERA CANTOR
Current occupation: Schoolteacher
Relationship: Friend and former girlfriend of Hank McCoy (Beast)
First appearance: X-MEN Vol. 1 #19
Other appearances: X-MEN Vol. 1 #22, 27, 31-32, 41, 47

TED ROBERTS
Current occupation: Unrevealed, former college student
Relationship: Former boyfriend of Jean Grey (Marvel Girl)
First appearance: X-MEN Vol. 1 #24
Other appearances: X-MEN Vol. 1 #25-28, 31, 34

CANDACE "CANDY" SOUTHERN
Occupation at time of death: Business executive
Relationship: Girlfriend of Archangel
First appearance: X-MEN Vol. 1 #31
Other appearances: X-MEN Vol. 1 #32; UNCANNY X-MEN #132, 146, 169

WILLIAM ROBERT DRAKE
Current occupation: Unrevealed
Relationship: Father of Bobby Drake (Iceman)
First appearance: X-MEN Vol. 1 #44
Other appearances: X-MEN Vol. 1 #46; UNCANNY X-MEN #289-290

X-MEN
EIGHTH LINE-UP
BLUE TEAM

ROGUE
JUBILEE
PROFESSOR X
PSYLOCKE
WOLVERINE
CYCLOPS
GAMBIT
BEAST

X-MEN'S SUPPORTING CAST

MADELAINE BEATRICE DRAKE
Current occupation: Unrevealed
Relationship: Mother of Bobby Drake (Iceman)
First appearance: X-MEN Vol. 1 #44

DR. MOIRA MacTAGGART
Current occupation: Research scientist, head of Mutant Research Center, Muir Island, Scotland
Relationship: Associate and former lover of Professor Xavier
First appearance: X-MEN Vol. 1 #96

LILANDRA NERAMANI
Current occupation: Majestrix (Empress) of Shi'ar Empire
Relationship: Lover of Professor Charles Xavier
First appearance: X-MEN Vol. 1 #97

ELIZABETH "BETSY" WILFORD
Current occupation: Stewardess
Relationship: Former girlfriend of Peter Rasputin (Colossus)
First appearance: X-MEN Vol. 1 #98

DR. PETER CORBEAU
Current occupation: Scientist, head of Project Starcore
Relationship: Friend of Professor Charles Xavier
First appearance: INCREDIBLE HULK Vol. 2 #172

MISTY KNIGHT
Current occupation: Private investigator
Relationship: Former roommate of Jean Grey (Marvel Girl)
First appearance: MARVEL TEAM-UP #1

CORSAIR (CHRISTOPHER SUMMERS)
Current occupation: Interstellar adventurer
Relationship: Father of Scott and Alex Summers (Cyclops and Havok)
First appearance: X-MEN Vol. 1 #104

CH'OD
Current occupation: Interstellar adventurer
Relationship: Ally of Corsair and X-Men
First appearance: X-MEN Vol. 1 #104

X-MEN
EIGHTH LINE-UP: GOLD TEAM
ART BY: BARRY KITSON/JOSEF RUBINSTEIN

X-MEN'S SUPPORTING CAST

SENATOR EDWARD KELLY
Current occupation: United States Senator
Relationship: Former political adversary
First appearance: UNCANNY X-MEN #133

DR. VALERIE COOPER
Current occupation: Member of the Federal Commission on Superhuman Activities, government liaison with X-Factor II
Relationship: Former adversary, now ally
First appearance: UNCANNY X-MEN #176

LOCKHEED
Current occupation: Member of Excalibur
Relationship: Companion of Shadowcat
First appearance: UNCANNY X-MEN #166

STEVIE HUNTER
Current occupation: Physical education instructor
Relationship: Trainer at Xavier's school
First appearance: UNCANNY X-MEN #139

HEPZIBAH
Current occupation: Interstellar adventurer
Relationship: Ally of Corsair and X-Men
First appearance: X-MEN Vol. 1 #107

RAZA
Current occupation: Interstellar adventurer
Relationship: Ally of Corsair and X-Men
First appearance: X-MEN Vol. 1 #107

NEREEL
Current occupation: Chieftain of the Savage Land Fall People
Relationship: Former lover of Colossus
First appearance: X-MEN Vol. 1 #115

MARIKO YASHIDA (DECEASED)
Occupation at time of death: Oyabun (leader) of Clan Yashida of the Yakuza (crime family)
Relationship: Fiancee of Wolverine
First appearance: UNCANNY X-MEN #118

X-RAY™

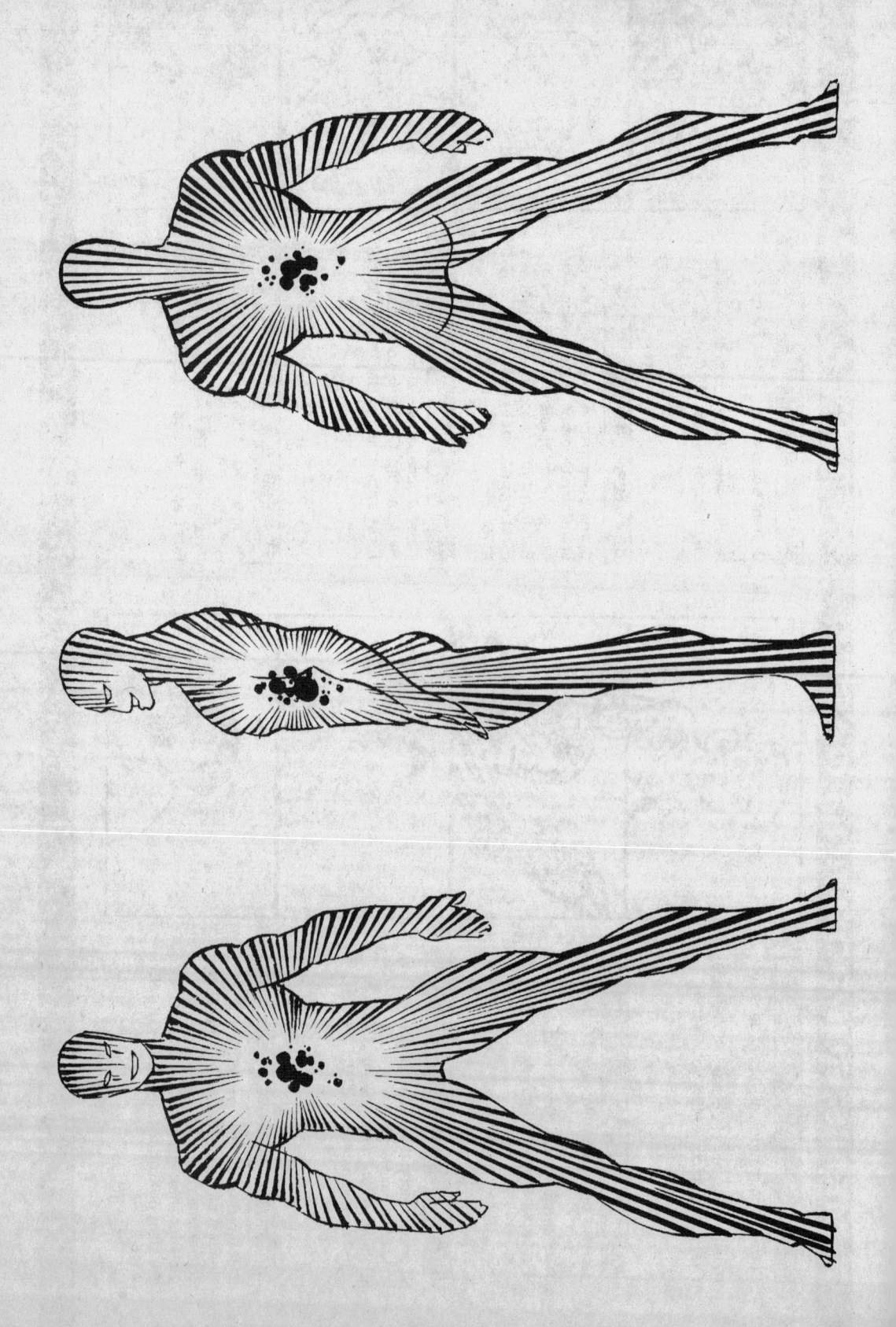

X-RAY

BIOGRAPHICAL DATA

Real name: James "Jimmy" Darnell
Other current aliases: None
Former aliases: None
Dual identity: Publicly known
Current occupation: Professional criminal
Former occupation: Propulsion fuel scientist
Citizenship: United States of America
Legal status: Criminal record in the U.S.
Place of birth: Unrevealed
Marital status: Single
Known relatives: Ann Darnell (alias Vapor, sister)
Known confidants: The U-Foes (Vector, Vapor, Ironclad)
Known allies: The U-Foes
Major enemies: The Hulk, Avengers West Coast
Usual base of operations: Mobile
Former bases of operations: Nevada
Current group membership: The U-Foes
Former group membership: None
Extent of education: Master's degree in engineering

PHYSICAL DESCRIPTION

Height: 5' 9"
Weight: 195 lbs., (as X-Ray) 0 lbs.
Eyes: Brown, (as X-Ray) White
Hair: Brown, (as X-Ray) None
Other distinguishing features: X-Ray's body is made of hard radiation.

POWERS AND ABILITIES

Intelligence: Above normal
Strength: Athlete
Speed: Athlete
Flight speed: Directed motion hovering
Stamina: Athlete
Durability: Superhuman
Agility: Normal
Reflexes: Athlete
Fighting skills: Moderate experience in hand-to-hand combat
Special skills and abilities: None
Superhuman physical powers: Aside from the above listed attributes, X-Ray has the power to convert his physical form into quasi-solid radiation. In this form he can levitate and project various wavelengths of radiation, including one that in some as yet unexplained way carries a concussive force. While in his X-Ray form he is virtually invulnerable to physical injury.
Superhuman mental powers: None
Special limitations: X-Ray cannot reassume his physical human form.
Source of superhuman powers: Exposure to cosmic radiation

PARAPHERNALIA

Costume specifications: None
Personal weaponry: None
Special weaponry: None
Other accessories: None
Transportation: Flight under own power
Design and manufacture of paraphernalia: Inapplicable

BIBLIOGRAPHY

First appearance: INCREDIBLE HULK #254
Origin issue: INCREDIBLE HULK #254
Significant issues: INCREDIBLE HULK #254 (with teammates duplicated original rocket flight of the Fantastic Four through cosmic ray belt and gained superhuman powers, battled Hulk, fell unconscious when powers went out of control); INCREDIBLE HULK #275-277 (revealed to have recovered; with U-Foes, defeated Hulk; exhibited captive Bruce Banner on national TV, defeated when Banner was freed and transformed into the Hulk); INCREDIBLE HULK #304-305 (with U-Foes, escaped special government prison and was accidentally "deflected" into "Crossroads" dimension by Vector; battled and defeated Hulk with help of alien "Puffball Collective," trapped in dimension inhabited by creatures that eat radiation); AVENGERS #304 (escaped back to "Crossroads" dimension with U-Foes, escaped back to Earth through dimensional warp unintentionally created by mutant Charles Little Sky, battled Avengers and Puma, defeated by Thor); AVENGERS WEST COAST #53 (with U-Foes, freed from the Vault; attacked Avengers West Coast, mistakenly believing they had killed Vector, battled original Human Torch, escaped)

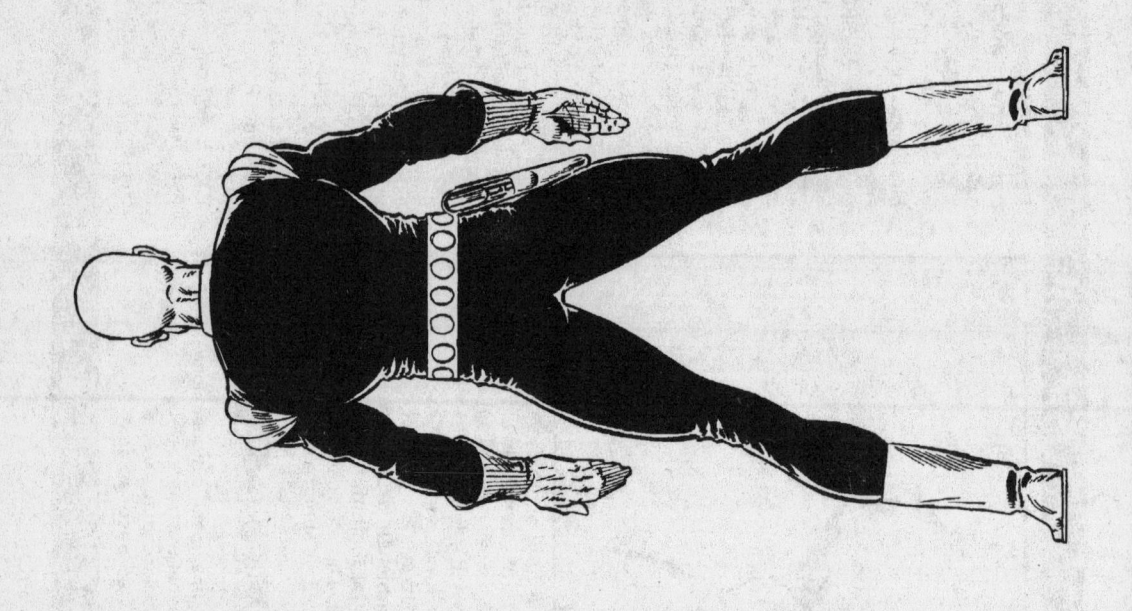

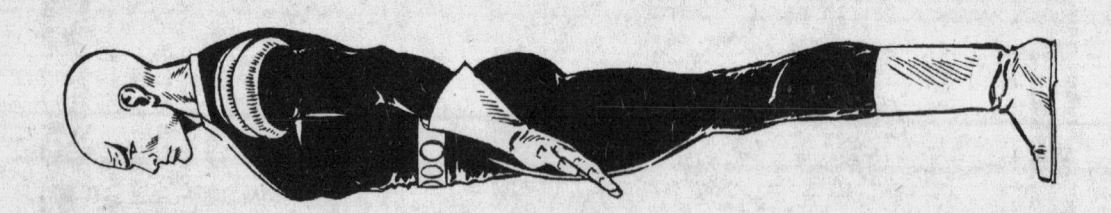

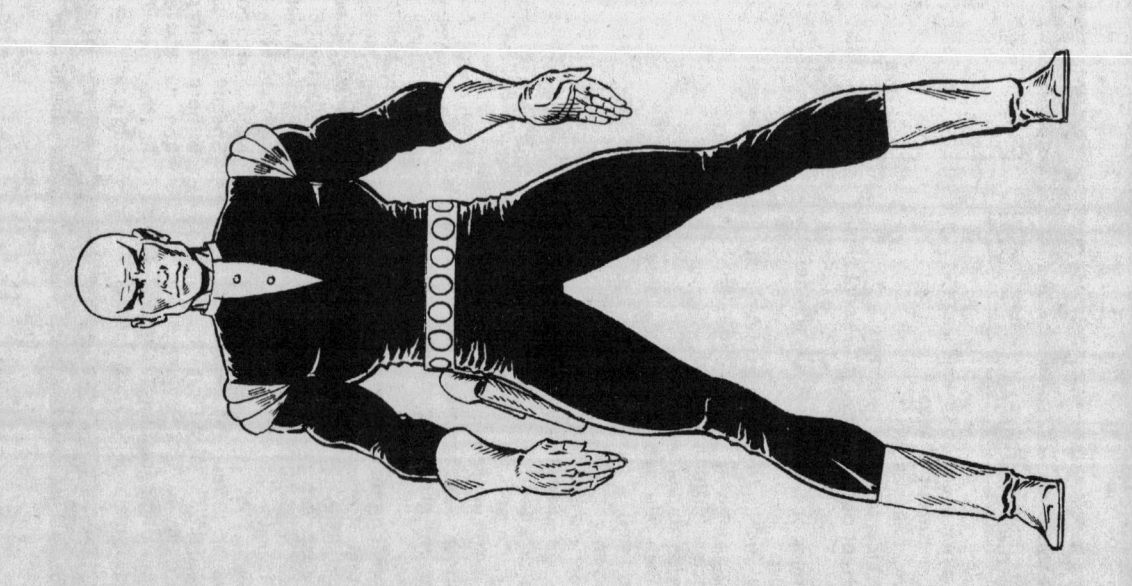

YANDROTH

YANDROTH

BIOGRAPHICAL DATA

Real name: Yandroth
Aliases at time of death: None
Former aliases: Scientist supreme
Dual identity: None; the general populace of Earth was unaware that Yandroth was an extradimensional alien
Occupation at time of death: Nihilist
Former occupation: Criminal scientist, would-be conqueror
Citizenship: An unnamed extradimensional alien planet
Legal status: No known criminal record
Place of birth: An unnamed extradimensional alien planet
Place of death: New York City
Cause of apparent death: Injuries received when hit by a truck
Marital status: Presumed single
Known relatives: None
Known confidants: None
Known allies: Voltorg (destroyed), the Omegatron (destroyed)
Major enemies: Doctor Strange, Victoria Bentley, Namor the Sub-Mariner, the Valkyrie, Namorita, the Defenders
Base of operations at time of death: Port Promontory, Maine
Former base of operations: An unnamed extradimensional alien planet; the Dimension of Dreams; an unnamed mystical dimension
Group membership at time of death: None
Former group membership: None

Extent of education: Ph.D. in physics (alien equivalent)

PHYSICAL DESCRIPTION

Height: (original body) 6'; (female body) 5' 6"
Weight: (original body) 180 lbs., (female body) 125 lbs.
Eyes: (original body) Grey, (female body) Blue
Hair: (original body) Bald, (female body) Brown
Other distinguishing features: None

POWERS AND ABILITIES

Intelligence: Genius
Strength: Normal
Speed: Normal
Stamina: Normal
Durability: Normal
Agility: Normal
Reflexes: Normal
Fighting skills: Average hand-to-hand combatant
Special skills and abilities: Vast knowledge of various sciences, including advanced physics, computer science, and robotics; some knowledge of mystic lore
Superhuman physical powers: Ability to exist in independent astral form after physical death; ability to manipulate the forces of magic for a limited number of effects, including the extrasensory ability to perceive beings in invisible astral form; (as spirit) Ability to possess the mind of any living human with similar brain patterns
Special limitations: (as spirit) Inability to affect the physical world without possessing a physical form, inability to possess the minds of more than half a dozen beings at once
Source of superhuman powers: (natural mental powers) Yandroth is a member of unrevealed alien race, (additional powers) Manipulation of the forces of magic

PARAPHERNALIA

Costume specifications: Alien fabrics
Personal weaponry: Q-ray blasters (capable of firing bursts of flame, concussive force, or disintegration beams), gloves equipped with mechanisms to fire brain implants
Special weaponry: Disintegrators, ultra-spectrum lasers, force-shield belt, anti-gravity devices
Other accessories: Voltorg (a 15' robot armed with "atomic electrodes" capable of incinerating solid steel), the Omegatron (a computer intelligence created by a combination of science and magic and enfused with Yandroth's own personality, programmed to to protect its own existence and to detonate every nuclear stockpile on Earth simultaneously on command; microscopic brain implants (capable of altering victims' brainwaves so as to be identical to Yandroth's, thus enabling him to possess them)
Transportation: Interplanetary teleportation devices
Design and manufacture of paraphernalia: Yandroth

BIBLIOGRAPHY

First appearance: STRANGE TALES Vol. 1 #164
Origin issue: Yandroth's origin is as yet unrevealed.
Significant issues: STRANGE TALES Vol. 1 #164-168 (with his robot Voltorg, battled Dr. Strange; lost within Dimension of Dreams); MARVEL FEATURE Vol. 1 #1 (gained magical knowledge in alien dimension, returned to Earth, physical body died, thus activating the Omegatron; as Omegatron, battled Dr. Strange, Namor the Sub-Mariner, and the Hulk; placed under time displacement spell by Dr. Strange); DEFENDERS #5 (as Omegatron, released from time displacement spell, battled Namor, the Hulk, Valkyrie, and Namorita; destroyed); DEFENDERS #119 (possessed an unnamed female chemist; as Yandroth II, battled the Defenders, defeated)

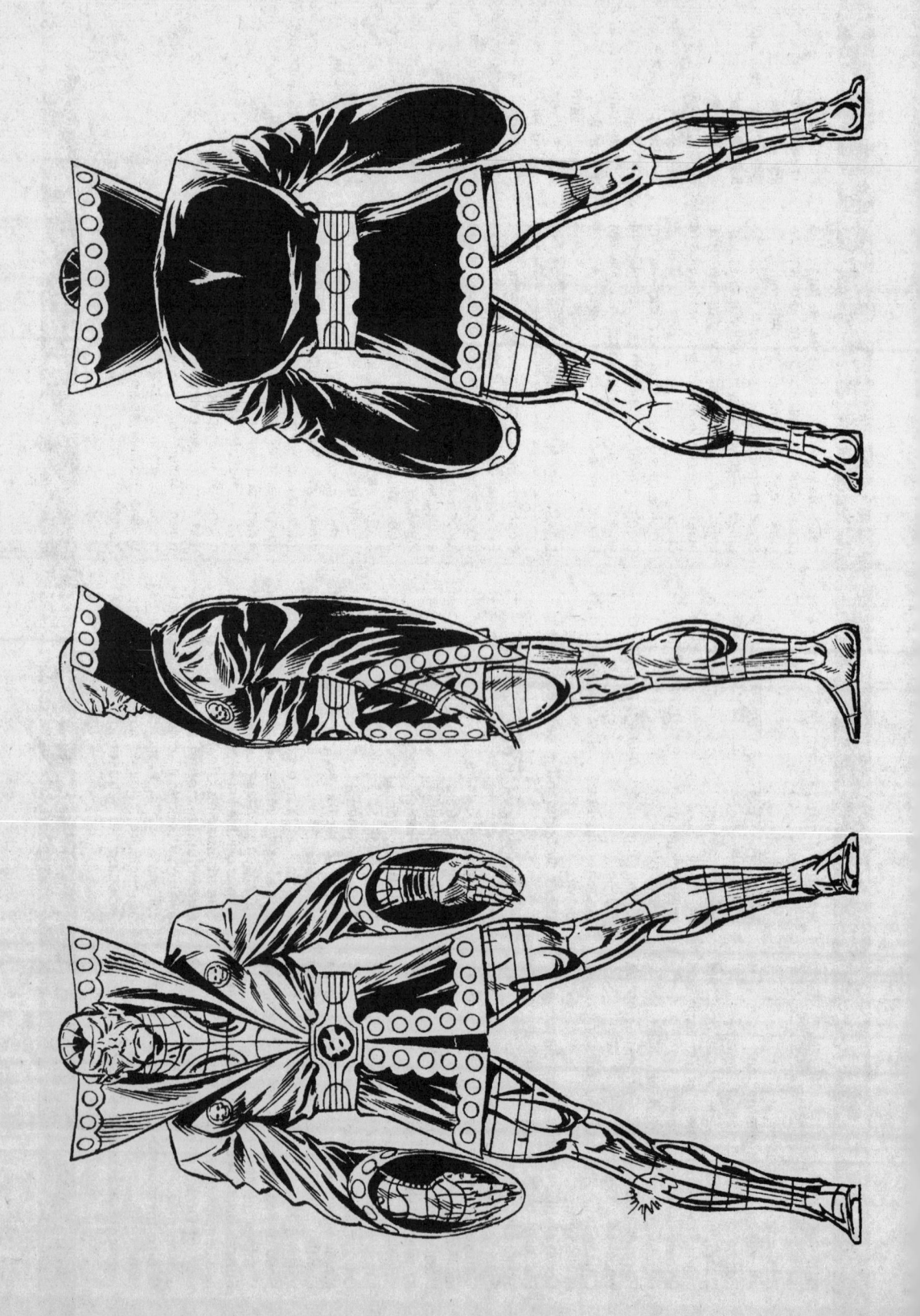

YELLOW CLAW™

YELLOW CLAW

BIOGRAPHICAL DATA

Real name: Unrevealed
Other current aliases: None
Former aliases: Bhagwan Sri Ananda
Dual identity: None
Current occupation: Would be conqueror
Former occupation: Unknown
Citizenship: People's Republic of China
Legal status: No criminal record
Place of birth: Somewhere in mainland China
Marital status: Married many times
Known relatives: Suwan (grandniece, deceased)
Known confidants: None
Known allies: Fritz Von Voltzman (alias Karl von Horstbaden, presumed deceased), Hop Sung, the Great Video, Skull Face, Electro I, Cold Warrior
Major enemies: James "Jimmy" Woo (deceased), 50's "Avengers" (Marvel Boy I, 3-D Man, Venus, Gorilla-Man, Human Robot), Captain America
Usual base of operations: Various hidden bases throughout the world
Former bases of operations: Various
Current group membership: None
Former group membership: None
Extent of education: Extensive knowledge in various sciences and black magical lore

PHYSICAL DESCRIPTION

Height: 6' 2"
Weight: 210 lbs.
Eyes: Brown
Hair: Bald
Other distinguishing features: None

POWERS AND ABILITIES

Intelligence: Extraordinary genius
Strength: Athlete
Stamina: Athlete
Durability: Athlete
Agility: Peak human
Reflexes: Peak human
Fighting skills: Master of Chinese martial arts, expert hand-to-hand combatant
Special skills and abilities: Genius in biochemistry and genetics, proficient in robotics, considerable knowledge of black magical lore
Superhuman physical powers: Able to manipulate magical forces to create certain effects, including reanimating the dead
Superhuman mental powers: Ability to psychically influence sensory perceptions of others, enabling him to cast extremely realistic illusions
Special limitations: The Yellow Claw's extended life-span is dependent on the continued efficacy of his life-prolonging elixirs
Source of superhuman powers: (physical powers) Manipulation of the forces of magic, (mental powers) unknown, (extended life span) chemical elixirs

PARAPHERNALIA

Costume specifications: Body armor
Personal weaponry: Various, as needed
Special weaponry: Id paralyzer (creates slaves subjects to his telepathic control), mind-amplification helmet (harnesses psychic energies of his mind-slaves as destructive force), other specialized technology as needed
Other accessories: Gigantic and hideously mutated creatures of his own design, created by biologists in his employ
Transportation: Various, as needed
Design and manufacture of paraphernalia: Yellow Claw

BIBLIOGRAPHY

First appearance: (historical) YELLOW CLAW #1, (as a telepathic "voice") STRANGE TALES #160, (robot Yellow Claw) STRAGE TALES #161, (actual Yellow Claw) CAPTAIN AMERICA #164
Origin issue: Yellow Claw's origin is as yet unrevealed
Significant issues: INVADERS #41 (IN 1942, encountered Lady Lotus in New York's Chinatown); YELLOW CLAW #1-4 (in mid-1950s various schemes to conquer America foiled by FBI agent Jimmy Woo and grandniece Suwan); WHAT IF Vol. 1 #9 (in late 1950s, recruited team of superhuman minions, abducted president Dwight D. Eisenhower, battled 50s "Avengers"); STRANGE TALES #160-161, 162-167 (sent troops to invade Liberty Island and activate Id paralyzer, foiled by Nick Fury and Captain America; Nick Fury and SHIELD battled robots of Yellow Claw and cohorts); CAPTAIN AMERICA #164-167 (transferred spirit of Princess Fan-le-tamen into Suwan, caused her to become evil, battled Captain America, the Falcon, Nick Fury, and the SHIELD; betrayed by Suwan; transferred spirit of Fan-le-tamen to himself, destroying Suwan, escaped); IRON MAN #69-71, 75, 77 (took part in Black Lama's contest of super-villains, defeated and killed Mandarin; battled Iron Man; abandoned Black Lama's contest, escaped); NOVA #13-18 (attempt to destroy New York City using a tidal wave; foiled by Nova I, Nick Fury, and SHIELD); AVENGERS #204-205 (planned to father sons by various genetically superior women, then sterilize mankind and rule the world; foiled by the Avengers); MARVEL FANFARE #31-32 (attempted to destroy New York City; foiled by Captain America, Frog-Man, Spider-Man, Human Torch, Angel, Beast, and Iceman); NICK FURY AGENT OF SHIELD Vol. 3 #12-14 (recruited Madame Hydra II as his new heir, battled Nick Fury and SHIELD; witnessed defeat of Madame Hydra's forces; responsible for reunion of Fury and Dum Dum Dugan)

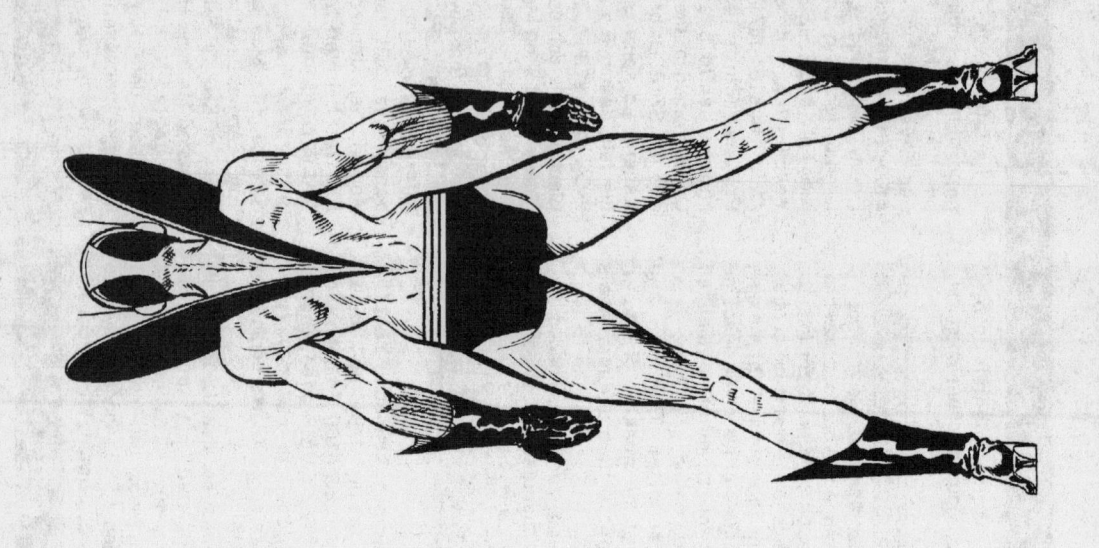

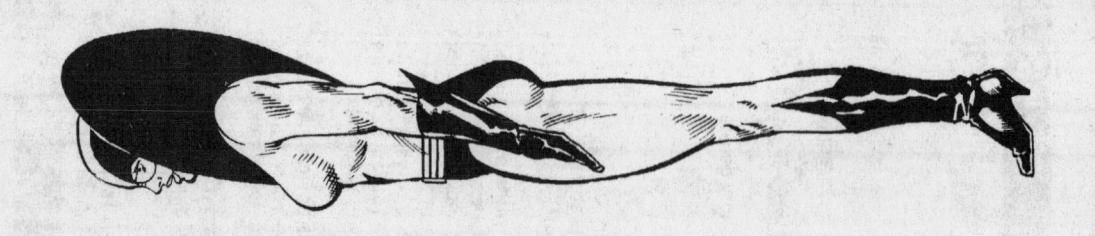

YELLOWJACKET ™

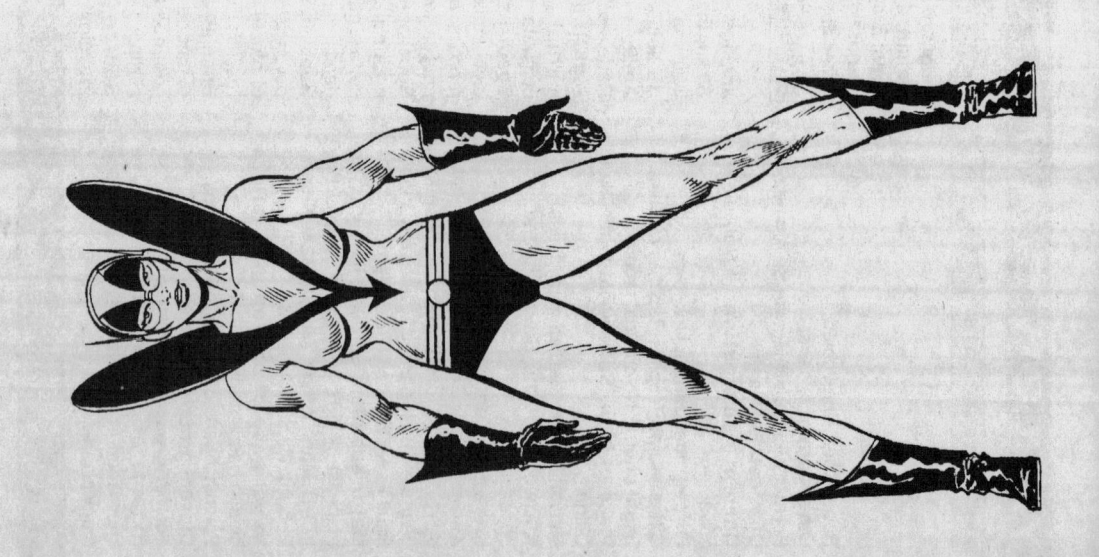

YELLOWJACKET II

BIOGRAPHICAL DATA

Real name: Rita DeMara
Other current aliases: None
Former aliases: None
Dual identity: Publicly known
Current occupation: Professional criminal
Former occupation: None known
Citizenship: United States of America
Legal status: Criminal record in U.S.
Place of birth: Unrevealed
Marital status: Unrevealed, presumed single
Known relatives: None
Known confidants: None
Known allies: Superia's Femizons, (formerly) Masters of Evil IV (Baron Zemo II, Moonstone II, Whirlwind, Tiger Shark, Absorbing Man, Titania, Screaming Mimi, Grey Gargoyle, Mister Hyde, Goliath IV, Blackout I, Fixer, Wrecker, Bulldozer, Piledriver, Thunderball)
Major enemies: (formerly) Wasp, the Avengers, Fixer II, Captain America, Paladin
Usual base of operations: New York City area, Superia's Island
Former bases of operations: None known
Current group membership: Superia's Femizons
Former group membership: Masters of Evil IV
Extent of education: Unrevealed

PHYSICAL DESCRIPTION

Height: 5' 5"
Weight: 115 lbs.
Eyes: Blue
Hair: Reddish-blonde
Other distinguishing features: None

POWERS AND ABILITIES

Intelligence: Normal
Strength: Normal
Speed: Normal
Flight speed: Winged flight limit
Stamina: Normal
Durability: Normal
Agility: Normal
Reflexes: Normal
Fighting skills: Fair hand-to-hand combatant
Special skills and abilities: Expertise in cybernetic technology
Superhuman physical powers: None
Superhuman mental powers: None
Special limitations: None
Source of superhuman powers: Inapplicable

PARAPHERNALIA

Costume specifications: Helmet contains subatomic "Pym particles" which she can release by mental command cybernetically through helmet's circuitry, enabling her to shrink in size to one-half inch in size and return to normal; helmet also contains manual override controls. Costume made of synthetic stretch fabric
Personal weaponry: Costume equipped with "disruptor sting" blasters enabling her to shoot electrical bolts from her gloves; can generate enough electricity to severely damage a car in a single blast
Special weaponry: None
Other accessories: None
Transportation: Costumes permits flight through unknown means
Design and manufacture of paraphernalia: Henry Pym, modified by Rita DeMara

BIBLIOGRAPHY

First appearance: AVENGERS #264
Origin issue: Yellowjacket II's origin is as yet unrevealed.
Significant issues: AVENGERS #264 (clashed with Wasp, became terrified upon shrinking; captured); AVENGERS #273-276 (alongside Masters of Evil IV, took over Avengers Mansion); SOLO AVENGERS #12 (freed from prison by the Fixer II, aided Black Knight III against Fixer II); AVENGERS ANNUAL #17 (aided Avengers against High Evolutionary); CAPTAIN AMERICA #389-391 (served as member of Superia's Femizons)

YMIR™

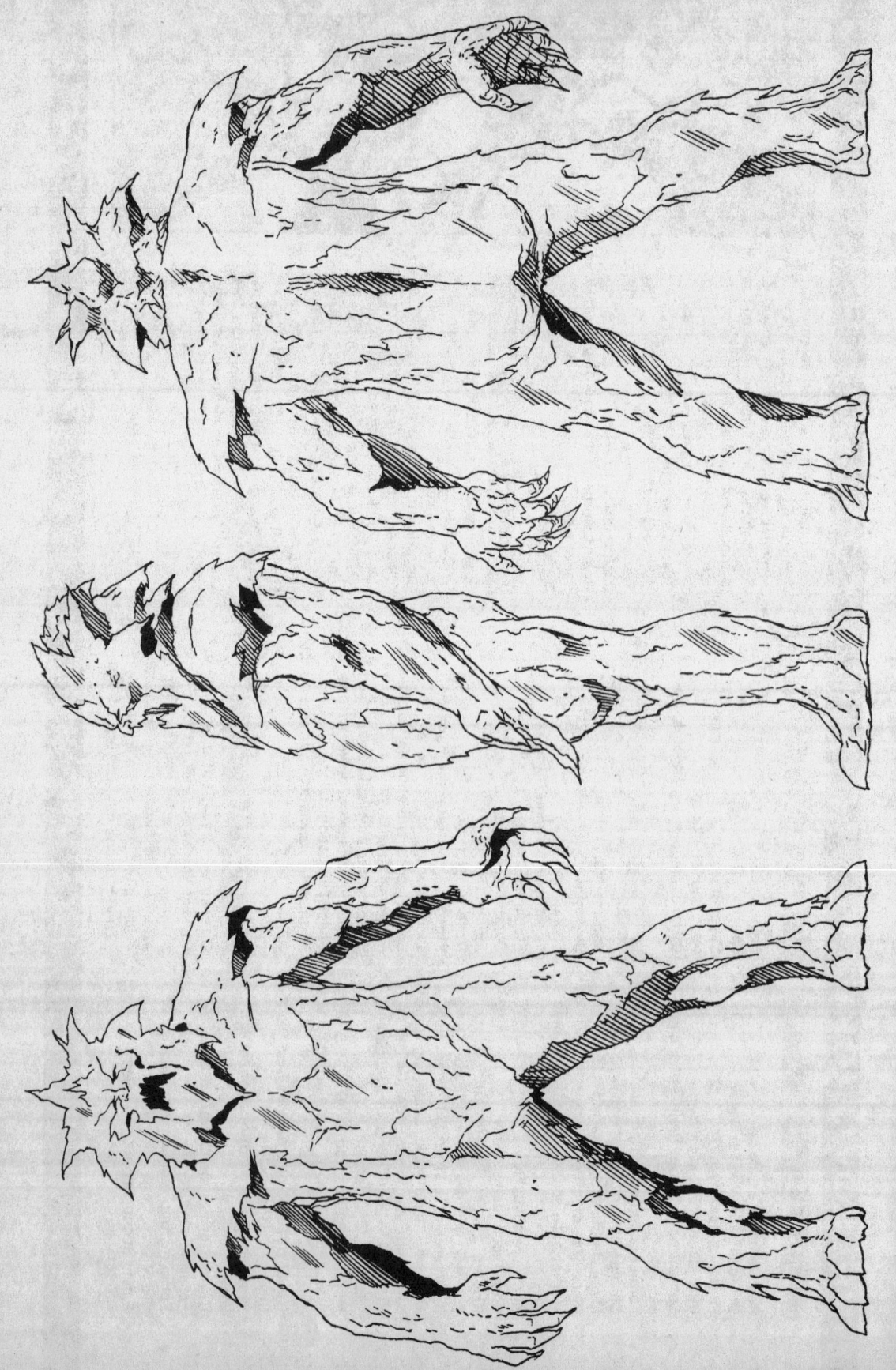

YMIR

BIOGRAPHICAL DATA

Real name: Ymir
Other current aliases: Auregelmir
Former aliases: None known
Dual identity: None; the general populace of Earth is unaware of Ymir's existence except as a mythological character.
Current occupation: Monarch of the Ice Giants
Former occupation: None
Citizenship: Niffleheim, dimension of Asgard
Legal status: No known criminal record
Place of creation: Above the Well of Life in the dimension of Asgard
Marital status: Inapplicable
Known relatives: Ice Giants, Frost Giants (progeny), Utgard-Loki, Loki (descendants)
Known confidants: None
Known allies: Ice Giants, (former) Frost Giants, Storm Giants, Sons of Satannish
Major enemies: Thor, Odin, Vidar, Surtur, Doctor Strange, Avengers, gods of Asgard, Frost Giants, (former) Vili, Ve
Usual base of operations: Niffleheim
Former bases of operations: None
Current group membership: Ice Giants
Former group membership: None
Extent of education: Inapplicable

PHYSICAL DESCRIPTION

Height: Variable, ranging to over 1000'
Weight: Variable
Eyes: White
Hair: None
Other distinguishing features: Since Ymir is an Ice Giant whose body continually generates intense cold, Ymir's body is always thickly covered with snow and ice.

POWERS AND ABILITIES

Intelligence: Normal
Strength: Incalculable
Speed: Superhuman
Stamina: Godlike
Durability: Demi-godlike regenerative
Agility: Superhuman
Reflexes: Superhuman
Fighting skills: Fair hand-to-hand combatant, no formal training, relies on brute force
Special skills and abilities: None
Superhuman physical powers: Aside from the above listed attributes, Ymir's body continually generates intense cold, and he can freeze anything by touching it. Ymir is fully immortal and can neither age nor die. Ymir's body greatly resembles ice, and although it can be shattered, he can then mentally cause his body to reform.
Superhuman mental powers: None known
Special limitations: Like all Ice Giants, Ymir's size is dependent on the presence of cold temperatures. If it were not for his ability to generate intense cold, Ymir's body would shrink and melt when exposed to intense heat.
Source of superhuman powers: Ymir is the eldest and most powerful member of the otherdimensional race of Ice Giants

PARAPHERNALIA

Costume specifications: Inapplicable
Personal weaponry: Carries an enormous ice-covered club that may be made entirely of ice. Also can create and hurl gigantic ice-spears.
Special weaponry: None
Other accessories: None
Transportation: None
Design and manufacture of paraphernalia: Inapplicable

BIBLIOGRAPHY

First appearance: JOURNEY INTO MYSTERY #97
Origin issue: JOURNEY INTO MYSTERY #97, THOR ANNUAL #5
Significant issues: JOURNEY INTO MYSTERY #98 (recounted how long ago Ymir led Ice Giants in attack on Asgard, was defeated and entrapped by Odin); DOCTOR STRANGE Vol. 1 #177/AVENGERS #61 (brought to Earth by Satannish, wreaked havoc and battled Avengers in Wakanda, was sent back to Niffleheim when Doctor Strange manipulated Ymir and Surtur into attacking each other); MARVEL SUPER-HEROES Vol. 2 #5 (allied himself with Frost Giants and Storm Giants in attack on Asgard, was defeated by Thor and Vidar); THOR #419, 421-425 (sought to destroy Asgard and Universe, battled and then joined forces with Surtur, was defeated by Thor wielding Odin's power, imprisoned in in the otherdimensional Sea of Eternal Night)

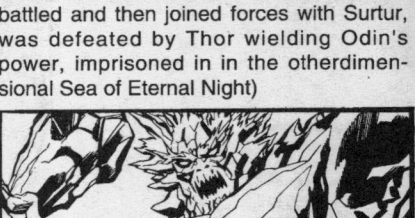

YONDU

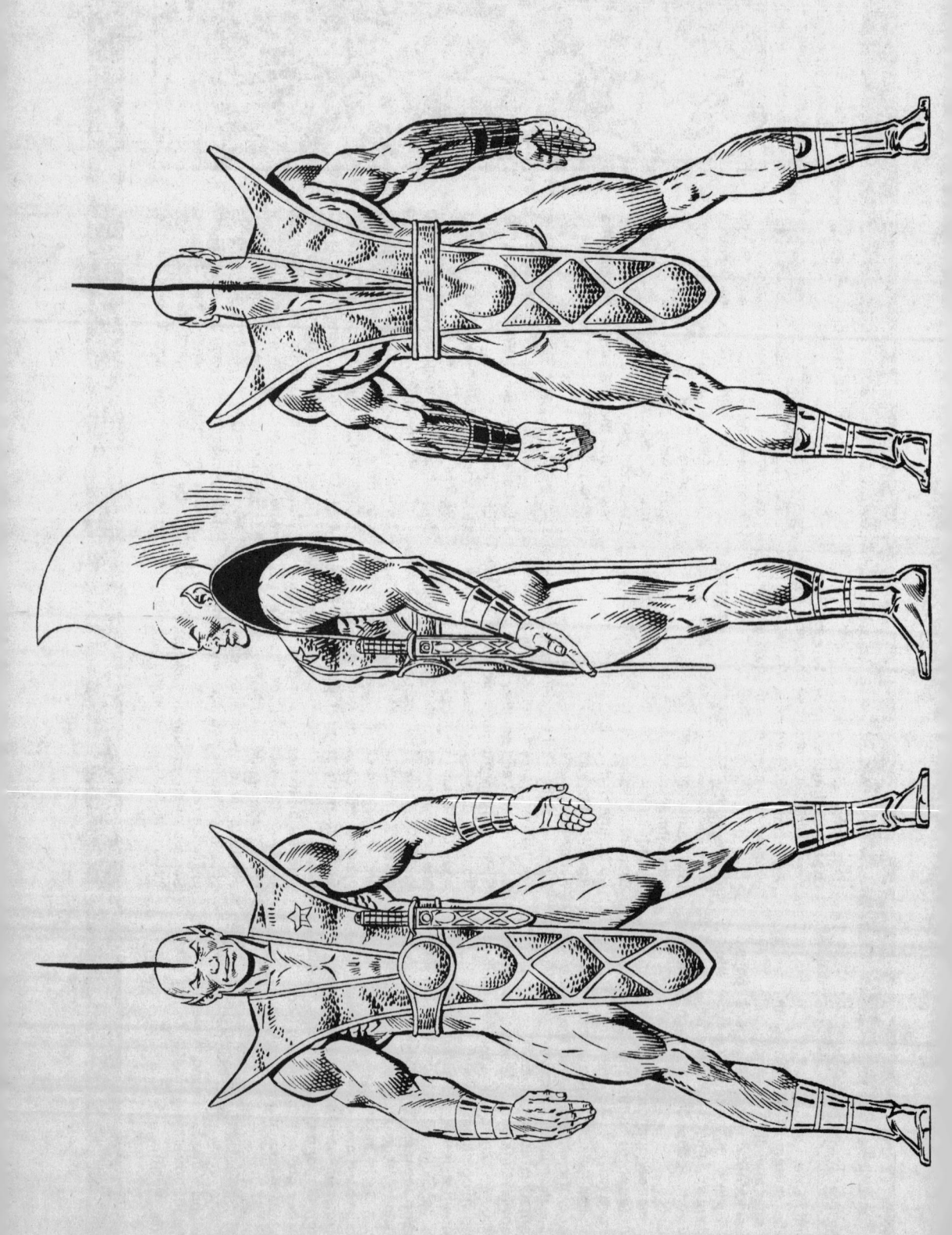

YONDU

BIOGRAPHICAL DATA

Real name: Yondu Udonta
Other current aliases: None
Former aliases: None
Dual identity: None
Current occupation: Adventurer
Former occupation: Hunter, warrior, freedom fighter
Citizenship: Planet Centauri IV, Beta Centauri System, circa 3015 A.D.
Legal status: No criminal record
Place of birth: Plysa Forest, Centauri IV
Marital status: Single
Known relatives: None
Known confidants: Vance Astro
Known allies: The Guardians of the Galaxy, the Defenders, the Avengers, the Fantastic Four, Spider-Man, Thor, Captain America, Firelord, Mainframe, Dargo, the Commandeers, Silver Surfer, Dr. Strange, Krugarr, the Spirit of Vengeance
Major enemies: The Brotherhood of the Badoon, Korvac, Minions of Menace, Overkill (Taserface), the Stark, Force II, Malevolence, Rancor, the Punishers
Usual base of operations: Mobile throughout the Milky Way Galaxy aboard the starship *Captain America II*, former Avengers sub-basements, New York City
Former bases of operations: Mobile throughout the Earth solar system aboard the starship *Captain America I*, space station *Drydock*, and the starship *Freedom's Lady*
Current group membership: Guardians of the Galaxy (Charlie-27, Martinex, Yondu, Nikki, Starhawk, Aleta, Replica, Talon)
Former group membership: Avengers (honorary)
Extent of education: Unrevealed

PHYSICAL DESCRIPTION

Height: 6' 2" (with crest) 7' 1"
Weight: 210 lbs.
Eyes: Blue
Hair: None
Other distinguishing features: Blue skin, bright red crest, right hand replaced by weapons concealment appendage

POWERS AND ABILITIES

Intelligence: Normal
Strength: Enhanced human
Speed: Athlete
Stamina: Athlete
Durability: Athlete
Agility: Athlete
Reflexes: Athlete
Fighting skills: Excellent hand-to-hand combatant, expert archer, able to control the flight of his yaka arrows by high-pitched whistling
Special skills and abilities: Highly skilled hunter and tracker, extensive knowledge of social and religious customs of natives of Centauri IV
Superhuman physical powers: Aside from the above listed attribute, none
Superhuman mental powers: Limited mystical sensory perceptions
Special limitations: Yondu's right hands has been replaced by a bionic device called a weapons concealment appendage. thus, he can no longer practice archery nor perform functions requiring him to grasp with his right hand.
Source of superhuman powers: Yondu is a member of the alien race of the planet Centauri IV

PARAPHERNALIA

Costume specifications: Alien materials
Personal weaponry: Formerly, a bow and yaka arrows (made of special sound-sensitive metal), dagger; currently, a weapons concealment appendage (a metal cup replacing his right hand, which can release from within itself a number of weapons, including a mace, a hatchet, a scythe, a barbed spear, and others; when not in use the weapons are concealed within the appendage at a reduced sized, until enlarged by Pym particles)
Special weaponry: None
Other accessories: None
Transportation: Various, most frequently aboard the starship *Captain America II*
Design and manufacture of paraphernalia: (costume, weaponry) Natives of Centauri IV, (weapons concealment appendage) Martinex

BIBLIOGRAPHY

First appearance: MARVEL SUPER-HEROES Vol. 1 #18
Origin issue: Yondu's origin is as yet unrevealed.
Significant issues: MARVEL SUPER-HEROES Vol. 1 #18 (in 3007 A.D.), helped form the Guardians of the Galaxy to fight the Badoon conquest of Earth's solar system); MARVEL TWO-IN-ONE #5 (in 3014 A.D., teamed with time-traveling Thing, Captain America, and Sharon Carter to retake New York City from Badoon forces); GIANT-SIZE DEFENDERS #5/DEFENDERS #26-29 (time-traveled to the 20th Century, met the Defenders; returned to 3015 A.D. with Starhawk and the Defenders to defeat Badoon invasion force); THOR ANNUAL #6 (teamed with time-travelling Thor, battled Korvac and his Minions of Menace); AVENGERS #167-168, 170, 173, 175-177 (traveled to present alongside fellow Guardians, assisted Avengers in battle against Korvac); GUARDIANS OF THE GALAXY #1-4 (in 3017 A.D., went on quest to find the lost shield of Captain America; battled Taserface and the Stark; defeated the Stark); GUARDIANS OF THE GALAXY #16 (right hand destroyed by Interface, replaced by Martinex with bionic appendage); GUARDIANS OF THE GALAXY #25 (discovered survivors of his race living on Centauri IV)

ZALADANE

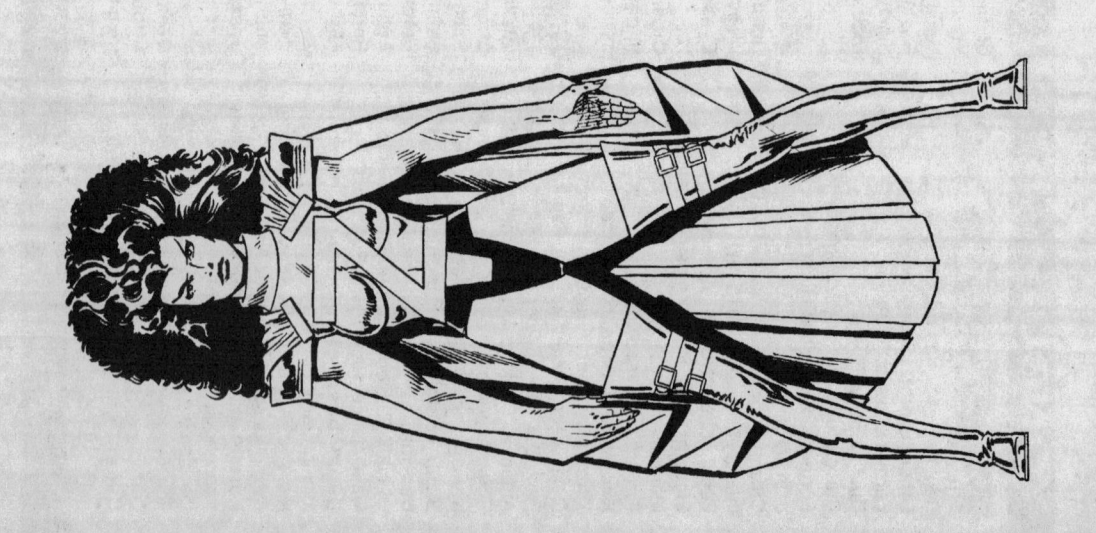

ZALADANE

BIOGRAPHICAL DATA

Real name: (Allegedly) Zala Dane
Other aliases at time of apparent death: None
Former aliases: Zala
Dual identity: Known to the Governments of the United nations and SHIELD
Occupation at time of apparent death: Empress and conqueror
Former occupation: High priestess
Citizenship: The United States and the Savage Land
Legal status: No criminal record
Place of birth: Unrevealed
Place of apparent death: Savage Land
Cause of apparent death: Impaled by object propelled by magnetic forces projected by Magneto
Marital status: Unrevealed, presumed single
Known relatives: Lorna Dane (Polaris, alleged sister)
Known confidants: None
Known allies: Savage Land Mutates, (former) Garokk, the High Evolutionary
Major enemies: Magneto, the X-Men, Polaris, Ka-Zar, Shanna the She-Devil, Nick Fury, Nereel
Base of operations at time of apparent death: The Savage Land
Former bases of operations: The Savage Land
Group membership at time of apparent death: Leader of the Savage Land Mutates
Former group membership: Queen of the Sun People
Extent of education: Unrevealed

PHYSICAL DESCRIPTION

Height: 5' 9"
Weight: 125 lbs.
Eyes: Blue
Hair: Black
Other distinguishing features: None

POWERS AND ABILITIES

Intelligence: Normal
Strength: Athlete
Speed: Athlete
Stamina: Athlete
Durability: Athlete
Agility: Athlete
Reflexes: Athlete
Fighting skills: Good hand-to-hand combatant, trained in combat skills of the Sun People
Special skills: Extensive knowledge of sorcery
Superhuman physical powers: Ability to control magnetic forces; ability to manipulate the forces of magic for an undefined variety of effects
Superhuman mental powers: Ability to control the minds of others
Special limitations: Unrevealed if any
Source of superhuman powers: Artificially induced mutation, training in sorcery

PARAPHERNALIA

Costume specifications: Body armor of an unknown composition
Personal weaponry: Spears
Special weaponry: Torch-bombs (chemically-filled incindiary bombs)
Other accessories: Various scientifically advanced equipment, including devices, such as the transmutator, belonging to the High Evolutionary
Transportation: Skysleds (advanced air vehicles); dinosaurs, pterodactyls, and diatrymas (giant flightless birds) trained to carry riders
Design and manufacture of paraphernalia: (scientific equipment) High Evolutionary and Brainchild

BIBLIOGRAPHY

First appearance: ASTONISHING TALES #3
Origin issue: Zaladane's origin is as yet unrevealed.
Significant issues: ASTONISHING TALES #3 (led Sun People in war to conquer the peoples of the Savage Land, army's weapons destroyed by Garokk, attempted to force Garokk to do her bidding but was attacked by him, seemingly destroyed); UNCANNY X-MEN #115-116 (magically transformed captive Kirk Marston into Garokk, endowing him with original Garokk's consciousness; aided Garokk in attempting to unite Savage Land tribes under his leadership, captured X-Men and Ka-Zar, thwarted by the X-Men); UNCANNY X-MEN ANNUAL #12 (assisted High Evolutionary in restoration of Savage Land, plotted with Savage Land Mutates to conquer Savage Land); UNCANNY X-MEN #249-250 (had Polaris abducted to Savage Land and stole her powers over magnetism, led army in attempt to conquer Savage Land, captured Ka-Zar, Shanna and various X-Men; defeated by them); UNCANNY X-MEN #274-275 (led army and Savage Land Mutates against Magneto, Ka-Zar, Rogue, Nick Fury and SHIELD forces; sought world domination, captured Magneto, Shanna, and Nereel; attempted to steal Magneto's powers over magnetism, defeated and apparently slain by Magneto)

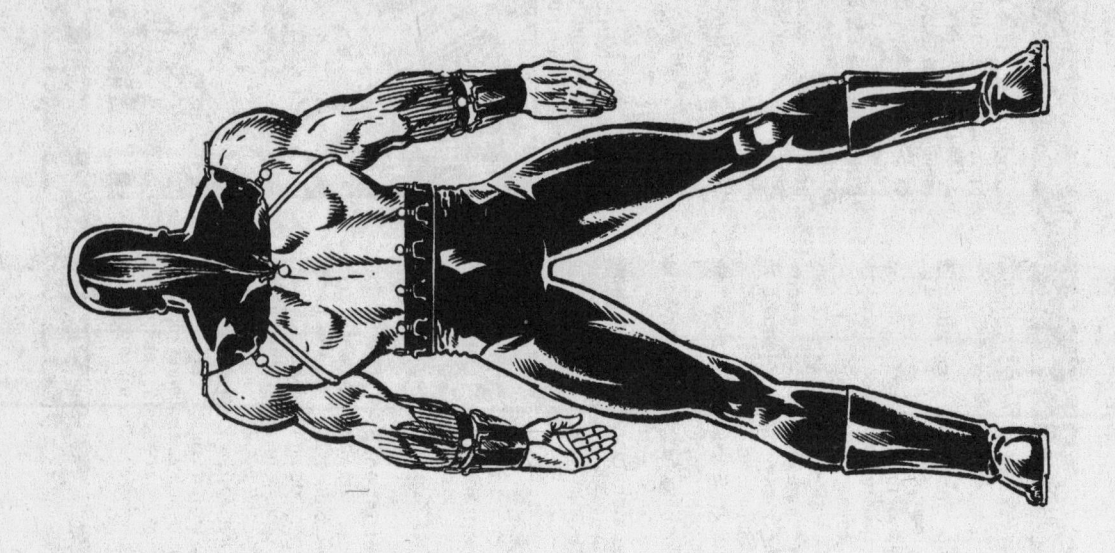

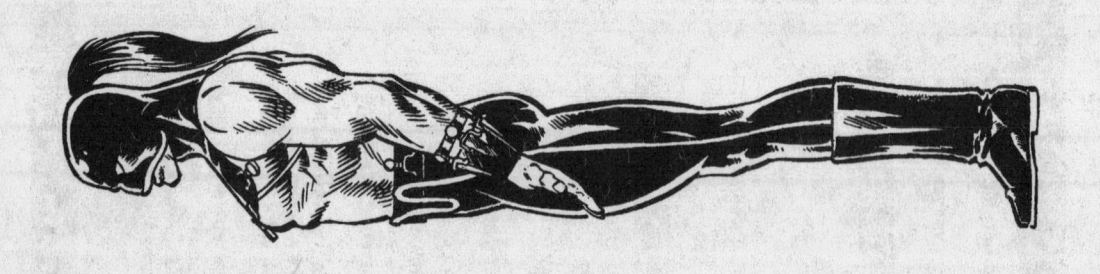

ZARAN

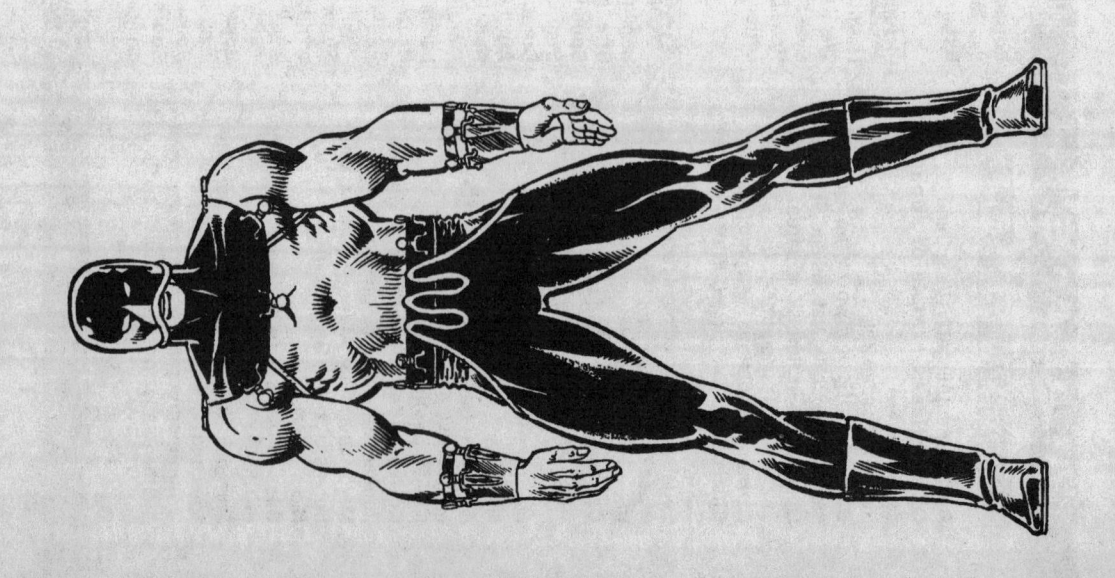

ZARAN

BIOGRAPHICAL DATA

Real name: Maximillian Zaran
Other current aliases: The Weapons Master
Former aliases: Unrevealed
Dual Identity: Secret
Current occupation: Mercenary, assassin
Former occupation: Agent of the British Secret Service: MI-6
Citizenship: United Kingdom
Legal status: Criminal record in the U.K.
Place of birth: Unrevealed
Marital status: Single
Known relatives: None
Known confidants: None
Known allies: Fah Lo Suee, Batroc, Machete, Shockwave, Razorfist, Baron Zemo II
Major enemies: Shang Chi, Captain America, Hawkeye
Usual base of operations: Mobile
Former bases of operations: London, England
Current group membership: Batroc's Brigade
Former group membership: British Secret Service: MI-6
Extent of education: British Secret Service training

PHYSICAL DESCRIPTION

Height: 6' 1"
Weight: 235 lbs.
Eyes: Blue
Hair: Red
Other distinguishing features: None

POWERS AND ABILITIES

Intelligence: Normal
Strength: Athlete
Speed: Athlete
Stamina: Athlete
Durability: Athlete
Agility: Athlete
Reflexes: Athlete
Fighting skills: Knowledge of all forms of armed and unarmed combat
Special skills and abilities: Extensive knowledge of ancient and modern weapons, including knives, bows, staffs, maces, spears, nunchakus, shuriken, and guns.
Superhuman physical powers: None
Superhuman mental powers: None
Special limitations: None
Source of superhuman powers: None

PARAPHERNALIA

Costume specifications: Leather with a variety of specialized clips, loops, and pockets for carrying weapons
Personal weaponry: Small sais (three pronged daggers) attached to gauntlets, collar and codpiece
Special weaponry: A bo staff/spear/blow gun
Other accessories: A wide variety of weapons as needed
Transportation: Various
Design and manufacture of paraphernalia: Unrevealed

BIBLIOGRAPHY

First appearance: MASTER OF KUNG FU #77
Origin issue: MASTER OF KUNG FU #77
Significant issues: MASTER OF KUNG FU #77-79 (employed by Sarsfield then Fah Lo Suee, battled Shang Chi three times, escaped); MASTER OF KUNG FU #87 (battled and defeated Shang Chi); CAPTAIN AMERICA #302-303 (joined Batroc's Brigade, employed by Obadiah Stane to steal Captain America's shield); WEST COAST AVENGERS #11 (battled Hawkeye, Mockingbird, and Iron Man alongside Shockwave and Razorfist); SOLO AVENGERS #3 (battled Hawkeye alongside Batroc's Brigade); CAPTAIN AMERICA #357-362 (Brigade employed by Baron Zemo II to acquire fragments of the Bloodstone, battled Captain America and Diamondback); MASTER OF KUNG FU #1 (employed by Shadow-Hand to recover elixer of Fu Manchu, battled Shang Chi)

ZARATHOS

ZARATHOS

BIOGRAPHICAL DATA

Real names: Zarathos
Other current aliases: None known
Former aliases: Ghost Rider I
Dual identity: None; the general populace of Earth is unaware Zarathos's existence.
Current occupation: Unrevealed
Former occupation: Demon
Citizenship: An extradimensional land of the dead, sometimes called "Hell"
Legal status: None on Earth
Place of birth: An extradimensional land of the dead
Marital status: Unrevealed
Known relatives: None
Known confidants: None
Known allies: (as Zarathos) Lillin, the Lillin; (as Ghost Rider I) Daimon Hellstrom (now Hellstorm), Champions of Los Angeles (Angel, Black Widow, Hercules, Iceman, Darkstar), "Legion of Monsters" (Morbius, Werewolf, Man-Thing), Phantom Rider I, Phantom Rider III
Major enemies: John Blaze, Mephisto, Centurious
Usual base of operations: Unrevealed
Former bases of operations: An extradimensional land of the dead; mobile on Earth; within the Soul Crystal
Current group membership: None
Former group membership: (as Ghost Rider I) Champions of Los Angeles, "Legion of Monsters"
Extent of education: Unrevealed

PHYSICAL DESCRIPTION

Height: 6' 2" (variable)
Weight: Variable
Eyes: Usually appear as empty sockets
Hair: None
Other distinguishing features: Resembles a flaming skeleton

POWERS AND ABILITIES

Intelligence: Normal
Strength: Superhuman Class 10
Speed: Enhanced human
Stamina: Immeasurable
Durability: Godlike
Agility: Athlete
Reflexes: Enhanced human
Fighting skills: Basic hand-to-hand combat skills
Special skills: Limited knowledge of magical lore
Superhuman physical powers: Aside from the above listed attributes, immortality, various inherent supernatural powers, and the ability to manipulate magical energies for a variety of effects.
Superhuman mental powers: None known
Special limitations: None
Source of superhuman powers: Demonic heritage and manipulation of the forces of magic

PARAPHERNALIA

Costume specifications: Inapplicable
Personal weaponry: None
Special weaponry: None
Other accessories: None
Transportation: Interdimensional teleportation; (as Ghost Rider I) Motorcycle
Design and manufacture of paraphernalia: Zarathos

BIBLIOGRAPHY

First appearance: MARVEL SPOTLIGHT Vol. 1 #5
Origin issue: GHOST RIDER Vol. 2 #77
Significant issues: GHOST RIDER Vol. 2 #77 (revealed to have been summoned by K'nutu to help his Indian tribe, defeated by Centurious and Mephisto and put under Mephisto's control); MARVEL SPOTLIGHT Vol. 1 #5 (grafted onto John Blaze by Mephisto to become Ghost Rider I); GHOST RIDER Vol. 2 #26 (began controlling personality of Ghost Rider I); GHOST RIDER Vol. 2 #43-44 (temporarily separated from John Blaze by the Crimson Mage); GHOST RIDER Vol. 2 #68 (gained additional control over Ghost Rider I, becoming more violent); GHOST RIDER Vol. 2 #74 (as Ghost Rider I, re-encountered Centurious); GHOST RIDER Vol. 2 #76 (identity first revealed, temporarily freed by Mephisto to to compete with John Blaze for his freedom); GHOST RIDER Vol. 2 #80-81 (battled Centurious, separated from John Blaze, trapped within the Soul Crystal with Centurious); AMAZING SPIDER-MAN #274 (temporarily freed from soul crystal by the Beyonder to prove humanity's faults to Mephisto, battled Spider-Man)
Note: The relationship between Zarathos and the demon in the current Ghost Rider (Daniel Ketch) has yet to be revealed.

ZAREK™

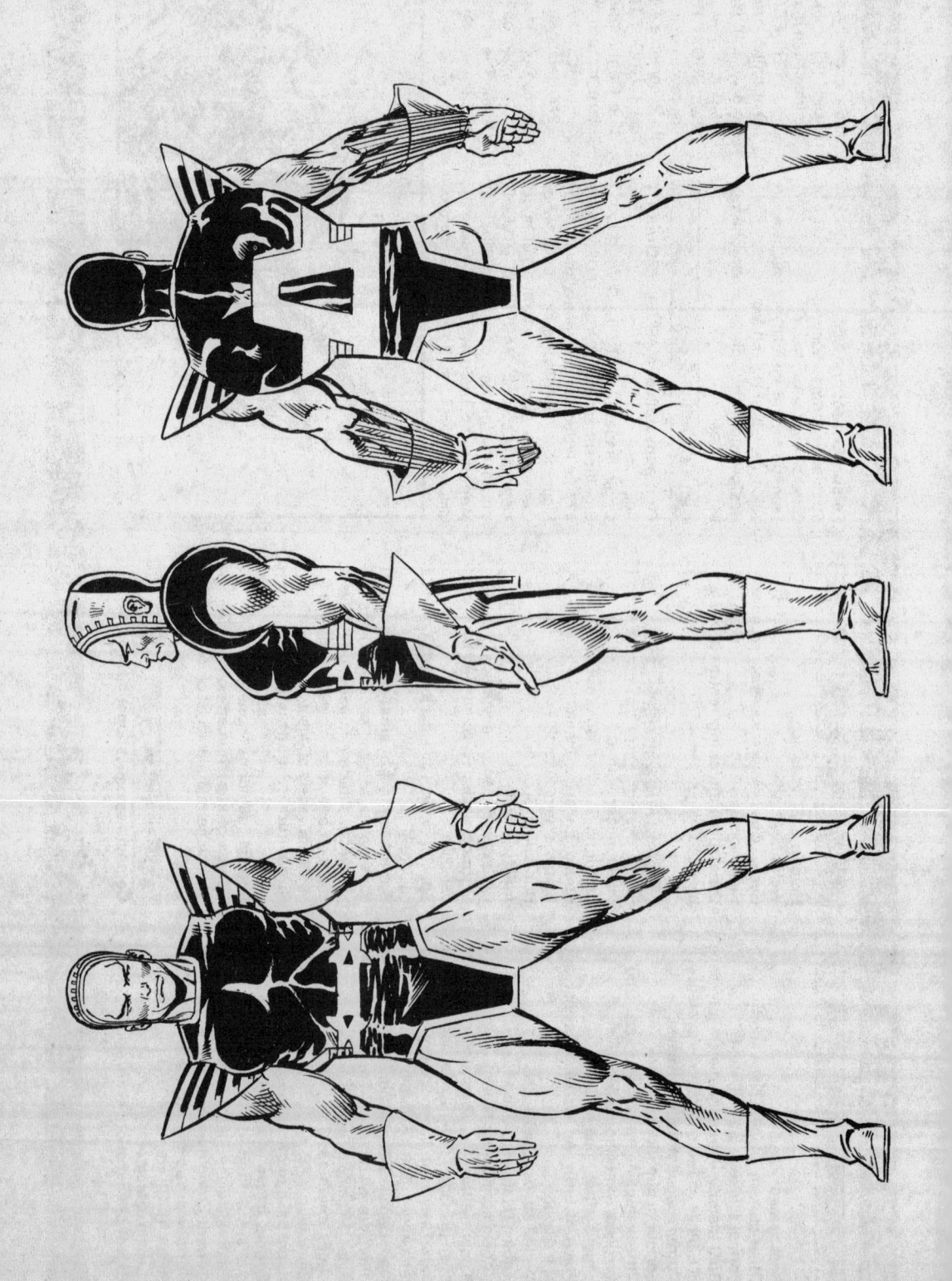

ZAREK

BIOGRAPHICAL DATA

Real name: Zarek
Other current aliases: None
Former aliases: None
Dual identity: None
Current occupation: Renegade
Former occupation: Imperial Minister of Kree Empire
Citizenship: Kree Empire
Legal status: Traitor to the Kree Empire
Place of birth: Unrevealed
Marital status: Unrevealed
Known relatives: None
Known confidants: None
Known allies: Ronan the Accuser, the Lunatic Legion
Major enemies: Captain Marvel, the Supreme Intelligence
Usual base of operations: The planet Kree-Lar
Former bases of operations: None
Current group membership: None
Former group membership: The ruling class of the Kree Empire, the Lunatic Legion
Extent of education: Unrevealed

PHYSICAL DESCRIPTION

Height: 6'2"
Weight: 250 lbs.
Eyes: Blue
Hair: None
Other distinguishing features: Like all genetically-pure members of the alien Kree race, Zarek's skin is pale blue.

POWERS AND ABILITIES

Intelligence: Normal
Strength: Enhanced human
Speed: Normal
Stamina: Enhanced human
Durability: Enhanced human
Agility: Normal
Reflexes: Normal
Fighting skills: Kree Militia training
Special skills and abilities: Extensive knowledge of the political intricacies of the Kree Empire
Superhuman physical powers: None; Zarek's superhuman strength is normal for a member of his race
Superhuman mental powers: None
Special limitations: None
Source of superhuman powers: Inapplicable

PARAPHERNALIA

Costume specifications: Alien materials
Personal weaponry: None
Special weaponry: None
Other accessories: None
Transportation: Various, including the faster-than-light starships of the Kree Empire
Design and manufacture of paraphernalia: Unrevealed Kree technicians

BIBLIOGRAPHY

First appearance: MARVEL SUPER-HEROES #18
Origin issue: Zarek's origin is as yet unrevealed.
Significant issues: MARVEL SUPER-HEROES #18 (chose Captain Mar-Vell to be Kree spy on Earth); CAPTAIN MARVEL #15-16 (conspired with Ronan the Accuser to overthrow Supreme Intelligence; defeated by Captain Mar-Vell); CAPTAIN MARVEL #38-41 (led band of Kree malcontents, the Lunatic Legion, in plot to use Captain Mar-Vell to destroy Supreme Intelligence; battled defeated by Captain Mar-Vell)

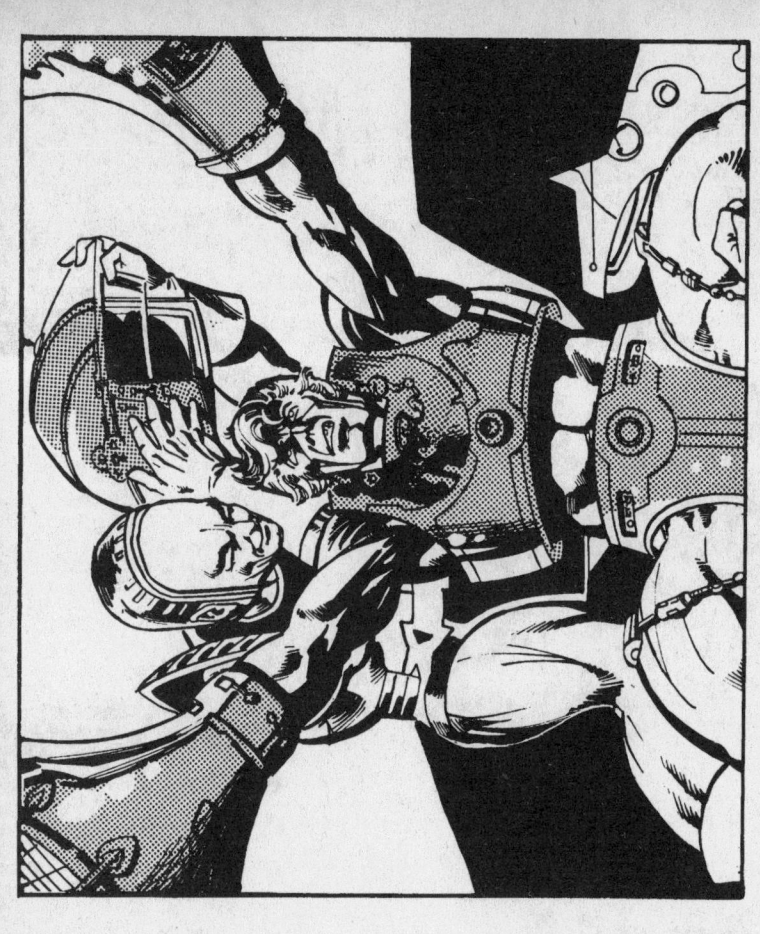

ZARRKO

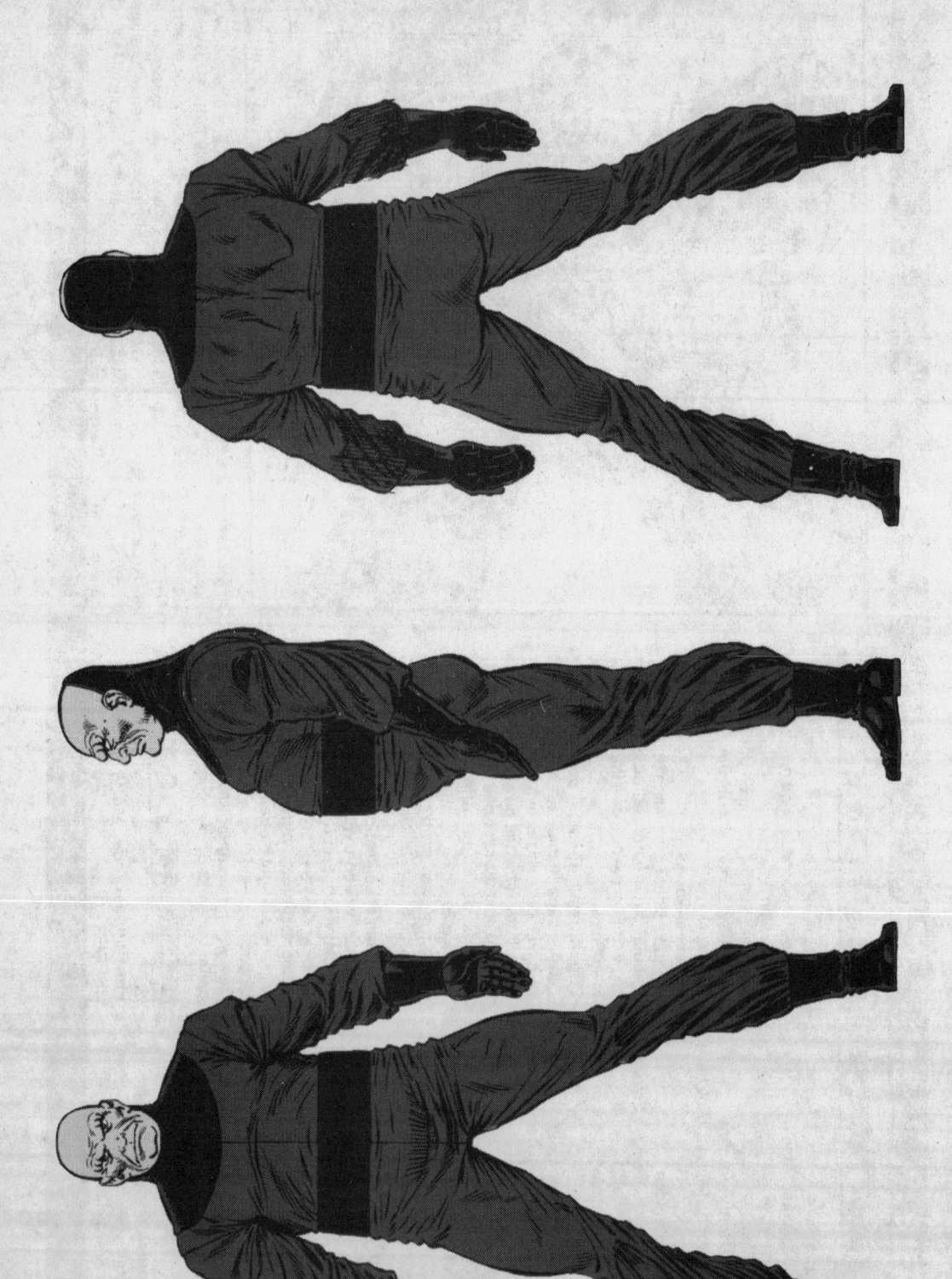

ZARRKO THE TOMORROW MAN

BIOGRAPHICAL DATA

Real name: Artur Zarrko
Other current aliases: The Tomorrow Man
Former aliases: None known
Dual identity: None; Zarrko's existence is not known to the general populace of present-day Earth
Current occupation: Conqueror, dictator
Former occupation: Civil servant
Citizenship: United States of the Americas, in an alternate future of the 23rd Century
Legal status: Criminal record in his own time era
Place of birth: Old New York
Marital status: Single
Known relatives: None
Known confidants: None
Known allies: (all former) Loki, Spider-Man, Iron Man, Thor, The Warriors Three (Hogun, Volstagg, Fandral), Mercurio, Uroc, Demonstaff, Grey Gargoyle, Cobra, Tyrus, Shatterfist, Executioner
Major enemies: Thor, Kang, the Time-Twisters
Usual base of operations: Various citadels on Earth of the 23rd and 50th Centuries
Former bases of operations: Unrevealed
Current group membership: None
Former group membership: None
Extent of education: Advanced studies in various applied sciences of his native time period

PHYSICAL DESCRIPTION

Height: 5'11"
Weight: 285 lbs.
Eyes: Blue
Hair: Bald
Other distinguishing features: None

POWERS AND ABILITIES

Intelligence: Genius
Strength: Normal
Speed: Normal
Stamina: Normal
Durability: Normal
Agility: Normal
Reflexes: Normal
Fighting skills: Minimal hand-to-hand combat skills
Special skills and abilities: Advanced scientific and technological skills
Superhuman physical powers: None
Superhuman mental powers: None
Special limitations: None
Source of superhuman powers: Inapplicable

PARAPHERNALIA

Costume specifications: Conventional materials
Personal weaponry: Various including force field projectors and radiation guns
Special weaponry: The Servitor, a giant robot with extraordinary strength capable of discharging concussive energy; time missiles containing "chronal radiation" which allegedly reverses the flow of time
Other accessories: Time-scope (a device able to peer through time)
Transportation: Time Cube, a time travel machine
Design and manufacture of paraphernalia: Artur Zarrko

BIBLIOGRAPHY

First appearance: JOURNEY INTO MYSTERY #86
Origin issue: JOURNEY INTO MYSTERY #86
Significant issues: JOURNEY INTO MYSTERY #86 (stole an experimental cobalt bomb to use in his own time, pursued by Thor I who recovered the bomb and caused Zarrko's ship to crashland); JOURNEY INTO MYSTERY #102 (memory restored by Loki, Zarrko returned to the 20th Century and coerced Thor I into helping him conquer the government of the 23rd Century; MARVEL TEAM-UP #9-11 (clashed with Kang when tried to conquer Zarrko's 23rd century, enlisted the aid of Spider-Man and Iron Man; defeated by Spider-Man and the Inhumans); THOR #242-245 (conquered an Earth in the 50th Century, encountered the Time-Twisters, used Servitor to enlist the aid of Thor and the Warriors Three to defeat them; journeyed with them to the "end of time" to thwart Time-Twisters' birth; when returned to 50th Century found himself deposed as ruler); THOR #438-441 (traveled to 2591 tricked Dargo, the Thor of that era into accompanying him to the 20th Century to battle Thor II and Beta Ray Bill; sought to use the energy unleashed by their hammers in the clash to activate the radical Time Stabilizer device to use to collapse all the time lines into one, left adrift in the time-stream)

Note: Zarrko's 23rd Century Earth is a different alternate future than the one Thundra comes from.

ZERO™

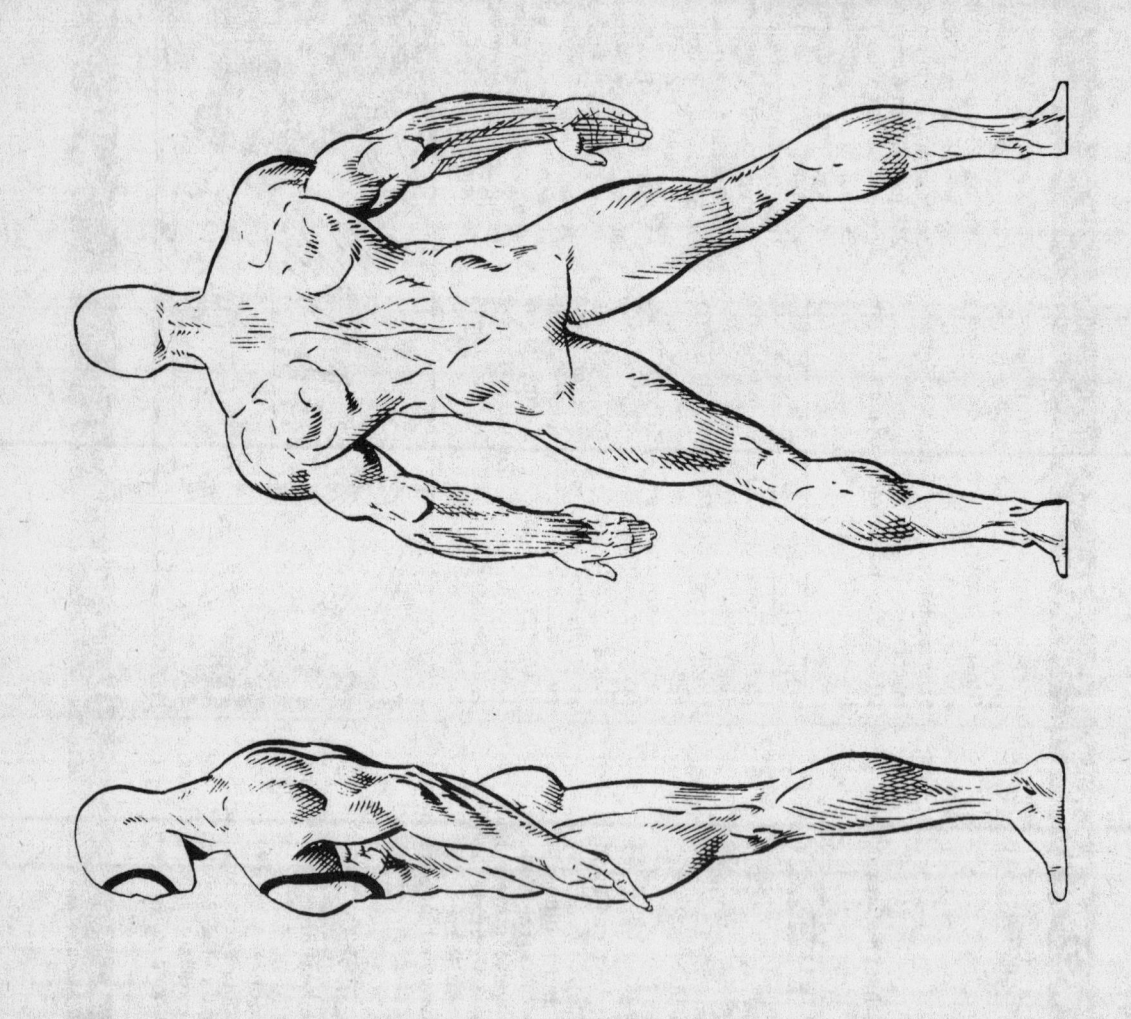

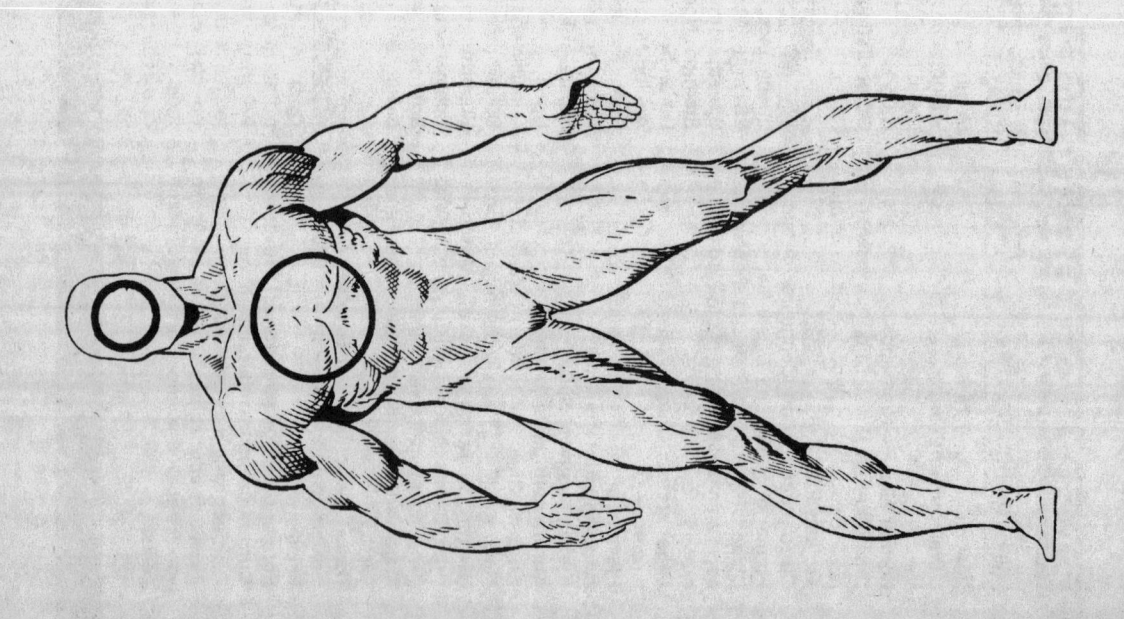

ZERO

BIOGRAPHICAL DATA

Real name: Unrevealed
Other current aliases: None known
Former aliases: None known
Dual Identity: Secret
Current occupation: Terrorist, servant of Stryfe
Former occupation: "Displacement unit" (teleporter) serving Stryfe
Citizenship: Unrevealed
Legal status: Unrevealed in his native time period, none in the 20th Century
Place of birth: Unrevealed, presumably in the Nor-Am Pact region, circa 40th Century A.D.
Marital status: Presumed single
Known relatives: None
Known confidants: None
Known allies: Stryfe, Mutant Liberation Front
Major enemies: Cable, X-Force
Usual base of operations: Unrevealed
Former bases of operations: Nor-Am Pact region in the 40th Century A.D. of alternate future; various bases of Stryfe on Earth and the moon in late 20th Century A.D.
Current group membership: Mutant Liberation Front
Former group membership: None known
Extent of education: Unrevealed

PHYSICAL DESCRIPTION

Height: 6'
Weight: 200 lbs.
Eyes: Unrevealed
Hair: Unrevealed
Other distinguishing features: None known

POWERS AND ABILITIES

Intelligence: Presumed normal
Strength: Presumed normal
Speed: Presumed normal
Stamina: Presumed normal
Durability: Presumed normal
Agility: Presumed normal
Reflexes: Presumed normal
Fighting skills: None
Special skills and abilities: None known
Superhuman physical powers: Ability to create teleportational warps through which he and others can travel
Superhuman mental powers: None
Special limitations: Zero cannot teleport to any location he has never been. He cannot keep a teleportational warp open for much more than a minute. Zero is mute.
Source of superhuman powers: Genetic mutation

PARAPHERNALIA

Costume specifications: Unknown fabrics from 40th Century A.D.
Personal weaponry: None
Special weaponry: None
Other accessories: None known
Transportation: Self-teleportation
Design and manufacture of paraphernalia: Unrevealed

BIBLIOGRAPHY

First appearance: NEW MUTANTS #86
Origin issue: X-FORCE #17
Significant issues: NEW MUTANTS #86 (teleported Mutant Liberation Front on an arson mission); NEW MUTANTS #87-88 (teleported Mutant Liberation Front members to safety after their liberation of Skids and Rusty Collins from federal custody); X-FORCE #1 (teleported Stryfe and Mutant Liberation Front members away from confrontation with X-Force); X-FACTOR #77 (teleported Stryfe and Mutant Liberation Front members on their mission to liberate the Nasty Boys from custody); CABLE: BLOOD AND METAL #1-2 (teleported Stryfe seven years ago, teleported Mutant Liberation Front members on museum thefts in present); X-MEN Vol. 2 #14 (brought genetic matrix from Stryfe to Mister Sinister); X-FORCE #16 (brought Cyclops and Jean Grey to Stryfe); X-FORCE #17 (revealed how Zero accompanied Stryfe in traveling from 40th Century to present)

ZEUS

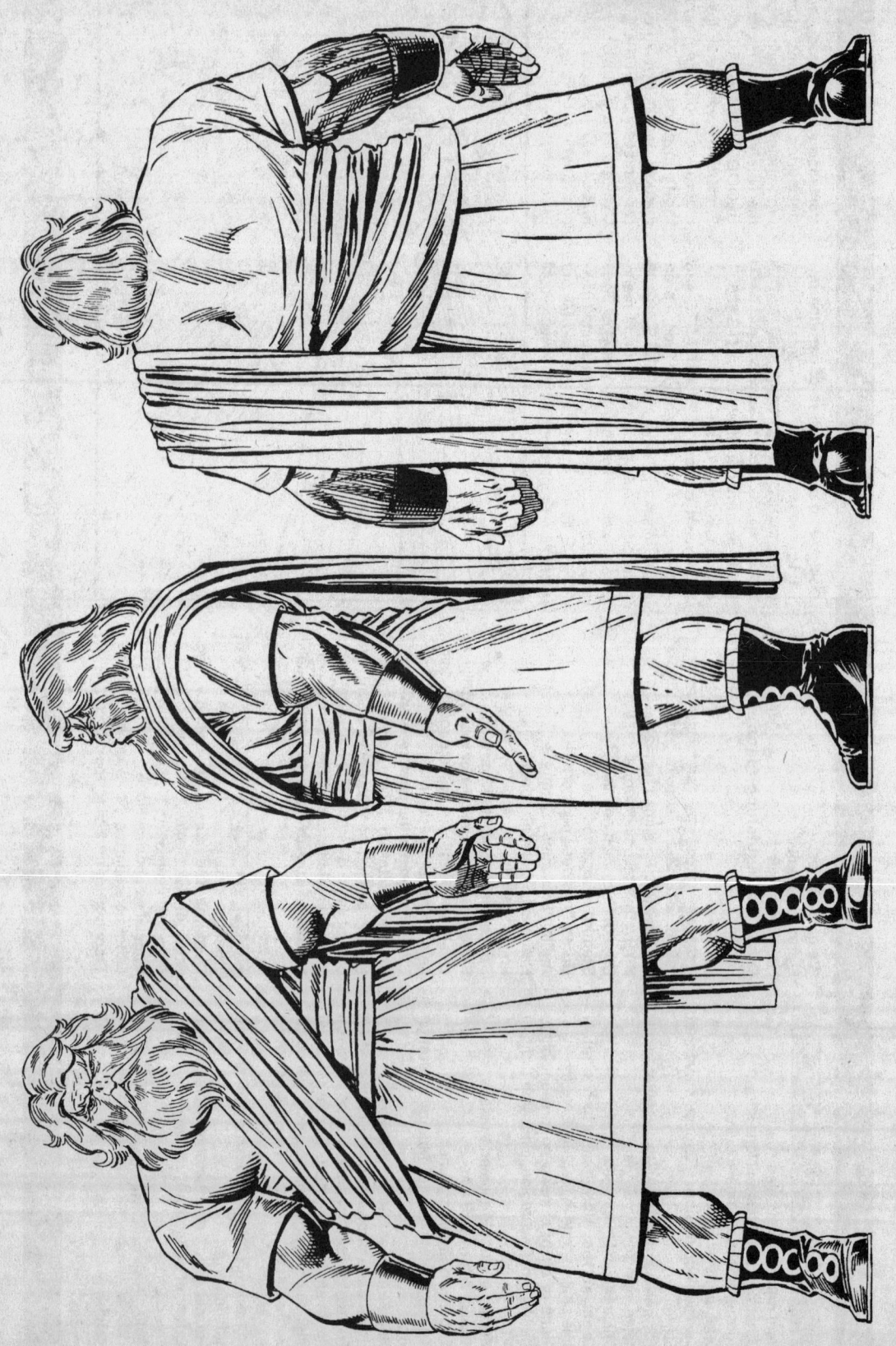

ZEUS

BIOGRAPHICAL DATA

Real name: Zeus
Other current aliases: Jupiter, Jove (his Roman names)
Former aliases: None known
Dual Identity: None in Olympus, believed to be a mythological character by the general populace of present-day Earth
Current occupation: Supreme monarch of the Olympian gods
Former occupation: Leader of the rebellion against Chronus and the Titans
Citizenship: Olympus
Legal status: No criminal record
Place of birth: Mount Lycaem, Arcadia (Greece)
Marital status: Married
Known relatives: Ouranos (grandfather, deceased), Gaea (grandmother), Cronus (father), Rhea (mother), Hera (wife/sister), Pluto, Neptune (brothers), Demeter, Hestia (sisters), Persephone (niece, sister-in-law), Apollo (son by Leto), Ares (son by Hera), Dionysus (son by Semele), Hephaestus (son by Hera), Hercules (son by Alcmena), Hermes (son by Maia), Athena (daughter by Metis), Artemis (daughter by Leto), Hebe (daughter by Hera), Helen of Troy (daughter by Leda, deceased), Venus (daughter by Dione), as well as numerous other children, Eros I (grandson) Atum/Demogorge, Thor I (sons of Zeus's grandmother Gaea)
Known confidants: Hera, Athena
Known allies: Hercules, Olympian gods, Cyclopes, Hekatonchieres (hundred-handed giants), Huntsman of Zeus, Odin, Thor I, heads of other Earth pantheons, Thena, Avengers, (former) Zuras (deceased), Champions of Los Angeles (disbanded)
Major enemies: Typhon, (occasional) Ares, Pluto, Hyppolyta, (former) Cronus and the Titans, Typhoeus, Otus and Ephialtes, Giants of Greek mythology, Third and Fourth Celestial host, Avengers, Enchantress
Usual base of operations: Olympus
Former bases of operations: Mount Ida, Crete; Dodona (site of oracle)
Current group membership: Gods of Olympus
Former group membership: None
Extent of education: No formal education

PHYSICAL DESCRIPTION

Height: 6' 7"
Weight: 560 lbs.
Eyes: Blue
Hair: Red
Other distinguishing features: None

POWERS AND ABILITIES

Intelligence: Normal
Strength: Superhuman Class 90
Speed: Superhuman
Stamina: Godlike
Durability: Demi-godlike regenerative
Agility: Superhuman
Reflexes: Superhuman
Fighting skills: Excellent hand-to-hand combatant, virtually invincible in hurling lightning bolts
Special skills and abilities: None known
Superhuman physical powers: In addition to the above listed physical abilities, Zeus possesses virtual immortality; the ability to manipulate vast cosmic/mystical energies for numerous purposes including powerful force bolts, creating interdimensional apertures, the power to generate great amounts of electrical energy and discharge it as lightning bolts, and the ability change his shape at will.
Superhuman mental powers: Limited precognitive abilities allowing him to see into alternate futures
Special limitations: None
Source of superhuman powers: Zeus is a member of the race of superhumans known as the gods of Olympus.

PARAPHERNALIA

Costume specifications: Olympian materials in a classical Greco-Roman style
Personal weaponry: None
Special weaponry: Olympian weaponry made by Hephaestus (Vulcan I) from virtually indestructible adamantine
Other accessories: None
Transportation: Interdimensional warps; mystical chariot drawn by magical horses capable of flight and traversing the dimensions
Design and manufacture of paraphernalia: Cyclopes, Hephaestus

BIBLIOGRAPHY

First appearance: (historical) RED RAVEN #1, (modern) JOURNEY INTO MYSTERY ANNUAL #1
Origin issue: Zeus's origin is as yet unrevealed.
Significant issues: JOURNEY INTO MYSTERY ANNUAL #1 (first met Thor I); THOR #129 (was unable to break Hercules "Olympian contract" with Pluto); AVENGERS #38 (exiled Hercules to Earth); AVENGERS #49-50 (exiled with other Olympian gods to another dimension by Typhon, rescued by Hercules, revoked Hercules's exile, sent Typhon to Tartarus); THOR #164 (thwarted Pluto's attempt to conquer Earth); AVENGERS #100 (overthrown by alliance of Ares and the Enchantress, restored to power by Avengers); THOR #221-222 (resisted failed attempt by Ares and Pluto to foment war between Olympus and Asgard); CHAMPIONS #1-3 (thwarted conspiracy by Pluto, Ares, and Hyppolita to overthrow him); THOR ANNUAL #5 (revealed pact made a millennia ago to end war between Asgard and Olympus); THOR #300-301 (revealed alliance with Odin and other Earth sky-gods against Celestials, imparted a portion of his power to resurrect Odin and Asgardians); NEW MUTANTS #81 (taught Hercules a lesson about his responsibility to mortals)

ZIRAN THE TESTER

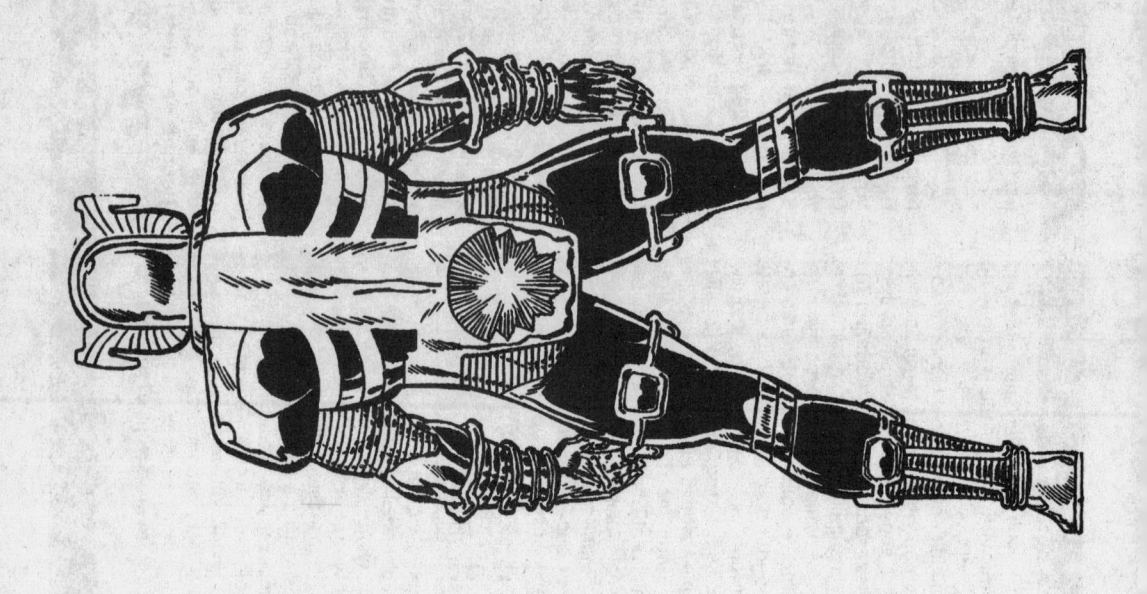

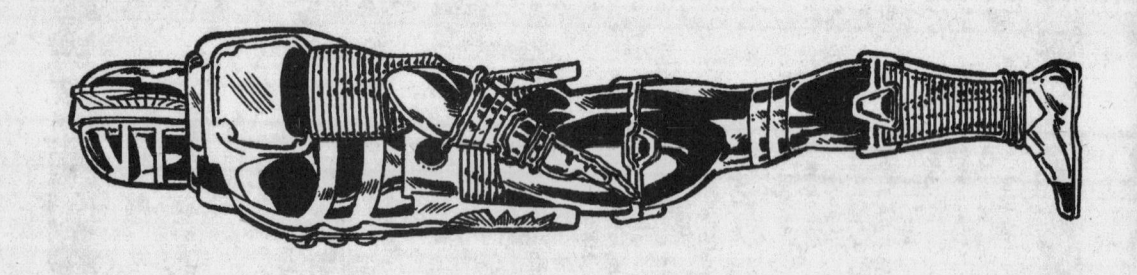

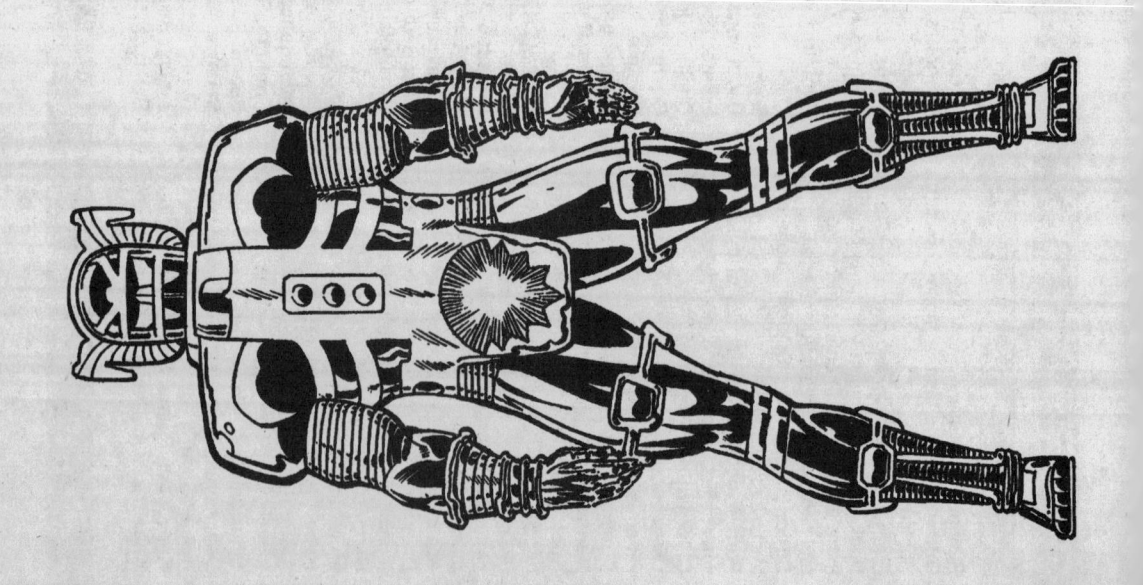

ZIRAN

BIOGRAPHICAL DATA

Real name: Ziran
Other current aliases: None
Former aliases: None
Dual identity: Inapplicable; the general populace of Earth is unaware of Ziran's existence
Current occupation: Experimenter, implementer
Former occupation: Unknown
Citizenship: Inapplicable
Legal status: Probably inapplicable
Place of birth: Unrevealed
Marital status: Unrevealed, possibly inapplicable
Known relatives: Unrevealed, possibly inapplicable
Known confidants: Unrevealed, possibly inapplicable
Major enemies: Unknown
Usual base of operations: Unknown, Celestials have moved throughout known space
Former bases of operations: Unknown
Current group membership: The Fourth Celestial Host
Former group membership: The First, Second, and Third Celestial Hosts
Extent of education: Unknown, perhaps inapplicable

PHYSICAL DESCRIPTION

Height: 2000' (approximately)
Weight: Unknown
Eyes: Unknown, perhaps inapplicable
Hair: Unknown, perhaps inapplicable
Other distinguishing features: Despite its immense size, Ziran apparently has the bodily proportions of a humanoid being evolved in Earth's atmosphere and gravity.

POWERS AND ABILITIES

Intelligence: Unrevealed, possibly immeasurable
Strength: Unrevealed, possibly immeasurable
Speed: Normal human
Flight speed: Unrevealed
Stamina: Unrevealed, possibly immeasurable
Durability: Unrevealed, possibly indestructible
Agility: Normal human, possibly below normal
Reflexes: Normal human, possibly below normal
Fighting skills: Unknown
Special skills and abilities: Unknown
Superhuman physical powers: Celestials are total enigmas, whose physical powers may be equal or superior to the most powerful physical beings in the known universe.
Superhuman mental powers: Unknown, probably telepathy and other psionic powers
Special limitations: Unknown, but the Celestials do not appear to have the capacity to time or dimension travel
Source of superhuman powers: Unknown

PARAPHERNALIA

Costume specifications: Unknown, possibly armament or tissue composed of unrevealed alien metal
Personal weaponry: Unknown
Special weaponry: Unknown
Other accessories: Unknown
Transportation: All Celestials can levitate. The Fourth Celestial Host travels through space by means of an immense mothership almost as large as Earth's moon. It is unknown if Celestials can convert themselves to energy for teleportation like the Watchers can.
Design and manufacture of paraphernalia: Unknown

BIBLIOGRAPHY

First appearance: ETERNALS Vol. 1 #19
Origin issue: Ziran's origin is as yet unrevealed.
Significant issues: ETERNALS Vol. 1 #19 (neutralized the rampant energies released when Druid activated a Celestial weapon hidden in the Pyramid of the Winds in the Arctic, encountered Ikaris and Sigmar of the Eternals); WHAT IF Vol.1 #23 (recounting of Ziran's testing and genetic coding of a protohuman being, resulting in the creation of the Deviant sub-species of humanity approximately one million years ago); THOR #300 (alongside assembled Fourth Celestial Host in Peru, confronted and resisted Odin animating the Destroyer, the Uni-Mind, and Thor, left Earth)

ZODIAC I

ZODIAC I

ORGANIZATION

Purpose: World economic and political domination

Modus operandi: Attempts to to extort enormous monetary sums by capturing and slaughtering innocent citizens on a massive scale

Extent of operations: United States

Relationship to conventional authorities: Nearly all of Zodiac's leaders were wanted and imprisoned by federal authorities for crimes including treason, subversion, extortion, and attempted mass murder.

Base of operations: None

Former base of operations: (Aquarius I, II) San Francisco, (Aries I) Atlanta, (Aries II, III) Chicago, (Cancer) Houston, (Capricorn) Detroit, (Gemini) Boston, (Leo) Los Angeles, (Libra) Honolulu, (Pisces) Miami, (Sagittarius) Washington, D.C., (Scorpio) Las Vegas, (Taurus) New York City, (Virgo) Denver

Known enemies: Avengers, Daredevil, Iron Man (James Rhodes), Nick Fury, Zodiac II

Known allies: None

MEMBERSHIP

Number of active members: 12 (not counting mercenaries and other henchmen employed by Zodiac

Number of reserve members: None

Organizational structure: Originally led by Aries I, then by Taurus I. Taurus instituted a system of rotating overall leadership by the twelve principal members, changing each month; each of the twelve Zodiac members also commanded a criminal organization based in his own city.

Known officers: See *Known former members*

Known current members: None

Known former members: Aquarius I, II, Aries I, II, III, Cancer I, Capricorn I, Gemini I (Joshua Link), Leo I, Libra I, Pisces I, Sagittarius I, Scorpio I (Jacob Fury), Taurus I (Cornelius Van Lunt), Virgo I

Known special agents: Spymaster I, Espionage Elite

Membership requirements: Each leader must have been born under the same zodiacal sign as that of the vacancy for which he or she was applying.

Note: All known leaders of Zodiac I are now dead, although Scorpio I's consciousness has inhabited a succession of android duplicates created by the sentient Zodiac Key.

HISTORY

Founder: Taurus I (Cornelius Van Lunt)
Other leaders: See *Known former leaders*

Major campaigns or accomplishments: Acquisition of Zodiac Key (sentient extradimensional power object), attempt to use Star-Blazer to murder one twelfth of Manhattan's population

Major setbacks: Failure of attempt to hold Manhattan for ransom, loss of Zodiac Key, murderous internal power struggle resulting in capture of entire leadership, murders of ten surviving Zodiac members by Zodiac II, death of Taurus.

TECHNOLOGY AND PARAPHERNALIA

Level of technology: Advanced, although Zodiac mercenaries mainly employed conventional weaponry

Transportation: Advanced aircraft of unknown design

Standard uniforms: Each of the twelve Zodiac leaders wore a costume patterned after his or her zodiacal sign. Zodiac mercenaries wore conventional uniforms

Standard weaponry: "Star-Blazer" hand weapons, powered by "stellar energy," fired unknown form of radiation

Standard accessories: None known

BIBLIOGRAPHY

First appearance: (Jacob Fury as Scorpio I) SHIELD Vol. 1 #1, (Zodiac as an organization) AVENGERS #72

Origin issue: SHIELD Vol. 1 #1, 5 (Scorpio I attempted assassinate SHIELD director Nick Fury); AVENGERS #72 (infiltrated by Nick Fury, posing as Scorpio; fought Avengers; escaped); AVENGERS #82 (Aries I led army in capture of Manhattan Island, ; thwarted by Avengers and Daredevil; Aries I died); IRON MAN #35-36 DAREDEVIL #73 (Aquarius I, Capricorn I, and Sagittarius I sought to recapture Zodiac Key, lost it to Brotherhood of the Ankh); AVENGERS #120-122 (led by Taurus I, attempted to kill all Manhattan residents born under the sign of Gemini as a show of power, thwarted by Avengers, Taurus I's faction attempted to kill Zodiac dissident faction, all twelve leaders captured by Avengers); IRON MAN #183-185 (Taurus I ordered Aquarius II and Aries III to kill Iron Man V, both failed); WEST COAST AVENGERS Vol. 2 #26 (led by Scorpio I in new android body, android Zodiac II massacred human Zodiac I, took over their criminal operations, Taurus I escaped); WEST COAST AVENGERS Vol. 2 #29 (death of Taurus I)

ZODIAC II

ZODIAC II

ORGANIZATION

Purpose: Terrorist activity against government and society of the United States
Modus operandi: Criminal activities based on astrological themes
Extent of operations: United States
Relationship to conventional authorities: Wanted for capture by SHIELD
Base of operations: (Aquarius III) San Francisco, (Aries V) Chicago, (Cancer II) Houston, (Capricorn II) Detroit, (Gemini II) Boston, (Leo III) Los Angeles, (Libra II) Honolulu, (Pisces II) Miami, (Sagittarius III) Washington, D.C., (Scorpio I) New Orleans, (Taurus III) New York City, (Virgo II) Denver
Former bases of operations: "Theater of Genetics," Belleville, New Jersey
Major funding: Unrevealed; the Zodiac androids have sometimes acted as paid mercenaries for various employers
Known enemies: Avengers, Defenders, SHIELD
Known allies: None

MEMBERSHIP

Number of active members: 12 (not counting mercenaries and other henchmen employed by each of the 12 Zodiac androids)
Number of reserve members: None; Scorpio I employs the Zodiac Key to create replacements for any members who are destroyed.

Organizational structure: Overall leadership by Scorpio I (Jacob Fury); each of the 12 android Zodiac members also command a criminal organization formerly led by his or her counterpart in Zodiac I
Known officers: Scorpio I (Jacob Fury)
Known current members: Aquarius III, Aries V, Cancer II, Capricorn II, Gemini II, Leo III, Libra II, Pisces II, Sagittarius III, Scorpio I, Taurus III, Virgo II
Known former members: Aries IV, Leo II, Sagittarius II, Taurus II
Known special agents: None
Membership requirements: Inapplicable
Note: All leaders of Zodiac II are androids (patterned after SHIELD's Life Model Decoys) created by Scorpio I (Jacob Fury) utilizing the Zodiac Key. Scorpio I himself is a human being whose original body died and whose consciousness has inhabited a succession of android duplicates created by the sentient Zodiac Key.

HISTORY

Founder: Scorpio I (Jacob Fury)
Other leaders: Aquarius III, Aries V, Cancer II, Capricorn II, Gemini II, Leo III, Libra II, Pisces II, Sagittarius III, Taurus III, Virgo II
Previous purpose or goals: Zodiac II members have sometimes acted as mercenaries for various employers in order to create further disorder in society.
Major campaigns or accomplishments: Massacre of Zodiac I's leadership, takeover of Zodiac I's criminal operations
Major setbacks: Capture and destruction of most of the original Zodiac II androids on two occasions, deactivation of the Zodiac androids in the Brotherhood of the Ankh's dimension

TECHNOLOGY AND PARAPHERNALIA

Level of technology: Advanced robotics, the Zodiac Key is a product of technology far in advance of Earth's.
Transportation: Unrevealed
Standard uniforms: Each of the twelve Zodiac androids wears a costume patterned after his or her zodiacal sign.
Standard weaponry: None; each of the Twelve Zodiac androids employs his or her own superhuman powers or individual weaponry
Standard accessories: None known

BIBLIOGRAPHY

First appearance: (Jacob Fury as Scorpio I) SHIELD Vol. 1 #1 (other Zodiac II androids; in shadow) DEFENDERS #49, (fully seen) DEFENDERS #50
Origin issue: DEFENDERS #48-50 (Scorpio I constructed android Zodiac members, plan thwarted by Defenders, Scorpio I committed suicide); DEFENDERS #63-65 (Libra II and Sagittarius II employed costumed criminals posing as Defenders to create chaos in New York City); IRON MAN #183 (Maggia employed Taurus II to wreck human Taurus I's headquarters, Taurus II defeated by Iron Man); WEST COAST AVENGERS ANNUAL #1 (Quicksilver employed Zodiac II to attack Avengers, Avengers defeated Zodiac II); WEST COAST AVENGERS Vol. 2 #26-28 (led by Scorpio I in new android body, android Zodiac massacred human Zodiac I, took over their criminal operations, battled West Coast Avengers, rendered inert when transported to dimension of Brotherhood of the Ankh)

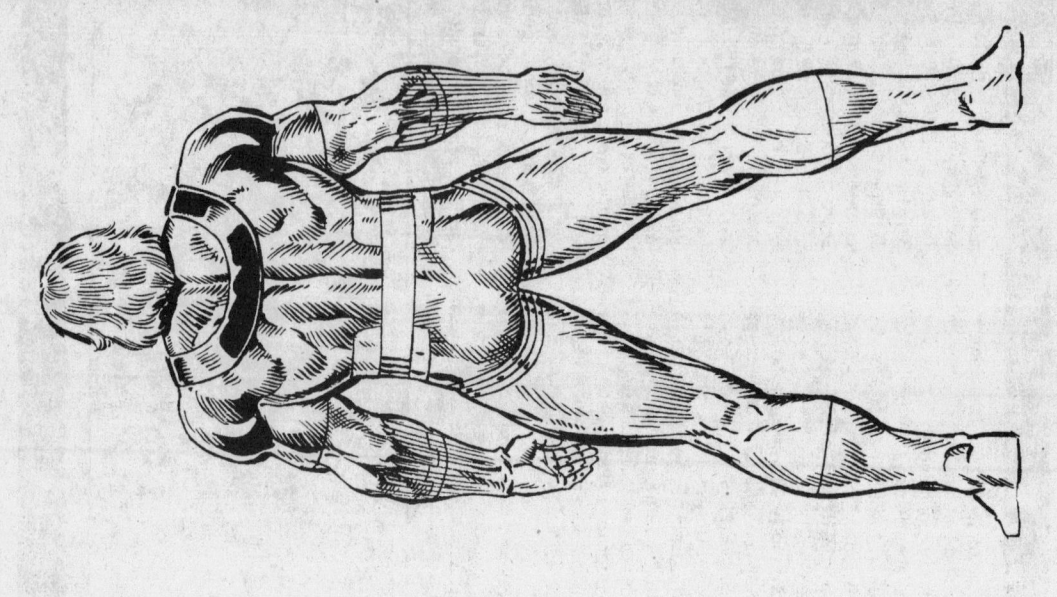

ZURAS

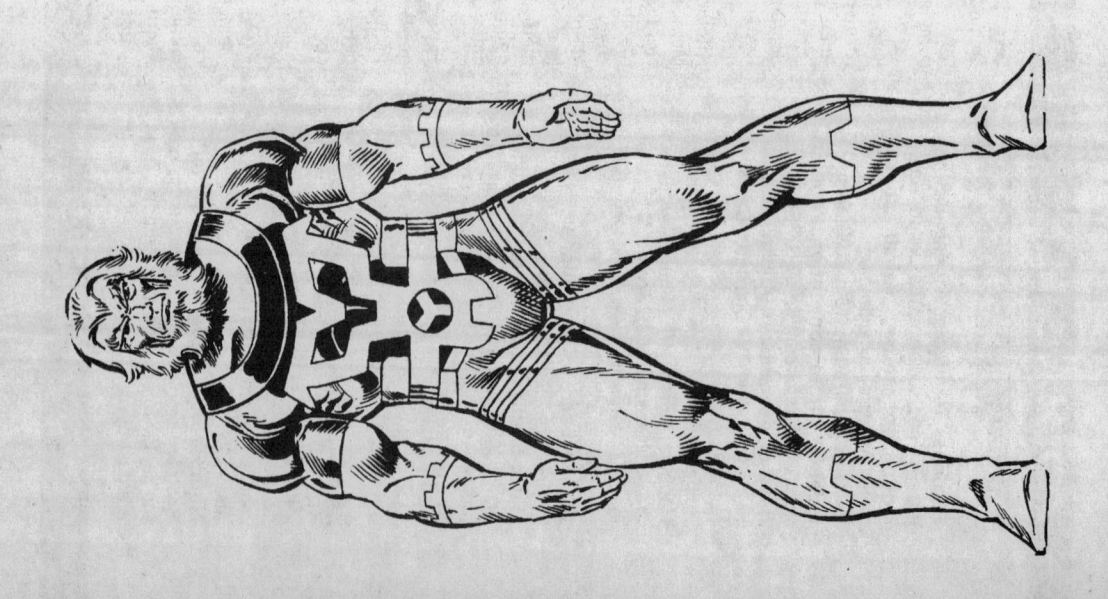

ZURAS

BIOGRAPHICAL DATA

Real name: Zuras
Aliases at time of death: None
Former aliases: Zeus
Dual identity: None
Occupation at time of death: Leader of the Eternals of Earth
Former occupation: Warrior
Citizenship: Olympia, city of the Eternals
Legal status: No criminal record anywhere on Earth
Place of birth: Titanos, first city of the Eternals, location unrevealed
Place of death: Peru
Cause of death: Attacking the Fourth Celestial Host while fusing with the Eternals in the Uni-Mind formation, Zuras was rendered brain-dead by a cosmic blast issued by Celestials Gammenon and Jemiah.
Marital status: Married
Known relatives: Kronos (father, deceased), Mentor (alias Alars, brother), Thena (daughter), Eros (alias Starfox, nephew), Thanos (nephew), wife's name unrevealed
Known confidants at time of death: Major Domo, Thena
Known allies: The gods of Asgard
Major enemies: Warlord Kro, the Deviant Empire, Dromedan
Usual base of operations: Olympia, Greece
Former base of operations: Titanos
Group membership at time of death: The Eternals of Earth
Former group membership: None
Extent of education: Unrevealed

PHYSICAL DESCRIPTION

Height: 6'2"
Weight: 300 lbs.
Eyes: Blue
Hair: Red
Other distinguishing features: A full beard

POWERS AND ABILITIES

Intelligence: Above normal
Strength: Superhuman Class 50
Speed: Superhuman
Flight speed: Subsonic
Stamina: Immeasurable
Durability: Godlike
Agility: Enhanced human
Reflexes: Enhanced human
Fighting skills: Due to his vast powers, Zuras never needed to develop hand to hand combat techniques.
Special skills and abilities: Extensive knowledge of ancient and arcane wisdom.
Superhuman physical powers: Besides his physical attributes above, Zuras possessed the ability to manipulate cosmic energy to augment his life force granting him great longevity and regenerative abilities, the projection of concussive force, heat and electrical energy up to a maximum range of 300 feet. He could also use cosmic energy to create force shields around himself, to levitate himself and/or others, and to psionically manipulate molecules so as to transform an object's shape. During his lifetime, Zuras was the only Eternal known capable of initiating the creation of the Uni-Mind (the collective life-form resulting from the physical and mental merging of a significant number of Eternals) by himself.
Superhuman mental powers: Telepathy, illusion-casting, limited teleportation
Special limitations: None
Source of superhuman powers: Above average development of the normal attributes of the race of Eternals through great discipline

PARAPHERNALIA

Costume specifications: Alien materials
Personal weaponry: None
Special weaponry: None
Other accessories: None
Transportation: Most frequently, levitation under his own power
Design and manufacture of paraphernalia: Inapplicable

BIBLIOGRAPHY

First appearance: ETERNALS Vol. 1 #5
Origin issues: CAPTAIN MARVEL #29 (as "Zeus"), WHAT IF Vol. 1 #25
Significant issues: WHAT IF Vol. 1 #25 (vied with brother Alars for leadership of the Eternals of Titanos; created first ritual of the Uni-Mind); ETERNALS Vol.1 #5 (gave permission to Makkari and Thena to fight Deviants); ETERNALS Vol.1 #10 (attempted to mind-probe Celestial craft; learned of coming Fourth Celestial Host); ETERNALS Vol.1 #11-12 (initiated first Uni-Mind fusion of Eternals in modern times to attempt to communicate with Arishem); ETERNALS Vol.1 #14 (ended Uni-Mind fusion); ETERNALS Vol.1 #15 (traveled to New York City; addressed public on the subject of the Celestial host on television broadcast); ETERNALS Vol.1 #16 (explored tomb of Dromedan the Brain-Snatcher); ETERNALS Vol.1 #17 (battled Dromedan); ETERNALS Vol.1 #18 (assisted U.S. State Department in the investigation of Celestial threat); THOR #287 (encountered Thor); THOR #291 (initiated second Uni-Mind fusion to probe Celestial mothership, battled Zeus); THOR #300 (initiated third Uni-Mind fusion to combat the Celestials, which disintegrated into component Eternals causing Zuras's brain death); THOR #301 (death revealed); IRON MAN ANNUAL #6 (Zuras's spirit left body)

ZZAXX™

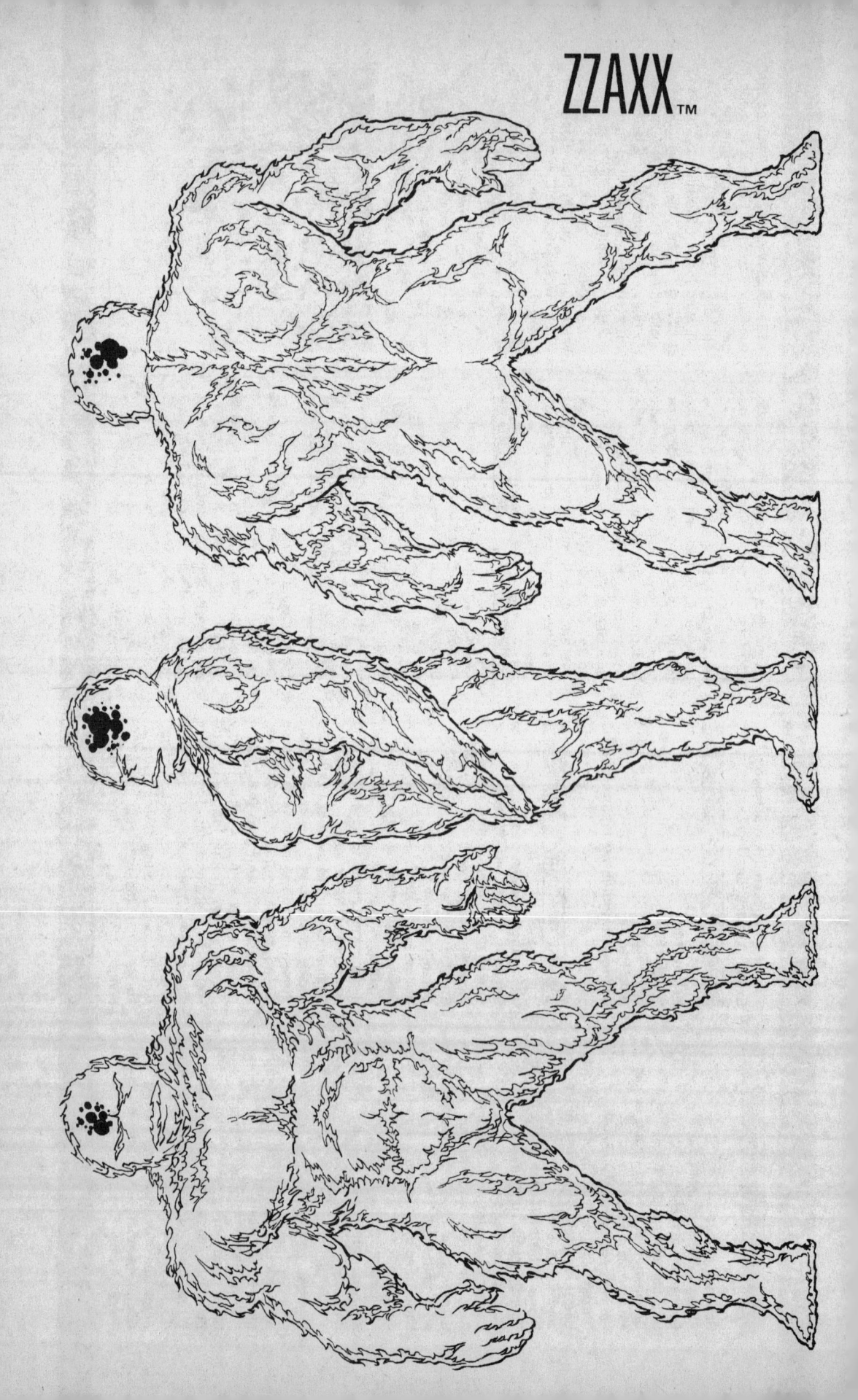

ZZZAX

BIOGRAPHICAL DATA

Real name: Zzzax
Other current aliases: The Living Dynamo
Former aliases: None
Dual identity: Inapplicable
Current occupation: Inapplicable
Former occupation: Inapplicable
Citizenship: Inapplicable
Legal status: Inapplicable
Place of creation: Consolidated Edison power plant, New York
Marital status: Inapplicable
Known relatives: Inapplicable
Known confidants: Inapplicable
Known allies: Graviton, Quantum, Halflife
Major enemies: The Hulk, Hawkeye, Power Man II, West Coast Avengers, Iron Man I
Usual base of operations: Mobile
Former bases of operations: New York City; Chicago, Illinois; Northwind Observatory, New York; Los Angeles, California; Gamma Base, New Mexico
Current group membership: None
Former group membership: None
Extent of education: Inapplicable

PHYSICAL DESCRIPTION

Height: 40' (maximum)
Weight: Negligible
Eyes: None
Hair: None
Other distinguishing features: Zzzax generally as a gargantuan mass of electrical "sparks", which is highly luminescent, whitish-yellow in color, and gives off the odor of ozone.

POWERS AND ABILITIES

Intelligence: Variable up to Normal
Strength: Superhuman Class 100
Speed: Inapplicable
Flight speed: Directed motion hovering
Stamina: Metahuman
Durability: Demi-godlike
Agility: Inapplicable
Reflexes: Normal
Fighting skills: Minimal
Special skills and abilities: None
Superhuman physical powers: Ability to fire blasts of electricity capable of incinerating everything in its path; ability to absorb other electromagnetic fields, including those of human brains, for subsistence
Superhuman mental powers: The ability to absorb thoughts, desires, and psionic energy from human brains whose electromagnetic fields it absorbs, thus adding to its intelligence and enabling it to mimic human emotions
Special limitations: Zzzax seemingly cannot absorb psionic energy from the Hulk. On rare occasions, Zzzax's consciousness can be supplanted by that of its intended victim (e.g., "Thunderbolt" Ross). Zzzax's constituent field can be dissipated by "short-circuiting" or "grounding" his electrical form
Source of superhuman powers: Zzzax is a form of electromagnetic intelligence, a psionically-charged electromagnetic field in humanoid form.

PARAPHERNALIA

Costume specifications: Inapplicable
Personal weaponry: None
Special weaponry: None
Other accessories: None
Transportation: Flight under own power
Design and manufacture of paraphernalia: Inapplicable

BIBLIOGRAPHY

First appearance: INCREDIBLE HULK Vol. 2 #166
Origin issue: INCREDIBLE HULK Vol. 2 #166
Significant issues: INCREDIBLE HULK Vol. 2 #166 (accidentally created in explosion at Consolidated Edison plant by terrorists, battled Hulk and Hawkeye, destroyed by Hawkeye); INCREDIBLE HULK Vol. 2 #166 (accidentally recreated in experiment at Soul Star Research, battled Hulk, destroyed); POWER MAN #47 (accidentally recreated during accident at Illinois Edison plant, attempted to transform Alexandria Knox into energy being, battled Power Man II, destroyed); INCREDIBLE HULK Vol. 2 #285 (accidentally recreated during construction of Northwind Observatory, battled Hulk, dissipated into space); WEST COAST AVENGERS Vol. 2 #12-13 (alongside Graviton, Quantum, and Halflife, battled West Coast Avengers, destroyed by Hawkeye and Wonder Man); INCREDIBLE HULK Vol. 2 #325-327 (transported by SHIELD to Gamma Base, absorbed "Thunderbolt" Ross's psionic energy during experiment, controlled by Ross's personality, battled Hulk II [Rick Jones]); INCREDIBLE HULK Vol. 2 #330 (Zzzax's energy within his brain used by Ross to destroy mutant mind-parasite); MARVEL COMICS PRESENTS #8 (accidentally recreated in test of Tony Stark's static electricity generator, freed of Ross's control, battled Iron Man I, destroyed)

INTELLIGENCE: Ability to think

Non-Sentient (instinctual behavior only)
Learning impaired (major mental deficiencies)
Below normal (minor mental deficiencies)
Normal (possessing an Intelligence Quotient that is approximately average)
Above normal (possessing a significantly higher than average IQ)
Gifted (possessing a significantly higher than average IQ and creative talents)
Genius (possessing an extremely high IQ and creative talents)
Extraordinary genius (possessing genius in multiple intellectual areas)
Superhuman (possessing genius in virtually all intellectual areas)
Immeasurable (alien, "omniscient")

STRENGTH: Ability to lift weight above one's head with arms fully extended

Below normal (cannot lift one's own body weight)
Normal (able to lift one's own body weight)
Athlete (able to lift from one's own body weight up to double one's own body weight)
Peak human (able to lift double one's own body weight to 800 pound range)
Enhanced human (able to lift in the 800 pound to 2 ton range)
Superhuman Class 10 (able to lift in the 2 to 10 ton range)
Superhuman Class 25 (able to lift in the 10 to 25 ton range)
Superhuman Class 50 (able to lift in the 25 to 50 ton range)
Superhuman Class 75 (able to lift in the 50 to 75 ton range)
Superhuman Class 90 (able to lift in the 75 to 90 ton range)
Superhuman Class 100 (able to lift in the 90 to 100 ton range)
Incalculable (able to lift in excess of 100 tons)

SPEED: Ability to move over land by running

Below normal (cannot attain 10-15 miles per hour)
Normal (peak range: 25-29 miles per hour)
Athlete (peak range: 32-36 miles per hour)
Peak human (peak range: 41-45 miles per hour)
Enhanced human (peak range: 61-65 miles per hour)
Superhuman (peak range: 111-115 miles per hour)
Subsonic (peak range: 250-500 miles per hour)
Speed of sound (able to reach the Mach 1: 770 miles per hour at sea level)
Supersonic (peak range: Mach 2 to Mach 4.6: 0.22-1.0 miles per second)
Orbital velocity (peak range: Mach 18.7 to Mach 23.3: 1-5 miles per second; when a runner reaches this speed he is no longer in contact with the ground and thus not running)

FLIGHT SPEED: Ability to move through open air or space by flying

Hover only
Directed motion hovering (peak range: 10-30 miles per hour)
Natural winged flight limit (peak range: 150-160 miles per hour)
Artificial winged flight (peak limit: 160-200 miles per hour)
Subsonic (peak range: 250-500 miles per hour)
Speed of sound (able to reach the Mach 1: 770 miles per hour; 0.22 miles per second)
Supersonic (peak range: Mach 2 to Mach 4.6 : 0.22-1.0 miles per second)
Orbital velocity (peak range: Mach 18.7 to Mach 23.3: 1-5 miles per second)
Escape velocity (Mach 32.7: 7 miles per second)
Sub-light speed (peak range: 80%-99.65% light speed: 150,000 to 185,620 miles per second)
Light speed (186,000 miles per second; cannot be attained by physical beings within Earth's atmosphere)
Warp speed (able to enter and traverse through warp space by transcending light speed, cannot be attained by physical beings within Earth's atmosphere)

WATER SPEED: Ability to move through water by swimming

Normal (peak range: 3-5 knots)
Athlete (peak range: 7-12 knots)
Peak human (peak range: 12-15 knots)
Enhanced human (peak range: 20-25 knots)
Superhuman (peak range: 50-60 knots)
Maximum (around 700 knots, detrimental environmental effects will occur, causing water to convert to plasma, etc.)
NOTE: 1 knot = 1.151 miles per hour.

STAMINA: Ability to sustain peak exertion before fatigue impairs performance

Below normal (unable to sustain for 1 minute)
Normal (able to sustain for 1 minute)
Athlete (able to sustain for several minutes)
Peak human (able to sustain for up to an hour)
Enhanced human (able to sustain for several hours)
Superhuman (able to sustain for up to a day)
Metahuman (able to sustain for several days)
Demi-godlike (able to sustain for weeks)
Godlike (able to sustain almost indefinitely)
Immeasurable (never tire due to self-generating energy)

DURABILITY: Ability to resist or recover from bodily injury or disease

Below normal
Normal (average resilience)
Athlete (conditioned metabolism enabling efficient healing)
Peak human (conditioned metabolism enabling extraordinarily efficient healing)
Enhanced human (skin, bone, and muscle augmented to make it stronger and harder than human; impervious to injury to a certain extent)
Enhanced human regenerative (skin, bone, and muscle retains human durability but body is able to heal near-lethal injuries by regenerating cells to a limited extent)
Superhuman (skin, bone, and muscle augmented to make it stronger and harder than human; impervious to injury to an extraordinary extent)
Superhuman regenerative (able to regenerate injured tissue and brain cells to an extraordinary degree; but not able to regenerate missing limbs or organs)
Metahuman (able to withstand extreme temperatures and pressures, and virtually all toxins, corrosives, punctures, and concussions without sustaining injury)
Metahuman regenerative (able to regenerate injured or missing brain cells, tissue, limbs or organs)
Demi-godlike (able to withstand all injury short of a direct nuclear explosion)
Demi-godlike regenerative (able to heal all injury short of a direct nuclear explosion)
Godlike (able to reconstitute body after total molecular disintegration)
Totally indestructible (absolutely cannot be injured)

AGILITY: Ability to to move the body with flexibility and coordination

Below normal
Normal (average)
Athlete (above average)
Peak human (significantly above average)
Enhanced human (beyond the natural limits of the human body)
Superhuman (significantly beyond the natural limits of the human body)
Metahuman (extraordinarily beyond the natural limits of the human body)

REFLEXES: Reaction time

Below normal
Normal (average)
Athlete (above average)
Peak human (significantly above average)
Enhanced human (beyond the natural limits of the human body)
Superhuman (virtually instantaneous)
Metahuman (instantaneous)

THE OFFICIAL HANDBOOK OF THE MARVEL UNIVERSE®: MASTER EDITION. Vol. 3, No. 5, 1991. Published by MARVEL COMICS, Terry Stewart, President. Stan Lee, Publisher. Michael Hobson, Vice President, Publishing. OFFICE OF PUBLICATION: 387 PARK AVENUE SOUTH, NEW YORK, N.Y. 10016. Copyright © 1991 Marvel Entertainment Group, Inc. All rights reserved. Price $3.95 per copy in the U.S. and $4.95 in Canada. No similarity between any of the names, characters, persons, and/or institutions in this magazine with those of any living or dead person or institution is intended, and any such similarity which may exist is purely coincidental. This periodical may not be sold except by authorized dealers and is sold subject to the condition that it shall not be sold or distributed with any part of its cover or markings removed, nor in a mutilated condition. Marvel Universe (including all prominent characters featured in this issue and the distinctive likenesses thereof) is a trademark of MARVEL ENTERTAINMENT GROUP, INC. Printed in CANADA.

SPECIAL GLOSSARY

accessories: Any article used or carried by the subject of the entry other than weaponry or transportation.

Adamantium: An artificially created alloy of iron that is most impervious substance found on Earth.

alternate earth: A world resembling Earth which coexists with Earth in another dimensional space.

alternate future: One of the possible future realities deriving from the present reality through a specific sequence of events.

android: An artificial being designed to resemble and mimic the form of a human being.

anti-matter: Matter composed of particles that have the opposite electrical charge as ordinary matter.

astral body: The sheath or form that contains a living being's life essence, consciousness, spirit, or soul.

astral projection: The ability to project one's astral body from one's physical body.

bionic: Of or having to do with an artificial simulation of a living thing or part of a living thing.

clairvoyance: The ability to perceive things without using the five physical senses.

confidants: Persons to whom the subject of the entry has revealed his or her secret identity or other highly confidential information.

cyborg: Cybernetic organism.

Darkforce: An unknown form of extradimensional energy that manifests as a non-reflective, highly opaque, black substance.

demigod: A humanoid being possessing almost godlike attributes, but was probably not worshiped. A demigod may be an offspring of a god and a human being.

demon: A godlike being who preys upon the living in some way, usually possessing some magical powers and living in other dimensions.

Deviant: A member of the evolutionary offshoot of humanity created through experiments performed by the alien Celestials, possessing no standard genetic physical characteristics other than humanoid form. Deviants tend to look monstrous.

dimension: A universe or realm containing space, time, matter, and energy.

Eternal: A member of the evolutionary offshoot of humanity created through experiments performed by the alien Celestials, possessing extraordinary life spans and a vast array of physical and energy manipulating powers.

god: A humanoid being with a longer life span and greater physical powers than human beings, whose kinsmen or self was was once worshiped by human beings.

Homo mermanus: An evolutionary offshoot of humanity who possesses gills and dwells underwater.

hyper-space: A realm of space existing outside of conventional space. Also called sub-space or warp-space.

levitation: The psionic or magical ability to screen the physical body from gravity and thus rise off the ground.

limbo: A generic term for various dimensions characterized by static or unchanging physical features. True Limbo exists outside the timestream itself.

magic: The art, science, and practice of utilizing certain unknown energies outside the electromagnetic spectrum.

metahuman: Characterized by skills, abilities, attributes, or powers that are as far beyond superhuman as superhuman is beyond human.

microverse: A parallel universe that may be reached from earth by reducing one's mass to a certain point, thereby creating a nexus. They are erroneously thought to exist within the atoms of our universe.

multiverse: A group of alternate universes that are related in some way.

mutagenic: Something capable of making cellular-level changes in an organism.

mutant: A being born with physical characteristics or the potential for them that are not possessed by either of its parents.

mutate: A being who acquires a physical characteristic by benevolent mutation from the exposure to a mutagenic substance.

Negative Zone: An anti-matter universe discovered by Dr. Reed Richards (Mr. Fantastic).

nexus: A point in one dimension through which access to other dimensions may be achieved.

Omnium: A steel alloy stronger than Titanium but weaker than Adamantium.

pantheon: A tribe, clan, or race of gods of common origin.

parallel world: A world that exists in another dimension whose reality never diverged from but is parallel to the reality of Earth.

personal weaponry: Instruments of offensive or defensive combat carried on the subject of the entry's person.

pocket dimension: A universe whose spatial size is limited.

precognition: The ability to psionically scan the various alternate futures and (sometimes) predict which one is most probable to manifest.

psionic: Pertaining to the mental manipulation of hypothetical subatomic particles called psions.

psychokinesis: The psionic ability to move or manipulate matter without physically touching it. Synonymous with telekinesis.

Pym particles: Theoretical particles discovered by Dr. Henry Pym that enables size-changing and shunting and accruing of mass extradimensionally.

radar senses: An extrasensory means of perception whereby the brain generates electromagnetic waves that bounce off of objects and travels back to the brain.

robot: A mechanical being capable of simulating certain human activities.

sentient: Possessing higher intelligence.

Subterraneans: Any of the offshoots of humanity who have adapted to living beneath Earth's surface.

superhuman: Characterized by skills, abilities, attributes, or powers that are outside the parameters of achievement by human beings.

special weaponry: Instruments of offensive or defensive combat used by the subject of the entry but not usually carried on his or her person.

telepathy: The psionic or physical ability to send and/or receive thoughts directly into other minds.

teleportation: The psionic ability to transport one's self or other people or objects from one point in space to another without physically having travelled the space in between.

time-line: The events of a particular reality that define its history. Also called reality line.

unstable molecules: A configuration of unknown atomic nuclei and electrons discovered or synthesized by Dr. Reed Richards (Mr. Fantastic) which is responsive to energized matter around it.

vampire: A magical creature who feeds upon the blood of living beings, created by a spell written by the demon Chthon in the book of the Darkhold.

Vibranium: A precious extraterrestrial metal found only in meteor deposits in the African nation of Wakanda and the Antarctic region called the Savage Land, capable of absorbing vibrations.

werewolf: A human being who can transform into a wolf or humanoid wolf through magic.

INDEX

ISSUE # / PROFILE	ISSUE # / PROFILE	ISSUE # / PROFILE	ISSUE # / PROFILE
5 Abomination	7 Black Knight	8 Colossus	12 D'Spayre
16 Absorbing Man	20 Black Knight	10 Constrictor	19 Earth-Lord
31 Agamemnon	14 Black Knight II	13 Contemplator	2 Eel
26 Aginar	9 Black Panther	20 Controller	7 Egghead
12 Aguila	17 Black Queen	6 Copperhead	9 Ego
3 AIM	10 Black Talon	1 Corsair	34 Eight-Ball
9 Air-Walker	25 Black Widow	25 Cottonmouth	3 Electro
10 Ajak	34 Blackheart	17 Count Nefaria	27 Electron
36 Ajax	8 Blacklash	1 Counterweight	8 Elektra
1 Anaconda	29 Blackout I	22 Crimson Commando	28 Elysius
32 Analyzer	30 Blackout II	5 Crimson Dynamo	20 Enchantress
17 Ancient One	36 Blackwing	33 Crippler	32 Enclave
12 Andromeda	28 Blade	12 Crossbones	33 Enforcers
14 Annihilus	4 Blastaar	21 Crossfire	14 Eon
30 Answer	24 Blaze, John	11 Crucible	17 Eson the Searcher
15 Ant-Man	5 Blizzard	30 Crusader	5 Eternity
27 Anvil	10 Blob	15 Crystal	36 Evilhawk
24 Ape-Man	23 Blonde Phantom	35 Crystal	4 Executioner
4 Apocalypse	13 Blood Brothers	28 Cutthroat	23 Falcon
19 Apollo	35 Bloodaxe	34 Cyber	32 Famine
21 Aquarian	2 Bloodstone, Ulysses	24 Cyclone	5 Fandral
13 Arabian Knight	31 Blue Eagle	16 Cyclops	18 Fang
34 Aragorn	1 Blue Shield	7 Cypher	13 Fantastic Four
22 Arcade	26 Boomer	5 Dagger	14 FF Replacements
20 Archangel	5 Boomerang	21 Dakimh	35 Fearmaster
11 Ares	9 Brother Tode	7 Daredevil	31 Feral
18 Arishem	17 Brother Voodoo	19 Daredevil in Action	13 Fer-de-Lance
23 Arkon	15 Brothers Grimm	16 Darkhawk	33 Feron
7 Armadillo	25 Bucky	6 Darkoth	25 Fin Fang Foom
28 Aron	18 Bulldozer	14 Darkstar	9 Firebird
27 Asp	13 Bullet	29 Dazzler	3 Firelord
6 Astronomer	6 Bullseye	25 Deadpool	7 Firestar
8 Attuma	22 Bushmaster	11 Death Adder	6 Fixer
29 Aurora	15 Bushwacker	24 Deathbird	20 Flag-Smasher
33 Avalanche	24 Byrrah	27 Deathlok	27 Foolkiller
15 Avengers 1st Lineup	26 Caber	35 Deathlok	16 Force
16 Avengers 2nd Lineup	3 Cable	17 Death-Stalker	26 Foreigner
17 Avengers 3rd Lineup	23 Cage	15 Deathurge	2 Forge
18 Avengers 4th Lineup	34 Caliban	33 Deathwatch	21 Fortune, Dominic
19 Avengers 5th Lineup	7 Callisto	34 Demogoblin	1 Foxfire
20 Avengers 6th Lineup	6 Cannonball	18 Demolition-Man	15 Frankenstein
22 Avengers 7th Lineup	2 Captain America	2 Destiny	12 Frenzy
32 West Coast Avengers 1st Lineup	14 Captain America in Action	31 Destroyer	34 Frog-Man
33 West Coast Avengers 2nd Lineup	20 Captain Atlas	4 Devastator	22 Fury, Nick
34 West Coast Avengers 3rd Lineup	10 Captain Britain	8 Devil Dinosaur	28 Galactus
35 West Coast Avengers 4th Lineup	5 Captain Marvel	27 Devos	21 Gambit
2 Awesome Android	34 Captain Marvel	13 Diablo	22 Gammenon
29 Balder	8 Captain Ultra	22 Diamond Lil	19 Gamora
11 Balor	32 Captain Universe	3 Diamondback	29 Gardener
21 Banshee	31 Cardiac	9 Doc Samson	3 Gargantua
7 Barbarus	29 Carnage	19 Doctor Demonicus	14 Gargoyle
20 Baron Blood	4 Carrion	20 Doctor Doom	15 Garrokk
3 Baron Mordo	29 Cassidy, Black Tom	26 Doctor Druid	6 Gatecrasher
16 Baron Strucker	27 Cat-Man	10 Doctor Faustus	18 Ghaur
4 Baron Zemo	33 Centurious	5 Doctor Malus	20 Ghost
23 Batroc	12 Centurius	4 Doctor Minerva	3 Ghost Rider
19 Battle Star	36 Cerise	22 Doctor Nightshade	15 Ghost Rider in Action
14 Beast	9 Chameleon	2 Doctor Octopus	27 Giant-Man
18 Beetle	14 Champion	23 Doctor Spectrum	33 Gideon
26 Belasco	36 Chance	35 Doctor Strange	11 Gilgamesh
27 Bengal	28 Changeling	28 Domino	24 Gladiator I
27 Beta Bill Ray	15 Charlie-27	35 Doom 2099	8 Gladiator II
35 Beyonder	24 Chemistro	1 Dormammu	17 Glob
21 Bi-Beast	29 Chief Examiner	32 Doughboy	23 Glorian
3 Big Bertha	19 Ch'od	30 Dracula	36 Goddess
36 Binary	26 Chondu the Mystic	8 Dragon Man	7 Goldbug
32 Bird-Man	30 Chord	34 Drake, Frank	12 Goliath
30 Bishop	23 Chthon	24 Drax the Destroyer	1 Gorgon
33 Black Archer	18 Clea	13 Dreadknight	10 Grandmaster
22 Black Bolt	11 Cloak	30 Dreadnought	16 Graviton
12 Black Cat	31 Coldblood	28 Dream Queen	27 Green Goblin
28 Black Crow	23 Collector	29 Dredmund Druid	9 Gremlin

ISSUE # / PROFILE	ISSUE # / PROFILE	ISSUE # / PROFILE	ISSUE # / PROFILE
2 Grey Gargoyle	14 Jetstream	19 Major Victory	27 Needle
26 Grey, Jean	10 Jigsaw	8 Makkari	32 Nefarius
30 Griffin	11 Jocasta	4 Malekith	26 Neptune
4 Grim Reaper	19 Jones, Rick	3 Man-Ape	11 Nezzar
34 Grizzly	24 Jubilee	28 Man-Beast	25 Night Thrasher
36 Grizzly I	1 Juggernaut	19 Mandarin	12 Nightcrawler
31 Gronk	35 Kala	31 Mandrill	5 Nighthawk
32 Growing Man	28 Kaluu	15 Mangog	8 Nighthawk
5 Guardian	8 Kang	8 Manslaughter	4 Nikki
25 Guardian	18 Kangaroo	5 Man-Thing	2 Nitro
15 Guardsman	21 Karkas	21 Mantis	30 Nobilus
26 Halflife	33 Karma	27 Marauders	6 Nomad
4 Hammer	12 Karnak	19 Marinna	13 Northstar
29 Hammer, Justin	7 Karnilla	16 Martinex	7 Nova
23 Hammerhead	3 Ka-Zar	7 Marvel Boy	19 Nova
7 Hangman	15 Killer Shrike	13 Master	20 Nuke
36 Hardcore	31 Killraven	21 Master Man	34 Null the Living Darkness
1 Harkness, Agatha	4 King Cobra	11 Master Order	21 Occult
32 Harriers	25 King, Hannibal	27 Master Pandemonium	29 Occulus
15 Hate Monger	17 Kingpin	29 Mastermind	11 Oddball
17 Havok	22 Kismet	32 Maverick	10 Odin
16 Hawkeye	24 Klaw	20 Maximus	15 Omega
21 Haywire	5 Knickknack	24 Medusa	34 Omega Red
3 Heimdall	10 Knight, Misty	28 Meggan	6 One Above All
6 Hela	16 Kofi	12 Melter	1 Oneg the Prober
12 Helio	27 Korath the Pursuer	29 Mentallo	19 Oracle
28 Hellfire Club	20 Korvac	14 Mentor	26 Orb
35 Hellstorm	23 Krang	32 Mephisto	2 Orka
25 Hepzibah	32 Kree	7 Mercurio	25 Osiris
30 Hera	11 Kronos	22 Merlin	9 Over-Mind
10 Hercules	2 Kubik	5 Mesmero	5 Owl
33 Hercules	14 Kurse	31 Micromax	32 Paibok
22 Hermes	17 Lady Deathstrike	16 Midas	17 Paladin
13 High Evolutionary	8 Lamprey	1 Midnight Sun	25 Peregrine
6 Hobgoblin	16 Lava Men	6 Mirage	9 Phantom Eagle
18 Hogun the Grim	2 Leader	25 Mirage	22 Phantom Rider
24 Horus	23 Left-Winger	10 Miss America	13 Phoenix
2 Howard the Duck	6 Leir	3 Mister Fantastic	24 Phoenix III
8 Hulk	29 Lightmaster	25 Mister Fear	8 Piledriver
33 Human Torch	9 Lightspeed	12 Mister Hyde	27 Pip the Troll
24 Human Torch II	20 Lilandra	4 Mister Jip	12 Piper
31 Hussar	34 Lilith	6 Mister Sinister	2 Plantman
27 HYDRA	21 Living Laser	23 Mockingbird	16 Pluto
11 Hydro-Man	28 Living Lightning	1 Modam	35 Polaris
9 Hyperion	31 Living Monolith	17 Modok	3 Porcupine
13 Iceman	4 Living Mummy	14 Modred	30 Portal
26 Ikaris	33 Living Tribunal	16 Mole Man	28 Possessor
6 Immortus	7 Lizard	31 Molecule Man	10 Poundcakes
30 Impala	10 Llan the Sorcerer	26 Molten Man	21 Power Broker
11 Impossible Man	1 Llyra	14 Mongoose	11 Power Princess
5 In-Betweener	26 Lockjaw	9 Moon Knight	31 Presence
33 Inertia	12 Loki	1 Moonboy	24 Prester John
25 Infinity	30 Longshot	18 Moondragon	15 Princess Python
21 Invisible Woman	32 Lord Chaos	15 Moonglow	36 Proctor
32 Ion	18 Lucifer	36 Moonhunter	6 Professor Power
24 Iron Fist	11 Lupo	2 Moonstone	18 Professor X
15 Iron Man	35 Lyja the Lazerfist	36 Morbius	35 Proteus
33 Iron Man	8 Machete	6 Mordred	14 Prowler
19 Iron Monger	24 Machine Man	33 Morg	7 Psycho-Man
18 Ironclad	9 Machinesmith	3 Morgan Le Fey	26 Psyklop
2 Isaac	13 Mad Dog	2 Mother Night	23 Psylocke
9 Isis	10 Mad Thinker	36 Ms. Marvel	1 Puck
23 It the Living Colossus	22 Madame Masque	34 Multiple Man	12 Puff Adder
7 Jack Frost	4 Madame Web	13 Mysterio	29 Puma
27 Jack O' Lantern	18 Madcap	26 Mystique	5 Punisher
12 Jack of Hearts	11 Madrox	3 Naga	34 Punisher 2099
34 Jack of Hearts	17 Maelstrom	17 Namor	17 Punisher in Action
8 Jackal	30 Magik	14 Namorita	4 Puppet Master
30 Janus	5 Magma	10 N'astirh	34 Pym, Henry
26 Jarella	7 Magneto	18 Nebula	36 Pyro
16 Jemiah	35 Magus	31 Nebula	25 Quagmire
21 Jester	20 Maha Yogi	1 Nebulon	20 Quantum

INDEX

ISSUE # / PROFILE	ISSUE # / PROFILE	ISSUE # / PROFILE	ISSUE # / PROFILE
13 Quasar	36 Siege	6 Thin Man	6 Whirlwind
5 Quasimodo	23 Silhouette	18 Thing	19 White Bishop
8 Quicksand	9 Silver Dagger	14 Thor	36 White Queen
2 Quicksilver	22 Silver Sable	21 Thor	11 White Tiger
31 Quill	25 Silver Samurai	17 3-D Man	3 Whizzer
23 Radioactive Man	12 Silver Surfer	17 Thunderball	22 Whizzer
30 Rage	20 Silvermane	3 Thunderbird	31 Wildheart
25 Rama-Tut	10 Siryn	35 Thunderstrike	21 Will o' the Wisp
32 Rampage	2 Sise-Neg	13 Thundra	25 Wind Warrior
28 Ramrod	9 Skids	13 Tiger Shark	26 Windshear
33 Rancor	30 Skrulls	34 Tigra	9 Wing, Colleen
26 Rattler	33 Slapstick	11 Tinkerer	27 Wingfoot, Wyatt
36 Ravage 2099	5 Sleeper	26 Titan	5 Wizard
27 Raza	31 Sleepwalker	5 Titania	18 Wolfsbane
3 Razorback	22 Slither	27 Toad	4 Wolverine
18 Razor-Fist	7 Slug	19 Tom Thumb	20 Wolverine (new uniform)
29 Reavers	27 Snowbird	14 Tombstone	16 Wolverine in Action
10 Red Ghost	30 Snowblind	32 Trapster	34 Wonder Man
17 Red Guardian	29 Solo	1 Trickshot	10 Wong
4 Red Raven	15 Space Phantom	2 Triton	8 Woodgod
7 Red Ronin	35 Specialist	24 Trump	17 Worm
24 Red Skull	5 Speed Demon	35 Turbo	30 Wraith
21 Red Wolf	21 Speedball	33 Tyler Stone	3 Wrecker
20 Redstone	14 Sphinx	1 Typhoid	9 Xemnu
34 Replica	1 Spider-Man	15 Tyr	23 X-Men 1st Lineup
33 Reptyl	33 Spider-Man 2099	8 Tyrannus	24 X-Men 2nd Lineup
14 Rhino	13 Spider-Man in Action	13 U.L.T.I.M.A.T.U.M.	25 X-Men 3rd Lineup
34 Rictor	14 Spider-Man's Web Shooters	29 U.S.Agent	26 X-Men 4th Lineup
19 Ringer	8 Spider-Woman I	21 Uatu the Watcher	27 X-Men 5th Lineup
13 Ringmaster	11 Spider-Woman II	7 Ulik	28 X-Men 6th Lineup
6 Rintrah	18 Spirit of '76	36 Ultimo	29 X-Men 7th Lineup
2 Rock Python	35 Spirit of Vengeance	19 Ultimus	30 X-Men 8th Lineup Blue Team
9 Rocket Raccoon	12 Spitfire	22 Ultron	31 X-Men 8th Lineup Gold Team
11 Rocket Racer	16 Spymaster	4 U-Man	10 X-Ray
15 Rogue	28 Squadron Supreme	10 Umar	30 Yandroth
36 Roma	16 Stallior	20 Unicorn	11 Yellow Claw
1 Ronan	22 Starbolt	12 Uni-Mind	16 Yellowjacket
12 Runner	1 Starfox	30 Union Jack	32 Ymir
20 Sabra	28 Starhawk	32 Union Jack	22 Yondu
16 Sabretooth	35 Starhawk	23 Unus	18 Zaladane
29 Sabretooth	6 Starlight	6 Ursa Major	3 Zaran
15 Sandman	25 Stellaris	28 Valinor	36 Zarathos
17 Sasquatch	7 Stilt-Man	7 Valkin	9 Zarek
19 Satana	24 Stingray	16 Vamp	20 Zarrko
12 Satannish	11 Storm	11 Vanguard	35 Zero
15 Saturnyne	1 Stranger	36 Vanisher	24 Zeus
23 Sauron	25 Strong Guy	4 Vector	4 Ziran the Tester
36 Savage Steel	26 Stryfe	10 Venom	19 Zodiac I
28 Scarecrow	3 Sunder	3 Venus	19 Zodiac II
9 Scarlet Witch	34 Sunfire	23 Vermin	1 Zuras
2 Scorpio	36 Sunspot	6 Vertigo	16 Zzzax
17 Scorpion	14 Super-Sabre	25 Vibro	
33 Scourge	26 Super-Skrull	9 Vidar	
18 Scratch, Nicholas	8 Supreme Intelligence	8 Viper	
22 Screaming Mimi	23 Supremor	17 Vishanti	
32 Senor Muerte	13 Surtur	31 Vision	
29 Sersi	21 Swordsman	32 Voice	
10 Seth	31 Talisman	2 Volcana	
4 Shadowcat	29 Talon	22 Volstagg	
30 Shalla Bal	35 Tamara Rahn	5 Vulture	
8 Shang-Chi	11 Tana Nile	31 War Machine	
4 Shape	23 Tarantula	15 Warlock, Adam	
7 Shaper of Worlds	9 Taskmaster	33 Warpath	
32 Shapeshifter	16 Tatterdemalion	28 Warstar	
19 Shatterstar	12 Taurus	29 Warwolves	
6 She-Hulk	24 Terminatrix	20 Wasp	
18 She-Hulk in Action	25 Terminus	1 Watchdog	
3 Shocker	22 Terrax	2 Water Wizard	
31 Shockwave	28 Terror, Inc.	35 Weapon X	
35 Shotgun	4 Texas Twister	14 Wendigo	
13 Shroud	10 Thanos	13 Werewolf	
14 Sidewinder	21 Thena	12 Whiplash II	